FAMILY BUSINESS SOURCEBOOK

3RD EDITION

A Guide for Families Who Own Businesses and the Professionals Who Serve Them:

Covering Succession Planning, Growth, Financial Issues, Management, Psychological Issues, Women in the Family Business, the Younger Generation, and other issues family businesses face.

Edited by

Craig E. Aronoff, Ph.D.

Dinos Distinguished Chair of Private Enterprise
Founder, Cox Family Enterprise Center
Kennesaw State College, Marietta, Georgia

Joseph H. Astrachan, Ph.D.

Wachovia Eminent Scholar Chair of Family Business
& Director, Cox Family Enterprise Center
Kennesaw State College, Marietta, Georgia

John L. Ward, Ph.D.

Clinical Professor
Kellogg Graduate School of Management at Northwestern University
& Wild Family Professor of Family Enterprise at
IMD, Lausanne, Switzerland

Family Enterprise Publishers
1220B Kennestone Circle
Marietta, Georgia 30066

Family Enterprise Publishers

Jane G. Aronoff, Managing Editor

***

FAMILY BUSINESS SOURCEBOOK 3rd Edition: A Guide for Families Who Own Businesses and the Professionals Who Serve Them: Covering Succession Planning, Growth, Financial Issues, Management, Psychological Issues, Women in the Family Business, the Younger Generation, and other issues family businesses face / edited by Craig E. Aronoff, Joseph H. Astrachan, John L. Ward.

P. Cm.

Includes index.

ISBN 1-891652-07-9

1. Family-owned business enterprises – handbooks, manuals, etc.
I. Aronoff, Craig E. 1951 -   II. Astrachan, Joseph H. 1961 -   III. Ward, John L. 1945 -

INTRODUCTION

Family business is a vibrant and growing area of interest today. The advantages of family businesses – sustainability, flexibility, concerns for employees, patient capital and unique organizational competencies – are increasingly recognized as real competitive advantages.

For family businesses, this means that family matters too. Many of the resources or talents that can differentiate a family-owned or family-controlled business from other forms of enterprise are embedded in the relationship between the family and its business. This is particularly true of the relationship between management and shareholders. Business schools, for instance, are engaging in a broader range of research and dialogue related to governance and the role of shareholders and boards. Three prominent families have recently highlighted the importance of ownership and stewardship by visibly changing the nature of their relationships with major US corporations. Consider the Ford family and the appointment of William Clay Ford Jr. as CEO of the Ford Motor Company during a period of turmoil at the large auto producer. Consider also the Hewlett and Packard families and their opposition to the merger between Hewlett-Packard and Compaq Computer. These families demonstrate that, for them, their involvement in the businesses that bear their names differs in fundamental ways from other investors – a difference worth fighting for. Family ownership and control is demonstrating that it is different and that it has influence.

After all, why did the Hewletts and Packards not just diversify the family portfolio and reallocate assets to other companies' equity in the pursuit of net-worth protection? Perhaps because the heirs care about the enterprise and instead of operating as an average shareholder-trader, they accept the responsibility of stewardship. They see the value of the legacy embedded in the enterprise and want to preserve it – not to arrest progress. They seek to create a future that wisely builds on a very worthwhile past.

In the media industry, an industry that has seen much family ownership replaced by corporate ownership, we have also witnessed singular ownership commitment in great enterprises during generational transitions and turmoil wrought by economic, natural and technological forces. The Ochs/Sulzberger family remains committed in its fourth generation to sustaining the quality and leadership of *The New York Times*. Katharine and Don Graham of *The Washington Post*, amply displayed this commitment during Watergate, the Pentagon Papers and a generational transfer of power. The Blethen family of *The Seattle Times* exemplified true stewardship responsibility when in a meeting with the fifth generation, the so-called "fifth edition", it recommitted itself to continuity in the face of a financially debilitating strike. The Ferre-Rangel family of *El Nuevo Dia* in Puerto Rico, has created a model for succession in Latin America by transferring power and the entrepreneurial spirit to a next generation that has to succeed with, and not fight against, the Internet and the convergence of multiple media forms.

The often quoted statistics remind us that most of the world of enterprise is still family business. Over 90 percent of businesses in the US, Italy, and Latin America, and over 80 percent of businesses in Spain and other European and Asian countries remain family owned and family-controlled. These same businesses, small and large, young and old, account for more than 50% of the gross domestic product of the world's most advanced economies, employ a majority of the working population and have created the bulk of new jobs in the last two decades. Perhaps only the extreme stereotype of nepotism stands in the way of full recognition and appreciation of these enterprises' significant contribution by the media, academic researchers, business schools and the government.

Only about one third of family businesses do not make it beyond the founding generation under the ownership and control of the same family and only about 10 percent survive the third generation. But then again, most companies do not enjoy long successful lives; less than 5% of the original *Fortune* 500 companies remain in the list (first compiled in 1965 or just 36 years ago). Still, in the past year alone, several top-ranked academic management journals (like the *Academy of Management Journal, Organizational Science* and the *Journal of Business Venturing*) have published articles exploring the unique agency costs, strategic resources, features and issues of family businesses. By becoming the subject of quality research in established academic periodical literature, family businesses are entering a stage where more knowledge of their unique challenges and advantages is being created with the prospect of very useful implications for practice. The *Family Business Review* itself, a pioneer in the field, has more recently published very innovative, fresh analyses and perspectives on family firms.

Clearly, much more work remains to be done comparing the performance of family-owned and management-controlled firms and contrasting the strategic, financial, management, human resource and governance practices each employ. It would not be surprising to us to have these explorations reveal that many of the management and governance practices used by great family businesses are worthy of application in the better understood and better documented management controlled firms. Regardless, the fact that family business is joining the mainstream of academic research in management, economics, law and the behavioral sciences bodes well for the ability to enhance its survival statistics.

Most of the articles included in this book were written in the last decade. These articles represent significant progress in our understanding of how uniquely advantaged family businesses are in their ability to compete globally. They also represent significant progress in pointing out to management, ownership and family practices that help mediate the relationship between a family and its enterprise. These articles focus on unique strengths and competencies of family businesses, and how to minimize vulnerabilities – like nepotism, family conflict, resistance to change and others. Leading, managing and governing family enterprises increasingly requires a unique set of skills, abilities and practices in the service of sustainability and continuity.

This is a very useful and practical book. It should be valuable to those who own, work in or are affiliated with a family business. The perspective derived from a wider appreciation of the issues and challenges facing other family businesses is an important step in creating the capacity to lead families and family-owned businesses. It should also be quite useful to service providers (consultants, attorneys, accountants, financial planners, family therapists) and partners in the value chain who depend on family-owned businesses for their distribution or sales. It is bound to be valuable to students and researchers seeking a thorough compilation of the multidisciplinary knowledge that represents the field of family business on subjects like:

Succession
Strategic Planning
Ownership and Stewardship
Taxes
Boards of Directors and Advisors
Leadership
The CEO
The CEO Spouse
Growth and Regeneration
Family Relations
Family-Business Relations
Culture and Values

The Next Generation
Women in the Family Business
Key Non-Family Managers
Family Meetings and Family Councils
Family Conflict
Family Business in the Global Society

I commend the editors on the wide net they have cast to provide the best in family business research and practice, gathered from academic periodicals representing several disciplines, from business journals and from many other trade and family business field publications. Read the *Family Business Sourcebook,* 3rd edition, reflect on its implications and then apply it to your own unique circumstances.

Ernesto J. Pozo
Professor for the Practice of Family Business and Director, Partnership for Family Business
Weatherhead School of Management
Case Western Reserve University
Cleveland, Ohio, USA

Craig E. Aronoff, Ph.D.

Co-founder and principal of The Family Business Consulting Group, Inc., Craig Aronoff is a leading consultant, speaker, writer, and educator in the family business field.

As the founder of the Cox Family Enterprise Center at Kennesaw State University in Marietta, GA, Aronoff invented and implemented the membership-based, professional-service-provider sponsored Family Business Forum, which has served as a model of family business education for some 150 universities world-wide. He holds the Dinos Eminent Scholar Distinguished Chair of Private Enterprise and is a professor of management in Kennesaw State's Coles College of Business.

As a consultant, Aronoff has worked with hundreds of family companies in the U.S. and abroad on issues including generational transitions; developing business and family governance processes and structures; finding and articulating family missions and values; facilitating decision making and conflict resolution; managerial development; family compensation and dividend policies; family meetings; and more. As an inspiring, informative and entertaining speaker on a variety of family business topics, he speaks regularly to trade and professional groups and has lectured at over 80 universities.

With co-author John L. Ward, Aronoff is perhaps the most prolific writer in the family business field. He has authored, co-authored or been editor of more than two dozen books, including the 15-volume *Family Business Leadership Series* and is executive editor of *The Family Business Advisor*.

Listed in Who's Who and widely acknowledged for his work in the area of family business, Aronoff has received, among other honors: the Family Firm Institute's Beckhard Award for Outstanding Contributions to Family Business Practice; The Freedom Foundation's Leavey Award for Excellence in Private Enterprise Education; and the National Federation of Independent Business Foundation's Outstanding Educator Award.

His present and past activities in civic and community organizations include: president of the Family Firm Institute (1992-94); president of the Marietta Kiwanis; vice chairman of the Cobb (County, GA) Chamber of Commerce; chairman of the Cobb Transit Advisory Board; member of the Marietta Planning Commission; and president of the Association of Private Enterprise Education.

Aronoff grew up in a family business. He received his bachelor's degree from Northwestern University, his Masters from the University of Pennsylvania, and his Doctorate from the University of Texas at Austin.

Joseph H. Astrachan, Ph.D.

A principal of The Family Business Consulting Group, Inc., Joe Astrachan holds the Wachovia Eminent Scholar Chair of Family Business and is Director of the Cox Family Enterprise Center at the Coles College of Business, Kennesaw State University in Marietta Georgia. He also holds a research chair at Loyola University Chicago's business school where he directs the research efforts of their well-known Family Business Center.

Astrachan is editor of *Family Business Review*, a scholarly publication of the Family Firm Institute (FFI) of which he is a former board member. He has been involved with such lobbying groups as The Committee to Preserve American Family Businesses, Family Businesses of America, and the Center for the Study of Taxation; is a member of the Academy of Management, Southern Management Association, National Association of Business Economists and the Family Business Network; a founding member of the Yale Program for the Study of Family Firms; a member of the team that designed and conducted several national research projects; and director of Kennesaw State University's Estate Tax Research Program.

Astrachan received the Richard Beckhard award, which is the Family Firm Institute's highest honor for contributions to the field of family business. He also received the International Family Business Program Association's Lifetime Achievement in Research Award. In addition, he is a founding board member and fellow of the International Family Business Research Academy.

Astrachan's presentations, consultations and publications concentrate on family businesses, succession, and the management of professional partnerships. He is author and co-author of several books, including: *Mergers, Acquisitions, and Employee Anxiety* (Praeger, 1991); *Family Business Sourcebook II; Making Sibling Teams Work: The Next Generation;* and *Developing Family Business Policies: Your Guide to The Future.* Astrachan is also editor of the *Family Business Bibliography,* is on the editorial review board of *The Journal of Small Business Management,* and is a consulting editor for the *Journal of Applied Behavioral Science.*

His extended family has owned businesses ranging from container and tanker shipping to pharmaceuticals. Astrachan earned his B.A., M.A., M. Phil., and Ph.D. degrees at Yale University, where he studied in the School of Organization and Management.

John L. Ward

John Ward teaches and studies strategic management, business leadership, and family enterprise continuity. He is an active researcher, speaker and consultant on succession, ownership, governance, and philanthropy. He speaks to numerous trade, professional and academic audiences each year and is a regular visiting lecturer at two European business schools.

Ward is the author of three leading texts on family business, *Keeping the Family Business Healthy, Creating Effective Boards for Private Enterprises,* and, with Randel Carlock, *Strategic Planning for the Family Business.* With Craig Aronoff and Arthur Andersen LLP, Ward publishes a monthly newsletter, *The Family Business Advisor.* Ward and Aronoff also author a collection of booklets, "*The Family Business Leadership Series,*" each booklet focusing on specific issues family businesses face.

Ward graduated from Northwestern University (B.A.) and Stanford Graduate School of Business (M.B.A. and Ph.D.). Previously he was the Ralph Marotta Professor of Private Enterprise and Associate Dean at Loyola University Chicago and, prior to that, a Senior Associate with Strategic Planning Institute (PIMS Program) in Cambridge, Massachusetts. He is the Co-Chairman of The Family Business Consulting Group and the Co-Director of The Center for Family Enterprises at Northwestern University. Ward also currently serves on the boards of several companies in the U.S. and Europe.

TABLE OF CONTENTS

CHAPTER 1
GENERAL OVERVIEW

The family business has been rediscovered as the embodiment of management practices and business values required for competitiveness. But family dynamics renders firms vulnerable to rivalries and jealousies. Managing the seeming contradictions within systems that combine family and business is the key to family business survival and success.

A minor industry has now developed in helping owners of family businesses deal with the contradictions confronting them. Consultants, therapists, financial planners and researchers have become fascinated with the dilemmas of family businesses. The thoughtful prescriptions of those who have developed expertise in service of family businesses are helping to improve the odds of survival and success. Planning and communication are critical. Commitment to family values is essential as well.

Dealing with the conflicts inherent in family businesses is valuable in a societal as well as a familial sense. Real differences exist between owner-controlled and manager-controlled enterprises with the former producing greater efficiency and return on investment.

No single definition of family business is accepted by all. Size, management quality or whether ownership is public or private are not good criteria. While multiple family member participation in ownership and management provides an objective definition, what sets family businesses apart has more to do with subjective criteria like values and attitudes. The authors suggest that a family business is one intended for future generations.

Just What Is A Family Business?

By John L. Ward and Craig E. Aronoff

"We don't view ourselves as a family business," said the 46-year-old president of a major firm whose father founded the company and serves as chairman and CEO, and whose brother is executive vice president. The three of them control nearly 25 million of the company's shares and dominate the board of directors. Nonetheless, the president explained, "We view ourselves as professionally managed."

On the other hand, the proud owner of a new quick-printing franchise operation says: "Sure, we're a family business. My wife works the counter and keeps the books. The kids help out after school. I work about 14 hours a day. Maybe when I can afford more employees, we'll be less of a family business."

In our opinion, both companies are family businesses.

With all the talk these days of family businesses, you would think they would be fairly easy to define and identify. Yet two questions we are asked most frequently are: "Just what is a family business?" and "How many family businesses are there?"

Some businesses avoid the "family business" label because they think the term connotes a lack of quality management. Others think that "family business" means small, "mom-and-pop" operations.

These attitudes are based on misunderstandings. Family businesses are not necessarily small. Our research shows that about one-third of the nation's 1,000 largest publicly traded manufacturing firms can be considered family businesses. About 10,000 to 15,000 privately held companies have more than 500 employees, and the vast majority of them are family firms.

Family businesses not only can be large, they also can be among the best performers. In 1988, when Fortune magazine evaluated its "500" list of the largest companies to determine which one performed best, it named a family business – Liz Claiborne Inc. Leonard Lauder, chief executive officer of the private cosmetics giant founded by his mother, Estee Lauder, maintains that public companies simply cannot perform as effectively as private companies with strong cultures and professional management.

So family businesses are not defined by size, quality of management, or whether ownership is private or public. It is awfully tempting to identify any business that considers itself a family business as one. But we are scientists, of a sort, and demand greater precision and quantification.

Most simply stated, a family firm is one that includes two or more members of a family that has financial control of the company. Sometimes, all family members are in the same generation: siblings, husband-wife teams, occasionally cousins. More often, businesses recognize themselves as family businesses when at least two generations are involved: an entrepreneur-parent and his or her children or occasionally a nephew or niece. By this definition, family members could be included in ownership, management, or employee roles – but family intensity increases if relatives actually work in the business.

Of course, even when the owner/manager is the only family member directly involved in the firm, the entire family is powerfully affected by what happens in the business and vice versa. Sometimes the owner/manager inherits the business and recognizes the family's legacy and tradition even if no other family member is currently involved.

No one knows exactly how many family businesses there are in the U.S. According to various estimates, from 75 percent to 95 percent of U.S. companies are family firms, and they generate from 40 percent to 60 percent of the gross national product. These numbers are difficult to nail down. The Small Business Administration has reliable data on privately controlled companies, so we know that about 500,000 have 20 or more employees, and several million more employ two or more people.

To refine the data further, our research shows that about 40 percent of all mid-sized private companies already have two generations of family members involved. Moreover, 80 percent to 90 percent of all entrepreneurs who have children in their late teens hope – usually quietly – that their kids will someday join them in the business.

Entrepreneurs rarely start a company to create a family business. But as a business and its owner mature, and as children reach an age when they can be envisioned as part of the business, the firm often evolves into a family enterprise.

But numeric definitions are unsatisfying because they do not touch the realities of family business. What sets a family business apart has more to do with values and attitudes.

Family businesses often are characterized by longer-term perspectives. Visions include not only personal accomplishments but also aspirations and goals for future generations. Indeed, we like to think of a family business as one intended for future generations. Such intentions give rise to the most critical family-business issues: long-term strategic orientation, careful estate-tax planning, and concern for leadership and ownership succession planning.

Ultimately, a family business presents a marvelous opportunity. It permits the character, energies, and resources of a family to be focused over the long term on building a profitable enterprise. The enterprise, in turn, can facilitate a family's growth and provide an outlet for family members' talents and creativity.

To start one's own business and be one's own boss has been a great motivational theme in this country. The successful transition of this entrepreneurial ideal to one's children has to be the next chapter of the American dream.

This article was originally printed in *Nation's Business*, February 1990.

Is family management contrary to American principles of freedom and equality? Is there real value in a tradition of family management? Does family influence contradict all precepts of professional management? Is it foolish to attempt to perpetrate family influence in any firm? Robert L. Donnelley poses these questions and then takes a dispassionate look at family business to identify some of its advantages and disadvantages.

The Family Business

By Robert G. Donnelley

...has both strengths and weaknesses. The important thing is to understand them.

- Is family management contrary to the fundamental American creed advocating free competition, equality of opportunity, and the best man for the job?
- Is the value of a tradition of family management largely illusory – a product of self-interested rationalization by the families involved?
- Does family influence contradict all precepts of professional management?
- Do the complexities and demands of today's business environment make it foolish to attempt to perpetuate family influence in any firm?

Doubts like these about the effectiveness – if not the morality – of family management of businesses are typical of prevailing attitudes among businessmen, consultants, and educators. In some enterprises, the family interest is a source of serious weakness. But whether the very presence of family members in an organization is per se an indication of mismanagement is definitely open to question. In fact, if one takes an objective look at the success of some family enterprises, he may wonder whether the effectiveness of the typical reward punishment system underlying nonfamily businesses has not been greatly overrated.

In this article, I will attempt to take just such a dispassionate look at family business and to identify some of its advantages and disadvantages, hoping that these will serve as guideposts for members of the business and financial community who wish to understand such enterprises more fully. I hope that this article will be of particular interest to those who are currently employed by, or are considering being employed by, or who now manage family firms.

What is a Family Business?

In this article a company is considered a family business when it has been closely identified with at least two generations of a family and when this link has had a mutual influence on company policy and on the interests and the objectives of the family. Such a relationship is indicated when one or more of the following conditions exists:
- Family relationship is a factor, among others, in determining management succession.
- Wives or sons of present or former chief executives are on the board of directors.
- The important institutional values of the firm are identified with a family, either in formal company publications or in the informal traditions of the organization.
- The actions of a family member reflect on or are thought to reflect on the reputation of the enterprise, regardless of his formal connection to management.
- The relatives involved feel obligated to hold the company stock for more than purely financial reasons, especially when losses are involved.
- The position of the family member in the firm influences his standing in the family.
- A family member must come to terms with his relationship to the enterprise in determining his own career.

In view of the fact that what are strengths in one company may be weaknesses in another, the most that any outsider can contribute to people within a particular firm is to provide insights that will help them understand their situations so they can then work out their own courses of action.

My observations are based on a study of 15 successful family companies, supported by personal interviews with family managers and other interested businessmen and educators.

Weaknesses to Avoid

Let us look first at the negative side of the picture, in terms of actual case examples, and then go on to examine the impressive instances where, in contrast, strengths have developed. Among the weaknesses of family management, the following seem most prevalent:

1. Conflicts occurring between the interests of the family and those of the enterprise as a whole.
2. A lack of discipline being exerted over profits and performance in all parts of the organization.
3. A failure to rise quickly to meet new marketing challenges.
4. Situations where nepotism rules unchecked by objective standards of meritorious managerial performance.

Conflicts of Interest

In a family company, the family almost always has the proprietary and/or management power to pursue its own objectives and aspirations, even when they are at variance with the best interests of the enterprise. By contrast, the competing interests and values of members of a "public" corporation check or condition those of the individual (and his family); and the corporate leadership tends to develop, perpetuate, and emphasize the institutional values of the firm over those of the individual through formal systems of measurement and incentive.

Of course, this situation in the public corporation does not always result in a balance. Sometimes, the organization will dominate the individual and his family. The popular concept of the organization man with his organization wife and children is an example of this danger. Such domination will sometimes directly affect the public interest, as was exemplified in the price-fixing case involving General Electric, Westinghouse, and some other producers of electrical equipment. While the public corporation may have problems, its corporate machine at least enforces in its members a sense of responsibility to the heads of the organization.

In a family enterprise, this organizational enforcement is not native to the system, at least as it applies to family members. The balance between family interests and company interests is usually a psychological one, stemming from the family's own personal sense of responsibility toward the firm. The fact that most successful family enterprises have developed elaborate institutional restraints on family prerogatives, backed in most cases by rigid family traditions, does not obviate this fact, for in each of these cases, the restraints had to be initially effected by the family members themselves. E. I. du Pont de Nemours & Company, Inc., almost universally considered the epitome of a well-administered, successful organization is an example:

> "Despite the fact that members of the du Pont family represent a substantial ownership interest in the company and are present in its management and policy making, family relationship, quite obviously, has not been the sole reason for promotion. This restraint on family prerogative, however, stems from Pierre du Pont's deliberate rejection, in 1910, of the "long-entrenched, inherited attitude that the firm was managed for the family and the family was to manage the firm...Pierre did appoint family members...to senior posts...but only after they had proven themselves managerially competent."[1]

In less successful organizations, however, the immunity from institutional restraint allows important company needs to be thwarted by family considerations. Such a situation may lead to one or more of the widely catalogued problems of family firms, including capital shortages, misguided financial secrecy, ingrown company policies, a lack of profit discipline, ineffective utilization of nonrelated management talent, nepotism, and, most seriously, family conflicts.

These abuses, moreover, are not unnatural, especially in a family that has failed to develop consciously a sense of company responsibility. Unlike the company value system, which ideally determines a person's authority, responsibility, status, and financial benefits on the basis of his demonstrated competence in accomplishing the goals of the firm, family norms usually stress the obligation of providing for the needs of the family. In the resulting confusion of values, company requirements may lose out to family obligations. Such a situation is demonstrated by the case of the Cole Hardware Company (the names of this and subsequent companies designated by an asterisk, and the individuals involved, are disguised, but they represent actual eases):

> Reasoning from his obligation to the other family members, Peter Cole, the president and sales manager, felt required to give his brothers and brother in-law positions in the firm, despite their incompetence. "The thing to do would be to let them out," he stated, "but I can't do that with my own brothers. Furthermore, if my brother-in-law isn't employed here in some sort of a job, I'll just have to find another way of supporting him."[2]

Cole's expressed obligation to his relatives is in direct contrast to an employer's normal responsibility which requires him to reward only performance and to penalize the lack of it. In the case of the Cole company, the president ignored the company need-a competent management group-to solve a family problem. This confusion of family interests with those of the firm is also the source of other problems in family firms.

In those situations where the company is considered the family exchequer, an excessive secrecy over financial matters may result, stifling the development of adequate business controls and sound planning techniques and allowing ineffective methods and policies to remain long undiscovered. Here is an example:

> In one large eastern family manufacturing firm, the family managers excluded – even from the treasurer – any knowledge of the company's financial position, because the family's financial interests were so interrelated with those of the business. In such a situation, the company treasurer was not able to perform even the most basic functions normally accorded the job.

Poor Profit Discipline

Another problem found in family firms (but also common to close corporations in general) is lack of profit discipline. Like a close corporation, a family company may tend to concentrate on product quality, excessive plant and equipment improvement, civic affairs, sales "empire building," and personnel relations beyond the contribution of these factors to the long-term profits of the company. This emphasis may lead to poor cost-control systems and other lax accounting procedures, or to management's unwillingness to take the necessary corrective action when company accounting procedures indicate that its "pet projects" are out of line.

Although the impact of this problem is hard to estimate statistically, the top officers of two major Chicago banks cited "good accounting systems" and the "willingness to take quick corrective action when costs are out of line" as the major differences between successful and unsuccessful family enterprises. And it is interesting to note that a recent comparison of a group of small companies (of which 80 percent are closely held) with their publicly owned counterparts revealed that those belonging to the closely held group generally had lower profit margins – one-half that of their publicly owned competitors. Since family firms are generally more conservative than public firms in their financial reporting, and since family firms, for competitive and tax reasons, may bury profits in many ways, these figures must be suspect.

Nevertheless, there is something to consider here for managers of family owned companies who may question the sharpness of their profit discipline.

How Prevalent is Family Ownership?

An estimated 20 percent of Fortune's list of 500 largest manufacturing companies show evidence of significant family management and/or proprietary interest.

In many industries – including chemicals, drugs, textiles, grain brokerage, meat packing, investment banking, glass making, liquor distributing, printing, publishing, advertising, and retailing – family-identified firms play a significant, if not dominant, role. These enterprises include such successful organizations as Du Pont, Seagrams, Cargill, Corning Glass, Upjohn, Firestone Tire and Rubber, Winn-Dixie Stores, Joseph Magnin, Cabot, Inc., and Lykes Bros. Steamship.

A 1955 Fortune survey of 175 of the largest U.S. corporations revealed the no less than 55 percent of the companies had close relatives or in-laws holding management jobs in the same firm.

A 1952 study based on a survey of 8,000 executives made by Professors W. Lloyd Warner and James C. Abegglen (Big Business Leaders In America, New York, Harper & Bros., 1955) revealed that two out of every five men whose fathers were top-ranking executives, and three out of every five men whose fathers were owners of large businesses, had positions in their fathers' companies. Significantly, these researchers found that the proportion of sons and major owners in the same firms as their fathers reflected an increase over that found in a survey conducted 24 years before. Professors Warner and Abegglen also noted a decline in the number of sons holding the top position of president or chief executive in the same firms as their fathers but found this "more than offset by the increase in sons among vice-presidents and below" compared with a generation ago.

Immobile Marketing

Too much involvement with family interest may prevent a company from capitalizing on new market developments or on major growth opportunities. This attitude is illustrated in the case of the Howard Wine Company:

> To meet a developing national market for its products, the company needed additional equity financing. Even though the firm's projected growth would have more than covered its equity dilution, the Howard family opposed the move, according to the financial consultant, solely because they felt "it wouldn't be right, having outsiders meddling in our affairs."

When a family identifies too closely with a particular product or function, another problem may arise: the company may be particularly vulnerable to the effects of changes in the market. Such a situation was true of the Hollowell Glove Company:

> Through the years, the father had trained his son to equate quality with a specific glove style. Despite a change in taste which made this particular style unacceptable, the son was unable to lead the firm in adapting to the new market condition. In this particular case, the son hopefully believed that customers would return to the old style and thought that any change in the product "would only cheapen the company's reputation for quality that my father took such pains to develop."

This problem does not exist in all family firms. Nevertheless, while some of the executives and business educators interviewed commended successful family companies in general for their "firm policy of defining their product and staying within the definition," many noted a wide-spread marketing weakness in family firms. As the president of a major Chicago bank put it:

> "With respect to the less successful enterprises, it is our observation that their production is usually fairly efficient. Their problems are most apt to center around marketing and the development of new and improved products. Thus, these companies tend to lag behind their competition and lose market position. Recovery of a deteriorated competitive position is a slow and difficult process which usually cannot be achieved by the management that permitted the deterioration to occur."

Excessive Nepotism

A less subtle problem of family companies is nepotism, which according to one dictionary definition is "the advancement of relatives on the basis of family rather than merit." So much has been written on this subject alone that there is danger of its being overly stressed in any discussion of family enterprises. As noted in Fortune, "The overriding fact is ...that competition and the demands of the marketplace soon take care of any company that relies on incompetent relatives in management."[3] Despite this fact, every family-identified firm must be concerned with possible favoritism built into its personnel policies, since popular opinion almost automatically suspects such an abuse in nearly all family businesses.

In firms where it is practiced, nepotism develops from the family's imposition of its own values and membership criteria on the business, regardless of the question of competence. When this occurs, the opportunities that can be offered to nonfamily management talent are restricted. This, of course, places the company at a disadvantage with respect to its competitors who can draw on wider markets for their personnel.

At the same time, nepotism weakens the firm's present managers, forcing them both to carry the dead weight of the incompetents and to assume the burden of the job left undone. Even more seriously, nepotism may lead to a management system that stresses family politics rather than accuracy. When this occurs, the essential task-orientation of the firm is destroyed considerably, jeopardizing the company's long-term prospects for survival.

The type of thinking that creates nepotism is also conducive to internecine feuds – the most serious problem in family enterprises. Arguments and serious differences of opinion are not unique to family firms. Nevertheless, the normal mechanism of inheritance can create strongly competing minority interests and disagreements which, when they do occur in a family firm, seem to involve the emotions of all the parties to an exceptionally high degree.

Tradition and company identification, as well as proprietary interest, cause each family member to view himself as a spokesman for the business, with a right to decide corporate policy equal to that of the other family members. Thus is created the paradox of one such company where the authority stemming from the position in the company is circumvented – so much so that the policies instituted by the president are challenged by the executive vice president.

When, in addition to nepotism, other abuses are present, the potential danger of family conflict is enhanced. In companies where out-and-out nepotism exists, the system of measurement and rewards based on family relationship rather than competence diminishes the institution's ability to cope with internal stresses and strains. Each decision becomes a subjective and highly charged "family problem," instead of a settlement based on the external objective standard of contribution to company goals. In the Everett Hardware Manufacturing Company:

> The senior executives, Paul and Peter Everett, agreed to treat their respective sons alike, despite the demonstrated greater competence of one of them. When the fathers died, however, the firm's operations became paralyzed, as

neither branch of the family allowed the other any control. Since the company was treated as a family inheritance rather than a family responsibility, the fathers provided no system of weighing the claims of the cousins. Such a system, however, became important when family harmony was lost.

Strengths to Seek

Even though these problems exist in some family firms, one should not overlook the significant advantages that may be realized by the organization that can successfully capitalize on the assets such a relationship supplies. After all, family self-interest is similar to any other human factor that competes with or otherwise interferes with corporate objectives. Parkinson's Law, for example describes a common bureaucratic situation in which a manager will satisfy his own need for prestige by adding superfluous employees. The situation in which workers restrict output despite a company's formal system of incentives and measurement is an example of powerful human forces at work on a lower level.

When, however, such self-interest is controlled in a family firm and the family equates its long-term best interest with that of the company, a rare harmony is achieved between the normally competing values within the individual and the organization. Reinforced and perpetuated by family pride, identification, and tradition, this unity of purpose has been a fundamental, though intangible, factor in the success of many family firms. It is also the basis of all the other advantages accruing to such an enterprise. Among these are the following:

1. The availability of otherwise unobtainable financial and management resources because of family sacrifices.
2. Important community and business relationships stemming from a respected name.
3. A dedicated and loyal internal organization.
4. An interested, unified management-stockholder group.
5. A sensitivity to social responsibility.
6. Continuity and integrity in management policies and corporate focus.

Personal Sacrifice

It is paradoxical that family interest, a source of financial weakness in some firms, is in other circumstances a major element of financial strength. Many family companies have been built on the tradition of minimal dividends and personal sacrifice, and family pride and loyalty have been responsible for continued operation through periods of hardship when considerations of profit and loss might well have dictated closing down. According to a noted business historian, it was just these factors that caused the early owning families behind Weyerhaeuser to sustain 40 years of losses so that the company could grow into an industrial giant.

The extent of this loyalty is evident in a wife's reminiscences of the early struggles behind another major industrial leader:

> "Our good times were always five years ahead. Whenever I wanted some new furniture, my husband said, 'Not now. We need a new machine.'"

In other cases, family pride and identification cause company obligations to be honored beyond the family's legal responsibility. The bankruptcy debts against many firms are repaid for these reasons. In one major company, the owning family even paid out of its own pocket the firm's obligations to its employees during a period of substantial financial losses.

Sometimes, a well-established family not only contributes financial support, but also draws upon management skills in its other organizations to help the firm in solving a serious problem. In several of the cases studied, particularly those dealing with closely held firms, this type of emergency pooling of resources is found to be quite prevalent. Take the case of the Roger Distributing Company:

Throughout the war years, this company had rapidly expanded by providing accounting and distributing services to industry. Most of its business, however, was tied up in one major account. In the post-war changeover to a new system of record-keeping, the company developed serious production and administrative difficulties in servicing this key account. Unsolved, these problems would not only have caused the company to lose a substantial amount of business, but would also have reflected on the firm's reputation in the industry. The necessary engineering help was found, however, in another company run by the Roger family. The owning family itself came to the rescue by making the necessary arrangements; it did not leave the solution up to the two competing management groups within the organization.

Much criticism is leveled against family executives who inherit plush administrative positions with little or no effort on their parts. Little credit, however, is given to the family manager who takes over an organization that is "too messy" or "too hopeless" to attract the so-called competent outsider. Witness the case of the Horwitz Machine Company, a small Midwestern manufacturer of heating products:

In this company, the nonrelated president attempted to ruin the firm so that he could own it outright. This action was instigated despite the favorable stock option plan provided the president on his acceptance of a position in management and without regard to the other employees or to the community within which the company was located. After a considerable personal investment, the family stockholders were able to squeeze out the president. When no one could be attracted to manage the company, an experienced family member undertook the job as part of his "family responsibility."

Valuable Reputation

In concluding its article on the Rothschilds, Time noted, "...to face the future, they [the Rothschilds] have one advantage from the past, the Rothschild legend – in itself a very bankable asset."[4]

Not only may a family's reputation have a beneficial influence on community relations, but it may have a direct and obvious impact on the company's operations. In many cases of struggling manufacturing companies, the owning family's reputation is an important factor in receiving loans from local banks. In spite of the uncertainty of these ventures, the banks believe that their risks are lessened in view of their past experience with the family.

Family ties may also be important in establishing the trust necessary to conduct business – especially in situations where the stakes are high and the companies involved are not protected by a unique competency, a special expertise, or by legal sanctions against a breach of faith. The fast-moving, risky field of investment banking seems to be an example of such a situation. Several New York investment houses are connected by family ties which may be important in the establishment of joint ventures where the returns may be substantial and the competitive relationships highly informs

In some cases, the benefit derived from a family relationship may be more subtle. In those areas of business where informal relationships are crucial to the conduct of the enterprise, the firm's identification with a family may have a direct bearing on is marketing activities. A closely held brokerage house, for example, may retain or attract customers because of its identification with a prominent family or families. Such a relationship may play a role in instances where all other factors are comparable or the results of the services provided are intangible.

Employee Loyalty

The value of a family relationship is not limited to the family's role in the firm's business and its public relations. Such involvement may also play a large role in the internal organization of the enterprise. To the small firm, family management can avoid disastrous executive turnover and ensure that the company's particular competitive skills will remain unique to it.

In recent years, business has become increasingly aware of the problem of the high turnover at the executive level. One New York consultant firm estimates that 75,000 to 100,000 of the nation's executives in middle and upper management change then jobs yearly. The size of this turnover led one writer to comment:

> "Although it cannot be shown in dollars and cents on a profit-and-loss statement, turnover at the executive level is …one of the most costly hidden items borne by the modern corporation."[5]

What is expensive to the large firm may be disastrous to the small one, where such turnover disrupts the management organization and threatens the firm's competitive livelihood. A nonrelated executive is held to a small firm only by his self-interest. If he finds an opportunity that suits him better, he will go elsewhere. If he joins a company in another area, he represents a considerable loss in terms of the time and expense spent in training him – resources that are severely limited in the small enterprise. More likely, he will join a competitive firm or go into business for himself and thus represent a major threat to his former company.

Unlike a large organization, the small firm does not have the security of size or of an extensive research and development program. Normally, its competitive strategy is based on the ability to perform certain services better than or faster than other, often larger, firms. Usually, a small company's resources are special techniques or product improvements which are not patentable. When one of its executives goes to work for a competitor, the small company may find its own techniques or product innovations used against itself and its position in the industry seriously jeopardized.

In contrast to the nonrelated executive, a relative is effectively blocked from the temptation of greener pastures. Once he decides to work in the family firm, the convergence of expectation, training, and family pressure ties him to the enterprise. If a relative does seek a job with another firm in the industry, his family connections, moreover, cause the firm's competitors to treat the relative with suspicion – another factor restricting his outside business opportunities.

Within the organization in general, a succession of competent family managers can develop a strong feeling for the company. Despite the current tendency of many observers to sneer at paternalism, several family companies apparently believe that relatives are particularly helpful in the area of employee relations, judging from the number of cases where relatives are used in this capacity. Such a finding seems to be supported by a Fortune article dealing with the pros and cons of hiring relatives. In noting that some companies consider the presence of family members an advantage when dealing with employees, the article quotes Charles Heinz, then vice president of industrial relations at H. J. Heinz Company, as saying, "I think the fact that I'm in the Heinz family helps make for a better climate in labor negotiations."[6]

In some family companies, the loyalty of employees and nonrelated managers to the family and the company is found to be particularly significant. Unlike the loyalty felt toward non-related managers, it is not lost when the recipient retires but tends to be carried over to his son and through him to the company. Sometimes, this loyalty is so great that the other company employees will actively attempt to perpetuate family control. In the case of a small metal-treatment company, for example, the employees [became actively concerned] about training the owner-manager's son because they did not want "outsiders" owning and managing the organization.

Management-Stockholder Unity

When a family closely identifies its own best interests with those of the firm, the company may realize a significant benefit from the resulting community of interest between stockholder and management groups. Such mutuality has been cited as the major defense of employee stock-ownership plans.

Not only is such a dual perspective nearly always automatically present in family managers, but because of the hold of family tradition, it normally extends beyond the sometimes limited self-interest of cashing in on a special stock option plan. Family members are usually extremely reluctant to sell their ownership in the family firm. This attitude seems to cause many such managers to place greater stress on the company's best interests in the long-term.

Because of their ownership influence, moreover, family managers may be less sensitive to criticism based on short-term performance, and may be freer to focus on the long-term aspects of the company moves. Many family executives, moreover, commented at length on moves that their firms made when considerations of short-term performance might well have dictated a more conservative policy. Several executives attribute their company's early emphasis on research and development to the ability to stress long-term goals.7

In some cases such as the following two examples, the assurance of a loyal stockholder interest apparently enables a firm to make key moves that critically affect its long-term strength.

- In the Hopwell Fabricated Material Company, according to the family president, such loyalty was a major factor in the firm's decision to embark upon a national merchandising campaign that caused the firm to dominate its field. "t its inception, the project called for annual expenditures equaling one-third of the companies annual sales," he said. "Without substantial stockholder support, the directors and the firm would have been much more conservative."

- In the Wray New England Printing Company, the president believed that family ownership was essential to his company's ability to "go for broke" in its fight to win the right to adopt technological improvements without prior union approval. This right was accepted only after a major strike which proved so costly in the short term that the owner-manager was convinced that the company would have failed without the stockholder support guaranteed by the family ownership interest. "We knew the family believed as we did, and were willing to take the risk," recounted a nonrelated manager about the situation. "With substantial outside stockholder interest, we might have viewed our responsibilities somewhat differently when faced with such severe losses."

The presence of a responsible family ownership interest may also play an increasingly important role in another respect. In companies where the family tie is primarily a proprietary one, the knowledge that there is an interested stockholder with enough stock to make his voice heard may make those charged with the management of the firm think extra long about their stockholder responsibilities. This role maybe a significant one in view of the increasing immunity of management from stockholder control where ownership is widely scattered. A substantial outside ownership interest ensures some review of management policies. When such an interest is tied to the firm by family identification, the protection afforded may be even greater, since the stockholder is less likely to sell out when difficulties arise

Besides these possibly unique advantages, several company managers believe that family-owned companies benefit, as do other forms of close corporations, from a greater flexibility than their more public competitors. Although such an advantage seems more attributable to the type of centralized organization that family ownership encourages than to family ownership per se, several family managers cited specific examples where their ability to move quickly on major policy decisions has resulted in important long-term gains. Because of this flexibility, a meat packing firm, for example, was able to make a major purchase of processing plant on six hours' notice, entering the processing part of the business at a very opportune moment.

This flexibility, however, may not always be an advantage, especially in cases where it interferes with good management principles. "A situation in which the family dominates the firm," noted one textile executive, "may encourage a 'yes man' management team and a captive board of directors, resulting in an improper review of company moves." Agreeing with this opinion, the executive of a family paper company observed, "Our family influence may enable management to move quickly, but every time we have, the results have been disastrous."

Similar to other forms of close corporations, family-owned companies may also have an additional advantage of secrecy. Although secrecy about company operations may interfere with management functions if carried to excess, several company executives cited the ability to restrict operational information as an important competitive advantage. A former family company, for example, based its decision to remain closely held partly on "the lessened ability of outside interests, particularly competition, to appraise the effect of company actions" which such ownership provided.

In some family businesses, as the following example shows, the ability to restrict information is considered crucial:

> In ten years the Lambrecht Machinery Company grew from one-fourth the size of its major competitor to two-thirds its size. "if our competitor had realized how rapidly we were expanding," the president said, "he would have prevented us. He knew we were establishing new plants but, without financial statements, he did not know how successful our ideas really were."

Social Sensitivity

Family pride and identification with the company may cause management to be more sensitive to its social responsibility and thereby contribute to the firm's long-term strength. The rigid profit consideration inherent in nearly all business organizations is a powerful one. Unchecked, it may lead to actions not always in the public's best interest.

When an individual employee is asked to participate in such actions, he may find himself in the untenable position of obeying his best judgment only at the sacrifice of his job and his family's security. But because of "the name on the door," a family management (many of the family executives interviewed believe) is less able to justify acts contrary to the communities best interests either to itself or to the public. Attitudes like the following are not uncommon:

> "How could I explain a price-fixing scandal to my son?" asked a paper manufacturer. "Such a situation would do considerable damage to the family's reputation, as well as that of the company."

As in the case of the other advantages cited, the importance of having a family name associated with a company is hard to substantiate statistically. While most executives interviewed agree in general that this is a potential advantage, almost all point out that whether or not it is realized depends on the family linked with the firm. "I have dealt with many a family," noted the treasurer of a large textile concern, "who had the ethics of thieves. And the conduct of their business reflected it "

Several executives were also quick to point out that this advantage may be diminishing in importance. "Twenty-five years ago," added the president of a large industrial material manufacturing company, "I would have agreed completely that social sensitivity was a strength of the family company, but today nearly every company has recognized the importance of a good reputation in the community."

Despite these qualifications the evidence appears to indicate that the family companies, because of the family involvement, tend generally to weigh the social aspects of decisions more heavily that do comparable public firms.

Continuity and Purpose

There is an overriding advantage that a succession of competent family managers can provide to a business enterprise – continuity and a deeply felt sense of corporate purpose. These two elements seem to be increasingly important in a society where change and the break-up of traditional institutions are normal.

Every company tends to have a number of corporate "myths" or traditions which entrench particular objectives and capabilities. When a family management tradition exists, these important myths are considerably strengthened by the families involvement in them, since each guiding principle becomes part of a continuum stemming back to the firm's founding, with the family manager providing the unifying factor between the company's past and its present.

While a family manager's most important contribution in this area may be an intangible one, a family association may have a major value in enabling a firm to absorb large-scale operational changes without disrupting important organizational values or the essential unity of the firm. For example:

- The chief executive of a large manufacturing concern believes that the presence of a family management tradition has helped his organization preserve its historical stress on quality despite an increasing mechanization in its production processes. The founder of the firm built the reputation of the company on its quality workmanship, and, according to the executive, the succession of family managers has tended to perpetuate this dedication to quality within the organization.

- The effect of family identification on a company's ability to absorb major changes was also noted by a nonrelated treasurer of a weaving firm. Since the war, his company has grown rapidly through acquisition. Despite this rapid growth, the treasurer believes that the sense of unity provided by the managing family, which traces its connection with the organization over three generations, has prevented a severe case of organizational indigestion. "Despite our growth and despite our absorption of many different firms," he added, "the diverse management elements have remained united through the mutual respect for the family members who head the company."

A family association, however, may be valuable for more than its influence on a firm's internal organization. Sometimes, this association may be directly related to a firm's unique competitive competency.

One steel company president noted that family management may be important in perpetuating the value of "personal service." When a firm is founded on the value of personal service (which often is linked to the activities of the original proprietor), its possibilities for expansion are limited. Yet the use of other family members may allow the firm to expand beyond one man's capabilities while still retaining the companies unique competitive ability. Such thinking underlies a well-known New England restaurant's stress on family management in its advertising.

In several other cases, family management seems to have been an element in a firm's public image. The Findlay Art Gallery, for example, prides itself in representing the experience of "three generations in art"; the Oscar Mayer Company, with sales of $279 million in 1963, communicates its emphasis on quality by referring to its family management in its motto: "A tradition of quality from our family to yours." A similar use of tradition is developed in a series of ads run by the H. J. Heinz Company. In these ads, Chairman Henry Heinz personally pledges the company to the maintenance of his grandfather's guiding principle of using only the finest quality ingredients. The tradition of family management and Chairman Heinz's ability to appeal to this tradition tend to reinforce the company's reputation for quality in the eyes of the public.

The family manager may also have several advantages in executive development over his non related counterpart. Among these may be dedication, experience, unusual access to management, and immunity from organizational pressures.

The point was repeatedly made by those interviewed that many sons and other family members will tend to work harder, to be more enthusiastic, and to be more loyal to the company than their nonrelated counterparts. Also, having grown up in the company environment, they may have an extensive knowledge of the company before they begin working. Once in the firm, they may benefit from a greater willingness on the part of senior management to spend time with them. Finally, family members may be able to develop themselves without jeopardizing their relations with others. A family supervisor noted: "Because I am in the family, I can set my own pace without others feeling that I am playing up to my boss." For these reasons, a family member, provided he is interested, may have an unusual opportunity in a family company to develop his management potential to the utmost.

Caveats to Consider

So far we have seen that the family participation is not always a source of weakness. What is weakness in one firm seems to develop, under competent management, into a major strength in another. But the experience of organizations where family participation is a source of strength indicates that this is true only when:

1. The family understands that its personal objectives can be realized only by the long-term success of the enterprise.
2. Family managers are willing to establish policies and formal restraints to ensure that family participation is limited to the extent of its contribution to the firm's long-term strengths.

The histories of many of the most prominent firms indicate that their present positions are in large part attributable to the recognition of the importance of these two factors. Such recognition, however, is often precipitated by a family or company crisis. In several cases, these conditions were met only after a family member had to be fired. In others, they were the result of the company's growth, which forced the family to come to terms with the needs of the enterprise. Paradoxically, by giving up some elements of control, the family apparently strengthened its own position of leadership and, at the same time, improved the firm's chances for profitable operation.

Checks on Favoritism

To ensure a positive balance between family and company interests the managements of most successful family firms seem to delineate clearly between traditional family prerogative and that belonging to management. While recognizing that the family association may give a relative some claims to employment and/or management preferences, many of these firms have ensured, through the establishment of formal checks as well as informal traditions, that these claims will not dominate. Here is a case in point:

> The Thompson Manufacturing Company is a large material processing firm. Its family executives believe that some family participation in management is important, because it adds to the firm's internal unity. This intangible strength is supported, moreover, by every practical consideration. Through their stock ownership, the family branches control the company, and the Thompsons believe that some family participation in management makes it more likely that this stock will be voted in the company's best interests. For these reasons, blood ties are a consideration in employment and in subsequent management selections.

> Nevertheless, this consideration has not been allowed to dominate, for the family executives believe that the right to manage has to be earned by family members in the same manner as by nonrelated employees. "A relative's name may get him in the door," noted the president, "but the rest is up to him." To ensure that such a condition is carried out, the company has a strict policy that, where sons are involved, all evaluation and supervision are under the control of others. The father is not even allowed to ask how well his sons are doing.

> In line with this personnel policy, the company exerts further control over family self-interest. A majority of the directors are not related to the Thompson family, although management encourages all family branches, including those not in management, to represent their stock on the board. When there is a company problem that involves family interest, such as management succession and compensation, these outside directors play an important role in ensuring that the needs of the enterprise are met despite sometimes conflicting family interests.

While allowing some family privileges, the owner-managers of the Thompson Manufacturing Company recognize the need to accept some limitations on family prerogatives in order to obtain a stronger management organization. Because of this willingness to take such action, the firm has risen to a position of dominance within an industry where family mismanagement is the rule.

Barriers to Employment

In the Thompson company, there are no special restrictions on family employment other than the general condition that the relatives measure up to the company's employment standards. Among companies studied, this situation tends to be the exception. Many of the family companies which recognize the importance of limiting family prerogatives tend to be more restrictive in their initial employment policies. A few family firms have even adopted a policy of employing no relatives at all.

The value of such a rigid policy, however, is uncertain. In general, the tendency to make exceptions to rules against hiring relatives seems to be most marked where the family retains stock control, such rules become self-defeating as the family becomes less willing to place company interests above family interests. In the more typical situation, families try to limit, but not eliminate, family employment.

In some companies employment restrictions are based on blood ties and/or age. Many families tacitly exclude in-laws, despite the fact that within several firms, including those where such restrictions are currently practiced, the experience with in-laws had in the past been favorable. In many of the companies studied, the firm is currently managed by the eldest son of the former chief executive. Such situations suggest that primogeniture exists in some companies. Since most of these sons are named after their fathers, the situation may be attributable to greater family expectation and pressure on such individuals to enter the firm.

In other companies, family members who wish to enter the family firm are required to measure up to standards more rigid than those applied to nonrelated management talent. A long-established family firm, located in New England, stipulates that a relative may work for the company only after he has been "invited in" by the present managers. Several companies require that family members be successful elsewhere before entering the firm.

One of the companies having such a condition is the Pillsbury Company, whose chairman, Philip W. Pillsbury, commented "I have had a policy of not having sons work for the company unless they have established themselves somewhere else for a period of years." In advocating such a policy, a family executive in a bank noted that this requirement provides the family member with an important business perspective and helps develop the individual's self-confidence.

The Thompson company is typical of a second approach to the problem of limiting family prerogatives. The managers hope that the family management tradition will be maintained, but they neither arbitrarily restrict nor force family participation in the company. The family management is especially careful not to pressure family members to join the business. The family helps its members who have outside interests to get started in other careers, and, because the stock of the company is publicly traded, no relative who embarks on another career is faced with the difficult problem of having his and his immediate family's financial well being under another's control.

Since the employment of relatives is not restricted in the Thompson company, the family managers give special attention to the problems of developing and objectively evaluating the administrative skills of the members entering the firm. Although some family companies establish special development programs for family members, the Thompsons are treated in a fashion similar to other management trainees. They participate in management development meetings and are required to work up through the normal levels of management.

Spurs to Performance

Establishment of impartial measures of the performance of family members is not unique to the larger firms such as the Thompson company. One family distributorship, for example, places its family employees on sales contracts, thereby making their compensation and success in the organization strictly dependent on their selling ability.

A similar approach can be noted in the case of a sporting goods manufacturing concern. In this firm, the son has been given complete responsibility over the development of a new product line. This project provides the son with valuable management experience, and at the same time it tests his competency in all phases of the operation. In another family firm, the trust officers managing the family trust have been specifically charged with evaluating the boss's son. If he proves not capable, they are required to sell the firm.

Executive Evaluation

While their methods vary, many of the more successful firms seem to realize that the best interests of both the firm and the family require objectivity in the executive development of family members. This objectivity is particularly important to the company because the family employees tend to personify the organization's chief vices and virtues to the public, to the company's customers, and to the entire staff of the firm.

From the viewpoint of the family member being evaluated, such objectivity may prevent the relatives from unwittingly discriminating against him. Henry Ford for example, allowed his son, Edsel, little management influence out of the misguided belief that he lacked the "toughness" necessary to run the company. History has indicated that the Ford Motor Company had outgrown the father's brand of "toughness" and that, at the time, the son's approach was what the company needed.

Thus, this type of objective appraisal may allow the family relative to be himself, rather than a junior edition of the senior family members, a situation which benefits both the company and the individual. Finally, when the family member is required to earn his position, his own doubts about his abilities are lessened, the challenge of a career with the firm is increased, and his problem of winning the acceptance and confidence of the organization is minimized.

Coexistent with the policy of limiting family prerogatives, wiser companies, such as Thompson, place strong emphasis on attracting and developing non related management talent. In the Thompson company policy was developed initially when growth pressures had convinced the family of the impossibility of filling all the management needs from within the family. Currently, nonrelated executives outnumber the Thompson family in top management and are widely represented in the executive committee. Nonrelated executives participate in a liberal stock option plan and, as the chairman noted, many of the nonrelated executives have made their fortune in the company. In the past, nonfamily managers have even been president of the company. Such willingness ensures that the company is well managed, regardless of the stage of executive development of family members. It also partly explains the company's reputation in its industry as a "good place to work."

The owning family's willingness to open top company positions to nonrelated management talent seems to be a common attribute of most of the longer lived family companies. Three of the five past presidents of a five-generation, $300-million manufacturing firm, for example, were not related to the owning family. A similar situation exists in a family bank studied, as well as in many of the longer-lived firms researched. When such opportunities are made available to all employees, regardless of family ties, the family company seems to have little problem in attracting the necessary executive talent.

Conclusion

Popular opinion has it that when family and business are interrelated, a less efficient business enterprise generally results. But a close examination of the subject suggests that this belief may be unfounded. It ignores the fact that effective administrative practice is founded on an understanding of all human relationships as they affect an organization and not on a denial of them. Where such understanding is present, the family firm has generally evolved organizational procedures and traditions, bordering on law, that have capitalized on those aspects of the interrelationship which are of direct value to the long-term interests of the firm and family.

The success of many family companies indicates that ignorance of the relationships involved and not family participation per se is a key factor in the success or failure of such firms. Understanding the contribution a family may make to the firm's long-term strengths, analyzing the weaknesses involved, and implementing organizational restraints to control such problems, all are aspects of the manager's problem in a family firm.

Notes

1. Alfred D. Chandler, Jr., *Strategy and Structure* (Cambridge, Massachusetts, Massachusetts Institute of Technology Press, 1962), p. 64.
2. C. Roland Christensen, *Management Succession in Small and Growing Enterprises* (Boston, Division of Research, Harvard Business School, 1953), p. 175.
3. Perrin Stryker, "Would You Hire Your Son?" *Harvard Business Review*, March 1957, p. 228
4. *Harvard Business Review*, December 20, 1963, p. 74.
5. Judith Dolgins, "A Good Man is Hard to Keep," *Dun's Review and Modern Industry*, May 1963, as quoted by *The Executive*, August 1963, p. 21.
6. Perrin Stryker, op. cit., p. 228.
7. See Arnold C. Cooper, "R & D is More Efficient in Small Companies," *Harvard Business Review*. May-June 1964, p. 75.

By demonstrating their reliability and willingness to make true commitments in the appropriate circumstances, family businesses earn confidence and trust. As a result, they often gain competitive advantage as preferred business partners. Trust reduces the cost and hassle of doing business. Commitment to trust, reliability and mutual benefit is the kind of old-fashioned thinking that ideally positions family firms for the future.

Trust Gives You The Advantage

By John L. Ward and Craig E. Aronoff

You've heard older people talk about it. "A man's word used to be his bond," they say. "Business was done on a handshake – on trust. But now, it's all lawyers and fast talk and sue, sue, sue! Those days when you could trust somebody are gone."

There was a time when business was based on relationships, often family relationships. "I knew your father. I knew your grandfather" – these were common statements that meant "I know your values, your background, your reputation, and how important your reputation is to you. So we can do business based on trust."

Today things are different. Too many organizations seem faceless and uncaring. Employees seem to come and go constantly. New management comes in or a policy is altered, and everything changes. People who make decisions aren't around to implement them.

We know of a dynamic family firm that was excited by the prospect of a lucrative new venture. Success, however, required a reliable, trusting relationship with a large supplier. The smaller firm hesitated.

"We've had bad experiences dealing with bureaucratic companies," lamented the family firm's leader. "They're too shortsighted. In the long run, they pay for it, but they don't seem to care."

The enthusiasm for the opportunity was further dampened by the family company's fear that the supplier might someday renege on the relationship.

Instead of moving profitably forward, the owners pondered questions such as: "Can we trust them? Are their key people all informed and in agreement? Or will they go into our business and compete with us?" Precious time ticked away, and legal fees piled up as the family business's executives waded through layers of the supplier's managers seeking real decision makers and sewing up an agreement that seemed airtight.

With a clear notion of their own history and values, the owners of the family firm longed, as they put it, "for the good old days, when business was done on the spot."

But business relationships are not determined by the times; they are determined by the leaders. Some firms have eschewed the kinds of policies and practices that build commitment, loyalty, and trust. However, family firms that retain such fundamental values as guides to decisions and operations find themselves at a strategic advantage.

Family enterprises that demonstrate their commitments to venture partners or to the communities where they do business win confidence and trust. They make commitments more quickly, and their commitments tend to be long-lasting. They require less hassle. Often, people recognize these advantages of dealing with family companies and therefore prefer to do business with them.

In family firms, decision makers are easily identifiable and often directly involved in the implementation of their decisions. Owners' actions are tempered by the recognition that their reputations-and those of their heirs-are on the line. What you see is what you get for a long time to come.

Because reliable, trusting relationships seem rare in today's business world, they are not taken for granted. Smart business people know that trust reduces the costs of doing business.

Rapid rates of change and today's intense competitive pressures for speed, efficiency, and flexibility are driving all kinds of businesses to a variety of close working relationships that require foundations of trust, reliability, and long-term orientations. Because family firms so often foster such values, they are seen as desirable participants in such partnerships.

Some of these relationships are relatively informal. Others include more formal joint ventures or a variety of subcontracted or cooperative arrangements. They are used for purposes such as:

- Sharing technology, so that the businesses involved can reach more customers more quickly before the technology is copied or becomes obsolete.
- Sharing sales forces to get more coverage and make selling less expensive.
- Sharing marketing programs, to make promotion, mailing, and advertising more cost-effective.
- Subcontracting manufacturing, so that the contracting company can reduce costs and capital expenditures and increase its focus on what it does best, such as design and marketing.

As we've said before in this column, having your family's name on the door of your business intensifies concerns for quality and service. As customers see these concerns demonstrated in products and services and in a caring attitude toward the community, their trust for your business builds, and your company, in turn, prospers.

Some consider family businesses to be hopelessly behind the times.

On the contrary, we find that commitment to trust, reliability, and mutual benefit is exactly the kind of old-fashioned thinking that ideally positions family firms for the future. "What you see is what you get" is an old idea – but an important old notion that's new again.

With the reputation of your family on the line, with your personal integrity behind every handshake, and with the economic future of your heirs at stake, owning a family business is not only a significant responsibility but also an opportunity for an increasingly valuable competitive advantage.

This article was originally printed in *Nation's Business*, August 1991.
Copyright 1991, U.S.Chamber of Commerce. Reprinted with permission of the authors.

Two studies presented in this article indicate both performance and policy differences between large owner-controlled and manager-controlled firms in the same industry. Firms controlled by their owners have both much higher rates of return on investment and lower dividend pay-outs. The owner-controlled firms appear more efficient, yet are gradually being eliminated. This becomes a problem of both private and public concern. Managers and directors can hardly ignore this challenge to their internal Operations: what goals are they attempting to achieve? And government officials should investigate a neglected ala of significance for public policy: should the relative social responsiveness of the two types of firms be considered in enacting taxation and antitrust laws?

Ownership and Management: The Effect of Separation on Performance

By R. Joseph Monsen

The separation of ownership from control in the large corporation has been recognized for many years. What has not been understood, however, is the effect of such separation on the performance of the firm. Evidence now indicates that large owner-controlled companies outperform manager-controlled ones in terms of return on investment by a significant degree.

A few economists in the past, including the author, have suggested that the separation of ownership from control of the corporation creates a quite different motivation between owners and managers. Such difference in motivation may be ascribed to goal conflict of owners and managers that exists in our modern economic system because of the asymmetry between risks and rewards. This asymmetry appears to take the form of greater incentives and rewards for owners than managers in terms of risk-taking. Since recent research has suggested that motivation has far greater consequences upon economic efficiency than economists or others have commonly supposed, differences in goals and motivations between owner-managers and nonowner-managers may indeed explain the differential performance between the owner- and manager-controlled companies.

If owners and managers are motivated differently do these differences affect corporate policy? In other words, we may ask whether owner- and manager-controlled companies are basically different in terms of goals, outlook, and policies, or are differentiated only because owner-controlled firms try harder to produce a higher rate of return on their investment? The research cited offers inconclusive proof on this point. However, some recent evidence suggests that there are very basic policy differences between owner-controlled and manager-controlled companies beyond mere return. The author has assembled data which show that dividend policies are very different between the two types of companies. It now appears that manager-controlled firms tend to have higher earnings/payout ratios than firms controlled by their owners. While the industry in which the firm is located has a significant effect upon its dividend pay-out, the type of control appears to be even more significant in explaining the difference in dividend policy.

Such differences appear quite understandable if we look at the goals and incentives of both owners and managers. Due to the tax differential between capital gains and dividend income, a preference for a smaller dividend pay-out and greater earnings retention is a reasonable policy for a company controlled by a wealthy owner-manager. Further, there are noneconomic reasons (desire to rule a financial empire or continuance of family name or tradition) that can supply other explanations as to why an owner-managed firm would prefer to finance itself through high retained earnings rather than risk loss of control by participating extensively in outside capital markets.

Thus it appears that overt policy decisions, such as dividend pay-out, are influenced significantly by what type manager controls the company. Differences between these two types of firms in both performance and policy suggest that fundamentally there are quite separate goals and motivations at work for owners and managers. Such differences in outlook result in distinctly different behavior patterns between the two types of firms.

If we admit such differences do in fact exist, what are the implications? A number of questions come to mind.

Is motivation really the crux of the issue? Is motivation sufficiently crucial for efficiency that it affects the firm as strongly as our data suggest?

Are professional managers themselves merely less proficient than the owner-managers in large firms? Are business schools training professional but inefficient managers? Could this account for the difference in performance and behavior we observed?

Would different compensation schemes for management alter their behavior and goals? If so, what kind of a system could be devised that might be successful?

Most critically for the economy, are current tax policies eliminating the most efficient firms, forcing them to merge with and become manager controlled? Is profit becoming less important to the largest corporations?

If owner-controlled firms are more efficient in terms of return on investment, are manager-controlled firms more responsive to the demands of workers, consumers, and government? Which is better? These questions will be explored briefly after we have examined in more detail several of the studies mentioned above.

Summary of Results

In an attempt to shed some light on the behavior of owner-controlled and manager-controlled large firms, 72 corporations were studied from Fortune's list of the 500 largest industrial firms by sales in this country for a twelve-year period (1952-63). Six firms (three owner-controlled and three manager-controlled) from twelve different industries were compared. A firm was considered owner-controlled if 10 percent or more of the corporation stock was owned by one party. An analysis of the data revealed that the owner-controlled group of firms outperformed the manager-controlled firms by a considerable margin. The net income to net worth ratio was 75 percent higher for owner-controlled corporations over the twelve-year period. This indicates that these firms provide a much better return on the original investment, and suggests a better-managed capital structure and more efficient allocation of resources.

The effect of the type of industry on the net income to net worth ratio was statistically significant but only one-third the strength of the control-type effect; the size of the firm was not a significant factor. No other effect, including the control plus industry interaction, was statistically significant, indicating that *the owner- or manager-control factor affects all industries tested.*

In an attempt to look at policy differences, particularly dividend policy, 69 owner- and manager-controlled firms were studied from among the 200 largest nonfinancial corporations in this country. Again, owner control was defined as a minimum of 10 percent stock ownership in the corporation by one party, and firms of roughly the same size and same industry were compared. Utilizing an analysis of variance statistical technique, as in the first study, the results were once again quite clear. The type of industrial classification to which a firm belonged did influence the firm's dividend pay-out ration. However, the ownership type of the company had an even stronger e£ fact, statistically, upon the dividend policy than the type of industry to which the firm belonged. Further, no evidence was found that industry interaction with ownership type produces special effects upon dividend payout ratios. Thus, the evidence supports the existence of distinct dividend pay-out policies between owner-controlled and manager-controlled firms of approximately similar size in the same industry.

These two studies support the idea that the type of control strongly affects both the performance and the policy decisions of a company. In this sense, the traditional economic approach addressing firms from this aspect as simply one aggregate of behavior is seriously oversimplified.

Why, in the first study, should the owner-controlled firms outperform the manager-controlled firms? And why, in the second study, should the two types have very different and distinct dividend policies? The answer that seems most convincing is that two quite different motivational incentive systems are at work, emanating from the pursuit of different goals. It would seem that our business system is not generally structured to provide the same set of motivations or goals for both owners and managers. As a result, the behavior of our largest firms differs widely depending upon what group controls them.

Some Practical Implications

Motivation

In the past, economists have tended to ignore the effect of motivation upon economic activity. Only recently have some studies been made which yield evidence that motivation is considerably more important in influencing efficiency in the economy as a whole than economists traditionally have believed. Thus, the effect of the modern separation of ownership from management may have a motivational impact upon the performance of the firm-perhaps of greater consequence than allocative efficiency, which has been the main concern of past economic efficiency studies.

If motivation does have a significant effect upon the performance of the firm, what factors influence motivation? Does the separation of ownership and control in most large corporations have an effect upon motivation of management? Does such motivational difference, if it exists, between owners and managers affect the behavior of the firm? The data of the studies we have cited here certainly do suggest that owner- and manager-controlled firms behave differently. The differences in goals and motivations that we have posited seem the most plausible explanation. However, while the differences in behavior of the two types of firms can be observed empirically, our motivational explanation, sound as it may seem, is not definitely established. We can in final analysis only suggest explanations that seem consistent with the data.

While traditional economic theory recognizes only one motive for firm management – to maximize profit – economic theorists have recently suggested that the large firm attempts to maximize sales, growth, or the management's own lifetime income. In fact, different types of firms may pursue one or a combination of these and other goals, and in the real world the owner-controlled firm appears more likely to fit the picture of the world painted by traditional economic theory. Distinguishing between types of firms is important because the behavior of each firm with respect to profits depends upon certain elements of its internal structure

The professional manager, unlike the owner-manager, is probably more responsive to pressures from the various constituent groups of the firm such as workers, consumers, suppliers, stockholders, and the government. The professional manager is apt to respond to conflicting demands from these groups by balancing one off against the other or by utilizing compromise as an issue-settling device. The owner-manager, who views each dollar given to workers, suppliers, consumers, or the government as coming from his own pocket, is less likely to compromise. Further, the position of the owner-manager is a good deal more secure regarding his tenure in office than that of the professional manager. For, although professional management is generally autonomous in the large corporation, an executive may be sidetracked or replaced if he makes a bad blunder. The owner-manager, because of his stock ownership, seldom faces this problem. The risk and reward system for owners and managers is therefore quite different.

Because of these basic differences in the security and financial reward of their respective positions, the strategy to maximize the income of an owner-manager may be considerably different from that of a nonowner manager. Given the same goal, to maximize their wealth, the strategy, policies, and performance of the firm would probably be quite different depending on whether the company was owner- or manager-controlled.

Further study may reveal that there are also differences in behavior between various subtypes of owner and manager-controlled firms. Mutually owned corporations are a specific category needing further research, for they appear to form a quite distinct category of their own. All told, if motivation is a major factor influencing firm behavior, we could hypothesize that wherever the motivations of corporate leadership patterns have a distinct character, firm behavior should reflect that fact. Finally, if motivations and behavior are different between groups of firms, should this cause any change in current tax or antitrust policies to either encourage or discourage certain forms of economic behavior?

Professional Managers Less Proficient?

Two questions are associated with the idea that owner-managers seem to be outper-forming professional (nonowner) managers. First, is there any reason to feel that the abil-ity level differs between the two groups? One is hard put to see why one group should be any more able than the other. If anything, one might suspect that the professional man-ager who has worked his way up in the company without benefit of family or financial interest might actually be more capable. However, we have already noted that the profes-sional manager's goals, motivations, incentives, and range of alternatives for company pol-icy might be quite different from that of owner-managers. Since there is no reason to believe otherwise, the latter factors, rather than intrinsic ability, would seem most likely to explain the behavior differences found in our data.

The other question that comes to mind is whether the business schools are training professional but inefficient managers. Again there is no particular reason to suspect that business schools only train nonowner-type managers. Yet the suspicion does remain that the modern business school has created its own ideology and technique of business man-agement that may, in effect, be stifling creativity and entrepreneurship. Are the business schools merely turning out business bureaucrats? Is this the type of individual who is ris-ing to positions of leadership in the major corporations? Frankly, the business schools have not examined their products or them program with this possibility in mind. Most of the major schools in this country seem largely concerned with justifying them present approach or system. Them own ideology has thus fan gotten in the way of them looking objectively at them impact and effect upon the business system – except to enthuse over it for fund-raising purposes.

It could well be that business schools are basically turning out business bureaucrats who know how to rise in the corporate bureaucracy but lack the motivation of owner man-agers. Therefore, nonowner managers may make decisions that prevent the company from performing as profitably as the owner-controlled firm. Why should they make such decisions? A number of possibilities can be suggested, many of which could be significant. Does the professional nonowner manager prefer to minimize risk? lead a quiet life? make the firm overly conservative by using compromise techniques in decision making? grow and merge for the sake of growth or his own vanity (and possibly higher salary in a larg-er company) rather than for potential return on investment? All of these possibilities cast the manager in a negative light. Yet the results themselves, in terms of lower return on investment, cast aspersions upon either the management-controlled firm's efficiency and competence or its goals.

Compensation Schemes

If we assume that the difference in performance between owner- and manager-con-trolled firms is due basically to different strategies to achieve their individual goals, then we must ask whether incentives can be developed that would tend to bring together the goals of both owners and managers in manager-controlled firms. Is it possible to devise incentives that would induce managers to maximize the rate of return on owner's invest-ment when they themselves are not major owners? It would be most interesting to inves-tigate whether the various compensation schemes of large companies are directly corre-lated with the performance of the firm as to rate of return. However, there now appears to be little major difference between the compensation schemes for officers of the coun-try's largest corporations, at least not enough to expect substantial differences in incen-tives. Could marginal differences in incentives and clear-cut goals of the corporation (par-ticularly constraints upon decisions) have a significant effect?

The problem may involve not only the goals of the corporation, but also the range of decision alternatives managers feel they possess. Altering incentives may do no good if the bureaucratic system of the corporation itself effectively prohibits managers from making the same kind of decisions that owner-controlled firms can make. If less risk, flexibility, and internal decision-making coherence is possible within the manager-controlled firms, altering incentive systems may have no appreciable effect upon present performance.

Let us assume, however, that manager-controlled firms would perform as owner-controlled firms if the compensation system is altered so that the manager income is largely related to the company's return on investment. Is there any chance that this might merely cause an overly great concern for short-run profits and that they might suffer in the long run? This is a possibility, of course. The twelve-year span of our original study on the rate of return on investment is hardly what might be called a long-run period. Yet, at the same time, this is not a short-run period as far as management tenure is concerned. Plenty of "birds would have come home to roost" during our period of observation if an overly great concern on short-run return was typical. Certainly some reflection of the damage to these firms might be evident within the space of twelve years.

A serious problem not previously considered is that owner-controlled firms may not pay sufficient attention to the interests of their public consumers, workers, suppliers, and the community. It maybe that, on the average, manager-controlled firms may not pay sufficient attention to the interests of their public-consumers, workers, suppliers, and the community. It may be that, on the average, manager-controlled firms are more responsive to the demands of the public and them communities. If this is the case, we then face the problem of having to decide between firms internally efficient or firms externally responsive to their constituency and environment. At present there is no way of empirically proving that the large managerially-controlled firm is consciously or even inadvertently accepting smaller rates of return on the owner's capital in order to satisfy demands from other groups upon the firm. Or, put another way, we have no evidence to determine whether the manager- or the owner-controlled firm is the most responsive to social demands of the public and its community environment.

It is possible, however, that just such a choice between (1) efficiency and social responsibility or (2) between the redistribution of return on owner's investment and the public maybe the crux of this issue. No investigations have yet been made that can answer this perplexing and disturbing questions.

Tax Policies

Our data reveal that the owner-controlled firms, which appear most efficient in operations in terms of return on investment (the usual definition of efficiency for firms), are gradually being eliminated from among the largest corporations. Tax policies make it very difficult to pass on working control of these large corporations. Further, the huge size of these firms, due to mergers and internal growth, make the money required for working control increasingly exorbitant. These factors, when coupled with division among heirs, tend to gradually eliminate the large owner-controlled firms from among the largest 200 or 500 corporations in this country. Further, the ranks of new owner-controlled firms among these top corporations are not replenished as easily as before due to the above reasons, particularly because smaller firms have to merge for competitive reasons, for owner's diversification of holdings, and for estate tax payment.

All told, the trend toward the elimination of owner-controlled firms seems inexorable, yet these firms may be the most efficient ones in our economy. By allowing them to disappear we may be reducing our over-all level of efficiency and economic growth. Since the trend is so pronounced and well-known, it may seem strange that there has been no research by government or private sources to determine whether policies which permit and promote this trend are sound for society as a whole.

Perhaps (just as antitrust laws prohibit mergers and practices that reduce competition within an industry) we should also prohibit the elimination of owner-controlled firms by manager-controlled ones. Competition is not the only major value. If, however, further research could provide additional evidence that manager-controlled firms were more socially responsible, such evidence might tend to offset our findings of greater efficiency on the pant of owner-controlled firms.

The entire area of government policy needs greater study to determine what the actual (rather than intended) effects of legislation and policy are upon the society and economy as a whole. At present our national policy is too haphazard and untested to be able to say with confidence that our values and goals are being furthered by present public policy. Further research in this area is badly needed, and should be sponsored by the government as well as by private sources.

Managers More Responsive to Society?

This, of course, becomes the crux of the issue of public policy changes. If it could be shown that manager-controlled firms are more responsive to the needs and demands of their public environment, then the gradual elimination of owner-controlled firms might be considered socially appropriate. Our society at this stage of development would probably opt for firms that would be more concerned about local community and social problems, the safety of their products, and the pollution of the streams and air they use. Such criteria might well rank with or above greater efficiency and return on the owner's investment in a society such as ours.

However, the firm that shows itself more efficient in its use of resources and shows a higher rate of return in the competitive market should benefit society materially by being able to produce more goods at less cost. Yet, in an affluent society where the problem is indifference rather than lack of resources, we might indeed be further ahead in terms of society's total welfare to exchange some efficiency for more social responsiveness .

The question we cannot answer at this moment, however, is whether the manager- or owner-controlled firm is the more socially responsive – if, indeed, there is any difference at all between them. If the owner-controlled firm proved to be socially more responsible – along with its superior efficiency record – our public policy would need to be drastically revised.

Property ownership in our society now appears to be of considerable significance in determining how resources are used. This is as true for the use and development of urban land in our major cities as it is for the use of corporate resource. Yet whether society should be encouraging certain types of ownership use and discouraging other types has not been clearly thought out in our public policies. Studies that are available have yet to be translated into relevance for tax policy, for example.

The implications of the studies mentioned here suggest that managers, owners, general investors, and the makers of public policy need to look carefully into the performance and policies of corporations where ownership control may provide different goals and motivations for different groups of firms. We have argued here that current public policies do not take these factors into account in the developing of tax or antitrust legislation and policy.

Conclusions

The studies discussed here offer empirical evidence that the separation of ownership from control has indeed produced different and distinct types of economic behavior. Both performance and policy differences are observable. Large owner-controlled firms in the same industry have much higher rates of return on investment and lower dividend payouts than manager-controlled firms. The first finding may or may not be the result of conscious policy; nonetheless, the performance differential is certainly there. The finding on dividend pay-out is the conscious result of policy decisions.

Our observation that the owner-controlled firm is more efficient but is gradually being eliminated was suggested by both Berle and Means in their original study nearly forty years ago and confirmed by Larner's recent one. Since this is a problem of both private and public concern, it should be investigated to see if the public policy which encourages it should be changed.

At the very least, managers, directors, investors, and government officials should give immediate attention to the reasons why owner-controlled firms have higher rates of return than comparable manager-controlled firms.

There may be considerable opportunities for increasing the rate of return in manager-controlled companies. Managers and directors can hardly ignore this challenge to their internal operations, and government officials should not let this opportunity pass to investigate a neglected area of significance for public policy. Could a case be made that manager-controlled firms should be constrained from acquiring owner-controlled ones? What would be the total effect upon our economy and society? The relative social responsiveness of the two types of firms could settle argument as to whether large owner-controlled firms should be gradually eliminated from our economy as present public policy encourages.

The main justification for the present public policy is either (1) that redistribution of economic power is encouraged by permitting managers to replace owner in controlling our largest firms, or (2) that manager-controlled firms have a higher social worth to society in some way, perhaps in greater social responsiveness to environmental problems. As we have said, the latter has yet to be established. Thus, this whole area of public policy needs investigation. It may well be that drastic changes in our taxation and antitrust laws need to be made. It is time, as well, that directors and management looked into their own motivation to determine what goals they are attempting to achieve and in what order of preference. The data here certainly cast suspicion on the assumption that manager-controlled firms are placing return on investment as their prime goal. If they are, they are inexplicably less efficient in pursuing this goal than the owner-controlled firms. It would seem more likely at this stage of investigation to posit motivational and goal differences between owner- and manager-controlled firms as the critical factors in influencing their performance and policies.

We can only hope that the studies cited here will create greater concern and further research. Both pubic and corporate policy may be badly in need of overhauling-how and where is the next question.

1. H. Leibenstein, "Allocative Efficiency vs. X-Efficiency," *American Economic Review*, LVI (June, 1966).
2. R. J. Monsen, J. S. Chiu, and R. J. Pulliam, "Dividend Policy and Corporate Control: Some Implications for the Theory of the Firm" unpublished.
3. R. J. Monsen, J. S. Chiu, and D. E. Cooley, "The Effect of Separation of Ownership and Control on the Performance of the Large Firms," *Quarter Journal of Economics*, LXXXII (August, 1968). The findings of D. R. Kamerschen in the June, 1968 issue of the *American Economic Review* appear inconclusive on this subject due to the design and methodology of the study.

The past decade has brought changes in our understanding of family businesses. This article identifies 10 "megatrends," which are evolving changes fundamental to understanding and working with family businesses. Identified trends include focusing on generational transitions rather than business succession; team management and ownership as a developing norm; the increasing importance of strategic planning in family business; increasing financial sophistication; increasing managerial professionalism; refining retirement; expanding roles for women; increasing sensitivity of professional service providers to family business; and increasing availability and quality of family business education and consulting.

Megatrends in Family Business

By Craig E. Aronoff

Introduction

The journalists who call seeking insights about family business often ask, "So, what's new in the world of family-owned enterprise?" "What trends do you see?" I am often tempted to answer, "What should be new in an institution that is as old as civilization?"

But with the multitude of professionals and scholars who now focus on family business (which, as I note later, is itself one of the major trends in the family business universe), there is reason to hope that original insights and knowledge might lead to changes in the "best practices" for family business. And, indeed, although it is not obvious on a day-to-day basis, if we can possibly step back and find the proper perspectives for measurement, we can discover – lo and behold! – the glacier has moved. In fact, there are changes and news.

Moreover, some of those changes are fundamental to our understanding of family businesses and how they work, justifying the term "megatrends." I offer 10 megatrends here. Perhaps there are more, or maybe I've included too many. Perhaps I am simply reporting on how my own understanding has evolved and thus projecting those changed perceptions onto the field. I do believe, however, that the collective consciousness about family business has changed in some rather profound ways.

Trend 1: Generational Transition Is Replacing Succession Planning

The old wisdom was succinct and to the point: The critical issue facing family business is to identify, develop, and install the successor to the business's top executive. "Family business succession" seemed the focus of everyone purporting to work with family firms. "Only 30% of family business survive the second generation for lack of succession planning" was the predominate insight and "how-to" guides and checklists proliferated.

But slowly, as the field gained experience, we began to recognize that the analogy of "passing the baton" from one runner to the next was terribly inadequate. Succession rarely involves only an incumbent and a successor. Instead, the process requires the perspective of a multigenerational time frame and takes place in a rich stew of social, cultural, financial, legal, strategic, moral, and other dimensions that resist neat, linear thinking. Indeed, when large-scale research permits correlations between various family business factors and multigenerational survival, succession planning is not shown as statistically significant. Strategic planning, an active board of directors, and frequent family meetings, however, do have significant correlations with success in passing the business from one generation to the next.

No longer satisfied with the notion of succession, many think leaders in the field now refer to generational transitions in family business. The changed perspective recognizes the importance of not just executive leadership, but of family and shareholder leadership as well. Moreover, the complexity of the simultaneous metamorphosis of personal, family, and corporate finances (including the effort to deal with the estate tax issue); strategic and structural changes in the business; relational, structural, and value changes in the family; altered expectations related to governance and accountability; and developments and changes experienced by key family member/owner/managers can only be encompassed by the broadest and deepest-possible understanding of the totality of "generational transitions" in family business systems.

Trend 2: Management Is Becoming a Team Effort

"You can only have one boss." "The buck stops here." "You must choose and install your successor." All these phrases represent common wisdom of the ages. But increasingly, particularly in second-generation family businesses, business leadership rests with a team. To some extent, this reality reflects the larger world of management thinking in which the team approach has become much more the norm.

Given this affinity that siblings and their parents have for equality, perhaps it is not surprising that team management is given a friendly reception in family business. What's new is the notion that installing a successor team can be an appropriate approach rather than a cop-out. For that matter, under certain circumstances and situations, installing a single omnipotent successor is clearly seen as the wrong approach. Indeed, according to the most recent Arthur Andersen/MassMutual survey, 42% of family business are considering co-presidents for the next generation. Even when one family member is selected as business leader, other family members in the business will likely act as members of the business leadership team.

The challenge, of course, is to assure that appropriately selected family management teams are properly developed and structured so that they can function effectively.

Trend 3: Ownership Is Becoming a Team Effort

As with executive leadership, benchmark advice on ownership has increasingly reflected a multiple rather than singular reality. Business-owning families have become more thoughtful about ownership goals and, therefore, are less likely to vest a single individual with ownership control as a knee-jerk reaction to potential conflict.

Alternatives to autocracy are more often recognized as ways of managing conflict. Accountability as a two-way street seems an increasingly accepted norm, backed up by family policies, family councils, and real boards of directors that include objective outsiders. Investing power with a single chief executive/controlling owner/patriarch is sometimes more a reflection of an entrepreneur's control needs than the appropriate process for assuring business and family success.

Trend 4. Strategic Management Is Becoming Important

Traditional views of family business evolved at a much less dynamic time in the history of our economy and society. When social and economic changes are slow, an entrepreneur can fill a need and, over time, perfect the process and organization used to produce or deliver a service or product. Having recognized a need and developed an efficient process for filling it, the elder generation could pass the necessary knowledge, contacts, and capital so that the next generation can enjoy their parents' niche. The voice of experience and the wisdom of the ages should be heeded in the grooming of the next generation.

Where strategies once lasted for generations and strategic evolution was slow, recognizing the speed of current socioeconomic transformation now has become a veritable cliché. Where once management was primarily about conformity and control, it is now about continuous innovation and improvement. As a result, comfort levels afforded by consistency and predictability are gone.

ARONOFF

29

Family businesses with traditions of entrepreneurship may have an advantage during these conditions of change. ("Make change your tradition!") But the dynamics of generational transition are further complicated by the velocity of required strategic change. Conflicts over business strategy, risk, and the appropriate managerial culture and style needed for success in a rapidly changing environment make transitions more difficult.

Family businesses that embrace the process of strategic change and view the younger generation as a resource to that process are much more likely to successfully navigate generational transition. Business strategy and strategic management have thus risen on the priority list of generation transition issues.

Trend 5. Financial Sophistication Is Becoming a Necessity

Financial management of the family business used to be straightforward. A business was bootstrapped or started with a loan from Uncle Harry and typically had as its goal making plenty of cash (but not profit) and getting and staying out of debt. Sophisticated financial management was for Wall Street, not Main Street.

With the Wall Street mentality now exploring every available market niche, ceding the skills of sophisticated financial management to the competition is dangerous. When continued competitiveness requires constant reinvestment and strategic risk, simply earning enough to provide family members a decent lifestyle cannot assure survival.

Family businesses must now go beyond "breaking even higher and higher" as a guide to success. Executives and nonactive stockholders need to know their way around profit-and-loss statements and balance sheets. ROI (return on investment), RONA (return on net assets), and EVA (economic value added) are concepts with which family businesses are becoming increasingly comfortable.

As investing activity has gained attention and exposure, family business executives can also expect more sophisticated questions from family stockholders. They too want to know more about their company's strategy, performance, and finances. As one family business leader recently said: "It's pretty scary when you find yourself in a sophisticated discussion with your family on valuation methodology. But then discussing it is a whole lot better than fighting over it."

Trend 6. Professional Management Is Replacing Entrepreneurial Management

As Collins and Porras suggested in *Built to Last* (1994), a business may be better off in the long run if it did not spring from an heroic founder. Entrepreneurial giants are a tough act to follow in so many ways!

Traditionally, family-member managers were contrasted with professional, "nonfamily" managers. That distinction is increasingly seen as irrelevant, at best, and dangerous, at worst. Family members are expected more and more to meet or exceed the highest levels of executive professionalism, including educational achievement and career success experienced outside the family business.

The result is management that is less idiosyncratic than can be found in entrepreneurial models. The founder is increasingly less likely to say to his successor, in effect, "sit here and learn how I do it." That founder too often had become a self-fulfilling prophet, claiming that "this business can't survive without me" and then proving himself right.

Professionalism rather than idiosyncrasy is increasingly the standard by which all family executives in family firms are judged. The family dimension means that professional management is married to family values, long-term perspective, and ownership with a human face. Family ownership and leadership do not excuse lack of discipline, accountability, consistency, or responsibility.

Trend 7. New Roles Are Defining and Replacing Retirement

"Set a retirement date, announce it publicly, and honor it," has been the traditional advice given to senior-generation chief executives of family businesses. "They'll carry me out feet first," has often been the incumbent's answer. Requiring retirement is good advice for those who will take it – but many will not, preferring to continue working or to semi-retire.

"I'm retired, more or less," said the eldergeneration leader. "I hate that," said his successor, "because I never know when he's retired more and when he's retired less."

Rather than focusing on retirement, family businesses increasingly focus on new roles for elder leaders – either outside or inside the business. A person who has devoted a lifetime to a business, deriving fulfillment and identity from it, must transition to something also filled with meaning and identity. And if the elder stays with the business, he or she is more likely to have a clear role and to actively clarify who the new leaders are by deferring to them. The one third of family business leaders who will hang around, increasingly pass the baton but stay on to watch, help, and cheer.

Trend 8. Women's Roles Are Continuing to Expand

The widow who becomes chairperson, the supportive wife who keeps the books, the behind the-scenes "chief emotional officer" are all stereotypical women's roles in family businesses. The blended business and family goals of family business systems, however, create a more flexible environment invested in the success of the next generation regardless of sex.

Historically, family businesses commonly had "no women" and "no wives" rules (whether formal or informal). In today's world of family ambition and increasing gender neutrality, women's roles encompass higher achievement in organizational hierarchies. Perhaps more importantly, women are more active in a wider range of roles. Sibling management and ownership teams usually and normally include women. Women who are not employed in the business are more likely to be educated, active, and impassioned owners whose insights and inputs are encouraged and honored rather than relegated to pillow talk." Common wisdom" now suggests inclusion rather than exclusion of spouses at family ownership meetings.

I don't suggest that gender issues have ceased to exist – they will continue as long as gender differences exist. But, in more and more families and in family businesses in general, gender is becoming a nonissue as it relates to leadership, ownership, and participation.

Trend 9. Professional Service Providers Are Becoming More Sensitive

Many if not most accountants, lawyers, bankers, and insurance professionals have long recognized that the majority of their clients are family businesses. At one time, they happily dealt with their clients' business issues, but usually considered family issues or issues at the juncture of family and business to be separate, distracting, dangerous, and discomforting. Confronted with family issues, their advice was to act rationally, or frequently they suggested selling the business before conflict could erode its value. Family conflict was often viewed as a threat to maintaining the client relationship or an opportunity to generate transaction fees.

These days, many professional service providers have become sensitive to and sophisticated in family business issues. They are more likely to recognize the diversity of family businesses and deal with them as unique systems. Increasingly they are willing to discuss the goals of individuals and families, eschewing the assumption that if family businesses do not fit into stereotypical motivational and reasoning patterns, they need to change their nature. Some professionals have gone so far as to educate themselves in family systems and hone their own listening skills. A few even embrace the notion that technical competence must be combined with a willingness to offer client-centered compassion that includes the ability to creatively respond to the process and the content of family business issues.

Unfortunately, in too many cases, the business service professionals' sensitivity is not to the real needs of family businesses but to family businesses as a market. Some advertise their family business expertise hoping to sell their traditional services and approaches to family businesses. Others, in fields ranging from psychiatry to financial planning, refer to themselves as family business consultants, but lack the required multidisciplinary competencies to be effective in that role. Still others have added services that family businesses use, such as accountants offering to facilitate family meetings – situations in which they are simply not qualified.

The good news is that more and better professional services are now available to family businesses than ever before. The bad news is that caveat emptor – let the buyer beware – has never before been as relevant or as important as it is today, from the perspective of family business consumers of professional services.

Trend 10. Family Business Education and Consulting Are Becoming Realities

Little more than a decade ago, universities routinely ignored the realities of family business. Now, more than 100 universities in the United States and throughout the world offer forums, seminars, courses, and research on family business. Where once the literature of family business consisted of a few articles and books, today an entire library could easily be devoted to what' written on family business. And what was once a handful of consultants devoting their careers to thoughtful service of family businesses, family business specialists are now practicing in most U. S. markets, and many work in all the world' developed economies. Family business owners have occasionally complained that they now receive too much attention!

Although millions of family businesses exist, only a small minority are likely to be consumers of products and services for the family business, and they will be consumers only at certain points in the lives of their businesses. The family businesses are changing and the family business field is continuing to mature, however, the family business marketplace will increasingly determine which institutions will gain the privilege of a family business's trust.

References

Collins, James C., & Porras, Jerry I. (1994). *Built to last: Successful habits of visionary companies.* New York: Harper Business.

CHAPTER 2
SUCCESSION

It has been said that the three most important issues confronting the family business are succession, succession...and succession. To remain a family business, each generation must be succeeded by the next, the ultimate management challenge.

Even among large, public businesses the effort to achieve family management succession remains amazingly strong in our society. This tendency is somewhat surprising in light of the myths that exist about family business succession and of what can be described as the succession conspiracy-forces aligned to resist succession planning.

To achieve familial succession, the generation in power must let go and the inheriting generation must desire involvement. Fortunately, guidelines and advice are available about navigating the succession process so that fewer family businesses will confront the reality of being the last generation.

While entrepreneur/parents are often ill-prepared and ill-suited to serve as teachers to next generation successors, the role is essential to multigenerational success. The article offers guidance on how to be a more effective teacher.

Chief's Toughest Job: Teacher

By Craig E. Aronoff and John L. Ward

If a business is to survive, someone must be prepared to carry it on. That simple truth pervades all management. After all, the manager's ultimate job is to develop his or her successor.

Management succession is especially critical in a family business. While entrepreneurs play many roles in their careers, none is more crucial or more difficult than that of teacher. And none is more important to the business's survival in the family.

Successful business owners get that way by doing many things well. They are great innovators and builders. They have incredible energy and resilience. Unfortunately, they are often lousy teachers, coaches, and counselors-especially of their own mature children.

It has been said that most self-made men are smart enough to employ college professors to train their sons. Indeed, we strongly recommend that entrepreneurs use both professors and nonfamily managers to guide significant aspects of a next-generation executive's development. The owner may delegate some – though certainly not all – of the teacher's duties, but they cannot be postponed indefinitely if the owner hopes for a smooth transition.

It is not surprising that entrepreneurs shun the responsibility of teaching. Entrepreneurs are usually ill-suited and ill-prepared for the teaching role. The personality required to start and grow a business eventually works against its continuity. Entrepreneurs are doers who do not see themselves as teachers. They are impatient. They take action, set and achieve goals, and control outcomes.

But teaching does not work that way. The art of teaching is the art of assisting discovery. It is patient. It demands activity by the student more than by the teacher. It requires letting go rather than control, standing aside rather than wading in.

Perplexed by this dilemma, one entrepreneur put it to us this way: "I need to feel I'm always accomplishing something. I need to see the concrete results of my labors. How do you know you're contributing if all you're doing is giving advice or responding to questions?"

His question reveals yet another difficulty of the teaching role. In the later stages of the entrepreneur's career, self-doubt and fear may grow. Reasserting one's value to the organization may lead to furious action.

Many founders cannot resist the temptation to spend their last years noticing things that are not yet perfect in their businesses and directing others to fix them. No one sees more that needs "fixing" than the entrepreneur who built the business and knows its every detail. The owner may even rationalize that he or she is meeting the responsibility to teach by being an excellent role model.

In reality, the opposite is true. Rather than putting the organization in the best shape for transition to new leadership, the owner may be undermining his or her future and destroying relations with the successor.

Eventually the business builder must recognize that he or she won't be around to attend to these problems. Sooner or later the owner must trust that the successor will do the job – and do it well.

In the meantime, by publicly pointing out problems and telling others to take action, the owner weakens the successor, shows to all in the company a lack of faith and respect in the successor's management capability, and raises doubt about the future.

Some entrepreneurs work hard to bite their tongues. They realize the consequences of taking personal action and circumventing a successor. But concerns over the business's imperfections build inside such entrepreneurs. At the first opportunity – perhaps when the successor approaches the entrepreneur for advice or, more likely, for reinforcement on a decision made – the founder deluges the successor with observations and recommendations.

As a result, the successor increasingly attempts to avoid the founder. The successor and the rest of the organization feel that the founder doesn't respect their abilities.

The founder in turn concludes that the successor lacks respect for the founder's experience. The founder may decide that the successor has character flaws or inadequate abilities. A cycle of vigilance and declining mutual respect sets in.

As the relationship between founder and successor disintegrates, the organization suffers. A power struggle ensues in which even in winning, the entrepreneur loses. What a sad final chapter in the career of a person who deserves nothing but honor and respect. The founder built a business but can't pass it on – at least, not smoothly.

We make several suggestions to founders – teaching techniques if you will – to help overcome this inherent problem in family firms:

- When you see a problem, don't tell others to fix it; wait for a private time to discuss it with your successor. Let him or her take action.
- Establish a regular meeting schedule to discuss problems with your successor.
- At other times, when your successor asks a question or shares a thought, respond only to the subject that has been raised. Don't dredge up other issues that you want to discuss. Save them for the regular meeting.
- Keep in mind that teachers – and great leaders – are known more by the success of their followers than by what they do themselves.

To successors: Be patient. Recognize how difficult it is for an entrepreneur to be a good teacher.

To founders: Take joy in knowing that the greatest gift you can leave your successor is your trust and respect.

You'll know how good a teacher you are by how often your successor seeks your counsel. Make that the action and achievement you seek.

This article was originally printed in *Nation's Business*, January 1991.

Copyright 1991, U.S. Chamber of Commerce. Reprinted with permission of the authors.

By examining the business continuity practices of family held firms in one industry, this article describes actual business practices and evaluates prescriptions offered by family business experts.

Selected Correlates of Business Continuity Planning in the Family Business

By Stewart C. Malone

The literature on family businesses presents a recurring theme: an owner-manager who through years of hard work has built a successful and valuable enterprise and then, by failing to address certain critical business continuity issues, endangers the long-term health or even the existence of the enterprise. Since most of the literature is confined to single case studies or illustrations, how prevalent is this problem? Since numerous authors have offered varying advice on how these business continuity problems can be resolved, how are we to judge the effectiveness of any of these prescriptions?

The focus of this article is the actual business continuity practices of family-held firms in one industry. In addition to surveying the practices these firms employ, this study seeks to examine certain prescriptions that have been offered by theorists in the field. The first underlying premise of this study is that, whether or not it is desired that the business continue in the family, firms that consciously plan for continuity are more likely to survive. A second premise is that the value of a going concern exceeds the value of one whose prospects are in disarray – that is, a firm with succession plans and managers in place, whether family or professional, is a more valuable asset than a firm requiring either replacement managers or a turnaround.

The Challenge of Business Continuity

Given Churchill and Hatten's (1987) "biological imperative" of aging, it is exceedingly easy to criticize family business owners for failing to plan for the continuity of the business. Even a relatively simple task, such as creating a will, may be ignored; Rosenblatt, de Mik, Anderson, and Johnson (1985) give examples of substantial problems resulting from the absence of a current will. But the owner-manager's will, which will dictate ownership (and possibly managerial control) of the family business, represents the maker's decisions regarding the personal competence, worth, and responsibility of his or her heirs. It is not easy to decide that child A is incompetent to run the business but that child B is competent. Even harder than making the decision will be telling children A and B of the decision. Likewise, the will probably represents the latest thinking on tax and estate law, an area of expertise that seems to change as soon as one comes to understand it. When viewed as a culmination of a multitude of decisions, even the basic will becomes a challenging task in the business continuity effort.

Review of the Literature

Multiple categories of factors are likely to influence the level of continuity planning in the family business (Handler and Kram, 1988). One such grouping would be the organizational characteristics of the business. Is the business large and successful, or is it a marginal performer? Does the firm's management actively plan for the future, or is it reactive? A second category of variables would be related to the current owner-manager. Certain demographic and psychological characteristics may influence the continuity planning effort. Given the complexity of family relationships, there exist a plethora of potential relationships, and the scope of this research is confined to a few that have been prominently cited in the literature.

Organizational Characteristics. Planning of the continuity of the family business can be influenced by any one of a number of factors, but a major consideration is certainly the size of the business. Timmons (1985) notes that the survival rate of small companies improves as the size of the business increases. In a study by Ambrose (1983), 71 percent of the terminated or transferred businesses had fewer than ten employees. The owner-managers of smaller companies may have fewer resources or less time to devote to such activities as planning, which are perceived as ancillary to primary duties. Likewise, smaller companies may be marginal financial performers. While the owners of these low performers may be satisfied with the income produced and may have a limited number of alternative career choices, they may well recognize that the business is not worth a major continuity effort. It also may be difficult to attract potential successors to the smaller business. The larger the company, however, the more likely it is to be an important financial asset to the owner-manager and his or her family. Given this significance, one would expect there to be a greater level of planning for continuity, whether or not the owner-manager wishes the business to continue to be managed by the family. This expectation is formalized as the first proposition of this study.

P1: There is a positive relationship between the size of the business and the level of business continuity planning.

Although planning for business continuity and management succession is critical for the long-term health of the business, a more general type of strategic planning has also been found to be beneficial for the smaller company. In an early empirical study, Mayer and Goldstein (1961) found lack of systematic planning to be a major reason for small-business failure. Robinson (1982) found that small firms that engaged in outsider-based strategic planning outperformed those that did not. Bracker (1982) concluded that small dry-cleaning firms that used strategic planning outperformed control groups on numerous economic criteria. In a later study, however, Robinson and Pearce (1984) found no significant differences in performance among fifty small banks, some of which engaged in planning and some of which did not. Sexton and Van Auken (1985) found that firms engaging in a higher level of strategic planning failed at a lower rate than firms engaging in less strategic planning.

While much of the research on strategic planning applies to smaller firms in general, an increasing body of literature pertains to the family-owned business, particularly in the area of management succession. Birley (1986) notes that one of the major issues faced by the firm is the question of choosing a successor. Ambrose (1983, p. 55) concludes that the family-owned business must "ultimately select between transfer [of ownership] and termination. Whichever is chosen, the task will be accomplished more successfully if the options are fully understood and the process is planned."

Since strategic planning involves devising a course of action to achieve some future desired state, and since the owner-manager's departure from the business is eventually inevitable, firms that engage in strategic planning will probably also prepare for the future continuity of the business. One would expect to see a "planning orientation" (Ward, 1987), addressing general strategic issues as well as business continuity issues in the planning process. This is the basis for the second proposition.

P2: There is a positive relationship between the level of strategic planning and the extent of planning for business continuity.

Obviously, planning for business continuity is contingent on many more factors than strategic planning. An encompassing and critical factor cited by Churchill and Hatten (1987) is the degree of family harmony. The literature on family businesses is replete with examples of acrimonious relations among family members. Many of these works discuss ways to reduce disharmony, treating it as a dependent variable. Rather than imputing causality, this study examines the relationship between family harmony and planning for the continuity of the business. A family business characterized by a high degree of harmony among family members is one of the most valued work environments, and continuity of such a business may be important to family members, irrespective of its financial performance. Likewise, the literature cites family businesses in which relationships are very poor, and the termination of these businesses may be the most desirable outcome for these family members. For example, the patriarch of the Bingham communications empire in Kentucky dismantled the highly successful family business after a family feud racked the firm.

Perceived family harmony is an exceedingly complex concept. For example, the level of harmony may differ according to whether one is looking at inter- or intragenerational relationships. Likewise, the absence of vigorous debate and disagreement, while indicating an apparent high level of harmony, may actually mask relationships where conflict and rivalries are merely submerged. Finally, there exists a question of whose perception of harmony is being examined. Many senior-generation owner-managers may simply be oblivious to or may severely underestimate the degree of conflict extant in their organizations and families. A complete examination of the harmony concept is well beyond the scope of this research, but its frequent mention in the literature leads to a third proposition.

P3: There is a positive relationship between the level of perceived family harmony and the level of planning for business continuity.

While planning for business continuity may be a prudent step, not only for ensuring the business's survival but also for conserving the family's assets, many owner-managers do not view it as a pleasant task. As one of Beckard and Dyer's (1983, p. 61) founders said, "It's preparing for your own death, and it's very difficult to make contact with the concept of death emotionally." If continuity planning is not an altogether enjoy able job, what makes an owner-manager undertake this task? One possible answer is the urging or the assistance of an outsider, yet there are few areas in which so much conflicting advice and evidence exist. Danco (1975) argues that outsiders force an owner-manager to address legitimate business issues that he or she may prefer to avoid. Likewise, Robinson (1982) found that firms that engaged in outsider-based strategic planning outperformed firms without this outsider perspective. Levinson (1971), Barnes and Hershon (1976), and Ward (1987) suggest that outsiders can provide an objective perspective that may defuse personal conflicts and enhance the business continuity effort. Outsiders may interact with the family business in a variety of roles, but Danco (1975) argues that a firm's board of directors should be composed of persons who are neither family members nor employees, and Ward and Handy's (1988) study reports a high level of CEO satisfaction with outside boards. Ford's (1988) findings failed to confirm many of the expected benefits of outside boards. Indeed, the results of Ford's study seem to indicate that a board of insiders was of greater perceived value than the traditionally advocated outside board. Some of the differences between Ward and Handy's (1988) study and Ford's (1988) may be explained by the different nature of the samples (that is, Inc. 500 firms versus more mature companies). Of greater interest here is the role that the presence of the board may play in continuity planning. In Ford's (1988) sample, there was some evidence of continuity planning, although not at a significant level. Likewise, Ward and Handy's (1988) boards reported little involvement in succession issues, but the authors surmise that the mere presence of the board helped to resolve these issues. Ward and Handy's findings, and certainly those of Ford, cause a significant amount of skepticism, but from the preponderance of prescriptive literature we advance the following proposition for testing.

P4: There is a positive relationship between the percentage of outsiders on the board and the level of business continuity planning.

Personal Characteristics. Since the business continuity effort is largely under the control of the current owner-manager (Lansberg, 1988), are there any personal characteristics that may have a relationship to business continuity planning? Handler and Kram (1988) provide a conceptual, multilevel framework for many characteristics, and Peay and Dyer (1989) show an empirical relationship between owner-managers' power orientation and succession planning. Given the certainty of aging and eventual death, the age of the owner-manager should be an important factor in continuity planning. As Lansberg (1988) notes, the need for succession planning is not typically seen until the owner-manager enters the later stages of life; if the owner-manager is relatively young, the perceived need for continuity planning may be minimal. As the owner-manager ages, and as friends and business colleagues succumb to various ailments, the idea of one's own mortality and the need to plan for one's replacement become far more salient.

P5: There will be a positive relationship between the age of owner-managers and the extent of business continuity planning.

Another personal characteristic that may influence the planning for business continuity is the owner-manager's locus-of-control orientation. Individuals who possess a highly internal locus of control tend to believe that they, rather than outside forces, control their fate. Subjects with an external locus-of-control orientation tend to view their condition as a result of luck, chance, fate, or the influence of powerful others. Miller, Kets de Vries, and Toulouse (1982) showed that CEOs with an internal locus-of-control orientation tended to implement innovative and proactive policies in small firms. For family firms, two alternative and opposing arguments can be made in regard to locus of control. The more traditional argument would be that a highly internal owner-manager would be proactive and advocate continuity planning, since his or her involvement would largely dictate the immediate future of the business. However, frequently cited factors, such as the fear of death, fear of loss of control, and loss of self-esteem, may alter this relationship in the family business context. The internal owner-manager faced with these negative outcomes may choose to maintain control indefinitely and avoid any continuity planning. Likewise, an individual who shows a highly internal orientation may believe that aging and death are largely under his or her control. Recognizing that alternative arguments can be made regarding this relationship, the following is proposed.

P6: The more internal the owner-manager's locus of control, the higher the level of business continuity planning..

Methodology

A questionnaire was constructed to examine the relationship between the variables already mentioned and planning for business continuity. Level of strategic planning was assessed with the five classification categories developed by Sexton and Van Auken (1982):

Strategy level 0: no knowledge of next year's sales, profitability, or profit implementation plans

Strategy level 1: knowledge only of next year's sales, but no knowledge of coming industry sales, company profit, or profit implementation plans

Strategy level 2: knowledge of next year's company and industry sales, but no knowledge of company profit or profit implementation plans

Strategy level 3: knowledge of company and industry sales and anticipated company profits, but no profit implementation plans

Strategy level 4: knowledge of next year's company and industry sales, anticipated profits, and profit implementation plans.

The extent of continuity planning focused on two different areas of succession planning. The first area concerned the legal aspects of estate planning, and respondents were asked to rate their plans on a five-point scale, describing the degree to which they had a current will that accurately reflected their wishes regarding the disposition of the business; had "keyman" life insurance or a buy-sell contract to pay estate taxes, buy out other stockholders, or compensate the company for the loss of the CEO's services; and possessed a recent valuation of the business (which was considered evidence that some estate planning had taken place).

The second area of continuity planning focused on the more personal aspects of the continuity effort. Again, respondents were asked to rate their companies on a five-point scale, saying whether they had a formally designated successor who would replace the current CEO in the event of death or disability and had clearly communicated the owner-manager's succession plan to heirs and employees. While the use of a five-point scale (1 = definite no; 3 = not sure; 5 = definitely yes) to measure what essentially should be yes/no questions may seem inappropriate, the construct being measured is not the actual presence of a current and valid will but the owner's perception of having a will that is both current and valid. Individual scores on each of the five questions were summed to yield a total score for business continuity planning. Cronbach's alpha for the summary score was 0.78.

The owner-manager's locus-of-control orientation was assessed with the scale developed by Rotter (1976). The composition of the board of directors was assessed as the percentage of nonfamily members and/or nonemployees relative to total board membership. Perceived family harmony is a complex construct and is likely to be multidimensional. Since the purpose of this research was not an in-depth examination of any one particular component of the continuity effort, respondents were asked to characterize the degree of harmony among family members involved in the business (1 = very disharmonious, 5 = very harmonious). The owner-managers were also asked what degree of confidence they had that the business would continue with the same level of performance should they die tomorrow.

A mailing list was compiled from the 1985 membership director of the North American Wholesale Lumber Association and was supplemented by companies listed in the 1986 *Lumbermen's RedBook*. A questionnaire was mailed to the owner-managers of 335 wholesale lumber dealers throughout the United States. Businesses that were obviously publicly held were excluded. A reminder notice was sent to each company three weeks after the original questionnaire was mailed. Usable responses were received from fifty-eight CEOs, producing a usable response rate of 19.5 percent. Companies ranged in size from 2 to 228 employees, and all of the respondents had other family members involved in their businesses as employees. While the questionnaires guaranteed the respondents anonymity, 26 firms voluntarily identified themselves, and telephone interviews were conducted with 25 of these companies.

Results and Discussion

Although it is generally assumed that continuing the family business is desirable, there is no reason to believe that continuing the business within the family is important to every owner-manager: 48 percent of the respondents indicated that continuity of the business in the family was either "desirable" or "highly desirable," while 26 percent rated family continuity as "undesirable" or "highly undesirable." Owner-managers who had founded their businesses tended to see continuity in the family as less desirable than those owner-managers who had either purchased or inherited their businesses. The degree of confidence in continuity that the owner-managers expressed was varied. Asked to rate their confidence that the business could continue with the same level of performance if the owner-manager were to die or be disabled tomorrow, 33 percent of the respondents indicated a "high" or "very high" degree of confidence, while almost 40 percent stated that their confidence level was "low" or "very low." Those owners who had higher levels of continuity planning exhibited more confidence in continuity than owner-managers with lower levels.

Business Size and Continuity Planning. Since a larger business generally represents a more significant financial asset to the owners than does a smaller business, a positive relationship was expected between the size of the business (number of employees) and the level of business continuity planning. The size of the company and the level of continuity planning were not related (r = +.216) at the .05 level of significance. This finding has troubling implications for heirs, employees, and even local communities. While the owner-managers of smaller companies may have good reasons for not planning for the continuity of their businesses in that the companies may be marginal performers or may be too small to attract successors, the owner-managers of larger companies may be risking serious financial losses to their families by not planning for the continuity of their businesses. It does not appear that lack of continuity planning is restricted to "mom and pop" types of businesses.

Strategic Planning and Continuity Planning. Family businesses and small businesses in general have been cited as engaging in little or no planning activity. Of the responding firms, 43 percent were classified in the lowest level of strategic planning (SL0), while fifteen firms (26 percent) were classified as high strategic planners (SL4). It was expected that firms engaged in higher levels of strategic planning would also be engaged in higher levels of business continuity planning, and the results indicated that strategic planning and business continuity planning are related (r = .336, p. > .01). While there are differences in the focus of strategic planning and continuity planning, there is enough overlap in certain areas (such as mission statements, financial investment policies, management development practices, and the like) that a discussion of a strategic plan will soon lead to the longer-term future of the business. It appears that Ward's (1987, p. 99) suggestion that "the intricate overlay of family and business plans requires that the family not separate strategic business planning from family planning" is an accurate description of the planning process in these firms.

Board Composition and Continuity Planning. The role of outsiders in the planning process has been generally considered beneficial, both in the strategic planning process (Robinson, 1982) and in planning for management succession (Ward, 1987; Danco, 1975; Levinson, 1971). The outsider-based perspective in this research is limited to the composition of the board of directors (Danco, 1975), but there are obviously many other roles in which an outsider could affect the planning process. Consultants, family friends, and business associates respected by the owner-manager may all be outsiders who could perform the same function as an independent board. Correlations between the outsider-dominated board and the continuity-planning level indicate a positive and significant relationship between these two factors (r = +.295, p > .05). It should be noted, however, that the positive correlation does not necessarily mean that outsider boards facilitate continuity planning. It may be just as likely that the willingness to have outsiders on the board is an indication of openness and flexibility on the part of the owner-manager. The willingness to discuss and review plans with nonemployees or nonfamily members may be the type of social control (Peay and Dyer, 1989) that makes continuity planning feasible.

Perceived Family Harmony and Continuity Planning. It was proposed that there would be a high level of business continuity planning in family businesses where a high degree of family harmony was perceived, and this relationship did exist (r = +.295, p < .05). As with many of the other results, alternative arguments regarding causality can be presented. A high degree of harmony in the family business may make the continuity planning process a more tolerable task, and the harmonious relationships may reinforce the importance of continuity planning in the owner-manager's mind. Alternatively, it is also possible that the planning effort serves to clarify ambiguous relationships and problems, thus serving to increase the level of harmony in the business.

Ward (1987) suggests that the cost of maintaining family harmony may be high in that new ideas and challenges are suppressed in the interest of family harmony. This research does not address that issue. Quite possibly, the harmony associated with the business continuity planning in this study resulted in continuity plans that were far less than optimal. However, the planning process itself may be the best method Of ensuring that pertinent issues are addressed and harmony is still maintained.

CEO's Age and Continuity Planning. While it was expected that older owner-managers would engage in higher levels of business continuity planning in anticipation of death and/or retirement, such was not the case (r = .069). This lack of planning as the owner-manager ages confirms Danco's (1975) viewpoint that many owner-managers ignore the increasing probability of death and the effect it will have on the organization.

Given that health considerations were a significant factor in Ambrose's (1983) owners' decisions to terminate their businesses, the advice to plan while still in good health seems particularly propitious. Heirs and potential successors may be disappointed if they expect the current owner-manager to begin planning for continuity at the "appropriate" time. For many owner-managers, the appropriate time will remain forever in the future.

Locus of Control and Continuity Planning. Previous research has shown an individual's locus-of-control orientation to be related to the proactiveness and futurity of his or her decision making (Miller, Kets de Vries, and Toulouse, 1982). The results (r = +.317, p < .01) indicate that internals were likely to engage in higher levels of business continuity planning than were externals. There was no significant difference in locus-of-control scores between founders and nonfounders. Since the alternative to continuity planning is to do nothing, the failure to plan effectively removes the current owner-manager from influencing the future of the business. Several respondents who had done little or no continuity planning stated that they could not anticipate all of the contingencies that might occur after their deaths and therefore had to rely on the goodwill of their survivors.

The relationship of locus of control and business continuity planning has two implications. First, it may be possible for outsiders to evaluate an owner-manager's predisposition toward business continuity planning. Second, it may be possible to alter an owner-manager's attitude toward business continuity planning by altering his or her locus of control through personal and organizational development programs (Jennings and Zeithaml, 1983).

Implications for Practitioners

The findings of this research confirm many of the generally held conceptions regarding family businesses, but there are at least three major implications for practitioners that bear attention. First, lack of planning, in both the business strategy and the business continuity areas, should not be considered to be an isolated case study or a spectacular "horror story." Twenty-five of the fifty-eight responding firms were classified as engaging in no strategic planning whatsoever. In terms of business continuity planning, twenty-four of the responding owner-managers did not even have wills that accurately reflected their current wishes. Second, while a will represents one of the most fundamental tools in the business continuity effort, the mean scores of the five factors used in the scale indicate that the interpersonal areas actually designating a successor and communicating the continuity plan to interested parties were accomplished less successfully than wills, valuations, and so on. While a will and a valuation may be important elements of continuity planning, these tools only represent the senior generation's wishes. The acts of selecting, developing, and communicating with successors are the actions that continue a business, not merely divide assets. Third, the high degree of correspondence between strategic and continuity planning suggests that efforts in strategic planning may pay dividends in continuity planning. Since strategic planning is not a concept restricted to family businesses, it benefits from the increased legitimacy of what Barnes and Hershon (1976) term the "outsider" perspective. Thus, it may be easier for family businesses to approach continuity planning via strategic planning than by tackling it directly as a family issue.

Implications for Future Research

Criticizing small businesses for inadequate planning has almost become a national pastime, but such criticism contributes little in terms of solutions. Robinson and Pearce (1984) note that small-business research should focus more on identifying and overcoming barriers to planning and less on these firms' lack of planning. The tasks faced by the owner-manager in planning for the continuity of the business are not trivial undertakings. Many of the owner-managers in this study mentioned that they were passing on successful businesses to their heirs, and the least the heirs could do was to sort out the loose ends. If owner-managers feel that they have substantially fulfilled their responsibility by bequeathing the business, a higher level of continuity planning is unlikely unless it offers some benefits to the current owner-manager. While most small-company planning research has traditionally used some measure of economic performance as a dependent variable, Robinson and Pearce (1983, 1984) note that other outcomes may also be valued. Results in this study indicate that owner-managers who had engaged in higher levels of continuity planning were more confident in the future of their businesses. Other, similar benefits certainly exist and need to be identified.

The results of this research suggest a number of question that could be addressed in future research. For example, given that an outsider-based board was associated with increased continuity planning, what is the mechanism by which this planning takes place? Given Ward and Handy's (1988) results, it apparently does not take place in formal board meetings. If this is true, does that mean it takes place in quiet conversations with the CEO, or does the mere presence of an outside board serve to facilitate the business continuity effort? Can Ford's (1988) finding be replicated in the family business context? If an internal locus-of-control orientation is associated with continuity planning, to what extent can planning be increased through efforts to shift the owner-manager's control orientation? Given the rather gross measure of family harmony used in this research, a number of questions arise. If the owner-manager's perception of family harmony is not widely shared in the family, how does this misperception affect the planning process (both strategic planning and business continuity planning)? Conflicts that are hidden or overlooked now may surface once the owner-manager is no longer in a position of power and may subsequently threaten the firm. Is Ward's (1987) admonition-that excessive emphasis on harmony may endanger the free flow of business ideas-empirically supported? If a certain amount of creative tension is required in the business, perhaps too great an emphasis on harmony will lead to very harmonious families and underperforming firms.

Finally, how does the owner-manager's continuity planning (or lack thereof) affect other family members and employees? One would expect continuity planning to have a positive impact on these parties, but only the owner-managers' perceptions were examined in this research. Additional focused research, exploring many of the other variables suggested in the literature, are needed to address these issues.

References

Ambrose, D. "Transfer of the Family-Owned Business." *Journal of Small Business Management*, 1983, 21 (1), 49-56.

Barnes, L. B., and Hershon, S. A. "Transferring Power in the Family Business." *Harvard Business Review*, 1976, 54, 105-114.

Beckard, R., and Dyer, W. G., Jr. "Managing Continuity in the Family-Owned Business." *Organizational Dynamics*, Summer 1983, pp. 5-12.

Birley, S. "Succession in the Family Firm: The Inheritor's View." *Journal of Small Business Management*, 1986, 21 (3), 36-43.

Bracker, J. S. "Planning and Financial Performance Among Small Entrepreneurial Firms: An Industry Study." Unpublished doctoral dissertation, Georgia State University, 1982.

Churchill, N. C., and Hatten, K. J. "Non-Market-Based Transfers of Wealth and Power: A Research Framework for Family Businesses." *American Journal of Small Business*, 1987, 11 (3), 51-64.

Danco, L. A. *Beyond Survival. A Business Owner's Guide for Success.* Cleveland, Ohio: The University Press, 1975.

Ford, R. H. "Outside Directors and the Privately Owned Firm." *Entrepreneurship: Theory and Practice*, 1988, 13 (1), 49-57.

Handler, W. C., and Kram, K. E. "Succession in Family Firms: The Problem of Resistance." *Family Business Review*, 1988, 1 (4), 361-381.

Jennings, D. F., and Zeithaml, C P. "Locus of Control: A Review and Directions for Further Research." *In Proceedings, Academy of Management.* Dallas, Tex.: Academy of Management, 1983.

Lansberg, I. "The Succession Conspiracy." *Family Business Review*, 1988, 1 (2), 119-143.

Levinson, H. "Conflicts That Plague the Family Business." *Harvard Business Review*, March/April 1971, pp. 90-98.

Mayer, K. B., and Goldstein, S. *The First Two Years: Problems of Small Firm Growth and Survival.* Washington, D.C.: U.S. Government Printing Office, 1961.

Miller, D., Kets de Vries, M.F.R., and Toulouse, J. M. "Top Executive Locus of Control and Its Relationship to Strategy Making, Structure, and Environment." *Academy of Management Journal*, 1982, 25, 237-253.

Peay, T. R., and Dyer, W. G., Jr. "Power Orientations of Entrepreneurs and Succession Planning." *Journal of Small Business Management*, 1989, 27 (1), 47-52.

Robinson, R. B. "The Importance of 'Outsiders' in Small Firm Strategic Planning." *Academy of Management Journal*, 1982, 25 (1), 80-93.

Robinson, R. B., and Pearce, J. A. "The Impact of Formalized Strategic Planning on Financial Performance in Small Organizations." *Strategic Management Journal*, 1983, 4, 197-207.

Robinson, R. B., and Pearce, J. A. "Research Thrusts in Small Firm Strategic Planning." *Academy of Management Review*, 1984, 9, 128-137.

Rosenblatt, P. C., de Mik, L., Anderson, R. M., and Johnson, P. A. *The Family in Business: Understanding and Dealing with the Challenges Entrepreneurial Families Face.* San Francisco: Jossey-Bass, 1985.

Rotter, J. B. "Generalized Expectancies for Internal Versus External Control of Reinforcement." *Psychological Monographs: General and Applied*, 1976, 80 (609), entire issue.

Sexton, D. L., and Van Auken, P. "Prevalence of Strategic Planning in Small Business." *Journal of Small Business Management*, 1982, 21 (3), 20-26.

Sexton, D. L., and Van Auken, P. "A Longitudinal Study of Small Business Strategic Planning." *Journal of Small Business Management*, 1985, 23 (1), 7-15.

Timmons, J. *New Venture Creation.* (2nd ed.) Homewood, III: Irwin, 1985.

Ward, J. L. *Keeping the Family Business Healthy: How to Plan for Continuing Growth, Profitability, and Family Leadership.* San Francisco: Jossey-Bass, 1987.

Ward, J. L., and Handy, J. L. "A Survey of Board Practices." *Family Business Review*, 1988, (3), 289-308.

The lack of succession planning has been identified as one of the most important reasons why many first-generation family firms do not survive their founders. This article explores some of the factors that interfere with succession planning and suggests ways in which these barriers can be constructively managed.

The Succession Conspiracy

By Ivan Lansberg

Max Weber, the great German sociologist, was among the first to identify the importance of having the founder of an organization turn over power to a successor who could solidify the administrative structures required for the continued development of the enterprise. Weber (1946) referred to this process as the institutionalization of charisma and saw it as one of the greatest challenges of leadership.

In family firms, the problem of succession and continuity acquires an even greater significance. Consider the following findings: Available estimates (Dun & Bradstreet, 1973) indicate that approximately 70 percent of all family firms are either sold or liquidated after the death or retirement of their founders (Beckhard and Dyer, 1983). The failure of these businesses to continue as family firms beyond the tenure of their founders has serious social and economic consequences.

The firms that are sold to large bureaucratic firms are subject to the self-interest and standardized bureaucratic policies of the purchasing organizations. Research suggests that many of the positive characteristics associated with family ownership and management, such as concern for quality, long-term investment perspective, and strong community relations, are easily lost as a result of acquisition by larger firms (Astrachan, this volume, 1988).

The liquidation of a family firm constitutes a loss not only to the proprietary family, which often has most of its assets tied up in the firm, but also to the employees and surrounding community, whose economic well-being depends on the survival of the business.

Demographic patterns suggest that the number of business owners confronting the realities of succession and retirement is rapidly increasing throughout the economy (Sonnenfeld, 1986). Today, there are more than 24 million Americans over 65 years of age. More important, this group constitutes the fastest-growing sector of the United States population (U.S. Bureau of the Census, 1977). In the coming decade, a large number of postwar business startups that weathered the economic and organizational challenges of their entrepreneurial years will face the exit of their founders.

The research that is available (Christensen, 1953; McGivern, 1974; Trow, 1961; Hershon, 1975; Barnes and Hershon, 1977, Tashakori, 1977; Ward, 1987; Dyer, 1986; Rosenblatt, de Mik, Anderson, and Johnson, 1985) shows that one of the most significant factors determining the continuity of the family firm from one generation to the next is whether the succession process is planned. Succession planning means making the preparations necessary to ensure the harmony of the family and the continuity of the enterprise through the next generation. These preparations must be thought of in terms of the future needs of both the business and the family.

First-generation family businesses are heavily dependent on the founders not only for their leadership and drive but also for their connections and technical know-how. Failure to plan for succession needlessly deprives the business of these crucial managerial assets (Christensen, 1953, Danco, 1982; Hershon, 1975; Tashakori, 1977; Beckhard and Dyer, 1983; Whetten, 1980). Moreover, if succession planning is avoided, the founder's unexpected death can force a major upheaval in the pattern of authority and ownership distribution. In this situation, conflict among the founder's heirs often becomes so intense that they are unable to make the strategic decisions needed to ensure the future of the firm.

Failure to plan for succession also threatens the family's financial well-being by leaving many thorny estate issues unanswered; a distressed sale of the firm is often the result.

Yet, in spite of all the rational reasons for planning the founder's succession, experience and research suggest that leadership succession is seldom planned in family businesses (Christensen, 1953; Trow, 1961; Hershon, 1975; Tashakori, 1977; Lansberg, 1985; Rosenblatt, de Mik, Anderson, and Johnson, 1985).

While much has been said about the high incidence and detrimental effects of the failure to plan succession, little attention has been given to the issue of why planning is so often avoided. This paper provides an analysis of the critical forces that interfere with succession planning in first-generation family firms. I describe the condition of the system as it approaches the succession transition and provide some preliminary explanations for why the planning process is so vehemently avoided in first-generation family firms. The basic argument is that each of the constituencies that make up the family firm experiences poignantly ambivalent feelings about the inevitable succession transition. This ambivalence prevents key decision makers from engaging constructively in planning for the exit of the founder. One underlying premise of this article is that gaining awareness of the reasons for resistance among the various constituencies is an important first step toward mobilizing the planning process. While my focus is predominantly on diagnosis, the last section considers intervention strategies that can help to mobilize the system in the direction of succession planning.

The ideas presented here arise from three sources: my own personal experience as the son of an entrepreneur who chose to plan his succession, my consultation with family businesses facing the succession transition, and my research on family firms that successfully completed the transition to the next generation and on firms that were either sold or liquidated.

Ambivalence Toward Succession Planning

The succession transition imposes a wide variety of significant changes on the family firm: Family relationships need to be realigned, traditional patterns of influence are redistributed, and long-standing management and ownership structures must give way to new structures. To further complicate matters, the timing of the succession transition tends to coincide with life cycle changes in the family as well as with changes in the firm's markets and products (Davis and Stern, 1980; Ward, 1987). These changes are anxiety provoking and create a need to resolve some of the uncertainties surrounding the future of the family enterprise. At the same time, resolving these uncertainties makes it necessary to address many emotionally loaded issues that most people would prefer to avoid or deny

People in family business adopt different ways of coping with their ambivalence toward succession planning. One common response is to compromise opposing feelings by enacting a number of self-defeating behaviors. For example, consider the case of a founder who chooses his oldest daughter to be his successor but undermines her authority by refusing to give her the coaching and training that she needs in order to perform competently in the top position (Rogolsky, 1988). Nominating his daughter as the successor addresses the founder's desire to "do something about the continuity problem. Passively sabotaging the daughter's professional development placates the founder's need to remain in control of the firm. The two sets of behaviors prevent any real movement toward the design of a feasible succession plan.

Another way in which people attempt to cope with their ambivalent feelings toward succession is by projecting the side of ambivalence that they feel least comfortable with onto others (Smith and Berg, 1987). In succession planning, such splitting tends to occur across generational lines, with the older generation becoming the primary defender of the status quo and the younger generation becoming the sole advocate of change. In these situations, each group enacts an opposing side of the ambivalence; together, they prevent the system as a whole from making any progress in planning for the future.

Consider the case of a founder who is repeatedly badgered by his oldest son about the absence of a succession plan. With every attack, the founder becomes increasingly defensive and moves to reassert his control over the family firm by procrastinating further. As the conflict escalates, the son becomes increasingly unaware of some of his own misgivings about the future (for instance, any doubts that he might have about his ability to perform competently in the top position or his fear of his father's death). Likewise, the founder loses sight of his reservations about preserving the status quo (for example, his secret yearning to retire from day-to-day operational management). The result of the struggle is that the two cancel each other out. Unless each of the critical actors comes to terms with the side of the ambivalence that is being denied, it will be difficult to reach the level of cooperation needed in order for planning to take place. Let us examine the issues that the succession transition raises for each of the constituencies that make up the family firm.

Stakeholders and Their Perspectives

In order to understand the impact of succession on a family firm, it is necessary to differentiate the perspectives of the various stakeholders that make up the system. Figure One constitutes a pictorial representation of a family firm. It depicts four basic constituencies: the family, the owners, the managers, and people external to the firm. (Similar frameworks have been developed by Davis and Tagiuri, 1986 and by Davis, 1983.)

Figure 1. The Family Firm System

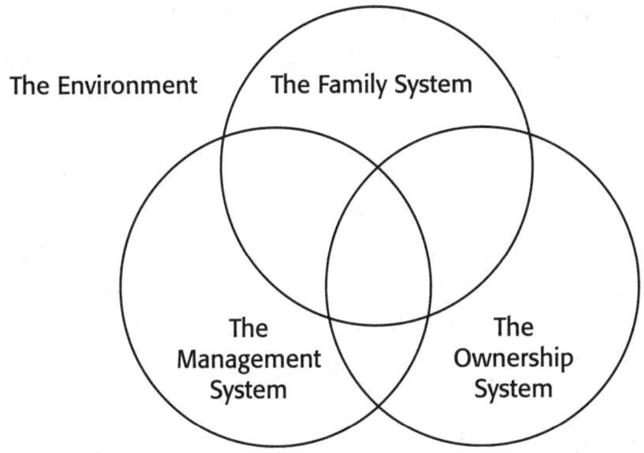

Each constituency tends to have different goals and expectations (Lansberg, 1983). For example, family members often view the firm both as an important part of the family's identity and heritage and as a source of financial security that will enable them to satisfy their life-style expectations. This view of the firm is rooted in their membership in the family and in a symbolic representation of the firm as a "mother" whose function is to provide nurturance and a sense of connectedness among family members. In contrast, those in management see their careers as tied to the firm and tend to regard the business as a vehicle for professional development and economic achievement. From their perspective, the firm's primary goal is not to look after the needs of family members but to generate profits and ensure them continued career growth. Accordingly, those involved in management expect that the firm's resources will be allocated to those who contribute directly to its growth. Finally, owners view the business predominantly as an investment from which they want to receive a fair return. Their expectations stem from an ownership right that is often difficult to exercise in the context of a family business. It is also important to note that individuals can belong to more than one group at the same time. It is, therefore, possible for the same person to hold conflicting views about the ultimate goals of the firm (Lansberg, 1983).

While I assume that each constituency will be ambivalent toward succession planning, my primary focus will be on the negative side of the ambivalence, because the available evidence indicates that the forces against planning tend to dominate in the majority of cases.

The Founder. Throughout the development of the family business, the founder tends to be the only person who is a dominant player in all three constituencies. (Throughout this article, I will be referring to founders as male, since the vast majority of entrepreneurs facing succession within the next decade are males, and our data is predominantly from male-run firms.) This position of centrality gives the founder a pervasive influence over the family firm system, making his own strongly felt ambivalence toward succession planning particularly problematic.

While founders are often aware of many good reasons for developing a succession plan, they also experience strong psychological deterrents to managing their exit. One difficult deterrent to succession planning is the founder's reluctance to face his own mortality. For a founder to plan succession, he must come to grips with death. This is not an easy task for anyone (Becker, 1973), least of all for an entrepreneur who typically has guided his life in the firm belief that he controls his own destiny (Gasse, 1983; Brockhaus, 1982). Succession planning forces founders to go through a kind of premature death ritual. As one founder I interviewed commented, "Planning my succession was like being actively involved in all of the arrangements for my own wake."

In her work on death and dying, Elizabeth Kubler-Ross (1969) proposes that the process of coming to terms with impending death follows a predictable sequence of stages: denial, rage, depression, negotiation, and finally acceptance. Succession planning requires that founders go through this difficult cycle at a time when they are still feeling strong and vital – when those around them continually remind them that they are the indispensable hub of the family firm. Under these conditions, it is very difficult for founders to move beyond the denial stage. Consider, for instance, Armand Hammer, the ninety-year-old entrepreneur who is legendary for his unwillingness to plan his exit from Occidental Petroleum, the firm he has run for the past thirty-one years. Asked by a *New York Times* reporter to comment on why he had not chosen a successor, he said, "'And if I pass,' – and here he paused, caught himself, and amended his statement – 'When I pass,' the board of directors will pick my successor. They are a good group." (Williams, 1984, pp. 1-3).

Frequently, founders develop a complex set of rationalizations and compromises that prevent them from engaging in succession planning. The most destructive maneuver is used by the founder who repeatedly goes through the motions of choosing successors only to undermine their authority and fire them after a given period on some capricious pretext.

Founders also resist succession planning because it entails letting go of their power to influence the day-to-day running of the business. In many cases, founders became entrepreneurs precisely because of a strongly felt need to acquire and exercise power over others. Surrendering power over the firm is thus experienced as the first step toward losing control over life itself. Founders' strong needs for power and centrality are evident in the way they structure their businesses (Hershon, 1975; Tashakori, 1980). Researchers have documented the tendency of founders to make themselves indispensable to their businesses by resisting the delegation of authority and insisting that they be involved in decisions that would be better handled at lower levels in the organization (Tashakori 1980; Hershon, 1975; Dyer, 1986). This self-reinforcing tendency for centrality leads many founders to develop an exaggerated image of the disastrous consequences that their retirement would bring. This image is frequently shared by others in the family firm, and it often becomes an integral part of the family firm's culture (Dyer, 1986; Schein, 1985). The gloomy outlook, in turn, creates a powerful rationale for avoiding succession planning and reinforces the founder's need to remain involved in day-to-day decisions. While it might be true that the founder is indispensable at any given point in the life of the family firm, the Act remains that the founder has the power to break the dependency cycle, since he is largely, though not entirely, responsible for perpetuating it.

The fear of losing control of the business is often compounded by the thought that retiring from the firm will lead to a demotion from one's central role within the family. As a successor in one company put it, "My father refused to let go because he feared that after retirement he would no longer be Papa-no longer the patriarch that all his children would look up to and depend on. He wanted to die ruling the family and the firm, and, unfortunately for all of us, he did."

It is interesting to note, in this regard, that even those founders who do plan their succession out of management of the business often retain ownership control of the firm until their death. They do so in spite of the considerable estate tax advantages of passing control of stock ownership to heirs while the founder is still alive.

In addition to the loss of power, founders also resist succession planning out of fear of losing an important part of their identity. For an entrepreneur, his organization defines his place in the community and in the world at large. Moreover, the firm forms an integral part of his sense of self (Levinson, 1971; McGivern, 1978). The business is often his most significant creation. And, unlike his children and, possibly, his wife, it is a loved one he can keep. Thus, founders suffering from the empty nest syndrome at home can become even more attached to their businesses (Rogolsky, 1988). At a time in life when the founder is struggling to come to terms with the meaning of his life's work, when there is too little time to redo some of his lid choices, the thought of separating from the organization is disturbing and painful. Even founders who have gathered the courage to forge ahead with a succession plan often find themselves disoriented after their plan is made public. In one family company that I studied, the founder worried that he would be ignored and cast aside by the financial community and by his business associates after he announced his succession plan. Whether or not he was invited to business gatherings and conventions became a major preoccupation, as did the title that he would put on his business cards. He also worried a great deal about whether he could keep his office in the company's building, even though he was still the sole owner of the firm.

Finally, as Levinson (1971) and others have indicated, founders struggling with succession often experience powerful feelings of rivalry and jealousy toward potential successors. Some psychoanalytic researchers have suggested that for a male entrepreneur the firm may constitute an unconscious representation of his mother. For example, Levinson (quoted by Goldman, 1986, p. 30), says, "The son symbolically defeats the father by starting his own business. He simultaneously builds and marries his organization; it represents the mother he could never win away from his father."

Succession triggers in the founder the same rivalry he experienced toward his father in the early stages of his life. This time, however, the struggle is reenacted with the successor, a younger rival who waits to take over the founder's place with his beloved organization. Simultaneously, the founder may be experiencing similar displacement in his daughters' affections through their choice of younger male partners (Rogolsky, 1988). These feelings become evident in a persistent distrust of the successor's competence and ability. In one company that I studied, the founder's mistrust and rivalry with his successor reached a point where the founder spent most of his time minutely documenting every decision the successor made in order to build a convincing case for not retiring. The fact that the company was actually making a sizable profit under the successor's leadership was not sufficient evidence of managerial competence. Instead, the founder argued that until the successor learned to take we of the details (like turning the lights off at night and using good grammar on internal memos) he would not be fit to assume the management of the firm. After a painful struggle for control, the successor left the company, and the founder has since repeated the cycle with two other successor candidates.

Most analysts of the succession problem limit their attention to the founder. While the founder is unquestionably the critical actor in succession planning, it is important to realize that the founder is not alone in resisting the planning process. The founder's own family frequently exerts strong pressures to avoid the emotion-laden issues of succession.

The Family. In order to understand the families reaction to succession planning and the reasons why its members might want to avoid the planning process, it is important to consider the stage in the lid cycle at which a family is likely to be at the time of succession. The need to start thinking about succession planning does not typically arise until the founder and his spouse enter the last stage in the life cycle (around age sixty). Family theorists (McGoldrick and Carter, 1982) have described some of the issues confronting married couples at this juncture in their lives. By this time, the last of the children has left home, and the couple is struggling to adjust to the vacuum produced by the empty nest. Unresolved marital difficulties that for years had lain dormant, masked by the continuous pressures of child rearing and business startup, reemerge during this period. The death or illness of the couple's parents, who are by now well into old age, exerts additional pressures. The thought of growing increasingly dependent on others is especially difficult for couples who place a strong value on managing for themselves.

Retirement and the changes of status that come with it further exacerbate these difficulties.. Couples at this stage resort to emotional strategies, such as denying the need to deal with succession, refusing to relinquish power, and reasserting their authority and centrality in both the family and the business hierarchies. For the offspring, this is also a time of stress and adjustment, as they are themselves adapting to the multiple demands of the adult world, including marriage and (for many) divorce, careers, and parenthood. In addition, the children are eager to establish their own financial independence and autonomy at this stage of their lives. These conditions make it unlikely that the offspring will be patient and supportive of the parents' attempts to assert their power over family members. On the contrary, the offspring may resort to displacing their own difficulties with succession onto the founder, who is viewed as the only obstacle to their own advancement within the firm. Often, those among the younger generation who most eagerly want to bring about the exit of the founder experience a good deal of unconscious guilt that leads them to sabotage their own chances of being effective successors.

Many of the developmental challenges of this stage interfere with the family's ability and willingness to engage in an open discussion of succession issues. For the founder's spouse, the succession transition creates a complex set of challenges and uncertainties. On the one hand, spouses may worry a great deal about the economic and emotional future of the family and continuously work to mediate conflicts that emerge between the founder and the next generation or among the siblings themselves. For this reason, spouses are often supportive of succession planning and in many cases serve as a powerful influence in mobilizing the founder to confront his difficulties in facing the transition. On the other hand, the founder's spouse faces a number of is sues that can deter her from addressing the succession issue. For the spouse, too, the firm constitutes an important center of activity and a major component of her identity (Rosenblatt, de Mik Anderson, and Johnson, 1985). Like the founder, she may be confronted with letting go of many important roles she has played in and around the business over the years. These roles vary significantly from firm to firm and include anything from running a part of the business or managing the company finances to helping employees with their family problems and organizing social activities for clients (Rosenblatt, de Mik, Anderson, and Johnson, 1985). At times, spouses can discourage succession planning because they fear that a substantive discussion of the future of the family business will disrupt the family's harmony. In one family business that I studied, the founder's spouse played the role of emotional guardian of the family, constantly shielding the family from the emotionally upsetting issues of succession. By actively discouraging any of the children from engaging in discussions about the future of the family business, the spouse enabled the founder to continue procrastinating on development of a succession plan. Sometimes, the founder's spouse resists bringing in an outside consultant because this would violate the privacy of the family and expose the family's dirty laundry to public view.

Many other family factors can interfere with the open discussion of succession. For example, as the result of such factors as gender and birth order, the parents can differ significantly in their preference for the children. These differences have a powerful effect on each parent's assessment of which child should be the founder's successor, and they heighten the chances that the choice will be experienced as preferential treatment. While the emotional response to the choice of successor is often mediated by such factors as the family's ethnic background and traditions (in particular with regard to primogeniture) as well as by the configuration of family coalitions and the developmental stages of the key participants, the decision tends to be emotionally loaded for the majority of business families.

In addition, most Western cultures have norms regulating family behavior that discourage parents and offspring from openly discussing the future of the family beyond the lifetime of the parents. This is particularly true of economic and financial matters, such as estate planning, an open discussion of which is typically viewed as a breach of etiquette or as denoting self-interest and a lack of mutual trust. These norms are functional in ensuring that relationships within the family are guided by personal caring, not by such motives as economic opportunism. However, when businesses are operated by families, the same norms can serve to discourage the necessary discussions of succession planning.

Other investigators have noted that many families have difficulty talking about inheritance and the economic future of the family. For example, Rosenblatt and his associates (Rosenblatt, de Mik, Anderson, and Johnson, 1985, p. 192) argue that the anxieties about succession and inheritance may also result from the fact that the stakes (financial and other vise) are high for the founder's heirs: "What people will inherit or fail to inherit is not only something of financial value but also an occupation, a status, and a place in the community." Families fear that an open discussion of these issues might only serve to fuel invidious comparisons among the heirs that could destroy the fabric of the family.

Finally, the younger generation sometimes avoids succession planning because it arouses strong fears of parental death, separation, and abandonment. In one case, an entrepreneur's adult son told me that "deep down inside" he did not even want to think about what life would be like in the absence of his parents. He feared that addressing succession would be so upsetting that it might actually bring about the death of his Other, who, incidentally, was in very good health. Given the anxiety that the succession transition generates, it is not unusual for family members to harbor very negative expectations of what would happen if succession issues were to be openly discussed in the family. While it is unquestionably true that families differ in their ability to cope with the stress brought about by succession planning, such fatalistic expectations often prevent even the healthiest of families from confronting the need to plan.

The Managers. The difficulties with succession are not limited to the founder and the family. The firm's managers are also confronted with difficult emotional issues that lead them to resist planning. This section discusses the senior nonfamily cadre of managers who constitute the upper echelons of the firm. This group is often composed of older managers who have worked with the founder from the start of the firm

Many senior managers are reluctant to shift from a personal relationship with the founder to a more formal relationship with a successor. In most cases, these managers have developed unique ties with the founder that extend well beyond the parameters of a contractual work arrangement. Over the years, the founder may have personally managed each senior manager's training, evaluation, and compensation and tendered personal favors to the managers and their families. For example, in several of the firms that I studied, the founder had helped secure loans to the senior managers for the purchase of their homes. For many senior managers, personal ties with the owner constitute the single most important advantage of having worked for a family firm over the years. The founder's succession may also confront the older managers with the reality of their own aging and retirement. In conflictual situations in which the founder and the younger generation are struggling for control, the older managers not infrequently side with the founder in favor of the status quo. The families of senior managers may also have personal ties to the founder and his family, so that the shifting hierarchy in the founder's family may stimulate changes in the families of senior managers. In many cases, several members of a single family are employed by the firm, so that a change in leadership can threaten the employment of these families as well. In some of the larger family firms, the senior managerial ranks include younger professional managers with shorter tenure in the firm who aspire to formalize the structure of the firm (Dyer, 1986). These managers are often eager to purge the firm of relatives both of the owners and of the other managers) who in their view are not contributing to the growth and development of the firm.

Regardless of his or her competence and skills, a successor is seldom able to replace the entrepreneur in the eyes of the older managers. With the chance of leadership, it is not only inevitable but also appropriate and necessary for many of the functions that the founder performed to become institutionalized (Greiner, 1972). Senior managers often expect that formal controls, such as budgets, management information systems, and personnel systems, will restrict their autonomy and influence. These expectations lead them to resist both the planning and the implementation of the succession transition. It is not unusual, therefore, to find the senior managers colluding with the founder and members of the family in avoiding serious discussions about succession.

The Owners. Besides the family and the senior managers, the owners also encounter difficulties addressing succession planning. In most first-generation businesses, the founder has given or sold some ownership interest to older managers, relatives, or both, either to give them an incentive to further their involvement with the business or to limit estate taxes. In these cases, the founder typically retains ownership control of the business. In larger firms, the founder has often secured the financial backing of outside investors who are given some share of the ownership in return for their investment. Typically, these outside investors are old friends of the founder and themselves owner-managers of other family firms in the community. Still other family firms are dealerships or franchises in which larger firms have a direct ownership involvement. Like other stakeholders in the family firm, the owners, in whatever capacity they serve, also experience difficulties actively engaging in or mobilizing the succession planning process.

For owners who work in the firm, whether they are family members or not, the difficulties typically stem from the way in which they acquire their share of ownership. Often, the founder has passed along some share of his ownership to these individuals as a paternalistic gesture of goodwill or in recognition of some special contribution that these people either have made or are expected to make. However, this gift or sale carries with it an implicit expectation of loyalty and allegiance to the founder that makes it very difficult for internal minority owners to raise questions about succession planning without appearing to be disloyal.

Outside minority owners who are old friends of the founder are often themselves involved in resisting succession planning with their own firms and as a result tend to avoid discussions of succession planning altogether. As one founder whom I interviewed put it, "The moment I announced I had finally decided to do something about succession, my partners and business colleagues jumped on me and told me that I was crazy. They inquired whether I had received bad news from my doctor. It took me a while to figure out that what I was doing confronted them with their own succession anxieties."

Not all founders have the wisdom to separate their own anxiety about succession from that of others. The problem of succession is a generational issue that confronts all members of the same cohort at about the same time. The reluctance of the founder's partners and peers to face up to succession often reinforces the founder's own resistance to planning his departure from the firm.

Family firms that belong to the dealer network of a larger firm are seldom constructively encouraged to plan for the succession of the founder. At best, large firms deal with the succession issues of their dealer principals by specifying in their contract that a "suitable successor" (*suitable* is usually left undefined) must be found in order for the franchise agreement to be renewed beyond the tenure of the dealer principal It is evident in many cases that the head office does not have much understanding of how the complex interaction of family and business affects the dealers' ability to cope with succession. In the parent organization management succession is typically handled through a formal process that has been institutionalized for a considerable period of time. Often the parent organization expects that dealers will approach succession with the same degree of bureaucratic rationality that is presumed to be used to handle management succession at headquarters. While the threat that the dealership agreement will be terminated does raise awareness of the need to do something about succession, the bureaucratic rationality imposed from headquarters actually serves to inhibit consideration of the way in which the personal dynamics of the founder and the founder's family might be interfering with succession planning. In addition the imposition of vague contractual limitations in the absence of supportive processes and structures serves only to increase the tensions that are characteristic of dealer-headquarters relations. Headquarters frequently becomes a target onto which the founder and others in the family firm can displace much of the anxiety and anger that they experience as a result of the succession situation.

The Environment. Resistance to the succession planning process is not limited to the individuals who are directly involved with the family firm system. Environmental forces also create barriers to succession planning. These forces consist of the clients and suppliers who have grown dependent on the founder as their primary business contact in the firm.

These people know that the founder is the person to whom they must speak when they want action. Although it is clearly in the client's long-term interest that the firm plan for its healthy continuation, clients and suppliers worry about losing their connection to the top and frequently side with the founder in avoiding the effort to plan succession. In one company that I studied, the founder had retired and moved a thousand miles away and was still getting and responding to daily calls from clients three years after his departure from the firm. In service businesses, in which the founder's personal network is one of the firm's most critical assets, the founder's connections can become a powerful reason for perpetuating centrality. In many cases, the founder's network results from a lifetime of shared experiences with members of his cohort who do not easily develop links with the successor and others of his or her generation.

It is worth noting here that our cultural values do not generally support leaders who plan their succession. In fact, until fairly recently, management scholars have not paid much attention to the generic problem of leadership succession. As Sonnenfeld (1986, p. 321) has indicated, "How a leader leaves of fine is as important to his or her constituents as how the office is acquired. Nonetheless, our attention is not balanced between these events. We hear regularly of the violent warfare surrounding prominent cases of corporate executive succession struggles, yet that is where the discussion begins and ends. The collective wisdom on leadership departures does not appear in the best-selling management guides, research reports, or classroom texts."

The stereotypes that we carry are of legendary leaders who have "died in the saddle" or "gone down with the ship," not of leaders who have thoughtfully planned their exit. Perhaps our own collective ambivalence toward authority interferes with our ability to come to terms with the fact that leaders do not just fade away-they die. In this context, succession planning is viewed more as a sign of weakness or as a deficiency of character than as an essential component of responsible leadership. Since founders view themselves as centrally responsible for the well-being of their families and their firms, they do not take such cultural messages lightly.

Mobilizing the Succession Planning Process

The preceding analysis presents a preliminary answer to the question, Why do so many first-generation family firms avoid planning the exit of their founders? The question is important because the lack of a succession plan is a critical factor in the failure of many family firms. I have painted a picture of a gridlocked system, in which critical stakeholders experience a great deal of ambivalence toward the planning process and consequently tend to procrastinate, compromise, or get stuck in nonproductive conflicts with one another. Although only some of the obstacles that I have identified may be operating in a given situation, it is critical for decision makers and consultants to be attentive to the ways in which these forces can interfere with stakeholders' willingness to participate in constructive planning for the founder's exit. An important first step in the effort to develop strategies for mobilizing the development of a succession plan is to diagnose the resistance from the perspective of each critical constituency.

This section suggests a number of interventions that can help to loosen the resistance toward succession planning. These ideas are aimed at those who may be able to help bring about change, including consultants, lawyers, accountants, directors, and other key decision makers directly involved with the firm. As the available data on the rarity of succession planning suggest, system-wide resistance to succession is a powerful force. Mobilizing the development of a succession plan requires a great deal of patience, skill, and persistence. It is important for those who attempt to bring about the design and implementation of a succession plan to have the credibility and legitimacy needed to work with all the critical constituencies. In recognition of the complexity of the problem, the ideas presented here should be viewed not as a recipe for "fixing" the succession situation but as suggestions that must be tailored to the specific conditions of any given case. They are based on the assumption that the family is a healthy one in which any conflicts and difficulties that do exist result not from serious pathology but from normal life cycle stressors (Walsh, 1982).

I shall first present some ideas that can help to mobilize the founder to undertake succession planning. Subsequently, I explore system-level interventions. Most of these suggestions are based on the idea that, in order to mobilize the system, we need to find ways of strengthening forces that favor succession planning while simultaneously weakening or redirecting the forces that work against it.

Working with the Founder. Given the centrality and influence of the founder, his willingness is a necessary, though not a sufficient, condition for effective succession planning to take place. At the very least, getting the founder to accept the need to plan should be an important priority during the early phase of any planned intervention effort. Let us examine what can be done to strengthen the founder's willingness to address succession, paying particular attention to his emotional and cognitive needs.

It is important to address the founder's emotional needs and insecurities about succession first, since these typically constitute a major obstacle to the development of a plan. The principal aim here is to create conditions that may help the founder to work through his most critical resistances to the planning process.

One option is to help the founder develop a support network of founders who have themselves done succession planning and as a result understand what the process entails. Conversations with these peers may help the founder to gain some perspective on his own resistances to succession. More important, comparing experiences with others increases the likelihood that the founder will understand his reluctance to let go as a common response of any founder faced with the succession transition-as a hurdle generic to the situation that can and should be overcome. Peers and elders who have successfully planned their succession and thereby ensured the continuity of the family business are most likely to transmit to the founder a sense of pride and accomplishment about having faced up to the challenges posed by succession.

Interestingly, many of the founders whom we interviewed who had planned their succession had recently had a close encounter with death, such as a heart attack, a near fatal accident, or the death of a close friend or relative. The interviews suggest that contact with death, either directly or vicariously, helped to mobilize these founders to face their own mortality and plan their succession. Being attentive to the occurrence of such events may help interveners to identify times when the founder is more receptive to the idea of planning his own succession. Once a founder has had time to grieve and work through the loss of a close friend or relative, he may be less guarded and more willing to come to terms with the consequences that his death could have on his own family and business. Here, too, a support network can help a founder to work through his fears by offering help from peers who have faced similar circumstances. For instance, founders who have planned their exit often envision the institutionalization of the firm as a realistic way of perpetuating their values and beliefs-a more tangible form of immortality. This perspective may help the founder to reframe the succession process as something that he would be doing for himself as well as for others. In addition, founders can also gain much from others who can serve as role models and describe the process they went through to plan their exit as well as their feelings about their new roles.

It is important for the family to understand how difficult and painful it is for the founder to let go. The entrepreneur is the symbol of strength and self-sufficiency in the family. This image may make it difficult for the family to perceive and empathize with the founder's difficulties around these issues. Helping family members to understand what succession means emotionally for the founder will help them to develop ways of supporting him through this painful transition. This process can take the form of helping the family to reframe "erratic" or "irrational" behavior as a natural reaction to the process of letting go. For example, a successor-to-be who is attentive to the founder's emotional difficulties with succession is more likely to react constructively to attempts by the founder to interfere with the transfer of power. By being firm and supportive rather than adversarial, the successor-to-be may help the founder to take the necessary steps.

Sharpening the founder's awareness of the need for planning is also important. Frequently, it is helpful to sensitize the founder to the degree to which the family business is dependent on him. The critical diagnostic questions at this stage are, What would happen today if the founder died unexpectedly? What is likely to happen in the family? What is likely to happen in the company? What would happen from the point of view of the ownership and estate taxes? How would the outside world (for example, banks, critical suppliers, clients) react? Typically, these questions help to create a sense of urgency about the need for planning.

It may also be helpful to strengthen the founder's sense of responsibility as a father and CEO by validating the fact that succession planning is the leader's highest duty. For example, it may be useful to expose the founder to case studies of family firms in which the founder assured the continuity of the family and the enterprise through a carefully planned and orchestrated succession.

The raising of awareness must be coupled with concrete ideas about what to do about the problem. The basic tasks involved in succession planning include:

- Formulating and sharing a viable vision of the future in which the founder is no longer in charge of the family firm.
- Selecting and training the founder's successor as well as the future top management team.
- Designing a process through which power will be transferred from the current generation of management to the next.
- Developing an estate plan that specifies how family assets and ownership of the enterprise will be allocated among the founder's heirs.
- Designing and staffing the structures appropriate for managing the change, including a family council, a management task force, and a board of directors.
- Educating the family to understand the rights and responsibilities that come with the various roles that they may assume in the future.

While it is beyond the scope of this paper to explore the preceding list in depth, it is important to stress that, unless the founder understands the specific tasks involved in succession planning, his resistance to the process is likely to be heightened.

It is also beneficial to help the founder to develop a clear vision of his future roles both inside and outside the family business. Founders who develop strong interests in activities other than management of the family firm have an easier time planning their succession. For some founders, this means pursuing new careers outside the firm. For example, a founder who longed to be actively involved in teaching became a highly successful management professor at a local college. Another retired to pursue a career in music. He is now the conductor of the town's symphony orchestra. Still another founded a consulting firm and spends his time advising other founders on the subject of family businesses and succession.

It is also important for founders to design the interim or transitional role that they will occupy after they turn over management of the firm to their successor. Clarifying this role helps to reduce uncertainty about the future and appeases the founder's fear that he will be totally disconnected from the firm on retirement. This transition role may vary significantly from one case to another. In some of the firms that we studied, the founders were out of operational management but continued to serve as chairmen emeriti in an advisory capacity on new projects or on overall policy matters. Others served as elder statesmen who worked to promote the firm in new and established markets. Still others managed to design an internal role well insulated from day-to-day management. One founder whom we interviewed is a highly successful engineer who invented an important manufacturing process. Basic research is his bust love. He turned over the running of the firm to his son (also an engineer) and, at age seventy, returned to the bench. Now eighty-three years old, he has developed a number of new patents since his return to research. Needless to say, there is a very real risk during the transitional period that a departing founder may infringe on his successor's territory and autonomy. It is important for the boundaries around the founder's involvement to be drawn very clearly and both the founder and the successor to monitor this aspect of the transition carefully. Clarifying future roles (both external and internal) facilitates succession planning by reducing uncertainties about the future. In addition, if the founder is drawn out of day-to-day management by his own excitement over new activities, the pain of surrendering power is mitigated by the attractiveness of the new challenges ahead.

Working with the Family. In order to help a family to overcome its resistance to succession planning, it is helpful to structure a process that brings together different subgroups of the family to discuss succession. The timing of these meetings is important.

During the early phases, it is important for the founder and his spouse to reach a mutual understanding about the necessity of planning. First, the couple should articulate what they would like to gain from the planning process. Together, the founder and his spouse constitute the leadership of the Emily business system. It is critical, therefore, that they develop a shared vision of the future. This vision should include a statement of their aspirations for themselves and the rest of the family as well as a list of the specific activities that they would like to share in the future. The primary aim is to help the couple to support each other throughout this process and to help them realize that they can be instrumental in achieving a good life in the future. This is important, because unless they feel empowered to design and implement a succession plan, it is unlikely that they will be able to exercise their leadership effectively and help others in the family and the firm come to terms with the challenges posed by succession. Sometimes, couples find it beneficial to seek marital counseling and advice on personal financial planning before they address succession planning. In these cases, helping the couple to make such a decision can be an important first step in mobilizing succession planning.

Once the founder and his spouse have had a chance to clarify their expectations and issues, it may be useful to create a family council. This group can be composed of all family members who are key to the future of the business, including the founder, his spouse, and children as well as other relatives who have a significant stake in the family business. The council comes together with the purpose of discussing issues that arise as a result of the families involvement with the business (Ward, 1987). These issues include, Should the family perpetuate the business, and if so why? How will family members in and out of the business benefit from perpetuating the firm? What are the family's shared values? How should these values be represented in the firm? How can the family give support to relatives who choose not to work in the business? Structurally, a family council should operate only as an advisory body to the company's board of directors. That is, the family council's function is to articulate the views of the family so that those in the board can make decisions and design policies that protect the overall values, needs, and wishes of the family owners.

For the family, the council provides a setting in which differences can be aired and worked through without interfering in day-to-day management of the business and without contaminating the family's non-work-related relationships. In the council, family members can articulate their expectations of one another and explore the specific roles that they expect or wish to play in the future. A family firm that I work with has made very effective use of such a family council. The council is made up of the founder, his wife, their children, and the children's spouses. In one of the early meetings of the council, each person wrote a description of himself or herself and the family business in five years. I encouraged them to think about this future scenario from the perspective of ownership, management, and family. Individuals then met with their spouses to share their individual expectations for the future. Each couple presented the conclusions from its discussions to the others. This was the first time that the family had come together to discuss their professional and family expectations. Moreover, the meeting served to clarify the views that family members had of one another. As one of the second generation participants commented, "This was very helpful, since it allowed me, for the first time, to appreciate the professional aspirations and the capabilities of my siblings."

The family council can also serve to bring together subgroups within the family that do not usually communicate. In one business, the founder and his son were the only family members directly involved in management; the other three siblings had long been kept in the dark about the true financial status of the firm. As a result, these family members had unrealistic expectations about the economic health of the business and about the financial benefits that it could provide. The family council made it possible for the founder and his son to educate the rest of the family about the financial constraints on the firm. This in turn helped those in the family who had not been involved with the firm to bring their expectations for the future into line with reality.

The family council is also a forum in which family members can come to terms with the end of an era in the family's history – that of the creation of the business under the leadership of the founder. Having an opportunity to discuss, enjoy, and mourn the pains and joys of this period in the life of the family helps to pave the way for succession planning. As numerous authors on human change have argued, the ability to achieve closure on a given period of life enhances successful transitions to the next phase (Bridges, 1980; Tichy and Devanna, 1986; Smith and Berg, 1987). Finally, a family council gives the next generation of leaders in the family an opportunity to become reacquainted with one another as adults. All too often, siblings unconsciously perpetuate early patterns of behavior. In family council meetings, siblings have an opportunity to rediscover one another by working on a common problem. The creation of the council may by itself be one of the most significant ways of mobilizing the system to engage constructively in succession planning.

Working with the Managers. Senior managers also need an appropriate forum in which to discuss succession issues openly and frankly. One option is to create a special task force whose mission is to develop a five-year management continuity plan. Ideally, such a plan addresses the problem of continuity not just in terms of finding a replacement for the founder but also in terms of training individuals to fill critical senior management positions in the future. In other words, such a group has primary responsibility for designing and staffing the management structures needed to institutionalize the firm. Thinking about continuity from a systemic perspective requires an assessment of the future needs of the family business. What kind of organization do we want to have in the future? What skills should top leaders have in order to manage this organization effectively? Do we have the people in place who can perform effectively in that future organization? If so, what kinds of training do they need in order to manage the future system competently? If we do not have the people internally, how will we go about recruiting appropriate candidates? These are some of the critical questions that need to be addressed.

In order to reduce resistance to addressing the critical issues, it may be helpful to structure some special incentives into the design of this task force. For example, the succession task force can be treated as a prestigious group in which only the founder's most trusted managers are invited to participate. In may also be useful to give members of this task force some financial incentives for their services.

It may also be beneficial to create some incentives for older managers to address their own retirement issues. These incentives can include an early retirement plan or career and outplacement counseling. In addition, it may be desirable to create incentives for managers to train and develop their replacements as an integral part of their regular job responsibilities.

Working with the Owners. The most effective way of mobilizing the owners to develop a succession plan is to activate the board of directors. Typically, family businesses underutilize their boards. Founders often assign board responsibilities only to inside employees. Often, these individuals are too dependent on the founder to be able to serve effectively as advisers.

A well-designed board of directors can provide a much-needed source of expertise and perspective during succession planning. More important, the board can serve a continuous monitoring function by overseeing that the transfer of management responsibilities from one generation to the next goes according to plan. When structuring a board, it is important to keep in mind that its primary function is to safeguard the interests of the owners by ensuring that the enterprise is effectively managed in keeping with its mission. It is important, therefore, for decision makers to be attentive to both the design and the composition of the board.

From the design point of view, it is desirable for the responsibilities of the board to be clearly articulated and for the board to have the power and authority necessary to fulfill its duties effectively. It is generally recommended (Ward, 1987; Danco, 1982) that such a board be predominantly staffed with outside directors who can provide an external and relatively unbiased perspective and that the size of the board be kept to a reasonable number (seven, plus or minus two). While this is sound advice, it is not always possible to structure an entirely external board. For one thing, many family firms cannot afford the cost of a totally external board. These businesses may have to work very hard at encouraging independence in the board by carefully selecting, training, and endorsing thoughtful insiders.

Ultimately, whether the board works effectively depends on the willingness of the founder to design it well and to abide by its recommendations. Some founders do use their boards effectively. For example, one founder in our study explicitly charged his board with the task of alerting him to any unconscious attempts on his part to undermine the design and implementation of a succession plan. In this case, the founder was aware of his own needs to resist the succession process and recognized the value of developing a process for monitoring his own behavior in the context of succession.

Finally, it may be helpful to bring together representatives of the family council, the succession task force, and the board of directors to work on specific problems If these exchanges are appropriately orchestrated, they can be an extremely useful way of educating people in the various groups about each other's needs and perspectives. For example, family members in the council who have never worked in the firm may learn about the professionalism and technical knowledge required to manage the business effectively. Managers have an opportunity to know the family as a whole and to get information about how the family is likely to treat management when the founder is no longer involved with the firm. It may also be useful to bring together the board from time to time. For example the board may benefit by hearing directly from family members about their values, goals, and expectations as these pertain to the mission of the family enterprise.

Summary

In this paper, I have analyzed the forces that interfere with succession planning in first-generation firms. My purpose has been to provide a set of hypotheses that can help us to understand the often cited failure of first-generation family firms to plan the exit of their founders. The central theme has been that the founder, the family, the owners, the senior managers, and other stakeholders typically experience poignantly ambivalent feelings toward succession planning. I have argued that these feelings cause the constituents in family firms to procrastinate in developing a plan. If they wait until the founder's death, it is often too late to rescue the firm, and the family undergoes tremendous stress.

The resistance to succession planning is difficult to change. Nonetheless, I have provided some suggestions for mobilizing the planning process. Figure Two summarizes these recommendations. I argue for a systemic approach to succession planning and for multiple interventions aimed at addressing the resistance of the founder and his spouse, the family, the senior managers, and the owners. Contrary to common practice, I maintain that is essential to develop structures, such as a family council, a board of directors, and a succession task force, that can involve those whose cooperation is critical for the development and implementation of a continuity plan. In the final analysis, it is very unlikely that a first generation family firm can mobilize itself for succession planning unless the founder is willing. In a very real sense, the founder retains his power to perpetuate or destroy his life creation right up to the very end.

Figure 2. Strategies for Mobilizing Succession Planning

Strategies for Mobilizing the Founder

- Help the founder to develop a supportive network of peers who can empathize and share leanings.
- Be attentive to timing, paying particular attention to how the founder is coping with his fears of death.
- Heighten the sensitivity of the family to the needs of the founder.
- Provide the founder with specific data about the steps involved in the development of a succession plan, and, if possible, get him to develop a timetable.
- Help the founder to design a role for the future that will motivate him to let go of his present involvement in operational management.

Strategies for Mobilizing the Family

- Help the founder and his spouse to develop a shared vision of the future.
- Help the found and his spouse to seek marital counseling if needed.
- Develop a family council that facilitates meeting of the family in which members discuss their values and expectations for the business and for one another.

Strategies for Mobilizing the Managers
- Create a succession task force and build in incentives that reward serious involvement in the development of a succession plan.
- Encourage planning for succession for senior managers as well as for the founder.

Strategies for Mobilizing the Owners

- Create a board of directors that is appropriately staffed and that provides an independent perspective that can safeguard the interests of the owners.

References

Barnes, L. and Hershon, S. "Transferring Power in the Family Business." *Harvard Business Review*, July-August 1976, pp. 105-114.

Becker, E. *The Denial of Death*. New York: Free Press, 1973.

Beckhard, R. and Dyer, W. G., Jr. "Managing Continuity in the Family Owned Business." *Organizational Dynamics*, Summer 1983, pp. 5-12.

Bridges, W. *Transitions: Making Sense of Life's Changes*. Reading, Mass.: Addison-Wesley, 1980.

Brockhaus, R. H. Sr. "The Psychology of the Entrepreneur." In C. A. Kent, D. L. Sexton, and K H. Vesper (ads.), *Encyclopedia of Entrepreneurship*. Englewood Cliffs, NJ.: Prentice-Hall 1982.

Christensen, C. R. *Management Succession in Small and Growing Enterprises*. Boston: Graduate School of Business Administration, Harvard University, 1953.

Danco, L. A. *Beyond Survival: A Business Owner's Guide for Success*. Cleveland, Ohio: University Press, 1982.

Davis, J., and Tagiuri, R. "Bivalent Attributes of the Family Firm." Unpublished manuscript, University of Southern California, 1986.

Davis, P. "Realizing the Potential of the Family Business." *Organizational Dynamics*, Summer, 1983, pp. 47-56.

Davis, P. Presentation at the annual meeting of the Academy of Management, Boston, 1984.

Davis, P. and Stern, D. "Adaptation, Survival and Growth of the Family Business: An Integrative Business Perspective." *Human Relations*, 1980, 30 (4), 207-224

Dun & Brad street. *The Business Failure Record: 1972*. New York: Dun & Bradstreet, 1973.

Dyer, W. G., Jr. *Cultural Change in Family Firms: Anticipating and Managing Business and Family Transitions*. San Francisco: Jossey-Bass, 1986.

Gasse, Y. "Elaborations on the Psychology of the Entrepreneur." In C. A. Kent, D. L. Sexton, and K H. Vesper (eds.), *Encyclopedia of Entrepreneurship*. Englewood Cliffs, NJ.: Prentice Hall, 1982.

Goleman, D. "The Psyche of the Entrepreneur." *New York Times*, February 2, 1986, p. 30.

Greiner, L. E. "Evolution and Revolution as Organizations Grow." *Harvard Business Review*, July-August 1972, pp. 37-46.

Hershon, S. A. "The Problem of Management Succession in Family Businesses." Unpublished doctoral dissertation, Harvard School of Business Administration, 1975.

Kubler-Ross, E. *On Death and Dying*. New York: Macmillan. 1969.

Lansberg, I. "Managing Human Resources in Family Firms." *Organizational Dynamics*, Summer 1983, pp. 3946.

Lansberg, I. "Family Firms That Survived Their Founders." Paper presented at the Annual Meeting of the Academy of Management, San Diego, Calif.. 1985.

Levinson, H. "Conflicts That Plague Family Businesses." *Harvard Business Review*, March-April 1971, pp. 90-98.

McGivern, C. "The Dynamics of Management Succession." *Management Decision*, 1978, 16, 32-46.

McGoldrick, M., and Carter, E. A. "The Family Life Cycle." In F. Walsh (ed.), *Normal Family Processes*. New York: Guilford Press, 1982.

Rogolsky, S. "Daughter Successors: Last Resorts or Lost Resources?" Unpublished manuscript, Yale School of Organization and Management, 1988.

Rosenblatt, P. C., de Mik, L., Anderson, R. M., and Johnson, P. A. *The Family in Business: Understanding and Dealing with the Challenges Entrepreneurial Families Face*. San Francisco: Jossey-Bass. 1985.

Schein, E. H. *Organizational Culture and Leadership: A Dynamic View*. San Francisco: Jossey-Bass, 1985.

Smith, K.K., and Berg, D. N. *Paradoxes of Group Life*. San Francisco: Jossey-Bass. 1987.

Sonnenfeld, J. "Heroes in Collision: Chief Executive Retirement and the Parade of Future Leaders." *Human Resources Management*, 1986, 25 (2), 305-333.

Tashakori, M. *Management Succession*. New York: Praeger, 1980.

Tichy, N., and Devanna, M. A. *The Transformational Leader*. New York: Wiley, 1986.

Trow, D. B. "Executive Succession in Small Companies." *Administrative Science Quarterly*, 1961, 6, 228-239.

U. S. Bureau of the Census. "Estimates and Projections of the Population: 1977-2050." *Current Population Reports*, July 1977, p. 25.

Walsh, F. Conceptualizations of Normal Family Functioning." In F. Walsh (ed.), *Normal Family Processes*. New York: Guilford Press, 1982.

Ward, J. *Keeping the Family Business Healthy: How to Plan for Continuing Growth, Profitability, and Family Leadership*. San Francisco: Jossey-Bass. 1987.

Weber, M. *The Theory of Social Economic Organization*. (T. Parsons, trans.) New York: Oxford University Press, 1946.

Whetten, D. A. "Sources, Responses, and Effects of Organizational Decline." In J. R. Kimberly and R. H. Miles (eds.), *The Organizational Life Cycle: Issues in the Creation, Transformation, and Decline of Organizations*. San Francisco: Jossey-Bass, 1980.

Williams, W. "The Uneasy Peace at Occidental." *New York Times*, September 9,1984, pp. 1-3 (business section).

From childhood, successors in family businesses are prepared in many subtle and direct ways for future leadership. This article presents a model of management succession in the family business that seems to account for the complexity of the process. The perspective adopted is one of long-term socialization.

The parent-offspring succession process is described in terms of seven stages: 1) pre-business, 2) introductory, 3) introductory/functional, 4) functional, 5) advanced functional, 6) early succession and 7) mature succession. The first three stages occur prior to the successor's full-time entry into the firm. The last two occur after the successor has assumed the leadership role. Each stage is described.

Management Succession in the Family Business

By Justin G. Longenecker and John E. Schoen

We recently visited the young president of a family-owned business. His father had founded the company in the late 1930s and retired several years ago due to a serious illness. At one point during our conversation, the president opened a desk drawer and produced a yellowed photograph.

As we looked at the picture, he said: "I guess I really have been preparing for the presidency since I was a little boy. See in the picture – that is Dad and me on a motorscraper at the factory in Illinois – it was just after World War II, and I must have been 6 or 7 years old.

In fact, with the exception of the two years I spent in the military, I have worked either on a part-time or full-time basis in the business since 1952. And believe me, some of the jobs Dad gave me were not much fun! On the other hand, I suppose those jobs made a better man out of me."

The comments of this young president and those of many other successors indicate an awareness of preparation for leadership that begins long before the successor enters the business, and that continues beyond the point of succession

A Model of Management Succession

Throughout childhood, adolescence, and adult years, successors are prepared in many ways, formally and informally, to accept the mantle of leadership at some time in the future. Some influences are subtle; others are more direct. Conditioning for future leadership includes specific training assignments prior to taking over the business, but it also includes much more. The process is apparently far more complex than would be indicated by a picture of transition based on a succession agreement between parent and child, followed by a brief orientation for the successor.

This article suggests a model of management succession that recognizes the complexities of the succession process.

The basic proposition may be stated as follows:

> Parent-child succession in the leadership of a family-controlled business involves a long-term diachronic process of socialization, that is, family successors are gradually prepared for leadership through a life-time of learning experiences.

The model provides an intuitively appealing explanation of successor preparation. Although some preliminary field studies have been conducted, no empirical data are presented here to support the model. It is desirable, of course, that the accuracy and practical implications of the model be explored by further research.

Limitations in Studies of Succession

Major studies of leadership succession have concentrated on the process by which the new leader, once selected, stabilizes himself in power.[1] These studies have been primarily concerned with short-run organizational effectiveness after the transfer of the leadership position.[2]

While analyses focusing on post-succession periods are useful, they also have several limitations. For example, the background and preparation of the successor for leadership have been ignored in most succession studies. In fact, the studies recognize neither the relationship between the development of the successor and his subsequent level of performance in the leadership position, nor the possibility of a developmental relationship between the incumbent and the successor.

Gouldner[3] and Guest,[4] however, have stated that managerial succession involves a number of stages and that analyses of succession should utilize the concept of stages. In a similar discussion, Grusky[5] noted the need to study succession as a developmental process rather than as an equilibrium process. According to these theorists, everything in succession does not occur at one time; some key variables are activated at different points in time. According to Gouldner, the limited time span and focus of inquiry found in the bulk of the succession research has contributed to an overly simplified view of managerial succession as an event rather than to its understanding as a long-term step-by-step process.

When a son or daughter succeeds a parent, it is clear that an extended relationship exists between the incumbent and the successor. To the extent that the relationship is directed toward the development of the child for the presidency of the organization, family succession can be described as a process of socialization. Indeed, the specialized learning of the successor and the relationship to the incumbent appears to occur both inside and outside of the organization and to extend over many years from the successor's childhood into his adulthood.

The central proposition of this article represents, therefore, an attempt to: (1) lengthen the time perspective of managerial succession, (2) emphasize the socialization or developmental aspects of succession; and (3) note the possibility of distinct periods of learning and activity for the successor. Although the term "father-son succession" is frequently used for the sake of simplicity, the description may apply equally well to father-daughter, mother-daughter, or mother-son succession.

Theoretical Foundations of the Succession Model

Although it has unique features, the proposed succession model has its antecedents in early succession theory. The long-term nature of managerial succession was emphasized by Davis when he observed that the transfer of leadership in business organizations may take a decade or more to complete.[6] Trow[7] and Christensen[8] also indicated that succession may involve an extended period of time and suggested the importance of the temporal dimension to the study of succession.

Stages in the succession process were mentioned by Trow,[9] Carlson,[10] and Levenson,[11] Christensen[12] and Davis[13] likewise described periods of selection and development for the successor prior to the transfer of the leadership position.

Socialization has been defined by Cogswell as the process by which individuals prepare for participation in a system or society.[14] Several contributors to succession theory including Grusky,[15] Levinson,[16] and Hodgson, Levinson, and Zaleznik[17] have used the concept of socialization in their discussions of successors and their development

The course of socialization, referring in this case to the development of the successor, is seen as a complex chain of events which ideally expose the individual to experiences that help him to perform successfully in the leadership position. The process of socialization typically requires the successor to fill several successive preparatory positions or roles. The successive steps necessitate the continued mastery of knowledge and skills as well as changes in the personal and social identity of the successor. In such a process of socialization, the incumbent (father) is typically cast as the chief socializing agent (developer) and the successor (son) as a novice (learner).[18]

Among the writers who describe the development of an individual as process of socialization, many offer insights to the dynamics of the incumbent-successor relationship. Branett and Tagiuri,[19] Crites,[20] and Edler,[21] imply the usefulness of the father-son or familial relationship in promoting the successor's interest and knowledge of the family business during his childhood and adolescent years, often culminating in a career choice to enter the organization. Similarly, the importance of the father-son relationship to the development of the successor after he formally joins the organization has been suggested by the writing of Becker and Strauss,[22] Brim,[23] Cogswell,[24] and Wheeler[25] in adult socialization.

In family business literature, there are also discussions of socialization and the long-term nature of father-son succession. Writers such as Levinson,[26] Calder,[27] Donnelley,[28] and Lazarus[29] described managers who began to indoctrinate and train their sons at an early age to replace them as the head of the family business. In such situations, childhood, adolescent, and adult model of father-son succession and socialization apparently occurred in the process of father-son succession. Thus, a systematic analysis emphasized a series of developmental steps or stages in family succession seems appropriate.

A Diachronic Framework for the Analysis of Father-Son Succession

Since the study of succession as a process differs from earlier succession studies, a new framework for analysis relating to stages in the process of father-son succession is required. Such a framework of analysis, organized on the basis of the "activities-learning experiences" of the successor, is presented in Figure 1.

The proposed framework represents a model of father-son succession and consists of seven stages including: (1) pre-business, (2) introductory, (3) introductory-functional, (4) functional, (5) advanced functional, (6) early succession, and (7) mature succession, as shown in Figure 1.

The stages are related to two important events in the family succession process: (1) the entry of the successor into the organization as a full-time employee and (2) the transfer of the leadership position to the successor. As shown in Figure 1, the "pre-business," "introductory," and "introductory-functional" stages are considered to occur prior to the successor's entry into the firm. In a similar manner. the "functional" and "advanced functional" stages relate to the development of the successor between becoming a full-time member of the organization and assuming the presidency. The last two stages of the typology, "early succession" and "mature succession," relate to activity and learning of the successor after the transfer of the presidency.

The first and last stages of the framework, "pre-business" and "mature succession," are included primarily to serve as boundaries for the actual process of a successor's development. In other words, the development of the successor for the presidency has a beginning and an end in each company although the exact points may be indeterminable and may occur with some variation among the organizations.

In one sense, the "pre-business" stage, therefore, simply establishes the boundary for subsequent stages in which substantial development occurs. On the other hand, the socialization of the successor may have started through a Ape of unplanned, passive orientation and conditioning that results from visits to the company and from play around equipment related to the business.

Like the "pre-business" stage, the "introductory" stage includes developmental experiences of the successor that occur before he is old enough to work in the family business. The "introductory" stage differs from the "probusiness" stage, however, in that the incumbent and other family members actively and intentionally introduce the successor to various facets and persons associated with the organization.

The "introductory-functional" stage begins when the successor first engages in part-time work in the family business and continues until he joins the organization as a full-time employee.

During this state, the successor completes his formal education and perhaps works as a full-time employee of other organizations or serves in the military service.

The successor enters the "functional" stage upon joining the family business on a full-time basis. This period includes the successor's initial assignment and all non-managerial positions held by the successor.

The "advanced functional" stage commences as the successor is promoted or brought into a managerial position by the incumbent and continues until the son succeeds his father in the leadership position. The successor may hold several managerial positions in the company before occupying the presidency.

When a son replaces his father as president of the family business, succession in the leadership position has, of course, taken place in the organization. On the other hand, a major conclusion of succession studies has been that the leadership role of an organization does not transfer as easily or absolutely between the incumbent and successor as does the leadership title. In a similar manner, Bailey[30] and Learned[31] have suggested that the development of a successor is seldom completed at the point he becomes president. Thus, the "early succession" stage denotes the period after the successor assumes the presidency, but before the time he masters the complexities of the position and gains the control associated with the leadership role.

The final or "mature succession" stage, then, serves as a boundary for the actual process of succession. That is, the major portion of a successor's development or socialization is considered to be completed when two conditions are met: (1) the successor has assumed the leadership role in the organization as well as the leadership position and (2) the successor is relatively autonomous in that role, particularly in terms of his relationship to his predecessor father. Since the determination of a "mature" successor is difficult to make and will vary in timing from individual to individual the "mature succession stage is defined as beginning two years after the transfer of the presidency.

Figure 1: Framework of Analysis – Stages of Father-Son Succession

Pre-Business	Introductory	Introductory-Financial	Functional	Advanced-Functional	Early Succession	Mature Succession
		Entry of Successor ‖		Transfer of Presidency ‖		
Successor may be aware of some facets of the organization or industry. Orientation of successor by family members, however, is unplanned or passive.	Successor may be exposed by family members to jargon, organizational members, and environmental parties prior to part-time employment in the firm.	Successor works as part-time employee in organization. Gradually, the work becomes more difficult and complex. Includes education and work as full-time employee in other organizations.	Successor enters organization as full-time employee. Includes first and all subsequent non-managerial jobs.	Successor assumes managerial position. Includes all supervisory positions prior to becoming the president.	Successor assumes presidency. Includes time successor needs to become leader of organization or more than "de jure" head or organization.	Successor becomes "de facto" leader of organization.

Summary

Management succession in the family-owned business involves a lengthy, almost life-long period of development. This article has proposed a model to identify seven stages of this succession process. These stages are, in turn, grouped according to two key events the entry of the successor into the business and the successor's assumption of the leadership position. Thus, the model conceptualizes management succession in the family-owned business as a long-term, diachronic process of socialization.

1. Bernard Levenson, "Bureaucratic Succession," in Amital Etzioni, ed., *Complex Organizations* (New York: Holt, Rhinehard and Winston, Inc., 1966), pp. 362-63.
2. Oscar Grusky, "Administrative Succession in Formal Organizations," *Social Forces*, Vol. 39 (December 1960), pp. 105-06.
3. Alvin W. Gouldner, "Comment," *American Journal of Sociology*, Vol. 68 (July 1%2), pp. 55-56.
4. Robert H. Guest, "Rejoinder," *American Journal of Sociology*, Vol. 68 (July 1962), p. 56.
5. Grusky, p. 106.
6. Stanley M. Davis, "Entrepreneurial Succession," *Administrative Science Quarterly*, Vol. 13 (December 1968), p. an
7. Donald B. Trow, "Executive Succession in Small Companies," *Administrative Science Quarterly*, Vol. 6 (September 1961), p. 232.
8. C. Roland Christensen, *Management Succession in Small and Growing Enterprises* (Boston: Division of Research, Graduate School of Business Administration, Harvard University, 1953), pp. 3-4, 11-14, 17-30.
9. Trow, 1961.
10. Richard O. Carlson, "Succession and Performance among School Superintendents," *Administrative Science Quarterly*, Vol. 6 (September 1961), pp. 212-13.
11. Levenson, 1966, pp. 363-67.
12 Christensen, 1953.
13. Davis, 1968, pp. 403-404, 407.
14. Betty E. Cogswell "Some Structural Properties Influencing Socialization," *Administrative Science Quarterly*, Vol. 13 December 1968), pp. 418 and 421.
15. Grusky,, 1960, pp. 106-110 and his "Managerial Succession and Organizational Effectiveness," *American Journal of Sociology*, Vol. 69 (July 1963), pp. 25-31.
16. Harry Levinson, "A Psychologist Looks at Executive Development," *Harvard Business Review*, Vol. 40, No. 5 (September-October 1963), pp.69-71.
17. Richard C. Hodgson, Daniel J. Levinson, and Abraham Zaleznik, *The Executive Role Constellation* (Boston: Division of Research, Graduate School of Business Administration, Harvard University, 1965, pp. 37-48.
18. Cogswell, 1968, pp. 419-21.
19. Rosalind C. Branett and Renato Tagiuri "What Young People Think About Managers," *Harvard Business Review*, Vol. 51, No. 3 (May-June 1973), pp. 106-18.
20. John O. Crites, "Parental Identification in Relation to Vocation Interest Development," *Journal of Educational Psychology*, Vol. 53 (1962), pp. 262-70.
21. Glen H. Edler, Jr., "Parental Power and Legitimation and its Effect on the Adolescent," *Sociometry*, Vol. 26 (1963), pp. 50-65.
22. Howard S. Becker and Anselm L. Strauss, "Careers, Personality, and Adult Socialization," *American Journal of Sociology*, Vol.62 (November, 1956), pp. 253-263, and Becker, "Personal Change in Adult Life," *Sociometry*, Vol. 27, No. 1 (March 1964), pp. 40-53.
23. Orville G. Brim, Jr. "Adult Socialization," in John A. Clauseu (ed), *Socialization and Society* (Boston: Little, Brown and Company, 1968), pp. 183-225, and his "Socialization through the Life Cycle," in Orville G. Brim, Jr. and Stanton Wheeler, *Socialization after Childhood: Two Essays* (New York: John Wiley and Sons, Inc., 1966), pp. 3-49.
24. Cogswell, op. cit., pp. 417-37.

25. Stanton Wheeler, "The Structure of Formally Organized Socialization Settings," in Orville G. Brim, Jr. and Stanton Wheeler, *Socialization after Childhood. Two Essays* (New York: John Wiley and Sons, Inc., 1966), pp. 53-116.

26. Harry Levinson, "Conflicts That Plague Family Businesses," *Harvard Business Review,* Vol. 49 (March-April 1971), pp. 91-93 and %-97.

27. Grant H. Calder, "The Peculiar Problems of a Family Business," *Business Horizons,* Vol. 4 (June 1961), pp. 96-97.

28. Robert G. Donnelley, "The Family Business," *Harvard Business Review*, Vol.42 (July-August 1964), pp. 102-105.

29. Charles Y. Lazarus, "From Family Management to Professional Management," *Indiana Business Paper* No. 8, n.d., pp. 3-5

30. Joseph C. Bailey, "Clues for Success in the President's Job," *Harvard Business Review,* Vol. 45, No. 3 (May-June 1967), pp. 97-104.

31. Edmund P. Learned, "Problems of a New Executive," *Harvard Business Review*, Vol. 44, No. 4 (July-August 1966), pp. 22-24.

According to Thomas Hubler, family businesses have a basic goal helping the "B.O.S.S." be successful. The elements of the "B.O.S.S." consist of the Business and its needs for success; the Other implying mutual commitment of members of the family business; the Self in which people are concerned for their own success, and the Shareholders which suggests consideration of the fulfillment of the needs of all key parties connected with the family business. He then outlines ten obstacles commonly faced by family businesses in their efforts to achieve success.

Ten Most Prevalent Obstacles to Family-Business Succession Planning

By Thomas Hubler

In a recent presentation at the University of St. Thomas Center for Family Enterprise Family Business Forum, John Davis, a family-business consultant, researcher, and educator, commented that their clients already know everything that consultants like himself teach. But to be successful, clients need to confront or deal with the obstacles inherent in family-business succession planning.

Of course, my first question was: What are those issues? As I looked back over my practice, I began to identify some common obstacles. But before I name these obstacles for discussion, I will describe the context in which I work with my clients.

In my work with family-business clients, the basic goal is to help the B.O.S.S. be successful. I begin my work with clients by helping them realize that they have to help the B.O.S.S. be successful so that they can successfully navigate the obstacles and deal with their issues.

At the initial client meeting, when I introduce this concept (which comes from *Collaborative Team Skills*, written by Miller and Miller, 1994), all heads turn toward the father. I announce to the father that he has just been demoted, and that the real boss around here is the four constituencies that make up the acronym. The **B** stands for the **B**usiness and what the business needs to be successful. The **O**, which is the most important part of the B.O.S.S. acronym, stands for the **O**ther. What do you want for the **O**ther and what does the **O**ther want? In the context of succession planning, each member of the family has to know that the others are committed to help each other be successful – it's a bilateral, mutual process. I use the common family vision to assist in this area. The first **S** is for self: What do I want for my**S**elf? This is the one area about which people are generally most concerned – themselves. To be successful, clients need to understand the systemic nature of family-owned businesses and that if they are to achieve personal goals (the **S**), they must create a win-win success for all four constituencies. The final **S** stands for the **S**takeholders, a group that usually includes the whole family, the employees, the customers, the vendors, and anyone else who is connected with the family business.

The ten obstacles described below are derived from my observations of client situations. These obstacles became stumbling blocks and obstructed the clients' ability to move from their current state to successfully navigate the succession planning process. I begin with Number 10, the most easily overcome obstacle:

10. The Tenth Obstacle Is Poor Expression of Feelings and Wants. In most family-owned business situations, the people most concerned do not express their feelings and wants. This omission is one of the major predictors of poor, ineffective communication. To communicate effectively, people need to be vulnerable, and that is the issue. In many family businesses, the family members do not have the capability, experience, or confidence to express their feelings and wants around the other daunting obstacles that follow. In some instances, their experience has been so frustrating and unproductive that they give up and are no longer willing to take the risk of vulnerability.

Also, both in our culture and in many families, we are taught not to express our feelings and our wants. Although family members have expectations of each other about what they want in an emotional sense, they are reluctant to express these expectations. Then, when their expectations are not met, they think it's because they're not worthy.

My solution is to engage clients in a communication training process that allows them to become more familiar with and confident about being able to express their feelings and wants. *The Collaborative Team Skills* workbook by Miller and Miller (1994), mentioned earlier, is an excellent resource for clients. They can quickly learn the skills necessary to transcend this obstacle.

9. When Differences Are Seen as a Liability Rather Than an Asset, it always creates a problem in family-owned business succession planning. Differences are really the key to an exciting and active life. Often, in family-owned businesses, differences are interpreted as "You don't love me" and "You don't care." In other instances, differences are personalized with the same kind of result.

Another example of this dynamic is the famous "Hubler's Speck of Dust Theory," which goes like this:

Family members often think about small business differences as issues they don't want to bring up with family members. Because they want to maintain family harmony in the context of family owned businesses, family members often inadvertently create the very problem they are trying to avoid by not discussing their business differences.

I use the Myers-Briggs Type Inventory as a resource tool to help people understand and objectify the notion of differences. I find that it helps me teach people in a positive way about their differences and how they can use the synergy among their differences to create a third or fourth way of doing things they otherwise would not have considered.

8. Indirect Communication is one of the most insidious problems in family-owned businesses. When differences occur, as they often do in succession planning, it almost always creates a problem if people do not talk with each other directly. Family members involved in the business often talk indirectly with other family members who are not involved. This creates a triangle that destroys the quality of family relationships. Again, I use the *Collaborative Team Skills* workbook, especially the chapter on "Styles of Communication," as a resource to educate clients about the pitfalls of indirect communication and to assist them in using direct communication for a win-win result.

7. Entitlement is often seen as a younger generation issue. Certainly that is true when younger generation people use their name as a way to achieve advantages over other people in the organization. When this occurs, it has a negative effect on morale.

In a recent client situation, the 30-year-old second-generation member of a family-owned business was encouraged by outside professionals to take over the sales department of his father's organization. Luckily, before he embarked on this self-destructive course, the son was able to do some career planning with our industrial psychologist. By having a discussion about expectations for his position and role with his supervisor and the director of sales, the son created a career plan and was able to realize how inappropriate and unrealistic his expectations were. As a result, the son was able to create a career plan that met his goals, the needs of the non-family managers, and his father's ambitions for his son's success.

Senior-generation members of family-owned businesses often have this same issue of entitlement. Founders and members of the senior generation can feel they are entitled to continue taking the primary responsibility of leadership. This sense of entitlement is often at the expense of their younger-generation adult children, who may be in their 40s and 50s and are still waiting for an opportunity to lead the company.

Clearly, the solution here is to work together to talk about the best interests of the B.O.S.S. and how we can continue to help the B.O.S.S. be successful. When family-business constituents have a common family vision, it alleviates the issue of entitlement and makes it much easier to create win-win succession strategies and solutions.

6. Scarcity is one of the most difficult issues in the context of family-business succession planning. What makes it so insidious is the fact that it is invisible because of the underlying assumption of the family that "there isn't enough to go around." This issue often manifests itself in the discussion of money, roles, and power.

In a family-owned business, there are two bottom lines. The first is the standard financial one. The second is invisible, the emotional bottom line. It is the lack of expression of appreciation, recognition, and love that is the underlying problem with emotional scarcity.

I have found two strategies that help with the issue of scarcity. The first is to have family members talk directly about what they expect from each other.

The second has to do with assisting clients to empower themselves to achieve their fullest potential, whether it is inside or outside the family business. In doing so, clients begin to understand the sense of abundance that exists in the world for all of us. A resource I have found to be particularly helpful to clients over the last eight years is the "Empowerment Workshop" offered by Gayle Straub and David Gershon. Clients who have participated in this workshop come away with a sense of abundance that allows them not only to be fulfilled but also to talk more directly about their emotional expectations from their families.

5. History is a big factor in all families, and it is certainly true in the context of family-owned businesses. A book on families, *The Way We Never Were* (Coontz, 1993), captures the essence of this concern with history. Though family history generally includes difficulties, we go out of our way to talk only about the good things, mistakenly trying to protect our children from our experiences in our own families of origin. But overlooking history is a major factor in family-owned businesses that are having a hard time creating their future. Soren Kierkegaard, the Danish philosopher, has been quoted as saying, "Life can only be understood backwards, but it must be lived forwards." Therefore, the full celebration of history is essential for continued family business success.

In my experience, not only do clients not celebrate their histories, they often take the positive aspects of their histories for granted and do not celebrate those, either.

4. Other-Oriented Regarding Change. Change is one of the most difficult aspects of life for all of us. My experience has been that even when it is positive, it is difficult. In the context of family-owned businesses, it is not unusual for people to expect others to change so that something good can occur. This expectation is a formula for disaster.

At a seminar for a trade association, I was presenting the classic family-business model of family and business in overlapping circles, which I consider to be one of the major problems and challenges in a family-owned business. A young man stood up and said, "The circles you are presenting are equal in size. If my dad were drawing these circles, his business circle would be very big, and his family circle would be very small. On the other hand, if my wife were drawing those circles, her family circle would be very big, and her business circle would be very small. So the next time you do the presentation, you may want to mention that."

As the young man was about to sit down, another participant asked, "What do your circles look like?" The young man said, "I'd rather not say." Basically he was caught in the middle between two people he loved. Just two weeks prior to the seminar, the father had called me and said, "I'm in a manufacturing business with my two sons. My oldest son is an engineer, and he's my successor. He's been absolutely terrific up until two years ago when he got married. My daughter-in-law is the problem. Can you come and fix her?"

Whenever I tell that story at seminars, the participants always laugh. It is quite an amusing story, but it is important because it demonstrates the issue of being other-oriented regarding change. The overlap of circles, which is an organizational problem in the context of family owned businesses, is experienced by family-business participants as an interpersonal issue. As a result, they often blame each other and expect the other to change.

The solution is self-responsibility – taking responsibility for what we successfully contribute to the family business and also taking full responsibility for our contribution to the problem. One of the major challenges in succession planning and family-owned businesses is helping clients take full responsibility.

3. Control. The issue of control, which is the very thing that makes owner-entrepreneurs successful, is also their Achilles heel. At seminars, I often cite Curt Carlson, Minnesota's most famous and successful entrepreneur, as an example of this. His struggle with the issue of control and the number of different people he has had in his organization as potential successors has been chronicled in the media very effectively. It has only been within the last few years, when Carlson Companies celebrated its sixtieth anniversary, that he has been able to deal successfully with that issue of control.

The reality is that it is not only the entrepreneurs, but also the family as a whole, who have to deal with the control issue. It is about change. As I mentioned earlier, change is difficult even when it is positive. It is a major, major issue for an entrepreneur who has spent the majority of his or her life closely involved with the family business.

When I was preparing for a recent presentation on aging and entrepreneurs, I began to realize that almost all of my clients were senior citizens. In thinking through the presentation, I began to realize how treacherous the succession planning process is, in that it can cause entrepreneurs to think that people are trying to change them and take away their companies.

Subsequently, I have been able to realize and work with entrepreneurs to help them develop a new dream. Entrepreneurs are driven by their dreams. Since it is not possible to change or control entrepreneurs, it does not make sense to continue to fight that battle. On the other hand, it is both possible and realistic to assist entrepreneurs and their families in developing new dreams in relation to their family, their business, their communities, their leisure time, and their philanthropy as a way to effectively deal with the issue of control.

2. Lack of Forgiveness. In the family businesses I have worked with in the last 18 years, when there has been a breakdown in family relationships, lack of forgiveness is number two on the list of those things that get in the way. It is impossible to go through life and be involved in a family business without inadvertently stepping on each other's toes. I have observed that those families that don't have the capacity to forgive each other for their transgressions clearly have a hard time being in business together.

To bridge this gap successfully, I have generally drawn upon and used my client's religious background, since most religions have a philosophy of forgiveness that is often helpful. I also suggest that clients read *A Little Book of Forgiveness* (Miller, 1994). It helps clients change their perspective about forgiving each other, and sometimes even themselves.

1. Lack of Appreciation, Recognition, and Love. Based on my experience with family-owned businesses, the number one obstacle is lack of appreciation, recognition, and love. When I read in the press about family-business catastrophes, or when I review in my ind where my own clients' breakdowns occur, lack of appreciation is often at the root. The senior generation desperately wants appreciation from their adult children, but they will deny to their dying day the fact that they want it and need it. At the same time, I have had clients who say, "What I really want is a little love around here." Younger-generation adult children have the same issue. They are still looking for recognition by their parents for their accomplishments and uniqueness. The lack of feeling recognized and appreciated underlies many of the problems in family-owned businesses. There is an implicit assumption that people are loved, but the fact that it is rarely if ever expressed often creates an obstacle.

The solution lies in teaching family members how to talk about their expectations of each other in an emotional sense, and how to express appreciation, recognition and love. Many families have a hard time doing this, and just take it for granted. From y experience, most families need to learn that the emotional bottom line in family-owned businesses is just as important – if not more important – than the financial bottom line. Appreciation, recognition, and love need to be expressed on a regular basis.

Over the years I have come to realize the importance of planning for success. As a result, it is critically important to incorporate a plan that addresses these obstacles. Addressing them proactively and in a positive way can only enhance a family business' opportunity for continued success and prosperity – both financially and emotionally.

References

Coontz, S. (1993). *The way we never were.* New York: Basic Books.

Miller, D. P. (1994) *A little book of forgiveness.* New York: Penguin Books.

Miller, S., & Miller, P. A. (1994). *Collaborative team Skills.* Littleton, CO: Interpersonal Communication Programs, Inc.

Myers, P., and Myers, K. D. (1977). *Myers-briggs type indicator.* Palo Alto, CA: Consulting Psychologists Press.

In the succession of a family business from one generation to the next, the corporation's ability to pay must be balanced with the needs of the individuals who own and operate it. Described here is an economic model and consulting tool for promoting a business-driven dialog that can result in the transferring of the business in a tax-advantageous manner while preserving the corporation's capital base.

Rough Corporate Justice

By Glenn R. Ayres

Introduction

Family business owners and their families understand that their enterprises are fundamentally different from their publicly traded cousins, and, for the most part, they would have it no other way. Basic in this distinction is how the two types of businesses cope with the inevitable stressors, or "pinch points," that all businesses and all families must confront.

One of the most critical pinch points is the succession of the family business from one generation to the next. With public companies, which usually have a clear line between management and ownership, succession is accomplished, at least in theory, by the board of directors, which selects the best-qualified person to lead the corporation. Succession is normally not a major capital-allocation issue and is managed without affecting the capital structure of the corporation. For most family businesses, however, succession is not only a highly charged emotional transition, but it also may put the capital integrity of the firm at risk.

Although a great deal has been written about training and selection of successors, estate planning for the owner/manager, and valuing family businesses, very little, if any, attention has been given to what the business needs and can afford. That consideration is essential if the capabilities of the family business are to be balanced with the needs of the individuals who own and operate it. Such a balance requires a flexibility that is gained only when a company's ability to pay exceeds the needs of its senior generation.

This paper explores that concept and suggests ways to promote a business-driven dialog that can meet the needs of all constituents in the succession process: the senior generation, the successor generation, and the business and its stakeholders. Although I developed the theory behind this concept, its transformation into an economic model and consulting tool is, to a great extent, the accomplishment of the Family Business Alliance, the multidisciplinary team referred to as the "we" in this paper (see acknowledgments).

Stages of a Family Business

A family business experiences a progression of phases as it passes through the generations. As Ivan Lansberg so perceptively points out in his work on "sibling partnerships" and "cousin consortium," a successful transition to multiple owners requires a shared vision (Lansberg, Gersick, Davis, & McCollom, 1997). We have found that this progression may occur smoothly from one phase to the next through the generations, or one phase may be repeated over several generations before the next one is entered. This progression has a great deal to do with family and business economics, but it deals even more with a family's governance philosophy, values, and its unique definitions of the benchmarks of success. Such a progression might look like this (Carlock, 1994):

Survival. This is the initial stage of any family enterprise and is characterized by the struggle for financial stability. Such a business is typically owned and operated by a single person or couple and represents the majority of the owner's net worth.

Stable. This phase characterizes an enterprise that is still probably owned and managed by a single person or couple, but it now has a stable product and customer base and has been profitable for a number of years. This type of enterprise is no longer being financed by the owner's compensation (or lack thereof), and, although the owner has begun to build net worth outside the business, its principal bank guarantor is the owner.

Professional. An enterprise in this phase of the progression has taken a fundamental step in a new direction. Ownership is probably spread among brothers and sisters (or even cousins), and although they are all involved in the business, they understand the distinction between their ownership and their management responsibilities. The business is likely experiencing fairly dramatic growth and revitalization with a blend of family and nonfamily managers leading the charge. Employment compensation is still the principal revenue source for family participants, but they also now have secure nonbusiness net worth and are no longer the principal bank guarantors for the business.

Institutional. In this final stage, the business is still privately held but now has a mix of family and nonfamily shareholders, and management has become a true "meritocracy." Family members may or may not be involved in management as their talents and interests dictate, but they take their shareholder responsibilities very seriously by ensuring that the board of directors is the true governing body of the organization and that it understands the needs and values of the shareholder base. Such a board will certainly have family members; however, it also will have management and independent representatives. Dividend income is now the principal revenue family members receive from the business, but they also have significant net worth exclusive of their family business stock interests. Preserving the corporation's capital structure and avoiding transfer tax dilution during future generational shifts in ownership are now the focus of the family shareholders.

From Survival to Institutional

Just what are the factors that make it possible for some businesses to move in three generations from "survival" to "institutional," whereas others never get past the "stable" phase? A quality product, solid management, and good people are obviously essential for getting out of the survival mode. But it is not all good practices, good engineering, and luck. In institutional family enterprises, the family members share three basic characteristics, regardless of their industry or tax situation:

They Understand and Are Committed to the Basics of Business Governance. Family members are first and foremost shareholders who understand that they are responsible for electing directors who will serve the best interests of the corporation while striving to meet the needs of all of the company's stakeholders, including its shareholders. As shareholders, family members also understand the limits of their authority and agree as a group that as long as they wish to keep the company private, they must leave governance to their board and day-to-day operations to their management team.

They Understand the Fundamental Competitive Advantage They Have over Their Publicly Traded Competitors and What They Must Do to Preserve that Advantage. Family members know that though they may not have access to the large pools of equity capital the public market offers, they have the ability to measure their success in decades, not fiscal quarters. They are also inherently more private in their dealings, capable of making faster decisions, and free to form organizational structures and strategic alliances that fit their needs rather than those dictated by the public market (Barnes & Kaftan, 1991).

They Understand the Critical Need to Build and Preserve their Capital Base. At some turning point in the history of these family businesses, a family value of "corporate stewardship" was created. Like the family farm, the business became something more than a personal financial scorecard; it became the financial (and, in all probability, the emotional) centerpiece of the greater family. This philosophical shift was founded on the idea "use the income as you need, but never spend the principal" (i.e., do not dilute the capital of the business or harm the land).

Preserving the Capital Base in a Succession

Most businesses that have progressed to the "institutional" phase have figured out how to transfer ownership down the generations without threatening the capital base every 25 to 30 years. A major deterrent to building and preserving an adequate capital base for family businesses is the senior generation's perception that they must somehow harvest their equity during the succession process. That perception is neither right nor wrong. Family businesses are sold every day to facilitate such harvesting, and, for the senior generation that built the enterprise, selling may well be a natural and highly appropriate culmination to a lifetime's work. But as well as the sale option works for the senior generation, it is not a particularly effective transfer tax strategy and may mark the end of the business as an economic resource for the family.

Access to a stable capital base is essential for the long-term success of most enterprises, especially in an economy with short product cycles that require nearly constant retooling and a highly competitive atmosphere that demands well-compensated, talented, and motivated people. No business can sustain its market position, let alone grow, when its capital base is dramatically diluted each time the mantle of ownership shifts from one generation to the next.

A simple example, unique to family businesses, illustrates this problem: Dad started a business that has now become a substantial enterprise. Like most entrepreneurs, he and Mom poured everything they had into the business. The years have been filled with financial risk, long hours, and an unflagging commitment to the enterprise. Today, the business is successful, and, at least on paper, Dad and Mom would be considered wealthy. A closer examination of the facts reveal, however, that Dad and Mom are still on the credit line at the bank; Dad's compensation, including "informal perks" that are run through the business, has not changed dramatically over the past decade; no richly funded retirement package waits in the wings, and, perhaps most distressing of all, the product life cycle in their industry has never been shorter and is getting shorter every day.

What's more, both the business and the family have put a great deal of time and effort into selecting an heir apparent for Dad – his daughter. She is very bright, earned an MBA from an outstanding midwestern university, is well respected in both the corporation and the industry, and, most important, is dedicated to the family enterprise as her life's work. Everyone, including the two siblings who are not involved in the business, is excited about where the business can go with her leadership.

Recently, Mom has begun to lobby for that long-promised retirement home in Scottsdale, Arizona. Meanwhile Dad, although not ready to retire completely, is proud of his daughter and eager to begin turning over the reins to her. Dad and his board of directors concur that it is high time they began planning the sale of his and Mom's stock to his successor.

Time for a reality check! Dad has the business appraised and finds that (on paper) he and Mom truly are among the well-to-do. Daughter begins doing spreadsheets on her personal cash flow and soon discovers that she will never make enough to buy Dad and Mom out; in fact, things are getting worse every day as the company continues to grow. The family lawyer suggests a redemption of Dad's and Mom's stock from the business, but their banker does not particularly like this idea unless the buyout is over a very long period of time and Dad stays on the corporate credit line until the process is complete. This option leaves Mom without the funds any time soon for the Arizona home and puts a tremendous debt burden on the corporation just when it needs to begin tooling up for the next product cycle.

In short, Dad and Mom have a tiger by the tail. The business provides a nice living for them day to day, but how do they ever get out? And what about the business? It has developed the next generation of stable, talented management, grown to a position of leadership in its industry, and demonstrated its ability to cope with a quickly changing marketplace. It has never been stronger, but it needs its capital to sustain this growth and prepare for the highly competitive years ahead.

To an outsider, the answer might seem easy: It is time to sell. But to many families in business, this is not a viable option (Ward, 1987). Mom and Dad did not run this business just for the money. They love it as their daughter has come to love it, and they are good at what they do. The answer for them is not to sell but to rethink the problem. The following model detailed in this paper is designed to help such families do this.

Measuring the Worth of the Business

This rethinking begins with considering how they measure the worth of their business. Unlike its publicly traded cousins, this business and these owners do not gauge their success on the market value of their stock. Profit, long-term profit, and good day-to-day livings for themselves and their employees are the benchmarks with meaning in the lives f family business owners. So why should the amount paid by a mythical ready-and-willing buyer for this business be the only measure of what the business is worth to this family? (The "price" would be its fair market value defined by our government shortly after the passage of the 1954 Internal Revenue Code in Revenue Ruling 59-60.)

The simple answer is that the institutions that purport to govern this economy all seem to push in that direction. Responsible succession planning certainly requires employing some measure of fair market value if for no other reason than it is the benchmark the Internal Revenue Service (IRS) uses. But it is only a benchmark; it is not an absolute truth.

There are almost as many opinions on what constitutes "fair market value" for a family business owner as there are appraisers ready to ply their trade and buyers ready to bid. A competitor may pay one sum because of the company's customer base or unique proprietary product; venture capitalists may pay another amount because they are not as familiar with the industry and, hence, must rely heavily on the business's management team; a large chain may pay yet a different price simply to remove this competitor from the marketplace; and the large public company may offer still another amount for the company's distribution network and physical locations. Fair market value is in the eye of the beholder: What a buyer will pay per share for 51% of a firm's stock may be 40%, 50%, or even 60% more than would be paid for only a 10% block of the stock.

Unless the owner/manager of the family business is willing to sell the majority of the company in an "arm's length" transaction, the fair market value of that stock can never be known. But who cares, anyway (except the IRS)? Everyone wants to keep it in the family, so what is required is some planning that works for both the family and the corporation.

A New Transition Yardstick

Fair market value, as traditionally defined, is a poor measure of the worth of the family business for the purpose of a successful intrafamily succession of ownership. A more realistic and even more accurate transition yardstick, however, may be NEED together with ABILITY TO PAY. This approach, which is the foundation of our model, is designed to help the senior generation prepare for the transition and provide the opportunity to talk about the coming change.

Balancing NEED with ABILITY TO PAY results in flexibility. Without such flexibility, the two generations may have to ultimately pay much more in terms of higher transition costs, such as income and estate taxes. Perhaps even more important, when the senior generation is forced to remain in "fiscal control" too long, that leaves little or no margin for error, thereby depriving the successor generation of the opportunity to make mistakes, an opportunity the senior generation had when it was starting out.

NEED is therefore a twofold concept. Monetarily, it is the sum of money the senior generation believes it "needs" to maintain the lifestyle it enjoys and to achieve its financial objectives in terms of community stewardship and "rough justice" (Ayres, 1990) for family members who have chosen not to participate in the business. NEED, however, also has a powerful social component that ties the vocational and social identification of the senior generation to the business during its transition plan. It is important to remember that NEED is not a cookie jar from which the senior generation can pull out whatever it wants, whenever it wants. Planning both the total economic harvesting and the period during which it will be done are critical because without such planning, the business cannot define its future.

On the financial side, the NEED concept begins with a private conversation between husband and wife about how much is enough. Wanting to be helpful, advisors often attempt to define this number for their clients and soon discover that they have offended the very people they are trying to serve. There is no way to get into other people's heads and make this judgment for them; they must answer this question for themselves. Advisors can, however, help set some goals, provide some tools to work with, and then get out of the way while the clients define this benchmark for themselves.

In some cultures discussions about money are some of the most sensitive, third only to those about sex and death, making many people very uncomfortable, even with trusted advisors (McGoldrick, 1982). They may fear the advisor will judge them if their expectation is perceived as too high, or they may even feel shame about their success when comparing it with other people's or even their parents' lot in life. This delicate matter requires sensitivity from an advisor who must respect clients' discomfort (even when cast in bravado) and avoid judgment when clients finally begin to share their financial needs.

One approach is to talk about the economics of succession and the needs of the business. Our intent with clients is to bring a reality check to the process that subtly sets some boundaries on the NEED definition while respectfully limiting unrealistic expectations. Next, we define a process clients can use to quantify the cash demands of their lifestyle in net worth terms. The goal here is to arrive at an annual or monthly dollar figure for maintaining their lifestyle, along with a date on which they will turn over leadership (we avoid the loaded word "retire"). Finally, we help them expand those results with their other economic goals. Some people may find parts of this process presumptuous, but our experience is that clients understand and appreciate it.

Defining NEED

Defining NEED involves five steps. The first step is a conceptual, not qualitative, discussion about the economic needs of the business. This includes some dialog on the competitive nature of the industry and how it relates to salaries, benefit packages, and training. We also discuss the position of the business in the industry relative to market share, how that has changed over the years, and what is needed to sustain (or re-energize) the company's growth. We review the debt burden the company carries, the status of personal guarantees, the need for working capital, and the need for what we call "energy capital" – the capital the company needs to stay technologically current, retain its proprietary products, sustain vitality, and grow. We try not to get too analytical at this stage because the clients must focus initially on their own NEEDS, not on those of the business. Ideally, after they have defined their own needs, they will initiate (or at least commission) a strategic planning effort from the corporate point of view that is not prejudiced by earlier assessments of corporate worth.

In the second step, we help clients identify their economic goals for their family and community, emphasizing their children and grandchildren; this is done in general, rather than specific, terms (see Jaffes, 1991). The economic "fairness" discussions occur at this point, and we get to glimpse their dreams for grandchildren's education and community stewardship, as well as their concerns for an aged parent, a favorite niece, or even an old and trusted friend. Keeping this discussion general often makes it easier to quantify these special needs once their own economic needs are better defined. The goal here is to learn how they feel about treating their children equally (ensuring that they understand the inherent contradictions in that phrase; see "Rough Family Justice," ibid.), what they see as their children's capabilities, and what they believe they want their legacy for their family and their community to be.

In step three, we introduce them to a budget-driven planning model and show them how to use it. Whatever the model, it should start with current living expenses and then move on to help them define what they NEED to accumulate outside the business to sustain that lifestyle after the succession. Using a comprehensive budget worksheet is an easy, often quite revealing way to capture current expenses: People at the higher socioeconomic levels often have no real grasp of how much they spend each year and on what. This process should be simple, as well as private.

In addition to filling out the worksheet, we want them to define what their post-succession lifestyle will look like. To do this well, they must think only about themselves for a little while. So many clients have lived such responsible lives for so long that even though they have no problem discussing the needs of their business, their children, or even their communities, they struggle to articulate what they personally want out of this transition. It is often helpful to ask them to define what their ideal job would be like after the succession; where they dream of living or traveling; how often they want to be in contact with the business; what they have always wanted to do but never had the time; and what non-economic needs the greater family or even the business may have that they would like to finally have an opportunity to address.

Table 1. Questions to Consider When Determining NEED

1. What assets do you have outside the business? This information is readily available from a current financial statement, which most clients in this situation already have.

2. What do you believe the rate of inflation will be during your retirement, and what rate of return would you like to use on your traditional investments?

3. What do you see as a target date for succession, and what, if anything, would you like to do for the company post-succession? If you do not see yourself with the company post-succession, will you still be working? If so, at what? Have you discussed these issues with your board of directors?

4. Do you have children or others who depend on you for economic support?

5. Which of your children do you envision being involved in the business as shareholders and/or managers? Has the family determined how children enter the business, and has the business determined how the children will be evaluated and promoted?

6. If all of your children are not destined to own the family business, what would you like to do for those children? How do you equate this with the economic opportunity afforded to the children who are involved?

7. Where do you intend to live, will you be buying a new home, and what will you do with your current residence?

8. Do you have any special goals you would like to meet regarding the community? Would you like to involve your greater family in meeting those goals? Have you discussed these issues with your family?

This "dreaming" is critical. Without it, the economic analysis will be fatally flawed because neither the advisor nor the company will have the data necessary to consider these special concerns. More important, unless the clients believe that the succession plan will work for them personally (both financially and emotionally), it simply will never get done.

The fourth step is the "sharpening and polishing" phase. Once the clients have done their dreaming and their lifestyle research, it is time to put all the NEED pieces together. Here, using their own work product, we help them extrapolate a vision of tomorrow. Economically, the result will be a post-succession lifestyle amount sufficient to also meet their planning goals. Emotionally, this will be a picture of what their role in the business will be like after the succession. To form a realistic picture, additional information may be needed, which can be drawn out by using such questions as those in Table 1.

Many of these questions will trigger for the advisor and, hopefully, the client the realization that some fundamental homework has yet to be done. Nevertheless, bringing this NEED analysis to as complete a conclusion as possible is advisable before starting the unfinished homework. The goal is to develop a sense of the doable for people who for years may have felt that short of selling the family business, succession planning was simply not possible. Both the senior and the successor generations need definable goals to develop the emotional energy necessary to sustain the process of succession through to completion. Assumptions naturally will change as family and business homework gets done, but without those initial believable goals, it is simply too easy to just go back to work with the intent of facing up to these concerns some day that all too often never comes.

The final step in the initial NEED process is to run the numbers. Whatever model is used, it should result in a figure that represents how much the client needs to set aside in nonbusiness assets to meet these basic needs:

Need 1: Maintain the lifestyle they have worked so hard to achieve.
Need 2: Attain the desired level of personal economic freedom.
Need 3: Leave the business confidently.
Need 4: Have sufficient resources to meet their special family and community needs.

In addition and equally important, we want a vision that can be articulated in business terms, of what the senior generation's involvement, if any, in the business may be after the succession.

Before moving on to the second half of the NEED-ABILITY TO PAY equation, it is important to acknowledge that this paper and the economic model presented here deals with the easiest part of the succession process – the economics of the transaction. For this or any other model to succeed, the truly difficult work of creating a shared family vision for the future of the business must come first, especially when the departing generation takes from the business significantly less than the fair market value. This implies the need for a cultural shift from building personal net worth to building corporate net worth. For this to happen, a certain threshold of personal wealth must already be achieved and the business in the future must have the capacity to provide future generations of owners with a reasonable return on their family business stock.

Rarely is this shift completed in one generation; it takes time, wise governance, good management, and perhaps some luck before a business and a family can progress from "professional" to "institutional." But the process must start somewhere. A look at the truly "institutional" family enterprises proves that one generation must see this status as an attainable goal, limit their own personal financial gain, and set in motion the process of building a family value system that says, "This will be our economic and social centerpiece for generations to come." The model presented here is an attempt to show how this process might get started.

Determining ABILITY TO PAY

Moving to the other side of the family-wealth, business-prosperity equation, the issue is one of balance. Once the NEED of the ownership generation is determined, the questions become, does the business have the ABILITY TO PAY? Can it afford to meet that NEED? ABILITY TO PAY is determined by the answers to the following questions:

1. Can the business generate sufficient resources for ownership succession to finance the ownership generation's NEED, while still meeting its own capital requirements?
2. Will lenders, suppliers, and other equity holders allow existing credit relationships to shift to the new ownership team without the personal guarantees from the senior generation?
3. Is the successor generation willing to suppress their own financial ambitions so that the "harvesting" of this NEED might take place?

ABILITY TO PAY is based on the future, not the past. Succession planning so that the business can afford to meet the ownership generation's NEEDS must be rooted in the fundamentals of long-term financial success. These basics are too often overlooked in traditional approaches to succession that focus on only the corporation's historical numbers and do not consider what the business should look like in the next generation. Basing ABILITY TO PAY entirely on the past violates the principle that the corporation is the engine that will make a prosperous future possible. It also violates the principle of stewardship to the corporation by both the ownership and successor generations. In this sense, the business is like a forest: If the cutting (or harvesting) is not selective, the forest will be lost.

Long-term business vitality centers on the ability to foster what we call "innovative development," which involves attracting and holding talented and motivated people and having access to sufficient capital to sustain long-term growth. These fundamentals are vitally important and all too frequently ignored by families in business together.

To continue to grow, to keep its manufacturing and distribution processes competitive, and to attract and hold skilled and motivated people, the corporation must have financial resources for: labor and management, marketing and selling, capital for new equipment, startup costs for new products, working capital investment, and research and development and modernization.

Innovative development is a type of modernization that has two equally important pieces: the creation of new tangible products or services and the creation of new processes that support that development. Innovative development can involve new tooling, new products, new operations, new uses for current products, new incentives for sales or manufacturing forces, new space – in short, a new approach that could lead to reinventing the business.

Most of our clients are not grounded in this aspect of business. They have instead capitalized on a highly valued work ethic, a commitment to customer service, and an intuitive wisdom that allowed them to make quick decisions to thwart problems before they ran out of control or to capitalize on new opportunities while others were still studying the problem. In other words, they have put their focus elsewhere. Likewise, many of our clients are still using 1950s or 1960s technology to fabricate their products or run their management information systems. Others are relying on a product that has been in the stream of commerce for more than 20 years. With the margins common in today's global market and with product life cycles measured in months rather than years, many of these clients are operating on borrowed time. Such organizations must now look to new distribution channels and at their manufacturing margins or risk falling by the wayside. This reality can be difficult to face from both a planning and an emotional perspective because many of these companies are driven by an entrepreneurial ethos that says, "I've always been successful doing it my way, and no one is going to tell me how to run my business." A serious problem also arises when Dad or Uncle Bill is the only innovator/inventor, and the next generation has neither those skills nor perhaps even an appreciation of their value. For such companies, the questions are, "Where is the new product to come from, and who will represent these sentiments in the planning arena?"

Attracting and holding talented and motivated people also require planning as well as money. All too often, the succession process comes at the same time that clients are struggling to convert their family businesses from traditional, entrepreneurially driven enterprises to more differentiated, managerially driven companies. These businesses are being affected by a variety of previously unused or at least underused disciplines, ranging from strategic planning to organizational development. All of this comes when there is a great deal of competition in the marketplace for people (both family and nonfamily) who can lead these businesses through these dramatic changes. The question often becomes one of how to attract and hold young talent in an organization still run by a dictator, no matter how benevolent.

One of the hallmarks of many of our successful clients is that they run "lean and mean" and are proud of it. This is not necessarily bad – even the public sector is trying hard to get back to the basics; but for many of these clients, this is more than a business strategy, it is part of their culture and deeply embedded in the owner/manager's need for control. But many of these businesses have simply grown beyond the ability of one person to make all the decisions. In addition the next generation of leadership often recognizes, as they attempt to go from an owner/manager model to one with multiple sibling or even cousin ownership, that a serious element of distrust (usually unspoken) arises when they are unwilling to subject management to the discipline of professional governance by a functioning, well-staffed, and impartial board of directors.

To maintain technical competitiveness, adequately staff the organization, and sustain growth, the business must also be able to obtain access to sufficient capital. Most clients' histories of capital use falls at one or the other end of a continuum. In many companies whose owners grew up during the Great Depression, debt is an evil to be avoided at all costs. Although one could argue credibly that the debt of these companies has not disappeared but rather has taken the form of diminished owner compensation or shareholder financing, the emotional reluctance to use debt financing remains powerful.

At the other extreme, everything is leveraged and always has been, and shareholder personal guarantees are a way of life. These companies, while not at all frightened by the prospect of discussing the use of debt financing, will often have little or no cash reserves, plan very little (perhaps because the prospect of facing this situation is so frightening), and believe with real conviction that anything is possible if one just has the guts to try. To make things work on both sides of the NEEDABILITY TO PAY equation, we must address not only the corporation's ABILITY TO PAY, but also the willingness of the senior generation to slow down or even eliminate its own personal debt-financed deals.

At either extreme, the task is to analyze what is truly possible in an atmosphere where change is inevitable. Nothing speaks louder for the need to begin this process early and to make it as inclusive as possible. It will take time to dig out the facts. Start slowly until confidence in the new methodology is gained, and sell the process to the company's principal stakeholders, not the least of which are its bankers, key suppliers, and major customers. In starting to estimate future levels of growth needed to sustain the company's goals, it is important to recognize that this is not a "gogo" time. Rather, it is a time to consolidate, strengthen the fundamentals, and give the principals in both generations breathing room to let all of this happen. Although no growth is probably a killer, growth must be kept under control and key stakeholders must know that this is exactly the plan, to avoid having a slowdown in growth look like a fundamental weakening of the business.

We have had significant success in getting both lenders and major franchisers to shift or even eliminate personal guarantees when we include them in this process. Once both generations feel good about the succession plan that has been laid out, we coach them on how to present this plan to their key stakeholders at the very outset of the implementation process and *before* any fundamental change in the underlying relationship is needed. These stakeholders are gratifyingly receptive to requested changes when such requests are conditioned on predictable events that are expected to occur *in the future*. For example, we encourage our clients to ask lenders to eliminate the personal guarantees of the senior generation or convert lending security from personal guarantees to an asset base only *after* the family has installed a new professional board of directors, strengthened their management team in key areas, upgraded their basic technology, and demonstrated an ability to sustain profits (even at a more modest level). Lenders, after all, are almost as terrified as their customers at the uncertainties of the succession process. But it is hard for the lenders to balk when the clients voluntarily offer this information along with an outline of a plan that trades increased compensation to the owners for a limited period of time for eliminating the potential for disastrous transfer tax liabilities. The key, of course, is to inform lenders early on about the company's intentions and to get *current* promises of *future* action only after the company has demonstrated its ability to attain the stated objectives.

Implicit in this model is the willingness of the senior generation to pass their equity (stock) on to the successor generation at little or no cost as this harvesting process becomes a functioning reality. In payment for this equity shift, the successor generation is willing to restrain their own economic demands on the business during this transition. Trust becomes a critical part of this equation, and such trust is best nurtured with the aid of a well-thought-out strategic plan that contains agreed-on targets for such NEED payments, the timing of corresponding gifts, and clearly understood benchmarks to ensure that the fiscal health of the business remains unimpaired.

Balancing the NEED-ABILITY TO PAY Equation

More often than not, owners and successors are surprised to learn that on this basis the business truly does have the ABILITY TO PAY. Even for companies that are a little soft on ABILITY, if this process is started early enough and supported by solid planning, many are capable of growing into this solution. The real trouble occurs when this process is delayed too long. If this happens, there simply may not be enough time for the senior generation to harvest sufficient resources without crippling the company with debt or forcing it into questionable quick-fix strategies. When the NEED-ABILITY TO PAY equation truly cannot be balanced, it is probably time to sell. But even this result is preferable to alternatives that are often marked by a clash of economic needs and feelings of entitlement when an economically realistic transition either cannot or does not occur. Even when a family business uses this process to discover that NEED actually does outstrip the corporate ABILITY TO PAY or that only a full fair market value harvesting of the equity buildup will satisfy the personal goals of the senior generation, uncovering these realities in a respectful, inclusive planning process is better than ignoring them until the successor generation becomes tired of waiting or the business is sold in a panic occasioned by ill health. Like so many concepts embedded in the art of family business consulting, this model simply provides another way to invite the family into a focused dialog about something that seems difficult to discuss: their wants, needs, and goals about money and all that it symbolizes.

The objective is to create additional, nonbusiness net worth for the successor generation over time to eliminate their dependence on the corporation to meet their NEEDS. Note that if the senior generation is still on the corporation's debt as personal guarantors, negotiations with the lenders will probably be necessary to eliminate or shift those guarantees to the successor generation before the senior generation can be expected to part with significant stock.

As the company initiates such a plan, actual equity must begin moving between the generations as the determined benchmarks are reached. This is important not only because it will enhance the level of trust between generations, but it will also send a strong signal to lenders, suppliers, key customers, and employees that the transition is moving forward on time and as planned. Like it or not, these key stakeholders are watching, and the success of the next generation in retaining their loyalty will have a lot to do with how smoothly this transition takes place.

From a transfer tax perspective, both generations would like this series of transfers to be as predictable and uneventful as possible. Prolonging the stock transfer to the next generation risks not only losing the use of earlier years' annual exclusions from the gift tax but also the accuracy of the valuation made for gift tax purposes, which may understate the IRS's view of the value of the enterprise. Because the IRS is still using the "fair market value" concept to value these transfers, delaying the shift of ownership may make the new structure more stable and hence subject to higher taxes on the stock being gifted. Discounting techniques, such as family limited partnerships, can and probably should also be used to help depress tax valuation throughout this process, but time is really the client's best ally. Get started early, make the transfers in small denominations, keep it on schedule, and avoid, if at all possible, a large transfer at the end of the transition. It is also probably a good idea for the shareholders to adopt a valuation mechanism or formula that can be consistently applied throughout. In so doing, however, it is vital to ensure that this mechanism addresses not only the parameters articulated by the IRS but also those unique to the business and its position in the marketplace.

The day is probably not far off when the valuation assumptions of Revenue Ruling 59-60 can be more realistically recast for the valuation of family-owned and closely held businesses. The essence of that ruling, and the appraisal art that has evolved to implement it, is that publicly traded companies already have taken into account through the actions of the public market all the variables that affect a given company's profitability and hence its value. Accordingly, as the theory goes, the best we can do is attempt to equate private companies with their publicly traded cousins. This, of course, has given rise to the appraisal methodology of determining dividend paying capacity through a series of simplistic profit and loss (P & L) and balance sheet adjustments (compensation norms, excess cash, inflated rents, etc.) and then comparing those results with supposed comparables that are publicly traded. Although this may do rough justice in some cases, particularly with the application of appropriate discounts for lack of marketability and (when applicable) minority interests, it is still overly simplistic and fraught with potential error.

The harvesting model described here is in its infancy and was designed as a planning tool, not as a valuation device. It may contain, however, the kernel of an approach that arrives at a more accurate "fair market value" of a private concern. The essential difference in these two approaches is that rather than looking just at excesses on the private company's financial statements for the purpose of determining "dividend paying capacity," we have attempted to dig a deeper, and, hopefully, more substantive trough that considers the fundamentals of long-term future success more accurately than by focusing only on short-term compensation and cash.

The Model Process for Guiding Family Businesses

At a small number of businesses with which we work, we discover that their internal financial people and senior management are conversant in and capable of documenting their conclusions on the topics that must be addressed in the ABILITY TO PAY part of the equation. They are usually in the process of setting a strategic direction for their firm that considers both the human and the economic realities of ownership succession. In such situations, we can quickly determine whether the equation can be balanced. If it can, we move on to determining how and when the harvesting should take place. Table 2 outlines a few techniques that might be used to help push additional resources into the hands of the ownership generation once ABILITY TO PAY is ascertained.

Most of our clients, however, do not have the internal expertise to determine their own harvesting capability or corporate ABILITY TO PAY. In those circumstances, we need a focused, respectful process to help guide the family and their business toward something they can confidently implement. The actual analysis of a client's situation is more sophisticated and customized than any simplistic model or outline we can offer at this point, but hopefully a discussion of the simplistic issues this planning encompasses will prove helpful.

One approach is essentially a four-step strategic-planning process that comprises numerical analysis as well as organizational and governance concerns. All these factors are inter-related, each having both financial and emotional components. Broadening the discussion to include all of these factors will bring up a wide variety of styles and points of view.

Table 2. Techniques for Giving the Ownership Generation Additional Resources

1. Increase compensation so that it's geared for a specific transition period to profits or sales to limit concerns about it being unreasonable.
2. Defer compensation and back it with a "rabbi trust" to provide the confidence that the dollars will be there.
3. Increase rents on (or even corporate purchase of) outside-owned real estate or equipment used by the business.
4. Set aside consulting compensation for post-succession assistance to the corporation and/or lump-sum payments for noncompetition covenants.
5. Upgrade pension and retirement benefits, perhaps including a limited employee stock ownership plan.
6. Change corporate form to enhance short-term cash flow to the senior shareholders.
7. Repay old shareholder debt.
8. Use the senior generation's unproductive or underproducing assets to fund split-interest charitable vehicles to increase cash flow and create a tax-absorbing charitable deduction.
9. Create passive income streams with equipment partnerships, royalty income, and directors' fees. .
10. Use an end-of-process, limited corporate redemption to put the plan over the top.

Step One, Bring All the Concerns Together. We try to make this process as inclusive as possible with representatives from senior management, the independent directors (if there are any – and, by the way, this is a good excuse to recruit a couple), sales, manufacturing, and human resources, along with the senior financial people, both internal and external. One of the side benefits of this process is that it provides an opportunity for the outside accountants to demonstrate in very real terms how some of their analytical skills also might be used in upgrading the company's basic management and financial tools.

Step Two, Gather the Expertise. This is a multidisciplinary exercise, because no one person or discipline has all the answers. Some consider it financial overload to have three or four outside consultants around the table during this process, but it is important to keep everyone informed about the progress and when and how the different skills of the consulting team can be helpful. We try to have everyone present at an initial planning meeting where we develop a primary planning team and identify when specific expertise will be needed as the process unfolds. For example, I might facilitate the primary planning effort with a team of four or five inside people and the outside accountant.

Typically a lawyer will not be there but knows what is going on and is prepared to modify estate planning and corporate compensation and benefits documents to dovetail with the process. Similarly, a consultant on the social sciences side is usually moving on a parallel path with a series of family council meetings to provide the family with the emotional confidence to allow this process to be supported by both generations involved.

Step Three, Encourage Dialog. With the permission of the senior generation, we try as early as possible to reveal both our underlying methodology and the implicit deal that we are trying to broker; that is, to let the senior generation harvest to a level that will sustain their own personal goals. In exchange, they will come to the table with whatever gift planning tools they can marshal to get this stock into the hands of the next generation at little or no cost. This dialog has the benefit of allowing the senior generation to share some of their most personal dreams with their own children (and it is truly amazing how seldom this occurs), but also of providing the planning team with a doable target for their efforts.

It is important for both sides to acknowledge that this harvesting process, if successful, will have been made possible through solid planning, restraint on what the senior generation could have taken from the business had they chosen to sell it, and the willingness of the successor generation to lead the corporation toward this goal while holding in check their own personal financial ambitions. There is plenty of credit to go around; do not forget to say it out loud.

Step Four, Run the Numbers. Although not strictly a numbers-driven process, it needs to be grounded in the numbers. This is where the abstract meets reality and where businesspeople develop their level of trust in the outcome. Next we examine how our basic ABILITY TO PAY model works.

Basic ABILITY TO PAY Model

Gathering Financial Data. We begin by gathering at least the last five years of financial statements, including balance sheets, income statements (P& Ls), cash flow statements (if available), and corporate tax returns. If we are fortunate enough to have industry statistics on debt ratios, profit margins, salaries, growth rates, and product life cycles, we pull in that information as well.

Analyzing Cash Flow. To start, we extrapolate from the raw data the firm's After Tax Cash Flow for those five preceding years. An easy task when cash flow statements are available, but even when they are not, it is not too difficult to rework the P& Ls by subtracting the noncash deductions. Regular debt financing should also be in this figure, as should a rough determination of annualized borrowing power if the client has never used their debt financing capability. We also add back any amounts that go to off-balancesheet entities that might be pulled back into the corporation during a reorganization, as well as the support of any family projects (for example, a subsidized hobby farm) that will be sold during this transition. We subtract from the available cash flow any amounts that have not been adequately serviced over the years, such as loans due shareholders. The average of this modified historical series (adjusted for any abbreviations that might have taken place in a single year, such as a major casualty loss or strike-enhanced revenues that spiked earnings) gives us our starting point and our first data entry number for our model.

Determining Research and Development Budget. The next number is one of the hardest to determine for any enterprise, but it is particularly difficult for growing family businesses: the Research and Development (R & D) budget. Few of the companies we work with have R & D departments to begin with. We use this term to include new product development as well as manufacturing and MIS process modernization. As a very rough starting point, we look at the last year's balance sheet entry for the accumulated depreciation figure and note how that figure has grown over the last five years. Even though this will not give us a final answer, it does provide some idea of how old the technology is and how long it has been since this sector received attention. If this figure is very crude, that recognition should give the group some impetus to dig a little deeper. We often find that after some dialog with our internal sources, it is most time-and cost-efficient to bring in an outside expert to estimate what and how long it will take to keep plant and equipment current and competitive. The external accountant usually can provide data on MIS. This investigative process gives us our second data entry number.

Analyzing Financial Status During Pro-posed Transition. Now we move on to Management (and, as necessary, governance) costs and attempt to predict what the organization will look like as it moves through this transition over the next several years. Growth will have a strong impact here, as will the need to provide more management depth for an organization that has traditionally run very lean. It is important to keep in mind here the cost of any outside help that is needed during this period, particularly in the areas of training and technology upgrades. If the client is an organization in which innovation has always been the sole responsibility of the senior generation, then a major hiring or engineering outsourcing commitment may be necessary. The end product translated as the new hires and the related cost of bringing them up to speed is our third data entry number.

Analyzing Cost and Impact of New Products. Akin to R & D, but not as difficult for the client to grasp, is the New Product Cycle Cost. Most clients have gone through the pain and expense of bringing a new product into production or adding a major new line to the sales inventory. As we explore this area, we take care to ensure that we have a sense of the research costs, what it takes to retool production facilities, train personnel, and how much time is involved. While many of our clients fail to adequately plan, this is one area where they probably have done some recent investigations. Even if they have not, a lot of good information is available from suppliers and industry sources. The cost and frequency of bringing new and upgraded products on line during this time frame is our fourth data entry number.

Determining Other Programmed Expenses. Every such analysis needs a space to add in the expenses that are unique to the particular company. Here, under the label of "Other Programmed Expenses," we add in any new strategic expenses the company sees itself investing in during this transition. Included here might be such things as a plant expansion, new sales outlets, or the continuation of a program of acquisitions. The cost of debt financing is included if it, too, will be a new element during this period. Other Programmed Expenses is our fifth data entry number.

Determining Available Resources. Our final raw data entry number looks at any balance sheet "Excess Cash," marketable securities, or other investment assets (not used in the operation of the business) that would be available for distribution or could be used to finance operations as a part of this succession plan. It is important not to overlook any loan covenants that may require that some or all of these "excess" resources remain on the balance sheet as security for the corporation's debt package. In some cases, it may also be prudent to look at the amount of inventory and/or raw material that is kept on hand and determine if some cash could be freed up by strategically cutting back in these areas. Finally, a review of receivable collection and payable cycles should be made to ensure that lazy or simply old habits are not unnecessarily delaying the receipt of (or distributing) needed working capital already due (or owed by) the company. This Excess Cash figure is our sixth and final raw data entry number.

Predicting Growth. Our next step is to add growth (or decline) percentages to these raw data entry numbers as the planning team believes appropriate. A positive percentage figure in cash flow will translate directly into increased revenues, so it is important to be sure that this relationship fits estimates of future performance. We find it is better to use modest percentage adjustments or no adjustment at all if we are unsure of how actual performance will track with our raw data. As a quick check, we use as guidelines historical sales, profits and return on asset ratios – information that we already have available. If the application of a positive percentage adjustment produces a result that significantly exceeds the historical figures, it is probably time to rethink the appropriateness of the adjustment.

In some areas, such as R & D and Other Programmed Expenses, it may be preferable not to add a percentage increase if they are short-term modernization expenses that probably will not reoccur during this succession process. In some cases, the entries for New Product Cycle Costs and Excess Cash even dictate a negative percentage adjustment. The effect of a negative percentage adjustment is simply to spread the cost of a large, up-front expense over a number of years (i.e., the larger the negative percentage, the faster the expense will disappear as time goes by).

Determining Harvesting Capacity. When all these data entry numbers and their corresponding percentage adjustments (if applicable) have been determined to the satisfaction of the planning team, they are then simply balanced out. The result is a Harvesting Capacity number (the amount of cash available after forecasted costs, over time); or what the company has the ABILITY TO PAY the senior generation annually in excess of the senior generation's current compensation and benefit package and still sustain profitable operations during this transition. When this figure is compared with the NEED analysis produced by the senior generation, it will very quickly be obvious if the equation can be balanced.

Three Illustrations

A Balanced Equation. Mom and Dad, ages 54 and 55, respectively, determined that in addition to their current, nonbusiness holdings, they needed to add $150, 000 in after-tax savings annually to meet their personal NEED objective within the next 10 years. The corporation's ABILITY TO PAY calculation showed that the business could continue to maintain a modest 5% annual growth, modernize as needed, and still distribute an additional $185, 000 annually to the senior generation. This equation was in balance, and the corporation had a modest cushion with which to work.

An Equation Out of Balance. Mom and Dad, ages 67 and 66, respectively, determined that in addition to their current, nonbusiness holdings, they needed to add $625, 000 in after-tax savings annually to those holdings to meet their personal NEED objective within the next three years. The corporation's ABILITY TO PAY calculation showed that the business could continue to maintain a modest 3% annual growth, modernize as needed, and still distribute an additional $200, 000 annually to the senior generation. This equation is out of balance. Even if the senior generation were willing to stay involved a little longer, there simply was not enough time to make up the difference. As frequently happens, this family waited too long to get started, and the senior generation probably failed to take enough money out of the business over the years to build an adequate nonbusiness nest egg. Here, the realistic options might include finding a new equity partner; doing a part-gift, part-sale transaction with the successor generation; splitting off an operating division and selling the balance; or simply selling the business outright.

An Equation Brought into Balance. Mom and Dad, ages 58 and 60, respectively, determined that in addition to their current, nonbusiness holdings, they needed to add $325, 000 in aftertax savings annually to those holdings to meet their personal NEED objectives within the next five years. The corporation's ABILITY TO PAY calculation showed that the business could continue to maintain a 6% annual growth, modernize as needed, and still distribute $175, 000 annually to the senior generation. This equation was initially out of balance, but in subsequent meetings of the planning team, Mom and Dad determined that they would remain involved for an additional two years and assist the company in a consulting capacity for three years beyond that date. The corporation also reworked its calculations and determined that it could maintain its marketplace position at a more modest 4% annual growth rate, thereby freeing an additional $50, 000 annually to distribute to the senior generation. With these adjustments, the equation was brought into balance.

Conclusion

Even when it ultimately proves impossible t balance the equation, in our experience this process promotes an essential dialog among the three constituents of the transition: the senior generation, the successor generation, and the business and its stakeholders. This fosters an understanding of the business fundamentals that are involved in a succession. This understanding takes a great deal of the mystery and, in some cases, the personal hurt out of a transaction that simply was not meant to be. When the equation does balance, the results are more predictable: Everyone feels good about the contribution that they have made to the process, and the business has taken a giant step toward becoming a long-term economic centerpiece for the family and a commercial institution.

It is my hope that the process presented here will help ensure the capital integrity of your client firms while satisfying the needs of both the senior and successor generations so that what is ultimately passed on is the future, not the past.

References

Ayres, G. (1990). Rough family justice, *Family Business Review, 3* (1), 3 –23.

Barnes, L. B. , & Kaftan, C. J. (1991). *Organizational transitions for individuals, families, and work groups.* New York: Prentice Hall.

Carlock, R. (1994). *The need for organizational development in successful entrepreneurial firms.* New York: Garland Publishing.

Jaffe, D. (1991). *Working with the ones you love.* Berkeley: CA: Conari Press.

Lansberg, I. , Gersick, K. E. , Davis, J. A. , & McCollom, M. (1997). *Generation to generation.* Cambridge, MA: Harvard Business School Press.

McGoldrick, M. (1982). *Ethnicity and family therapy.* New York: Guilford Press.

Ward, J. L. (1987). *Keeping the family business healthy.* San Francisco: Jossey-Bass.

CHAPTER 3
MANAGEMENT &
STRATEGIC PLANNING

The managerial issues confronting family firms differ somewhat from those facing non-family businesses. Personal and family goals, emotions, and impact on relationships are much stronger considerations in family business management and strategic planning.

This chapter deals with some of the management issues made especially thorny because the business is a family firm. How do you compensate family and non-family employees, and how do pay issues change over the life of the business? Why and when is employee turnover good for the family business?

Many family businesses fail to engage in meaningful strategic planning. Articles contained in this section seek to demystify the process, showing how to engage in strategic planning and how to adapt the strategic planning process to family and business goals.

This article reviews the literature on family business from a strategic management perspective. In general, this literature is dominated by descriptive articles that typically focus on family relationships. However, the literature does not usually address how these relationships affect the performance of a family business. Taking a strategic management perspective, we outline a new set of objectives for family-business research. We also identify some of the key issues and gaps that should be explored in future studies if research is to contribute to improving the management practices and performance of family firms.

Strategic Management of the Family Business: Past Research and Future Challenges

By Pramodita Sharma, James J. Chrisman, Jess H. Chua

Introduction

Currently, family-business research is largely descriptive rather than prescriptive. Most of the literature that has taken a prescriptive approach has done so from the perspective of how to improve family relationships rather than business performance. While a better understanding of the family in the family-business dyad is valid and useful, there are other goals that deserve to be pursued as well.

There have been a number of recent review articles on family business by scholars such as Friedman (1991), Handler (1989), Marshack (1993), and Wortman (1994). These reviews, while aware of the literature's orientation toward family rather than business issues, have largely taken the literature as is. In this article we review the family-business literature from a strategic management perspective with the purpose of examining the extent to which this literature deals with issues that might lead to improvements in the management practices and performance of family firms. Recent work has indicated a need for such a perspective (Harris, Martinez, and Ward, 1994; Wortman, 1994).

In this article we attempt to identify, as comprehensively as space allows, the important issues and directions in which future research can prove especially useful in strategic management. Since most of the research has not been conducted from the strategic management viewpoint, many studies fit only loosely into our framework. Unfortunately, with this extent of coverage, it is not possible to explore each topic in detail and do justice to all the researchers and theorists who have made contributions. For example, we exclude topics such as taxation, health, and family foundations. We include, however, some articles that deal with the relation between family and work, recognizing that these relations can have an important influence on the strategic management process in family firms. Thus, what follows is a discussion of the family-business literature's progress in strategic management issues rather than a review that analyses the contents and methodologies of relevant articles.

The next section provides a definition of family business and discusses a framework steeped in the paradigm of strategic management by which, we believe, progress in the field of family business toward improving family-firm performance can be judged. We then use this framework to discuss the family business literature and present an agenda for future research. We provide our conclusions in the final section.

The Strategic Management Process

Before describing the strategic management process and evaluating the literature on family business from this perspective, it is important to define what we mean by a family business. Following Chua, Sharma, and Chrisman (1996), we define family business as a business governed and/or managed on a sustainable, potentially cross-generational, basis to shape and perhaps pursue the formal or implicit vision of the business held by members of the same family or a small number of families. This definition is important from a strategic management perspective because it implies that there are goals being pursued, a strategy designed to fulfill those goals, and mechanisms in place to implement the strategy and control the firm's progress toward the achievement f its goals. This is what strategic management is all about.

It is important to point out that this definition is based on behavior instead of a list of components. It encompasses the nuclear-family-controlled firm and even the publicly held firm that is shaped and managed by two or more generations of a family that might not hold controlling interest in the firm. Therefore, a large number of shareholders, which is the legal criterion for classifying companies as publicly held, does not automatically disqualify a firm as a family firm. Consequently, we only discuss family versus non-family firms instead of family, closely held, or privately held versus publicly held firms. While this definition explicitly allows for multiple-family ownership, for expository convenience throughout the rest of this article we refer to the controlling family in the singular.

The basic strategic management processes for both family and non-family firms is similar in the sense that a strategy, whether implicit or explicit, must be formulated, implemented, and controlled in the context of a set of goals. In this sense, even performance is similar, since it should be measured with respect to achieving a set of goals. The differences are in the set of goals, the manner in which the process is carried out, and the participants in the process. For example, in family firms, the owner-family is likely to influence every step of the process (Harris, Martinez, and Ward, 1994), whereas in non-family firms, family influences are at best (or worst) indirect.

These similarities and differences hold substantial opportunities for family-business studies. The similarities provide the field with a general working model of the factors that should affect a family firm's performance. The differences, or possibility of differences, suggest that each aspect of the strategic management process in family firms needs to be carefully explored and compared to the processes used in other family firms and in non-family firms. Such comparisons promise to improve the management practices in both types of firms, since the cross-fertilization of ideas cannot proceed effectively without an understanding of what those differences are, why they have occurred, and their results.

Figure 1. The Strategic Management Process*

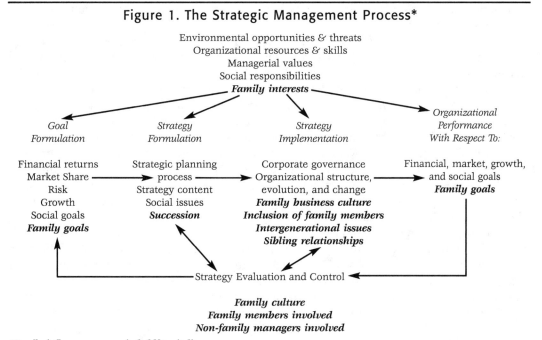

*Family influences appear in boldface italic

The strategic management framework with which we review the literature is based on a simplified model of the strategic management process (Andrews, 1971; Hofer and Schendel, 1978; Schendel and Hofer, 1979). Figure 1 provides a schematic diagram of this model. As the figure shows, the process is dynamic and interactive. Goals must be selected, strategies formulated to achieve those goals, and the chosen strategy implemented. Furthermore, at all stages it is necessary to select and evaluate alternatives, make decisions, and ensure that effective control processes are in place in order to make adjustments where needed. How well an organization accomplishes these tasks in light of the opportunities and threats in its environment, the resources it possesses or can procure, and the values and noneconomic responsibilities held by its managers, determine its performance.

Within this framework, the family business may differ from non-family businesses because the controlling family's influence, interests, and values have overriding importance. How this concentration of control, influence, and values affects the strategic decisions and performance of family firms should be of great interest to family firms, but has not yet been adequately explored. Using this model to set the agenda, we see that for future research to improve family business management, it must help managers do one or more of the following: more accurately define problems and opportunities concerning the environment or organizational capability; refine goals and objectives; generate better strategic decisions; improve the implementation of strategies, policies, procedures, and tasks; or facilitate the evaluation and control process.

This does not mean that we necessarily subscribe to what Hollander and Elman (1988) characterize as the "rationalist approach" to family-business management. Proponents of this approach (Cohn and Lindberg, 1974; Levinson, 1971) advocate the excision of family considerations from the business system. They argue that the two subsystems of family and business are so different that they cannot possibly co-exist except in the most unusual situations. In contrast, as shown in the bolded and italicized text in Figure 1, our approach accommodates family influences in various forms and in all parts of the process. Family interests and values are incorporated into the goals and objectives set for the firm. Family relationships influence the strategies considered. Succession within the family can be one of the most important strategies determining the longevity of the firm. Decision criteria are affected by family considerations built into the firm's goals and the choice of alternatives to consider. Family involvement in implementation creates its own dynamics, politics, and possibilities. Finally, family relationships and how the family perceives the role of non-family managers can make it easier or harder to constructively evaluate or control decisions and actions.

The key is to understand these influences and how to harness the potential strengths they convey, and to deal with the weaknesses with which they encumber the firm. In this sense, our view is closer to "systems theorists" such as Barnes and Hershon (1976), Hollander and Elman (1988), and McCollom (1988), who recognize the importance of both subsystems and seek ways to effectively integrate them. What we most want to accomplish with this approach is to connect studies of family businesses with the achievement of their goals and objectives, whether those goals be family-oriented or business-oriented.

As implied above, to gain a better understanding of how to improve the performance of a family business, two kinds of research are key. First, it is necessary to find out how a family business differs from a non-family business with respect to the strategic management process. Isolating these differences makes it possible to determine the reasons for them. Where differences affect performance positively, research should be targeted toward strengthening or exploiting them fully. Where they have a negative impact, research should be directed toward minimizing or eliminating their negative influences. As an added benefit, comparative research of this type allows researchers, consultants, and practitioners to appreciate the extent to which knowledge concerning business in general applies to family businesses in particular, and the reasons why it will or will not apply.

Second, studies that compare and contrast more and less successful family businesses are also essential. Comparative studies of this type will contribute further to our understanding of the family's influences on the strategic management process, how differences in those influences affect performance, and the coping mechanisms used by high-and low-performing firms.

We also recognize that not all family businesses, or non-family businesses, are alike, nor should they be. Thus, we realize the need to acknowledge the legitimate contingencies that cause one family firm to act differently from another. However, what we propose is nothing more than good science, because the classification and investigation of homogeneous populations of family firms is essential for progress in the field (cf. Chrisman, Hofer, and Boulton, 1988; McKelvey, 1982).

In all, we reviewed 204 family business related articles appearing in 32 journals from 1980 to 1994. Only about 37% (77 out of 204) of these articles are based on empirical research. They are catalogued in Appendix 1. Family firms' penchant for privacy and the early stage of the field's development could explain the relative paucity of empirical studies (Davis, 1983; Ward, 1987). The small number of empirical studies clearly emphasizes the need for more research.

Goals and Objectives

Due to family involvement, the goals and objectives of a family business are likely to be quite different from the firm-value maximization goal assumed for publicly held and professionally managed non-family firms. However, very few attempts have been made to identify these differences. Some authors believe that the family firm's goals could be family or business centered (Singer and Donoho, 1992). Other researchers see the goals as changing through the interaction of the needs of the family and the firm (Danco, 1975; Davis and Tagiuri, 1989; McGivern, 1989).

For example, Ward (1987) proposes a three-stage development model of the family business. In the first stage, the needs of the business and the family are consistent; the owner-manager makes all decisions. Although families are not necessarily monolithic units, at this stage of a family business's development, research on the motivations and characteristics of the founder can be particularly useful in providing some indication of the goals of family enterprises (Hollander and Elman, 1988). The current stream of research in this area (e.g., Dyer, 1986; Malone and Jenster, 1992) runs parallel to studies of the entrepreneur's characteristics, except that the entrepreneurship literature concentrates on the early life of the firm and the family-business literature deals with a firm in its later stages, especially when succession is imminent. Thus, a careful examination of entrepreneurial research may yield additional insights.

In the second stage, the owner-manager remains in control, but the growth and development of the family's children are of primary importance to the family. As a consequence, the goals of the family firm are likely to change, reflecting the greater importance of finding a place and securing a future for sons and daughters.

In the last stage, business and family needs can come into conflict. The business can become stagnant, in need of regeneration; the owner-manager can become bored or retire; and maintenance of family harmony can become the primary family goal. Again, business goals can change as a result of family needs or a desire to achieve a turnaround in the firm's economic performance.

The point of all this is that it is necessary to understand what the business's goals are, who sets them, and why the business selects particular goals. Researchers should also be cognizant of the differences in goals of family firms in these stages and avoid lumping such firms together for study. Otherwise, findings about behaviors, based on averages, represent none of the firms.

An indication of how a family firm's goals can differ and affect decision making can be gleaned from certain ethnic studies. In studies of immigrant Chinese and African-American family businesses, researchers (Dean, 1992; Wong, McReynolds, and Wong, 1992) found that succession is not a priority, because families view their firms as the means to prepare children for a professional career, not as a family legacy. Even though some family firms might not seek continuation of the business through succeeding generations, around a quarter of the articles we surveyed discuss succession.

It is unclear to us whether succession is a goal or a means to a goal. An empirical study on the goals of family business by Tagiuri and Davis (1992) found the following to be the six most important goals: to have a company where employees can be happy, productive and proud; to provide financial security and benefits for the owner; to develop new quality products; to serve as a vehicle for personal growth, social advancement, and autonomy; to promote good corporate citizenship; and to provide job security. It is interesting that none of these goals, and only one of the 74 goals included in that study, are directly concerned with the next generation. Extrapolating from this study, succession could be, in some circumstances, a strategy for achieving one or more goals rather than a goal itself. However, we must make such extrapolations with caution. Since 86% of Tagiuri and Davis's sample consisted of CEOs and 60% consisted of founders, a different sample composed of potential successors, spouses, other family members, or non-family managers could yield quite different results. Nevertheless, their findings underscore the importance of identifying and considering the goals of family firms before attempting to make prescriptive statements about how they should be managed.

It is clear from this discussion that a family business is more likely to have multiple, complex, and changing goals rather than a singular, simple, and constant goal. The paucity of research in this area indicates that the potential contribution of studies on goals and objectives could be substantial. Research that compares the goals and the manner in which they are formulated in family and non-family businesses or between those of family firms that are high or low-performing, large or small, young or old, run by the founder or by a later generation, in service or manufacturing industries, and so on, is clearly needed. It would also be useful to know how the goals that are chosen affect decision making and economic performance. Furthermore, we do not yet know whether family firms perform better in the traditional goals and objectives of non-family firms, or in the unique goals and objectives of family businesses. Nor do we know the extent to which family and business goals are compatible, when they are or are not, and why. There are also many questions on the influence of various family and non-family members, family relationships, and family objectives that deserve consideration. Finally, there may be a need to distinguish between the goals that the family harbors for itself and those that they hold for the family business, since the latter will likely incorporate considerations for customers, suppliers, and non-family employees.

Strategy Formulation and Content

Although more attention has been paid to the process of strategy formulation and the content of strategy in family businesses, we still know relatively little. Here too, the interaction of family and business makes strategy formulation a dynamic process, not amenable to simple or across-the-board solutions. For example, Post (1993) suggests that for family firms to remain successful, they must generate a new strategy for every generation that joins the business. This provides autonomy for the newly joining family members, thereby aiding the maintenance of good work relationships. Strategies recommended include starting a new venture or division of the business (Barach, 1984), internationalizing (Gallo and Sveen, 1991), and helping successors acquire skills that other family members do not possess (Wong, 1993). On the other hand, research on non-family businesses suggests that corporate entrepreneurship (Biggadike, 1979), first diversification (Hofer and Chrisman, 1989), and strategic change in general (Hannan and Freeman, 1989) can be risky. Family-business researchers have not yet come to grips with the problem of how a family should deal, simultaneously, with the possibly conflicting strategic needs of the family and the business. From a strategic management perspective, families are both a resource and a constraint. The literature is silent on the appropriate business strategies for different family configurations and dynamics, as well as for different business situations.

Strategic planning process. Family-business researchers who have focused on the strategic planning process espouse the benefits of strategic planning (Barry, 1975; Jones, 1982; Ward, 1988) and offer opinions on how it should be done. However, since the benefits of planning are by no means proven, research in this area would be valuable. There is much we do not know. We know little about how family firms scan their environments, assess their capabilities, or search for and evaluate alternative strategies; how the strategy formulation process is influenced by family considerations and interests; whether the alternatives considered are many or few, or better or worse than those generated by non-family firms; how the dynamics and politics of decision making are different in the family business; and which types of family influences are advantageous and which deleterious to the process.

Strategy content. There have been several comparative studies of the strategies and policies adopted by family and non-family firms (Covin, 1994; Doeringer, Moss, and Terkla, 1992). Trostel and Nichols (1982) discover no differences in the management processes or styles of publicly held and private companies, but the latter do have a higher rate of sales growth, place greater emphasis on asset utilization, charge lower prices, and employ accounting policies that help reduce taxable income. Unfortunately, since ownership is not necessarily the single feature distinguishing the family firm from the non-family firm, it is difficult to gauge the implication of these results for family-business research. For example, Kleinsorge (1994) found that family nursing homes provide a higher level of care but are less cost-efficient, have fewer assets, more liabilities, and lower occupancy rates than non-family nursing homes. Other studies find that family firms emphasize personal values over corporate values in customer service policies (Lyman, 1991), place more emphasis on growth potential than on short-term sales growth, and pay higher wages to employees (Donckels and Frohlick, 1991; Trostel and Nichols, 1982). On the other hand, other studies find little difference in the location preferences of family and non-family firms (Kahn and Henderson, 1992). These results are interesting, but we do not know what they mean in terms of achieving the goals of family and non-family firms.

The literature is by no means consistent on what strategies will be most effective for family businesses. For example, Gallo and Sveen (1991) and Swinth and Vinton (1993) arrive at opposite conclusions on the possible success of family businesses in global markets. Gallo and Sveen believe that family businesses are less globally oriented because of their slowness in making structural changes and their strong local orientation. Swinth and Vinton, on the other hand, believe that family firms share some important values across cultures and that these values should enable family firms to bridge cultural barriers more effectively than non-family companies. While both of these arguments have intuitive appeal, neither has been tested empirically.

In terms of strategic management, there is much that the results above do not tell us. We do not know if family firms follow different corporate, business, or functional level strategies from non-family firms in the same industry. Neither do we know whether these differences are justified by differences in resources, skills, or cultures; whether family firms are more or less likely to adopt innovative strategies; or whether differences in strategies between family and non-family firms lead to differences in profitability, growth, and survival.

Strategies and social issues. On the basis of a case study, Post (1993) argues that family businesses are more likely to get involved in environmentally friendly strategies because of their local orientation. Unfortunately, there is not enough empirical evidence to generalize this conclusion. With social issues, we need to know if the ethics and values of family business managers are similar or dissimilar to those in non-family businesses; what social policies are followed; how socially responsive family firms are; and whether it is easier or harder to implement socially responsible policies in these firms. How social responsibility, social responsiveness, and economic performance relate in family firms is another area worth investigating.

Succession. As we argued earlier, for some families, succession appears to be a strategy for achieving one or more goals rather than a goal itself. Handler and Kram (1988), Welsch (1993), and Handler (1994) have reviewed the literature on family business succession, so we limit our discussion to succession topics that have received the most attention in the literature.

The major portion of the family-business literature on succession has focused on the succession process. Subtopics include succession planning, succession timing, interest of the next generation, and who should choose the successor. The successor's characteristics have been studied mainly from the point of view of what they are rather than what they should be.

Managing the transition from one generation to another is a difficult process (Handler and Kram, 1988). Writers such as Ayers (1990) and Lane (1989) consider it the most important issue in family-business management, although this issue could occur only once in a few decades. In spite of this, succession planning seldom occurs in family businesses (Lansberg, 1988; Rosenblatt, deMik, Anderson, and Johnson, 1985). The reasons for this could include the reluctance of founders to let go, hesitancy to make possibly divisive decisions, or a perceived or real absence of a relationship between succession planning and goal achievement (e.g., Firnstahl, 1986; Levinson, 1971; Perrigo, 1975). Since business continuity is largely under the control of the current owner-manager (Lansberg, 1988; Malone, 1989), a large portion of the literature has focused on ways that individual can effectively plan and manage the process.

Issues in succession planning that need to be addressed by all owner-managers include ownership continuity or change, management continuity or change, power and asset distribution, and the firm's role in society (Beckhard and Dyer, 1983). These basic decisions help determine the degree and pattern of involvement for both family and non-family members (Barry, 1975; Weiser, Brody, and Quarrey; 1988). However, it is uncertain at this point what factors can contribute to the effectiveness of these options, let alone their relative importance or how they might work in combination.

Another vital issue in the succession process is the timing of succession. Davis and Tagiuri (1989) find that the life-stage combination of the father and son can either facilitate succession or aggravate the tensions that accompany it. This suggests that succession planning can help make succession smoother. It is conceivable, however, that a smooth succession, especially if it yields a compromise candidate, can have both positive and negative effects on the economic performance of a family business, but this is by no means established. It is also unclear whether results such as these can be generalized to situations involving female owners or successors (Dumas, 1989). Both Post and Robins (1993) and Lansberg (1988) believe that succession timing can be affected by the founder's "inner circle" if the people in that circle perceive leadership continuity to be in their best interest. How to mobilize this inner circle for the good of the firm is a question still waiting for an answer.

A third issue related to succession is concerned with making sure that the next generation is both interested in joining the family business and capable of managing it. Some research has been done, opinions are varied, yet there is much we do not know. For example, Ambrose (1983) suggests that early inclusion of potential heirs in the business helps develop their interest and increases their likelihood of joining. But when is the time appropriate for the business or the heir's career development? How will this affect the potential heirs' relationships with non-family managers? Ambrose also argues that the time demands of business leaves founders with less time to build relationships in the family and get the next generation interested in the business. It is unclear, though, how this will affect the performance of the family business. To take a strategic management perspective, researchers need to remove themselves somewhat from family considerations, unless, of course, they affect the performance of the business. Thus, when Beach (1993) observes that children are socialized into home-based businesses at a very young age, we must ask how this affects the children's attitudes or aptitudes and, ultimately, the business's performance.

The fourth issue addresses who should choose the successor. The recommendations vary from the founder, who knows the business best, to the family, the board of directors, outsiders on the board, and outside consultants.

Certain characteristics of a successor are believed to affect the smoothness and efficacy of a succession. These include sensitivity to the founder's needs (Lansberg, 1988), patience and diplomacy (Jonovic, 1989), understanding the organization's intricacies and culture (Horton, 1982), and congruence between the successor's power in the family and the business (Holland and Boulton, 1984). A strategic management perspective should lead us to wonder when and under what conditions these traits and behaviors of a successor translate into making more effective decisions and achieving family business goals.

The succession literature has paid more attention to the succession process than the successor. We might conclude from this that some researchers believe the process is more important than the outcome, or that a good process always leads to a good outcome. No one appears to have investigated how much of the subsequent performance of a family business is determined by the succession process and how much by the successor. In family-business research, this issue seems to be too important to be left as an assumption.

Within the strategic management framework, the prime objective of managing the succession process is to choose the best successor. This requires a definition of the best successor. It appears to us that "best" will depend on the goals of the family firm. If the family firm is most concerned with family harmony, then the successor who will contribute the most toward that goal is the best. On the other hand, if the family firm's goal is growth and profitability, another candidate might be preferable. Since the current literature on family firm succession does not explicitly tie prescribed actions and processes to the achievement of clearly stated goals, the prescriptions might not be well-founded.

Strategy Implementation

For successful strategy implementation, family businesses need to effectively handle two key sets of relationships that generally do not affect non-family businesses: those among family members and those between family members and professional managers (Horton, 1986). The emphasis here has been on the nature of these relationships and how to handle them. There needs to be some emphasis on connecting these observations with the performance of the family business.

Corporate governance. In a family business, the family and the business are so entangled that emotions are unavoidable (Alderfer, 1988). Consequently, family firms are often advised to appoint outside board members. For family firms that are not large enough to attract outside board members, family councils (Lansberg, 1988; Ward, 1987), review councils (Jonovic, 1989), or advisory councils (Tillman, 1988) are recommended.

Proponents argue that outside board members bring fresh perspectives and new directions (Jain, 1980); monitor the progress of the family business and act as arbitrators (Lane, 1989; Mace, 1971); help in the succession process by providing support for the newly elected leader (Harris, 1989); analyse perceived strengths and weaknesses more objectively (Mathile, 1988); help reduce the loneliness of the owner-manager (Gumpert and Boyd, 1984; Mathile, 1988); and act as catalysts for change (Mueller, 1988), sounding boards for the owner-manager (Heidrich, 1988), and low-cost consultants (Heidrich, 1988).

In contrast, Ford (1988) and Jonovic (1989) perceive outside directors as having less value. They cite reasons such as lack of knowledge about the firm and its environment, lack of availability, and a lack of authority and definable shareholder interest. Some argue that outside directors are obligated to the owner-manager and are therefore not free of political pressure (Alderfer, 1988). Furthermore, professional management teams, effective financial planning and control systems, and strategic planning efforts can significantly diminish the need for outsiders on the board (Jonovic, 1989).

Clearly, the issue of outside board members is much more complex than what the general statements convey. Studies (Jonovic, 1989; Harris, 1989; Ward and Handy, 1988) find that the type of board formed (outside, inside, or token) depends on the age, size, type, and complexity of the business; the nature of ownership; and the personality and experience of the CEO. In turn, the type of board formed will determine its role and functions. It seems likely that this contingency perspective also applies to the relation between governance and performance, although in the absence of empirical studies it remains speculative.

Family business culture. Dyer (1988) identified four types of family-firm cultures that provide a framework for analyzing relationships between family members and non-members. Dyer's classification of paternalistic, laissez-faire, participative, and professional cultures is based on different assumptions about human nature, relationships, and the environment. What is still needed, however, is research that identifies the cultures associated with superior performance in different situations, how to recognize when a firm's current culture is inappropriate, and the best mechanisms available to family businesses for moving from one type of culture to another.

Reiss (1982) uses a classification that concerns itself with the relationship among family members. This classification recognizes three types of families: consensus-sensitive, interpersonal distance-sensitive, and environment-sensitive. Davis (1983) suggests that excessively consensus-sensitive families become "enmeshed" under stress, making individual decision making and actions difficult. On the other hand, the connections between family members are so loose in the interpersonal distance-sensitive family that they cannot act in concert. Therefore, he and Hoffman (1981) conclude that the environmentally sensitive family is ideal. In her research on three department stores, however, McCollom (1988) concludes that we must be cautious about suggesting an ideal relationship for family businesses because families can adopt different relationships at work and at home to achieve stability. We would go further in stating that it is unlikely that any one type of relationship among family members is ideal in all situations from the perspective of the business, even if relationships at home and at work are similar. Again, there are so many variables and so many contingencies involved in influencing the performance of a family business that it is exceedingly risky to assume that ideal patterns of family relationships can be found. Research could make more progress, we believe, if it identifies these contingencies and takes them into account in family-business studies. Also, from a strategic management perspective, we are concerned more with the trade-offs that the family firm encounters in the different patterns of family relationships and how they affect the firm's short-and long term performance.

Ethnic studies underscore the impact of culture on the way strategies are implemented in family businesses and the need to take a contingency perspective in research. Ethnic groups that have been studied include Chinese (Chau, 1991; Wong, McReynolds, and Wong, 1992; Wong, 1993); Japanese (Wong, 1993); Latin Americans (Lansberg and Perrow, 1991); Jewish (Rothstein, 1992; McGoldrick and Troast, 1993); Italians, African Americans, Irish, Germans, and Anglo Saxons (Dean, 1992; McGoldrick and Troast, 1993; Salomon and Lockhart, 1980); and Native Americans (Stallings, 1992). These studies suggest that methods of conflict resolution and the importance attached to education, value systems, and the participation of women vary widely among different ethnic groups. Differences among family businesses in terms of their culture and decision making can exist according to their size, age, generation in control, type of business, and so on. These differences need to be investigated and accounted for. More importantly, from a strategic management perspective, we need to understand how and why culture affects strategy implementation, and the subsequent impact the method of implementation has on the performance of the family firm.

Inclusion of family members. In implementing strategy, a family firm has the choice of using family or non-family members. Lansberg (1983) advises that all relatives be given opportunities to learn, but only the most competent should be taken into the firm. A strategic management perspective could take this as a starting point, but should also consider the political aspects of the inclusion or exclusion of family members in the business (MacMillan and Jones, 1986).

In general, research has found that family members are more productive than non-family members (Rosenblatt, deMik, Anderson, and Johnson, 1985; Kirchhoff and Kirchhoff, 1987). However, in examining compensation practices, Rosenblatt et al. conclude that family members believe they are overworked and underpaid, while Kirchhoff and Kirchhoff suggests that family members are given higher salaries and perquisites. This contradiction deserves more study, because if not recognized and dealt with, the apparent discrepancy between perceptions and reality can lead to problems in strategy implementation.

By contrast, in a study of home-based business workers, Heck and Walker (1993) discover that family members and unrelated workers are more productive than related workers (e.g., cousins). They warn that relatives who depend on family ties for employment could be the least competent. Although it suggests a hiring strategy for family businesses, such research has yet to be replicated in larger family businesses. We also know little about the political ramifications of denying relatives employment opportunities. Since hiring decisions are among the most important human resource decisions a firm can make, further studies of this issue, in the context of a firm's performance, are clearly needed.

From a strategic management perspective, the study of women in family businesses is another fruitful area for research. Various studies report that women are not generally considered for the job of chief executive in family businesses (Hollander and Bukowitz, 1990; Salganicoff, 1990; Upton and Sexton, 1987). Other researchers suggest that female members' positions as the caretakers of family concerns can give them a better understanding of the family business than the male members have (Hollander and Bukowitz, 1990). Women, for their part, have been advised to acquire appropriate business skills, training, and experience (Salganicoff, 1990). How best to train and deploy female family members in the business, the political implications of their inclusion, exclusion, and career opportunities, and the impact of all this on the performance of family firm, are areas that deserve more attention.

Intergenerational issues. Although they are closely akin to succession, we have classified intergenerational issues as part of strategy implementation rather than strategy formulation because of their potential impact on the day-to-day operations of the firm. Much of the research done in this area has been on relationships between fathers and sons, which Levinson (1971) observes is ambivalent at best. Researchers report that founders are generally authoritarian, unwilling to share power (Birley, 1986; Donckels and Frohlick, 1991; Geeraerts, 1984), and strategically conservative (Levinson, 1974). On the other hand, sons are generally impatient for strategic change, personal independence, and an opportunity to prove their worth (Seymour, 1993). Most of the family business literature seems to assume that conflict is unhealthy and disruptive. This may be true. However, conflict can also be a driving force for change. Before passing judgment, research from a strategic management perspective could examine the extent and types of conflicts that occur in the context of both family and business situations. More importantly, such research could investigate the impact of conflicts on strategy implementation and firm performance.

Dumas (1989) concludes that the father-son relationship cannot be generalized to the father-daughter dyad. She suggests that the father-daughter relationship is more harmonious and different in nature. Daughters willingly assume the role of caretakers, both of the father and the business. As a consequence, they are less likely than sons to be in conflict with their fathers over the issues of power and control. This insight is very important because it provides a basis for comparative research on intergenerational relationships. Is – or when is —conflict or accommodation preferable in the context of strategy implementation? By careful matching father-son and father-daughter situations in similar businesses, research may be able to answer such questions.

When a leader does let go, departure styles may vary. Sonnenfeld and Spence (1989) identify four departure styles of leaders: monarchs, generals, governors, and ambassadors. They suggest that the best departure style for a family business leader is that of the ambassador, who leads the organization to moderate levels of growth, recognizes the time to step down, and maintains contact with the organization as advisor. While the ambassador style can appear to be conceptually superior, this has not been empirically proven. And whether it is or not, the existing literature provides few clues as to how a departing leader can be persuaded to follow the appropriate departure style, or how successors can minimize the deleterious effects of a leader who cannot be so persuaded.

Sibling rivalry. Friedman (1991) argues that although competition for parental love and attention spurs sibling rivalry, it is the parents' response that is the major influence on the children's relationships with one another. Suggestions to resolve dysfunctional sibling relationships include encouraging open communication and discussions among the siblings about the roots of their rivalries, establishing empathy by inviting them to imagine their roles reversed, and encouraging them to redefine current relationships (Friedman, 1991; Lundberg, 1994). From the point of view of a family's business, however, we do not know if or when sibling rivalry is dysfunctional for the family business. Researchers have assumed that what is good for family harmony is good for the business, but this is not necessarily the case. While understanding what is good for the family is important, family businesses also need to understand the trade-offs involved in maintaining family harmony. This is where the strategic management perspective comes in. For example, Levinson (1971) suggests that if children are each provided with an operation to lead, sibling rivalry can be abated. This may or may not work, because the success or failure of each operation depends on more than family harmony. For example, if location is the key to success, sibling rivalry can increase as a result of the competition to be in charge of the operations with the best locations. The fragmentation of operation and control or the diversification of a family business can also impact the firm's profitability and competitiveness.

Organizational structure, evolution, and change. Research suggests that the family business is less horizontally differentiated and more reliant on informal controls than nonfamily firms (Daily and Dollinger, 1992; Geeraerts, 1984). As a result, the family firm can be more successful in businesses that require a lean and responsive structure (Harris, Martinez, and Ward, 1994). Most of the studies on the family firm's organizational structure, evolution, and change, however, are concerned with the transition to professional management.

Hollander and Elman (1988) identify three different approaches adopted by researchers to formulate evolutionary models. The first approach relates the firm's developmental stages to the family's generational progression (e.g., Barnes and Hershon, 1976). The second focuses on the interaction between the firm's needs and the life stages of individuals crucial to the firm (Danco, 1975; Davis and Tagiuri, 1989; McGivern, 1989). The third views the interaction of three sets of life cycles: firm, family, and key individuals (Ward, 1987). In an empirical study of 41 businesses, Holland and Oliver (1992) find support for the three-stage model proposed by Ward (1987). The underlying theme in all these models is that the delegation of responsibility and power to nonfamily members varies significantly in the different stages.

A family business could need to professionalize and delegate authority because of growth, lack of management skills within the family, preparation for succession, or to change the norms and values of the business (Matthews, 1984; Dyer, 1989). However, owner-managers could be reluctant to delegate control because of a lack of formal training, insufficient knowledge of management techniques (Dyer, 1989), fear of losing control (Perrigo, 1975), or a belief that professionalization is an unnecessary, expensive overhead. A strategic management perspective could lead to other questions and avenues for research. For example, if some family firms lack the skills or the will to successfully make the transition to professional management, should they even try to do so? Are there other alternatives, and if so, what are they? Also, when business needs and family desires conflict, which is more important for the short-and long-term performance of the firm?

Summary. As the discussion above clearly illustrates, the family-business literature describes the influences of family on strategy implementation. Unfortunately, however, it stops short of showing how a particular family influence helps or hinders the firm's achievement of its goals and objectives. For example, we do not know if family firms with outside board members actually make better —or even different —strategic decisions than those without them. Since experience has shown that life-cycle models do not apply to every business (Dhalla and Yuspeh, 1976), we need to understand the conditions that cause differences in family firms' evolutionary patterns and which of these conditions has the greatest implications for organizational performance. Studies also need to be directed toward understanding from the perspective of the business how effective the intervention strategies suggested actually improve sibling relationships are, and if there are gender differences. Despite the behavioral orientation of much of the literature, we still know too little about how family dynamics impact non-family members of the business, or if these pressures act as contributors or constraints to the effective implementation of strategy. Studies that chronicle the authoritarian system of the founder-managed family business could make a more significant contribution if they also showed us when the authoritarian system is effective or dysfunctional, and whether these instances differ for the family business and the non-family business. In sum, more work is required before we will know what kind of organization structures, systems, and processes are likely to be most effective for family businesses, and whether these differ according to the situation.

Strategy Evaluation and Control

Besides making strategic decisions and implementing them, an organization must also set up appropriate administrative and operating mechanisms to control and evaluate its performance vis-à-vis its goals and objectives. If family businesses have goals, strategies, and structures that are different from those of non-family businesses, they are also likely to evaluate —or will need to evaluate —performance differently. However, the literature tells us very little about whether strategic decisions and performance are evaluated and controlled differently in the family firm, or if such differences are justified. The notable exception in this regard is in the area of financial control, where tax minimization is the guiding principle (Trostel and Nichols, 1982). Articles by rationalists that address this issue argue for the separation of the family and the business, thus recommending that family firms use the same set of evaluation and control systems employed by non-family firms (Levinson, 1974). Unfortunately, we do not know the answers to the following vital strategic management questions: Are there differences in the types and use of strategic evaluation and control systems between high-and low-performing family businesses? Are the predominant systems similar or different from those used by nonfamily businesses? How important are the differences, if any? How do family members influence the design and use of strategic evaluation and control systems? Is the influence positive or negative?

Conclusion

In this review we have attempted to describe, from a strategic management perspective, the issues that currently dominate the study of family businesses. As this review shows, many studies have concentrated on issues that have a major impact on family relationships but an unclear impact on the performance of the business.

Our objective is to outline an alternative direction for family-business research. Using the concept of strategic management, we detail some of the key issues that must be resolved if we are to achieve the primary goals of business research: the improvement of management practice and organizational performance.

To date, it appears that the knowledge accumulated about family businesses has made relatively little progress toward achieving these goals. Specifically, questions that remain to be answered include those that ask what are the goals, strategies, and implementation methods of family businesses? How do these compare with those of non-family businesses and among high-and low performing family businesses?

In finding the answers to these questions, researchers should first keep in mind that family businesses are not a homogeneous group. What works for one family in a specific situation will not necessarily work for another family in a different situation. Therefore, it is important to make it clear what types of families, businesses, and business environments are being studied. Second, researchers should also recognize that family and business goals, and the strategies needed to achieve these goals, are not always compatible. As a consequence, family firms are confronted with implications and trade-offs that might not be readily apparent. Studies that identify these trade-offs and inform family-business managers about their implications can make a great contribution.

A third, related, point is that family-business research needs dependent variables. Whether these be family harmony, economic performance, or goal achievement matters less than the identification, explicit recognition, and inclusion of these variables to measure the outcomes of decisions and actions. It appears to us that investigations of goals and objectives and the determinants of performance hold the most promise for contributing to the advancement of the field, if for no other reason than that these topics have not received sufficient attention in the past.

Insofar as family-business consultants and family-business managers are concerned, our review of the literature from a strategic management perspective suggests several implications. First, the family-business literature has been very good about identifying and diagnosing family problems, and quite informative about how these problems either originate in, or spill over to, the business. It is replete with solutions for dealing with family problems, and some of those solutions seem quite reasonable. What the literature has not dealt with is how those problems and their solutions affect the strategic management processes of a family business, its economic performance, or the achievement of its goals and objectives.

Second, although the family-business literature acknowledges that the family business is a system composed of a family and a business, it has not yet come to grips with the trade-offs involved in dealing with the needs of the two subsystems. The working hypothesis appears to be that what is good for the family is good for the business, but the hypothesis has never been tested.

Third, although the field recognizes that different types of families exist, not much has been done to determine which differences really matter, or what they imply, in terms of effective family business management. Thus, our advice to consultants and family-business managers is to proceed with caution when applying the findings of previous research. Do not assume that what was a problem for one family business will be so in another, or that what worked in the past will work in the future. Instead, use the literature as a guide to problem diagnosis, as an aid for understanding why a particular solution worked, and how the solution can or cannot be adapted to fit a particular set of needs. Do not assume that what is good for a family is good for its business, or vice versa; instead, realize that there are usually trade-offs between the needs of the family and the needs of the business that are involved in any decision, and seek to understand them in order to make decisions that are most likely to result in a desirable outcome mix.

In sum, the message of this article can be stated as follows: While the importance of the family cannot be denied, the business is no less important. How the family affects the operation and management of the business and how the influence of the family can be directed toward more productive and profitable outcomes are certainly research objectives worth pursuing. To achieve these objectives, researchers need to take a strategic management perspective, concentrating on comparative studies that will eventually lead to prescription rather than description. Until such a refocusing takes place, progress in the field will continue to be confined to the family in the family-business dyad.

Appendix. Summary of Empirical Articles Reviewed

Author(s) and Date	Sample (Respondents) Studied and Response Rate (When Available)	Key Finding
Tagiuri & Davis (1992)	524 participants (86% CEOs, nearly 60% founders) in Smaller Company Management Program at Harvard Business School	**Goals and Objectives** Six most important goals of family firms are having a company where employees can be happy, productive, and proud; financial security and benefits for the owner; developing new and quality products; a vehicle for personal growth, social advancement, and autonomy; good corporate citizenship; and job security.
Ambrose (1983)	86 businesses terminated between 1976 & 1981; 53 owners & 33 children	**Strategy Formulation and Content** To increase the chances of an effective transfer of business to the next generation, the children should be involved when they are young.
Barnes (1988)	Several hundred participants of Owner/President Management Program at Harvard Business School	Dealing with incongruent hierarchies (when a daughter or younger son takes over as CEO of family firms) involves a major shift in expectations, perceptions, and behavior of family members and employees. Restructuring is time consuming and only day to day actions and behaviors can bring the two hierarchies into line.
Barry (1975)	25 firms in British printing industry	Family business owners have four options: continuing both ownership and management, retaining ownership but letting go management, abandoning ownership and retaining management control, and evolving as a more bureaucratic firm.
Beach (1993)	31 firms (6 family day-care providers, 10 shoe stitchers, 15 families of home workers)	Family acts as a filter affecting the operation of home based businesses. Children may be involved at four different levels: play, watch, and help; assistance with simple tasks; regular unpaid assistance; and regular paid assistance.
Covin (1994)	223 students (115 undergraduates and108 graduates)	Family firms perceived as competitive as nonfamily firms. Lack of formalization perceived as major weakness. Graduate students viewed career in family firms less favorably than undergraduates. Gender not a significant influence on perceptions.
Davis (1968)	25 firms in Mexico	Three patterns of entrepreneurial succession were observed: strong father, weak son; conservative father, progressive son; branches of a family, each with distinct challenges.

Author(s) and Date	Sample (Respondents) Studied and Response Rate (When Available)	Key Finding
Doeringer, Moss, & Terkla (1992)	Fishing crew and captains at 2 New England ports	Study examines two systems of employment and pay – kinship and capitalist. Capitalist systems resemble standard competitive firms. Kinship systems are based on work guarantees and labor adjustments. For labor intensive industry (fishing) kinship system is highly effective.
Goldberg & Woolridge (1993)	254 CEOs	Effective successors score significantly higher on self confidence and managerial autonomy. Birth order is not related to the success of succession. When owners lack confidence in the successor's ability or willingness to control, the reluctance to let go becomes higher.
Handler (1992)	32 next generation family members	The study identifies the various factors that influence the quality of succession of family firms. Two factors identified were individual influences (including personal need fulfillment, and personal influence) and relational influences (mutual respect and understanding, sibling accommodation, commitment to family business perpetuation, and separation strains due to family involvement).
Holland & Boulton (1984)	Firms (number not mentioned) in food processing industry	Family firms can vary in terms of size and ownership management structures. Based on the degree of family involvement, family businesses can be classified as prefamily, family, adaptive family, or postfamily. The managerial orientation of an individual in a family business depends upon his/ her power in the family and in business.
Jones (1982)	69 firms; Response rate 34. 5% (69 out of 200)	The study compares firms engaged in strategic planning to those that are not. Planning firms engage in environment scanning, identify future opportunities through research, and involve a number of organizational members in planning activities. These firms are more successful than nonplanning firms.
Kahn & Henderson (1992)	990 firms (435 family & 555 non-family firms); Response rate 44%	Comparing location preference of family and nonfamily firms, study finds mixed support for the notion that family firms seek locations that improve the family's quality of life. Nonfamily firms seek locations that lower the cost of operation. All firms rank the proximity to markets and customers as most important factor in determining location preference.

Author(s) and Date	Sample (Respondents) Studied and Response Rate (When Available)	Key Finding
Kaye (1992)	10 case studies	Structural family dynamics can place one sibling (usually youngest son) in an outsider role, because this individual is brought up in a more affluent environment than other family members. This individual is trapped in business and can display a tendency to be defensive. Family members feel obliged to carry him along.
Kleinsorge (1994)	34 nursing homes (10 family owned and 24 non-family owned) in Oregon	Family owned nursing homes provide more high level care but are less efficient in providing care, have lower occupancy rates, have lower assets and higher liabilities, spend less on patient care and more on salaries than do non-family owned nursing homes.
Lansberg & Astrachan (1994)	130 individuals from 109 family businesses Response rate 36%	The effect of family adaptability and cohesion on management succession planning and training are mediated by the family's commitment to the business and the quality of the relationship between the owner-manager and successor.
Lyman (1991)	78 business managers and 48 family members in family owned businesses	In terms of the differences in customer service among family owned and non-family owned firms, study finds that family business managers have a more personal orientation, trust their employees to a greater extent, and show less reliance on formal written policies.
Post (1993)	Case study of Boston Park Plaza Hotel	Study finds that the commitment of the top management team, communication and creative thinking, and reward systems are necessary elements in successfully meshing the spirit of ownership with that of responsibility.
Post & Robins (1993)	40 case studies of political leaders	When a leader is taken ill, contradictions between patient comfort and those of leaders' competence must be managed. Four factors that determine the relationship between the leader and his inner circle are factors associated with the disease, leader's reactions to the illness, social and political environment, and medical management of the leader.
Prince (1990)	18 law firms	Three mechanisms for resolving interpersonal conflicts within the family business include litigation, arbitration, and mediation. Study argues that mediation is the only effective method for conflict resolution in family businesses.
Ward (1988)	2,020 firms from public data sources	Six interdependent steps that are important for strategic planning process are an assessment of family's commitment to business, business health, business alternatives, family and personal goals, selection of business strategy, and family's interests and capabilities.

Author(s) and Date	Sample (Respondents) Studied and Response Rate (When Available)	Key Finding
Welsch (1993)	183 (59 family and 124 nonfamily) firms	Study finds no significant differences in large industrial family and nonfamily firms in terms of the rational, political, or bureaucratic dimensions of management succession.
Barnes & Hershon (1976)	35 companies (200 participants)	**Strategy Implementation** Study identifies three stages through which a company passes: entrepreneurial, specialized functions, and divisional operations.
Berenbeim (1990)	20 U. S., Latin American, & European firms	Study describes three stages in the transition of a business towards professionalization: coalition to establish firm, ascendancy to authority, and founder's departure.
Birley (1986)	61 potential inheritors (MBA & BBA students)	Study finds that family business owners adopt an authoritarian style, and that sibling position is not correlated to the willingness to return to family business. Gender was found to be related.
Burke, Weir, & DuWors (1980)	85 senior administrators of correctional institutions	Greater occupational demands can lead to less marital satisfaction, decreased social participation, and increase in psychosomatic symptoms amongst wives of senior administrators.
Cambreleng (1969)	Case study of a sales & service company	Clear policies and open communications are useful for dealing with the presence of nepots in family firms.
Crouter (1984)	55 employees in a manufacturing plant	Family life influences the morale, stability, and productivity of work force. Women with young children reported high family to work spillover.
Daily & Dollinger (1992)	104 small manufacturing firms Response rate 21%	Nonfamily firms are larger, older, pursue increase in growth and size, and rely more on internal controls. Study finds no statistically significant differences in performance of family and nonfamily firms.
Davis & Tagiuri (1989)	89 father/son pairs	The quality of work relationship between father and son varies as a function of their respective life cycle stages.

Author(s) and Date	Sample (Respondents) Studied and Response Rate (When Available)	Key Finding
Dean (1992)	234 African American firms Response rate 34%	African American business owners are preoccupied with survival and management issues, do not benefit from community associations, and report little family work conflict. Succession is not a primary concern, because business is used as a foundation for professionalization of children.
Donckels & Frohlick (1991)	1,132 small and medium businesses in 8 European countries	Study develops a holistic model that includes four subsystems of family, management, equity, and business. Family firms are more stable, pay higher wages, and have a more conservative attitude towards business, than nonfamily firms.
Donnelley (1964)	15 family businesses	Family firms generally have valuable reputation, loyal and dedicated family members, and are sensitive to continuity and integrity. Challenges include nepotism, lack of managerial talent, and lack of discipline. Policies to regulate family firms can be helpful.
Dumas (1989)	18 family businesses in California(40 family members)	Study examines similarities and differences in problems faced by male and female inheritors in family businesses. While sons have a desire for autonomy, daughters take a more submissive role as caretakers and need help with empowerment.
Dyer Jr. (1988)	40 family businesses	Study identifies four types of cultures of family businesses: paternalistic, laissez faire, participative, and professional. For a successful transition, owners must analyze their firm's culture and plan a change in culture if necessary.
Ewing (1965)	918 executives Response rate 34%	Nepotism not as prevalent as it is believed. Executives do not support it but do not dismiss it blindly, either.
Ford (1988)	35 privately held companies (325 CEOs & 91 board members)	Outside directors are perceived as more effective than insiders.
Francis (1991)	250 large U. K. firms	Stages of control through which the firms pass are members of family, transition to professional management, and control by financial institutions.
Geeraerts (1984)	142 small & medium Dutch businesses	The size of an organization and its structure is modified by the status of its management. Firms controlled by professional managers are more horizontally differentiated, formalized, and have higher internal specialization than family managed firms.

Author(s) and Date	Sample (Respondents) Studied and Response Rate (When Available)	Key Finding
Goffee & Scasse (1985)	12 firms in general building and personal services	Proprietors can be reluctant to delegate control and may resort to "quasiorganic" structures. In this form of organization, control is passed to the executives, though owners maintain proprietorial prerogatives, e.g., arbitrary intervention.
Gumpert & Boyd (1984)	249 owners Response rate 83%	Small business ownership is closely associated with loneliness. Remedies include rearranging work environment, participating in peer group activities, and being attentive to family and friends.
Hayes (1981)	350 family and nonfamily businesses	The advantages of working in a family business are warmer relationships, greater latitude in decision making when accepted as an insider. The challenges include lesser professionalization, unclear lines of authority, and nonavailability of stock options to nonfamily members.
Heck & Walker (1993)	508 home based business owners	Study examines the differences in the business output of paid, unpaid, and contracting workers. It finds that paid and contracting family workers or unrelated workers achieve highest levels of output in family owned home businesses.
Holland & Oliver (1992)	41 family businesses	Study supports a three stage development model of family businesses. The three stages are controlled by owner-manager, control shared by family members, and professionally managed firm. The transition from family to professional management may not be as conflict ridden as is generally believed.
Jain (1980)	120 small and medium companies	Outside directors can be very helpful to small companies in development of public relations, mediation on a wide range of internal issues, and providing expertise indifferent areas. The study discusses roles and responsibilities of these directors, as well as sources for finding these directors.
Kirchoff & Kirchoff (1987)	647 small firms	Study finds family members are more productive than nonfamily members in family businesses. However, as percentage of revenue in these firms, the profitability does not increase as the wage and salary expense increase.
Landes (1993)	Case studies of 2 merchant banking firms	The family firm's identity, separate from the family, must be guarded or it will be lost over time.

Author(s) and Date	Sample (Respondents) Studied and Response Rate (When Available)	Key Finding
Lansberg & Perrow (1991)	25 family businesses in 9 Latin American countries	Latin American economies are dominated by large family firms (grupos). These grupos are favored by governments, lack of competition, generally have highly skilled and educated family members, and adopt socially responsibly policies. However, they face challenges such as lack of governance mechanisms.
Liebtag (1984)	20 firms in U. S., Europe, and Latin America	Timely withdrawal of founder from active management of the company and handing it over to professionals is the most critical factor in transforming a family firm to a professional company.
Lyman (1988)	73 business women (39 family business, 34 nonfamily business)	Study examines interpersonal networks of women in family and nonfamily firms. The women associated with family firms describe contact with family at work as a necessity, and seldom mention nonfamily contacts. Nonfamily business women consciously attempt to separate their work and family lives.
Malone (1989)	58 CEOs of family operated wholesale lumber dealerships Response rate 19.5%	Level of strategic planning, perceived family harmony, presence of outsiders on the board of directors, and the internal locus of control of owner-manager are positively associated with higher level of continuity planning. Study finds no significant correlation between the size of business or age of owners and level of continuity planning.
McCollom (1988)	Case study (3 department stores owned by a family)	Study sees the two subsystems of family and business as interdependent. In family firms, the two subsystems seek stability through reciprocal adjustments. An enmeshed family achieves stability by using a differentiated work environment.
McCollom (1990)	Case study (3 department stores owned by a family)	Clinical methods offer a distinct advantage for research in family firms because of structural, role, cultural, and task complexity.
McCollom (1992)	565 organizational stories in one family owned retail business	Study determines relations between family and business by use of narratives and stories. The stories of owners focus on security issues and frustration with incompetent employees. Those of employees focus on relationships with colleagues, frustration with management, and difficulties in dealing with customers.

Author(s) and Date	Sample (Respondents) Studied and Response Rate (When Available)	Key Finding
McGivern (1989)	2 case studies	Study identifies five main variables influencing succession process: stage of organizational development based on the succession issue's importance, motivation of owner-manager, extent of family domination, organizational climate, and business environment.
Mintzberg & Winters (1990)	Case study of a family owned retail business	Over a period of 57 years, the company goes through an entrepreneurial and planning mode. In entrepreneurial mode the owner is fully in charge, but in planning mode procedures replace vision, and strategy making becomes an extrapolation of status quo.
Navin (1971)	105 companies	Most companies appear to have five stages of development: initiator, founder, founder's heirs, technicians, and professional managers.
Owen & Winter (1991)	187 households with home based businesses	Study finds that women are less disrupted by home based businesses than men. Businesses that require more time of family members are perceived as more disruptive. Respondents using established managerial practices perceive less disruption. Marketing and agricultural workers perceive most disruption. Business income and age do not influence perceived disruption to family life.
Rothstein (1992)	45 Jewish sons in family business Response rate 82%	Jewish families have lower rates of marital disruption compared to the general population, greater expectations of higher education from their children, and strong value systems.
Salganicoff (1990)	91 women in family businesses	Woman joining family businesses can be mutually advantageous. Women should be taught appropriate skills and given training, and work in other organizations before joining the family business. They should be encouraged early to gain know how and feeling for the business.
Salomon & Lockhart (1980)	81 German, 91 Irish farm families	The families that maintain future orientation and plan for transfer of holdings are successful in maintaining rich and respectful family relationships.
Schein (1983)	3 case studies of organization founders	While considering effective succession, founders must have knowledge about the organizational culture.

Author(s) and Date	Sample (Respondents) Studied and Response Rate (When Available)	Key Finding
Schwartz & Barnes (1991)	262 family businesses Response rate 30%	The study strongly supports the inclusion of outsiders as members of family firm boards. Outsiders provide unbiased views and help in establishing networks. However, they are not very helpful in terms of day to day operations or the resolution of family tensions.
Seymour (1993)	105 family firms Response rate 38%	Study finds that the quality of work relationship between the owner-manager and the successor has a positive relation to successor training. However, there is no association between quality of relationship and succession planning. Considerable differences exist in successor and owner ratings. Owners rated succession training and planning higher than did successors.
Sonnenfeld & Spence (1989)	About 400 CEOs Response rate 67%	Based on their heroic mission and stature, study finds four different departure styles among the CEOs: monarchs, generals, governors, and ambassadors. While the monarchs and generals feel more attached to the stature of their role as CEOs and remain in close contact with the organization, the ambassadors and governors are more satisfied with their achievements and maintain a distance from the business after their retirement. The challenge for the departing leader is to plan an ambassador like departure and ensure objective involvement in succession process.
Upton & Sexton (1987)	29 family firms	Study finds that daughters hold stereotypical female positions in family businesses.
Ward & Handy (1988)	147 family companies	48% of firms in the sample have outsiders as directors on their boards. Firms find that having outsiders on the board is useful for advice and counsel, and for accountability of management. Only 2% of the respondents report the usefulness of the board in succession planning.
Welsch (1991)	Family firms from Spain (750), Germany (501), and Great Britain (8,000)	Study reanalyzes three previously conducted studies and compares demographic factors on family businesses.
Whisler (1988)	73 companies (59 privately held, 14 publicly held)	Outside directors can be helpful when a company is in transition towards professionalization. These directors play three roles: preceptor, technical advisor, and arbitrator.
Willmott (1971)	79 British companies	Study finds the influence of work on family life in terms of working hours, and taking work, strains, and worries home.

Author(s) and Date	Sample (Respondents) Studied and Response Rate (When Available)	Key Finding
Wong, McReynolds, & Wong (1992)	100 individuals from 53 families	Patterns of family structure, kinship ties, information networks, financial cooperation, and aspiration levels are helpful for the survival of first generation Chinese immigrant businesses. To second generation Chinese, family business is not an attractive career option.
Wong (1993)	32 cotton spinning mills	Study finds Chinese family businesses pass through different stages of development: emergent, centralized, segmented, and disintegrative. These stages are discussed and compared with those of Filipino and Japanese firms.
Rowe, Haynes, & Bentley (1993)	620 family owned home businesses	Strategy Evaluation and Control The profitability of home based businesses depends on two factors: characteristics of the owner (education, need for achievement, family situation, gender, education), and the business (organizational context, structure, age and size of firm, location, marketing efforts). Personal and family characteristics are more powerful variables in determination of profits than those of business.
Trostel & Nichols (1982)	10 matched pairs of privately and publicly held companies	Study finds privately held companies attain a higher rate of actual growth in sales, place greater emphasis on asset utilization, employ accounting policies that help in reducing taxable income, than publicly held companies. There are no significant differences in the degree of formalization in planning, education of managers, or ratio of administrative and professional personnel to sales.
Trow (1961)	108 small and medium firms	Study finds a strong association between planning for succession and subsequent profitability of the firm. When manager's son is perceived incompetent, succession is delayed. In cases of unplanned successions, study finds subsequent profitability is associated positively with successor's ability.
Verdin (1986)	58 employees of a family owned chain of retail shoe stores	Setting challenging goals and providing regular feedback helps in improving the sales performance in small businesses.
Winter & Fitzgerald (1993)	321 owners of home based businesses, 211 still in business in 1992	About 33% of home based businesses close after three years. Only 20% have economic reasons. Others cite health, employment, and family reasons.

References

Alderfer, C. P. (1988). Understanding and consulting to family business boards. *Family Business Review, 1* (3), 249-261.

Ambrose, D. M. (1983). Transfer of the family-owned business. *Journal of Small Business Management, 21* (1), 49-56.

Andrews, K. R. (1971). *The concept of corporate strategy*. Homewood: Irwin.

Ayers, G. A. (1990). Rough family justice: Equity in family business succession planning. *Family Business Review, 3* (1), 3-22.

Barach, J. A. (1984). Is there a cure for paralyzed family boards? *Sloan Management Review, 25* (1), 3-12.

Barnes, L. B. (1988). Incongruent hierarchies: Daughters and younger sons as company CEOs. *Family Business Review, 1* (1), 9-21.

Barnes, L. B., & Hershon, S. A. (1976). Transferring power in the family business. *Harvard Business Review, 54* (4), 105-114.

Barry, B. (1975). The development of organization structure in the family firm. *Journal of General Management*, Autumn, 42-60.

Beach, B. (1993). Family support in home-based family businesses. *Family Business Review, 6* (4), 371-379.

Beckhard, R., & Dyer, W. G., Jr. (1983). Managing continuity in the family owned business. *Organizational Dynamics, 5* (1), 5-12.

Berenbeim, R. E. (1990). How business families manage the transition from owner to professional management. *Family Business Review, 3* (1), 69-110.

Biggadike, E. R. (1979). *Corporate diversification: Entry, strategy, and performance*. Cambridge: Harvard University Press.

Birley, S. (1986). Succession in family firm: The inheritors view. *Journal of Small Business Management, 24* (3), 36-43.

Burke, R. J., Weir, T., & DuWors, R. E., Jr. (1980). Work demands on administrators and spouse well being. *Human Relations, 33* (4), 253-278.

Cambreleng, R. W. (1969). The case of the nettlesome nepot. *Harvard Business Review, 47* (2), 14-34.

Chau, T. T. (1991). Approaches to succession in East Asian business organizations. *Family Business Review, 4* (2), 161-179.

Chrisman, J. J., Hofer, C. W., & Boulton, W. R. (1988). Toward a system for classifying business strategies. *Academy of Management Review, 13*, 413-428.

Chua, J. H., Sharma, P., & Chrisman, J. J. (1996). Defining the family business as behavior. *Proceedings of the Administrative Sciences Association of Canada*, 1-8.

Cohn, T., & Lindberg, R. A. (1974). *Survival and growth: Management strategies for the small firm*. New York: AMACOM.

Covin, T. J. (1994). Perceptions of family-owned firms: The impact of gender and educational level. *Journal of Small Business Management, 32* (3), 29-39.

Crouter, A. C. (1984). Spillover from family to work: The neglected side of work family interface. *Human Relations, 37* (6), 425-442.

Daily, C. M., & Dollinger, M. J. (1992). An empirical examination of ownership structure in family and professionally managed firms. *Family Business Review, 5* (2), 117-136.

Danco, L. (1975). *Beyond survival: A business owner's guide for success*. Cleveland: University Press.

Davis, J. A., & Tagiuri, R. (1989). The influence of life-stage on father-son work relationships in family companies. *Family Business Review, 2* (1), 47-74.

Davis, P. (1983). Realizing the potential of the family business. *Organizational Dynamics, 5* (1), 47-56.

Davis, S. M. (1968). Entrepreneurial succession. *Administrative Science Quarterly*, 402-416.

Dean, S. M. (1992). Characteristics of African American family-owned businesses in Los Angeles. *Family Business Review, 5* (4), 373-395.

Dhalla, N. K., & Yuspeh, S. (1976). Forget the product life cycle concept. *Harvard Business Review, 54* (1), 102-112.

Doeringer, P. B., Moss, P. I., & Terkla, D. G. (1992). Capitalism and kinship: Do institutions matter in the labour market? *Family Business Review, 5* (1), 85-101.

Donckels, R., & Frohlick, E. (1991). Are family businesses really different? European experiences from STRATOS. *Family Business Review, 4* (2), 149-160.

Donnelley, R. (1964). The family business. *Harvard Business Review, 42* (3), 93-105.

Dumas, C. (1989). Understanding of father-daughter and father-son dyads in family owned businesses. *Family Business Review, 2* (1), 31-46.

Dyer, W. G., Jr., (1986). *Cultural change in family firms: Anticipating and managing business and family transitions.* San Francisco: Jossey-Bass.

Dyer, W. G., Jr., (1988). Culture and continuity in family firms. *Family Business Review, 1* (1), 37-50.

Dyer, W. G., Jr., (1989). Integrating professional management into a family owned business. *Family Business Review, 2* (3), 221-235.

Ewing, D. W. (1965). Is nepotism so bad? *Harvard Business Review, 43* (1), 23-39.

Firnstahl, T. W. (1986). Letting go. Harvard Business Review, 64 (5), 14-18.

Ford, R. H. (1988). Outside directors and the privately owned firm: Are they necessary? *Entrepreneurship: Theory and Practice, 13* (1), 49-57.

Francis, A. (1991). Families, firms, and finance capital: The development of U. K. industrial firms with particular reference to their ownership and control. *Family Business Review, 4* (2), 231-261.

Friedman, S. D. (1991). Sibling relationships and intergenerational succession in family firms. *Family Business Review, 4* (1), 3-20.

Gallo, M. A., & Sveen, J. (1991). Internationalizing the family business: Facilitating and restraining factors. *Family Business Review, 4* (2), 181-190.

Geeraerts, G. (1984). The effect of ownership on the organization structure in small firms. *Administrative Science Quarterly, 29,* 232-237.

Goffee, R., & Scasse, R. (1985). Proprietorial control in family firms —Some functions of "quasi-organic" management systems. *Journal of Management Studies, 22* (1), 53-68.

Goldberg, S. D., & Woolridge, B. (1993). Self confidence and managerial autonomy: Successor characteristics critical to succession in family firms. *Family Business Review, 6* (1), 55-73.

Gumpert, D. E., & Boyd, D. P. (1984). The loneliness of the small business owner. *Harvard Business Review, 62* (6), 18-24.

Handler, W. C. (1989). Methodological issues and considerations in studying family businesses. *Family Business Review, 2* (3), 257-276.

Handler, W. C. (1992). The succession experience of the next generation. *Family Business Review, 5* (3), 283-307.

Handler, W. C. (1994). Succession in family businesses: A review of the research. *Family Business Review, 7* (2), 133-157.

Handler, W. C., & Kram, K. E. (1988). Succession in family firms: The problem of resistance. *Family Business Review, 1* (4), 361-381.

Hannan, M. T., & Freeman, J. (1989). *Organizational ecology.* Cambridge: Harvard University Press.

Harris, T. B. (1989). Some comments on family boards. *Family Business Review, 2* (2), 150-152.

Harris, D., Martinez, J. L., & Ward, J. L. (1994). Is strategy different for the family owned businesses? *Family Business Review, 7* (2), 159-176.

Hayes, J. L. (1981). All in the family. *Management Review,* July, 4.

Heck, R. K. Z., & Walker, R. (1993). Family-owned home-businesses: Their employees and unpaid helpers. *Family Business Review, 6* (4), 397-415.

Heidrick, G. W. (1988). Selecting outside directors. *Family Business Review, 1* (3), 271-285.

Hofer, C. W., & Chrisman, J. J. (1989). The strategic management of first diversification: A new perspective, I. In L. Fahey (Ed.), *The Strategic Planning Management Reader,* Englewood Cliffs: Prentice-Hall, 206-214.

Hofer, C. W., & Schendel, D. (1978). *Strategy formulation: Analytical concepts.* St. Paul: West Publishing.

Hoffman, L. (1981). *Foundations of family therapy*. New York: Basic Books.

Holland, P. G., & Boulton, W. R. (1984). Balancing the family and the business in a family business. *Business Horizons, 27* (2), 16-21.

Holland, P. G., & Oliver, J. E. (1992). An empirical examination of the stages of development of family businesses. *Journal of Business and Entrepreneurship, 4* (3), 27-38.

Hollander, B. S., & Bukowitz, W. R. (1990). Women, family culture, and family business. *Family Business Review, 3* (2), 139-151.

Hollander, B. S., & Elman, N. S. (1988). Family-owned businesses: An emerging field of inquiry. *Family Business Review, 1* (2), 145-164.

Horton, T. P. (1982). The baton of succession. *Management Review*, July, 2-3.

Jain, S. K. (1980). Look to outsiders to strengthen business boards. *Harvard Business Review, 58* (4), 162-170.

Jones, W. D. (1982). Characteristics of planning in small firms. *Journal of Small Business Management, 20* (3), 15-19.

Jonovic, D. L. (1989). Outside review in a wider context: An alternative to the classic board. *Family Business Review, 2* (2), 125-140.

Kahn, J. A., & Henderson, D. A. (1992). Location preferences of family firms: Strategic decision making or "home sweet home"? *Family Business Review, 5* (3), 271-282.

Kaye, K. (1992). The kid brother. *Family Business Review, 5* (3), 237-256.

Kirchhoff, B. A., & Kirchhoff, J. J. (1987). Family contributions to productivity and profitability in small businesses. *Journal of Small Business Management, 25* (4), 25-31.

Kleinsorge, I. K. (1994). Financial and efficiency differences in family-owned nursing homes: An Oregon study. *Family Business Review, 7* (1), 73-86.

Landes, D. S. (1993). Bleichoders and Rothschilds: The problem of continuity in the family firm. *Family Business Review, 6* (1), 85-101.

Lane, S. H. (1989). An organizational development/team-building approach to consultation with family businesses. *Family Business Review, 2* (1), 5-16.

Lansberg, I. (1983). Managing human resources in family firms: The problem of institutional overlap. *Organizational Dynamics, 12* (1), 39-46.

Lansberg, I. (1988). The succession conspiracy. *Family Business Review, 1* (2), 119-143.

Lansberg, I., & Astrachan, J. H. (1994). Influence of family relationships on succession planning and training: The importance of mediating factors. *Family Business Review, 7* (1), 39-59.

Lansberg, I., & Perrow, E. (1991). Understanding and working with leading family businesses in Latin America. *Family Business Review, 4* (2), 127-147.

Levinson, H. (1971). Conflicts that plague family businesses. *Harvard Business Review, 49* (2), 90-98.

Levinson, H. (1974). Don't choose your own successor. *Harvard Business Review, 52* (6), 53-62.

Liebtag, B. (1984). Problems tracked in transition from owner to professional management. *Journal of Accountancy*, October, 38-40.

Lundberg, C. C. (1994). Unravelling communications among family members. *Family Business Review, 7* (1), 29-37.

Lyman, A. R. (1988). Life in the family circle. *Family Business Review, 1* (4), 383-398.

Lyman, A. R. (1991). Customer service: Does family ownership make a difference? *Family Business Review, 4* (3), 303-324.

Mace, M. L. (1971). *Directors: Myth and reality*. Boston: Division of Research, Harvard Business School.

MacMillan, I. C., & Jones, P. E. (1986). *Strategy formulation: Power and politics*. St. Paul: West Publishing.

Malone, S. C. (1989). Selected correlates of business continuity planning in the family business. *Family Business Review, 2* (4), 341-353.

Malone, S. C., & Jenster, P. V. (1992). The problem of the plateaued owner manager. *Family Business Review, 5* (1), 25-41.

Marshack, K. J. (1993). Coentrepreneurial couples: A literature review on boundaries and transitions among copreneurs. *Family Business Review, 6* (4), 355-369.

Mathile, C. L. (1988). A business owner's perspective on outside boards. *Family Business Review, 1* (3), 231-237.

Matthews, G. H. (1984). Run your business or build an organization? *Harvard Business Review, 62* (2), 34-44.

McCollom, M. (1988). Integration in the family firm: When the family system replaces controls and culture. *Family Business Review, 1* (4), 399-417.

McCollom, M. (1990). Problems and prospects in clinical research on family firms. *Family Business Review, 3* (3), 245-262.

McCollom, M. (1992). Organizational stories in a family-owned business. *Family Business Review, 5* (1), 3-24.

McGivern, C. (1989). The dynamics of management succession: A model of chief executive succession in the small family firm. *Family Business Review, 2* (4), 401-411.

McGoldrick, M., & Troast, J. G. (1993). Ethnicity, families, and family businesses: Implications for practitioners. *Family Business Review, 6* (2), 283-300.

McKelvey, B. (1982). *Organizational systematics: Taxonomy, evolution, classification.* Berkeley: University of California Press.

Mintzberg, H., & Waters, J. A. (1990). Tracking strategy in an entrepreneurial firm. *Family Business Review, 3* (3), 285-315.

Mueller, R. K. (1988). Differential directorship: Special sensitivities and roles for serving the family business board. *Family Business Review, 1* (3), 239-247.

Navin, T. R. (1971). Passing on the mantle. *Business Horizons, 14* (5), 83-93.

Owen, A. J., & Winter, M. (1991). Research note: The impact of home-based business on family life. *Family Business Review, 4* (4), 425-432.

Perrigo, A. E. B. (1975). Delegation and succession in the small firms. *Personnel Management,* May, 35-37.

Post, J. E. (1993). The greening of the Boston Park Plaza Hotel. *Family Business Review, 6* (2), 131-148.

Post, J. M., & Robins, R. S. (1993). The captive king and his captive court: The psychopolitical dynamics of the disabled leader and his inner circle. *Family Business Review, 6* (2), 203-221.

Prince, R. A. (1990). Family business mediation: A conflict resolution model. *Family Business Review, 3* (3), 209-223.

Reiss, D. (1982). The working family: A researcher's view of health in household. *American Journal of Psychiatry,* November, 1412-1420.

Rosenblatt, P. C., deMik, L., Anderson, R. M., & Johnson, P. A. (1985). *The family in business: Understanding and dealing with the challenges entrepreneurial families face.* San Francisco: Jossey-Bass.

Rothstein, J. (1992). Don't judge a book by its cover: A reconstruction of eight assumptions about Jewish family businesses. *Family Business Review, 5* (4), 397-411.

Rowe, B. R., Haynes, G. W., & Bentley, M. T. (1993). Economic outcomes in family owned home-based businesses. *Family Business Review, 6* (4), 383-396.

Salganicoff, M. (1990). Women in family business: Challenges and opportunities. *Family Business Review, 3* (2), 125-137.

Salomon, S., & Lockhart, V. (1980). Land ownership and the position of elderly in farm families. *Human Organization, 39* (4), 324-331.

Schein, E. H. (1983). The role of the founder in creating organization culture. *Organizational Dynamics, 5* (1), 13-28.

Schendel, D. E., & Hofer, C. W. (1979). *Strategic management: A new view of business policy and planning.* Boston: Little Brown.

Schwartz, M. A., & Barnes, L. B. (1991). Outside boards and family businesses: Another look. *Family Business Review, 4* (3), 269-285.

Seymour, K. C. (1993). Intergenerational relationships in the family firm: The effect on leadership succession. *Family Business Review, 6* (3), 263-281.

Singer, J., & Donoho, C. (1992). Strategic management planning for the successful family business. *Journal of Business and Entrepreneurship, 4* (3), 39-51.

Sonnenfeld, J. A., & Spence, P. L. (1989). The parting patriarch of a family firm. *Family Business Review, 2* (4), 355-375.

Stallings, S. L. A. (1992). Research note: The emergence of American-Indian enterprise. *Family Business Review, 2* (4), 413-416.

Swinth, R. L., & Vinton, K. L. (1993). Do family owned businesses have a strategic advantage in international joint ventures? *Family Business Review, 6* (1), 19-30.

Tagiuri, R., & Davis, J. A. (1992). On the goals of successful family companies. *Family Business Review, 5* (1), 43-62.

Tillman, F. A. (1988). Commentary on legal liability: Organizing the advisory council. *Family Business Review, 1* (3), 287-288.

Trostel, A. O., & Nichols, M. L. (1982). Privately held companies and publicly held companies: A comparison of strategic choices and management processes. *Academy of Management Journal, 25* (1), 47-62.

Trow, D. B. (1961). Executive succession in small companies. *Administrative Science Quarterly, 6*, 228-239.

Upton, N., & Sexton, D. L. (1987). Family business succession: The female perspective. *Proceedings of 32nd annual world conference of the ICSB*, 313-318.

Verdin, J. A. (1986). Improving sales performance in a family owned business. *American Journal of Small Business, 10* (4), 49-61.

Ward, J. L. (1987). *Keeping the family business healthy: How to plan for continuing growth, profitability, and family leadership*. San Francisco: Jossey-Bass.

Ward, J. L. (1988). The special role of strategic planning for family businesses. *Family Business Review, 1* (2), 105-117.

Ward, J. L., & Handy, J. L. (1988). A survey of board practices. *Family Business Review, 1* (3), 289-308.

Weiser, J., Brody, F. & Quarrey, M. (1988). Family businesses and employee ownership. *Family Business Review, 1* (1), 23-35.

Welsch, J. (1991). Family enterprises in the U. K., the Federal Republic of Germany, and Spain: A transnational comparison. *Family Business Review, 4* (2), 231-261.

Welsch, J. (1993). The impact of family ownership and involvement on the process of management succession. *Family Business Review, 6* (1), 31-54.

Whisler, T. L. (1988). The role of the board in the threshold firm. *Family Business Review, 1* (3), 309-321.

Willmott, P. (1971). Family, work, and leisure conflicts among male employees. *Human Relations, 24* (6), 575-584.

Winter, M. & Fitzgerald, M. (1993). Continuing the family-owned home-based businesses: Evidence from a panel study. *Family Business Review, 6* (4), 417-426.

Wong, B., McReynolds, S., & Wong, W. (1992). Chinese family firms in the San Francisco Bay areas. *Family Business Review, 5* (4), 355-372.

Wong, S. L. (1993). The Chinese family: A model. *Family Business Review, 6* (3), 327340. The original article was published in *British Journal of Sociology*, 1985, 36 (1), 58-72.

Wortman, M. S., Jr. (1994). Theoretical foundations for family-owned business, a conceptual and research based paradigm. *Family Business Review, 7* (1), 3-27.

The second most frequently raised concern in family businesses relates to compensation of family members. Each stage of family business evolution creates predictable dilemmas about pay. Here's how family businesses deal with compensation at each stage.

Pay Issues Vary with Family Business Stages

By John L. Ward and Craig E. Aronoff

Compensation ranks second only to succession as one of the thorny issues facing family businesses. Understanding the changes family businesses go through as they pass from the first to second and subsequent generations of family ownership is one way of anticipating potentially contentious questions about pay. Each of the three stages in family-business evolution – the founding or entrepreneurial stage, the sibling ownership stage, and the "cousin" or "family dynasty" stage – raises new issues of family participation, team-building and shareholder unity. Similarly, each of these new stages tends to create certain predictable questions about pay.

Here is a summary of some of the pay issues most common to businesses in each stage.

The Entrepreneurial Stage

Compensation can seem simple when the business is run by the founder or by one offspring of the founder, and the next generation is only beginning to enter the business. At this stage, parents set the culture and the tone of any discussions about compensation. Attitudes toward saving on taxes, family gifting, phantom jobs and other pay practices are conveyed and absorbed uncritically by offspring. With one or two people in unquestioned control, few conflicts erupt.

One issue that may arise is whether parents have sufficient savings to ensure their security in retirement. If parents lack an adequate retirement cushion, that needs to be communicated to the next generation and resolved. Estate planning can raise the same issues.

If parents are financially secure independent of the business, they also need to let the next generation know that. The way the message is conveyed, however, can either enhance or distort children's understanding of compensation. If children are allowed to believe that the business owner's salary was the sole source of the wealth accumulated over the years, they may form unrealistic expectations about their own income potential in the business. On the other hand, the business owner can use the opportunity to inform children about the difference between compensation and dividends or other sources of wealth.

The Sibling or Second-Generation Stage

A large number of second-generation family businesses today are owned and managed by a team of siblings. Some embrace a "partnership vision" whereby two to four siblings co-own and co-lead the business with very few, if any, inactive family shareholders or non-family shareholders. Some prefer to choose a new leader from among several siblings.

Complaints about compensation often arise at this stage, but that does not necessarily mean that the underlying resentments or inequities did not exist before. It may mean only that the presence of older family members was such a powerful influence that younger members did not focus on, or feel free to express, their questions or concerns.

Several issues are common. Do the children view the family business as a money tree rather than a proving ground? How does the family deal with differences in lifestyle? Are children prepared for the fact that multiple siblings will lead the business in the future, and for the questions about compensation that raises? If a son enters the business as expected and is awarded an artificially high and ever-increasing rate of pay, what happens 15 years later when another son opts for a family-business career and begins wondering why he can't earn the same exalted salary? What perks are fair and how will they be allotted? How will information about compensation be communicated among family members?

Ideally, the parent generation has already shaped the pay expectations of second-generation leaders as they enter the business. In one family business, the principle that siblings would be paid differently based on the nature of their jobs and their backgrounds, among other things, was accepted. Yet all were aware that the policy posed risks to the team's relationships. When the three sisters in the business began speculating about pay behind each other's backs, they were offered a chance to meet to discuss their questions, with the help of the outside board's compensation committee. The sisters' right to privacy was respected; the meeting was presented as a voluntary team-building effort, and no one was pressured to participate. All three chose to take part, and the result was a candid, relaxed exchange.

One by one, the sisters discussed their pay, the reasons for it and any frustrations with it. The youngest was making more than the middle sister because she was paid at the median for her graduating class at an outstanding journalism school. But her bonus potential in her current job is limited, she told her sisters.

The older sister admitted some discomfort over her lower pay, but supported the principles behind it. Her job offered more bonus potential, and she told siblings of her plans to increase her base pay by expanding her job responsibilities .

The middle sister said she was happy with the broad management, line and strategic responsibility afforded by her job. Though her bonus was up to 25 percent of her pay, she said she would like even greater incentive opportunities .

After each had spoken, all discussed with directors some key characteristics of jobs that justify higher pay levels. They also talked about threats to their team relationship. Though odds were against harmony, all the sisters said they were committed to making it work. "If we fail, I would feel I had failed," one sister said.

The discussion defused suspicions and heightened the sisters' commitment to teamwork. It also underscored to each how important their relationship was to each of them and laid the groundwork for honest, open and mutually respectful communications in the future.

The Third-Generation or "Cousin" Stage

Toward the end of the sibling stage or at the third generation of family-business ownership, a new era begins. At this point, the business usually no longer employs all shareholders. The family business begins to resemble a public company. It becomes increasingly important for the managers of the business to be fair to all family members.

The advent of owners who lack day-to-day contact with the business can raise issues that transform the compensation system – or sometimes, wreak havoc with it. Family shareholders may begin to suspect that their siblings or cousins in the business are overpaid, at the expense of their dividends or shareholder value. They may begin speculating or trying to conduct their own independent pay assessment.

Family members not in leadership roles rarely appreciate the unique emotional burdens of leadership. They usually underestimate top managers' sense of stewardship for their interests. They also don't realize the degree to which top executives "live the job" mentally and socially, reflecting on business problems and attending business-related gatherings during their "time off." The person who understands these unspoken pressures best is the top executive's spouse. And he or she is likely to resent any indignation that may arise among siblings about executive pay. Therein lie the seeds of conflict that can eventually pull apart a family business – and a family.

These pressures often lead second- or third-generation family businesses to move toward a rational, open and professional compensation plan similar to those embraced by publicly held companies. At this stage, an external source of information and advice, such as a compensation consultant, an active outside board or both, is often necessary to win the trust of active and inactive shareholders alike.

Other questions arise at this stage about how to reward both owners and employees fairly. As growth in the family dilutes individuals' equity stakes, managers may need additional incentives, beyond their existing ownership of shares, to build shareholder value. This may lead to a long-term incentive plan tied to measures based upon increases in shareholder value.

Reprinted with permission from *Family Business Compensation* by Craig E. Aronoff and John L. Ward. Copyright 1994, Family Enterprise Publishers.

Strategic planning is particularly important in family businesses because it is the secret to keeping the business in the family long term. Family firm strategic planning involves the needs and interests of both the family and the business. As members of the next generation assume leadership, strategic planning is a key to regenerating the business while implementing their program. As generations change, so do priorities. So must strategy, most often by building on the strategic foundation set by the previous generations.

To engage in strategic planning, write down three or four key words representing business goals. Then take a long-term view, understand the company's environment, get the management team involved, and focus on the company's strengths in relation to its environment. Examples given of families and family business using strategic planning include: a snack food maker, a funeral home chain, a supermarket, a cabinet maker and an automotive dealership.

Strategies for Family Firms

By Sharon Nelton

When Michael W. Rice succeeded his father as president of Utz Quality Foods, Inc., it was a nice little potato chip and pretzel company with 325 employees and an annual growth rate of five to 10 percent. From its location in Hanover, Pa., it served three markets: Baltimore, Washington and south-central Pennsylvania.

Now, nearly eight years later, Utz is a *bigger* nice little company with 550 employees and an annual growth rate of more than 20 percent.

Why has this family business, founded by Rice's grandparents in 1921, grown and prospered so?

Because Rice, 43, did some strategic planning.

First, he decided he wanted more rapid growth. "My grandfather and father were content with a slow rate of growth," he says. "They liked to control things very closely and felt that if they grew faster, they'd lose the control. I felt that if you developed your managers properly, you could achieve growth but still maintain the quality and basic strength that got you where you were."

He expanded the company's geographic reach to encompass Virginia. He added new products, including corn chips and other corn snacks, because he could see that corn-based snacks were gaining popularity in the mid-Atlantic region. He stepped up marketing and, to make Utz more manageable, he bought out a sister's interest in the company, leaving himself and his mother, Arlene Utz Hollinger, as sole owners.

One thing he did not change was quality. Utz snack foods are more costly to produce, but Rice believes he has a better product than most of his competitors.

Rice has proved to himself what a number of other business owners are coming to learn – that strategic planning in family businesses pays off. Most of the planning concepts involved apply to non-family enterprises, too.

Strategic planning should not be confused with day-to-day operational planning, advises William P. Anthony, professor of management at Florida State University.

In his recently published *Practical Strategic Planning* (Quorum Books, Westport, Conn.), he says it includes five key elements:

- Long-term focus, usually three to five years but sometimes as long as 20.
- An understanding of the outside environment in which the business operates.
- Involvement of top management.
- Commitment of large amounts of organizational resources.
- A setting of direction for the organization by focusing on its identity and its place in a changing environment.

Anthony says a good strategic plan can help a company answer such questions as: Are we growing enough? Are some of our products and services obsolete? Should we add new ones? What type of personnel should we hire?

Charles Gueli Jr., 40, chairman of the Gueli Organization, a diversified family-owned business in New York, says he found that when members of his family simply talked about their hopes and dreams for the company, it often made them better prepared to take advantage of opportunities that arose. Since making that discovery a few years ago, Gueli has instituted more formal planning procedures and is working to improve them.

Matthew J. and Richard J. Lamb, brothers who own Blake-Lamb Funeral Homes, Inc., in Oak Park IL, have turned to strategic planning to help them remain competitive in a fast-changing industry. They are also using it to help ensure that their business stays in the family.

Marvin "Mickey" Weiss has used strategic planning to weather the bad times that have beset the steel industry in northern Indiana, where Wise Way Super Food Centers, his independent supermarket chain, is located. Over a 2 1/2 year period, he phased out the four least profitable of his eight stores, losing only a third of his volume in the process. Now the company is ready to expand again.

Other families do strategic planning because their business has reached a stage when plans must be made if the business – and consequently the family – is not to suffer. Herb H. and Kenneth Seilkop of Economy Pattern & Castings Company, a Cincinnati firm that serves the foundry industry, say they finally decided they had to grow.

"We're too big to operate as a little company and too little to operate as a big company," Ken says of the $4.5 million sales firm. He and his brother have brought in an outside board of directors to help them clarify and achieve their strategic objectives.

Harvey J. Beaudin did no strategic planning for Miles Fox Office Products Company, in suburban Detroit, throughout the 1970s. Even during Detroit's darkest days, the office supply industry was booming – and it still is. Miles Fox (named after the founder) grew fast enough to absorb three of the four Beaudin children and has now outpaced even their ability to manage it without becoming more professional. It had 16 employees and revenues of $660,000 in 1968, the year Beaudin bought it; now there are more than 70 employees and annual revenues of $12 million. The Beaudin family is using strategic planning to create a more professionally run organization.

"A strategic plan is a business' formula for success," says John L. Ward, professor of free enterprise at Loyola University of Chicago and author of *Keeping the Family Business Healthy*, to be published by Jossey-Bass, of San Francisco, next fall.

Michael J. Kami, of Corporate Planning Inc., a Lighthouse Point, Fla., consulting firm, suggests that the phrase "strategic planning" be abolished because it smacks of reports that are put together and then ignored. He prefers to call it "strategic management with strategic thinking."

He explains: "'Management' is doing something, and 'thinking' means don't be stupid."

Though strategic planning in publicly held corporations is concerned only with the needs and interests of the business, John Ward points out that there is a second dimension to such planning in family businesses: the needs and interests of the family.

With time, for example, Mike Rice may find that planning does more than help the Utz company improve its performance. It may also help him, his mother and his wife, Jane – Utz's public relations director – transfer leadership of the company to the fourth generation.

Fewer than 15 percent of family businesses stay family-run that long, according to Ward. "The average life expectancy of the once very successful family business is 55 years," he says. After that, they either close or change hands.

"Perpetuating the family business is the most difficult, most challenging management task that anybody can undertake," contends Loyola University's Ward. He has conducted research on 200 family businesses, and, he says, "The secret to keeping the business in the family is to take the long view – to think and plan strategically."

Ward is interested in helping family businesses avoid living out the "shirt sleeves to shirt sleeves in three generations" syndrome in which the first generation builds the business, the second maintains it, and the third loses interest in it. Sometimes, the second generation milks the business, consuming all its wealth so that nothing is left for the third generation.

Family businesses that have been most successful over the years, Ward says, are those that have found ways to regenerate themselves with new strategies each time they reach a plateau.

In a family business, "you're dealing with two different issues," says Matt Lamb, board chairman of Blake-Lamb Funeral Homes. "A family is forgiving; a business is bottom-line oriented. How do you really meld those two together and still have a successful business and a loving family?"

Business people like the Lambs, who include the future of the family itself in their strategic planning, find it not only results in a better business but also makes it easier for family members to clarify their roles in and out of the business, helping them to face directly such touchy issues as who will own and run it.

Matt and Dick Lamb bought their 106-year-old funeral home company from their father, who had acquired it from the founding Blake family in 1928. The $7-million-a-year firm includes 11 metropolitan Chicago funeral homes.

The brothers began to formalize strategic planning about five years ago.

"We had gotten very aggressive in acquisitions, but we really felt the need to have an overall picture of where we were going and where the industry was going," says Dick, 45, the president. A decade ago, the Lambs began to see their industry moving from one of family-owned companies to one made up of large conglomerates.

In the past couple of years, competition from the conglomerates has become more and more aggressive, and the environment, says Matt, 54, has become "hostile to a family-type, small operation. One of the main decisions that we had to make was whether we wanted to sell out or to persevere in this kind of environment."

They decided to persevere.

But they wanted help, and two years ago they created an advisory board of three Chicagoans in unrelated fields: Schwinn Bicycle Company president Edward R. Schwinn, Jr., because of his experience in running a family company that had undergone many changes in recent years; Ronald L. Taylor, president of the Keller Graduate School of Management, who could bring an academic overview to the operation; and Mark A. Levy, a restauranteur and real estate developer, for his knowledge in acquisitions, service, quality control and personnel development. Levy is in business with his brother, a fact that was important to the Lambs, who wanted to know more about how other brothers with different interests get along in a rapidly growing company.

"The most important thing the advisory board does for us," says Dick, "is to make us focus on the really important things for our future rather than strictly on putting out fires today."

"We found we could no longer just be in the business of providing caskets, limousines, funeral facilities and funeral services. We found that in the light of the changing environment, changing competition and new ideas, we were really in the business of providing services to families at the time of a death."

Their board has helped them build on the strength of outreach services that they were already offering, such as programs to help people cope with the death of a loved one. They have also moved into joint ventures with cemeteries and a flower company. And they are developing a computer software business-management package and insurance programs that they expect to market to new customers – other funeral homes.

Blake-Lamb is growing 25 percent a year, but the Lambs are keeping in sharp focus the vision of their company as one that can respond to new ideas and still treat grieving clients as individuals.

Simultaneously, the Lambs have been paying attention to developing the company's future management. Three of Matt's four children have chosen to join the company, and one of them, Rosemarie Lamb, 29, has already been singled out as the successor in leadership. As chief operating officer, she is running the company on a day-to-day basis, and Matt and Dick are beginning to involve her in developing the programs for growth as well.

Within the past few years, Matt's family has periodically held structured meetings in which both family issues and business issues are discussed. They get such items on the table as why one family member is paid more than another and why the oldest daughter was chosen chief operating officer.

"Everyone has to leave their egos and prejudices outside the room," says Matt. "Then you just get into it. There is never anything unsaid between us."

Dick's five children are younger, the oldest being 20, and it remains to be seen whether any will join the family business. The family does not have formal meetings yet, but there are discussions around the dining table. Dick says, "The issues at this point are, 'Should I go into the business?' 'What happens if I don't go into the business – will you still love me?'"

Still open is the question of future ownership of the company – an issue the Lamb brothers say is hard to get into while the company is growing so fast. With nine children between them, however, the growth and increasing complexity of the company may make ownership decisions easier. Because the company has more facets to it and more subsidiaries, Dick says, ownership can be "shared in ways that were not possible for us in the past."

Another set of brothers who are conscious of the need to account for the family in their strategic planning are the Seilkops of Economy Patterns & Castings in Cincinnati. But their problems are quite different. It is uncertain whether anyone from the next generation will take over Economy.

Herb is 57, and neither of his two children, now in their 30s, expect to join the family business. Ken is 48; his older daughter, a college sophomore, has expressed interest in joining the company in an accounting position someday, while the younger, a high school senior, has indicated no interest.

Because of the uncertainty, the Seilkops have taken several steps to assure the continuity of the business. For the time being, their plan calls for the company to remain in the family but to be run by professional management if Ken and Herb are not available to run it. They have brought in an outside board of directors empowered to see that the company has good management. And they have identified their vice president, C.B. Green, as their successor, if the board approves.

In families where succession is uncertain or family members are especially young, reliance on trusted lieutenants like Green can be vital. At 27, Donald Weiss is the youngest of four Weiss children and the only one involved in Wise Way food stores. He is the clear-cut successor. But his father, Mickey Weiss, is 63, leaving a larger-than-usual generation gap and, although Mickey plans to be around awhile, there is some question about whether there will be enough time for him to train the younger generation.

"When there's a case where there's a big gap in ages, like my own," says Don, "non-family business members are very important – both for filling the gap between generations and also bringing in some professional management expertise." Mickey recruited managers from other chains who, Don says, have contributed their experience and given the company stability. Mickey and Don also rely heavily on their long-time vice president, Patrick O'Malley, who handles day-to-day operations. Don, who has a Columbia University M.B.A., has been able to learn much about the supermarket business under the tutelage of these valued managers.

Ask family business owners if they can recall a time when lack of strategic planning hurt the business, and most will say yes.

Mickey Weiss thinks he missed an opportunity by not getting into discount supermarkets earlier. He and his son will try to recoup by making their next store, now in the planning stages, a discount operation.

Ken and Herb Seilkop at Economy Pattern & Castings believe they missed out on good acquisitions they could have made if they had started strategic planning earlier.

Inability to come up with a new strategy, in fact, caused Wolferman's, a grocery chain based in Kansas City, Mo., to close its doors. It began as a downtown grocery store in 1888, when Kansas City streets were filled with horses, wagons and cowboys, and became the premier grocery chain in the area, offering high quality products, charge accounts and home delivery.

"It was a high-overhead business – that was one of our problems," says Fred Wolferman, whose grandfather and great-grandfather founded the company. After World War II, supermarkets came on strong, getting better at merchandising. The need for stores like Wolferman's dwindled. The stores were liquidated in 1972, four years after Fred Wolferman, now 41, went to work for the company.

"It would have taken a radical reorganization of the business to adapt it to the changing market." he says.

But he did keep a piece of the company: the famous, extra-thick English muffins that the family had been producing since the early 1900s. He went into the industrial real estate business, but he also went into partnership with the head of the old company's bakery to continue producing muffins for wholesale.

When his partner retired in 1976, Fred Wolferman quit the real estate business and went into muffins full-time. His wife, Kristie, is not actively involved in the business, but she came up with the strategic idea that put the company back on the map again. Do mail order, she urged.

Fred placed the first mail order ad in *Bon Appetit* in 1977, "and darned if it didn't sell a lot of muffins," he says. The ad launched Wolferman's into a venture that increases 30 percent to 40 percent a year, helping to boost the revitalized company's annual sales from $600,000 in 1981 to more than $4 million last year. Now getting back into retailing, Fred recently opened two stores, each combining a restaurant with a specialty food shop.

Loyola's John Ward observes that among the family businesses that survive over the long term, you see a change in strategy with each new generation. The new leadership does not necessarily abandon the old strategy but often adds to it.

The Gueli Organization was launched as a woodworking company in Brooklyn 40 years ago by Charles Gueli, Sr., a master craftsman who learned his trade in Italy. When Charlie, Jr., joined the company in 1964, it was basically the same woodworking business his father had started, doing $800,000 a year in sales with the help of 50 Old World craftsmen. "They could build cabinetry better than anyone and always had a backlog of work," Charlie recalls.

Inadvertently, the company began to do other kinds of construction-related work, such as painting or drywall simply because it was asked to do so by contractors who did not want those jobs themselves.

Only when Charlie was well-versed in the business did the Guelis actually start to seek clients for the new areas of work they were getting into.

Since Charlie, who has been chairman since 1976, joined the business, it has grown to seven companies involved in such fields as construction, architectural management and maintenance, all extensions of the original woodworking operation. Charlie's brother, Robert, joined the Sum in the mid-1970s, to be followed by Robert's wife, Connie, who is in sales, and a cousin, Charles A. Gueli, who opened a Washington office and helped the company get started in the real estate development field, its big new growth area.

Charlie, Jr., feels the company has found its real estate niche in smaller commercial projects in suburban locations. In just three years, its holdings have grown to $35 million. The Gueli Organization itself is doing $30 million in annual sales and has grown to 140 employees.

Another successor who brought a new strategy to a company is Thelma Hausman Dunlevy, 55, who became president of Hausman Motor Company, a Louisville, Ky, Jeep dealership, after her father died in 1982.

Charles Hausman had been in business for 60 years and, says Dunlevy, "he had earned the community's respect for his integrity." That was an image she did not want to change, but she did begin to advertise much more aggressively and make the company more visible by sponsoring community events and participating in trade and community organizations.

Sales of new Jeeps jumped from 35 to 70 the year she took over. Now the dealership sells 100 annually, even though, because of the demographics of the area, the manufacturer's projections indicate sales should be only 32.

The Hausmans might have lost the opportunity to keep the business under family management if Dunlevy and her sister, Joan H. Campbell, who is office manager, had not pushed their way into the business. Dunlevy says their father was a "warm and loving patriarch." Their mother, Loretta W. Hausman, now 83, has been involved in the business in the office since the 1940s. Dunlevy says she and her sister, with their mother's help, convinced their father "that we could serve as a bridge to carry the business on into the fourth generation.

Even as small children, says Dunlevy, the sisters planned how they would run the company when they were grown up. It was a long time before Dunlevy's ambitions were realized, "because women weren't supposed to get into sales." She became a teacher first and did not join the family firm until 1977. Only six months before Dunlevy's father died could her mother persuade him to incorporate. Dunlevy and her sister got stock for the first time, and also for the first time, she says, "the tax lawyer, accountant and banker became acquainted with the daughters."

Now that it is her turn, Dunlevy is not leaving succession to chance. Seven of the 13 Hausman employees are family members, including three of Dunlevy's six children. Two of them, sons, are being groomed to take over. Meanwhile, Dunlevy says, "Mother, my sister and I have worked hard to show one and all that women can pick up the torch and carry it."

Members of the younger generation speak with special appreciation of parents who face up to the succession issue and start planning it early.

Richard M. "Rick" Beaudin, 31, president of suburban Detroit's Miles Fox, says "one of the things you've really got to give credit to my father for" is that he drew up a buy-and-sell agreement with his children as soon as Rick graduated from high school. "He wants to make sure the company stays with the family," says Rick.

By helping his son get a bank loan, Mickey Weiss has made it possible for Don to buy one of the WiseWay stores.

To begin the strategic planning process, Mike Kami advises, family business owners should collect their thoughts at 2 o'clock in the morning, when it is quiet and put down three or four words that are most important for the business or for themselves.

He says: "Maybe it's 'security' or maybe it's 'power.' Maybe it's 'lots of money' or 'give my son or daughter a career.' What is the absolutely most important?"

Suppose you choose "lots of money." Then, says Kami, "maybe the plan should be to make the company profitable short-term and sell it to a conglomerate. If you say you want power, then you may want to run a good company and use the money to run for political office."

Once you have made the big decisions, he says, "then, derivatively, you make the little decisions." But your decisions cannot be contradictory, he warns. For example, you must choose either "quality" or "cheap," because each calls for a completely different strategy.

Family businesses tend to change leadership only every 25 or 30 years, notes John Ward. He says this can be a problem in a world where non-family firms change leadership more often and where, studies indicate, the average business life cycle (the move from startup to maturity to early decline), which once tended to last 30 or 40 years, has dropped to less than 20.

It is not feasible for a family business to change leadership every 10 or 15 years, Ward says. But today's rapid pace does mean that a family business can no longer wait from one generation to another to change its strategy. "We need to see family business leaders who are able to bring to fruition two or three new strategies to their business every generation," says Ward.

For some family business leaders, this may be difficult, if not impossible.

For others, it is the perfect situation. Ward finds that some people are not satisfied by building one business to a point where they are wealthy and socially accepted. They like to keep on charging, because they love the challenges of managing and of change – even more than they love the products and services they have created.

Perhaps that is what keeps Mickey Weiss going. Since he started WiseWay in the early 1940s, he has outlasted the national supermarket chains that came and went in his Indiana area. He has outlasted many of his independent grocery competitors. Now, with the help of his son, Don, he is preparing to outwit and outlast his discount competitors.

Mickey would never have been content to stop at age 45 and live comfortably on what he had built, says Don. "He is not a person who is happy with the status quo."

Whether new strategies are introduced by one high-energy business owner, by the younger generation or by top-notch non-family managers, they must be frequent enough and timely enough to meet the challenge of competition and change, experts say. At the same time, the leaders of enterprise must be deft enough to meet family needs.

Sums up Loyola University's Ward: "The future of any family business depends on two key factors. There must be an atmosphere that encourages personal growth and harmonious succession. And there must be effective management with both short- and long-range views."

Neither factor, he cautions, comes about by accident. They require planning, commitment and investment of money and time now to reap the benefit in the future.

This article was originally printed in *Nation's Business*, June 1986.

Copyright 1986, U.S. Chamber of Commerce. Reprinted with permission of the publisher.

Most family-owned businesses struggle to survive beyond a single generation. Strategic planning – for both business and family – can help to strengthen the family enterprise and extend its lifespan. The author offers a six-step process toward implementing strategic planning: family commitment; business health assessment; identification of business alternatives; family and personal goal consideration; selection of business strategy; and assessment of family interests and capabilities.

The Special Role of Strategic Planning for Family Businesses

By John L. Ward

Strategic planning for family-owned businesses differs from planning for other types of companies largely because the family firm must incorporate family issues into its thinking.

Family concerns and preferences can influence the choice of business strategy and often make the family reluctant to embrace more formal goal-oriented discussions and decisions. Further, family considerations can limit the strategic aggressiveness of the family firm.

While our research revealed several reasons for this hesitation among family businesses, it also pointed to the critical need for strategic planning and the special benefits to those who undertake it.

That research consisted of three studies of strategy in family firms. Ward (1987) has detailed information on this research. In the first study, 200 privately owned firms that were at least five years old and that employed at least twenty people in 1924 were selected at random from the *Illinois Manufacturers Directory*. (The year 1924 was selected because 1919 was the earliest date of meaningful data.) Interviews at the surviving firms in 1984 documented the family ownership and leadership succession patterns and the evolution of the companies' strategies.

The second study compared the strategies and results of firms that were closely held or family-controlled with the strategies and results of public firms not controlled by families. For this study, we subdivided the PIMS data base (Strategic Planning Institute, Cambridge, Massachusetts) into 300 business units of privately controlled firms and 1,500 units of publicly held firms not controlled by families and studied their strategic profiles to determine the extent to which private companies selected different strategies, competed in different environments, and obtained different results. We explored hypotheses on the long-term orientation of private and family-controlled companies, the emphasis on quality, and so on.

In the third study, we recruited twenty family firms to apply the strategic planning framework to their own businesses. Each business assessed its industry, market, and environmental threats and opportunities. Each firm also assessed its strengths and weaknesses. As a result of these assessments, the businesses selected strategic alternatives that were most appropriate to their situations. Then, they described their current strategies. In nearly every case, their current strategies were less aggressive than their self-determined strategic potential. Last, each family identified the factors that it believed to have contributed to the conservativeness of its choices. The explanations included questions bearing on estate tax and personal financial liquidity and uncertainty over the eventual success of future family leaders.

With this paper, I hope to stimulate research exploring the special role of strategic planning in the family firm; to provide professionals who serve family businesses with some insights on how families in business approach strategic planning; and, most important, to outline a strategic planning framework for the family business. I want to encourage a formal approach to strategic planning. Many contend that strategic planning is merely one quick vehicle to "strategic thinking" – conscious regular attention to key issues affecting the future of the business. They argue that formal planning is not necessary if "strategic thinking" is present, especially for smaller firms. I prescribe a formal process for three reasons: First, not all family businesses are small. Second, for most family businesses, strategic planning is the necessary groundwork for active "strategic thinking." Third, formal planning meetings and review help to promote the healthy, open, shared decision-making so often needed in the family enterprise. Brandt (1981) and Steiner (1969) are two good references on formal strategic planning.

This paper begins with an argument urging strategic planning in family businesses. Then, I define this process for families and identify the particular questions they must address. Next, I illustrate how family issues often influence the choice of business strategy, and I outline a strategic planning framework integrating family and business. I then suggest several unique competitive characteristics of family companies that can influence the choice of business strategy. I conclude by noting the reasons that I believe explain the reluctance of family business owners to plan and the additional benefits of planning specific to family businesses.

The Need for Strategic Planning

A family that perpetuates its company from generation to generation is rare. The study of 200 family-owned Illinois manufacturing firms found that only 13 percent lasted through the third generation. Of these, just a small minority – 3 percent (N = 3) – actually prospered, as evidenced by an increase of 10 percent or more in their employee base over the sixty years between 1924 and 1984. The results of this study are summarized in Figure 1.

There are several possible explanations for the high failure rate. First, many family businesses are small and lack the staff and financial strength of larger companies. Second, the family itself can become a stumbling block as the rigors of business sharpen such problems as sibling rivalry and generational succession. Relatedly, the funding of family estate planning, retirement, divorce, and other personal projects often tempts business owners to harvest the company's profit rather than to reinvest it in additional business growth. Third and most important, many owners of family businesses lack a conceptual framework for assessing their company and planning for its future. They often do not take advantage of modern analytical tools that can help them to conquer the challenges of family business continuity. The most critical of these tools is planning – to guide both the company and the family.

Figure 1. Life Expectancy of 200 Successful Privately Owned Manufacturing Firms 1924-1984

No longer surviving	80%
Same name still surviving as independent companies	20%
Of the 20% still independent:	
Sold to outsiders	5%
Went public and no longer controlled by the founding family	2%
Still owned by the same family as in 1924	13%
Of the 13% still owned by the same family	
Grew significantly	3%
Did not grow	3%
Declined	7%
Of the 80% that did not survive:	
Ceased when 0 to 29 years old	33%
Ceased when 30 to 59 years old	36%
Ceased when 60 to 89 years old	16%
Ceased when 90 years old and over	15%

My research noted one important pattern among the family firms that had not only survived but prospered: these firms had renewed or regenerated their business strategies several times over the sixty years studied. They added new strategies to their past ways of doing business as market and competitive pressures required response. For example, one food service distributor began in the early 1900s with its founder selling fresh fish to restaurants from a seaport's docks. With the advent of refrigeration technology, the company began using coolers to store and truck fresh and frozen fish and frozen vegetables. Next, the company enlarged its geographic range and added warehouse space for dry goods in order to compete more effectively. Now, the firm is exploring national markets and even export opportunities. Another successful firm began as a stationery supplier to businesses. Then, the firm added furniture to its line, which also moved the business into interior design services. Now, the company is opening multiple outlets for retail stationery, gifts and cards, and it is considering the acquisition of a discount office furniture retail store. The key point from these examples is that prospering firms plan actively and add new strategies to their businesses as their environments change. The successful firms in our research pursued change continually.

The research noted another important pattern that was related to the family: Often, the new business strategies came about as a result of changing family influences. In some cases, the new directions were an expression of a successor's interests. In other cases, the plans provided sibling partners with opportunities to "do their own thing" or to obtain some "healthy distance" from each other.

I believe that the best way both of addressing the changing environment and of coping with shifting family circumstances and needs is through a strategic planning process that incorporates both.

What is Planning?

The term *strategic planning* typically refers to the process of developing a business strategy for profitable growth. It is designed to create insights into the company and the environment in which the company operates. It provides a systematic way of asking key business questions.

Such an inquiry challenges past business practices and opens the way for choosing new alternatives. The result should be a well-prepared strategic plan – usually a written document that spells out specific steps to improve customer satisfaction, increase profit, and revitalize and prepare the company for the next generation. The plan also states the chosen mission of the business, identifies the direction of future growth, and describes programs that can help to achieve that growth. It thus indicates ways in which the business can compete more effectively.

This approach to strategic planning does not assume that business growth occurs automatically. Instead, it assumes that growth occurs only if specific steps are taken to encourage it. The purpose of the planning process is to determine these steps by asking three questions: in what markets do we want to compete? how can we compete effectively in those markets? and how aggressively do we want to reinvest our corporate and family resources?

The approach advocated here is similar to the sort of strategic planning practiced by most companies. However, the family business must consider the other dimension: the preparation not only of a business strategic plan but of a family strategic plan. The family plan spells out long-term personal and professional goals for family members. It also establishes a process whereby family goals and issues can be explored at regular intervals.

Family strategic planning addresses four questions: *First*, why is the family committed to perpetuating the business? For example, why not sell the company? What benefits does the family see in keeping the business? *Second*, how does the family see itself and the company in years ahead? Does the family envision that many family members will be active in the firm, or will they be passive owners? Does the family see the business creating spin-off ventures for family members? *Third*, how will the family build or maintain strong relationships, resolve conflicts and work for harmony? How will the family and the business resolve questions of family compensation? *Fourth*, what are the specific steps required to accomplish the family's personal and professional goals each year? Is this the year to discuss and establish rules, such as expecting outside work experience? Will the family begin regular "family fun" activities, such as group vacations?

Answers to these questions are important, because in a family enterprise they shape business strategy in ways that other companies do not need to consider. Should family members in the company work together in one business and location or apart in separate businesses and locations? How much money does the family need from the company? Are older family members confident that their sons and daughters can run the company well? In its strategy, the company's plan must reflect these considerations.

This weaving together of business and family plans represents a special challenge for the family business, because it means that the business and the family plans are highly interdependent. The business plan requires the family to determine the extent of its commitment to the company. That commitment depends on the prospects for the business that the planning process reveals. As a result, the family cannot separate strategic business planning from family strategic planning. It must undertake both in a connected and simultaneous way.

Realizing the Company's Full Potential

Some owners resist the idea of combining family with business. They believe that business decisions are best and most cleanly made when the decision makers ignore the personal interests of the family. But, those who subscribe to this school of thought should consider the following: In 1982, we studied twenty family concerns representing a variety of industries and locales that were willing to share their planning process with us. The owners were asked to assess their companies through a comprehensive, strategic planning process. Much to their surprise, the majority of the business owners discovered that they were performing below their strategic potential. That is, they were pursuing strategies less ambitious than their own business assessments would justify.

For example, a company supplying food vending machines and products to businesses was the leader in its market. It was very profitable, and it faced no particular competitive or technological threats. Yet, for several years the firm had been plodding along doing nothing different except refining operational procedures, such as developing sales commission systems and computer programs that provided more detailed information on delivery and repairs. Although the opportunities for growth – in new cities, in cafeteria food service, in new product lines, and other areas – were bountiful, the company did not have a vision. The stagnation came from wanting to limit the possibility of dispute among the three brother owners, to wait until the plans and capabilities of the next generation were clear, and to avoid a business spending commitment while their own personal financial plans were unaddressed.

Owners offered two explanations for the disparity between their strategic potential and their actual – less ambitious – strategic choices. First, they were unsure of the way in which family members might influence their businesses. For example, they did not know whether all members would want to work together under a single roof or whether they would prefer to work apart in autonomous business divisions. They did not know whether those in the business would have to provide financially for those outside the business. They did not know whether they as parents might wish to set cash aside for the new ventures of entrepreneurially-minded offspring.

Second, owners were unsure of their own commitment to the company's future. They were unsure because they had not explored or settled such key issues as the amount of money available for new projects or the amount of managerial talent that potential successors possessed. As a result of these uncertainties – all related to their families – the owners selected more cautious, conservative business strategies. They did this despite self-avowed confidence in the underlying strengths of their companies.

This study demonstrates that family issues strongly influence the choice of business strategy in a family business. Family issues shape business judgement whether the fact that they do is formally recognized or not.

How Planning Begins

When a family business faces almost any setback, a specialist in strategic planning may well be called in. The problem can be characterized in such terms as these: "We're not as innovative as we should be." "We're losing profitability." "We're wasting a lot of energy debating where we should be going." The first efforts of the planner, as he or she begins to intervene, are usually to profile the current situation, using financial analysis or competitive analysis or customer analysis, and to interview the senior managers on what they see as the key strategic issues facing the firm.

The first entry into the business can offer insights on its health and aggressiveness. The interviews often uncover all sorts of family business issues, such as uncertainty about succession, rivalries among family members, and discrepancies between position and performance.

In any case, the planner or consultant looks for opportunities to generate enthusiasm about the planning process. The hesitancy to undertake strategic planning often results from fear that it is an unfamiliar process and that it may reveal confidential data, expose weak management communication practices, and surface past errors and current family issues. The planner is asked to propose a process that gets strategic planning going.

Step One: The Commitment of Family

In a family business, the ideal starting point for the planning process is the family itself. The first step is for the family to establish its level of commitment to the future of the business and to planning as a way of securing that future. Is the family willing to sacrifice short-term material gains in order to invest money in the company? Will family members spend the time it takes to build a business? Can they work together? Do offspring have the necessary qualities of leadership? Are parents willing to let go of the company when the time comes?

If family members reach a consensus on these issues, they can write a preliminary statement of commitment. Such a statement might say, "We are fundamentally interested in the long-term future of this business. We want this business to last forever. And, we wilt do what it takes to accomplish that!" Whatever the resolve and rationale, the family's statement of commitment is a necessary first step. As Figure 2 shows, the rest of the planning process flows from this commitment.

Step Two: Assessing the Firm's Business Health

Next to the family's commitment, the foundation for planning lies in a financial and market analysis of the business. Such an analysis is common in firms that practice strategic planning. It shows whether the company is gaining or losing market share, using cash efficiently or inefficiently, and increasing or decreasing its productivity. Such analysis has an additional significance for the family business. Among other uses, it reveals whether the family is reinvesting sufficiently in the business to help ensure a vital future or whether it is financing personal needs at the expense of the company.

Natural forces within the family business probably encourage disinvestment from the business over time. So-called excess cash from the business is often used to reward the family for years of sacrifice with an improved standard of living. Or, it is used to meet such perceived needs as retirement and inheritances or to retire debt or reward loyal employees.

Most successful families are unaware of the damage done by these financial "harvesting" practices. They assume that all is well if profit is strong and sales are rising. They think they can afford high levels of personal spending. Yet, successful businesses must have a certain amount of reinvestment if they are to continue to grow. In fact, the longer family members want the business to live and the more prosperity they want to enjoy in the years ahead, the higher their rate of current reinvestment must be. Families that spend the company's profit elsewhere set in motion forces that silently weaken the firm, often in ways that will not show up on the bottom line for years. At that point, it may be too late

Figure 2: The Interdependence of Family and Business Planning

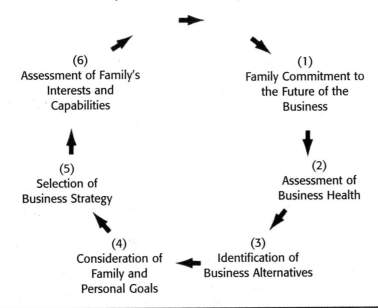

to reinvest and turn the company around.

Financial analyses uncover potential soft spots. They illustrate just how much money is going into such areas as family bonuses and how much is being plowed back into the enterprise. The most important of these analyses figures the rate of reinvestment in the business.

Approaches to the calculation of rate of reinvestment range from figuring debt-to-equity ratios to judging the number of strategic experiments under way. One of the most useful approaches compares the return to the owner with the return to the business. This approach figures family salaries, bonuses, and perquisites as a percentage of the total sum available for future business opportunities. That sum is typically measured by net income before taxes.

To figure the percentage, owners divide family salaries plus perquisites by that sum. Family salary and perquisites should usually be no more than 33 percent to 50 percent of operating income for mid-size companies with more than twenty employees. If the figure is significantly higher, the family is milking the business for short-term gain. It is withdrawing more funds than public companies typically pay out in dividends to their shareholders.

To be sure, milking or harvesting the business may be desirable for some families. Perhaps a family has concluded that the future of the company is dim or even hopeless for reasons beyond its control. If that is the case and the family still wants to find a long-term, prosperous role for itself in business, the family should harvest profit and seek other ventures in which its members can invest. But, if the family has concluded that its firm is a satisfactory investment, the harvesting of profit clearly compromises the future vitality of the family business.

Step Three: Identification of Business Alternatives

The next step is to identify possible business alternatives; enter new geographical areas, increase the quality of service, hire strong managers to generate sales or improve productivity, and so on. At this stage, family businesses can consider some of their possible uniquenesses or advantages.

Truly clever strategies capitalize on market insights and the relative competitive strengths that the individual business enjoys. Good family businesses will share some strengths by the very fact that they are family businesses. The following insights were supported by the study that compared the strategies and performance of nearly 300 family companies with the strategies and performance of 1,500 public companies.

Many family firms enjoy the benefits of a long-term orientation. They rarely have outside shareholders to whom they must justify quarterly performance in sales and earnings; no stock market will judge them harshly if they increase expenses for worthwhile strategies. They can afford to focus their vision on the future. They also tend to have a flexible organization, with fewer bureaucratic layers that can stall a needed market response. The company's motivation for quality, born of having the family's own name on the door or in the board room, often produces quick service and top-notch products. The company is adaptable to smaller markets. It is often willing to invest in people. And, if the family provides a unified culture at the top of the organization, it becomes easier to establish business direction and to get everyone pulling together in that direction. Clear direction increases a company's chances of success.

The strengths just listed have clear implications for the strategic direction of any family business. The strategies that are suitable to these particular strengths include exploiting smaller markets, market niches, ethnic or regional markets, declining or more mature markets that yield profit through personal effort, and emerging markets. Smaller companies can also emphasize craftsmanship or customized services or products.

These strategic directions suggest that the smaller family business does best by seeking out the "hidden customers" – the buyer whom others have somehow overlooked or ignored. Of course, big and small companies alike desire that customer. But, the family business has some specific advantages that can help it to win even when it competes with companies that have larger staffs, more financial clout, or both. Its very smallness gives it the ability to respond quickly. The personal involvement of the owner tends to seal the loyalty of employees and customers alike. And, if it is physically close to its market, there is the potential for such extra services as emergency delivery and personal tracking of customers' tastes.

These possibilities also suggest some relative weaknesses of the smaller family business, such as limited access to large amounts of capital, naivete of management, or inattention to cost-cutting measures. In the business strategic planning process, I encourage attention to the relative strengths and weaknesses of family ownership. Explicit recognition of these characteristics should improve the choice of strategy.

Reluctance of Family Business Owners to Plan

The planning process outlined in this paper often seems threatening to business owners. Many think of planning as a straitjacket that will constrain their instinctive survival skills and limit business flexibility. The nature of the planning process also requires these independently minded business owners to share decisions – and private financial statements – with others in the company. These statements represent power and information that many owners would rather keep to themselves.

Others object to planning because they think the future is too uncertain to make the effort worthwhile. Rapidly changing markets, an unpredictable economy, and the unclear career interests of offspring are just a few of the unsettled issues that they foresee.

Perhaps the greatest threat is the association of planning with change. This association seems to create nearly unresolvable dilemmas, because change requires compromises. For example, satisfying the demands of customers for a new product may require the business to divert money from successful projects that have a guaranteed return to experimental activities whose return is unknown. Executing the changes suggested by planning also often requires business owners to tailor their products to specific customers in specific markets. Such tailoring destroys the "Be All Things to All Customers" principle that guides so many businesses in their early years, a principle that is especially attractive to the business owner who sees a variety of customers and products as a way of diversifying risk from any one category of product or customer.

Executives in non-family businesses are often exposed to more businesses over time, and they may have more experience with sophisticated planning systems. More important, they are less likely to see the stability of the business as critical to the preservation of their own family wealth and well-being. In any case, my experience suggests that the mature business owner who owes his or her personal wealth and life-style to a strategy that he or she has built or designed is reluctant to change the successful formula.

Benefits of Planning

As we have seen, formal planning helps to prevent family businesses from "under-shooting" their strategic potential by articulating assumptions and perceptions. Planning encourages commitment from family members as a part of the process. It provides techniques that help managers to assess the company's rate of reinvestment and assure that the business is retaining sufficient cash for a solid future.

The very nature of planning requires a variety of people to be invoked. Those who report directly to the chief executive will contribute to the business plan. Members of the immediate, and often, the extended family will be involved in the family strategic plan. As a result, the planning process increases business knowledge throughout the company and the family and provides outstanding training for offspring, who are the successors and future leaders of the company.

Planning provides one other key benefit. Because it requires the participants to answer tough questions about competition and reinvestment, the planning process helps all managers and family members to develop a common understanding – that is, the same assumptions – about the world in which the company operates. Consequently, at the very least, business planning should encompass everyone who reports to the business owner and every family member with a key management role in the present or future.

Such a common undertaking is critical, because conflict in family businesses is often caused by differences in basic assumptions of values, especially among family members involved in guiding the business's direction. For example, consider the father and son who are arguing about whether to install up-to-date manufacturing equipment. The argument may be less about the value of technology than it is about the relative value of change and consistency. The young often argue for change; the old, for the status quo. Typically, they will not attempt a straightforward resolution of such underlying differences. Instead, they may begin to argue about personalities or management styles. Such discussions can easily cause emotional pain. The original objective – to decide whether or not to install new equipment – is forgotten.

The Special Role of Personal Values and Family Communications

Even within families, values are bound to vary. They shape the choice of goals, modify the ability to tolerate risk, and influence ideas about teaching and learning. They show up in family decisions that in turn mold business strategies and the approach to strategic planning. How much money does the family need for security? The answer to this question affects the level of investment in a business strategy. To what degree should family differences be openly discussed and tolerated? The answer to this question affects the ability to debate business facts and perceptions. How close should family relationships be? The answer to this question affects decisions on geographic expansion.

All these questions are critical examples of how family factors influence the choice of strategy in a family business. Answering these questions can lead to conflict. Understanding that there is no absolute right or wrong in many of these issues is one step toward compromise. Strategic planning is a valuable tool that helps to build such qualities as the ability to work toward consensus, team management, and shared decision-making. It identifies the fundamental business and family assumptions in a constructive way.

Strategic planning strengthens the ability to share decisions and value orientations. Both are critical requirements for success in perpetuating the family business. So, in addition to providing a framework for evaluation and choice of a business direction and family goals, strategic planning is a process that prompts healthy communication on critical family business issues.

Conclusion

To keep a family business moving forward requires a spirit of reinvestment; a confident eagerness to commit funds for the sake of future family benefits. Motivating the family requires a compelling vision – a commitment to a family dream – that everyone shares. When such a commitment has been made, the family can aggressively invest family funds in a business strategy.

There are many challenges to sustaining a family's emotional investment in an enterprise from generation to generation. Deliberate strategic planning is one key to success. It helps to create motivation that can sustain the family and business through inevitable differences in individual perspectives. Good planning releases energy that the family can use to fulfill the dream of many family businesses: creating and sustaining a healthy family enterprise for the next generation.

The insights gained from the three studies outlined at the start of this paper and from personal experience suggest how strategic planning in the family business differs from planning in nonfamily business. It is clear that business and family strategic planning promote continuity in family businesses.

References

Brandt, S. C. *Strategic Planning in Emerging Companies.* Reading, Mass.: Addison-Wesley, 1981.

Steiner, G. S. *Top Management Planning.* Ontario: Collier-Macmillan, Canada, 1969.

Ward, J. L. *Keeping the Family Business Healthy: How to Plan for Continuing Growth, Profitability, and Family Leadership.* San Francisco: Jossey-Bass, 1987.

Planned, accepted turnover of mid- and top-level managers is essential if a family business is to avoid stagnation, frustration and lack of opportunity for next-generation growth and development.

Employee Turnover Has Its Good Side

By Craig E. Aronoff and John L. Ward

Jim O., a 56-year-old business owner, learned that his 45-year-old administrative vice president would be leaving. He would become executive vice president at a similar firm owned by one of Jim's good friends in another state. Jim congratulated his employee on his advancement and called his friend to tell him that he had hired a good person.

Charlie L. faced a situation similar to Jim's, but when he found out, he lectured his departing operations manager about loyalty. He offered a 10 percent raise and promised the employee that if he would stay, a higher position would open up.

What Jim realizes – and what Charlie does not – is that turnover can be good for a family business.

Most family business owners are more like Charlie. Since starting their businesses, they have struggled and suffered with a shortage of good people. When key employees leave, family members personally have to pick up the slack, returning to duties they thought they had put behind them. There's a feeling of going backward.

As a business strengthens, it can better endure turnover. But why not avoid turnover altogether? What could be more valuable to a family business than its employees' commitment? Overpaying long-term people a little to reward their loyalty is a common practice in family businesses because it saves the agony and cost of replacing them. But there is a hidden danger.

As a business matures, its growth rate slows. Time, employee loyalty, and retention inevitably conspire to reduce opportunities to add new people.

When Charlie's business was young and growing, he built a team of like-minded folks seeking opportunities. As the business matured, the managers aged together. With the company's executives all about the same age, how much room is there for younger people, including Charlie's children, to be promoted? With mature executives reinforcing each other's views, how receptive might they be to ideas or changes?

Our experience is that this situation results in organizational stagnation. To see whether your business might suffer similar problems, make a drawing of your organization chart as a pyramid of ages.

Charlie's business might look like this:

Seven Top Managers
Average Age 56

Five Middle Managers
Average Age 42

Two Management
Trainees
Average Age 27

Because Charlie's business is overloaded with mature executives still several years from retirement, there can be no movement. In time, several concurrent retirements will leave the company with too few people eligible for promotion into key slots.

Charlie will wonder what happened to initiative, ideas, and energy. He'll be even more upset if his son is the next employee who gets frustrated and leaves. That is the price of too little turnover.

Now let's take a look at Jim's organizational age profile. It looks like this:

Three Top Managers
Average Age 56

Five Middle Managers
Average Age 42

Six Trainees and
Lower Managers
Average Age 27

While Jim's company is run by mature top management, several younger people are being tested for potential. As senior executives retire, several candidates are available from within. New ideas are in good supply, and the vast majority of the managers don't have a vested interest in the status quo.

There's another advantage. Jim has two children among the six in the lowest age bracket. They have a peer group to work with and to be compared with. They have older, intervening managers with whom they can sharpen their skills. They can experience orderly development and follow a career path to the top of the organization.

How can your company be more like Jim's? The answer is turnover – planned, accepted turnover.

Start with the 42-year-old middle managers. Assess them not on their past contributions but on their clear potential for top management. If that potential is lacking, now is the time for them to find other jobs. As the years pass, finding a new position becomes more difficult. They are likely to stagnate – and your business will too.

A company can't expect to keep all of its younger managers. Consequently, more are needed than there are positions above them to fill.

Obviously, you will seek only very good people. Some will leave for better opportunities. Therefore, there should be turnover of good people.

Our ideal is a nice, evolutionary progression. Several good younger people, including your children, are hired, and the best ones move up as middle managers are promoted to executive positions that become vacant through retirement. A good organization is prepared for the future, and the family successor has a good team in place when he or she takes over.

Developing executive talent requires vision, energy, and courage. The organizational pyramid has to be imagined many years ahead. Recruiting, performance reviews, and coaching have to be taken seriously. Since loyalty and stability are highly valued in family businesses, it takes courage to implement programs that shake up people (as turnover inevitably does), even in the best future interests of the company and its employees.

Turnover of good people can be a good thing. Obviously, you want to keep the very best for yourself. But you can't recognize the best unless you have several candidates to compare, candidates who have had ample opportunity to grow in your organization.

Should stock be used as part of key nonfamily managers' compensation in family businesses? This article explores the pros, cons and alternatives.

Equity Compensation for Key Employees

By David K. Carlson and Ross W. Nager

If you seek to hire and retain top quality nonfamily managers, you'll eventually face the question of using stock as part of your key managers' compensation. Answering that question involves economic, tax and personal considerations when evaluating alternatives.

The Pros

Competition for talented, dedicated and creative managers remains intense. Family businesses must compete with public company compensation packages, which frequently include some form of equity participation. In fact, recent publicity over stratospheric salaries in the face of declining profits is leading public companies to rely more on equity.

The logic is simple. If the business performs well, the manager profits from stock value appreciation. Of course, the reverse is also true. Equity ownership tends to give the employee a longer-term perspective, while cash bonuses tend to focus on annual profit performance. Since family businesses usually focus more on long-term growth, aligning the manager's fortunes with stockholder objectives seems to make perfect sense.

For the cash-hungry family business, there is an added benefit. Handing out stock certificates does not require cash, so equity can seem to be a "cheaper" way to compensate key people.

The Cons

Despite the incentives to award equity, in our experience, family businesses rarely do so. The primary reason is devotion to the personal desire to restrict ownership to family members. But there are other reasons.

When a public company manager quits or is terminated, he or she can keep the stock or sell it on the exchange. Either way, the company makes no cash outlay. Most private companies don't want ex-employees as stockholders. Buying back the stock requires the business to shell out nondeductible cash. A buy/sell agreement must be in place before stock is distributed to require the ex-employee to sell at previously agreed on terms. Valuation formulas put forth in the buy/sell agreement can alleviate potentially severe disputes if the formula is perceived to be fair by both sides.

Public companies typically grant stock or options that employees can sell after five to ten years. To delay cash strains, family companies typically restrict stock redemptions until employment termination or death. Ownership of noncontrolling, nonmarketable stock provides tarnished golden handcuffs at best.

Finally, stock ownership increases employee scrutiny of family actions. The employee-owner has a vested interest in family employment and compensation issues, strategic direction, and other issues. While this interest can be beneficial, it also can produce complexity and conflict.

The Phantom Alternative

Family businesses often use phantom stock to provide the benefits of equity without the drawbacks. Phantom stock is a kind of longer-term cash bonus plan tied to stock performance.

Under a written phantom stock plan, selected employees are awarded participation units. Each unit is analogous to a share of stock, but it is not actual stock. A modest number of units is awarded annually based on employee performance.

Unit value typically is established by a formula which approximates stock value. If the business prospers, the unit increases in value. Units are usually awarded at no cost and the employee's bonus is based on increases in formula values after the unit is granted.

If golden handcuffs are desired, the plan can vest only after a certain period of time. The corporate desire to delay payment, however, should be balanced with the morale-boosting benefit of providing at least some cash prior to the employee's retirement or death.

Actual payment under a phantom plan requires cash. However, the unit buy-back payment is deductible as a compensation expense. Dividends paid to actual shareholders also are often paid to phantom owners. Phantom dividends are also treated as deductible compensation.

While phantom stock owners have neither voting nor other ownership rights, they can become concerned over family actions to the extent they affect the valuation formula.

Should you provide stock to a key executive? Would phantom stock be a better approach? Providing a longer-term incentive than salary and annual bonuses makes business sense, particularly in family businesses with longer-term perspectives.

Consider the pros and cons of each approach from all perspectives – family, business and employee. Rarely is any compensation technique perfect. However, by addressing and prioritizing your objectives and using a process of elimination you'll be more likely to select the most acceptable approach. Use your advisors to fine tune the plan. Then, make sure your key people fully understand the objectives and rules.

CHAPTER 4
OWNERSHIP ISSUES

Wearing the owner's hat requires family business principals to consider matters ranging from capital structure to dividend policies to stewardship. This chapter explores several important issues faced by nearly all family businesses, including appropriate levels of owners-return on investment and responsibilities to minority shareholders.

Other articles look at financial options available to owners of family businesses – such as employee ownership or going public. Ideally, however, family business owners want to maintain ownership in the family. This goal requires transfer of the business from one generation to the next in a manner most positive and least injurious to the family and the business through estate planning that is both sensitive and smart.

Family businesses gain a competitive advantage by enjoying lower capital costs produced by the "family effect" of a satisfied, trusting, closely knit shareholder group. Because such owners are often less demanding of current financial return, family firms can adopt longer-term strategies or exploit niches inappropriate for other firms. Family conflict can reverse this advantage. This article discusses an equation developed to explain and predict the effect of family harmony on the business's cost of capital.

[RF + b(MR-RF)] • (1 + IP) • (1-FE)

Craig E. Aronoff, Francois de Visscher, and John L. Ward

Finance experts observing family businesses often note that such enterprises can benefit from relatively low capital costs. Lower capital costs can allow family firms to adopt longer term business strategies or exploit niches insufficiently profitable for larger businesses with higher short-term required returns on capital.

When conflicts develop within families, however, or when circumstances force family businesses rapidly to become liquid, capital costs can escalate dramatically. Indeed, a capital situation that had been a competitive advantage can quickly become a fatal liability to a family firm.

While those of us who work with family businesses have long had a "gut" understanding of these financial realities, François M. de Visscher, president of de Visscher & Co., recently encapsulated these crucial relationships in the formula above. Greenwich, Connecticut-based de Visscher & Co. is a financial advisor to family businesses specializing in designing liquidity options for family shareholders or capital options for their businesses, thereby facilitating financial transitions. He calls his concept the "Family Shareholder Return Formula," and developed it in collaboration with Maurits Bruel of Groningen University, the Netherlands. François postulates that the family shareholder's expected annualized rate of return is predicted by the firm's provision of liquidity to its shareholders and the degree to which family members' non-financial values are met by the family business (the "Family Effect"). Let's explore François' equation:

The first part of the equation applies to any business. "RF" stands for risk free rate of return – what one would earn on U.S. Treasury securities, for example. Since any business investment necessarily contains risk, investors normally expect a higher rate of return, "MR," a market rate of return. The return premium is further influenced by the volatility of a particular investment relative to the market as a whole – the risk of an investment being priced poorly in relation to the market when an investor would like to sell. This concept is well known in the investing world as "Beta," represented by the "b" above. The first part of the equation, [RF + b(MR-RF)] simply says that a business's required rate of return will be the risk-free rate of return plus the difference between the market return and the risk free rate of return modified by the volatility of the investment relative to the market.

de Visscher explains that, for example, when the 10-year treasury yields around 7% (RF = 7%), and market return premium is around twice that rate (MR = 14%), and if a family firm is 20% more volatile than the market as a whole (say Beta = 1.2), the expected rate of return should be [.07 + 1.2(.14-.07)] = .154 or 15.4%.

This rate of return, however, must be adjusted by two critical variables: liquidity and the "family effect." The first variable, which is the second part of the equation, deals with the "illiquidity premium (IP)." Most family business investments, in the absence of a ready market for the stock, are simply illiquid. Investors find it difficult or costly to turn their investment into money and hence typically demand a premium – the less liquid, the more the premium. François explains that illiquidity can cause the expected rate of return to as much as double. Hence IP can vary from 0 to 1. A liquid investment would have no impact on the expected rate of return: If IP = 0 then (1 + 0) = 1 and [.07 + 1.2(.14-.07)] • 1 = 15.4%.

The most familiar impact of the "illiquidity premium" is seen in the common "discount for lack of marketability." A dramatic impact of this reality is the so-called "fire sale" that occurs in response to large, unexpected needs for liquidity (as in estate settlements). Because higher rates of return are demanded for relatively illiquid investments, the price of the investment is severely diminished. When IP approaches 1, the value of the investment can be reduced by nearly half: If IP = .9, then (1 + .9) = 1.9 and [.07 + 1.2(.14-.07)] o1.9 = 29.26%. An investment yielding 15% and priced at $100, would drop in value to $50 to cause the same dollar amount to yield 30%.

This suggests that family businesses need to address the matter of liquidity. Eventually, family business owners must answer the question "what is this piece of paper (stock certificate) worth?" The answer often comes in the form of some kind of dividend as well as the ability to sell stock. Indeed, we find the illiquidity premium's proof in what family members say when programs are implemented to provide a formula for pricing and a method for redeeming stock. "Now that I know I can sell it, I no longer feel the need to," is often the response. In other words, liquidity takes the pressure off.

The final part of the equation is most fascinating to students of the dynamics of family businesses. de Visscher's equation suggests that the "family effect (FE)" can reduce shareholders' expected rate of return to zero or, on the other hand, entirely remove a family business' capital cost competitive advantage.

In terms of the equation, a family whose members were all perfectly satisfied with the family business would make no demands of it for short-term returns. In this case FE = 1, and therefore (1-1) = 0. Even under conditions of high illiquidity, the equation suggests the elimination of capital costs: [.07 + 1.2(.14-.07)] · 1.9 · 0 = 0.

As time and generations pass, the likelihood is continuously reduced that family members' increasing disparate needs will be fully met. They become less likely to restrain their financial demands. As the "family effect" dissipates over the generations, the expected return to capital goes up. This strongly suggests, however, that actions successfully undertaken to keep the family closely connected and strongly committed to clear goals and values will directly impact costs of capital. Good family relations really is like money in the bank.

We thank François for so succinctly expressing the relationships between a family business's capital costs, its provision of liquidity to its shareholders and perhaps most critically, its responsiveness to its owning family's values and needs. We encourage family businesses to use the formula to estimate their own expected rates of return and to take actions that would tend to sustain or lower capital costs.

When the employment of a shareholder in a family business is terminated or when dividends are not paid to inactive members, disputes often arise that can lead to litigation. In the past, minority shareholders have not had much leverage in these situations. However, developments of the past decade have substantially enhanced the position of minority shareholders. recognizing this, professionals in the family business area may be able to mediate disputes before the polarization that leads to litigation occurs.

A Legal Perspective on Shareholder Relationships in Family Businesses: The Scope of Fiduciary Duties

By Moni Murdock and Charles M. Murdock

Happy families are all alike; every unhappy family is unhappy in its own way.
– Leo Tolstoy

Thus does James O'Toole open his acclaimed book, *Vanguard Management* (O'Toole, 1985, p. 14). He then questions whether this view holds true when analogized to business and basically concludes that it does not. On the family side, its wisdom is equally open to question. It is almost as if the converse were true: There are many ways in which families can be happy, while unhappy families have many elements in common. These include problems of respect, communication, abuse of power, tensions over fairness, and inability to resolve conflict.

What is clear is that, if the family deteriorates, the business often will be weakened or destroyed. However, families in a family business often manifest the ability to make significant changes. The interplay of the family and the business, while it is often the source of conflict (Davis, 1990), can also be a catalyst for growth. This is why many family therapists are successfully bringing their systems expertise to bear in the family business arena.

This opportunity for stability and growth represents the carrot in the well-worn metaphor, but the family business system also contains a stick: If problems are not resolved, litigation can arise. The Shoen family of U-Haul fame (or infamy) recently made the front page of the *Wall Street Journal* when family disintegration led to litigation and, at last report, $5 million in legal fees ("U-Haul's Patriarch," 1990). While not all litigation is as disruptive or expensive, it is impossible to litigate in a friendly or inexpensive way As Voltaire once said, he had been ruined only twice in his life: once when he lost a lawsuit and once when he won (Levinson, 1971).

This article reviews litigation of the past decade that has involved shareholders of closely held and family businesses to identify the situations that lead to litigation in a family business and to discuss the legal principles involved. We will also suggest what family business consultants can do to help to prevent these problems. With this background, professionals will be aware of the legal consequences when relationships do not work out. We hope that such awareness will assist them in motivating their clients to a strategy of growth rather than destruction. In a consulting context, it is often helpful to ask clients what they see as the logical consequences of their present tack. If it is moving toward litigation, they had better steer a different course.

How Do Problems Arise?

Problems in a family business generally arise out of the interaction between the family system on the one hand and the corporate structure on the other. A family business is a system that by definition has more than one player. The players can be intergenerational-the founder and one or more offspring-or intragenerational-two or more siblings. This article assumes that the players are shareholders. With respect to the nature of the shareholdings, legal problems generally develop in one of two contexts: There are two players, the shares are equally divided, and deadlock develops. Or either there are two players in a majority-minority model, and the minority holder believes that he or she is not being treated fairly, or there are three or more players, and someone in the minority becomes the odd person out. This second scenario typically involves either an active person who is fired or an inactive person who receives no return. The first scenario can have majority-minority overtones when one 50 percent shareholder is in control and uses the deadlock situation to perpetuate control to the disadvantage of the other 50 percent shareholder. This can occur when one of two active shareholders dies, and the survivor uses the deadlock to prevent the spouse of the deceased shareholder from obtaining any benefits while continuing to draw a salary and run the company.

Most disputes involving principals in closely held businesses pertain to power or money. Corporations involve a tripartite allocation of power: the shareholder level, the board of director level, and the officership or key employee level. Money and power effectively reside at the officership level. Shareholder power and director power are basically a means to an end: to be elected as an officer and thereby draw a salary and participate in day-to-day management. The primary function of shareholders is annually to elect directors. Occasionally they are involved in approving a fundamental change, such as amending the articles of incorporation or approving a merger or sale of substantially all the assets of the corporation. The board of directors in turn elects the officers and sets their salaries, makes major policy decisions, and declares dividends. But closely held corporations generally seek to distribute earnings in a tax-deductible form, such as through salaries or bonuses, and rarely declare dividends (C. Murdock, 1990). While the board makes policy decisions, the officers make the day-to-day decisions that are key to the effective functioning of the business.

Thus, while shareholder power is key to electing directors, and control of the board of directors is key to electing officers and establishing compensation, the real game is played at the officer level, because it is at this level that meaningful compensation is paid and that meaningful decisions are made. Accordingly, the goal for most participants in family-owned businesses is to be employed-to draw a respectable salary and to participate in the day-to-day operations of the business. Shareholder status as such-particularly if one is in a minority position-avails little if no dividends are declared. An asset that has no current return contributes little to the living of the good life.

Membership on the board of directors can be, but seldom is, an end in itself. This is because the board of directors rarely functions as a board, notwithstanding the statutory mandate to the contrary. Annual meetings are often not held, or if they are, they are a mere formality. Too often, the minutes of annual meetings prepared by the corporation's lawyer are headed "consent in lieu of meeting" and bear a remarkable resemblance from year to year. What this means is that no meeting was held and that the lawyer submits a piece of paper for signature each year or sometimes after the passage of several years.

However, if the board fulfills its statutory mandate and meets quarterly or bimonthly to review operations, deal with policy, and hold officers accountable, this is a responsible and significant activity that can warrant substantial compensation. Thus, directorships as well as officer ships can provide a mechanism to achieve a return on investment. Moreover, directorships provide a mechanism to obtain information, a critical need for shareholders in family and other closely held businesses. Finally, it is more difficult to take advantage of someone sitting in the same room with you – in fact, sitting across the table. Evil is most easily done anonymously or at least at a distance.

Obviously, the triggers that can generate animosity and eventually litigation are actions – or, in the case of dividends, nonactions – that deprive a person of power and/or money. At the shareholder level, if cumulative voting, which permits representation on the board of directors proportional to stock holdings (Model Business Corporation Act, 1985), does not exist, a shareholder controlling a majority of the shares could elect all the directors and thus foreclose minority participation on the board. In some jurisdictions, from a statutory standpoint, such a shareholder could also remove any unwanted director, even if no cause for removal existed. But the actions that generally trigger problems are those taken at the board of director level. It is the board that declares dividends, authorizes officers' salaries, and hires or fires key employees. Inactive shareholders may resent the failure of the board to declare dividends while at the same time it awards handsome salaries or bonuses to shareholders who are employed. Or a shareholder who was employed is either fired or excluded from a bonus, or his or her compensation and duties are markedly circumscribed.

When disputes arise between those who are in control and those who lack control, who comes out the winner is often a function of whether the duty of care or the duty of loyalty is implicated. Those in control argue that their actions are in the best interests of the corporation, that the business judgment rule protects their actions, and that no duty of care – with respect to which the plaintiff has the burden of proof-has been breached. Those on the outside are watching a different film. They allege that the majority acts in the best interests of the majority, that those in control have fiduciary duties of loyalty to the corporation and of fairness to the minority, and that the burden of proof is on the majority to justify their self-dealing actions. The distinction between the duty of care and the duty of loyalty is discussed in the next section. The discussion that follows also traces the evolution of minority shareholders' complaints from a focus on the director's duty of care, to a focus on the breach of the duty of loyalty to the corporation, to a focus on the breach of the duty of fairness that the majority owes to the minority.

The Duty of Care and the Business Judgment Rule

Under the common law, fiduciaries, including corporate directors, owed two major duties with respect to property under their control: to manage it carefully and not to use it for their personal benefit. These duties are generally referred to as the duty of care and the duty of loyalty. They developed in the context of trust law before being imported into the law of corporations. Importing the duty of care into the world of corporations resulted in some uneasiness among the judiciary. While directors are under a duty to exercise care in managing the business, and their acts are subject to challenge in the courts, the judiciary has long recognized that judges are ill-equipped to run a business. Accordingly, the courts have developed the business judgment rule pursuant to which courts defer to the judgment of directors. Thus, a challenge to director action predicated on a purported breach of the duty of care is rarely successful.

Courts defer to the judgment of the board of directors because "the authority and responsibilities vested in corporate directors, both by statute and decisional law, proceed on the assumption that inescapably there can be no available objective standard by which the correctness of every corporate decision may be measured, by the courts or otherwise. Even if that were not the case, by definition the responsibility for business judgments must rest with the corporate directors; their individual capabilities and experience peculiarly qualify them for the discharge of that responsibility. Thus, absent evidence of bad faith or fraud...the courts must and properly should respect their determination" (*Auerbach v. Bennett*, 1979, 1000).

Generally, the business judgment rule is asserted as a defense to a claim by minority shareholders that the directors have breached their duty of care. Many activities of which a disenchanted shareholder might complain are within the sphere of activity with which the board of directors normally deals and with respect to which the business judgment rule normally is applicable: liquidity and personnel. For example, the declaration of dividends affects liquidity, and firing an employee or determining not to give an employee a raise or bonus has an impact both on liquidity and on personnel issues.

A minority shareholder seeking to challenge such actions as these has little likelihood of success if the challenge is predicated on a breach of the duty of care by the directors in control. Not only does the shareholder have the traditional burden of proof normally borne by plaintiffs and the task of overcoming the presumptions established by the business judgment rule, but such a plaintiff also has the nearly impossible task of proving injury to the corporation. The duty of care is owed to the corporation, and recovery for such breach is premised on injury or loss to the corporation. How can the corporation be hurt by not declaring a dividend or not paying a bonus – actions that enhance rather than adversely affect the cash position of the corporation? While firing a truly key employee might hurt the business of the corporation, it is rare that an employee is so valuable that he or she cannot be replaced.

The Duty of Loyalty and Self-Dealing

A more fertile approach for a disgruntled shareholder is to examine the situation to determine whether the facts disclose a breach of the duty of loyalty to the corporation. Classic examples of duty of loyalty issues are transactions involving self-dealing or conflicts of interest by a director or officer in which one person is on both sides of a transaction; transactions involving the personal appropriation or usurpation by a director or officer of an opportunity that properly belongs to the corporation; and transactions in which a director or officer competes with the corporation.

It is rare that a family-owned or closely held business will not be replete with conflicts of interest. Most obvious is the decision to compensate the company's officers. Since the officers, or at least the president or CEO, are usually directors, there is a clear conflict between their role as directors in authorizing compensation, where their responsibility is to get the best talent at the most reasonable cost to the corporation, and their role as recipients of compensation, where their desire is to get the best compensation with the fewest strings attached.

Unfortunately, some courts have tended to take a duty of care type analysis when compensation to an officer-director has been challenged under a duty of loyalty or conflict of interest theory. This is because courts realize that a main consideration in organizing a business is to provide employment for the shareholder-investor. However, these courts fail to realize that there are two parts to the employment decision: whom to hire and at what price. Accepting the legitimacy of a director's determining to hire himself or herself-a conflict of interest because a more qualified employee might be available-does not resolve the issue of the price at which he or she should be hired.

The statutory mandate with respect to a director's establishing compensation for himself or herself is that he or she is entitled to reasonable compensation. However, one person's reasonableness is another person's unreasonableness. In other words, reasonableness is a range, not a point. Two constituencies have a direct stake in the reasonableness of compensation: the shareholders and the tax collector. The stake of the shareholders is predicated on the fact that the earnings distributed as compensation to officers reduce the earnings that can be distributed to shareholders as dividends. The stake of the tax collector stems from the fact that compensation is deductible from business income in determining the corporation's taxable income; thus, the higher the compensation, the lower the taxes collected.

However, reasonableness in the corporate context is distinct from reasonableness in the tax context, and different policy considerations are applicable. In shareholder litigation, an accountant will often testify that the corporation has been audited and that the I.R.S. approved the reasonableness of the officers' compensation. Thus, the accountant will conclude, there is no basis for a shareholder to challenge the officers' salary as unreasonable. This is a non sequitur. The fact that an I.R.S. agent does not challenge a salary does not mean that the salary is reasonable. An audit has aspects of horse trading. On a cost-benefit analysis, there may be other issues within the corporation that an agent sees as having more potential for generating additional tax dollars. In addition, from a cost-benefit perspective, the agent must weigh the time spent in auditing this corporation with the potential tax revenues to be generated from the next corporation on the audit list. The agent may simply not want to do the detailed analysis necessary to establish that compensation is unreasonable when he or she has easier targets to challenge.

Over the past decade, courts have become much more insightful in recognizing that compensation to shareholder officers is really bifurcated: Part of it is compensation for services, and part of it is really a return on investment or, in other words, a distribution of earnings. This recognition has been articulated by courts that have grappled with attempts by minority shareholders to have the corporation dissolved or to be bought out because those in control have acted oppressively and thwarted the reasonable expectations of the minority shareholders. In the related area of valuation, both courts and commentators have recognized that compensation to shareholder officers can be "nonfunctional" and added such compensation back into earnings when valuing a business on a multiple of earnings (C. Murdock, 1990).

Compensation matters are not the only transactions that often pose conflicts of interest in closely held corporations. It is not unusual for directors to own the property on which the corporation conducts its business and to lease such property to the corporation. If the lease payments are excessive, directors are benefiting themselves at the expense of the corporation. In contrast to the duty of care situation, the defendant director here has the burden of proving that the transaction was fair to the corporation. The fact that the defendant has the burden of proof substantially increases the likelihood that he or she could be liable to the corporation. If the defendant could have had the transaction approved by disinterested directors, this would have the effect in some jurisdictions of returning the burden of proof to the plaintiff. However, if other family members comprise the board of directors, it is unlikely that they would be considered disinterested.

Another situation that often gives rise to conflict of interest occurs when a director sells stock to or buys stock from the corporation. If the sale price is too high or the issuance price is too low, the corporation is injured.

While the likelihood of success for a disgruntled shareholder increases substantially in a duty of loyalty situation, it is still a limited remedy from the standpoint of a minority shareholder, since the real plaintiff in either a duty of care or a duty of loyalty case is the corporation itself. Although such litigation is usually initiated by a minority shareholder, he or she brings the lawsuit on behalf of the corporation. It is the corporation to whom the duty of care and the duty of loyalty are owed, and it is the corporation that is injured. Thus, even if the suit is successful, there is no direct benefit to the minority shareholder. Neither the duty of care nor the duty of loyalty, as traditionally developed, can protect the minority shareholder from being fired or assure the minority shareholder of a return through the declaration of dividends.

This does not mean that duty of loyalty litigation cannot be useful for a disgruntled minority shareholder. Since it is a weapon that halts directors from benefiting themselves to the detriment of the corporation, the threat of such litigation has not only a disciplinary effect on directors and those in control, but it also gives the minority shareholder some leverage that might lead to a negotiated buy out at a reasonable price or to some other acceptable accommodation.

Nevertheless, further developments in the law were necessary if there were to be remedies for actions that directly affected a minority shareholder but did not necessarily injure the corporation.

Fiduciary Duties for Controlling Shareholders

While a few early decisions had alluded to the existence of a fiduciary duty of fairness owed by majority or controlling shareholders to minority shareholders, it was not until the mid 1970s that two landmark Massachusetts decisions, *Donahue v. Rodd Electrotype Co. of New England, Inc.* (1975) and *Wilkes and Wilkes v. Springside Nursing Home, Inc.* (1976), fully developed this concept in the context of a closely held corporation. These two cases have often been cited in decisions from other jurisdictions.

In *Donahue*, the widow of one of the founders held 50 shares, and the Rodd family held 200 shares. As part of a plan in which the senior Rodd passed control of the corporation to his children, the corporation redeemed 45 of his shares for $800 per share but denied the widow's request to have her shares redeemed also. While selective repurchases of corporate stock have generally been upheld, the Donahue court analogized shareholders in a closely held corporation to partners and held that they owed fiduciary duties to each other. In an insightful opinion, the court recognized that the majority had disadvantaged the minority by means of the selective (read *discriminatory*) redemption from two perspectives: First, the majority had created a market for the majority's stock but denied the same market (namely, the corporation) to the minority. Second, the majority had engaged in a preferential distribution of corporate assets to itself to the exclusion of the minority. The court adopted an equal opportunity rule and required the corporation either to purchase the widow's shares or to rescind the Rodd purchases.

In *Wilkes*, plaintiff was one of four shareholders, each of whom had designated responsibilities in connection with the corporation for which they were compensated. Plaintiff had a falling out with one of the other investors, and his salary was terminated. At their next meeting, the shareholders did not elect him to be either an officer or a director. The court found that the majority shareholders had breached their fiduciary duty to plaintiff by frustrating the purpose for which he had helped to organize the corporation, namely, to obtain a return on his investment. The court stated that "the denial of employment to the minority at the hands of the majority is especially pernicious in some instances. A guaranty of employment with the corporation may have been one of the 'basic reason[s] why a minority shareholder has invested capital in the firm.' The minority shareholder typically depends on his salary as the principal return on is investment since the 'earnings of a close corporation...are distributed in major part in salaries, bonuses, and retirement benefits.'...[B]arring him from corporate office...[also] severely restricts his participation in the management of the enterprise" (*Wilkes and Wilkes*, 1976, at 663).

The court tempered its holding somewhat by recognizing that, when a minority shareholder alleges a breach of fiduciary duty by the majority, the majority is entitled to demonstrate that it had a legitimate business purpose for its actions. But even if a legitimate business purpose can be demonstrated, the minority shareholder must have the opportunity to demonstrate that the majority's business purpose could have been achieved by an alternative action less harmful to the minority. However in *Wilkes*, the majority could not establish any business purpose in firing plaintiff. Accordingly, he was entitled to his lost income after he was fired.

While these two cases have been characterized as "pioneer[ing] in developing an effective cause of action for minority shareholders who have been denied their fair share of benefits in close corporations" (*Sugarman v. Sugarman*, 1986, 7), subsequent cases have pointed out three limitations to the *Donohue* and *Wilkes* approach. The first is that it is applicable only to a closely held corporation. There are many family businesses in which gifts or bequests to children and grandchildren have created a substantial number of shareholders. If the jurisdiction in question has a statute defining close corporations as those with fewer than n shareholders, this could be a problem. The second qualification is that the relation between the parties must be analogous to a partnership relation. Thus, one court – erroneously, we believe – has held that a 5 percent shareholder was more like an employee than a partner and that his termination was not wrongful (*Harris v. Mardan Business Systems, Inc.*, 1988). The third limitation is that there is no wrongful conduct if there is a business purpose for defendants' actions and if plaintiff cannot show a less harmful alternative to respond to the business purpose supporting defendants' actions.

The decision in *Harris* may be supportable under this third limitation. Plaintiff had been induced to leave his position with 3M to oversee the U.S. operations of defendant. When sales and morale deteriorated, plaintiff was terminated. However he was offered alternative employment at the same salary as a regional sales manager, which he declined. In effect, defendant had a business purpose in removing plaintiff from his original position. Under the *Wilkes* less-harmful alternative test, plaintiff could claim that there was a lesser position that he was capable of filling. But defendant preempted this possibility by offering plaintiff a position as regional sales manager. When plaintiff declined, he was left without a remedy.

While the position of minority shareholders has been improved by judicial recognition that those in control of a corporation owe fiduciary obligations to minority shareholders not to injure the minority through misuse of that power, the minority shareholder is still exposed to the possibility of further wrongful conduct in the future. For example, the issue left unresolved in *Wilkes* was his status in the future. If he was not rehired, he would be faced with the prospect of new litigation to recover additional lost salary. If he was rehired, he could expect unpleasant assignments and possibly an attempt to justify a lower salary because of alleged incompetence. In other words, this business marriage will probably be contentious and litigious in the future. Better that the parties should split! Is there an appropriate remedy in such a case? If so, the minority shareholder can retrieve his or her investment in the corporation and go on to more pleasant business opportunities.

Dissolution: An Exit Strategy

Almost all states have statutes that permit a court to dissolve a corporation when the actions of those in control are illegal, oppressive, or fraudulent (Model Business Corporation Act, 1985). When a corporation is dissolved, its assets are sold, its creditors are paid off, and the equity is distributed to its shareholders. Thus, a formerly locked-in shareholder can retrieve his or her investment or at least his or her pro rata share of the net assets-if the shareholder can prevail upon a court to dissolve the corporation.

For this to be a worthwhile remedy, the minority shareholder must confront three obstacles: He or she must convince the court that the conduct of the majority is "oppressive," he or she must overcome the judicial concern that dissolution is a "drastic" remedy, and he or she must realize value upon dissolution equivalent to the value of the live corporation as a going concern.

The last two concerns are interrelated. Courts have looked on dissolution as corporate death. Thus, it is a "drastic" remedy. If the corporation were to be "killed," society would be the lesser. A provider of products or services and a source of employment would be lost. What would be distributed to the shareholders would be the "dead" asset value of the corporation, not the going concern or "live" asset value. For example, if a real estate brokerage corporation were to be dissolved, some courts would foresee that all that shareholders would realize is the liquidation or under-the-hammer value of the desks, file cabinets, and desktop computers. The going concern value would be lost.

In reality, if the business is viable, the assets will not be sold in a piecemeal liquidation but rather as an entity with going concern value. The real assets of this hypothetical business are its lease (location), its employees, and its file cabinets-not the metal of which they are made but the paper (customer files) within their drawers (C. Murdock, 1990). The buyer will be one or more of the existing shareholders, a competitor, or possibly an unrelated third party.

However, the problems just set forth are never faced unless the minority shareholder can demonstrate that the actions of those in control are oppressive. Courts in different states and even decisions in the same state over time have differed in their conclusions about what constitutes oppressive conduct. Thus, an Illinois court has found oppression and granted dissolution where defendant managed the corporation to the exclusion of the other shareholder and withdrew excessive salaries (*Compton v. Paul K. Harding Realty Co.*, 1972), while a Missouri court denied relief to a widow of one of two brothers who controlled a corporation, even though, in the ten years after her husband's death, the surviving brother and his son had received salaries and bonuses while assets were being sold to generate cash and the book value of the company dropped 10 percent (*Fix v. FLY Material Co., Inc.*, 1976). The corporate impotence of the widow and the failure to provide her with any return on her investment did not quite drop, according to the court, to a level of oppression.

The Development of Alternative Remedies and the Recognition of "Reasonable Expectations"

In the 1970s, both courts and legislatures began dealing with the concern that dissolution was a "drastic" remedy by providing alternatives to liquidation when oppressive conduct had been demonstrated. Among the remedies provided were the power to declare dividends or rescind bonuses or appoint a provisional director or custodian. However, the most welcome alternative remedy was the authority for a court to order the corporation or controlling shareholders to buy out the complaining minority shareholder. While this may at first glance appear to be an onerous burden for the corporation or the majority, from a practical standpoint such a remedy does not differ significantly from the situation in which dissolution is granted, and the majority buys the assets at a judicial sale for their going concern value (C. Murdock, 1990).

The development of less "drastic" alternatives to dissolution appears to have broadened the scope of conduct that today can be found oppressive. Syllogistically, this would seem reasonable: If the remedy is drastic, then the conduct necessary to justify the remedy must also be drastic. However, if the remedy is less drastic, then the conduct necessary to justify such a less drastic remedy should in turn be less drastic. In any case, there is no question that courts have been more liberal in the 1980s in giving relief to minority shareholders who charge that those in control have treated the minority unfairly.

In 1979, the New York legislature enacted a bill providing for a buy-out of a minority shareholder as an alternative to dissolution when the shareholder alleges oppressive conduct by the majority (*N.Y. Business Corp. Law*, 1986). Shortly thereafter, the first significant suit applying this legislation was brought (*In re Topper*, 1980). Plaintiff had left stable employment of twenty-five years to become a one-third shareholder in two pharmacies. In addition to uprooting himself and his family, he invested his life savings and executed personal guarantees for loans to the corporation. He initially received a $30,000 salary, which was increased to $75,000. But within a year from the time when the business was organized, he was fired. The court, in holding for the plaintiff, stated that "unlike their counterparts in large corporations, minority shareholders in small corporations often expect to participate in management and operations. Furthermore, there generally is an expectation on the part of some participants that their interest is to be recognized in the form of a salary derived from employment with the corporation. These reasonable expectations constitute the bargain of the parties in light of which subsequent conduct must be appraised" (*In re Topper*, 1980, at 365).

This construction of reasonable expectations as the standard by which to measure whether the conduct of those in control has been oppressive, thereby justifying a judicially ordered buy-out or other alternative relief to dissolution, has become the touchstone for subsequent decisions, both in New York and in other jurisdictions.

Three years later, the highest court in New York, the Court of Appeals, considered a similar fact situation and gave its blessing to the reasonable expectations test (*In re Kemp & Beatley, Inc.*, 1984). There were eight shareholders, two of whom were no longer employed. In the past, de facto dividends based on stock ownership had been paid in the form of extra compensation bonuses. After the employment of the two shareholders was terminated, the extra compensation was still paid, but it was not based on stock ownership. The court affirmed the reasonable expectations test in defining oppression and concluded that "*Kemp & Beatley* had a-longstanding policy of awarding de facto dividends based on stock ownership in the form of extra compensation bonuses...[There was uncontroverted proof that this policy was changed either shortly before or shortly after petitioners' employment ended. Extra compensation was still awarded by the company. The only difference was that stock ownership was no longer a basis for the payments" (*In re Kemp*, 1984, at 1180).

The following year, the reasonable expectations test was applied in a different context: A nonactive shareholder complained that the refusal of those in control to declare dividends frustrated her reasonable expectations (*In the Matter of Maybelle Mintz*, 1985). Plaintiff had acquired 30 percent of the stock of the corporation from her husband, who had been employed by the corporation until 1968, when he suffered a series of strokes. Both plaintiff and her husband were over seventy. The corporation had paid dividends totaling $1.5 million in 1970 and 1971 but thereafter declared none. It did purchase shares from another shareholder in 1977 for $1.4 million. The rationale of the corporation for not paying dividends was that it was developing a twenty-acre apartment complex and paying off a mortgage on a Brooklyn shopping center.

Under a duty of care type analysis, these reasons probably would have protected the directors from any liability, because such a decision was within their business judgment. With respect to plaintiff's claim of oppression, the trial court dismissed her petition without a hearing. However, the appellate court reversed the trial court and recognized that those in control may be attempting to force her to sell her shares below their fair value, or they may have received dividends in the form of compensation from which she was excluded. The court concluded:

> A review of the allegation in the record before us reveals a substantial number of factual issues regarding whether the actions of the corporate directors have served to defeat the reasonable expectations of petitioner as to her investment. When the initial investment in the corporation was made by petitioner's husband it appears that, in addition to regular dividends, his family benefited from compensation received for his efforts in the management of the business. Now it is alleged that while certain Of the other original investors continue to receive substantial benefits from the corporation through salaries and the like, petitioner-although the largest single corporation stockholder-and her family, have received no return on the investment for over twelve years. The record also reveals a number of other allegations regarding the corporate operation which call into question the good faith and judgment of the directors in freezing all of the cash surpluses of Astoria for all of these years (*In the Matter of Maybelle Mintz*, 1985, at 4921).

In addition to New York, courts in Alaska, Montana, New Jersey, New Mexico, North Carolina, North Dakota, and Texas have all either adopted or favored the reasonable expectations test to determine whether conduct by those in control is oppressive.

While reasonable expectations may appear in the abstract to be as open-ended as the concept of oppression, it can easily be focused on specific facts. For example, that shareholders often invest in a closely held corporation to provide a job for themselves is almost self-evident. If there is any doubt, the proposition can be confirmed empirically by surveying representative businesses. In addition, the conduct of the parties prior to the onset of disagreement provides insight into their expectations at the time when they entered into the relationship. If all three shareholders were employed by the business since its inception, it is reasonable to conclude that employment was one of their expectations in joining together.

Finally, a critical difference between the reasonable expectations test in a buy-out situation on the one hand and a duty of care or duty of loyalty or shareholder fiduciary duty case on the other hand is the focus and the remedy. The latter situations focus on the wrongdoing of the defendant and, often, on whether the defendant's actions can be justified by business considerations. The reasonable expectations test focuses not on the wrongdoing of the other party but on determining the basis of the bargain between the parties-the explicit or implicit conditions pursuant to which the parties associated themselves together-and on fulfilling such entitlement.

Conclusion

In trying to judge whether conduct is wrongful, courts have taken some very substantial and positive strides in adopting a reasonable expectations test. In so doing, however, courts have had to deal with the task of determining what were the expectations of the parties. Courts have lamented that the "bargain of the parties is often not reflected in the corporation's charter, bylaws, nor even in separate, signed agreements" and that "the parties' full understanding may not even be in writing" (*In re Topper*, 1980, 365).

Here, then, is an area where family business consultants can be helpful. Much has been written about the importance of family mission statements. These should consider such critical issues as succession, employment and management, compensation and ownership, and family harmony and responsibility (*Ward*, 1987). These issues are often the same issues that arise in family litigation. Better for the family to decide them before the fact than for a judge to decide them after the fact.

But the value of a mission statement, for example, is far more than the conclusions that ultimately find their way onto a piece of paper. In reality, the real product is the process. What is desirable is not a document that can resolve litigation but a process that can prevent litigation. When family members come together in a collective, collaborative effort to deal with critical issues and resolve them in a manner that is fair and acceptable to all involved, the tensions and the strains that lead to litigation are far less likely to get out of hand.

In order for process to work and to be able to forestall litigation, several key elements must be in place (M. Murdock, 1990): a coming together of all the adult family members, an environment that fosters mutual trust and respect, a mechanism to facilitate the understanding of differences, the identification of family values and rules, the development of communication patterns without judging or assuming, the toleration of conflict in the short run, and the resolution of conflict in the long run.

Too often, when families attempt to do this on their own, the old Chinese proverb holds true: Lots of noise at the top of the stairs; no one coming down. Patriarchs need to shift gears from imposing to proposing and perhaps even to relenting. For a vision to have power, it must be shared; it cannot be imposed.

Thus, professionals working with family businesses can render a real service in creating the safe environment in which families can work through tensions to arrive at mutually acceptable positions to which members can commit. From the perspective of cost-benefit analysis, it is better to work with family professionals on the front end than with legal professionals on the back end.

References

Davis, J. "Spouse Troubles." *Family Business*, Oct. 1990, p. 32.

Levinson, L. *Bartlett's Unfamiliar Quotations.* Chicago: College Book Co., 1971.

Model Business Corporation Act, Annotated. Englewood Cliffs, NJ.: Prentice Hall, 1985, suppl. 1990.

Murdock, C. "The Evolution of Effective Remedies for Minority Shareholders and Its Impact upon Valuation of Minority Shares." *Notre Dame Law Review*, 1990, 65, 425-489.

Murdock, M. *Family Mission Statements.* Presentation to the Harris Trust & Savings Bank of Chicago Family Conference, Sept. 15, 1990.

New York Business Corp. Law. Secs. 1104-a, 1118. New York: McKinney, 1986, suppl. 1988.

O'Toole, J. *Vanguard Management: Redesigning the Corporate Future.* Garden City, N.Y.: Doubleday, 1985.

"U-Haul's Patriarch Now Battles Offspring in Bitterest of Feuds." *Wall Street Journal*, July 16, 1990, p. A1.

Ward, J. *Keeping the Family Business Healthy: How to Plan For Continuing Growth, Profitability, and Family Leadership.* San Francisco: Jossey-Bass, 1987.

Legal References

Auerbach v. Bennett, 393 N.E.2d 994 (N.Y. 1979).

Compton v. Paul K. Harding Realty Co., 285 N.E.2d 574 (1972).

Donahue v. Rodd Electrotype Co. of New England, Inc., 328 N.E.2d 505 (Mass. 1975).

Fix v. Fix Material Co., Inc., 538 S.W.2d 351 (Mo. Ct. App. 1976).

Harris v. Mardan Business Systems, Inc., 421 N.W.2d 350 (Minn. Ct. App. 1988)

In re Kemp & Beatley, Inc., 473 N.E.2d 1173 (N.Y. 1984).

In re Topper, 443 N.Y.S.2d 359 (N.Y. Sup. Ct. 1980).

In the Matter of Maybelle Mintz, 493 N.Y.S.2d 488 (1985).

Sugarman v. Sugarman, 797 F.2d 3 (1st Cir. 1986).

Wilkes and Wilkes v. Springside Nursing Home, Inc., 353 N.E.2d 657 (Mass. 1976).

What should a business pay its owners? While different family businesses have decidedly different answers to this question, having a clear policy to govern its decision is extremely helpful. This article aids business owners as they think through the implications of business, family, and personal needs for dividend policies.

Thinking About Dividend Policies

By Craig E. Aronoff

We've had several occasions recently to deal with the matter of appropriate levels of reward paid by the business to shareholders. Whether we are dealing with an S corporation's distributions or a C corporation's dividend, the issue revolves around competing uses for "excess" funds.

The founder of a firm made no distinction between salary and dividends in his wholly-owned S corporation, but when he began to compensate two sons in the business and gift them stock, the distinction became real in a hurry. Other manager/owners of an S corporation were considering retirement security, but were concerned that bonuses to themselves would impact distributions on stock gifted to their children. The next generation's lifestyles depended on expected funds. The third generation in a C corporation struggled with the proper amount to pay as a dividend since most of the more than a dozen family stockholders were not in the business. These and other situations commonly found in family businesses cry out for dividend policies-yet few family firms even know how to begin the process of creating one.

Dividend policies rest on numerous considerations. Tax considerations often drive dividend actions in C corps, but taxes are not the focus of this article. For now, let's look at dividends from the simultaneous perspectives of business needs, family needs, and the personal needs for funds.

If a family is committed to maintaining a healthy firm, business needs usually should be considered first when determining how "extra funds" should be used. The first concern should be to question whether extra funds are really "extra."

It is easy to make a business more profitable in the short term by cutting costs, reducing staff or foregoing expenses. While it is stylish to get businesses "lean and mean," owners/ managers must be careful not to overdo it-affecting a slow, if unintentional, liquidation of the company.

Before deciding that funds are available for distribution, please ask yourself these questions:

- Has the lifelong security of incumbent family owner/managers been accomplished?
- Does the business have adequate reserves to weather difficult times?
- Are its equipment and buildings up-to-date and in good shape? Do we have needs for capital expenditures that we are not funding?
- Are we devoting sufficient resources to our sales and marketing efforts? If you are looking for ways to generate profits and dividends, cutting advertising expenses, for example, is an easy solution but may sacrifice future revenues.
- Do we have sufficient management depth? Many family businesses "do it themselves" in managerial and executive roles and too slowly develop middle managers. Indeed, the common complaint we hear about not having time to plan is often a symptom of inadequate investment in managerial resources.
- Are we adequately funding our strategy? Obviously, our choice of strategy is impacted by the family owner's tolerance for risk, desire for growth and alternative uses for funds, but the question remains: Do we know where we want to go as a business, and are we investing in what we need to get there?
- Are we investing in "strategic experiments" which may shape the future of our business in ways we are not yet sure of? Some family businesses that we greatly admire actual-

ly budget for exploring and developing new ideas with the full knowledge that a certain percentage of the experiments will not work out. In the short term, such actions can negatively impact profits and dividends.

Family Needs

As family businesses move into second, third or later generations and ownership is spread among more people, the family develops collective needs which require funding. Examples of collective family needs include: expenses related to family meetings and family governance including the cost of family business consultants and education; funds for family philanthropy; and funds to provide liquidity for shareholders.

When one person controls the business, funding for such needs usually comes from the firm or from that individual's pocket (often viewed as one and the same).

When many people-and especially non-family-are involved in ownership, money must flow out of the business before family needs can be dealt with.

Rather than distributing all stock to individual owners, family businesses sometimes establish trusts to hold stock and to use distributions of funds for the general purposes of the family. Other businesses appropriately budget expenses related to family meetings, family business consultants and the like as shareholder relations, training or management development. Families add to corporate reserves and budget specific amounts to provide a means by which individuals wishing to sell shares can do so.

The point is this: These uses of funds can (and we would argue, should) make less money available to be paid out as dividends to individual stockholders.

Distributions to Individual Owners

While there are certainly gray areas and room for discussion, our view is that distributions on individual shares in family businesses should be paid only after business and collective family needs are met. Our bias is to keep dividends relatively low. Family member owners rapidly become habituated to lifestyles afforded by whatever level of dividend is provided. Non-employed shareholders often do not understand the business's continuous need for funds and may pressure managers to make more money available through distributions. Under such circumstances, family business executives are in a very difficult position relative to making appropriate decisions.

We are not suggesting eliminating dividends. Too many family businesses have member/owners who see their stock as "just a piece of paper." Similarly, too many have executives who resist accountability to shareholders because they are "just family." Dividends can make ownership more meaningful while creating a certain level of accountability.

We do suggest that owners both inside and outside of the family business gain understanding and information about business and family needs. Then a meaningful dividend policy can be established, viewed as fair by all. Family owners can then more fully commit themselves to business and family well-being. Ultimately, business and family well-being contribute to individual well-being, even if dividends are somewhat reduced in the process.

Reprinted with permission from *The Family Business Advisor*, March 1994. Copyright 1994, Family Enterprise Publishers.

The fourth-generation leader of Johnson Wax explains the enduring advantages of family businesses. They include secrecy, stability, flexibility and generosity. Focus on multi-generational success is something that public corporations cannot afford.

Why We'll Never Go Public

By Samuel C. Johnson

There are distinct advantages to being a family corporation. especially when you are competing against public firms. Public companies do have some advantages, principally, unlimited access to the public equity financial markets and the ability to make acquisitions with stock. Also, in some cases the public market is the only way minority family shareholders can diversify investments or settle their estates. But the burden of dealing with thousands of shareholders with diverse expectations, as well as worrying about a potential takeover, encumbers the chief executive of virtually every public corporation.

The preeminent edge for a family firm, if it is totally private, may well be secrecy from your competition, a cherished privilege among private CEOs You can even liken this to a game of poker. Take a public and a family corporation that are roughly the same size, with comparable market shares for competing products: the private firm can hold each and every one of those cards tight to its vest – right through the betting and until it's time to lay them down. But the public firm has to expose the majority of its cards almost from the start, keeping only a proprietary ace or two until its hand is called.

The private company can see many of the strengths and weaknesses of its public competitor and act accordingly. Curiously enough, the private player doesn't even have to show much of its hand when the moment of truth arrives. And if it wins. it simply takes the money off the table, with the public company never really knowing the amount.

Some people assume that public companies represent the benchmark of better business – that if you want profits to soar, it's best to operate as a public enterprise. But it is difficult to compare earnings between the two. A public company does its utmost to enhance short-term earnings, those numbers that appear in quarterly and annual reports, those columns of black ink that keep shareholders content and quiet. But a family-controlled company measures its success in terms of years and decades, not merely quarter by quarter. It can accept lower earnings in lieu of stiff tax liabilities; certain tax wrote-offs are viewed as long-range opportunities, not as drawbacks. Comparing the performances of public and private firms – given the different arenas in which they function – can produce dubious results.

Logically, one might think public companies would show higher profit margins. But a study of public and private earnings conducted by the University of Southern California business school – one of the few ever attempted since acquiring data on private firms is so difficult – concluded that private companies had earnings margins substantially higher than those of public corporations. The private outfits also earned higher assets.

Essentially a private company can conduct its business free from public scrutiny. Your competitors, moreover, have little idea of how strong you are, where problems might lie, or even If you're winning. They can figure your share of a given market though Nielson and SAMI reports, but they don't have any notion of your bottom line. More important, they don't know how other parts of your enterprise affect the company, positively or negatively. In sum, you are a downright mysterious entity.

A CEO of a public company is beholden to literally thousands of individuals and interests. The time he spends actually managing the business, trying to make money, is cut appreciably by the necessity of taking to the road to pump the company's stock, meeting with security analysts, talking to investment bankers, and informing *Wall Street Journal* reporters and other newsmen. He must also spend countless hours with government agencies. And when shareholders call to complain about the company's quarterly earnings report, or even to compliment the CEO, he's forced to talk with them.

The outright financial costs of SEC compliance are also high. Indeed, were we totally public, we clearly would be forced to spend hundreds of thousands of dollars every year on legal fees, registration fees, filing requirements, publishing quarterly and annual reports, and so forth. When Congoleum Corp. was public (it went private in 1980), its chairman figured that all the requirements of being a public corporation cost his company in the neighborhood of $1 million a year.

A private company is also free from the vagaries of the stock market ups and downs that sometimes, through no fault of the management, can send shudders through a corporation. How well these fluctuations are accepted depends a lot on the common sense of the shareholders. A large number of public shareholders are a more volatile audience than a few members of one's family.

The best situation, in my view, occurs when the majority of the stock in a private company is concentrated in the hands of one family member, who is then free to make the decisions that are in the best long-term interest of the company. If there are periods of poor performance, one hopes the family and employee shareholders are understanding, aware that short-term profits must sometimes be sacrificed for the firm's future health.

A truly public company that has thousands and thousands of shareholders is a different matter. Most of the time the inside management group has enough control: shareholders supportively sign their proxies, inside managers and board members control nomination committees as well as the agenda of the annual meeting, and so on.

Nonetheless, they do take lumps from dissidents, suffer serious inquisitions if earnings don't meet expectations, and are picked at by securities analysts and government agencies, if they are not taken over by a hostile raider or even one who seems friendly. But usually the management endures.

A better scenario is a public company controlled by one or a small group of family or management shareholders, where there is access to the public market for acquisitions or additional capital, but no fear of internal strife or outside takeovers. The worst situation I can imagine is being CEO of a public company that is heavily family-owned, in which no more than 5 percent of the stock is concentrated in any member's hands. There you have the disadvantages of public scrutiny without concentration of control. Not only do you have to argue with Wall Street, but also with uncles, cousins, and nieces.

While we at Johnson are free from the uncertainties of the stock market and the family bickering that's described above, we do care about the value of our stock. Shares are sold to our key executives on a select basis; a formula regulates the value according to the company's performance. We don't get the huge upward or downward swings that you see in the stock market, but then I genuinely feel that the performance of the company is a better measure of long-term stock value than the psychological enthusiasm of the market.

Family ownership of a company is usually an advantage over public ownership, provided there is enough concentration of ownership in one or two members. Management of such private organizations can, to be sure, take several forms. Professional management, brought in by the family owners, often serves a company's interests best.

In a family enterprise that does not bring in outside management, one hopes that ownership – and perhaps more important, control – is vested in the most talented member of the family. Should this go on for generations, it results in a continuity of management and management philosophy. When good things are passed along, they gain even more credibility with age.

Johnson Wax was one of the first companies to institute profit sharing, a practice established by my grandfather. My father initiated a no-layoff policy during the Great Depression of the thirties. For many years the company has been committed to giving 5 percent of pre-tax profits to charity. My father followed through with those ideas, as have I.

Not long ago I received a letter from one of our employees, a mechanic I, frankly, had never met, who had been working for the company for 23 years. He said he had been reading about the layoffs at companies in our area in the local newspaper, the *Racine* (Wisconsin) *Journal Times*. "I just felt moved to write you a letter and say 'Thank you' for all the good years that I've had at the company." I don't believe that kind of feeling is engendered in many public companies.

The vast majority of our people know we're not going to change direction and abuse them. And in turn, I know I can count on their loyalty. There have been only a couple of times when I've had to go in front of the employees and ask them for exceptional efforts, when I've said, "Honest to God, help us and pitch in." Invariably, they have responded.

They also know that competitive realities at times require restructuring, and while no one wants to be among those whose jobs are cut out, everyone knows that those affected will be treated fairly.

Of course, if the company founder is a miserly, tough old goat. and his disagreeable ways are genetically and psychologically transmitted to the next generation of management, then you're talking about continuity with no redeeming social value. However, when a family member is placed in control of a company, and everyone knows clearly who the boss is, and who will still be the boss five or ten years hence, then there's a palpable air of stability.

When it comes to hiring at S. C. Johnson & Son, having the owner-manager's name on the building is a big plus. Since the average tenure of a public CEO is a little more than six years, a skilled, next-level professional manager in search of a secure position can't be sure whom he will be working for several years down the line. A new CEO is likely to change the way a company does its business, making his mark as quickly as possible. Professionals are aware of this. Moreover, they know when they join a public company they risk being the victim of a takeover and purge a year or two later. But in a private company, they can settle into their jobs, work steadily with the same top management, use their talents to the fullest, and see a well-functioning relationship stay that way.

There's an old and often-repeated scenario that goes like this: The first generation starts the company, the second builds it up, and the third generation screws it up. Well, I represent the fourth generation at Johnson, and my father certainly didn't screw it up during his turn.

My great-grandfather, who was in his fifties when he started the company, got the enterprise rolling. My grandfather was really the initial builder; he diversified the fledgling product line of waxes and polishes. My father took a regional manufacturer of waxes and polishes and turned it into an international company. If there is any major contribution I've made, you might say it's diversification, expanding the product line even more – into insecticides, personal-care products, industrial products, financial, commercial and home services – and expanding foreign operations from 11 to 45 countries.

Not only is it important that the next generation bring something new to the enterprise, it is equally important that they feel the great personal satisfaction that results from contributing a new dimension to the business, which they often do in spite of those who prefer the status quo.

None of us were clones of our fathers or mothers in management style, the scope of our ideas, or any facet of our lives. Yet each of us built upon what we believed to be the positive parts of the family heritage. In a public firm, or even a private one controlled by professional management, a successor is less likely to build on the heritage of someone he worked for and may not even have liked, to boot. Change may be refreshing, but a company that makes radical shifts every five years, without foundation or consistency, grows schizophrenic and suffers.

Untalented, misdirected, and poor CEOs of public corporations do not however, last as long as similar managers in a family company. If the CEO of a public company is doing a terrible job, Wall Street is going to drive him out. The stock will fall so low that some raider may be tempted to make a bid or come in with a lineup of opposing shareholders' votes at the annual meeting and simply chuck the CEO (that is, if the directors don't do it first – it doesn't happen often enough). Strangely, a family corporation can likewise end up placing a family member in control who turns out to be – putting it mildly – incompetent.

This is why I believe that one of the prime requirements for a healthy, family-owned company is a strong and independent board of directors. It should contain members who are well-recognized professionals, high-level business people who are not family members.

If I go around the bend the day after tomorrow, and as a result the company begins to suffer, my independent board can say, "Sam, we think it's time to turn it over to the next generation or give your seat to professional management until the next generation is properly groomed."

One can't forget that I could, in turn, just call a special board meeting and fire all the independent directors. But this is unthinkable and would incur the wrath of the rest of the family and the management – not to mention possible lawsuits. Successful boards are collegial bodies, and the practical point of the matter is that a CEO/owner simply doesn't fire a group of people of the caliber chosen for the board of a respected private company.

However, a family company can reach a point in its history when the lines of succession are not clear. Our firm has been fortunate in that there has been only one logical successor in each generation. (The fact that the stock was concentrated by archaic, male-chauvinistic or age-biased principles won't hold today, but that – offering no apologies – is how it has been up until now, a situation that may change after my tenure is over.) When a strong leader departs, and several people fight to take that place, it's obvious how messy the situation can become.

A public company may indeed have the edge in succession over a private, family-managed business unless the private company can hand concentrated control from one individual to another.

This will not be the case with the next generation of Johnson. There are two boys and two girls in our family, and we face the risk of losing that "concentration." But today I can add an important caveat. Our business has become diversified, and even though there are several family members who may take leadership roles, I envision no major problems, primarily because of that business diversity. Authority – and in some cases, ownership – can be split along the lines of the greatest talent or interest on the part of our children. While it isn't the easiest trick to manage, it can be done. For example, we spun off Johnson Worldwide Associates, a group of companies that makes products for the outdoor leisure market, which has become a family-controlled, public company.

I don't believe, though, that it's sound to have siblings competing. This can be avoided by spreading authority to various parts of the operation. Our firm currently has some existing separation of businesses; unit companies each serve as bases of operation, reporting all the way to an executive vice-president There is some sharing of manufacturing facilities, but the system works well. So, should the family need to "break up" the company, either in terms of spheres of management authority or ownership, the structure is already in place. We may take more segments of the company public to allow family shareholders to diversify, to bail out their estate, or to allow that segment to acquire additional companies for stock. In any event, family control should prevail.

The family-controlled firm also has the mechanics to make decisions faster than public corporations. This again goes back to having one person, with clear authority, in charge of each major unit of the company. It's the mark of a well-run company.

A good example is our decision in 1975 to take fluorocarbons out of our products. We had done some homework on the matter, but when it became apparent that keeping them in the products would harm our reserve of consumer trust and loyalty, we made the commitment to remove the propellant within a week. Bang.

On occasions when we have been beaten to the market for a new product – as in the case of lemon-scented furniture polish – we have been able to come up with a quick counter punch I would have preferred to be the innovator of the lemon idea, but you can't always be the first. We ultimately won that battle, though. Sometimes, you have to play catch-up, and it's important to do that as well as being an innovator.

Lastly, a family firm can do things of social or cultural value that a public company might be reluctant even to consider, if only for fear of shareholder fury. Granted, many major public companies give millions of dollars to the humanities. the arts, charity, education, and public television, among other causes. This has been recognized over the last decade or so as necessary "corporate responsibility "

However, public firms that are about the size of Johnson Wax frequently have shareholders who don't view philanthropy as necessary; they don't see funding an art exhibit as anything but a cut in their dividend check. We, on the other hand, can do things that enhance the communities in which we live and work without having to explain it to thousands of people.

Being part of a family company compels you to think of the community. You certainly do not want to dump toxic wastes on a site that your children or grandchildren may one day occupy.

As I explained, the private company has an edge over public firms because of secrecy. But this can be taken too far. You don't need to cloak your operation as if you're in the Kremlin. I read where an official of one private corporation said: "It will be a cold day in hell before [his company] talks to the press." That's ridiculous. A CEO can talk about his business without giving away secrets. Isolating oneself and belligerently refusing to become part of the greater public does a disservice to the corporation and the community.

Each generation In a family-owned company probably adapts to and creates change, to win under the conditions of the business and society of the day. The one constant is the focus on the long-term success of the company, for the next generation and ones even further down the line. It can be said that this is more a matter of pride than success for the family pocketbook. And it's a luxury that public corporations – with all the pressures that being public creates – simply cannot afford.

A Father's Question: Where's the Wax?

I can remember when I was the first new-products director of the company back in the fifties. My father, who recognized the need for new products because the wax business wasn't growing, told me, "Sam, it's up to you to find some thing new."

After a few months, I came up with a proposal for a new product – a Johnson's aerosol insecticide. He looked skeptically at the prototype can and commented, "Don't you know we don't make any product without wax in it"

"We could put some wax in it" I answered, "but I doubt if it will improve the insecticide."

"What's better about it than the competition's products?"

"It's an aerosol," I noted.

"There are other aerosols on the market," he responded.

"Well," I said. "We've got a nice label."

"There are other nice labels out there. What's really better about it?"

"It's very good formulation. but I doubt that it's better than what's out there." I admitted. His final comment was, "When you come up with something that's really better, then well talk about getting into the insecticide business."

It was a great lesson. I went back to the lab, authorized further research, and discovered that all of the insecticides then on the market were solvent based, and they smelled bad. Also, if you used them near house plants, the solvent (not the insecticide) killed them. We reformulated the insecticide into an aqueous system that could be used safely on plants and didn't smell like kerosene. We named it "Raid House and Garden Insecticide." It was a winner, and we're now the world's largest producer of insecticides. If you're going to get into a new field, you have to have a better product, one the consumer recognizes as demonstrably superior to that of your competitors.

An agency theory framework is used to test the effects of founding family control on firm performance, capital structure, and value. Both the finance and management literatures regarding the relationship between firm control and firm value are explored. Controlling for size, industry, and managerial ownership, the results suggest that firms controlled by the founding family have greater value, are operated more efficiently, and carry less debt than other firms.

Founding Family Controlled Firms: Performance, Risk, and Value

By Daniel L. McConaughy, Charles H. Matthews, and Anne S. Fialko

While it has generally been accepted that family-controlled businesses differ from professionally managed firms, little empirical research has been done to support and advance our understanding of this premise (Daily and Dollinger 1991). The small amount of existing research, however, does suggest that there are key differences. For example, Fama and Jensen (1983) propose that family controlled businesses should be more efficient than professionally run firms because the costs of monitoring are less in a family controlled firm. Daily and Dollinger (1991) found that there are a number of valid differences between non-family controlled firms and family controlled firms. Non-family controlled firms tend to be larger, have lower mortality rates, use different strategies, and rely more on formal control systems than do family controlled firms.

In the United States, it is estimated that as much as 60 percent of the Gross Domestic Product is generated by family-controlled businesses (Bellet et al 1995). Often these are thought to be "microfirms" (Carsrud 1994) – mom and pop operations. It is estimated, however, that family owned businesses make up approximately 35 percent of Fortune 500 firms (Carsrud (1994). Furthermore, some estimate that in 80 percent of all businesses, a controlling family has a significant say in the company's strategic direction (Carsrud 1994; Kets de Vries1993). Yet little attention has been given to the effect of family control on the business, and only recently has the definition of a family business been systematically addressed.

A review of both the finance and management literatures regarding the relationship between firm control and firm value suggests three general research questions: (1) Do founding family controlled firms (FFCFs) have a greater value than other firms? (2) Are FFCFs run more or less efficiently than other firms? And (3) Are FFCFs less risky than other firms?

Related Literature

Efficiency, Risk, and Principal-Agent Conflicts

The finance literature has little to say about how family control affects how a firm is operated. Research has focused on the impact of ownership control on corporate value, following the leads of Jensen and Meckling (1976) and Fama and Jensen (1985). Empirical work has focused on the effect of the increased ownership concentration associated with corporate takeovers on corporate efficiency (for example, see Kaplan 1989; Smith 1990; Muscarella and Vetsuypens 1990; and Gibbs 1993), and the relationship between ownership structure and capital structure (for example, see Masulis 1988; Grossman and Hart 1986; and Leland and Toft 1996).

The terms "ownership control," "ownership concentration," and "management (managerial) ownership" are used some what similarly in the literature and deserve a brief comment in the interest of clarity. In a corporation, shareholders are the owners, and ultimately they can determine the course of the firm. The extent of the shareholders' influence (ownership control) depends on their relative stakes in the firm as well as on how actively they participate in the activities of the firm. A shareholder with 50 percent of the shares plus one more share can exercise total control the firm if he or she wants, because this individual can outvote all the other shareholders combined. However, an individual does not need this level of ownership to exercise is a great deal of influence over the firm, because influence can also depend on how credible the shareholder is, and how concentrated the other shareholdings are. "Managerial ownership" can be viewed as a proxy for how much influence the "owner/managers" exert and is often used in studies that examine "principal-agent" conflicts. These topics are discussed in more detail below.

Jensen and Meckling (1976) brought the issue of misalignment between the interests of managers and those of owners to the forefront. Using agency theory as a basis for developing a model of corporate structure, the authors define the agency relationship as "a contract under which one or more persons (the principal(s) engage another person (the agent) to perform some service on their behalf which involves delegating some decision-making authority to the agent" (Jensen and Meckinling 1976, p. 308). They define agency cost as the sum of (1) the monitoring expenditures incurred by the principal; (2) the bonding expenditures incurred by the agent; and (3) residual loss. Jensen and Meckling then hypothesize that the larger a firm becomes, the larger its agency costs become due to the increased monitoring necessary in a large firm. However, they argue that agency costs can be reduced by increasing the level of managerial ownership in order to reduce monitoring costs. Lower agency costs are associated with higher firm values, other things being equal. Morck et al. (1988) and McConnell and Servates (1990) present some evidence that firm values are positively related to the degree of managerial ownership at lower levels of ownership. The relation weakens at higher levels, suggesting that high levels of managerial ownership may shield entrenched managers from the discipline of the market for corporate control.

Jensen and Meckling (1976) acknowledge that several considerations are missing in their analysis, among which is their assumption that they were dealing with only a single investment financing decision. In other words, they did not deal with any long-term financial issues. Second, they did not consider the relationships among owner-managers and outside equity holders.

The empirical literature regarding corporate takeovers adds support to the agency theory position that more concentrated management ownership leads to greater firm efficiency. Takeovers concentrate ownership and control among a small group of managers and buyout specialists. This concentration is generally followed by improvements in operating efficiency and increases in firm value. Kaplan (1989), Smith (1990), Muscarella and Vetsuypens (1990), and Phan and Hill (1995) all found evidence of improved efficiency following a buyout. The research on corporate efficiency and changes in value after takeover suggests that reduced agency costs due to the concentration of control created by the takeover are responsible for the improvements.

The Jensen and Meckling (1976) position, however, is not uniformly accepted. Demsetz (1983) and Demsetz and Lehn (1985) argue that the level of managerial ownership varies systematically as the managers try to maximize the firm value. Demsetz and Lehn (1985) suggest that the forces affecting ownership structure are optimal firm size, effective control of managers by owners, government regulation, and the firm's ability to provide amenities to owners. Thus, according to these researchers, the level of managerial ownership does not affect firm value.

However, when Hill and Snell (1988) adjusted profit rates for industry differences, they found that although greater concentration of stock ownership did lead to greater firm profitability, the relationship was mediated by firm strategy. Daily and Dollinger (1991) demonstrated that there were differences between family controlled and non-family controlled firms with respect to firm size, firm age, firm strategy, and internal control systems. They found family controlled firms to be smaller, to have higher mortality rates, to use different strategies, and to rely less on formal control systems than did non-family controlled firms.

Fama (1980) suggests that the separation of ownership and control can be an efficient form of economic organization. He suggests that the labor market for managers functions as assurance that managers act in the best interests of the firm. Most recently, Cho (1998) found support for the Demsetz and Lehn (1985) contention that managerial ownership is a function of firm characteristics. His study of Fortune 500 firms in 1991, using a two-stage regression methodology, found that firm characteristics are unrelated to managerial ownership, but that managerial ownership is related to firm characteristics.

Tosi, Katz, and Gomez-Mejia (1997) suggest that the agency theory approach oversimplifies the complexity of the agency relationship. Morris (1989) suggests that no separation between ownership and management can offset the positive long-term orientation of the business. In addition, family differences and role conflict can lead to behavior that does not support the best interests of the firm. Psychological conflict within the family (such as sibling rivalry, autocratic behavior, and nepotism) can offset the benefits of reduced monitoring (Kets de Vries 1993). Family emotions can also cloud financial vision in such issues as succession planning (Morris 1989). Clearly, the literature raises more questions concerning performance, risk, and firm value than it answers. Nevertheless, a persistent theme suggests that family ownership and control are beneficial in mitigating the principal agent conflicts that afflict firms run by professional managers without founding family oversight.

Ownership Control and Managerial Risk Aversion

Capital structure can affect the risk of a firm and, therefore, the risk to which managers are exposed. Capital structure is viewed broadly here as the proportion of debt to equity rather than as specific types of securities used to finance capital investments. In evaluating capital structure, managers must consider the risk of the business and the time frame of the financing decisions.

Masulis (1988) suggests that managers prefer having less leverage than shareholders in order to reduce the risk of their undiversified investment in the company. Grossman and Hart (1986), modeling the stockholder-manager conflict, found that increased leverage reduces managers' discretion over corporate decisions and reduces agency costs associated with managerial discretion. Phan and Hill (1995) found that increased debt is associated with increased emphasis on efficiency goals.

Risk is generally defined in the finance literature as the probability that the actual return on an investment will deviate from the expected return (Van Horne 1980). In general, a firm will be more or less risky depending on its capital structure (Van Horne 1980). Overall, conventional decision theory considers investment choice to be a trade-off between risk and expected return (March and Shapira 1987).

However, the management literature suggests that the concept of risk is not nearly so straightforward for managers. Managers do not consider risk to be a probability concept, nor do they attempt to reduce it to a single quantifiable construct (March and Shapira 1987). Furthermore, individuals have been found to treat risk as a dynamic factor, using the perspective of change in value rather than total value to evaluate a decision and to separate gains but not losses from the initial outlay (Hollenbeck et al.1994). To add to the complexity, because managers also consider personal risk when making decisions regarding firm risk (May 1995), they may use only approximate time frames in their planning rather than the accurate time forecasts called for in financial models (Simon 1993).

The nature of risk has also been found to be shaped by the time horizon (Bernstein 1996). For example, Walsh and Seward (1990) suggest that managers are most interested in firm performance during the period in which they are compensated. Family businesses, however, are generally considered to have a longer-term perspective than public organizations (Kets de Vries 1993). Oswald and Jahera (1991) found that high levels of inside ownership were associated with higher excess returns. They state, "The higher levels of inside ownership implies improved decision-making resulting in higher earnings and dividends..." (p.325). Oswald and Jahera conclude that having individuals in the firm with vested interests is beneficial to the long-term performance of the business. Thus, closely held firms would be expected to move more cautiously than diffusely held firms. Agrawal and Nagarajan (1990) found that there is significantly greater family involvement in corporate operations of all-equity firms than in leveraged firms.

Mishra and McConaughy (1999) examined why family controlled firms use less debt.

After controlling for a variety of factors that affect cross-sectional debt levels among all firms, they found that family control and not managerial ownership, is related to debt levels. This calls into question studies of managerial ownership and firm characteristics that do not control explicitly for family control. They conclude that the founding family's aversion to the risk of a loss of control motivates the use of less debt.

Family Control and Firm Value

The literature cited clearly suggests that the level of equity held by a firm's efficiency, profitability, and capital structure and, therefore, its value. However, if the management is composed of members of a founding or controlling family, does that change the level of management influence? Not only do family controlled businesses differ in structural areas (Daily and Dollinger 1991), but the dynamics of family businesses are different than those of a public corporation because of the added dimensions of the family relationship (Rosenblatt et al. 1985; Kets de Vries 1993) and the time horizon (Kets de Vries 1993; Walsh and Seward 1990). With regard to the firm's value, the mix of a firm's financial claims (such as debt and equity) have an effect because any changes to that mix affect the firm's cash flow and therefore its value (Jensen and Warner 1988).

Thus far, the empirical evidence that family control affects the value of the firm consists primarily of supplementary detail found in more general studies or else it has dealt with specific issues. The evidence fails to provide an overall view of the relationship of founding family control with firm value. In a seminal study of the relationship between the level of managerial ownership and the value of large firms, Morck, Scheifer, and Vishny (1988) found that the Tobin's Q measure of firm value increases when the founding family holds one of the top two positions for firms incorporated after 1950. Johnson et al. (1985) found that the sudden death of founder-CEOs leads to a stock price increase. While examining the effects of the death of blockholders, Slovin and Sushka (1993) found that founder status does not have any significant effect. Stultz (1988) found a curvilinear relationship between managerial ownership and firm value. Initially, values rise as ownership becomes more concentrated and monitoring costs decrease; however, as management become more insulated, firm values decrease. McConaughy et al. (1998) found that family control is associated with higher firm performance. They suggest that families have better incentives to maximize firm value. Like Morck et al. (1988) they found that younger founder-controlled firms are more valuable after controlling for the investment opportunities. However, they do not address the impact of the risk preferences of FFCFs.

Of course, there are both benefits and problems associated with family control. Benefits include a more clearly defined culture because the family spirit determines the prevailing values, norms, and attitudes (Kets de Vries 1993) and the family members' extensive knowledge of the firm since they have known it from early childhood (Kets de Vries 1993). Referring specifically to closed organizations, Fama and Jensen (1983) suggest that family relationships among owner/managers should reduce agency costs as well as provide quasi- (economic) rents. DeAngelo and DeAngelo (1985) suggest that family control serves to monitor and discipline managers. Kole (1997) observes that family controlled firms are less likely to have any explicit incentive compensation plan. McConaughy (2000) found that founding family CEOs in family controlled firms earn less and receive less incentive pay than non-family CEOs in family controlled firms after controlling for size, managerial ownership, and tenure. His results are consistent with the family incentive alignment hypothesis, namely that founding family managers have more incentives than non-family managers. This is consistent with Fama and Jensen's (1983) hypothesis that family control improves monitoring. In other words, more effective monitoring in family controlled firms reduces the need to "incentivize" CEOs to reach a high level of performance. On the downside, Morris (1989) suggests that the lack of separation of ownership from management causes family businesses to suffer from cloudy financial vision. Furthermore, the complex psychological nature of family relationships can lead to a confusing organizational structure in which authority and responsibility are not clearly defined (Kets de Vries 1993).

To summarize, family control through share ownership may provide incentives for operational efficiency at the exposure to higher risk from the shareholdings. Thus, we can broadly illustrate the research framework as one that examines ownership, its relation to performance and capital structure, and then the impact of these on firm value. Figure 1 depicts this framework.

Hypotheses

In spite of the mixed empirical results, the literature reviewed here reveals that ownership structure affects the efficiency and capital structure of a firm and that these in turn affect firm value. The arguments for explaining increased efficiency in a family controlled or closely held firm are derived from agency theory. The reduced costs of monitoring, resulting from having owners involved in firm management, are thought to increase the firm's efficiency. Capital structure is assumed to be affected by risk profile and time frame. Family owners are generally assumed to take a longer-term outlook and to be less willing to take risks, especially if their control allows them access to economic rents which could be irretrievably lost if financial distress resulted in a change of control. The increased efficiency of the firm can also lead to increased cash flows, which also influence the firm's capital structure.

Existing research supports the premise that family-controlled firms (Kets de Vries 1993; Daily and Dollinger 1991). The next step is to determine whether the value of founding family controlled firms is indeed greater than that of other firms. Fama and French stress the importance of the market-to-book equity ration (ME/BE) in measuring value, asserting that "strong firms with persistently high earnings" have high Me/BE ratios (Fama and French 1996, p.56; 1992). The ratio is similar to the Tobin's Q used by Morck, Scheifer, and Vishny (1988) and McConnell and Servaes (1990) in assessing firm value. This measure also serves as an overall performance measure. Thus, our first hypothesis:

> H1: Founding family controlled firms (FFCFs) have higher market-to-book equity ratios than non-founding family controlled firms (NFFCFs).

Since this increased value is result of the assumed increased efficiencies suggested by agency theory and the capital structure preferred by owner-managers, elements of a firm's operations must be examined to determine whether FFCFs operate more efficiently than non-FFCFS. Higher operating efficiency suggests better management. Efficiency can also be viewed as a proxy for lower agency costs.
Thus:

> H2 :FFCFs have more favorable operating ratios than NFFCFs.

As the amount of debt in a firm's capital structure increases, the firm becomes increasingly risky (Van Horne 1980). Managers in FFCFs have a heavy investment in their firms in terms of both financial investment and human capital. They also have a likelihood of receiving quasi-rents from their positions. Thus, FFCFs would be expected to finance more conservatively than non-FFCF's, using less debt and relying more on retained earnings. Thus:

> H3:FFCFs choose capital structures that involve less risk than NFFCFs.

Research Methods

Founding family controlled firms are defined to be public corporations whose CEOs are either the founder or a member of the founder's family. Through biographical sketches of CEOs provided in "*The Business Week* CEO 1000," 219 such firms were identified. Managerial ownership data come from the June 1987 Disclosure and are calculated as the percentage holdings of officers and directors as reported in proxy statements. The remainder of the data comes from the COMPUSTAT database for 1986 through 1988. The stock prices are year-end closing prices. The 1986-1988 averages are calculated using only those firms that have data for all three years.

Figure 1. Research Framework

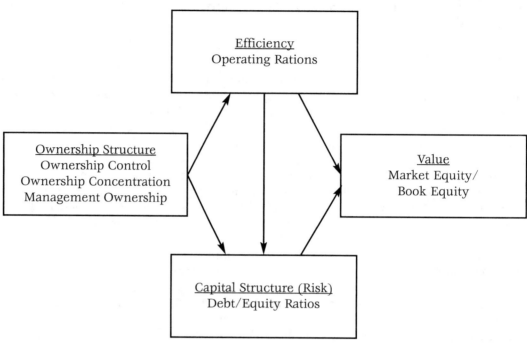

The matched pairs methodology was used to control for size, industry, and ownership effects. Using COMPUSTAT, screens were run for public companies whose 1987 sales were plus or minus 25 percent of each FFCF, initially using the four-digit SIC classifications, then three-and finally two-digit classifications. Next, data were obtained on the percentage of the firms owned by officers and directors of the FFCF firms and the potential controls. When proxy data were unavailable, data from SEC forms 3 and 4 were used.

In order to separate the effects of family ownership and control from non-family management ownership, two sets of control matches were formed using size, industry, and ownership data for the FFCFs and the potential control firms. One set, the "ownership match," contained the firms closest to each FFCF in terms of size, industry, and managerial ownership. These are referred to as the Closely Held Firm (CHF) group. The other control set, the "diffuse set" was also matched in terms of size and industry but also contained the firms with the lowest percentages of managerial ownership in the size and industry class. These are referred to as the Diffusely Held firm (DHF) group.

Because exact ownership matches were not available, an attempt was made to match the ownership level of the ownership control firms with the five ranges used by Morck, Scheifer, and Vishny (1988): 0-5 percent ownership; 5.01-15 percent ownership; 15.01-25 percent ownership; 25.01-50 percent ownership; and over 50 percent ownership. A slight variation was added: the two highest ranges were subdivided. When a match could not be found, an attempt was made to find a firm with managerial ownership within 10 percent of that of the FFCEF.

After forming matched pairs, the data set contained 109 ownership matches and 128 diffuse matches. Eighty-five FFCFs had both ownership and diffuse matches. The sample was tested for an ownership effect with the FFCFs and each set of controls. A second test was conducted to determine whether there was an ownership effect between the two control groups. Comparisons were made using multivariate matched pairs analysis and trend analysis to determine whether the differences between the family controlled firms and each of the control groups were significant.

Dependent variables used to compare firm values between groups were *Market/equity to book equity (ME/BE) ratio* and *stock return*. The dependent variables in the comparison of operating efficiency were broken down into areas of productivity, profitability, asset utilization, and working capital management. Productivity was measured using *sales*

Table 1. Descriptive Statistics

	A		B		C	
Characteristics	Founding Family Controlled Group	Non-Founding Family Controlled Group	Founding Family Controlled Group	Diffusely Held Group	Non-Founding Family Controlled Group	Diffusely Held Group
Number (n)	109	109	128	128	85	85
Mean Sales ($ million)	1,283	1,278	1,442	1,391	1,373	1,324
Standard Deviation Sales	1,819	1,842	2,316	2,272	2,046	1,915
Median Sales ($ million)	610	632	579	515	573	529
Mean Ownership (percent)	12.8	12.3	20.7	2.6	12.9	2.1
Standard Deviation	11.9	3.1	19.5	2.9	13.4	2.5
Median Ownership	9.1	6.7	13.1	1.6	7.6	1.5
Founder Controlled (n)	73	NA	83	NA	NA	NA
Founder's Family Controlled	36	NA	45	NA	NA	NA
Median Earnings/Price Ratio	0.065	0.075	0.063	0.066	0.060	0.067
Difference[a]/(n)	-0.010		-0.003		-0.007	
	[58]		[68]		[35]	
Median Beta (1986-1988)[b]	1.225	1.125	1.300	1.200	1.175	1.150
Difference[a]/(n)	0.100		0.100[c]		0.025	
	[62]		[71]		[32]	

[a]Differences are the difference between the sample firm's median and the control firm's median. Significance levels are based on one-tailed Wilcoxon signed-rank tests.
[b]Individual year-end betas are calculated using five years of monthly data.
[c]$p < .05$ level

growth, *sales per employee*, and *cash flow per employee*. Profitability was assessed using *net profit margin*. Asset utilization was measured using the *total asset turnover ratio*, while *working capital/sales* was used to assess working capital management. The dependent variables used to compare firm financial structure were *total debt/total assets* and the *cash dividend payout ratio*.

Because several variables were used to represent several of the constructs, the question of whether to use a multivariate or univariate approach arose. A check of sphericity showed that the sphericity assumption necessary for matched pairs repeated measures was violated in most instances, making the issue somewhat complex (Stevens 1996). Furthermore, the assumption of univariate normality was violated for some variables, indicating that the assumption of multivariate normality was not met (Stevens 1996). Therefore, a nonparametric, univariate method, the Wilcoxon signed-rank test, was used to assess differences between FFCFs and each control group. This test is a substitute for the t-test in paired samples (Snedecor and Cochran 1989).

Results

Part A of Table 1 compares the characteristics of the FFCF group with those of the NFCF group. Part B of Table 1 compares FFCFs with DHFs. Part C of Table 1 compares the two control groups. Each control group includes firms that are of similar size and from the same industry but that differ in the percentage of managerial ownership.

Table 1 shows that the matching process appears to have worked well. In each panel, mean sales levels for the samples and controls are much the same. Median sales levels differ more because of the skewed nature of sales volume within industries. Managerial ownership percentages for the FFCF sample and the ownership control group are comparable, while they are dissimilar for the FFCF sample and the diffuse control group.

While there was no conscious effort to match earnings/price (E/P) ratios, the groups are also similar across this dimension. In no case is there a statistically significant difference between the FFCFs and the control firm's E/P based on a one-tailed Wilcoxon signed-rank test. However, there is a significant difference between the median E/Ps of the ownership and diffuse control groups.

The FFCF sample and the control groups have similar median betas. Betas for the

Table 2. Comparison Between Founding Family Controlled Firms and the Control Group Matched on Size, Industry, and Managerial Ownership

Measure	1986	1987	1988	1986-1988
Value				
Sample Median (Market Equity/ Book Equity)	2.26	1.94	9.97	2.06
Difference from control[a]	0.64***	0.66***	0.65***	0.64***
Number (n)	69	69	69	59
Sample Mean Stock Return	0.34	0.166	0.042	0.584
Control Mean Stock Return	0.211	0.046	0.111	0.35
Difference from control[b]	0.129**	0.120*	-0.069	0.234**
Number (n)	104	91	83	83
Sample Standard Deviation	0.445	0.448	0.321	0.642
Control Standard Deviation	0.472	0.392	0.482	0.788
Difference from control[c]	-0.027	0.056	-0.161***	0.146**
Number (n)	104	91	83	83
Operating Efficiency	0.139	0.165	0.321	0.209
Difference from control[a]	.012***	.070***	.068***	.043***
Number (n)	109	101	97	97
Sample Median Sales/Employee ($thousands)	107.9	113.5	115.6	107.2
Difference from control[a]	8.9	4.3	1.8	0.6
Number (n)	96	94	77	77
Sample Median Cash Flow/Employee ($thousands)	11	12.2	12.3	13.3
Difference from control[a]	4.4***	5.3***	5.0**	6.2***
Number (n)	88	86	71	71
Sample Median Gross Margin	0.365	0.364	0.350	0.360
Difference from control[a]	.069***	.069***	.958**	.068***
Number (n)	89	89	78	78
Sample Median Net Margin	0.063	0.069	0.067	0.066
Difference from control[a]	0.021***	0.027***	0.024***	0.023***
Number (n)	106	107	93	95
Sample Median Total Asset Turnover	1.100	1.090	1.115	1.070
Difference from control[a,b]	-0.070	-0.125	-0.130	-0.162
Number (n)	109	104	86	80
Sample Median (Working Capital/Sales	0.215	0.212	0.204	0.212
Difference from control[a]	0.014	0.027	0.500**	0.017*
Number (n)	77	77	66	66
Risk				
Sample Median (Total Debt/Total Assets)	0.158	0.206	0.200	0.196
Difference from control[a,b]	-0.078**	-0.032**	-0.071***	-0.062***
Number (n)	107	107	96	96
Sample Median (Short-term Debt/Assets)	0.014	0.018	0.016	0.021
Difference from control[a]	-0.023***	-0.017**	-0.022***	-0.019***
Number (n)	106	107	96	96
Sample Median Cash Dividend Payout Ratio	0.154	0.151	0.186	0.149
Difference from control[a]	-0.090**	-0.096***	-0.103***	-0.146***
Number (n)	76	78	67	58

[a]Significance level based on one-tailed Wilcoxon signed-rank test.
[b]Significance difference between sample and control means based on two-tailed paired sample t-test.
[c]Significance difference between sample and control standard deviations based on two-tailed F-test.
*$p < 0.10$
**$p < 0.05$
***$p < 0.01$

FFCF firms are generally slightly higher. Only in one case, however, is there a statistical difference. In part B, the difference between the sample firms' median beta of 1.3 is significantly different from the 1.2 median beta of the diffuse control group's at the 0.05 level.

The differences between sample and control group statistics were tested using Wilcoxon signed rank tests for the median values on all but the stock market returns. The mean differences for stock market returns were tested using a two-tailed t-test, while the significance difference for the standard deviations on stock returns was tested using a one-tailed F-test. When significant, the results of these tests allow us to note that there are differences between FFCFs and the control group.

Comparison of Firms by Value

Table 2 presents the comparison between the FFCF sample and the control group matched by size, industry, and percentage of managerial ownership. Table 3 presents the comparison between the FFCF sample and the control group matched by SIC classification and size. Table 4 presents the results of the comparison of the two control groups. As expected, the FFCFs have higher ME/BE ratios and provide higher stock market returns than similar closely held firms in which managers are not family members.

The first comparison in Table 2 illustrates that FFCFs sell at higher ME/BE premiums than do NFCFs. Each $ 1 of FFCF book value sold for $2.06, a premium of about $0.64 over the control groups. This difference is significant at greater than the 0.001 level for each of the years 1986, 1987, and 1988 and for the three-year average. Thus, Hypothesis 1 is supported.

The two sets of control groups were very similar along most dimensions (Table 4). Statistically, firms in both control groups sell for the same ME/BE ratio (except for 1987 when they are different at the .10 level) and generate similar stock market returns. This indicates that it is family ownership rather than management ownership that explains the difference in firm value.

Comparison of Firms by Efficiency

As expected, the FFCFs exhibit attributes that suggest they are better run than similar closely held firms in which managers are not family members. The FFCFs generate higher sales growth (an additional 4.3 percent per year on average), higher gross and net margins on sales, and more cash flow per employee than do CHFs. Each of these differences is significant at the 0.01 level, showing support for Hypothesis 2. It is interesting to note that these differences are not the result of higher-volume operations. The FFCFs' sales per employee, while minimally higher, are not significantly different from those of the ownership-match firms. The total asset turnover is lower for the FFCFs, but the difference is not statistically significant.

In further support of Hypothesis 2, the data in Table 2 suggests that FFCFs exhibit a more conservative management style. FFCFs have more working capital per dollar of sales volume, use less debt (particularly short-term debt), and pay out a considerably smaller portion of earnings as dividends. The differences in the working capital-to-sales ratios are relatively modest. FFCFs carry working capital equal to 21 percent of sales – an average difference from the controls of 1.7 percent over the 1986 to 1988 period. This difference is significant at the 0.10 level and appears to be driven by the 5 percent difference in 1988 which is significant at the 0.05 level. The differences for 1986 and 1987 are not significant.

The hypotheses are again supported by the comparison with the diffusely held firms. The FFCFs have attributes that suggest they are also better run the diffusely held control group. In general, the results in Table 3 duplicate the results in Table 2. Where there are differences, they arise from some of the differences in the two control groups.

Statistically, the two sets of controls generate similar sales growth and similar profit margins. There are two notable differences between the two sets of controls:

(1) the ownership-matched firms generate higher total asset turnover ($p < .01$) than the diffusely held firms; and (2) in two years (1986 and 1988), the manager-owned firms have a lower working capital-to-sales ratio than the diffusely held firms, implying more aggressive capital management.

Comparison of Firms by Capital Structure

Hypothesis 3 is also supported. The differences in finance operations between the

Table 3. Comparison Between Founding Family Controlled Firms and the Control Group Matched on SIC Classification and Size

Measure	1986	1987	1988	1986-1988
Value				
Sample Median (Market Equity/ Book Equity)	2.16	1.08	1.94	2.11
Difference from control[a]	0.66***	0.61***	0.43**	0.54***
Number (*n*)	85	83	70	70
Sample Mean Stock Return	0.358	0.181	0.018	0.595
Control Mean Stock Return	0.205	0.047	0.214	0.459
Difference from control[b]	0.153*	0.134**	-0.196***	0.136
Number (*n*)	120	101	94	94
Sample Standard Deviation	0.480	0.441	0.342	0.696
Control Standard Deviation	0.383	0.367	0.399	0.623
Difference from control[c]	0.097**	0.074**	-0.057*	0.073*
Number (*n*)	120	101	94	94
Operating Efficiency				
Sample Median Sales Growth	0.165	0.163	0.37	0.239
Difference from control[a]	0.059***	0.052***	0.135***	0.084***
Number (*n*)	128	115	112	112
Sample Median Sales/Employee ($thousands)	116.5	122.2	132.8	127.0
Difference from control[a]	8.1 **	12.9*	12.6	13.9*
Number (*n*)	112	107	82	82
Sample Median Cash Flow/Employee ($thousands)	12.0	14.0	16.5	14.7
Difference from control[a]	4.8**	6.8**	6.6*	6.7**
Number (*n*)	106	100	78	78
Sample Median Gross Margin	0.407	0.416	0.377	0.399
Difference from control[a]	0.099***	0.89***	0.061***	0.094***
Number (*n*)	105	102	90	90
Sample Median Net Margin	0.061	0.064	0.067	0.064
Difference from control[a]	0.020***	0.022***	0.019***	0.023***
Number (*n*)	125	125	108	107
Sample Median Total Asset Turnover	1.115	1.115	1.115	1.078
Difference from control[a,b]	0.050	0.100	0.075	0.061
Number (*n*)	125	122	91	92
Sample Median (Working Capital/Sales)	0.239	0.255	0.253	0.264
Difference from control[a]	0.054**	0.170*	0.086*	0.070**
Number (*n*)	88	87	72	72
Risk				
Sample Median (Total Debt/Total Assets)	0.175	0.204	0.230	0.210
Difference from control[a,b]	-0.059**	-0.025	0.004	-0.017
Number (*n*)	126	124	108	108
Sample Median (Short-term Debt/Assets)	0.014	0.018	0.017	0.020
Difference from control[a]	-0.021***	-0.014***	-0.011**	-0.017***
Number (*n*)	125	123	106	108[a]
Sample Median Cash Dividend Payout Ratio	0.117	0.115	0.141	0.117
Difference from control[a]	-0.158***	-0.009**	-0.076*	-0.148***
Number (*n*)	83	79	70	59

Significance level based on one-tailed Wilcoxon signed-rank test.

[b]Significance difference between sample and control means based on two-tailed paired sample *t*-test.

[c]Significance difference between sample and control standard deviations based on two-tailed F-test.

*p < 0.10

**p < 0.05

***p < 0.01

FFCF group and the closely held control group are significant. Over the 1986 to 1988 periods, the median debt/asset ratio for FFCFs is 19.6 percent, while that for the ownership match is 6.2 percent higher. This difference is significant at greater than the 0.0001 level. Individual year differences range from 3.2 percent to 7.8 percent and are significant at the 0.01 and 0.05 levels. As expected, the FFCFs have more conservative financing than similar closely held firms in which managers are not family members.

The difference in the use of short-term debt is even more pronounced and just as statistically significant. FFFCFs carry approximately one-half the relative amount of short-term debt than the firms in the ownership match control group. The FFCFs' short-term debt-to-sales ratios are approximately half those of the ownership match firms. The median short-term debt-to-sales ratio for the FFCFs over the 1986 to 1988 period is 2.1 percent while that for the ownership match is 4.0 percent, a difference of 1.9 percent ($p < .01$). The differences for the individual years range from 1.7 percent to 2.3 percent and are significant at either the 0.01 or the 0.05 levels.

In contrast, the results presented in Table 4 indicate that, statistically, the two sets of control firms finance similarly. As with value, it appears to be the family relationship rather than management control that accounts for the differences in capital structure.

Discussion

The Wilcoxon signed rank tests merely indicate whether there are significant differences between two groups in terms of the dependent variable (Snedecor and Cochran 1989). We must be careful not to imply causality in relationships among the variables. Further, each hypothesis was tested with several univariate tests. Using the Bonferroni inequality test, the overall alpha level (probability of at least one false rejection when the null hypotheses are true) for Hypotheses 1 and 3 is 3.6, while that for Hypothesis 2 is 8.4 (Stevens 1996).

The results show that FFCFs perform better on a wide variety of measures. However, these tests also indicate that there are differences between FFCFs and NFCFs that are not just due to decreased monitoring costs associated with management ownership. FFCFs have greater working capital per dollar sales volume than NFCFs, generate higher sales growth than NFCFs, and carry less debt than NFCFs. They are financed more conservatively, consistent with the notion that CEOs of FFCFs are more risk averse, perhaps because they have more to lose (quasi-rents). Finally, the family controlled firms have greater market value/book value ratios than either control group as a result of higher performance combined with less risk.

The absence of differences between the two control groups has important implications. Financial theory leads us to expect a closer alignment of managerial and shareholder interests in the closely held firms. This alignment should reduce agency problems and improve operating results and market returns. Without family control, the anticipated improvements in results and returns do no occur. Recent research by Cho (1998) and Kole (1997) suggest that managerial ownership is endogenous to the firm (depends on firm characteristics). Cho found that firm characteristics explain managerial ownership levels but not the converse. Kole found that managerial ownership levels do not explain the presence of incentive pay plans but that family controlled firms are less likely to have incentive plans.

Thus, it appears that the key to reduced agency costs is not the concentration of ownership in top management but the characteristics of the group in whom ownership in concentrated. Founding family control yields the results anticipated by agency theory, while management control in the absence of the founding family ties does not.

This research demonstrates that firms controlled by the founding family (FFCFs) are generally run more efficiently than other firms, carry less debt than other firms, and have greater value as measured by the Market Equity/Book Equity ratio than other firms. It also suggests that it is the family control of the firm rather than management ownership that is the key to these differences.

This research also suggests that further analysis is warranted. Several questions emerge from this study. First is the causal nature of the relationship. Might increased efficiency be caused by the structure of the firm or some other characteristic of the FFCF

Table 4. Comparison of Ownership-Matched Control Group with Diffusely Owned Control Group

Measure	1986	1987	1988	1986-1988
Value				
Sample Median (Market Equity/				
Book Equity)	1.62	1.38	1.46	1.47
Difference from control [a]	0.12	0.16*	0.15	0.03
Number (n)	43	42	36	36
Sample Mean Stock Return	0.219	0.044	0.130	0.400
Control Mean Stock Return	0.190	0.053	0.178	0.463
Difference from control[b]	0.029	-0.009	-0.048	-0.063
Number (n)	80	70	59	59
Sample Standard Deviation	0.474	0.326	0.409	0.761
Control Standard Deviation	0.392	0.343	0.408	0.662
Difference from control[c]	0.082*	-0.017	0.001	0.099
Number (n)	80	70	59	59
Operating Efficiency				
Sample Median Sales Growth	0.118	0.081	0.247	0.161
Difference from control[a]	0.03	-0.017	0.003	0.002
Number (n)	83	68	64	64
Sample Median Sales/Employee	98.2	111.7	118.2	110.5
($thousands)				
Difference from control[a]	-7.4	-2.4	-5.7	-3.9
Number (n)	76	74	51	51
Sample Median Cash Flow/Employee	7.2	7.7	8.2	7.8
($thousands)				
Difference from control[a]	-0.8	-0.1	-1.6	-0.8
Number (n)	73	70	50	50
Sample Median Gross Margin	0.303	0.294	0.322	0.297
Difference from control[a]	-0.005	-0.034	-0.003	-0.003
Number (n)	72	70	55	55
Sample Median Net Margin	0.042	0.045	0.044	0.045
Difference from control[a]	-0.001	-0.004	-0.009	-0.003
Number (n)	85	82	64	64
Sample Median Total Asset Turnover	1.100	1.100	1.175	1.132
Difference from control[a,b]	0.110**	0.075***	0.240**	0.059**
Number (n)	83	77	55	56
Sample Median (Working Capital/Sales)	0.196	0.177	0.140	0.175
Difference from control[a]	-0.053*	-0.039	-0.047***	-0.027
Number (n)	66	63	50	50
Risk				
Sample Median (Total Debt/Total Assets)	0.259	0.238	0.260	0.238
Difference from control[a,b]	0.027	0.009	0.039	0.048
Number (n)	83	80	62	62
Sample Median (Short-term Debt/Assets)	0.049	0.039	0.039	0.041
Difference from control[a]	0.008	0.001	0.013	0.000
Number (n)	82	81	63	62
Sample Median Cash Dividend Payout Ratio	0.267	0.258	0.188	0.28
Difference from Control[a]	-0.052	0.037	0.017	0.029
Number (n)	50	53	36	29

Significance level based on one-tailed Wilcoxon signed-rank test.
[b]Significance difference between sample and control means based on two-tailed paired sample t-test.
[c]Significance difference between sample and control standard deviations based on two-tailed F-test.
*$p < 0.10$
**$p < 0.05$
***$p < 0.01$

rather than reduced monitoring costs? Is it caution that causes founding family controlled firms to assume less debt or is it lack of access to financial markets? While it makes sense that the greater efficiency and less debt found in FFCFs would lead to greater value, the nature of the statistical analysis used here does not allow for causal inference. Results thus far suggest that further examination of the data would be useful.

Second, the differences in the management of FFCFs between founders and their descendents need to be more fully explored. Family control is not necessarily the same as found control. The nature of these differences raises several questions. Do both descendent controlled family firms have the same differences with non-founding family controlled firms found in this study? Are descendent controlled family firms managed more or less efficiently than founder controlled family firms? Do descendant firms carry more or less debt than founder firms? do founder controlled family firms or descendent controlled family firms have greater value in terms of market-to-book equity ratios and stock market returns? The findings presented here suggest that these are questions worthy of investigation.

References

Agrawal, A., and N.J. Nagarajan (1990). "Corporate Capital Structure, Agency Costs, and Ownership Control: The Case of All-Equity Firms," *Journal of Finance* 45 (4), 1325-1331.

Bellet, W., B. Dunn, R.K.Z. Heck, P. Parady, J. Powell, and N.B. Upton (1995). "Family Business as a Field of Study," found at http://nmq.com/fambiznc/cntprovs/orgs/cornell/articles/real/ifbpa.htm.

Bernstein, P.L. (1996). *Against the Gods: The Remarkable Story of Risk*. New York: John Wiley & Sons, Inc.

Carsrud, A.L. (1994). "Meanderings of a Resurrected Psychologist or, Lessons Learned in Creating a Family business Program," *Entrepreneurship: Theory and Practice* 19 (1), 39-48.

Cho, M.-H. (1998). "Ownership Structure, Investments, and the Corporate Value," *Journal of Financial Economics* 47, 103-121.

Daily, C.M., and M.J. Dollinger (1991). "Family Firms are Different," *Review of Business* 13 (1), 3-5.

DeAngelo, H., and L. DeAngelo (1985). "Managerial Ownership of Voting Rights: A Study of Public Corporations with Dual Classes of Common Stock," *Journal of Financial Economics* 14, 33-69.

Demsetz, H. (1983). "The Structure of Ownership and the Theory of the Firm," *Journal of Law and Economics* 26, 375-390.

Demsetz, H., and K. Lehn (1985). "The Structure of Corporate Ownership: Causes and Consequences," *Journal of Political Economy* 93 (6), 1155-1177.

Fama, E.F. (1980). "Agency Problems and the Theory of the Firm," *Journal of Political Economy* 88 (2), 288-307

Fama, E. F. (1980). "Agency Problems and the Theory of the Firm," *Journal of Political Economy* 88(2), 288-307.

Fama, E.F., and K.R. French (1992). "The Cross-Section of Expected Stock Returns," *Journal of Finance* 47 (2), 427-465.

_____(1996). "Multifactor Explanations of Asset Pricing Anomalies," *The Journal of Finance* 51 (1), 55-84

Fama, E.F., and M.C. Jensen (1983). "Separation of Ownership and Control," *Journal of Law and Economics* 26, 301-325.

_____(1985). "Organizational Forms and Investment Decisions," *Journal of Financial Economics* 14, 101-109.

Gibbs, PA. (1993). "Determinants of Corporate Restructuring: The Relative Importance of Corporate Governance, Takeover Threat, and Free Cash Flow," *Strategic Management Journal* 14, 51-68.

Gossman, S., and O. Hart (1986) . "Corporate Financial Structure and Managerial Incentives," in *The Economics of Information and Uncertainty*. Ed. J.J. McCall. Chicago, IL.: University of Chicago Press.

Hill, C. W.L., and S.A. Snell (1988). "External Control, corporate Strategy, and Firm Performance in Research-Intensive Industries," *Strategic Management Journal* 9(6), 577-590.

Hollenbeck, J.R., D. R. Ilgen, J.M. Phillips, and J. Hedlund (1994). "Decision Risk in Dynamic Two-Stage Contexts: Beyond the Status Quo," *Journal of Applied Psychology* 79(4), 592-598.

Jensen, M.C., and W.H. Meckling (1976). "Theory of the Firm: Managerial Behavior, Agency Costs, and Ownership Structure," *Journal of Financial Economics* 3, 305-360.

Jensen, M.C., and J.B. Warner (1988). "The Distribution of Power among Corporate Managers, Shareholders, and Directors," *Journal of Financial Economics* 20, 3-24

Johnson, W.B., R.P. Magee, N.J. Nagarajan, H.A. Newman, and G.W. Schwert (1985). "An Analysis of the Stock Price Reaction to Sudden Executive Deaths: Implications for the Managerial Labor Market," *Journal of Accounting and Economics* 7(1), 151-178.

Kaplan, S. (1989). "The Effects of Management Buyouts on Operating Performance and Value," *Journal of Financial Economics* 24(2), 217-254.

Kets de Vries, M.F.R. (1993). "The Dynamics of Family Controlled Firms: The Good and Bad News," *Organizational Dynamics* 21(3), 59-71.

Kole, S. (1997). "The Complexity of Compensation Contracts," *Journal of Financial Economics* 43, 79-104.

Leland, H.E., and K.B. Toft (1996). "Optimal Capital Structure, Endogenous Bankruptcy, and the Term Structure of Credit Spreads," *The Journal of Finance* 51(3), 987-1019.

March, J.G., and Z. Shapira (1987). "Managerial Perspectives on Risk and Risk-Taking," *Management Science* 33 (11), 1404-1418.

Masulis, R.W. (1988). "Corporate Investment and Dividend Decisions under Differential Personal Taxation," *Journal of Financial and Quantitative Analysis* 23(4), 369-385

May, D.O. (1995). "Do Managerial Motives Influence Firm Risk Reduction Strategy?" *Journal of Finance* 50(4), 1291-1308

McConaughy, D., M. Walker, G. Henderson, and C. Mishra (1998). "Founding Family Controlled Firms," *Review of Financial Economics* 7(1), 1-19.

McConaughy, D. (2000). "Family CEOs vs. Non-Family CEOs in the Family-Controlled Firm: An Examination of the Level and Sensitivity of Pay to Performance," *Family Business Review* 13(2), 121-131.

McConnell, J.J., and H. Servaes (1990). "Additional Evidence on Equity Ownership and Corporate Value," *Journal of Financial Economics* 27 (2), 595-612.

Mishra, C., and D. McConaughy (1999). "Founding Family Control and Capital Structure: The Risk of Loss of Control and Capital Structure: The Risk of Loss of Control and the Aversion to Debt," *Entrepreneurship Theory and Practice* 23 (4), 53-64.

Morck, R., A. Scheifer, and R.W. Vishny (1998). "Management Ownership and Market Valuation," *Journal of Financial Economics* 20(1), 293-315

Morris, D.M. (1989). "Family Businesses: High Candidates for Financial Distress," *Small Business Reports* 14(3), 43-45.

Muscarella, C., and M. Vetsuypens (1990). "Efficiency and Organizational Structure." *Journal of Finance* 45(5), 1389-1413.

Oswald, S.L., and J.S. Jahera (1991). "The Influence of Ownership on Performance: An Empirical Study," *Strategic Management Journal* 12(4), 321-326.

Phan, P.H., and C.W.L. Hill (1995). "Organizational Restructuring and Economic Performance in Leveraged Buyouts: An Ex Post Study," *Academy of Management Journal* 38(3), 704-739.

Rosenblatt, P.C., L. deMilk, R.M. Anderson, and P.A. Johnson (1985). *The Family in Business.* San Francisco, Calif.: Jossey-Bass.

Simon, H.A. (1993). "Strategy and Organizational Evolution," *Strategic Management Journal* 14, 131-142.

Slovin, M.B., and M.E. Sushka (1993). "Ownership Concentration, Corporate Control Activity, and Firm Value: Evidence from the Death of Inside Blockholders," *Journal of Finance* 48 (4), 1293-1321.

Smith, A. (1990). "The Effect of Leverage Buyouts," *Business Economics* 25(2), 19-25.

Snedecor, G.W., and W.G. Cochran (1989). *Statistical Methods*, eight edition. Ames, Iowa: Iowa State University Press.

Stevens, J. (1996). *Applied Multivariate Statistics for the Social Sciences*, third edition. New Jersey: Lawrence Erlbaum Associates.

Strultz, R.M. (1988). "Managerial Control of Voting Rights: Financing Policies and the Market for Corporate Control," *Journal of Financial Economics* 20, 25-54.

Tosi, H.L., J.P. Katz, and Gomez-Mejia (1997). "Disaggregating the Agency Contract: The Effects of Monitoring, Incentive Alignment, and Term in Office on Agent Decision-Making," *Academy of Management Journal* 40 (3), 584-602.

Van Horne, J.C. (1980). *Financial Management and Policy*, fifth edition. Englewood Cliffs, N.J.: Prentice-Hall.

Walsh, J.P., and J.K. Seward (1990). "On the Efficiency of Internal and External Corporate Control Mechanisms," *Academy of Management Review* 15(3), 421-458.

Directors of family business can encourage effective ownership by following this seasoned guidance.

Developing Effective Ownership in the Family-Controlled Business

By John L. Ward

Family businesses are by definition family-owned or controlled. Clearly, the family's goals as a group of owners must support the strategy of the business. To align the goals of owners with the strategy of the company, directors (including owners serving as directors) must understand family business patterns. They must also understand governance fundamentals, including their own role.

The family business is by definition family-owned or controlled. Therefore, the family's goals as a group of owners must support the business's strategy. Why is this so tough?

- First, unlike management, ownership has no standardized job description, required training, or special qualifications. Through purchase, inheritance, or gifting, family members become shareholders with all the rights and responsibilities of ownership, no matter what their training, experience, or qualifications.
- Second, shareholders, in most cases, are shareholders for their lifetime.
- Third, shareholders have the right to elect the board of directors and therefore influence the selection of management, the direction of the company, and even the company's continued existence.
- Fourth, and perhaps most significant to the future character of the family business, shareholders gift or sell stock to the next generation of owners, thereby shaping the future ownership group.

To align the goals of owners with the strategy of the company, directors (including owners serving as directors) must understand family business patterns and the forces shaping them. They must also understand governance fundamentals, including their own role. Finally, directors need to understand stewardship.

Family Business Ownership Patterns

Business families potentially move through six possible ownership patterns:
- entrepreneurship
- owner-managed
- family partnership
- sibling partnership
- cousins' collaboration
- family syndicate (see Figure 1).

It is important to realize that the six ownership configurations are not necessarily linear – not every family business goes through them or completes them. In fact, the family firm may skip phases or circle back into a phase because of family ownership decisions or actions. An owner-manager may transfer majority ownership to his or her children but personally continue to control the firm's business direction. This business remains in the family partnership phase until the parent's death.

Sometimes families will agree that the business should be owned by the family member who serves as CEO or only by the family members employed in the firm. In these cases, the business would continually recycle itself in the owner-managed phase or the sibling partnership phase.

Family ownership issues can also be mediated by family actions. Some families work hard to maintain the connection and identification of future generations with the business and its heritage. These families may never become disinterested owners even when they reach the family syndicate phase.

Factors Shaping Ownership Patterns

The interaction of life-cycle forces and family ownership decisions determine the family business's ownership configuration. The different ownership configurations have unique ownership groups and characteristics.

Life Cycle and Ownership Patterns

The family's movement through the individual and family life cycles directly influences the family ownership configurations. Life-cycle events such as birth, marriage, retirement, and death create the potential for changes in the ownership group. Examining the life cycle helps to identify its impact on the family business and demonstrates the need for ownership education programs.

The family needs to anticipate and plan for individual and family life-cycle transitions because they create changes in personal goals, financial situations, and investment objectives. Different lifecycle stages are associated with behaviors that directly impact the family business system. Life-cycle transitions often trigger events for changes in ownership. The founder's retirement or 65th birthday will often coincide with the transferring of stock to the next generation of family members.

Family Ownership Decisions and Ownership Patterns

Family decisions on ownership transfer can have significant ramifications for the future of the family business.

The following ownership structure scenarios demonstrate how different family decisions on the transfer of ownership to the next generation can affect a business. The first scenario is equal distribution to all heirs, the second scenario is distribution to males, and the third scenario is distribution only to family members employed by the firm.

Scenario One: Distribution of ownership to all family members. This example demonstrates ownership that is based on a family decision of equal family ownership across each generation. The founding couple divided their stock equally among their three children and this tradition has been followed by succeeding generations. By the fourth generation, this decision results in the single heir in Branch B controlling 33 percent of the company's stock. The remaining ownership is split among the other 13 members of the fourth generation based on the number of family members in their branch.

Scenario Two: Ownership based on a family tradition limiting ownership to male family members. This family decision creates an ownership structure that is based

Figure 1. Four Generation Genogram With Possible Ownership Configurations

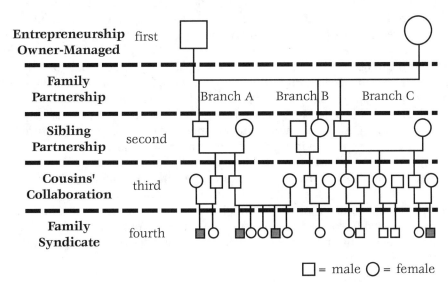

on a family agreement that allowed stock to be transferred only to male descendants of the founder. Using this model of ownership transfer, the son in Branch C (see the shaded squares) will control 50 percent of the stock after four generations. His three cousins in Branch A will control the remaining 50 percent.

Scenario Three: Distribution based on employment in the family business. The final ownership structure demonstrates the effect of an ownership agreement that is designed to maintain control with family members who are employed by the firm. The family's ownership agreement contains two stipulations.

First, ownership is based on employment and the corporation redeems all shares at the employee's retirement or death.

Second, each family employee is allocated shares annually based on their compensation using an ownership distribution formula.

Under this plan, senior family executives with long tenure own a larger share of the company's stock. This plan effectively redistributes the ownership to each new generation or branch of family employees and prevents a concentration of ownership. It also allows family members to join the family business and earn ownership even if their parents were not involved with the family business. Third generation family members could become significant owners even though their parents had no ownership in the business.

The three scenarios demonstrate that ownership patterns can vary dramatically, depending on the family's ownership decisions. There are no "right or wrong" outcomes, but each decision does result in different ownership characteristics and varying levels of commitment to family business ownership. If a family makes no effort to plan the relationship between the family's future vision and its ownership structure, then a new ownership pattern may undermine family continuity.

Family Ownership Forces

As the family matures and the ownership group changes, three ownership forces affect the characteristics of the ownership group. These three forces create changes in the characteristics of the ownership group resulting in the different ownership challenges that family businesses face. They include:
- the participation of multiple generations of family members
- an expanded potential number of owners, and
- the separation of management and ownership roles.

An important theme in all family businesses is the participation of multiple generations of family members.

Multiple generations of family members. The involvement of two or more generations in owning and managing a business creates the potential for conflict.

First, sharing power is required and this means that the senior generation has to learn to accept a change in their business and family roles. At best this is difficult, because of the hierarchies of the family and business structure. How well power is shared and leadership is transferred creates a pattern that will be replayed in future generational transitions.

Second, there can be conflicts over personal or business priorities between the generations. As senior shareholders mature, they become more conservative and their personal motivations, financial goals, and tolerance for risk change. As they begin to plan for retirement, their goals become more focused on financial security. At the same time, the successor generation is concerned more about business growth and creating future wealth. The two generations have age appropriate risk/return criteria that may cause conflict over strategic choices and investment opportunities.

Expanded ownership group. As time passes, most families increase in size. A third- or fourth-generation business family can have a large and diverse group of shareholders. This larger shareholder group means a diffusion of ownership, often resulting in more shareholders with smaller ownership positions. Another important consideration is the separation of management and ownership, which deserves special emphasis in the family business.

Separation of Management and Ownership Roles

In their 1932 book on *The Modern Corporation and Private Property*, Adolf A. Berle, Jr., and Gardiner C. Means noted a new and troubling separation of ownership and management in large public companies. The famous Berle and Means commentary on this separation has influenced much of modern corporate governance theory and practice in public companies. However, separation of ownership and management is not an issue for public companies only; it is a core issue in the family-owned business as well.

As the ownership group expands, it becomes increasingly unlikely that a large percentage of the owners will work for the business. The diversity of individual interests and the business's requirements for professional management force many owners to find careers outside the family business. This separation of ownership and management roles fundamentally changes the firm's decision making. By necessity, decision making and management discussion have to become more formal as management – and ownership roles – separate.

The management-ownership separation also creates a split in owners' views on strategy or reinvestment decisions. A 40-year-old family executive and shareholder sees an investment in the company as positive for his or her own career and ownership interests. However, his or her cousins who are not employed by the family business might not be so pleased to learn of a new strategy that cuts dividends for the next two years to fund a long-term growth opportunity.

Multiple generations, growing numbers of family owners, and increased separation of management and ownership roles typically accompany the family's move through the life cycle. These forces shape the ownership issues and challenges facing the business and, therefore, the ownership programs that the business must eventually develop.

The characteristics of the family ownership group change in several key ways:
- the level of information-sharing changes
- the percent of family members employed in the business changes
- the family's level of business experience changes
- connections among family members change
- the relationship between family members and the business's founder changes
- the degree of wealth concentration changes, and
- the degree of ownership concentration changes.

For example, in early ownership configurations (owner-managed and family partnerships), all these issues are of low intensity because of the ownership characteristics. The relationships between management and ownership are strong and in many cases overlapping. Later in the life cycle they are less directly connected. And as the ownership characteristics change, the owners' need for ownership programs increases. The family must increasingly depend on proactive ownership programs to address issues such as the owners' potential lack of accurate information and defuse any conflict that might arise.

Each ownership configuration creates different challenges for the business family concerned about creating an effective ownership system. To meet these challenges, directors need to focus on four essential issues:
- ownership education
- ownership agreements
- estate plans, and
- overall governance design.

Understanding Ownership Fundamentals

If shareholders are prepared for ownership roles and responsibilities, it more likely that they will be willing and able to address the future challenges they will face. An owner, especially one who is not employed by the family firm, has two main challenges: understanding shareholder responsibilities and knowing the business.

No one doubts the importance and value of training and development activities to ensure qualified family managers and leaders. However, families typically do not pay similar attention to ownership education among members who are not as involved in the business. This is particularly unfortunate as the business grows, because the shareholders' role becomes a more powerful factor in the firm's long-term success.

The value of ownership education increases as the ownership moves toward the cousins' collaboration or family syndicate phases. Owners who take the time to participate in the training will not only gain insight into the nature of the business but will also find that it creates a relaxed, productive way to talk business with their parents and other senior family members. Senior family members also can use these sessions to develop an understanding the next generation's expectations.

Family members may have different definitions of what ownership in the company means. Here are some questions that they may want to discuss:
- What are the rights and responsibilities of family business owners?
- How does the family balance the capital demands of the business with the family's liquidity needs?
- How do they strengthen the family's role on the board?
- Is it time to identify a board strong outside directors?
- How do they improve the effectiveness and participation of the ownership group?
- Who should decide on the CEO's compensation and review his or her performance?

Shareholder Responsibilities

Understanding the responsibilities ownership – especially for those family members not employed in the business – is absolutely crucial to the family business board. Family owners concerned about improved family and business performance need to consider broad responsibilities:
- understanding the ownership role, and
- balancing individual interests the shared interests of the other business and family stakeholders.

Shareholders concerned about the consequences of their actions need to understand their responsibilities as they decisions or take actions regarding family business.

Understanding the ownership role.

Being a capable and informed shareholder requires study and preparation. The following questions provide a brief overview of what it means to be a capable shareholder:
- Do I consider the rights of other stakeholders?
- Do I have the *business knowledge*, information, and understanding to participate meaningfully in shareholder meetings and contribute to shareholder decision making?
- Do I understand my family *business's culture* and how to contribute to it?
- Do I appreciate the role of the board of directors?

Considering Other Stakeholders

Owners need to understand how their actions and demands will affect other stakeholders in the family business. Traditional business theory asserted that a business should be run for the benefit of the shareholders, with their interests placed above all others. That is changing. A concern for ethics and the realization that all interests are interrelated has led to a broader approach. A stakeholder is anyone who is affected by the business's actions – not just shareholders. Typically stakeholders include employees, customers, owners, suppliers, partners, banks, and the community at large.

Business Knowledge

Developing a working knowledge of the business can be especially challenging when one's career is not in business. Ownership education must be designed to inspire basic business thinking and an understanding of the family business and how it operates. It must be conducted in a way that encourages learning and participation, particularly from the most inexperienced owners.

Key topics include:
- family and business vision
- financial goals and family investment expectations

- business strengths and weaknesses
- external opportunities and threats
- industry and market trends, and
- current situation and performance.

Organizational Culture

All organizations, and particularly families and family firms, have deeply ingrained cultures that dictate the way things are done. The future owners owe it to themselves and the company to try to understand the culture of their family business – first to protect what is of value, and second to understand how to influence change.

Many next-generation owners, however, do not know the family business system and consequently fail to understand its unique culture. They eagerly propose new ideas, seeking to introduce changes that reflect their personal identity, training, or experience.

What these individuals must realize is that change in a family business is typically evolutionary, not revolutionary. This evolution should be a process of gradual movement based on agreed-upon core values. A new culture will result from new practices and behaviors built on the business' existing culture.

As the future owners observe and listen, they should keep in mind the following questions:
- How is the business different from others?
- What does the family add?
- What is unique about the history, values, or experience?

When the inquiry is finished, future owners should be able to define the culture of the business in a few paragraphs. To make sense of the business's culture, start by asking the following:
- Who makes what decisions?
- How much are the people and the company's history respected?
- What does the organization celebrate that is, innovations, loyalty, performance, risk taking, and so on)?
- What stories are told around the organization about the founder? About the family?
- What do the people who like to work at the business share in common?
- How are power and authority handled in the family and business?
- How does the organization structure hinder or support communication?
- Is the formal or informal organization more powerful?

Governance Responsibilities: The Role of the Board

Governance is a fundamental responsibility of effective ownership. In the family business context, governance takes on a double importance, requiring governance structures for both the business and family. As the family grows and ownership expands, there is an increased need for planning formal governance structures for both systems.

Family Business Governance

On the business side, senior managers and shareholders will recognize the need for a functioning board of directors when they feel that the business's size and complexity requires additional expertise. As the number of non-employed shareholders increases, the board must increasingly represent the interests of a growing group of owners.

Yet the next generation of owners have to educate themselves so that they can create an efficient governance structure for the board to follow. The well-governed family business is focused on the shared family and business vision, not bogged down in debates about operations or family issues. This topic deserves special emphasis.

Effective governance is the fundamental responsibility of ownership. Family business governance requires parallel family and business thinking to support the development of planning, decision-making, and problem-solving structures for both the family and business systems. Most businesses have a board of directors (or supervisory boards) that oversee management actions, allocate capital, and participate in the strategy process.

Family councils are the family's "board." They provide a governance structure to support consensus decisions, coordinate family actions, and provide leadership.

Sharing information and coordinated action between the family council and board of directors is often required because of the overlap in the family and business systems. These groups may simply offer counsel to each other, or, on difficult decisions, they may both be asked to participate in the decision-making process. Sharing decisions and plans related to family agreements, ownership transfers, management succession, and business strategy ensures that the family and business policies and plans are complementary. The family council and board of directors are forums for that sharing.

Board of Directors

A family concerned about creating an effective business governance structure needs to consider decisions about the board's purpose, key tasks, and structure.

Purposes and tasks. In any company, the board of directors must do the following: protect the company's assets, ensure that capable management is in place, and support strategies that create shareholder value. In a family business, the board also serves as a link between the family and senior management. That means the board may be involved in mediating ownership, investment, or career issues created by the overlap of business and family systems.

The board is elected by the shareholders and legally represents them in directing the corporation. The board of directors typically comprises top management, family members, and, in the best cases, experienced businesspeople from outside the company. Ideally, a board will have a majority of independent, outside directors and will elect its own chairperson. The critical tasks of the board include:
- monitoring the firm's performance and assessing the CEO
- providing support and counsel to the senior management team
- contributing to the strategic planning process
- providing mentoring to family employees on careers and family relationships
- acting as a link between the family shareholders and the management team, and w representing the needs of non-family stakeholders in the decision-making process.

In addition to its formal governance roles, the board can also support the family's relationship with the business. The board can play an invaluable role in management succession decisions and provide objective counsel about which candidate may have the skills and talents needed to manage the business in the future.

The board may also be structured as a training vehicle for future-generation owners and directors. The future leaders may hold non-voting slots on the board if the company chooses to structure its board that way. An effective board with outside members also demonstrates to the next generation the family's commitment to professionalism in ownership and management – and new ideas.

Family decisions on creating boards. Developing a functioning board, especially with outside directors, is a major task that must support the shared future vision. Therefore, the family should carefully discuss why they feel creating a board will add value to their family and business. This discussion will identify several issues that the family should consider:
- the board's role and decision-making authority
- the composition of the board (the mix of management, family, and outsiders)
- the selection process for members
- a method for evaluating individual members' performance, and
- how to compensate board members

A board, when well conceived and given clear authority and responsibility, is an invaluable tool. The opposite is also true. A board comprising family members designed to counteract a strong CEO's authoritarian rule only creates another venue for conflict and negative feelings. The board's role should be clearly identified and discussed by shareholders and the senior management team.

There may be a reluctance to authorize a board of directors with outside members or even younger members of the family. For this reason, some families choose to begin their governance activities with a board of advisors who provide a new level of objectivity but without the formal or legal structure of a board.

Family Council

Family governance structures typically evolve from informal family meetings. As the number of family members increases and the influence of the senior generation decreases, it becomes difficult to organize and conduct regular family meetings. The large number of family members may also reduce the effectiveness of the meeting process. At this time, the family should consider developing a representative family council to formalize the planning and decision-making actions that are on the family meeting agenda. The creation of a family council is a logical step to complement the business governance provided by the board of directors.

Purposes and tasks. Typically, the transition to a family council represents a need for a more professional approach to addressing and resolving family issues. The family meeting often continues but on a less frequent schedule, typically annually or semi-annually, focusing on educational, social, and informational activities.

A multi-generational family business or one with a large number of members may also benefit from the representational approach that opens up participation to more of the family. Younger family members, those who are not employed by the business, or those not currently shareholders, may find that a representative family council is more open to hearing their ideas and addressing their concerns. The nomination or election of family council members also creates leadership opportunities for a more diverse group of family members.

The family council's purposes can vary by family needs but typically addresses family planning, decision making, and resolving problems or conflicts. Specific projects often include: developing family education, revising family and ownership agreements, resolving family conflicts, and enforcing the family's code of conduct. Examples of ongoing family council tasks include the following list of responsibilities:

- leading the development of family plans
- reviewing business strategy
- transmitting family values and the family vision
- offering a family forum for sharing ideas
- encouraging family participation and commitment
- supporting the family's ownership education programs
- developing family leaders from the next generation
- monitoring family and business interactions, and
- implementing family plans and programs.

Families that plan on using a family council should consider the responsibilities of the council in relation to the family and the model of representation.

Family decisions on creating a family council. If the family council evolves from a tradition of family meetings, then the family will have accepted the idea of shared planning and decision making. Family members will have experienced the value of working together to create understandings about critical issues.

The transition to a family council will be supported because the family appreciates the need for the change and feels that the entire family will still have influence on critical decisions. The family's concern over the council's decision-making authority can be addressed by providing a ratification procedure at the annual family meeting.

A more difficult issue is deciding how to select a representative group to serve on the council. Historically, family meetings may have been organized by the senior generation that played a leadership role in conducting family meetings. Some families may want to ensure representation from different branches of the family or seek a balance between family members employed inside and outside the business. Other families will try to maintain a balance based on generations of the family. Some very successful families try to avoid constituent council make-up and instead seek the best candidates regardless of family branch or generation.

Stewardship as a Family Ownership Value

Stewardship, as an overriding theme in family values and vision statements, suggests that each generation will pass on a family business that is healthier and more valuable to future generations. Stewards recognize that they are making decisions for their children's children and therefore consider the long-term interests not only of the owners, but also all the firm's stakeholders.

Families can encourage stewardship by reviewing important actions based on future outcomes and consequences. Discussing what stewardship values mean to the family during family and business planning sessions, at family council and family meetings, and at board meetings creates awareness throughout the system.

Summary

Ownership education programs and board or family council meetings can be therapeutic for families caught up in the everyday stresses of managing and governing a business. These processes provide a structure and an objective framework for communication on sensitive topics, which builds family trust. Parallel planning concepts also encourage a type of communication that is more acceptable to businesspeople because the output is a strategic plan while integrating the family's aspirations and values.

Early in the planning process, family managers, owners, and the rest of the family may not be ready to share or hear constructive criticism. But even in conflict, a shared vision and focus is being created. Eventually, families will reach consensus faster based on the painful process of airing all their views. At that point, it is more likely that planning programs programs will reflect a shared future vision, rather than focus on differences in short-term goals.

It is important to develop agreements on a wide range of ownership and governance topics before ownership is transferred. These family procedures become the basis for effectively directing the actions of the family and its relationship with the business. The worst circumstance for any family business is a conflicted family or shareholder group.

Educated and well-informed owners are important to the planning process when management needs to make investments that require patient capital. The owners need a sound understanding of business and finance concepts, an appreciation of the responsibilities of management, boards, and shareholders, and an appreciation of the family business's culture. These areas of knowledge are important to becoming active and effective shareholders.

CHAPTER 5
TAXES:
TRANSFER, GIFT AND ESTATE

Like family dynamics or business strategy, planning for tax liabilities can determine a family business's multi-generational success. Tax structures, effective tax planning, and the impact of family relationships on tax planning (and vice versa) are all topics addressed in the chapter.

While taxes pose huge challenges to business survival across generations, these articles suggest two critical insights. First, while tax planning can be very complicated, techniques are available to reduce the burden and provide for payment. Second, but equally important, the goal of eliminating taxes is often at odds with effective family functioning. Reading the articles in this chapter reminds us of the importance of the effort to balance family and business goals.

For a business family, forms of estate planning include business continuity, personal financial security, equitable treatment of the next generation and tax savings. This article suggests means and processes by which a business family can successfully engage in estate planning. Succession hazards are pointed out so they may be avoided.

Estate Planning for the Family-Owned Business: It Is Not Really "Mission Impossible"

By Glenn R. Ayres

Estate planning, or perhaps more accurately for the family-owned business, ownership planning, is all too often shrouded in legal and tax mysteries and conducted exclusively in the confines of the professional's office. There is an almost tangible aura of confidentiality surrounding these efforts and a stifling seriousness associated with dealing with such emotionally-loaded topics as "money," "death," and "family."

Even if it does get "finished," the task may be seen as thoroughly distasteful and as a result the planning is often incomplete or frequently languishes for years without adequate review or update.

It does not have to be this way. However, the process of change has to be initiated by the business owner. Most lawyers, accountants, financial planners and trust officers have been taught to operate as experts, not as process consultants. The client presents a problem and they have one, two, or a dozen immediate solutions waiting on the shelf or in the word processor. The priority is to get the job done, bill the file and go on to safer, other work.

Financial experts struggle daily to keep abreast of an ever-evolving tax system; their markets are extremely competitive; and it is their perception that they get paid for results, not talk. Spending much time in the murky and emotional waters of death, money and family simply doesn't make good economic sense when they hear the client say over and over again, "keep it simple and get this done as quickly as possible."

The first order of business, then, is for you, the family business owner, to change the ground rules. The client is always in control of the relationship and if that control is exercised, most professional advisors will welcome an open and direct approach rather than one which is critical and guarded.

Begin with a review of your priorities before the first visit and then clearly establish those priorities with your consultant. Certainly tax planning is important, but viewed from a family business perspective, the following list might be a lot more productive:

1st Priority – Continuity of the Business
2nd Priority – Your Personal Financial Security
3rd Priority – Equitable Treatment of the Next Generation
4th Priority – Tax Savings

Continuity of the Business

Continuity of the business, seen both as a family and a business issue, deserves top billing. Viewed in this way, questions of management and ownership can be separated and the topic of succession planning broadened to deal with all aspects of what is good for the company. It is fair game in this contest to talk about selling the business, involving non-family employees, or even utilizing outside management resources. In short, by placing continuity of the business at the top of your priority list you have put this area back into the contest of business planning. This is an area you know well and one in which you have participated, if not directed, for years. Solid answers in this area will direct and focus the rest of the estate planning process.

Your Personal Financial Security

It is amazing how often this priority is left off the list entirely. Yet the best tax advice is utterly useless if it runs counter to your own needs and desires. The vast majority of estate plans, no matter how sophisticated, do not save a penny of taxes for the current generation so it is vitally important that you assess your own needs early on in the process. Consider this abbreviated list:

- What does your life style demand in the way of financial support?
- How large a reserve do you need to feel safe, comfortable and independent?
- When the business no longer occupies you on a full time basis, what will it cost to pursue the activities and interests you have?
- What is your personal risk tolerance? Can you step back and let someone else make the big business decisions, even if you are not at risk financially?
- Do you have responsibilities or financial commitments to others outside the business?

Equitable Treatment of the Next Generation

Note this does not say *equal* treatment. Your children are not fungible and you have never treated them "equally." Parents strive to treat their children as unique individuals, each with their own business, family and personal goals. Why all of a sudden must everything be divided down to the last penny and piece of silver?

Perhaps this problem of absolute equality stops more good planning from going forward than any other single factor. Most surprising to many parents is the realization, usually brought to time by their own children, that the children neither want nor expect absolute equality. "Of course Bill and Sue should ultimately get the business," voices a brother, "they've been working there all their lives and a good measure of our family's success has to be attributed to their involvement and commitment."

Even without the next generation's recognition of fairness as opposed to equality, the concept needs to be accepted if the first and second priorities are to be achieved in most planning situations. Almost invariably the business represents the most significant element in your balance sheet, and unless a sale, merger, or public offering is a part of the plan, it simply will not be possible to effectuate absolute equality in your estate plan and still serve the best interests of the business. And this is not to say that there are not a number of ways a healthy business can financially serve non-action family members. But the goal must not be equality at all costs.

Assuming the business is sufficiently sound to permit some financial participation by non-active family members, it is important not to saddle involved family members with the uncontrolled "arm chair quarterbacking" of a non-involved parent or sibling. Such second guessing can, with good planning, be turned into active and knowledgeable board participation, but passive policy making is touchy business at best. If attempted, it should be carefully structured, involve outside directors, and include some dear lines of responsibility in addition to a system of evaluation for both board members and management.

All of this protecting of the active family members is not just for the benefit of management. On the flip side, a gift of a minority interest that does not carry enough weight to influence management is not a great bonanza to non-active shareholders. Family or closely held company stock normally pays no dividends; there is no market for the stock: and it often represents an appreciating asset on a non-active child's balance sheet that will someday cause an estate tax problem with no off-setting financial gain.

If the financial benefits from the company are to be used to assist non-active family, consider structuring those benefits around passive assets, like land or equipment, or use the business to bolster your own non-business resources so that your future gifts will not impact on the management structure. Listed below are some ideas the financially healthy company might employ

1. *Net-Net Lease:* Assuming the real estate used by the company is owned outside the corporation, giving this property, subject to lease, to a spouse or non-active children creates a passive income stream for the owner while assuring the company that it will

have predictable costs it can rely upon. The "net-net" feature in such a lease merely places the burden for maintenance, insurance and taxes on the company rather than the non-active owners. (Equipment leasing is yet another variation on this theme.)

2. *Recapitalization:* While recent legislation has limited some of the tax benefits of capital reorganization, it is still a viable way to separate passive income (dividends) from corporate control (voting rights). This technique permits the splitting up of the corporate stock into blocks that typically carry with them corporate control (voting common stock) and blocks that have no vote, but rather carry an annual dividend stream (preferred stock). Used judiciously, this is one way for the current generation to replace some of their salaried income with dividend income while allowing day to day control to pass to the now active generation. Such dividend paying preferred stock can also be given to the next generation of non-participating family members, while at the same time allowing those active in the business a free hand in running its affairs. (In the partnership context, the use of a family partnership can serve much the same purpose.) As with all major planning devices, care must be taken to insure that the operational as well as the tax ramifications are well understood prior to implementation.

3. *Insurance:* This type of asset can be used by the business to retire the senior generation's stock or the policies can be owned directly or in trust by non-active children as a substitute for corporate assets.

4. *Corporate Benefit Packages:* Concepts like deferred compensation, profit sharing, pension plans and even bonus plans, can play an important role in building non-business assets for the use of a surviving spouse or non-active children pursuing other career options.

   Used most creatively this type of asset serves as a substitute for a stock buy-out between generations by using business dollars generated by son's management efforts to build a fund for mom and dad. Done in this manner, the stock can now be gifted to the active son rather than sold; dad and mom have replaced an illiquid asset with a highly liquid one, and a pool of divisible funds has been created for use in planning for the children not involved in the business.

5. *Consulting Agreements:* These contracts permit the senior generation or other children involved in related enterprises, to tap into corporate compensation in a programmed and complimentary manner that takes into account their individual skills while at the same time not being an intrusion on management.

Tax Savings

Taxes should be one of the tests of whether the plan is, or is not, workable. However, they must not be the focus of the planning. In many respects, estate taxes are equivalent to the cost of the project. Like any cost factor, if the price is too high, another alternative will be chosen. The only real distinction here is that "not buying" should not be considered an option.

This part of the analysis should be left to the expertise of your lawyer or accountant. First decide what is in the family's best interest, and then look at the tax cost of the project. If the cost is too high, a framework will then exist for you and your advisor to discuss alternative techniques. The objective is to lower the cost without doing serious damage to how you want your affairs and the affairs of your business ordered.

Through this process you will gradually work down from an ideal plan that is too expensive to a compromise plan. It will be an affordable plan that still carries out your essential wishes. Keep in mind that the most tax effective plan is really not very cost effective if it results in a ruined business, an impoverished spouse, or conflict between the brothers and sisters.

Having settled on your new list of priorities, one other new ground rule needs discussing: Confidentiality. There is probably nothing as private in our legal traditions as the preparation of a will. This is neither incorrect nor inappropriate in many situations, but for the family business owner the maintenance of strict confidentiality that excludes the family makes the job a whole lot tougher. Consider:

- The impact the business is having and has had on your entire family.
- Whether it is to go to all the children or none of them.
- Whether your spouse will succeed you or sell out.

The disposition of a family-owned business affects everyone in the family. Your daughter may fear working for her mother who has not been involved in the business, or your son maybe looking for other options if he doesn't get some signal from you soon. The family owned business is truly more than a business; it has been part of your lives together and even the most passive of children need to be heard on this issue. Equally important, you need to know their thinking if business continuity and family harmony are to be achieved through your decisions.

Business owners say, "But, I can't discuss this topic at home, it would be World War III!" But if you do not exercise the leadership to solicit views and facilitate some collective understanding of these issues as only a parent can do, it will just as surely be World War III after you are gone.

No one is suggesting that estate planning discussions are easy, particularly if the family does not manage their differences well already, but any old probate hand will tell you that fights which erupt during the probate more often than not will leave permanent scars. Opening these discussions to your entire family may, in the final analysis, be the most important legacy of all.

If you choose to involve your family in the estate planning process, help is available. Your lawyer, accountant, financial planner or trust officer will be pleased to participate in a planning process that has clear priorities and an openness initiated by you. Such an advisor may be able to solicit more candid responses from your family than even you can and he or she can set the tone for the process by making it clear that this is your planning. The participation of your children is to be encouraged and welcomed, but the ultimate decisions must remain your own. As a third party, the advisor can also often facilitate discussions that would not be productive or even possible for a family member. And, of course, the advisor has the technical skill to help you translate your business and family decisions into an effective estate plan and explain the operation of that plan to your family and management team.

Such a process can take any number of forms, but here is one suggested format:

1. Hold an initial meeting with your advisor where your priorities are laid out, your tentative business decisions communicated, and your family concerns expressed.
2. Schedule interviews between your advisor and the next generation (and perhaps selected non-family employees) to solicit their views, goals and concerns.
3. Hold a family planning meeting chaired by you and facilitated by your advisor where the concerns and objectives of the family are reviewed in a non-personal way and where the advisor presents the outline of an estate plan designed to address these issues.
4. Have the advisor prepare the documents necessary to memorialize this plan. Schedule a review and approval meeting for the two of you.
5. Convene a family signature conference where the instruments are executed with your family present. Have the advisor explain their operation and impact on the business and individual family members.

Yes, it costs more up-front to do it this way, and yes, it may at first be more than a little intimidating to all concerned. But carried through to completion in an open and respectful manner this kind of planning will produce an estate plan that addresses your priorities and has the support of the entire family, whether they are involved in the family owned business or not.

Certainly Uncle Sam will change the rules on us again, children will change their minds, and you may even decide to move to Phoenix. But updating your estate planning will never be as difficult or as mysterious as it once appeared and it certainly won't be viewed as "Mission Impossible."

Family-Owned Business Succession Hazards

Owners of family-owned businesses, like everyone else, find it difficult to openly confront the emotionally sensitive topics of death and money. Estate and succession planning can only be done if both subjects are discussed in detail Avoidance easily sets in.

Avoidance is also fostered by complexity. Family business owners are surrounded by complexity. Protection of self and spouse, distribution to offspring, and tax considerations are essential concerns, but only if the business continues to exist. The priorities of continuity, protection, distribution and taxes are often in conflict with each other. Avoidance can be a line of least resistance when trying to sort out the confusion.

Avoidance results in failure to take action, secrecy, poor communication and incompleteness. The result can be a harsh and undesired emotional and economic legacy for future generations. The cost of avoidance is high.

Use the following list of "Succession Hazards" to check out your avoidance of estate planning.

1. "Doing nothing at all." An unprepared family in the midst of grief has to deal with the task of taking over business operations and sorting out the legal hassles.
2. "Behind closed doors." Secret discussions with legal advisors mean surprises for the survivors at a time when emotions are already spent and surprises are not easily managed.
3. "Equality at all costs." Confusing expressions of love and affection with the distribution of assets may burden the business and leave wounded feelings.
4. "It's no one's business." Neglecting to take into account the impact of decisions on the lives of the next generation and overlooking the possibility of communicating about needs and wishes can leave loved ones feeling discounted and unimportant.
5. "Our family has always done it this way." Tradition may mean issues of competence, interest and suitability are overlooked, hurting the business and thereby neglecting talent and interest within the family.
6. "No one else can do it right." Difficulty in valuing differences and in recognizing the contributions of others can rob the business of potential growth and creativity and can prevent appreciation and validation from being felt among family members.

Buy-Sell agreements are contracts among shareholders specifying rights and actions under various circumstances. Such agreements are crucial to family businesses with more than one shareholder. The following article explains how they work.

Understanding Buy-Sell Agreements

By David K. Carlson

Transitions in family businesses can be difficult, threatening destructive conflicts. Death, retirement, voluntary or involuntary separation from the business, divorce, or just the desire to sell one's shares in the business can cause stress in the family and in the firm. The business can suffer because its principals' attention and energies are diverted or because of unexpected demands for funds.

As with many difficult family business circumstances, their possibility can be anticipated and planned for. Potential for conflict is reduced if the parties agree in advance about how situations will be handled. That is what buy-sell agreements are all about.

A buy-sell agreement is a contract specifying certain ownership rights among the owners of corporate stock or a partnership interest. In general, it focuses on shareholders' rights to transfer stock in the business to other people, what circumstances activate those rights, and how such transfers might be accomplished.

Most buy-sell agreements restrict who may be an owner of the business. In family businesses, it is often understood that only lineal family members (or possibly spouses) can be shareholders. Buy-sell agreements formalize such understandings with a contractual agreement not to sell or give any shares to anyone outside of an identified group without prior approval of the other family shareholders. Most buy-sell agreements permit share transfers only to a spouse, child, grandchild, or trusts established for them, or to the company itself. Those receiving shares are also bound by the agreement.

Some buy-sell agreements are mandatory. They *obligate* shareholders (or their estates) to sell shares in a family business upon the occurrence of a triggering event. Identified buyers are *required* to purchase upon that event. Triggering events may include death, disability, retirement, reaching a certain age, or even a divorce. For example, an agreement could require that upon death or retirement, either the shareholders or the corporation must purchase a shareholder's stock in the business – no ifs, ands or buts.

Voluntary buy-sell agreements *do not require* a shareholder, or his estate, to sell shares because of a triggering event. Shares in the family business can be retained, sold, willed or gifted within the class permitted in the agreement.

Separation from the company, either voluntarily or through retirement, is particularly important as a specified triggering event. Use of this triggering event can limit the ownership to individuals actively employed by the business. This feature is very common where shares of stock are either given or sold to non-family employees. Such buy-sell agreements work both to maintain family control and to reduce potential conflicts between active and non-active owners.

Buy-sell agreements also provide a method for pricing shares sold. Too often, federal estate tax considerations rather than fairness to all parties, drive the establishment of a pricing mechanism.

The IRS can throw out unreasonably low buy-sell established prices, but that same price can be binding to the estate of a shareholder. The result: less money to pay higher estate taxes.

Generally, a buy-sell agreement either puts forth a formula price felt to be indicative of a company's appropriate value, or directs that one or more outside appraisals be obtained when a triggering event occurs. Common formulas for purchase prices include: book value, book value adjusted to the fair market value of certain assets and liabilities, a multiple of earnings, a multiple of weighted earnings over a period of time, or a combination of book value and a multiple of weighted earnings.

The appropriateness of any of these formulas is determined by the nature of the business. For example, book value of a pure service business may be totally inappropriate – while the fixed assets of the business are relatively small substantial net income may be generated. Where a formula purchase price is to be used, it is always advisable to consult with an appraisal firm or valuation expert to assist in the development of a formula that will be truly reflective of your business' continuing value.

Having a mechanism to determine price may not be valuable if the terms and means of payment are not specified. Where retirement is a triggering event, or life insurance is unlikely to cover the full purchase price payable upon a shareholder's death, the agreement should allow the purchaser to pay in installments over time at a fair interest rate. With a death-triggered purchase, the initial payment should be equal to any life insurance used to fund the agreement.

The agreement should tell what to do if more than one shareholder experiences a triggering event. For example, if two shareholders (or more) die within a payout period, the agreement should indicate how available funds should be split among those entitled to payouts.

Finally, a buy-sell agreement should identify buyers of shares. A *redemptive buy-sell* obligates the business itself to redeem shares. In this case, the business would obtain any life insurance used to fund purchase obligations. A *cross-purchase buy-sell* obligates remaining stockholders. Each shareholder would, if possible, obtain life insurance on the remaining shareholders and bear a proportionate obligation to buy the shares of any retired or deceased shareholder. Generally, cross-purchases cease to be practical if there are more than three or four shareholders within the group, or if any are uninsurable.

Buy-sell agreements are as important to businesses with more than one shareholder as wills are to individuals. They provide solutions to potential conflicts before the conflicts arise and thus, save tremendous time, pain and expense. Moreover, well constructed buy-sells can protect both individual shareholders and the business by providing a way to achieve liquidity while keeping demands for funds manageable.

Don't wait for conflicts to make reaching a buy-sell agreement impossible. If you don't have one, call your business advisor now and develop a shareholders' contract supporting your family business goals.

Reprinted with permission from *The Family Business Advisor*, February 1992. Copyright 1992, Family Enterprise Publishers.

The Tax Code is enormously complex, due in no small part to the provisions that deal with related-party translations. Anyone providing tax consulting services to a family business must be extremely well-versed in the family attribution and aggregation rules (which appear throughout the Code) and the related-party transaction rules, which prevent perceived abuses that a family acting as a unit might be able to accomplish. This article will explore what every tax adviser to family businesses ought to know before structuring any transaction involving family members, or family members and the business.

Planning Around the Problems of Transactions Involving Family Members

By Gary A. Zwick

Controlled Groups

Family attribution can have a big impact in the area of controlled groups. A controlled group is defined in Sec. 1563(a) to include, but is not limited to, corporations that are commonly owned as brother-sister entities. In a brother-sister group of corporations, five or fewer individuals own at least 80% of the value of the outstanding stock and there is more than 50% common ownership between the two companies. If corporations are deemed to be members of a brother-sister controlled group, they will be aggregated for purposes of making use of the lower tax brackets on income below $100,000, and they will be tested as one corporation for purposes of rules relating to whether the uniform capitalization rules of Sec. 263A must be met[1] and as one entity for purposes of determining whether qualified plans meet coverage and provision of benefits tests. (There are other consequences to being a member of a controlled group but these are the most commonly confronted.)

In determining whether there is common ownership between corporations, certain family members are treated as one individual. Sec. 1563(e) sets out the attribution rules in this context. Generally, husbands and wives who work in the same business are treated as one individual for purposes of testing their ownership. However, if the husband owns one business and works separately in his business, and a spouse owns the other business and works separately in her business, there is no common ownership of the two corporations relative to the couple's interests. Each must also not be an officer or director of the other's corporation.

In addition, children and grandchildren are aggregated with parents and grandparents under two sets of rules. If the lineal descendant is under the age of 21, his stock ownership is attributed to the parent or grandparent in all circumstances. If the lineal descendant is age 21 or older, the parent or grandparent will be deemed to own that descendant's stock only if the older generation himself also owns, directly or indirectly, more than 50% of the same corporation. There can be no double attribution in the family area and, therefore, stock attributed to one spouse as a result of this latter rule is not also attributed to another spouse who either is or is not working in the business

Example 1: Father, *F*, owns 100% of corporation *X*. Corporation *Y* is owned 50% by *F* and 50% his daughter, *D*.

Scenario 1: *D* is 18 years old. *X* and *Y* are members of a controlled group.

Scenario 2: *D* is 25 years old. In this case, *X* and *Y* are not members of a controlled group.

Scenario 3: Same as Scenario 1, except 100% of *X*'s stock is owned by a trust for the benefit of *P*. *X* and *Y* are members of a controlled group.

Scenario 4: *X* is owned 100% by *F*'s spouse, who is not at all involved with *Y*. *F* is also not involved with *X*. There is no controlled group in this case.

Scenario 5: *X* is owned 79% by *F* and 21% by *F*'s brother. There is no controlled group in this case.

Qualified Retirement Plans

A qualified plan is one of the last remaining tax shelters available to small business owners. There are very few other vehicles that provide an immediate tax deduction on funding, deferred income to the recipient and tax-deferred build-up of the assets in the fund. In exchange for these benefits, the Code mandates that these plans not discriminate excessively in favor of highly compensated individuals, including substantial owners of the business.

One of the rules designed to help prevent this discrimination treats husbands, wives and lineal descendants under the age of 19 who work in the business as if they are one person for purposes of certain limits on contributions and benefits in qualified plans.[2]

> *Example 2*: *H* and *W* are two unrelated individuals working in the same business. Each makes $200,000 per year in compensation. *X Co.* has a profit-sharing plan to which it contributes 15% of their pay. For the calendar year 1991, *X* contributes 15% of *H*'s pay, or $30,000, to the plan. A similar amount is contributed on behalf of *W*. Together they have received a contribution of $60,000 to the plan. In 1992, *H* and *W* get married. Again, each earns $200,000 in compensation. However, because they are husband and wife they must be treated as one person for purposes of the limitation on compensation that may be taken into account in a plan. Therefore, *H* and *W* are deemed to have earned $114,430 each (a pro rata portion of the $288,860 compensation limit for 1992), and each receives only a $17,165 contribution to the plan for 1992. Thus, getting married has cost *H* and *W* over $25,000, as a family, in profit-sharing contributions every year.

Interestingly, the Sec. 415 limits that prohibit one individual from receiving more than a $30,000 contribution to a defined contribution plan do not require the same family aggregation. Thus, the total maximum contribution to a defined contribution plan (which is the lesser of 25% of pay, or $30,000) would allow a husband and wife in a best case scenario to receive a total contribution of $57,215 in 1992.

In situations in which a husband and wife can control their relative compensation, a qualified plan contribution on a family basis can be maximized by monitoring each spouse's compensation. If the company has a 25% money purchase pension, no additional contribution is available to either spouse after their compensation exceeds $120,000. Thus, if a couple's total compensation is less than $228,860 (in 1992), capping compensation at $120,000 for one spouse produces the largest contribution. For 15% profit-sharing plans, the cap is $200,000.

> *Example 3*: *X Co.* has a 25% money purchase pension plan. If *H* has $120,000 of wages and *W* has $60,000 in wages, the plan contributions will be $30,000 and $15,000, respectively, for a combined $45,000 contribution. If, instead, *H* is paid $150,000 and *W* is paid $30,000, the contributions will be only $30,000 and $7,500 for a total of $37,500 on the same overall compensation of $180,000. Thus, by controlling relative wages, the family's plan contribution can be increased on the same total family compensation.

Caution: Maximizing plan contributions may increase overall payroll taxes. In addition, the reasonableness of each spouse's compensation relative to his or her contribution to the company may limit flexibility. Careful planning is required.

Sec. 401(k) plans have a similar rule with regard to aggregating family members. However, with respect to the Sec. 401(k) feature, the effect of the rule is to cut back the amount that may be deferred from a family business owner's compensation as a percentage of the deferral for the nonhighly compensated.

> *Example 4:* X Co. has four employees. Employee *A* is the owner of the business, employees *B*, *C* and *D* are unrelated and are not highly compensated. *X* has a Sec. 401(k) plan and *B*, *C* and *D* on average elect to defer 2% of their compensation. The Sec. 401(k) rules will permit *A* to put as much as 4% of his pay, up to a maximum of $8,728 (in 1992), into the Sec. 401(k) plan.
>
> If, instead, *B* is the son of *A* (regardless of age for Sec. 401(k) plan purposes) *A* and *B* together are treated as one person. Therefore, although *B* is not by himself a highly compensated individual, he is considered a highly compensated employee by virtue of his relationship to his father. Also, *A* and *B* are treated as one person for purposes of determining how much they may contribute to the Sec. 401(k) plan. Thus, if *C* and *D* elect to defer an average of 1% of their compensation to the plan, *A* and *B* together may only defer 2% of their combined pay into the Sec. 401(k) plan. This results in a cutback for both *A* and *B*.[3]

For purposes of the Sec. 401(k) rules, family members include the employee, his spouse, lineal ascendants or lineal descendants, and the spouses of such lineal ascendants or descendants.[4] Under rules contained in proposed regulations before Aug. 8, 1991 (the adoption date of the final Sec. 401(k) regulations), family members were tested both separately and in the aggregate to see which resulted in the lower overall deferral. Mercifully, the final regulations have simplified this test.

Installment Sales

There are situations in which an intrafamily sale, particularly on the installment method, can have both estate planning and income tax planning benefits. While these transactions can be accomplished, there are special rules that affect the use of the installment method when the buyer and seller are members of the same family, commonly controlled entities or include individuals and their controlled entities. In addition, special rules have an impact on the use of the installment method when a transaction is between individuals and a controlled entity and the sale is of depreciable property.

Sec. 453(e) prescribes rules for installment sales between family members in order to avoid abuses. This section was amended in response to the landmark *Rushing*[5] decision, in which a husband and wife made an installment sale of corporate stock to a trust for the benefit of their children. Very soon after the installment sale was accomplished, the trust received proceeds from the sale of the corporation's assets in liquidation of the corporation. The assets were sold to an unrelated third party. Thus, while the trust was able to hold and invest the entire cash proceeds, the parents were able to defer the gain on the sale through the use of the installment method.

The rules of Sec. 453(e) provide that when an individual uses the installment method and sells any property to a related party, and that related party disposes of the property while there are unpaid installments, the gain on the sale to the original seller may be accelerated. For this purpose, related parties include the spouse, child, grandchild, parent, grandparent, brother, sister, controlled corporations and partnerships. In addition, a grantor-fiduciary relationship and a fiduciary-beneficiary relationship for trusts qualify as relationships for these rules.[6]

If the property sold by the original seller is a marketable security that is traded on an established securities market, the installment method is not available in any event.[7] If the property sold by the original seller is not a marketable security, the related party must wait at least two years before reselling to an unrelated third party. If the two-year rule is met, there will be no acceleration of the installment payments to the original seller. If the sale to the unrelated third party is within two years of the original sale, the original seller will accelerate gain to the extent a related party receives proceeds on the sale to the third party.[8]

For purposes of this rule, installment reporting is required to be accelerated if the property is sold or otherwise disposed of in a taxable transaction. If, however, it established that neither disposition had as one of its principal purposes the avoidance of Federal income taxes, such as the disposition being a like-kind exchange or tax-free contribution of property to a corporation or partnership under Sec. 351 or 721, no acceleration is required.

Although these related-party transaction rules were designed to prevent family units from taking advantage of the Code to accomplish deferrals when none existed, there arc significant loopholes that present planning opportunities. The most obvious one is the two-year rule, which is easily planned around. An individual with a significant and appreciating piece of property may sell that property to a related family member on the installment method and defer gain while freezing the value in his estate and still allow that family member to wait two years and resell the property for cash, taking advantage of rules similar to those in the *Rushing* case.

In the case of an installment sale of depreciable property, Sec. 453(g) provides an even harsher rule than previously discussed. It disallows entirely the use of the installment method on sales of such property to related parties. Although the result is harsh, mercifully it defines related parties in a much narrower way than does the general related party rule. Related parties for purposes of the depreciable property installment sale rule are limited to individuals and corporations or partnerships in which they own more than 50%, an individual and any trust in which he and his spouse are more than remote contingent beneficiaries, and two or more partnerships in which the same persons own, directly or indirectly, more than 50% of the capital or profits interests.[9]

Read together with the general rule of Sec. 453(i) (which prohibits the use of the installment method on the portion of gain attributable to depreciation recapture), this means that family members and related parties must be careful when structuring installment sales to be sure that they do not fall into any traps.

> *Example 5:* B owns a building worth $500,000. The original cost was $200,000, and depreciation taken to date is $100,000. Of the total gain of $400,000, all $100,000 of the depreciation taken is subject to recapture under Sec. 1250. B sells the property to his son or a trust for the benefit of his son, on the installment method, calling for annual payments of $100,000 for five years, plus interest. B may not recognize the recapture income on the installment method. It is all recognized as income in year 1. The rest other than interest on the note, is capital gain and return of basis recognized on the installment method. If, in year 2, B's son sells the property to a third party, B will recognize income as if the cash received by his son were received directly by him if greater than the amount he actually received. Thus, if B's son received $550,000 in year 2 on the sale, B would accelerate all of his gain and recognize it all in year 2, even though his son continues to pay him in annual installments. Had B sold the property to a corporation in which he owned more than 50% of the stock, no installment reporting would be allowed because the building is depreciable property.

Recent case law also has had an impact on thc tax treatment of installment sales between family members when the installment note is self-canceling on the death of the seller. In *Frane*,[10] the Tax Court held that the notes were canceled within the meaning of Sec. 453B(f) on the death of the obligee and treated as if disposed of other than by sale or exchange. Thus, gain was recognized by the decedent to the extent the face amount of the obligation exceeded the decedent's basis. Despite this seemingly adverse decision, planning opportunities still exist for properly structured self-canceling installment notes.

Capital Gain Versus Ordinary Income

Although the maximum tax rate for ordinary income relative to long-term capital gain income is only about a 3% differential, there have been times when the difference was far greater. If certain legislative proposals are passed, that difference will become larger and more important in the future. In addition, if individuals have capital loss carryovers or other attributes such as disallowed investment interest expense, there may be a great deal of difference between whether a gain on a sale generates capital gain or ordinary income.

Under Sec. 1239(a), if a sale is between certain persons and a related entity, and if the sale is of depreciable property, the resulting gain on the sale will be treated u ordinary income. For this purpose, related parties include any person and an entity in which he or a member of his family owns more than 50%, and a person and any trust in which such person or his spouse have more than a remote beneficial interest. For the rules related to controlled entities, family includes a spouse, brothers and sisters, ancestors and lineal descendants. Thus, if a father sells a depreciable asset to his son's wholly owned corporation, the entire gain will be ordinary income.

Remember that this rule affects only the sale of depreciable property and only produces a different result than under normal tax rules when the amount of gain exceeds what would ordinarily be depreciation recapture (which is already taxed as ordinary income). Again, the definition of a related party is relatively narrow and can, therefore, be planned around in most cases. However, a lack of planning can produce some unwanted surprises.

Loss Transactions

Sec. 267 prohibits the current use of a loss on a sale between related parties. When a transaction comes under Sec. 267, the selling party cannot recognize the loss on the transaction. It is suspended and potentially usable by the related-party purchaser when the property is ultimately disposed of to an unrelated third party.

These rules apply to the sales of all types of property. They treat the family as a single unit. Thus, a loss cannot be recognized on sales within the family unit because for this purpose it is treated essentially as if no sale had occurred. Only after the property leaves the family unit can the loss be used; and it may be used only by the family member who finally sells the property to an outsider and only to offset a gain on the sale.[11]

For purposes of this section, the definition of related party is extremely broad, encompassing family members who are spouses, ancestors, lineal descendants and siblings.[12] In addition, it includes related entities in which any individual owns, either alone or together with his family, more than 50% of that entity.[13] Other attribution rules too numerous to list are enumerated in Sec. 267 and may influence other situations beyond the scope of this article.

Therefore, any sale of property between such entities and those owners or the family of those owners cannot produce a recognized loss to the entity. Similarly, a sale from an individual to an entity that is related within these rules cannot generate a recognized loss to the individual. The interplay of the family attribution rules and the attribution rules between entities and individuals can produce surprising results.

> *Example 6:* H owns a parcel of land for which he paid $30,000. H's son owns a 51% interest in N, an S corporation. The other 49% is owned by unrelated third parties. If H sells the land to N for $20,000, he may not use the loss. If N later sells the land for $40,000, its recognized gain is only $10,000. If the sale is for $25,000, N will recognize no gain or loss on the transaction and the overall $5,000 loss is not allowed at all. However, if the land was owned by a corporation that is a member of a controlled group with N, and it sold the land to N for $25,000, the full $5,000 loss would be utilizable under a special rule in Sec. 267(f)(2) when the property is sold outside of the controlled group.

Accrued Expenses Between Related Parties

Rules similar to the loss disallowance rules affect family businesses whose books and records are kept on the accrual method of accounting. The accrual method generally requires an entity to recognize income when earned and deduct expenses when the amounts are incurred and not when they are actually received or paid. In many businesses, this is the only way to clearly reflect income. While this method usually requires income to be recognized earlier than it would be on a cash basis, it also allows certain expenses to be deducted before they might otherwise be on a cash basis.

During the 1970s and early 1980s, when tax and interest rates were high, many small businesses recognized that the ability to take a deduction in a business entity without having to immediately pick up the income by a shareholder-employee presented tremendous monetary savings. Officer and shareholder compensation, rental and other expenses paid to owners presented just such a deferral opportunity. A common technique was for a family business using the accrual method to use a fiscal year ending in October, November or December. The company could declare a bonus to a family member shareholder that was in recognition of services performed during a particular fiscal year but was not payable until 2 and 1/2 months after the corporation's year-end. The corporation was able to deduct the bonus in one year but the shareholder was not required to pick up the income on the bonus until paid, which would be in the next calendar year. Thus, while the deduction would benefit the corporation, the shareholder would not have to pay tax an the income until April 15 of the year following the year in which the bonus was declared.

In 1984, Congress moved to close this technique for many family-owned businesses. The rules of Sec. 267 now state that when an individual or his family owns more than 50% of a business entity, the entity may not deduct wages or other expenses accrued to that individual or a family member until the year in which they are paid. As mentioned above, individuals who are members of the same family are all treated as one individual for purposes of determining whether 50% of the company is owned by such person. For this purpose, family is defined to include a husband and wife, lineal descendants, lineal ascendants, brothers and sisters. This is the same definition used for loss sales between related persons or entities. However, persons owning any stock in an S corporation, any interest in a partnership, or more than 10% of a personal service corporation are also considered related to those entities for this purpose only.[14] Note that in-laws are not related for these purposes. Thus, a significant deferred planning opportunity exists when married family members can have their spouses own stock.

If a brother and sister own 50% each of a corporation that is on the accrual method, any salary declared for either may not be deducted by the corporation until the year in which that compensation is actually paid. However, if the brother's stock is owned by his wife, the salary may be accrued as long as it is paid within 2-1/2 months of the corporation's year-end.[15] Additionally, if, for example, an individual works for an S corporation in which his father owns even 1% of the stock, the corporation may not accrue salary to that person until it is paid.

Family businesses must be particularly aware of these rules and be sure that when a deduction for compensation or other payments such as rent is of critical importance, the amount is actually paid before the end of the fiscal year of any related business entity.

Compensating Family Members

There is no general requirement in the Code that an individual be compensated for services rendered. However, in family situations, Congress is concerned about the potential for shifting income among family members on an arbitrary basis. Thus, in certain family-owned businesses there may be a requirement to pay reasonable compensation when a family member provides services to the business. In the case of an S corporation, Sec. 1366(e) states that if one member of a family owns stock in an S corporation, services provided by a family member must be compensated for reasonably. For example, assume a father and son both own stock of an S corporation. The son is a minor who does not work in the business. If the father performs services for the business, he must receive reasonable compensation for those services. Thus, in a business in which service is the main source of income and the father's efforts are the sole means of earning an income, there will be little ability to shift income to the child owner under Sec. 1366. Similarly, when capital is furnished by one family member, reasonable compensation for the use of that capital must be provided to that individual.

In the partnership area, rules similar, but not identical to those in the S corporation area require that reasonable compensation be paid to family members working in the business or providing capital.[16] However, the definition of family members is exactly the same for both, it includes a spouse, ancestors, lineal descendants and any trust primarily for the benefit of such persons.

Taxation of Regular Corporations and Their Shareholders

Family attribution is particularly problematic in the area of taxation of shareholders and corporations. Sec. 318 includes attribution rules applicable to family members.[17] Whenever Sec. 318 applies, individuals who are spouses, parents, children and grandchildren are treated as one for some purposes. Note, however, that siblings are not treated as part of the family. In addition, for some purposes, a showing of family hostility may operate to negate these attribution rules. However, there is no dear sailing or safe harbor on this point.

The family attribution rules figure prominently when a shareholder removes money or other property from a C corporation with earnings and profits (E&P) and wishes to have that amount treated as other than a dividend, e.g., if a shareholder wants to redeem all or a portion of his shares and have that redemption be treated as a sale or exchange. Under Sec. 302(b)1, there are four situations in which money or other property may be distributed to a shareholder with respect to stock and have it be treated as a sale or exchange rather than as a dividend.

1. A distribution that is not essentially equivalent to a dividend.
2. A distribution that represents a substantial reduction in the shareholder's interest in the corporation.
3. A distribution that is a complete termination of the shareholder's interest in the corporation.
4. A distribution that represents a partial liquidation of the business of the corporation tested at the entity level.

Thus, in most cases, there must be a significant difference in the actual and constructive ownership of the stock the shareholder owns in the corporation before and after the redemption. Generally, the shareholder must reduce his share of ownership either significantly or completely for the transaction to be treated as a sale. In determining how much the individual owns in the corporation both before and after the transaction, the individual's direct and indirect percentages of ownership are taken into account. Indirect ownership is ownership through related entities and family members. Since an individual is deemed to own the shares owned directly by or for the benefit of lineal ascendants, descendants or a spouse, there may be situations when, after a redemption, an individual's percentage ownership of a corporation will not be reduced.

> *Example 7:* H and W are unmarried individuals who own 50 shares each of corporation X's 100 outstanding shares. If X redeems 25 of H's shares, H's ownership in X is reduced from 50% before the redemption to 33-1/3% after the redemption. Ownership has increased from 50% before the redemption to 66-2/3% after the redemption. This redemption qualifies as a sale or exchange.
>
> If H and W are married, each is deemed to own 100% of X. H owns 50% of X outright and 50% via family attribution under Sec. 318(a)(1)(A)(i). If H now redeems 25 shares, be is the owner after the transaction of 33-1/3% directly

and 66-2/3% of X via family attribution. H has not reduced his ownership of X. Thus, the transaction will be treated as a dividend and not as a sale or exchange.

As Example 7 illustrates, family attribution can prevent a transaction from qualifying for sale or exchange treatment in many situations. However, there are some situations in which family attribution may be waived: Under Sec. 302(b)(3), if an individual redeems 100% of his stock and would not qualify for sale or exchange treatment under any other subsection of Sec. 302(b) by virtue of family attribution, he may agree to waive family attribution. Under Sec. 302(c)(2), the redeeming shareholder must enter into an agreement with the IRS that is attached to his income tax return, which states that he will not have an interest in the corporation other than as a creditor for 10 years after the redemption takes place. In such a case, the family attribution rules are not applied to determine the indirect ownership of that shareholder in the corporation. This agreement is particularly useful when a family member wishes to transfer ownership of the business to the nest generation or when a surviving spouse who inherits stock wishes to cash out in favor of other family members.

At the present time, when ordinary income and capital gains rates are close to being the same, the distinction between dividend treatment and capital gain treatment in a lifetime redemption is important only if either the redeemed shareholder has a high basis in his stock or the redeemed shareholder has current or carryover capital losses. However, the distinction between capital gain and dividend income becomes extremely important when shares are redeemed on, or after, the death of a shareholder.

> *Example 8:* H dies owning 50% of Corporation X. At his death, the stock is worth $1,000,000 but had a cost basis to H during his lifetime of $1,000. X has $2,000,000 of E&P. There is a buy/sell agreement that requires the X stock to be redeemed on the death of either of the two shareholders for fair market value (FMV). On H's death, X pays his estate $1,000,000 in exchange for the stock. If the redemption of H's stock qualifies under Sec. 302(b) as it will if H is unrelated to the other shareholders of X, the redemption will be treated as a sale of the stock for $1,000,000, which produces no gain or loss to the estate by virtue of the step-up in the stock's basis to $1,000,000 under Sec. 1014.
>
> If, however, the redemption fails the rules of Sec. 302(b), it will be treated as a dividend. The estate will have $1,000,000 of dividend income unreduced by the basis of the stock and it will also have a capital loss on the disposition of the stock of $1,000,000. This loss can be used only to offset capital gain and up to $3,000 per year against other income.

As noted above, a complete redemption of a shareholder's stock will result in sale or exchange treatment when the redeemed shareholder is not attributed stock from another shareholder or when the attribution rules may be waived. Also as noted above, when the attribution is from other family members, it may be waived if certain conditions are met. However, in the case of redemptions at death, the stock is often being redeemed from an estate or a trust that has beneficiaries who are family members of the decedent. If those family members also own stock in their own right, a problem may arise that results in the same harsh dividend treatment outlined in Example 8.

> *Example 9:* Assume the same facts as in Example 8, except that when H died, owning 50% of X, the other 50% was owned by his son, S. S is a beneficiary of H's estate. The buy/sell agreement calls for the purchase of the stock from the estate on H's death. Before H's death, he owned 50% of the stock outright and the other 50% via family attribution. On his death, H's estate owns 50% of the stock outright and the other 50% via attribution under Sec. 318(a)(3)(a). This rule attributes stock from a beneficiary of an estate or trust to the entity. Thus, if the stock held by the estate is redeemed by X, the estate will be from own-

ing 100% actually and constructively before the transaction to 100% actually and constructively afterward. This is because 100% of the outstanding stock after the redemption will be owned by a beneficiary of the estate whose stock is attributed to the estate. Thus, if not properly planned for, the redemption will be dividend creating $1,000,000 of ordinary income and a $1,000,000 capital loss to the estate.

The "entity" attribution between the estate or trust and the family member beneficiary cannot be waived unless the entity and each related family member meet the rules prohibiting involvement with the corporation for a 10-year period.[18] Therefore, unless no family members have any involvement with the business, none of the exceptions of Sec. 302(b) apply. In Example 9, the easiest way for the estate to rid itself of the entity attribution is for the son to receive his entire distribution from the estate and, thus, cease to be a beneficiary before the actual redemption of the stock. Another way is to plan so that the buy/sell agreement does not compel the redemption at a time that entity attribution would apply. This would occur when the buy/sell agreement requires a cross-purchase in which the stock could be purchased by the son directly. Since the source of the funds is not the corporation directly, there would be no need to test for dividend treatment. Another way to plan would be to allow the corporation to redeem the stock from the beneficiaries. In that case, the stock would be distributed outright to the estate beneficiaries and then redeemed. Any stock distributed to a family member who does not otherwise own stock or work in the business could qualify for sale or exchange treatment on redemption by waiving family attribution. If that family member owns stock in his own right, however, a redemption of the inherited shares only may fail to qualify as a sale or exchange because of the general attribution rules.

The family attribution rules of corporate taxation are quite complex and provide many traps. There are many other areas that are beyond the scope of this article, such as transactions between entities owned by family members that might require testing for dividend treatment under Sec. 304. Practitioners must keep their eyes open for any potential situations, particularly those that seem too good to be true.

Antichurning Rules

In the past decade, depreciable lives of fixed assets have generally been reduced over those permitted before 1981. In addition, in many instances, the methods used for depreciating those assets have been accelerated relative to those prior depreciation methods. Although the modified accelerated cost recovery system (MACRS) method is often less liberal than the ACRS method used before 1987, there still may be some older assets whose depreciation deductions are so limited that a disposition of the property to a family member to take advantage of the new depreciable lives and methods might make economic sense. However, the rules of Sec. 168(f)(5) prohibit what is known as "churning" of property in order to get shorter depreciable lives.

> *Example 10*: A mother, *M*, owns an apartment complex acquired in 1980, which is being depreciated straight line over a 40-year life. If that property is disposed of to a third party in 1992, the purchaser would depreciate that property over 27-1/2 years. Instead, *M* might consider selling the property to her daughter, *D*, so that *D* could depreciate the property over a shorter life. However, the antichurning rules prevent *D* from using MACRS for this property since it was previously depreciated under an old straight-line method. *D* must use the same method that *M* used and, this, will be required to depreciate the property over a 40-year life using the straight-line method.

The antichurning rules apply when property is sold by an entity or an individual to a related entity or individual. Related individuals for this purpose include a spouse, ancestors, lineal descendants and siblings.

Also, if an entity is owned more than 10% by the purchaser or if the seller owed more than 10% of the purchaser, the antichurning rules will apply. While there seems to be very little to be gained these days by churning property in this fashion, the rules do exist and must be adhered to.

Chapter 14 Valuation Rules

Whenever gift or estate planning is being done in the context of a family business, the new valuation rules under Secs. 5701 to 2704 (which replace repealed Sec. 2036(c)) must be considered.

In enacting these rules in the Revenue Reconciliation Act of 1990, Congress was reacting to a proliferation of planning techniques that were designed to allow taxpayers to reduce or avoid estate or gift tax on assets they had acquired and transferred to younger generation family members without giving up control or income from the property during life. From the classic technique of preferred stock recapitalization, other innovative ideas soon followed, such as partnership freezes and split-interest purchases. All of these techniques used either IRS valuation tables or very subjective valuation techniques to accomplish what the IRS argued was a repeal of the Federal estate tax. While the IRS continued the attack on these techniques on a case-by-case basis and recorded some significant victories, taxpayers continued to win the war.

The new valuation rules are designed to take the valuation games and Internal Revenue tables out of the equation and to treat most transfers from one family member to a second-generation family member as if the property was given outright at its full FMV at the time of the transfer.

Thus, under the new rules, a parent may recapitalize stock of a corporation into preferred and common shares and transfer the common shares to a child as under prior law. However, unless the parent retains a regular cumulative dividend at a fixed rate, the parent will be treated as having transferred the full value of the stock as if it had not been split into common and preferred shares. If, at a later date, the preferred shares are transferred, credit will be given to the donor for the gift tax paid on that portion of the value. If the donor decides to retain a cumulative preferred FMV dividend, the IRS will allow the gift value for the common stock to be reduced by the value of the retained preferred shares. This is because the dividend will be paid or will be required to be included in the estate of the donor and the preferred stock will have real value on the grantor's death based on this required income stream.

For purposes of the rules for preferred stock recapitalizations and other entity freezes, family is defined under Sec. 2701(e)(1) generally to include
- the transferor's spouse;
- a lineal descendant of the transferor or the transferor's spouse; and
- the spouse of such lineal descendant.

Thus, an uncle may use a prior law preferred stock recapitalization or partnership freeze with respect to his nephew without causing these rules to apply. However, the same cannot be done with his son or his son's spouse.

Another technique covered by these rules is the transfer in trust. Prior to the new valuation rules, individuals could transfer income-producing property into a trust and retain an income interest for a period of years. If, for example, an income interest was retained for a 10-year period at which time the corpus would go to a family beneficiary, that income interest was valued at approximately 61% of the total corpus based on IRS tables and assuming a 10% interest rate. Thus, a family-business owner previously was able to transfer S stock into a grantor retained income trust (GRIT) and retain the income from the S stock for 10 years and make a gift valued at only 39% of the stock's value. If the donor lived longer than the term of years, the property was removed from his estate. If the grantor did not outlive that 10-year period, the value of the property would be brought back into the grantor's estate.

Those rules proved to be extremely favorable to individuals wanting to make gifts of property and transfer significant appreciation to a younger generation, particularly when little or no income was being generated by the property. Congress decided, therefore, that this "loophole" should be closed unless the donor was willing to retain an income interest that is stated in terms of either an annuity or a unitrust interest at current interest rates. Thus, the donor is required to receive annual distributions of a significant amount in exchange for a reduced gift tax value for the property. Again, the Government will allow a lower gift value because of the real value of the retained interest. The annuity or unitrust interest guarantees that the donor retains real value. For purposes of these rules, family is defined more broadly than for the freeze techniques. In this case, family is defined under Sec. 2702(e) to include

- the transferor's spouse;
- any ancestor or lineal descendant of such individual or such individual's spouse;
- any brother or sister of the individual, and
- any spouse of any individual included in the second and third descriptions.

The new Chapter 14 valuation rules also have an impact on buy/sell agreements between family members and other similar option-type arrangements. Under prior law, a buy/sell agreement that set a price that was fair at the time the agreement was entered into, was binding on the shareholder during his lifetime and at death, and was a bona fide business arrangement met the test for fixing value for estate tax purposes. Thus, a parent wishing to transfer ownership of a business to a child without incurring a large estate or gift tax could enter into a buy/sell agreement with a formula valuation based in whole, or in part, on book value and mitigate the effect of the corporation's appreciation on the estate. The Service attacked these arrangements extensively but had mixed success. The new rules require that a buy/sell agreement state a buyout price that is FMV at the time of the buyout. The new rules do not preclude the use of a formula in the buy/sell agreement. However, any formula that is heavily dependent on book value will be suspect. Agreements that will pass muster include those which provide for regular appraisals or a buyout at the appraised FMV to be determined at the time of the triggering event or some formula that would presumably meet the requirements of Rev. Rule. 59-60,[19] the bible of valuation rules for closely held businesses.

While the above rules are highly complex, they do allow for some planning in the transfer of a family business from one generation to the next. An outright gift of a pro rata portion of all of the outstanding shares of stock or ownership interests in the entity to a younger generation family member will be acceptable to the IRS. This is because it does not allow a first-generation taxpayer to maintain a disproportionate frozen interest while giving away appreciation. It is also true that a first generation taxpayer may give away an appreciation right and maintain a frozen interest if he is willing to pay gift tax on the value unreduced by the retained interest. In many situations, violating the Chapter 14 rules can still be very beneficial.

Some techniques that still work after the implementation of Chapter 14 include private annuities (which never had broad appeal but do have beneficial uses in certain situations), grantor retained income trusts for personal residences, tangible property trusts and grantor retained annuity and unitrusts.

Minority Discounts

Family aggregation has not been very successfully used by the IRS in the use of minority discounts. While the new Chapter 14 rules affect the valuation of family business entities for purposes of determining what portion of the property has been given away and for fixing estate tax value, the fundamental rules of valuation contained in Rev. Rule. 59-60 still apply for purposes of determining FMV. A long-accepted element of value is whether or not the stock or other ownership interest being transferred represents a majority interest in the entity. For obvious reasons, a majority interest is worth more than a minority interest in a business. Therefore, when a minority interest in a company is transferred, a typical practice of appraisers is to discount the value of that ownership interest for the fact that there is a lack of control over the business. Similar discounts are available for lack of marketability of the closely-held stock. These discounts can run as high as 35% or more of the total value of the company.

When an owner of a business transfers a minority interest in that business to another family member, the courts have been reluctant to apply a family attribution concept even when the family unit owns a majority interest and even when the transferor owns a majority interest. This is true despite the IRS's contrary position In Rev. Rule. 81-253.[20] Thus, the value of a gift of stock in a family business in which the recipient is by himself a minority owner after the transfer should be entitled to a discount even if the recipient's family owns all of the stock of the corporation. Similarly, when the owner of a family business transfers enough ownership to another family member to bring his actual ownership of the stock down below 50%, the value of the stock retained by the donor should be entitled to a discount because it represents a lack of control of the corporation even when all of the other ownership interests are held by family members.

Part of the reason for the reluctance to impose family attribution is that there is no statutory provision in the Code that requires it. Except when the facts of the case are so extreme that the transaction is viewed as a sham, the courts have not attributed family ownership and probably would have a hard time doing so absent statutory guidance. This may be in part because of the problems of the definition of family and the factual inquiry as to whether the family operates as a unit or are hostile to one another. However, a recent decision indicates that some form of family attribution may be imposed when the facts clearly indicate a tax avoidance motive. In *Murphy*,[21] the owner of a family business had been advised for years by her accountant and attorney to give enough stock to family members to bring her ownership of the corporation that she held at her death below 50%. At the time when it became clear that the individual was on her deathbed, a transfer of a very small amount of stock was made to the taxpayer's children. On her death, her estate applied a minority discount to the value of her shares. The Service challenged this discount and the court upheld the Service, falling just short of applying the family attribution concept. However, this significant victory for the IRS provides the seeds of future attacks imposing a family attribution rule in the minority discount area.

Generation-Skipping Transfers

Wealthy families have long known that the Government, via the federal estate tax, can appropriate a large portion of a family's wealth before it can pass to younger generations. In order to avoid this harsh result, wealthy individuals have in the past made transfers directly to their grandchildren and great-grandchildren, skipping middle generations and, thus, avoiding at least one and sometimes more levels of tax.

> *Example 11:* T is a wealthy individual. In his will, T leaves $1,000,000 to F, his grandchild. F's parents are deceased. Assuming T is in the maximum estate tax bracket of 55%, the tax on this bequest would be $550,000, leaving $450,000 after tax to pass to F.

> If, however, F's father, J, is living at the time of T's death and T leaves the $1,000,000 to J, assuming no growth, J will have $450,000 after tax on T's death and then, on J's death, another $247,500 tax will be due. Thus, F will have only $202,500 after the second tax if he is forced to inherit his grandfather's wealth via his father.

The first transfer is known as a generation-skipping transfer (GST) because it "skips" a generation. Such a "skip," if permissible, could save estate taxes on a grand scale for the very wealthy. For this reason, Congress enacted the generation-skipping tax that, for transfers generally after Oct. 22, 1986 (with exceptions), taxes these direct skips as if the intervening generation had inherited the property and then passed it to the next generation after paying estate tax in the highest marginal tax bracket.

> *Example 12*: Assume in Example 11 that T leaves the $1,000,000 in trust paying income only to J, with the $1,000,000 corpus going to F on J's death. The result under current law will be identical to the result under old law (in

Example 11, where the property was left outright to *J*, who died and passed it on to *F*). *F* ends up with $202,500.

Example 13: The result is different, however, if *T* decides to leave the property outright to *F* while *J* is still living. In this case, it is treated as if *J* received the property and gave it to *F* after paying gift tax from his own separate assets. Therefore, *F* will have $290,000 available after the generation-skipping tax, but the entire tax payable will be due on *T*'s earlier death, rather than partially payable at *J*'s later death. Therefore, while the tax is lower, some of it is paid earlier.

The GST is a potential trap for the accumulation and transfer of family wealth even for relatively modest estates. Any time a transfer can occur (whether intended or not) by one individual to another who is two or more generations younger, this double tax, which can exceed the value of the gift, must be considered.

Some common situations in which a generation-skipping transfer can occur include:
- Leaving property outright to a grandchild or great-grandchild when the lineal ancestor is still living.
- Leaving property in trust to a child with remainder to a grandchild when the property will not be included in the child's estate.
- Leaving property in trust to a child, but the child dies before he is able to vest in the property, thus allowing the property to go to the grandchild.
- Leaving property in trust and the trustee may and does pay out amounts for the benefit of a grandchild.

Each person is allowed to transfer up to $1 million during his lifetime to individuals who are two or more generations younger. This $1 million exemption may be allocated among various transfers to make maximum use of the safe harbor. However, this is often easier said than done. The generation-skipping transfer exemption must be allocated judiciously and in a timely fashion, and estate planning documents should include appropriate language to allow for the most flexible planning.

Individuals should also not assume that the GST exemption of $1 million per person is sufficient, even in modest estates. Life insurance, whether held personally or in trust, can take taxable GSTs up to the limit and beyond very quickly. Making maximum use of the GST exemption and elections to allocate the exemption is of utmost importance and the strategy should be reviewed from time to time.

Employee Stock Ownership Plans

Employee stock ownership plans (ESOPs) are qualified plans that are primarily invested in stock of the employer. Their purpose is to spread ownership of a business to rank-and-file employees. In exchange for giving up ownership to the rank and file, the Code allows the owner of the business to obtain certain very important tax benefits on the sale of stock to the plan. One of those tax benefits is that, under Sec.1042, the owner may take the proceeds of the sale of stock to the ESOP and within a 15-month period, beginning three months before the sale and ending 12 months after the sale, reinvest that money in the stock of any domestic corporation including a new closely held corporation and defer the tax on the gain. This tax benefit is so significant that it has generated a great many transactions involving ESOPs in the last several years.

However, in order to take advantage of this "rollover" of gain, under Sec. 409 the stock sold to the ESOP may not be allocated to the account of a participant who is a 25% owner. A 25% owner is an individual who, either alone or through attribution, owns at least 25% of the stock of the corporation. This includes the stock owned by the selling shareholder just before the sale.

In testing whether an individual owns 25%, either actually or by attribution, all members of a family are treated as one and are deemed to own the shares of their other family members. For this purpose, family includes a spouse, ancestors, lineal descendants and siblings. This is in addition to attribution of stock owned by various entities in which the

25% owner or his family have an interest.

Thus, it is not possible for a shareholder to sell stock to an ESOP and gain rollover treatment under Sec. 1042 when members of his family or other significant shareholders and their families will receive an allocation of stock under the plan. Those individuals are permitted to be participants in the ESOP, but any amount allocated to their accounts must be made in cash or property other than stock of the sponsoring corporation sold to the ESOP in a rollover transaction. This requirement makes sense considering the stated purpose of the Government to diversify ownership to rank-and-file employees. If these family aggregation rules were not there, it would be possible for owners of corporations to gain very large tax benefits without moving ownership of their corporations outside of their own families.

Conclusion

Practitioners need to be aware of situations in which family attribution can have an adverse impact on transactions and plan around the problems accordingly. Some of these situations are not readily apparent because they do not all require a tax avoidance motive. While family businesses face the economic hurdles of the 1990s, tax professionals will face the challenge of avoiding tax traps for these family businesses.

Notes

(1) Modifying the 80% test to substitute more than 50%.
(2) Sec. 401(a)(17).
(3) Sec. 401(k)(3).
(4) Secs. 401(k)(5) and 414(q)(6)(b).
(5) *W.B. Rushing*, 441 F2d 593 (5th Cir. 1971)(27 AFTR2d 71-1139, 7101 USTC 19339).
(6) Sec. 453(f)(1).
(7) Sec. 453(k)(2).
(8) Sec 453(e)(1).
(9) Sec. 453(g)(3).
(10) *Est. Of Robert E. Frane*, 98TC No. 26 (1992).
(11) Sec. 267(d).
(12) Sec 267(c)(4). However, under Sec. 267(g), a sale between spouses would be entirely a nonrecognition event by virtue of Sec. 1041.
(13) Sec. 267(b)(2).
(14) Sec. 267(a)(2), flush language, and (e).
(15) Sec. 404(b).
(16) Sec. 704(e).
(17) Sec. 318(a)(1)(A).
(18) Sec. 302(c)(2)(C).
(19) Rev. Rule. 59-60, 1959-1 CB 237.
(20) Rev. Rule. 81-253, 1981-2 CB 187.
(21) *Est. Of Elizabeth B. Murphy*, TC Memo 1990-472.

Dynasty trusts are efforts to protect key assets against estate taxes for multiple generations. They have particular importance to families owning substantial businesses. This article explains such trusts and their use.

The Dynasty Trust: Protective Armor for Generations to Come

By Pierce H. McDowell, III

A curious phenomenon to those of us who follow such matters is that many of the trusts created by wealthy families in the latter part of the last century or the early years of this century, are now terminating. A news account of the recent sale of the *Boston Globe*, for example, noted that the sale was prompted by the impending expiration of family trusts that owned the newspaper and that had allowed control to remain in the same family since 1872. Another interesting case was provided by Lucius P. Ordway of St. Paul, MN, an early investor in Minnesota Mining & Manufacturing (3M), who created a family trust in 1917. The trust terminated in 1979 when the Last of Ordway's five children died, and the trust funds were distributed to his grandchildren, one of whom filed a disclaimer of her share, prompting a long-running dispute with the Internal Revenue Service that the United States Supreme Court this past June agreed to hear. Another example, not stretching quite as far back in time, is provided by William Randolph Hearst, who in his 125-page will created a family trust to own one-third of the stock of Hearst Corp. That trust will expire with the death of the last of Hearst's eight grandchildren alive when he died in 1951, an event estimated to occur around the year 2035. Cases such as these raise a question that is more than a mere curiosity for estate planners, namely, what if a trust could be created to last forever?

The Dynasty Trust Concept

The basic premise underlying the federal transfer tax system is that property is to be taxed each time it passes from one generation to the next. Thus, transfers made either during an individual's lifetime or at his death to his children will be subject to transfer tax. In the same manner, the property which the children have received from their parents will, unless it is consumed by them during their lifetimes, again be subject to tax when they transfer it to their own children. The result, from the perspective of a grandfather who wishes to pass his property down to his grandchildren, is that property will be taxed twice before this process is completed.

his scheme of taxation was successfully avoided in many instances by wealthy families who placed their wealth in trusts, so that no estate tax was incurred on the death of an individual whose only interest in the trust was a life estate. To reduce or eliminate the use of trusts as estate tax avoidance devices, Congress enacted the Federal Generation Skipping Transfer Tax (the "GST Tax"). In its current form, the GST Tax imposes a tax at the highest marginal estate tax level on certain "generation-skipping transfers." Such transfers can include a "direct skip" from a grandparent to a grandchild or "taxable terminations" or "taxable distributions" from trusts to persons who are "skip persons" with respect to the transferor of the trust property (that is, occupy a generation at least two removed from the transferor).

Congress has granted limited relief from the GST tax in Code Sec. 2632(a), which provides for an exemption from the GST tax in the amount of S 1,000,000 per individual. This exemption allows affluent persons to use, albeit to a lesser extent, the same strategy used by the Rockefellers and the Vanderbilts for generations to avoid estate tax. The technique commonly used for this purpose is an irrevocable perpetuities trust – also called a "dynasty trust" – for the benefit of a settlor's descendants. In the typical case, the trustee will be given discretion as to whether income or principal should be distributed. It is usually anticipated that only limited distributions will be made, so that trust principal will be preserved for future generations.

The dynasty trust is funded with property to which the settlor allocates all or a portion of his or her GST exemption. The settlor's spouse may take part in the funding of the trust, allowing a total GST exemption of $ 2,000,000 to be allocated to the trust. Once exempted, the property transferred to the trust, as well as any appreciation on the property and all accumulated income from the property, will remain forever free from federal transfer taxation – but only for as long as the property remains in the trust, typically for as long as the rule against perpetuities allows.

The rule against perpetuities provides that a trust may not postpone the vesting of interests beyond a certain period, which is usually defined as 21 years after the death of the last to die of certain identified lives in being at the time the trust was created. A vested interest is one which gives the beneficiary ownership and possession of the trust assets and requires termination of the trust, either immediately or at some specified future time. Once the trust property vests in a beneficiary, transfer tax will occur at that beneficiary's generation level – at rates as high as 50 percent under current federal law (scheduled to return to 55 percent under pending legislation)(1) – and this will drastically reduce the amount of property that remains for future generations.

A dynasty trust may be created either during the settlor's lifetime or at his death. If lifetime funding is used, there can be more property held in the trust by the time the settlor dies than could have been placed there if the initial trust funding occurred at the settlor's death. Lifetime funding of the dynasty trust also has the advantages of locking in the benefit of the current $600,000 unified credit exemption equivalent for gift and estate tax purposes, which may be reduced in the future (although last year's proposal in this regard did not become law), and removing the gift tax funds from the settlor's estate. The settlor may be reluctant to fund her dynasty trust fully during her lifetime, since to do so will involve the payment of gift tax. Often the trust will be funded only to the extent of the available exemption equivalent – $600,000 for an individual settlor or $1.2 million for a married settlor whose spouse agrees to split the gift. Sufficient property to absorb the balance of the $1,000,000 GST exemption amount is then transferred to the trust at the settlor's or the spouse's death.

The growth of assets within a dynasty trust can be likened to the French riddle of the lily pad. On the first day there is just one lily pad in the pond. The next day the lily pad doubles. Thereafter each of its descendants doubles. In 30 days, the pond completely fills with lily pads. When is the pond exactly half full? Answer: On the 29th day. Unfortunately, just when the dynasty trust dollars are about to achieve their greatest proliferation – in the trust's "29th day" – the trust normally must terminate, exposing the dollars to confiscatory transfer taxes all because of the rule against perpetuities.

The Truly Perpetual Trust

The rule against perpetuities exists in some variant in virtually all states. In these states the term "dynasty trust" is something of a misnomer, since the trust will in fact end when the perpetuities period expires. A few states – Idaho, South Dakota and Wisconsin – have no rule against perpetuities. If a dynasty trust is established in one of these states, the trust can in theory last forever. As long as the trust continues, the trust assets will be exempt from federal transfer taxation due to the GST exemption that was allocated to the trust when it was created.

This article will consider South Dakota as the model situs for a dynasty trust. It is the author's view that a South Dakota dynasty trust is preferable to one established in any other state. In addition to the advantage of having no rule against perpetuities, South Dakota also has no state income tax and, moreover, offers a very favorable business climate. (The latter factor is one of the reasons why a recent Money magazine article named Sioux Falls, South Dakota, as the best place to live in the United States.) It is possible, though, that favorable results may be obtained in the other jurisdictions mentioned, and their laws will be mentioned briefly.

Applicable Statutes

South Dakota repealed its rule against perpetuities in 1989. South Dakota does have a rule against suspension of the power of alienation. S.D. Cod. L. Sec. 43-5-1. This statute provides that the power of alienation may not be suspended for a period longer than the continuance of the lives of persons in being plus 30 years. The statute also provides, though, that while the suspension of the power to alienate trust property is within the ambit of the statute, a violation of the rule is avoided if the trustee has the power to sell, or if there is an unlimited power to terminate in one or more persons in being. S.D. Cod. L. Sec. 43-5-4.

As long as the settlor of the South Dakota Dynasty Trust grants the trustee the power to scll trust assets, the trust's existence will not be limited by the rule against suspension of the power of alienation. The power of sale does not mean that the trustee is required to distribute the sale proceeds to the beneficiaries, or even to sell the trust assets at all.

Another pertinent South Dakota statute provides that, while the income from real estate may be accumulated for a beneficiary under age 21, such accumulation must terminate when the beneficiary reaches age 21. S.D. Cod. L. Secs. 43-6-4 through 43-6-6. Ordinarily the terms of a dynasty trust will require, or at least authorize, the accumulation of trust income. Thus, it would be necessary to fund the South Dakota Dynasty Trust with assets other than real estate in order to avoid the effect of this statute.

Alternatively, the trust instrument could contain provisions reminding the trustee of the existence of the statute and providing guidance for the trustee based on the settlor's wishes. The trust might, for example, require that no real estate be held by the trust unless the income from it will be paid out. The Case Study Comparison presented below is a case study comparing the results achieved by three identical dynasty trusts established in South Dakota, Illinois and New York. Illinois and New York were selected as the comparative states because they represent low-income-tax (Illinois) and high-income-tax (New York) states. The case study is based on the following facts:

> Assume that in 1993, a 70-year-old Settlor establishes a Dynasty Trust by lifetime gift for the benefit of his descendants with $1,000,000 of cash and exempts the entire trust with his GST exemption. It is his intention that the trust last for the longest possible time permitted by law. At the time the trust is created, he has a 45-year-old child and a 20-year-old grandchild living. Under mortality tables used by the Internal Revenue Service, the grandchild has a life expectancy of about 62 years. Therefore, in a state where the rule against perpetuities applies to the trust, the longest expected period of time that vesting of the trust can be postponed, assuming the grandchild is the youngest identifiable life when the trust is created and he lives to his life expectancy, is 83 years (62 + 21). Assume further that at the end of the 83 years, there will be a great-grandchild living in whom the trust will vest, and that the great-grandchild will die two years later (i.e., in the 85th year after creating the trust). Finally, assume that the cash will be invested in marketable assets that will earn a 5 percent current yield over the trust term, that trust assets will appreciate at the rate of 7 percent annually over the term, and that the trust portfolio turns over (is sold and reinvested) at a rate of 20 percent annually.

The critical question is: What will each dynasty trust be worth, and hence what amount of property will each make available to the family, following the great-grandchild's death in year 85? In either Illinois or New York the trust must vest in the great-grandchild at the end of the 83-year term. As a result, the trust property will be subject to gift or estate tax at the generation level of the great-grandchild before it passes to the next generation. In contrast, because the South Dakota trust can postpone vesting indefinitely beyond the 85th year, no vesting in the great-grandchild is required. Therefore, no transfer taxation at that generation level will occur.

Based on the facts described above, the performance of the South Dakota trust by the end of the 85-year period, compared to the performance of the other two trusts, is as follows:

After-tax Income Generated:
South Dakota: $1.4 billion
Illinois: $1.3 billion
New York: $871 million
Appreciation In Trust Assets:
South Dakota: $1.0 billion
Illinois: $934 million
New York: $622 million
Value Available to Family:
South Dakota: $1.9 billion
Illinois: $777 million
New York: $488 million

It can be seen that the South Dakota trust will provide over 240 percent more value than the Illinois trust and almost 390 percent more value than the New York trust. Why does the South Dakota trust produce so much more overall value to the family at the end of the 85-year period – $1.9 billion compared to $777 million for the runner-up Illinois trust? The answer is its avoidance of the devastating federal transfer tax. The South Dakota trust, unlike the Illinois and New York trusts, need not terminate and expose its assets to such tax after 83 years.

Exhibits A, B and C illustrate graphically the comparative results just discussed. This comparison is based on the assumption that all trust income is accumulated and no principal invasions occur over the illustrated term. Total accumulation and retention is not required for a dynasty trust; discretionary invasion provisions for family beneficiaries are commonly used. While total accumulation is unrealistic to expect for most dynasty trusts, the relative advantages of the South Dakota trust over the same trust created in another state should remain about the same even if discretionary income and principal distributions are assumed, so long as some degree of accumulation or appreciation occurs.

The benefits of the South Dakota trust will not end after the 85-year period assumed in the example. Because the South Dakota trust need never terminate, the benefits will continue to compound over future generations. It is easy to imagine that the relative benefit of the South Dakota Dynasty Trust over a couple of hundred years could reach into the multiple billions of dollars.

Exhibit A: Dynasty Trust Analysis

Total Aggregate After-Tax Income of Trust Over 85 Years

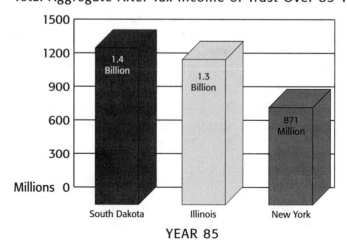

Exhibit B: Dynasty Trust Analysis

Total Aggregate Appreciation of Trust Assets Over 85 Years

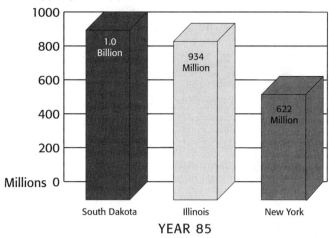

YEAR 85

Exhibit C: Dynasty Trust Analysis

Total Aggregate Value of Trust At End of 85 Years

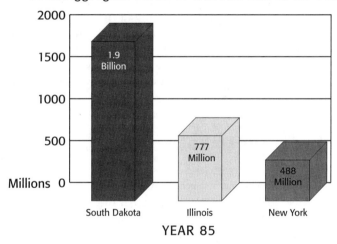

YEAR 85

Exhibit D: Dynasty Trust Analysis

Total Aggregate Value of Trust At End of 85 Years

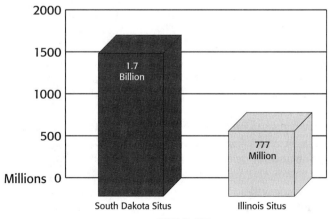

YEAR 85

No South Dakota Income Tax

Another advantage to South Dakota situs for a dynasty trust is that there is no state income tax in South Dakota. Indeed, in the November 1992 election an initiative to impose a state income tax was resoundingly defeated. The lack of a state income tax distinguishes South Dakota from the two other states that have no rule against perpetuities – Wisconsin and Idaho.

In the case of a non-resident settlor or non-resident beneficiaries, if income taxation in the domiciliary state can be avoided, locating the trust in South Dakota can produce a more favorable income tax result, at least as long as income and gains are accumulated in the trust. If the grantor had an asset which had substantially appreciated in value and which was to be sold, the asset could be contributed to the South Dakota trust, and the trust could then sell the asset without any state income tax on the gain, thus preserving principal.

It is possible that a South Dakota Dynasty Trust may be characterized by the taxing authorities as a "resident trust" for income tax purposes in the state where either the settlor or the beneficiaries reside. Because South Dakota has no income tax of its own, however, no additional tax burden is imposed on the trust due to its location in South Dakota. To illustrate, assume an Illinois resident creates a dynasty trust governed by South Dakota law. Since the settlor is an Illinois resident when the trust becomes irrevocable, the trust will be treated as a resident trust for Illinois income tax purposes and thus subject to Illinois income tax. Nevertheless, because the South Dakota trust can avoid transfer taxation, it will provide a total of $1.7 billion to the family at the end of 85 years compared to $777 million if the trust were governed by Illinois law. This compares favorably to the $1.9 billion provided by the "pure" South Dakota trust (i.e., one created by a South Dakota settlor or one in which the income tax of the settlor's domiciliary state could be avoided). In other words, an Illinois settlor who creates a South Dakota Dynasty Trust can obtain 90 percent of the benefit provided by the "pure" trust ($1.7 billion divided by $1.9 billion). These results are illustrated in Exhibit D.

A Trust Situs In South Dakota

How does a non-resident settlor ensure that his dynasty trust will have a South Dakota situs so that it will be governed by South Dakota law and accordingly not be subject to the rule against perpetuities? Generally, the settlor of a trust that is funded with personal – as opposed to real – property may designate the state whose laws he wishes to govern the validity and construction of the trust, as long as the state has a substantial relationship to the trust. See Restatement, Conflicts of Law, 2d, Secs. 268 through 270; *Wilmington Trust Co. v. Wilmington Trust Co.*, 24 A. 2d 309 (DE, Ch. 1942). Whether a particular state has a "substantial relationship" to the trust is a question of fact. A favorable determination can usually be obtained if the designated state is the one where the trustee maintains its place of business or where the trust assets will be administered. In most cases, this should be equally true whether the trust is established under a will or during the settlor's lifetime. In the typical case, the settlor will choose a South Dakota bank as trustee and deliver the assets to the bank for administration in South Dakota.

On the other hand, the validity and construction of a trust of real estate is normally determined by the law of the state where the property is located. Thus, a non-resident settlor who wishes to establish a South Dakota Dynasty Trust should not fund it with out-of-state realty interests.

As to existing trusts, it should be possible to move the situs to South Dakota, assuming that the trust instrument provides for such a change (eg., by permitting the trustee or the beneficiaries to change the situs) or at least does not prohibit a change of situs. Of course, if the existing trust was created in a jurisdiction where the rule against perpetuities applies, the trust instrument will most likely contain a savings clause providing for vesting or termination of the trust at the end of the perpetuities period. Insofar as the trust interests will terminate or vest as provided in the trust instrument despite the change of situs, no significant benefit would be achieved by moving the trust to South Dakota.

South Dakota Inheritance Tax

On beneficiaries. The South Dakota inheritance tax will not apply upon the death of any beneficiary of the trust. This is because no beneficiary has any vested right in the trust assets unless the assets have actually been distributed to him or her.

On non-resident settlor. Transfers by a non-resident to a South Dakota Dynasty Trust, whether made *inter vivos* or by will, are not subject to South Dakota inheritance tax, provided the state in which the settlor resides extends reciprocity to South Dakota residents for similar transfers made by them and provided further that the trust's assets are intangibles. S.D. Cod. L. Secs. 10-4-4 and 10-4-5.

On resident settlor. Under the South Dakota inheritance tax statute, transfers which are intended to take effect in possession or enjoyment at the death of the settlor are subject to the tax. S.D.Cod. L. Sec. 10-40-2(3). Although there appears to be no South Dakota authority on point, case law from other jurisdictions suggests that such an inheritance tax might be imposed where the trust income cannot be distributed during the settlor's lifetime. Eg., *Estate of Crowell*, 56 Cal. App. 3d 564, 128 Cal. Rptr. 613 (1976). The dynasty trust will ordinarily not prohibit distributions during the settlor's lifetime, so this case law should not be controlling. Moreover, other (non-South Dakota) case law indicates that such an inheritance tax would not apply if the settlor had divested himself of all interests in the trust property, even if distributions were deferred until the time of the settlor s death. Eg., *In re Heine's Estate.* 100 N.E. 2d 545 (Probate Ct., Hamilton Co., Ohio 1950).

If the transfer is made by the South Dakota resident within one year of his death, or is made via a testamentary dynasty trust, the transfer will be subject to the South Dakota inheritance tax. S.D. Cod. L. Secs. 10-40-1(1), 10-40-2(1). (The statute creates a refutable presumption that transfers within one year of death were made in contemplation of death.)

Other Jurisdictions

As mentioned above, there are two other jurisdictions in which the rule against perpetuities does not apply. These states also are candidates for the situs of a perpetual trust, although they both have the disadvantage of a (relatively high) state income tax.

Wisconsin. The rule against perpetuities is not recognized in Wisconsin. Wis. stats. Ann. Sec. 700.16(5). The state does have a rule against suspension of the power of alienation which is similar to that of South Dakota. Wis. Stats. Ann. Sec. 700.16(1)-(4). Wisconsin has a state income tax which has a marginal rate of 6.93 percent on taxable income over $ 15.000.

Idaho. Idaho does not recognize the rule against perpetuities. *Locklear v. Tucker*, 69 Idaho 84, 203 P.2d 380 (1949). By statute in Idaho the power to alienate real property cannot be suspended for longer than a period determined by lives in being at the creation of the limitation plus 25 years. Idaho Code Sec. 55-111. An exception is allowed for a contingent remainder in fee on a prior remainder in fee which takes effect if the persons to whom the first remainder is limited die before age 21 or otherwise have their estate determined before majority. Idaho Code Sec. 55-202. Idaho's state income tax reaches a rate of 8.2 percent on taxable income over $ 20,000.

Delaware. Although the common law rule against perpetuities does not exist in Delaware, by statute a perpetuities period is provided under which vesting can be postponed for as long as 110 years. Del. Code Ann. Sec. 25-503. For purposes of the rule, powers of appointment are deemed to have been created at the time the power is exercised, and no interest is void under the rule unless it is void if created at the date of exercise of the power of appointment. Del. Code Ann. Sec. 25-501. Delaware has a state income tax with a marginal rate of 7.7 percent for taxable income over $ 40,000. Ill.

Drafting Considerations

"Single Pot" Trust v. "Family Lines" Trust. The dispositive terms of the South Dakota Dynasty Trust can take any one of many forms. The trust may be structured as a "single pot," i.e., a continuing sprinkle trust in which principal and income are available to all descendants in the trustee's discretion. The "single pot" approach gives the trustee the flexibility to treat, for example, all grandchildren equally, whereas they would be entitled to only their respective parent's share if a separate, *per stirpes* trust approach were used. The single pot trust may be easier to administer insofar as it will tend to be larger. In particular, the advantage of economies of scale may more easily be achieved for purposes of investments.

The settlor may prefer instead an approach which breaks the trust out along family lines. A separate trust would be created for the benefit of each child and that child's lineal descendants. This approach avoids the conflicts that might arise when different children (or their descendants) compete for a share of the "single pot." Moreover, it encourages additional contributions to the trust, since the person making the contribution will know that her contribution will be earmarked for her family's share of the trust. The main disadvantage of separate trusts for each family line is that it tends to cause a proliferation of smaller trusts which are difficult to administer and can add to administrative fees.

Corporate or individual trustee. A dynasty trust is an ideal candidate for a corporate fiduciary. A corporate fiduciary provides continuity of management, which is of the utmost importance in a perpetual trust. Moreover, a corporate fiduciary offers neutrality, which can become important where various family members are involved. The trust will extend over many generations, most of whose members are not even known at the time that the settlor establishes the trust, and friction may develop between the various beneficiaries. A corporate fiduciary also offers professional management and is more likely to be aware of changes in tax, trust and other laws over the course of the many years that the trust will be in existence.

The settlor may feel uncomfortable naming a corporate fiduciary as the sole trustee of the dynasty trust. An individual, either a family member or a trusted adviser, may be named to act as co-trustee. Alternatively, one or more individuals may be given the right to remove the corporate fiduciary for appropriate reasons.

Special powers of appointment. It is often desirable to give at least some of the beneficiaries special testamentary powers of appointment that will enable them to change the dispositive terms of the trust. Such changes may be appropriate where circumstances arise that were unknown to the settlor at the time the trust was created. Usually the settlor will want to limit the potential appointees of such powers to his descendants and perhaps the spouses of descendants. The use of special powers of appointment is easier with the "family lines" approach as opposed to the "single pot" approach. If special powers of appointment are given in a "single pot" trust, the power might extend to a pecuniary amount.

A special power of appointment does not cause the property subject to the power to be includable in the power holder's taxable estate. Under the Proposed Regulations for the GST tax, however, the exercise of a non-general power of appointment is treated as a transfer subject to a federal estate tax or gift tax with respect to the creator of the power if the power is exercised in a manner that may postpone or suspend the vesting, absolute ownership or power of alienation of an interest in property for a period, measured from the date of creation of the trust, extending beyond any specified life in being at the date of the creation of the trust plus a period of 21 years (plus if necessary a reasonable period of gestation) or, alternatively, the 90-year period under the Uniform Statutory Rule Against Perpetuities. Prop. Regs. Sec. 26.2652-1(a)(4).

This proposed regulation has been criticized on the grounds that its purpose is unclear. As long as the proposed regulation exists, however, it may present an obstacle to the use of powers of appointment in the South Dakota dynasty trust That is, any exercise of the power to appoint the property in further trust would have to comply with the regulation, and this would effectively limit the duration of the trust to the perpetuities period specified in the regulation. It is hoped that this proposed regulation will be withdrawn (*see*

Covey, ed., *Practical Drafting* (U.S. Trust), p. 3132) or at least clarified in way that will make it inapplicable to states that do not have perpetuities restrictions.

Trustee's power to terminate or amend. The trustee should be given the power to terminate or amend the trust if the continuation of the trust in its original form would be unduly burdensome or otherwise unwise. Termination or amendment could also be authorized if tax or other legislative changes make the continuation of the trust inadvisable. The settlor might state explicitly his purposes in creating the trust and authorize the trustee to terminate or amend the trust if such purposes were being thwarted for any reason.

Charitable gift-over. Any well-drafted trust includes a provision for the possibility that the time may come when no beneficiary of the trust is living. In view of the expected longevity of the South Dakota Dynasty Trust, the use of a charitable gift-over becomes especially important. Since a termination due to lack of beneficiaries could occur literally hundreds of years in the future, it would be advisable to name several alternative charitable takers. Better yet, the settlor could state in detail her charitable intent so that this intent can be carried out by the trustee if none of the charities named by the settlor is in existence when termination occurs.

Trust assets. The trustee should be relieved of the duty to diversify trust investments. The lack of a diversification requirement is especially important insofar as an interest in a family business may be the main asset of the South Dakota Dynasty Trust. Real estate should be discouraged. Non-South Dakota real estate in particular would be inconsistent with South Dakota situs for the trust

Life insurance may be a suitable asset for the trust, in order to provide leveraging. Insurance could be acquired on the life of one or more very young beneficiaries, with very positive results. If insurance is contemplated, it is advisable to include language authorizing its acquisition and retention as a trust asset and detailing the trustee's duties with respect to this asset, including appropriate exculpatory language. If "Crummey" withdrawal powers are included in the trust, the trustee should be sensitive to the possibility that the power holder can become the "transferor" for GST tax purposes as to amounts in excess of the "5 & 5" limitation.

Spendthrift clause. One of the main advantages of a dynasty trust is that it allows protection against a beneficiary's creditors and a beneficiary's estranged spouse seeking alimony or support upon dissolution of marriage. For this reason it is advisable to include spendthrift language in the trust. While the South Dakota Supreme Court has not ruled on the validity of spendthrift trust provisions, the federal Court of Appeals for the Eighth Circuit concluded in a 1980 decision applying South Dakota law that the South Dakota Supreme Court would enforce the spendthrift provision at issue. *First Northwestern Trust Company of South Dakota v. Comm'r*, 622 F.2d 387 (8th Cir. 1980). Moreover, by statute in South Dakota, the beneficiary of a trust holding real estate may be restrained from disposing of his interest. S.D. Cod. L. Sec. 43-1012. The spendthrift clause may be superfluous in view of the discretionary nature of the trust, but it is an added safeguard. If the trustee's discretion is tied to a standard, creditors might be able to reach trust corpus, in which case spendthrift language would be useful. The trustee should be authorized to withhold distributions from any beneficiary who has creditor or marital problems.

Other drafting points. The trust instrument should contain language authorizing the trustee to refuse to accept property if the addition of the property to the trust would cause the trust to lose its zero inclusion ratio for GST tax purposes.

If the settlor expects that one or more descendants who are disabled may be beneficiaries of the trust it would be advisable to include "supplemental needs" provisions to protect the trust principal from the reach of governmental or other care providers.

It is important that the trust instrument grant the trustee the power of sale so that there will be no violation of the rule against suspension of the power of alienation in South Dakota. The trust instrument might also contain cautionary language regarding investment in real estate so that the trustee does not inadvertently become subject to the state's statute limiting accumulation of income from real estate.

The trust should of course contain provisions regarding South Dakota situs and South Dakota governing law.

The term "spouse" as used in the trust instrument should be defined in such a way as to take into account possible divorces and remarriages of beneficiaries.

The trust may be drafted as a "defective" trust, i.e., as a grantor trust for income tax purposes. This will cause trust income to be taxed to the grantor. This could be advantageous as it could reduce the grantor's taxable estate and serve to enlarge trust principal.

The perpetual trust may also be a suitable vehicle for the "incentive trust" espoused by some practitioners. See R. Adams, "The Future of the Golden Rule," *Trusts & Estates* (Jan. 1993) p. 10. The basic concept here is that trust distributions are keyed to the amounts that a beneficiary earns through his own employment. The incentive trust encourages beneficiaries to work and not become layabouts dependent on the trust for survival. As trust principal mushrooms over the generations, the incentive trust features of the South Dakota Dynasty Trust could become extremely important.

Conclusion

A truly perpetual trust such as the South Dakota Dynasty Trust brings into focus even more clearly than the nonperpetual dynasty trust an important truth in estate planning, namely, that property held in trust is generally more beneficial than property held outright. Most people think that outright ownership is preferable because of the control that it gives. Such control is illusory, however, in a world where asset value may be eroded by such factors as litigation from creditors or divorce settlements and, most certainly of all, by taxes. In this world, which is the world of the 21st century, the South Dakota Dynasty Trust offers protective armor for generations to come.

Footnote

1. This article was written prior to the re-enactment of the 55 percent highest marginal tax rate. All examples are based upon a 50 percent rate.

The United States repealed estate and generation skipping taxes in 2001. But as Ross Nager explains, it's not that simple. The tax is eased slowly and with many complications and, according to the legislation passed, goes away only for one year 2010. This article helps readers to understand and cope with the uncertainty introduced by tax changes.

Estate Tax Repeal?

By Ross W. Nager

In 2001, Congress repealed the estate and generation skipping taxes and enacted a host of income tax reduction measures. President Bush quickly signed the legislation into law. The bad news is that the estate tax repeal and all of the other tax reduction provisions will self-destruct at the beginning of 2011.

In this article, I will explain what Congress did and did not do. Plus, I'll provide some thoughts about the impact on estate planning. This legislation is a classic example of political sausage making. So, I caution my tender-stomached readers to take some antacid before continuing.

Byrd Droppings

The starting point is a provision buried on page 291 of the legislation and, accordingly, obscured from many reporters and constituents. The entire "Economic Growth and Tax Relief Reconciliation Act of 2001" is subject to the Senate's so-called "Byrd rule," which "sunsets" legislation after 10 years. "Sunset" means that the entire legislative package expires after 10 years.

The reason is that the requisite 60 Senators did not vote to override the Byrd rule. So, on January 1, 2011, we will have a rebirth of the income and estate tax law as in effect before this legislation. We will experience a terrific dream for about 10 years and then wake up to the old reality. Perhaps the rebirth should be called a "sunrise."

(Named after Senator Robert Byrd, the 1990 Byrd rule actually was well-intentioned because it keeps the Senate from enacting long-term spending and deficit-enhancing bills without the approval of a greater-than-majority vote. However, in this case, I am reminded of what inevitably happens if you stand on a dock throwing bread crusts to seagulls in the air *above* you.)

Shoot the Byrd

So, the estate tax is repealed after December 31, 2009. The Byrd rule restores current law effective for deaths after December 31, 2010. So, start planning now. Die in 2010 and there is no estate tax. Screw up your timing by dying before or after 2010, and Uncle will get his due.

You and your advisors will want to shoot this Byrd due to the confusion and complexity that it creates. Congress undoubtedly will sort this out over the next 10 years, although permanent estate tax repeal is but one of an infinite number of possibilities. In the meantime, dealing with the uncertainty of virtually certain law changes in the interim will ensure with certainty that your advisors will be able to provide college education for their children and grandchildren. I will present more thoughts on interim planning and expectations later.

Gift Tax Survives

Don't expect to circumvent this silliness by giving everything away during 2010. Congress had the foresight to prevent that planning. It did not repeal the gift tax – *ever*. This is particularly odd because, in the beginning, Congress enacted the estate tax and decided that it was good. It took Congress several years to figure out that even stupid people could avoid the estate tax by making gifts while alive. So, it enacted the gift tax. Over a half century later, Congress decides to have gift tax, but no estate tax. Weird!

I have heard no social policy rationale for a gift tax and not an estate tax. In fact, Congress simply needed to reduce the cost of responding to the popular rallying cry (that it created) to repeal the "Death Tax." Since Congress did not rally the people around the evils of taxing gifts, it conveniently decided to keep the gift tax.

New Rates and Exemptions

Subject to possible different interpretations by the IRS, the chart is my attempt to illustrate the estate, gift and generation skipping tax rates and exemptions, along with the family business exclusion.

Year	Current Estate and Gift Tax Exemption	New Gift Tax Exemption	New Estate Tax Exemption	Family Business Exclusion*	New GST Exemption	New Maximum Gift, Estate and GST*** Tax Rate
2001	$675,000	$675,000	$675,000	$625,000 million	$1.06 million	55% over $3
2002	$700,000	$1 million	$1 million	$300,000	$1.06 million**	50% over $2.5 million
2003	$700,000	$1 million	$1 million	$300,000	$1.06 million**	49% over $2.0 million
2004	$850,000	$1 million	$1.5 million	Repealed	$1.5 million	48% over $2.0 million
2005	$950,000	$1 million	$1.5 million	Repealed	$1.5 million	47% over $2.0 million
2006	$1,000,000	$1 million	$2 million	Repealed	$2 million	46% over $2.0 million
2007	$1,000,000	$1 million	$2 million	Repealed	$2 million	45% over $1.5 million
2008	$1,000,000	$1 million	$2 million	Repealed	$2 million	45% over $1.5 million
2009	$1,000,000	$1 million	$3.5 million	Repealed	$3.5 million	45% over $1.5 million
2010	$1,000,000	$1 million	Estate tax repealed	Repealed	GST repealed	35% for gifts over $500,000
After 2010	$1,000,000	$1 million	$1 million	$300,000	$1.06 million**	55% over $3 million****

* Under both the current and new laws, the family business exclusion is $1.3 million minus the estate tax exemption.
** Indexed for inflation after 1997, so amounts should be higher in 2002, 2003 and after 2010.
*** The GST rate is a flat rate equal to the maximum estate and gift tax rate.
**** Applies to gifts, estates and generation skipping transfers.

Family business owners actually get no overall estate tax exemption increase until 2004. The reason is that in the current law, $1.3 million family business exclusion phases down as the estate tax exemption phases up. So, the 2002 increase in the estate tax exemption to $1 million is offset by a decrease in the family business exclusion to $300,000.

Beginning in 2006, the estate tax exemption consumes all of the lower estate tax brackets. So, if you die in 2006 or later years, every dollar of your estate over the exemption will be taxed at the highest stated percentage. Similarly, in 2010, there effectively will be a flat 35% gift tax rate because the $1 million exemption will consume all lower gift tax brackets.

Some commentators have indicated that the top gift tax rate is tied to the top income tax rate beginning in 2010. The statutory language actually fixes the gift rate at 35%.

Although 35% is consistent with the new law's income tax rate reductions, the gift tax rate actually is not tied to the income tax. Given Congress' proclivity to raise, rather than lower income taxes, that may be a good thing.

Rates and exemptions are only a part of the story.

Look Ma, No Basis

Estate tax exemption increases, rate reductions and ultimate repeal grabbed the headlines thanks to Congress' Memorial Day tax legislation. There are other significant changes that can affect your estate planning. Some are good and some are, well, not so good.

Basis Step-Up

If you die under current law, your heirs inherit your assets with a new basis equal to fair market value at your date of death. This "basis step-up" rule frees heirs from the pain of paying income tax on any appreciation in assets held at your death. For example, that family business you capitalized with just the shirt off your back can be sold by your heirs at its gazillion dollar date-of-death value and they pay no capital gains tax.

Recently minted heirs discovered that the law works both ways. Suppose you bought dot.com stock in early 1999 and hold it until your death. Your big built-in capital loss will die along with your investment-prowess embarrassment, because the basis will be stepped down at death.

Carryover Basis

The estate tax dies at the stroke of midnight December 31, 2009, unfortunately taking basis step-up with it. At that point, a new concept will enter our lexicon - carryover basis. Carryover basis simply means that heirs inherit property with the decedent's cost basis beginning in 2010.

A planning opportunity arises. If you have appreciated property and a spouse, you should die by December 31, 2009, and leave your estate to your spouse. There will be no estate tax thanks to the marital deduction, but your spouse will get a basis step-up. Your spouse should then plan to die during 2010, passing the property to the heirs before the estate tax returns in 2011.

Murky Basis

That's the best of all worlds, assuming you are motivated solely by taxes. But, if either you or your spouse do not like or cannot guarantee compliance with this plan, there are some other carryover basis considerations:

- The good news is that each decedent will have a freebie $1.3 million "basis increase amount" to allocate among assets held at death. The bad news is that your heirs will be able to quarrel over who gets what asset AND who gets how much of the basis increase amount! Incidentally, no asset's basis can be increased above date-of-death fair market value (FMV).
- At death, any unused capital loss and net operating loss carryovers increase the $1.3 million increase amount. Unrecognized losses on property worth less than basis at the date of death also add to the $1.3 million basis increase amount.
- Under current law, a surviving spouse receives a basis step-up (or down) even though no estate tax is due. After 2009, carryover basis comes into play for bequests to spouses. However, there is a $3 million basis increase amount that may be allocated to property passing to a surviving spouse. (The $1.3 million basis increase amount also can be used for property passing to a spouse.)

Did you notice the references to "FMV?" Despite estate tax repeal, date-of-death appraisals and IRS valuation disputes will continue to play a vital role in the administration of an estate. The battle simply will shift from FMV for estate tax calculation to FMV for income tax basis determinations.

Wills in Turmoil

Currently, estate tax minimization drives how most married couples divide up assets at death. This tax-driven economic splitting of assets between spouse and descendents does not necessarily coincide with what is appropriate for the family.

The welcome increase in the estate tax exemption could screw up your estate plan's economics without you even being aware of it. For example, the typical will provides for a family trust to use the lifetime exemption, with the rest of the estate passing to the surviving spouse, possibly in trust. The will most likely accomplishes this by "formula" language, which automatically increases the funding of the family trust as the exemption increases.

Before the recent legislation, you may have been comfortable with the family trust receiving $675,000 (increasing to $1 million in 2006) and your spouse receiving the rest. However, the new law increases the exemption to $1 million next year and then ratchets it up to $3.5 million in 2009. Do you want to shift that much away from your spouse into the family trust? Is your spouse comfortable with that? Are the terms of your family trust consistent with this dramatic increase in its funding?

What does this have to do with carryover basis? The carryover basis regime likely will cause attorneys to develop wills that divide assets to maximize the use of the $1.3 million general basis amount and $3 million spousal basis amounts. The complexity may be mind boggling, because the will would need to consider not only the division of value among the spouse and descendents, but also the selection of specific assets to assure that the full basis increase amount can be used.

For example, leaving $1.3 million of asset value to your kids won't use the entire $1.3 million basis increase amount unless those assets have zero basis. So, taxes will continue to drive testamentary plans, but the focus will shift from estate tax to income tax savings.

Murky Future

Will carryover basis ever see the light of day and, if so, will it stay with us? We older folk remember that Congress enacted carryover basis in the mid-1970s and repealed it a few years later because the complexity was overwhelming. For example, imagine the practical problems for heirs finding and proving the basis of property bought many years ago by someone who is no longer around.

One certainly could question Congress' wisdom in failing to learn from past mistakes. But, for estate tax repeal to become and remain a reality, carryover basis probably must become a reality. Why? The simple answer is that carryover basis will raise a lot of tax dollars for the government and, therefore, is critical to reducing the overall cost of killing the death tax. A secondary reason is more of a philosophical point. Death is not a legitimate reason to allow families to avoid tax on income and gains. The current law basis step-up is accepted under this philosophy only because the estate tax rate is so high.

You Might Like It!

Now, I recognize that some family business owners will cheer carryover basis. The capital gains rate is lower than the estate tax rate. The tax on the gain isn't due until the asset is sold and cash presumably is available.

For senior generation family members who want the business to remain in the family, carryover basis may be the best of all worlds. The estate tax goes away as an incentive for the kids to sell the business. Plus, carryover basis will act as a disincentive because a sale will trigger a big capital gains tax. Nirvana!

On the other hand, the capital gains tax disincentive might keep disgruntled or disinterested heirs from selling their business interests. The result could be one less option for releasing tensions within the family.

Generation Skipping Relief

Deeply buried in the estate tax repeal legislation is significant relief from some of the complexities and traps inherent in the generation skipping tax (GST). Unfortunately, despite Congress' good intentions, the new rules do not cover all situations and could give you a false sense of security.

So, if you have (or plan to create) trusts that might some day benefit your grandchildren, grandnieces and grandnephews, or people more than 37.5 years younger than you (other than your spouse), these new provisions merit attention.

The Time Bomb

A potential problem exists with gifts to trusts that could someday benefit your grandchildren. A common estate planning scenario is a trust that is primarily for the kids for their lives, with the remainder passing to your grandchildren.

Gifts to these trusts plant a potentially devastating time bomb that will explode in the future either when a child dies or when distributions are made to a grandchild. Why? Those are two events that trigger the generation skipping tax (GST). Those events deem property to pass from you to the grandkids, "skipping" your kids in the process. The particularly nasty fact is that the tax (currently 55%) will be based upon the value of the trust at the time of the triggering event, not the historical value of your gifts, potentially including decades of income and appreciation.

These trusts often are structured to qualify for the *gift tax* annual exclusion, so many people tend to ignore them and just add $10,000 per year per donee. Life insurance trusts often follow this pattern when you pay the annual premiums on behalf of the trust. Unfortunately, thanks to a devious Congress in 1988, these trusts rarely qualify for the GST annual exclusion. Unless you take action, each year's gift adds more blasting powder to the GST time bomb.

The way to avoid the GST is to allocate part of your $1.06 million GST exemption each time you make a gift to the trust. The problem is that you must affirmatively elect to allocate the exemption by filing a statement in a gift tax return each year. The election statement is necessary even though the gift tax annual exclusion otherwise precludes the need for a gift tax return.

If you discover the problem years after the gift, you can make a "late" exemption allocation election. However, the late election eats up exemption based upon the potentially much higher value of the trust's assets at the time you file it.

Defusing the Bomb

Recognizing that many people are blissfully unaware of the problem (and the resulting huge bucks at stake), the American Institute of CPAs fought for years to get legislative relief for failures to allocate the exemption. Thanks to their efforts, the recent tax bill offers some relief.

The new law reverses the election concept for gifts to some trusts beginning this year. Now, your GST exemption will be allocated automatically to gifts to *some* trusts that have children and more remote descendents (technically, "skip" and "non-skip" persons) as potential beneficiaries.

However, Congress decided that the new automatic allocation should apply only if there is a likelihood that a significant portion of the trust will pass beyond the kids. The idea is to reduce the risk of wasting exemption if the trust likely will benefit only kids. Therefore, the automatic allocation does not apply if the trust instrument requires more than 25% of the assets to be distributed to the kids before age 46 (or meets certain other technical requirements).

This arbitrary restriction on automatic allocation means that many trusts remain unprotected. Examples include:

- Trusts created by people who think the kids will require more than 45 years of maturity before being entrusted with more than 25% of their largess;

- Trusts that require more than 25% to be distributed to the kids before age 46, but that retain some assets ultimately passing to grandkids;
- Trusts created before 2001 if you did not allocate exemption previously and the trust might pass to the grandkids (because the new law does not cure the problem for pre-2001 gifts); and
- Charitable lead and charitable remainder trusts.

To Allocate or Not to Allocate

You waste your GST exemption if you elect to allocate (or the new law automatically allocates) it to a trust and nothing ultimately passes to your grandkids. This creates an interesting dilemma for gifts to a trust that will distribute to your child at, say, age 35. Chances are that he will live that long so allocating the exemption likely would waste it. On the other hand, if the actuaries are wrong and he dies before 35, Uncle Sam will confiscate the lion's share of the grandkids' inheritance.

The new law helps with this dilemma, but with many "ifs." If...

- You did not allocate exemption for past gifts to a trust,
- Your child(ren) and grandchild(ren) are potential beneficiaries, and
- Your child dies *while you are still alive*...

...then you may elect to retroactively allocate your exemption as if you had done so at the time the gifts were made. The problem is that you must survive your child for this relief to be available. So, the allocation remains a dice roll, but the odds are slightly more in your favor.

Authorizing Forgiveness

The new law directs the IRS to be more understanding when taxpayers ask for relief from past GST mistakes. If granted, "relief" means that you may retroactively allocate GST exemption to prior years' gifts based upon the date-of-gift value as compared to a late election's current asset value.

The relief takes two forms. First, good-faith efforts to allocate exemption will be accepted even though election technicalities, like the form was improperly prepared, were deficient. Second, the IRS is authorized to grant relief if "relevant circumstances" (such as the terms of the trust instrument) indicate that you intended the trust to benefit the grandchildren and, therefore, would have wanted to allocate GST exemption had you known about the issue.

This relief is supposed to be available for pre-2001 failures to allocate exemption. You should act promptly to address the need to request relief, since the IRS probably will require the request to be filed within a reasonable time after you discover a problem.

Severing Stops Bleeding

There are a few additional goodies that give attorneys and accountants goose bumps. For example, the new law allows trustees to sever a trust that is partially GST exempt and partially nonexempt. Division into two parallel trusts (one exempt and one non-exempt) can greatly improve the ability to plan for and reduce GST taxes. It is relevant to people who do not have enough GST exemption to cover all their gifts and bequests to trusts.

By the way, if all this talk about grandkids makes you worry about the family's ability to qualify for the 15-year payout of estate taxes, you can rest easy. Congress has increased to 45 (from 15) the number of shareholders (in addition to your family line) that your company may have and still qualify for the extended payout term. So, you can encourage your kids and siblings' kids to give you more. (Grandkids, grandnieces and grandnephews, etc. that is!)

Naturally, all of these rules are complex, so check with your advisors.

A Glimpse of the Future

Now, the big questions. Will the estate tax really go away? And, what should you do about your estate plan given what Congress has done?

The answers can be found in the murky goo of federal budgeting and politics. Let's dive in and sort this mess out as logically as possible.

The starting point is predicting future legislation. Congress must and will do something about the notorious "sunset" provision, which returns the estate tax to its full glory beginning in 2011.

Federal Budget

The key to predicting Congress' next step is money, plain and simple. Will Congress have the dough to repeal the estate tax once and for all? Unfortunately, the answer most likely is "no." One tip off is the shenanigans Congress pulled just to get us into the current fiasco.

Congress stole from the future and is already being "busted" for its actions. During much of the tax-reduction debate, the economy was booming. Budget estimators created rosy 10-year predictions showing huge budget surpluses. Politically, tax reduction became a certainty. Then came the sudden downturn in the economy, which hit much of corporate America by surprise. Our legislators ignored the potential decline in tax revenues and plunged ahead.

Only now are budget estimators beginning to factor the downturn into their thinking. Predicted future surpluses have vanished. It doesn't take a genius to see that promised tax reductions might vanish, too.

Even with the expectation for a continued booming economy, Congress had trouble paying for the tax cuts. That is the reason for the complex, long-term phase-ins both the income and estate tax rate reductions, marriage penalty relief, etc. The lack of tax revenues in the near term necessitated delaying these tax cuts, thereby deferring the cost to the fisc. Congress hoped that a continued (or renewed) economic boom would allow tax revenues to rise in time to pay for the tax reductions as they phase in. They stole from the future without regard to whether the money would be there.

States Get Stuck

Congress also stole from the states. Under current law, the U.S. shares its estate tax revenues by granting a credit for the states' inheritance taxes. The credit is very generous (reaching 16% of estate values exceeding about $10 million). Most people hardly notice it because the total estate tax doesn't change; the executor simply splits it into two checks, one for Uncle and one for the state.

Beginning next year, the credit rapidly phases down through 2004. Since most states simply assess an inheritance tax equal to the federal credit, they get the shaft. Don't expect the states to take this lying down. The inheritance tax is a significant state revenue source. They probably will increase their inheritance taxes to compensate for the federal changes. If they maintain their total tax revenue and the feds give a smaller credit, guess what that means for you!

Even worse, in 2005, the federal credit is replaced by a deduction. Because a deduction is worth less than a credit, your total death tax burden actually can rise despite the federal rate reductions and increasing exemption.

Congress had to pull these kinds of tricks to create tax reductions *in a booming economy*. What are the chances of rectifying these shenanigans in a depressed economy? Could Congress permanently repeal the estate tax if we went back to the same booming economy that we had a year or two ago? Don't hold your breath!

Politics Won't Help

Keep in mind that all of the income tax and other provisions in the legislation also sunset. A paltry $53 billion is needed to extend the estate tax repeal for just one year to 2011. That's a half trillion dollars for a 10 year extension of repeal. Put that in the context of 2001's $1.3 trillion of *combined* income and estate tax cuts over 10 years. So, absent huge amounts of revenues that did not exist even in the rosy economic projections, Congress will have to pick between repealing the estate tax for a relatively few people or reneging on the income tax reductions for a far larger constituency.

Of course, which political party controls the presidency and Congress will be important. But, regardless of whether it's elephants or donkeys, there will be a huge difference between the political dynamics last summer and those likely to exist when Congress finally faces this issue.

The family farm and small business lobbies, which spearheaded the estate tax repeal debate, are not likely to be as vociferous the next time. Why? The estate tax exemption, which rises to $3.5 million ($7 million for a married couple) in 2009, will remove all but a paltry few from the estate tax. Those lobbies are likely to be satisfied with simply keeping most of their constituents off the tax rolls by making that exemption permanent. They also will be far more interested in the pent up demand for business tax breaks, which were passed over this summer. And, there will be an increased outcry over the distastefully costly and complex carryover basis regime, which has become the trade-off for estate tax repeal.

So, dear readers, betting the ranch on the estate tax going away for good is an extreme long shot. Some will use the possibility as an excuse to put off their estate planning, possibly as a cover up to avoid facing the difficult family and business issues that have forestalled action in the past. That part of the goo has been a frequent topic in this column and newsletter, so I won't get into it at this point.

However, none of us are getting younger and few of us can afford to wait for either the tax or personal issues to resolve themselves. Unfortunately, the morass created by the 2001 legislation requires reconsideration of your current plan even if you just want to stick with what you have now.

Acting in the Face of Uncertainty

What should you do about your estate plan in light of estate tax repeal, the sunset of that repeal and the uncertainties created by the related law changes?

Unfortunately, no single answer applies to everyone. Sweeping generalizations are dangerous. Among other things, your decisions should consider:

- Your expectations as to Congress' future actions – Will repeal become permanent? If not, how will it mutate over time?
- The size of your estate now and in the future – Will your estate be below the expected higher exemption or will rapid appreciation exacerbate your ultimate tax burden?
- Personal objectives – Does the new law surreptitiously alter your heirs' sharing of your estate?
- Your and your spouse's ages and current and future health status - Will you live to see repeal if it happens? Will you be competent to change your will when Congress re-addresses the sunset provision?
- Willingness to accept tax and financial risk – Can you accept gift tax risk to continue lifetime planning? Can your business afford the estate tax if repeal does not happen and you fail to address the problem in the interim?

These mind boggling uncertainties may push you to inaction. However, inaction might be the worst action for you. Perhaps the best way to resolve this thorny problem is to attack it piecemeal. Start with the basics and, depending upon the size of your estate and your personal situation, progress to the more complex planning strategies.

Testamentary Documents

Congress may have stealthily changed your family members' economic sharing of your estate, especially if you are married. The only way to make sure that you like the change is to review your will (and revocable trust if you have one).

The increasing estate tax exemption affects wills that divide the estate between the surviving spouse and other family members (typically via a trust for the children). Many married couples' wills use a "formula clause" geared to the amount of the estate tax exemption. The exemption amount, which can pass tax-free, goes to a family trust. The remainder is left to the surviving spouse, thereby using the marital deduction to defer estate tax until the survivor's death.

As the exemption phases up, the family trust's share of the total estate increases. For example, assume that your estate is worth $3 million. The chart shows the potentially dramatic shift from your spouse to the family trust, depending solely on the year of your death. The amounts in parentheses apply if your estate is larger than $3 million. If your estate is less than $3 million, the marital share is wiped out sooner. For example, if your estate is worth $1.4 million, your spouse gets nothing if you die in 2004.

If you die in:	Family Trust Receives Estate Exemption Amount	Surviving Spouse Receives Remainder
2001	$675,000	$2,325,000
2002 – 2003	$1,000,000	$2,000,000
2004 – 2005	$1,500,000	$1,500,000
2006 – 2008	$2,000,000	$1,000,000
2009	$3,000,000 (up to $3.5 mil)	None (excess over $3.5 mil)
2010 (estate tax repealed)	$3,000,000 (entire estate)	None (None)
2011 and later (old law restored)	$1,000,000	$2,000,000 (excess over $1 mil)

Taking advantage of the increasing exemption makes sense from an estate tax standpoint, but your spouse may not appreciate it! At a minimum, you should determine whether the terms of the family trust permit adequate distributions to your spouse given the decreasing size of the marital share. You simply need to have your will checked to see whether and how the increasing exemption affects your testamentary intent.

Attorneys continue to grapple with drafting wills that deal with the vagaries of increasing exemptions, changing asset values, and estate tax repeal and its sunset. The state death tax credit phase-down and conversion to a deduction, along with guesswork as to the states' future legislative reactions, also are giving attorneys fits. Many have thrown up their hands with trying to minimize carryover basis issues, or at least have decided to finesse them until someone figures out how to handle the problem.

Many attorneys have started drafting wills with one dispositive plan if there is an estate tax and another if there is no estate tax. I expect that these early "models" will become outdated as the profession comes up with better mousetraps.

Huddle with estate planning and legal counsel and decide how best to proceed. Expect to have to readdress your testamentary documents periodically as the legislative scene changes.

Life Insurance

It probably is unwise to cancel life insurance policies betting on estate tax repeal. Insurance also may continue to be required to fund buy/sell agreements or to pay capital gains taxes due to asset sales under the carryover basis regime.

For new policies, consider term insurance rather than some form of more expensive whole life insurance. However, be sure that the term policy can be converted, without a medical exam, to a more permanent policy if the estate tax does not go away. Have your agent run projections of future years' premiums assuming conversion at various later dates. That will help you determine whether you can afford the increased premiums should you decide to convert the policy.

Life insurance trusts continue to make sense to protect the proceeds from estate tax. If you use term insurance, consider the gift and generation skipping consequences of future premium increases, whether caused by a future conversion to a permanent policy or simply by keeping the policy in force as you age.

Annual Gift Program

Don't forget the basic blocking and tackling of using your $10,000 annual gift exclusions, along with the payment of descendents' qualified medical and educational costs. Failure to do so results in annual lost opportunities to reduce your estate, which will be important unless estate tax repeal becomes reality. There is little downside risk.

Most advisors continue to recommend using the lifetime gift exemption, which increases to $1 million in 2002. In fact, next year's big exemption increase offers a significant opportunity to use more sophisticated techniques to leverage additional wealth to younger generations.

Larger Estates in the Face of Uncertainty

Although the increasing exemption will remove many people from the estate tax rolls, people with larger estates (and those who hope to join those privileged ranks) face some additional issues and opportunities in light of estate tax "repeal."

Using Both Spouses' Exemptions

Both spouses' estate tax exemptions increase beginning in 2002. However, if you own everything, your spouse's exemption will be wasted if he or she dies penniless. Consider giving a portion of your estate to your spouse currently to enable use of the exemption in that event.

Larger Gifts and Transfers

There are some differences of opinion concerning the appropriateness of techniques that could result in a taxable gift in excess of the lifetime exemption. Some pundits have suggested that advisors will be subject to malpractice claims if they counsel their clients to take a gift tax risk. The rationale is that, if the estate tax ultimately disappears, paying gift tax to transfer assets during life will be stupid.

Frankly, sweeping generalities like these are *themselves* stupid. They are based solely on the potential for the estate tax to go away, a dubious possibility at best. They ignore:

- The lost opportunity to shift a decade's growth out of the estate by acting now, rather than waiting until the law becomes clear. Keep in mind that, assuming just 7% annual appreciation, your estate could double in value just waiting for Congress to decide what to do with the estate tax.
- The potential for a person to die before 2009, failing to have actively addressed estate tax reduction opportunities in the interim.

Many of the more sophisticated lifetime planning techniques risk additional gift tax if challenged by the IRS. For example, a gift or intra-family sale of a large family partnership interest can result in an unintended gift in excess of the lifetime exemption if the IRS successfully challenges the valuation discount. (See the discussion of family limited partnerships in my March 1997 column and "perfectly defective trusts" in my May and June 1995 columns.)

These types of techniques supercharge lifetime planning, but do take on more risk of a gift assertion and resulting tax. Most advisors have come to accept the gift tax risk associated with these transactions. The only real change is the remote possibility that the estate tax will be repealed, making the risk of that gift tax unnecessary. Put this in the context of my discussion over the last several months of the odds that the estate tax will go away.

There likely will be a somewhat greater interest in the use of grantor retained annuity trusts (GRATs), which were discussed in my September and October 1995 columns. This technique provides a unique opportunity to incorporate an adjustment clause to defeat an IRS assertion of gift tax if you have undervalued the property placed in the GRAT. However, for many people, the advantages of the perfectly defective trust will still outweigh the disadvantages of the GRAT.

Opportunity Transfers

It makes sense to continue to take advantage of opportunities to shift high-appreciation-potential investments to younger generations. The classic opportunity is one in which your contacts, buying power, influence and abilities create a greater-than-ordinary chance of success. Perhaps you can mitigate the children's risk by loaning part of the capital to a kid-owned investment entity. If the deal goes south, you take much of the hit through your then worthless loan. Another example is having your children own real estate, which is leased to the business, thereby providing a reasonably assured investment return.

Renewed Importance of Trusts

For larger estates, the new law creates an additional motivation to use multi-generation trusts. Because the gift tax survives estate tax repeal, your children will be able to transfer only $1 million to their descendents through lifetime gifts. If you pass your property to a trust that can make distributions to all of your descendents, your kids' gift exemptions are not required for the trust to make distributions to your grandchildren. You may think that $1 million is plenty for your children to sprinkle among their children. However, since the $1 million exemption is not indexed for inflation, $1 million may not go very far a few decades from now.

Plus, assets that you place in trust for your descendents most likely will be protected from the estate tax if Congress reinstates it after you have left the scene. Your kids then will not have to deal with the hassles and costs of estate planning to pass the property to their descendents.

I wish I had an earth shattering observation to help you deal with the increasing uncertainties that we face in our daily lives. Unfortunately, it's just not that easy. We must have plans and take actions that consider both positive and negative outcomes. That is true for the estate tax as well.

Reprinted with permission from *The Family Business Advisor*. Copyright 2001, Family Enterprise Publishers.

CHAPTER 6
PROFESSIONALIZING
THE FAMILY FIRM

Business growth or successful generational transition ultimately requires an evolution from an entrepreneurial to a professionally managed organization. This evolution occurs not only in terms of managerial practices, but also in terms of the firm's cultural values.

Professionalization of the family firm helps to overcome the emotional and psychological contradictions inherent in family business systems.

Business growth or successful generational transition ultimately requires an evolution from an entrepreneurial to a professionally managed organizational system. This article offers guidelines for small-to-medium-sized companies seeking to make the transition. A successful transition should be planned and executed carefully and gradually in four stages: analysis and evaluation of existing business strategy; formalization of decision-making and information systems of the firm; selection and training of key individuals and development of middle management; and constant monitoring of change to insure a smooth transition.

The Transition to Professional Management: Mission Impossible?

By Charles W. Hofer and Ram Charan

Since the pioneering work of Schumpeter[23], the study of entrepreneurship and enterprise development has attracted considerable interest in both academic and professional circles. This interest has been further stimulated by later research that showed the significant impact entrepreneurial activity has had on technological growth[14]. Until recently, this interest was channeled into two related, but separate lines of inquiry. The first focused on various characteristics of the entrepreneur. Here the hope was to find those traits or other factors that differentiated successful entrepreneurs from other individuals, for if this could be done, our limited national and organizational resources could be more effectively directed to those persons most likely to succeed. The second line of inquiry involved an examination of the evolution of new enterprises over time. Here the purpose was to discern those characteristics that distinguished successful from non-successful enterprises at each "stage of their development."

The importance of such work is further accentuated by the ever unfolding sequence of current events that increasingly dramatize the limitations on our natural and organizational resources and the consequent need to use them wisely. Such constraints make it critical that we increase our understanding of the enterprise development process so that we can reduce the extremely high failure rate of new ventures and thus reduce the amount of resources we need to allocate to risk-taking activities. At the same time, we also need to further improve our knowledge of the downstream aspects of enterprise development because recent research has indicated that, after the starting difficulties have been overcome, the most likely causes of business failure are the problems encountered in the transition from a one-person, entrepreneurial style of management to a functionally organized, professional management team. Accomplishing such transitions is a difficult task, however, especially because of the psychological makeup and personality traits of most founding entrepreneurs[3 6 8]. It is, in fact, so difficult that Barnes and Hershon[2] have concluded that the best way to make such transitions in organizational evolution is to pursue them when the entrepreneur retires or dies and a new generation of management takes over the direction of the organization. While this may be so, the need to improve our use of organizational resources demands that we develop models for successfully making such transitions without resorting to such a drastic expedient. It is the purpose of this paper to present one such model.

Enterprise Development and Evolution

There are, of course, already numerous models of organizational development and growth. Starbuck, for example, identified models of organizational growth that he felt could be grouped into four broad categories, i.e., "cell division models; metamorphosis models; will-o'-the-wisp models; and decision making process models."[26]

In the policy area, most of the organizational development and growth models proposed to date would combine characteristics of Starbuck's cell division and metamorphosis categories. Because of this overlap, we have found it more useful for our own research to reclassify such models into one of the following four categories: (1) life cycle models, (2) stages models, (3) evolutionary models, and (4) transition models.

The life cycle models, including those of Steinmetz[28] and Kroeger[171], represent organizational development and growth as following a pattern directly analogous to biological life cycles. While intuitively appealing, such models have a number of weaknesses. First, organizations do not display the time consistency of development found in biological models. Thus, few of these models stipulate when one phase of the life cycle ends and another begins, even though such specification is necessary for improving management practice. Second, the development portrayed by such models is invariant in sequence, yet most studies of organizational development indicate no such invariant sequence in real life. And, third, not all organizations die as postulated by such models or at least not in time periods relevant to the entrepreneur. The stages models, including those of Filley[12], Scott[24], Buchele[3], Lippett and Schmidt[19], Salter[22], Thain[26], Collins and Moore[10], and Straus[29], attempt to get around these difficulties by postulating a series of "stages" through which organizations evolve over time. Unlike the life cycle models, however, the movement of an organization from one stage to another in these models is dependent on a number of factors other than time. Thus, it is not necessary that an organization ever move out of Stage I, and, even if it does, there is no prescribed time at which this must occur. Equally important, organizations need not go through every stage, and there are several possible sequences in which they may move from stage to stage. These models also permit several alternatives to death for the alternate development of the firm. The two most critical weaknesses of stages models are that, with one or two exceptions, they do not indicate the details of the process or the problems involved in making the transition between stages, and that they do not agree on a common set of stages. Thus, Straus has only two stages, while Buchele has seven. Moreover, their stages do not simply collapse into one another. Instead, Collins and Moore, Fllley, and Buchele present several stages that precede Stage I of the Scott, Salter, and Thain models, while the latter contain at least one or two stages that follow the last stages of the Collins and Moore and Buchele models. Nonetheless, the stages models are a great improvement over the life cycle models, even though more research is needed so show that the patterns of organizational structure and systems they recommend for each stage do indeed produce better organizational performance than other patterns of structure and systems for that stage of development.

The evolutionary models of organizational development and growth proposed to date are both stronger and weaker than the stages models. Their major weakness is that while they contain most of the "stages" of development described by the stages models above, they propose an invariant linking of the different stages in the same way the life cycle models linked the different phases of the life cycle. In fact, Greiner[15] goes so far as to propose that "each phase is both an effect of the previous phase and a cause of the next phase." And, as we noted above, this proposition does not square with actual field observations even though there are some organizations for which it may be true. The strength of these models is that they explicitly recognize the existence of, the importance of, and the difficulty of the transitions between stages. Unfortunately, however, they do not go on and develop any detailed models of how these transitions may be accomplished. This limitation is especially critical since the management problems encountered in making such transitions are more severe than those involved in selecting the optional structure and systems once the transition is accomplished. Similarly, more scarce resources are consumed by the firms that fail while trying to make these transitions or that retard their growth because they fear they will be unable to make the transition than are lost by firms which continue to operate with an inefficient structure once the transition is completed.

One problem in developing transition models is that it may be necessary to construct a different model for each different transition that is possible between different stages. Christensen[6], for example, has developed a model that focuses on the problems of management succession in entrepreneurially managed firms. Among the different transitions that are possible, probably the most difficult to achieve and also perhaps the most important for organizational development is that of moving from a one-person entrepreneurially managed firm to one run by a functionally organized, "professional" management team. Little research has been done on this topic, and most of what has been done has focused on the non-behavioral aspects of the transition. One exception is Barnes and Hershon's work[2] on the management succession-organizational development linkages in closely held firms. In general, they conclude that it is much easier to move from one stage of organizational development to another at the same time that a transition is made in the top management of the organization than at any other time. They also note that such transitions are more easily achieved from the second generation onward as each succeeding generation has some appreciation for the problems of such transitions since they went through such an experience themselves. Except for timing and perspective, however, Barnes and Hershon offer no further prescriptions for how such transitions might be accomplished Nonetheless, their observation that the psychological makeup and personality traits of the entrepreneur pose equal, if not greater, barriers to the transition to professional management than do limitations on organizational resources and environmental opportunities is a major contribution to the development of improved models of this process.

The Entrepreneurial Process of Decision Making

Before beginning a discussion of our propositions on how to most effectively implement the transition to professional management, it is necessary to examine the key characteristics of entrepreneurially managed firms that will need to be modified in the transition process. The most important of these are: (1) a highly centralized decision making system, (2) an over-dependence on one or two key individuals for its survival and growth, (3) an inadequate repertoire of managerial skills and training, and (4) a paternalistic atmosphere.

It is impossible, of course, to centralize all decision making in any firm. Typically, though, most decisions about the acquisition and allocation of capital resources, the selection and compensation of key personnel, pricing, purchase of raw materials, development of new products, loans and credit arrangements, labor negotiations, and diversification are made by one or two individuals including the entrepreneur him/herself in the Stage I firm.

At the same time, these individuals usually also get heavily involved in many of the day-to-day operating activities of the firm. This characteristic of the entrepreneurial firm permits it to respond quickly to environmental opportunities and threats. However, it also inhibits the development of subordinates' decision making skills-a situation that oft-times makes the organization too dependent on the top few individuals. Another possible danger arising from this tendency of the top individuals to get heavily involved in day-to-day activities is that such activities will begin to cut into the time the entrepreneur and his/her top executives should be spending on strategic decision making.

The failure to develop subordinates, coupled with the entrepreneur's personal limitations, and the fact that the entrepreneur usually feels he/she cannot afford to hire high-salaried functional personnel generally produces a number of major gaps in the range of skills possessed by the entrepreneurial firm. For example, since its inception fifteen years ago, Lawn King Products, Inc., a $40 million mideastern organization that manufactures and markets garden tractors, has been highly dependent on its owner/president's personal abilities for its high brand image and extensive distributor dealer network. Additionally, it is the owner himself who does all the selling. However, in recent times the owner has been feeling the limitations of his lack of knowledge and training with regard to broader marketing concepts, internal control through accounting and competitive strategies against larger companies, and this has begun to show up in the company's performance.

The final key characteristic of entrepreneurial firms is their highly paternalistic climate. Because they are small and have a relatively stable group of "core" employees, these firms develop a high sense of family among their members. In addition, the entrepreneur, through his/her attitudes and actions, encourages every employee to seek his/her advice whenever problems of a personal nature arise. Though the loyal paternalism that results from such behavior does account for part of the success of the entrepreneur in developing his/her company and personnel, it can also have long-term counter-productive effects.

Before proceeding to describe our model, it should be noted that the four characteristics discussed above are often important and in many cases essential to the success of the small, entrepreneurially managed firm at least up to a point. Beyond that point, however, they can become barriers to the Sum in its efforts to capitalize on further market opportunities. For example, Breitman & Company, a manufacturer and marketer of women's belts and handbags, expanded its sales and profits over 3300 percent during its first 10 years of operations because of the genius of its president as a designer and the selling talents of its vice president. During this time neither man changed his style of management and the company continued to use the same systems and procedures it had developed at start up. Over the next four years, however, its profits remained constant even though sales more than doubled because of the increasing inefficiency of these systems, and less than two years later the firm went bankrupt when its costs had risen even more and its sales had dropped sharply because of customer dissatisfaction with its ever increasing delivery times.

Moreover, when these characteristics start turning into barriers, they begin to tax the physical and mental capabilities of the entrepreneur. It is, therefore, at this juncture that he/she must realize that the mode of managing his/her business requires a change from entrepreneurial to professional management.

A Model for the Transition to Professional Management

A professionally managed Stage II firm is one which has a functional organization structure based on its current needs, permits delegation of appropriate day-to-day decision-making authority to its subordinate managers, utilizes formal information analysis and the intra-firm consultative process to make administrative decisions, reflects in its routine operations stable corporate and business strategies that recognize both the long and short-term needs and goals of the organization, is free from excessive dependence on any particular individual or individuals for their skills and talents, and displays a certain degree of interchangeability among its components.

Given the characteristics of the typical entrepreneurially managed Stage I firm described above, it is not likely that successful transitions to professional management will occur very often unless they are planned carefully and implemented gradually.

The transition itself will usually involve five or more of the following seven steps See exhibit 1 for a conceptual overview of the process.

1: *The entrepreneur him/herself must want to make the change and must want it strongly enough to make major modifications in his/her own task behavior.*
2: *The day-to-day decision making procedures of the organization must be changed.* Specifically, participation in the decision making process should be expanded, and the consultative process should be introduced. Greater emphasis should also be placed on the use of formal decision techniques.
3: *The two or three key operating tasks which are primarily responsible for the organization's success must be institutionalized.* This may involve the selection of some new people to supplement or replace those 'indispensable' individuals who have performed these tasks in the past.
4: *Middle level management must be developed.* In general this means that specialists will need to learn to become functional managers while functional managers are learning to become general managers.
5: *The firm's strategy should be evaluated and modified if necessary to achieve growth.*
6: *The firm's organizational structure and its management systems and procedures should be modified slowly over time to fit the company's new strategy and senior managers.*
7: *The firm must develop a professional board of directors.*

In general, the transition process is slow since it involves organizational and personal learning and because it is necessary to preserve old strengths while developing new ones.

It must also be handled carefully because of all the psychological contracts that will have been built up over time.

Moreover, the relative importance of these steps varies as is indicated by the following set of propositions about the transition process:

P1: If the entrepreneur does not want to change, the probability of successful transition is almost nil.

P2: If the entrepreneur is unwilling to change his/her day-to-day behavior, the probability of a successful transition is very low.

Some support for these propositions is provided by the experiences of Breitman & Company which was unable to make a successful transition in spite of successfully completing steps 4-5 of the transition process because its top managers were unwilling and unable to make such changes in their behavior. At the same time, several other steps of the transition process are also critical to successful transitions as is indicated in the following propositions:

P3: If the day-to-day decision making procedures are not changed and the top two or three key operating tasks are not institutionalized, the probability of a successful transition is almost nil.

P4: If sufficient numbers of middle managers are not developed, the probability of a successful transition is very low.

P5: If the firm's strategy is not consistent with moderately large and rapid growth, the probability of a successful transition is almost nil.

Some support for propositions P4 and P5 comes from the experiences of the Blakeston & Wilson Company which went bankrupt because of strategy problems and a lack of effective middle level managers even though its top management was so enthused about growth prospects that it easily met propositions P1 and P3 as well as P7 below.

P6: If a firm's top management is desirous of growth and willing to change its behavior and if the firm changes its day-to-day decision making procedures, institutionalizes key tasks and adopts a strategy consistent with moderately rapid growth, then the probability that it will successfully complete the transition process is quite high.

P7: Firms that try to complete the transition process too quickly or that take excessive time to complete it are less likely to be successful than firms that proceed at an intermediate rate.

Propositions P6 and P7 are supported by the experience of the Wilton Oil Equipment Company which met the conditions stipulated in propositions P1, P2, P3, and P4 but which did so only after a prolonged period of time so that it did not enjoy the measure of success it might have had.

Testing the Model

Quite clearly it is not acceptable to use single item anecdotal observations such as those above to test either individual propositions or the conceptual scheme from which they were derived. On the other hand, we were reluctant to establish the type of large scale research program that would be needed to comprehensively test each of our propositions until we were more confident of the general validity of our model. Consequently, we decided to test our ideas on a small scale basis first to see whether they appeared to have sufficient validity to warrant a more complete testing program.

As our sample, we chose ten different case studies on the transition process that are currently available from Harvard Case Services. We then asked a three person group to evaluate the degree to which each of the case studies supported or contradicted our propositions. (See Table 1)

Since not all cases provided direct evidence with respect to the validity of the different propositions, the sample size for most of the propositions was insufficient to permit strong statements about the statistical validity of the proposition even though, in all cases, the evidence that was available did support the propositions. On the other hand, taken as a group, our data provided rather strong support for our overall conceptual model i.e., 26 out of 29 directly relevant observations are supportive of the propositions developed from

Table 1. Propositions on the Transition Process

COMPANIES	P_1	P_2	P_3	P_4	P_5	P_6	P_7
Dansk Designs	V_w	V_w	V_w	V_w	V_w	V_s	N_s
Breitman	V_s	V_s	V_s	V_s	X	V_w	V_s
Wilton Oil	V_w	V_w	V_w	V_w	X	X	V_s
Vappi	V_w	V_w	V_w	V_w	V_w	V_s	X
Solartron Electronic Group	X	X	V_w	N_w	V_w	N_s	V_s
Vermont Tubbs	N_w	N_w	V_s	V_s	X	V_w	V_s
Blakeston & Wilson	V_s	V_s	V_s	V_s	V_s	V_w	V_s
Duralast	N_w	V_s	V_s	V_s	V_s	V_w	V_s
Hedblom	V_w	V_w	V_w	V_w	V_w	V_s	N_s
Superb Biscuits	V_w	V_w	V_w	V_w	X	X	V_s
Saltwater Farms	V_w	V_w	V_w	X	V_w	X	V_s
Total — V_s	2	3	4	4	2	3	8
Total — V_w	6	6	7	5	5	4	0
Total — N_w	2	1	0	0	0	0	0
Total — N_s	0	0	0	0	0	1	2

Key:

V_s indicates the situation provides strong direct evidence that the proposition is valid.

V_w indicates that the situation provides weak, indiret evidence that the proposition is valid.

N_w indicates that the situation provides strong, direct evidence that the proposition is not valid.

N_s indicates that the situation provides weak, indirect evidence that the proposition is not valid.

X indicates that the situation neither supports nor refutes the proposition.

our model while 33 of the 36 tangential observations also support our propositions.

One could question of course, whether one should duster the data relating to different propositions together as we have done. Clearly such a procedure would be inappropriate if all propositions were not related to each other in any way. However, since they were all developed from the same conceptual scheme, such a grouping gives a rough test of the statistical validity of the conceptual scheme as a gestalt even though the sample size for each individual proposition precludes making any final judgments about the statistical validity of our propositions on an individual basis.

Summary and Conclusions

Overall, this preliminary study suggests that our conceptual model of the transition process involved in moving from a one person entrepreneurial style of management to that of a functionally organized team of professionals is a useful tool for predicting whether such transitions will be successful It also indicates that it may be possible to assist the entrepreneur who would like to make such a change to do it successful by, i.e., that it is not necessary to wait for a new generation of management to take over before making such changes as Barnes and Hershon suggest. On the other hand, it would be inappropriate to put excessive faith in our model at this time since our sample size was not large enough to produce statistically significant results for any individual proposition.

Perhaps equally as important as the initial testing of our model however, was the idea of testing the validity of our conceptual scheme in the aggregate. It would be incorrect to suggest that such a procedure should ever be considered as a substitute for the large scale testing of a model and its associated hypotheses – it is not! However, in those circumstances in which a series of propositions are all derived from one model or conceptual scheme, this procedure provides a way to get some rough assessment of the overall validity of the model or conceptual scheme before incurring the high cost associated with gathering a large-scale sample.

The Next Steps

Since this study has indicated that our conceptual framework may have merit, the next steps are to sharpen up the individual propositions and to develop the larger scale sample needed to test each proposition individually. When gathering this sample, we will need to take care that we get observations on a variety of different types of organizations since our present sample consisted mostly of manufacturing firms. In addition, we shall also need to get data on those situations not in the public record in which the transition was not successful since such firms are likely to be smaller than those we have studied and may indeed have different needs and requirements during the transition process.

Exhibit 1. A Schematic Representation of the Transition Process Showing the Relative Time Dimensions Involved in the Change

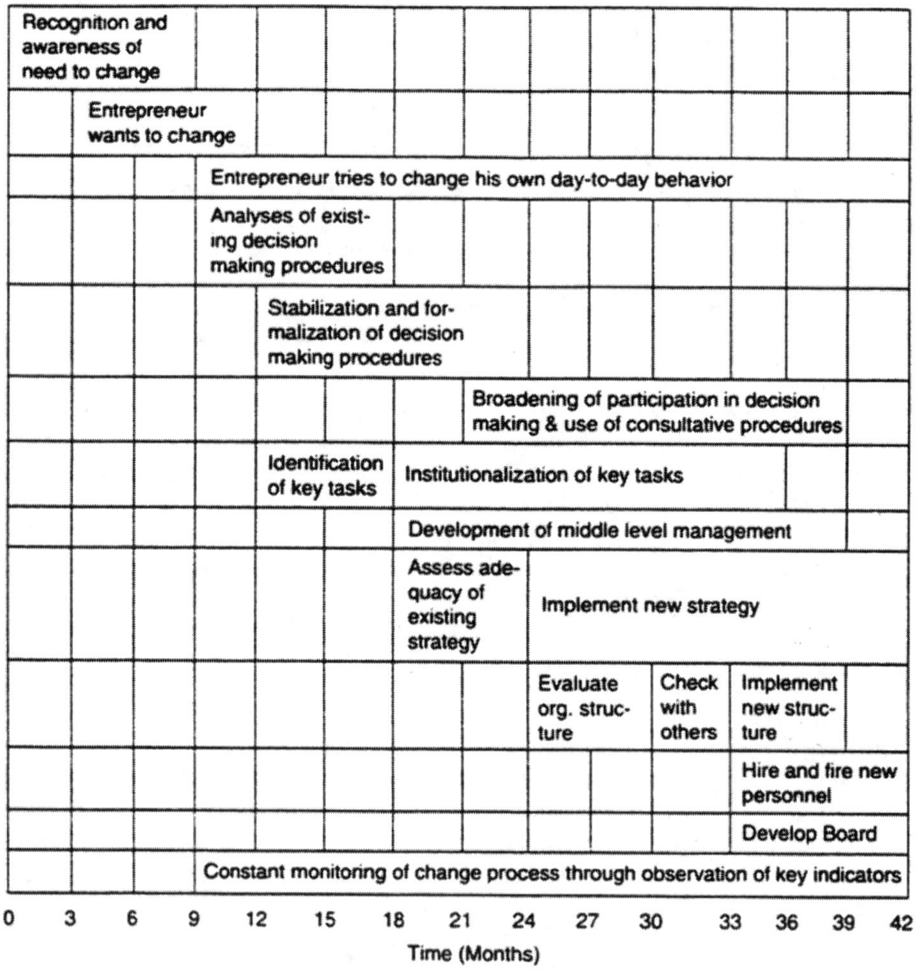

Recognition and awareness of need to change

Entrepreneur wants to change

Entrepreneur tries to change his own day-to-day behavior

Analyses of existing decision making procedures

Stabilization and formalization of decision making procedures

Broadening of participation in decision making & use of consultative procedures

Identification of key tasks | Institutionalization of key tasks

Development of middle level management

Assess adequacy of existing strategy | Implement new strategy

Evaluate org. structure | Check with others | Implement new structure

Hire and fire new personnel

Develop Board

Constant monitoring of change process through observation of key indicators

0 3 6 9 12 15 18 21 24 27 30 33 36 39 42
Time (Months)

References

1. Ansoff, H. I. and R. G. Brandenberg. "A Language for Organizational Design: Parts I and II." *Management Science*, 17(12): 705-31.
2. Barnes, L. B. and S. A. Hershon. "Transferring Power in the Family Business." *Harvard Business Review*, 54(4): 105-114 (July/August, 1976).
3. Buchele, R. B. *Business Policy in Growing Firms*. Scranton, Pennsylvania: Chandler Publishing Company, 1967.
4. Cannon, J. T. *Business Strategy and Policy*. New York: Harcourt, Brace and World 1968.
5. Chandler, A. D., Jr. *Strategy and Strategy and Structure*, Cambridge: MIT Press, 1962.

6. Christensen, C. R. *Management Succession in Small and Growing Firms*, Boston: Harvard University. 1953.

7. Clarke, P. *Small Business*. Sydney West Publishing Company, 1973.

8. Clifford, D. K "Growth Pains of the Threshold Company." *Harvard Business Review*, 51(5): 143-154 (September/October, 1973).

9. Cohn, T. and R. A. Lindberg. *Survival and Growth: Management Strategies for the Small Firm*. New York: AMACOM. 1974.

10. Collins, O. and D. C. Moore. *The Organization Makers*, New York: Appleton-Century-Crofts, 1970.

11. Dun and Bradstreet. *The Business Failure Record Through 1972*, (New York: Dun and Bradstreet, 1973), p. 9.

12. Filley, A.C.A *Theory of Small Business and Divisional Growth*. Unpublished doctoral dissertation. Ohio State University, 1962.

13. Glueck W. F. "An Evaluation of Stages of Corporate Development in Business Policy," Paper presented to the Midwest Academy of Management, Kent, Ohio, April 26, 1974.

14. Gough, J. W. *The Rise of the Entrepreneur*. New York: Schocken Books, 1970.

15. Greiner, L. E. "Evolution and Revolution as Organizations Grow," *Harvard Business Review*, 50(4): 37-46 (July/August, 1972).

16. Kotler, P. "A Theory of Market Evolution." Unpublished working paper July 23, 1976.

17. Kroeger, C. V. "Managerial Development in the Small Firm." *Business Horizons*, 17(1): 41-47 (Fall, 1974).

18. Levinson, H. "Conflicts that Plague a Family Business." *Harvard Business Review*, 49(2) (March/April, 1976).

19. Lippett, G. L. and W. H. Schmidt. "Crises in a Developing Organization." *Harvard Business Review*, 45(6): 102112 (November/December, 1967).

20. McGuire, J. *Factors Affecting the Growth of Manufacturing Firms*. Seattle: Bureau of Business Research, University of Washington, 1963.

21. Mueller, D. C. AA Life Cycle Theory of the Firm." *Journal of Industrial Economics* 20(3): 199-214 (July, 1972).

22. Salter, M. S. "Stages of Corporate Development." *Journal of Business Policy*, 1(1): 23-27 (Autumn, 1970).

23. Schumpeter, J. A. *The Theory of Economic Development*. New York, Oxford Press, 1961.

24. Scott, B. R. Stages of Corporate Development-Parts I and II. Boston: Harvard Case Services, #9-371-294 and 5.

25. Starbuck, W. "Growth and Development." In March, J. (ed) *Handbook of Organizations*. Chicago: Rand McNally, 1965.

26. Thain, D. H. "Stage of Corporate Development." *Business Quarterly*, Winter 1969, pp. 33-45.

27. Steinmetz, L. L. Critical Stages of Small Business Growth." *Business Horizons*, February 1969, pp. 29-36.

28. Straus, G. AAdolescence in Organizational Growth: Problems, Pains, Possibilities." *Organizational Dynamics*, 2(4): 1-12 (Spring 1974).

A study of forty family firms shows that the family business's culture helps to determine success in the firm's survival into the second generation. Researcher W. Gibb Dyer of Brigham Young University found four common family business cultures: participative, laissez-faire, participative, and professional.

In the first generation 80 percent of family businesses were found to be paternalistic and 10 percent each were laissez-faire and participative. Only one firm had a professional culture. In succeeding generations, two thirds experienced cultural change, the majority becoming professional cultures. Since paternalistic cultures do not prepare the next generation well for leadership responsibilities, successful leadership transfer generally appears to require evolution from paternalistic culture to one of the other three available patterns.

Culture and Continuity in Family Firms

By W. Gibb Dyer, Jr.

In today's turbulent times, family firms lead a tenuous existence. Few are able to survive beyond the first generation. The reasons for the demise of these firms include poor economic conditions, lack of capital and resources, and incompetent management. However, my study of more than forty family firms indicates that the culture of the family business plays an important role in determining whether the firm continues successfully beyond the first generation.

In this paper, I will describe the kinds of cultures found in the business side of the family firm (as opposed to the culture of the family or the board of directors), outline the advantages and problems associated with each cultural pattern, and discuss how one might go about changing the culture if that is deemed to be necessary.

Culture and Continuity

To gain an understanding of why some family firms succeed and others fail, my research team and I systematically examined the histories of more than forty family firms. Some firms were rather well known, such as du Pont and Levi Strauss, while others were much smaller mom-and-pop businesses. We gathered data from a variety of sources, such as corporate histories, annual reports, methods of former leaders, interviews, and minutes of board of directors meetings. As we gathered data from these sources, we began to create "maps" of the cultures of the firms in our panel. Dyer (1986) describes the method. By studying these firms historically, we sought to discover the kinds of cultures found in these firms and to determine the kinds of cultural patterns that tended to be associated with family firms that had been successful over time.

What is Culture?

The culture of any group can be viewed on four levels: artifacts, perspectives, values, and assumptions (Schein, 1985; Dyer, 1986). Artifacts are the more tangible aspects of culture. They are physical – the dress, physical layout, company logo, and other emblems used by a group; verbal – the language, jargon, stories, and myths shared by the group; and behavioral – the common rituals, ceremonies, and behavioral patterns. Artifacts are the most visible manifestations of culture, but to fully understand a culture, one must decipher the shared meanings behind them.

Artifacts can be thought of as the symbolic representations of the next level of culture, socially shared perspectives. A perspective is "a coordinated set of ideas and actions a person uses in dealing with some problematic situation" (Becker, Gear, Hughes, and Strauss, 1961). Perspectives are the norms and rules of conduct that the group deems acceptable for handling such problems as developing a new product, giving a performance appraisal, hiring and training new employees, or gaining a promotion.

While perspectives are situation specific rules, values are broader principles, such as Serve the Customer, Be Honest, or Do Not Question Superiors.

Values are both formal and informal and they can often be found in the "philosophy" espoused by the group. Since groups do not always act in accordance with espoused values, distinguishing between the ideal and real values is critical in doing a cultural analysis.

At the foundation of the culture are the group's basic assumptions. The other three levels of culture are based on this most fundamental level Assumptions are the premises on which a group bases its world views and on which the artifacts, perspectives, and values are based In family firms, certain kinds of assumptions are often found regarding the nature of relationships, human nature, the nature of truth, the environment, time, the nature of human activity, and whether preferential treatment should be given to certain individuals. Figure 1 describes these categories of assumptions and the kinds of orientations associated with each category. In each of the firms that we studied, we mapped the firm's artifacts, perspectives, and values and then made inferences regarding the underlying pattern of assumptions.

Figure 1 Categories of Cultural Assumptions

1. **The Nature of Relationships.** Are Relationships. Are between members of the organization assumed to be primarily lineal (that is hierarchical), collateral (that is, group oriented), or individualistic in nature?
2. **Human Nature.** Are humans considered to be basically good, basically evil, or neither good nor evil?
3. **The Nature of Truth.** Is truth (that is, correct decisions) discovered from authority figures, or is it determined by a process of personal investigation and basting?
4. **The Environment.** Is there a basic belief that humans can master the environment, that they must be subjugated by the environment, or that they should attempt to harmonize with the environments
5. **Universalism/Particularism.** Should all members of the organization be evaluated by the same standards, or should certain individuals be given preferential treatment?
6. **On Nature of Human Activity.** Are humans basically active (**doing** orientation)? Are humans passive and unable to alter existing circumstance (**being** orientation)? Or, is a person's primary goal the development of self as an integrated whole (**being-in-becoming** orientation)?
7. **Time.** Are members of the organization primarily oriented to the past, the present, or the future?

Cultural Patterns In the Family Business

The cumulative set of assumptions that a group holds is called the cultural pattern of the group. Indeed, the core of any culture is this pattern of interlocking assumptions that creates a unique belief system. Because basic assumptions are the key to understanding culture, my research team used them to broadly define the kinds of family business cultures that they found. We observed four common business cultures: the paternalistic culture, the laissez-faire culture, the participative culture, and the professional culture. Figure 2 presents the basic assumptions underpinning these cultures.

The orientations outlined in each category indicate how leaders of family firms use very different assumptions in operating their businesses. For example, the paternalistic pattern is founded on assumptions that emphasize personal and charismatic characteristics of the founder and family, while the professional pattern emphasizes impersonal rules as the means of getting work done. In the next four sections, I will describe each pattern in detail and identify its strengths and weaknesses.

Figure 2. Cultural Patterns of the Family Business

	Paternalistic	Laissez-Faire	Participative	Professional
Nature of relationships	Lineal (hierarchical)	Lineal	Collateral (group orientation)	Individualistic
Nature of human nature	People are basically trustworthy	People are good and trustworthy	People are good and trustworthy	People are neither good nor evil
Nature of truth	Truth resides in the founder family	Truth resides in the founder/ family although outsiders are given autonomy	Truth is found in group decision making/ participation	Truth is found in professional rules of conduct
Orientation toward the environment	Proactive stance	Harmonizing/ proactive stance	Harmonizing/ proactive stance	Reactive/ proactive stance
Universalism/ particularism	Particularistic	Particularistic	Universalistic	Universalistic
Nature of human activity	Doing orientation	Doing orientation	Being-in-becoming orientation	Doing orientation
Time	Present or past orientation	present or past orientation	Present or future orientation	Present orientation

The Paternalistic Culture

The *paternalistic* pattern was the most common culture in the family firms that we studied. In this pattern, relationships are arranged hierarchically. The leaders, who are family members, retain ad power and authority and make all the key decisions. The family distrusts outsiders and closely supervises the employees. Moreover, family members are afforded preferential treatment. Employees are assumed to have a "doing" orientation; that is, they are supposed to carry out the families orders without question. The stance toward the environment tends to be proactive in developing new markets or products. However, the family may also create a particular market niche and prefer to stay within it. The paternalistic firm also seems to have one of two orientations around the time dimension. Some paternalistic firms tend to be oriented to the past. Carrying on the founder's and families legacy is the primary aim of the owning family. Thus, time-worn traditions are at the center of the culture. Other paternalistic firms tend to be very present oriented. Although they maintain some traditions, they focus on current problems and needs and quickly change to meet new threats.

One company that illustrates the paternalistic pattern was National Cash Register under the direction of John Patterson. Patterson and his family controlled the firm for almost a half century. Patterson charted his own course after he bought the company for $6,500 in 1884. He did not follow the advice of local business leaders and rarely listened to his subordinates. He believed that salesmanship was the key to success and developed the most sophisticated training school for salesmen at the time. His salesmen wore white shirts and dark suits – a forerunner of the IBM image. In fact, Thomas Watson received his initial training at NCR Patterson often acted in what many would consider to be an arbitrary and capricious manner: He would give an employee a raise one week and fire him the next. He had his top managers arrive for work early in the morning for horseback riding and calisthenics. He viewed himself as a pioneer and a conqueror – he rode a white horse because Napoleon did. He claimed to be an expert in topics ranging from health to religion. He also created one of the first "welfare" industrial organizations in the United States, building parks, theaters, and other amenities to bring the employee's entire family into the NCR fold. As one observer at the time described Patterson, "he was so intent on helping that often he insisted on minutely regulating the lives of those with whom he came in contact. He was perfectly willing to override the objections of the individual if he believed that the individual's objections were against the best interests of both the individual and of society. He thought there was only one best way of doing anything and that everyone ought to be taught that best way and then be forced to follow it" (Crowther, 1923, p.9). John Patterson built an amazing empire with this cultural pattern until his death in 1922.

The paternalistic pattern tends to work well when the leader of the family business has the necessary expertise and the information needed to manage all aspects of the business. In this kind of culture, there is little uncertainty regarding who makes the decisions. Thus, decisions can be made quickly, and resources can be mobilized to meet competitive threats. Since the leaders in a paternalistic culture are often highly charismatic figures, there tends to be high commitment on the part of the followers to carry out the leader's vision. This commitment has a positive effect when a business is small and struggling for survival.

However, a number of potential problems are associated with the paternalistic culture. First, the business often relies too much on the leader for direction. Hence, the firm is in jeopardy if the leader dies or is incapacitated. Second, training and development for the next generation are often neglected. Third, the leader may not be able to manage ambiguity or complexity as the business grows or as the environment becomes turbulent. Fourth, since the leader makes all the key decisions, many members of the family business may have feelings of incompetence or powerlessness. Given these potential problems, the paternalistic culture generally is best able to succeed when the business is small and the environment is fairly stable. As the firm grows, the leader's family matures, and as the environment becomes more volatile, the family business culture often must evolve into a new cultural pattern.

The Laissez-Faire Culture

We have called another cultural pattern that we have studied the laissez-faire culture. This pattern is similar to the paternalistic pattern in many ways. Relationships are hierarchical, family members are afforded preferential treatment, and the employees are expected to achieve the family's goals. Moreover, the orientations of these two cultures toward the environment and time are similar. Where they differ is in their assumptions about human nature and the nature of truth. In the laissez-faire culture, employees are seen as being trustworthy, and they are given responsibility to make decisions. While the ultimate truths regarding the firm's mission and goals rest in the hands of the family, employees are given a great deal of authority and discretion to determine the means of achieving those goals. As a result, the laissez-faire firm is quite unlike the paternalistic firm, where the family determines both the ends and the means

Levi Strauss and Company has historically followed this laissez-faire tradition (Cray, 1978). The founder's daily routine emphasized the responsibility that he delegated to his subordinates. Levi Strauss would typically leave for his morning walk to work at nine o'clock and arrive around ten-long after the store was opened Trusted employees opened the store. He would check the sales figures for the previous day and spend the rest of the day chatting with his salesmen, who called him by his first name. He left the store in the late afternoon to visit a local tavern and have a drink with some friends. Employees stayed until closing time, and the trusted bookkeeper locked up the store.

The Strauss family and their descendants have also been known for their willingness to take care of their employees during times of trouble. For example, the family paid the doctor bills of one employee who became ill with diphtheria. They also gave him $1,000 to pay his debts. This employee eventually became the plant manager. Thus, from Levi Strauss down to the current leadership of the Haas family, the family has attempted to provide a secure place of work for employees, and it has provided overall direction and guidelines, but it has allowed employees great latitude in making decisions and influencing company affairs.

DYER, JR.

The laissez-faire culture is more amenable to business growth and individual creativity than the paternalistic pattern is, since the family delegates a great deal of responsibility to employees. Such a pattern is appropriate if the family is not able or willing to oversee all the day-to-day activities of the business, and the business requires employees to use their initiative and change quickly in order to meet new conditions.

The major danger of the laissez-faire culture is that employees may not act consistently with the family's basic values and assumptions. Such was the case of Levi Strauss. Although the company was able to grow very rapidly by giving autonomy to plant managers, it began to have serious problems with product quality in the 1970s when some plants produced garments that did not meet the company's standards. Without appropriate review, employees working in a laissez-faire culture can lose sight of the company's goals, and the business can run out of control.

The Participative Culture

The third pattern that we studied is the *participative* culture. This cultural pattern is relatively rare in a family firm. We found only four organizations in our panel that had developed such a pattern at some point during their history. The participative pattern is based on assumptions that vary dramatically from the first two patterns that I have described. Relationships tend to be more egalitarian and more group oriented. The status and power of the family tend to be de-emphasized. Employees are deemed to be trustworthy, and the family attempts to give employees the opportunity to magnify their talents. "Doing" is not enough. Employees must accomplish their work in such a way that other people will be involved and personal growth and development will result. Participative cultures tend to be proactive in managing their environments. They attempt to get at the truth and to make proper decisions by eliciting employee input. No one is assumed to have all the answers. The participative culture is present-focused but also oriented toward the future. Nepotism and other forms of favoritism are formally disdained.

One of these unique participative cub turns is found at W. L. Gore and Associates. Founded by Bill Gore, a scientist from du Pont who developed a variety of applications of Teflon, the company has created a culture that seems to have a number of advantages: high commitment and morale, the ability to respond quickly to changes in the environment, and the ability to innovate.

To create this kind of culture, all 4,000 people who work for the company are called *associates* rather than *employees*. Terms like *boss*, *manager*, and *supervisor* are replaced by words like *leader* or *sponsor*. This practice is intended to de-emphasize the use of titles and status symbols and to create a feeling of community. There are no job descriptions to speak of, nor are there organization charts. The associates become part owners of the company after one year of service. Bob Gore, Bill's son and the current president, constantly reinforces the belief that status, rules, and hierarchy inhibit communication and group decision making (Pacanawsky, 1985). Hence, the Gore family is committed to an egalitarian climate, and it has attempted to foster a sense of freedom and responsibility in employees that is seldom found in a family firm.

In a participative culture, employees are generally able to be creative to develop their talents and abilities. Through participation in decision making, they become more able to understand and internalize the values of the company, and they are more committed to the decisions that are made. Such a pattern seems to succeed in environments that are complex and changing and that require employee input from many levels in order to make the right decisions.

The major weakness of the participative culture is also found in its decision making processes. It often takes a great deal of time to come to a participative decisions. Important decisions can be delayed or undermined by the process of gathering input from employees. Hence, the challenge of those working in a participative culture is to differentiate between the decisions that need to be made rapidly with minimal discussion and the decisions that must receive more time and employee participation.

The Professional Culture

The term *professional culture* is not intended to mean that this type of organization is more professional than the others but that this cultural pattern is generally found in firms where the owning family decides to turn the management of the business over to non-family, professional managers. The professionals often bring with them a set of assumptions that are quite different from those in the other three patterns. Relationships are individualistic, meaning that employees focus on individual achievement and career advancement. Competition is keen in this kind of culture. Professional managers often take a rather impersonal, neutral stance toward employees, who are evaluated on their ability to contribute to the profits of the business. The owning of family's involvement in the business that characterizes the other cultures often disappears with the advent of professional management. The professionals rely on their years of professional training to make rational decisions. The result typically involves the creation of various programs to improve efficiency and cut costs. Employees are encouraged to do their jobs quickly and efficiently; personal development of employees is a secondary concern. Since professional managers are frequently brought into a family firm in order to turn it around, they may find themselves in a reactive mode – forced to put out fires – or they may take a proactive stance in cutting costs by instituting "modern" management techniques, restructuring the company, or laying off employees.

One company that developed this professional pattern was International Harvester. Founded by Cyrus McCormick at the turn of the century, International Harvester was run in the paternalistic tradition of the family. When the company fell on hard times in the 1970s, the president Brooks McCormick (a descendant of Cyrus), hired Archie McCardell, chief operating officer at Xerox, to turn the company around. McCardell replaced the previous management with his own team (see Harvard Business School Case no. 9-381-053) and encouraged the new managers to compete with one another in carrying out his cost-cutting programs. Bonuses and other incentives were given to those individuals who succeeded. *Efficiency and cost control* were the watch words of the McCardell regime. Unfortunately for McCardell, the impersonal nature of the cost-cutting programs created a great deal of ill will among union members and precipitated a bitter strike. Eventually, the union ended the strike, but it was able to force the board of directors to fire McCardell. Thus, the assumptions of the professional culture proved to be short-lived at International Harvester.

The advantage of the professional culture is found in the new ideas and management techniques that the professional managers can often bring to the firm. The outsiders can often improve the firm's accounting, marketing, or other operating systems and make the business run more efficiently. Furthermore, they have fewer ties to the past, and thus they are able to see new possibilities that can move the firm in new directions.

The major weakness of the professional culture is that it tends to alienate the employees who were used to working for the family under a different set of assumptions. Absenteeism, turnover, unhealthy competition among individuals and among departments, low morale, and low commitment are often the negative side effects of the change to professional management.

Ensuring Continuity in the Family Firm

The preceding descriptions of family business cultures illustrate the variety of culture in family firms. While not every family firm may fit exactly the patterns of assumptions listed in Figure 2, we were able to categorize the family firms in our panel according to the four patterns.

The paternalistic pattern was the pattern most commonly found among the family firms that we studied. This procedure was particularly true of first generation firms: Approximately 80 percent of the firms in our panel had a paternalistic culture in the first generation. The firms with participative and laissez-faire cultures each accounted for 10 percent, and only one firm was deemed to have a professional culture in the first generation. In succeeding generations, more than two-thirds of the paternalistic firms experienced cub turn change, the majority becoming professional cultures. It would seem that in order for the family firm to transfer leadership to the next generation successfully, the paternalistic culture must evolve into one of the other three patterns. Paternalistic cultures do not prepare the next generation well for leadership responsibilities and give them little chance to develop their leadership skills. The experience of the firms in our panel suggests that family firm cultures do indeed change as new leadership takes over.

As we have mentioned, all cultural patterns-not just the paternalistic pattern – bring their own set of problems and challenges for management, and they may need to change in order to meet new conditions in the external environment, in the business, or in the owning family. For example, family firms that face an increasingly turbulent environment often need to foster assumptions of the participative culture in order to respond quickly to changes, develop new ideas, and improve decision making. Companies experiencing the negative effects of nepotism may need to move to professional management. Family firms experiencing rapid growth generally must delegate authority and responsibility to nonfamily employees, thus becoming more laissez-faire in nature.

At some point in time, most leaders of family firms are faced with the question: How do I change the culture of my business to make it more effective? The answer to this question can be threatening, because leaders of family firms often must change their own assumptions and behaviors. The experience of most family firms is that such assumptions change only when there is a major crisis in the firm. However, if the leaders wait for a crisis to occur before they begin to change, the outcome is generally not favorable either for the family or for the business. That is why many family firms fail. Despite this rather pessimistic assessment, there are some actions that leaders of family firms can take to initiate culture change. These activities can include analyzing the culture and planning for change, changing the assumptions of the leaders, or developing new leadership through the use of hybrids and outsiders. The planned change approach represents a method for changing the culture incrementally, while the other two approaches represent more drastic remedies where change is more abrupt.

Analyzing the Culture and Planning for Change. One method for changing culture is, first, to create a Rapt of the organization's artifacts, perspectives, values, and assumptions; second, to determine the consequences of this cultural pattern; and, third, to plan for change (Schein, 1985; Wilkins, 1983; Dyer, 1986).

To conduct such an analysis and change effort typically involves the creation of an action-research team involving members of the organization as well as outside consultants. The insiders help the outside consultants to understand the subtle nuances associated with the culture, while the outsiders-often by asking "dumb" questions about surprises they encounter-attempt to make the more tacit dimensions of the culture overt.

This inside/outside team interviews individuals and observes behavior at various levels and locations throughout the organization. Usually both an insider and an outsider conduct the interviews in order to foster joint inquiry. The team lists what appear to its members to be the significant artifacts of the culture, then attempts to discover the routines and rules of the culture that make up the perspectives shared by members of the organization. Often such questions as who succeeds and who fails here? What are sins in this organization? and How are decisions made here? are used to gather data (Dyer, 1986). Career histories are also useful, inasmuch as interviewees often discuss the kinds of problems they encountered as they attempted to adapt to the culture. The team also attempts to uncover organizational subcultures groups holding different beliefs – by asking interviewees which individuals or groups hold opposing views. Often, the problems in family firms are the result of subcultures in conflict, such as the first generation versus the second generation or family members versus nonfamily employees.

When the more overt artifacts, rules, and norms are discovered, the research team must begin to build hypotheses about the company's values and tacit assumptions. As mentioned earlier, these more tacit beliefs must be inferred, since members of the organization may be unable to articulate them clearly. This is particularly true of members of the owning family. What we can hope that the action-research team will arrive at is a map of the culture that lists the key artifacts, perspectives, values, and assumptions. Once this has been done, the team can identify the kind of cultural pattern – paternalistic, laissez-faire, participative, professional, or some other – that prevails.

Once the culture map has been created, the action-research team can begin to focus on the question, what are the consequences of this kind of culture for the company now, and what will they be in the future? The team should attempt to articulate how the culture helps or hinders the organization's strategy and its effectiveness, as well as how it affects employee motivation, productivity, and development. Through this analysis, the tea n can begin to pinpoint where the problems are and whether there is a need for change.

If change is needed, the team then can develop specific actions that reflect a different set of assumptions. For example, succession planning and estate planning can be used to push a family firm to become more future oriented New guidelines for decision making and delegation can move the firm to become more participative in nature. Reward systems can be altered to discourage nepotism. Conflict management mechanisms, such as asset management boards, can be set up to manage family disagreements (Beckhard and Dyer, 1983).

If this approach to change is used, it needs support from the family and top management if it is to succeed, because the changes may reflect new assumptions, and they may be strongly resisted. Change in the way power is distributed often accompanies culture change. Some are likely to gain and others to lose in the process. I have found it useful in generating support for any proposed changes to include key members of the family and nonfamily employees in the action-research team. Although such an approach can seem quite attractive, I have found through working with a number of family and nonfamily businesses that attempts to change via this method are easy to resist, undermine, and misunderstand. Thus, we must look at other change strategies as well.

Changing the Leader's Assumptions. One of the greatest problems facing leaders of a family firm is their lack of awareness of the impact of their assumptions and behavior on those around them and of the kinds of cultural patterns that their behavior promotes. Since the leaders of family firms have often created the culture, the culture can change if the assumptions of the leaders change. By becoming aware of their own assumptions and the impact of their assumptions on those around them, leaders can begin to take the often painful steps needed to change them.

To gain such self-awareness, family leaders can do a number of things. For instance, they can sit on the boards of directors of other family firms. By observing the problems of others, they can gain insight into their own. They can also find competent board members and advisers for their own company who can help them to grapple with difficult problems and give them honest feedback on their performance.

Leaders can use data gathered via interviews, questionnaires, and group meetings to obtain feedback about themselves. Outside consultants can also help leaders to understand how their behavior affects their business and their family. In one family firm that we studied, I gave the president of the company a detailed description of the culture. One of the main problems seemed to be the difference in management style and philosophy between the president, who favored a participative culture and his chief operating of fixer, who was attempting to foster the assumptions of a professional culture. Of this study, the president said: "I got it the study at the office one day and took it home to read. While I usually sleep soundly, I woke up at one o'clock in the morning and began to read, finishing it at dawn. It was gripping to read, like a novel. While there were few surprises about how I ran things, the differences the professional manager had made did surprise me. I hadn't appreciated how different our styles really were." Using this new information, the president eventually fired the chief operating officer and took steps to correct some serious problems.

In some cases, workshops, seminars, or sensitivity training sessions offered by specialist organizations can also prove helpful. A number of organizations have been created to provide the heads of family firms with information and programs to help assess their problems.

Therapy and counseling are other alternatives for those who seek insight, experience anxiety or depression, or find serious schisms in their families. In one family firm, the son of the founder was constantly plagued by the ghost of his father and by employees who reminded him that his father "wouldn't have done it that way." To deal with this pressure, the son enlisted the help of a competent therapist. The therapist finally convinced the son that the business was his – not his father's. Armed with this insight, the son has been able to change the culture and expand the business. His anxiety and fears have also been alleviated. Therapy is often the only way in which individuals and families can gain insight and help with serious emotional or psychological problems.

Change Through Hybrids and Outsiders. If the family leader is unwilling or unable to change his or her own assumptions, there are alternative ways of changing the firm's basic values and assumptions. One option that Edgar Schein (1985) has discussed is to promote individuals who share most of the basic values and assumptions of the leaders but vary on one or two dimensions. These individuals are enough like the leader to gain acceptance but different enough to introduce change. For example, a new manager could share all the assumptions of the leader of a paternalistic firm with the exception of the assumption about human nature. The new manager could believe that people can be trusted and given responsibility. If such hybrids are promoted and encouraged, the culture can eventually change to become a laissez-faire or participative culture.

If the culture needs to be changed more quickly, replacing the top management with outsiders who have different assumptions is another option. This method of introducing change is often used during crisis periods where a quick turnaround is needed. We have seen a number of cases where professional managers quickly changed the culture when they were brought in to solve a crisis. The disadvantage of this approach is the fact that many of the traditions, routines, and skills that had helped the firm in the past can be lost. Also, long-term employees who are passed over for promotion may become disgruntled and demoralized when outsiders are placed in leadership positions.

Conclusion

It is difficult to change the culture of any business, and to attempt any of the activities that have just been described requires leadership that is committed to change. Since the leaders largely create and shape the cultural patterns of the business, they must understand the effect of those cultures and take steps to ensure that they foster cultural patterns that will allow the business and family to grow and thrive. Family business cultures can either contribute to success or be a major stumbling block. To understand and manage the opportunities inherent in family business cultures is not easy, and it is not often done in family firms, but it is essential for leaders who wish to ensure the continuity of their businesses and the well-being of their families.

References

Becker, H.S., Geer, B., Hughes, E. C., and Strauss, A. L. *Boys in White*. New Brunswick, N.J.: Transaction Books, 1961.

Beckhard, R., and Dyer, W. G., Jr. "Managing Continuity in the Family-Owned Business." *Organizational Dynamics*, 1983, 12 (1), 5-12.

Cray, E. *Levi's*. Boston: Houghton Mifflin, 1978.

Crowther, S. *John H. Patterson: Pioneer in Industrial Welfare*. New York: Doubleday, 1923.

Dyer, W. G., Jr. *Cultural Change in Family Firms:Anticipating and Managing Business and Family Transitions*. San Francisco: Jossey-Bass, 1986.

Pacanavsky, M. Personal communication, June 29, 1985.

Schein, E. H. *Organizational Culture and Leadership: A Dynamic View*. San Francisco: Jossey-Bass, 1985.

Wilkins, A. L. "The Culture Audit: A Tool for Understanding Organizations." *Organizational Dynamics*, 1983,2 (2), 24-38.

Despite their diversity, all family firms exist on the boundaries of two qualitatively different social institutions: the family and the business. Each has its own distinct, often contradictory, notes of conduct. These structural contradictions affect the founder's ability to effectively manage the firm, particularly as it matures and grows. The founder experiences psychological stress as a result of conflicting social norms. Specific conflict areas confronting family business owners include: selection of employees, compensation, equity, performance appraisal, and training and development.

The author recommends that founders gain understanding of the contradictions confronting them, make others in the system more aware, and then to affect the separation of management and ownership.

Managing Human Resources in Family Firms: Problem of Institutional Overlap

By Ivan S. Lansberg

Since the early beginnings of capitalism, the family has constituted a primary vehicle of economic production. In spite of the any significant technological changes that have taken place since those early times, recent surveys show that the family remains a critical force behind many modern work organizations. In the United States alone, for example, over 90 percent of all corporations (including 35 percent of the *Fortune* 500,) are either owned or controlled by a family.

Yet, despite the prevalence of family businesses, our understanding of this type of organization remains rather limited, particularly with regard to its fundamental structure. In response to this state of affairs, this article examines some basic sociological properties of family firms, focusing on how structural contradictions that are built into their fiber affect the founder's ability to effectively manage relatives who work in the business. The article also provides some practical guidelines for entrepreneurs who head family firms.

Institutional Overlap: A Fundamental Problem

Family firms come in many shapes and forms, ranging from the local AM and PM store to the huge multinational In addition, family firms vary widely in their missions and strategies and in the markets in which they operate. Despite this diversity, however, one undeniable fact holds true for all family firms: These organizations exist on the boundaries of two qualitatively different social institutions-the family and the business. Each institution defines social relations in terms of a unique set of values, norms, and principles; each has its own distinct rules of conduct.

These institutional differences between family and business stem primarily from the fact that each exists in society for fundamentally different reasons. The family's primary social function, on the one hand, is to assure the care and nurturance of its members. Thus social relations in the family are structured to satisfy family members' various developmental needs.

The fundamental *raison d'etre* of the business, on the other hand, is the generation of goods and services through organized task behavior. As a result, social relations in the firm are, on the whole, guided by norms and principles that facilitate the productive process.

In their formative years family firms often benefit from the overlap between family and business principles. During this stage, the firm's social dynamics are still highly organic, with all employees reporting directly to the founder/entrepreneur. The informal nature of familial relations is frequently carried over into the firm, serving to foster commitment and a sense of identification with the founder's dream. In addition, during these early days the family often provides the firm with a steady supply of trustworthy manpower.

As the business matures, however, and more complex organizational forms emerge, institutional overlap between family and firm begins to generate conflicts in the organization. Typically, these conflicts manifest themselves in the form of normative contradictions whereby what is expected from individuals in terms of family principles often violates what is expected from them according to business principles.

The Founder

In most family firms, the person who experiences these institutional contradictions most strongly is the founder (usually the founder/father), who sits at the head of both the family and the task systems. Typically the founder finds him – or herself operating under conditions of high normative ambiguity in which incongruent values, norms, and principles erode the ability to manage effectively.

Take, for instance, the following case:

> Harry Peterson is the founding father of a highly successful service business. Now 65 years old, Harry is beginning to consider the prospect of retirement. In so doing, he confronts the difficult task of picking his successor. Harry knows the importance of technical expertise in determining the success of a chief executive officer (CEO) in his business. Harry's son has worked in the business for the past five years. While being bright and hard working, his son lacks the technical knowledge to assume the responsibilities that such a position would require. From a business point of view, Harry feels he should choose one of his senior managers to succeed him. This person is highly competent as a professional and is well acquainted with all the technical aspects of the business. From a parental perspective, however, Harry feels that he should give the job to his son. After all, the son deserves an opportunity to follow in Harry's footsteps and develop into a full-fledged professional. What should Harry do?

Although these problems are structural in nature – that is, they result from conflicting social norms existing independently of the founder – he or she often experiences personal psychological difficulties as a result of the conflicting pressures. Founders frequently experience a great deal of stress from "internalizing" the contradictions that are built into their jobs as heads of the family firm.

Moreover, the psychological stress induced by this conflictive situation reduces the entrepreneurs ability to manage effectively and sets the stage for the firm's eventual downfall, which typically occurs about the time when the founder leaves the business. It is interesting to note that the average family firm exists for approximately 24 years, a period that happens to coincide with the average tenure of most founders.

Human Resources Problems

Contradictions between the norms and principles that operate in the family and those that operate in the business frequently interfere with the effective management of human resources in family firms. Let's examine some characteristic ramifications of this institutional overlap.

Problems of Selection

Typically, relatives feel entitled to "claim their share" of the family business; they flock to the firm demanding jobs and opportunities regardless of their competence. The rationale rests on the family principle that unconditional help should always be granted to relatives who are in need. From a business standpoint, however, the founder knows that the firm cannot be allowed to become a welfare agency. The hiring of too many incompetent individuals (whether they are "family" or not) would certainly threaten the effectiveness and possibly even the survival of the business.

Founders often find themselves in the difficult situation of having to choose between either hiring (or firing) an incompetent relative or breaking up their relationship with some part of the family.

Problems of Compensation and Equity

In the area of compensation, remuneration of relatives who work in the firm also creates difficult problems for the founder. The conflict here again is structural in nature and exists "independent of the founder's will." Let us examine some research findings that shed light on the dynamics underlying the giving and getting of rewards in the family and in the business.

Sociologists tell us that the norms and principles that regulate the process of giving and getting (that is, the exchange of goods and services) in the family are qualitatively different from the norms and principles that regulate the same process in the firm. The exchange of resources in the family is guided by implicit affective principles that focus each person's attention on the needs and long-term well-being of the other, rather than on the specific value of the goods and services being exchanged.

By contrast, the process of giving and getting that operates in the firm is regulated by economic principles that oblige individuals to be explicit about both the market value of the goods and services exchanged and the time frame within which the exchange will take place. Hence the notion of "A fair day's work for a fair day's pay."

Given the problems inherent in mixing the principles of exchange in family and business, it comes as no surprise that many founders have difficulty discussing terms of compensation with their relatives. This is particularly the case with their children who work in the firm. As a result, compensation for relatives is often based on ambiguous principles deriving from a hybrid of family and business criteria and they generate all sorts of dysfunctional processes in the firm.

For instance, contrary to commonly held beliefs about nepotism, studies have shown that founders tend to under-reward their relatives who work in the firm. While this practice is relatively harmless during the formative stages of the firm, it creates considerate problems in the mature family business. Under-rewarding relatives, regardless of their competence, may lead to a situation in which incompetent family employees are retained while competent family employees are driven to seek employment elsewhere.

Founders repeatedly justify such under-compensation by arguing that family members Shave an obligation to help outs in the business. Moreover, founders frequently feel that rewarding relatives in terms of market rates would be perceived as favoritism by non-family employees. Clearly, both of these rationales reflect some confusion about principles of exchange that should operate in the context of the firm.

In compensation, the problems created by the institutional overlap of family and business are not limited to incongruent principles of exchange. Perhaps one of the most difficult problems faced by the founder in this area stems from the fact that family and firm are regulated by different norms of fairness.

In the context of the family, two dominant norms of fairness operate. In vertical family relationships – that is, the relationship between parents and their children – the dominant norm of fairness is the concept of need. Parents have a moral obligation to allocate their resources so that the children's needs are met. In horizontal family relationships, such as the relationships among siblings, equality is the dominant fairness norm. Thus it is assumed that in allocations among siblings, each individual is entitled to an equal share of resources and opportunities.

However, the norm of fairness that operates in the firm is based on the concept of merit. Ideally, the level of rewards an employee receives is determined by his or her competence in accomplishing organizational goals. Given the fundamental task orientation of the business, it is more functional in this context to allocate resources so that those who are most productive receive proportionally larger shares of the resources available in the system.

The mixed nature of family business makes it difficult for founders to resolve allocation problems in way consistent with both the norms of fairness that operate in the firm and the norms of fairness that operate in the family.

The clash between the principles of fairness that operate in the family and in the firm lies at the heart of the problem of nepotism. Seen from the overlapping systems perspective, nepotism occurs when the ground rules that define fairness in the task system are violated that is, when family are given rewards and privileges in the firm to which they are not entitled on the basis of merit and competence.

Problems in Appraisal

The institutional overlap between family and firm also interferes with the appraisal process. Frequently, founders experience many difficulties when trying to evaluate the performance of a close relative who works in the firm, particularly when it comes to objective evaluation of their own children.

First of all, the very concept of appraisal (that is, objective assessment of an individual's contribution and worth) in the context of a family system seems a preposterous idea. In a family system individuals are, by definition, seen as ends in themselves. The standing of an individual in a family is determined more by who the individual "is than by what the individual "does." Applying a set of objectively derived criteria to evaluate a family member's performance goes against the very principles that regulate and define social behavior in the family.

In the firm, on the other hand, the process of appraisal seems fully congruent with the requirements of a system whose primary function is economic productivity. In this context, looking at individuals more as means than ends enables us to identify those who contribute most to the achievement of organizational goals.

It is not surprising therefore, that a founder faced with having to assess the managerial competence of his or her own offspring experiences a great deal of stress because it is not possible simultaneously to do justice to the norms and prescriptions that operate in the family and in the business systems. Moreover, the founder's difficulties in making such appraisals are frequently compounded by informational problems. These problems emerge when nonfamily employees cover up a relative's incompetence – either to curry favor or to avoid "crossing" the founder.

Problems in Training and Development

The clash between family and business principles also impacts the founder's ability to manage effectively the training and development of family members. In this instance, founders frequently find it difficult to separate individual needs from organizational needs. From a family point of view, the relative's training should focus on "whatever is best for him or her." From a business point of view, training should emphasize learning experiences that will increase the individual's ability to attain organizational goals. Very often, however, individual relatives' needs do not coincide with the firm's needs. Moreover, founders are frequently willing to invest organizational resources in ventures that, while being risky or even outright incompatible with the organizations core mission, are intended to provide their offspring with an opportunity to grow and develop.

Coping Mechanisms

Caught in the midst of these conflicting institutional prescriptions, founders often have trouble adopting clear and explicit management criteria. This is particularly true in these areas of human resources management in which family and business principles come directly into conflict. To cope with the stressful double bind in which they find themselves, many founders adopt one of two strategies.

One is to adopt decisions that compromise between conflicting family and business principles. These compromises, however, often lead to decisions that are suboptimal from a management point of view. For example, one founder who was unable to choose between his son and a professional manager as his successor decided to split the office of chief executive into two distinct offices, giving one to his son and one to the professional manager. In this case the founder's "solution" led to a power struggle between the two that threatened the firm's long-term survival.

Another coping strategy for dealing with the institutional contradictions that confront them is to indiscriminately oscillate between family and business principles. Founders often arbitrarily behave strictly in accordance with business principles in some instances and strictly in accordance with family principles in others, without laying down a set of criteria or guidelines that specify when family or business principles are appropriate. This constant oscillation between business and family principles often leads to discontent both among employees and among relatives, all of whom perceive the founder as being inconsistent and unpredictable in his or her managerial approach.

Solutions To These Problems

It is evident from the foregoing analysis that the institutional contradictions facing the founder are built into the very nature of these organizations, so the problems entailed can never be fully resolved as long as the firm remains a family business. From our perspective, the best that founders can hope for is to develop procedures for managing more constructively the contradictions inherent in their role as founders.

As an important first step toward the development of constructive coping strategies, founders need to gain the awareness that a fundamental part of the stress they experience is environmentally induced Research evidence on what is typically referred to as "role conflict" suggests that understanding the problem's structural roots would significantly reduce their stress and enhance their ability to manage these institutional contradictions more effectively.

Similarly, founders need to make significant others (both in the family and in the firm) aware of the contradictions that are built into the family firm's strum turn Shifting the problem's source from the founder to the system would stimulate the formulation of procedures for separating family and business issues and would set the stage for collaborative problem solving among all the parties concerned.

The key to developing effective procedures for managing these contradictions is the separation of management and ownership. Basically, this entails examining the relatives who work in the firm from two distinct perspectives: an "ownership" perspective and a "management" perspective. From an ownership perspective, relatives would be subject to all the norms and principles that regulate family relations; from a management perspective, relatives would be affected by the firm's principles. Let us briefly examine how this separation would work in terms of the various human resources problems discussed earlier.

First of all, the separation of ownership and management issues in terms of personnel selection would call for accepting into the firm only those relatives who, on business grounds, were thought to possess the skills needed to perform effectively on the job. Hence from a management perspective relatives would be treated just as others are treated when they apply for a position. From an ownership point of view, on the other hand, relatives interested in working in the firm would be given the opportunity to acquire the necessary skills to meet the firm's standards. These opportunities could take many forms, including sponsored apprenticeships in other firms, formal educational training, and so forth. The funds to cover the necessary training expenses would come from the family=s assets rather than from the business. In this way relatives could be taken care of in a manner consistent with family principles without necessarily compromising the firm's sound management standards.

Second, in terms of the compensation process, a similar distinction between management and ownership needs to be made if we want to develop more constructive ways of managing the institutional overlap. In this case the separation of management and ownership would entail rewarding relatives working in the firm strictly on the basis of business principles. Any additional rewards, advantages, or opportunities for relatives would be allocated under the ownership umbrella quite independently from the relatives' standing in the firm. For instance, under these conditions a founder wishing to provide a son or daughter with an expensive life style would make the necessary income available to him or her by way of stock dividends, not by inflating the offspring's salary beyond his or her professional worth in the market. Such an arrangement would ensure honoring the offspring's privileges as an owner while maintaining an effective merit-based reward system.

With regard to the appraisal process, the separation of ownership and management implies that relatives working in the firm would be subject to evaluation on professional grounds, like everyone else working for the firm. To deal with the potential conflicts between family and business principles, the appraisal of family members would include the opinions of subordinates, peers, and superiors rather than just the potentially biased opinion of founder or family.

Finally, the separation of management and ownership has important implications for managing the training and development of family members who work in the firm. From a management perspective, it is important to plan explicitly the career and training paths of relatives in the business. Moreover, as would have to be the case for nonfamily employees as well, career paths for relatives would have to mesh with the organization's overall goals. Any relative working in the firm whose interests and needs fail to mesh with the organization's goals would have to reconsider his or her employment in the business. From an ownership point of view, these individuals would be entitled, as members of the owning group, to claim a share of the family assets to invest in pursuing their professional objectives outside of the firm. The size of their share of family assets would, of course be determined by family and not by business principles.

Selected Bibliography

To my knowledge, one of the most complete sources on family firms to date is Pat Alcorn's *Success and Survival in the Family-Owned Business* (McGraw Hill 1982). This work is geared to a managerial audience and covers a broad range of issues from entrepreneurship to succession. Other classics in family businesses include: Harry Levinson's "Conflicts that Plague Family Businesses" (*Harvard Business Review*, March-April 1971); "Transferring Power in the Family Business" by Louis B. Barnes and Simon A. Hirshon (*Harvard Business Review*, July-August 1976).

Readers who might be interested in a more theoretical treatment of the conflicts generated by institutional overlap are directed to Robert K. Merton's classic, *Sociological Ambivalence and Other Essays* (The Free Press, 1976). Another classic sociological work that deals with the nature and consequences of structural conflicts is *Organizational Stress: Studies in Role Conflict and Ambiguity* by Robert L. Kahn, Donald M. Wolfe, Robert P. Quin, J. Diedrick Snoek, and Robert A. Rosenthal. (John Wiley and Sons, 1964).

Other relevant articles in the social/psychological literature include: M. S. Clark's and J. Mills's "Interpersonal Attraction in Exchange and Communal Relationships" (*Journal of Personality and Social Psychology*, January 1976), M. Deutsch's "Equity, Equality and Need: What Determines Which Value will be Used as the Basis of Distributive Justice?" *Journal of Social Issues*, Justice Motive in Social Behavior Issue, Volume 31, Number 3, 1975), and C. C. Peterson, "Distributive Justice Within and Outside the Family" (, May 1975).

CHAPTER 7
BOARDS OF DIRECTORS IN THE FAMILY FIRM

Owners of family businesses usually cherish their independence. Often, the last thing they want to do is share information with outsiders or justify their actions and decisions. Yet to improve family business's chances for survival and success, creating a meaningful board of directors containing respected outsiders is a widely offered prescription from those who work extensively with family businesses.

The planning essential for long-term success can be stimulated and guided by outsiders selected for their particular expertise and overall business acumen. They can provide invaluable contacts. Perhaps most importantly, the board helps with thorny questions related to succession.

While the percentage of family businesses with meaningful outside participation is still small, those who have them say that their boards are extremely valuable. Those who have not set up outside boards raise common concerns and excuses. Here are some of the most frequently expressed and the authors' answers to them.

10 Myths About Outside Boards

By John L. Ward and Craig E. Aronoff

"The best thing we ever did was put independent, outside directors on our board," says one family-business owner. We know. "I sure wish I'd done it sooner. It would have saved us a lot of grief and a lot of money."

Family-business owners tell us again and again about the tremendous benefits they gain from having CEOs of other companies on their board. They praise the strategic stimulation they receive. They recognize the value of objective perspective on family business topics such as succession, family compensation, and shareholder involvement. Most of all, they appreciate the empathetic counsel they get as they struggle with the loneliness of leadership.

We wonder, then, why so few family businesses have outside boards. Our research suggests that no more than 5 percent to 10 percent of medium-sized private companies have the three or so outside directors necessary to have a creative, effective board. Here are the excuses we hear most often – and how we respond:

1. *No one that good would serve on my board.* Business owners are often too humble to believe they can attract the CEOs of other, usually larger, dynamic companies. However, in our experience, When one business owner approaches another wanting help with the interesting challenge of board membership, the second owner is inclined to say yes.

   Business leaders know how much board membership benefits them. As they learn about your business, they think about their own. They enjoy learning from other leaders on the board.

2. *I don't even know people who would serve.* That's very frequently true – and that's a good thing. Usually, the better you know board candidates, the less appropriate they are. Start by defining the background and experience you are looking for, not by confining yourself to people you know. When what you're looking for is clear, then your friends, suppliers, and professional advisers (banker, lawyer, accountant, consultants) will be eager to help you identify candidates.

3. *The current family and employee directors will feel hurt.* If existing board members are asked to leave, they may feel disappointed. But they should understand why the change is being made. Board meetings should be only one channel for keeping key people informed and involved. Executive committee meetings should fill that need for key managers; family meetings do it for family. Occasionally invite key managers or family members to board meetings. Share agendas and minutes with them. They shouldn't have to be on the board to be in the loop.

4. *I can't keep meetings interesting enough.* You surely have at least one important strategic question every three or four months. That's the best agenda possible. If you struggle to identify important issues, ask the directors for help. Let them propose some topics for discussion.

5. *I might need to remove a director – that would make me very uncomfortable.* Dissatisfaction with outside directors is far more rare than you might think. One of our surveys shows that only 1 percent of directors were replaced each year because the CEO was unhappy with the board member. Still, we recommend clear, limited terms (two to five years) and a mandatory retirement age, such as 65 to 68. Exceptions can be made when warranted.

6. *Boards are too much work.* Preparation typically takes three or four hours per quarter. However, the financial and management reports you develop for board meetings should be valuable to management as well. Preparation also forces some "strategic reflection," which owners tell us is very valuable in its own right.

7. *We're growing too fast. A board will slow us down.* Your board should include other "fast-growth" CEOs. They will encourage you to slow down if they think it's for the good of the business. Fast-growth companies need good boards the most. They can help anticipate the problems and requirements of your growth.

8. *Directors' liability insurance is too much hassle and expense.* Few existing boards have – or need – directors-and-officers insurance. Corporate indemnification is often quite sufficient. The unprotected exposure for directors of private companies is infinitesimal. In our research, we've found no example of a director's personal penalty. If liability is still a serious concern, form an "advisory council" of the same people to serve the same purpose.

9. *Outside directors don't want to be drawn into resolving family conflict.* Correct, they don't. But we find that the mere existence of a distinguished, respected, outside board lessens family conflict dramatically. And when there is a conflict, the board encourages resolution; it doesn't – and shouldn't – resolve family conflicts itself.

10. *I don't want to give up control.* This is the most frequent underlying concern. Business owners perceive that control rests with the board. In reality, it rests with the shareholders.

As you see, the objections of business owners to having a board are based more on myth than fact. Real obstacles exist – such as family politics or a partner's lack of enthusiasm. In those cases, we recommend starting with an advisory council and letting the concept prove its own value.

In our opinion, an outside board is the best investment you can make in the future of your business and in your family's security.

This article was originally printed in *Nation's Business*, April 1993.

Copyright 1993, U.S. Chamber of Commerce. Reprinted with permission of the authors.

While few pieces of advice are relevant to all family businesses, having and using a board of directors that includes powerful outsiders is a general prescription. Boards contribute mightily to family businesses' strategies, continuity and communication. This article describes the benefits of having excellent outside directors.

Outside Directors: How They Help You

By Craig E. Aronoff and John L. Ward

An active, effective board of outside directors is, we believe, the single greatest resource for the family business. Dozens of business owners who are committed to continuously developing their firms while maintaining family control have told us that having an outside board is the best thing they have ever done.

We typically avoid making broad generalizations, but on this subject, our experience causes us to make some categorical statements. A "good" board will improve your company's strategy. A "good" board will help assure your company's continuity. Board meetings provide important forums for communication. They stimulate planning.

Boards also help in other ways. We've seen business founders racked with doubt about their successors' capabilities or about their own roles subsequent to a transition. By providing a knowledgeable, objective, and understanding perspective, outside board members offer tremendous emotional support.

We've seen many successful transitions that would not have been accomplished without the outsiders on the board. We've seen the failure of transition attempts that would have succeeded had a good board been in place. The board can overcome the fears that most often stall the transition process by providing commitment and momentum for one generation letting go and the next taking over.

When second-, third-, or fourth-generation family firms are co-owned and co-managed by several or many family members, outside directors add strength to the continual search for consensus. Board discussions elevate the quality of discourse.

When some family owners are in the business and others are not, outside directors provide the necessary objectivity for addressing issues such as dividends, titles, compensation, and performance.

We've seen the process of developing appropriate policies change from family feuds to rational deliberation when outside board members were brought into the discussion.

What does a "good" board look like? It includes three or four currently active chief executives whom you respect and who have business and personal experience relevant to the key issues you face. Their only interest in your business is that it grows stronger and lasts longer. The establishment of such an outside board brings many advantages to a family business. Among them:

Fresh, creative perspective. Boards brainstorm ideas and explore embryonic thoughts without the risk that employees might overreact to the topics before they are developed. The breadth and depth and differences of the directors' own experiences bring tremendous creativity.

Objectivity. With no vested interest in you or the business, an outside board is the best source of honest feedback and opinion.

Clarified roles. Family business owners often confuse their various roles. Sometimes they just can't tell whether their thinking represents family, manager, or owner perspectives. Directors can help them see which "hat" they seem to be wearing on a given topic.

Accountability. Outside boards provide discipline and accountability for company leaders, resulting in higher standards and better performance.

Affirmation and confidence. Business owners experience increased self-confidence to take new risks because outside directors usually affirm their thinking and reinforce their abilities.

Promise of continuity. The mere existence of an outside board tells all impacted by the organization that responsible succession planning is a priority. Fears that the business will be sold are diminished. Bankers, customers, suppliers, and others feel reassured. Spouses or heirs have help in case of a crisis.

Symbol of openness. The existence of a board also tells the organization that business leaders are open to new ideas and that their thinking can be challenged.

Despite these tremendous advantages we find less than 5 percent of all mid-size family firms have such an active, outside board. Why?

Most often, business owners just have not imagined the possibility. They think of a board as a fancy governance system for a public company or an honorary relationship in a community organization – not as a resource for the private company.

Often they see the potential but are too humble to believe they can attract highly respected CEOs to be directors. We have consistently found that many private company CEOs will respond positively to an invitation from a well-prepared, well-intended business owner.

Family business leaders sometimes feel overwhelmed by the amount of work they think effective board management will require. In our experience, it takes about 10 days to set up an effective board and another day per quarter to prepare for each meeting. Again, however, those who make the commitment consider it to be perhaps their very best investment.

We have seen boards fail, but only when they are established without adequate thought to their purpose. When family-business chief executives are so committed to their own impulses that they can't take counsel or feedback even from those who have their best interests at heart, a board may not click. Even if they've had such experiences, business owners approaching generational transitions should reconsider the contributions outsiders can bring.

The greatest threats to family-business continuity are strategic myopia and lack of proper succession planning. No one knows that better than successful CEOs of other businesses. Nothing can help you address these threats more than putting CEOs on your board.

This article was originally printed in *Nation's Business*, October 1992.

Copyright 1992, U.S. Chamber of Commerce. Reprinted with permission of the authors.

Conclusions based on research presented in this article show that small business owner/managers who don't plan penalize their business' sales, profitability and productivity. To effectively plan, however, smaller business should take advantage of outsiders to facilitate strategic planning. The study concludes that small businesses should incorporate outsiders into their planning and strategic decision making on a regular, repetitive basis.

The Importance of "Outsiders" in Small Firm Strategic Planning

By Richard B. Robinson Jr.

Small firm owner/managers do not engage in systematic planning. Planning in the small firm is: (1) often done on an ad hoc, problem basis (Golde, 1964); (2) frequently only a mental activity of the owner/manager (Still, 1974); (3) informal, sporadic, and closed (Still,1974); and (4) often relying on advice from random acquaintances with less skill and/or less experience than the owner himself (Rice & Hamilton, 1979).

Although small business owners avoid planning, numerous authors extol the virtues and benefits planning would bring to the small firm (Gilmore, 1971; Steiner, 1967; Still, 1974). Limited empirical evidence is available to support these contentions (Chicha & Julien, 1979; Gasse, 1979; Potts, 1977; Trow, 1961).

Key Component: The Outsider

A considerable body of prescriptive literature has evolved in small business planning that emphasizes the important role of "outsiders in improving the effectiveness of strategic planning in small firms. Unfortunately, only limited empirical evidence has been gathered to support such an idea. (Outsiders generally refer to consultants, lawyers, accountants, bankers, board of directors.)

Trombetta (1976) and Robinson (1979b) examine outsiders involved in small firm planning. Each author offers a case study of a small firm that utilized a consultant in its planning and strategy development. Both authors report a favorable response by the small firm manager, a thorough planning effort, and the adoption of actions that resulted in subsequent increased sales. Unfortunately, their conclusions are quite limited due to their single firm samples. Smith's (1978) dissertation looked at the effectiveness of one type of outsider planner-the Small Business Institute (SBI) program. Studying a stratified sample of 42 small firms receiving SBI assistance, Smith found that less than half of the clients gave favorable ratings to the value of SBI assistance. Yet, he also found that 60 percent of the firms implemented one or more of the SBI recommendations. Smith's study is of limited use, however, because "client's perception of SBI value" and "number of recommendations implemented" were the only effectiveness measures employed. Anderson's (1970) dissertation is another study tangentially addressing issues relative to the use of outside planners in small firms. Studying 75 small service firms, he found that 19 firms had Small Business Administration (SBA) loan guarantees and had utilized the management assistance officer (MAO) program of the SBA. Over half of these firms indicated that the SBA-MAO contributed nothing to the firm's success. Given the findings of Anderson (1970) and Smith (1978), Potts' (1977) dissertation might lead one to conclude that outside planners are potentially useful as long as they are not from the SBI or SBA-MAO. Potts compared successful and unsuccessful small businesses on their use of outside accounting services. Though both firms used such services, "successful firms made a significantly broader use of outside accounting services in a 'total planning activity'...had a more positive outlook towards such services...and placed greater importance upon these services" (1977, p.115). Again Potts' perceptual "effectiveness" measures restrict the extent to which definitive conclusions can be drawn.

A growing number of authors argue that outsiders are important participants in small firm strategic planning. Several reasons are offered. Golde (1964) suggests that most large corporations have full time planning staffs, but small firms cannot afford this luxury. Other authors offer this same argument (Buchele, 1965; Cohn & Lindberg, 1972; Krentzman & Samaras, 1960). They suggest outsiders as a remedy for this disadvantage. Still (1974) and Gilmore (1971) go further, suggesting that outsiders can improve the quality of decision making and the likelihood of repetitive use of systematic planning by small firms. In addition, they argue that planning interaction will cause small business managers to take planning seriously and become more motivated to allocate the time necessary. Buchele suggests that planning with Outsiders can get the small businessman away from day-to-day operations, thus allowing him the chance to plant (1965, p.129).

Other authors suggest outsiders as a means to compensate for small firms managers' lack of planning skill Sexton and Dahle argue that outsiders can supplement "limited entrepreneurial capacity...imperfect or insufficient information" presenting impediments to small firm planning (1976, p.164). Timmons, Smollen, and Dingee (1977) suggest that outside consultants can supplement inadequate skills in both the process of planning and the content of strategies. Timmons feels that outsiders can help difficult planning issues that concern family problems, difficult decisions, and trade-offs. Wheelwright (1971) reports that computer simulated consulting in strategic planning evokes more "creative and high payoff strategies" from small firm managers participating in a management development seminar.

Golde, one of the earliest proponents of using outsiders in small firm planning, makes the following observation:

> Outside people may be very valuable aides to planning. Company directors, accountants, lawyers, bankers, or advertising agencies frequently prove helpful. In most cases, the help these people can provide is more in developing the planning approach than in actually doing major chunks of company planning. The cost of such outside help is likely to be minimal or nonexistent if these people are already servicing the company in some fashion. If more concrete help of a sizeable nature is required, it is always possible to call in an outside management consultant...Formal use of an outsider in planning has one other helpful effect...the (day-to-day) pressures on a small-company executive are immense, and the executive typically responds to the strongest pressures. An outside person can become the one who continually gives firm reminders that time must be spent on planning (1964, p. 154).

Cohn and Lindberg (1972) surveyed 197 small and large firm executives about their perceptions of the critical difficulties in managing small versus large companies. Cohn and Lindberg found that although the skills, time, and staff necessary for planning are not major issues in large firms, they represent 98 percent of the planning-related management difficulties in small firms.

When these authors refer to outsiders, they discuss two basic types. Mainer (1968) and Buchele (1965) make reference to a board of directors for the firm. Following Golde's suggested "outside types of people" (1964, p.154), they perceived that small firms should include outside people with vested interest in the firm's performance in a board of directors role. Such people include primarily bankers, lawyers, and accountants with whom the firm does business.

Krentzman and Samaras (1960), while recognizing the importance of outside assistance in planning, apparently prefer consultants over the composition of a board of directors as previously described. They suggest:

> The board of directors represents real resource...A well-informed, hard working, practical-minded outside board can be a precious asset, although...its members often do not have the time to help the manager in executing their good suggestions. Securing such a board is no easy task, of course, since they

are rare among small firms...A firm's banker, lawyer, and accountant are often called on to serve in what is essentially a consulting capacity...but, except by circumstance, they lack the rounded view possessed by consultants...who are experienced in a range of problems...The executive of a small business is probably far better informed about the specifics of "his own industry" than are most advisors. What he needs is not only creative advice but on-the job assistance in carrying out...resolution on immediate crisis situations and establishment of long-range planning techniques which will minimize future crises and maximize future opportunities...(1960, P.90).

Buchele supports consultants for small business planning. He suggests that consultants "often have insights that escape insiders, can see a possibility that the insiders cannot see...and offer realistic assessment of the firm's strengths and weaknesses" (1965, p.125).

The costs of such outsiders, whether directors or consultants, appears to be seen as prohibitive by many small firm managers (Krentzman & Samaras, 1960). Several authors see this perception as erroneous (Buchele, 1965; Drucker, 1977; "The Role of the Consultants," 1975). Nonetheless, given the strong support many advocates have offered for the potential of consultants to improve planning in small firms, increasing emphasis is being placed on government supported consulting assistance ta small firms.

SBA sponsored programs received the most attention. These include the SBI, MAO, and Services Corps of Retired Executives (SCORE) programs. Studies by Anderson (1970) and Smith (1978) cast doubt on the ultimate effectiveness of the SBI and MAO approaches. The SBI program, using undergraduate students as consultants, was seen to be of more benefit to the student than to the small businessman. SBI and SCORE are both quite limited in resources and therefore lack the capacity to meet potential small business planning demands (Krentzman & Samaras, 1960). Anderson (1970) suggests that the MAO program places greater emphasis on policing SBA loans and loan guarantees than on management assistance. Fogel goes so far as to suggest that "the SBA could best help small businesses by helping them plan..not by giving them loan-guarantees" (1979, p. 9).

Small Business Development Center Program

Recognizing the need for staff specialists and planning consultants in small firms, as well as the hesitancy or inability of small firm owner/managers to procure such services through conventional sources, the Small Business Development Center (SBDC) program was inaugurated in 1977 on an experimental basis in eight states (Flewellen & Bramblett, 1978; 1979). These centers attempt to meet this outsider need more effectively by providing free, comprehensive managerial planning consultation to small businesses in a manner patterned after the Agricultural Extension Service (Flewellen & Bramblett, 1978). The SBDC programs are staffed by MBA students, Ph.D. students already holding the MBA, and full-time professionals (holding the MBA). A major prerequisite at the University of Georgia SBDC is prior business experience in order to become a "staff consultant" (Flewellen & Bramblett, 1978; Robinson, 1979a). These staff consultants are available for "in-depth consulting...regarding the problems, critical decisions and planning...of the small firm manager" (Robinson, 1979a, p.124). SBDC staff consultants also engage in the transfer of specific information (for example, the types of business licenses that are needed for X business) and in continuing education seminars. The present study is concerned one with SBDC assistance of an in-depth nature with business owners or managers.

SBDC consultants assist the manager in analyzing and making strategic decisions regarding the client firm. Hofer and Schendel (1978) identify three major levels of strategy: corporate strategy, business strategy, and functional area strategy. For small firms, corporate and business level strategies are synonymous. Furthermore, in the small firm, the interdependence of business and functional area strategies is often inseparable when facing critical strategic problems. SBDC consultants consistently address a wide range of functional area problems or strategies (financial, marketing, personnel, control, etc.) in addition to the overriding business level strategy (for example, should a motel operator increase emphasis on his campground and gradually phase out the motel operation?) in their role as outsiders in the firm's strategic planning. In the aggregate, the range of problems or strategic issues addressed by SBDC consultants is broad. This is consistent with the idea that the content of strategic planning (or strategic management) in small firms must focus thoroughly on both business level and functional area strategy. Therefore, the assistance rendered by SBDC consultants in in-depth SBDC cases provides a logical operationalization of outsider-based, small firm strategic planning as it has been advanced in the literature

Hypotheses

The overriding research question guiding this study asked: Is there a difference in the effectiveness of small firms engaging in outsider-based strategic planning (OBSP) and that of similar small Sums that do not engage in such planning? The study compared the effectiveness of small firms that had engaged in OBSP (in-depth SBDC assistance) and two, small firm control groups that did not engage in OBSP. The experimental and control groups were compared over matching pro and post-OBSP time periods. Two hypotheses were tested:

Hypothesis 1. The profitability of small firms engaging in OBSP is not significantly different from a matched sample of small firms from RMA Annual Statement Studies (1978, 1979) during pre- and post-OBSP time periods.

Hypothesis 2. The change in effectiveness of small firms engaging in OBSP will not be significantly different from that experienced by a random sample of small firms in a bookkeeping service control group over matching pre- to post-OBSP time periods.

Method

The focus of this study was to examine the impact of outsider-based, strategic planning on the effectiveness of small firms in an attempt to ascertain whether strategic planning, and particularly outsider-based strategic planning, is of value in the small firm. A firm was defined as small if it met each of the following restrictions.
1. less than 50 employees
2. less than $3 million in annual sales
3. independently owned and operated

Sample

The sample included 101 small firms that had received SBDC strategic planning consultation (outside-based strategic planning) and two control groups not engaging in outsider-based planning. The first control group was a matched sample of small firms from *RMA Annual Statement Studies* (1978). The firms in this control group were matched with SBDC sample firms by type of business (SIC code) and annual sales. The second control group was a random sample of 61 similar small firms from the files of a northeast Georgia bookkeeping service. Files were identified that were similar to the SBDC sample by type of business (SIC code), annual sales, and number of employees. A random sample, every third folder, was selected. Table 1 provides a breakdown of the SBDC sample and the two control groups by type and characteristics of the firms.

Chi-square goodness of fit tests were used to examine the representativeness of the SBDC sample with the two control groups, the small business population in Georgia, and the small business population in the United States. Three dimensions of representativeness were examined: (1) percentage distribution of the three categories of firms, (2) percentage distribution of specific types of firms (by SIC code) within each category, and (3) mean/median annual sales and number of employees. The chi-squares ranged from 1.01

Table 1. SBDC and Control Group Samples

Characteristic	Retail	Service	Manufacturer	Overall
Number in sample				
SBDC	48	40	13	101
RMA[a]	48	40	13	101
BKS[b]	31	30	--	61
Mean annual sales				
SBDC	$250,310	$181,730	$473,676	$251,904
RMA	$228,752	$152,451	$422,798	$225,710
BKS	$226,052	$118,594	--	$165,827
Mean number of employees				
SBDC	5.4	5.8	13.4	6.6
RMA	--	--	--	--
BKS	6.0	5.2	--	5.8

[a]RMA Annual Statement Studies (1978) sample.
[b]Northeast Georgia bookkeeping service sample.

to 5.35, with none reaching significance at the .05 level. Therefore, a thorough pattern of representativeness was present between the SBDC sample, the control groups, and the populations. This level of representativeness avoids what has been a major deficiency in previous policy research with small firms – a pervasive use of samples composed exclusively of manufacturing firms.

The SBDC sample and the two control group sample were compared on one additional dimension: profitability before engaging in outsider-based strategic planning. If pre-OBSP profitability was significantly lower in the OBSP group than in the control groups, then a subsequent finding of significantly higher improvement in OBSP firms' effectiveness might be attributable as much to normal recovery as to OBSP impact.

To compare the OBSP group with the RMA control group, net profit divided by sales was used as the measure of profitability. A correlated samples *t-test* was used to examine mean differences. The results are shown in Table 2. The pre-OBSP profitability of SBDC firms and RMA control group firms was not significantly different.

A similar procedure was followed to examine the pre-OBSP profitability of SBDC firms and BKS control group firms. Two measures of profitability were available in this case: net profit divided by sales (NPOS) and net profit plus compensation divided by sales – return on sales (ROS). A *t-test* was use owner d to compare the SBDC and BKS means on each profitability measure. The results are provided in Table 3. The profitability of SBDC firms was not significantly different from the BKS firms during matching pre-OBSP time periods on either measure of profitability.

Table 2. SBDC Versus RMA: Pre-OBSP Profitability

	Mean NPOS[a]%	t	df	p
SMDC	4.40	-.84	100	.41[b]
RMA	6.04			

[a]NPOS = net profit before taxes/total sales.
[b]No significant difference between SBDC firms and RMA firms on pre-OBSP profitability

Table 3. SBDC Versus BKS: Pre-OBSP Profitability

	Mean NPOS[a]%	t	df	p
SBDC	7.18	-1.66	149	.11[c]
BKS	10.85			

	Mean ROS[b]%	t	df	p
SPDC	16.63	-1.39	143	.17[c]
BKS	20.52			

[a]NPOS = net profit before taxes/total sales.
[b]ROS = (net profit before taxes plus owner compensation)/total sales.
[c]No significant differences between SBDC firms and BKS firms on either measure of pre-OBSP profitability.

Operationalizing Outsider-Based Strategic Planning

SBDC strategic planning consulting, described earlier in this paper, provided the means to operationalize OBSP in this study. The OBSP firms (experimental group) engaged in in-depth SBDC consulting. The two control groups' firms did not engage in SBDC consulting.

A decision rule was employed to identify SBDC-served firms that had engaged in in-depth SBDC consulting (OBSP). To be included as an OBSP firm, the SBDC consulting (in that firm) had to meet each of the following criteria:

1. address business level strategy issues
2. include thorough analysis and decision making in two or more functional areas
3. involve 10 or more contact hours between client and consultant(s)
4. include three or more substantive, contact periods.

This decision rule reflects the basic characteristics of small firm strategic planning, particularly OBSP, identified earlier in the literature review

Operationalizing Small Firm Effectiveness

The assessment of organizational effectiveness has received considerable attention in management literature. For a thorough, general summary of this literature, see Cunningham (1977). For a thorough summary relative to the small firm, see Robinson (1980a, 1980b). One major debate is between the use of organizational goals versus a systems approach to an accurate assessment of effectiveness. Another debate centers around the use of "hard" measures (such as profit, sales, market share) versus "soft" measures (such as job satisfaction or social responsibility) in assessing effectiveness. One consistent theme in this literature is that organizational effectiveness is a multivariate phenomenon. In the present study, effectiveness generally was operationalized as a multivariate phenomenon. In the comparison of OBSP firms with RMA firms in Hypothesis 1, effectiveness was operationalized with only one measure: net profit before taxes divided by sales (profitability). A multivariate operationalization was not feasible due to the limited nature of Robert Morris Associates data (number of employees and owner compensation were not available). In Hypothesis 2, effectiveness was operationalized as a multivariate concept.

Table 4 presents the measures used to operationalize effectiveness in this studs

Grows Profitability and Productivity. Friedlander and Pickle's (1968) in-depth study of small firms suggested that effectiveness as measured by improvement in profitability and growth in sales appears significantly associated with increased effectiveness as measured by satisfaction of community, customer, and employee needs. Studies by Alves (1978), Edmister (1970), and Gnu (1973) support Friedlander and Pickle. Each found a measure of profitability, productivity, and a measure of change in sales to be the most significant com-

Table 4. Operationalizing Organizational Effectiveness

Dimension of Effectiveness	Variable Used to Operationalize Each Dimension	Formula Employed to Measure Each Variable		
Growth	Percentage increase (decrease) in total sales	Total sales for post-OBSP time period (adjusted for inflation)	[–]	Total sales for matching pre-OBSP time period
		Total sales for matching pre-OBSP time period		
Profitability	(Hypothesis 1) Absolute increase in net profit before taxes/total sales (NPOS)	NPOS for post-OBSP time period	[–]	NPOS for matching pre-OBSP time period
	(Hypothesis 2) Absolute increase in (net profit before taxes plus owner compensation)/total sales (return on sales - ROS)	ROS for post-OBSP time period	[–]	ROS for matching pre-OBSP time period
Productivity	Absolute increase in sales/employee	Sales/employee for post-OBSP (time period adjusted for inflation)	[–]	Sales/employee for matching pre-OBSP
Employment	Percentage increase in the number of full-time equivalent employees (FTEs)	Number of FTEs for post-OBSP time period	[–]	Number of FTEs for matching pre-OBSP time period
		Number of FTEs for matching pre-OBSP time period		

ponents of discriminant equations between successful and unsuccessful small firms. Furthermore, all three studies concluded that return on sales was a more powerful measure of profitability than return on investment in small firms because specification of "investment" is inconsistent on small firm balance sheets.

Finally, each study employed sales per employee (total sales divided by number of employees) as a measure of productivity.

Social Responsibility. The small business sector of the economy creates more jobs than any other. Between 1969 and 1975, 14 million Americans joined the civilian work force and 9 million jobs were created. During that time there was no net increase in employment among the 1,000 largest U.S. corporations. Of the nine million individuals in the new jobs, three mid lion went to work for state and local governments, and the remaining six million went to work for small business (*Fact Book on Small Business*, 1979). Small business plays an important role in U S. society as a source of employment Therefore, increasing number of employees was used in this study to reflect the social responsibility dimension of small firm effectiveness

Absolute Change Versus Percentage Change. The concern of this study was the comparative improvement in effectiveness over a specific time period between OBSP and non-OBSP firms. The four effectiveness measures were taken for matching pre-OBSP and post OBSP time periods on all firms (with the impact of inflation on sales controlled for). The focus of analysis was the increase or decrease (change) in effectiveness (four measures) for OBSP and non-OBSP firms. Two effectiveness measures, sales and number of employees, were measured as "percentage change" from pro to post-OBSP time periods in order to control for differences which might have been attributable to size if "absolute change" were used. For example, two firms (A and B) might experience an identical $100,000 increase in sales and an increase of 4 employees over the two time periods measured.

However, if firm A had $200,000 in sales and 5 employees during the pre-OBSP time period while firm B had $1 million in sales and 45 employees, the relative accomplishment of firm A is considerably greater than firm B. The use of "percentage change" controls for this size distortion in sales and number of employees. There is danger in the percentage change approach, however, if one group is predominated by very small farms (by sales) and the other by large (small) firms (again using sales). As reported earlier, this danger was examined via median sales and number of employees. No significant differences in the distribution of firms by sales or employees between the OBSP and non-OBSP groups existed.

Profitability (return on sales) and productivity (sales per employee) are ratios. The potential for distortion due to size differential does not exist. Therefore, absolute change was used to measure increase or decrease in these effectiveness measures

Statistical Analysis

Hypothesis 1 was tested using the correlated sample truest. Hypothesis 2 was tested using one-way multivariate analysis of variance (MANOVA) with Duncan's multiple range test as an a posterior follow-up to isolate sources of overall differences (*Statistical Analysis System*, 1979).

Table 5. Results: Hypothesis 1

	Mean Sales	Mean NPBT[a]	Mean NPOS[b]%	t	df	p
Pre-OSBP time period						
OBSP firms	$252,724	$10,018	4.40	-.77	200	.44[c]
RMAfirms	$225,710	$13,683	6.04			
Post-OBSP time period						
OBSP firms	$279,959	$24,636	8.79	2.31	200	.03[c]
RMAfirms	$226,110	$13,877	6.09			

[a]Net profit before taxes over the time period in which total sales were generated.
[b]NPOS = (net profit before taxes)ltotal sales.
[c]Although the profitability (NPOS) of OBSP and RMA firms was not significantly different before OBSP, OBSP firms had a significantly (.05 level) higher profitability than RMA firms after engaging in OBSP (p. < 03)

Results

Hypothesis 1: Hypothesis 1 was rejected The results of the test of this hypothesis are present in Table 5. Although the profitability of OBSP firms and RMA firms was not significantly different during the Pre-OBSP time period, the OBSP firms were significantly more profitable than RMA firms during the post-OBSP time period. Small firms that engaged in OBSP had a significantly higher increase in profitability (NPOS) than did the matched sample of RMA firms. These findings were consistent in each of the three types of firms (retail, service, and manufacturing).

Hypothesis 2: Hypothesis 2 was rejected. The results of this hypothesis are presented in Table 6. Small firms engaging in OBSP had a significantly higher improvement in effectiveness than did the random sample of BKS firms. The Duncan's follow-up proce dure found three sources (at the .05 level) of this overall significant difference: sales, profitability (ROS), and number of employees. These findings were consistent for both types of firms, although the differences were more pronounced in service firms.

Table 6 Results: Hypothesis 2

MANOVA: F(4, 140) = 4.40   P = .002

Duncan's Follow-up procedure:

	Sales[a]	ROS[b]	Employees[c]	Productivity[d]
Pre-OBSP time period				
OBSP mean	$270764	16.23	5.82	$41,768
BKS mean	$290,197	20.52	5.83	$54,977
Post-OBSP time period				
OBSP mean	$297.955	17.76	6.40	$45,869
BKS mean	$296.910	18.21	6.12	$58,091
Change				
OBSP	29.1%	1.53	20.9%	$ 3,299
BKS	3.9%	-2.31	5.4%	$ 3,144
Significant differences				
	SD@.05	SD@.05	SD@.05	NSD

[a]Total sales or revenue for matching pre - and post-OBSP time periods

[b]Return on sales = (net profit before taxes + owner compensation)/total sales.

[c]Number of full-time equivalent employees.

[d]Sales per employee over pro- and post-OBSP time periods.

[e]Using Duncan's New Multiple Range Test to isolate sources of overall difference found in the MANOVA procedure.

Discussion

The results of this study support the authors who have urged small businesses to utilize strategic planning. Small business owner/managers who continually "do not have enough time to plan" are penalizing their business' sales, profitability, and productivity. Indeed, this study would suggest that they are penalizing society by denying the potential for increased employment. In each hypothesis, small firms engaging in outsider-based strategic planning experienced significantly higher increases in effectiveness than did their control group counterparts not engaging in such planning. This appears to be the case whether the firms were retail, service, or manufacturing firms

If small businesses are to utilize strategic planning as an effective management tool, a major necessity (based on this study) is the comprehensive inclusion of outsiders in the planning effort. Apparently, outside planning consultants supplement the owner's lack Of planning orientation, skills, time allocation, and commitment. The tentative conclusion of this study is that small businesses should incorporate outsiders into their planning and strategic decision making on a regular, repetitive basis.

Strategic management/business policy theory and research has expanded considerably over the last fifteen years. Unfortunately, small firms have been basically ignored in this expansion. This study suggests small business to be a fertile area for policy research. Indeed, the role of outsiders suggests a specific difference in strategic planning in large versus small firms. A recent study found that "the degree of openness in long-range planning processes is directly related to the degree of environmental complexity and instability for large firms, but inversely related for small firms" (Lindsay & Rue, 1980, p.402). Apparently firm size is a critical contingent variable in any evolving contingency approach to business policy. If so, the smaller end of this size contingency deserves considerably more attention in business policy research than has been given to date.

Several possible extensions of this research may be considered:

1. Is there a possibility that those business owners who choose to work with an outsider (or SBDC) have somewhat different qualities, such as openness to ideas or greater commitment to economic success? Though not specifically considered in this study, this condition may have some relationship with the decision to use an outsider, the nature of the relationship, and the subsequent impact.

2. Replication to confirm whether or not the outsider is an important aspect of strategic

planning in small firms deserves further research.

3. What level of involvement should the outsider take? Determine what the content role of the outsider should be.

4. Is the use of outsiders (or the nature of their involvement) contingent on environmental circumstances, life cycle considerations, or other variables?

5. Determine whether different types of outsiders (such as SBDC, SBA, lawyers, accountants, consultants, business colleagues) are more effective. And is this continent on different factors or formats?

6. Determine at what point formal strategic planning emerges as an identifiable function in small business within different environmental circumstances (Lindsay & Rue, 1980). Building on this suggestion by Lindsay and Rue:

    a. At what point does the outsider be come an important determinant of the emergence suggested?

    b. If the outsider planner expedites this emergence, is there a critical point(s) in the stages of development at which the payoff is greatest?

    c. Is there a critical point(s) at which the outside planner should lessen or terminate involvement?

Efforts to develop a greater understanding of strategic management in small firms must be undertaken if a truly contingent approach to business policy is to be developed. Lindsay and Rue's suggestion that "small firms should be considered as a separate class in this and future related studies" (1980, p. 402) is a positive, understated challenge to future policy research.

References

Alves, J.R. *The prediction of small business failure utilizing financial and non-financial data.* Unpublished doctoral dissertation, University of Massachusetts, 1978.

Anderson, D.C. *Factors contributing to the success of small service-type business.* Unpublished doctoral dissertation, Georgia State University, 1970.

Buchele, R. B. *Business policy in growing firms.* San Francisco: Chandler Publishing Company, 1965.

Chicha, J. & Julien, P.A. *The strategy of SMBs and their adaption to change.* Trois-Rivieres, Quebec: University of Quebec at Trois-Rivieres, 1979.

Cohn, T. & Lindberg, R.A. *How management is different in small companies.* New York: American Management Association, 1972.

Cunningham, B. Approaches to the evaluation of organizational effectiveness. *Academy of Management Review,* 1977, 2, 463-474.

Drucker, P.F. Helping Small business cope. *Wall Street Journal,* April 21, 1977, 30.

Edmister, R. O. *Financial ratios as predictors of small business failure.* Unpublished doctoral dissertation, Ohio State University, 1970.

Factbook on small business. Washington D.C.: National Federation of Independent Business, 1979.

Flewellen, W. D. , & Bramblett, L.R. The small business development center act. Testimony before the senate select small business committee, United States Senate, 96th Congress, April 5, 1979.

Fogel, I. Importance of planning in small business. *Proceedings of the International Council on Small Business,* 1979, Quebec City, Canada, 20-1, 20-9.

Freidlander, F., & Pickle, H. Components of effectiveness in small organizations. *Administrative Science Quarterly,* 1968, 13 (3), 289-304.

Gasse, Y. Management techniques and practice in small manufacturing firms. *Proceedings of the International Council on Small Business,* 1979., Quebec City, Canada, 16-1 to 16-15.

Gilmore, F.F. Formulating strategy in smaller companies. *Harvard Business Review,* 1971, 49 (2), 71-81.

Golde, R. A. Practical planning for small business. *Harvard Business Review,* 1964, 42 (3), 147-161.

Gru, L. G. *Financial ratios, multiple discriminant analysis, and the prediction of small corporate failure.* Unpublished doctoral dissertation, University of Minnesota, 1973.

Hofer, C. W., & Schendel, D. *Strategy formulation: Analytical concepts.* St. Paul, Minn.: West Publishing Co., 1978.

Krentzman, H. C. & Samaras, J. N. Can small business use consultants? *Harvard Business Review,* 1960, 38 (3), 5764.

Lindsay, W. M., & Rue, L. W. Impact of the organization environment on the long-range planning process: A contingency view, *Academy of Management Journal,* 1980, 23, 385-404.

Mainer, R. The case of the stymied strategist. *Harvard Business Review,* 1968, 46 (2), 36-45.

Potts, A. J. *A study of the success and failure rates of small businesses and the use or non-use of accounting information.* Unpublished doctoral dissertation, George Washington University, 1977.

Rice, G. H. & Hamilton, R. E. *Decision theory and the small businessman.* College Station: Texas A & M University, 1979.

RMA annual statement studies. Philadelphia: Robert Morris Associates, 1978.

RMA annual statement studies. Philadelphia: Robert Morris Associates, 1979.

Robinson, R. B. Business information and consulting services: UGA-SBDC. Paper presented at the annual meeting of the Southwest SBI Association, Houston 1979a 127-138.

Robinson, R. B. Forecasting and small business: A study of the strategic planning process. *Journal of Small Business Management,* 1979b, 17(3), 19-27.

Robinson R. B. *An empirical investigation of the impact of SBDC-strategic planning consultation upon the short-term effectiveness of small business in Georgia.* Unpublished doctoral dissertation University of Georgia, 1980a.

Robinson R. B. The measurement of organizational effectiveness for business policy research in small and growing firms. Proceedings of the *Southern Management Association Annual Meetings,* New Orleans, 1980b, 142-145.

The role of the consultant. *Viewpoint,* Fall 1975. 3. 14-16.

Sexton T. N. & Dahle, R. D. Factors affecting long-range planning in the small business firm. *Marquette Business Review,* 1976, 20(2), 158-165.

Smith, S. B. *The small business institute program: A study of its effectiveness.* Unpublished doctoral dissertation, University of Southern California, 1978.

Statistical analysis system. Raleigh, N. C.: SAS Institute. 1979.

Steiner, G. A. Approaches to long range planning for small business. *California Management Review,* 1967, 10(3), 3-16.

Still, T. W. *An exploratory investigation of strategic planning behavior in small businesses.* Unpublished doctoral dissertation, Florida State University, 1 974

Timmons, J. A., Smollen, L. E., & Dingee, A. L. *New venture creation: A guide to small business development.* Homewood, Ill.: Richard D. Irwin, 1977

Trombetta, W. L An empirical approach to marketing strategy for the small retailer. *Journal of Small Business Management,* 1976, 14(4), 55-59.

Trow, D. B. Executive succession in small companies. *Administrative Science Quarterly,* 1961, 6(3), 232-239.

Wheelwright, S. C. Strategic planning in the small business. *Business Horizons,* 1971, 14(3), 51-58.

The debate over the usefulness of outside board members in family businesses goes on. Two of the three empirical studies on this issue tend to disagree on their value. Using a sample of 262 family business firms, drawn from the Business Week Newsletter for Family-Owned Businesses, this study surveyed CEOs to learn of their attitudes toward inside and outside board members. The findings strongly support the inclusion of outsiders and suggest that the more outside board members the better and the more inside family members the worse, but only where CEO desire, careful selection, and shared expectations are part of that outsider membership.

Outside Boards and Family Businesses: Another Look

By Marc A. Schwartz and Louis B. Barnes

Over the years, we have seen ongoing debates, but little research, on the value of outsiders as members of family business boards of directors. Advocates claim that outside directors are essential to the workings of the board and to the owner families because of their objectivity and because inside directors are beholden to the presiding CEO or their own narrow interests. Proponents of outsiders argue that family members and insiders do not offer much beyond what they might contribute in family discussions or management meetings (Mace, 1971; Danco and Jonovic, 1981; Jacobs, 1985; Ward, 1989). However, the issue is not clear-cut. One recent empirical study supports that conclusion (Ward and Handy, 1988). Another disputes it (Ford, 1988). John Nash, president of the National Association of Corporate Directors, estimates that fewer than 10 percent of family businesses have outside board members beyond the company attorney (Ward, 1988).

Not surprisingly, writers on family business call for more and better studies on the topic. John Ward, one of the researchers just mentioned, made such a plea as guest editor for the *Family Business Review* issue on "Establishing and Managing Boards of Directors." Ward (1988, p. 225) wrote, "To our knowledge, no researchers have examined actual board structure or practice in a scientific sample of private U.S. firms, much less in a sample of family companies." Consequently, we decided to take a look into the matter for ourselves. The results are described in this article.

Some Definitions

As in any field of inquiry, definitions vary. One early study defined a family firm as one where controlling ownership was held by an individual or by members of a single family (Barnes and Hershon, 1976). That study also required the company to be managed by a member or descendant of the founding family. This definition is stricter than most, but it is the one we have adopted. It requires that both management and ownership control be in the hands of family members. Even so, only 5 of the 322 companies that ultimately provided data in our survey were discarded for failing to meet this criterion.

For our purposes, an outside director is one who is neither a member of the controlling family, an active or retired employee, a retained professional adviser, nor a close family friend of the CEO's. We found ourselves agreeing with Dance and Jonovic (1981), who believed that retired company executives and close professional advisers should be considered insiders due to their involvement and possible conflicts of interest. Clayton Mathile (1988), a family business owner writing on the topic, seemed to agree. He noted that "in forming my board, I made the classic mistakes, inviting my attorney, banker, and insurance man...I learned that the worst thing that an owner can do is to have friends and personal advisers on the board. The second worst thing that the owner can do is not to have a board at all" (Mathile, 1988, p. 231).

From our perspective, outsiders included CEOs of other family or public companies, retired executives from other firms, or unassociated business or professional people.

The Debate on Outsiders as Board Members

To the best of our knowledge, only three empirical studies have closely addressed the issue of inside versus outside boards of directors in privately held companies-this despite many opinions on the topic. In combination, the three studies raise almost as many questions as they answer.

One study was reported by Thomas Whisler (1988), who found that what he called growing"threshold" sized firms with outside directors had faster growth rates than those with no outside directors. However, he felt that it would be presumptuous to give the outside directors total credit for this growth rate, since he was unable to control for a variety of other variables in his sample of seventy-three firms.

A second study was conducted by Roger Ford (1987, 1988), who used surveys and some follow-up interviews with a sample of privately held firms. He concluded that outside directors were neither as influential nor as effective as the advocates of outside boards had claimed.

The third study was done by John Ward and James Handy (1988). It, too, relied on a survey of privately held firms, but it did not conduct follow-up interviews. Some of the firms in this study would qualify by our standards as family businesses. Its conclusions were just the opposite of Ford's (1987, 1988).

All three studies raise relevant questions. Ford (1987, 1988) gathered survey data from 214 chief executive officers and ninety-one board members from *Inc.* magazine's "*Inc.* 500" firms.[1] Even though he expected to find that outside board members had more influence on CEOs than inside board members, the data showed just the reverse. Ford (1988, p. 54) concluded that "data from the Board Member Survey and follow-up interviews (with CEO and board members from seven firms)...supported the general finding that inside boards may be more influential or important to the firms than their mixed or outside board counterparts."

In contrast, Ward and Handy (1988) found support for outside boards. Their study included surveys from 147 CEOs (66 ran family businesses) who were members of a midwest association called the Executive Committee.[2] They disputed Ford's (1987, 1988) focus on influence as the key measure of board member value to a company. However, they applied the term outside board to any board with two or more outsiders, including retired company executives, company attorneys, accountants, or consultants. Despite rebuttals and counter rebuttals over methodologies, meanings, and conclusions, the debate goes on.

Research Questions

With some of these events in mind, we tried to make our research questions theoretically and practically meaningful. We had four key questions: Are CEOs more satisfied with their boards of directors if they include outside directors? If so, is there an optimum number of outsiders? Are larger and/or older firms more likely to have an outside board than their smaller and newer counterparts? What are the primary areas in which CEOs perceive outside directors to be of most and least help?

We were also interested in learning how the presence of family members impeded or helped family business boards. Respondents for the study came from approximately 1,100 CEOs who subscribed to the *Business Week Newsletter for Family-Owned Businesses*, at that time the largest periodical directed exclusively toward family-owned businesses.[3] For the purposes of this study, the newsletter provided an ideal sample. The questionnaire response rate was about 30 percent or 322 forms altogether. Sixty of these were incomplete or useless, leaving us with 262 companies.

We assumed that companies with nonfunctioning and/or inside boards of directors would be least likely to respond. We also suspected that our respondents would be more likely to have outside directors than family firms in general and that they would probably use outsiders more often than firms not responding. We made the same assumption of the chief executive officers who expressed a willingness to be interviewed. Nevertheless, only 31 percent of the responding companies had outsiders, as we defined them, on their boards.

Exhibit 1. Questionnaire on the Use of Boards of Directors in Family Firms

1. Would you classify yourself as a(n): ____first-generation entrepreneur
   ____ family business successor ____nonfamily professional manager
2. What proportion of ownership is controlled by family members?
   What proportion is controlled by family members in management?
3. If the company is currently managed by the founding family, which family generation is currently managing the company? If not, at what generation did the company move into nonfamily professional management?
4. How old is your company?
5. What was your average revenue over the last three years?
6. How many employees are in your company?
7. How many of these employees are members of the founder's family?
8. What is the geographical spread of your company?
   ___ local ___ regional ___ national ___ international
9. What type of business are you involved in?
   ___ heavy/light manufacturing ___ high/low technology ___ service
   ___ consumer goods ___ other
10. How many individuals are on your board of directors?
    a. How many directors are family members in management?
    b. How many directors are family members not in company management?
    c. How many directors are in management but outside of the family?
11. If you have any individuals on your board from outside both company management and the family, what are the occupations of these "real" outside directors? (If you have no such members, please skip to question 12).
    a. How old was the company when it first brought in these outside directors?
    b. Which members of either management or the family were most eager to bring in these outside directors?
    c. Which do you find to be the areas in which outside directors are of most help?
    d. Which do you find to be the areas in which outside directors are of least help?
12. Would you say your board has been:
    ___ extremely valuable   ___very valuable   ___ valuable
    ___ not so valuable   ___ a waste of time
13. What advice would you offer to other CEOs concerning family boards?
14. What would you do differently with your board if it could be done?
15. Who do you seek for advice in issues relating to business?
16. Who do you seek for advice in issues relating to the family in business?
17. Do you have an advisory board of outsiders other than a board of directors?
18. How many boards outside of your own do you sit on?
19. Would you be willing to discuss in confidence your experiences with boards of directors in more detail by phone?
20. If yes, please leave your name and phone number. Thanks.

One point to bear in mind is that the survey data represented CEO perceptions. Because they were perceptions, the responses could reflect biases or self-fulfilling prophecies. For example, a CEO who had outside directors on the board might feel compelled to justify his choice by endorsing them as effective and valuable. However, as we shall see, need to justify apparently did not prevent CEOs with only inside boards from being critical. Consequently, the defensiveness effect can probably be discounted.

Nevertheless, we tried very hard to keep our requests and survey questions as neutral as possible. The *Business Week* announcement to its subscribers of the research request simply noted that, "while consultants often advise business owners to fill director slots with outsiders who can bring to the enterprise missing expertise and can mediate disagreements among family members, there is little empirical data on how directors actually work in such firms...[This research] wants to know how much directors contribute and who besides directors are sources of advice" ("Top of the News," 1989, p. 2).

Table 1. Company Characteristics (N = 262)

	Percentage
Chief Executive Officer	
Family business successor (N = 207)	79
First-generation entrepreneur (N g 55)	21
Size of Firm by Number of Employees[a]	
Fewer than 75	31.8
75 to 149	18.7
150 to 224	9.0
225 to 299	6.4
300 to 374	7.1
More than 374	26.2
Size of Firm by Annual Revenue over the Past Three Years[b]	
Less than $20 million	53.2
$20 to 39 million	16.9
$40 to 59 million	10.5
$60 to 79 million	5.2
$80 to 99 million	3.0
More than $99 million	9.7
Character of Business[c]	
Manufacturing	29.6
Service	24.7
Consumer goods	9.7
Distribution	7.9
Technology	4.1
Construction	3.4
Other	20.6
Age of Firm	
Less than 19 years	10.1
20 to 39 years	26.6
40 to 59 years	27.0
60 to 79 years	6.5
80 to 99 years	9.4
More than 100 years	10.5
Family Generation of Present Management[d]	
Less than second generation	22.1
Less than third generation	44.6
Less than fourth generation	22.1
Fourth generation or more	8.2

[a]Two companies did not report number of employees.
[b]Three companies did not report average revenues.
[c]Other includes five different businesses as well as firms designated as being in more than one industry type.
[d]Three companies did not report family generation of present management. The five companies under nonfamily professional management are not included.

In addition, many of the survey questions were deliberately open-ended so as not to influence respondents. (Exhibit 1 presents a copy of the survey questionnaire.) In addition to the survey data, seventeen CEOs and eight outside directors were interviewed at length for additional explanations and interpretations of the data.

Company Characteristics

The survey asked each chief executive officer to describe certain company characteristics. We used these data to help us understand the company's CEO, size, business, age, and generation characteristics. Table 1 displays the information about company characteristics.

Table 2. Board Structure

	Number	Percentage
Inside boards	181	69.1
All-family board	92	35.1
Family-management board	48	18.3
Quasi board	41	15.6
Outside boards	81	30.9
One outsider	21	8.0
Two outsiders	30	11.5
Three outsiders	16	6.1
Four outsiders	5	1.9
Five or more outsiders	9	3.4
Total	262	100.0

Board Size and Structure

The study divided boards of directors into two major categories, inside and outside. An inside board contained only family members, close friends, adviser professionals, or past or present employees of the company. (For the purposes of this study, *professionals* include accountants, lawyers, and consultants.) An outside board included at least one individual who did not meet these criteria. To allow for a more detailed analysis, we divided these main headings into further subcategories. Inside boards included the all-family board, the family-management board, and what we called the *quasi* board. The all-family board is composed entirely of family members. The family-management board contains at least one family member and at least one representative of company management. The quasi board consists of at least one professional or retired company executive and any combination of family members and company management. (The *quasi* designation recognizes that professionals and ex-employees are treated as outsiders in some previous analyses and that they should therefore not be separated from family members and present management.) Outside boards were divided into five subcategories-one outsider, two outsiders, three outsiders, four outsiders, and five or more outsiders-to test Ward's (1989) conjecture that "the presence of two or more outsiders is a critical demarcation." Table 2 shows the data on these board structures.

The data show that more than two-thirds (69.1 percent) of our surveyed firms had inside boards of directors. The figure is probably lower than would be found in the general population of family businesses. (We assumed that CEOs with outside boards would over respond.) Yet, even in our sample, more firms had all-family boards (35.1 percent) than had outside boards (30.9 percent). It is interesting to note that most of the outside boards (22.9 percent) had more than one outsider. This suggests that, once a CEO decides to obtain outside directors, he or she seeks more than token representation.

Some additional patterns appear when company size and age are examined in conjunction with board structure. For example, the size of the firm seemed to dictate board structure to a certain extent. The larger-sized firms in our sample – those with approximately $50 to $100 million in revenue or 400 to 1,000 employees – had a higher percentage of outside boards. This may support Whisler's (1988) findings with regard to threshold companies.

In this middle-upper range, businesses involved in service industries were somewhat more likely to have outside boards than others. This finding should be further explored. Our data show that firms on the extremes-either very small or very large ones-were less likely to have outside boards. For small firms, this finding might be explained by cost considerations as well as by the reluctance of CEOs to open the business to outsiders. Interview data from the largest firm in our sample (a multi billion-dollar company) told us that the CEO felt that the family holdings were too diversified for a single board. Instead, he had replaced his outside board of directors with an advisory board of executives from related industries whom he called on informally, depending upon which busi-

Table 3. Board Size as a Function of Board Structure and Firm Size

Board Structure	Firm Size	Board Size
Inside Boards	(N = 181)	5
Fewer than 100 employees	(N = 82)	4
100 to 500 employees	(N = 62)	5
More than 500 employees	(N = 37)	6
Outside Boards	(N = 81)	7
Fewer than 100 employees	(N = 25)	6
100 to 500 employees	(N = 26)	7
More than 500 employees	(N = 30)	8

Note: Board sizes for subcategories are mean scores. The values given [or the main headings of inside and outside boards are medians as well as means. The difference between the means for the main headings is significant to $p < .0005$.

ness needed help. First-generation entrepreneurial firms were as likely as others in general (30.9 percent) to have outside boards. Most of the seventeen first-generation companies with outside boards in our sample had only one outsider on the board. However, the oldest firms, which included firms with fourth-generation ownership, were more likely to have outside boards. There is no noticeable difference between other age or generation groupings. Finally, CEOs who sat on the boards of other companies were no more likely to have outsiders on their own board than were CEOs who did not sit on other boards, contrary to Ward and Handy's findings (1988). Thus, 63.8 percent of our CEOs with outside boards sat on other boards, but so did 60.3 percent of those with inside boards.

Table 3 shows how board size varies with the inside or outside nature of the board and company size. Inside boards generally had fewer members than outside boards. On the average, inside boards contained four family members and one additional company insider. Outside boards typically had three outsiders, two or three family members, and one or two additional persons. The larger size of outside boards was not due simply to outsiders. There seemed to be fewer family members as well, suggesting that these outside boards included both outsiders and nonfamily insiders. Board composition, when considered in conjunction with inside or outside members, suggests that there is no easy middle ground. Most boards were heavily dominated either by family or by outside members.

Value of the Board

An important question in this study asked CEOs to rate their boards on perceived value. We used this overall board value satisfaction rating to minimize the insider-outsider distinction and the effects of the wide variance in business contexts.

The value responses show very significant differences when they are analyzed according to inside-outside board structure. The responses were made on a Directors-type scale from 1 to 5. A value of 1 is least positive.[4] Table 4 shows the board value data.

Clearly, there is a large difference between the value satisfaction ratings given by CEOs with inside boards and the ratings given by CEOs with outside boards, and the difference is highly significant statistically. The most prevalent board, the all-family board, received the lowest average value rating of all (2.16). From there on, the outlook gets brighter. The data show increasing value satisfaction as the board becomes more subject to influence from outside members. The one exception occurs when the five CEOs with boards including four outsiders rate their boards less enthusiastically than CEOs with either three outsiders or five. The nine companies with five or more outsiders on the board gave the highest rating of all with a 4.78 average. This finding tends to support Ward and Handy's (1988) conclusion that the more outsiders on a board the better.

The data also show that the less family dominated the board is, the more valuable it is perceived to be by CEOs. This implies that family members, especially those not involved in company management, were unwanted, or certainly not valued, as board

Table 4. CEO's Board Value Rating as a Function of Board Structure

	Mean Value	Significance Level
Inside boards (N = 181)	2.32	p < .0005
All-family board (N = 92)	2.16	
Family-management board (N = 48)	2.20	
Quasi board (N = 41)	2.73	
Outside boards (N = 81)	3.83	p < .0005
One outsider (N = 21)	3.48	
Two outsiders (N = 30)	3.7	
Three outsiders (N = 16)	3.94	p > .05
Four outsiders (N = 5)	3.80	
Five or more outsiders (N = 9)	4.78	

Note: Significance levels were conducted as t-tests for differences between two means for two groups of the same sample, $H^0 = X^2 X^1 = 0$, where X^2 is the mean value rating for inside boards and X^1 is the mean value rating for outside boards. The last significance level shown in the table compares boards with two or fewer outsiders with boards containing three or more outsiders.

members by their CEOs. On the average, CEOs with inside boards rated their boards (2.32 average) closer to the not so valuable rating of 2.00 than to the valuable rating of 3.00, which suggests that firms with inside boards lose more than they gain in the eyes of their CEOs.

This difference between the value ratings for inside and outside boards looks even stronger when we turn the data around and examine the responses for inside and outside boards by ratings. Table 5 details these scaled ratings given by CEOs.

When the data are presented in this manner, it is easy to see that CEOs with inside boards give a median response of not so valuable, while the median response for CEOs with outside boards is very valuable. Table 5 also shows the inside-outside data to be at almost opposite extremes. A majority of CEOs with outsiders on their board (65.4 percent) rated the board's value at the upper end of the scale, while almost as large a majority of the CEOs with inside boards (56.9 percent) rated the board's value at the lower end. Only seven CEOs with outside boards (8.6 percent) gave less than a valuable rating, while only 11.6 percent of the CEOs with Inside boards rated their boards as very valuable or extremely valuable. Not one CEO with an outside board rated the board as a waste of time, though forty-two CEOs with inside boards (23.2 percent) did. Only six CEOs with inside boards (3.3 percent) claimed their boards were extremely valuable, in contrast to twenty-one CEOs with outside boards (25.9 percent).

Moreover, six of the seven outside boards given a not so valuable rating were in companies with fewer than 100 employees, and six of these seven CEOs had only one outsider on the board. These findings would seem to provide further support for the claim of Ward and Handy (1988) that two outsiders on a board provide a crucial demarcation. It also reinforces the idea that boards with fewer outsiders will be rated less valuable than those with more. To be sure, boards with only one outsider imply that the desire of the CEO to really "open up" the company to outside perspectives is weaker than it is where boards have more outsider strength. In addition, two or more outside board members imply a critical mass intensity that is lacking when only one person represents an outside perspective.[5] Several outside board members said that they welcomed the company of other outsiders on the board. Others wished that they had such company.

The seventeen CEOs whom we interviewed were asked to describe why they had given their board the value ratings they had. Many who had boards with outside directors noted the presence of outsiders. Common responses included: We gain due to the broader perspective from outsiders. The presence of outsiders enhances the functioning of the board. Outsiders help us to see the forest and not the trees. An outside board gets you to explain actions in a way you can't do with insiders, particularly those insiders with whom

Table 5. Scaled Value Ratings by Board Type

	Inside Boards		Outside Boards	
	Number	Percentage	Number	Percentage
Waste of time	42	23.2	0	0.0
Not so valuable	61	33.7	7	8.6
Valuable	57	31.5	21	25.9
Very valuable	15	8.3	32	39.5
Extremely valuable	6	3.3	21	25.9

Note: Rounding prevents the percentages from totaling 100.

you've worked for twenty years.

These interview data strongly support the view that outsiders are a key factor in the board's positive rating. It is interesting to note in this regard that CEOs who gave lower ratings tended to have inside boards. They responded with statements such as these: The board simply functions as a rubber stamp. The board really doesn't add anything to the company.

Such a devaluing of their board and of insider contributions was accompanied by an unwillingness to use the board more than they did. Some implied that it was impossible to remove unwanted or unhelpful family members from a board. These CEOs reported that insiders provided no board benefits beyond those available in other contexts. Some of them admitted that they did not use their boards very effectively, while CEOs with outsider boards said that their outside members helped force such activity. Inside boards often provided no such challenge.

Role of Outsiders

We asked the CEOs whom we interviewed to describe the areas in which outside directors were of most and least help. Table 6 lists the responses in order of frequency from highest to lowest.

The unbiased, objective views provided by outsiders were valued most by CEOs, while assistance with day-to-day operations was deemed least helpful. These were by far the most frequent positive and negative responses. Indeed, three of the four areas in which outsiders were seen as least helpful involved detailed knowledge of company or technical information-categories similar to those judged by Ford (1988) as associated with what he called *ineffectiveness*. Our findings suggest that Ford (1988) did not look far enough. His conclusion that outside directors were not effective because they lacked specific knowledge narrowed the focus while neglecting outsider helpfulness with general outlooks and issues. In addition, his sample of *Inc.*'s high-growth companies might have exaggerated the problem. His sample of CEOs might have wanted greater detailed technical information because of the stage of their company's development. It is an empirical question worth more research.

Nevertheless, in our sample, detailed company or technical data from board members were apparently neither expected nor highly valued. Instead, board members were apparently valued more for their general perspectives. This does not mean that outside board members were disparaged if they possessed relevant company or technical information-only that it was less valued than their general objectivity.

Both Dance and Jonovic (1981) and Ford (1988) suggest that outside board members can provide two other useful functions: acting as company or family arbitrators and mediators and helping to choose the CEO's successor. Supposedly, the outsider can help during periods of critical controversy and transition. However, in our study, as in Ward and Handy's (1988), mediation and arbitration and choice of successor were viewed as areas in which outsiders were less helpful. People other than outside board members (for example, family members, family friends, consultants) were evidently considered more useful during those periods. CEOs valued outside board members more for their business acumen than for their family assistance. Our interviews with outside directors suggested that

Table 6. Outside Directors' Areas of Most and Least Help

Most Help	Least Help
Unbiased, objective views	Day-to-day operations
Accountability of management	Issues of family conflict
Network of contacts	Technical expertise
Asking challenging questions	Very specific matters
Long-term perspective	
Setting executive salaries	

they, too, valued their own objectivity and did not wish to get involved in family dynamics. One said, "I shouldn't be involved there. It's not my business, and I should be where I can be more objective than they are."

The outside directors thus seem to have viewed themselves more as silent supporters than as active participants when it came to family tensions and conflicts. As we have noted, this finding runs counter to the commonly held view that outside directors should mediate actively and arbitrate family tensions and conflicts. It, too, needs further research.

Challenges of Changing to an Outside Board

We asked CEOs for advice with regard to family business boards and what they would do differently with their board if it were possible. The most common advice was to make more use of outsiders. Related responses stressed increasing the number of outsiders, decreasing the number of family members, and keeping professionals employed by the firm off the board. Other responses suggested keeping the board small, meeting more often, and keeping the family in a control position. Not surprisingly, CEOs with outside directors were most likely to recommend the use of outsiders. Other CEOs answered that they would like to include outsiders on their board but that they had been unable to do so due to family opposition or other family-based difficulties.

There were a number of reasons why some of these CEOs resisted an outside board. Several feared that such things as stock options for outside directors would dilute their control, and they had not looked into alternative compensation possibilities. Some CEOs said that they might prefer the vehicle of the advisory board to the board of directors in order to reduce liability risks as well as to keep control. Others said that the family would never go along with the idea.

Further Implications

Three other criteria for success with outsider boards became clear to us as we studied the data. Each is easier said than done. First, until a CEO honestly wants outside directors, steps to include them are not, and possibly should not be, taken. The risk with delay, of course, is that it potentially prolongs narrow thinking and paralysis. The CEO's desire to open the board to individuals outside the company and the family's willingness to listen to them are the first criterion.[6] With regard to openness to outsiders, one CEO observed that "a strong-minded founder should not have an outside board. My father did, and it was a mistake. The CEO has to be open and maintain open communication with the board, or the directors will realize their efforts are useless, and they will not be committed." A woman CEO in a large, successful company commented, "I'm glad I'm not as strong-minded about the board as my husband was. He didn't want anyone to have any knowledge or say about what went on in the company." And a male CEO observed, "As much as the family agenda needs to be supported by the board, the board agenda needs to be supported by the family."

Once a real commitment to outside directors is made, there is a second crucial criterion. This one involves the search and selection process for the new outsiders. Family members and management are often too involved in the company to bring a sufficiently broad perspective to such situations. Outside directors, our data show, can add value to this search. A poorly chosen outsider will add little to the board and can even be a detriment. One CEO reported that he replaced an outside director because the director exerted so little effort and commitment to the success of the firm. Another commented. "In order to be totally open, which you must be, you have to be careful in hiring. You must create the commitment on the part of the outsiders to do the work."

While critical selection is the second key ingredient, neither CEO nor board members should assume that any individual has a permanent seat on the board. One CEO acknowledged that after twenty years his outsiders "virtually became insiders because they had been around and involved for so long." In theory, this kind of tenure may sound good, but the outsider's main strength-a more objective perspective-is lost. It is important for the CEO to realize that, as Dance and Jonovic (1981) note, tenure on a board is not for life.

Our third rule is that the CEO should clarify and exchange expectations with the new outside members and periodically with the old ones. As with commitment and selection, this rule poses a potential trap. Low, inappropriate, or false expectations can result in a misuse of all board members. Our data suggest that CEOs with outside directors best used their boards for advice, counsel, and accountability. Those with inside boards treated them more as an obligation than as a resource.

Ward and Handy (1988) have remarked that outside and inside boards differ in expectations of the board's role. We might add that the self-fulfilling nature of these expectations can seriously affect a firm. A CEO's expectations will directly and strongly influence his or her perceptions of an outside director's value. Appropriate mutual expectations by both CEO and director are as important as the other two criteria. By establishing these expectations, a CEO can help to determine a director's real value to a firm. Worse yet, if outsiders are not carefully selected, and especially if they are not wanted, their value is likely to reflect these reduced or misguided expectations.

Ford's (1988) study provides an example of CEOs with poor-fit, and possibly inappropriate, expectations. According to our data, CEOs find it less than optimal to expect outside directors to have detailed company knowledge and time availability. Indeed, such close-up strengths may even be regarded as flaws, since our outside directors were seen as most helpful when they could provide unbiased, objective views; establish the accountability of management; and create an outside network of contacts. As one CEO stated, "Having realistic expectations of what outside directors can do is crucial."

The eight directors whom we interviewed strongly agreed with these CEOs. They stressed the importance of a CEO's desire for outside perspectives as well as the need for shared expectations. As noted earlier, two of the directors whom we interviewed were the only outsiders on their respective boards. They commented that at times they "were fighting an uphill battle" and that they could be more effective if there were additional outsiders on the board who could add cumulative weight.

Conclusion

This study has returned to several research issues raised in earlier studies on family business boards of directors. We applied the inside-outside question to an entirely family business sample. Three conclusions seem relevant: First, the CEOs of firms with outside directors on their boards are more satisfied with their boards than CEOs whose firms do not include outsiders. CEOs in firms with more outside directors were more satisfied than those with fewer. One outside director is better than none but not as good as two or more. Second, outside directors are perceived as most helpful in providing unbiased views, forcing management accountability, and establishing networks of contacts. They are of least help in day-to-day operations, resolving explicit family tensions, and working with very detailed company issues. Third, there is a perception of reduced board value and of increased constraints on the CEO as the number of family members increases While the central finding that outside directors can greatly benefit family firms is strongly supported, the data do not indicate that outside directors are highly useful in all family firms. We suggest that three interdependent conditions need to be met before that can be true. First, there must be an honest desire on the part of the CEO, and preferably of family members as well, for an outside board with open communications. Second, a selection process that seeks and assures the choice of competent outsiders is needed. Third, there must be realistic, shared expectations about the contributions that outside directors can make.

Our study suggests also that outside directors are not best used in detailed company or family conflict matters. Instead, they serve better as objective judges of the business and its overall performance. If more help with day-to-day operations or family mediation is part of the CEO's expectations, then the performance of outside directors is likely to fall short. In effect, do not ask outsiders to get too involved in inside issues, either business or family. They may then lose their greatest advantage: their perceived objectivity. Moreover, while our data suggest that outsiders should definitely be included on family boards, they do not address the importance of having outsiders in a majority position on the board. That study still needs to be done.

Finally, an old question needs to be raised again with some aspects of this study in mind. Why do so few family firms survive beyond first generation family ownership and management?[7] Our data suggest that there are potentially great benefits for both entrepreneurs and heirs in developing outside boards if a CEO can meet the three criteria just described. Although an outside board is not ideal for every family business at all times, our data show that outside directors were as highly regarded by first-generation entrepreneurs as they were by CEOs of succeeding generations, although they made fewer explicit comments on the topic. Three of the seventeen entrepreneurs who had outside boards did say that moving to outsiders "the sooner the better" was important. This finding should provide a serious basis for thought to any first-generation entrepreneur who is interested in the longer-term success of his or her company. Entrepreneurs can benefit from, and work with, outside director advisers, however strong-willed the entrepreneurs may be. Keeping outsiders off a board may simply serve personal vanity at the expense of business survival. The age-old dilemma is getting the self-directed, first-generation entrepreneur to want such outside advice. Possibly this article can help to develop further research and debate on that issue as well as others.

Notes

1. The ninety-one board members represented thirty-five firms. However, all the *Inc.* 500 firms were high growth, privately held, but not necessarily family-managed firms; a majority had been in business for an average of six to ten years. It may not have been a good representative sample of family business firms.
2. The Executive Committee, an organization composed of company presidents from Illinois, Minnesota, and Wisconsin, is headquartered in Milwaukee.
3. A privilege received with gratitude from Dan McCrary and Dan Moskowitz of McGraw-Hill, publishers of *The Business Week Newsletter for Family-Owned Business*.
4. For the reader's information, the ratings were: 1 = waste of time, 2 = not so valuable, 3 = valuable, 4 = very valuable, 5 = extremely valuable.
5. The finding is reminiscent of the famous experiments on conformity and deviation by Solomon Asch (1952). A single-voice perspective was much more apt to be silenced or subdued than one strengthened by another similar perspective.
6. The interest of the CEO in having outside direction and the family's willingness to listen were suggested in an informal discussion with Professor Miguel Gallo at the Instituto de Estudios Superiores de la Empresa, University of Navarra, Spain.
7. Even though 95 percent of American (and probably a higher percentage of foreign owned) businesses are family owned or controlled, only 25 percent of these businesses survive into the second generation, and fewer than 15 percent make it to the third generation (Barnes and Hershon, 1976; Ward, 1987).

References

Asch, S. E. *Social Psychology*. Englewood Cliffs, NJ.: Prentice Hall, 1952.

Barnes, L. B., and Hershon, S. A. "Transferring Power in the Family Business." *Harvard Business Review*, July-Aug. 1976, pp. 105- 114.

Danco, L. A., and Jonovic, D.J. *Outside Directors in the Family Owned Business*. Cleveland, Ohio: Center for Family Owned Business, 1981.

Ford, R H. "The Value of Outside Directors: Myth or Reality." *Business*, Oct.-Dec.1987, Pp. 44-48.

_____"Outside Directors 44-48. and the Privately Owned Firm." *Entrepreneurship Theory and Practice*, Fall 1988, pp. 49-56.

Jacobs, S. L. "A Well-Chosen Outside Board Gives Owners Peace of Mind." *Wall Street Journal*, Jan. 21, 1985, p. 21.

Mace, M. L. *Directors: Myth and Reality*. Boston: Division of Research, Harvard Business Schools 1971.

Mathile, C. L'A. Business Owner's Perspective on Outside Boards." *Family Business Review*, 1988, 1 (3), 231-237.

"Top of the News." *Business Week Newsletter for Family-Owned Business*, Dec. 22, 1989, p.2.

Ward, J. L. *Keeping the Family Business Healthy: How to Plan for Continuing Growth, Profitability, and Family Leadership*. San Francisco: Jossey-Bass, 1987.

_____"The Active Board with Outside Directors and the Family Firm." *Family Business Review*, 1988, 1 (3), 223-229.

_____"Researching Inside Versus Outside Directors: A Rebuttal to the Rebuttal." *Family Business Review*, 1989, 2 (2), 147-149.

Ward, J. L., and Handy, J. K. "A Survey of Board Practices." *Family Business Review*, 1988, 1(3), 289-308.

Whisler, T. K. "The Role of the Board in the Threshold Firm." *Family Business Review*, 1988, 1(3), 309-321.

The survey reported in this article begins to examine how boards of various firms are structured. It may serve as a road map for those evaluating or establishing boards. The primary purpose of this article is to present the results of a survey on how privately controlled companies use and structure their boards.

A Survey of Board Practices

By John L. Ward and James L. Handy

Business owners or leaders considering boards face several basic questions: Why would someone serve on my board? Who should serve on my board? How should I structure and manage the board? Even those who are eager to establish an active board with outside members can be deterred or frustrated by these questions. This paper focuses on the last of these three questions: How should I structure and manage the board? While there are ample data on board makeup, compensation, size, and other & factors for large, publicly traded companies, virtually no such data exist on actual board practices in small and private firms. The last study we know of is the one by Jain (1980). Consequently, we surveyed the boards and practices of 147 privately controlled companies. We hope that the data presented here are useful both to those seeking to establish an active board and to those already using an active board.

Survey Participants

The sample of firms that we surveyed was not random. If we had surveyed a random cross-section of all U.S. firms, we would expect fewer than 5 to 10 percent to have an outside board. Our purpose was not to study board status in a cross-section of firms but to gain enough insight into firms with active boards to provide useful information to business owners who are establishing or managing their own active boards.

Our sample of 147 useful responses – and 20 not useful – was drawn from a mail survey of about 350 members of The Executive Committee, an organization headquartered in Milwaukee, Wisconsin, that serves company presidents in Illinois, Minnesota, and Wisconsin. Our respondents were more likely to have outside boards, to structure them professionally, and to seek advice and counsel from them. Nevertheless, more than half of the firms in our sample did not have an outside board, and we believe that those who responded to the survey were more likely to have an outside board than those who did not respond. Table 1 describes the 147 firms that provided useful responses, and Table 2 provides information about their chief executive officers (CEOs).

Comparing the backgrounds of CEOs and their firms and boards is an area for future study. We saw one interesting pattern. The firms that seem more likely to have outside boards are older companies, firms with third- or fourth-generation family owners, firms whose CEOs have advanced degrees, and firms whose CEOs have had personal experience on other companies' boards. CEO age and character of the business seem not to be related to board behavior.

Typologies and Hypotheses

To facilitate our examination of the data, we developed several classifications. For example, we distinguished three types of boards – outside, inside, and token; three types of companies that used boards – entrepreneurial, family, and widely held; and three types of functions of boards – reporting, approving, and advising. Thus, our first aim in this article is to define these terms and others in ways that may be useful to future research or further thinking about board behavior. We will pay special attention to the category *family business board*, because family businesses face particular issues pertaining to board structure and practice.

Table 1. Survey Respondents: Companies (N = 147)

Company Size		Company Ownership	
Fewer than 100 employees	32%		
100-199 employees	27%	Entrepreneurial Ownership	40%
200-299 employees	10%	Founder-owned	21%
300-399 employees	8%	Acquirer-owned	12%
400-499 employees	3%	Partner-owned	7%
More than 499 employees	20%		
		Family Ownership	37%
Character of Business		Successor-owned	23%
Industrial mfg	50%	Owned by several family members	
Industrial service	16%		14%
Consumer goods mfg	16%		
Consumer service	10%	Widely Owned	23%
Financial institution	7%	Investor group-owned	3%
Wholesaler	5%	Employee-owned	6%
		Publicly owned	13%
Age of Company		Nonprofit	1%
Less than 21 years	29%		
21 -40 years	26%		
41 -60 years	20%		
61-80 years	14%		
81 - 100 years	6%		
More than 100 years	5%		

Note: Sums not totaling 100% are due to rounding errors.

Table 2. Survey Respondents: CEOs (N = 147)

CEO's Age		CEO's Length of Service as CEO	
30-40 years	10%	1-5 years	34%
41-50 years	40%	6-10 years	24%
51-60 years	33%	11-15 years	16%
61-70 years	14%	16-20 years	12%
More than 70 years	3%	More than 20 years	14%
Median = 51 years		Median = 9 years	
Mean = 51.65 years		Mean = 11.20 years	
CEO's Relation to Founder		CEO's Higher Education	
None	39%	High school	10%
CEO is founder	29%	Bachelor's degree	
Son	16%	(4 years of college)	60%
Son-in-law	3%	Master's degree	24%
Grandson	7%	Ph.D. or professional	
Great-grandson	5%	degree (J.D. or M.D.)	6%
Great-great-grandson	1%		
Personal Service on Other Boards			
None	21%		
One board	22%		
Two boards	17%		
Three boards	15%		
Four or more boards	25%		

Note: Sums not totaling 100% are due to rounding errors.

Second, we will attempt to identify some key variables affecting board makeup, practice, and performance. Interpreting the data suggested a framework of hypotheses for future research. For example, to explain board behavior and structure, three variables seem important: company size, form of ownership, and CEO background. We will offer several propositions for further studies

Finally, we will discuss how to judge board performance or satisfaction and examine several common concerns or dilemmas that companies face with their boards.

Types of Boards

For the purposes of discussion and to stimulate debate over the proper makeup of boards, we propose several definitions.

The ideal board consists only of outside directors plus the CEO. One or two others can replace the outsiders but only if they are substantial equity partners. In this spirit, the CEO has a majority of independent outsiders to provide oversight and also the maximum amount of valuable counsel on key business issues. There is little risk that board discussions will be tempered by the presence of managers or family who are not substantial owners.

Very few of the businesses in our survey (5 percent) had such an ideal board. Ninety-five percent of the boards included one or more nonshareholders-managers, a higher percentage (18 percent) had majority boards, in which the majority of members were independent outsiders. We can surmise that these boards allow for a majority of independent outside opinions.

Many other firms in the survey had the benefit of outside perspective. Twenty percent of the total had what we called a minority board – one on which there were at least two outsiders, though not a majority. Five percent gained outside perspective through the use of advisory boards. In sum, nearly half of the boards that we surveyed (48 percent) had two or more outsiders. Later, we will suggest that the presence of two or more outsiders is a critical demarcation. Table 3 provides data about these and several other types of boards. In our typology, inside boards are those with no more than one outsider; the other members are owners, managers, or family members. In the family board, most members are family members who are not shareholders. In the management board, most members are company managers. In the stockholder board, most members are stockholders

We propose that an effective board is most likely to include as much independent, outside perspective and as little potential role conflict between the board function and that of inside management or paid advisers as possible. For that reason, we recommend that the reader closely examine the data presented for the seventy outside boards in the study.

Table 3. Types of Boards (N = 147)		
	Number	Percent of Total
Outside Boards	70	48
Ideal board	8	5
Majority board	27	18
Advisory board	8	5
Minority board	28	20
Inside Boards	51	34
Family board	8	5
Management board	13	9
Shareholder board	30	20
Token Boards	26	18
Total	147	100%

Note: Sums not totaling 100% are due to rounding errors.

Typical Board Practice

These are the questions most commonly asked by business owners or leaders about board structure: How many should be on the board? Where do you find them? How often do we meet? How much should we pay? How do we structure the pay? How long should each term of election be? What do we do about liability and insurance? How should we allocate meeting time?

Tables 4 and 5 summarize the survey responses to these questions. Table 4 includes responses from the seventy outside boards and examines the impact of size on board structure. The most typical or median board has six members, three or four of whom are outsiders. The board meets quarterly for about four hours each time, and it usually has one other unscheduled meeting per year. Compensation is generally about $1,000 per meeting. Table 5 summarizes the data for all 147 boards studied – those in Table 4 plus the inside boards. The overall data suggest that the average practices of the total sample of boards resemble the average practices of the outside boards

Thus, it appears that all functioning boards look essentially the same. This finding has two possible interpretations: Either active boards do not take full advantage of their particular strengths and potential or all boards more or less follow what they believe to be the normal practices of public company boards. From our personal experience, boards are under-utilized because companies lack understanding of their potential as resources. Later in this paper, we will discuss this issue further.

Much larger differences in practice can be observed when we focus on size of firm. We divided firms into seven groups: those with 0-19, 20-99, 100-199, 200-299, 300-399, 400-499, and 500 or more employees. There were very minor differences among most of these groups, but enough variation among small (fewer than 100 employees), medium (100-499 employees), and large (more than 499 employees) firms to justify delineation by these categories. Size of firm had the most critical impact on size of the board, director compensation, and liability insurance limits and costs.

In general, it appears that board practice is quite informal. Rarely are search firms used to help find directors. Most often, there is no defined term of office or mandatory retirement policy. As the companies included in this study are probably more sophisticated than most and as the percentage of firms in this sample with active boards is quite high (nearly 50 percent), it seems little has been done to professionalize the boards in small and medium-size firms and private companies.

Board Meetings

A frequent criticism of board meetings is that they focus more on reports of past activities than on key issues for the future. In a private company, there is possibly even more opportunity to design the meeting so as to address challenging questions that can help the CEO in his or her job. Table 6 shows how respondents described the (typically) sixteen hours that they spent per year in board meetings.

Surely some reporting at meetings is necessary. However, minimizing the reporting, which in our sample took fully one-half of the meeting time, would be beneficial. One way of lessening reporting time is by providing more written background material in advance of the meeting. Then, any questions or issues on that information can be handled by exception. Our personal experience indicates that reporting can be structured so that it takes less than 25 percent of the total meeting time, thereby leaving approximately three hours at each meeting for discussion in depth of one or two critical issues.

We did notice one pattern in board agendas that was related to size of firm: Larger companies spent more time on strategic issues. Smaller businesses devoted more time to CEO reports.

Role of the Board

Perhaps the greatest difference between outside and inside boards in our study lies in the expectations that they have about the role of the board. The CEOs with outside boards

Table 4. Typical Board Practice: Outside Boards Only (N = 70)

	Small (17) (< 100 employees)	Medium (33) (100-499 employees)	Large (20) (> 499 employees)	Total (70)
Number of Board Members[a]	5	6	7	8
Nonshareholder outsiders on board	57%	58%	52%	56%
Number of Meetings per Year				
Regular meetings[a]	4	4	4	4
Special meetings[b]	0.75	1.03	1.05	0.97
Length of Meeting in Hours[a]	3	4	4	4
Source of Contacts to Find Outside Board Members				
Personally known[b]	82%	73%	80%	77%
Search firm[b]	12%	6%	10%	9%
Other business owners or professionals[b]	6%	21%	10%	14%
Annual Compensation[b]	$2,465	$2,872	$8,400	$4,228
Meeting fee[b]	56%	40%	31%	42%
Retainer[b]	31%	16%	19%	21%
Meeting fee plus retainer[b]	13%	44%	50%	37%
Committee meeting extra fee in dollars[b]	180	160	426	246
Use of preferred compensation	12%	22%	47%	27%
Term of Office				
No term[b]	65%	61%	42%	57%
One year[b]	18%	27%	32%	26%
Two years[b]	6%	3%	0%	3%
Three years[b]	11%	9%	26%	14%
Mandatory Retirement Age Policy				
None[b]	94%	90%	58%	82%
At age 65[b]	0%	7%	26%	10%
At age 70[b]	6%	3%	16%	8%
Liability Protection				
Company indemnification	86%	71%	74%	75%
Shareholder indemnification	7%	32%	21%	28%
Carry D&O insurance[b]	36%	46%	63%	49%
Limits of coverage in millions of dollars[b]	2.0	4.3	6.0	4.6
Annual premium in dollars[a]	[c]	24,111	82,286	[c]

Note: Sums not totaling 100% are due to rounding errors.
[a]Median response
[b]Mean response
[c]Insufficient data

see the benefit of using their boards for what we believe to be the two best purposes: advice and counsel, and accountability. The CEOs with inside boards seem to see them more as an obligation (that is, as a requirement or as something to be seen by others) than as a resource. The responses to the open-ended question "Why do you have a board?" Please discuss" can be categorized as follows:

	Inside Boards	Outside Boards
Legal requirements	46%	14%
Image to outsiders	12%	3%
Advice and counsel	23%	47%
Provide direction	8%	11%
Accountability of management	10%	21%
Resolve differences	1%	1%
Succession planning	0%	2%

Note: Sums not totaling 100% are due to rounding errors.

Table 5. Typical Board Practice: All Boards Surveyed (N = 147)

	Small (17) (< 100 employees)	Medium (33) (100-499 employees)	Large (20) (>499 employees)	Total (70)
Number of Board Members[a]	4	5	7	5
Nonshareholder outsiders on board[b]	31%	38%	40%	37%
Number of Meetings per Year				
Regular meetings[a]	4	4	4	4
Special meetings[b]	0.74	1.36	0.43	1.19
Length of Meeting in Hours[a]	2	3	4	3
Source of Contacts to Find Outside Board Members				
Personally known[b]	47%	48%	62%	50%
Search firm[b]	4%	3%	10%	5%
Other business owners or professionals[b]				
	49%	49%	28%	45%
Annual Compensation[b]	$1,825	$2,805	$8,258	$3,926
Meeting fee[b]	63%	39%	23%	42%
Retainer[b]	25%	21%	23%	23%
Meeting fee plus retainer[b]	12%	40%	54%	35%
Committee meeting extra fee in dollars[b]				
	100	120	300	177
Use of preferred compensation[b]	11%	21%	44%	24%
Term of Office[b]				
No term	68%	63%	54%	63%
One year	23%	31%	25%	27%
Two years	2%	1%	0%	1%
Three years	7%	5%	21%	9%
Mandatory Retirement Age Policy[b]				
None	98%	94%	61%	88%
At age 65	0%	5%	21%	7%
At age 70	2%	1%	18%	5%
Liability Protection				
Company indemnification	67%	68%	74%	69%
Shareholder indemnification	18%	20%	22%	20%
Carry D&O insurance[b]	18%	32%	59%	35%
Limits of coverage in millions of dollars[b]				
	2.0	3.5	8.5	5.0
Annual premium in dollars[a]	[c]	19,958	111,600	[c]

Note: Sums not totaling 100% are due to rounding errors.
[a]Median response
[b]Mean response
[c]Insufficient data

Interestingly, few CEOs see an important role for the board in succession; it appears that the CEO takes full personal responsibility for that, even in family firms. It is also clear that almost no one sees the board in the role of active mediator or arbitrator of disputes. This, we believe, is healthy. In our experience, once the board in a private company starts taking sides-especially in a shareholder dispute – the board becomes ineffective and really more part of the problem than part of the solution. Instead, we find that the mere existence (not the actual involvement) of an active board helps conflicting parties to put their differences in perspective and gives them an impetus either to put the problem aside or to resolve it between themselves.

Because most CEOs who have active boards see the board's role as primarily one of providing advice and counsel, it seems all the more important to structure board meetings and agenda so that members can spend more time on key issues than on reporting.

Committees and Attendees

Use of board committees was prevalent among survey respondents. Of the boards that had two or more outsiders, about 46 percent had at least one board committee, 25 percent

Table 6. Board Meeting Agenda: 70 Outside Boards

Activity		Percentage of Board Time
Listening to Reports		49
Recent financial results	21	
Reports from key managers	12	
Report from CEO	16	
Approving Board Decisions		18
Formal duties (compensation, titles, dividends, other)	7	
Strategic decisions (acquisitions, strategic plans; other)	11	
Discussing Critical Issues		33
Strategic issues	16	
Organizational issues	9	
CEO priorities	2	
Family business succession	2	
Other	100%	100%

Note: Sums not totaling 100% are due to rounding errors.

had two committees, 16 percent had three, and 7 percent had four. The most common types were audit and compensation committees. About half the companies with committees had one; most had both. About one third of the companies with board committees had executive committees. Rarely did a company have a strategic planning committee (only two) or a human resources committee (only four).

For companies with outside boards, pay for committee work varied greatly. While the average pay per committee meeting was $250, about one third (32 percent) had no committee compensation. For companies with more than 499 employees, compensation for committee meetings was most typically $500 per meeting per director; less than a quarter (22 percent) had no compensation for committee meetings. About 91 percent of the outside boards regularly invited nonboard members to attend meetings. Those most often invited were the company controller/financial officers (in 33 percent of all active boards), the senior sales and marketing officer (15 percent), heads of operations (11 percent), and the outside attorney (7 percent). Less than the anticipated proportion of manufacturing people (eleven firms) and of technical research and engineering people (three firms) were invited. In only a very few companies were relatives or wives invited to observe.

For family businesses, we believe that an opportunity is being missed for family members – especially spouses – to learn about the board process and to become more bonded to the directors, which can be valuable in the case of death or disability of the CEO/owner. There are two other ways of building the relationship between the board and the business owner's family: Some firms hold social events introducing spouses and family. Others schedule informal "fireside" conversations between the board and interested family members.

The majority of active boards meet four times per year. Approximately 10 percent meet three times per year, 10 percent meet five times per year, 10 percent meet six times per year, and 10 percent meet twelve times per year. Meetings are most likely to be held at the place of business (82 percent).

We feel that meeting more than four or five times per year runs the risk of making meetings more operational in nature than they should be. Surely boards that meet monthly must work to resist that tendency. We also like to encourage companies to consider meeting away from the office in order to minimize interruptions and maximize confidentiality.

Board Members

Among the active boards, the typical (that is, the median) board makeup is six members: three outsiders, the CEO, and two managers or one manager and the firm's attorney or a retired officer. Table 7 provides data about the backgrounds of outside directors.

Half of the outsiders were presidents of other companies, as those who have written

Table 7. Backgrounds of Outside Directors (N = 232) President of another firm

President of another firm	52%
Senior executive of another firm	17%
Retired executive[a]	10%
Professionals	21%
Attorneys	12%
Consultants	5%
Academics	3%
Others	1%

Note: Sums not totaling 100% are due to rounding errors. [a]Almost all the retired executives had retired from the firm they served as directors.

about boards usually recommend. Danco and Jonovic (1981) and others urge business owners to seek risk-taking peers (that is, other business owners) for their boards. Typical length of service in the board for outsiders is eight to ten years.

From our survey, more board members were insiders (N = 333) than outsiders, even on the active boards. Besides the CEO, who served on virtually every board in our study, the most prevalent responsibilities of other insider board members were:

Senior general manager	35%
Finance	26%
Sales and marketing	16%
Operations or production	12%
R&D or engineering	4%
Other	7%

We have already noted the relative infrequency with which senior operations and technical people are asked to attend board meetings. Here, we see how relatively rare it is that senior operations or technical persons are on the board itself. This observation is even more striking when we recall that 66 percent of the companies in our survey are industrial firms and that 61 percent of the total are manufacturing firms. As technology and manufacturing become perceived as more fundamental to the company's strategy and performance, we might expect more representation of those functions in board deliberations. Perhaps we might even begin to see a committee of the board focused on these issues. There was none in our survey.

Liability and Insurance

This paper does not intend to offer counsel on matters of board liability or insurance but to share what survey respondents reported on their understanding of their insurance and liability status.

Private and small firms often mention threats of liability and the cost or unavailability of insurance as obstacles to the establishment of an active board. Many perceive that good directors are reluctant to serve for fear of possible liability. Some people suggest that using advisory boards might help to overcome these concerns. We attempted to explore these questions in our survey.

Only about one-third of the companies surveyed had directors and officers' (D&O) liability insurance. However, about two-thirds of the largest firms (more than 499 employees) were insured. Predictably, the most common protection of any form was corporate indemnification. Such indemnification promises directors that the company will pay any legal costs if directors are named in a lawsuit. It is likely that more companies than reported had corporate indemnification, but the person who filled out the survey did not realize it. Between 20 and 25 percent of the firms had shareholder indemnification, in which shareholders promise to pay the costs. For family businesses with several shareholders, this protection might be considered more often.

Our study showed that the average cost of insurance in the medium-sized firms was

Table 8. D & O Insurance Premiums

	Medium (100-499 employees)	Large (>499 employees)
Number of private firms	60	22
Number of public firms	10	6
Insurance premium for private firms[a]	$16,000	$35,000
Insurance premium for public firms[a]	$23,000	$100,000

[a]Median response

about $20,000. Insurance, then, when bought, represents about the same expense as board compensation (cost for six members at $3,000 to $4,000 per year is $18,000 to $24,000). For medium-sized private firms, board costs, with some rough estimates for travel and meal expenses and materials, might be expected to total $25,000 without insurance and $50,000 with insurance. The cost of insurance for the larger firms in our survey was much higher. Most of this variance can best be explained by the fact that many of the larger firms are publicly traded. Table 8 presents our data on the cost of insurance.

Private companies often perceive the cost of a board, especially the cost of insurance, as a reason for not having a board. Advisory boards are sometimes recommended as one way of eliminating the expense of insurance and encouraging reluctant outsiders to participate (Fox, 1982). Because we share some of these advocates' enthusiasm, we were surprised to find only eight advisory boards among our 147 survey firms.

Perhaps the best way of justifying the perceived cost of a board is to say that, on the basis of our survey, for private companies that had insurance, the total cost of having a board was between $20 and $25 per employee per year-probably much less than 0.1 percent of the company's total payroll expense.

Family Business Boards

As many experts suggest, the challenge to family business ownership is to manage the conflicting roles of family, management, and ownership.

Nowhere is the overlap of perspectives more likely to be evident than in the boardroom. There, all roles are present.

A family business can design its board in many ways. The firm can choose to form a majority or ideal board that lets objective, business-oriented directors (that is, directors who assume the role of representing all the owners) influence direction and decisions. As an alternative, the family business can include a few outside directors with family members to provide counsel and to mediate family business issues. We refer to this type of board as an *outside board*. Or, the owning family can allow the board to be the arena in which several family member-owners – especially owners from different branches of the family-determine the family's future business direction and financial and succession policies without the help of outsiders. Such an all-family board is sometimes referred to as an *asset board*.

Each of these possibilities requires unique sensitivities that are not documented in the literature and that are not found in the experience of big, public companies and their board conduct.

To investigate the prevalence of difference configurations of family involvement on the board, we recorded the experience of the sixty-six businesses in our survey that had family members other than the CEO on their hoard. Table 9 summarizes our findings in this area.

Fifty-six of the firms had family members who were also shareholders on their board. Forty-two had family members who were also employees of the firm on their board. As Table 9 shows, family CEOs were much more satisfied with their boards when two or more outsiders accompanied family members.

Table 9. Boards with Non-CEO Family Members (N = 66)

	Number	Percentage	Board Value as Seen by CEO[a]	Significance[b]
Outside Boards with Shareholder Family Included	16	29	2	
				$p < .01$
Inside Boards with Shareholder Family Included	40	71	3	
Outside Boards with Family Managers Included	14	33	2	
				$p < .01$
Inside Boards with Family Managers Included	28	66	4	
Total Boards Including Family Members in Addition to CEO	66	100%		

Note: Sums not totaling 100% are due to rounding errors.
[a]Based on a Likert scale where 1 = Tremendous, special value, 2 = Very helpfully valuable, 3 = Useful addition, 4 = Not as valuable as expected, and 5 = Sadly not worth it.
[b]Statistical significance tested by median test (Siegel, 1957).

Satisfaction with the Board

We attempted to evaluate the CEO's satisfaction with the board in three ways. First, we asked CEOs to assess the value that the boards had to their firms. As Table 10 shows, CEOs who had outside boards were more satisfied than CEOs who had inside boards

To further our understanding, we examined the relationship between number of outsiders and perceived board value. The correlation was strong. In fact, the value to firms of the board that had a majority of outsiders was more than 50 percent higher than the value ascribed to all other types of boards.

The other interesting relationship bearing on the perceived value of the board involves the background of the CEO. CEOs who were nonfamily professional managers were more satisfied with their boards than entrepreneurs or family business successors. This is a curious finding, because in a sense the nonfamily professional manager is more vulnerable to the board than is either the entrepreneur, who by definition has total control, or the family successor, who probably has significant stock control. One possible explanation for this finding is the nonfamily professionals' familiarity with boards and the help that boards can provide. Some support for this explanation is found in survey data that show quite conclusively that CEOs who served on boards of other firms were more likely to have more outsiders on their own boards and to find value in their own boards. Perhaps this consideration suggests that outside exposure and involvement for CEOs has value – at least if one believes that outside boards are desirable.

Fifty-six of the firms had family members who were also shareholders on their board. Forty-two had family members who were also employees

Enthusiasm for boards in companies that have outside boards is consistent regardless of the size of the firm. Smaller firms with outside boards are just as pleased as larger firms who use outside boards. In short, one key to satisfaction may be to increase the number of outsiders regardless of the size or type of firm.

Another possible measure of the CEO's satisfaction with the board-a substantial source of anxiety to those who are considering the establishment of a board-is how often they feel the need to remove or replace a director. In our survey we asked CEOs how many times in the last ten years they had wished to replace a director, how many times in the last ten years they had actually removed a director, and when was the last time they had removed a director.

Table 10. Board Value to Firm

	Inside Boards	Outside Boards
Tremendously valuable	6%	18%
Very valuable	33%	49%
Useful	29%	21%
Not as valuable as expected	26%	10%
Not worth it	6%	2%
Median value (on the Likert scale above) as perceived by CEO $p < .001$	3	2

Note: Sums not totaling 100% are due to rounding errors.

The results indicated that CEOs were generally satisfied with their directors. More than half (59 percent) had never wished to replace a director within the past decade. During that ten-year period, the companies that we surveyed had actually replaced only sixty-eight directors – that from a pool of 565 directors. In other words, on average, only about I percent of the director positions were replaced each year as a result of CEO dissatisfaction. CEOs also seem to take the action to replace someone-however uncomfortable it may be – when they become dissatisfied. Virtually every company had replaced every director that it was believed needed replacing.

The last thing we did to assess CEOs' satisfaction with their boards was to ask what advice they would offer to other CEOs and what they would do differently if they could. This inquiry was open-ended, and we attempted to classify the responses in a useful way. Responses came from all those surveyed (N = 147). Here is their advice in order of frequency of mention:

Increase the number of outsiders	49%
Get better expertise and balance into the board via more outsiders	29%
Give outsiders more influence	17%

Clearly, these responses indicate that CEOs have a positive attitude toward boards and toward having outsiders on boards.

Respondents noted two ways in which boards could be improved. Eleven percent urged that boards be kept smaller. Several suggested keeping board size to seven or fewer. Second, some CEOs with outside boards (7 percent) urged the establishment of formal terms of office. This advice can probably be explained by a desire to have some rotation or change of membership and a belief that terms help to promote it. As we noted earlier, for nearly two thirds of our survey participants, board members did not have formal terms of office.

Framework for Future Board Research

This survey set out to collect information on the structure and practices of boards in small and medium-size companies. A very high percentage (86 percent) of the companies in our survey were privately owned. More than one third (37 percent) were owned by family business descendants, and 40 percent were owned by entrepreneurs who someday may pass ownership on to family or who already have other family members in the firm. In the private firm, the decision to form an outside board and the structure that it has are voluntary. The business owner can almost always do as he or she wishes. These facts raise several questions for research:

- What kind of CEO is likely to choose to form a board?
- When does a board best help the firm?
- What types of boards work best?
- How does board structure depend on the personality or background of ownership or on circumstances facing the company?
- What types of boards are perceived as most satisfactory?

Figure 1. A Framework for Research on Boards

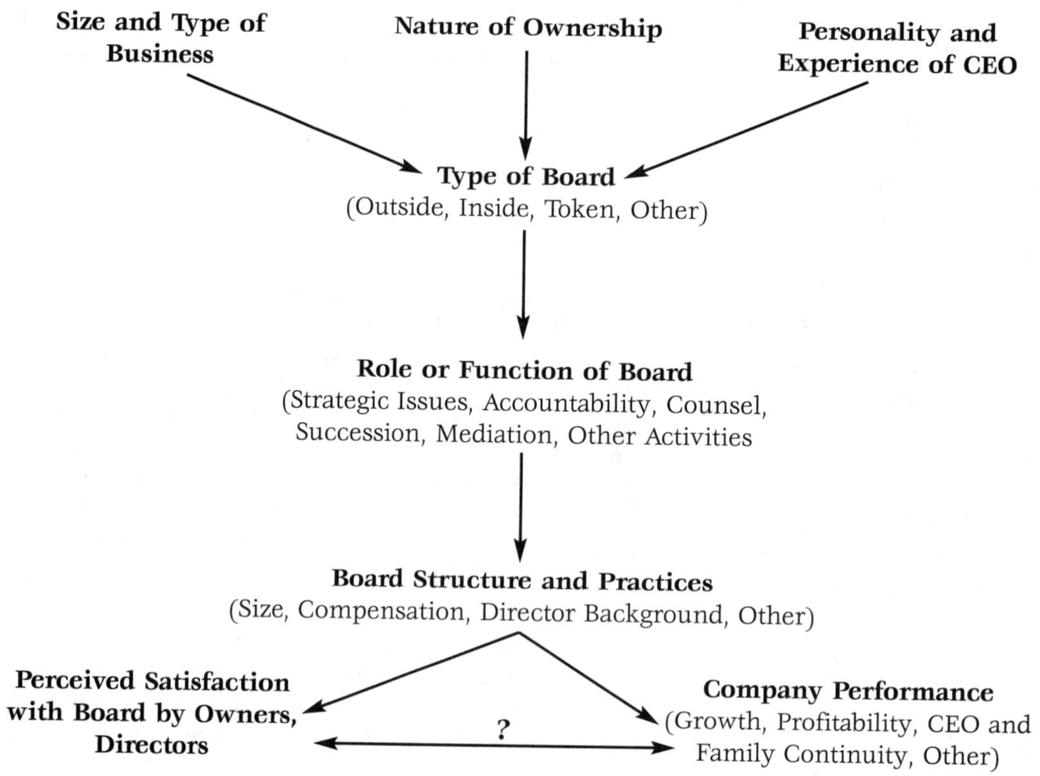

Figure 1 illustrates the framework for future research on boards that these questions suggest. Of course, this framework implies numerous possible hypotheses for further consideration. Our sample suggests several interesting hypotheses that future research could explore:

- As the company size increases, so does the number of boards on which the CEO serves.
- Larger companies have more board members.
- Larger companies and publicly traded firms have a higher percentage of outsiders on the board.
- Larger companies pay higher director fees.
- Larger companies have higher limits and premiums for D&O insurance.
- Larger companies have longer board meetings.
- The CEOs of larger companies see more value in their boards.
- Entrepreneurial owners have smaller boards.
- Entrepreneurial owners have fewer regular and special board meetings.
- Entrepreneurial owners have fewer outsiders on the board.
- CEOs of publicly traded firms wish to remove and actually do remove directors from the board.

Concluding Discussion

The purpose of this study is to explore board practices-especially of the firms that have outside boards. We found that even in this sample of successful companies and nonfamily professional CEOs, there were very few majority boards and that far more had inside than outside boards. For those who are already convinced of the value of outside boards, we hope that the data in this article are helpful in structuring and managing their boards. This exploration also raises some questions for future consideration:

- What do the boards in a random sample of all small or private or family firms look like? Is the conventional wisdom that only 5 to 10 percent of all private companies have outsiders on their boards correct?

- What is the relationship between a firm's performance and the nature of its board?
- How do companies with multiple family member-owners use and structure their boards, and how satisfied are they with their boards?
- Do the directors and the CEO have the same perceptions of their board's worthiness?
- To what extent is the liability issue an obstacle to the formation of active boards for private companies? What are the public policy implications?

In addition to the data on boards that we provide, we hope that our effort to define types of boards and types of firms and to identify the variables that affect choice of board practice and performance will be useful for future studies and research.

References

Danco, L. A., and Jonovic, D. J. *Outside Directors in the Family-Owned Business.* Cleveland, Ohio: University Press, 1981.

Fox, H. W. "Quasi-Boards: Useful Small Business Confidants." *Harvard Business Review,* 1982, 60 (1).

Jain, S. K. "Look to Outsiders to Strengthen Small Business Boards." *Harvard Business Review,* 1980, 58 (4), 162-175.

Siegel, S. *Nonparametric Statistics for the Behavioral Sciences.* New York: McGraw Hill, 1957

An active board of directors can benefit almost any firm with 50 or more employees, as long as the members are chosen for what they can contribute to the strategic needs of the business. The article explains how to build an effective board and find board members who can make a real contribution.

Recruiting The Board For You

By John L. Ward

Outside directors are one of the richest and least-used resources available to private companies today. By most estimates, only a small fraction of private firms in the United States have boards with outsiders on them. More often, boards are composed of shareholders, family members, and figureheads who meet to rubber-stamp resolutions. In some firms, lawyers write fictional minutes of meetings that never took place.

Business owners' fears about active outside boards usually turn out to be unfounded. In the last few years, I've interviewed more than 20 business owners with active outside boards. All felt that their outside directors help them tackle major issues without robbing them of control, independence, or any meaningful measure of privacy.

It is true that sometimes unusual tensions among shareholders weigh against inviting outsiders to serve. In one family business, for instance, the 62-year-old CEO and his wife, the company's financial executive, were eager to hand the business over to their daughter, who was working in the company. But the daughter's second marriage, to a man also employed in the business, was troubled, and the parents' energies were consumed by the struggle to hold it together.

Clearly, this was a no-win situation for outside directors. The family needed to resolve its internal problems before it could focus on the problems of the business and deal effectively with a board.

In most cases, however, an active board can benefit almost any firm with 50 or more employees. For professional service firms, the threshold is even lower, at about 20 employees. Smaller firms can benefit from forming an informal two- or three-member advisory council that includes respected peers or the corporate lawyer, accountant, or consultant.

Ideally, the board should be in place before the company reaches major – and sometimes predictable – corporate transitions. Often, for instance, a company hits an "entrepreneurial plateau" at about 40 to 80 employees, where the business outstrips the entrepreneur's ability to run it alone and, as a result, stagnates or loses its strategic focus. At this point, the owner often experiences burnout and badly needs energy from an active board.

A board can also be particularly helpful during a change in corporate leadership. The continual guidance of trusted, experienced outside directors can provide a kind of insurance policy, guaranteeing that the transition will be smooth and orderly. A broadening of ownership, a change in industry structure, or the onset of new forms of competition, technology, or regulation can pose similar challenges, taxing even the most vital and skilled manager.

Give Key Shareholders a Veto

The board should be kept relatively small, with usually no more than seven members. The ideal board consists of only outside directors, plus the CEO as chairman. One or two insiders may supplant the outsiders, but only if they are substantial equity partners.

Of course, anyone who is a major stockholder, or who represents a branch of a family with major stock holdings, has a right to a seat on the board. These partners in the business cannot be excluded. If ownership is dispersed among several branches of a family represented by four different directors, then outside directorships will probably have to be limited to three or four, to keep the board a manageable size.

If branches of the family each have substantial shareholdings, voting trusts can be established, with designated trustees representing each branch on the board. This can help unify shareholders and avoid politicking and maverick activity by dissatisfied or restless individuals with small holdings.

Especially in the first round of director selections, the CEO should make sure that all key shareholders are comfortable with the nominees. The veto concept should apply here: If a shareholder or family member is not confident from the beginning that a candidate will be a good, trustworthy director, then the CEO should reject that candidate without grilling the shareholder or family member on his or her reasons.

At the same time, the CEO should guard against letting the selection process deteriorate into a contest among various constituencies. This can yield a constituency board, with each director feeling a sense of responsibility to a particular shareholder group. This setup can cause major problems in the event of a shareholder dispute.

To see that everything goes smoothly, the business owner can sometimes designate a trusted associate or outsider-a consultant, a director, an accountant, attorney, or banker-to act as an objective facilitator for the board selection process.

Who Should Not Be Asked to Serve

"Whom do I leave off?" is the first question many business owners ask when establishing an active outside board. "How can I possibly include on my board all the deserving candidates – my customers, my suppliers, my old friends, my banker, my accountant, my lawyer, my family, my vice-president of sales...?"

The answer: Leave them all off.

Politics, bolstering egos, repaying debts, conveying thanks, rewarding performance, satisfying interest groups ideally, none of these factors should play a role in selecting directors. Instead, the CEO should design the board with one purpose in mind: to meet the needs of the company as well as the needs of the CEO as the leader of the business. Let us look at the strengths and weaknesses of various kinds of outside board candidates:

Top-management directors. The widespread practice of reaching into top management ranks for directors has significant drawbacks for the CEO intent on making the most of the board.

The presence of senior managers can inhibit board discussion of such confidential matters as succession, management compensation, organizational development, and so on. It also can reduce opportunities for the business owner to be truly candid – to doff his or her "employer" hat and discuss deep-seated doubts, fears, and questions.

This does not mean that the insiders should be excluded from board meetings. The controller or other top executives may be included in most, or even all, board sessions. But management insiders should always be present by invitation; that preserves the CEO's right to ask them to excuse themselves when sensitive issues arise.

Competitors. Competitors or potential competitors should never be directors, for obvious reasons. Directors serving on competitors' boards should be ruled out, too; the law prohibits interlocking directorates, "wherein the same people serve on the boards of competing companies."

Consultants. The services of these professionals are already available to the business owner, and they bring to the boardroom an inherent conflict of interest. "These people work for you. They're not the right people to challenge you," says Richard Kent, an entrepreneur and experienced director.

Some business owners find that it pays to make exceptions for advisors who have broad exposure to top executives of a wide range of businesses. These professionals often develop executive skills and can be a valuable resource, even if they lack experience in starting or running a company. Paid advisors should not dominate the board, though.

Friends. Friends are harder to find than directors, and their counsel is usually freely available anyway. Why jeopardize a good friendship by subjecting it to the stresses of the boardroom?

One business owner faced a dilemma after naming a longtime family friend to his board. When the business owner asked the director to step down after several years to permit him to bring some fresh perspective to the board, the director called him the next day. "Henry, I couldn't sleep last night. I was hurt." the director told him. "I've been with the family all these years. Do you mind if I sit in the back of the room at the board meetings and just listen?" This awkward and painful situation led the CEO, against his better judgment, to retain the director.

Retirees. While retirees can be excellent directors, the CEO should be cautious about overusing them. One reason is that retirees sometimes lose touch with the mainstream of business. Another is that directorships can become too important to them. If holding seats on corporate boards is a major source of stimulation and ego support, the retiree can become so fearful of losing the directorships that his judgment is compromised.

Academics. In some cases, people from universities, schools, charities, think tanks, or other organizations can be excellent directors. Arguably, they also tend to be more available than corporate CEOs. Nevertheless, the performance-driven business owner takes a risk when he enlists someone without experience in running a profit-making organization.

People who hold other directorships. Candidates who already serve on several boards are also risky recruits. First, the business owner may have to offer high fees in order to compete for their services in the marketplace for directors. Second, the appeal of the learning opportunities afforded by board membership dims for the person who already serves on several. That means he or she may reject the invitation to serve.

Other CEOs, entrepreneurs, and business owners. "Risk-taking peers," in the words of Léon Danco, a leading family business consultant, often make the best directors. People from larger private companies who have weathered the crises or surmounted the hurdles that still lie ahead for your company are the best candidates of all. They offer the business owner unparalleled experience, perspective, and empathy.

However, business owners should avoid any CEO on whose board they serve and any CEO who holds a directorship that overlaps with their own on another board. Overlapping directorships risk compromising the director's independence and creating an incestuous situation.

Division heads. Heads of divisions or subsidiaries of big public companies can be good directors. But, as a rule, the business owner should avoid functional vice-presidents, such as heads of marketing or research. If marketing expertise is what you need, for example, find the CEO of a marketing-driven company.

First, Identify Your Strategic Goals

Preparing a board prospectus is the first step in organizing an effective board. This one-page to three-page document can be a helpful tool in recruiting director candidates, and it can assist the business owner in networking with lenders, advisors, and others who might know attractive director prospects.

The introductory section of the prospectus usually gives a concise overview of the company, including its size in terms of sales and employees, its relative strengths and weaknesses, and its major strategic goals or challenges. This section should convey a sense of the company's industry, competition, customers, and market. And while the prospectus need not reveal a great deal of financial information, it should offer director candidates a clear sense of the business context.

The second component of the prospectus – the board profile – describes the criteria for board members in terms of experience, skill, and understanding. To reach that point, most CEOs find it useful to ask several preliminary questions.

What is your industry profile? The first step is to thoroughly examine the driving forces in your industry. What is the nature of the competition? Is it fragmented, oligopolistic, or undergoing fundamental change? At what stage of development are the industry's principal markets? Are they new, maturing, or expanding internationally? What is the nature of your customers and their buying decisions?

How powerful a role do suppliers play in your industry? What are important characteris-

Contents of the Board Prospectus

A typical prospectus used in recruiting board members covers the following points:

I. OVERVIEW OF THE COMPANY
- Industry
- Most important products and types of customers
- Size
- Nature of ownership (two brothers as founding partners, third-generation family business with 15 shareholders?)

II. BOARD PROFILE

A. Character of Business
- Stage in life cycle (rapidly growing, mature)
- Relative strengths or weaknesses (highest-quality producer in the region, need to develop more cost consciousness?)
- Strategic thrust (developing an international presence, seeking to grow by acquisition, committed to increasing market share?)

B. Purpose(s) of the board

Most common examples:
- Brainstorm and examine alternative strategic directions in an industry facing maturity and intensifying competition.
- Stimulate professionalization of management and organizational development.
- Aid in developing the succession process.
- Serve as counsel to spouse and/or successors in case of death of CEO. Encourage increased self-discipline and accountability for president and organization.
- Provide counsel and support to successor(s).
- Develop board strength to support future financing needs or public offering.

C. Personal criteria
- Desired background, personal characteristics, and experience of board candidates.

III. STRUCTURE OF THE BOARD
- Number of outsiders and owners on board
- Number of meetings
- Time commitment
- Participation in committees or family business activities
- Honorarium or compensation: amount and form of payment – (per meeting or per quarter? in cash, stock, or deferred compensation?)
- Director liability provisions
- Term of office

---

tics of the regulatory environment? Of your competitors? What changes are underway in the competitive environment? And what is the state of technology in the industry?

What is your strategic profile? This step requires a look at the company's current stance and direction in relation to its industry. What is its market-share position? Where is its competitive advantage in differentiating its product or service from others, or in operating at a lower cost? You should consider the labor and capital demands of the business, as well as the role of marketing, R&D, and customer service.

What are the keys to success? The industry and strategic profiles flow naturally into an analysis of the keys to success for the business. Based on the company's current position in a changing industry, what types of tasks, decisions, people, and systems are needed to ensure its success? Does prosperity depend on securing more shelf space from powerful distributors? Does the business require a more highly motivated, fully utilized sales force? Is raising private capital to expand the company's retail branch outlets crucial?

What will be the main sources of future growth? This analysis of future challenges is a logical extension of the previous three steps. Here, the CEO identifies the most promising new markets or new products, as well as the most important threats to success, including competitive and environmental issues. An analysis of the resources that will likely be needed to secure the future is needed to build a useful board profile.

How will the company's ownership profile affect its future direction? Many business owners seek directors with some understanding of the special ownership and management issues faced by the private business. To that end, it can be helpful to build an ownership profile, describing the relationships among owners, future ownership plans, and so on. A nearly universal question is: How important to us is maintaining private ownership? Another common issue is: How should we address the needs of the growing number of family members who are not working in the business? Basic to this step is an examination of how ownership of the company is likely to evolve in the years to come. Many business owners also include a description of their management style and culture.

Once the business owner has answered these questions, it becomes easier to identify other businesses that demand analogous skills of their executives, and to reach across industry lines to identify candidates who have already reached the goals that are still only objectives for your business. Let's look at a few examples of how this kind of strategic analysis has helped owners identify director candidates.

The funeral home chain. This privately held firm has a dominant share of its market. It offers a relatively high-priced, high-quality service to buyers who only require it infrequently. The business is both capital- and labor-intensive, maintaining a wide variety of sites and employing people at a broad range of salary levels.

The keys to success for this company include dealing effectively with a wide range of employees and customers. The firm also needs to be able to coordinate countless details of complex events and to respond quickly to customers' changing priorities. An ability to manage many locations simultaneously and to maintain a good word-of-mouth reputation with people who make only infrequent, expensive purchases is crucial as well.

In working on their strategic profile, the business owners identified several challenges. Tough new competition was emerging from lower-priced competitors as well as from a giant, publicly held chain, and the company needed new sources of private capital to compete. Rising real estate prices and the growing popularity of such burial alternatives as cremation were also forcing the company to redefine its industry and identify new sources of growth.

The owners' analysis yielded several interesting analogies in other industries:
1. Hospital executives face the same intense capital and labor demands.
2. Festival, meeting, and concert planners, who organize complex events in timely fashion, face the same pressures to please a diverse and fickle public.
3. Hotel and airline operators have similar capital, labor, and service requirements.
4. Restaurant chains, auto dealers, and computer store chains face similar site- and capital-management challenges.

This exercise left the funeral home chain owners at a good starting point to begin screening candidates for their board. Eventually, they developed a list of 25 candidates with expertise in analogous areas, weeded the list down to 10, met with 6, and, finally, invited 3 outside directors into their business.

The specialty bakery. One of the challenges in this business is to create and exploit demand for holiday-related products – Christmas cookies, Valentine's Day cookies, and other impulse items. One place where this business owner looked for potential directors was in the greeting card business – which must also "invent holidays" and capitalize on consumer fads. Both businesses require flexible work forces able to redouble their efforts before holidays; both require nimble and creative new-product development and the ability to work with powerful retail outlets.

At the same time, product development at the bakery demands a talent for inventing, licensing, and marketing fanciful consumer products. The CEO found analogous skills in an executive of a successful firm that markets collectibles.

Another director that he recruited was the head of a food service concern with its own line of branded perishables for the supermarket deli case. This entrepreneur had expertise in management of perishable products, new-product development, and distribution, as well as broad food industry knowledge.

The hardware chain. This retail business requires many locations and constantly faces new forms of competition, ranging from Sears, Roebuck & Co. to Builders Square Inc. Yet its structure enables it to realize some economies of scale through centralized buying, pricing, accounting, billing, and data processing services. In structuring his board, this business owner looked for analogous expertise among owners of furniture store chains, flower shops, and other similarly structured businesses.

Beyond the strategic profile, the business owner may also be looking for peers with experience in general management, ownership, or succession issues. One might seek a CEO who has demonstrated skill in managing third-generation shareholder issues. Another might look for a CEO who has successfully selected and groomed a successor from among several siblings. Still another might seek an entrepreneur who has installed professional management systems in his or her fast-growing company.

Aim High

Once the strategic profile is complete, the business owner will want to identify some personal criteria for directors. A few obvious ones should be at the top of the list. Such simple criteria as integrity and courage of conviction can be crucial to a board's success. A desire to learn is an especially appealing trait in directors, and so is a strong team player instinct. Confidentiality, discretion, and tact also show up often on this list.

Another dimension that may be important is entrepreneurial initiative. "A person who has spent his whole career at a company like Ford Motor Co. usually has no sense of what it means to be running a $3 million firm," says William Nance, a former Vlasic Foods Inc. executive and an experienced director.

Some CEOs might wait to find people who have shown that they can sustain a successful family business, or people who have thrived in business partnerships. Others might look for directors who are active in political, civic, and social affairs or who have accumulated significant personal wealth. Experience with wealth can yield valuable lessons, as well as comfort, to the business owner seeking candidates with a similar outlook.

Still others may seek a broad age distribution among directors, perhaps to provide young successors with highly successful peers and role models. Others may strive for a balance between people who are primarily rational and analytical and those who are strongly creative and intuitive. CEOs who have never experienced an effective board might also want to look for people who have served as directors of other successful companies.

In a board search, the business owner should set high standards, seeking out the very best people he or she can find. Candor and thoroughness in the selection process can greatly improve the chances of success. A cross-check of candidates' qualifications with mutual acquaintances is a must. But in the end the business owner has to trust instinct, look for good chemistry, and give top priority to his or her own needs and the requirements of the business.

This article is excerpted from *Creating Effective Boards for Private Enterprises: Meeting the Challenges of Continuity and Competition* by John L. Ward. Copyright 1991, Jossey-Bass Inc.

While family governance may seem to be an oxymoron, Harry Martin maintains that stable family governance is achievable when families set up procedures that take into account both oversight of family assets and cultivation of family members' human needs. This article outlines six steps to successful family governance.

Is Family Governance an Oxymoron?

By Harry F. Martin

Introduction

The short Webster's dictionary definition of *governance* is, "to exercise authority over; to influence the action of." The definition of *oxymoron* is, "speech in which antithetical incongruous terms are combined." This paper examines whether successful governance of wealthy families is even possible.

Successful long-term family governance only appears to be an oxymoron because relatively few multigenerational businesses and wealthy families are able to achieve it. However, stable family governance is achievable as generations pass and family members multiply. The reason effective family governance is elusive for wealthy families is that it requires establishment and maintenance of the following values and practices:

1. Culture and structure of open family communication
2. Valuing overall family over individual or family branch needs
3. Importance of demonstrated competence in assigning responsibilities
4. Effective generational succession plan for survival of family and its wealth
5. Creation of family conflict management processes
6. Creation and maintenance of an effective family governance plan

Families are capable of setting up the procedures required to achieve successful long-term governance. The governance plan can continue to function well through periods of family growth in terms of number of descendants and wealth. A solid governance plan not only takes into account the need to provide oversight for the family wealth or business, but also considers the need to cultivate and honor the human needs of family members. The human side should not be sacrificed in the interests of maximizing investment return. Over the passage of generations, the family governance model should also be subjected to review if changes are required to keep it relevant.

Before moving into the governance process, let's acknowledge the bedrock framework that a family must establish before good governance can occur: good parenting. To demonstrate why solid parenting in previous generations is required before creating a viable family governance plan, consider the following analogy. Imagine trying to transplant our American democratic socialpolitical system to a country with no history of respect for human rights or individual expression, no experience with any form of stable government except chaotic, despotic rule, and no history of working together to postpone immediate self-gratification for longer term mutual gain to society. Without long preparatory effort, our democratic model would never get off the ground in such a country because the cultural-political background required to sustain it is missing.

Good parenting in wealthy/business families establishes the framework in which a sound governance model can work. Good parenting means that certain values required to execute a family governance model over time are present, including:

- Valuing the contribution and individuality of each family member while setting high standards of family work ethic and discipline for all
- Valuing open communication between family members –a spirit of transparency
- Accepting the value of merit in determining roles of family members in governance and business
- Valuing the concept that the interests of the overall family and its business or wealth

are more important than selfish individual or family branch needs
- Playing by rules established in the family's governance model

Lasting Family Governance Plan Process

This section outlines the process required to create a lasting family governance plan. Note that the process does not begin with the family governance model itself; that key stage appears last, after establishment of a number of important prerequisite values and processes. The six steps of the process follow the order of values and practices mentioned above.

1. Culture and Structure of Open Family Communication. A culture of open family communication, reinforced by structured processes, is an integral precondition to creating a successful family governance process. Other key areas of family life must have an open communication culture or process. After all, a viable family governance process cannot survive in an atmosphere of ignorance and distrust.

The first place to start is communication between the family members themselves about family matters. In smaller first-and second-generation families, this communication can be achieved through annual family meetings guided by a good communication process for both family and family business matters. Families that have grown to a multigenerational stage may require a formal structure, such as a family council and/or a family office. The council meets several times a year to discuss family issues, including performance of the family company or investments. Such meetings provide an open forum for family members to discuss outstanding matters with each other. The council may have key functional responsibilities, such as nomination of family directors to the company board. The family council can also serve as an educational and mentoring facility for the younger generation. Most important, it helps to create and sustain a culture of mutual trust within the family.

The second area of open communication requires a regular flow of information from the family company or investment-philanthropy structure to family members. The closed mode of keeping key financial data from all but a small circle of family members should be avoided. Why should shareholders of a family business receive less information than shareholders of a public company, who get quarterly financial reports? How can a meaningful family governance process be put into place in a culture of secrecy?

These two communication processes among the family members and between the family and its business or wealth structure create the knowledge and competency required by family members who will have responsible roles in the family governance model. Along with the accumulated experience of being exposed to financial results or philanthropic grants and discussing them with other family members comes some of the understanding required for good governance. Company and investment performance results become more familiar subjects for the family rather than unknown, distant data.

What is really at the heart of this entire communication process is the creation of trust among family members. Openness and inclusion creates family trust, and family trust creates family harmony.

2. Valuing Overall Family over Individual or Family Branch Needs. Few issues are as destructive to effective family governance as emphasizing individual or family branch interests over the greater good of the overall family, its company, or its investments. It is common to observe in multigenerational families that long, simmering real or imagined grievances suffered by one family branch translate into that branch regarding its governance role as a struggle for power against other branches. Once well entrenched, these fractional attitudes are hard to eradicate.

The essence of successful governance of any entity is that the shareholders do not represent their own narrow interests, but the interests of all of the shareholders to ensure the best future for the organization. It is important to emphasize continually this theme of focusing on the stewardship of the entity being governed rather than on one's immediate needs. The addition of outside, independent directors to the family company, investment process, or philanthropic endeavor can also be helpful in educating family members in their broader responsibility as directors.

The most powerful argument against selfish interests is that they can kill the goose that laid the golden egg. For example, what is the good of a family business furnishing jobs for or promoting unqualified family members if this results in a steady erosion of the company's value?

3. Importance of Demonstrated Competence in Assigning Responsibilities. Any sound governance process requires demonstrated competence in its directors, at least in a majority of the board members, concerning issues confronting the entity. Whereas family representation is important, without competence in the governing body, an entity will falter. The family culture required to recognize this truism must be developed. The principle of competency or "best to the top" should affect not only which family members are selected to a governance board, but also whether independent, nonfamily directors are required.

There are structural ways in which a family can reinforce the culture of required competency, including written requirements of experience and skill for family member participation on boards. The same principle can be introduced into the family company, investment process, or philanthropies by creating written standards of employment and advancement applicable to family members. All of this is valuable in creating a culture that recognizes that a family member's role in governance is subject to certain competency standards required to ensure the effectiveness of the governance process.

One educational process should precede the effort to ensure that family directors have the competency required: a continuing effort to educate family shareholders in their responsibility to follow and understand their company's or investment fund's challenges and ongoing performance. Informed, participating family shareholders will build the foundation for competent family directors.

So far, we have discussed family governance as it applies to entities like a family business, investments, or philanthropy, where professional skills and experience are required. An equally important part of the family governance process includes governance of the family itself. This is an area where other competencies are crucial, including the ability to deal in a fair, balanced manner with family issues, including conflicts. A spirit of maturity and sensitivity in dealing with family members, particularly those from other branches or generations, are additional valuable traits. The wisdom of the seniors is extremely helpful here, and family councils and offices may have required retirement dates that are much older than those of business boards. The family should endeavor to create a culture and practice that recognizes the importance of choosing family members with these useful character traits for boards where family, rather than business, issues are the main focus.

4. Effective Generational Succession Plan for Survival of Family and Its Wealth. No family governance plan can be successful over time without the creation of a meaningful generational succession plan. It seems that more havoc is wreaked in families and their businesses by the lack of such a plan than by any other negative force. The origin of a lack of a meaningful generational succession plan is usually a controlling patriarch or matriarch who has dedicated his or her life to the business with good results, but cannot contemplate, much less provide for, sharing his or her power and control. Sons and daughters are played off against each other or discouraged until none of them may be actually prepared to run the business or investments. Succession plans advanced by consultants are ignored or toyed with to allow the passage of time without results.

A controlling family CEO can, thus, prevent the creation of an effective family governance simply by failing to invest genuine power in the governance board. All of the meaningful responsibility remains with the patriarch or matriarch. Family members or outsiders may serve on the board, but the controlling senior deliberately limits their role. The family wealth is then at risk when the family CEO is disabled or finally passes on. Family members suffer personally, particularly the children, who are never allowed to develop the competencies and confidence required for future leadership of the family or its wealth. The situation is aggravated when the family CEO holds a controlling block of stock and the family must suffer in silence or simply leave the scene.

One constructive approach to address this problem is for the family to appreciate that the company has become the entire world of the family CEO, who put so much skill and effort into building the company. Perhaps the family can assist in finding alternative vehicles for the founder/builder to use his or her energies and talents in later life.

A well-established solution is to have mandatory retirement ages for the CEO and board members. Mandatory retirement at age 65 for a CEO and 70 to 72 for board members is common. Often, the best way to select the most qualified family member or other candidate for the top spot is to form a board committee comprised of nonfamily members to make the eventual selection. The process can take several years of careful consideration of candidates, including nonfamily members.

The family governance role in the crucial succession process will be important even if family board members themselves do not choose the next CEO. Family values of work ethic, best to the top, and employment standards focusing on ability and competence can set the stage for a future family member's secession to the CEO role. The governance process can also provide promising family members in the company with the advantage of constructive mentoring from key company officers.

Another important issue is the need for a succession plan for rotation of family and other members on the family council, family office board, or company board. Provisions should be made for younger and middle family members to be eligible and prepared for membership on these boards when appropriate. Without such a process, there is no meaningful overall family participation in a governance role that is reserved solely for a few senior family members.

Suppose the younger generations are admitted to key family boards only when one or two key senior family members die. How can they perform their governance roles well with no preparation over the prior years? In a culture that excludes younger and middle-generation family members from the governance process, such members become cynical or disinterested, losing interest in the family's future.

Let me now share a special message with my consulting colleagues. We family practitioners do a pretty good job of helping functional families establish and carry out workable family governance plans. We often have considerable trouble doing so with dysfunctional families, particularly those where an autocratic patriarch or matriarch controls the company and/or family. One of our limitations here is that many of us may need to be liked and find open confrontation with an overbearing personality difficult. This position can lead to a powerful family member merely using us to postpone indefinitely the sharing of power or control. We can be led and may ourselves lead codependent family members through futile processes where decisions are postponed forever, obviously unprepared successors are appointed who can never succeed, or no successor is ever adequately prepared.

Our mission is not to be liked; our mission is to help our clients change their behavior. I believe that we have a professional responsibility in these cases either to resign and/or to inform junior affected family members that their future opportunities are limited until the controlling family member actually dies. The best options for their developing lives may be either to confront the controlling family member in a group or simply to move on elsewhere to achieve their potential.

5. Creation of Family Conflict Management Processes. To be successful over generations, a family governance process must be able to survive the inevitable points of family conflict that arise. Therefore, it makes sense to anticipate these conflict areas while creating family values and processes designed to avoid or minimize them. The following are some of the troublesome areas along with accompanying solutions.

Angry, isolated family members. This is a classic risk area in wealthy families. These are the people who tend to bring lawsuits against the family, its trusts, or its company. The family value of treating each family member with respect and listening to their complaints goes a long way to alleviate these risks. When people feel included and can voice their complaints, it is often possible to work out solutions. The family governance model should provide for long and open processes of communication when any major family decision is required, such as selling the family company. Everyone should be encouraged to attend these meetings, especially those family members who may oppose the action proposed.

However, the greater family should not be held hostage to a distinct minority in moving the family, its company, or its investment process forward. The open communication process should not allow one or a small minority of family members to hold up indefinitely a decision for needed change. After appropriate due process, a family majority, or supermajority, should be able to approve the change and have it enacted.

No liquidity available for family shareholders. This is another constant risk point. The family governance process should provide for a transparent liquidity procedure with fair independent appraisals. If the family company or its investments limit the amount of liquidity that can be provided at any one time, then these limits should be explained to the family. The key is to have a predictable liquidity process informing the family when and how they can obtain needed cash from their shareholdings.

Anger regarding why certain family members were appointed or promoted within the family governance, company, investment, or philanthropic structure. We previously considered some of the governance standards effective in dealing with this normal human reaction of jealousy, particularly virulent in family situations. Here we need clearly established family values and written standards favoring competency and merit. It also helps if the governance structure, either directly or by approving recommendations by family company management, acknowledges regularly that certain family members demonstrate the qualities required for more responsibility. This information can be appropriately communicated to the family at venues such as family council meetings, thus avoiding surprises that fuel family jealousy.

Anger regarding family company dividend policies. The need for and interest in dividend flow can be vastly different between a nonworking shareholder and a shareholder in a responsible family business position. A process of education regarding the company's need for retained earnings to sustain its growth and competitiveness adds helpful balance to this issue. Outside advisors can add credibility to such family discussions.

Use of skilled, trusted family advisors to mediate family conflict. Family conflict is unavoidable no matter how prudently a family prepares its governance. At times of inevitable difficulty, family advisors who have built credibility with a wide range of family members over the years can be invaluable. They can move between family branches and generations with calming advice in a manner that would not be possible for involved family members. Wise families recognize this and not only give their trustees, consultants, lawyers, and family office heads the status to operate effectively within the family, but also request their help in sensitive situations, where appropriate.

6. Creation and Maintenance of an Effective Family Governance Plan. Applying the earlier dictionary definition of governance, we see that by the governance process, the family both "exercises authority over" and "influences the action of" the groups it governs, i. e., the family, its businesses, wealth, philanthropy, and so on. This process of control is the whole shebang; this governance process covers just about every overall family activity and every communal family asset. It even reaches into individual family behavior. No wonder it is so important. Effective family governance consists of and requires for its success so many distinct family value models, so many family structural procedures, so much persistent hard work and selfless commitment from many family members over succeeding generations.

Why, then, is there no universally applicable family governance model? The fact is, you can't simply push a button on your PC and obtain the model that will be perfect for your family. What you can and should do is follow the good parenting practices required for a solid family base and then work through the six values and practices described above to create your own family governance model. The effort to establish a family governance plan for a receptive, highly functional first-/second-generational family will be quite different from the effort required to help a difficult multigenerational family (which may have ignored many of the above suggestions) create a meaningful governance plan.

The examples of two great American families continuing their legacies well into their fifth and sixth generations illustrate how good family governance can perpetuate a family's wealth and values for well over 100 years. The Cargill-Macmillan family continues its role shepherding Cargill, the largest privately owned company in the United States, not by positions in senior management, but by its governance responsibilities on the Cargill board. Similarly, the Rockefeller family continues its key role in its philanthropic foundations and investments through its influence as directors of these varied entities.

A lasting family governance plan can, therefore, prevent the shirtsleeves-to-shirtsleeves syndrome while creating family harmony. It demands enormous commitment, patience, and hard work from the family. Whatever the effort, it is worth it.

Reprinted with permission of the publisher from *Family Business Review*, June 2001. Copyright 2001, Family Firm Institute.

CHAPTER 8
FAMILY BUSINESS GROWTH

Among the challenges confronting family businesses is a tendency toward stagnation. Absent demands of public stockholders, family business owners can grow comfortable or even complacent in their economic niche. When the niche begins to close, however, change and growth are required for survival. To achieve growth, yet another family business paradox must be overcome. Entrepreneurship must be professionalized to be sustained--but professionalism must not destroy the entrepreneurial spirit.

To keep a family business healthy across several generations, owners must arrest the normal process of product life cycle decline by implementing management practices to support growth and transgenerational entrepreneurial activity. Through strategic exploration, organizational development, financial restructuring and behavioral change, the stage can be set for renewal and growth. Changes in reward or information systems, diversification or specialization in business where in-house expertise already exists or other approaches can stimulate necessary regeneration. The article provides numerous examples and cases, as well as useful guides to creating organizational cultures that support interpreneurship, financial restructuring options, overcoming barriers to interpreneurship.

Managerial Practices That Support Interpreneurship and Continued Growth

By Ernesto J. Poza

A bottle manufacturer and distributor in Detroit has been revitalized by every single generation. Its founder built a business around the recycling of glass bottles in the late 1800s, when bottles were handblown and expensive. The second generation entered the business in 1915, and by the early 1920s it was distributing bottles to the largest beverage manufacturers and bottlers in the United States.

When the third generation of family entrepreneurs took over the business, they added plastic bottles to the line, because plastic bottles were rapidly gaining favor with bottlers. One generation later, this venture had become old hat and relatively unprofitable, so in the early 1980s the fourth generation decided to go directly to retail customers with new plastic bottles. A division was formed to support the pursuit of this vision. Today, the new division sells plant misters to K-Marts, nurseries, and drug store chains nationwide (Posner, 1985).

How did this company make its vision of growth and regeneration happen? This article reviews the management practices that help to implement changes that support growth and entrepreneurial activity across generations of managers and owners. These managerial practices are the bricks and mortar with which families build organizations that will last beyond a lifetime. This article considers strategic exploration by family and firm, organizational change and development approaches, financial restructuring, and behavioral changes in the family system. These measures set the stage for renewal and growth. Specific interventions, such as the implementation of business teams, changes in reward and information systems, and diversification or specialization in businesses where technology and market knowledge already exist in-house, can then stimulate interpreneurship and appropriate business growth. Figure 1 outlines the steps to build interpreneurship into a business.

The practices and interventions considered in this article are the result of some years of consultation to family businesses and many more years of observing the risks of decline that such businesses face. On several occasions, interventions have been no more than informed experiments aimed at finding a way of reversing decline and regenerating the business The discussion is also grounded in literature on family business and entrepreneurship and in the author's experience in organizational development and strategic management consultation. The discussion is also grounded in the existing literature on family business and entrepreneurship and in the author's experience in organizational development and strategic management consultation.

Figure 1. Creating the Culture That Supports Interpreneurship

Setting the Stage	Identifying and Managing Barriers To Change	Specific Interventions	Outcomes
Strategic exploration	Absence of growth vision	Specialization	Profitability
Organizational change and development	Distance from customers, employees operations, and the competition	Diversification Entrepreneurial approximations	Growth Family harmony
		Task and business teams	
Financial restructuring	Nervous money and short-term focus	Reward system changes	
Family system change	Large overheads and perception of high social (image) risk	Information systems	
		Family venture capital company	
	Obsession with data and logic	Ownership equity structures	
	Inappropriate boundaries between management, owners, and the entrepreneur	Human resource policies and practices	

Interpreneuring: The Concept

A business can be said to be interpreneuring when it organizes for and supports a revitalization of the business just prior to or during the tenure of the next generation. The motive for interpreneurship can be growth, leadership, fun, profit, or the perpetuation of important personal or family values. The word interpreneurship is derived from entrepreneurship. Much as intrapreneurship refers to in-house entrepreneurial activity (Pinchot, 1985), interpreneurship refers to intergenerational entrepreneurial activity

Instead of pursuing growth and interpreneurship, many family businesses find themselves at the end of the founder's career with large cash reserves and assets but no stakes in the future of the business or the family. The founding entrepreneur who is interested in interpreneuring chooses to pursue growth rather than to address the later years through traditional estate and succession planning-or avoiding such planning. By funding a family venture capital firm or through joint ventures with other firms, the founder supports entrepreneurial activity by the second generation and beyond.

Peter Drucker (1985, p. 170) asserts that he knows of "no business that continued to remain entrepreneurial beyond the founder's departure, unless the founder has built into the organization the policies and practices of entrepreneurial management. If these are lacking, the business becomes timid and backward within a few years at the very latest." Drucker compares Walt Disney Productions and McDonald's with companies that built entrepreneurship into their structure: "Within a few years after the death(s) of these founders, [McDonald's and Walt Disney Productions] had become stodgy, backward-looking, timid, and defensive." In contrast, says Drucker, Procter and Gamble and Johnson and Johnson, who put the appropriate policies, practices and structures into place, "continue to be innovators and entrepreneurial leaders decade after decade, irrespective of changes in chief executives or economic conditions."

Setting the Stage for Interpreneurship and Continued Growth

Setting the stage for interpreneurship usually includes changes in strategy, organization, business finances, and the family. For example, after a careful study of its marketplace and a thorough review of its organization, a well-known consumer technology retail chain in the Midwest, here called Midwest Electronics, embarked on a transformation aimed at revitalizing the business. The second-generation brothers envisioned a new position in the marketplace for the company. They restructured the organization to support increased customer orientation in the stores, and they made changes in their sibling behavior to increase the effectiveness of their shift toward greater customer orientation at headquarters.

The need for these changes was far from obvious to the brothers; they were too close to the problem to see it. But the eldest, the current president, was not getting what he wanted from the organization either in advertising copy or in product availability at the stores. The two younger siblings headed advertising and merchandising. The president called in a consultant to conduct an organizational review of the operation.

After much discussion and a significant amount of shuttle diplomacy on the part of the consultant, a consensus emerged about the need to change the organizational structure and the roles and responsibilities of the brothers. These changes, it was hoped, would help to change sibling behaviors that were causing frustration and disharmony in the family and in the business.

Midwest Electronics developed a new mission and positioning statement that focused the business on value-added customer service, following the strategic redirection called for by a recent customer study. At the same time, Midwest Electronics regionalized retail operations. This move removed one layer of headquarters retail staff and made it possible for store managers, who in the past had drowned in paperwork, to emphasize sales and customer service activities. Finally, they gave overall responsibility for retail stores to the very able and motivated younger brother. He had previously been second-guessing every decision made by the nonfamily retail operations manager.

In their changes of strategy, organization, and family behavior, the brothers have purposefully taken steps to bring about changes in both the family and the firm that support growth and interpreneurship.

Strategic Exploration. Management initiatives concerning strategy are often led by a successor to the founder-entrepreneur who acts as strategy czar. Through this managerial approach, a business can focus on its mission, examine its strengths and weaknesses relative to the competition, and map its future accordingly. Strategic analysis and planning tap the future orientation of the next generation and sometimes increase the entrepreneurial propensity of the founder. However, even an entrepreneurial and intuitive founder can have difficulties supporting or participating in a strategic planning process if the process is forced upon him by an aggressive, forward-looking second generation. It is important for the second generation to be sensitive to the needs of the founder at this late stage of his life (Lansberg, 1988). Framing the interpreneurial effort as a natural progression that builds on the founder's legacy and acknowledges the contribution that the founder has made can ease the transition to the next phase of growth.

Organizational Change and Development. Changes in strategy are often accompanied by changes in structure and vice versa. In growth-seeking businesses, the objective in changing the structure is to provide the various product, business, technology, or geographic units with sufficient autonomy that they can operate with plenty of exposure to the competitive environment. The intent is to have new ventures operate as if in a free-market environment. Some of these innovative organizational approaches also help to institutionalize the process of growth.

In family-owned businesses, structural reorganization can also be aimed at developing managerial skills in successors and at reducing conflicts between potential successors (often siblings) or between founder and successor. The firm is split into separate functional areas, divisions, or geographical regions, each of which is headed by different family (and perhaps some nonfamily) managers.

Figure 2. Financial Restructuring Options

Financial Restructuring Technique	What it is
Real Estate Trust	A trust made up of a variety of real estate holdings. Although the tax benefits of trusts have been severely limited by recent tax laws, they can still provide an equitable distribution of the estate for family members not active in the business.
Preferred Stock Recapitalization	The creation of a higher-dividend-yielding stock with preferential redemption rights to replace some of the common stock issues. It allows for increased income to a founding generation, for example, while giving voting control via the common to the next generation.
Stock Swap	Similar in nature to the preferred stock recapitalization but involving exchanges of different classes of stock some higher-yielding, others with capital gain appreciation potential.
Buy-Sell Agreement	An agreement between parties, often parents and offspring or siblings, to buy each other out under certain conditions and at a certain price. Often funded by life insurance in the event of the death of one party.
Private Annuity	An arrangement between the heir or heirs to a family business and the parents by which the children issue an annuity providing regular interest income to the parents in exchange for operating control of the business.
Installment Sale	Partial sale of stock over several years aimed at transferring control.
Limited Partnership	Provides siblings with a claim to a distinct portion of the assets while the general partner retains control. Often, the earlier generation can provide developmental and collegial opportunities for the next generation.
Holding Company or Capital Corporation	A portfolio of assets contained in a constellation of corporations, each with its own stock, and an ownership relationship with the "holding" or capital corporation.

But, there is more to organization than structure. Some firms have created new communication and coordination mechanisms, such as quarterly business review meetings for the family. Other businesses have emphasized management development for owners and other members of the organization. And, a family business can negotiate role changes that allow greater differentiation among roles within the business and the family. In family firms, differentiation between family and business roles is essential.

Other organizational development approaches used to promote continued growth include steering committees, asset boards, outside boards of directors, in-house management education for family members, the hiring of nonfamily professionals to complement and educate family members, and venture review boards that evaluate the interpreneurial plans of the next generation.

Financial Restructuring. Financial reorganization is perhaps the approach most often used to set the stage for new ventures in the family business. It has the clearest tax and economic consequences. Its popularity may also be due to the fact that, in contrast to other forms of business and family consultation, legal and accounting expertise have been relatively accessible to family firms. Figure Two summarizes the financial restructuring techniques now available: real estate trusts, preferred stock recapitalization, stock swaps, buy-sell agreements protected by life insurance policies, private annuities, installment sales, limited partnerships, and multiple corporations with a holding company or family capital corporation model. While these techniques are still allowed under current tax legislation, recent changes in the law make expert tax advice necessary. In several instances, the time required for full implementation has been extended This requirement has the effect of lengthening the founder's planning lead time. New tax legislation continues to provide strong incentives for employee ownership, and it has spurred the use of employee stock ownership plans (ESOPs) as an ownership succession mechanism.

Family System Change. A family in business shares the culture of the family and the culture of the firm. By culture, we mean the pattern of basic assumptions, values, symbols, and perspectives that underlies behavior (Schein, 1985). The basic cultural patterns in the organization center on the nature of leadership-paternalistic, laissez-faire participative, or professional-and they are heavily influenced in first generation firms by the personality of the founder (Dyer, 1986). Cultural patterns in the family can be characterized as patriarchal, collaborative, or conflicted (Dyer, 1986). The combination of the cultural patterns of the firm, the family, and the board of directors creates a powerful dynamic that has significant consequences for the business' ability to be interpreneuring. The absence of consensus on what constitutes a desirable future or on how to get there can subject the business to prolonged periods of paralysis in which no interpreneurial activity is possible.

Family culture can also determine the extent of differentiation among family members: between parents and offspring and among the siblings. For example, a son or daughter may face a hard struggle in establishing his or her own leadership style and world view while working under the shadow of a parent who is also a boss. To the extent that principles of equality overshadow each individual's unique abilities and strengths, individuation and role differentiation among siblings may be difficult to achieve. These obstacles, in turn, often blunt the interpreneurial potential of next-generation family members, because they make it difficult for an individual to harness his or her energy and creativity.

Before we review managerial practices that weave interpreneurship into the fabric of an organization, let us examine the barriers to interpreneurship.

Barriers to Interpreneurship and Continued Growth

Most obstacles to interpreneurship can be labeled bureaucratic in nature. Bureaucracy, or the natural hardening of organizational arteries that comes with age, plays a part in slowing down growth. Unhealthy family dynamics and inappropriate managerial practices and organizational structures also put on the brakes. This section examines some barriers to interpreneurship.

Absence of a Growth Vision. Most entrepreneurs feel impelled by forces that they themselves often do not understand. Some call it heart; others call it passion or a crazy obsession. If neither the preceding nor the following generation in an organization has a vision of long-term growth, the possibility of interpreneurship is very slim.

Distance from Customers, Employees, Operations, and the Competition. Family businesses like Mars, Kings Supermarkets, and Kollmorgen stay close to their customers by engaging with them on new product ideas, product enhancements, and related opportunities. Von Hippel (1982) was the first to document the use of this practice; he called it the customer-active paradigm. In much the same way, companies committed to interpreneurship avoid anything that distances people within the organization, be it reserved parking spaces, titles, walls, privileged information, or "silver spoons." Families committed to interpreneurship are obsessive about communications and promote the personal growth and professional development of family members and nonfamily managers and employees.

Nervous Money and Short-Term Focus. Patience and timing are important skills whenever money is invested. New strategic directions are quite fragile until they take root and develop their own momentum and a critical mass of support. It takes time and money to regenerate the vitality of any business. Creating a venture capital arm and reorganizing the company into separate growing and mature divisions can help to overcome the obstacles imposed by nervous money and a short-term focus.

Large Overheads. The previous generation of owners or managers should not spare the interpreneur the pain of creating something new. Limiting the funding accorded to any new venture promotes creative "scrounging" or "bootlegging" by the interpreneur, replicates external market conditions, and sharpens the focus of the interpreneur's creative process. However, constricted funding also means that the interpreneur's project area should be shielded from the burden of the mature corporation's overhead expenses. Just as the entrepreneur usually starts in a low-overhead, inexpensive, and inelegant office space, the interpreneur should be allowed the freedom to start with a minimum of previous financial commitments. For similar reasons, the interpreneurial area should be minimally staffed, especially in regard to support personnel; in this way, it imitates the start-up situation of a firm composed of peer professions.

Perception of High Social (Image) Risks. While Exxon is not a family business, it provides a good example of the barriers to entrepreneurial activity posed by external perceptions. When Exxon changed the name of Jersey Enterprises to Exxon Enterprises, entrepreneurial employees felt both the constraints and the social pressure to perform in ways acceptable to Exxon. In his study of entrepreneurial management, Howard Stevenson (1985) of the Harvard Business School found the increased weight of what he called "social contracts" bearing down on managers in ways that prevented full consideration of opportunities. Trusteeship of resources and constituencies takes priority over adventurousness. Families in business are often highly visible in their own communities and need to create boundaries that allow them to free up time and resources to enable them to experiment without high social risk. Locating new businesses in different cities and giving them different names can help in this respect.

Obsession with Data and Logic. Computers have made the bias toward data and logic increasingly easy to pursue. The quantity and sophistication of financial software and the misuse of fashionable statistical process control methods throughout the entire business. Interpreneurs need the freedom to follow their hunches. Since control is probably still vital to the established segments of the business, it may be appropriate to cordon off an area for the interpreneurs that is not as controlled as the rest of the business.

Inappropriate Boundaries Between Management, Owners, and Interpreneur. It is difficult for people who wear different hats in different settings to be perceived appropriately in each setting. Is John the successor treated as John the son or as John the aggressive interpreneur? And, how can preconceptions and their accompanying role expectations be managed? When the boundaries between family and business are unclear, the family relationships may seem to be threatened by interpreneurial changes in the business.

Joseph Schumpeter (1934), an early writer in entrepreneurship, described entrepreneurship as the process of "creative destruction." The difficult destruction that is needed within a business to create something better is even harder to accomplish when the business system is entwined with a family system. A brother who is the chief executive of the family business may have to balance the task of interpreneuring with managing the shifts in his relationship to a younger brother who works in the business that occur as the business is reorganized. Executing the responsibilities of an interpreneur while meeting relationship expectations or psychological contracts based on the son role can create serious dilemmas. Such dilemmas can paralyze individuals and bring interpreneurial activity to a halt.

Interventions Aimed at Increasing Interpreneurship and Promoting Growth

After setting the stage, recognizing existing barriers, and considering necessary changes in strategy, organization, finances, and the family, owners have to intervene directly in these areas. Interpreneurship requires overcoming the barriers listed earlier and shaping the systems and structures that will institutionalize the process of renewing or revitalizing the business. Figure Three relates requirements to interventions that can be used in the process of creating an interpreneurial culture. This section discusses the interventions outlined in Figure Three.

Diversification or Specialization. Unless the original market niche is growing, a growth strategy often requires diversification or further specialization. A must for successful diversification is knowledge of the market and the product and manufacturing process technology involved. A policy of every growth-seeking entrepreneurial organization should be to "stick to its knitting," or commit only to ventures in which the company has accumulated knowledge about a kind of customer or a technology. Ideally, the company has accumulated knowledge about hath

Many studies have explored diversification, its outcomes, and the conditions under which it is most likely to be successful. Unrelated diversification or diversification into businesses or industries not related to the initial core business is generally riskier. Research on diversification (Rumelt, 1982; Roberts, 1985) clearly shows that diversification that sticks to its knitting pays off. Most diversification outside the products, manufacturing processes, and markets that a firm knows well fails.

But, the risks of unrelated diversification have been exaggerated, because owners and managers in search of growth have often behaved like bankers or venture capitalists, not like obsessed entrepreneurs. Putting sweat equity into something that you care enough about to support financially, on a shoestring, is very different from investing in a diversified portfolio of stocks

Several rules based on this research should help diversification efforts First, do not diversify unless you have to in order to grow or preserve the profitability of the business or to offer interpreneurial opportunities to a promising next generation. Second, do not think of acquisitions, mergers, or new ventures unless the profit margins in the new businesses are at least as good as they are in the business in which you are already engaged. Third, if you are going to diversify via equity positions, mergers, or acquisitions, distinguish between investing and committing to growth through new ventures. A company that spent several million dollars in twelve companies through the early 1980s had returns exceeding $200 million in cash and stock but not a single profitable major new business unit.

Fourth, do not diversify quickly into an area of business whose market or technology are alien to your firm. The batting average is good only when you know both, and it drops as you steer farther away from your company's area of expertise. An insurance company lost a lot of money when it diversified into construction. The son of the company's founder developed a new interest in construction as a result of managing a construction project for the company. Father and son colluded on this ill-fated diversification move for different reasons. The founder wanted to give the son a territory in which the son could pursue his own interests without interfering with the founder's domain, while the son was driven by the need to differentiate himself from his father. In the absence of product, manufacturing process, and market knowledge, venture capital investments, joint ventures, or licenses are better interpreneurial strategies.

Fifth, set up a competent venture review board. Many of the benefits of diversification observed in conglomerates may be due to the supervision provided by top management with strategic oversight responsibility to a unit of a larger corporation (Lauenstein, 1985). While units of conglomerates must justify their decisions to higher-ups, family businesses often lack supervision by outside authorities.

Sixth, specialization is another very viable strategy, especially if you find most of your profits coming from only one or two of your product lines. While this strategy seldom

Figure 3: Creating an Interpreneurial Culture

	Requirements	Interventions
Strategy	Knowledge of product and manufacturing process technology	Specialization
	Knowledge of market	Diversification
	Overcoming absence of growth vision	Entrepreneurial approximations
Organization	Role differentiation and separation between family and business and between owners and managers	Task and business teams
	Focused structures	Reward systems
	Communication and problem solving	
	Overcoming distance from customers and employees	
Finance	Creating an information-rich decision-making environment	Information systems
	Funding of new ventures	Family venture capital company
	Overcoming obsession with data and the "nervous money" syndrome	
Family	Equity structures that support "focused" organization structure and a distinction between active and inactive owners	Ownership equity structures
	Commitment and sense of ownership by nonfamily employees	Human resource policies and practices
	Overcoming inappropriate roles and boundaries between founder, family and business Overcoming perception of high social risk	

leads to growth in the volume of sales, it often results in increased profitability and focus, a great foundation for renewed growth. Specialization typically cashes in on customers' needs for higher quality and customer service even if higher prices are the result. This is well-known strategic territory for many family businesses.

A final word of caution: Venturing into new businesses is, obviously, not an easy task. The casualty rate is high. But, the guidelines provided here should help.

To summarize the advice just given on diversification:

- Do not diversify unless you have to
- Do not acquire, merge, or venture except for better profit margins
- Distinguish between passive investments and active business ventures
- Stay with familiar markets and technologies
- Set up a competent venture review board
- Consider specializing in quality, high-service niche
- Remember that new ventures are risky.

Entrepreneurial Approximations. Perhaps least found and yet quite promising for inter-preneuring and continued growth are the formation of venture capital firms (such as the Rockefellers' Venrock), the formation of new ventures divisions within businesses (often headed by successors), and the creation of ownership and reward systems that encourage long-term growth of the firm.

American Research and Engineering, a family business in Chicago, has set up a trust to enable the next generations to engage in entrepreneurial activity. Recognizing that the family business is often shaped by the personality of its founder and that it may therefore prove a poor fit for the succeeding generation, the founder created a venture trust. The trust, guided by the family philosophy "You get out of life what you put in," enables any child in the family to be funded in a business venture of his or her own choosing. The individual must present a business plan for review by a board of family members, who decide whether or not to fund it. If the plan is accepted, the interpreneurial family member receives the start-up funds in exchange for 49 percent of the shares of the company.

With 51 percent of the shares, the interpreneur owns the company and returns to the family trust a dollar for every dollar of profit that the new company retains. This return helps to fund children, cousins, nieces or nephews down the road (Liataud, 1983). Changes in tax laws make the counsel of expert advisors acquainted with the particular situation a requirement in implementing funds of this sort.

Another excellent example of the creation of an entrepreneurial approximation is that of Mars, Inc. The founder, Frank Mars, made arrangements for his son, Forrest Mars, to start a new business in England. Forrest traveled abroad with several thousand dollars of family venture capital and the recipe for Milky Way, which in England became the Mars Bar. The European company grew at a very fast pace and in 1964 bought out its American counterpart.

One study (Biggadike, 1979) found that it takes an average of eight years for a corporate venture to reach profitability and about ten to twelve years before its return on investment (ROI) equals that of mainstream business activities. However, when independent entrepreneurs start businesses, they reach profitability in four years (Weiss, 1981). The contrast between these two studies points to two things: the need for medium- to long-term financial support of any new venture sponsored by a business or family and the need for better entrepreneurial structures within established companies (Drucker, 1985).

Forming joint ventures with other entrepreneurial businesses, where financial support of the other firm's more promising research and development is exchanged for stock or licensing agreements, is another interpreneurial strategy.

The family's ability to assess the quality of investments and its willingness to invest in them for the long term are critical to its ability to sponsor new ventures. Some families will never be able to act as venture capital firms for the next generation. But, many more could than currently do if they would commit to a vision of growth and interpreneurship during the high profitability years of the family business.

Task and Business Teams. Another organizational innovation that supports continued growth is task and business teams. Organized around a particular task or business unit-for example, new product development or business for a particular major customer – such teams are composed of representatives of various departments and top management as needed. Planning, doing, and reviewing are all responsibilities of these teams. Usually embedded in the context of a functional organization, they help a firm to become more responsive to change, more adaptable to rapid growth, and more efficient in the deployment of human resources.

An Ohio firm started these cross-functional teams along customer lines. Its concern was that rapid growth would lead to deterioration in product quality, on-time delivery, and manufacturing cost control. With a production manager acting as a team leader and a team composed of representatives from engineering, finance, quality assurance, personnel, purchasing, and distribution, the firm has significantly improved on-time delivery and shortened order-to-delivery cycles. These improvements have reduced the amount of cash tied up in work in process. The plants now operate with a strong customer focus. Top management periodically meets with the team to review accomplishments and do what it can to support continued improvement.

Still experimenting with interpreneurship and Undergoing the test of time is Kollmorgen Corporation, a $350-million family business headquartered in Stamford, Connecticut. Bob Swigget, its chairman of the board, believes that in order to achieve innovation and growth a company must maintain a "free-market environment for every individual in the company (Kollmorgen Corporation, no date). That way, he argues, "each employee is exposed to the risks and rewards of the market." He or she succeeds or fails on the basis of skills and abilities in meeting this responsibility. And, Kollmorgen believes that the best way of encouraging such entrepreneurial commitment is to break a company into small, autonomous product or profit center teams.

Kollmorgen found its vision of the future operating within its own confines in the Proto (for *prototype*) Department. The Proto Department was a thirty-five- member unit that could turn around an order for a new type of circuit board in one to three weeks. It generally took six to ten weeks for other departments to produce a new board. The Proto Department was also the most profitable unit of the company. Nevertheless, it took top management several years to realize that this small renegade department had all the components of what is now the Kollmorgen philosophy: small groups of committed individuals acting autonomously to serve the customer, often innovatively, and the resultant payoff in profitability and growth.

Kollmorgen's compounded rate of growth between 1974 and 1984 was a staggering 18 percent. Since then, in perhaps the worst electronics industry recession in twenty years, the company's profit margins have narrowed, and its growth has slowed. But Kollmorgen intends to continue to grow, if at a slower rate, and to produce a 20 percent return on equity for its shareholders. While other families in business could develop and promote a vision like that of Kollmorgen, family interests and desires need to complement the aspirations that have been set for the business. As a result of these other interests, rates of growth may not be as aggressive. Marriott, another family-controlled business, has also been able to maintain annual revenue growth rates at about 20 percent.

Reward Systems. Pay is a strong incentive for risk taking and growth. This is particularly true in family businesses where career opportunities for nonfamily members may be limited. Thus, to support the growth strategy that Kollmorgen managers had set for themselves, a new bonus plan was set up. This plan was to be driven by return on net assets (RONA). RONA also gave individuals throughout the company a handy way of keeping score. Individuals in a division that had a reasonably good year would end up with a bonus amounting to 15 percent to 20 percent of their gross annual salary. Within six months of implementation, receivables and inventories had been reduced by $11 million. On the long road to growth and continued entrepreneurship, significant short-term improvements were also evident. Kollmorgen shows that long-term business growth and short-term effectiveness go together.

Information Systems. Keeping up-to-date measures of company performance, when coupled with dividing the large enterprise into small business units, provides timely information to every employee about inventories, costs, customer wants, and competitor moves. This contact with the market creates an information-rich decision making environment in which strategies and decisions are constantly updated and tested on the basis of new information.

Knowing the competition is particularly important in guiding growth and interpreneurship, because competitive information may contain the seeds of opportunities available to the business. At the Detroit bottle manufacturer and distributor mentioned at the beginning of this article, the thirty-year-old fourth-generation president of the plastic bottles division frequently comes into the office with samples or cardboard displays of new product ideas. Combing through product show and hardware and discount store shelves daily, he begins his days back at the office by laying out competitive product information for all to see. He tells everybody what is going on in the marketplace, what customers are thinking, and what new products he is considering. This practice has particular value for family-owned businesses. Because of the close attachments of family life, a family business may focus predominantly on internal indicators and ignore, deny, or minimize external information that has serious implications for market competitiveness.

Ownership Equity Structures. The family capital corporation model mentioned earlier is a particularly attractive ownership structure because it can accommodate the needs and preferences of different individual owners. This financial structure can contain all the assets of the family, both active business interests and passive assets (such as real estate and stocks in public companies). Issuing several classes of preferred and common stock can help different owners to achieve their objectives without disrupting the continuity of the active business. For instance, Class A preferred stock could be nonvoting, low par value, with a high dividend preference and liquidation preference after Class B preferred-perfect for a nonmanaging owner. Class B preferred could then have liquidation preference over all stock classes, dividend preference after Class A, and voting rights that lapse at death, and be convertible to common stock. The common stock could have voting rights and receive all capital appreciation and possible future control.

A number of entrepreneurial privately held and family-owned businesses have chosen to distribute some equity to employees in the conviction that the best way of getting people to behave like owners is to make them owners. After all, it is the families "real" ownership of a business that is often discussed as a competitive advantage of tenacious family businesses with their long-term perspective (Ward. 1987).

A study of American Business Conference companies (Clifford and Cavanaugh, 1985) revealed that, in the best-performing of these mid-size companies (as measured by sales growth, return on equity, assets, and jobs created), 31 percent of the stock was owned by employees themselves. In contrast, less than four percent of the equity in the larger pool of *Forbes* 100 companies is employee owned.

Another study of companies with stock ownership plans (Conte and Tannenbaum, 1978) found a statistical correlation between employee ownership and profitability. Other things being equal, the greater the equity the employees owned, the greater the company's degree of profitability.

Human Resource Policies. There are a variety of other ways of increasing psychological ownership and commitment to growth among employees. Human resource policies that demonstrate caring, recognize individual differences, and promote respect and dignity, when coupled with management that supports its people with the right tools, raw materials, and information, promote high involvement and behavior that resembles that of proprietors. Some of the innovations in manufacturing organizations over the last twenty years support this claim (Poza and Markus, 1980; Poza, 1983). Gain-sharing and profit-sharing bonus plans that financially reinforce the attitude that "we are in this together" also help to create a sense of commitment that resembles that of equity ownership (Lawler, 1981).

The Politics of Survival for Interpreneurs

The founder of a graphic design and media services firm is transforming the company into an employee-owned organization as it moves to the hands of a second generation in order to preserve the high quality of its designs and services beyond the first generation. A high-commitment, peer-based professional organization is the founder's legacy to the next generation. And, his son has been an active codesigner of the entire transformation and regeneration of the business.

Today, this company relies on project teams led by team leaders for its creative tasks. The overall management of the business depends on weekly management team meetings and a series of management committees: finance, personnel, and marketing. These committees report to the Member Group, as the management team is called. A board of directors, which includes two outsiders, meets twice a year to review the firm's financial performance, provide management advice, review the firm's annual budget and financial goals, and monitor its strategic direction.

One way in which interpreneurs have achieved major breakthroughs is by starting small with broad goals, proceeding slowly and experimentally, and shying away from the spotlight in the early stages. There are good reasons for this pattern of success.

Politicians and strategic managers know that one way of minimizing early resistance to change is by keeping the vision broad. A broad vision makes it difficult for others to polarize around details. A broad vision encourages those who join to elaborate and shape the details, and it allows room for mistakes. With time, the number of new adherents and the objective results provide the critical mass that enables the new idea to withstand the opposition.

Interpreneurs and their advisers need to keep the new idea or new venture simple and small: Conceive of it as a series of successive approximations to the interpreneur's total vision. Clearly define, bound, and structure the new venture unit. Keep it separate from the rest of the company, preferably as a small team of peers in a simple, inexpensive setting (the classic garage, basement, or trailer). Dare to venture only on the basis of need. Make sure that others see the need for higher profit margins or that they have a quest, an obsession; get an "angel" for the venture. Recognize that both money and sponsorship are key. And, keep commitments flexible or negotiate agreements that prevent premature evaluation and undue pressure for early positive results.

A Case Example

S. C. Johnson and Son, Inc. is now stimulating growth after years of lethargy. This two-billion-dollar consumer products giant, best known for its Johnson Wax line of products, is being run by a fifty-nine-year-old member of the fourth generation, Samuel C. Johnson, chairman and chief executive officer. Johnson is currently stimulating growth through a series of new policies, structures, and practices all aimed at promoting interpreneurship by the fifth generation. Within the last several years, Samuel C. Johnson has instituted a matrix organizational structure to promote interdepartmental cooperation between such functions as manufacturing, marketing, and finance. He has also created four business teams: personal care, home care, specialty chemicals, and insecticides. The purpose here is to promote responsibility and other behaviors akin to those of owners and to reduce the bureaucratic layers of management.

Johnson Wax has overhauled the compensation system to promote pay for performance, a concept quite alien to this traditionally paternalistic company. To improve knowledge of technology, it has increased the R&D budget and hired a new chief scientific offer. Finally, Samuel C. Johnson recruited and hired his son S. Curtis Johnson III to head a venture capital unit that is investing in both related and unrelated businesses.

All this change making to facilitate interpreneuring comes out of a recognition that growth and innovation must be supported at a critical juncture for the company. Samuel C. Johnson's father had recognized a similar need a generation ago when he backed S. C. Johnson's idea for a new business unit, the Raid line of insecticides. It is currently one of the company's most profitable product lines.

This recommitment to growth and interpreneurship appears well timed both for the business and for the family. In the late 1970s, as a result of diversifying too far afield from what Johnson managers knew best – personal and home care products – the firm suffered financial losses from a string of acquisitions in the leisure and recreational equipment business. Recoiling from this and several other market blunders, S. C. Johnson and Son, Inc. headed for protected waters-core businesses in which it had technical and marketing expertise-only to find that more aggressive competition had moved in. Lethargy had resulted in uncompetitive production costs and higher prices on the shelves, which caused profit margins to erode and market share to decline. On the family front, we find a fifth generation whose members had gone through college and were ready to make a contribution without knowing what context they could make it in. But, with Samuel C. in his fifties and S. Curtis and other members of the fifth generation in their late twenties or early thirties, the probabilities of enlisting the next generation for continued entrepreneurship are, psychologically speaking, the best they will ever be (Davis, 1983).

Time will judge the effectiveness of this case of interpreneurship, yet many of the elements are present: changes in organization that promote greater autonomy and free-market dynamics, including the use of business teams; changes in reward systems; additions to the company's knowledge of technology and markets; new information systems; and a venture capital led by an entrepreneur at heart, S. Curtis Johnson. The entrepreneurial fifth generation Johnson admits he likes the freedom to explore opportunities that is built into his job. This ability to explore and commit, with passion, to new opportunities is at the heart of interpreneurship and continued growth.

Summary

Strategic exploration and planning by family and firm, organizational change and development, financial restructuring, stock ownership, and behavioral changes in the family system all set the stage for interpreneurship and continued growth. Task of business teams, changes in reward and information systems, diversification or specialization in areas where knowledge of technology and markets already exists, and in-house entrepreneurial approximations are interventions that support interpreneurship and continued business growth. While the evidence is not yet extensive, comprehensive and consistent use of several of these interventions appears to be effective in stimulating interpreneurship.

The choice of interpreneurship practices will have to be guided by the business and family cultures as well as the firm's technical and marketing expertise. Many entrepreneurs and interpreneurial families, particularly those involved in highly successful businesses, have so much of their identity and social status defined by the original product, service, or market served that choosing to expand in new directions creates extreme tension and discomfort. Much more than money is at stake. The choice will also depend on the degree to which the firm has already used interpreneurial structures, policies, and practices, on its financial status, and on general economic conditions. Interpreneuring is most likely to succeed when the business possesses a culture that is well suited to the ambiguity and risk taking of entrepreneurial activity; management supports the new venture with structures, policies, and practices that separate the young venture from the old businesses and shelter it from corporate burdens (such as high overheads) that it cannot carry, those who commit financial resources to the new venture take a long-term investment perspective; and the family culture supports new ventures.

This article can do no more than provide a glimpse of a powerful set of growth opportunities available to family businesses everywhere. The author is aware of at least a dozen experiments in interpreneuring now under way in the United States and Latin America. Research aimed at determining the patterns of success and identifying the sources of difficulties and failure is badly needed.

References

Biggadike, H. R. "The Risky business of Diversification." *Harvard Business Review*, 1979, 57 (3), 103-111.

Clifford, D., and Cavanaugh, R. *The Winning Performance: How American Mid-size Companies Succeed.* Toronto: Bantam Books, 1985.

Conte, M., and Tannenbaum, A. "Employee-Owned Companies: Is the Difference Measurable?" *Monthly Labor Review*, 1978, 101 (7), 23-28.

Davis, P. "Realizing the Potential of the Family Business." *Organizational Dynamics*, Summer 1983, 12 (1), 47-56.

Drucker, P. *Innovation and Entrepreneurship.* New York: Harper & Row 1985

Dyer, W. G., Jr. *Cultural Change in Family Firms: Anticipating and Managing Business and Family Transitions.* San Francisco: Jossey-Bass, 1986.

Kollmorgen Corporation. Company philosophy statement, no date.

Lansberg, I. "The Succession Conspiracy." *Family Business Review*, 1988, 1 (2), 119-143.

Lauenstein, M. C. "SMR Forum: Diversification the Hidden Explanation of Success." *Sloan Management Review*, 1985, 27 (1).

Lawler, E. E. *Pay and Organization Development.* Reading, Mass.: Addison-Wesley, 1981.

Liataud, J. "Entrepreneurship and the Family." *Loyola Business Review*, 1983, 4(1).9-12.

Pinchot, G. *Intrapreneurship: Why You Don't Have to Leave the Corporation to Become an Entrepreneur.* New York. Harper & Row, 1985.

Posner, B. G. "The 100-Year-Old Startup." *Inc.*, September 1985, pp. 79-85.

Poza, E. "Twelve Actions to Strong U.S. Factories." *Sloan Management Review*, 1983, 25 (1), 27-38.

Poza, E., and Markus, M. L. "Success Story The Team Approach to Work Restructuring." *Organizational Dynamics*, Winter 1980, 8 (3), 2-25.

Roberts, E.B., and Berry, C. A. "Entering New Businesses: Selecting Strategies for Success." *Sloan Management Review*, 1985, 26 (3), 3-17.

Rumelt, R. P. "Diversification Strategy and Profitability." *Strategic Management Journal*, 1982, 3, 359-369.

Schein, E. H. *Organizational Culture and Leadership: A Dynamic View.* San Francisco: Jossey-Bass, 1985.

Schumpeter, J. A. *The Theory of Economic Development.* Cambridge, Mass. Harvard University Press, 1934.

Stevenson, H. H. "A New Paradigm for Entrepreneurial Management." In J. J. Kokao and H. H. Stevenson (eds.), *Entrepreneurship: What It Is and How to Teach It.* Boston: Harvard Business School 1985.

Von Hippy, E. "Get New Products from Customers." *Harvard Business Review*, 1982, 60 (2), 117-122.

Ward, J. L. *Keeping the Family Business Healthy: How to Plan for Continuing Growth, Profitability, and Family Leadership.* San Francisco: Jossey Bass, 1987.

Weiss, L. A. "Start-Up Businesses: A Comparison of Performances." *Sloan Management Review*, 1981, 23 (1), 3753.

Most family businesses simply don't grow. This paper explores the reasons for and theories behind business stagnation and proposes a set of "best practices" that can revitalize a firm and enhance its performance.

Growing the Family Business: Special Challenges and Best Practices

By John L. Ward

According to popular perception, family-owned businesses don't grow. No less an expert than Leon Danco of the Arthur Andersen Center for Family Business, the founding father of the field of family business, supports this notion. He said that family businesses fail because they allow themselves to be destroyed, slowly but surely, by the action – or more accurately, *inaction* – of their owner-managers. The businesses fail because, more often than not, these people never make the decisions needed to ensure the vitality of their companies in an ever-changing, even more complex world (Danco, 1980).

Contrary to popular perception, however, family-owned businesses can grow. Although they face several inherent challenges, family business can expand by following some simple, yet critical, steps.

This paper examines the special challenges to growing a family firm and then proposes a growth model for overcoming them. It concludes with a detailed review of the management best practices that can enable family firms to implement the model daily while ensuring long-term growth and prosperity.

Lack of Growth: Folklore and Fact

The notion that family-owned businesses do not grow is supported by folklore as well as fact. The adage "from shirtsleeves to shirtsleeves in three generations" expresses the widespread perception that family firms do not survive over the long term.

As for the facts, a study of the fastest growing companies in the United States by the public accounting firm Coopers & Lybrand (Jones, Cohen, and Coppola, 1988) found that only 1% were firms run by family successors to founders, whereas 80% were led by their entrepreneurial founders. In a 1995 MassMutual Life Insurance survey of more than 1, 000 family-business owners, growth was ranked sixth among seven possible business goals, with much higher priority placed on increasing profitability, reducing debt, and increasing family wealth outside of the business (Greenwald, 1995).

Some of the most frequently quoted statistics on family business come from 1987 study of a sample of family firms in Illinois (Ward, 1987). It found that over a sixty-year period, only 15% of the sample survived as independent business owners. Two-thirds of those that did survive did not grow at all through the decades. Similar results were found in a more recent study of European firms by the London-based accounting firm Horwath Group (Benson, Crego, and Drucker, 1990).

Challenges to Growth

There are many theories on why family firms do not grow and rarely survive over the long term. The following are those most frequently seen:
- Growth is difficult for all long-established firms, family owned or not, because of maturing markets, intensifying competition, and changing technology. The business life cycle identified by Joseph Schumpeter (1990) is the natural order for all businesses.
- Once-effective personal paradigms eventually constrain successful entrepreneurs. As the business environment and requirements for success change, entrepreneurs can become particularly inflexible by clinging to habits of past success and avoiding deci-

sions that might threaten their image or economic security.

- Inherited security or wealth deprives next-generation family members of the hunger and drive they need to be successful entrepreneurial business leaders. They often prefer the pleasures of leisure, artistic expression, and time with family and friends.
- Children growing up in a family dominated by a successful, hard-working, self-reliant, decisive entrepreneur do not learn vital social skills of cooperation, shared decision-making, and unselfish collaboration. They also lack a parental role model for the teamwork and servant leadership skills so necessary for the next generation to work together or even to own a business together as a partnership of siblings.
- Even good business growth cannot satisfy the economic wishes of family that is growing both in size and lifestyle expectations. Excellent linear revenue growth of 5% to 10% per year rarely keeps up with the linear growth in numbers of family members: Two parents (or more) might have several offspring who likely have even more children among them. An added burden is the frequent hope of most generations to live a lifestyle at least as expensive as that of its forebears.
- As families expand and acquire in-laws, the diversity of personal goals and values makes it unlikely that there can be consensus for business decision-making and common commitment to business ownership. Building a shared vision for the future and reconciling inevitable conflicts become increasingly difficult, if not impossible.

All of these theories hold some intuitive appeal, as stories supporting each appear regularly in the media. Family-business owners themselves acknowledge their validity. In questionnaires to speech audiences, owners rank the six most powerful challenges to their firms' long--term growth in this order:

    (1) Maturing business life cycles and increasing competition
    (2) Limited capital to fund both family needs and business growth needs
    (3) Weak next-generation business leadership
    (4) Entrepreneurial leadership's inflexibility and resistance to change
    (5) Conflicts among sibling successors
    (6) Disparate family goals, values, and needs

Maturing Business Life Cycles

Although all businesses struggle with Schumpeter's inevitable business life cycle, family-owned firms have some special burdens. Family firms frequently pride themselves on their loyalty to employees and their strong culture and traditions (Dyer, Jr., 1988). Both practices can create resistance to change, however. As an example, family firms carry loyalty too far by retaining long-standing suppliers and advisors who are past their prime and are no longer appropriate to the needs of the business.

Another problem is that most family-business leaders know and own just one business. When it matures, they have few options but to hold on to declining asset. Most prefer to nurse the business along rather than shift their focus to new growth possibilities because the business is their creation, their identity, and their comfort (Lansberg, 1988). Low profitability reinforces this inherent unwillingness to change by increasing dependence on the historic core business.

As the business matures and the adventures of growth wane, declining business energy and resources fuel a downward cycle. The business becomes less able to attract and retain dynamic family and non-family leadership, the business leader's dependence on and appreciation for those remaining grows, and paternalistic rewards such as steady bonuses and recognition for tenure increase. These typical challenges of business maturity frequently are exacerbated in businesses owned for a long time by the founding family.

Limited Capital

Like all businesses, family firms must satisfy the growing expectations of shareholders. Unlike their non-family counterparts, however, they face the challenge of providing capital to pay their owners' death taxes. Many surveys show that the value of the typical family firm represents about 80% of the family's total assets, and when the senior generation dies, the owning family faces the most onerous death tax rate in the world (Ward, 1987).

Further complicating the capital crisis is the desire by some members in growing family to renounce their ownership position. Along with cash for their shares, they seek personal independence, privacy, and emotional freedom. Although providing cash to such family members sacrifices needed capital for business growth, the remaining business owners often are highly motivated to comply and avoid family disharmony or potentially nasty fights over dividends, corporate direction, and valuation shares for redemption (Ayers, 1990).

Weak Next-Generation Leadership

Many surveys show that one third to one half of all family businesses don't have available next-generation successors (Arthur Andersen, 1995). Those that do still face the reality of unlikely business growth because following in the footsteps of a very successful person who also is a parent or relative is, for many, an intimidating prospect. The next-generation leader must cope with many doubts and pressures:

- How can I make my mark in the land of a legend?
- How can I show respect for predecessors, yet remain my own person and foster change as a leader?
- How do I deflect the notoriety of a famous name and the constant comparisons with my namesake?
- How do I accept the responsibilities of leadership and for the welfare of others when the beneficiaries are my loved ones?
- How do I replace as leader of the family a person of an older generation who had not only the power of a parent or a senior, but also the authority of earned business success?

The odds of personal failure and the inevitability of disappointing others deeply affects the next-generation leader's style and decision making. Often, the result is a reluctance to take risks. Without risk-taking, however, the prospects for business growth wane.

Although many point to the lack of hunger and drive in the next generation as a primary cause of risk avoidance and business stagnation (Kets de Vries, 1993), these outcomes are just as often due to concern for the expectation of others. Many a successor has proclaimed, "If it were all my business and all my money, I'd take the risk. But it's not. I have to be careful to protect the welfare of the family, the inheritance of others, and the family name..."

In many other situations, no heir is interested or qualified to be the business leader. Besides motivation, successors need a special set of skills to manage with a particular strategy at a precise time in the development of the business, the environment, and the organization.

Inflexibility and Resistance to Change

Business psychologists have observed that successful leaders with very successful business strategies become fixated on that formula for success (Danco, 1975). As times and requirements for success change, the architect of the past strategy becomes inflexible, stifling growth.

Other classic entrepreneurial characteristics also block growth opportunities. For example, many entrepreneurial personalities reject planning as managerial practice, often arguing persuasively that it brings more disadvantages than advantages (Mintzberg, 1994):

- Planning requires sharing information. Entrepreneurs frequently prize secrecy.
- Planning forces entrepreneurs to respond to the ideas of others and to defend their own views. Entrepreneurs often relish ambiguity.
- Planning increases the opportunity for conflict among management and family. Entrepreneurs tend to avoid negatives and conflicts.

- Planning concentrates limited resources in a more focused manner. Entrepreneurs prefer spreading risk among many products, customers, and lines of business.
- Planning implies long-term commitments. Entrepreneurs like to keep as many options open as long as possible.

Reluctance to plan makes growth more unlikely (Ploster, 1994). In addition, over time, a business owner's personality changes, becoming more conservative and risk averse (Backley, 1994). With age, business owners also become increasingly concerned about responsibilities such as the financial security of their spouses, the welfare of family members not yet well settled, and even their own retirement. To assure maximum personal security and control over economic resources, business owners cling to the voting power of ownership and strive to protect extra strength on the balance sheet.

This keen concern for security and control reduces successors' motivation and frustrates their use of resources for business growth. It also limits useful estate planning options that could provide more financial resources in the future for growth.

Sibling Successor Conflict

Studies show that, more often than ever, U. S. family firms are owned by team of siblings (Nelton, 1996). Nearly half of all business owners expect to pass on leadership and ownership to two or more of their offspring.

The challenges facing sibling partnership teams are unique. Relationships among siblings are intense, and if serious discord occurs it frequently is fatal to the existing ownership structure. Approximately half of all sibling partnerships result in a split-up (Ward and Aronoff, 1992), which not only disrupts the management process and business climate, but usually consumes tremendous capital and growth potential as one or more partners are bought out by the other(s).

For a sibling partnership to work, the teammates must continually invest in their relationship. They must be able to compromise, talk things through, and follow a code of mutual understanding. Fundamentally, they must "agree to agree, "because it is more vital to preserve the sibling relationship than to make optimal business decisions (Ward and Aronoff, 1992). In fact, it is better to short-change business growth if it preserves the strength of the partnership. Good partnerships can overcome average business decisions, but bad partnerships will destroy even the best business.

The survival and success of the sibling partnership team comes largely from the interpersonal skills the siblings learn as youngsters at home. The climate of an entrepreneur's home is usually not a good breeding ground for those skills, however. The stereotype of the autocratic entrepreneur is based in fact: Entrepreneurs usually come home exhausted from the challenges of the day, seeking tranquillity and being intolerant of more stress and conflict. Their offspring are not encouraged to work out their conflicts because the business "boss" comes home and tells them how to behave...or else.

Scholars of healthy families suggest that shared decision-making is at least as important as any skill (Aronoff and Astrachan, 1996). Siblings of autocratic, controlling, impatient entrepreneurs do not have adequate opportunity to learn this skill. Once the siblings mature, conflict among them diverts energy from feeding the fires of business growth.

Disparate Family Goals

Sibling and cousin-owned family businesses share an important challenge: How to reconcile the different goals, needs, and values of several family members. As families expand and grow older, goals and values inevitably become more diverse.

For most non-family-owned businesses, shareholders come and go as the nature of the investment suits their expectations. For most family-owned businesses, on the other hand, the investment is liquid, carries emotional significance, and represents most of the shareholders' wealth. Consequently, family shareholders struggle over whether to retain their investment.

If they choose to sell, they feel disloyal to their heritage and worry about getting full value for their shares. If they choose to stay with their investment, they feel they deserve special rewards and acknowledgment (Murdoch and Murdoch, 1991). Rewards may include hefty and consistent dividends, while acknowledgment may include involvement in business governance or extra efforts made to communicate information to them about the business.

Both bring challenges to growth. Providing capital for share redemption draws funds from building the business, and paying dividends diverts profits from reinvestment. Time spent earning shareholder commitment diverts energies from day-to-day business.

Firms that are fortunate enough to have family shareholders who are steady and content with their investment can focus on long-term strategies. More often, however, the different goals and needs of various owners hurt prospects for growth.

The most serious threat to growth occurs when some family members feel the business is unfair to their cause or does not exemplify their beliefs. These owners attack management relentlessly. Just as detrimental are family owners who feel mistreated by previous generations and focus their resentments on current family managers who they perceive as unfairly privileged representatives of their forebears.

Summary

Most well-established family firms do not grow. Several popular theories illustrate the special challenges to growth that are unique to family-owned firms. When asked why their family business does not grow, business owners rank the causes in order of importance as (1) business maturity, (2) limited capital, (3) ill-suited successors, (4) entrepreneurial inflexibility, (5) sibling conflict, (6) disparate goals and values.

The first four causes are mostly related to business issues. Curiously, when I ask audiences of families who own businesses what they think are the greatest threats to the growth and survival of *other* people's businesses, the results are very different. The two most troubling issues are the last two, both of which are primarily issues of family relationships.

In short, family-business owners know that family problems pose the real threats to their futures. The most serious threat is disparate goals and values, followed by sibling team interpersonal conflict. Wise family-business leaders invest substantial energies to nurture and strengthen family-member harmony, trust, and satisfaction.

Avoiding Stagnation: The Growth Model

For most family-owned businesses, the path to survival is one of stagnation. How do these firms survive when they do not grow for so many years? The answer is in examining two unusual circumstances that benefit non-growing survivors.

First, the non-growing firms that have survived have kept ownership in one person's hands, rather than evolving into sibling partnerships or firms held widely by a variety of family members. In general, ownership by one family member who leads the business significantly increases the chances of growth and survival.

Second, the nature of their businesses and industries have spared them much competitive or technological change. In sum, most of the long-lasting survivors have avoided many of the business and family challenges faced by both family and non-family businesses (Ward, 1987).

In contrast, the family firms that have grown the most over time follow different but no less predictable path: Each generation of leadership brings to the business new strategic ideas that build on underlying, long-held competencies developed for earlier strategies (Hamel, Jr., 1994). In addition, ownership control rests with one family manager, or if not one, as few as possible (Stoy Hayward, 1989).

A good example of this growth model is Rosenbluth Travel, a $1.3 billion Philadelphia-based firm that is more than one hundred years old. The first generation founder began by arranging steamship passage for immigrants. To succeed, the business developed excellent skills in customer service and in accounting for customers' monies.

A later generation shifted the focus to leisure travel. The same skills were important to success: providing outstanding personal service and applying the data processing and record-keeping talent to analyze customers' needs and rate structures.

The current-generation leader added a new dimension, corporate travel. This new strategy draws on the firm's historic skills. Besides providing good customer service to corporate accounts, Rosenbluth maintains excellent recordkeeping and data processing in order to deliver on its "lowest possible fares" promise to its customers.

While the growth model exemplified by Rosenbluth accurately reflects the experience of most long-growing family firms, it does not explain the day-to-day management practices that spark that growth. Nor does it explain the leadership practices necessary to hold together more complicated forms of family ownership, such as sibling partnerships or more widespread family ownership. The next section outlines the best practices needed to make the growth model succeed.

Best Practices

Family-owned firms that grow through the decades must address each of the following requirements in order to promote expansion and overcome the special challenges inherent in family firms.

Assure Fresh Strategic Insights. Long-term growth requires ongoing sources of fresh strategic insights. In most industries, strategies must change every few years, if not continuously. Efforts to stimulate new thinking are particularly important for family-owned firms, because few successors have much breadth or variety of outside experience and most managers and leaders have long tenures. Family-business leaders can create an atmosphere that fosters and welcomes new ideas if they:

Promote strategic experimentation. Growing companies constantly test and stretch their current strategic limits (Mintzberg and Waters, 1990). They revise products, explore new markets or channels of distribution, refine the marketing mix of pricing and promotion, and create new ways to add value or differentiation. New insights come most often from the trial-and-error experiments with current strategy, and experimentation helps jolt family firms out of the complacency that comes so naturally to many successful individuals and firms.

Budget strategic expenses. To assure that strategic development is a highly conscious process, successful firms establish a "strategic budget"that clearly identifies initiatives to promote strategic development (Mintzberg and Waters, 1990). Strategic expenses are spent on efforts that, for example, promise to increase market share volume in future years or to build new lines of business. They do not include costs to maintain and protect the status quo. Many family firms find that setting up a strategic budget provides helpful tension to preserve needed funds in the family business against the temptation to pay increasing dividends or family-member bonuses and perks.

Provide serendipity capital. Creative managers need discretionary funds to explore and experiment with new ideas and to react to new circumstances that were not anticipated in the annual operating budget process. Some outstanding growth firms include such discretionary funds for each manager as part of their operating budgets. Managers are encouraged to spend these funds for the sake of the future, which creates a climate of experimentation and motivates creative, dynamic managers to achieve their best.

Use independent directors on the board to challenge strategic assumptions. The greatest way to avoid stagnation and decline is to have an absolute business mission. Business leaders who are committed to growth urge their independent outside directors to challenge the relevance of their mission and the validity of the assumptions underscoring it. Successful business leaders know that no one can challenge their thinking and the direction of the business better than highly respected outside directors.

Encourage global experience for next-generation business leaders. A famous study by Professor Miguel Gallo (Gallo and Point, 1994) of IESE in Barcelona found that the most successful international family firms were those in which the leaders' offspring had significant work or educational experience outside of their home country. However, most family-owned firms run a high risk of limiting international growth opportunities because successors often do not gain significant outside external experience.

Attract and Retain Excellent Non-Family Managers. Long-term growth demands a pool of talented non-family managers, but most family firms do not take this resource fairly enough. They are reluctant to invest in future talent when they are unsure of the effects of strong non-family managers on the family members' career paths. Frequently, business owners are too modest to believe they can attract people of the highest caliber (Tanner, 1994). To combat their tendencies, family business leaders must:

Emphasize merit in personnel decisions. The best non-family managers need to feel that they are valued, appreciated, and compensated on the basis of merit.

Provide opportunities for the best managers to accumulate personal wealth. Few family firms give stock or stock options to their key executives (Carlson and Nager, 1993). More often, they are given opportunities to participate in "phantom stock" plans or to invest alongside family members in special arrangements such as a new venture or a real estate opportunity.

Assure career growth opportunities for the best non-family executives. Talented non-family managers need assurance that they can continue to grow as professionals. Too often, the company's organization chart and the likely career paths of young family members do not give them that assurance. In response, some family firms restrict family members from entry into the business until they have ample, successful external experience. They also work hard to create more top management leadership positions than could be filled by family members alone.

Create a Flexible, Innovative Organization. Constant strategic experimentation requires a flexible, innovative organization that can:

Share business information openly. As noted earlier, secrecy is a common trait of business owners. They fear disclosing financial success, because it leads to demands by valuable employees, and financial failure, because it drives away good people. But without information and trust, creativity and loyalty are limited. Successful family-owned firms grow by sharing vital information among a large number of managers.

Champion change and celebrate new ideas. For innovation and flexibility to flourish, teamwork must be a part of the company's culture. Growing companies de-emphasize heroic leaders as the reasons for success (Danco, 1994). Instead, they credit the organizational team and the habit of past innovation that extends to the founding of the business itself.

Constantly change some things. The best way to encourage innovation is to foster positive feelings about change. One popular approach to increasing comfort with ongoing change is to tinker regularly with management systems and processes, such as compensation bonus systems, information systems, organizational roles and structure, and reporting and personal performance review processes (Nelson, 1994).

Create and Conserve Capital. As the family grows, as death taxes arise, and as new strategies require increased financial resources, the demands for more capital are high. However, conserving as much cash as possible for the business is critical for growth. To help resolve the dilemma between family financial needs and growth's fiscal requirements, long-lasting, growing family firms become adept at creating and conserving capital. Among their strategies:

Use other people's money. Growing firms use more debt (Tennenbaum and Trien, 1992). They also are creative in securing capital from others who want to invest in the business's success, sometimes by offering ownership shares and opportunities for joint ventures.

Manage strategy to be less capital intensive. Over time, long-growing family firms shift their strategy to require less capital for growth (Flamholtz, 1986). They de-emphasize aspects that require significant capital (such as real estate or totally integrated production) and emphasize those that require less capital (such as servicing and franchising).

Quickly establish a share redemption plan and dividend policy. The sooner the formula for redemption is established, the less capital it will require. Long established redemption plans usually are less contentious and designed to give the business ample time and favored terms to make payouts. In addition, clear dividend policies usually lead to more content and less demanding shareholders (*Family Business Advisor*, 1994).

Implement estate plans early. Family-business experts agree that one of the best ways to conserve capital is to lessen the bite of death taxes by implementing the estate plan and its funding mechanism(s) as soon as possible (Blackman, 1994). The sooner the plan is implemented, the more taxes that can be saved. Prompt action also minimizes the cost of necessary insurance.

Prepare Successors for Leadership. Successors to family firms face unique job requirements that require specific skills to maximize their chances of leading business growth. Most of the education for successors is either unsupervised, on-the-job training or formal course work at a university or college (Cohn, 1992). Both neglect some critical aspects of the job of CEO of a family firm. To fill the gaps, family business leaders must:

Support the successor in developing a culture of change in the business. For family successors of successful parents, leading organizational change is extremely difficult. Promoting change is usually perceived as an indictment of the past or a criticism of the predecessor. Predecessors can help by focusing on how the company team contributes to the firm's success and by discouraging credit for themselves.

Promote good mentoring for the successor. Successors benefit from several mentoring experiences: working elsewhere before entering the family firm; learning how to cope with the expectations of the outside world of civic organizations, charities, and trade associations; and learning how to create a common strategic vision for the company and the owners.

Set a date to transfer both responsibility and control to the next generation. Successors can be inhibited by uncertainty over the date of succession. Predecessors who establish the date far in advance usually are more calm and prepared for retirement, and their successors are more motivated and committed to be the leaders the business and its growth require. Nothing frustrates the growth of a family firm more than the unwillingness or inability to empower and to entrust the next generation with control and authority (Jaffe, 1990).

Exploit the Unique Strategic Advantages of Family Ownership. Much of the early part of this paper outlined the disadvantages and special challenges to growth for many family firms. Successful family-owned companies know there are special advantages, too, and they strive to shape strategies that exploit them, such as:

Seeking investments that reward patient capital. Family firms have a unique opportunity to be long-term oriented. Security analysts can't punish their long term thinking. For a strong family, long-term value is much preferred to short term results. Highly successful family firms can therefore be more consistent in their business-building efforts and react less to bumps in the economy or their industry. Such efforts can include research and development, brand name development, market expansion, and even investments in out-of-fashion businesses, such as savings and loans and metal platers.

Build strategy around relationships. For the family-owned business, reputation is all-important (Donnelley, 1964). With the family name on the door and with the realization that future generations will be known, in part, by today's decisions, families in business have every advantage in dealing with each other. Mutual trust can lead to exciting new growth opportunities: More and more global alliances are being established by family firms.

Concentrate on businesses in which fast decision making is a plus. While quick decision-making certainly is a function of small firms, it also is a function of family firms. Decreased organizational politics and the resonance of ownership with managerial leadership allow family businesses to respond when quick decision-making is required.

Conclusion

While the prospects for long-term growth are limited for all family-owned businesses, enough of them have grown over long-enough periods to demonstrate the best practices just described. Although such practices are powerful tools that both permit and facilitate growth, two other conditions also are important for long-term growth: the motivation of leadership to follow these practices and the commitment of the owning family to support the sacrifices necessary for growth.

Figure 1. The Pyramid of Ownership Motivations

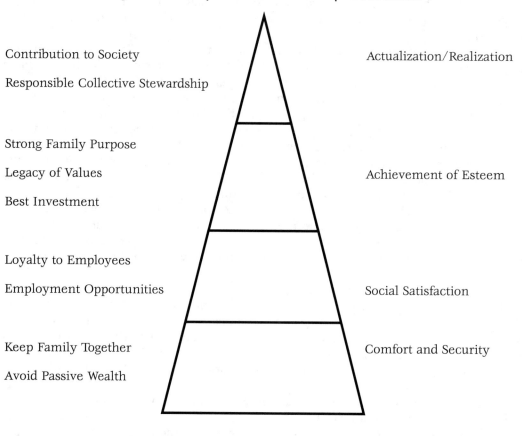

Contribution to Society

Responsible Collective Stewardship

Actualization/Realization

Strong Family Purpose

Legacy of Values

Best Investment

Achievement of Esteem

Loyalty to Employees

Employment Opportunities

Social Satisfaction

Keep Family Together

Avoid Passive Wealth

Comfort and Security

Masters of Growth. The family business leaders who are personally driven to grow their businesses by following the best practices are a special breed. As exceptions to the many theories of stagnation addressed in this paper, my experience indicates that they represent only 7% to 10% of all family business leaders in the world.

Studies of who these "masters of growth"are and what drives them show that they share several characteristics. Their personal mission is to build an enduring institution that will last and be even more successful in the future (Tagiuri and Davis, 1992). They build and test a personal philosophy of management that attempts to make their organization a self-managed system (Guzzo and Abbott, 1990). They are willing to be role models for their beliefs, not out of vanity, but because they know it is the best way to get good feedback on their philosophy and thinking (Mintzberg and Waters, 1990). They also realize that public accountability is a great motivation for themselves and for others in the company (Mintzberg and Waters, 1990). These "masters"see themselves as stewards of capital and do not feel a sense of personal ownership (Danco, 1975). Instead, they believe it is their responsibility to pass on the business and its leadership in better condition than when they found it.

Committed Family Purpose. The "masters of growth"have tremendous personal energy and passion for growth. Eventually, however, they begin to focus on the goals and needs of family members to determine whether there is the desire and commitment to continue enthusiastically.

The "best practice"that is most important to long-term family business growth is the process of holding family meetings to define family purpose and mission, family values, and the motivations and rationale for continued business ownership. If good consensus emerges, the path to long-term business growth is quite secure.

There are several motivations for committed long-term family ownership, as presented by the Pyramid of Ownership Motivations (Figure 1). The pyramid attempts to reflect

Maslow's Hierarchy of Motivational Needs (Maslow, 1954). The reasons at the base of the pyramid do not seem to provide sustainable, long-term commitment to ownership continuity (i. e., providing family members with employment or withholding liquid wealth from future generations). The motivations toward the top of the pyramid are more compelling and durable reasons for continuing the family business another generation (i. e., assuring the business's contributions to society or perpetuating a legacy of family values).

References

Arthur Andersen & Co., S. C. (1995). Research Findings. *American Family Business Survey,* Chicago.

Aronoff, C. E. & Astrachan, J. H. (1996). How to make better decisions. *Nation's Business, 84* (1), 39 –40.

Ayers, G. R. (1990). Rough family justice: Equity in family business succession planning. *Family Business Review, 3* (1), 3 –22.

Backley, C. (1994). Learning money personality helps achieve business success. *The Family Business Report, 4*(2), 1.

Benson, B., Crego, E. T., & Drucker, R. H. (1990). *Your Family Business: A Success Guide for Growth and Survival.* Homewood, IL: Dow-Jones-Irwin.

Blackman, I. L. (1994). Two magic bullets...or How to beat the tax collector. *National Petroleum News, 86* (2), 44.

Carlson, D. K., & Nager, R. W. (1993). Equity compensation for key employees. *Family Business Advisor.* (January).

Cohn, M. (1992). *Passing the Torch: Succession, Retirement, and Estate Planning in the Family-Owned Business.* New York: McGraw-Hill.

Danco, L. A. (1975). *Beyond Survival: A Business Owner's Guide.* Cleveland, OH: The University Press.

Danco, L. A. (1980). *Inside the Family Business.* Cleveland, OH: The University Press.

Danco, L. A. (1994). Why few firms outlive their founder. *Tire Business,* 8.

Donnelley, R. G. (1964). The family business. *Harvard Business Review, 42* (4), 10 –11.

Dyer, W. Gibb, Jr. (1988). Culture and continuity in family firms. *Family Business Review, 1* (1), 37 –50.

Family Business Advisor. (1994). Thinking about dividend policies. *Family Business Advisor, 3* (3), 1.

Flamholtz, E. G. (1986). *How to Make the Transition From a Entrepreneurship to a Professionally Managed Firm.* San Francisco: Jossey-Bass.

Gallo, M. A., & Point, C. G. (1994). Internationalizing family firms. *Family Business Advisor, 3* (4), 1.

Greenwald, Matthew and Associates (1995). Research Findings. *MassMutual Life Insurance Company,* 47.

Guzzo, R. A., & Abbott, S. (1990). Family firms as utopian organizations. *Family Business Review, 3* (1), 23 –34.

Hamel, L. H., Jr. (1994). The first generation. *Family Business Report,* (November), 7.

Jaffe, D. (1990). *Working with the Ones You Love.* Berkeley, CA: Conari Press.

Jones, S., Cohen, M. B., & Coppola, V. V. (1988). *The Coopers & Lybrand Guide to Growing Your Business.* New York: Wiley.

Kets de Vries, M. F. R. (1993). The dynamics of family controlled firms: The good and the bad. *Organizational Dynamics, 21* (3), 59 –71.

Lansberg, I. (1988). The succession conspiracy. *Family Business Review, 1* (2), 119 –143.

Maslow, A. H. (1954) *Motivation and Personality.* New York: Harper.

Mintzberg, H. & Waters, J. A. (1990). Tracking strategy in an entrepreneurial firm. *Family Business Review, 3* (3), 285 –313.

Mintzberg, H. (1994). *The Rise and Fall of Strategic Planning.* New York: The Free Press.

Murdoch, M., & Murdoch, C. M. (1991). A legal perspective on shareholder relationships in family businesses: The scope of fiduciary duties. *Family Business Review, 4* (3), 287–301.

Nelson, R. (1994). Creating an energized workplace. *Leader to Leader, 5* (Summer), 34–39.

Nelton, S. (1996). Team playing is on the rise. *Nation's Business, 84* (6), 53 –55.

Ploster, J. (1994). Keeping a family business moving. *The Cleveland (OH) Plain Dealer: Financial and Estate Planning Section.*

Schumpeter, J. A. (1990). Essays on entrepreneurs, innovations, business cycles, and the evolution of capitalism. *The Journal of Economic History, 50,* 246 –247.

Stoy Hayward & Associates (1989). *Staying the course: Survival characteristics of the family owned business.* Report conducted by the Graduate Students of the London School of Business, 22 –23.

Tagiuri, R., & Davis, J. A. (1992). On the goals of successful family companies. *Family Business Review, 3* (1), 43 –62.

Tanner, F. L. F. (1994). Do you have an effective compensation plan for you key employees? *Family Business Forum Quarterly, 7* (3), 8.

Tennenbaum, B. H., & Trien, J. W. (1992). How to woo your banker. *Family Business Magazine,* (Summer), 31 –36.

Ward, J. L. 1987. *Keeping the family business healthy: How to plan for continuing growth, profitability, and family leadership.* San Francisco: Jossey-Bass.

Ward, J. L., & Aronoff, C. E. (1992). Sibling partnerships. *Nation's Business, 80* (1), 52–53.

CHAPTER 9
PSYCHOLOGICAL ISSUES

Given the complications of family relationships being played out in a business structure, psychological dimensions are basic to family business systems. Articles in this section deal with the application of psychological therapy to family firms. The psychological problems that can confront business families range from the stress associated with passing the business to the next generation to substance abuse by family members. Ultimately, how and how well families cope depends on the family paradigms – the core beliefs through which family members experience their world.

In this article, a psychoanalyst looks at the behavior patterns in family firms and finds "good news and bad news." Family business's advantages and disadvantages are explored.

The Dynamics of Family Controlled Firms: The Good and the Bad News

By Manfred F.R. Kets de Vries

That business was built specifically for my family. Anybody who wants to come in, there's an open place for him. If the business is destroyed as a result of that, so be it.

– Sam Steinberg

Once upon a time, there was a potter who made the most beautiful pottery in the world. Everyone who saw his pottery immediately fell in love with it and wanted to buy it. As a result, the potter's shop flourished and became known far and wide. After some time, demand for his product became so great that he found it impossible to do all the work himself. The potter started a factory and hired people to help. As the years went by, he employed more and more workers. Eventually, the potter spent all day managing the factory. He no longer had time to make pottery. Sometimes he longed for the good old days when things seemed so much simpler and he did everything himself. He didn't really like to be so dependent on others, since very few people could live up to his standards of excellence.

Fortunately, his children were now older and had begun giving him a hand. They became increasingly helpful in managing the business. Although the potter was reluctant to let go, he began to realize that he really had no choice. His health and endurance were no longer what they used to be. But he wanted to keep the business in the family. He liked to see the family name on the building. For him, the business was a way of keeping the family together. After all, the reason for having worked so hard was to create a better life for all of them.

When the potter died, he left the company to his two sons and only daughter. The pottery plant and the sales outlets continued to prosper under their guidance. More and more plants opened. The operation expanded across borders and diversified into related products such as glass, crystal and silverware.

When the children's children became older, they were also brought into the business. Unfortunately, with so many family members around, things started to go downhill. The original family cohesiveness began to unravel. There were periods when those who could remember times past would think nostalgically of the good old days, when the old man was in control. Everything had seemed so much simpler then; everyone knew who was in charge!

The cousins and siblings began to argue about money, shares, power, and the responsibilities: who would get what and who made what. Envy reared its head. Eventually, what had started as mere bickering degenerated into bitter feuding. The two brothers and the sister, their wives, husband, and children spent all their time and energy fighting. Employees were forced to choose one of the many factions. Soon the most capable employees began to leave. Product quality decreased, and customers stopped buying.

In the end, the strife led to bankruptcy for the company and the loss of the family members' personal fortune. Thus ended the potter's dream – the family having gone from rags to rags in three generations.

The people in this fairy tale did not live happily ever after. Clearly, they had made a mess of things – an all too common scenario for many family businesses. The problem is that family businesses have a built-in Achilles' heel. Two systems interact – the family and the business – and these two systems are not necessarily compatible. On the contrary, examples of destructive family feuds are not hard to find. Consider how vendettas, shareholder fights, and lawsuits divided the Gucci family, one of Europe's great mercantile empires. Or recall the power struggle between the Steinberg sisters, the inheritors of the large Canadian shopping center emporium, a fight that eventually ripped the family firm apart. Or think about the feud over money power and honor at Gallimard, France's most prestigious publishing house.

Although the statistics vary, it seems that only three out of ten family firms make it through the second generation, and only one in ten through the third. Analysts have estimated the average lifespan of an entrepreneurial firm at only twenty-four years, the usual length of time the founder is associated with it.

Some people may say, who cares? Why all this concern about family firms? Isn't all the "real action" in publicly held corporations? Those who play down the importance of family firms are making an enormous mistake. According to some estimates, 80 percent of all businesses are family controlled, in the widest sense of the term, in that the family has a significant say in the company's strategic direction and the appointment of a new CEO.

Nor does the argument that these figures are misleading because they mainly apply to mom-and-pop stores hold water. For example, in the U.S. one-third of the Fortune 500 companies are family controlled. Family businesses account for the majority of jobs in most Western societies. In the U.S., some 40 percent of the gross national product comes from family corporations.

Given the importance of family businesses to national economies, it is surprising that so little attention has been given to what affects this type of firm. Managing family firms raises a host of questions. This article addresses two: What contributes to the problems these firms experience? Are there special dynamics characteristic of family firms? This article is based on my work with family firms and in-depth interviews with over 300 executives associated with family firms as owners, owner-managers, family members, or managers.

There is clearly "good news" and "bad news" when it comes to working in a family business. Exhibit I summarizes the advantages and disadvantages.

The Good News

For family members, one of the obvious advantages of working for a family firm is the sense of being in control of their destiny. Running something in which one has a personal stake certainly creates a greater feeling of independence. Moreover, the narcissistic pleasures should not be underestimated. There is something to be said for seeing one's name on the building, particularly if it is a well-known brand name. This can have other beneficial side effects. As the family member of a media conglomerate once mentioned, "The name I have has certainly helped me to get access to top executives of companies, persons who under other circumstances would have kept their doors shut." Nor should we underestimate the possible financial benefits. There is always the possibility of becoming really successful. And these benefits represent only the tip of the iceberg.

The Long-Term Perspective

In general, family firms tend to have a longer term view of their business. They are not fly-by-night operations. This means that family owner-managers may have a different outlook vis-a-vis their employees, their customers, the community, and other important stakeholders, and this may positively affect the quality of their product. The fact that the owners have their name on the building makes them more conscious of their standing in the community and more jealous of their reputation.

In many instances, the company and its products affect the identity of family members. To be associated with defective or inferior products becomes a reflection on the self. Thus, the family will find it singularly unattractive to go for short-term financial gains if doing so will tarnish the company's standing. When a family has been producing wine for many generations, like the house of Torres in Spain, or publishing books, like the Bonnier family in Sweden, members want to be proud of the product.

Exhibit 1. Advantages and Disadvantages of Family Controlled Firms

Advantages	*Disadvantages*

• Long-term orientation
• Greater independence of action
  – less (or no) pressure from stock market
  – less (or no) takeover risk
• Family culture as a source of pride
  – stability
  – strong identification/commitment/ motivation
  – continuity in leadership
• Greater resilience in hard times
  – willing to plow back profits
• Less bureaucratic and impersonal
  – greater flexibility
  – quicker decision making
• Financial benefits
  – possibility of great success
• Knowing the business
  – early training for family members
	• Less access to capital markets may curtail growth
	• Confusing organization
	  – messy structure
	  – no clear division of tasks
	• Nepotism
	  – tolerance of inept family members as managers
	  – inequitable reward systems
	  – greater difficulties in attracting professional management
	• Spoiled kid syndrome
	• Internecine strife
	  – family disputes overflow into business
	• Paternalistic/autocratic rule
	  – resistance to change
	  – secrecy
	  – attraction of dependent personalities
	• Financial strain
	  – family members milking the business
	  – disequalibrium between contribution and compensation
	• Succession dramas

Moreover, compared with publicly held corporations, family firms are not the slaves of Wall Street, haunted by quarterly results. They are under less pressure; there is less public scrutiny, and they have greater independence of action. The fact that family firms do not have to divulge as much information as publicly held corporations can be a competitive advantage: It is not as easy for competitors to know what they are really up to. Those who have tried to get information about famous but secretive family corporations, such as Mars (the confectionery manufacturer), Michelin (the tire maker), or C & A (the department store chain) know what this means.

Also, privately held companies worry less about takeover threats. There is less need to create elaborate schemes with "poison pills" and "golden parachutes." Executives can save their energy for other causes. Finally, family firms tend to be more resilient during hard times, given their greater willingness to plow profits back into the business.

The Family Culture

This long-term outlook can be reinforced by greater certainty about what kind of leadership will prevail in the firm. With effective succession planning (a subject we will discuss later), everyone knows who is next in line. This can mean peace of mind and, consequently, less political behavior in the company.

The family spirit will very much determine the prevailing attitudes, norms, and values in the company. The values family members express create a common purpose for employees and help to establish a sense of identification and commitment. In well-run family firms, the employees feel like part of the family. Access to senior management comes easier. There is often less bureaucracy and thus quicker, more effective decision making.

The kind of corporate culture that permeates Herman Miller Inc., the furniture manufacturer, has become legendary. This company has repeatedly been listed as one of the best managed companies in America. The company was started in 1923 by D.J. De Pree, who was succeeded first by his son, Hugh, and then by Hugh's son, Max. At Herman Miller

Inc we find a group of people strongly committed to the beliefs and ideas of the senior family members, particularly Max De Pree. Employees share the family's outlook toward customer service, quality, and productivity. This is a covenant that works both ways. The family has a strong belief in the potential of people. This belief is backed up by a set of rights that determine the psychological contract between workers and management.

Included in the "ground rules" for working at Herman Miller Inc. are the right to be needed, the right to be involved, the right to understand, the right to affect one's own destiny, the right to be accountable, and the right to appeal.

This focus on rights goes beyond mere talk – it affects everyone's wallet. The company has a longstanding Scanlon Plan entitling workers to a share of the financial gains resulting from their suggestions for improving design, customer service, quality, and productivity. When Herman Miller Inc. went public, management established a stock option plan. Without exception, all regular employees who have worked in the firm for at least a year own stock. There are even "silver parachutes" for all employees in the case of an unfriendly takeover, not just golden parachutes for top management.

Herman Miller Inc. also exemplifies a family firm that is less bureaucratic than an equivalent publicly held corporation. The family culture makes the firm much less impersonal. Encouraging employees to feel like part of the family facilitates access to senior management. Even the lowliest production worker has no difficulty knocking on Max De Pree's door. Such an atmosphere expedites decision making and leads to greater flexibility of procedure and action.

Knowing the Business

Another important competitive advantage can be found in the extensive expertise family members have. After all, they have been in contact with the business from early childhood onward. Breakfasts, dinners, walks, family gatherings, and summer jobs create opportunities to learn more about the business.

One executive recalled how as a child he would take long walks with his father, during which they would visit stores to look at competitors' products. Afterwards, his father would ask him which products he liked most, and this would lead to lengthy arguments about each product's quality. This man felt that the expertise he gained during those informal outings proved invaluable later in life.

This kind of knowledge may give family members a head start, compared with executives entering the business later on. Early training like this helps to explain the sometimes puzzling appointments of very young family members to senior positions. Actually, such "age inappropriate" appointments can have a beneficial effect, in that they may lead to a rejuvenation of an arteriosclerotic group of top executives.

The Bad News

Obviously, there cannot be only good news. On the debit side, the "technical" difficulties that dog family ownership spring immediately to mind. Tax code covering inheritance, for example, can create problems that threaten the continuation of the firm. Another obvious problem is that family corporations usually have greater difficulty obtaining access to capital markets. This may inhibit growth.

The organization of family firms frequently strikes the outsider as messy and confusing. Authority and responsibility may not be clearly defined; jobs may overlap; executives may hold a number of different jobs. The decision-making hierarchy may be completely ignored, existing only to be bypassed.

When one interviews people in family firms, however, one quickly discovers that many of the key problems are of a psychological nature. They center on issues such as the fit between the senior executive's leadership style and the company's stage of development, the overflow of family conflicts into the business, coalition politics among the family members (which detract from the substance of the business), and, last but certainly not least, the question of succession.

All these problems can turn into high drama. At times, life veers between soap opera and the extremes of Greek tragedy. Cronos, King Laius, Jocasta, Medea, and Oedipus are regular guests on the family cast list. As we see these problems recurring again and again, they deserve closer examination.

The Question of Nepotism

Family logic often overrules business reason. In many instances family members are welcomed regardless of their ability to contribute to the business. Senior owner-managers often show a remarkable capacity for closing their eyes to the weaknesses of their beloved sons or daughters.

Working under a person who is clearly incompetent places a non-family member in a highly unattractive position. When there is an imbalance between contribution and credit, feelings of equity cannot be maintained. An absence of fair play can undermine one of the pillars of corporate culture: the need for trust. Lack of trust will influence the company climate, affecting job satisfaction, motivation, and performance.

This situation is particularly ironic if, as is often the case in many family firms, family members demand a high level of commitment from the non-relatives. Such demands are acceptable if management gives non-family members due credit for work well done. However, they may be unacceptable if the existing incentive system is heavily biased toward non-contributing family members. In this case, it becomes difficult to attract capable managers, a development that may endanger the company's future. The people who are willing to stick around may not be the ones the company needs most.

Consider the example of a well-known international firm in the clothing business. The president of this company (encouraged by his wife) was completely blind to the incompetence of his only son. Having survived a severe coronary attack, he placed his son, who had been busy flunking out of every school he had been sent to, in a senior position. The son's behavior soured the atmosphere. One of his worst habits was to lay the blame for whatever mistake he had made (forgetting appointments, not following up on clients, allocating resources poorly) on others; it was never his fault. Eventually, many of the more competent employees could take it no longer and left the company. When the son (against all advice) acquired a firm with outdated product lines and obsolete machinery, the company went into the red, and this finally opened the father-president's eyes. He realized what had really been going on and reasserted his control.

The "Spoiled Kid" Syndrome

This story provides a good example of the "spoiled kid syndrome." In the typical scenario, the principal protagonist is the hardworking entrepreneur completely obsessed by his business. He works day and night, thinking about nothing else. Obviously, this lifestyle leaves him very little time to devote to his family (he is usually a man). Although he is aware of what he is doing, he cannot help himself. The demands of the business (or at least his perception of them) are too overwhelming. He rationalizes his behavior by saying that he is doing it in the best interests of the family. He cherishes the notion that, because of his efforts, everyone will be better off later on. He fails to realize, however, that he may be cannibalizing that very future: There may be no "later on." We often see these men gradually becoming estranged from their wives and children.

This kind of behavior leads to feelings of guilt. A common way of dealing with such feelings is to start bribing the family members, a kind of pay-off for not being available emotionally or otherwise. The pay-off may start with a big teddy bear when the children are young and metamorphose into sports cars, jewelry, expensive vacations, or condominiums. Unfortunately, these gifts will never replace the attention that was missing during childhood. At the same time, for the giver, handing out material possessions becomes a way of making up for hardships that he himself experienced. He is giving to his children what he once longed for himself.

In trying to create a better life for their offspring, such people are full of good intentions. Unfortunately, possessions, rather than a set of well-internalized values, feelings of affection, and mutual respect, become the overriding criteria. And this pursuit of material possessions may eventually turn out to be a Faustian bargain.

The Steinberg family feud, which captured headlines in many newspapers, provides a prime example. The daughters of Sam Steinberg, who built up a shopping center empire, battled for control of the business. In their book, *Steinberg: The Break-up of a Family Empire*, journalists Gibbon and Hadekel concluded from their interviews with the principal players that "the girls were spoiled rotten," having been lavished with clothes, cars, and condos in Florida. According to Gibbon and Hadekel, "When it came to his daughters, his pockets were deep; there was nothing they couldn't have. They would never know the life Sam Steinberg had lived growing up in a crowded, unheated flat on The Main."

We could ask how much attention Sam Steinberg and his wife Helen had paid to the more intangible needs of their daughters. They seem to have given little value to education, business training, and social responsibility. The notion that authority and responsibility should be awarded only in recognition of proven accomplishments did not apply to Steinberg's family members. His daughters wielded enormous power as the company's major shareholders, and their poor understanding of the business had catastrophic consequences. Moreover, the rivalry between the sisters, suppressed while their father was alive, made the situation far worse and led eventually to the company break-up.

The War of the Roses

A parent's emotional unavailability can have lasting repercussions on children. They may start to fight for whatever little quality time is available, and they soon become expert judges in who has preference in the "love equation." These early feelings of envy and jealousy are not easily resolved and will likely remain troublesome throughout life.

In the process of growing up, siblings often separate and choose their own courses in life. With time and geographical distance, residual childhood irritants and resentments are less likely to flare up. However, joining the family firm breaks this pattern. Parents may use emotional blackmail to induce their children to go into the business. Consequently, in one way or another, family members may be stuck with one another. They may feel trapped. And they may end up in a vicious circle of endlessly repeating conflicts-a continuation of the old emotional "games" of childhood.

Publicly held organizations may not be paragons of rational behavior, but family firms, given the greater likelihood of emotional drama, are most certainly not. Irrational decision making can become rampant. Old wounds may be reopened; others may never have had an opportunity to heal. Decisions may be made on an emotional basis only, rather than according to sound business sense.

Family members may become trapped in situations of highly concentrated risk, not just financial but emotional. When love has been a scarce commodity and object of competition during the developmental years, the stage is set for internecine strife. Family and business disputes tend to become confused. Since these disputes have their origin in early childhood, they can become extremely messy and far more difficult to disentangle than would be the case in publicly held corporations.

A good example of numbing fraternal strife is the saga of the Horvitz brothers, heirs to one of America's largest fortunes: a $700 million newspaper, cable television, and real estate empire. After the father died, the fight over who would gain control of the business began in earnest, reaching a new crescendo when the mother, who had acted as peacemaker, died soon after. Accusations and counteraccusations flew. Fistfights were par for the course. Lawsuits led to years of legal wrangling. As a son of one of the three brothers said, "Decisions were based on how the brothers felt when they were twelve."

Factional infighting can become extremely complex in family firms that have survived a number of generations and are run by large families. Obviously, maintaining a cohesive family unit becomes more difficult as the generations spread out. The danger is that too much time will be spent on conspiratorial activities and not enough attention paid to the substance of the business. When envy overpowers reason, the politics of succession may become a major pastime.

King Laius Revisited

In addition to the problem of the entrepreneurial father's emotional unavailability, we must also consider the effects of his often domineering behavior. (Again, these phenomena are more applicable to men than to women.) It is not easy to live in the shadow of a captain of industry, and the eldest son often bears the brunt of entrepreneurial aggression. Children born later, or children of second marriages, tend to have a much easier time. The entrepreneur perceives them less as a threat to his power base and more as a symbol of his potency and vitality.

In his autobiography, *Father, Son & Co.: My Life in IBM and Beyond*, Thomas Watson, Jr., of IBM recalls coming home from school in tears (he was not much of a student) saying that he *couldn't do* – referring to the general expectation that he, as the oldest son, would take over the business from his father, Thomas Watson, Sr. He had always found it difficult to live up to his father's expectations. He saw his father as a giant of a man who made him feel inconsequential He was convinced that he was lacking in some way and always felt a deep uncertainty about his ability to deliver.

Watson Jr. recalled bouts of depression as a child, often accompanied by asthma attacks. His childhood experiences worsened when he noticed how everyone would bow and scrape and ingratiate themselves in his father's presence. He compared his father to a blanket, smothering everything. He recalled how he and his father had terrible fights, which frequently led to the brink of estrangement. Later on, as president of IBM, Watson Jr. would perform a ritual on the anniversary of his father's death; he would take stock of what the company had accomplished and tell his wife that he had managed yet another year alone.

Many entrepreneurs seem to have experienced a symbolic Oedipal victory in gaining the major portion of their mother's love and affection, bypassing their fathers. However, they will not allow a similar triumph for their own sons. Instead, some entrepreneurs will go to great lengths to belittle their sons, continuously cutting them down to size. Consequently, some sons may give up, do poorly at school, and behave irresponsibly. They become the antithesis of their fathers, either temporarily or permanently.

Of course, in describing these psychodynamic processes it should be stressed that they do not necessarily happen consciously. Whether conscious or unconscious, the experience is emotionally devastating.

The first Henry Ford and his son Edsel had a particularly destructive relationship, characterized by an enormous amount of ambivalence. Henry Ford was in the habit of building his son up at times, then going out of his way to humiliate him. One of Edsel's major frustrations came from his father's continuous rejection of his well-thought-out plans to improve products and conditions in the company. Instead, Henry Ford preferred to listen to people who were brutalizing the work environment. Edsel never found the nerve to stand up to his father, who preferred to portray his son as weak, incompetent, and "too fond of cocktails and decadent East Side living." The strain of this relationship led to medical problems for Edsel, and the stress probably contributed to his stomach ulcer and premature death. According to the biographer R. Lacey, in his book *Ford: The Men and the Machine*, when Edsel died, his wife, in a fit of anger, told her father-in-law that he had killed his own son.

The example of the Fords is not unique, although most father-son relationships do not come to this kind of tragic ending. In comparison, father-daughter, mother-daughter, and mother-son relationships seem to be less prone to conflict in a business context. However, given the current scarcity of case examples of female company presidents, it may be wise to suspend judgment for the time being.

The Ghost of the Padrone

Family firms are prone to autocratic rule. As I have already mentioned, founders tend to be domineering personalities. After all, without their dominance and persistence the company would never have taken off. Their presence and their behavior give the company its particular flavor. In many such companies, a paternalistic attitude may prevail. But what started off as well-meaning may end up as not only stifling but also, at times, perverted.

A good example of this is the house of Krupp, a 400-year-old dynasty that armed

Germany during four major wars. For generations, members were guided by Alfred Krupp's *Generalregulativ*, the company constitution laid down in 1872. This document detailed the absolute obligations of the *Kruppianer* (Krupp employees). It said, among other things, that the house of Krupp was entitled to receive from its workers full and undivided energy, punctuality, loyalty, and love of good order. On the other hand, a *Kruppianer* who ran up debt would be sacked; any man five minutes late would lose an hour's wages; troublemakers would be dismissed forever. But the *Kruppianer* were entitled to health services, an emergency relief fund, pension schemes, low-cost housing, non-profit retail outlets, and homes for the aged. In terms of its social welfare policy, Krupp was undoubtedly ahead of its time. But this paternalistic attitude became a grotesque travesty during WW II, when the company willingly used almost 100,000 prisoners of war and concentration camp inmates as slave laborers.

The Krupp dynasty may be an extreme example of paternalistic, autocratic rule. However, lesser examples are not hard to find. One can hypothesize that people willing to work under such conditions may possess many of the characteristics of the dependent personality. These companies will attract "yes-men" – hardly the kind of people to move the company forward.

A company haunted by the "ghost of the *padrone*" can often be secretive, conservative, and traditional Consequently, it may become too inward looking, ignoring developments in the environment. Naturally, such an attitude does not foster change and can seriously threaten the firm's survival.

Milking the Business

When a number of family-member employees add little or no value, the company risks turning into a kind of welfare institution. It gives family members "something to do" without actually engaging them in any productive work. Most companies cannot afford to have too many of these people around. Apart from the financial strain, unproductive hangers on can lead to serious morale problems.

In one consumer products company, three of the five family-member employees drew large salaries, used company-chauffeured cars and planes, and lived in company-financed luxury apartments. However, the occasional hours they spent at the office did more harm than good. They spent most of their time at the hunting lodge or on the golf course, both of which were financed through company memberships. When the economy turned sour and the company went into the red, these individuals refused to accept the new reality-in spite of warnings by a company adviser. In a due course, the company went bankrupt.

The Succession Conundrum

Of the many problems associated with family firms, the most insidious center on the question of succession. And of the various roadblocks to succession planning, one of the most profound is the difficulty many people have in accepting their own mortality. It is not easy to confront the ultimate narcissistic injury: the disintegration of the body. Some presidents of family firms (particularly founder-owners) act as if death were something that happens to everyone except themselves. Talking about their death is taboo. Raising the topic is viewed as a hostile act, and may be interpreted as a wish to have the person in question dead. Although children, in moments of anger, may have wished their parents dead (which in turn may have resulted in strong feelings of guilt), as adults they often choose to suppress or even repress such thoughts altogether. This conspiracy of silence can be augmented by the fear of abandonment. The children may wonder whether they will be able to cope without their parent being around. If there are several children, they may worry about who is going to be the *primus inter pares*. Some may be afraid – and often for good reasons – that there will be open conflict when the parents are no longer there to act as arbiters. All these issues may mean that they prefer to let matters slip rather than face succession problems head-on.

The firm's symbolic value may also aggravate succession problems. For many founder-managers, the enterprise becomes part of their core identity. They largely depend

Exhibit 2. Barriers to Succession Planning in Family Firms

Founder/Owner	*Family*
• Death anxiety	• Death as taboo
• Company as symbol	– Discussion is a hostile act
– Loss of identity	– Fear of loss/abandonment
– Concern about legacy	• Fear of sibling rivalry
• Dilemma of choice	• Change of spouse's position
– Fiction of equality	
• Generational envy	
– Loss of power	

on the company as a measure of their self-esteem and may be intensely anxious about whether their successors will respect their legacy or destroy what they built up so carefully. Shakespeare's tragedy *King Lear* vividly dramatizes this sort of crisis.

Choosing a successor from among one's children can be extremely difficult. It shatters the fiction that all the children are equal. Singling someone out may lead to discord. Many owner-managers, faced with the necessity of making a choice, prefer to let the matter be, and procrastinate.

It is very difficult for some people to let go of the power that comes with the job. They may have become addicted to all the tangible and intangible benefits attached to it. Think only of Serge Dassault of Dassault Enterprises, the French airplane builder, who was 61 before he took over the chairmanship from his father. Thomas Watson, Sr., of IBM handed over control to his son only when he was 82 years old. Armand Hammer of Occidental Petroleum is another notorious example of a person who seemed to have experienced great difficulty in grooming a crown prince.

In the process of letting go, the operation of generational envy (i.e., the envy parents feel toward the emerging abilities of their children) should not be underestimated. Many owner-presidents display high artistry in finding reasons for crushing or humiliating their children. At the heart of this process – mentioned earlier in the context of Oedipal rivalry – is their concern about their waning physical powers.

In some instances, it is not only the CEOs who have problems in letting go, but also their spouses. The latter may have grown accustomed to the perks and vicarious recognition that come with the job. (Exhibit 2 presents a summary of the barriers to succession planning.)

Facilitating Forces

Fortunately, several powerful forces operate against these barriers. Tax legislation is one example. Unless the estate is to be burdened by high inheritance taxes-which may endanger the continuation of the company-it is better to take some preventive steps and transfer ownership to the next generation in plenty of time.

Another effective (but hardly attractive) force is the aging process itself and the health problems that accompany it. A cynic could claim that nothing helps clear a stalemate about succession as effectively as a mild coronary attack When one is lying in the hospital, it becomes more difficult to deny the possibility of death. In such situations, spouses, confidants, or board members can often give the extra push needed to help the person overcome his or her reluctance to let go.

A more positive force is the founder's wish to see the business continue. In theory this seems obvious. To act on the desire, however, is a different matter. It takes a certain amount of maturity and wisdom to make it happen. One needs to have acquired a sense of generativity. Instead of being envious of the younger generation, the founder needs the capacity to take vicarious pleasure from seeing young men or women do things on their own.

The Theater of Choice

The family has a considerable number of options available when deciding on succession. Each option, however, has complications. Should the rule of the primogeniture be applied? What if the oldest child is not the most capable one, or is not really interested in the business? If some form of nepotism is going to be inevitable in family firms, one should at least make the effort to pick the best family member available.

Will daughters be eligible? Choosing a daughter can make the situation quite messy. The sons-in-law may want to get in on the act. If both daughters and sons-in-law work in the firm, real problems arise in the case of divorce. And then there is the problem of names. A married daughter will probably have changed her name, which can disrupt the symbolic, emotional value many people attach to names and the company identity. (Consequently, daughters and sons-in-law are often unwelcome in family firms.)

There are other more imaginative, but not always practical, solutions to dealing with the problem of succession. One can, for example, cite instances of shared management, or some form of management rotation. But with this strategy comes the threat of organizational paralysis. On the other hand, if it works well, the complementarity of individual skills can yield enormous benefits. To make this work, a lot of trust is needed among the different family members.

There are interim solutions, of course. A typical one is to put a trusted employee in the saddle for a specific period of time. This person may be appointed as trustee of the family heirloom until a family member is groomed to take over. Of course, a more dramatic solution is to bring in professional management. At times, only a neutral non-family member can balance the interests of the different factions within the family unit.

Given the potential for family strife to spill over into the company, another popular and effective solution is to divide the business. One tactic puts each child in charge of a division or department. A more Draconian approach splits the business into separate companies and gives one to each family member. The added value is frequently much higher if this option is chosen. Moreover, it is often the ideal solution for keeping potentially quarrelsome family members apart. Other possibilities are selling the business, going public, or choosing liquidation.

Of course, the final issue is who should make the choice of successor. Should it be the outgoing president? a family council? the board of directors? all the parties combined? Should one give the children the opportunity to choose among themselves? There is no perfect solution. However, because very powerful psychological processes can affect the out-going president's judgment, it is important that he or she not be the only decision maker.

Managing for Survival

The family council can play a crucial role in preventing the company from becoming one of the casualties of the family drama. The council must define the rules of the game for the whole family.

As a caveat, it should be said that although such councils are the right forum for discussing certain key issues, decisions eventually have to be made. In business life more than in many other situations, speed is a competitive advantage. Unfortunately, coalition politics, speed, and effective decision making do not usually go together. Although a certain amount of politicizing is an inevitable part of organizational life, it should be kept to a minimum. Unless there is one domineering family member (because of personality or seniority) or a dominant coalition with complementarity of interests, there is a danger that family councils will begin to resemble elective politics, leading to situations where compromise candidates, not leaders, gain the upper hand.

In an effective family council, the first task is to decide what members want to accomplish. What is the overall family vision? Are they going for continuity of the family regime? Do they want to go public? Do they want to sell the business? Do they want to divide the business? Decisions have to be made about all these issues.

The council can articulate certain rules as well. For example, how should non-active family members be dealt with? How can people get out and cash in their shares? Is there going to be some kind of shotgun clause as a way of getting a fair price in case of serious disagreements?

How are family members going to be selected for promotion? Who is going to decide who is most suitable to occupy senior positions? As we have seen, parents can be remarkably myopic when it comes to their offspring. It is extremely important that the council establish specific criteria in order to select the company's future leadership.

A carefully thought-through management development program can smooth succession planning. This kind of program takes account of two elements: what the company will require in the future, and what the members of the next generation expect for themselves. In that context, the council can find answers to key questions. How long, for example, should it take for a family member to assume a senior position? What experiences should he or she have before assuming that role? What will the compensation be like? Should future officers acquire some outside experience before committing themselves to the family firm? Doing so will be invaluable for self-esteem; it will prove to the individual and his associates that he is capable of making it on his own, not just because of family connections.

The family firm can pick up a number of important lessons from practices in public companies.

In order to prevent organizational myopia, it is a *sine qua non* that outsiders should be welcomed and trusted. Without the help of outsiders, the manpower supply soon becomes awfully slim. Consequently, the human resources management systems in the family firm should be compatible with those of public companies. For reasons of equity, and in order to avoid destructive envy, it is extremely important to design incentive systems for non-family members.

Other standard company practices should be observed. Strategic planning should become a matter of course. Roles and responsibilities should be clearly defined. Having well-defined boundaries and clear division of labor will go a long way toward preventing conflict.

Family management should strive to build a corporate culture that is relatively open and minimally politicized. It should be a culture in which people are not afraid to speak their minds and where, through delegation, they have a certain amount of control over their lives. True management professionalism can only occur when people have the feeling that non-family members are also eligible for senior management positions.

In order to keep the company on course, an independent-minded board of directors will be needed. The importance of professional advisers should also be emphasized. They can take on the role of border guards, helping to keep family dramas playing on stages outside the company. And family firms usually have enough high drama to keep an audience on the edge of their seats.

As those who have experience with family firms know all too well, maintaining a separation between business and personal lives can be an uphill struggle. One certainly does not risk being bored. When things go well, they can go very well, although the opposite is also true.

For the psychologically minded, family firms offer a tremendous variety of issues. The excitement lies in detecting patterns. In that respect we might well recall the words of Tolstoy, who wrote in his novel, *Anna Karenina*, "All happy families resemble one another, every unhappy family is unhappy in its own way."

Five strategies for coping with the stress created by the intergenerational transfer of the family farm were identified in a population of Midwestern families. These strategies were then associated with measures of psychological well being and perceived ease in making the farm transfer decision. Parents had higher psychological well being than their children, even though fathers reported the transfer decision to be somewhat more difficult that did sons. Use of family discussion was positively associated with personal well being for fathers. Daughters-in-law were especially lacking in effective coping strategies.

Coping Strategies Associated with Intergenerational Transfer of the Family Farm

By Candyce S. Russell, Charles L. Griffin, Catherine Scott Flinchbaugh, Michael J. Martin, and Raymond B. Atilano

Farm families routinely cope with high levels of stress caused by the dual demands of work and family life. Members must work together in an interdependent fashion because they experience an overlap in the physical space used for work and domestic life, and they must cope also with relative isolation from contacts and activities off the farm (Rosenblatt *et al.*, 1978).

Additional stressors include seasonal variations in work demands and income, infrequent days off, high accident rates (Rosenblatt and Anderson, 1981), and economic vulnerability (Rosenblatt and Keller, 1983). Added to these is the stress of transferring the farm as the older generation retires. This shift in control from one generation to the next is both a business and family issue. The younger generation may be striving for self respect, autonomy, and a greater share of responsibility, while the older generation is striving to maintain control of decision making and respect for past accomplishments (Rosenblatt and Anderson, 1981).

The study reported here focuses on the coping strategies used by farm families during the process of deciding how to transfer the farm from one generation to the next. Data were collected from parents, the sons who were receiving the farm. and the sons' wives.

Literature Review

The McCubbin *et al.* (1980) review of family stress research over the last decade raises the challenge to learn more about the nature of critical transitions in the family system. Of particular interest is the role of family resources, including coping strategies, social support, and family problem solving, which lead to successful negotiation of critical transition points. Research efforts to date have primarily focused on the coping repertoires of three populations: military families, who cope with varying periods of separation (Hill, 1949; McCubbin and Lester, 1977; McCubbin *et al.*, 1976); corporate business wives, coping with repeated short-term separation (Boss *et al.*, 1979); and families, who cope with chronic illness (McCubbin *et al.*, 1982). The stress that is encountered when intergenerational farm transfer occurs offers another unique population for extending the understanding of family adaptation to stressful normative events in the developmental life cycle. This transfer process involves critical role changes and task realignments, which are expectable at certain points in the family life cycle. Yet, this remains an under-researched topic of special importance to farm families and those professionals working with farm families (Hedlund and Berkowitz, 1979).

McCubbin (1979) directs us to consider coping as an *active* process of adaptation, and therefore involves variables which maybe "taught" to families under stress. Much of the literature has followed Hill's (1949) classic ABC-X formulation of family stress research. Here, major attention has been given to (1) identification of family stressors and the "pile-up" of stressors, (2) assessment of family resources, (3) the family's perception or definition of the event, and (4) the role of the social network as a family resource and mediator of stress. Only a handful of researchers have attempted to shed light on the reasons why some families are better able to adjust and manage chronic stressors than others.

McCubbin (1979) has identified several coping strategies common to wives who cope with their husbands' occupationally induced separations. These include expressing feelings, reducing anxiety through alcohol or drugs, maintaining family ties, belief in God, establishing independence and self sufficiency, building interpersonal relationships, living up to the employer's expectations, and keeping active in hobbies. Pearlin and Schooler (1978) have done similar work in identifying the structure of coping among individuals facing marital, parental, and occupation-related stressors. These personal coping styles include self reliance, controlled reflection, positive comparisons, negotiation, selective ignoring and optimistic faith. While farm families are coping with high levels of togetherness rather than repeated separations (as in the McCubbin work), certain coping strategies (such as belief in God, expression of feelings, advice seeking) reappear in the work of Pearlin and Schooler and may be of more general applicability, including intergenerational farm transfer.

The Stress of Intergenerational Farm Transfer

Most farm families desire to bring members of the next generation into the business in some manner leading to a transfer of ownership (Bratton and Berkowitz, 1976; Hedlund and Berkowitz, 1979b). Titus *et al.* (1979) suggest that family disputes over inheritance cases are more common among farm families because beneficiaries may need to maintain the estate intact in order to maintain profitability, and emotional bonds to the land may be very strong. Inheritance serves as a vital entry point into farming for persons who are likely to be heavily socialized toward agriculture as a career. Bratton and Berkowitz (1976) report intergenerational assistance to beginning farmers in 15 of 21 families in their sample, emphasizing the complexity and variety of transfers that were found. For these reasons, intergenerational transfer of the family farm has been reported as a major stressor in the lives of farming families (Hedlund and Berkowitz, 1979b; Rosenblatt and Anderson, 1981, Rosenblatt *et al.*, 1978; Titus *et al.*, 1979). Hedlund and Berkowitz (1979b) report intergenerational transfer "problems" in 75 percent of their sample, although only 30 percent met their definition of "stressful" as "resulting in dysfunctional task or interpersonal performance."

The intergenerational transfer of the farm brings together numerous "critical role transitions" (Hill and Joy, 1979) within a unique economic and social context. Interpersonal friction may arise as the family attempts to accommodate a younger generation and phase out the older. The younger generation may be striving for feelings of self-respect, autonomy, and a fair share of responsibility, while the older generation may be striving to maintain decision making, psychic and physical territory, and the respect merited by greater experience and by precedence and investment in the enterprise (Rosenblatt and Anderson, 1981) as they near retirement. Other potential difficulties relate to sibling rivalry and competition, which are reported as stressful in 20 percent of the Hedlund and Berkowitz (1979b) sample.

Wives of both generations report role stress as they attempt to mediate conflict. Hedlund and Berkowitz (1979b) find stresses relating to the wife in 60 percent of their sample, leading them to suspect that wives often attempt to play a peacemaker role. Interestingly, when open conflict is reported within the marriage or between siblings, the wife's role stress is lower (Hedlund and Berkowitz, 1979a). Kohl (1976) suggests that wives fill a powerful "switchboard" position. Barnes and Hershon (1976) also document this sort of coping strategy in family businesses where the wife plays an important "bridging" role between father and son in helping a transition to occur. Though stressful for the wife, this "switchboard" or "bridging" role may be a useful way of organizing in families where communication between father and children is not open. Berkowitz and Perkins (1984) find that husband support is an important factor in the amount of stress experienced by their wives. Therefore, if the wife feels supported by her complex role in the family, her own stress level is likely to be lower.

Additional literature highlights the importance of open communication in families involved in intergenerational farm transfer. Communication which is "open and free"... [and where] feelings, opinions, and ideas of all family members are heard and understood" (Hedlund and Berkowitz, 1979b:240) is frequently mentioned as a mediating factor. Bratton and Berkowitz (1976:9) report that families who are able to achieve intergenerational continuity "were able to communicate about needs, desires, and future possibilities. They could talk about options without making the children feel obligated to stay on the farm." Openness of the communication and decision-making style appear to be related to level of stress. Hedlund and Berkowitz (1979b) report a significant relationship between shared decision making and lower marital and intergenerational stress. Furthermore, in issues surrounding inheritance, Rosenblatt and Anderson (1981) and Titus et al. (1979) report that the likelihood of bitter feelings and conflict is lower when the disposition of property is clearly discussed in advance with all involved parties.

Several sources suggest that farm families may be likely to use distancing as a coping mechanism. Distancing may be accomplished by family members working off the farm, living off the farm, or expanding the operation (Rosenblatt and Anderson, 1981). For instance, farm wives in the Hedlund and Berkowitz (1979b) sample who reported low levels of stress had strong involvements outside the farm. In both the Boss et al. (1979) study of corporate executive wives' coping patterns in response to routine separation averaging eight months in military families, the wife's response of establishing independence and self-sufficiency emerged as a basic coping strategy.

The role of social support networks has received much attention in the family stress literature as another major variable affecting families' abilities to manage stress. Cobb (1976) defines social support as information that communicates an esteem, understanding, and belonging. Social support may also include information about problem solving and new social contacts who may help. The importance of developing and maintaining supportive relationships with the community emerges as a major predictor of successful adaptation to stress (McCubbin, 1979). However, little attention has been given in farm family literature to the possible function of community support networks, perhaps, because of the perception of the relative isolation of farm families.

The present study is designed to identify the coping strategies that are associated with managing stress produced by the transfer of the family farm from one generation to the next. It builds upon the literature reviewed above by assessing the effectiveness of those coping strategies that have previously been associated with occupationally and/or family-induced stress. More specifically, the research investigates the "B" or "resource" factor in Hill's (1949) ABC-X model by exploring resources that families use to keep the disruptive effects of intergenerational farm transfer to a minimum. Furthermore, the specific coping strategies identified as resources represent the three categories of coping behaviors McCubbin (1979) identified in his integration of individual coping behaviors into family stress theory. These are: (1) management of family stability and individual anxiety, (2) procurement of social support, and (3) direct attack upon the stressor event through individual and collective family effort.

Method

Sample Selection

The sampling frame includes families where an intergenerational transfer decision has been made within the last five years. The transfer was between the parent generation and child generation, and at least one of the children was 18 years of age or older.

Furthermore, farming was the primary occupation of the donor generation at the time of the transfer decision. Finally, at least one member of the donor generation was still alive.

In order to represent the state of Kansas as adequately as possible, ten counties from each of the five geographic regions of the state (Northwest, Southwest, South Central,

Northeast, and Southeast areas) were randomly selected. Agriculture professionals provided names of families they believed met the screening criteria. From these names, families were randomly selected and contacted by telephone to determine their eligibility, to secure their cooperation, and to generate names and addresses of children in the receiving generation.

One hundred fifty-seven eligible families were contacted. Of these, 113 (72 percent) were unwilling to participate.

Respondents Compared with Non-respondents

Completed questionnaires were received from 81.9 percent of the parents, 81.3 percent of the children and 75 percent of their spouses. Phone follow-ups were done with non-respondents to get reasons for nonreturn and responses to a few crucial questions, including perceived ease of transfer. With phone follow-ups, the response rates were 95.4 percent, 92.8 percent, and 90.2 percent for parents, children, and spouses, respectively.

The most frequent reason given for not returning the questionnaire was "didn't get around to it," followed by low perceived relevance of the questionnaire for self. Daughters-in-law who did not return questionnaires reported significantly more difficulty with the farm transfer decision than did their mail-responding counterparts ($F = 2.38$; 7,371 d.f.; p .05). Inmost respects, however, nonrespondents did not differ from respondents in background or in their perceptions of the farm transfer decision.

Sample Description

The analyses are limited to those families where a son who was receiver of the farm was also on the farm. This selection procedure maximizes the homogeneity of the receiving group since fewer females than males were receivers, and receivers who lived off the farm were usually involved in non-farm occupations as well. The daughters-in-law included in the analyses were married to the sons targeted for analysis and thus were also living on the farm. The analyses are based, then, on 86 fathers, 91 mothers, 89 sons, and 73 daughters-in-law, representing 92 intergenerational families. Each of the five demographic areas of the state was represented in the sample, with each region representing between 15 and 25 percent of the total. If each region were equally represented, its share would have been 20 percent of the total.

The parents were typically about 60 years of age with a high school education or an additional year of college or vocational training. The sons averaged 31 years of age (range 20 to 53) with two and one-half years of education beyond high school. The daughters-in-law averaged 30 years of age (range 18 to 48) and had two to six years of education beyond high school.

The predominant farm structures were "individual ownership" (31 percent) and "corporation" (24 percent). Other structures included "informal partnership" (18 percent), "legal partnership" (12 percent), a "combination of the above" (8 percent), or "other" (8 percent). The average farm size was 1,989 acres (range 130 to 12,000), devoted to pasture and/or crops. Typically, the farm had been in the family for three generations.

Instrumentation

Thirty-five items representing methods of handling stress created by the farm transfer issue were factor analyzed in order to identify statistically independent coping strategies. Relevant items from the McCubbin *et al.* (1981) Family Coping Inventory (FCI) and Pearlin and Schooler's (1978) Occupational Coping Responses were adapted and included in the original pool of 35 items together with additional items specific to the farm transfer experience.

Included in these items was information on membership in farm organizations, attendance at estate-planning workshops, specialization in a particular aspect of the farm operation, involvement in activities off the farm, open discussion of competition between two or more family members, discussion of parents' retirement needs and goals with the children, and parents making it dear to children that their choice of occupation is their own decision. The items adapted from the McCubbin *et al.* (1981) and Pearlin and Schooler (1978) inventories were more general ones, including areas of social support, emotional expression, faith, positive comparison, negotiation, learning new behaviors, ignoring, escape, and isolation. The original 35 items are available upon request from the first

Table 1. Terminal Five-Factor Solution (Varimax Rotation) on Coping Strategies (N = 390)

Factor I[a]	Factor II[b]	Factor III[c]	Factor IV[d]	Factor V[e]	Item
0.40340	0.14367	0.20678	0.16370	-0.08147	Purchasing nearby land
0.35838	0.11172	0.18455	0.16717	0.09564	Specializing in a particular aspect of farm operation
0.53212	0.01045	-0.02555	-0.00844	0.09314	Membership in American Ag. Movement
0.45920	0.05648	0.04839	0.09970	0.02486	Membership in National Farm Organization
0.54615	0.13679	0.03693	0.11818	0.05419	Membership in Wheat Growers Association
0.68584	0.03166	0.04687	0.20172	0.02755	Membership in Kansas Livestock Association
0.14837	0.76776	0.15778	0.11471	-0.05844	Talking with my children (parents) about the Farm Transfer Decision
0.19570	0.81430	0.15986	0.13132	0.04654	Discussing management of the farm with my children (parents)
0.04430	0.53279	0.16136	0.20587	0.09339	Discussing retirement needs and goals with my children (parents)
0.14786	0.19729	0.62403	0.12431	0.02090	Believing in God
0.14786	0.20883	0.77419	0.09559	0.09570	Telling myself I have many things to be thankful for
0.07294	0.05378	0.48511	0.05936	0.14256	Keeping problems to myself
-0.02186	0.04989	0.48529	0.13744	0.08517	Becoming more involved in activities off the farm
0.10254	0.19613	0.08356	0.68975	0.23760	Consulting Extension Agents
0.14701	0.17506	0.12163	0.66140	-0.00101	Attending Estate Planning Workshops
0.19191	0.07760	0.11807	0.50212	-0.01079	Membership in Farm Management Association
0.29361	0.04660	0.21764	0.42730	0.00450	Membership in Farm Bureau
0.01211	-0.05064	0.15349	0.10018	0.64615	Allowing myself to become angry
0.17256	0.11920	0.14467	0.01301	0.70128	Getting angry at the whole economy

[a]Factor I = farm management, mean = 9.09, SD = 14.64, Eigenvalue = 4.05466; 50.6% of variance, Alpha = 0.66.
[b]Factor II = discussion, mean = 8.39, SD = 6.19, Eigenvalue = 1.25051; 15.6% of variance, Alpha = 0.78.
[c]Factor III = individual coping, mean = 11.46, SD = 8.00, Eigenvalue = 1.11930; 14.0% of variance, Alpha = 0.71.
[d]Factor IV = professionals, mean = 7.22, SD = 9.50, Eigenvalue = 0.82021; 10.2% of variance, Alpha = 0.71.
[e]Factor V = expression of anger, mean = 2.71, SD = 5.00, Eigenvalue = 0.762060; 9.5% of variance, Alpha = 0.65.

author. Respondents checked each item as "not used," "not helpful" "minimally helpful "moderately helpful," or "very helpful." The factor analysis was based on degree of helpfulness, which could range from one to four. Three hundred and ninety questionnaires from the total sample of farm families, including siblings of the sons targeted for further analysis were used for the factor analysis.

The terminal five-factor orthogonal solution with varimax rotation (see Table 1) revealed the following coping strategies: a Farm Management factor, which includes membership in farm organizations, Discussion, Individual Coping, Use of Professionals, and Expression of Anger. The scales ranged from two to six items, with internal consistencies ranging from 0.65 to 0.78. The items falling within each style together with their factor loadings are listed in Table 1. Personal well being was assessed by the Campbell *et al.* (1976) Index of Well Being. This is a nine-item semantic differential scale composed of general affect and life satisfaction items with a reported internal consistency of .89 (Campbell *et al.*, 1976:50). This is the scale used by the Institute for Social Research in its series of cross-national studies of adult well being. It distinguishes between employed and unemployed segments of the population and between divorced and married adults (Campbell *et al.*, 1976-51). Campbell and his associates (1976) report a correlation of .26 with their measure of "fears and worries" (p. 58) and .35 with their Index of Personal Competence (p.60).

Perceived ease of making the transfer decision was measured with a single Likert-type item: "How easy was it for you to handle the farm transfer decision?" Responses ranged from "very difficult" to "very easy." The item was significantly correlated with reported life satisfaction (r = .20, p .007) and with satisfaction with farming lifestyle (r = .22, p .003).

Research Questions

The data were analyzed separately for four groups: fathers, mothers, sons who were to receive the farm and were also living on the farm, and their wives. The following research questions were addressed: (1) Which coping strategies are reported to be most helpful? (2) Which coping strategies are used most? (3) Are there significant differences in use of coping strategy according to family position? (4) Is the use of coping strategies associated with personal well being and perceived ease of making the transfer decision?

Results

Use of Coping Strategy by Family Position

Each item in each coping factor was scored as either "used" or "not used." However, since the number of items per scale ranged from two to six, weighted scores are displayed in Table 2 in order to cancel the effect of unequal number of items per scale.

The two coping strategies reported to be used most were Individual coping and Discussion. This was true regardless of family position. Expression of Anger was the next most frequently used coping strategy among daughters-in-law, while Use of Professionals was the third most frequently used style among fathers and mothers. Farm Management was reported as a coping strategy by more males than by females.

Scheffe's test (Winer, 1971) of multiple comparisons was used to assess the significance of differences at the .05 level in use of the five coping strategies by the four groups included in the sample. Daughters-in-law reported using Discussion (F = 18.30; 3,327 d.f.; p .01) significantly less than all other family members. Daughters-in-law also consulted Professionals (F = 3.79; 3,319 d.f.; p .01) significantly less than either parent. Mothers reported significantly less use of Farm Management (F = 3.48; 3,310 d.f.; p .05) strategies than did sons, while sons used Expression of Anger (F = 4.41; 3,327 d.f.; p .01) significantly more than their fathers did.

Helpfulness of Coping Strategy by Family Position

As with scores on the use of coping strategies, scores for perceived usefulness were weighted in order to cancel the effect of an unequal number of items per scale. The two styles reported to be most helpful, regardless of family position, were Discussion and Individual Coping. Expression of Anger was reported to be the least helpful coping style, except for daughters-in-law, while Use of Professionals and Farm Management were intermediate in helpfulness (see Table 3).

Mothers reported use of Individual Coping to be significantly more helpful than was true for sons (F = 4.38; 3,327 d.f.; p .01). Fathers, mothers, and sons reported Discussion to be significantly more helpful than did daughters-in-law (F = 21.47; 3,327 d.f.; p .001). Daughters-in-law also found Professionals to be significantly less helpful than either parents (F = 5.73; 3,319 d.f.; p .001). Finally, mothers reported Farm Management strategies to be significantly less helpful than was true for sons (F = 3.61; 3,310 d.f.; p .01).

Relationship of Coping Strategies to Personal Well Being and Ease of Transfer

Table 4 displays correlations between the use of each coping style and the dependent variables of personal well being as measured by the Campbell *et al.* (1976) scale and perceived ease of making the farm transfer decision.

Among fathers, Discussion was significantly related to well being (r = .23, p .05) but was negatively associated with perceived ease (r = -.22, p .05). Also among fathers, Expression of Anger was associated with low levels of well being (r = -.20, p .05) and with reports that the transfer decision was a difficult one (low ease) (r = -.30, p .01).

Among mothers, perceived ease was negatively associated with Use of Professionals (r = -.24, p .05). Use of Professionals was also used by sons when the farm transfer decision was perceived to be difficult (r = -.21, p .05). In addition, sons who used Expression of Anger as a coping strategy were significantly more likely to score low on personal well being (r = -.35, p .001). Daughters-in-law who used Professionals and Expression of Anger as coping strategies were also likely to score lower on personal well being (r = -.25, p .05 and r = -.29, p .01, respectively).

Table 2. Use of Coping Strategy by Family Position in Weighted Scores*

	Fathers (N = 86)	Mothers (N = 91)	Sons (N = 89)	Daughters-in-law (N = 73)	Overall x
Farm management	2.00	1.57	2.32	1.79	1.92
Discussion	5.08	5.20	5.06	3.52	4.72
Individual coping	4.95	5.33	5.27	5.27	5.21
Professionals	3.33	3.36	3.15	2.42	3.07
Expression of anger	2.10	2.31	3.30	2.91	2.67

*Scores were weighted, based on number of items in each scale: Farm management (1.0), Discussion (2.0), Individual coping (1.5), Professionals (1.5), Expression of anger (3.0). The reader should note that these are not standard scores and therefore should not be used to compare any one individual's score to group means.

Discussion

In reviewing the frequency and perceived usefulness of each of the five coping strategies identified in this population, it is striking that they are generally ordered in a sequence reflective of the basic values of rural America: self reliance (Individual Coping), family (Discussion), and then community (Professionals). However, sons and daughters-in-law are more likely to use Expression of Anger before using Farm Management strategies or turning to the community for professional consultation. Both members of the younger generation appear to turn to Expression of Anger in the face of limited power vis-a-vis the parent generation.

In this population, the mothers and daughters-in-law present an interesting contrast. If we can apply the results of earlier research to this group of farm families, the women in the older generation may be highly involved in the transfer as "bridges" between father and son (Barnes and Hershon, 1976) and as mediators of conflict (Hedlund and Berkowitz, 1979b). The younger women, who have married into the family more recently, may hold the least involved family positions, and they certainly were the least likely to report themselves as having a "great deal of influence" on the transfer decision (F = 62.24; 3,328 d.f.; p .001). Given their position of low influence, it is not surprising that the daughters-in-law present a profile of coping strategies where use of Individual Coping is primary. As a relative newcomer to the family and possibly even to farming, the daughter-in-law may not be aware of, accepted by, or comfortable with established agricultural support systems. Furthermore, if the daughters-in-law perceive themselves as having less influence on the transfer decision than others, it is not surprising that they are significantly less likely to consult farm professionals or even engage in family discussion around the transfer issue …or to find them helpful when these strategies are attempted.

Low influence, however, does not mean low involvement. To whom the farm is transferred, by what means, and the timing of that transfer may be of great importance to the daughter-in-law. While the younger women reported using fewer coping strategies than others and reported some strategies to be less helpful when they were used, both sons and daughters-in-law scored significantly lower than the parent generation on our measure of personal well being (F = 11.81; 3,335 d.f.; p .001).

This suggests that daughters-in-law may occupy an especially vulnerable position; one that is highly stressed, but one with relatively more limited access to or familiarity with coping strategies and social support.

Openness of discussion within the family has been highlighted in the literature as an important predictor of success in making inter-generational farm transfers (e.g., Bratton and Berkowitz, 1976). In our research, the Discussion coping strategy was significantly associated with reports of personal well being for fathers, though *negatively* associated with perceived ease of making the transfer decision. At least two interpretations of these data are possible. First, fathers faced with especially difficult transfer decisions may use

Discussion in such a way as to support personal well being when they are under stress. Second, those fathers with high levels of personal well being may be the ones who dare to open up Discussion despite the difficulty of the issue. Either way, it is important to point out that fathers rank Discussion number one in the hierarchy of helpfulness of coping strategies. Furthermore, while others rank family Discussion high in helpfulness, fathers are the only ones for whom this coping strategy is significantly associated with personal well being.

It appears from these data that use of the five coping strategies by other family members reveals more about their stress than about their well being. Mothers who seek Professionals are low on perceived ease. Among sons, consultation with Professionals is also significantly negatively associated with ease of the transfer decision. The more difficult the transfer, the more they consult. However, these efforts are only reported to be moderately helpful, ranking below the helpfulness of family Discussion and Individual Coping. Those sons who report Expression of Anger as a coping strategy are significantly more likely to report low levels of perceived personal well being, and this coping strategy appears at the bottom of the list so far as helpfulness is concerned. Daughters-in-law with low levels of perceived well being are significantly more likely to use Expression of Anger and consultation with Professionals as coping strategies, both of which are ranked midway in their list of strategy helpfulness.

In sum, the receiving generation appears to be more stressed than the parent generation, probably because they have less control in the situation and are less well supplied with helpful coping strategies. This is particularly true of daughters-in-law. It is somewhat

Table 3. Perceived Helpfulness of Coping Strategy by Family Position in

	Fathers (N = 86)	Mothers (N = 91)	Sons (N = 89)	Daughters In-Laws (N = 73)	Overall x
Farm management	5.51	4.03	5.91	4.39	4.96
Discussion	16.42	17.00	14.84	9.74	14.50
Individual coping	15.21	16.64	14.22	14.75	15.21
Professionals	9.50	9.54	7.76	5.81	8.15
Expression of anger	3.24	3.81	4.98	5.16	4.30

*Scores were weighted, based on number of items in each scale: Farm management (1.0), Discussion (2.0), Individual coping (1.5), Professionals (1.5), Expression of anger (3.0). The reader should note that these are not standard scores and therefore should not be used to compare any one individual's score to group means.

Table 4. Perceived Helpfulness of Coping Strategy by Family Position in Weighted Scores*

	Fathers (N = 86)		Mothers (N = 91)		Sons (N = 89)		Daughters In-laws (N = 73)	
	Well being	Perceived ease	Well being	Perceived ease	Well being	Perceived ease	Well being	Perceived ease
Farm management	.03	-.11	.11	-.10	.05	-.15	-.11	.01
Discussion	.23*	-.22	.06	-.14	-.06	-.15	-.11	.01
Individual coping	-.02	-.14	-.02	-.09	-.07	-.04	-.16	-.15
Professionals	.16	.09	.01	-.24*	-.15	-.21*	-.25*	-.03
Expression of anger	-.20*	-.30**	-.17	-.12	-.35***	-.15	-.29**	-.06

* = Significant at .05 level.
** = Significant at .01 level.
*** = Significant at .001 level.

surprising that distancing through nonfarm involvement was not identified as a coping strategy among these families. This may be because of the strong emotional tie family members feel to the land. A pattern of expressing anger was used by some, though it was generally one of the least helpful of the strategies respondents reported using. Following the thinking of Rosenblatt and Anderson (1981), one might speculate that if family members were to use distancing through nonfarm involvement, they might use Expression of Anger less often as a coping strategy and perhaps would experience less stress and perceive greater personal well being.

Implications

The findings of this study would appear to be particularly helpful to persons attempting to aid farm families through this stressful transition period. Interventions that would encourage families to engage in open discussion between both generations (particularly the daughter-in-law) might be useful. This type of approach might help the receiving generation to feel that they have some control over the situation, ease the stress level, and contribute to their overall feelings of well being. Within the donor generation, the wife might be the most likely person to serve a "bridging" function by suggesting that the family discuss the intergenerational transfer as a complete unit, excluding no one. Another approach to helping families through this transition period might include an attempt to strengthen the coping styles of the individual family members. Family members who are able to deal with their own stress may be able to assist each other through the stressful period and avoid the "pile up" of stressors within the family.

Professionals such as attorneys, farm management organizations, and estate planners need to be aware that critical psychosocial transitions are occurring within the farm family at the same time that economic transitions are occurring within the farm business. One approach that is commonly used from a business standpoint to reduce the uncertainty of the intergenerational transfer is incorporation. Salamon and Markan (1984), however, have suggested that incorporation may succeed in reducing the amount of role ambiguity in the farm family but may also be a tool to exploit or enforce authority over the younger generation and thereby increase their stress level. In our sample, sons involved in corporations and partnerships are somewhat more likely to perceive the transfer decision as difficult than those involved in individual ownership (X = .88; 2 d.f.; p .06). This relationship just misses the traditional .05 alpha level but supports Salamon and Markan's position and is worth investigating in future research.

Psychologists and family therapists working with farm families need to be sensitive to the unique implications of the joint business-family nature of the family farm and the stress that is created as a result, particularly around the intergenerational farm transfer issue. Future research needs to focus specifically on successful intervention strategies for working with families who are experiencing difficulty with intergenerational transfer decisions.

References

Barnes, L. B., and S. A. Hershon, 1976, "Transferring Power in the Family Business." *Harvard Business Review*, 54 (July-August): 105-14.

Berkowitz, A. D., and H. W. Perkins, 1984, "Stress Among Farm Women: Work and Family as Interacting Systems." *Journal of Marriage and the Family*, 46 (February): 161-66..

Boss, P.G., H. I. McCubbin, and G. Lester, 1979, "The Corporate Executive Wife's Coping Patterns in Response to Routine Husband-Father Absence." *Family Process* 18 (March): 79-86.

Bratton, C. A., and A., D. Berkowitz, 1976, "International Transfer of the Farm Business." *New York's Food and Life Sciences Quarterly* 9 (April-June): 7-9.

Campbell, A., P.E. Converse, and W. L. Rodgers, 1976, *The Quality of American Life*. New York: Russell Sage Foundation.

Cobb, S., 1976, "Social Support as a Moderator of Life Stress." *Psychosomatic Medicine*, 38 (September-October):300-14.

Hedlund, D., and A. Berkowitz, 1979a, "Farm Family Research in Perspective: 1965-1977." Ithaca, New York: Cornell University Agricultural Experiment Station, *Rural Sociology Bulletin* 79.

Hedlund, D., and A. Berkowitz, 1979b, "The Incidence of Social-Psychological Stress in Farm Families." *International Journal of Sociology of the Family*, 9 (July-December): 233-43.

Hill, R., 1949, Families Under Stress. New York: Harper and Row.

Hill, R., and C. Joy, 1979, "Conceptualizing and Operationalizing Category Systems for Phasing of Family Development." Unpublished Manuscript, University of Minnesota.

Kohl, S. B., 1976, *Working Together: Women and Family in Southwestern Saskatchewan.* Toronto: Holt, Rinehart and Winston of Canada.

McCubbin, H.I., 1979, "Integrating Coping Behavior in Family Stress Theory." *Journal of Marriage and the Family* 41 (May): 237-44.

McCubbin, H., and G. Lester, 1977, "Family Adaptability: Coping Behaviors in the Management of the Dual Stressors of Family Separation and Reunion." Paper Presented at the Military Family Research Conference, San Diego, California.

McCubbin, H., B. Dahl, G. Lester, D. Benson, and M. Robertson, 1976, "Coping Repertoires of Families Adapting to Prolonged War-Induced Separations." *Journal of Marriage and the Family*, 38 (August): 461-71.

McCubbin, H., C. Joy, A. Cauble, J. Comeau, J. Patterson, and R. Needle, 1980, "Family Stress and Coping: A Decade Review." *Journal of Marriage and the Family*, 42 (November): 855-71.

McCubbin, H. I., R. S. Nevin, A. E. Cauble, A. Larson, J. K Comeau, and J. M. Patterson, 1982, "Families Coping with Chronic Illness: The Case of Cerebral Palsy." Pp. 169-88 in H. I. McCubbin, A. E. Cauble, and J. M. Patterson (eds.), *Family Stress, Coping, and Social Support.* Springfield, Illinois: Charles C Thomas.

McCubbin, H., and J. Patterson with A. E. Cauble, A. Larsen, J. K Comeau, and D. A. Skinner, 1981, "Systematic Assessment of Family Stress, Resources and Coping Tools for Research, Education, and Clinical Intervention." St. Paul, Minnesota: University of Minnesota, Department of Family Social Science.

Pearlin, L., and S. Schooler, 1978, "The Structure of Coping." *Journal of Health and Social Behavior*, 19 (1): 2-21.

Rosenblatt, P., and R. Anderson, 1981, Interaction in Farm Families: Tension and Stress." Pp. 147-65 in R. Coward and W. Smith, Jr., (eds.), *The Family in Rural Society.* Boulder, Colorado: Westview Press.

Rosenblatt, P. D., and L. O. Keller, 1983, "Economic Vulnerability of Significant Attributes of Farming to Family Interaction." *International Journal of Sociology of the Family* 8 (January-June): 89-99.

Salamon, S., and K. K.. Markan, 1984, "Incorporation and the Family Farm." *Journal of Marriage and the Family*, 46 (February): 167-78.

Titus, S., P. Rosenblatt, and R. Anderson, 1979, "Family Conflict Over Inheritance of Property." *The Family Coordinator*, 2 (July): 337-46.

Winer, J. B., 1971, *Statistical Principles in Experimental Design.* New York: McGraw-Hill.

Addictive behavior, no matter the substance, is often embedded in the family. It is rare for substance abuse to appear in only one member of a family or in one generation This reality, combined with the destructiveness of drug abuse on any business, calls attention to the compounded effects of drug abuse in family firms. David Bork suggests that families must support those seeking to overcome their addictive behavior.

Drug Abuse in the Family Business

By David Bork

Drug abuse in any business is destructive and complicated, but in a family business, it is even more devastating. Alcohol and other drugs can be a family's biggest competitor for profits and business longevity. And the problem is compounded because of the close personal relationships and the perceived stigma of admitting a problem within the family's ranks.

The Beser family owned a chain of specialty retail shops. Richard Beser resented his "take-charge" brother, Edward, and retaliated by becoming drunk at all family functions. When Edward was chosen as the father's successor in the business, it was the final blow to Richard's ego, and he moved his family to another state. His father, depressed about the break in the family, had a stroke.

The family members blamed Richard and cut off communication with him. Further, he was denied revenues from the company, both by his father's will and by his brother. Soon after, Richard died in an auto accident, but his wife and other family members were never certain he had not committed suicide.

Charles Harwood indulged in both alcohol and marijuana as a college student. When he joined his father's manufacturing firm, his drinking problem became increasingly severe.

But Harwood's father ignored the obvious symptoms and never referred to them. Louis Harwood had always used alcohol as a relaxant and as a business/social tool. He had many three-martini lunches and sometimes imbibed heavily after hours. If he occasionally took a day off to "rest," no one regarded it as a recuperative period from anything except overwork.

The names and businesses here are fictitious, but they are based on cases that are very real: As the Harwood case suggests, addictive behavior, no matter the substance, is often embedded in the family. It is rare for substance abuse to appear in only one member of a family.

Often family members tend unwittingly to keep an addicted family member in a dependent position, to infantilize him, to see him as weak and to encourage him to escape frustrations rather than overcome them. In this way, families act in collusion to perpetuate substance use. This collusion may take the form of only token concern with alcoholism or even active support of the drinking behavior.

As damaging as the addiction problem may be, recovery may present a threat to other family members, friends and associates. Focus must be placed on the entire social system that supports and derives rewards from the addictive behavior. Treatment is often based on "unlearning" destructive behavior and altering patterns that reinforce the addiction. Within the family, such change involves major shifts in power allocation and reward systems and demands new forms of communication.

The recovering "problem carrier"s may want to reoccupy the powerful, influential roles that are now occupied by others. If Richard Beser had not been an alcoholic, he might have been a serious contender for the succession and thus a threat to his brother's position. Had Louis Harwood admitted his son's drinking problem, he would have had to examine his own drinking patterns. Thus, others in a family may even encourage the addiction in order to ensure the status quo.

Some families are able to face what must be done, however.

Foster Ellison, his wife and two other partners ran a rapidly expanding telecommunications business. Ellison's college reputation as a heavy, but not problem, drinker followed him into business, where major sales agreements were negotiated in the warmth of good restaurants and mellow wines. Long periods of work and growing conflicts among the partners resulted in a serious attack of hypertension for Ellison.

His wife dealt with the disability by increasing his life insurance-not by insisting that he alter his lifestyle. Startled by this pragmatic attitude, Ellison sought medical advice, which included a rigid diet, shorter work hours, and an end to both smoking and drinking.

Three brothers – Johnny, Pat, and Sam Moser – continued the "booze and build" tradition of their hard-working father and grandfather when they joined the family construction business. They added two new substances, cocaine and marijuana. When Pat began to make major, costly mistakes, Johnny and Sam discovered he had a drug problem that siphoned off more than they "allowed" for drug and alcohol.

One day Johnny was almost killed in a job-related accident. He was hospitalized for several months, which forcibly dried him out and gave him a long time to think. He resolved to stop drinking, and his decision to stop led Pat and Sam to do the same.

The one thing that kept the brothers on their new path was the support they gave each other. None wanted to see the other two fail. All went into treatment, and they encouraged employees with addiction problems to do so, even paying for their treatment when necessary.

Several years later, the Moser business was not only clean of abusive substances but headed toward its highest profits ever.

Families need to support those who seek to untangle themselves from addictive behavior. In the end, a family in business needs to ask itself if what it has built is in danger of being destroyed by substance abuse.

This article was originally printed in *Nation's Business*, December 1986.

CHAPTER 10
CHANGE AND CONFLICT
IN FAMILY BUSINESS

Nothing is constant in life but change and the only thing that is everywhere the same is that there are differences. The inevitable realities of changes and differences lead to inevitable conflicts in family businesses.

This section explores changes experienced during the life cycles of family firms. To an extent these changes can be managed, but at other times changes or differences lead to unavoidable conflict. Rivalries develop. Differences provoke animosity because consistency was anticipated.

Methods are available to render conflict less destructive. Sometimes these methods can be reduced to rules. In other cases attention to how individual goals work with family goals and a real commitment to information-sharing can help to resolve conflict-- sometimes before it begins.

When a shared business retards the life-cycle development of both generations, it may not be possible for consultants to "restore" their system to health as a family business, because it is unhealthy for such families to be in business together at all. Fantasies of saving their family business, or "succeeding" in passing it to the next generation, are misguided at best. The author argues that when parents' ego development is inadequate, normal individuation makes them and their children so anxious that the business functions like an addiction. A primary role of the consultant is to recognize such cases, diagnose them carefully, and intervene in ways that encourage the next generation to explore a wider range of options.

When the Family Business Is a Sickness

By Kenneth Kaye

Introduction

Family business therapists and financial/legal advisors hope to add to one another's understanding and not contradict one another's recommendations. Yet we survey the territory with different eyes. The latter group focuses more on success in terms of earnings, shareholder equity growth, and wealth retention; the therapists (of whom I am one) look at success in terms of individual and family development.

Across all our professions, however, most of the rhetoric about family business assumes that the desire of a next generation to enter and eventually take over their parents' enterprise is a good thing. Their firms and their families are described as suffering from various internal and external sources of stress, which unfortunately often interfere with their "success."

The mantra of the family business industry is that "...only about one third of family firms *survive* to the second generation; at least two thirds *fail* to make it that far, and five sixths *fail* to make it to the third generation." Note the value laden assumptions we reinforce every time we use those words *succeed*, *survive*, and *fail*. No one has calculated how many of the "failures" were actually terrific success stories, creating liquidity that opened new paths of opportunity for the next generation; or, conversely, how many that "made it" through a transition trapped their successors in misery.

We therapists have bought into those assumptions no less than the business and legal consultants. We address ourselves to problems such as the perfectionist with the controlling nature that makes empowering others so difficult for many entrepreneurs; the frustration felt by successors trying to establish their competence and credibility under the shadow of a strong parent; effects on marital, sibling, and in-law relationships when a subset of family members interact frequently and intensely; the confusion between entitlement as an owner (present or future) and expectations as a manager; etc. Note that each such problem is assumed to afflict a system that is intrinsically worth fixing and preserving. These are problems we try to resolve so as to enable our clients to "succeed" in keeping their business in the family, rather than "fail" to pass it on.

When serious problems arise, the family business is treated, for all practical purposes, as a patient. Accountants, attorneys, financial planners, therapists and business consultants come to the bedside like a team of doctors, attributing the patient's condition to a combination of unfortunate causes and working heroically to restore the patient's health. The prescribed treatment is to improve decision-making processes and long-range commitments by all concerned parties, with the help of experts in succession planning. We, the experts (regardless of professional discipline) tend to assume that the patient – the family's continuity in their business – must be saved. Because a family business is intrinsically good for its owners, its employees, its customers, and its community, it must be made healthy enough to survive.

That rhetorical picture may be consistent with our clients' dreams, but it isn't always true. On the contrary, in many cases the family business is not the patient, but an illness afflicting the family. These are cases in which keeping it going means keeping the family sick. *These owners use their business to retard the normal development of their children and themselves.* Their health as a family business cannot be "restored" because it isn't healthy for them to be a family business.

The first part of this article describes families who relate to their businesses in unhealthy ways, as if it were an addiction. Then I offer an explanation of this phenomenon in terms of developmental psychology and family systems theory, specifically arguing that parents whose own ego development is inadequate tend to create family-shared apprehensions about individual differentiation, and who thus may be inclined to use a business (unconsciously, and tragically) as a growth retarding drug. In the final section, I discuss consultation to such families.

Because such cases are far from rare, one of the consultant's primary roles is to be able to recognize them, diagnose the problem, and intervene to encourage exploring a wider range of options for the next generation. Otherwise, a family owned business can enable a dysfunctional family to maintain its dysfunction over decades, for generations; resisting individuals' efforts to achieve healthier roles and relationships; denying and distorting chemical or process addictions (for example, gambling); perpetuating conflict; justifying exploitation; and excusing incompetence. Foolish parents and spoiled children can use a family business to cover a multitude of sins, especially the sin of claiming helplessness and victimization in the face of what is really their own self-destructive behavior. And because, like an addictive drug, the family business creates a "high" with delusions of grandeur and power, it creates a market for the services that exploit those delusions, and thereby, unfortunately, feeds the addiction.

Of course, there are also many healthy families in business. The achievement of a successful enterprise, the fun of managing it together, and the opportunity to use wealth beneficially excite their members in common cause and personal fulfillment, across generations. They are neither addicted to nor stifled by their enterprises – but this article is not about those families.

Context

Three directions influenced me to look at the cases where family business is a sickness. One was a series of astonishing statements by experienced family business consultants, about the high incidence of substance abuse among their clients. For example, Fredda Herz Brown (1994) remarked that virtually all her clients had one or more substance-abusing members. Leslie Dashew (1995) said she found, if not alcohol or drugs, then gambling or some other addiction in practically every case. And Tom Hubler (1995) pointed out that "a family business is the ultimate enabler" to all kinds of addictions and dependencies. Such comments made me understand why one of the pioneers in our field, David Bork (1986), courageously put alcoholism at center stage by using an alcoholic family as the case example for his book, *Family Business, Risky Business*.

No one has yet gathered data on whether substance abuse is much more prevalent in family firms than in U.S. society generally. Regardless, when a business family does have a substance-abusing member, is the substance addiction a cause or a symptomatic result of family and business problems? In my experience, the business itself is usually that family's primary drug, and various other dependencies follow.

The second influence on my thinking came from consultants who questioned the reasons some people enter a family business. For example, John Messervey writes:

> Many enter the business as a means to resolve family issues of power, control, conflict and intimacy. These may include father-son conflicts, unresolved sibling rivalry or marital issues, and several dozen other challenges plaguing the family. So, the family business becomes the arena for desperately expected change, for repeated patterns of behavior and for acting out unspoken family conflicts. (Messervey, 1996)

"Desperately expected change" naturally leads to angrily experienced disappointment. Bernie Liebowitz's early insight has described many of my clients very well:

> Throughout their association in the FOB, both father and offspring appear to have been in a silent conspiracy not to allow underlying conflict to emerge and be resolved, even though when they started, each had hoped there would be a resolution that would satisfy everyone. (Leibowitz, 1986)

Leibowitz observed that family businesses are most often formed by people trying to resolve a problem in their relationship with a particular relative, or to fix a dysfunction in their whole family. Tragically, it doesn't work. It only perpetuates the problem, and sometimes makes it worse.

The third influence was my background as a developmental psychologist, which led me to interpret this tragedy in families as a matter of inadequate *differentiation*, or *individuation*. Successful human development is a balancing act between family attachments and the formation of a self. Family attachment is a strong instinctive motive, yet it works against individuation.

The three lines of thinking that converge in this paper are inherently intertwined, because addiction can be best understood (in family systems) as a failure of differentiation. Over identification with a business is an example of a process addiction. What begins as a desperately sought solution becomes an even bigger problem; the enterprise itself becomes the drug of choice, with the whole family addicted to keeping some members in business together at all costs.

Unlike some of my colleagues, I see quite a few families who are free of chemical dependencies, gambling problems or other addictions. I cannot even say that I see workaholism in every case. Although they wouldn't come to me if they didn't have conflict, many are "clean-living," dedicated entrepreneurs with strong core values and cohesive families – sometimes *too* cohesive. Sometimes I see an addiction-like overidentification with a business, both generations clinging to it as if they were chemically dependent on it, even as it tears them apart.

Later in this article, I return to the problem of too-cohesive families, and the idea that people might be drawn into family business in hopes of solving interpersonal problems. I argue that when a family business does become a process addiction, it may be a symptom of parental over control and resistance to children's individuation. First, however, we need to summarize some features that process addictions share with chemical dependence in families.

Troubling Similarities

Schaef and Fassel (1988) point out that addictive organizations have essentially the same symptoms as do individual addicts and their families. Table 1 provides a synopsis for this discussion of the behaviors that have been widely observed in addicted individuals and their families. Alcoholism is the most researched dependency illness, and the characteristics in Table 1 will be familiar to anyone who has worked with alcoholic families. However, they also characterize other chemical addictions, as well as non-chemical addictions such as anorexia nervosa, bulimia, or gambling.

It is left to the reader to judge whether some of these characteristics are true of family firms he or she has known.

Progressive dependency and tolerance are the defining characteristics of any addiction. People are addicted to a substance or to a process when they will not give it up even though it is ruining their lives. *Tolerance* means that they tolerate more of it than the average person would – not that it doesn't affect them. The word *progressive* refers to the fact that it takes increasing doses to give them the "buzz" or other result they seek. *Codependents* are people who enable an addict to maintain his or her addiction.

Dependency is a central issue in many family firms. Inability to leave is the surest sign that a business is an addiction rather than a healthily shared enterprise. Just as a person is an alcoholic when drinking is no longer a pleasure, but a necessity, someone is

Table 1. Characteristics of Addiction

1. Progressive dependency and tolerance
2. Denial
3. Defensiveness, projection, judgmentalism, invalidation of others' perceptions or ideas, dualistic (black-white) thinking, self-centeredness, isolation, tunnel vision, forgetfulness
4. Perfectionism and obsessiveness
5. Dishonesty, secrets, ethical deterioration, spiritual bankruptcy
6. Grandiosity, seduction, manipulative disinformation
7. Chronic stress, chronic depression, crisis orientation, negativism, fear, frozen feelings, external referencing (no feelings or perceptions of one's own)

addicted to the family business when, without joy or fulfillment, they persist in spite of pain. The way out seems more terrifying than the dependency is crippling. I described some entrepreneurs' children as "prisoners of the family business" (Kaye, 1992), but in truth their parents, siblings, or spouses are equally trapped.

Denial is among the most human mechanisms of mental life, used by normal, healthy, optimistic people every day. In the addicted personality, it predominates over realistic judgment, not only protecting the illness, but guaranteeing its progression. The force of denial leads to the confused thinking and illogic faced by anyone who tries to confront addicts rationally.

Whole families engage in denial in many ways. Families of workaholics can deny their disease easily, because workaholism carries no shame in our society. But their disease progresses, and until the organization faces reality, the individual cannot begin to recover. Similarly, prisoners of a family business suffer from their relatives' and friends' denials about the problem.

The third cluster of symptoms in Table 1 (the set beginning with *defensiveness*) has to do with shutting out information that threatens the addiction. Addicts and any codependent family members or coworkers are as quick to blame, criticize, and judge others as they are to defend vigilantly (proactively) against criticism of themselves. Often, in a family business, it is the norm to attribute interpersonal problems to "personality conflicts," implying that nothing is fundamentally wrong with the system. Thus its members cannot benefit from conflicting views as opportunities to challenge themselves and promote continual adaptive growth (Kaye, 1994).

Self-centeredness, isolation, and *tunnel vision* are common in addicts as they tune out possible threats to their status quo and as their chosen drug subsumes their world. Similarly, many business founders and successors have a remarkably narrow world view. The constant pressures of competition in a market economy naturally incline them to see government and labor unions as their enemies, inheritance as the only legitimate entitlement, and wealth itself as proof of predestination. Those precepts may become entangled with their faith, or even (for some) function as religious principles. Good versus evil: Business ownership and tax avoidance are family values, while social welfare and regulation equal moral decay. Market protectionism is a patriotic virtue, but the same patriots advocate free trade when it comes to offshore cheap labor.

When speeches and newsletters on family business pander to the successful entrepreneur's sense of moral superiority (for example, with rhetoric about the rapaciousness of the IRS), they do both his family and society a disservice.

The first three clusters of symptoms in Table 1 probably lead to the fourth, and also the fifth, cluster. *Perfectionism* and *obsessiveness* result from a felt shortage of love, respect, or money (a surrogate for love and respect). The young child thinks, "If only I were more perfect, my parents would be happy and would value me." The grown-up child thinks, "If I achieve perfection (in my weight, my work, my social status, the cleanliness of my home, or whatever), *then* I'll be worthy of love." Many adults who are not addicts themselves, but were children of alcoholics, suffer from perfectionism, excessive self-criticism, workaholism, and rigidity.

Again, there is a parallel with family business: Scarcity of their father's attention and approval leads some adult children of entrepreneurs to workaholism and perpetual dissatisfaction with themselves. This underlies many sibling conflicts in family firms. Too little of what they need from either or both of their parents in childhood creates siblings who, as adults, will be chronically distrustful and jealous of one another. ("You were always the favorite.") This may explain why even some extraordinarily wealthy adults squabble like children over matters involving relatively few dollars.

Many of the symptoms in Table 1 are related to the need to control. For example, adult children of alcoholics make poor team members, according to Schaef and Fassel (1988), because they are poor listeners, have difficulty giving and receiving criticism, and have an excessive need to control. Carrying the baggage of painful childhood experience into business relationships, their anxiety around authority figures takes the form of resistance or defiance, often passive- aggressively. Similarly, we see passive-aggressive behavior in not a few children of bossy entrepreneurs.

Codependents, on the other hand, are sensitive listeners, compliant, eager to please. "Co-dependents would rather care for someone in a way that leads to that person's death," wrote Schaef and Fassel (1988), "than to take the risk of seeing and speaking the truth and possibly offending him or her." In some business families, the favored successor may be the member least likely to challenge dysfunctional norms.

The fifth cluster includes *dishonesty* and *ethical deterioration* as well as the addicts' *spiritual bankruptcy*, which has been discussed explicitly by Hubler (1995) among other family business consultants. Religious faith is not equivalent to spiritual strength. Quite the contrary: Religion can be a process addiction in itself, especially if parents are dogmatic and authoritarian instead of supporting each child's individualized growth in spirit and character.

The illusion of control through *secrets* in some (not all) business families is also a characteristic of addicts and their families.

Both the perfectionist tendencies and the dishonest tendencies are probably involved in creating the sixth set of characteristics in the literature. *Grandiosity* is frequently a characteristic of addicts. As they live on the verge of greatness, the promise of spectacular achievement or fortune keeps them from seeing how they are wasting their lives. The promise of the future takes attention away from current problems, denies current feelings, and devalues the ordinary self. The loftier and more unattainable the promise, the more probable that the organization becomes a rigidly grandiose denial system:

> The very fact of having goals frequently can be enough to con employees into believing that everything is all right in the organization. The mission is like a household god. As long as it is in its shrine, the organization is protected, even if what it is doing has little to do with the stated mission. (Schaef and Fassel, 1988)

Shared grandiosity plays into the seduction noted by addiction counselors as well as by consultants to addictive organizations:

> Loyalty to the organization becomes a fix when individuals become preoccupied with maintaining the organization. When loyalty to the organization becomes a substitute for living one's own life, then the company has become the addictive substance of choice . . . The issue is not benefits per se, but the way the organization and individuals use them to stay central in the lives of workers and consequently to prevent people from moving on and doing what they need to do. (Schaef and Fassel, 1988)

Seduction often takes a form that might be termed *manipulative disinformation*. Members are trapped in the family business, for example, by assurances that they can leave any time. Relatives are led to believe they have been promised management roles or financial rewards, then later accused of misunderstanding.

Finally, all of the above combined with desperation and unrealistic expectations naturally lead to *chronic stress, depression*, etc. Codependents are at especially high risk for workaholism (which ranks among the most resistant of addictions to treatment) and consequently for ulcers, colitis, back pain, high blood pressure, and eating disorders. *Frozen feelings* and *external referencing* mean not knowing how one feels except in terms of what others want or expect one to feel. The person has no boundaries, no self, and consequently no true recognition of others as selves with distinct feelings, perceptions, and desires.

> Most of these people want to be doing something else. When we challenge them to explore other opportunities, they respond that they cannot afford it. We should not miss the real message here:…they cannot afford to take the risk of being fully alive. (Schaef and Fassel, 1988)

Schaef and Fassel were writing about workaholic employees of corporations, but could they not just as well be describing prisoners of family business?

Surely we can identify some, if not all, the problematic behavior listed in Table 1, in many family business systems. It is even clearer how similar family firms in pain are to families in chemical dependency if we describe the *progressive* course of addiction to family business. I trace the downward decline in Table 2, showing how it ends in a hopeless abyss. I drew the "crucial" and "chronic" phases of this table (with only a few word changes) from a poster widely used by substance abuse counselors, called a Jellinek chart. They use this to help members of addictive families recognize how far their illness has progressed, and where they are headed if they keep ignoring the problem. Earlier, in what I call the "relief" phase, the business might be used much like social drinking as an escape, complete with "peer pressure." Note that the risk factors for family business addiction are identical to those for substance abuse. (We turn to the "phases of recovery" side of the Jellinek chart later in this paper.)

Individual Development in the Nonindividuated Family

So far, I have only pointed out *similarities* between addictive families and a significant number of business-owning families. If indeed they appear to share similar symptoms, is it possible that the same processes might account for such developmental disturbances, irrespective of the substance or institution of choice?

Table 2. Phases of Addiction to the Family Business

1. Risk factors	Inadequate self esteem Inadequate skills Inadequate permission to differentiate (be an individual)
2. Relief phase	"Peer pressure:" sibling and/or parental encouragement "Escape:" The family firm is a way to avoid competing in the real world Tolerance – > dependence Guilt – > denial and excuses
3. Crucial phase	Remorse, failure of resolutions Grandiose, aggressive behavior Loss of other interests Money troubles, denial of responsibility, blaming Lifestyle, inflated to compensate for emptiness, traps family member in the business
4. Chronic phase	Loss of tolerance (too late) Lengthy "intoxications:" obsession with the business Physical and moral deterioration Self-loathing – > hopelessness
5. "Hits bottom"	

The function of normal parenthood is to develop independently self-supporting offspring. In developmental psychology, we call the progress of children toward self-support *differentiation*, or *individuation* (interchangeable terms). Healthy adult children are separate, distinct people – even as they enjoy numerous interdependent connections with one another and with the other generations of their extended families.

The field of family-business therapy has now progressed to the point where we can draw a powerful conclusion: Contrary to the course of normal life-cycle development, family-owned and -managed enterprises are often used to resist the differentiation and development of children who join the business, and sometimes even of children who don't.

I am saying that *individuation and the family business are at odds*. This conclusion runs directly counter to the family-business literature, which assumes that because processes of individuation in healthy families minimize destructive conflict and increase the chances of good succession, helping members to individuate should be good medicine for the less healthy family firm. On the contrary, I am concerned about the way family business succession in a less healthy family can be the means of resisting differentiation – maladaptively. In those cases, members' individuation threatens rather than supports the family business system.

The literature, unfortunately, often equates success with succession. For purposes of this discussion, we will *not* assume that succession to the next generation means the family business has succeeded. On the contrary, succession sometimes occurs as a result of developmental failure in a family, and (conversely) a thoroughly successful outcome for a family business can sometimes involve a decision to dispose of it. We are interested in the relationship between individuation and family business success – not necessarily succession.

What Is "Individuation"? "Individuation" is a lifelong developmental process that begins in the first year of life, soon after an infant begins to feel attachments to specific people. The infant becomes aware that relationships with parents, siblings, and other caregivers are vital for a body's physical and emotional survival. This translates into the importance of being needed and valued by those caregivers, which in turn leads to the question, in effect, "Who am *I* and how am I *distinct* from those people, relationships, and their expectations of me?" By the end of the second year, with the blossoming of language, the question manifests itself in the stage parents call "the terrible twos," which is really the beginning of a lifelong quest for balance between attachment and individuation.

Theories about the self are almost as old as the field of psychology: about 100 years. From the early writers like James (1890), Cooley (1902), and Mead (1934) to Maslow (1954) and more recently Loevinger (1976) and Kegan (1982) as well as the school of psychoanalysis called "self psychology" (Kohut, 1971; Galatzer-Levy and Cohler, 1993), virtually all theories understand the self as deriving both from a person's dependence upon "significant others" and his or her need to differentiate from those others. In other words, one needs to be *both* a separate person *and* a member of the family/group/community/profession/organization.

In one of the seminal papers in the field of family therapy, Bowen (1972) wrote of his struggle to differentiate from his own family, which happened to own a business. Bowen was the only sibling who had not stayed or returned home to work in the business. Although successful in his career as a psychiatrist, he found himself unable to avoid being drawn into his family's conflicts surrounding their business roles and their failure to grow as individuals.

Too much self-differentiation would not be adaptive for human development. We are a social species, and the family is our basic economic and cultural unit. It is the molecule. Just as molecules are composed of atoms, families are composed of individual people, but it is the structure and nature of the bonds connecting those people, and the dynamic forces operating among them, that make them who they are. Furthermore, what constitutes a "healthy" balance between individual differentiation and family cohesion varies across societies and across cultures within a society – a fact we shall need to keep in mind in the section on treatment, below.

On the other hand, too much resistance to differentiation is equally maladaptive. Without the freedom and without the support of one's family to pursue individual talents and dreams, creativity and growth are stifled. Conflict becomes chronic. People lack the flexibility to keep up with changing demands of their economic environment. For that reason alone, a business that serves the function of retarding its owners' development is not one whose family ownership continuity should be encouraged.

What Is Success? Confining ourselves to intergenerational family enterprise, let us define "success" in the long run, if and when:

1. Both generations feel that the younger generation has made significant contributions to the business.
2. They either passed the baton or made a good decision to sell the business, in which case they worked together to maximize its value.
3. The process of getting there was personally rewarding for them, individually as well as collectively.
4. There were no serious personal casualties along the way.

An example of failing to meet the first criterion is the family whose business never serves as a place where children can be validated as adults and appreciated by their parents. The second type of failure characterizes a business whose equity value is held down by a history of poor teamwork, poor leadership, or poor management of this family resource. An example of the third type is one in which financial success has been achieved at the expense of the members' personal satisfaction, enjoyment of their relationships, or their moral values. The fourth type of failure is found in a family business that makes its owners and most of their children happy, but which contributes to one member's arrested development, chemical dependence, or other form of lifelong alienation.

The families that I would call addicted to their business have failed in most, if not all four, of those criteria.

A Set of Cases

My prior training and experience tends to attract more than my share of clients whose family firms are in crisis, or who want to avert an impending crisis. Hence, I would not claim that the number of families I see, in which members of the second generation are trapped in the business to their detriment, is a representative number; only that such cases are not rare.

At the time of writing I have had consulting engagements with 64 two generation family business cases of sufficient duration to categorize them. (This excludes corporate management teams, non-family-business partnerships, single generation owners, and some members of two-generation families who consulted me briefly or without including other key members.) By the four criteria listed above, at the onset of consultation only about one quarter of those 64 business families appeared to be family relationship success stories. Table 3 indicates how many (over the course of, or following consultation) either achieved a promising succession to the next generation or made a decision they felt good about, to sell the business.

A cautionary note concerning the data in Table 3: The classification reflects my subjective evaluations rather than a blind coding scheme. Furthermore, many of these families are still in process of addressing their issues, either with me or with other kinds of advisors. Some fled from addressing them as soon as they came to light; still others, I hope, made positive steps after I lost touch with them. Nonetheless, I present my "best guess" numbers as a stimulus to other consultants: In how many cases do I feel my efforts were successful? Table 3 answers that question for this consultant only. Again, I emphasize: It tells nothing about the population of all family firms.

Clearly, among those clients who had no crippling conflict when they sought my help as a transition-planning facilitator, all of those I kept track of made good progress. I was less effective with families who, in my own opinion, needed to create an alternative path for one or more members because those members' unhappiness, lack of realistic preparedness, and/or symptomatic behavior created a serious detriment to the business

Table 3. Classification of 64 Two-Generation Family Business Engagements

Type of Case	Consultant's Idea of Success	Results to Date
16 cases (25%) • At least one capable business person in the successor generation, with the interests and ability to carry the company on AND • Basic trust among family members who work in the business.	**Succession** Effectively planning toward business succession and eventual disposition of parental assets in a way that meets the needs and desires of both generations.	• Excluding 4 unknown, 100% (12 cases) made good progress toward succession.
26 cases (41%) • At least one capable business person in the successor generation, to whom the torch could be passed BUT • One or more persons or relationships a significant obstacle to business or family teamwork.	**Liberty and Succession** It's hard to imagine the family business functioning profitably; OR harmoniously unless the unhappy member is liberated from it in a fair and constructive way.	• Excluding 4 unknown, 32% (7 cases) made good progress toward "liberty and succession." • At least 3 cases of catastrophic family breakdown.
22 cases (34%) • no capable manager(s) in the next generation, for the size and complexity of their business OR • Members' capabilities nullified by dysfunctional family relationships.	**Sale** From the standpoint of family harmony and individual development, these families probably should sell their firms when the present generation is ready to retire.	• Excluding 3 unknown, 11% (2 cases) made good progress toward planned sale to employees or outsiders. • At least 8 cases of catastrophic family breakdown.

team. About a third of that group achieved what seemed to me a healthy outcome for all members. I was *very* ineffective with parents whose best course of action (again, in my own opinion) was *not* to pass the torch to their children. Only two of those, so far, have decided not to do so – 11%.

To answer the more cheerful question expressed above, more than 40% of the cases (21 of 53) did make decisions – either succession or sale – to all members' satisfaction. However, from the 32 cases who remained stuck as their problems deteriorated, we can conclude that unhappy, poorly collaborating families show great resistance to altering their course, even when working with a consultant who candidly airs his doubts about their family business's prospects for succession to the next generation.

Regardless of how skewed this particular sample may be, other consultants surely encounter such families. We therefore need a theory about how they got where they are and what keeps them stuck.

Individuation in Entrepreneurial Families

It is not correct to say that family business success depends on good differentiation. Anecdotal case reports and a very small amount of statistical evidence suggest that the two variables are positively correlated (e.g., Swogger, 1991; Kaye, 1992; Lansberg and Astrachan, 1994). Nonetheless, to infer from that fact a linear cause and effect (inadequate individuation leads to problems in the business) would be fallacious. Probably the direction of effects is the other way around. Lansberg (1997) breaks radically from the traditional view in our field (e.g., Friedman, 1991; Swogger, 1991) when he writes, "A successful family business may, in fact, delay the process of individuation." My suggestion is even more unsettling: Some people bring their offspring into a business or come to work with their parents *in order to retard* individuation.

Should we regard the child's individuation problem as an accidental by-product of the economic organization? No, because the family is a social system. What looks like an accidental result is, I believe, the dysfunctional system's *purpose*. Individuation is a problem for these families because parents brought children into a business *hoping (perhaps unconsciously) to delay their individuation*. Table 4 shows where I agree and disagree with the family business literature's view of individuation.

Step III in the two theories is the same systemic postulate. The process is circular, as the children's immaturity or inadequacy confirms the parents' low opinion of them. Step II in the old theory, however, is a linear cause-effect inference from the apparent correlation between individuation problems and family business problems. The new theory rejects that inference in favor of the key assumption that runs from Step I through IV: Some families are so drawn to involve sons, daughters, and other relatives in their business that it looks as if they were *trying to prevent* healthy individual growth and family adaptation.

Table 4. Systemic Relationship Between Individuation and Family Business Conflict

Accepted Wisdom (mix of linear and systemic)	New Theory (systemic)
1. Entrepreneurs by nature may have a tendency to be over-controlling as well as ineffective at building children's self-esteem, confidence, etc. On top of that, running a business sometimes leads parents to neglect children's needs for individuation.	1. People who are uncomfortable with a normal degree of individuation in their children's development find the prospect of bringing them into a business particularly attractive. They can use the family business system to maintain excessive cohesion or connections without actually meeting the young adults' developmental needs.
2. Whatever the causes of poor individuation, it creates problems when the next generation has to work together, resolve conflicts, pursue careers, choose leaders, etc.	2. The whole family shares rarely spoken fears about what might happen to some or all of its members, and to their relationships, if individuation is allowed to go too far. Conflict serves the function not of differentiating them but of locking them in problem maintenance cycles that protect them from the risks of change.
3. Those problems in turn become obstacles to the parent's letting go. Added to the parent's own resistance to separating from the business, systemic resistance keeps the would-be successors underperforming and unempowered.	3. Same as accepted wisdom at the left
4. Most or all family members are unhappy with their lack of progress toward succession.	4. Most or all family members are relieved about the maintenance of their painful but familiar equilibrium.

In systems theoretical terms: All open systems, including human social systems, assimilate energy and matter from their environment in order to maintain equilibrium with the energy they expend. Sometimes they change adaptively to resist entropy (breaking up and losing the informational value they bring to one another as a system). But systems don't always manage to do that. Sometimes the demands of the environment are greater than the systems' capacity for adaptation, so they try to stave off destruction by rigidly resisting change.

Differentiation is an aspect of ego development. (*Ego* is the internalized capacity for self-regulation as well as the experience of oneself as a whole person). It is not just a psychoanalytic concept; other disciplines give it the same importance under different names. For example, the philosopher Macmurray (1957) discussed the development of a self as agent rather than just an object to others. There is a developmental progression, from primitive aims and primitive forms of attachment to others, toward the balanced attachment and higher aims of the individuated self (Maslow, 1954; Loevinger, 1976; Vaillant, 1977; Kegan, 1982). Vaillant showed that the types of defenses people use can be hierarchized and correlated with a broad range of success measures. All the classic authors on the subject of self or ego development (all the way back to James, 1890) agree on a developmental hierarchy. An individual's primitive aims include *seeking to belong to*, and support, norms of the group; whereas *self-actualization* is a higher, more developed aim. Similarity to and connection to the group provides the necessary condition for development, but:

> It largely is differentiation from others that challenges and determines our activity...It is as if each individual felt his significance only by contrasting himself with others. (Simmel, 1950 translation,)

Of course, all those classic authors were western, mostly American, authors. Self-actualization is an American concept, and it could be argued that we "baby boomers" and our children are excessively preoccupied with it. This article does not consider other cultures; however, even if the balance point between individuation and attachment motives is shifted for different cultures, both motives exist: The need to find the right balance is universal in human development. Within every set of cultural norms, some families find a more comfortable balance than others.

Ego Development, Individuation, and Addiction to the Business

Table 3 indicates that among the 48 clients who, I felt, needed to liberate at least one member (if not the whole next generation) from the business, at least two thirds have not managed to do so – or have managed not to do so. What long-term family processes made their business entanglement more like an addiction than a pleasure?

We must probe a little further into developmental psychology for a theory about causal processes in families that will eventually become "stuck" in the family business.

I have said that the symptoms of family business dependence are similar to those of chemical dependence (Table 1) and that their etiology is similar (Table 2). Chemical dependence begins first with a reason to use the drug – peer pressure, a way to avoid dealing with something, or both. Gradually, tolerance (the required dose) and dependence increase. So it is with family business dependence: It begins with family pressure or avoidance of challenges outside the family, or both. Then tolerance (the level of rewards or privileges needed from the business in order to believe oneself satisfied) increases. The young person becomes trapped in the business, as doors to alternative career paths close.

It is easy to understand what motivates sons or daughters (or in-laws) whose parent, through a combination of overt and subtle messages, and perhaps a financial package the child can't refuse, pressures them to come work in the business. But *what motivates the parent?* A desire to give his children wonderful opportunities? Surely that is part of it, but the opportunities are so narrowly defined that we suspect a more selfish motive. Is it just the

Figure 1. Hypothesized Effects Among Ego Development, Individuation, and Addiction.

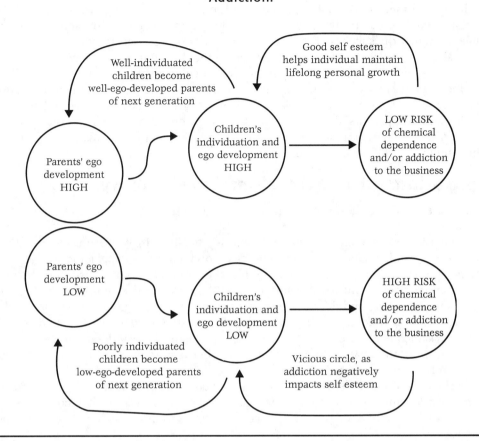

need for trustworthy help, the fear that non-family managers will steal from him? Sometimes. Often, however, a motive seems to be that of keeping children and grandchildren close, or bringing them back home after an experimental period of living too far away.

If any of those essentially selfish motives is at work, we have to postulate poor ego development on the parent's part. Permission for a child to differentiate into a healthy, secure individual requires ego development on the part of his or her parents. The parents have to let go.

In other cases, it is not the parent but the child who instigates and presses to come into the business, overcoming parental reservations. The "employer of last resort" scenario happens when the son or daughter has failed elsewhere, or withdrawn in fear of failing. Severe lack of self-esteem can often be traced back to childhood, when parents didn't do all they could to build the child's confidence in his or her ability to make it in the outside world.

It should be pointed out that self-esteem varies, to some extent, congenitally; although parents affect it, children aren't equally easy to equip with self esteem. Let us concern ourselves here, however, with those parents who did significantly less than they could have done for their children's self-esteem before those children ever came to work in the business. Again, we would have to postulate poor ego development on the parents' part. Not all adults are whole enough (mature enough or "big enough") to devote themselves to building individuated self esteem in their children. Some need to keep the children dependent and relatively undifferentiated.

This leads us to a testable theory: "Prisoners" or "addicts" of the family business – sons, daughters, in-laws – who stay in the business despite being manifestly unhappy, unsuccessful, locked in chronic conflict, and perhaps ungrateful, not only have low self-esteem and inadequate adult differentiation from their families, they also have parents or parents-in-law with poor ego development who resisted the children's differentiation.

Unfortunately, I have found no literature on ego development among entrepreneurs. The theory outlined in Table 4 (right-hand column) suggests a hypothesis (Figure 1): If consultants could do a family audit, assessing the parents' ego development, we ought to be able to predict the success of their family business succession. In other words, I would hypothesize that my clients' fates, as indicated by the different cells of Table 3, might have been predicted by a good test of the parents' ego development.

Is individuation only an issue for children in family firms? No. It is an issue in normal development that seems to be especially difficult in this context. We all work on our relationships with our parents all our lives, but the family business can force a risky degree of overlap. When the performance pressure never ends, it is harder to balance love and duty against individual self-actualization.

Implications of the Developmental Theory

Let me summarize the implications of this argument before turning to the treatment perspective:

1. Individuation *is* necessary for family business transition in Western societies. (Family business is as old as *homo sapiens*, whereas individuation is especially problematic in modern times and in America. Healthy members of any society must individuate to a considerable degree, but we also suffer from the myth of individualism, which glorifies excessive autonomy and denies the primacy of teamwork, organizations, and families.)
2. Family business systems, by their nature, run the risk of overly resisting individuation.
3. Such resistance leads to conflict, which increases fears about individuation.
4. Unfortunately, the resistance may be justified, because individuation may well endanger family business transition.
5. Only those family businesses that *don't have to do so* will succeed over generations. In other words, families whose members had other paths on which they could have succeeded are the only ones with the capacity to thrive in business together over generations.
6. Many of those that *cannot* pass their enterprises successfully to the next generation are those families that can least afford not to – because their children are ill-equipped for success elsewhere.
7. The role of a family therapist as family business consultant should not be to increase the number of families engaged in succession, but to *narrow* the number to just those for whom healthy reasons to be a family business outweigh the unhealthy motives.

The mission of the Family Firm Institute and the mission statements of many firms serving owners of closely held companies explicitly or implicitly suggest that their purpose is succession for the sake of succession. Indeed, the words *success* and *succession* are often used synonymously. We say we abhor tax driven planning, yet we are guilty of a comparable blindness: Our avowed mission seems to be succession-driven rather than health-driven. Instead, we should be in the business of helping entrepreneurs discover whether their overlapping family and business roles yield more advantages than disadvantages (Tagiuri and Davis, 1996). And we should be helping families liberate themselves from the fear of differentiation (Kohut, 1971; Pinsof, 1995).

Treatment

The foregoing sections have pointed out the strong similarities between dysfunctional family business systems and the process of addiction, and explained how a family's business can become its drug.

Such a perspective may seem pessimistic, yet I arrived at it after enjoying ten years of satisfying work with business-owning families. Even the 50% of my clients who still have serious problems have usually accomplished some changes we can both feel good about.

Thus I feel positive about most of the people who are in family businesses, and optimistic about new prospects. The reason I can feel so optimistic about the outcome of their

Table 5. Phases of Recovery (Individuals or Whole Family)

1. "Hits bottom"

2. Acknowledgment	Honest desire for help
	Learns addiction can be arrested
	Leaves the business
	Awareness of spiritual emptiness
3. Realistic thinking	Sees possibilities of new way of life
	"Regular nourishment taken:" Explores
	new sources of personal satisfaction
	Diminishing fears of unknown future
	Self-esteem returns (or begins)
	No more desire to escape
	Natural rest and sleep
	Family and friends appreciate efforts
4. Appreciation	New circle of stable friends
	New interests develop
	Application of real values
	Increased emotional control
	Care of personal appearance
	Therapy and group support continue
	with increased insight on past
	Enlightened and contented personal
	identity

work with me is that I don't try to help them improve their relationships *so they can stay in business together*. More often than not, the healthiest outcome is for the family business to assist at least one member, if not all of them, into the career equivalent of a recovery program.

The treatment model for an alcoholic family may be the most appropriate model to use with many family firms. Like alcoholic beverages, family business isn't poisonous if taken in moderation. In fact, family enterprise was the normal means of survival during our species evolution and for most of human history, and still is the norm outside the industrialized countries. But, like alcohol dependence, once it becomes symptomatic, it has to be regarded as a pathology: *No other problems will be treatable if the addiction is ignored.*

Just as an alcoholic family needs to be told that their concern (for example) about one child's school failure or eating disorder cannot be constructively addressed until they face the truth about the parent's addiction, so a family business consultant needs to tell his or her clients that their desired succession planning would be a waste and a sham if they refuse to face the painful truth regarding codependencies, self-defeating expectations of entitlement, addictive obsessions with work, lying, or grandiose fantasies about the future. Unless their business represents a healthy life for the successors, the family business consultant is like a bartender, listening sympathetically to the drunkard's tale of woe while continuing to "serve" the system. Untreated addictions are progressive and fatal.

Readers familiar with the Jellinek chart mentioned earlier will recognize that Table 5 corresponds verbatim to the other side of that chart, which shows the challenging climb to recovery.

The treatment process is difficult, frustrating, and not always successful, but its chances are better with the following guiding principles:

Be aware of the risk factors. The earlier a consultant can recognize the risk factors listed in Table 2, the better his or her chances of helping to shift the family system from the downward slope shown in the bottom of Figure 1, to the upward slope shown at the top.

Respect the people, not the business. Don't assume that our job is to save the family business. Help clients examine whether the business is playing a healthy role in their lives. If not, then a successful outcome may be to get one or more members *out* of the business; possibly to help the whole family see ending their business relationships as something other than "failure." Whether they stay in business or not, it is our job to help them explore all their options more realistically.

Don't pathologize enmeshment. A lack of differentiation, or a high degree of individual subordination to the needs of the family, isn't necessarily dysfunctional. In a way it's like sexual mores: What goes on between consenting adults in the privacy of their homes is no one else's business. Therefore, as consultants, we cannot assess the health of a family business based on some sort of individuation score. The concept should be applied only where people experience unhappiness and frustration in their family business. Person A may be less individuated from her family than person B is from hers; but suppose A is happy with her life. Suppose it is culturally appropriate, in her world, to build an identity within rather than beyond the family of origin; suppose it suits her personality. B's level of individuation, though greater than A's, may be frustrated by a family system that endorses the individualistic society's messages about achievement, but at the same time, dysfunctionally, sabotages the individual's attempt to reach out for it. Only in B's case, not in A's, is there reason to consider the family business *possibly* an unhealthy environment.

Don't diminish the crisis. It creates the motive and opportunity for radical change. Keep a sense of urgency, to achieve the clients' sincere recognition of their enmeshment in a codependent system. Challenge their denial. They have to want to help themselves; refuse to continue lying to themselves, each other, and others; and be willing to undergo pain. Schaef and Fassel discuss "the myth that rules will alleviate the disease of the addictive system." (1988, p.165) One of the quotations from their book earlier in this paper raises the disturbing question whether we as consultants sometimes urge mission statements, rules, and structures *codependently* – in our own misguided attempt to create the illusion of control.

Family members will want to avoid painful historical and emotional questions about what led them down destructive paths in the first place. They will prefer to make small changes in working roles. Often small changes *are* the best steps toward resolution, but sometimes they are only Band-Aids® over infected wounds or internal hemorrhages. Keep alive the question of whether being part of the business is really good for each member – until that question is definitely answered.

This is not to say that goals, mission statements, and rational procedures are bad things to urge on our clients. They may be important diagnostically, to see if the system is capable of implementing consistent rules. They seldom, if ever, constitute the whole cure.

Reframe the problem. When offering opinions, be sure they don't sound like judgments, which would only elicit defensiveness. It is crucial not to stigmatize people. If parents' personality defense mechanisms or entrepreneurial obstinacy have led to family problems, recognize that their conscious intentions were good. They have also led to business success.

It also helps to point out how widespread these problems are in our society. *Many* people have made the understandable human error of hiring a family member in hopes of giving that person a new start; or of forming a business partnership in hopes of turning a bad relationship into something better. Many people have walked the recovery road, too, with great success.

Create a safe environment for change. Take responsibility for the consultation, not for the outcome. Our responsibility is to create conditions for system members' constructive discourse about their concerns. If their discussion leads to anyone's leaving the business, they will need a safe context for dealing with that, too. (Just as we expect severe withdrawal symptoms in a person recovering from chemical dependence, it's not too far-fetched to view withdrawal from the business as an equivalent to detoxification.)

You're not telling them anything they don't know. You merely give voice to *the* *message the clients came to you to hear an expert say*. Say what has to be said about the course they are on, even if it is sad or frightening to contemplate.

Don't be the rescuer. As White and Whiteside (1995) admonished consultants who work with alcoholic families, beware of system pressure on the consultant/therapist to become the over-responsible, controlling counterfoil to the out-of-control, under-responsible members. Our clients' respect for our knowledge and expertise is seductive because we want to be heroes; that aspect of our personalities drew us into our professions in the first place. But rescuing others, even if it were possible, disempowers them. We are not in charge of their lives.

They will need other support (peer and professional). Recovery is a process, not a quick fix. Therefore, giving up the addictive agent – in this case, the family business – is only a first step for the family member or members involved. The consultant who facilitates that step, like one who facilitates an alcoholism intervention, need not be the same one who will do the follow-up counseling. But it surely is our job to do everything possible to get the "recovering" client into an ongoing relationship with a career counselor, therapist, self-help group, or whatever appropriate resource will remain in touch with the course of recovery.

Behavior change will not be enough without increased understanding. Just as an addict needs to explore and develop a personal story ("Why I'm an addict" "What my addiction has done for me as well as to me"), so our clients will need cognitive change. Be skeptical about action decisions that are reached too quickly.

Substitute healthier habits. The good news is that when family business is an addiction, it is a process addiction (like bulimia, or gambling) rather than a substance addiction like alcoholism. It is curable, not just treatable. The cure is to substitute healthier habits, in this case a new career for the individual or a new way of defining their identity as a family.

Conclusion and Warning

The good news is that most patients treated for process addictions (along with their family systems) do recover. As Table 5 suggests, the recovering family business system or recovering individual family business member can usually move on to a better life as an individuated person. They don't pine for the conflicts and anxieties of the former life in their family business.

On the other hand, the family business sickness is more dangerous than other addictions in one important way: The family business addicts' world is attractive and rewarding to the consultant. The same money that can seduce a young person away from her own independent career path and personally fulfilling lifestyle may also co-opt a consultant into affirming the client's self-deluding beliefs and self-destructive denial system. It is not only legal and financial advisors whom I challenge to consider whether the pecuniary attractions of their clients sometimes lead them to feed rather than confront that denial system. Even those of us who act as therapists, with years of clinical family therapy experience, can easily fall into the trap of treating the family business as our wealthy "patient" whose life is precious. In cases when a business is not the patient but the sickness itself, that is inexcusable.

References

Bork, D. (1986). *Family business, risky business.* New York: AMACOM.

Bowen, M. (1972). On the differentiation of self in the family. In M. Bowen (Ed.), *Family Therapy in Clinical Practice* (pp. 467-528). New York: Jason Aronson.

Cooley, C. (1902). *Human nature and the social order.* New York: Scribner's.

Dashew, Leslie. (1995). Personal communication.

Herz Brown, F. (1994). Personal communication.

Friedman, S. (1991). Sibling relationships and intergenerational succession in family firms. *Family Business Review, 4*(1), 3-20.

Galatzer-Levy, R., & Cohler, B. (1993). *The essential other: A developmental psychology of the self.* New York: Basic Books.

Hubler, T. (1995). *Obstacles to family change: Our role in discovering them, naming them, and working with them.* Paper presented at the conference on Psychosocial Dynamics of Family Business, Evanston, Illinois.

James, W. (1890). *The principles of psychology* (Vol. 1). New York: Holt.

Kaye, K. (1992). The kid brother. *Family Business Review, 5*(3), 237-256.

Kaye, K. (1994). *Workplace wars and how to end them: Turning personal conflicts into productive teamwork.* New York: AMACOM.

Kegan, R. (1982). *The evolving self.* Cambridge: Harvard University Press.

Kohut, H. (1971). *The analysis of the self.* New York: International Universities Press.

Lansberg, I. (1997). *Managing succession and continuity in family companies.* Boston: Harvard Business School Press.

Lansberg, I., & Astrachan, J.H. (1994). Influence of family relationships on succession planning and training: The importance of mediating factors. *Family Business Review, 7*(1), 39-60.

Leibowitz, B. (1986). Resolving conflict in the family owned business. *Consultation, 5*(3), 191-205.

Loevinger, J. (1976). *Ego development.* San Francisco: Jossey-Bass.

Macmurray, J. (1957). *The self as agent.* London: Faber and Faber.

Maslow, A. (1954). *Motivation and personality.* New York: Harper and Row.

Mead, G. H. (1934). *Mind, self, and society.* Chicago: University of Chicago Press.

Messervey, John. (1996). Personal communication.

Pinsof, W. (1995). *An integrative problem centered approach to family business problems.* Paper presented at the conference on Psychosocial Dynamics of Family Business, Evanston, Illinois.

Schaef, A., & Fassel, D. (1988). *The addictive organization.* New York: HarperCollins.

Simmel, G. (1950). *The sociology of Georg Simmel.* In K. Wolff (Ed. and Trans.). New York: Free Press.

Swogger, G. (1991). Assessing the successor generation in family businesses. *Family Business Review, 4*(4), 397-411.

Tagiuri, R., & Davis, J. (1996). Bivalent attributes of the family firm. *Family Business Review, 9*(2), 199-208.

Vaillant, G. (1977). *Adaptation of life.* Boston: Little, Brown.

White, C., & Whiteside, M. (1995). *Alcohol and the family business: An uneasy partnership.* Presentation at the Family Firm Institute, St. Louis.

It is always difficult to move from small entrepreneurships to large management structures. But a family-operated firm may have twice the difficulties, as family interrelationships complicate the changes This examination of such computations describes methods of overcoming growth problems in family businesses including redefining management, focusing on the family and engaging in strategic planning.

Life-Cycle Changes in Small Family Businesses

By Richard B. Peiser and Leland M. Wooten

Every successful small business must sooner or later face the problems of growth and expansion. Where family businesses are concerned, normal growth problems are compounded by the difficulties of separating family relationships from business decisions.

One of the crucial tests of a successful small business is its ability to make the transition from the entrepreneurial stage to the administrative stage in its development. This transition frequently occurs in family businesses by transition from the first generation to the next – a transition which many family businesses do not survive. In this article, we examine the process of managing life-cycle changes, both in the firm and in the family, so as to provide growth and development beyond the state of entrepreneurship.

The Project-Oriented Family Firm

The types of small businesses discussed in this article have several common features. First, a family is deeply involved in the affairs of the business, having in most cases founded it. Most of the firms which survive as long as the second generation of both the family and the enterprise have come to grips with problems of growth, purpose, personal conflict, succession, and a whole host of family issues ranging from the mundane to the bizarre.

A second characteristic of the firms discussed here is that they are in the process of transition, both in the firm and in the family. Businesses go through life-cycles; so do the families playing the dominant roles in managing these firms. It is this overlap of family life-cycles on top of business life-cycles that provides a central issue in making a successful transition.

A third characteristic of these small businesses is their project-oriented nature. While family businesses are found in every industry, they are particularly important in a number of project oriented industries such as real estate, construction, and various consulting services. Day-to-day activities are centered around individual projects rather than around continuous activities such as manufacturing or retailing. Often, they are firms in easy-entry and easy-exit industries because the time frame of management is short-term and project-oriented.

The project nature of these firms offers some opportunity for smoothing the problems of transition between generations because it provides a way to give the second generation experience and responsibility. However, it also adds another difficulty to the transition – namely, the ease with which project oriented firms can be divided. If transition difficulties become too severe, one solution is to divide the firm up among the family members. Because this represents a reasonable possibility, the transition from the founding generation to the next is more complicated than in nonproject-oriented family business.

Firm and Family Life Cycles

A number of typologies have been used to describe the various stages of a firm's life-cycle.[1] One such typology describes three stages of evolution for a small business: survival-the firm's founding stage in which it struggles to stay alive; success-a period in which the growing company breaks out of resource process; and take-off-a period in which the company evolves toward a big organization. All three of these stages come under Henry Mintzberg's category of a "simple structure."[2] The life-cycle crisis frequently comes at a point when the firm is in the "success" stage. As Churchill and Lewis describe, in the success stage the company may either prepare for growth or may decline as the owner begins to disengage himself.

Paralleling the firm's life-cycle is the life cycle of its owners. In family businesses, the life-cycle of the founding member or founding generation has particular significance because of the need for successful transition of power from the founding generation to the next. This transition is complicated by the very spirit that often makes the firm successful in the first place, the entrepreneurial spirit of its founders.

This entrepreneurial spirit creates particular problems for the passing of power between generations: "For the entrepreneur, the business is essentially an extension of himself, a medium of personal gratification and achievement above all."[3] If the firm is to survive, he must find a way to disengage himself. However, the multifaceted aspects of family relationships-father-son, brother-brother, mother-child-may make the process of disengagement more perilous than it would be for the founder in a non-family business.

The life-cycle crisis often occurs at the time when the second generation has developed enough expertise to assume major responsibility in the general management of the firm but the first generation is not prepared to share that responsibility. While this point may occur during any of the three firm life-cycle stages, it typically occurs during the second stage when the firm has reached a plateau of success. What happens at the crisis point is crucial because it determines whether a successful transition is made to the second generation. If the founding generation cannot relinquish sufficient responsibility, then the second generation may break away from the family business. Of course, the original firm may survive, but not in the form which its founders envisioned, and not in a form which perpetuates the family's fortunes with the firm.

The timing of the second generation's involvement may be crucial to the occurrence or seventy of the type of life-cycle crisis described here. The second generation may acquire the needed experience to run the business at a time when the founding generation is ready to step down or to become more involved in outside activities such as public service. If so, then the life-cycle crisis may not be severe and a relatively smooth transition is apt to occur.

More often, however, timing is not optimal, and many pressures occur which threaten to pull the firm apart. Consider the following case:

> Jim, a developer who has built a number of buildings in his community over the last ten years, is in his late forties. He is one of the leaders in the community and has . an increasing amount of his time to community activities. In so doing, he has slowed his development activities and is spending more time managing his current holdings and less time working on new ventures.

> Jim's son, Junior, entered the business five years ago and has worked in all areas of the firm, from construction to leasing and management. Junior is eager to pursue new, innovative multi use projects, but Jim is reluctant to undertake major new commitments.

Jim's firm is in a life-cycle phase that parallels his own. His energies are being concentrated outside the business, and the business is in a holding pattern. Whether the business enters a success-growth phase instead of a sub cess-decline stage depends on whether Jim is able to turn over responsibility to his son and on whether Jim is willing to let Junior initiate projects and incur risks that Jim no longer would undertake on his own. If Jim does not, then the business may continue in a holding pattern while Junior becomes increasingly frustrated, or Junior may simply give up and go elsewhere.

As the principals in a family business age, their needs and goals change. The first generation tends to become more conservative, but their need for stability and for holding on to what they already have runs directly counter to the needs of the second generation who want their turn to prove themselves. In non-family businesses, this presents less of a problem because the business management tends to revolve around more people, and the transfer of power from one principal to the next does not involve the same sort of conflicts formed by family familiarity.

When Goals Collide

The life-cycle crisis is frequently precipitated when goals of the founding generation and those of the second generation collide. Goal congruency exists when the personal goals of each individual are consistent with the business goals of the firm and when the personal and business goals of each individual are consistent with those of the others. This does not mean that every member of the family must share all the business goals of each family member. What it does require, however, is that a level of understanding and tolerance exist in the organization such that diversity becomes a strength rather than a seedbed for conflict.

In the early stages of a firm's development, goal congruency is rather high, giving the firm a sense of what it wants to accomplish in the future. In fact, goal congruency is seldom a problem at this stage, and any failure of the firm is more probably caused by misjudgment of the entrepreneur rather than by the lack of goal congruency.

Lack of goal congruency comes later in the life of the firm, after the firm has achieved a measure of success. The problem can appear in several forms. The founder's interests may move in directions away from the firm, and what is best for the founder may cease to be what is best for the firm. At this point, many non-family businesses move in the direction of professional management. In family business, as other family members become ready for general management, goal congruency not only becomes a problem between each family member and the firm, but also between the family members themselves. In other words, family members must share the same general goals for the firm. Furthermore, if authority is shared, they must agree in how the firm should best proceed toward those goals.

In the example above, the energy level of the fist generation was declining as Jim spent more time in community activities. As a result, the firm was in a holding pattern, sustaining past levels of activity but generally static in terms of growth. The second generation (or younger brother) enters the firm and develops the competence and expertise to take over the firm's leadership at a time when the fist generation's goals are changing. A crisis occurs when the disparate goals of the two generations create conflicts. The firm can either begin a new phase of growth with the second generation taking leadership, or it can decline as existing projects wind down, or it can dissolve with each generation gong its separate way.

External business pressures such as prosperity or recession may significantly contribute both to the timing of the life-cycle crisis and to its outcome. Recession may force the firm to narrow its scope at a time when the second generation is eager to expand. Despite the reduction in economic prospects, a declining economy may hold the firm together as opportunities outside the firm are reduced. On the other hand, a vibrant economy may bring the life-cycle crisis to a head as the second generation sees opportunities for growth that the fist generation would prefer to pass over.

Symptoms of the Life-Cycle Crisis

The absence of goal congruence frequently shows itself in many small ways, irritating family members and distorting the purpose of the organization. The focus of the family members changes from a strategic perspective to one of managing minutia. When more and more time is being spent making decisions, and when the firm is being pulled in different directions by the family, it is time to stand back and take stock of where the firm is and where it is going. But this is especially difficult to do in family firms where relationships developed over a lifetime make open communication cumbersome.

A number of symptoms of the life-cycle crisis, shown in Figure 1, signal the growth of a situation which could easily become a very serious developmental crisis for the firm.

Figure 1. Symptoms of a Life-Cycle Crisis

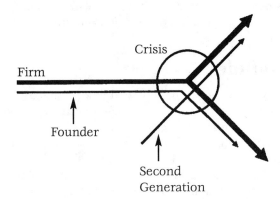

- Increased levels of interpersonal conflict, leading to a belittling of each other's goals.
- Attention to short-term profits rather than long-term goals.
- Ill-defined management procedures emphasizing the short term.
- No defined process for integrating new family members.
- No career plans, offering the younger generation no enticement.
- Failure to tap available financial resources from the external environment.
- Difficulty in valuing diverse contributions of family members to the firm, using conformity to avoid the strengths of diversity.
- Leveling off of growth and/or profits, probably an indicator of a lack of shared long-term goals.

Consider the following case, in which the facts have been changed only slightly, involving the interaction of three brothers.

> Three brothers run a successful apartment construction business. The two eldest, John and Paul, founded the business and have built it up over ten years. The third brother, Richie, is eight years younger than Paul.
>
> Richie has been in the business three years and wants to try building an office building. John and Paul are satisfied with what the firm is doing now. They do not feel that Richie has enough experience to build an of fine building and they are upset with his work habits. Richie likes to party at night and come to work at 9:30 or 10:00, although he tends to work late.

Paul is upset with both John and Richie because he feels that he is doing more work than the others. The eldest brother, John, spends almost one-half of his time as president of the local Apartment Builders Association.

The brothers own equal shares of the business. To equalize their time, Paul suggested some time ago, and the other brothers agreed, that each of them should start keeping a time card. However, Paul is the only one doing so, and he is getting more frustrated and upset every day.

The three brothers are caught up in "fire-fighting" activities of running a business. Each brother is at a different stage of his personal life-cycle, and a lack of goal congruency is causing them to lose sight of strategic issues and to focus instead on daily minutia and the irritating work habits of the others.

Their firm has enjoyed a history of success, but activity has leveled off. Whether they enter a growth stage or a decline stage depends on their ability to deal successfully with the life-cycle crisis. The business is primarily a reflection of the needs of the three brothers. However, their needs are different, and Richie's position as the "baby in the family" makes it difficult for him to achieve equal status with the other brothers. Typically, each brother feels he is carrying an unfair share of the total workload.

This firm is encountering many of the problems shown in Figure 1 which are symptomatic of a life-cycle crisis. The indicators obviously point to the need for change and suggest some type of intervention in the day-to-day activities of the firm. Before the intervention takes place, however, the managers of the firm should have a clear picture of the exact nature of the issues they are facing. These issues, shown in Figure 2 are essentially threefold in scope.

Management Issues. These usually provide the first indicators of the life-cycle crisis. In the early years of the firm, management issues did not pose problems because the entrepreneur founder simply made all the important decisions. With more family members in management, responsibilities and accountabilities are often ill-defined. For example, in the case described above, the three brothers had divided authority along functional lines so that each brother was involved at some point in every project, and all important decisions (and most minor ones) were made collectively. If a project fell behind schedule, the brothers blamed one another for the delay. A first step in the clean-up process may be a careful delineation of responsibility and accountability, one that makes responsibility dear and identifies success or failure with each individual.

This redefinition of responsibility is designed to replace the old system, a personalized authority system of the entrepreneurial stage. When the second generation (or younger brothers) becomes involved, some mechanism is needed to let them be successful on their own. At the same time, some mechanism is needed to reduce the personalized authority of the first generation, characterized by their over-involvement in every project. A more formal project management structure provides the appropriate mechanism to produce the required changes in behavior and responsibility. Yet once the cleanup process begins, it will inevitable lead to the emergence of a second set of issues, that of new family roles.

New Family Roles. Many small businesses have the luxury of dealing with the goal congruency crisis without the complicating aspects of family involvement. Not so here. Family involvement gives a personal quality to the crisis since the family itself must change as the firm enters a new stage of development. This can be especially hard since family roles are conditioned by a lifetime of family interaction. Suddenly, younger brothers or children must be met on equal terms-a transition which may be easier said than done. Perceptions of one another, as well as of one's own capabilities, must often be changed, but it can be difficult for family members to interact on the basis of job performance rather than prior family relationships. Conflict resolution may be necessary as maybe matching each member's aspirations for his or her life-cycle to organizational goals.

Development Stage. This involves the joint evolution of the firm and the family. The resolution of strategic management issues requires that the changing nature of family roles be recognized at the same time. It is virtually an impossible task in most situations of this type to begin a process of extrapolating the firm into the future if the key members of the organization have not begun to grapple with the task of linking changes in the family with changes in the firm.

Assuming that the members of the firm recognize the symptoms of a life-cycle crisis, what can be done to resolve the problems flowing from these issues, and more importantly, what about the resolution of the life-cycle crisis itself?

Resolving the Crisis

The issues point to the need for some type of intervention into the day-to-day activities of the firm. In most cases a third party outside the organization or an outside board member could best manage the processes of confronting the problems at hand and defining a new direction. Businesses get mired down by the conflicts within the family; not often will someone within the firm be objective enough to stand back and examine the problems without bias. Consultants are not always clothed in time-honored virtues in the

Figure 2. Critical Issues of Goal Congruency

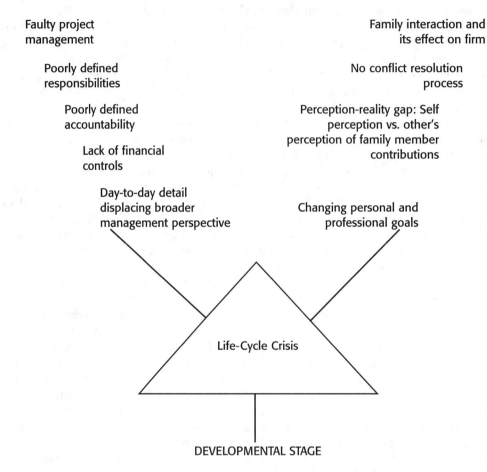

MANAGEMENT ISSUES

Faulty project
management

Poorly defined
responsibilities

Poorly defined
accountability

Lack of financial
controls

Day-to-day detail
displacing broader
management perspective

FAMILY ISSUES

Family interaction and
its effect on firm

No conflict resolution
process

Perception-reality gap: Self
perception vs. other's
perception of family member
contributions

Changing personal and
professional goals

Life-Cycle Crisis

DEVELOPMENTAL STAGE

- Increasing reluctance to be innovative, a classic risk-avoidance posture.
- Failure to exploit the reputation of the firm for developing new business – a withdrawal strategy.
- Increasing difficulty in making consensus decisions, a key indicator showing the lack of goal congruence.

eyes of the small business community, but some form of outside intervention is strongly recommended. What, then, is the role of the outside intervener?

Information may not be as widely shared in a family as some would think. For example, entrepreneurs often keep in their heads most of the information about certain problems and management procedures, and particularly about future personal and professional goals. As the organization begins to expand, this becomes both an untenable and a deeply imbedded source of conflict. Therefore, the primary goal of the intervention and background data cop Section will be to create a public forum in which the key members of the organization can wrestle with issues and solve problems. In the schema defined here, data should be collected in the following ways:

1. In-depth interviews should be conducted with key members of the organization.
2. Organizational-profile instruments can develop perceptions about such things as organization structure, leadership characteristics, or problem-solving styles.
3. Each key member of the organization should list what he or she sees as the problems, challenges, and future directions of the firm.

Once data are collected, the consultant or outside board member must exercise influence in the feedback process. He must be able to demonstrate expertise in three areas of concern to small family business: conflict resolution, response to management problems, and strategic planning. While the latter two functions are traditional management consultant skills, the first function, conflict resolution, may seem to the family members far more important than the development of a business plan.

Conflict resolution begins with the in-depth interviews. If conflicts exist, the consultant can easily draw out the nature or source of the conflict since it will probably be foremost on the minds of the participants. Sometimes conflict may be resolved simply by opening up new lines of communication. However, it may be rooted in misperceptions of one another or of one's own capabilities, or in the problems of goal congruency mentioned earlier. The process resembles that in family counseling, so there is no magic formula guaranteeing success.

Assuming that major conflicts are resolved, the next step is interpreting the data and feeding it back to the participants, in this case according to the scheme suggested in Figure 2. The goal is to engage the key members of the firm in responding to issues raised, and more importantly, in solving the management problems.

The third step involves strategic planning. The consultant must help the organization develop a procedure which allows the wheels of the firm to turn more smoothly. This planning phase requires linking the short-term strengths of the firm to its potential for long-term growth. An action agenda is drawn up and individuals commit their energies to the task of pointing the Organization in new directions. In this stage, new risks will be taken but managed in a different way.

This important activity can be structured by an action agenda, a type of planning process in reverse. The normal procedure followed in planning for change is to go from the general to the specific-that is, to think first about broad goals before reaching any commitment to action. However, in the crisis depicted in this article, a slow movement away from a rather stagnant situation is necessary. As such, a few simple refinements in the management system of the firm are an appropriate first step, allowing the organization to regain a sense of direction and movement. With this in mind, the following steps are recommended:

1. Redefine project management. As we noted, one of the characteristics of these firms is a project-oriented nature. Yet the management structure is often organized along functional rather than project lines to keep the entrepreneur the only one with the "big picture." If several family members function as equals, as in the case cited, there is a tendency toward management by consensus. Functional organization (finance, sales, production, and so forth) gives every family member responsibility while making it harder to divide up the firm. Of course, if the consensus breaks down, so does the management.

As a first step in refining the management system, everyone in the organization should be aware of the various current projects. Second, as a management team, family members should define a set of objectives committing individuals to short-term performance goals. These objectives should be measurable, time bound specific, and realistic. This is not a rigid system of management by objectives, but rather a simple attempt to involve the key decision makers in the process of defining and evaluating performance. Therefore, the third step is to define check points around which evaluation can be assessed Individuals should accept responsibilities for project objectives suited to their abilities, and be evaluated on the basis of accomplishment of those objectives. Such a more formal, yet still flexible, system of managing the day-to-day affairs of the business makes job performance more explicit by giving those responsible for successful projects credit and by pinpointing responsibility for failure.

It should be noted that members of the family may be averse to true project management for two reasons: first, because it does clarify success and failure; and second, because it may simplify breaking up the Arm along project lines if the life-cycle crisis remains unresolved Nevertheless, if a principal source of conflict is the perception of unequal workloads and unequal contributions to the firm, then objective measurement of contribution is an essential step in reducing conflict and improving decision making.

2. Focus the family upon itself in both an affective and rational manner. The emotional aspect of a family business can be an important dimension of its success. The family business may in fact have a built-in advantage little explored in the literature and probably little appreciated by the family members themselves. In short, the conflict resolution process described above is not merely designed for encouraging people to bury the hatchet; rather, it is a critical procedure whereby the family can again focus on the subjective feelings, emotions, and intuitions which bond the family together and form an important organizational rationale for staying together rather than being a divisive force.

Secondly, the focus shifts to the rational aspects of family contributions to the firm. With the data collected around family issues, the firm can deal with the thorny issues of perceived work loads, career goals, and personal goals. It should be no surprise to any family business that these perceptions and goals change over time. In fact, if they don't, then the firm has another indicator of the loss of dynamism and another piece of data suggesting the future may be beyond the evolutionary capabilities of the firm. Therefore, the firm must begin to look beyond the dominant roles played by each family member in the past to developing a more sophisticated notion of diverse career paths and contributions. Indeed, the perception of some family members that others are not contributing as much to the firm's success as they did in the past is a major source of conflict. One can never lose sight of the traditional key functions in the organization, such as project management or sales, but one must also never fail to accept new roles and functions as the organization and the family evolve into different stages of development.

Everyone need not perform the same function, such as project manager, in order to have contributed equal value to the firm. Once again, a diverse approach to contributions and rewards is absolutely critical. The cost/benefit evaluation of activities may suggest that some activities are more important than others. The family needs to rethink how it has valued certain activities in the past. If in the past, projects were virtually found on the doorstep of the organization, in the future the function of bringing new projects into the firm might be elevated to a new importance. This part of the action agenda should aim at a redefinition of both the affective and rational contributions of the family so they can rediscover those bonds which will help them confront the next stage of development. To complete this process, the action agenda must next look at strategic plans for the future.

3. Make strategic plans. The strategic planning process goes beyond the daily routines of the firm and looks at critical issues in the future. Once the firm has "cleaned up" its management procedures so that decisions are again being made, and once the family issues are being addressed, then it is time to look ahead. In doing so, those plotting the future should answer a number of questions.

- What is the current strategy? What are the problems with this current strategy? Is the company having difficulty implementing the current strategy? Is the current strategy no longer valid? Does it lack competitive advantage? Does it fail to exploit the firm's distinctive competencies?
- What are some alternative strategies? Which ones are acceptable? How do present competencies limit alternative strategies? Which alternatives offer the best competitive advantages? Which ones minimize the creation of new problems?
- Which new strategies are most appropriate? What are the long-term implications of these new strategies? What new skills are needed?
- What are the implications of these new strategies on family participation in the business? How will responsibilities be shared with nonmembers who will have a larger role in the firm? What value will be attached to the diverse roles which will be played by various members of the family? How will consultive management procedures be different from the paternalistic ones of the past?

We have tried to add to the literature on small businesses by taking a contextual approach – that is, small businesses are varied, with a rich diversity of problems and potential contributions to our economic well-being. We have discussed the life-cycle crisis unique in one kind of firm-the project-oriented family business.

What makes the life-cycle crisis so important is that it maybe the most critical test to the family business's survival once the early stages of the firm's growth are past. The heart of the crisis is the interrelationship between the personal life-cycles of the family members with respect to one another and to the life-cycle of the firm.

While the life-cycle crisis may range widely in terms of its severity, we believe that it is a crisis that is faced sooner or later by virtually all family businesses. By recognizing that it is a common malady, with common symptoms and cures, we hope that more family businesses may pass successfully through the crisis and into a new success-growth stage.

References

1. Neil C. Churchill and Virginia Lewis, "A Typology of Small Businesses: Hypothesis and Preliminary Study," Southern Methodist University, *Working Paper* 82-103,1982. See also Larry E. Greiner, "Evolution and Revolution as Organizations Grow," *Harvard Business Review*, July-August 1972: pp. 37-46.

2. Henry Mintzberg, "Organization Design: Fashion of Fit?" *Harvard Business Review*, January-February 1981: pp. 103-116. Mintzberg's other categories – machine bureaucracy, professional bureaucracy, divisionalized form, and adhocracy – all describe larger firms with some form of post-entrepreneurial structure.

3. Harry Levinson, "Conflicts That Plague Family Businesses," *Harvard Business Review*, March-April 1971: pp. 90-98.

Conflict resolution is a special area of concern to those who work in or with family businesses. Conversely, family business issues offer special challenges to both the professional mediator who seeks to resolve and the social scientist who seeks to understand chronic, destructive, or crippling disputes.

Penetrating the Cycle of Sustained Conflict

By Kenneth Kaye

Analysis of a family's chronic cycle of escalating and retreating from conflicts is a powerful tool for breaking the cycle, resolving conflicts, and improving relationships.

The purpose of this article is to suggest how family business consultants can apply a conflict-resolution model that is derived from theories of family and family-like systems. Although the sustained conflict cycle, or "problem maintenance system" (Pinsof, 1983) is the theoretical basis of some techniques used by family therapists, the two specific techniques explained here can be applied by any consultant or by family business members themselves. Toward the end of this article, criteria are suggested for when and how mental health professionals should be involved in consultations with families in conflict.

Orientation

The simplest models of conflict resolution assume that people really are fighting about what they say they are fighting about. This may often be true of disputes between strangers who happen to transgress one another's rights or threaten one another's interests, but it is rarely the case between spouses or among relatives or longtime business partners. Furthermore, many approaches to conflict assume that people normally behave rationally: if they behave irrationally, it must be because they do not have adequate information or do not communicate clearly with one another. This article does not make that assumption. Finally, while most models assume that people want to resolve their problems, human beings are actually more interesting than that. Sometimes we only want excuses not to resolve our real problems.

This article makes three claims. Its first proposition is that conflicts *within* organized groups of related or mutually dependent people are fundamentally different from conflicts between separate parties. Although kinship or marriage relationships do add extra dimensions to within-group conflicts, the fundamental distinction is between all types of conflict within groups (including, for example, incidents among co-workers) and conflicts between disputants who lack any long-term relationship (as in a product liability suit). Unfortunately, most models of conflict resolution view disputes as arising between clearly separate parties or at interfaces between nonoverlapping groups. Therefore, these models are usually inadequate for understanding or helping to resolve conflicts among the members of a closely held firm.

This article's second proposition is that within-group (or within-system) conflicts follow a dynamic pattern. Some features of that pattern are generic; for example, it is usually circular. Nevertheless, each family or family-like group of people creates and sustains conflicts that have their own characteristic sequences, repeated time after time. Analysis of a group's chronic pattern is a vital and powerful tool for resolving its conflicts and improving members' interaction.

The third proposition advanced here is that such conflicts are not merely defensive on the part of each individual against the others. They are also collusively defensive in that the members collaborate-often instinctively and unconsciously-to protect their whole system from something that threatens them even more than conflict with one another does. It often requires an outsider to discern their unspoken, hidden, barely hinted at apprehensions. Enabling the participants to discuss their real fears is the key to resolving their conflicts because, in most cases, they have been using conflict to forestall coming to terms with those undiscussed issues.

Definitions

We use the word *system* (short for *social system*) for any group of people with some shared history or knowledge of one another's actions and some shared intentions: people trying to get somewhere together. Thus every family, every business, and every group of two or more co-workers is a system. Human systems are characterized by communication, by rules (norms), and by being *open* (which means that they adapt to changing conditions, including other surrounding and intersecting systems).

Human systems do not often operate the way well-oiled machines do. Conflict is a normal, healthy aspect of all systems. One can easily distinguish, however, between conflict that drives a system toward its objectives, toward constant reevaluation and new objectives, and conflict that mires the system down. This article uses the word *conflict* in the latter sense. When we speak about resolving conflict, we mean getting the truck out of the ditch and onto the road, not shutting off the engine.

Related-Party (or Within-System) Conflict

Negotiation and mediation specialists look for win/win solutions. Some of the techniques used to facilitate win/win solutions apply to related-party and separate-party disputes alike. For example, probably all mediators spend time clarifying the messages exchanged between parties. Another thing we do is to block people from reacting to their own assumptions. We force them to check those assumptions with one another: "I hear you saying _____." "Is this what you intended to say?" "Is that how you think George would react?" A third tactic, used regardless of whether the parties are related, involves separating the points on which they essentially agree from those that require negotiation. Another is to emphasize the costs of prolonging the dispute, as against the benefits of settlement (Simmel, 1950; Deutsch, 1973; Blake and Mouton, 1984).

Notwithstanding their similarities to other kinds of conflicts, within group disputes (of which family business disputes are quintessential examples) have some special features that call for special handling. The most important distinguishing feature is that the parties to the dispute cannot walk away from it easily. Separate organizations, or individuals with little relationship to one another, have the option of settling a dispute financially and ending their relationship. That is not a satisfactory solution for parties who must continue to work together or who are related to one another by kinship or marriage. Another feature of conflict within groups is that the parties usually share some long-term goals, which override their separate interests and even override their common material interests. One of those goals may be to strengthen their relationship (Miller and Rice, 1970; Lewin, 1948; Weber, 1947). Moreover, the parties typically hold simultaneous memberships and play roles in several intersecting systems, not just the one in which the lines are drawn for a dispute. This may be true in all kinds of disputes (Coser, 1956), but the likelihood of an individual's identifying with two or more factions is much greater in within-group disputes.

Because family business conflicts have these special features, no matter which members are involved (parent and child, sibling, spouse, in-law, members in the business, members out of the business) and no matter what kinds of issues are at stake (inheritance, management, growth, power, role definitions), family conflicts are never linear problems, with a cause leading directly to an effect, and they are never traceable to one party's behavior. They always turn out to be what we call *circular* or *systemic*. This simply means that the members react to one another's problematic behavior (irresponsibility, aggression, refusal to delegate, withdrawal) in such a way as to maintain, prolong, or exacerbate the very things they are upset about. To make this point clear, let us back up to a simpler model of conflict and see its limitations.

Rational Communications Model

A conflict-resolution model that fits many situations where the parties have no personal relationship with one another (other than their current conflict of interests) is represented in Figure 1 by two balloons with both fluid and solid content. The two parties interact only in the sense that they negotiate joint passage, without giving up what is important to them and without forming a permanent relationship. An example might be a dispute between two ranchers over water rights. The parties' core needs are compatible; they can accommodate one another once they become willing to be flexible about less important matters. With good negotiation skills or the help of a good mediator, they may

Figure 1. Rational Communications Model of Conflict Resolution

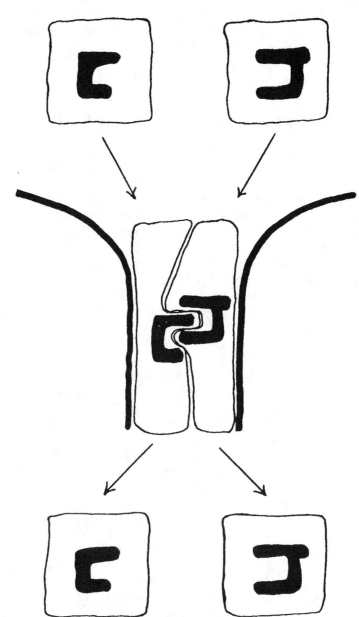

Find a win/win solution by improving the parties' communication, so that they can work together to clarify their points of agreement and negotiate compromises where their interests collide.

discover that where they had thought there was only room for one of them to succeed, both can do so. This model is based on two assumptions:

ASSUMPTION RC-1. It is primarily inadequate communications that make parties' interests appear incompatible and also make each party react defensively, emotionally, and irrationally. This situation tempts them toward rights- or power-based (win/lose) resolution.

ASSUMPTION RC-2. Rational people revise their behavior when they see better ways to achieve their objectives.

These assumptions lead to a fairly well established approach to resolving conflicts: get both sides to state their priorities clearly, improve their communication so that they can work together to clarify their points of agreement, and negotiate their points of disagreement by means of compromise, trade-offs, and compensations.

Two examples of this approach are Blake and Mouton's (1984) "interface conflict-solving model" and Fisher and Ury's (1981) "reconciling interests" approach. Both seek win/win solutions, as opposed to the win/lose outcomes typical of appeals to rights or the lose/lose outcomes of power-based resolution (for example, warfare). The effort to reconcile mutual interests through rational, constructive communication is often successful, but this model applies only when the parties' ostensibly endorsed interests are more potent than their hidden reasons for maintaining their problem. What can be done about the unarticulated, the unconscious, the unacknowledged?

Rational Interactions Model

A more realistic model of conflict between parties who have any kind of relationship with one another – even a brief one – is shown in Figure 2. Instead of picturing two or more parties with independent intentions that may or may not be compatible, this model acknowledges that people trigger one another's behavior and interact as a system. In fact, their perceptions, beliefs, and attitudes interact, and each of these is affected by the other person's behavior and, in turn, shapes the perceiver's own subsequent actions (Bateson, 1972; Coser, 1956; Deutsch, 1973). A responds to his or her perception of B's intentions in a fashion that elicits a response from B that is very likely to confirm A's perception. B's behavior is partly an outgrowth of B's perception of A's intentions. Each party's defensive or preemptive maneuvers are perceived as offensive by the other. Thus each participates circularly in maintaining and escalating the conflict while blaming the other. As Figure 2 indicates, the fact that A and B comprise an interacting system creates the risk of their

---

Figure 2. Rational Interactions Model of Conflict Resolution

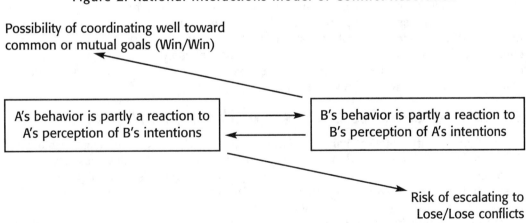

In addition to improving communications, point out to each side how it is contributing to the problem. By clarifying their own and one another's intentions, the parties reduce the risk of escalation and learn to coordinate their behavior more adaptively.

escalating to a lose/lose conflict. (The twenty-five-year arms race between the United States and the Soviet Union was a classic example of such risk; other illustrations can be found in such places as Northern Ireland and the Persian Gulf.)

The sensitivity of A and B to one another's behavior also has a promising aspect, however. It implies the possibility of change, so that they can learn to coordinate their efforts toward common or mutual goals (win/ win). Unfortunately, in the absence of a mediator, both parties are usually afraid to lower their defenses.

What assumptions does this model make?

ASSUMPTION RI-1. Rational people revise their behavior when they realize it is counterproductive (same as RC-2).

ASSUMPTION RI-2. Insights about their interaction system help the parties communicate more constructively in the future. In fact, conflicts are not resolved in any lasting way unless the system of interaction changes.

When Blake and Mouton (1984) focus their clients on improving mutual understanding so as to avoid similar disputes in the future, and when Ury, Brett, and Goldberg (1988) help their clients design systems to cut the time and other costs of inevitable conflicts, they move beyond reconciling clients' interests in specific disputes. They are leading their clients' systems to change.

To the standard "clarify and compromise" approach, the rational interactions model adds some techniques that are widely used in family therapy. In addition to improving communication, the mediator points out to each side how it has been contributing to the problem. By checking their perceptions of one another's intentions, taking responsibility for clarifying their own intentions, and learning to trust one another, the parties work their way free of an "arms race" type of escalating loop. A therapist or other professional consultant tries to build up the system's own capacity to coordinate adaptively and resolve future conflict earlier, with less turmoil.

This model is much more sensitive than the rational communications model to the fact that conflicts arise through interaction. Thus, when applied to families, work groups, or any other organization, the rational interactions model holds that for conflict to be resolved, the system of interaction must change.

Nevertheless, this model is superficial. It offers little guidance on the specific aspects of the system's interaction that a change agent ought to focus on. In fact, the model has two weaknesses. The first weakness is that it does not explain why conflicts sometimes escalate and sometimes de-escalate spontaneously. What determines the direction of a particular conflict, in the absence of intervention? (See Figure 2.) In the same way that an understanding of the human circulatory system's disease processes and health-restoring processes gives medical scientists clues to the design of treatments, an understanding of social systems' natural processes of breakdown and restoration would provide crucial clues for the design of interpersonal interventions. (A few researchers actually are studying interaction processes in business negotiations; see Putnam, 1985.) The second weakness is that this model does not necessarily probe beneath the surface of the disputants' conscious, expressed motives. A better model expands this one, at the price of greater complexity but with the benefit of more power to explain and change conflictual behavior when it arises within a set of relationships.

Sustained Conflict Cycle (Equilibration) Model

All family conflicts follow habitual patterns. To know a family's unique pattern of conflict is to know its members so intimately as to be able to predict their crises. This is possible because conflict is not something that happens to them; it is something they suffer to sustain because it serves some function in their system. One of our first tasks is to figure out, in each case, what that function may be.

A way of analyzing conflict in any system and then changing the system could be called the *sustained conflict model.* Unlike the notion of a family system (a useful metaphor, but not an explanatory theory; see Kaye, 1985), this model yields testable hypotheses about conflict in family systems, as well as practical procedures. It is founded on three assumptions:

Figure 3. Sustained Conflict Cycle

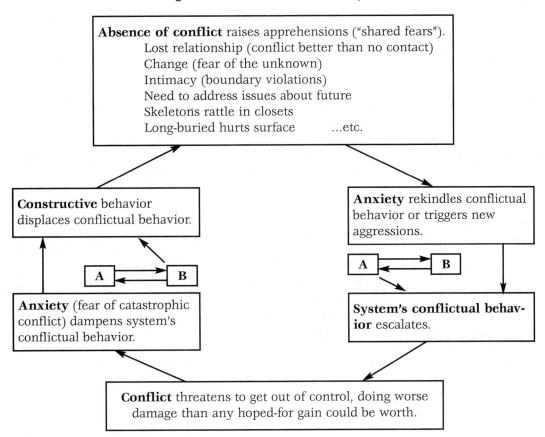

Absence of conflict raises apprehensions ("shared fears").
Lost relationship (conflict better than no contact)
Change (fear of the unknown)
Intimacy (boundary violations)
Need to address issues about future
Skeletons rattle in closets
Long-buried hurts surface   ...etc.

Constructive behavior displaces conflictual behavior.

A → B

Anxiety (fear of catastrophic conflict) dampens system's conflictual behavior.

Anxiety rekindles conflictual behavior or triggers new aggressions.

A → B

System's conflictual behavior escalates.

Conflict threatens to get out of control, doing worse damage than any hoped-for gain could be worth.

A's and B's interaction system undergoes a natural cycle between too much and too little conflict.

ASSUMPTION SC-1. Individual members collaborate to sustain the conflict, at a comfortable equilibrium between too much conflict and too little.

ASSUMPTION SC-2. When a conflict grows too intense, it raises members' anxiety about the destructive effects, and this anxiety motivates them to cool down.

ASSUMPTION SC-3. The strange-sounding idea of too little conflict is explained by shared fear: as conflict cools, its absence is alarming because it raises members' anxieties about deeper, more catastrophic possibilities. ("I don't like it," says the Hollywood cowboy, cop, or soldier, "it's too quiet.") Those anxieties trigger defensive mutual offenses, which, if they do nothing else, serve to distract the whole system from whatever significant challenge or tough issue or painful acknowledgment it really ought to be addressing.

This conflict-resolution model incorporates the rational communications and rational interactions models already described, but it adds the concept of *equilibration*. At the center of this model are the major combatants (see Figure 3). A's and B's interaction system undergoes a natural cycle, between too much and too little conflict.

The downward arrows on the right side of this cycle correspond to the one toward the lower right of Figure 2, escalating the conflict to the brink of Armageddon. The upward arrows on the left side of the cycle show the members, of their own accord, defusing their conflict. That portion of Figure 3 corresponds to the upper left of Figure 2: the possibility of coordinating better. In other words, the sustained conflict cycle model hypothesizes that both escalation and de-escalation occur naturally – in each case, just until the level of conflict deviates too much from those levels of sustained conflict at which the system is used to functioning (Bateson, 1972). The key task for a consultant, therefore, is to support the intrinsic processes that are constructive (those on the left side of Figure 3) and then disabuse the members of whatever expectations have led them in the past to elect to renew their conflicts. That task is what leads us to probe their shared fear. This article postulates, as a testable hypothesis, that when people who should have common cause appear to be mired irrationally in win/lose or even lose/lose conflicts, they are often acting in concert to avoid another outcome, perhaps only dimly or even unconsciously imagined, that scares them more than the apparent costs of their fighting.

How can the absence of conflict raise apprehensions? What might those awesome apprehensions (shared fears) be? Some possibilities are listed in the top box of Figure 3. One is loss of family contact: isolation, loneliness, death. Another may be simply the fear of change, of the unknown. Family members may fear (probably correctly) that, in order to address issues about the future, it will be necessary to broach some subjects that they traditionally have treated as taboo, or perhaps they fear that candor may engender intimacy and violate walls that they built long ago around certain emotions. Sometimes skeletons rattle in closets, or long buried hurts may reemerge. The sustained conflict model suggests that some such apprehensions lie at the root of group members' having maintained their conflict over a long period. This is a special application of Pinsof's (1983) "problem maintenance cycle" (a model that applies to a variety of family problems, including, for example, sexual dysfunction in marriage or children's failure in school).

Why would family members behave so irrationally as to sustain their conflict indefinitely? The answer is their shared, almost conscious concern that if the problematic behavior were to stop, a worse catastrophe of some sort might ensue: Dad would have a heart attack, or the sisters would never speak to one another again, or the business would not stay in the family. An effective way to resolve these conflicts involves tracing the problematic cycle of family interaction and elucidating the shared anxieties that underlie it, and then enabling family members to put their apprehensions on the table, where they can be examined and weighed realistically, usually for the first time.

The major combatants are also surrounded by other family members, managers, and shareholders, who all contribute negative and positive feedback (see Figure 4). Charting a conflict, as in Figure 4, can provide outside consultants or even executives themselves with the keys to unlock the cycle and create opportunities for more constructive interactions.

These two major concepts-the sustained conflict cycle, and the idea of shared fear-lead to the following method of conflict resolution:

1. Form an alliance with the system, validating (or "normalizing") its members' fears and resistance to change. For example, a consultant says, "You're quite right to be concerned about that. It's a risk to be guarded against."
2. Call attention to the positive behavior already present (indicated by arrows in the left half of Figure 4). This action reinforces the system members' confidence in their ability to replace conflict with constructive communication.
3. Encourage reality testing and cost-benefit analysis regarding shared fears, correct or incorrect perceptions, and maladaptive behavior (indicated by arrows on the right side of Figure 4).

How does one do that? One does not make a frontal assault ("Why do you behave that way?" "What are you afraid of?"); rather, one poses a tactful surrogate question ("What would happen if..."): "What do you think might happen if George reported directly to Sally?" "What might your father's reaction be if you were to tell him that's the way you feel?" "What if we were to put that topic on the table for discussion?" "What would you guess we might be talking about today if you *hadn't* got into that 'big to-do over nothing'?"

Asking for a concrete (although speculative) prediction is invariably more effective than requesting an interpretive analysis of whatever block stands in the way of members' adopting the consultant's suggestions. The individual's prediction turns out to be the very "catastrophic expectation" (Pinsof, 1983) that, untested, has led him or her to persevere in problematic behavior or to avoid a constructive solution.

Furthermore, it is often a shared catastrophic expectation, coinciding at least partially with other system members' apprehensions. Thus the consultant must use "what if" questions with one individual after another, comparing expectations and encouraging mem-

Figure 4. Sustained Conflict Cycle

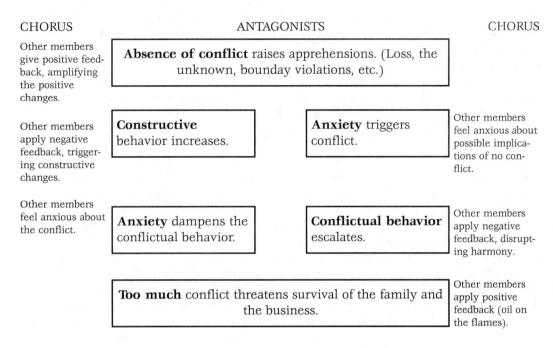

| CHORUS | ANTAGONISTS | CHORUS |

Absence of conflict raises apprehensions. (Loss, the unknown, bounday violations, etc.)

Other members give positive feedback, amplifying the positive changes.

Other members apply negative feedback, triggering constructive changes.

Other members feel anxious about the conflict.

Constructive behavior increases.

Anxiety triggers conflict.

Other members feel anxious about possible implications of no conflict.

Anxiety dampens the conflictual behavior.

Conflictual behavior escalates.

Other members apply negative feedback, disrupting harmony.

Too much conflict threatens survival of the family and the business.

Other members apply positive feedback (oil on the flames).

Includes the contributions of other family members, who alternately incite or dampen the principal antagonists' conflictual behavior.

bers to check their assumptions about one another's expectations: "What do you think might happen if George reported directly to Sally?" (Answer: "She would...") "Have you ever discussed that possibility with George or Sally?" ("No.") "What do you think they'd say?" Note that this can be done recursively – "what if" in response to the answer to a "what if," in response to the answer to a "what if," almost ad infinitum. As a result, system members not only see new options for constructive action but also begin to incorporate this way of questioning themselves in their routine discourse.

Table 1 summarizes those features of within-group or "family" conflicts that have implications for resolution facilitators. Some of the indicated intervention techniques fall properly within the professional field of family therapy; others, however, are useful, safe, and often indispensable techniques for any consultant or problem-solving leader. The two cases that will be discussed in the remainder of this article benefited from the tracing of sustained conflict cycles and the elucidation of shared fear. In the first case, it was important that the present author is a licensed psychologist and family therapist. In the second case, that was not important.

Application by Family Therapists

A mental health professional, as distinct from a legal, managerial, or financial professional, emphasizes emotion, the unconscious, personal history, and biological considerations whenever they are relevant. He or she sensitively pursues intimate, perhaps traumatic, aspects of a family's past, if those experiences bear on its members' assessment of present and future reality. Yet the approach discussed here is problem-centered, which means that we solve the problem, if possible, in the here-and-now, and in specific steps that our clients can take in the future. In that respect, we are like other consultants, but we are also prepared to move back to the past and down into the intrapsychic level of experience, as far as necessary. Clarification of shared fear is one of the tools with which we can move to those deeper levels. I shall now illustrate the analysis of a sustained conflict cycle in a family business with which I was involved primarily as a therapist. (All clients' names throughout this article are pseudonyms.)

Ted Spyros, after losing his pancreas to cancer, had been told that he would probably die within six months. Ted was still alive a year later, but his hours at his wholesale food business were restricted by frequent pain from gastrointestinal complications that he was not healthy enough for surgery to correct. Ted and his wife, Grace, were a strong, loving couple with unshaken religious faith. They had two reasons for seeking my help. One was their twin sons' arguing with one another and with Ted. The aggravation that this arguing caused not only reduced Ted's ability to manage his physical pain but also made Ted doubt his sons' ability to manage the business. The couple's other reason for seeking help, which emerged after several sessions, was concern about the future of all four children after Ted's death.

This was a close family, in the worst sense (see Figure 5). Family members fought with one another every time they met – especially the twins, John and Jimmy, thirty-one, who worked together. All four children, unmarried, were in touch with their mother every day and with their father several times each week. The elder daughter, Peggy, thirty-three, was a schoolteacher, extensively involved with her students' extracurricular activities (chaperoning trips to Europe, directing musicals); her schedule permitted no time for dating. By the norms of her Greek-American heritage, she should already have been married ten years before. The younger daughter, Tammy, twenty-nine, had once been a beauty but was now obese, depressed, and unemployed. She and Jimmy still lived in their parents' home. The parents worried about the younger daughter's apparent destiny as a spinster even more than they did about her older sister's (Peggy, at least, enjoyed some professional success). Ted and Grace worried that their daughters would never marry and that their sons would never get along. They feared that the impact of Ted's illness was cementing those dire fates.

John's and Jimmy's fighting was a sustained conflict. To all appearances, the twin brothers were enemies, yet they never really did anything to hurt one another except to disagree and argue, as Ted described it, "until who yells loudest." Ted himself was an arguer from way back. In one of our meetings, Peggy complained, "You do it, too, Dad. Before you got sick, you'd argue with them until you were blue in the face."

"Well," Ted said, "maybe I would at one time, but I don't have the stamina for it now. I just get angry and walk away."

The men's arguments followed a clear cycle (see Figure 6). Whenever Ted had had a bad night and did not come to the office in the morning, one of the two brothers would criticize the other, and a volatile argument would ensue. Ted would be drawn into the argument, either by telephone or later, when he came to work. He sometimes took sides in the brothers' dispute but more often staked out his own position, always emphasizing his views by yelling at the son or sons with whom he disagreed. If the argument lasted into the evening or the weekend, one or both sisters was sure to get into the act, telling the brothers to stop acting like babies. This action would provoke louder shouting. Eventually, Ted would go into a coughing fit, one or all of the women would chastise the brothers for "goading" him, and the argument would be dropped-unresolved.

Figure 5. Structure of the Spyros Family

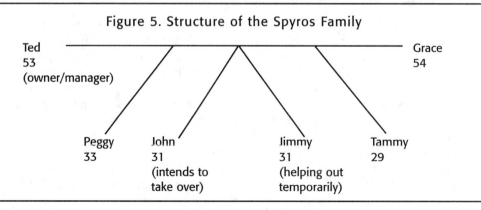

Figure 6. Sustained Conflict Cycle in the Spyros Family

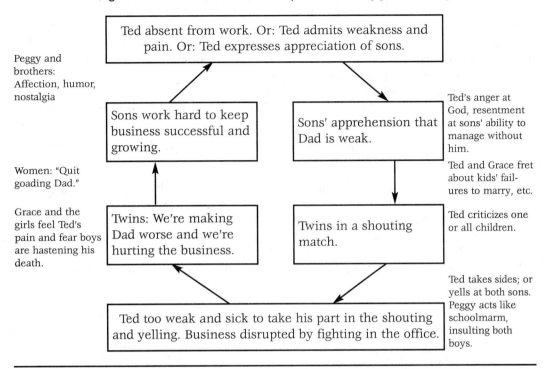

Peggy and brothers: Affection, humor, nostalgia

Ted absent from work. Or: Ted admits weakness and pain. Or: Ted expresses appreciation of sons.

Sons work hard to keep business successful and growing.

Sons' apprehension that Dad is weak.

Ted's anger at God, resentment at sons' ability to manage without him.

Ted and Grace fret about kids' failures to marry, etc.

Women: "Quit goading Dad."

Grace and the girls feel Ted's pain and fear boys are hastening his death.

Twins: We're making Dad worse and we're hurting the business.

Twins in a shouting match.

Ted criticizes one or all children.

Ted too weak and sick to take his part in the shouting and yelling. Business disrupted by fighting in the office.

Ted takes sides; or yells at both sons. Peggy acts like schoolmarm, insulting both boys.

A comparison of Figure 6 with Figure 4 shows how simple it is to apply the present method to a particular conflict. As in a crossword puzzle, one starts by filling in the obvious or easiest cells: perhaps what the conflict is like at its worst point, or how it seems to start. The intermediate steps in the cycle soon come to light: What does this lead to? What usually provokes that?

Diagraming the Spyros brothers' conflict cycle (Figure 6) made several things clear, first to me and then to the family members. First, whenever Ted's physical condition became obvious, the whole family collaborated to draw him into an argument. He then reacted as the tough, vigorous dad they had known all their lives. For a short time, they could deny the inevitable. Then, after the fight had escalated too far for Ted to win by out-yelling his sons, his wife and his daughters would attack the twins, who would leave each other alone for a while. Soon, however, the very fact that their father was too sick to function as his old self must have stirred sadness and panic in John and Jimmy, and the cycle repeated itself.

Also shown in Figure 6 is another observation: in my meetings with the family, whenever Ted alluded to his illness, and especially when he expressed love, gratitude, or praise for his sons' hard work in the business, his sons attacked him. In one session, for example, Ted told me, "These guys have done a heckuva job coming in under the circumstances."

Jimmy said, "How come you never tell us that?"

"I've told you that," Ted protested.

"No, you haven't," Jimmy said. "I don't recall you ever saying that."

"That's not the point, Dad," John interjected.

Ted ignored John and replied to Jimmy in a calm, sincerely caring voice that apparently clashed with the sons' and daughters' memories of the tough guy he used to be.

"Well, if I didn't say it so you heard it, I apologize. I especially appreciate what you've done, Jimmy, because you only came to work because of the situation that exists. I know you wouldn't be there if I were pulling my weight, and I appreciate that."

"We've totally gone off the point," said John, while Jimmy muttered in imitation of their father, criticizing and bossing everyone around in a gruff voice exactly opposite to the voice that had offered the warm, sincere praise I had just heard. Jimmy's mocking performance was accompanied by menacing body language, which seemed quite unlikely to have been produced recently by the frail, prematurely aged father slumped on the couch in front of me.

Another thing apparent in Figure 6, by its omission, is that uttering the words *cancer* and *death* seemed almost taboo as far as the younger generation was concerned. Ted and Grace used those words when they met with me privately. In our meetings with their children, however, they referred only to "the situation" and "the circumstances." The adult children knew the truth-that Ted had no expectation of living until Christmas but all their references to his health were of the "How are you feeling today?" variety. In fact, they goaded him not to be so gloomy about his pain. At one point, the following remarkable exchange took place:

JIMMY: All right, you had a bad night, you were up a lot last night, so you didn't feel well, and you didn't come in this morning. You'll be better tomorrow.
TED: How do you know?
JOHN: How do you not know?
GRACE: When Dad isn't feeling well, I don't think he should be goaded.
JOHN: Ma, I don't think I'm goading anyone. I'm trying to run a business. [John changed the subject.]

The family acted as if our meetings were about anything but death, yet that was precisely what they were about: the sons were fighting to drive away the Angel of Death.

Having formed a mental picture something like Figure 6, I began to explore what might happen if the family members were to acknowledge their grief and discuss the problems that lay ahead. I interrupted one of their shouting matches and asked everyone around the room what he or she was feeling. Ted felt "angry." All three women felt "aggravated." Jimmy felt "accused," and John felt "happy-because all these arguments and our personalities are finally getting dealt with." I then said I was feeling sad about Ted's prognosis and surprised that none of them was aware of feeling that.

"I wonder," I said, "whether maybe it's easier to argue over day-to-day irritations than to think about the future." A textbook line: we therapists do not try to be original, just effective. And this was. The family members indicated, by their expressions more than by their words, that they were ready to be led gently to the point.

I asked, "What might your family be like a year from now, or whenever, if Dad's not around?"

Peggy said, "I'm afraid we'll fall apart as a family."

She thought that if her two brothers were not forced to work together, both would distance themselves from the family. Furthermore, she thought that none of the four adult children had enough in common with the others to sustain a relationship, were it not for the parents' role as a central exchange. Thus it was not Ted's death alone but also the confrontation it forced with aging and the loss of the parents' generation (and, in fact, the young people's own acceptance of adulthood) that, for Peggy, was the real underlying issue. This feeling was shared, to varying degrees, by other family members .(John voiced a different version of the fear: "Ma will fall apart.")

Putting those fears on the table gave family members the opportunity to confirm or disconfirm them. In fact, the children's fears that their mother would break down and their family would fall apart were unrealistic. Grace was a pragmatic, capable person. An office manager for a large checkclearing firm, she managed seventy-five employees, about five times the number who worked for her husband and her sons. It reassured her children immensely to hear her say that her life was not over at fifty-four.

After Ted's death, John and Jimmy did not become close friends or effective business partners, but they did break out of their habitual cycle, and they began to talk about more serious matters. Jimmy pursued his own career, while continuing to live with Grace and Tammy, and John arranged to purchase the business from Grace, at an appraised price, over a period of years.

Application by Other Consultants

One need not be a therapist, or even an industrial or organizational psychologist, to analyze a sustained conflict cycle or to use "what if" questions. In some cases, I would argue, the work I do could just as well be done by a financial or a legal consultant who took a few minutes to analyze the sustained conflict cycle. In the case just discussed, I showed the family members their cycle (Figure 6) as an entree into discussing their grief and the younger generation's fears. Everything I did up to that point, including charting and the "what if" questions, would have been equally appropriate for any consultant to do. The transition to the work on emotional relationships could have been handled through a referral to a family therapist. This is an important point because nontherapist consultants do encounter cases where these two techniques are sufficient to get on with the job, and where a family therapist is either not needed or not what family members want. It would be a mistake to hesitate in using these techniques for fear of where they could lead. The place to draw the line between the work of a business consultant and that of a therapist is after the analysis of a cycle of sustained conflict.

Flanagan & Sons, an electrical contracting firm, worked primarily on new and rehabilitated office buildings, hotels, and factories. Tom Flanagan had founded the company twelve years earlier, at forty-nine. Before that, Tom had been in the field for thirty years. His last job, before he started his own business, had been as a project supervisor for a much larger contractor. His first employee had been his twenty-one-year-old son Bill, already an experienced electrician with a union card. The company's annual revenues had grown steadily, to about $2 million.

At the time they engaged me as a consultant, Flanagan & Sons' principal employees and noninvolved family members were as shown in Figure 7. Bill, now thirty-three, had left the firm more than a year earlier. Mickey, the principal nonfamily member, had worked for Tom nearly ten years. Sons Tom Jr. and Patrick had both joined the firm about four years before. Daughter Kathy, an attorney with a large law firm, did much of the family business's legal work.

A succession plan for Flanagan & Sons was already in place, and it was the principal underlying problem. Mickey, Tom Jr., and Patrick had signed contracts with Tom Flanagan to buy 74 percent of his stock, in equal shares, over a three-year period. Because there were no other stockholders, Tom would retain 26 percent ownership, and each of the younger men would eventually own a little less than 25 percent. (Originally, their shares had been smaller because Bill had been part of the plan.) To enable Mickey, Tom Jr., and Patrick to buy Tom's stock, the company was paying them $75,000 each in annual bonuses for those three years.

Figure 7. Structure of the Flanagan Family

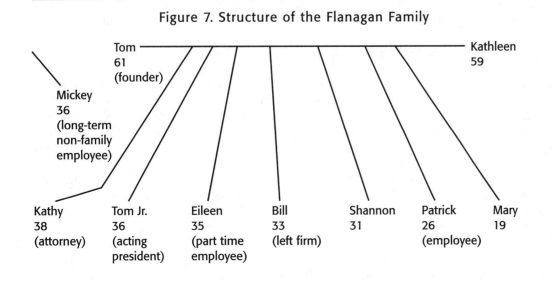

Figure 8. Sustained Conflict Cycle in the Flanagan Family

Tom Jr. is allowed to take on responsibility. He begins to represent the next generation of ownership.

Wives, sisters, daughters are pleased by the men's reconciliation.

Tom Jr. comes back, with a good attitude.

Tom Jr.: Patrick is getting equal rewards for much less work.
Patrick: Why should I take orders from my brother?
Unarticulated: Was Bill right? Our "succession plan" is a bad deal?

Dad: I can't trust Tom Jr. (Unarticulated: He's too much like me.) I must be fair to Patrick; and Mickey has always been loyal.

Wives, sisters, daughters urge restraint.

Tom Jr.: If I don't back to work right away, Dad will fire me.
Patrick: With Dad back in town, the future is uncertain. And he expects me to work harder.

Wives: Look out for our financial interest!

Kathleen (mother) and **Susan** (Tom Jr.'s wife) worry about husbands' hotheadedness and mutual hurt.

Patrick and Tom Jr. fight.

Dad asks Patrick or Mickey whether Tom Jr. is doing all he should be doing.

Tom Jr. and Dad yell at each other.
Tom Jr. accuses Patrick of using marijuana;
Tom Jr. is demoted and/or quits.

Dad returns to office.

Bill had quit in anger over this take-it-or-leave-it succession plan. He did not like the inclusion of Mickey as an equal partner with the three brothers; in any case, he felt the plan was unsound. Their father viewed it as a gift, "buying himself out" of the business, but Bill saw it as Tom's bleeding the business dry and only then turning over what was left.

Tom Jr. had a different complaint. Ten months into the plan, his father had moved to Florida and left the business in his charge, only to return three months later in an emergency. That emergency-a fistfight in the office-had been created deliberately by Patrick (in Tom Jr.'s view). Tom Jr., the eldest son, was ten years older than Patrick but had no more seniority in the company. For several years after his dishonorable discharge from the Army, for drug use, Tom Jr. had not communicated with anyone in the family. Eventually, he went through a successful recovery program, married a woman with three children, and fathered three more. He and his wife were ardent participants in Alcoholics Anonymous and Al-Anon.

The incident that triggered Tom's return from Florida was repeated several months later in another incident between the two brothers. This was the one that led the Flanagans to seek a consultant. In both cases, Patrick and Tom Jr. had come to blows, but both incidents fit a pattern that had occurred frequently, with less physical violence (see Figure 8): whenever Tom Jr. took on significant administrative responsibility-"stopped working with the tools," as they put it-Patrick resented his brother's assumption of authority. Tom Jr. criticized Patrick for leaving "early"-at 4:30 P.M., when the other wage-earning employees went home. Patrick took offense (or Tom Jr. took offense at his younger brother's reply), and verbal jabs, if not punches, were thrown back and forth until Tom Jr., who had inherited his father's temper, would do something hotheaded that Mickey or Patrick could report to the father.

The next step was that Tom would demote his son back to "working with the tools." Tom Jr. would then have to prove himself reliable all over again, and another target date would be set for the father's departure to Florida. Twice in the past year, Tom Jr. had quit for a week or two before coming back, at his mother's and his wife's urging, to accept his demotion.

When I first met with him, and then with his father, Tom Jr. had left abruptly once again. This time, however, his dissatisfaction with the terms of the buyout contract he had signed was complicating the situation. He had read it carefully and realized for the first time that if he quit, the stock he had "purchased" from his father to date would simply remain in limbo while Patrick and Mickey continued to acquire the rest. Since neither they nor the company would have to buy it back from him, he had nothing with which to start a business of his own. Furthermore, he believed that he had paid income tax on the $75,000 bonus (actually, the tax had been withheld before the stock-purchase payment). In any case, if he quit, he would have no compensation in the near future for the hard work he had put into his father's business. If the business went to pot under his brother Patrick's immature, irresponsible direction (the outsider Mickey, was great in the field but not a candidate for front-office management), then Tom Jr. would never get anything out of the business. If he did not quit, however, he might only be setting himself up for the same dilemma a year hence, when twice as much accumulated equity would be at stake.

My sketch of their conflict, along the lines of Figure 8, led me to support Tom Jr.'s insistence on reopening the whole succession plan. I advised Tom Sr. privately that he needed to make a decision. Was it his purpose to maximize his financial return for retirement purposes, or to pass along a successful business to Mickey and one or more of his sons? If the company were to grow and prosper in their hands, he could not go on defining the problem as Tom Jr.'s "making up his mind whether he wants to be a company president or a street fighter." He would have to retain leadership long enough to break his sons out of that cycle. Showing him the chart (always an effective visual aid), I said that I believed that Patrick was as much a troublemaker as Tom Jr. was, but that the real cause of the trouble was their inadequate preparation for his retirement. I tactfully pointed out his own role in perpetuating the problem-his demoting Tom Jr. to Patrick's level every time the brothers had a fight (which gave Patrick an incentive to pull his brother's trigger), instead of rewarding both sons for managerial development.

Unfortunately for the company, but perhaps fortunately for Tom Jr., his father continued to blame him for the battles between the two of them and between the brothers. As a psychotherapist, I could not help seeing Tom's unresolved anger, disappointment, and hurt at his son's misspent youth. I saw his resistance to acknowledging that Tom Jr.'s volatile temper was a carbon copy of his own, and I saw that Tom Jr. had reopened the wounds that his brother Bill had inflicted by rejecting their father's ownership transfer plan. I ended up keeping these insights largely to myself, however, for this family was not interested in them; the family members simply wanted to know whether the take-it-or-leave-it plan could work or not; I thought not.

Family conflicts sometimes echo patterns belonging to the family's cultural heritage, even generations after the migration to America. It is interesting to observe that Irish fathers usually did not decide until late in life which son would inherit the land (McGoldrick and Pearce, 1981). Today, Tom Flanagan Sr. is still running his business. The firm did buy back Tom Jr.'s stock. Patrick and Mickey now own a majority of the shares, but the future is less clear than it seemed three years ago.

Tom Jr. benefited from seeing the cycle he had been trapped in. He found a good hourly electrician's job with the large firm where his father had worked for thirty years. In less than a year, he was promoted to the front office. His brother Bill has a similar managerial position with a construction company. They have talked about starting a business together, when the time is right.

Consultant or Therapist?

The Flanagans required a consultant essentially to manage a necessary confrontation. Charting the cycle gave me a map through the conflict and a vivid picture with which to confront the parties. If Tom Sr. had allowed me to do so, I could have moved into a family counselor's role (or referred him to an appropriate professional) to help deal with the emotional issues between him and his sons. Still, it did not require a therapist to see that Tom Sr.'s succession plan was ill advised and unequitable. One need not be a mental health professional to make good use of analyzing sustained conflict cycles and shared fear.

In general, I do not believe that an expert on family systems should be a member of every professional team advising business owners on succession matters. Obviously, attorneys and accountants must always be involved, and each case will call for other organizational and financial consultants but not always for a therapist. When can these methods be used by anyone who is analyzing the organization? When is it better to bring an expert on family systems on the scene?

Often a nonpsychologist can trace a sustained conflict cycle on the basis of what the involved parties report. Any consultant can fill in the diagram and use the arrows (see Figure 4) for guidance on the parties' shared apprehensions and their healthy adjustments. If there are blanks in the cycle, "what if" questions can be used. Clients themselves, and their consultant's relationship with them, will make it clear if and when the issues call for a process person rather than a technical adviser.

An attorney or financial adviser can often ask "what if" questions, clarify consistencies and inconsistencies among different individuals' answers, and even suggest constructive actions. For example, "You ought to tell your son" is not an intervention that requires a therapy license. Where one should draw the line is at the point of offering to intervene in emotion-laden communications. "Can I help you say that to your son?" or "I'm surprised none of you expressed your grief and fear" would probably be inappropriate for an attorney to say, just as it would be inappropriate for me to give estate planning advice. When there is work to do on the other side of that line, the attorney or other professional should consider whether to bring a psychologist consultant into the case or simply refer the client to an appropriate treatment program or a private mental health professional. Before making either suggestion, it may be best to call the person or the program one has in mind for the client, discuss the problem anonymously, and get specific advice for making the referral responsibly, effectively, and tactfully in the particular situation.

Why do consultants do that less often than they should? For example, in the case of a family, one of whose members appears to have a drinking or drug problem, why are consultants shy about confronting the problem? But "why" is the wrong question. If we ask, "What would happen if...?" we may learn that many consultants fear offending their clients. Our next question should be whether what they gain by not offending their clients is really worth more, in the long run, than what they lose by not helping their clients.

There are cases in which one sees the sustained conflict cycle but cannot seem to elicit the parties' shared fear, even when they have been interviewed privately. That is a situation in which one probably does need a coconsultant who is a family therapist. The terminology causes confusion here, because even when a family therapist is consulted, it does not necessarily mean that the family needs to engage in therapy. It means that the family needs a consultant who is trained and experienced in therapeutic counseling with many kinds of families in all kinds of distress, including but not limited to business-owning families.

It should be pointed out that not all clinical psychologists, not all clinical social workers, and only a small number of psychiatrists are formally trained to work with family systems. Conversely, designations like *family therapist*, *family counselor*, and *family systems specialist* may, unfortunately, be used by people with little or no clinical training. Other professional consultants and their clients should ask detailed questions about our certification and experience, just as we would probe a legal or financial consultant's experience and knowledge about closely held businesses before referring anyone to him or her.

Summary

Family business disputes are often examples of a type of conflict whose most significant features do not fit the prevailing dispute-resolution models. Members of a family (or, in fact, of a familylike group of co-workers) quite often are fighting about deeper issues than the ones they claim to be incensed about. Clear communication is at least as crucial within family systems as it is between any other disputing parties, but it is never true that family members need only understand one another's positions, common interests, and respective differences to work rationally together toward an optimal resolution. Often, unfortunately, their reasons for sustaining their conflict-reasons probably not even clear to themselves-are stronger than their ostensible desires to resolve it.

Fortunately, while disputes among people who have long-term relationships with one another add an extra dimension, by contrast with the average contract negotiation or tort litigation, such disputes have their own chronic, repeated dynamics, which an observer or interviewer can chart. The chart, once filled in, shows the typical course of conflict escalation in this group, including who does what to whom and what function the conflict serves. It also shows what the members normally do to keep the conflict within bounds, which is information that a consultant can use to strengthen the system's healthy resources.

My background in problem-centered family systems therapy has taught me to ask questions of the form "What would happen if...?" This is an unthreatening way to make constructive suggestions. It is also the least provocative way to explore any shared fears or assumptions that have kept family members laboring on the stationary bicycle of stultifying conflict. Although other consultants to family businesses will neither want nor be expected to operate as therapists, the analytical tool of the sustained conflict cycle, as well as the interviewing device of the "what if" question, can be incorporated into any skilled consultant's repertoire, without danger of the consultant's overstepping the boundaries of his or her own professional expertise.

References

Bateson, G. *Steps to an Ecology of Mind*. New York: Ballantine, 1972.

Blake, R. R., and Mouton, J. S. *Solving Costly Organizational Conflicts: Achieving Intergroup Trust, Cooperation, and Teamwork*. San Francisco: Jossey-Bass, 1984

Coser, L. *The Functions of Social Conflict*. Glencoe, 111.: Free Press, 1956.

Deutsch, M. *The Resolution of Conflict: Constructive and Destructive Processes*. New Haven, Conn.: Yale University Press, 1973.

Fisher, R., and Ury, W. *Getting to Yes: Negotiating Agreement Without Giving In*. Boston: Houghton Miftlin, 1981.

Kaye, K. "Toward a Developmental Psychology of the Family." In L. L'Abate (ed.), *The Handbook of Family Psychology and Therapy*. Vol. 1. Homewood, 111.: Dorsey Press, 1985.

Lewin, K. *Resolving Social Conflicts*. New York: Harper & Row, 1948.

McGoldrick, M., and Pearce, J. "Family Therapy with Irish-Americans." *Family Process*, 1981, 20, 223-241.

Miller, E. J., and Rice, A. K. *Systems of Organization: The Control of Task and Sentient Boundaries*. New York: Barnes & Noble, 1970.

Pinsof, W. "Integrative Problem-Centered Therapy: Toward the Synthesis of Family and Individual Psychotherapies." *Journal of Marital and Family Therapy*, 1983, 9, 19-35

Putnam, L. "Bargaining as Task and Process: Multiple Functions of Interaction Sequences." In R. L. Street, Jr., and J. N. Cappella (eds.), *Sequence and Pattern in Communicative Behavior*. London: Edward Arnold, 1985.

Simmel, G. *The Sociology of Georg Simmel*. Glencoe, lil.: Free Press, 1950.

Ury, W. L., Brett, . M., and Goldberg, S. B. *Getting Disputes Resolved: Designing Systems to Cut the Costs of Conflict*. San Francisco:Jossey-Bass, 1988.

Weber, M. *The Theory of Social and Economic Organization*. New York: Oxford University Press, 1947.

The job of operating a family-owned company is often grievously complicated by friction arising from rivalries involving a father and his son, brothers, or other family members who hold positions in the business, or at least derive income from it. Unless the principals face up to their feelings of hostility, the author says the business will suffer and may even die. He offers advice on how relatives can team to live with their peculiar situation, but the one real solution is developing professional management.

Conflicts That Plague Family Businesses

By Harry Levinson

In U. S. business, the most successful executives are often men who have built their own companies. Ironically, their very success frequently brings to them and members of their families personal problems of an intensity rarely encountered by professional managers. And these problems make family businesses Possibly the most difficult to operate.1

It is obvious common sense that when managerial decisions are influenced by feelings about and responsibilities toward relatives in the business, when nepotism exerts a negative influence, and when a company is run more to honor a family tradition than for its own needs and purposes, there is likely to be trouble.

However, the problems of family businesses go considerably deeper than these issues. In this article I shall examine some of the more difficult underlying psychological elements in operating these businesses and suggest some ways of coping with them.

They Start With the Founder

The difficulties of the family business begin with the founder. Usually he is an entrepreneur for whom the business has at least three important meanings:

1. The entrepreneur characteristically has unresolved conflicts with his father, research evidence indicates. He is therefore uncomfortable when being supervised, and starts his own business both to outdo his father and to escape the authority and rivalry of more powerful figures.2

2. An entrepreneur's business is simultaneously his "baby" and his "mistress." Those who work with him and for him are characteristically his instruments in the process of shaping the organization.

   If any among them aspires to be other than a device for the founder-that is, if he wants to acquire power for himself he is soon likely to find himself on the outside looking in. This is the reason why so many organizations decline when their founders age or die.

3. For the entrepreneur, the business is essentially an extension of himself, a medium for his personal gratification and achievement above all And if he is concerned about what happens to his business after he passes on, that concern usually takes the form of thinking of the kind of monument he will leave behind.

The fundamental psychological conflict in family businesses is rivalry, compounded by feelings of guilt, when more than one family member is involved. The rivalry may be felt by the founder – even though no relatives are in the business – when he unconsciously senses (justifiably or not) that subordinates are threatening to remove him from his center of power. Consider this actual case:

> An entrepreneur, whose organization makes scientific equipment and bears his name, has built a sizable enterprise in international markets. He has said that he wants his company to be noted all over the world for contributing to society.

He has attracted many young men with the promise of rapid promotions, but he guarantees their failure by giving them assignments and then turning them loose without adequate organizational support. He intrudes into the young men's decision making, but he counterbalances this behavior with paternalistic devices. (His company has more benefits than any other I have known.)

This technique makes his subordinates angry at him for what he has done, then angry at themselves for being hostile to such a kind man. Ultimately, it makes them feel utterly inadequate. He can get people to take responsibility and move up into executive positions, but his behavior has made certain that he will never have a rival.

The conflicts created by rivalries among family members – between fathers and sons, among brothers, and between executives and other relatives – have a chronically abrasive effect on the principals. Those family members in the business must face up to the impact that these relationships exert and must learn to deal with them, not only for their own emotional health but for the welfare of the business.

I shall consider in turn the father-son rivalry, the brother-brother rivalry, and other family relationships.

Father-Son Rivalry

As I have indicated, for the founder the business is an instrument, an extension of himself. So he has great difficulty giving up his baby, his mistress, his instrument, his source of social power, or whatever else the business may mean to him. Characteristically, he has great difficulty delegating authority and he also refuses to retire despite repeated promises to do so.

This behavior has certain implications for father-son relationships. While he consciously wishes to pass his business on to his son and also wants him to attain his place in the sun, unconsciously the father feels that to yield the business would be to lose his masculinity.

At the same time, and also unconsciously, he needs to continue to demonstrate his own competence. That is, he must constantly reassure himself that he alone is competent to make "his" organization succeed. Unconsciously the father does not want his son to win, take away his combination baby and mistress, and displace him from his summit position.

These conflicting emotions cause the father to behave inexplicably in a contradictory manner, leading those close to him to think that while on the one hand he wants the business to succeed, on the other hand he is determined to make it fail.

The son's feelings of rivalry are a reflection of his father's. The son naturally seeks increasing responsibility commensurate with his growing maturity, and the freedom to act responsibly on his own. But he is frustrated by his father's intrusions, his broken promises of retirement, and his self-aggrandizement.

The son resents being kept in an infantile role – always the little boy in his father's eyes – with the accompanying contempt, condescension, and lack of confidence that in such a situation frequently characterize the father's attitude. He resents, too, remaining dependent on his father for his income level and, as often, for title, office, promotion, and the other usual perquisites of an executive. The other's erratic and unpredictable behavior in these matters makes this dependency more unpalatable.

I have observed a number of such men who, even as company presidents, are still being victimized by their fathers who remain chairmen of the board and chief executive officers.

"Why Don't You Let Me Grow Up?"

Characteristically, fathers and sons, particularly the latter, are terribly torn by these conflicts; the father looks on the son as ungrateful and unappreciative, and the son feels both hostile to his father and guilty for his hostility.

The father bears the feeling that the son never will be man enough to run the business, but he tries to hide that feeling from his son. The son yearns for his chance to run it and waits impatiently but still loyally in the wings-often for years beyond the age when others in nonfamily organizations normally take executive responsibility-for his place on the stage.

If the pressures become so severe for him that he thinks of leaving, he feels disloyal but at the same time fears losing the opportunity that would be his if he could only wait a little longer. He defers his anticipated gratification and pleasure, but, with each postponement, his anger, disappointment, frustration, and tension mount. Here is a typical situation I know of:

Matthew Anderson, a man who founded a reclaimed-metals business, has two sons. John, the elder, is his logical successor, but Anderson has given him little freedom to act independently, pointing out that, despite limited education, he (the father) has built the business and intuitively knows more about how to make it successful.

Though he has told John that he wants him to be a partner, he treats John more like a flunky than an executive, let alone a successor. He pays the elder son a small salary, always with the excuse that he should not expect more because someday he will inherit the business.

He grants minimal raises sporadically, never recognizing John's need to support his family in a style fitting his position in the company.

When John once protested and demanded both more responsibility and more income, his father gave Henry, the second son, a vice presidential title and a higher income. When Henry asked for greater freedom and responsibility, Anderson turned back to John and made him president (in name only). The father, as chairman of the board and chief executive officer, continued to second-guess John, excluded Henry from conferences (which of course increased John's feelings of guilt), and told John that Henry was "no good" and could not run the business.

Later, when John sought to develop new aspects of the business to avoid the fluctuations of the metals market, his father vetoed these ideas, saying, "This is what we know, and this is what we're are going to do." He failed to see the possible destructive effects of market cycles on fixed overhead costs and the potential inroads of plastics and other cheaper materials on the reclaimed metals business.

The upshot was that profits declined and the business became more vulnerable to both domestic and foreign (particularly Japanese) competition. When John argued with his father about this, he got the response: "What do you know? You're still green. I went through the Depression." Once again Anderson turned to Henry – making the black sheep white, and vice versa.

Angered, John decided to quit the business, but his mother said, "You can't leave your father; he needs you." Anderson accused him of being ungrateful, but he also offered to retire, as he had promised to do several times before.

Despite his pain, John could not free himself from his father. (Only an ingrate would desert his father, he told himself.) Also John knew that if he departed, he could not go into competition with his father, because that would destroy him. But John shrank from entering an unfamiliar business.

Nevertheless, from time to time John has explored other opportunities while remaining in the business. But each time his father has undercut him. For instance, John once wanted to borrow money for a venture, but Anderson told the bankers that his son was not responsible

Now, when John is middle-aged, he and his father are still battling. In effect John is asking, "Why don't you let me grow up?" and his father is answering, "I'm the only man around here. You must stay here and be my boy."

"He's Destroying the Business"

The son also has intense rivalry feelings, of course. These, too, can result in fierce competition with his father and hostile rejection of him, or abject dependence on him.

Sometimes the competition can lead to a manipulative alignment with the mother against him. Consider this actual case:

Bill Margate, a recent business school graduate, knew that he would go into his father's electronic components business. But he decided that first he should get experience elsewhere, so he spent four years with a large manufacturing company. From his education and experience, he became aware of how unsophisticated his father was about running the business and set about showing the senior Margate how a business should be professionally managed.

Margate can do no right in Bill's eyes, at least not according to the books which he has read but which his father has never heard of. Bill frequently criticizes his father, showing how ignorant he is. When Margate calls his son "green," Bill retorts, "I've forgotten more about managing a business than you'll ever know."

Bill's mother is also involved in the business; she has been at her husband's side for many years, though their relationship is less than the best. Mrs. Margate dotes on her son and complains about him to her husband, and she encourages Bill in his attacks on his Other. When Bill undertook several ventures that floundered, she excused the failures as being caused by his father's interference

But whenever the father-son battle reaches a peak, Mrs. Margate shifts allegiance and stands behind her husband. So the senior Margate has an ally when the chips are down, at the price of a constant beating until he gets to that point.

The struggle for the business has remained a stand-off. But as the elder Margate has grown older, his son's attacks have begun to tell on him Bill has urged him to take long Florida vacations, but Margate refuses because he fears what would happen when his back is turned. For the same reason, he does not permit Bill to sign checks for the company.

Now Margate has become senile, and Bill's criticism of him continues, even in public. "He's destroying the business," Bill will say.

However, Bill cannot act appropriately to remove his father (even though he is now incompetent) because of his guilt feelings about his incessant attacks. That would destroy his father, literally, and he cannot bring himself to do it.

"The Old Man Really Built It"

The problem for the son becomes especially acute when and if he does take over. Often the father has become obsolete in his managerial conceptions. The organization may have grown beyond one man's capacity to control it effectively. That man may have been a star whose imagination, creativity, or drive are almost impossible to duplicate. He may also have been a charismatic figure with whom employees and even the public identified.

Whatever the combination of factors, the son is likely to have to take over an organization with many weaknesses hidden behind the powerful facade of the departed leader. For these reasons many businesses, at the end of their founders' tenure, fall apart, are pirated, or are merged into another organization.

The Ford Motor Company, at the demise of Henry Ford, was a case in point; a completely new management had to be brought in. Henry Ford II was faced with the uncomfortable task of having to regenerate a company that appeared to have the potential for continued success, but which, according to some, could easily have gone bankrupt.

While the son is acting to repair the organizational weaknesses left by his father, he is subject to the criticism of those persons who, envious of his position, are waiting for him to stumble. They "know" that he is not as good as his father. If he does less well than his father, regardless of whether there are unfavorable economic conditions or other causes, he is subject to the charge of having thrown away an opportunity that others could have capitalized on.

The scion cannot win. If he takes over a successful enterprise, and even if he makes it much more successful than anyone could have imagined, nevertheless the onlookers stimulate his feelings of inadequacy. They say, "What did you expect? After all, look what he started with." To illustrate: Tom Schlesinger, the president of a restaurant chain, inherited the business after his father had built a profitable regional network of outlets with a widely known name – a model for the industry.

Tom has expanded it into nearly a national operation. He has done this with astute methods of finance that allow great flexibility, and with effective control methods that maintain meal quality and at the same time minimize waste. By any standards he has made an important contribution to the business.

But those who remember his father cannot see what Tom has done because the aura of his father still remains. They tend to minimize Tom's contribution with such observations as, 'Well, you know, the old man really built that business "

Tom cannot change the attitude of those who knew his father, and he feels it is important to keep lauding his father's accomplishments in order to present a solid family image to employees, customers, and the community. But he is frustrated because he has no way of getting the world to see how well he has done.

Brother-Brother Rivalry

The father-son rivalry is matched in intensity by the brother-brother rivalry. Their competition may be exacerbated by the father if he tries to play the sons off against each other or has decided that one should wear his mantle, as I showed previously. (In my experience, the greatest difficulties of this kind occur when there are only two brothers in the organization.)

The problem is further complicated if their mother and their wives are also directly or indirectly involved in the business. Mothers have their favorites-regardless of what they say-and each wife, of course, has a stake in her husband's position. He can become a foil for his wife's fantasies and ambition.

The rivalry between brothers for their father's approval, which began in childhood, continues into adult life. It can reach such an intensity that it colors every management decision and magnifies the jockeying for power that goes on in all organizations. Consider this situation:

Arthur, five years older than his sibling, is president, and Warren is an operating vice president, of the medium-sized retailing organization which they inherited. To anyone who cares to listen, each maintains that he can get along van well without the other.

Arthur insists that Warren is not smart, not as good a businessman as he; that his judgment is bad; and that even if given the chance, he would be unable to manage the business.

Warren asserts that when the two were growing up, Arthur considered him to be a competitor, but for his part, he (Warren) did not care to compete because he was younger and smaller. Warren says that he cannot understand why his older brother has always acted as if they were rivals, and adds, "I just want a chance to do my thing. If he'd only let me alone with responsibility! But he acts as if the world would fall apart if I had that chance."

Every staff meeting and meeting of the board (which includes nonfamily members) becomes a battle between the brothers. Associates, employees, and friends back off because they decline to take sides. The operation of the organization has been turned into a continuous family conflict.

The Elder...

Ordinarily, the elder brother succeeds his father. But this custom reaffirms the belief of the younger brother (or brothers) that the oldest is indeed the favorite. In any event, the older brother often has a condescending attitude toward the younger. In their earliest years the older is larger, physically stronger, more competent, and more knowledgeable than the younger merely because of the difference in age, as in the case I just cited.

Only in rare instances does the younger brother have the opportunity to match the skills, competence, and experience of the elder until they reach adulthood. By that time the nature of this relationship is so well established that the older brother has difficulty regarding the younger one as adequate and competent.

Moreover, the eldest child is earlier and longer in contact with the parents, and their control efforts fall more heavily on him. Consequently, older children tend to develop stronger consciences, drive themselves harder, expect more of themselves, and control themselves more rigidly than younger ones. Being already, therefore, a harsh judge of himself, the eldest is likely to be an even harsher judge of his younger siblings.

...And the Younger

The younger brother attempts to compensate for the effects of this childhood relationship and his older brother's en forts to control him by trying to carve out a place in the business that is his own. This he guards with great zeal, keeping the older brother out so he can demonstrate to himself, his brother, and others that he is indeed competent and has his own piece of the action for which he is independently responsible.

If the brothers own equal shares in the organization and both are members of the board, as is frequently the case, the problems are compounded. On the board they can argue policy from equally strong positions. However, when they return to operations in which one is subordinate to the other, the subordinate one, usually the junior brother, finds it extremely difficult to think of himself in a subservient role.

The younger one usually is unable to surmount this problem in their mutual relationship. He tends to be less confident than his brother and considers himself to be at a permanent disadvantage, always overcontrolled, always unheeded. Since the older brother views the younger one as being less able, he becomes involved in self-fulfilling prophecies. Distrusting his younger brother, he is likely to overcontrol him, give him less opportunity for freedom and responsibility – which in turn make for maturity and growth – and likely to reject all signs of the younger brother's increasing competence.

If for some reason the younger brother displaces the older one, and particularly if the latter becomes subordinate to him the younger brother is faced with feelings of guilt for having attacked the elder and usurped what so often is accepted as the senior brother's rightful role.

Intrafamily Friction

The problems of the father and brothers extend to other relatives when they, too, become involved in the business. In some families it is expected that all who wish to join the company will have places there. This can have devastating effects, particularly if the jobs are sinecures.

The chief executive of a family business naturally feels a heavy responsibility for the family fortunes. If he does not produce a profit, the effect on what he considers to be his image in the financial markets may mean less to him than the income reduction which members of his family will suffer. So he is vulnerable to backbiting from persons whom he knows only too well and whom he cannot dismiss as faceless. Consider this case:

Three brothers started a knitting business. Only one of the brothers had sons, and only one of those sons stayed in the business; he eventually became president. The stock is held by the family. Two widowed aunts, his mother, his female cousins (one of whom was already widowed), and his brother, a practicing architect, depend on the business for significant income

When business is off, the women complain. If the president wants to buy more equipment, they resist. If they hear complaints from employees or merchant friends, they make these complaints known at family gatherings. The president is never free from the vixens who are constantly criticizing and second-guessing him.

Perhaps more critical for the health of the business are the factional divisions that spring up in the organization as associates and subordinates choose the family members with whom they want to be identified. (Often, however, those who take sides discover that in a crisis the family unites against "outsiders," including their partisans, who are then viewed as trying to divide the family.)

If the nonfamily employees or board members decide not to become involved in a family fight and withdraw from relations with its members until the conflict is resolved, the work of the organization may be paralyzed. Worse yet, the dispute may eventually embroil the entire organization, resulting in conflicts at the lower levels, as employees try to cope with the quarrels thrust on them.

Now the business has become a battleground that produces casualties but no peace. Such internecine warfare constitutes a tremendous barrier to communication and frustrates adequate planning and rational decision making.

A business in which numerous members of the family of varying ages and relationships are involved often becomes painfully disrupted around issues of empires and succession. Its units tend to become family-member territories and therefore poorly integrated organizationally, if at all.

As for succession, the dominant or patriarchal leader may fully expect to pass on the mantle of leadership to other, elder relatives in their turn. He may even promise them leadership roles, particularly if he has had to develop a coalition to support his position.

But for both realistic and irrational reasons he may well come to feel that none of the family members is capable of filling the role. He cannot very well disclose his decision, however, without stirring conflict, and he cannot bring in outside managers without betraying his relatives or reneging on his promises.

On the other hand, he fears what would happen if he died without having designated a successor. He may decide that the only way out is to sell the business (at least each relative will then get his fair share). But that solution is costly-it signifies not only the loss of the business as a means of employment, but also the betrayal of a tradition and, inevitably, the dissolution of close family ties that have been maintained through the medium of the business.

Facing Up To It

What can be done about these problems?

Most entrepreneurial fathers seem unable to resolve their dilemma themselves. They tend to be rigid and righteous, finding it difficult to understand that there is another, equally valid point of view which they can accept without becoming weaklings. Well-meaning outsiders who try to help the father see the effects of his behavior and think seriously about succession usually find themselves rejected. Then they lose whatever beneficial influence they may have had on him.

Several approaches have worked well. In some instances, sons have told their fathers that they recognize how important it is to the father to run his own business, but it is just as important for them to have the opportunity to "do their own thing." They then establish small new ventures either under the corporate umbrella or outside it, without deserting their father.

In a variant of this approach, a father who heads a retail operation opened a store in a different community for each of his sons. They do their buying together, with appropriate variations for each community, and maintain a common name and format, but each son runs his own operation while the father continues to run his.

In still another situation, the father merged his company into a larger one. Each of his two sons then became president of a subsidiary, and the father started a new venture while serving as a policy guide to his sons.

The Son's Role

Whether such alternatives can work depends in part on how the son conducts himself. He must be honest with himself and consider his paternal relationship candidly. He must take steps like these:

- He must ask himself why he chose to go into the family business. Most sons say it is because of the opportunity and the feelings of guilt if they had not done so. Often, however, the basic reason is that a powerful father has helped make his son dependent on him, and so his son is reluctant to strike out an his own.

  He rationalizes his reluctance on the basis of opportunity and guilt. Struggling with his own dependency, he is more likely to continue to fight his father in the business because he is still trying to escape his father's control.

- Having examined this issue, and recognizing whatever validity it may have for him, the son must realize how often his own feelings of rivalry and anger get in his way. The more intense the rivalry, the more determinedly he seeks to push his father from his throne and the more aggressively the latter must defend himself. The son must therefore refrain from attack.

- He must quietly and with dignity, as a mature man, apprise his father of the realities-that he needs an area of freedom and an independent medium to develop skills and responsibilities. He can do so within the company framework or, if that is not feasible, outside it. In his own self-interest, as well as the companies, he must be certain that he gets the opportunity.

- He must not allow himself to be played off against his brother, and he must not allow his guilt to be manipulated. By the same token, he himself must become involved with others in manipulation.

- He must honestly recognize and respect his father's achievement and competence. To build a business is no mean task, and usually the father still has useful skills and knowledge. Furthermore, the son should recognize the powerful psychological meaning of the business to his father and not expect him to be rational about his relationship to it.

If the son is still unable to make choices about what he wants to do, then, despite his pain and his father's reluctance to seek help, he himself must do so. Only he can take the initiative to relieve his anguish. Here is an example of how a group of sons has taken the initiative:

In Boston, a group calling itself SOB's (Sons of the Boss) has been formed to encourage men in that position to talk over common problems and share solutions. After educating themselves about the psychological dimensions of their situation, the group will make it a practice from time to time to invite their fathers as a group to discuss their problems openly. Then fathers and sons will get together separately.

This procedure may enable fathers and sons to realize that their particular problems are not unique to themselves, and to obtain support from those in a similar predicament.

Another approach for a son would be to ask his father to read this article and then discuss it privately with a neutral third party of their choice, to develop a perspective on their feelings and behavior. Having done so, a father is then in a better position to talk with his son, in the presence of the third party.

The third person must use his good offices to subdue recrimination. At the same time he must foster the father's expression of his fears over losing control, being unneeded, and suffering rejection, as well as the son's concerns about being over controlled, infantilized, and exploited.

If meeting with the third party fails to help, the next step is consultation with a psychologist or psychiatrist. There are rare instances, usually when conflict becomes severe, in which father and son are willing to go to a professional together or separately. In such cases it is often possible for the father to begin to make compromises, learn to understand his and his son's motivations, and work out with him newly defined, more compatible roles. Usually, however, such an effort requires continued supportive work by the professional and strong desire on the part of both men to resolve their differences.

If all these measures fail, those who work with patriarchs must learn to tolerate their situation until the opportunity arises for a change.

Fraternal Spirit

With respect to the brother-brother conflict, it is important for brothers to see that in their relationship they recapitulate ancient rivalries, and to perceive clearly the psychological posture each assumes toward the other.

Once they understand these two issues, they must talk together about them. They should try to discuss freely the fears, worries, anger, and disappointments caused by each other. They should also be able to talk about their affection for each other.

Since there is love and hate in all relationships, theirs cannot, by definition, be pure. They should not feel guilty about their anger with each other, but they do need to talk it out. Having done that, they then must consider how they can divide the tasks in the organization so that each will have a chance to acquire and demonstrate competence and work in a complementary relationship with the other.

A brother cannot easily be subordinate at one level and equal on another. If a brother is an operating executive subordinate to the other, he gets into difficulty when he tries to be an equal on the board of directors. If more than one brother is on the board, then only one, as a rule, should be an operating executive. Of course, such rules are unnecessary if the brothers work well together.

If the brothers still cannot resolve their conflicts, then it becomes necessary to seek professional aid. If that does not help, they should consider being in separate organizations. In such a case, the big problem is the guilt feelings which the departing brother is likely to have for deserting the other and the family business.

Toward Professional Management

Where there are multiple and complex family relationships and obligations in a company, and particularly problems about succession, the best solution is a transcendent one. The family members should form a trust, taking all the relatives out of business operations while enabling them to continue to act in concert as a family.

The trust could allot financial support to every member who desires it to develop new business ventures on behalf of the family, thus providing a business interest that replaces the previous operating activity. This also helps maintain family cohesion and preserve the family's leadership role in the community.

In general, the wisest course for any business, family or nonfamily, is to move to professional management as quickly as possible. Every business must define its overriding purpose for being, from which it derives its objectives. Within this planning framework, the business must have a system for appraising the degree to which it and its components are achieving the goals that have been set.

All organizations need to rear subordinates in a systematic manner, thus creating the basic condition for their own regeneration. I know of no family business capable of sustaining regeneration over the long term solely through the medium of its own family members.

Where there is conflict, or inadequately rationalized territories, members of the family should move up and out of operations as quickly as possible into policy positions. Such movement recognizes the reality of ownership but does not confuse ownership with management.

It also opens the opportunity for professionally trained managers to succeed to major operating roles, instead of having to go to other organizations as soon as they are ready for major responsibility. The more competitive the business situation, the more imperative such a succession pattern is.

More than others, the family members need to have their own outside activities from which they can derive gratification equal to what they can obtain in the company. Otherwise they will be unable to let go and will continue to be barriers to others. Moreover, they will make it difficult to recruit and develop young persons with leadership potential who, as they mature, will see the inevitable barriers.

A number of family businesses have handled these issues wisely and have become highly professional in their management. The Dayton-Hudson Corporation and E. I. du Pont de Nemours are examples. Family members in both organizations must compete for advancement on the same terms as nonfamily managers. This practice is reinforced, at least at Dayton-Hudson by a thorough performance appraisal system which includes appraisal of the chairman and president by a committee of the board.

Concluding Note

It is very difficult to cope with the problems of the family business. That does not mean, however, that one should merely endure them. There is no point in stewing in anger and guilt, since chronic irritation is only self-flagellation. It solves no problems; it only increases anger and hostility and paves the way for explosion, recrimination and impaired relations.

The family member can do something about such problems, as he can with any other. If reasonable steps to solve the problems do not work and he continues to feel bound to the organization his problem is largely psychological To free himself to make choices about what he wants to do, he must talk his feelings out with his rival in the organization which is best done in the presence of a neutral third person. Sometimes professional help is necessary.

This will reduce sufficiently the intensity of the emotions generated by the problem so that he can see possible alternatives more clearly and make choices more freely. That is better than the years of agitation that usually accompany such problems, unless of course the rival needs to expiate his guilt by continuing to punish himself. In that case, it is his problem and not necessarily that of the family business.

Notes

1. For two thoughtful views of the subject, see Robert G. Donnelley, "The Family Businesses," *Harvard Business Review*, July-August 1964, p. 93; and Seymour Tilles, "Survival Strategies for Family Firms," *European Business*, April 1970, p. 9.
2. See Orvin F. Collins, David G. Moore, and Darab B. Unwalla, *The Enterprising Man* (East Lansing, Michigan State University Bureau of Business Research, 1964).

CHAPTER 11
FAMILY RELATIONS

What makes family businesses different from other businesses is the inclusion of family and the relational bonds among family members. This section explores family relationships as a component of family business systems and deals with constructively managing those relationships. Productive family relationships begin with the recognition and tolerance of differences among family members.

Rather than viewing family matters as disruptions of rational business practice, a more systemic, coevolutionary perspective offers greater understanding and insight. The integration of family and business cultures plays a powerful role in the satisfaction experienced by family members from their involvement in the family business.

Families place restraints on their businesses which affect business strategy and can cause conflicts in the family/business relationship. How such conflicts are managed depends in part on the manager's power base and interpersonal skills. However, if the family has developed consensus around its goals and values and explicitly recognized its commitment to the family and the business, the environment of family relations can be positively affected.

Family businesses are reported to consist of overinvolved family relationships. Overinvolvement often leads to conflict when late adolescents attempt to develop their own identity, separate from the home, and choose an occupation. This study examines differences between family-and non-family-business offspring in relation to psychological overinvolvement, and career choice and development. Analyses of assessments completed by 248 undergraduate college students does not support the belief that family business members are overinvolved with each other, but does suggest implications for the career development of family business offspring.

Effects of Family Business Membership and Psychological Separation on the Career Development of Late Adolescents

Christopher J. Eckrich, Teri A. Loughead

Introduction

Late adolescence, from the age of 18 to the early 20's, is a period of tremendous transition as children prepare for and choose an occupation, and eventually gain independence by leaving home. This is a necessary process in the formation of a healthy identity that occurs when young adults recognize and accept their own values, beliefs, ideas, and goals (Erikson, 1968). The formation of a vocational identity is one of the strongest determinants of the identity formation process, generally culminating in an occupational choice or a decision to pursue further education that will lead to a career in a specific field (Waterman, 1985).

Children who are raised in families in which one or both parents own a family business are believed to generally experience both internal and external pressure to work in the family firm (Beckhard and Dyer, 1983). The internal pressure arises because their identities have been formed to include the family-business heritage, while external influences generally stem from parents wishing to pass on the organizations they worked so hard to create (Kepner, 1983). When late adolescents choose to work in their parents' businesses, the choice can put them in environments ill-suited to their interests or abilities, resulting in dissatisfaction and eventual frustration with their work environments (Holland, 1985). Evidence suggests children from business-owning families seem to enter into the business without considering the impact that working for their parents might have on their overall career paths or on their sense of self. While working with their families could provide unique opportunities for social support, it is thought that these children tend to question their ability to succeed on their own and experience confusion about their identities (Kepner, 1983).

Currently, there is anecdotal evidence suggesting that family-business children, defined here as children of business-owning families, experience unique career development patterns. Despite all that has been written about family owned organizations, however, there is a dearth of empirical research comparing children from family-business owners with children of those who are not. Additionally, a review of the literature reveals little documentation on the career development of these late adolescents, and particularly on how they make occupational choices. Because the decisions they make have tremendous implications for their own careers as well as the future management and leadership of their family businesses, it is critical to better understand their career decision-making processes. Thus, the purpose of this research is to examine whether late adolescents who are members of business-owning families experience family dynamics and career development patterns different from non-family-business children.

Hypotheses Development. Recently there has been interest in family influences as salient variables in children's vocational development (Savickas, 1989). Healthy families adapt to changing circumstances both to maintain family continuity and concurrently support the psychosocial growth of each family member (Beavers, 1982; Minuchin, 1974). However, dysfunctional enmeshed families, or those in which independence of thought and feeling are perceived as threatening the integrity of the family, are likely to discourage young adults (covertly or overtly) from developing a sense of psychological separateness (Bowen, 1976; Kerr and Bowen, 1988). This in turn likely inhibits the necessary independent career decision-making and implementation tasks (Blustein et al., 1991). Literature related to college student adjustment suggests that late adolescent development is negatively impacted by enmeshment in the family system (Kenny and Donaldson, 1991; Lopez et al., 1988). The absence of psychological separation from parents is believed to result in the adolescent's inability to foreclose on a career choice, meaning that they fail to execute a decision about which career to pursue (Blustein et al., 1991).

While this logically flows from a family systems theoretical perspective, the theoretical expectations of an interacting family and business system run somewhat counter. In a family business, the business represents not only the livelihood of the family (Miller and Rice, 1988), but also the embodiment of family rules and values in the organization (Hollander and Bukowitz, 1990). The importance of family values and traditions is perhaps the most influential variable children consider when making initial career choices (Bratcher, 1982). A choice away from the organization can appear as a choice away from all the family represents. Because the family business system is so dominant in the child's development, a lack of psychological separateness is considered to lead to a choice to remain in the business rather than inhibit choice of an occupation (Beckhard and Dyer, 1983; Penick and Jepsen, 1992). In other words, the child has foreclosed on, or adopted, an identity that is roughly equivalent to what his or her parents had intended (Marcia, 1966, 1980).

Therefore, we hypothesize, first, that membership in a family business can moderate the relationship between psychological separation from parents and the tendency to foreclose on a career choice.

Specifically, we presume that as psychological separation decreases, family business children commit more quickly to a career choice without exploring occupations.

Second, we hypothesize that family-business children have a greater tendency to foreclose on a career choice than non-family-business children.

The tendency to foreclose on a career choice is the degree of openness one has towards the process of considering multiple career options.

> **Vocational Identity.** Vocational identity means the possession of a clear and stable picture of one's goals, interests, personality, and talents. This characteristic leads to relatively untroubled decision-making and confidence in one's ability to make good decisions in the face of inevitable environmental ambiguities. (Holland, Daiger, and Power, 1980, p. 9)

When enmeshed families exert influence over their children's career development process, restricting career exploration and hindering identity development, then vocational identity development is thwarted (Bratcher, 1982; Holland, Daiger, and Power, 1980; Lopez and Andrews, 1987; Zingaro, 1983). Empirical research supports the lack of psychological separation from parents as being associated with lower vocational identity among high school students and college students (Lopez et al., 1988; Penick and Jepsen, 1992).

These theoretical assumptions are opposite of what might be expected from children of an enmeshed business-owning family. Based on anecdotal evidence, children are expected to forgo the career exploration process and quickly commit to their career choice within the family system (Bork, 1986; Kepner, 1983). Rather than career indecision, entry into the business could be difficult to avoid (Beavers, 1977; Beckhard and Dyer, 1983; Kepner, 1983). This remains an important point, as the vocational identity construct (Holland, Daiger, and Power, 1980) appears to significantly tap the indecisiveness construct (Fuqua and Newman, 1989).

For this reason, we hypothesize that vocational identity and commitment to career choices among late adolescent family business members increase as family enmeshment increases.

Answers to these hypotheses can provide both practitioners and researchers with valuable information about the nature of career development among family business members.

Research Methods

Our study utilizes a survey research design based on the work of Dillman (1976). During the eleventh week of the semester, we gave all participants a packet of assessment instruments. We randomized the order of tests to control for testing effects and informed participants that the research was intended to examine families and career development. Participants completed the packets at their leisure; packets were collected at the beginning of the subsequent class period.

Participants. Participants consisted of 423 undergraduate students, primarily juniors and seniors, at a large midwestern public university. The study targeted juniors and seniors because this is the age at which individuals typically engage in the career decision-making process and strengthen vocational identities (Ginzberg et al., 1951; Ginzberg, 1984; Super, 1990). Also, this age group provided access to family business owners' children whose career decisions could impact the future management and leadership potential of their family firms.

A total of 274 packets were returned, of which 248 provided usable responses, for a response rate of 65%. Demographic characteristics of the sample are identified in Table 1.

Instruments. Five assessments were used: a demographic data sheet, the *Psychological Separation Inventory*, the *Vocational Exploration and Commitment Scale*, the *Tendency to Foreclose Scale*, and the *Vocational Identity Scale*.

Table 1. Demographic Characteristics of Total Sample

Age (Mean)	21
Gender:	
Female	63.7%
Male	36.3%
Major:	
Agriculture	11.7%
Business	29.4%
Consumer family sciences	9.3%
Education	4.8%
Liberal arts	36.7%
Science	4.0%
Other	4.0%
Race:	
African American	3.6%
Asian American	3.2%
Caucasian	89.5%
Hispanic American	1.2%
Native American	1.2%
Other	1.0%
Parents Married	75.1%
Parental Combined Income:[a]	
Over $90,000	12.9%
Between $60,000 and $90,000	36.4%
Between $40,000 and $60,000	39.6%
Below $40,000	11.1%

[a]Data collected only for participants reporting incomes of both parents.

We used the *Psychological Separation Inventory* (PSI; Hoffman, 1984) to measure the components of the psychological separation process as defined by Blos (1979). Higher scores on the PSI represent greater psychological separation between children and their parents. The PSI scales essentially measure two dimensions: affinity for and conflict with parents.

The first of these is a general identification with or affinity for parents (PSI Combined), and measures an individual's ability to direct his or her own affairs without parental assistance; freedom from an overly excessive need for approval; emotional support or closeness with parents; and differences in attitudes, values, and beliefs from those of the parents (Rice, Cole, and Lapsley, 1990).

The second factor measures conflictual independence (PSI Conflict), which is an individual's freedom from anxiety, resentment, mistrust, guilt, and responsibility towards parents (Hoffman, 1984). Chronbach's alpha coefficients for the PSI Combined and the PSI Conflict scales were found to be 0.97 and 0.93, respectively.

We used the *Vocational Exploration and Commitment Scale* (VECS), a subscale of the Commitment to Career Choices Scale (CCCS; Blustein, Ellis, and Devenis, 1989), to measure commitment to vocation. The VECS measures progress in the commitment to a career choice by using a seven-point Likert-type format (Chronbach's Alpha = 0.91). In creating this 19-item scale, we integrated Super's (1957) and Harren's (1979) theoretical approaches to the career choice commitment process. We used expert judgments from vocational psychologists to refine a list of theoretically derived items.

The *Tendency to Foreclose Scale* (TTFS), another subscale of the Commitment to Career Choices Scale (Blustein, Ellis, and Devenis, 1989), measures the tendency to foreclose on a career choice. The TTFS is a nine-item scale in which low scores represent an open approach taken towards the commitment process, and high scores indicate a closed and dogmatic approach to the commitment process (Chronbach's Alpha = 0.83). We constructed the TTFS in the same theory-based manner as the VECS.

We used the *Vocational Identity Scale* (VIS) in *My Vocational Situation* (MVS; Holland et al., 1980) to measure vocational identity. The VIS indicates clarity of goals, interests, personality, and talents (Holland et al., 1980). Chronbach's Alphas have ranged from 0.85 to 0.87 in previous studies (Healy, Tullier, and Mourton, 1990; Ross and Spencer, 1988).

Limitations of the Present Study. Due to the nature of the sample and data gathering, there are several limitations in this study. First, the large percentage of Caucasian participants may limit the generalizability of the findings. Second, the sample is predominantly female. Although we used preliminary analyses to examine gender differences, it is possible that the results were impacted by the high percentage of female participants. The family-business literature has frequently described the different experiences that sons and daughters encounter in their families and businesses. This study does not propose differences for men and women during hypotheses development, but the possibility of differing career development variables based on gender presents an opportunity for future inquiry.

In this study, we do not consider the impact of marital separation and divorce on participants. Therefore, there is no way to determine the impact of recent or past family turmoil on the measures. It is quite possible that parental marital strife impacted children's perception of career options or obligations, or influenced perceptions of psychological separation from parents. Especially in situations of conflict, where parent is pitted against parent, choice towards or away from the business may be more a function of loyalty towards a particular parent than a well-conceived career decision.

The design of the study itself presents several limitations. The correlational nature of this study does not permit causality to be examined. Also, the limitations of using self-report measures have been well documented (Mitchell and Jolley, 1988). A longitudinal design that employs both self-reporting and observational methods of data collection is indicated for the future.

Data Analyses and Results

Descriptive Characteristics. The family-business group consisted of 66 participants, and the-control group had 182 participants. Chi-square tests showed no differences between the family business group and the comparison group based on sex, class, race, parents' marital status, or whether the participant had experienced pressure to enter into any specific occupation. We found a significant difference between groups for majors, $X^2(3, N = 216) = 20.96$, $p < 0.001$. The family-business group had a higher percentage of agriculture majors than expected. Conversely, the comparison group had a smaller percentage of agriculture majors than expected. This finding is likely the result of including students recruited from a farm management course in the sample.

We also found a significant difference for participants' response to the question, "Which parent is the breadwinner of the family?", $X^2(2, N = 245) = 6.35$, $p < 0.05$. The disparity occurred between the two groups with respect to retired fathers as having been the primary breadwinner: No family-business offspring identified a retired father as having been the primary breadwinner.

We assessed several demographic characteristics for the family business group. Fathers were reported as founders by 53% of the group, grandfathers by 31.8%, followed by mothers at 6.1%. Compared to a recent national survey of family businesses (MassMutual, 1994), a higher percentage of parents were reported as founders. However, it should be noted that the current research employed a less restrictive definition of family business, utilizing Ward's (1987) definition as a business in which the management and control of the organization could be passed on to the next generation. The average duration of parental employment in the family business was 20.1 years; the average duration of business operation was 29.9 years. Business size averaged 34.5 employees, with 90% of the sample reporting less than 50 employees. Financially, 53% of respondents reported businesses as performing above average by, and 16.7% reported below-average performance.

Various demographic characteristics are summarized in Tables 2 and 3.

Gender Considerations. The present study makes no differential predictions based on participant gender. Still, because the process of separating from parents is thought to be different for men and women (Hoffman, 1984; Josselson, 1988; Levinson, 1978) and the family-business literature frequently reports experiential and developmental differences for sons and daughters (Bork, 1986; Dumas, 1989; Kaye, 1992), gender differences on the

Table 2. Demographic Characteristics of Business for Family Business Group

Founded by:	
Father	53.0%
Mother	6.1%
Grandfathers	31.8%
Other	9.1%
Number of family members in business:	
(Mean)	3.12
1 to 2 members	40.9%
3 to 4 members	39.45%
5 or more	19.7%
Years of parental employment in business (mean)	20.1
Years of business operation (mean)	29.9
Business size in employees (mean)	34.5
Financial performance:	
Above average	53.0%
Average	30.3%
Below average	16.7%

Table 3. Demographic Comparison for Family Business and Non-Family Business Groups

	Family Business (n=66)	Non-Family Business[a] (n=182)
Business size (mean)	34.5	9,837
Both parents working in same business	35.0%	10.2%
At least on sibling working in same business	43.9%	9.1%
At least one extended family member in same business	54.5%	26.7%
Can enter business if I want	62.1%	35.4%
Will enter business	18.2%	8.9%
Will probably not enter the business	65.2%	79.5%
Am being pressured to enter the business by		
Father	13.6%	2.3%
Mother	4.5%	1.1%
The following would like me to enter the business		
Father	37.9%	16.5%
Mother	24.2%	8.9%
The following would prefer I not enter the business		
Father	39.4%	60.3%
Mother	57.6%	64.3%
I will experience distress if I do not enter the business	13.6%	1.1%
I will let someone down if I do not enter the business	13.6%	1.7%

[a]Instead of asking non-family-business group members about the family business, they were asked about their parent's company or field.

dependent measures were examined. The only significant difference found between men and women occurred on the Psychological Separation Inventory Combined scale $F(1, 225)$ = 4.38, $p<0.05$. Males scored significantly higher than females, indicating that males are apparently more psychologically separate than females. In summary, the results of the preliminary analyses indicated no difficulties in combining the data for hypothesis testing.

Comparison of Groups. Family-business children are similar to non-family-business children in the following constructs, since we found no statistically significant differences on measures of psychological separation (PSI), the tendency to foreclose on a career choice (TTFS), or progress in the commitment to a career choice (VECS) between family-business members and non-family-business members.

The groups differed significantly on the measure of vocational identity. A comparison of means suggested family-business children had lower vocational identity than that of the non-family-business children, meaning that family business children's interests, personality, talents, and goals were less well established (Holland, Daiger, and Power, 1980).

Examination of Moderating Effects. As Table 4 shows, there are mixed results on the hypothesis predicting a moderating effect on the relationship between psychological separation and tendency to foreclose on a career choice based on parental occupation type. The adjusted R^2 is significant when we enter the PSI Combined by Parental Occupation Type interaction (A1 x B) into the model. An interaction effect for the PSI Combined by Parental Occupation Type cross-product indicates that Parental Occupation Type indeed moderates the relationship between PSI Combined and TTFS. However, an examination of the adjusted R^2 increment (incremental adjusted R^2 =0.012) suggests that the finding lacks practical importance.

We obtain unstandardized regression coefficients for each separate parental occupation type entered into the regression equation (Baron and Kenny, 1986), based on the dummy coding procedure outlined by Cohen and Cohen (1983), to examine the nature of

Table 4. Hierarchical Regression Analyses for Tendency to Foreclose on a Career Choice (TTFS)

	R2 Overall	Adj. R² Overall	Adj. R² Increment	Full Model F	p	Beta	p
PSI COMB (A1)	0.03388	0.030	0.03	7.82	0.006[b]	-0.280	.0[b]
POCT (B)	0.03390	0.025	.0	3.90	0.022[a]	-0.494	0.032[a]
A1 X B	0.05527	0.042	0.012	4.31	0.006[b]	0.513	0.026[a]
PSI CONF (A2)	0.06030	0.056	0.056	14.31	.0[c]	-0.302	.0[c]
POCT (B)	0.06030	0.052	.0	7.13	0.001[c]	-0.546	0.168
A2 X B	0.06840	0.056	.0	5.41	0.001[b]	0.546	0.168

Note: N = 225. Adj. R² = adjusted R²; POCT = parental occupation type; PSI COMB = PSI combined scale; PSI CONF = PSI conflict scale. POCT was coded with two dummy variables (Cohen &Cohen, 1983). Beta is the standardized regression coefficient.
[a] = p < 0.05, [b] = p < 0.01, [c] = p < 0.001

the PSI Combined by Parental Occupation Type interaction effect upon TTFS. This interaction is graphed in Figure 1.

Increases in psychological separation are associated with decreases in tendency to foreclose on a career choice for non-family-business members and slight increases in tendency to foreclose on a career choice for family-business members. For family-business children, increases in appropriate separation from parents are associated with a more closed approach to the career decision-making process. For non-family-business children, increases in separation from parents are associated with a more open approach to career decision making.

The second test (of family business membership as a moderator between psychological separation and tendency to foreclose on a career choice) showed some relationship between TTFS and PSI Conflict (Table 4). However, examining the beta weight suggests that there is not a significant interaction between conflictual independence and Parental Occupation Type, indicating that Parental Occupation Type does not moderate the relationship between PSI Conflict and TTFS. Based on the results of the separate regression analyses, using PSI Combined and PSI Conflict as independent variables, conclusions are

Figure 1. Interaction Between PSI Combined and Tendency to Foreclose Scale by Group

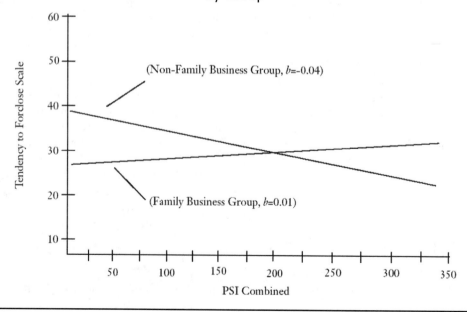

Table 5. Hierarchical Regression Analyses for Vocational Exploration and Commitment Scale (VECS)

	R2 Overall	Adj. R² Overall	Adj. R² Increment	Full Model F	p	Beta	p
PSI COMB (A1)	0.012	0.010	0.010	3.33	0.070	-0.109	0.172
POCT (B)	0.023	0.014	0.004	2.60	0.076	0.114	0.625
A1 X B	0.023	0.010	.0	1.73	0.162	-0.024	0.918
PSI CONF (A2)	0.077	0.073	0.073	18.55	.0[c]	-0.169	0.024[a]
POCT (B)	0.083	0.075	0.002	10.07	.0[c]	1.070	0.006[b]
A2 X B	0.110	0.098	0.023	9.14	.0[c]	-1.001	0.010[b]

Note: $N = 225$. Adj. R^2 = adjusted R^2; POCT = parental occupation type; PSI COMB = PSI combined scale; PSI CONF = PSI conflict scale. POCT was coded with two dummy variables (Cohen &Cohen, 1983). Beta is the standardized regression coefficient and is not bound by a range of -1 to 1 (Neter, Wasserman, & Kutner, 1990).
[a] $= p < 0.05$, [b] $= p < 0.01$, [c] $= p < 0.001$

mixed as to whether Parental Occupation Type moderates the relation between psychological separation and the tendency to foreclose on a career choice. Since only one psychological separation component revealed a moderating effect and that effect was small, we advise caution in interpreting this finding.

There is also partial support for the results of the analyses that predicted that family-business membership as having a moderating effect on the relation between psychological separation and progress in the commitment to a career choice. This is shown in Table 5.

Although PSI Combined does not predict VECS, PSI Conflict does appear to predict VECS. The interaction between Parental Occupation Type and conflictual independence from parents accounts for a significant, unique variation in predicting participants' progress in the commitment to a career choice. Increases in conflictual independence from parents are associated with greater increases in commitment to a career choice for

Figure 2. Interaction Between PSI Conflict and Vocational Exploration and Commitment Scale by Group

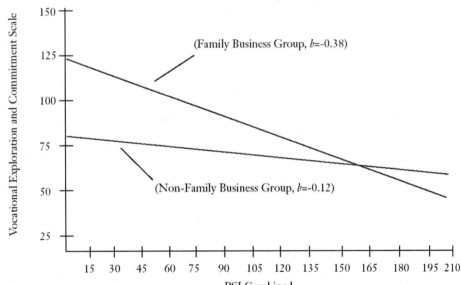

Note: Lower scores on the Vocational Exploration and Commitment Scale indicate a greater degree of commitment.

Table 6. Hierarchical Regression Analyses for Vocational Identity Scale (VIS)

	R2 Overall	Adj. R² Overall	Adj. R² Increment	Full Model F	p	Beta	p
PSI COMB (A1)	0.004	.000	.0	0.90	0.345	0.021	0.789
POCT (B)	0.019	0.011	0.011	2.20	0.113	-0.288	0.216
A1 X B	0.022	0.009	.0	1.64	0.180	0.171	0.463
PSI CONF (A2)	0.043	0.039	0.039	10.15	0.002[b]	0.140	0.066
POCT (B)	0.056	0.048	0.009	6.67	0.002[b]	-0.697	0.078
A2 X B	0.066	0.053	0.005	5.22	0.002[b]	0.590	0.134

Note: N = 227. Adj. R² = adjusted R²; POCT = parental occupation type; PSI COMB = PSI combined scale; PSI CONF = PSI conflict scale. POCT was coded with two dummy variables (Cohen &Cohen, 1983).
[b] = $p < 0.01$

family-business children than for non-family-business children. Once again, however, caution is advised in interpreting these results, since the incremental addition of the adjusted R² was not very large (incremental adjusted R² =0.023). The beta weight in the interaction term indicates that Parental Occupation Type moderates the relation between conflictual independence and progress in the commitment to a career choice. This is illustrated in Figure 2.

Increases in freedom from conflict over the separation process are associated with stronger increases in commitment to career choice for family-business children than for non-family-business children.

The results of the hypothesis predicting that family business membership could have a moderating effect on the relationship between psychological separation and vocational identity receives no support, as indicated in Table 6. Parental Occupation Type does not moderate the relation between conflictual independence and vocational identity.

Discussion

This study's findings reveal that late adolescents with a parent working for their own family's business may have slight deficits in vocational identity compared to those whose parents work for a non-family business. In other words, late adolescents from families who own their own business have a less clear sense of their abilities, talents, and interests in a career than do late adolescents from non-family-business homes.

Possible explanations for this finding lie in the characteristics of family businesses and their leaders. As Table 3 shows, there are notable demographic and descriptive differences between the family-business group and non-family-business group. One obvious difference is the absence of retired, primary breadwinner parents in the family-business group versus 8% in the non-family-business group. This finding may reflect the inability of family-business leaders to relinquish control of the business, which frequently occurs during the succession process (Barry, 1989; Beckhard and Dyer, 1983). It is possible that tensions surrounding this transition may focus children's energies on the leader and away from their own development, resulting in lower vocational identity.

Other demographic differences concern family involvement in the workplace. A much higher percentage of the family-business group than the non-family-business group reports both parents as working for the same company (35% versus 10.2%), a sibling working in the firm (43.9% versus 9.1%), or an extended family member employed in the enterprise (54.5% versus 26.7%). Additionally, a higher percentage of family-business members say they can enter their parent's firm if they choose (62.1% versus 35.4%), and the percentage of family-business children who intend to enter the firm of their primary breadwinner parent is twice that of the non-family-business group (18.2% versus 8.9%). Nearly six times as many family-business children report pressure from their fathers to join the business (13.6% versus 2.3%), and four times as many family-business children perceive similar pressure from mothers (4.5% versus 1.1%). The percentage of family-business-group members who experience distress by not joining their parent's firm is 12 times greater than the non-family-business group (13.6% versus 1.1%). Interestingly, the percentage of family-business children who report paternal pressure to join the family firm is identical to the percentage of family-business children who say they would experience distress if they did not join the firm. A subsequent examination of the relation between perceived paternal pressure to join the firm and perceived distress by not joining the firm reveals a significant correlation ($r = 0.60$, $p < 0.001$).

Considered together, these observations support previous contentions that late adolescents from families in business are exposed to greater familial involvement in the workplace, thus potentially blurring the line between work and family (Barnes, 1988; Galagan, 1985; Kepner, 1983). Secondly, the observations suggest that late adolescents from families in business perceive a greater opportunity to follow the career paths of parents, but also perceive stronger internal and external pressures to engage in these paths. The significant difference on vocational identity between the groups may also reflect the centripetal, or inward focus (Beavers, 1977) that is said to occur in family-business families (Davis, 1983; Miller and Rice, 1988). By directing energies towards familial involvement, the family-business adolescent may forgo opportunities to become more aware of his or her skills, talents, and interests, thus resulting in lower vocational identity development (Holland et al., 1980).

However, if there is a greater focus on the family, this focus does not manifest itself through greater perceived overinvolvement with parents. Overinvolvement can be thought of as an absence of psychological separation to the degree that children are not free to make decisions independently, hold beliefs and attitudes that are different from parents, or function without excessive parental approval and emotional support (Rice, Cole, and Lapsley, 1990). Overinvolvement can also include excessive guilt or resentment towards parents (Hoffman, 1984). In this study, the family-business and non-family-business groups do not differ in the levels of reported psychological separation from parents. Despite strong theoretical and anecdotal evidence documenting parental overinvolvement in family-business families, family-business children do not appear any more overinvolved with their parents than are non-family business children.

We find significant interactions between parental occupation type and psychological separation for both the tendency to foreclose on a career choice and progress toward committing to a career choice. This suggests that family business membership has an impact on the career development process. As family-business children become more conflictually overinvolved with their parents, they are less likely to commit to career choices. Overinvolvement with parents appears to inhibit the necessary tasks involved in committing to career choices. One way to interpret this is that family-business children may not commit to career choices because they do not want to commit to the family business, or perhaps they do not wish to commit to a career choice away from the family. Though we theorize here that increased overinvolvement could lead to greater commitment for family-business children, lack of commitment must not be confused with absence of a career choice. If a family-business member refrains from occupational choice commitment, they may still end up working for the family by default. In essence, where refusal or inability to commit may lead to indecision for non-family-business children (Lopez and Andrews, 1987), it is quite possible that this same refusal or inability to commit among family business children directs their career path to the family enterprise.

Demographic factors also influence the choice to enter the family business. In our study, many of the family firms represented are quite small (mean = 34.5). Particularly when a family firm is small, the number of siblings can impact the individual's expectation level for entry into the business. There may not be room in the firm for more than one child. If the child is an only child and the parents seek family involvement, the amount of self-applied and parental pressure to enter the business can be high, whereas a large family has several children who can fill this need. Conversely, a later child could be freer to choose other occupations if an earlier child entered the firm and the business could not support another employee. Though this study does not consider them as variables, company size, birth order, and family size can each exert strong influences on late adolescents' career decision-making processes.

Parental Occupation Type also moderates the relation between psychological separation and the tendency to foreclose on a career choice. Compared to non-family-business children, family-business children take a more closed, dogmatic approach to career decision making when there is more separation from parents. It may be that as non-family-business children gain independence from parents, there is an increased understanding of available career options to which they become more open. The family-business adolescent's more closed approach to career choice-making can reflect the modeling they encounter regarding decision making. Family-business founders and leaders tend to be autocratic and dogmatic in their approach to managing (Hollander and Elman, 1988). Family-business children may have learned through mastery modeling (Bandura, 1986) that a closed approach to making decisions, including their career decisions, leads to success.

Ironically, all three significant findings of the aforementioned studies contraindicates their earlier formulations. Evidence suggests that family-business children score higher on vocational identity than do non-family-business children. Furthermore, increases in parental overinvolvement were theorized to associate with increases in tendency to foreclose on a career choice and increases in commitment to career choices for family-business children, relative to non-family-business children. Instead, we find that family-business children possess lower vocational identity than do non-family-business children, and increases in parental overinvolvement are associated with decreases in commitment to career choices. Furthermore, the tendency to foreclose on a career choice is nearly unresponsive to increases in parental overinvolvement for the family-business group, but is associated with decreases in the non-family-business group. The presence of three significant counterhypothetical findings suggests that they are not simply anomalies. Erikson's (1959, 1968) theories of identity development may suggest a singular explanation.

Late adolescents require earned successes and accomplishments to develop strong ego identities. Failure to do so can result in an inner questioning of the individual's true identity (Erikson, 1959). Studies report that family business children experience identity problems and question their ability to succeed outside of the family organization, particularly when there is an overcontrolling parent/owner (Barry, 1989; Galagan, 1985; Miller and Rice, 1988). This appears to reflect identity underdevelopment. Commitment to a vocational choice could be difficult for children who have not yet settled upon identities (Erikson, 1959). For family-business children, the decrease in vocational commitment that was observed as parental overinvolvement increased suggested identity development difficulties, which made commitment to a career more difficult.

Implications. There is a need for family-business owners to take specific actions to better ensure appropriate identity development among their children, especially vocational identity development. Business-owning parents can accomplish this by fostering open communication about the business and their expectations for family members who wish to enter the firm. Open communication allows children to learn about business needs, compare their abilities and talents to those needs, and actively develop skills where they find deficiencies. Vocational identity develops as children compare their skills against objective criteria. Parents can further this process by supporting their children in seeking outside professional assistance to accurately assess their interests, abilities, and personality traits. Parents can also encourage or require the establishment of goals that provide direction in skill development, task accomplishment, and the development of the personality characteristics needed to succeed. This is especially important for children who seek to enter into the firm.

Children can also take responsibility for developing their vocational identities. Participating in self-assessments and establishing goals, even if those goals are somewhat unrealistic at first, can provide a greater sense of self control. Whether or not they intend to work in the family firm, taking action to learn about occupations or businesses other than the family firm will allow children to recognize where their interests and motivations lie. Talking to adults in a variety of professions can help identify workplace realities. Finally, late adolescents from business-owning families have a responsibility to sit down with their parents and pointedly ask about expectations surrounding the family firm. In this study, 38% of the family-business group were not sure if they could enter the family business; 38% were unsure if their mothers wanted them to join the business; and 46% were not sure if their fathers wanted them to join the firm. It is quite likely that many of these individuals could achieve greater self-definition by having a realistic understanding of their options regarding family-business employment.

This study demonstrates that late adolescents in family-business families do not, as some have argued, experience greater overinvolvement with their parents than do other children. The frequently reported overinvolvement among family-business members could reflect the manner in which data are collected. The family-business literature is replete with articles from consultants who were brought in to help resolve existing problems, and research has typically been conducted in organizations that are known to have high family involvement. It may be that overinvolved family businesses tend to receive outside assistance, and the dynamics in these firms have led to theory formation. Rather than generalize these findings to all family businesses, efforts are needed to systematically determine the impact on children in problematic family enterprises versus those that report no problems.

The results have implications for family-business consultants and counselors. These advisors may wish to alert family-business leaders about the potential risk of exerting great influence to pressure children into the firm unwillingly. The parent/owner may get them to join the company, but the lack of commitment to the choice may transpire into a less enthusiastic and unsatisfied employee. When providing counsel to family-business children, advisors should also be aware that these children have lower vocational identity, which means that their sense of self may be diminished. Encouraging parent/owners to provide opportunities for their children's self-definition is recommended.

References

Bandura, A. (1986). *Social foundations of thought and action: A social cognitive theory.* Englewood Cliffs, NJ: Prentice-Hall, Inc.

Barnes, L. B. (1988). Incongruent hierarchies: Daughters and younger sons as company CEOs. *Family Business Review, 1* (1), 9-21.

Baron, R. M., &Kenny, D. A. (1986). The moderator-mediator variable distinction in social psychological research: Conceptual, strategic, and statistical considerations. *Journal of Personality and Social Psychology, 51* (6), 1173-1182.

Barry, B. (1989). The development of organizational structure in the family firm. *Family Business Review, 2* (3), 293-315.

Beavers, W. R. (1982). Healthy, midrange, and severely dysfunctional families. In F. Walsh (Ed.), *Normal Family Processes.* New York: Guilford.

Beavers, W. R. (1977). *Psychotherapy and growth: A family systems perspective.* New York: Brunner/Mazel.

Beckhard, R., &Dyer, W. G., Jr. (1983). Managing continuity in the family-owned business. *Organizational Dynamics, 12* (1), 5-12.

Blos, P. (1979). *The adolescent passage.* New York: International Universities Press, Inc.

Blustein, D. L., Ellis, M. V., &Devenis, L. E. (1989). The development and validation of a two-dimensional model of the commitment to career choices process (Monograph). *Journal of Vocational Behavior, 35* (3), 342-378.

Blustein, D. L., Walbridge, M. M., Friedlander, M. L., &Palladino, D. E. (1991). Contributions of psychological separation and parental attachment to the career development process. *Journal of Counseling Psychology, 38* (1), 39-50.

Bork, D. (1986). *Family business, risky business: How to make it work.* New York: American Management Association.

Bowen, M. (1976). Theory in the practice of psychotherapy. In P. Guerin (Ed.), *Family therapy* (pp. 42-90). New York: Gardner Press.

Bratcher, W. E. (1982). The influence of the family on career selection: A family systems perspective. *Personnel and Guidance Journal, 61,* 87-91.

Cohen, J., & Cohen, P. (1983). *Applied multiple regression/correlation analysis for the behavioral sciences.* Hillsdale, NJ: Lawrence Erlbaum Associates.

Davis, P. (1983). Realizing the potential of the family business. *Organizational Dynamics, 12* (1), 47-56.

Dillman, D. A. (1976). Mail and telephone surveys: The total design method. New York: Wiley-Interscience.

Dumas, C. (1989). Understanding of father-daughter and father-son dyads in family owned businesses. *Family Business Review, 2* (1), 31-46.

Erikson, E. H. (1959). *Identity and the life cycle.* New York: W. W. Norton &Company.

Erikson, E. H. (1968). *Identity: Youth and crisis.* New York: W. W. Norton &Company.

Fuqua, D. R., & Newman, J. L. (1989). An examination of the relations among career subscales. *Journal of Counseling Psychology, 36* (4), 487-491.

Galagan, P. (1985). Between family and firm. *Training and Development Journal, 39* (4), 68-71.

Ginzberg, E. (1984). Career development. In D. Brown and L. Brooks (Eds.), *Career choice and development* (pp. 169-191). San Francisco: Jossey-Bass.

Ginzberg, E., Ginsburg, S. W., Axelrad, S., & Herma, J. L. (1951). *Occupational choice: An approach to a general theory.* New York: Columbia University Press.

Harren, V. H. (1979). A model of career decision-making for college students. *Journal of Vocational Behavior, 14* (2), 119-133.

Healy, C. C., Tullier, M., &Mourton, D. M. (1990). My socational situation: Its relation to concurrent career and future academic benchmarks. *Measurement and evaluation in counseling and development, 23* (3), 100-107.

Hoffman, J. (1984). Psychological separation of late adolescents from their parents. *Journal of Counseling Psychology, 31* (2), 170-178.

Holland, J. L. (1985). *Making vocational choices: A theory of vocational personalities and work environments.* Englewood Cliffs, NJ: Prentice-Hall.

Holland, J. L., Daiger, D. C., & Power, P. G. (1980). *My vocational situation.* Palo Alto, CA: Consulting Psychologists Press.

Hollander, B. S., & Bukowitz, W. R. (1990). Women, family culture, and family business. *Family Business Review, 3* (2), 139-151.

Hollander, B. S., &Elman, N. S. (1988). Family-owned businesses: An emerging field of inquiry. *Family Business Review, 1* (2), 145-164.

Josselson, R. (1988). The embedded self: I and thou revisited. In D. K. Lapsley & F. C. Powers (Eds.), *Self, ego, and identity: Integrative approaches* (pp. 91-108).

Kaye, K. (1992). The kid brother. *Family Business Review, 5* (3), 237-256.

Kenny, M. E., & Donaldson, G. A. (1991). Contributions of parental attachment and family structure to the social and psychological functioning of first-year college students. *Journal of Counseling Psychology, 38* (4), 479-486.

Kepner, E. (1983). The family and the firm: A coevolutionary perspective. *Organizational Dynamics, 12* (1), 57-70.

Kerr, M. E., & Bowen, M. (1988). *Family evaluation: An approach based on Bowen theory.* New York: W. W. Norton and Company.

Levinson, D. J. (1978). *The season's of a man's life.* New York: Alfred A. Knopf.

Lopez, F. G., & Andrews, S. (1987). Career indecision: A family systems perspective. *Journal of Counseling and Development, 65* (2), 304-307.

Lopez, F. G., Campbell, V. L., & Watkins, C. E. (1988). Family structure, psychological separation, and college adjustment: A canonical analysis and cross-validation. *Journal of Counseling Psychology, 35* (4), 402-409.

Marcia, J. E. (1966). Development and validation of ego identity status. *Journal of Personality and Social Psychology, 3* (5), 551-558.

Marcia, J. E. (1980). Identity in adolescence. In J. Adelson (Ed.), Handbook of adolescent psychology (pp. 159-187). New York: Wiley.

MassMutual. (1994). *1994 Research findings.* Springfield, MA: Author.

Miller, E. J., & Rice, A. K. (1988). The family business in contemporary society. *Family Business Review, 1* (2), 193-210.

Minuchin, S. (1974). *Families and family therapy.* Cambridge, MA: Harvard University Press.

Mitchell, M., & Jolley, J. (1988). *Research design explained.* New York: Holt, Rinehart, and Winston, Inc.

Neter, J., Wasserman, W., & Kutner, M. H. (1990). Applied linear statistical models: Regression, analysis of variance, and experimental designs. Boston: Irwin.

Penick, N. I., & Jepsen, D. A. (1992). Family functioning and adolescent career development. *Career Development Quarterly, 40* (3), 208-222.

Rice, K. G., Cole, D. A., & Lapsley, D. K. (1990). Separation-individuation, family cohesion, and adjustment to college: Measurement validation and test of a theoretical model. *Journal of Counseling Psychology, 37* (2), 195-202.

Ross, T. J., & Spencer, F. (1988). Reliability and utility of MVS for a psychiatric population. *The Career Development Quarterly, 37* (1), 70-77.

Savickas, M. L. (1989). Annual review: Practice and research in career counseling and development, 1988. *Career Development Quarterly, 38* (2), 100-135.

Super, D. E. (1957). *The psychology of careers.* New York: Harper & Row.

Super, D. E. (1990). A life-span, life-space approach to career development. In D. Brown and L. Brooks (Eds.), *Career choice and development* (pp. 197-261). San Francisco: Jossey-Bass.

Ward, J. L. (1987). *Keeping the family business healthy: How to plan for continued growth, profitability, and family leadership.* San Francisco: Jossey-Bass.

Waterman, A. S. (1985). Identity in the context of adolescent psychology. In A. S. Waterman (Ed.), *Identity in adolescence: Processes and contents* (pp. 5-24). San Francisco: Jossey-Bass.

Zingaro, J. C. (1983). A family systems approach for the career counselor. *Personnel and Guidance Journal, 62* (1), 24-27.

Too many family business owners keep too many secrets. Why? Some fear competitors gaining knowledge. Others fear spreading bad news or worry that if the extent of success is known, others will want a bigger piece of the pie. Still others worry about losing control.

But playing it too close to the vest restricts effective team building, injures initiative and job effectiveness, and reduces trust and motivation. It also leads to family conflict.

To combat the tendency to be overly secretive, develop a strategic plan to share with the organization, institute performance appraisal systems which stress two-way communication, and encourage open communication among family members.

Do You Keep Too Many Secrets?

By Benjamin Benson

Family-business owners have a reputation for being secretive. But keeping secrets is not always best for your business – or your family.

Picture a football coach trying to inspire his team at halftime:

Coach: We can win this game if we all pull together as a team.
Player: It would help, Coach, if we knew where the goal line was.
Coach: Don't worry. I'll let you know when you're getting close.
Player: But we don't even know the score.
Coach: You don't have to know it. Just do your job.

It sounds ridiculous, doesn't it? Yet versions of this dialogue are played out daily in countless family businesses. Ask the boss about his views on religion, politics, or sex, and you may get candid answers. Just don't bring up any forbidden topics, such as the company's financial statements or his plans for the business. Instead of clear signals from management, employees must depend on the company grapevine, with all of its distortions.

And don't think that this attitude is directed only toward employees. A son working in his family's firm once told me: "I'm committing my life to this business, yet I don't know Dad's plans for retirement, his thoughts about a successor, or who will own the stock when he dies. I don't dare bring it up, though, because it will make me look unappreciative and greedy."

Of course, this behavior doesn't apply to all owners. Many are able to build open, effective organizations.

Why, then, do so many others play it so close to the vest? Is it out of fear that competitors would benefit if they had access to inside information? Or that employees would leave if they knew how bad business was – or would want a bigger piece of the pie if they knew how much money the business was making?

Despite the risks they have taken, some owners feel guilty about accumulating a disproportionate amount of wealth compared with their employees. Others have an inordinate need for control. When the business is in its infancy, they get involved in every aspect of the operation, down to the smallest detail. When it gets too big to allow that level of involvement, they maintain control by being the almighty source of information, the "keeper of the secrets."

Such behavior prohibits the team building that is essential to creating a lasting business.

People need information to do their jobs properly; in well-managed businesses, information is complete, timely, straightforward, and widely disseminated.

Research shows that the secretive approach leads to low employee morale, substandard performance, and ultimately, to the loss of high performers who tire of mind-reading and guessing games.

It also leads to family conflict as misconceptions develop and ill feeling festers.

I believe many owners would change their secretive styles if they realized how destructive such styles are to their enterprises and their families. If you are one of those owners, here are some ways for you to begin:

Create a strategic business plan. Many owners find it difficult to share their vision for the company with employees and family members because they often don't have a clear picture themselves. You can start to shape your company's future by creating a strategic business plan – a living document that will drive daily operations for the next three to five years, subject to periodic fine-tuning and modification.

Begin with a retreat of two or three days with your key managers. Together, establish goals, identify strategies, and assign responsibilities (with timetables). This process will help you to focus your resources in an organized way, and you won't have to rely on "seat-of-the-pants" management.

When its content is communicated throughout the organization, your strategic plan can be a real "turn-on" as employees get a clear understanding of the company's goals and how their jobs fit into the greater picture.

Be a Listener. Many owners are better at giving orders than at listening. The company of one such owner was experiencing a sales decline. Members of the sales force knew why but could not bring themselves to tell the boss. "He doesn't want to hear anything that conflicts with his view of the situation," one salesman lamented.

Overemphasis on secrecy usually works both ways, and if you are secretive, you may be cutting off important upstream information.

Make it easy for your employees to share their views with you and to disagree with you. After all, they may be right.

Establish two-way performance evaluations. Many bosses assign a task and say, "If you mess up, you'll hear from me. Otherwise, assume you're doing OK."

If you want to enhance employee performance and commitment, there's a better way: Establish a performance evaluation process with a written evaluation for every employee, including family members. It begins with a definition of their job responsibilities and objectives – arrived at with their participation-and is periodically followed by a constructive assessment of their progress.

All employees want to know what is expected of them, how they are doing, and how they can improve their performance. This is vital information, too and it should be shared, not kept inside the head of the business owner.

Encourage open communication in the family. You don't have to carry the entire burden of the family/business relationship. It's your family's responsibility, too.

Developing a family "constitution" that defines the family's relationship to the business can be an important step in opening the lines of communication.

Encourage discussion. Listen to your family's concerns. Meet the important issues head-on and establish policies concerning them.

These may include the family's ultimate plans for the business, management succession, the owner's retirement plans, rules regarding family members' participation in the business, and plans for the next generation's ownership of stock.

If you can face up to these issues together as a family, you stand 3 better chance of keeping misunderstandings from heating up into severe conflict.

These suggestions probably involve more structure than you are accustomed to, and if you're inclined to be secretive, they may make you uncomfortable.

However, as you move toward the openness recommended here, you will probably find that it can have a profound and positive influence on the success of your business and the harmony of your family.

This article was originally printed in *Nation's Business*, August 1989.

Copyright 1989, U.S. Chamber of Commerce. Reprinted with permission of the publisher.

Families and businesses develop structures and cultures. In a family business these cultures over-lap and reflect each other. The founding generation of a family firm should establish ground rules and define the integration of their two cultures. Satisfaction with involvement in the family business is related to the fit between family and business values. Subsequent generations must redefine family business culture to adapt to changing times. Adaptation is stimulated when fam-ily business systems are forced to deal with crises, often beginning around seemingly minor issues with major consequences An example illustrates the cultural evolution of a complete fam-ily-business system.

Building Successful, Enterprising Families

By Susan Golden

What's satisfying about being a family member of a family business? What makes it work for you? What's your definition of being a successful family business?

As a family therapist accustomed to meeting families when they are in trouble, I am better at seeing pitfalls than windfalls. Interviewing family business members has given me an appreciation of the rich variety of the kinds of successful family businesses at dif-ferent stages of development. Just as each family has its own organization and 'culture' developed across generations, businesses also develop an organizational structure and cul-ture.

When an organization is a family business, the two cultures overlap and resect back on each other. There is an exchange back and forth. The task of the first generation of a family business is to set the ground rules and define the integration of these two cultures.

Family businesses are special cultures because they share a fundamental belief in the interdependence of family members, stressing and valuing family connectedness. As a result the action and perceptions of one member can have enormous implications for other family members. The task of the founder is to develop a stable and coherent ideol-ogy for the business that will enable the family to work together to build the business.

Satisfaction with being an on-going part of the business is often related to the level of fit between family values and the nature of the business. A book manufacturer described his satisfaction with his career in his fourth generation family business as related to the fact that he sees it as a clean business, where he values the product, meets and works with interesting, diverse and bright people. This contrasts with the satisfaction expressed by a second generation owner of a scrap metal business. He commented that his family has always been good at making do, making the most of things. They enjoy working with messes and turning them into something constructive and lucrative, and find the industry fits with their enjoyment of a lot of conflict and the intensity which is part of the process.

These themes are then integrated into the family culture its definition of itself. The choice of the kind of business that the family founds amounts to the selection of a work environment that the family will seek to control, and that will, in turn, greatly influence the environment of the family. Subsequent generations must eventually redefine the cul-ture of the family business for it to continue to successfully adapt to changing times.

Interviewing family business families, I have been struck by the centrality of the fam-ily culture in determining the business' vulnerabilities and strengths. Davis and Stern from the Wharton School describe the importance for family businesses of establishing a valid legitimizing structure; a set of values, norms and principles which generate behav-ior, which is jointly adapted to the needs of both the family and the business task system. Another term for this is the family business's paradigm.

Crises can serve an adaptive role in the development of this legitimizing structure or paradigm in the family business.

A crisis presents an opportunity to restore family cohesion and to revise the rules of the family culture, shifting the definition of what the family and business are about in response to the changing needs and stages of development. If these changes are adaptive, and new family business rules emerge, the family and business can be strengthened. Obviously crises can also result in loss of all kinds. The family paradigm in the well functioning family is shaped by the crisis it encounters. The seeds of the paradigm are evident in the family business founder's story of "how we came to be, who we are and what we are about." The first revision is evident in the story of the business' first crisis, as family and business goals begin to shift in response to actual experience working together. It is modified as new solutions to the challenge of perpetuating the family business emerge. The paradigm provides cohesion, differentiates this business from other businesses, reaffirms values, provides directions, goals and priorities.

In successful family businesses there exists:

1. a fit between the task of the business and the paradigm of the originating family.
2. a paradigm which contains rules for how things are done here, guidelines for dealing with crisis, with conflict between future growth versus a maintenance approach, as well as for continued belonging (who we are, what we can be, the kind of business and people we are).

There are rules about trust and mistrust which determine the role of outsiders, spouses, non-family employees, and rules for screening and bringing in new ideas, allowing for subsequent maximization of good fit for outsiders brought into the system. There are rules for handling differences, areas of conflict and risk-taking and finally, the paradigm contains the seeds of the model of succession that will work for the family (based on family precedents for separation and differentiation).

The following example illustrates a small second generation business's use of a crisis to lay the groundwork for movement to the next developmental stage. This service business was founded as a mom and pop shop with the husband running production and his wife doing the books, controlling the money. The family had eight children, six sons.

At the time of interviewing, the father had been semi-retired for four years because of a stroke. The mother still ran the books and was the conduit for information on the business to her husband. The three oldest sons then drew up a legal partnership agreement that established rules based on fairness and performance that would enable the younger siblings to qualify for partnership.

The evolution of this document was consistent with the family goal of staying together, and shared value of fairness, and the ethos that any family member who wants to and works hard, can join the business. However, this document was developed with the expectation that the business could potentially expand to meet the needs of all family members, supporting three to eight families. While the business tripled in size in four years, it was unclear whether it would have the capacity to expand eight-fold to accommodate the family goal of keeping everybody in the business.

At the time of the founding, the goal of the business was to simply provide a living for the family. By the second generation the goal had become to keep the family working together as a team, particularly the sons. The family values of working hard, staying together, mutual responsibility, pride in quality teamwork and fairness were central to the development of the second generation's horizontal structure. The questions they faced in this generation were: How do you earn your place? Can you be your own person? Can the business support this expanded family?

Minor crises do not always generate minor consequences. Revision of the family paradigm often begin around seemingly small issues, preparing the way for work on major changes and differences. While many of the sons and their wives were entering the parenthood years, the mother who controlled the money in the business and her oldest daughter who worked in the office, experienced their minor disagreements and tensions escalate into a major family blow-up. There was a great deal of conflict in this usually how conflict family, pressure to take sides, and ultimately the lining up of all family members and their spouses on either the mother's side or the daughter's side. Finally, the daughter decided to leave the company, the first family member to leave. Her husband stayed on as an employee.

The crisis over the daughter served to clarify aspects of the family ethos, and lay groundwork for several important upcoming family issues: 1) the conflict between the family need to perpetuate connection and all continuing to work together, with the business's need for disconnection, (i.e. acknowledge increased competition for scarce resources, worry that the payroll wouldn't be able to support all family members, raising the possibility of either restructuring or splintering) and 2) the issue of succession, who would take over the mother's role.

The crisis outcome reaffirmed: that it is possible to leave the business by rehearsing a leave-taking crisis with a less central family figure, the oldest daughter; and that the succession issue was premature. The father was ill and out, but the mother was still central and the sons would side with her.

The crisis was an impetus to revise the goal of the business of keeping the brothers working as a team. It fostered decisions which served to differentiate more dearly separate spheres of control for the brothers, reducing the threat of too much increased conflict by simmering down areas of greater competition. Also, shortly after the crisis, the brothers decided that the middle son would take over the task of working more closely with the mother, gradually taking over the books and beginning for the computerization of more company functions.

The brothers then worked together to develop plans for expansion, use of new technologies to broaden the base of the business, and made two decisions which served to create a healthier distance between them. One brother began to set up out of town contracts. The group also decided to build an addition to their office space that would provide more privacy and separate offices for the first time.

The work out of town perpetuated another crisis when it coincided with the birth of a new baby in the family and there was a period of increased tension with the wives. Through the crisis the wives formed a stronger coalition, advocating for their needs, pressing for more home involvement and structured, predictable vacations for their spouses. This surfaced issues to differentiate more dearly points of conflict between the business's needs and the differing needs of the individual nuclear family units.

Some of the signs of well functioning on the part of the family were their ability to use the crisis to reaffirm basic family values and an ethos of balancing the needs of the business, the extended family and individual family units; and their ability to use the crisis to develop adaptive strategies for innovation and expansion, hence, family and business survival; and finally, their ability to begin to surface the upcoming issues of some brothers or sisters leaving the business, of the mother's movement out of the business and out of her role as information link to father, and of differential role expectations.

The family was able to begin to recognize and legitimate the wives' roles by helping the sons establish dearer boundaries from their family of origin and the business. They were able to begin to air conflict and establish rules as they entered a stage requiring greater conflict and differing visions of the future.

The family's areas of vulnerability seemed to be the possibility that they might be distracted from key conflictual issues by creating tension and false fights between the wives, and that the younger, unmarried family members would choose spouses that challenged the rules of the system and wanted more involvement. Thus far, the brothers had chosen wives with independent professions who did not want to be part of the business, and could buffer financial crises when the company had trouble meeting payroll.

Without marriages, family businesses cannot continue. But the integration of outsiders into the family and the business through marriage, introduces complex dynamics and concerns. This article suggests means by which new spouses and family businesses can cope effectively.

Marrying Into Family Business

By Sharon Nelton

Marriage is both the blessing and the curse of a family business. Without marriages and the children they produce, businesses wouldn't be family businesses. But marriages can lead to divorce, remarriage, stepparents, stepchildren, problems with in-laws, and, consequently, uneasiness or outright conflict in a family firm and occasionally a threat to the business itself. The business, on the other hand, can be so demanding that it strains a marriage – sometimes to the breaking point.

It's natural to have some fears when someone in your family is getting married. In a business family, says John Ward, a professor of free enterprise at Loyola University Chicago, those fears are more likely to be concerns about "emotional alliances" than about the possibility of divorce and the financial impact it might have on the business. "The important problem is that the daughter-in-law is going to side with her husband against her father-in-l aw if there's a father-son problem or against the husband's brother in a sibling-run business," says Ward.

How can a family business cope with the issues that marriage raises? It helps first to look at things from the viewpoint of the "outsider." What can you expect if you are marrying into a family business?

There are benefits. You may be marrying into wealth. You may have opportunities such as working in the business and even sharing in its ownership. And you may enjoy the love of a family that is strong, close-knit, and exciting, as business families often are.

But that business family may also include what San Diego psychologist Ken Druck calls"a very powerful, nurturing system." If you have not come from such a strong family, he says,"you may become infatuated with this system. You may want to just immerse yourself in it."

There is a lot of interaction in such families because their members deal with one another at work as well as after hours. For the new in-law, says Druck, this can be overwhelming. "There's going to be more to manage."

Among the things to be managed will be pressure to conform to the family norms, according to David Bork, a nationally known family-business consultant based in Aspen, Colorado. Says Bork: "Very often, what happens is that you are expected to take on a role similar to the same-sex person in the family that owns the business." If no women in the family are involved in the business, for example, a new daughter-in-law would probably be discouraged from having an active role.

Before you marry into a family business, you should have a very strong sense of yourself and your own value, Bork counsels. Then, with your new spouse, he adds, you must "really focus on establishing a sense of identity as a couple apart from the business."

For some, marrying into a family business results in relocation. Monica Geocaris grew up in rural St. Francis, Kan. After college, she did secretarial and administrative work for eight years in Denver. There she met and fell in love with a law student, John Geocaris. Following their marriage, they went to John's hometown, Chicago, so that John could join his family's restaurant and beer-distribution business.

"It was a bit of a culture shock," says Monica Geocaris. Now she was living in a house in the suburbs of a big city, and her identity had become "John's wife," she says. "I felt a little bit misplaced."

New in-laws may feel they are regarded with suspicion. And they are. "The moment that the daughter-in-law comes into the family, she's on trial," says Ward. "Everybody is hypersensitive to all the subtle signals she may be giving as to whether she's 'with us or against us.' "

Because she's in a new culture and she's just trying to take it all in, that daughter-in-law may seem reserved. But the strong business family, says Ward, may be wondering: "Why aren't you joining us faster? Why aren't you committing yourself to us?"

Isolation can be another problem. Ten years ago Robin Raymond left an established business as a portrait photographer in her beloved Chicago to marry a widower, George G. Raymond Jr., head of the Raymond Corp., a manufacturing and distribution firm in Greene, N.Y. The tiny upstate town revolved around the Raymond Corp., a 1,500-employee public company partly owned by the Raymond family.

While she made friends, Robin felt she didn't have "real acceptance." And she missed the cultural events available in Chicago. After 2 1/2 years, the Raymonds moved to Binghamton, 18 miles away, and until his recent retirement, George commuted to Greene.

When sons or daughters work in the family business, they may feel they have something to prove, and therefore they may spend an extraordinary amount of time at work. And the less time they spend at home or with the children, the more their spouses can come to resent the business.

Sons or daughters may also bring home all the problems they have at work-such as disagreements with Dad or a sibling. If you're the husband or wife, you may be tempted to take sides with your spouse. But if you do, warns Ken Druck, you may find yourself in a position "that may polarize you against one or several family members." The best way to be supportive, adds Druck's wife, Karen, also a psychologist, is not to try to tell a spouse what to do but to ask good questions. Instead of agreeing with a son who complains that he's not earning enough money, for example, a wife might say, "Honey, if this wasn't a family business, what do you think you should be earning?" Then the son can start exploring the issue himself.

One of the hardest decisions a newcomer may have to make is whether to join the family business. Many families put pressure on their children and their children's spouses to work in the firm. For some in-laws, the business can be a perfect fit. Barbara Baylor used to teach music in school. Now she is part owner of Country Cupboard, a $7.5-million-a-year restaurant and inn that she helped start with her husband and members of his family in Lewisburg, Pa., in 1973. She says she finds her business career "much more satisfying" than teaching.

Monica Geocaris also enjoys her role as account executive for Little Lady Foods Inc., a frozen-pizza business in a Elk Grove Village, IL, that the Geocaris family acquired in 1985. She likes the work, and she likes the flexibility she works three days a week so that she can spend some time with her two young children.

At the same time, she finds that she's harder on herself than she would be if she worked for another company. Her husband is president of the 80-employee firm. "When you come in as the boss's wife, you feel a certain pressure to perform better than a non-family member might,"she says.

Family-business experts advise new in-laws to acquire outside experience before they join the family firm. Says David Bork, "I would stress the importance of being well-qualified before you get caught up in the business. There's no substitute for competence in family businesses."

Being competent gives you more than confidence; it minimizes the tendency of non-family employees to believe that you got your job just because you are a family member. Others advise that you make sure there's a real job there with sharply defined responsibilities. Otherwise, relatives will be doing the same tasks as you are, and, says Monica Geocaris's father-in-law, Angelo Geocaris, you will be "underfoot all the time." Having separate responsibilities also avoids rivalry, points out Barbara Baylor's husband, Gary, who is president of Country Cupboard. Young people marrying into a family business are not the only ones who create concerns. If, after a divorce or the death of a spouse, the business owner remarries, a host of fears and ill feelings can surface.

Robin Raymond jokingly refers to herself as the "wicked stepmother" of the family business. George Raymond's three children, already adults when she married him, were still suffering over the death of their mother the year before. Robin had visions "that I would be able to tie up a lot of the wounds of a grieving family."

But that was not to be. While the children didn't seem anxious about having to share the family business or wealth, they regarded the marriage and their stepmother with hostility. "I think they were mad at me," George says. They had lost a mother and perhaps he muses, they now thought they were losing their father, too.

For some children, however, the appearance of a stepparent poses a real obstacle to inheritance or position in a business. One son had started working in his father's construction business as a teenager and had worked his way up to vice president by his early 30s. But his father died unexpectedly at age 52 and, to the surprise of the son, left everything to his second wife. She became president, and the son left to start his own firm.

With today's high rate of divorce, the possibility of a business owner's remarrying is one that can hardly be ignored. Bruce Monning, an attorney with the Dallas firm of Vial, Hamilton, Koch & Knox, says: "The big fears there are what are wife No. 2's motives and what is Dad's ability to balance his desire for happiness for the rest of his life with what the children perceive to be an obligation to perpetuate the wealth for their benefit."

Starting some early communication; may ease the situation, he suggests. "When the children see that Dad is enamored of Betty Boop or whomever,": he says, they should work together to establish a strategy for approaching their father and letting him know what their concerns are. They should also have a goal in mind regarding legal steps their parent might be willing to take to protect them. It might mean giving the children an interest in the business or a premarital agreement in which the second spouse relinquishes any claim to the business.

In a healthy family there's usually opportunity for informal give-and-take, says Monning, and discussing such issues might be addressed "in more spontaneous and less staged a manner."

Good communication is also important in handling other situations arising from relationships. Country Cupboard was started by Gary and Barbara Baylor, by Gary's sister and brother-in-law-Carole and Robert Hamm – and by Gary's parents. Gary recalls that his father, now retired, used to freeze Bob Hamm out of business discussions.

"My dad would pretty much decide what he wanted to do, and my brother in-law had to fall in behind us, and that was a great source of difficulty," says Gary. Now the two couples are running the business, and Bob Hamm is part of the inner circle. "The fact that we do communicate, we do sit down, we do listen, we do share, and we try to bring in everybody's point of view and get commitment and get consensus helps the system to work," says Gary.

And although George Raymond's children did not welcome his second wife to the family, Robin reports that some progress is being made with those relationships. "They've become a lot more forgiving, finally," she says. More important, she and George have been able to talk about the problem. "He understood, and he never let his children's feelings interfere with our relationship."

Communication before marriage helps, too. The couple should anticipate as many problems as possible and discuss how they will be handled. And, says Barbara Baylor, the one marrying into the business needs to ask questions such as: "Can I live within the constraints of what the family business requires? Can I live with the long hours? Can I live with the relationship that I'm going to have to develop in the business with my in-laws?"

Baylor says she knew just what she was getting into. She and Gary met when they were in fifth grade, and Barbara knew Gary's family very well before she married him. "For me, it turned out very nicely."

Families with businesses need mission statements for their families as well as businesses. The family mission statement is a document that lays out your family's goal of working together as a family in business, spells out the benefits and pledges the family to the goal Otis hammered out through discussion, clarifying areas of consensus and conflict Concerns are aired and discussed at a family meeting. If the business is seen as worth the family's commitment, write it down. The process can energize the family forbears to come.

A Family Needs a Mission Statement

By John L. Ward and Laurel S. Sorenson

Why does succession have to be so painful? Can our sons and daughters work together? Will our family business last?

These questions worry every family business. They come down to one issue: Is it worth it?

In times of doubt, it's helpful to open the desk drawer and take out a piece of paper that says "Yes! It is worth it," and goes on to say why.

This piece of paper is a family mission statement. Separate from the business mission statement, it lays out your goal-your dream, really-of working together as a family in business. It spells out the benefits. And it pledges your family to make the dream come true.

To be sure, coming up with such a statement isn't easy. Sometimes, even deciding to stay together in business is difficult. Uncomfortable questions must be asked-and answered-to make that happen. When should the business pass from one generation to the next? Who is welcome in the business? What qualifications must they have? What compensation do they deserve? What titles should be bestowed? How should ownership be distributed? What returns do owners deserve? How shall business decisions be made?

Any of these issues may spark a debate that will threaten your dream. Yet if your family has a commitment, you have a much better chance of resolving the debate than a family without it. A mission generates enthusiasm. It encourages solutions. And it diverts squabbles into more productive channels.

"Energies once devoted to sibling rivalry are now put to better use," says a manufacturer of specialty-meat products, who last year spent 16 hours over six months with his wife and four children (three work in the company) to develop the family's mission statement. "We now have a common understanding of the commitment we must have to the business. And we know what each of us can expect in return."

Preparing your mission statement means, first of all, getting the family together after hours in a conference room, the family den or even a vacation retreat. The setting doesn't matter, as long as the atmosphere is casual and the time is not constrained.

The leader of the discussion might begin by summing up the uncomfortable questions outlined above. "Family businesses inevitably have these tensions," he might add. "So this has got to be something we really want to do. Otherwise, it's not worth it. So do we want to do it? And if so, why?"

You can expect family members to exchange nervous glances. A few throats will be cleaved. Then comments will start to surface.

Some will be uncertain: "It's a lot of responsibility. I'm not sure I can work for Dad. What if fighting about the business tears the family apart?"

Others will be more positive: "I want to work for myself. Let's keep it alive for the kids. I think it's great working together as a family."

Airing concerns might take more than one meeting. But eventually, your family will arrive at a consensus. Then-if the answer is yes-you can set your dream down in a short document that everyone can refer to in the months ahead.

The specialty-meat manufacturer, for example, took just two sentences to summarize the family's decision. "We have a mutual commitment and obligation to family security and development. Perpetuating the family business will encourage independence and opportunity for self-actualization for all employees-family and non-family alike."

One of the best family mission statements we've seen comes from a family that has been in the newspaper business for those generations. Five sets of parents and all thou children met on three Saturdays over the course of a year at a local hotel.

Sticky issues that they examined ranged from developing retirement programs for parents to equalizing voting control among the families. Yet, they decided, strong emotional ties to the paper and to their hometown made the work worth the effort. Two "children" (in their 30s) volunteered to draft the decision as a letter between the generations.

"To our parents," the one-page epistle began. "We resolve to keep our company in the family as long as possible. We ask you to hand down a precious legacy. It's not money. It's not fancy cars and fat salaries. It's an opportunity to maintain a tradition of journalistic excellence

"You have instilled in us a tremendous pride in our business and in our family. It's because of this pride that we ask you to entrust us with this valuable inheritance."

The signatures of 19 of the younger generation lay below the last line.

You don't have to be a professional writer to get your point across. If your family agrees the business is worth the effort, just say so, in a brief letter to yourselves. Explain why. Then ask everyone to sign.

And keep in mind that it won't work to copy some other family's statement.

The process you go through in coming to agreement on your own is more important than the words you finally commit to paper, because if usually draws family members closer together. Once you've agreed to a mission statement, you'll find that it gives you energy and hope for years to come.

This article was originally printed in *Nation's Business*, October 1987.

Research on the work relationships of fathers and sons permitted the authors of this article to develop a model of the dynamics of father-son interactions in family business. Fathers' and son's greatest complaints with each other are listed as are the seven aspects of work relationships that determine relationship quality. The importance of work relationship context, relationship history and the interaction of respective life stages are explained.

Life Stages and Father-Son Work Relationships

By John Davis and Renato Tagiuri

Since the dawn of history fathers and sons have worked together with varying degrees of happiness and success. Stories of father-son conflict as well as inspiring tales of loyalty and triumph are numerous. While these stories hold important lessons for fathers and sons working together today, there is little knowledge based on systematic research of these work relationships. Family members often find themselves in multiple roles when they work together. They are simultaneously relatives, partner, superior, or subordinate, and probably co-owners. Thus this work relationship is much more complex than that of two unrelated people.

The Work Relationship Model

Our research on these work relationships has helped us develop a model to understand the dynamics of these interactions. The first major lesson of our model is that there are always two separate points of view in any relationship and one needs to take into account both parties' perspectives to understand their interpersonal dynamics. Consider for example, what fathers and sons complain about most often in their relationship (based on a survey of 89 father-son pairs).

What do Fathers complain about most often?
- My son is too much in a hurry to take over responsibilities.
- My son is not ready yet for more responsibility.
- He wants to change the way we do things, the way I know works.
- He wants to take too many chances and risk the company, which I, and my father before me, built from nothing with so much effort and so many sacrifices.
- He does not appreciate what I have accomplished.
- He does not trust my judgment and experience.
- He is better educated than I am, but I have graduated from the University of Hard Knocks. Most of what he knows is from books, or worse, from professors; and professors do not know how to get things done.
- He wants to change the goals and objectives of the company (e.g., diversify).
- He wants to push aside the middle-level managers who have been loyal to me since we began, who came with me and trusted me when I had nothing!

What do Sons complain about most often?
- My father is stuck in his ways of doing things. He does not understand what needs to be done nowadays.
- Father does not give me any authority. When he does, he countermands it, goes over my head.
- Father does not respect my judgment.
- Father does not treat employees in a respectful, professional way.
- Father does not recognize that he is no longer able to run the show.
- Father uses the work situation to teach me how to live. It makes me feel like a little boy all over again.

Clearly fathers and sons pay attention to different things in their work associations. Our work (Davis, 1982; Davis and Tagiuri, 1981; Tagiuri and Davis, 1982) indicates that there are a small number of aspects that strongly influence he quality of work in a relationship between any two people; whether it is healthy (productive, comfortable, and enjoyable) or unhealthy (unproductive, difficult, and painful). To understand a work relationship, consider, through each party's eyes, the following aspects, here stated in question form.

1. To what extent do we have AGREEMENT on goals? Each person will have his/her own understanding of what they want to accomplish working together. Do they agree about the purpose of being together? Do they agree on the goals of the company? Its strategies? If two people do not agree on what they and the company are supposed to accomplish by being together, this is likely to lead to serious conflict.

2. What is the DIVISION OF RESPONSIBILITIES between the two? Are their respective responsibilities *clearly* understood and agreed upon? Is there much *overlap* in responsibilities? Does the way the responsibilities are divided up help *get the job done*? Does it support each person's concept of himself/herself? Not surprisingly, most people want clearly defined responsibilities that overlap only a little with another's responsibilities to agree with how they see themselves.

3. Who has what kind of POWER in the relationship? On what does each persons' power depend? (e.g., on authority, title, knowledge, charisma, connection with a powerful person)? Has authority been allocated in proportion to responsibility? How does each person use his/her power (to get the job done, to coerce the other, or in some other way)? People typically want enough power to get their job done, and they want others to use their power for productive and not abusive purposes.

4. What are the SIMILARITIES and DIFFERENCES between the two persons in their objectives, abilities, traits, and work styles? Given the purpose of the relationship, in what ways is it better for them to be different? Consider similarity, complementarity, and incompatibility:

   For two persons working together, similarity in punctuality, for example, probably favors harmony. Differences that are complementary for achieving the work objectives also help the relationship. Thus if the task of the pair is to coordinate the production and marketing functions of an organization, it helps the relationship if one member is strong in one function and the second in the other. However, if one party wishes to take the work in a direction contrary to the wishes of the other, this incompatibility is likely to place great stress upon the relationship.

5. What SENTIMENTS does each hold for the other? Doe they like, love, trust, and respect each other? Do they dislike, or hate each other? To what extent does each respect and

Figure 1. Important Aspects of Work Relationships

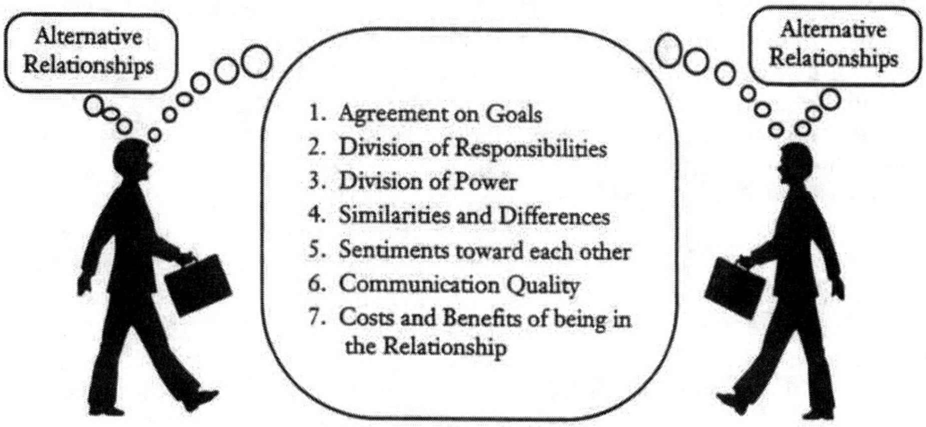

Alternative Relationships

1. Agreement on Goals
2. Division of Responsibilities
3. Division of Power
4. Similarities and Differences
5. Sentiments toward each other
6. Communication Quality
7. Costs and Benefits of being in the Relationship

Alternative Relationships

trust the other's (a) character and honesty, (b) competence, and (c) judgment? Are they indifferent?

Relationships are more satisfying and usually more productive when people feel positively toward each other. But even in work relationships where the parties initially like and trust each other, other aspects mentioned in this note can damage the relationship.

6. The ability and willingness of both parties to send and receive messages is an important determinant of how a pair will get along. How well does each relative listen to the other and control his own tendency to prejudge the other's remarks? How carefully does each person speak, write, and in other ways COMMUNICATE to increase the other's ability and willingness to understand the sender's message as the sender understands it?

7. What are the COSTS and the BENEFITS of the relationship for each person? That is, what is each giving and receiving as a result of the work relationship and how does this measure up to what each can comfortably give and what each wants? Does each person profit from the relationship? If one or both members feel short-changed, and believe they contribute more than they benefit from the relationship compared to what they expected, they will be disappointed, resentful, and possibly uncooperative.

One should remember that although we may not be conscious of it, we evaluate our relationships in part on their own merits and in part by comparison with ALTERNATIVE RELATIONSHIPS that are available to us. One should not lose sight of the fact that even if the characteristics of a relationship seem healthy, either party may be dissatisfied with it if it does not "measure up" to other relationships in which he/she could be participants.

These seven aspects and, hence, the quality of work relationship area, themselves, influenced by:

1) *the current context* of the work relationship – the situation in which the relationship exists – which takes into account the organization structure, the technology, the strategy, the pressures on the company, the stage of the company's development, what is happening in the firm's environment, and what is going on in the family;

2) the *history* of the two individuals and their relationship, the period of history into which the father and son were born (their respective generations), and most important, their mutual experience within the family; and

3) the respective *life stages* of the individuals involved.

While we need to understand how all of these elements in concert affect the quality of a father-son work relationship, this report examines how the father's and son's respective life stages interact to influence the quality of how they work together in their family company. More specifically, this is an inquiry into the hypothesis that *The quality of the work relationship between a father and son will vary depending upon their respective stages of life.*

When both members of a pair go through periods of life in which certain social interactions are relatively easy, then we predicted that their work relationship would be relatively harmonious. Conversely, when both members are in life stages when interactions tend to be difficult, then we assumed that their work relationship would be relatively problematic. We call the overlap of individuals' life stages a Life-Stage Intersect. One life-Stage Intersect, for instance, is when the father is in his mid-life transition, normally during his forties, and his son is in his adolescence, normally during his teen years.

We take into account the Life-Stage Intersect of a father and son to explain the quality of the father-son work relationship. By quality we mean "how well" they work together and we measure this, from the perspective of both parties, along four dimensions: (1) the ease of their work interaction; (2) the enjoyment they derive from their work relationship; (3) how much they get done working together; and (4) how much they learn from working with each other. By "the quality of the work relationship" we refer to a combination of these four components.

We postulated here that the quality of a father-son work relationship depends, in part, on the degree of compatibility of the strengths, interests, tasks, attitudes, and behaviors that result from the life stage each person is in. We believe certain life stages for the father mesh very well with certain life stages for the son and that these intersects produce relatively good work relationships. Other periods in the father's and son's life (i.e., other Life-Stage Intersects) involve the two men in incompatible tasks and behavior and result in relatively problematic work relationships.

Here we report the results of 89 father-son pairs who gave us rich questionnaire data on their work relationship. To help describe the findings of this study, let us introduce the Life Stage Matrix. It shows the father's and son's ages divided into intervals. According to life cycle theory, the age periods 17-22, 34-50, and 61-70 are times when interpersonal relationships, and probably work relationships, can be relatively difficult. On the other hand, the age intervals 23-33 and 51-60 should be relatively more conducive to harmonious interactions. On the basis of what we know about these male life stages, we would expect that two cells of the Life Stage Matrix would have relatively poor work relationship quality, and one cell would have relatively good quality.

We find that the data support the hypothesis that the quality of the work relationship between father and son depends to some extent on the interplay of their respective life stages. Figure 3 shows that five zones (A, B, C, D, and E) can be distinguished in terms of the quality of the work relationship. In Zone A, the quality is mixed (+ /-). In Zones B and D the quality is good (+), while in C and E it is poor (-).

While we had no firm expectations based on life stage theory of what the quality of the work relationship would be when the father reaches the age of 70 or above Zones D and E are consistent with what we know to be a problematic period for the son (between 40 and 50) and the difficulties we would expect to arise in a work context when the father is in his late seventies, shown in Figure 3 by a dotted line (Beveridge, 1089; Buhler, 1955; Freud, 1924; Gould, 1972; Sonnenfeld, 1988). Let us now examine in some detail the dynamics in each of these zones.

Zone A. Our data indicate that a work relationship between a young father and a young son is of mixed quality (+ /-). Consider first the father's situation. Although few men perceive the forties as a time of acute crisis, most men experience some turbulence during this period. During his forties, a man begins to face that there is an end to life and

---

Figure 2. Life Stage Matrix and Predicted Quality Zones for Father-Son Work Relationships

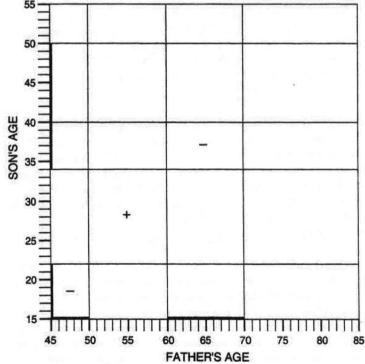

to reconsider what to do with his future. Vaillant (1977) reports that men experience a heightening of basic drives such as sexuality (as in adolescence), and Levinson (1978) and Gould (1978) stress the sense of urgency felt at this time. Men often believe that their lives up to this point have been wasted, that they have not contributed enough to the world or found real fulfillment themselves. The sense of urgency created by the feeling that time is running out and by the questioning of "who" they are and what they want out of life makes this an emotionally charged time. Gould (1978) and Levinson (1978) each give 45 as the typical end of what the latter author calls the Mid-Life Transition. In our opinion, however, it is very likely that the Mid-Life Transition extends to the end of the forties. To begin with, the age boundaries given for the stages are only approximate. Second, Gould (1978) believes the pressure that mid-life fathers feel is related to the transition occurring in their families, when the children grow up and leave home. If this is so, having one's son in the company might delay or extend this period of transition, because of his dependency upon the father as employer.

Consider next the son. Young men in their teens and early twenties are still in the process of separating from their family, or trying to establish their identities, and often still have strong conflicts with their parents (Erikson, 1950; Vaillant, 1977: Levinson, 1978; Gould, 1978). Energies and instinctual drives are at a high point during this period; memories of early and recent conflicts with the father are fresh. This is an emotionally charged time for the son as well. To go to work for one's father right after high school or college extends father's control over one's life at a time when, according to life cycle theories, a young man can least tolerate the dependence. Working with one's father probably prolongs time needed for separating from one's parents and making the transition into adult-

Figure 3. Actual Quality Zones for Father-Son Work Relationships

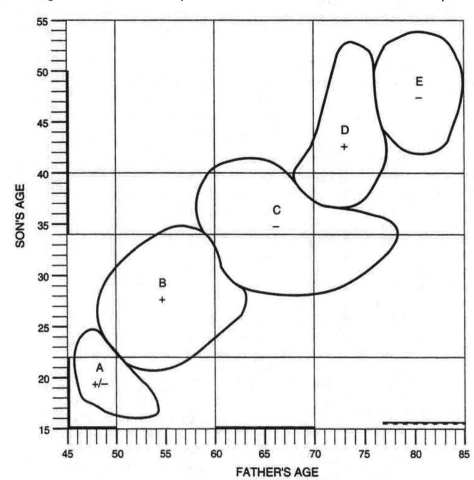

hood. Although for a son the family company can be a vehicle for independence – permitting a faster career path, a larger income, perquisites, and the like – it is also an extension of the family. Entry into the family firm before establishing his independence away from the family may have a regressive or retarding influence on a young man. The issues and tensions of adolescence can thus be extended into the twenties.

Father and son in their respective life stages have much in common – high energy, identity questioning, and the appraisal of life. These similarities lead to tension in the relationship and are accompanied by relatively poor quality of work interactions. Because this is a relatively emotionally charged time for both men, it is possible that each will distort messages the other sends and regard many of the other's actions as threats to meeting his own strongly felt needs. At the very least, communication between father and son is likely to be poor in this life stage intersect.

The son, at this point in his life, probably has several career opportunities and, at the very least, may not feel the need to make the work relationship with his father succeed. Worse, his desire for freedom could make him resent any implicit or explicitly pressure by the family to join the firm. If his responsibilities are limited and his performance and behavior are closely supervised by the father, he is likely to feel overwatched, held back, and resent it. He may also be isolated from other employees, who are suspicious of the boss's son or resent his advantages in the company. This would be upsetting for a young man still seeking peer approval.

Sons joining their fathers right out of college are likely to have high expectations, some created by the father, about what they will be able to do n the business and want to put into practice some concepts and book learning that may not be grounded in the reality of the specific business of the family company. To fathers, these "new ideas" may appear as a lack of appreciation for his valuable experience, and they may veto them on emotional grounds. Fathers may not recognize that peer relationships during high school and college and the mild hierarchical classroom atmosphere – where democratic ideals, speculation, and experimentation are encouraged – do not prepare the son to "accept his place" in the company and to apply the "proven methods" of the father. In this period, Levi et al. (1972) find that sons, at this time of identity testing and separation from the family, can exacerbate a mid-life father's sense of control.

Levinson (1978) says that mid-life men try to find a way to give their lives meaning that will live after them and that for most men, work is the most significant component of their life structure and the major source of their legacy. Founders or heirs of companies, who probably feel more attached to their organizations than do most men, and have the power to mold a company legacy, in this period of life would become more determined than ever to leave their stamp on their organizations.

The owner-manager may then tend to assert his power over others and fight with those who exacerbate his self-questioning and reduce his feeling of control over his legacy. Work at this stage could be a source of stability for the father, and the son's testing of father's competence and authority at work could be extremely threatening, and reduce the quality of the work relationship. Many types of relationships being with a "honeymoon" period, where each party tentatively accepts the other while they come acquainted. Gabarro (1979) shows this is true for work relationships as well. We might expect that this "honeymoon" effect would offset the life stage influence at least for a short time, but we do not see any indication of this in our data. Perhaps fathers and sons already know each other very well when they begin to work together, and instead of "easing into" their respective work roles by spending some time gathering impressions of one another, they immediately begin to test each other's limits in this new situation. The testing of limits could be a very important aspect of defining the work relationships as the father and son have already established mutual family roles.

Zone B. Starting again with the father, the period beyond the Mid-Life Transition and until at least age sixty is recognized as a time of tranquility. Vaillant's study of the life cycle identifies a stage occurring during the fifties (between Erikson's stages of Generativity and Integrity) that he calls "Keeping the Meaning versus Rigidity" (1977); what he means is that having weathered their children's and their own second coming of age, men in this period become more tranquil and place more emphasis on doing things carried on rather than replaced. The challenge in this stage is to try to get one's way without becoming rigid.

Levinson (1978) and Gould (1978) describe men beyond the Mid-Life Transition as less competitive, as less apt to idealize and condemn others, being less controlled by external stimuli, valuing possessions less, being more objective and philosophical, and better able to respond to the developmental needs of their children and other young adults. In this period men have both the experience and inclination to teach younger people. It is here that they are more likely to become effective mentors.

Let us now turn to the son. For men the period between the ages of 23 and 28 is not considered to be particularly stable. They usually have the concurrent desires to choose among alternative options and keep as many open as possible. Internally they desire stability. They also feel external pressure to grow up, define their direction, get married. At the same time, their youthful vitality creates in them a strong sense of adventure and they try to keep open the many opportunities that life offers them (Levinson, 1978). Erikson (1950) and Vaillant (1977) regard this as a period when men test their identity in relationships, and Levinson finds that most men at this age believe their lives are headed in the wrong direction and have trouble building an initial life structure apart from their parents.

While these factors might lead us to expect great tension for a father-son dyad, in this period young men search for mentors who can help them define and work out their plan (Levinson, 1978). According to Gould (1978), they strongly desire competence and increasingly desire recognition and advancement. Between 28 and 33, a man usually makes a lasting occupational choice and before the end of this period he has begun to commit himself to a life plan (Levinson, 1978). During this period, according to Levinson (1978) and Vaillant (1977), men become more settled and materialistic, strive for competence, and increasingly desire recognition and advancement.

Our key reasons for expecting harmonious father-son work relationships in Zone B are that the father is emotionally able during this time to understand and tolerate the son's instability and that the son wants to learn and grow in competence at the same time the father wants to teach and help the younger generation develop. The instinctual drives of both men in Zone B are less strong than in Zone A, and the two are less emotional, and communications between them becomes easier.

As the son increasingly focuses his life, he comes less interested in alternative work opportunities. This probably raises the value of his work relationship with the father, and the desire to make it work.

The father is also less concerned about possessions and external stimuli when the son is becoming more materialistic and eager for recognition. It is probably relatively easier for the father in this period to regard and recognize his son. Importantly, his is a time when both men are likely to be physically and intellectually strong and capable of contributing to the business. It is more likely then that the father and son will feel that rewards, recognition, responsibilities, and authority are divided fairly between them.

The compatibility in this period seems due to the father's willingness to teach, support, and promote his son and the son's eagerness to grow and the fact that he is not threatening the father's position at this time. Both the 23 to 28 and the 29 to 33 age periods for a son seem compatible with a father in his fifties and we will feel that the stability of the father during this time and his important task of teaching his son, will offset some of the tension the son brings to the work relationship.

Zone C. Little has been written about the adult male life cycle beyond age fifty, but we are aware of the difficulties many men have with retirement. In their sixties, they are mindful of the eventual loss of meaningful activities and associations when they leave their companies. For the owner-manager, retirement is not prescribed and often occurs simultaneously with his death. Nevertheless, the social norm is for retirement to occur during a man's sixties. Even those men who plan to retire in this period of life probably want to stay at the helm and demonstrate their skills and authority until they step down.

According to our data, the typical retirement age of 65 – a transition year for many life state theories – is not accompanied by a marked difference in the quality of father-son work relationships. Although many owner-managers claim to retire around age 65, involvement with their firms often continues for several years afterwards.

The son, meanwhile is in his late thirties, say between 34 and 40, when men strive to attain competence, recognition, advancement, and security (Vaillant, 1977; Levinson, 1978). Approaching 40, these tasks become very pressing. Between the ages of 36 and 40, he urgently seeks independence and recognition. He must become "his own man," and the urgency he feels brings about a resurgence of the little boy in the man. The boy's elemental struggles with dependence, sexuality, and authority come to the forefront in this period and relationships with mentors – as well as with wives – are likely to be stormy and may be terminated (Levinson, 1978). The resurgence of strong emotions regarding his dependence on his father could stimulate very negative sentiments toward his father (such as a lack of trust).

It seems likely that the father-son work relationship in this coincidence of life stages will be difficult since the son's renewed struggle with authority would overlap with the father's desire to demonstrate the continuing value of his own authority, skills, ideas, and leadership. The son probably resents reporting to his father in this time.

The son's emotional state can lead to distorted communication between the two men. Sons probably feel held back in their desire to change how the company is run; fathers can oppose the attempt and also feel appreciated. There may be serious conflicts over the goals of the company during this time, the father wanting to keep the company on a steady course which the son considers wasteful or disastrous, and the son desiring to alter the direction of the firm, which the father considers reckless.

The son may regard responsibilities and authority in the company as inequitably distributed. The father, his son might argue, is no longer keeping up with the times or putting in the effort to make decisions, and yet he still has the final say. The son having worked for several years in the family firm, or perhaps in other organizations feels by now very competent. Believing that he has a number of options (alternative relationships) in life besides working for his father makes him feel more comfortable about challenging his father. Such tensions are probably more intense in companies that do not permit the son to manage an activity essentially independent of his father's control.

The son wants to continue to grow and as he nears forty his need to be on his own and achieve his personal goals becomes very pressing. But in the typical smaller company he cannot satisfy his need for independence while his father is still in charge. If the father did not have his own need to demonstrate his vigor in this period, some mutual accommodation might be found. Instead, what often ensues is a fight for the control of the firm.

Zones D and E. Because we know less about the adult male life stages after the sixties we have less of a understanding of what occurs in Zones D and E. What appears to be true in these zones is the father's age influences the quality of work relationship more than does the son's age. When sons are in a turbulent period and the father is not (essentially Zone D) quality is relatively good. One the other hand, when fathers are in a turbulent period, and the son is not (the upper part of Zone E), quality is relatively poor. This could reflect less acceptance of relationship problems on the part of the son. Future investigation of these later life stages will hopefully clarify the issues and concerns of the two men.

Differences in Quality Ratings by Fathers and Sons

The ratings of the quality of the relationship given by fathers and sons generally agree. Both father and son report positive and negative changes in the quality of their work relationship at about the same time and do not differ much on the degree of change in the quality. Both fathers and sons identify the father's sixties and the son's late thirties as the worst period.

Sons, however, consistently rate the work interaction less favorably or more harshly. This clear finding has many possible explanations. Fathers may discount tension in the father-son work relationship because they feel more responsibility for the way things are. The father probably feels justifiably accountable to some extent for the actions of the son he has raised, and tends to excuse him. A son, on the other hand, probably feels much less responsible for his father's behavior even though people associate him in their mind with his father. Sons could therefore feel accountable but not responsible and try to distance themselves from their fathers by being harsher in their evaluation. Also it may be that people in general become less critical and more tolerant with age, having had more experience with the frailty of human nature.

It could be that the son's more critical rating stems from the resentment often felt by people in dependent positions. Sons are dependent on their fathers from the time of birth and their resentment begins at a very young and pre-verbal age – a feeling that is likely to continue to exist unconsciously into adulthood. Sons' more critical ratings could reflect a reserve of resentment against their fathers, which fathers do not feel to an equivalent extent.

There could also be a stage-of-life explanation for some of the father's more positive ratings. This leniency phenomenon is particularly true where the fathers are over sixty. At this stage on typically tires to make sense of one's life and look back on it with satisfaction. Fathers, therefore, may be less willing to focus on what is going wrong or what has gone wrong in the work relationship.

One particular father, who works with three sons, suggested that the difference in ratings occur because sons are better at hiding what they do wrong than others, who therefore have fewer grounds for criticism in their sons than the sons in the parent.

In comparing how fathers and sons rate their work relationship we find that the fathers' quality ratings are less closely related to changes in life stage than are those of the sons. Perhaps fathers perceive the changes but deny them to themselves or just deny them to us. It could also be that fathers do not perceive strong changes because they are more lenient with their sons than the sons are with them, and consistently rate the work relationships highly. Fathers might also be less sensitive to changes in work relationship quality because they themselves go through fewer changes after age forty than their sons go through between ages twenty and forty. By the time these fathers are forty, most are in charge of their firms, they are married and have children, and most have done significant work on their "dreams" (as Levinson might put it). For the son, many of these important components of the life structure, these major milestones that mark changes in life, have still to appear. It is very likely that as sons experience changes in their lives they perceive changes in the quality of their work relationships with their fathers. Some sons, for instance, reported that their work relationships improved when they got married. Could these findings possibly imply that perceived changes in the relationship are strongly linked to how much the perceiver himself is changing?

Reasons for Harmony and Conflict

The questionnaire asked, "Why have you and your father (or son) worked well together and/or have had problems working together over the last years (or during the last few years of the ended work relationship)?" We asked the subjects to consider goals, work habits, personalities and temperaments, the work situation, and other factors. If we assume that the reasons given for harmony and conflict in the work relationships reflect the needs that have to be satisfied in the relationship then it seems as if fathers and sons were both similar and different in their needs. Mutual respect and understanding are considered by both fathers and sons to be key reasons for compatibility. The importance of respect for the other's skills, commitment, and contribution to the company is strongly evidenced. It is curious that the sentiments of liking and loving one another did not show up very often in their free responses. But perceived concern with building and maintaining good family relations correlates with both the father's and the son's ratings of the quality of their work relationship. Beyond this level of agreement, fathers and sons want different things from their work relationships. The father wants his son to identify with him, to have similar goals for the company, to have the same attitudes about work, to think as he does. But he also wants his son to respect his authority and position. He wants his son to be a good apprentice, to learn from him but not to surpass him.

The son wants his father to recognize his capabilities. He wants to grow in ability and responsibility, make his own way and, in the process, make his father proud of him. These particular goals do not seem to change much as a function of age for either father or son. In some Life Stage Intersects it is possible for them to have what they want and in other intersects they must adjust their expectations or be at odds. Their goals are much more likely to be realized by both in Zone C.

The reason most often given by fathers for the difficulties in working with their sons is that the latter challenge them in many ways. If the son is not seeking his father's position in the company (the son may want the father to retire), the son is trying to change things, complains about being held back, has a different style, takes too much credit, or is critical of his father. Problems occur in the work relationship for many reasons including poor early relationships in the family, adverse economic conditions, and difficulties with other mangers who are members of the family. But most of the problems, as seen by the father, occur when son steps out of the "good apprentice" mold. Sons attribute problems in the work relationship mostly to their fathers. According to son, difficulties arise when the father impedes the son's progress, the father cannot let go of the company, will not reduce his control of the company, resists change, is headstrong, holds the son back, interferes in the son's life.

Our understanding of these data is that the father associates the quality of his work relationship with their opportunity to grow. Thus, they do not necessarily wish to overthrow their father, but do not want to be held back. The fight with father for control of the company comes because it is the only way they feel they can continue to grow personally, if they stay in the company. Perhaps there is something about the psychology of fatherhood that inhibits collegiality with the son. Fathers do want their sons to grow and progress. In fact, some of what the sons view as growth, the father may see as a challenge to his power in the company, and perhaps in the family. Then, too, what the father regards as the continuation of a successful management strategy the son may interpret as an attempt to hold him down.

Implications for Fathers and Sons

The findings of this research have many implications for father-son work relationships in family companies. Perhaps the most important is that swings in the quality of the work relationship depend to some extent upon the respective life stages of the two parties, and therefore can be anticipated and prepared for. The more the father and son realize that their needs will change over time and that their expectations in their work relationship will also change, the less they will blame each other for incompatibilities.

It could also be that the generation into which the father and the son were born accounts for the tension or incompatibility between them. The fathers now in their sixties were in their teens or perhaps twenties at the time of the Great Depression and their values, as a result, could be very conservative. Their sons, now in their mid to late thirties, were in their late teens or early twenties during the Peace Movement of the 1960s and may not have the older generation's respect for authority. It could be therefore that the tension that we are noticing results not from a life stage influence so much as from earlier experiences in their respective lives. We found, however, that there is low correlation between the difference in the ages of father and son and the quality of the work relationship, a finding that casts doubt on this alternative explanation.

The evidence seems strong that the son should not start working with the father right out of college. Not only do most sons need to have time to establish their own identifies away from their families, but a father's own self-questioning and internal conflict in his forties should not be exacerbated by the son's presence.

Given that work relationships are best when both father and son are in relatively stable stages, we would recommend that sons join their fathers at work after their early twenties and after their fathers have gotten beyond their troublesome forties. Employment in another firm for a few years can provide the son with many management skills, enable him to find himself in a less emotionally charged work situation, and postpone his entry into the family firm until he and his father are at a more appropriate stage of life. Beyond the more immediate conflicts that may occur because of premature entry, there is evidence that sons who have not proven themselves in other work settings find it difficult to overcome a lifelong feeling that their success may be due solely to the protective environment of the family firm.

It seems reasonable to us that sons in their thirties should be given separate areas of responsibility to the extent that the operation of the company and the son's competence permits. It could very well be that the conflict between son and father over the control of the business occurs because authority is regarded by both men as an "all or nothing issue." That is, the son could believe that if he is to have any control over his life, he must have his father completely out of it. The father, likewise, could believe that if he is to control his son he must control him in a very strong way. We are led to believe that the overriding issue that develops between fathers and sons in Zone C is *not* displacing the father by taking over the company, but rather escaping the father's shadow and reach. It might be that fathers and son could coexist in the family company well into the father's seventies, if the father relinquished some authority in the company to his son. In some cases that might mean that the father assumes the Chairmanship position and turns over operational responsibilities to the son. In other cases he could delegate to the son a division of the company to run while the father maintains his own operational responsibilities in other parts of the firm. Inevitably, however, father eventually must retire. With no involvements other than work in the company, retirement can be a frightening prospect and clinging to work is understandable.

Especially because of the highly sensitive nature of these work relationships, it is important for fathers and sons to cultivate an ability to look at themselves and the other objectively, but still with empathy. Increased sensitivity to the other may be achieved in a number of ways, not the least of which is becoming more in touch with oneself.

Direct communication between father and son, where each talks about himself – his current goals, interests, tasks, and even fears – and avoids commenting on the other (unless requested) is the most intimate way to maintain the process of adjustment to one another. Consultation with a third party, respected by both father and son, is another way to facilitate an exchange of information between them. Alternatively, a seminar on these work relationships and particularly on the influence of life stage on their association might be very helpful for encouraging a father and son to discuss what they want from each other and in their lives in general.

As our research makes so clear, fathers and sons should keep in mind the importance that respect has for each of them in the relationship and take care that they do not lose the other's esteem. They should be aware, also that power is the key determinant of quality in their work relationship. What upsets both men are challenges to or limitations placed upon their "deserved" power. Father and son should each understand from what bases his power derives and be sensitive to how the other feels power should be apportioned.

Responsibility for the quality of the father-son work relationship lies with both men. But it is the fathers who can most influence this relationship. The father is often emotionally attached to his company, so to the child, and this relationship competes with his attachment to his son. The father must decide which child (son or company) means more to him. In the best father-son work relationships we have studied, the father demonstrates a strong desire, unqualified by his attachment to his company, to see his son grow into all that he can be.

References

Beveridge, W. E. "Retirement and Life Significance: A Study of the Adjustment to Retirement of a Sample of Men at Management Level." *Human Relations*, 1980, 33 (1), 69.

Buhler, C. "The Curve of Life as Studied in Biographies." *Journal of Applied Psychology*, 1955, 19, 405-409.

Davis, J., *The Influence of Life State on Father-Son Work Relationships in Family Companies*. Doctoral Dissertation, Harvard University, Graduate School of Business Administration, 1982.

Davis, J., and Tagiuri, R. "The Incidence of Work Relationships Between Relatives in the Family Business." Unpublished paper, Harvard Business School, 1981.

Erikson, E .H. *Childhood and Society*. New York: Norton, 1950.

Freud, S. "Dostoevsky and Patricide." In J. Strachey (ed.), *The Complete Psychological Works of Sigmund Freud*. Vol. 21, London: Hogarth, 1924.

Gabarro, J. "Socialization at the Top: How CEOs and Subordinates Evolve Interpersonal Contract." *Organizational Dynamics*. Winter 1979:3-23.

Gould, R. "The Phases of Adult Life: A Study in Developmental Psychology." *American Journal of Psychiatry*, 1972, 129(5), 521-531.

Gould, R. *Transformations: Growth and Change in Adult Life*. New York: Simon & Schuster, 1978.

Levi, L. D., Stierlin, H., and Savard, R. J. "Fathers and Sons: The Interlocking Crisis of Integrity and Identity." *Psychiatry*, 1972, 35.

Levinson, D. J., *The Seasons of a Man's Life*. New York: Knopf, 1978.

Sonnenfeld, J. *The Hero's Farewell: What Happens When CEOs Retire*. New York: Oxford University Press, 1988.

Tagiuri, R., and Davis, J. "Note on Work Relationships." Unpublished paper, Harvard Business School, 1982.

Vaillant, G. E. *Adaption of Life*. Boston: Little, Brown, 1977

Trust patterns in family-owned businesses are frequently catalyzed by one person. Such individuals are sometimes, but not always, family members who initiate, maintain, and help create higher trust for both the family and the organization. These Trust Catalysts often have little or no formal hierarchical authority in the business. To examine their influence on trust levels, we conducted in-depth interviews with more than 60 people from seven multigenerational companies and backed these findings with data from earlier pilot case studies. Their practices helped us to understand how trust develops, operates, and even expands within family business systems.

The Trust Catalyst in Family-Owned Businesses

Kacie LaChapelle, Louis B. Barnes

Introduction

Few would doubt the powerful impact that both trust and mistrust exert on our personal and professional lives, a belief that recent literature on the subject increasingly supports (Horton & Reid, 1991; Whitney, 1993; Baird & St-Amand, 1995; Fukuyama, 1995; Zand, 1996; Shaw, 1997). But there are no guarantors of trust in either families or organizations. Longstanding family feuds, marital difficulties, and courtroom battles, whether warranted or not, often follow the loss of trust. In this regard, the Bingham, Steinberg, Berkowitz, and Haft families come to mind.

On the other side, we hear far too little about the solid examples of long-term trust in family enterprises. Organizational trust typically survives either temporarily or in isolated group settings, always fragile and at risk. Yet both past research and topical writers suggest that organizations whose leadership successfully builds ongoing trust are healthier, more effective, and more successful in the long run (Kegan & Rubenstein, 1973; Likert & Likert, 1976; Driscoll, 1978; Cook & Wall, 1980; Barnes, 1981; Butler & Cantrell, 1984; Goldstein, 1984; Bennis & Nanus, 1985; Butler, 1991; Horton & Reid, 1991; Drucker, 1992; Dyer, 1992; Kouzes & Posner, 1993; McFarland, Schindler & Thomas, Senn, & Childress, 1993; 1993; Whitney, 1993; Hosmer, 1995; Bennis & Goldsmith, 1997; Shaw, 1997).

Further data that trust becomes a critical issue – in leadership, effective performance, quality of life, and continuity in family owned businesses – are provided in a recent study involving in depth interviews with more than 60 owners and members of seven family firms (LaChapelle, 1997). In that research, the role of trust was explored by examining family and company histories, norms, values, and membership transitions, as well as each family's espoused and observed leadership practices. These data suggest that relatively high and low degrees of trust within these businesses, not surprisingly, begins with family members who serve as a constellation of role models for other non-family employees. Organizational trust grows from these family constellations that create the standards others come to expect and replicate for themselves.

Within these family constellations, sometimes aided by outsiders, there often exists a single individual who initiates and helps create higher trust within both the family and the business. We began to refer to these individuals as Trust Catalysts – people who take a role in creating and maintaining trust within and beyond the family. The role is typically paradoxical because, despite the immense power surrounding trust, it often takes hold softly and informally over time. In addition, Trust Catalysts value the total family entity while also promoting the rights of individual members – sometimes a very difficult feat.

Who the specific catalyst is varies from situation to situation. Wives and/or mothers frequently take on this role, regardless of whether or not they participate formally in the business. Sometimes it is another relative, an outside consultant, or a board member who helps bridge the gap between the boss (father) and subordinates (children) or between siblings and other subordinates. Very often, the critical question becomes who in the eyes of others can initiate and sustain such a role? During major transition periods, as formal authority and ownership moves from one generation or family figure to another, new Trust Catalysts emerge from the younger generation, or a new outsider assumes the role previously taken on by an elder. Over time, trust as a value within the family can become an important cornerstone for succeeding generations of the family business.

Perceptions of Trust: Four Relational Characteristics

> Trust is difficult to define...It is like pornography, though. You know it when you see it. – *Bob Marr, CEO of The Marr Companies*

> Trust is one of those fundamental notions that is claimed to be understood by everybody, yet which is hard to explain or precisely define. (Taylor, 1989)

> The vast array of definitions given in the literature bear witness to this fact. (Baird and St-Amand, 1995)

Bob Marr, like most of the participants in our study, recognized that trust is in the eye of the beholder. It is either perceived or not. Throughout our interviews, people struggled to define trust in reasonably precise terms. For one person, it was when the trusted party's "word is gold." For another, it was when "you can bank on what they say," leading to credibility, believe ability, and ultimately trustworthiness. Even recent writers on trust suggested that it is a highly subjective and difficult phenomenon to measure (Hosmer, 1995; Bennis & Goldsmith, 1997). In effect, if we do not perceive trust in the behavior of others, it does not exist.

As Baird and St-Amand (1995) suggested, trust has been investigated using a wide variety of definitions and theoretical constructs including theories of expectancy, perception, risk preference, paradox, commitment, roles, decision making, and the overall psychodynamics of the family. But in our judgment, the most meaningful approaches depend not only on the actor, but also on the perceptions of the actor. Rotter's seminal work (1996), for example, noted that "positive expectations of another person's behavior" are a major determinant of trust. In that sense, trust involves relational characteristics, not just personal attributes. Yet the terms most often cited in the literature involve personal attributes and behavior, such as ability, availability, benevolence, caring, compassion, competence, confidence, consistency, discreteness, fairness, integrity, loyalty, openness, predictability, receptivity, reliability, and support (Deutsch, 1960; Cook & Wall, 1980; Butler & Cantrell, 1984; Bennis & Nanus, 1985; Mishra & Morrisey, 1990; Butler, 1991; Williams, 1992; Hosmer, 1995; Mayer, Davis, & Schoorman, 1995).

Such word lexicons mostly deal with individual attributes, not interpersonal relationships. As we learned from our respondents, such words convey little meaning unless the other party perceives them as real. Over time, using shared experiences, trust can be reinforced, although almost never solidified, because of needs for occasional repair and periodic testing. In early research, Barnes (1981) described his concepts of trust as predictability and caring, in the context of an ongoing reciprocity:

> ...Much of our initial behavior in...situations is an effort to search for, test out, and initiate a tentative sense of trust or mistrust. When other people see this initial behavior as both predictable and caring, they develop an expectation of future hope which accompanies trust. Such early search behavior also invites similar responses from others. This exchange creates the giving and getting in return behavior that (Erik) Erikson pictures (as essential to trust) and which pervades all cultures in what sociologists call the norm of reciprocity.

In a later paper, Barnes (1989) added:

One party typically initiates the process – sometimes at some peril, sometimes not. Parents may initiate trust relationships with their children, but often the initiation of trust requires early gestures that will reduce threat but put oneself at risk – gestures like self-effacing humor, more humble questions than erudite answers, overlooking potential slights or insults, disclaiming credit, or making repeated attempts to behave in nonjudgmental ways. Valid trust begins when these efforts become reciprocal, stronger, and ongoing – a two way street involving both giving and receiving gestures.

Based on our own data, aligned with a survey of literature definitions, we expanded the salient characteristics of trust beyond Barnes's Predictability and Caring to include two other dimensions: Character and Competency.

- Character captures a number of concepts inherent in the basic values of integrity, honesty, and credibility; being perceived as a "good" person.
- Competency involves skills, expertise, and performance that implies generally sound judgment and decision making abilities.
- Predictability refers to follow-through, kept promises, and a history of consistent responses and behavior.
- Caring is demonstrated through supportive acts that convey genuine interest in the wellbeing of others, as well empathy and understanding.

Bennis and Goldsmith (1997) followed up on this line of thinking in a recent book highlighting the importance of the role of trust in leadership of successful organizations. They wrote: "Competency, Congruity and Consistency, and Caring – those are the qualities a leader (family) must embody in order for trust to be created in a group."

By Congruity, Bennis and Goldsmith were referring to Integrity, which closely matched our concepts of Character. Competency, Congruity, and Consistency are also in accordance with our attributes, though here again we need to emphasize the importance of reciprocal perceptions. If the reciprocal loops become ignored or broken, the way is open for mistrust to emerge. In our studies, if the positive reciprocities were reinforced, then trust developed and continued. We shall now try to show how we applied, sometimes without success, these Four Relational Trust Characteristics using Trust Catalysts in the situations we studied.

The High-Status Friend as Trust Catalyst

In a now almost forgotten article, Morton Freilich (1964) described a "natural triad" in kinship and complex systems that involved the triangular relational pattern of a high status authority (HSA), a low-status subordinate (LSS), and a high-status friend (HSF). Because of the almost inevitable tensions between the LSS and the HSA, particularly as perceived by those in the LSS position, the LSS often seeks out an HSF for support. This is a person who potentially provides less threat and more Caring. If found, the HSF can become an effective bridge between the HSA and an LSS but only with the HSA's encouragement. In other words, the primary Trust Catalyst needs the support and approval of the high-status task leader, often the father/boss in a family business. Given that support, the HSF can become a Trust Catalyst for both the family and the organization, introducing and reinforcing exchanges of Character, Competency, Predictability, and Caring.

The Marr Companies

In the case of the Marr Companies, the four Marr sons had inherited ownership of a fifth generation $30 million-a-year construction business of which their Uncle Bob had become CEO after their father died. The brothers all claimed that a solid basis of trust began with their family upbringing. Each spoke of a commitment to do his best and work hard in his own areas of responsibility and to serve the company in ways that would guide it into the future. Each wanted to give the business the same level of dedication and devoted work ethic that had been handed on to them. As a family, the sons emphasized that the importance of trusting one another was a paramount feature of their business interactions.

However, the primary Trust Catalyst was Uncle Bob, the CEO, who had initially acted as a buffer between his nephews and their father, Dan. Bob had no children of his own and often acted as an unofficial big brother or HSF for his nephews. He stated:

> My brother, Dan, was a firm taskmaster for the kids. All the Marrs had conflicts with their sons historically. My grandfather had fired his son at one point. I thought Dan would have learned from that, but he treated his own sons worse. I tried to buffer the boys from their father. There was a mutual respect between them and me, more like an employer-employee relationship.

The younger generation acknowledged and respected Bob's role. Their common perception was stated by one of them:

> Bob was always more of a communicator than Dad. He [Bob] has a mentoring philosophy. He gives information, even though he sometimes needs to be prompted. As is usually the case, our generation has pushed the envelope, pushing for expanded horizons and new opportunities. Bob was held back by his father and was holding back the reins on us. We've had respect for each other's position. However, Bob used to make many more decisions than he currently makes. Over the years, we've made more. He makes the ultimate decisions, but that should be his role, as CEO. I've had twenty-five years working with Bob. Our thinking styles are very similar in terms of what is best for the family, the business, and the community. We have that stewardship philosophy.

Bob gradually did transfer increased responsibility, knowledge, and authority to his nephews. Some years earlier, he began a series of quarterly dinner meetings with "the boys" that he called the "Uncle Bob meetings." The dinners presented an opportunity for everyone to discuss business issues and concerns. Bob wanted to provide an environment that encouraged the next generation's leadership, who were then in their thirties and forties, to take on more responsibility while he still maintained ultimate authority as CEO. Bob also had his own views of how control and direction should evolve:

> You don't have to own the stock to control the business. I never gave control over to them. I made the decisions and told them, "When it's your company, you can make the decisions." I know they don't anticipate twenty years from now having their decisions vetoed by their children, nephews, or nieces. When the boys used to get aggressive about certain issues, I would say, "This is not a democracy or a stockholders meeting. We're not voting. We're here to discuss options, then I make the decision." I would take input from other people, but my role is to make the decision. However, as the boys entered their thirties and forties, I've become more passive. I've been trying to cut my own role down and am preparing to move on.

If we go back to our earlier criteria for trust relationships – the Four Relational Characteristics: Character, Competency, Predictability, and Caring – trust grew as each nephew perceived Uncle Bob's Character, over time, in their relationships with him. Trust became reinforced as the nephews collectively tested and shared these Character attributes with one another. Uncle Bob was first deemed acceptable in terms of moral standards and values in their eyes. Having a common family background helped, but Bob's being initially their (HSF) uncle, and not the authority figure (HSA) father, also lent him credibility as a Trust Catalyst, partly because his Character stood up under their scrutiny, over time.

In addition, Bob's record of experience in the business and the company's success helped give him an air of Competency. He hadn't led his nephews or others astray with poor judgment or foolish behavior, nor had he avoided task responsibilities. Instead, his capabilities and skill sets encouraged task completion, further reinforcing their impressions of his Predictability, Character, and Competency.

As uncle and nephews were able to count on one another over time, trust relationships also grew with collective histories of positive Predictability. This Predictability reflected both Character and Competency experiences, which could have sewn negative seeds of mistrust if their prior relationships had been different. As we have come to think of it, Predictability lets us rely on the trusted party, who acts in an expected manner with congruent words and actions (Stevenson, 1997). Although the Marr brothers usually interacted daily, they often worked in different locations, making Predictability especially important. Though ownership was shared equally, operational decisions tied to profit were often made independently. David, youngest of the four Marr brothers, stated:

> We have diverse roles. I buy equipment [worth] up to a million dollars. I might give my brothers and uncle a brief overview and they might have minor questions, but they don't "third degree" question me. We reciprocate. They all do their jobs well, and I know they check things out before they decide something. That's helped our survival because there is no stepping on toes. Employees appreciate that too. There's continuity – different styles – but the same goals.

It is important to note that the Predictability of trust implies the kind of positive expectations that David Marr had described. Negative Predictability leads to neither a high level of trust nor maintenance of trust, particularly when the fourth dimension, Caring, is perceived as absent.

Examples of Caring – a perceived concern for the well-being of others – were many and varied within the Marr Companies data. Brothers, uncle, and non-family members all provided examples of mutual support, suggesting that when each felt valued and cared for trust developed and grew within the organization. Several non-family members commented on this:

> They think enough of the employees to take care of them financially. Bob is a firm believer in the safety of our employees and property of others. There is a lot of caring about us here. – *vice president and 21-year employee*

> The trust is high. We do our own thing and aren't questioned. We have freedom. They don't second-guess what we're doing, as a rule. There are many things I need to discuss with Bob or Danny. We work together as a team, in confidence. Employees are treated fairly. They are very loyal, there is a lot of longevity here. – *sales manager with 33 years at the company*

> The bosses you can trust will deal with and relate to you on the same wavelength, with respect. They have a manner of talking with you, not at you. When people talk with you as an equal, it opens the door for sharing information and responsibilities in an environment of open communication and team work. – *controller of two months*

In the cases we examined, the individuals who functioned as Trust Catalysts did not simply pursue their own self-interests. The Marr family members asked employees about their lives, both in and out of work, and they also apparently shared and disclosed personal information about themselves. This sharing of personal and business lives, once thought taboo in most businesses, has recently been deemed more appropriate. For many years, the word was never to mix professional and personal issues at work, a mandate that family businesses, in particular, may have violated. Such notions may be changing because concerns for both personal and professional issues may expand the opportunity for trust relationships and organizational well-being. The dual concerns represent an acknowledgment by family and non-family members that Caring for the whole human being may be a critical ingredient in organizational life (Bailyn, Fletcher, & Kolb, 1997).

In contrast to the Marr case, what happens when family members cannot develop trust among themselves, with no one to successfully catalyze the effort? There are times when a Trust Catalyst is available but does not always succeed. Both generational and sibling transitions often become mired in conflict. Some don't succeed for product, market, technology, financial, or other external reasons, but others fail because they cannot make the step from owner-controlled status to that of a younger generation owner, sibling partnership, or cousin consortium (Ward, 1987; Gersick, Davis, McCollom-Hampton, & Lansberg, 1996). One company that was apparently moving in that direction was Hobson Industries.

The Evolution of Mistrust – Hobson Industries

Trust relationships are fragile – hard to come by and extraordinarily easy to lose. The role of Trust Catalyst is not an easy one, often because catalysts may lack formal authority. Hobson Industries was a company that revealed heavy doses of familial mistrust. Although the entrepreneur's wife, and the mother of the second generation, Grace Hobson, tried to play the catalyst role, she was unsuccessful. Grace Hobson was immobilized by history and by her husband's persistent philosophy of founder supremacy and parental mistrust. When Grace tried to build bridges of trust to other family members, her husband, Theodore, undercut them. Over time, she gave up.

The erosion of trust had been developing within the family, particularly between Theodore Sr. and his son Theodore Jr. (Teddy). Seeds of mistrust occurred even before Theodore Sr. proclaimed his credo of rugged individualism and competitive aggression to his children. Theodore Sr.'s own childhood set the stage. His early defenses seemed to come from his parents, sister, and brother. Theodore spoke of not being wanted as a child – "an intrusion in the lives of my parents" – who were in their mid-forties when he was born. His suspicion was confirmed by his older sister years later. In addition, parents, brother, and teachers told Theodore that he did not measure up intellectually to his brother's genius-level IQ, MIT doctorate, or physical attributes. "I grew up in the shadow of my older brother," Theodore stated. Many years later, Theodore felt unfairly treated again. His father's estate went largely to Theodore's older sister. Presumably, she needed it more than Theodore did.

Theodore Sr.'s guiding philosophy emphasized "winning" out on issues of business and financial success. He believed that his ability to overcome adversity, outsmart the competition, and ignore the antagonism of others and would, in the end, "show them all" by coming out ahead. Although quite possibly an admirable competitive perspective, these qualities seemed to provide little basis for establishing trust or continuing family management in Hobson Industries.

In the same vein, Theodore raised his three sons and daughter in an environment that encouraged the tensions and adversity that he felt would lead to success. Like their father, younger sons Teddy and Evan were wrestling team captains and champions. Theodore Sr. described a time when Teddy, in his late teens, didn't win a match and was sitting under the bleachers sobbing. When Theodore approached his son to tell him he did well, Teddy quickly hauled off and punched him. About his father, Teddy stated: "He used to praise me for beating the crap out of people. I always had to fight."

In addition, Theodore Sr. encouraged his sons to settle arguments by fighting them out in the family living room. Despite daughter Julia's outside career success, she resented her brothers' gaining the family business opportunities and financial rewards. She began to distance herself from the family, who eventually stopped getting together as a whole. As suspicions increased, the locks on the family home were even changed.

These antagonistic relationships also permeated the business environment. Disputes and rivalries remained unresolved as pressures increased, thus affecting both operational procedures and long-term business strategies. Profits declined and turnover was very high, even though sales were a healthy $19 million. Neither Teddy nor his older brother Peter felt that their father had much confidence in their Character or Competency. In addition, they felt that Caring for their well-being was a low priority. In their perception, though Theodore Sr.'s behavior was Predictable, it was negatively so.

In an effort to improve the situation, a non-family senior manager was hired who both father and sons liked and respected, offering some hope as a potential Trust Catalyst. Unfortunately, the patterns of conflict and mistrust were too deep. The manager, along with the other non-family managers, found himself unable to change the dominant atmosphere that just got worse. In fact, after serving 18 years in the business, Theodore Jr. was fired by his father.

The Hobson case suggests that good intentions alone do not create trust. Grace Hobson and the new outside manager, both noble in their hopes for family harmony, met with seemingly insurmountable barriers in the form of Theodore Sr.'s background, his founder-supremacist convictions, and his behavior. Grace frequently tried to build trust between her husband and her children but failed because her efforts were mostly viewed as intrusions. According to her, she was often caught in the line of fire and became worn out after losing one battle after another. Unable to support her son Teddy at the expense of her relationship with her husband, the relationship between Grace and Teddy also became strained and, eventually, almost nonexistent.

To be sure, Grace had no formal position from which to gain the compliance of her husband or children. But neither did people in other companies who were able to take on the Trust Catalyst role. Theodore Sr.'s need to win seemed to play a stronger role, preventing him and others from creating or sponsoring trust relationships. He wanted to stand clear of entangling cooperative relationships with family members, company employees, town officials, or even the state government, all of whom experienced Theodore Sr.'s self-righteous wrath at one time or another. Though others would argue that the family and the company had a deep need for more trust, it never came.

What can be said about this supposed need for trust? In some other long-neglected literature on relational leadership in groups, researchers talked about the dual importance of Task Roles and Socio-Emotional or Maintenance Roles (Bales, 1950). Focusing on Task alone, as in the Hobson case, fails to provide sufficient amounts of either social satisfaction or task performance. At Hobson Industries, quality was low, turnover was high, and though revenues increased each year, profits did not. Neither groups nor organizations seem to function well without attention to the maintenance-of-membership processes that encourage trust. It brings to mind another comment made by one of the participants in our study: "When I can trust someone, I can relax...and to some extent, that's true whether the trusted one is a secretary, a boss, or a coworker."

Where trust is reciprocal, there is little need to second-guess others' motives. "I can relax" means that there are also feelings of security and safety. Such a "family feeling" apparently creates a more inclusive Caring and personal environment in which trust can flourish.

Mother and Wife as Trust Catalyst – Hillside Plastics

Take another case in which a wife and mother became the primary Trust Catalyst. The company was a family business called Hillside Plastics. Janet Haas, the wife and mother, took on that role while her husband, Dick, assumed the role of leader. He became the HSA, and she, the HSF. Unlike Theodore Sr. , Dick Haas appreciated and valued his wife's initiating the Character, Competency, Predictability, and Caring behaviors that created trust relationships within both the family and the company. Janet's Trust Catalyst role became particularly clear in the way that Dick, the children, and non-family managers described her.

From the very beginning, Janet Haas was involved in the business, trying to help it as well as her husband survive. Dick Haas spent three years as a dedicated, hard-working employee of and investor in Hillside Plastics. When he was 31, Dick had open-heart surgery but returned to work seven days later to find that his employer had lost all interest in the business. Such a situation might have discouraged any husband and father of three young children to support, but it was particularly difficult for Dick. He had cashed in his life insurance policy to put money into Hillside, not realizing that he had invested more than anyone else. During one sleepless night in May 1969, Dick made a profound decision:

that somehow he would make a go of the business, even though they were unable to afford the mortgage payments on their home. The Haases moved into an old farmhouse soon after Dick took over the company.

Janet viewed her role as that of supporter, family peacemaker, and people person with strong humanistic values. She also provided critical work support, returning to the office many evenings after her young children were asleep to resume her administrative and bookkeeping duties, sometimes until 3:00 A. M. Dick often worked three days and nights virtually nonstop. Despite their efforts, the bank declared the company bankrupt several years later. Dick realized that the business he'd worked so hard to hold on to could be closed down any day. While Janet did a lot of praying, Dick recalled:

> I would go into work and try to make it for 15 minutes at a time. If I could make it 15 minutes with no one shutting me down, I'd go another 15 minutes. Then I'd work most of the night to make enough products to ship the next day. I guess I owed so many people so much money, they couldn't shut us off.

Janet formally took on the role of human resources manager in 1980. She was described by employees as "gifted, caring, attentive, compassionate, and very interested" in the people she interacted with. Janet, herself, noted: "I'm a helper. I like helping others to succeed. The excitement for me is in dealing with the people. Dick worries about the business."

During the 1980s, the three Haas children – Peter, Kate, and Greg – joined the business. Each contributed significantly to the growth of Hillside Plastics, which in 1997 approached $10 million in sales. According to all family members, expanding the business and maintaining family working relationships provided a constant challenge, requiring enormous investments of time, energy, and commitment.

Throughout these periods of growth and transition, Janet facilitated communication between her husband and children as well as between non-family managers. Although Dick as CEO never considered communication his strong suit, he was described as a visionary entrepreneur who knew what he wanted but didn't always know how to bring it about. His children said that they either needed to learn how to pry information from him faster or become better mind readers. It was often unclear to others what Dick expected from them or how he felt about the jobs they were doing.

One thing, however, was clear: Dick trusted his family and gave them every opportunity to contribute, learn, grow, and even fail. That approach was one he said he never regretted. The Haases all agreed that learning to communicate more effectively with each other was absolutely essential in working together productively. According to Dick, "Janet made us communicate. It probably never would have worked without that. I was glad, at least most of the time, that she was there facilitating." The three children agreed, and daughter Kate noted:

> With sales doubling in three years, the biggest thing that's held us together was successful meetings – not nasty, but sometimes intense. We'd communicate in ways that real feelings came out. Sometimes it was difficult. We'd even come out of meetings crying on occasion, but I don't see any other way. Mom had always pushed meetings, and I pushed meetings. Dad was not really a "meeting person," and it took a while to determine what we wanted to get out of the meetings. It promoted shared decision making.

After Kate married, she continued working part-time for the business and, like her mother, became instrumental in helping to facilitate communication and trust among family members and others within the company. Whether deliberately or not, she began taking on the role of second-generation Trust Catalyst. Kate apparently valued that role: "You have the chance to move from being just your parents' child, to being an adult in your own right, and to understand your parents as human beings more objectively, with compassion, understanding, acceptance, and greater clarity."

Non-family managers at Hillside echoed the importance of trust for the company as well as for the family:

> I'm always amazed at how unbelievably high the level of trust is here. Trust is built over time, as a relationship develops. It either comes about or it doesn't through your shared experiences. The way I've seen people operate here, I've never seen anything that makes me feel I can't trust. Trust is when people believe in you; that you are doing the best you can at what you are asked to do. I see they trust me implicitly. – *non-family manager and employee of 10 years*

> Trust is something you give. Some people exhibit qualities, but it comes from the giver. That means letting a person make mistakes and not crucifying them. People then work at trusting the one who trusts them. Recognizing one's own part in the process and taking steps in dealing with an area of low trust involve being conscientious when you are communicating with someone. Trust requires acting as a trustworthy person. It's not based on whether I like you or not; it's based on how reliable you are. I can dislike someone, but still trust them, in terms of knowing what they will do in a given situation. I think it's the values of the family here that make it work, and their maturity. They are very conscious of their own limits and take responsibility for their own actions, which make for good role models and a good working environment. – *non-family manager of seven years*

Another Mother and Wife as Trust Catalyst – Rattler's Restaurants

It doesn't always work that way. A Trust Catalyst's success is never guaranteed, nor is that person's presence necessarily appreciated, as noted in the Hobson case. At Rattler's Restaurants, appreciation came, but the family continued to struggle (Gersick, 1997). Paul DeAngelo and his son, Jeff, moved into an era of shouting and fighting once Paul's wife – Jeff's mother – died of cancer. The company controller, a non-family member, observed:

> As visionary as Paul was, Mary was more of a realist. She kept us all grounded. Last week we bought some expensive technology to take food photographs for marketing. We all laughed that if Mary were here, she would have killed us. She was really a nice person. I never realized, but I always used to value her personal advice on everything. She was a friend. She would have been happy to have one restaurant, where it was safe. After all, in Michigan she saw things fall apart. Most women would not have stayed around. Paul would never have gotten his second chance.

> She had a lot of sympathy for Jeff, but she always supported Paul, at least in the office. She stayed out of their arguments. Jeff is more like his mother than his father. When I was handling the money, Paul would come in and say, "I want to do this or that," and I would never say no. But Mary wouldn't stand for that. If we didn't have the money, she wouldn't spend it. Her death – I don't think I've ever dealt with it – the company took some time out for about 6 months. Mary was always the buffer between Paul and Jeff. They never saw eye to eye about anything. She was the one who mediated.

And another employee, the office manager, commented:

> Mrs. D was diagnosed with cancer in July of 1995, and died in February '96. It was really hard. She came first. Now, every decision I make, I think, "What would Mrs. D do?" She was really running the business. She signed the checks,

talked to everyone. She talked to Mr. D, talked to Jeff – when she was going through chemo, she wasn't here, and everyone was looking around and realizing how many things she took care of. She was in the office every day.

Mary DeAngelo played a critical role in helping the task leaders, like her husband, Paul, soften and clarify their own expectations, roles, and chains of command. As may sometimes be the case with Trust Catalysts, those who worked with Mary did not fully appreciated her until she was gone.

The Son-in-Law as Trust Catalyst – The Rugg Manufacturing Company

Five generations of family leadership in the Rugg Manufacturing Company included several different configurations of family involvement. At the time of our study, Rugg had about $20 million in sales and was doing well. Two of the current four family owners, including the company president, Mike Fritz, were sons-in-law of former presidents of the 154-year-old firm.

Mike Fritz joined Rugg in 1972 and rose through the ranks. Steve Peck, the senior vice president of manufacturing, another in-law, began his career at Rugg in 1982. Fritz helped the other owners expand the family's trust values that were initiated in earlier generations, while professionalizing the business and creating systems where there were none. The espoused stewardship philosophy of the fifth generation served as a basis of a business strategy that Fritz and the other owners took very seriously.

Making a successful transition to the fifth generation required Mike Fritz and Tom Fitch, treasurer and controller, to gain the trust of the three fourth-generation owners still active in the business. Tom's uncle, Al Rugg, had invited Tom to join the business in 1987. Al, Bill Rugg, and Tom's father, David Fitch, each took turns running the company until 1992 when Mike took over. According to 32-year-old Tom:

> Dad saw the direction Mike and I wanted to go in, that of establishing corporate divisions, guiding, and dispersing resources to divisional areas. To accomplish that, we had to do a lot of difficult things. Dad had hired a number of good people who were very loyal to him. He allowed us to choose key people for those positions. I think it got to the point where Dad trusted our way of thinking better than his own. He realized our philosophy was that we thought of ourselves not as owners but as stewards whose job it was to get the company from the fourth to the sixth generation and leave it better than we got it. I also feel very comfortable with Al's trust in my abilities. Bill has trust in me too, but would go in a different direction than I would. Trust is the cornerstone to the ongoing success of the business.

The fifth generation's approach also emphasized an inclusive family work ethic that relied on building long-term relationships with employees, customers, and vendors. Mike Fritz referred to these as "good and ethical practices operating within an atmosphere of respect and trust." A gain-sharing program for the more than 80 employees guaranteed that when minimum profit levels were reached, everyone received a portion of those profits. By developing task groups of people working together to solve problems and make improvements, the owners helped to implement further trust building. In addition, the company's financial information was shared with all employees. Employees also received 12 weeks of training that helped show the relevance of each employee's specific contributions to the business. By including employees in the overall strategy of the business, actively seeking participation, and giving information to everyone, employees claimed that Rugg increased the trust levels between members of the company while also building added morale and commitment.

The Successor's Role as an Evolving Trust Catalyst

Replacing Peter Picknelly Sr. seemed nearly impossible in the eyes of his management team. Even the brightest and most-talented offspring would pale in comparison, as was the case with Peter Jr. Typically, Peter Sr. began work at 6:00 A. M. seven days a week, almost every day of the year. His entrepreneurial vision built Peter Pan Bus Lines and a series of real estate acquisitions into thriving enterprises. His work ethic (Character) and Competency were well-known in the community and admired, if not envied, by those who worked for him.

Peter Sr. did not, however, arrive at this pinnacle of success without help. His management team showed enormous dedication to the success of the organization and without exception seemed grateful to the elder Picknelly for the opportunities he provided for their career development. Despite his reputation for being overly blunt and often intimidating, his managers shared a Caring rapport with their boss that made them comfortable about approaching him for advice or support, even on personal matters. According to one of those managers:

> Trust is a level of comfort that someone is being genuine. You know where the person is coming from. You don't have to second-guess them. I don't have to question my relationship with Peter Sr. We have been through so many things together over the last decade. When he gives his word, it is gold. I know I can trust that. When he makes a decision, I can trust that and proceed on a course of action.

Peter Jr. (along with younger brother Paul and older sister Mary Jean), rose through the ranks of the bus company but not always easily. The children knew their father mainly through his working in the business. Peter Jr. stated: "All I ever wanted to do was work at Peter Pan, and I've always done that." In 1991, when Peter Jr. was in his early thirties, Peter Sr. began relinquishing control of the business. In this case, an outside advisor initially became a Trust Catalyst, helping to facilitate a succession plan in which Peter Jr. would take over the bus company and younger brother Paul would serve as president of the hotel and office plaza that had recently been acquired.

The advisor noted that, at the time, "Peter Jr. was young, single, and driving his Lotus all around town. He created an image that made people question whether he really wanted to or would be able to run the bus company." As Trust Catalyst, the advisor worked with and coached both brothers in solidifying their new roles and helping them learn to better manage their relationships with their father and senior managers.

Over time, emerging from his father's formidable shadow, Peter Jr. developed and gained confidence in his own style and approach. Although many of his strengths and qualities differed from those of his father, he too began to earn respect from his peers and others – even his father. This platform of success grew as Peter Jr. established his own identity and eventually assumed a new role as a Trust Catalyst within his family and increasingly with the managers and employees of Peter Pan.

The family background of the Picknelly children had not facilitated trust as a value in a traditional sense. Their father divorced their mother when the children were young and dedicated his life to his business. Consequently, the three children grew up taking care of each other. Although Picknelly Sr. did not assume the typical role of a father, he did, however, open his world – the business – to his children. Mary Jean had provided a Caring and nurturing force that helped cement the bond between her siblings, but her influence in the business was limited by the perception that she was not as dedicated a performer as her brothers and father. In this way, Peter Jr. assumed the greater role as Trust Catalyst. He acted as a sounding board and always lent a Caring ear. According to Mary Jean: "I trust Peter. If I tell him something in confidence, even if he goes and tells Dad, it's done in a caring way. Then he'll come back and let me know. He won't do anything to hurt you. If my father wants to know what is going on with me, he'll go to lunch with Peter."

Trust Beyond The Family. Through his refined listening skills and openness, Peter

Jr. became both the student and the teacher. Dedicated and thorough in his approach to decision-making and planning processes, he was also highly inclusive of his valued management team. He often expressed his appreciation and respect for the company's employees. Trust Catalysts, like Peter, exemplify a broad concern for the needs and feelings of others – not simply their own dominant needs. His extended sense of Caring reached beyond family ties into the organization where he seemed to talk with people in ways that expressed genuine interest and respect. According to Peter Jr. , he often included employees in other aspects of his life:

> The management team is like my extended family. I socialize with them. Some people have a problem with that. They are concerned that you can't separate the roles, but it has never been a problem. In fact, I think it has helped create a bond with people where, if I ever need to, I can say "what's going on here," and hold people accountable. I think it's even easier because people know I genuinely like and respect them. I couldn't imagine having had the christening of my babies without inviting the people from work.

Even here, though, roots of trust are never completely firm, particularly during periods of rapid growth (or decline) when managerial relationships shift. At Peter Pan, growth was accompanied by some doubt. As one non-family manager with a long history at Peter Pan remarked:

> When there's trust, you don't have to second-guess anyone's decisions. You empower them to make decisions. You feel loyalty – that they care about you and the best interests of the business. They are not just out for their own benefit. Trust levels have diminished some since we've gotten bigger. Several middle managers have been brought in, and there is some competition. Are they going to get Peter Jr.'s ear on every issue?

Outside Advisor Trust Catalysts – The Fielding Oil Company

Although the Fielding family's background showed relatively high trust, that was put to a severe test during the sibling succession struggle between eldest son, Bill, and youngest son, Rob, 14 years Bill's junior. Not the least of which was its impact on other family and non-family employees in the $80 million-a-year company. An "us versus them" feeling seemed to arise between family and non-family members when non-family members felt forced to take either Bill's or Rob's side. Non-family members also felt caught between long-term loyalties and task integrity, as when non-family employees received conflicting instructions or feedback from family members. Under these conditions, organizational trust was truly jeopardized. The resulting ambiguity, confusion, and resentment began to erode Fielding's historical pride in performance, cooperation, and loyalty.

Fielding presented still another example of the impact family values and interactions have on the culture and continuity of the business. The four second-generation brothers who shared ownership of the company also shared pride in how their parents had built the business to provide opportunities for their future. Eldest brother Bill, 67, stated: "Our father fostered a culture of 'givers' through his example. That's been essential – the willingness to give for the benefit of everybody with the objective being success. We learned about human relations, how to treat people, from our father. He was a friend to customers."

The Fielding brothers identified strongly with their family name and a desire to continue it into the next generation and beyond. Youngest brother, Rob, spoke with great conviction about his family's values in a way that implied inherent trust:

> The most important decision in the history of the company was in 1957 when my parents turned the business over to my brothers and made a provision for

me to eventually join them. They didn't have to do that, but they did. And they did it largely without a guarantee. Our representation to them was "we'll take care of you," and to this day, we take care of them. We come from a world that has to do with aunts and uncles, brothers and sisters. It is a cultural thing. We have religious roots and a heavy emphasis on forgiveness. That's why we brothers are still together here. We are not perfect by a long stretch. About the only thing we have perfected, however, is the ability to forgive one another. That is the good thing that we do.

Despite this legacy, marked tensions began to occur between Bill and Rob. While in control of the company, Bill functioned as the primary Trust Catalyst. That changed in the late 1980s when Rob challenged Bill for more control and wanted to become the HSA. The 14-year difference in age also posed conflict. Bill had assumed the strong patriarchal role in both the family and business as soon as their father retired. He stated: "Rob and I are really a generation apart. We have different views and different values. The 1980s were really quite difficult. Rob started to feel his oats. He wanted to get in and run the company. He talks a different language than I do. He has a different vocabulary and a different perspective on things."

Rob was the only one of the four brothers who had graduated from college. He also had earned an advanced degree. With education and experience came confidence, and Rob took on the role of the task-centered change agent who wanted to keep things moving. He increasingly challenged Bill's judgment and, not surprisingly, encountered increasing resistance. Rob saw this as groundless rejection by his older brothers. Eventually, the gap grew so large between Rob and two of his older brothers that Rob proposed that he leave if he wasn't given more control over the business. He gave notice in 1987 and announced plans to leave the following year.

For two months, Rob received no response from Bill. When Bill finally did reply, he said nothing in advance and suddenly announced in a meeting that Rob would take over as president and that Bill would become chairman of the board of directors. Rob became president on January 1, 1988, but the conflicts began again when Rob sought his brothers' agreement on their future plans for retirement. Continuing disputes over operational and management issues further undermined relationships.

The idea of forming a board of advisors was originally presented to the Fieldings by a family business consultant they'd hired in 1984. According to that person, Bill's initial response was, in effect, "Over my dead body. We're used to doing this ourselves, our own way." After all, he probably reasoned that if they couldn't trust each other, how could they trust an outsider?

By 1991, the company had still not resolved the sensitive retirement and stock-ownership issues involving all three older brothers. Finally, the brothers agreed to form a board to assist in planning the future of the business and to help the brothers unravel their own problems. Of necessity, objections were temporarily put aside, though not forgotten. Four advisory board members were sought, each with expertise in a key area.

Over time, the board played a significant role. Not only did the Fieldings establish direction and policies for the business, but they found ways to deal with the retirement and stock-ownership issues. The board became the new Trust Catalyst. In the words of Frank Fielding, a third-generation successor: "The board sucked three-quarters of the emotion out of the family stuff. Having objective, outside people changed the dynamic of the brothers." Before that could occur, though, things got worse. According to Frank, non-family members in the company paid a high price during this period of low trust:

> The succession process took two years, during which there was a lack of focus and an upheaval in the company. It was virtually leaderless during that time. Growth halted, profits shrank, and morale problems grew. It was a real low point. Rob had become president and had a cadre of people reporting to him in all different areas, and this group took on a life of its own – against Rob, as a result of lack of direction.

Rob was consumed with the succession problems, and no one was minding the store. It was split between upper-management upstairs and employees downstairs (not family versus non-family). It was the multiple-boss syndrome – a who-do-people-listen-to kind of dilemma. Lower level employees were confused. The brothers were telling people different things. No one knew who the boss was.

The family business consultant, who had originally proposed the idea of forming a board, became a director when the board was finally formed. He became a Trust Catalyst for Fielding; presenting and encouraging neutrality, Caring, and Competency. In the advisor's words:

> The idea of the board was to work toward consensus. It was essential for outside board members to have everyone's interest in mind. This can be a difficult balance to manage. Bill was a hands-on type of leader; a doer who was decisive and knew what he wanted. Rob was a more process type of guy who puts things in context. But their family background favored conflict avoidance at all costs. Developing plans for the older three brothers' retirement was very complex. Trust was a powerful binder for them. It is like a gold thread in a fine fabric that gives it its beauty.

Such tales of trust and mistrust are never completely over. With the critical issues behind them, however, the Fielding brothers' relationships improved dramatically. According to Rob, Bill eventually went on to become a highly constructive elder partner. During Fielding's critical sibling transition, previous Character, Competency, Predictability, and Caring role modeling had to be reshaped and sustained by people outside the family – something that occurs in countless family business situations when tensions get too high. With an appropriate sense of timing, outsiders may step into the Trust Catalyst role that no family member can fill at that time. Outside board members, consultants, or family friends may also establish those HSF footholds of trust that remind family members of the trust issues that are in jeopardy. Under such conditions, family members may collectively find it easier to trust an outsider than each other, which, in itself, may provide the basis for a new beginning with a new family member as Trust Catalyst.

Conclusion

It is easy to imagine how further empirical research in family businesses could extend the tentative findings of this study. To begin with, survey research could further establish the presence, frequency, and role characteristics of Trust Catalysts. Do they really exist on the scale that we observed in successful family organizations? And do failing businesses show a marked decline or absence of such people? Further research must also be done on the relational characteristics of HSA individuals and their HSF counterparts.

Family businesses, almost more than any other kind of enterprise, pack intense emotions into predicaments and problems that can leave the people involved wondering whether the effort is worth it. History also shows that many entrepreneurs sell their businesses rather than get into the difficulties brought about by succeeding family involvement in the business. Whether it is succession, rivalry, favoritism, or power, family business arenas, both large and small, seem worthy of some of Shakespeare's greatest dramas. Whether the model is Lear, Hamlet, or Macbeth, the play goes on as one generation or family member struggles to please, challenge, surpass, or succeed the previous one.

But unlike Shakespeare's characters, family business members often have the power to modify the script before it is finally written. Even though there will always be predicaments and problems, disaster is not inevitable. Cures and progress can result from the ways in which families build, structure, and tend to relationships. Sometimes that means pruning the business of some family members, as Rob Fielding tried to do, eventually with Bill's help. Sometimes it means establishing procedures for promotion, replacement, and succession that won't rip the family apart, as in the Marr, Hillside, and Peter Pan situations. And sometimes it means encouraging the kind of family relationships that build effectiveness in both business and family. That kind of effectiveness, this paper proposes, can best evolve when trust is created, appreciated, valued, and subscribed to by all parties. But a culture of trust, we suggest, must be encouraged by those family members who focus on the task dimensions of the business.

Establishing high-trust relationships with non-family employees, as we have seen, is a critical requirement for long-term family business performance and continuity. Many family participants in our studies, however, revealed concerns about their ability to build trust with and successfully integrate non-family members into their organizations. It was typically stated that trust comes more easily within families. But even when a relatively high level of trust exists within the family, there is no guarantee that it will extend to non-family employees. How can trust be created, particularly with new employees who do not share the bond and history of family background? In the absence of trust, an us-versus-them situation can develop between family and non-family members of the organization. Trust Catalysts seem aware of the importance of bridging this gap as they utilize the Four Characteristics of Trust – Character, Competency, Predictability, and Caring – to extend relationships with non-family members of family businesses.

Equally important, conclusions from this study suggest that organizational trust may have small beginnings – one person who serves as an appreciated Trust Catalyst and helps to create exchanges of Character, Competency, Predictability, and Caring that introduce, receive, and expand that person's tentative offerings of trust. In our study, the Trust Catalysts were often not the CEOs or task leaders of the family business. Instead, they might have been on the fringes of central business purposes, sometimes people without formal lines of authority, but who were trusted and sponsored by those who did have that authority. These HSFs were able to work with the sponsorship of a CEO's HSA.

Ironically, these Trust Catalysts are probably just as important in explaining both family and business success as are the more famed family business leaders who typically gain most of the public credit for a company's success. Though dutifully referenced in public pronouncements by their more famous sponsors ("I couldn't have done all of this without the help of...") it seems time for them to receive greater recognition from a wider audience who more fully understands the importance of what they so often quietly do in their own families and organizations.

References

Bailyn, L. , Fletcher, J. K. , & Kolb, D. (1997). Unexpected connections: Considering employees' personal lives can revitalize your business, *Sloan Management Review, 38*, 11–19.

Baird, A. , & St-Amand, R. (1995, May). *Trust within organizations*, Monograph, Issue 1. Ottawa: Public Service Commission of Canada.

Bales, R. F. (1950). *Interaction Process Analysis: A method for the study of small groups.* Reading, MA: Addison-Wesley.

Barnes, L. B. (1981). Managing the paradox of organizational trust. *Harvard Business Review, 59*, 107– 116.

Barnes, L. B. (1989). *Managing interpersonal feedback* (Course Note 9-483-027). Boston: Harvard Business School.

Bennis, W. , & Nanus, B. (1985). *Leaders: The strategies of taking charge.* New York: Harper & Row.

Bennis, W. , & Goldsmith, J. (1997). *Learning to lead: A workbook on becoming a leader.* Reading, MA: Addison-Wesley.

Butler, J. K. Jr. (1991). Toward understanding and measuring conditions of trust: Evolution of conditions of trust inventory. *Journal of Management, 17*(3), 643–661.

Butler, J. K. , Jr. , & Cantrell, R. S. (1984). A behavioral decision theory approach to modeling dyadic trust in superiors and subordinates. *Psychological Reports, 55*, 19–28.

Cook, J. , & Wall, T. (1980). New work attitude measures of trust, organizational commitment, and personal need fulfillment. *Journal of Occupational Social Psychology, 53*, 39–52.

Deutsch, M. (1960). Trust, trustworthiness, and the F scale. *Journal of Abnormal and Social Psychology, 61*, 138–140.

Driscoll, J. (1978). Trust and participation in organizational decision making as predictors of satisfaction. *Academy of Management Journal, 21*(1), 44–56.

Drucker, P. (1992). *Managing for the future: The 1990's and Beyond.* New York: Truman Talley Books.

Dyer, W. G. (1992). *The entrepreneurial experience.* San Francisco: Jossey-Bass.

Erikson, E. (1950). *Childhood and society.* New York: Norton.

Freilich, M. (1964). The natural triad in kinship and complex systems. *American Sociological Review, 29*(4), 529–540.

Fukuyama, F. (1995). *Trust: The social virtues and the creation of prosperity.* New York: Free Press.

Gersick, K. A. , Davis, J. A. , McCollom-Hampton, M. , & Lansberg, I. (1996). *Generation to generation: Life cycles of the family business.* Boston: Harvard Business School Press.

Gersick, K. A. (1997, July). *Rattler's restaurants* (Case # N9-498-009). Boston: Harvard Business School.

Goldstein, J. (1984). *How to start a family business and make it work.* New York: M. Evans & Co.

Horton, T. R. , & Reid, P. C. (1991). *Beyond the trust gap.* Homewood, IL: Business-One Irwin.

Hosmer, L. (1995). Trust: The connecting link between organizational theory and philosophical ethics. *Academy of Management Review, 20*(2), 379–403.

Kegan, D. & Rubenstein, A. (1973). Trust, effectiveness, and organizational development: A field study in R& D. *Journal of Applied Behavioral Science, 1,* 498–513.

Kouzes, J. , & Posner, B. (1993). *Credibility: How leaders gain and lose it, why people demand it.* San Francisco: Jossey-Bass.

LaChapelle, L. K. (1997). *The role of leadership and continuity of family-owned businesses.* Unpublished doctoral dissertation, Union Institute, Organizational Behavior.

Likert, J. , & Likert, R. (1976). *New ways of managing conflict.* New York: McGraw-Hill.

McFarland, L. , Senn, L. , & Childress, J. (1993). *21st century leadership: Dialogues with 100 top leaders.* Los Angeles: Leadership Press.

Mayer, R. , Davis, J. , & Schoorman, D. (1995). An integrative model of organizational trust. *Academy of Management Review, 20*(3), 704–734.

Mishra, J. , & Morrisey, M. (1990). Trust in employee/ employer relationships: A survey of west Michigan managers. *Public Personnel Management, 19*(4), 443–461.

Rotter, J. (1966). Generalized expectancies for internal vs. external control of reinforcement. *Psychological Monographs, 80.*

Schindler, P. , & Thomas, C. (1993). The structure of interpersonal trust in the workplace. P*sychological Reports, 73,* 563–573.

Shaw, R. B. (1997). *Trust in the balance.* San Francisco: Jossey-Bass.

Stevenson, H. H. (1997). *Do lunch or be lunch.* Boston: Harvard Business School Press.

Taylor, R. (1989). The role of trust in labor-management relations. *Organization Development Journal, 7*(2), 85–89.

Ward, J. L. (1987). *Keeping the family business healthy.* San Francisco: Jossey-Bass.

Whitney, J. O. (1993). *The trust factor: Liberating profits and restoring corporate vitality.* New York: McGraw-Hill.

Williams, R. (1992). *Preparing your family to manage wealth.* Marina, CA: Marina Pacific Institute.

Zand, D. (1996). *The leadership triad: Knowledge, trust, and power.* New York: Oxford University Press.

There has never been greater interest in the governance of business families by those families themselves. Alden G. Lank and John L. Ward look at numerous European and North American family businesses to provide insight and advice on developing governance processes and making them work.

Governing the Business Owning Family

By Alden G. Lank and John L. Ward

Governance* as a serious field of study in business academic circles has been around for barely a decade. In this relatively short period, we have learned a considerable amount about the nature and importance of good governance of the corporation. It is only in the last five years or so that the focus has started to turn to the governance of the family enterprise per se. Hence our knowledge base is considerably less in the latter case. When it comes to the governance of the family, the literature is extensive and the area has been researched for many decades. Yet, somewhat surprisingly, we know relatively little about the governance of the business owning family that shares the characteristics of any other family but, in addition, has unique (and complicating) features specific to it. This addition complexity derives from the overlapping of the family system and the business system that the family owns wholly or in part.

Our recent experience working with owning families indicates clearly that there never has been a greater interest in the governance of business families. We are often asked, amongst many other related questions:

- What kinds of governance institutions or bodies do we need?
- What purposes should they serve?
- What should be the content of the underlying Family Protocol and how should it be drafted?

These queries reflect not only the void in the governance literature noted above but also a dawning awareness that successful business families (ones who continue in the ownership role over the generations) have been paying attention to governance all along. Furthermore, as families decide to perpetuate their philanthropic interests and/or to increase their desire and ability to act as as responsible long-term stewards of capital, it becomes evident that this will not be possible without the creation of governance bodies and enabling protocols. Indeed, we would predict that there is a positive correlation between the wish and need for formalized (as opposed to de facto or informal) governance bodies and written (as opposed to implied or verbal) protocols and the following:

- The size of the family
- The wealth of the family
- The number of non-active vs. employed (in the family firm) members of the family
- The strength of the desire to remain an owning family
- The size of the business owned
- The later the stage of the company
  Stage 1 – Owner-Managed
  Stage 2 – Sibling Partnership
  Stage 3 – Cousin Consortium**

Of course, these are hypotheses that remain to be further tested by ourselves and others and, inevitably, there will be and should be differences between owning families in the

---

*We define "governance" as "systems and structures to direct, control and account for" whatever organization is being examined – such as a corporation, a family enterprise, a business owning family, a family, etc. See Fred Neubauer and Alden G. Lank, *The Family Business: Its Governance for Sustainability*, London: Macmillan Business, 1998, pp. 60, 71.

types of governance bodies and the nature of the underlying protocols. There are few general rules and each family must tailor-make its governance approach to its own particular needs. The remainder of this article will focus on the basic types of governance bodies and their roles, the key issues that must be addressed (usually to be reflected in the Family Protocol) and what can be done to maximize the chances of successfully governing the business owning family over time.

Typical Governance Bodies and Their Roles

Business families thrive when they have a compelling sense of purpose and pro-active policies to help achieve that purpose. Assuring these two ingredients is the central function of the Family Council – arguably the most important governance body that the family can create.

For smaller families the Family Council may be comprised of the entire family.*** Others restrict membership to only direct descendants of the founder. As the family grows larger, the Family Council often becomes a constitutionalized representative body of the family – chosen either by appointment or election. We refer to the family at large as the Family Assembly. If the Family Assembly develops a formal organization with a constitution, we refer to that as the Family Association. Whenever the Family Assembly gets together or the Family Association meets, such a gathering is commonly referred to as a "family meeting."

The Family Council is like the symphony conductor, directing the many elements of the family to achieve the family's purpose. The score the Family Council shapes and/or implements is the Family Protocol. While the content of such Protocols varies tremendously among different families, a not untypical list of themes is the following:

A Typical Table of Contents of a Family Protocol
- Family Mission and Vision
- Family Values and Principles
- Family Commitment to Ownership
- Family Business Policies
  - Family Personnel Policy
  - Shareholders' Agreement
  - Family Code of Conduct
  - Family Member Conflict of Interest Statement
  - Governance of the Family Business
- Family Constitution (including the family governance bodies, their roles, composition, structure, etc.)

For a business-owning family, the Family Council needs to address and to balance three key dimensions: the family as family, the family as employees and the family as owners. The important topics of each dimension follow. As the family grows in size and complexity, the different topics can be addressed by sub-groups or committees under the over-all coordination of the Family Council.

A rather full-blown family governance system is portrayed in Figure 2. Very few families have all the elements of the model but we believe it is helpful to have a model in mind to facilitate the work of the Family Council. For each of the topics of family governance listed, a reference number (reflected in Figure 2) is provided to indicate the most typical governance body that addresses the topic. Again, each family will have to decide the most logical locus for its own special case.

**See John L. Ward, *Creating Effective Boards for Private Enterprises: Meeting the Challenges of Continuity and Competition*, San Francisco: Jossey-Bass, 1991.

***Sometimes the Family Council and the Council of Elders (its name evokes its composition) are one and the same. Other times the Council of Elders is advisory to the Family Council, Family Assembly and/or Family Association or it can act as ombudsman for the entire family.

Figure 1

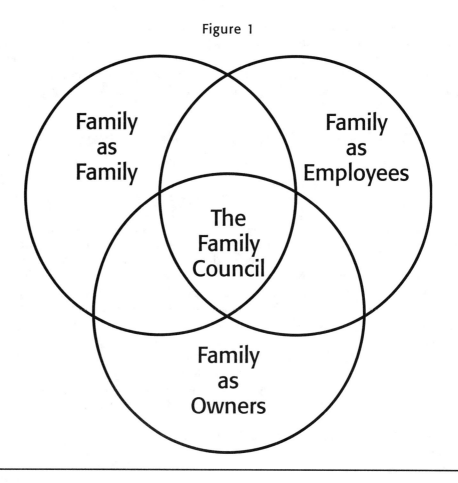

Family As Family

The Family Council seeks to assure that family needs, rights and responsibilities (as outlined in the Family Protocol) are honored in addition to its general coordinating role concerning Family as Employees and Family as Owners. It aims to achieve strong bonds of social cohesion. What follows is a sampling of topic areas.

Develop Social Relations (2)

A social committee can promote family reunions, fun times at family meetings and entrench family traditions (e.g. Founder's Day, joint vacation trips, etc.).

Manage Family Heirlooms (4)

The Family Office often looks after precious family assets such as the family compound, family museum or family archives.

Articulate Family History (2)

The social committee or the communications committee may undertake the task of publishing the family history and keeping it up to date. Occasionally, a special family history committee may be appointed for this purpose.

Provide Shared Services (4)

The Family Office can also arrange for individual tax services, personal financial planning, insurance and real estate advice, personnel services for household help, legal record management and many other services.

Support Families-in-Need (1)

Some families leave such issues to individuals and so specify in the Family Protocol. Others, however, use collective family resources to help those with special needs. The Family Council or Council of Elders should also be supporting the emotional needs of family members in times of distress.

Offer Education (2)

Many families offer interpersonal skill development programs such as listening skills,

Figure 2. Family Governance Model

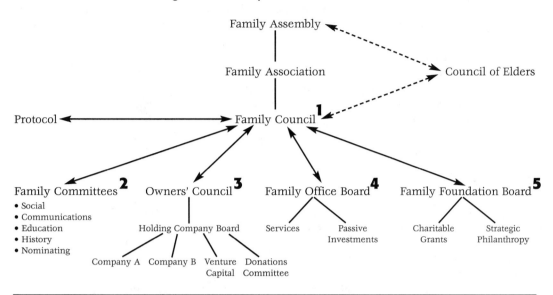

presentation skills, consensus development skills, etc.**** Some families have an education fund that provides financial support for higher education, private education or personal development seminars.

Facilitate Family Communications (2)

A communications committee can produce a family newsletter, manage the family website or publish and distribute private essays and letters. Members of the committee can also lead family sharing sessions at family meetings. The first task is to identify what information the family needs and wants.

Resolve Conflict (1)

The Family Council or the Council of Elders is typically the body that addresses family conflicts. Many families have formalized (in the Protocol) conflict resolution mechanisms (i.e. mediation or arbitration) that may involve respected non-family members.

Identify Future Family Leaders (2)

Some large families have nominating committees whose task is to ensure a flow of qualified family leaders for the various governance bodies.

Family As Employees

As the family owns a business, it is to be expected that some, if not many, family members will wish to become employees of the company. Thus, we believe it is vitally important the the Protocol include a section on the Family Personnel Policy. This will specify the "rules of the game" concerning the rights and responsibilities of and conditions which must be met for a family member to join and remain with the family firm. One of the key issues here is whether family employees will be treated exactly the same as non-family employees or whether special privileges accrue to the status of being a family employee.

Provide Professional Development (2)

Families often recognize the need for professional development beyond the human resource programs offered by the business. Family employees can benefit from special sources of performance appraisal (objective feedback often being very difficult to obtain within the firm) and from special education on the issues connected with being a family employee. The firm's Board of Directors can play a critical role in these areas but often needs to be encouraged or assisted by the family's education committee.

****See Sharon Krone and John L. Ward, The Family University: Personal and Professional Education for the Extended Family, *The Family Business Network Newsletter*, no. 23, May 1999.

Nurture Family Interest (2)

The education committee is also the most likely forum to encourage and oversee summer jobs, internships and other forms of business exposure for younger family member as they consider their vocational interests and career options.

Handle Grievances (1)

In the course of a family member's career in the family firm, there may be occasions when he or she feels improperly or unfairly treated. Some families leave such matters to be handled by the line organization. Others have charged a sub-committee of the Board of Directors (comprised of family and non-family members) with this task. A common approach is to give this job to the Family Council or the Council of Elders that can play either a mediation or arbitration role.

Family As Owners

There are at least two dimensions to ownership: the legal and the emotional. The formation of an Owners' Council can be of great help in administering the legal (rights and responsibilities) requirements of ownership. The Council works to provide a unity of voice amongst the owners and to assure that ownership is a proactive force in the governance of the business.

Too often a fragmented family ownership group creates a vacuum for the abuse of power by corporate management with the acquiescence of a disinterested Board of Directors. At least as often, an undisciplined family ownership constituency frustrates management effectiveness and discourages efforts to attract excellent independent directors. While the Owners' Council (in small families this could be comprised of all shareholders) must be selected by the shareholders and the Family Council usually by the Family Assembly or Family Association, these two central governing bodies must work together in the best interests of the family and of its business.

Define the Business Governance Structure (3)

The controlling owners need to decide what form of corporate governance they want. They need to address the size of the Board of Directors, the make-up and role of the Board (e.g. majority family?) and the design of subsidiary Boards.

Guide the Director Selection Process (3)

The company's Board (as well as the family) looks to the owning family members to participate in or ratify the criteria for corporate directors and the selection of the directors.

Define Owners' Goals, Values and Vision (3)

It is ownership's responsibility to make explicit its expectations (hopefully with one voice) to the Board of the business. The Family Council often plays a key role in articulating the family's values in this regard and these will form an important part of the Family Protocol.

Assure Shareholder Information System (3)

In concert with the Company's Board and, possibly, management's shareholder relations staff, the Owners' Council defines the frequency and content of the information flow to the family shareholders (and in conjunction with the Family Council to the other family members) about the business. This task is critical if the family's commitment to the business is to be strengthened.

Overseeing the Internal Stock Exchange (3)

Many families have found it necessary to establish some form of internal stock exchange to allow members to buy and sell shares within the confines of the family. This process has to be supervised and often this task is given to the Owners' Council if not the business' shareholder relations officer.

Maintain Relations With Other Shareholders (3)

If the family does not own all the shares, a strategy is needed for relating to the other shareholders so as to enhance the probability of the family's wishes being accepted while maintaining fruitful and mutually advantageous relations with the non-family shareholders.

Define and Oversee the Company's Charitable Charter (3)

One ownership goal that needs specific delineation is the form in which the company gives back to society and this should be determined by the Owners' Council. Sometimes the family, through the Family Council, actively administers corporate giving. Other times, this is a corporate function undertaken in line with the owners' wishes.

Manage Collective Family Philanthropy (5)

Some families fund a separate Family Foundation from corporate profits. Others endow or have endowed a Family Foundation with shares of stock or other family capital. Many believe that family philanthropy helps unify the extended family and helps owners cope with the emotional challenges of inherited wealth. The Family Protocol often provides guidelines for family collective giving.

Aid in the Acceptance of Wealth (2)

Ownership can result not only in considerable individual wealth but also inherited privilege and power. How to deal positively with these matters and avoid the many potential dysfunctional results can be an important role for the education committee.

Prepare Family for Ownership and Governance (2)

Another of the family's educational roles can be to provide the family (whether or not currently employees, directors or owners) with an understanding of the rights and responsibilities of ownership and to develop family members for directorships. Sometimes, in collaboration with the company's Board, the education committee can organize "Junior Board" learning experiences.

Common Critical Issues

The effective operation of any family governance system rests on being able to find answers to several challenging questions. Sometimes these questions are addressed in early versions of the Family Protocol. Often, the issues only emerge as the family grows and evolves through the generations. In either case, a process is needed and, once again, experience shows that the Family Council often takes the lead. By making recommendations for ratification by the Family Assembly or Family Association, approved texts can then be added to the appropriate sections of the Family Protocol. What follows are some of the key issues which families must confront.

Who Is Family?

Defining the rules of inclusion and exclusion is a complex task for many families. What finally evolves is typically a function of the family's culture, its historical experience and the ethnic or national culture in which it is anchored. Issues beyond pure membership include eligibility for leadership roles of in-laws, young children, ex-spouses, stepchildren, adopted children, ex-owners, small or never-been owners.

How To Vote?

Families also struggle with how many votes a person has in any matter that has to be voted upon. Are votes allocated on a per capita, per stirpes or per share basis?

How To Select Leaders?

Some families have open elections for each family leadership position. Others have a slate of officers developed by the Family Council or the family nominating committee. They can follow a leadership ladder where last year's Family Council vice president, for example, automatically becomes next year's president, etc. Related issues include defining terms of office and how to "deselect" or discharge a family member from office. Can they also be selected for professional executive or staff functions (e.g. president of the Family Office or executive director of the Family Foundation). The family also needs to consider whether its philosophy is to encourage broad involvement with rotations or strictly merit criteria for family governance roles.

How To Involve Family?

Families struggle with the balance between individual autonomy and collective conformity. For example, does the family put social pressure on family members to participate and to serve? On the other hand, does the family honor those who are not interested or prepared to carry their fair share?

How To Compensate?

Are family governance positions (e.g. chair of the Family Council, Chair of the Family Foundation or Family Board Office) eligible for compensation and if so using which benchmarks? Are family members reimbursed for personal travel and/or research and/or development expenses associated with their involvement in family governance activities?

How To Fund?

Raising monies to fund the family's activities also creates many questions. Some families charge their members dues; others feel that the business should pay for Family Council type costs in the interests of shareholder relations or efficient tax planning.

How To Start?

Creation of the first governance bodies and the underlying Family Protocol normally requires a family "champion" who sells the necessity to other interested family members sometimes with the help of an external facilitator. Task forces are then set up to draft proposals for submission to the family (however defined) or some subset thereof. Families vary in terms of the approval procedures used – all the way from no vote (i.e. consensus) to simple majority to "super majority."

Maximizing Success

Up to this point in the article we have tried, based on our experience, to be largely descriptive about the governance of the business owning family. In this last section, we shall try to be more normative in terms of what families should do to maximize the success of their governance approach. These are very personal reflections based on the many successes and failures we have seen in business families. Our hope is that our conclusions will stimulate both debate and better practice. Here are the principles that we believe will help to maximize success.

1. Ensure that the Family Protocol has been developed in such a way as to maximize consensus. This implies creating the conditions that will allow the family to feel psychological ownership of the resulting document. It also means that the Protocol should specify the process for its re-examination as conditions change.
2. Be clear in regard to the objectives, structure, process to be followed, authority and responsibility of any governance body.
3. Avoid overlap between any governance bodies but encourage dialogue between all bodies.
4. Encourage each body to pursue "fair process" – valuing consistency and ensuring procedural justice.
5. Build a clear supervisory system to ensure that each governance body is accomplishing its objectives within the parameters established by the Protocol.
6. Be prepared to revise the mandate of any body and have a process for so doing.
7. Have a vehicle for family members to question the workings of any body in the extreme case even a grievance committee.
8. Avoid over-centralization of power across the governance bodies in the hands of a single individual or clique whenever possible. While competence should be the major criterion for serving on governance bodies, remember that these bodies can be excellent training vehicles, e.g. for younger members of the family. Serving on them can play a major role in keeping the members of the family united and giving them the feeling of connectedness to the family and its business.
9. Maximize openness of communication between each body and the larger family group, e.g. publishing of minutes, reporting back annually to the Family Council or the Family Association, publishing articles in the family newsletter or on the website. When this is

not possible or advisable, have the family accept the necessity of confidentiality (e.g. if there is a grievance of one family member against another, the body having the right to arbitrate may decide that the decision should only be reported to the parties involved).

10. Provide mechanisms for appropriate and timely communication between the family and the Board of Directors and the management of the family's enterprise. The family Council and the Owners' Council should consider this one of their key responsibilities.

11. Use non-family experts to increase the effectiveness and efficiency of family governance bodies. They can provide an independent perspective, outside accountability and wise counsel. Some families have appointed "independent advisors" to the Family Council or the Owners' Council. Non-executive, non-family members of the business Board can also serve on the Boards of the Family Office or Family Foundation.

12. Search for opportunities to learn from other families' experiences with their governance systems. Every family can learn from others' successes and failures.

Conclusion

The governance of the business owning family is a highly complex task. Yet, it cannot be avoided if the family is to achieve cohesion and a sense of shared purpose. Without a well-articulated governance system it is highly doubtful that the family will be able to perpetuate itself as owners of a business enterprise. Despite the many complexities involved, many families have found to their pleasant surprise that the very process of developing governance bodies and their underlying Family Protocol have brought the members closer together and reaffirmed their commitment to both the family and its enterprise.

This article was published in the *Family Business Network Newsletter*, No. 26, May 2000. Reprinted with permission.

Family meetings develop family unity through the creation of perceived shared beliefs. The article presents a model with strategic implications showing how shared beliefs lead to collective action, which leads to outcomes and then the reassessment of the shared beliefs. Finally, the article reports on initial research on the reliability of instruments developed to explore one aspect of this model: The creation of shared beliefs through family meetings. The initial results suggest that perceptions of shared beliefs may be an important stimulant of collective family activity.

Research Note
Perceptions Are Reality: How Family Meetings Lead to Collective Action

By Timothy G. Habbershon and Joseph H. Astrachan

Introduction

Prior research and theory have identified major causes of business, family, and succession problems as family conflict (Kaye, 1991; Harvey and Evans, 1994), lack of clarity about goals and values (Tagiuri and Davis, 1992; Harris, Martinez, and Ward, 1994), and family communication and behavioral patterns that lead to misinterpreted information (Lansberg and Astrachan, 1994; Whiteside, Aronoff, and Ward, 1993). Family business practice and theory suggest that family meetings can have a beneficial effect on family involvement in the business (Ward and Aronoff, 1994; Gersick, Davis, McCollom-Hampton, and Lansberg, 1997) and that they should be the starting point for all family business planning (Ward, 1987). The implicit assumption of these two streams of thinking is that when unity about goals, desires, and actions is achieved through family meetings, it becomes the basis for positive outcomes in a family business.

In this article, we test this assumption and develop a competing theory that we adapted from Langfield-Smith's (1992) work concerning the development of shared beliefs or "collective cognitions." We posit that it is the degree to which family members believe group unity exists, rather than the actual level of group unity, that predicts, and indeed may motivate, collective behavior. This will come as no surprise to many who work with families. Families can often be observed as agreeing far more than they perceive. We further suggest that the effectiveness of family meetings is not found in simply generating consensus around a set of family beliefs, but in creating a forum for processing individual beliefs. We contend that those beliefs are reflected by their perceptions of group agreement on critical family and business issues. Through the family meeting as a "collective encounter" experience (Langfield-Smith, 1992), individual group members reassess their beliefs in the light of information and outcomes, and develop new degrees of shared beliefs through reframing and renegotiation. This in turn leads to renewed collective action.

We study the reliability of instruments developed to measure perceptions of agreement that family members have on a number of critical dimensions. These dimensions are drawn from prior theory and research and include community involvement, family, company performance, and stakeholder goals. Some initial research results are presented on how various factors seem to impact perceived family agreement, hinting at a fluidity in individual perceptions of agreement

Finally, we examine the strategic implications of this research. Our findings suggest that coordinated family action that uses new information to continually reassess and modify its thinking may lead to better performance and increase the probability of long-term family business survival. It may be that the content and actual level of agreement about shared beliefs at any given instant is not as important as both the frequency with which they are collectively reassessed, and the level of perceived agreement among family members about their beliefs. This proposition supports the aphorism that action is better than inaction.

Shared Beliefs

The concepts of shared beliefs, meanings, and sense-making have all been used to describe aspects of organizational culture (Schein, 1984; Gagliardi, 1986; Dyer, 1986). It is generally agreed that individuals within an organization must share a certain level of cultural beliefs and values if a group is to function coherently (Pfeffer, 1981, Smircich, 1983a; Trice and Beyer, 1984). However, the nature and degree of the shared beliefs necessary for collective action has been the subject of significant debate.

One theory asserts that organizations are systems of shared meanings, and that organizational action is the product of consensus among organizational participants (Van Maanen, 1979; Smircich, 1983b). Weick (1979) presents a competing theory, holding that only minimal shared understanding is required, because common ends and shared meanings are outcomes of organized action or exchange. Weick's theory requires only the recognition of some basic agreement among the parties about their interdependence and about the means of enacting their relationship (Donellon and Bougon, 1986).

Building on the theoretical work of Weick (1979), Langfield-Smith (1992) developed a mediating theory. She finds that while groups do not maintain a consensus of shared beliefs as a basis for collective action, they do develop "collective cognitions" that are more "...transitory social artifacts of the group subscribed to in varying degrees by the members of the group at a particular point in time" (p. 360). She suggests that when individuals function as members of an organizational group, there will be some overlap in the content of their individual belief systems. The degree of overlap is developed through social interaction, termed a "collective encounter." In a family-business context, these shared beliefs could be expressed during a family meeting as they become realigned during dialog and the exchange of new information. Langfield-Smith (1992) holds that collective encounters are necessary for developing and maintaining the shared beliefs that lead to collective action.

Perceptions of Group Agreement as Shared Beliefs. Langfield-Smith (1992) developed her theory on "collective encounters" as a result of earlier work on collective cognitive maps (Langfield-Smith and Lewis, 1989). Cognitive maps are a diagrammatic representation of an individual's beliefs about a particular domain. Collective cognitive maps are an attempt to capture and map the shared beliefs of a group, that is, the extent to which the individuals' maps overlap. Collective cognitive maps can be ascertained by using either an aggregating method (combining the individual maps to make a group map) or a congregate, workshop method (eliciting collective beliefs from the group while they are meeting). In her workshop study, Langfield-Smith concluded that collective cognitive maps could not be established as enduring artifacts, since they can change rapidly. She stated that because of the transitory social and perhaps political nature of group belief systems, collective beliefs should be referred to as "collective cognitions." We can see the rapidly changing nature of family beliefs clearly during a succession process, when one generation and the next are often at odds.

While we agree with Langfield-Smith's theoretical conclusions, we believe that collective cognitions can be measured at a given point in time. We posit that because she was attempting to interactively elicit and measure individual agreement with the actual content of a belief structure, Langfield-Smith could not accurately assess the group's sense of reality. Additionally, simply combining individuals' levels of agreement with a defined belief may not reflect the group's collective beliefs. Eliciting agreement on actual beliefs in emotionally charged or conflicted groups is also difficult. Conversely, as is commonly seen in some family businesses, in tightly knit or emotionally enmeshed groups, individuals might not be able to express disagreement with either the group's long-standing beliefs, or with the beliefs of more powerful individuals or coalitions (Davis, 1950; Bettenhausen and Murnighan, 1985; Cobb, 1991).

Figure 1. Group Action as a Function of Perceived vs. Actual Agreement

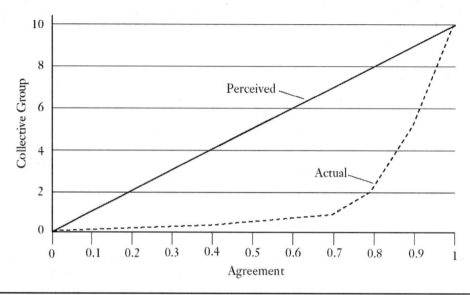

Perceived group agreement on a belief may be a better indicator of the "real" shared belief structure of groups in a relational and political context. Perceived group agreement may also be a better predictor of a group's organizational actions, upholding the axiom that "perceptions are reality."

The theory behind this paper is that as individual family members' perceptions of group agreement converge, it indicates that the group perceives itself as agreeing. By measuring the convergence or divergence in individual perceptions of group agreement, we can capture the collective cognitions or shared beliefs of the family at a given point in time. Collective actions of a group thus flow from its perceptions of unanimity, which is to say, from its shared belief structures.

Cooperative collective action requires that members of a family believe they agree. From experience, we understand that when group members think they agree, they are more apt to trust one another's intentions. As trust increases, so does the expectation that family members' future actions will be mutually supportive. If a family member does not perceive a high level of agreement, then he or she is more likely to expect that the actions of others will interfere with their own. Consequently, that person will be less likely to act cooperatively. Furthermore, if perceived agreement is lacking, individuals may feel that the group has different or opposing goals and beliefs. These feelings may leave family members wondering whether there is a unified course of action, or, in organizational terms, whether they have a shared-belief structure. We therefore suggest that we can and should assess the collective mind of groups or families by examining group members' perceived level of group or family agreement about a belief, rather than focusing on individual agreement with the actual content of the belief.

Previous work suggests that actual agreement about clearly articulated beliefs is crucial to organizational action in a family business (Ward and Aronoff, 1994). We have noted that the actual beliefs are not as important as the perceived level of agreement on the beliefs. Though we do not test this supposition directly, we assert that actual agreement is only relevant when there is a relatively high level of perceived agreement. We have seen anecdotal evidence of this in our consulting work. We often see family members who present themselves as disagreeing – and they truly do believe they disagree – but to us as outside observers, there appears to be a great deal of actual agreement; particularly on the core values and beliefs of the group.

Because the perceptions of group members are continually shaped by the social process (Janis, 1971; Bettenhausen and Murnighan, 1985), and because individual behavior follows perceptions (McGrath and MacMillan, 1992), even in groups in which core

Figure 2. An Iterative Model for Collective Action

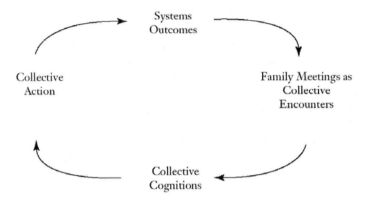

beliefs remain a stable guiding force, collective actions are born of collective individual perceptions of group unity. That is to say, perceptions of agreement mediate the collective actions that might be expected to flow from a consensus around the core beliefs.

The anticipated relation between actual group agreement and perceived group agreement and their affect on group action is shown in Figure 1.

Only at high levels of perceived group agreement do we expect to see a tendency towards collective action. We also note that at high levels of actual group agreement, perceived group agreement is implicit. We can expect that collective action will increase in proportion to increases in perceived group agreement. In family businesses, organizational action and outcomes thus become a direct function of the alignment of perceptions among family members. This alignment of perceptions can result from family meetings. Building on this theoretical relation between the alignment of group members' perceptions with collective action, we present a model that suggests how family meetings lead to collective action in family businesses.

An Iterative Model for Collective Action

Figure 2 places Langfield-Smith's (1992) theory in an iterative model. The figure shows how the collective encounters generate collective cognitions that lead to collective action and systems outcomes. An essential component of this model is the iterative cycling back to the collective encounter or family meeting. System outcomes provide an opportunity for family members to evaluate the results of their beliefs and the opportunity to observe the extent to which they all pulled in the same direction. This is our first step in developing a theory that describes the function and purpose of family meetings within the family-business system. Family meetings are recurring occasions for processing transitory col-

Figure 3. A Model of Perceptions of Family Agreement and Collective Action

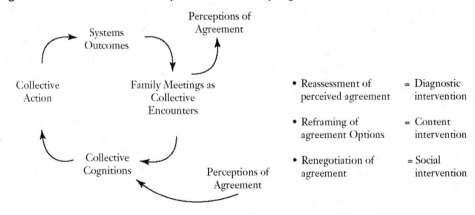

lective beliefs of family members. They are not simply single occasions for developing consensus around a core set of family or business beliefs.

Figure 3 continues the development of the model, adding the measurement of perceptions of family agreement as the means for assessing the degree of collective cognitions. The theory behind this instrument-based (see Appendix 1) cognitive mapping is that as family members' perceptions of group agreement converge, it is an indication that they perceive themselves as a unit. Thus, they establish their de facto degree of shared beliefs or their collective cognitions.

Measuring family members' perceptions of group agreement at the start of a collective encounter presents the family with a benchmark of their shared beliefs. This diagnostic benchmark can then lead to renegotiation and a new perception of common beliefs. The post-encounter measurement of family members' perceptions of agreement reflects the new collective thinking.

The extent to which family members perceive they share beliefs can predict the extent to which they will engage in independent and collective action. The more they perceive group agreement, the more likely they are to act and to act in concert. Action begets outcomes, and the cycle repeats.

In many families and business decision-making groups, the reassessment of shared beliefs and the negotiation of new ones never occurs, even during family meetings. Normally, the group proceeds straight from system outcomes to new collective action. Often, this action is dictated by an overriding sense of the family business's cultural beliefs, or by a single powerful force, such as a patriarch who may believe that everyone in the family agrees with his or her pronouncements. In either case, the intended collective action may not reflect the group's true perceptions, which causes a breakdown in action or creates underlying systems conflict.

We propose that the development of collective cognitions and shared beliefs can occur by using family meetings as collective encounters. Figure 3 presents three types of activities that can facilitate the development of common beliefs.

The Diagnostic Intervention is designed to assess the commonly held beliefs or differences among group members. The diagnostic process is a reassessment stage, allowing family members and the group as a whole to determine their degree of perceived agreements. By having family members understand their commonalities and differences, they can readjust their individual views to be more consistent with the general group view (Hackman, 1976). The diagnostic feedback may actually facilitate the social process activity in which the individual's group identification shapes his or her perceptions of reality (Smith, 1982; Alderfer, 1977). The diagnostic instrument also allows family members to express their views on agreement, making potential "choice shifts" (Butler, 1992) without risking the social conformity constraints normally found in groups (Davis, 1950; Bettenhausen and Murnighan, 1985). The diagnostic intervention adds the powerful component of individual and group awareness to the family meeting, thereby transforming it into a social process capable of realigning expectations and perceived family agreement.

The Content Intervention (e.g. , family business education) allows group members to consider new belief options. This in turn creates an opportunity for reframing and gaining perspective on their agreement and disagreement. This intervention most often takes the form of an educational session in which an expert provides views on family-business life that allow group members to place themselves in a larger context of family businesses. The content intervention fulfills one of the traditional functions of family meetings (Ward, 1987; Gersick, et al. , 1997). However, by creating the expectation that its purpose is to generate reframing options, it increases its social process significance.

The Social Intervention is the actual renegotiation of beliefs through dialogue. Drawing from organizational learning theory, we see dialogue as a vehicle by which individuals access a larger, collective pool of knowledge, "...going beyond any one individual's understanding" and developing "...a new kind of mind which is based on common meaning "(Senge, 1990). In this dialogue, group members restate their positions and develop compromises or new solutions together. In the process, the group develops a greater sense of perceived agreement about the beliefs under consideration. The social interaction is not framed as a debate in which people try to win. Individuals are asked to suspend their assumptions while communicating them freely (Senge, 1990). The continuous re-establishment of collective cognitions creates a sustained condition for generative or "double-loop" learning (Argyris, 1982) to take place.

Combining the three interventions, the education from the content intervention, the feedback gained from the diagnostic instrument, and the interactive exchange through the social intervention, creates a synergistic interaction between content and process (Schein, 1984; Ketchen, Thomas, and McDaniel, 1996). Establishing a continuing, structured process for reassessing, reframing, and renegotiating a family's perceptions of agreement creates a mechanism for maintaining their shared belief structure. Family meetings acknowledge that within the social context of family-business relationships, an individual's or coalition's shared belief structures are transitory, and that perceptions of family agreement may constantly change. As these family meetings become coupled with successful outcomes, the family-business system incrementally learns how to create the cohesiveness necessary for having efficient businesses, healthy families, and fulfilled individuals.

Table 1. Construct Operationalization

Construct and Main Sources	Items
Company Performance Goals Lumpkin & Dess (1996) Hoy, Verser, & Champy (1994) Daily & Dalton (1993) Moravec (1996) Lansberg (1983) Poza (1988)	Overall performance goals: sales, asset growth, profitability, ROI, debt to equity, levels of innovation, R& D spending, business reinvestment, concentration/dilution of ownership; strategic direction of business; leader selection process; leadership development programs; importance of loyalty to employees; non-family professional management roles; board of directors role; importance of non-family/non-employees on board of directors; effectiveness of company hierarchy
Family Goals Dyer (1986) Gersick, et al. (1997) Harvey & Evans (1994) Kaye (1991) Ward (1987) Lansberg & Astrachan (1994) Whiteside, Aronoff, & Ward (1993); Holland & Boulton (1984) Aronoff & Ward (1992) Tagiuri & Davis (1992)	Communication, family harmony, family togetherness goals; opportunities for future generations; importance of keeping the business in the family; importance of keeping family control of the business; family values; family mission statement; ability to challenge other views; role of in-laws; role of extended family; when to sacrifice for the business; when to sacrifice for the family
Community Involvement Danco & Ward (1990) Brody & Strauch (1990) Astrachan, (1988)	Community involvement goals: of business, of family members, community service of business; philanthropic; desired reputation of business in the community; involvement in trade and professional associations
Benefits to the Stakeholder Ward (1987) Monsen (1969) Murdock & Murdock (1991) Handler (1992) Schwartz & Barnes (1991) DeVisscher, Aronoff, & Ward (1995) Aronoff & Ward (1993)	Level of dividends; shareholder agreements; liquidity policy; entering and employment policy; promotion and advancement policy; board of directors membership policy; outside opportunities resulting from business associations; personal pride derived from association with business; involvement in shareholder decisions; knowledge necessary for stakeholders; compensation levels and policies; ownership in the next generation

Methods

As a first step toward investigating the embryonic theory on family meetings, we developed a questionnaire to measure perceptions of family agreement on several goals: community involvement, family, company performance, and stakeholder. The items in the questionnaire are based on prior theory and research and the authors' experiences with family businesses (Table 1). Questionnaire items are reproduced in Appendix 1.

To validate the instrument, we collected data from family members during three family meetings, and from 219 participants during two family-business seminars. The usable instruments totaled 132. The data were collected at the beginning of each event. Eighty-seven of the participants also completed questionnaires at the end of each event. The meetings and seminars were educational in nature and did not include family dialogue based on the assessment data.

We sought to validate each of the constructs tested by drawing on previous field work and review of the literature. Additionally, we performed a factor analysis on all items, showing Eigen values of over 1. 0 for each of the constructs. Instrument reliability was further supported by calculating Chronbach coefficient alphas for each construct. All alpha coefficients were above the 0. 7 level advocated by Nunnally (1978). The means and reliabilities of each scale are reported in Table 2. The scales have high reliability and correlation, giving the impression that perceived group agreement may be primarily an overall state and secondarily related to the specific goal being explored by the items.

In addition to the reliability analysis, we conducted a brief exploration into how the scales correlated with some typical explanatory variables, such as age and company size (Table 3).

Table 3 shows that several possible explanatory variables correlate with the scales. Perceived agreement about company performance goals decreases with firm revenue size and business age. Those family members of larger, older companies perceive less overall agreement on company performance goals. This suggests that as the company grows, agreement about what the company should be doing is harder to achieve. This may be due to the increasing complexity of the company. It also indicates that as the company ages and families grow in complexity, family members perceive less agreement. In addition, perceived agreement about stakeholder benefit goals also decreases with the age the company and its size as expressed by the number of employees. Again, as the company grows

Table 2. Agreement Scales

Scale	Mean	S.D.	Chronbach Alpha	Correlations		
Community involvement goals	21.2	4.6	0.82			
Company performance goals	77.7	11.3	0.91	0.53		
Stakeholder benefit goals	56.5	10.5	0.86	0.48	0.72	
Family goals	56.1	9.2	0.76	0.55	0.47	0.55

Table 3. Scale Correlates*

Selected Correlates	Company Performance Goals	Community Involvement Goals	Family Goals	Stakeholder Benefit Goals
Revenues	-0.37			
Employees				-0.27
Family managers			0.32	
Business age	-0.15			-0.25

*only significant correlations reported (p < .01)

in complexity and perhaps in ability to provide benefits, there is a perceived greater disagreement among family members.

The most notable finding is that as the number of family members in the business grows, perceived agreement about family goals also increases. Because more family members are working in the business, they may have more extensive common language, communication, shared experiences, and a sense of the exigencies of the business that increase their perceived group agreement. This can be interpreted as suggesting that greater family interaction increases perceived family agreement. If the rest of the model on which this research is based has validity, then this finding would suggest that greater family interaction improves the likelihood of collective family action and intended organizational outcomes.

In addition to the above analyses, repeated measures analyses of variance were conducted. These analyses indicate a significant difference among individual perceptions of family agreement for all scales between rounds one and two. This suggests that there is a change in perceived levels of family agreement due to an educational intervention. We find additional support for this because there is no significant correlation among scale responses between rounds one and two.

Conclusions

This research provides initial support to the idea that perceived agreement among family members can be measured. It supports the theory concerning the impact of collective encounter (family meetings) on collective cognitions (shared beliefs) in family-business groups. The research demonstrates the reliability of scales concerning goals in community involvement, company performance, family, and stakeholder benefits. It also provides initial support to the notion that family meetings may increase perceived family agreement among family members.

The authors recognize that there are many limitations to this study. It is offered to develop theory, to stimulate discussion and further research, and to provide an instrument others might use in their work with, and research on, family businesses.

There is much research yet to be done. The effectiveness of different family meeting interventions (diagnostic, educational, and interactive) on changes in levels of perceived agreement should be a top priority. It should be a great help to those working with family businesses to have an understanding of which intervention works most effectively, and under what conditions. In addition, the model needs further exploration and testing. In this new model, long-term performance rests on the idea that perceived agreement among family members directly impacts the level of collective action and system outcomes. If this is true, it would indicate that changing agreement levels could have a great impact on business activity and perhaps family business success.

Appendix 1

AGREEMENT QUESTIONNAIRE

Company performance

Rate your perceived level of agreement among family stakeholders about the following issues:

(Scale is one to five, one being no agreement and five being total agreement, or not known because not discussed, or not known because I don't understand the issue, or not applicable)

1) Overall company performance goals
2) Sales goals
3) Asset growth goals
4) Profitability goals
5) Return on net assets goals
6) Return on investment goals
7) Debt to equity goals

8) Strategic direction of the business
9) Goals regarding level of innovation (products, processes, structures, lines of business)
10) Research and development spending goals
11) Business reinvestment goals
12) Process for selecting leaders
13) Leadership development programs
14) Goals for concentration/dilution of ownership
15) Importance of loyalty to employees
16) Role of professional non-family management
17) Role board of directors
18) Importance of non-family/non-employees on board of directors
19) Effectiveness of company hierarchy

Benefits to you as a stakeholder

Rate your perceived level of agreement among family stakeholders about the following issues:

(Scale is one to five, one being no agreement and five being total agreement, or not known because not discussed, or not known because I don't understand the issue, or not applicable)

1) Level of dividends
2) Shareholder agreements (policies about acquiring and disposing of stock)
3) Liquidity policy (policy around stock redemptions)
4) Policics about cntcring and employment in business
5) Policies about promotion and advancement in business
6) Policies about becoming a member of the board of directors
7) Level of opportunities outside of the business that arise because of your association with the business
8) Level of personal pride derived from association with the business
9) Who should be involved in shareholder decisions
10) T what extent should shareholders be involved in shareholder decisions
11) Level of knowledge and education about the business necessary for family stakeholders
12) Compensation levels and compensation policies for family members in the business
13) Plans for disposition of ownership in the next generation

Family goals

Rate your perceived level of agreement among family stakeholders about the following issues:

(Scale is one to five, one being no agreement and five being total agreement, or not known because not discussed, or not known because I don't understand the issue, or not applicable)

1) Communication goals
2) Family harmony goals
3) Family togetherness goals
4) What are the opportunities for future generations in the business
5) Importance of keeping the business in the family
6) Importance of keeping family control of the business
7) Family values
8) Family mission statement
9) How much one can challenge other's views
10) Rolc of in-laws in the business
11) Role of extended family in the business
12) When should family members make sacrifices for the business
13) When should the business be sacrificed for the benefit of family

Community involvement

Rate your perceived level of agreement among family stakeholders about the following issues:

(Scale is one to five, one being no agreement and five being total agreement, or not known because not discussed, or not known because I don't understand the issue, or not applicable)

1) Community involvement goals for the business
2) Community involvement goals for family members
3) Philanthropic goals
4) Desired reputation of the business in the community
5) Goals for community service for the business
6) Importance of involvement in relevant trade and professional associations

Company characteristics

1) Number of full-time employees
2) Approximate annual revenues
3) Estimated market value of business
4) Age of business
5) Number of generations involved in business since business founded
6) Number of family shareholders
7) Percentage of stock held by family
8) Size, in percent, of largest ownership position held by an individual family member
9) Number of family members in management of business
10) Number of family members, who are not managers, employed in business
11) Number of family on board of directors
12) Number of family on board of directors who are also employed in the business
13) Primary industry

Respondent characteristics

1) Relationship to founder
2) Title
3) Gender
4) Age

References

Alderfer, C. P. (1977). Group and intergroup relations. In Hackman, J. R, & Suttle, J. L. (Eds.), *Improving life at work* (pp. 227-296). Santa Monica, CA: Goodyear.

Argyris, C. (1982). The executive mind and double-loop learning. *Organizational Dynamics*, Autumn, 5-22.

Aronoff, C. E., & Ward, J. L. (1992, April). The critical value of stewardship. *Nation's Business*, 49.

Aronoff, C. E., & Ward, J. L. (1993). Family business compensation. *Family Business Leadership Series*, Marietta, GA: Business Owner Resources.

Astrachan, J. H. (1988). Family firm and community culture. *Family Business Review*, 1 (2), 165-189.

Bettenhausen, K., & Murnighan, J. K. (1985). The emergence of norms in competitive decision-making groups. *Administrative Science Quarterly*, 30, 350-372.

Brody, D., & Strauch, C. (1990). Who are the family foundations? Findings from the foundation. *Family Business Review*, 3 (4), 337-346.

Butler, J. K., Jr. (1992). Effects of initial tendency and real risk on choice shift. *Organizational Behavior and Human Decision Processes*, 53, 14-34.

Cobb, A. T. (1991). Toward the study of organizational coalitions: Participant concerns and activities in a simulated organizational setting. *Human Relations*, 44, 10.

Daily, C. M., & Dalton, D. R. (1993). Board of directors leadership and structure: Control and performance implications. *Entrepreneurship, Theory & Practice*, 17 (3), 65-81.

Danco, L. A., & Ward, J. L. (1990). Beyond success: The continuing contribution of the family. *Family Business Review*, 3 (4), 347-355.

Davis, K. (1950). *Human science*. New York, NY: MacMillan.

De Visscher, F. M., Aronoff, C. E., & Ward, J. L. (1995). Financing transitions: Managing capital and liquidity in the family business. *Family Business Leadership Series*, Marietta, GA: Business Owner Resources.

Donnellon, A., Gray, B., & Bougon, M. G. (1986). Communication, meaning, and organized action. *Administrative Science Quarterly*, 31, 43-55.

Dyer, W. G., Jr. (1986). *Cultural change in family firms: Anticipating and managing business and family transitions*. San Francisco, CA: Jossey-Bass.

Gagliardi, P. (1986). The creation and change of organizational cultures: A conceptual framework. *Organization Studies*, 7, 117-134.

Gersick, K. E., Davis, J. A., McCollom-Hampton, M., & Lansberg, I. (1997). *Generation to generation: Life cycles of the family business*. Boston, MA: Harvard Business School Press.

Hackman, J. R. (1976). Group influences on individuals. In Dunnette, M. D. (Ed.), *Handbook of industrial and organizational psychology*. Chicago, IL: Rand McNally.

Handler, W. C. (1992). Succession experience of the next generation. *Family Business Review*, 5 (3), 283-307.

Harris, D., Martinez, J. I., & Ward, J. L. (1994). Is strategy different for the family owned business? *Family Business Review*, 7 (2), 159-174.

Harvey, M., & Evans, R. E. (1994). Family business and multiple levels of conflict. *Family Business Review*, 7 (4), 331-348.

Holland, P. G., & Boulton, W. R. (1984). Balancing the 'family' and the 'business' in family business. *Business Horizons*, Mar/Apr.

Hoy, F., Verser, T. G., & Champy. (1994). Emerging business, emerging field: Entrepreneurship and the family firm. *Entrepreneurship, Theory & Practice*, 19 (1), 9-23.

Janis, I. L. (1971). Groupthink. In Hackman, J. R., Lawler, E. E., and Porter, L. W. (Eds.), *Perspectives on behavior in organizations*. New York, NY: McGraw Hill.

Kaye, K. (1991). Penetrating the cycle of sustained conflict. *Family Business Review*, 4 (1), 21-44.

Ketchen, D., Jr., Thomas, J. B., & McDaniel, R., Jr. (1996). Process, content and context: Synergistic effects on organizational performance. *Journal of Management*, 22 (2), 231-257.

Langfield-Smith, K. M. (1992). Mapping the need for a shared cognitive map. *Journal of Management Studies*, 29 (3), 349-368.

Langfield-Smith, K. M., & Lewis, G. P. (1989). Mapping cognitive structures: A pilot study to develop a research method. Working Paper No. 14. Melbourne, Australia: University of Melbourne, Graduate School of Management.

Lansberg, I. (1983). Managing human resources in family firms: Problem of institutional overlap. *Organizational Dynamics*, 12, 39-46.

Lansberg, I., & Astrachan, J. H. (1994). Influence of family relationships on succession planning and training: The importance of mediating factors. *Family Business Review*, 7 (1), 39-59.

Lumpkin, G. T., & Dess, G. G. (1996). Clarifying the entrepreneurial orientation construct and linking it to performance. *Academy of Management Review*, 21 (1), 135-172.

McGrath, R. G., & MacMillan, I. (1992). More like each other than anyone else?A cross-cultural study of entrepreneurial perceptions. *Journal of Business Venturing*, 7, 419-429.

Monsen, J. R. (1969). Ownership and management: The effect of separation on performance. *Business Horizons*, 12 (4), 46-52.

Moravec, M. (1996). Bringing performance management out of the stone age. *Management Review*, 85 (2), 38-42.

Murdock, M., & Murdock, C. M. (1991). A Legal perspective on shareholder relationships in family businesses: The scope of fiduciary duties. *Family Business Review*, 4 (3), 287-301.

Nunnally, J. (1973). *Psychometric theory*. New York: McGraw-Hill.

Pfeffer, J. (1981). Management as symbolic action: The creation and maintenance of organizational paradigms. *Research in Organizational Behavior*, 3, 1-52.

Poza, E. J. (1988). Managerial practices that support interpreneurship and continued growth. *Family Business Review*, 1 (4), 339-358.

Schein, E. H. (1984). Coming to a new awareness of organizational culture. *Sloan Management Review*, 25, 3-16.

Schwartz, M. A., & Barnes, L. B. (1991). Outside boards and family businesses: Another look. *Family Business Review*, 4 (3), 269-285.

Senge, P. (1990). *The fifth discipline: The art and practice of the learning organization.* New York: Doubleday.

Smircich, L. (1983a). Concepts of culture and organizational analysis. *Administrative Science Quarterly*, 28, 339-368.

Smircich, L. (1983b). Organizations as shared meanings. In Pondy, L. R., Frost, P. J., Morgan, G., & Dandridge, T. C. (Eds.), *Organizational symbolism*. Greenwich, CT: JAI Press.

Smith, K. K. (1982). *Groups in conflict: Prisons in disguise.* Dubuque, IA: Kendall/Hunt Publishing Co.

Tagiuri, R., & Davis, J. A. (1992). On the goals of successful family companies. *Family Business Review*, (4) 1, 43-62.

Trice, H. M., & Beyer, J. M. (1984). Studying organizational cultures through rites and ceremonials. *Academy of Management Review*, 9, 653-669.

Van Maanen, J. (1979). On the understanding of interpersonal relations. In Bennis, W., Van Maanen, J., Schein, E., & Steele, F. I. (Eds.), *Essays in interpersonal communication* (pp. 13-42). Homewood, IL: Dorsey.

Ward, J. L. (1987). *Keeping the family business healthy: How to plan for continuing growth, profitability, and family leadership.* San Francisco, CA: Jossey-Bass.

Ward, J. L., & Aronoff, C. E. (1994, September). How successful business families get that way. *Nation's Business*, 42-43.

Weick, K. E. (1979). *The social psychology of organizing*, 2d ed. Reading, MA: AddisonWesley.

Whiteside, M. F., Aronoff, C. E., & Ward, J. L. (1993). How families work together. *Family Business Leadership Series*, Marietta, GA: Business Owner Resources.

CHAPTER 12
WOMEN IN THE FAMILY FIRM

Women are becoming more involved in the business side of family business. Increasingly they move into executive roles in family firms. Special issues confront women assuming leadership roles, not the least of which are the positive and negative aspects of such responsibility on the women involved. While additional potential successors can further complicate succession planning, women may bring special skills to the firm. Socialized nurturing skills can be translated into management skills. Daughters are better than sons at avoiding intense rivalries and power struggles with father. A woman's involvement is not always a matter of choice, however. Many a woman has stepped into a dead husband's role. A woman married to the family firm's founder should be prepared for her contingent role.

A study of 702 women in family-owned firms in Canada has identified paths to participation and leadership taken by women in family-owned firms. Some of the key factors contributing to participation and leadership are presented in a descriptive framework. Implications of this study for practice and research are presented.

Women's Pathways to Participation and Leadership in the Family-Owned Firm

By Colette Dumas

Introduction

Women are a prominent entrepreneurial force, owning 36% of all U. S. businesses, according to the National Foundation for Women Business Owners. That comes to approximately 8 million businesses producing a total of $2.28 trillion in annual revenues (Nelton, 1996). Moreover, these businesses employ 18.5 million people or 27% of all U. S. employees (National Foundation for Women Business Owners, 1996).

Despite their impressive contributions, very little is known about women as founders and successors in the family-owned business and in the entrepreneurial domain (Brush, 1992). This is particularly unfortunate because hypothetically women could own about a third of all family businesses since, by some estimates, 90% to 95% of all businesses in the United States are family controlled (Shanker & Astrachan, 1996). In addition, within the next five years, the leadership of 42% of the family businesses in the United States is expected to change (28%) or begin to shift (14%), as CEOs retire or semi-retire (Nelton, 1997). Women may play significant roles in these firms in the next century, as either founders or leaders of family businesses.

This study intends to determine the effect women have on family businesses and increase the knowledge and understanding of women' participation and leadership in family-owned firms by examining the factors that affect women' participation in the family firm, the paths they are taking to leadership, and their characteristics and those of their firms. What follows is an overview of the current thinking and research about women in family-owned firms.

Literature Review

Research conducted over the past 15 years has increased our knowledge of family-owned firms. Unfortunately relatively little empirical research has been conducted on women and their participation in family-owned businesses. I have organized the research along two main themes: barriers to participation and to leadership in the family business, and opportunities for participation and leadership.

Barriers to Participation and Leadership. Women in family-owned firms have often been invisible successors – previous research indicates that they are rarely considered serious contenders for succession (Dumas, 1989b). This invisibility is part of traditional family business configurations, which have focused on the male founder and his heirs. The "strength of traditional family roles, both within society and within individual families, kept women's business contributions from being acknowledged" (Lyman, Salganicoff, & Hollander, 1985). In a study of married couples working together, Marshack (1994) found that although wives are still invisible in the leadership of the family business, they are fundamental to the day-to-day running of the business and the family.

Sociological theories argue that social structures (workplace, family, and organized social life) affect women's access to entrepreneurial opportunities (Aldrich, 1989). Occupational segregation, under-representation in upper-level management, and expectations about traditional family roles can restrict women to certain industrial sectors and also affect their motivation and goals for their business ventures (Aldrich, 1989). Women who work in family businesses face issues similar to those faced by all businesswomen (Starr & Yudkin, 1996). They also have problems that are unique to their situation, such as conflict over roles and loyalties; relationships with parents, siblings, and nonfamily members; and struggles for power and authority (Dumas, 1992; Salganicoff, 1990). In addition, the contributions of some women in family firms may not be recognized because of their roles as informal advisors or mediators for family members who formally run the business (Gillis-Donovan & Moynihan-Bradt, 1990; Hollander & Bukowitz, 1990).

Hollander and Bukowitz (1990) studied the impact family culture has on opportunities for women within the firm and the resulting effect on the family business. The authors found that primogeniture was an internalized part of the decision-making process, which resulted in the elder son assuming the leadership role. Salganicoff (1990) also noted that gender bias in family culture can influence the decision-making process, including the choice of successor. In a study of 91 women, Salganicoff discovered that only 27% expected to enter the family business. The reasons those 27% gave for wanting to join the business included helping the family, filling a position that no one wanted, and being dissatisfied at another job. I found (Dumas, 1989) that the women studied did not plan a career in the family business but came into the business to help the family in a time of crisis or because other options were less desirable.

Frishkoff and Brown (1993, p. 66) reported that women in the family firm belonged to the "outward division of labor in the family business." That division refers to the split within the family of the domestic responsibilities, which belong to the wife, and the business responsibilities, which belong to the husband. As more women become involved in family business, they challenge the norm of transferring leadership from the father to the first-born son (Barnes, 1988; Dumas, 1989a, 1989b, 1990). According to Barnes and Kaftan (1990), daughters in the family firm must confront severe challenges in acceding to power because they frequently face skepticism from both parents and siblings, who see them as incompetent or ignorant about the business. Fathers put up the most resistance, placing more pressure on daughters who take over the business than on sons (Barnes, 1988). I found (Dumas, 1989a) that daughters are usually overlooked as potential successors unless a family crisis creates the opportunity for them to take the leadership role.

Several researchers found role conflict problematic for women in the family business because of their struggle with the expected family role versus the expected business role (Hollander & Bukowitz, 1990; Dumas, 1990). Freudenberger, Freedheim, and Kurtz (1989) indicated that women in family businesses are uncertain about how to behave. They fear becoming as successful as the men in the business because they may be seen as too masculine and aggressive. Unless they can individuate from their families, they remain unable to realize their business roles. Iannarelli (1992) identified some key differences between the way daughters and sons are socialized for succession. Daughters spend less time in the business, develop fewer skills, and are less frequently encouraged professionally than their male siblings. In a study of nine families, Keating and Little (1997) identified gender as the most important factor that determined the successor. These authors discovered that there was an implicit rule that daughters could not be family business successors. Instead, they were encouraged to train for other careers, whereas sons were encouraged to join the family business for an apprenticeship. In a study of 30 next-generation family members, Dumas, Dupuis, Richer, and St. Cyr (1995) discovered that more women than men sought training to work outside the family farm. These women did not believe they would take over the farm, even though more women than men pursued careers in agriculture outside the family business.

In yet another more recent study, Harveston, Davis, and Lyden (1997) found that gender plays a role in succession planning. Male and female business owner/managers operate under different predictive processes when making succession plans and are influenced by different individual, organizational, and resource issues. Therefore, these authors proposed that gender-specific models of organizational succession should be considered, and that considering gender could better identify and evaluate variations that drive succession processes. In her study of 23 family business members, Cole (1997) identified several themes related to gender issues and leadership: invisibility of women in family business-es where members and others ignore the woman's professional capabilities; different deci-sion-making processes in which women take more time to make business decisions than men; and different concerns and issues in which women worry about adequate child care and balancing work and family more than men.

Opportunities for Participation and Leadership. Cole (1997) also found that the women she interviewed identified opportunities. They believed their positions in the company reflected high levels of respect and responsibility. In addition, several women were poised to take over the family business, even with an older brother in the business. Another study (Dumas, 1992) found that daughters were able to successfully work with their fathers to take over the family firm because they had been socialized to collaborate throughout their lives. In addition, Jaffe (1990) found that the women in his study saw that the family business represented a great career opportunity.

Family firms offer a variety of opportunities for women including flexible work sched-ules and access to traditionally male-dominated industries that would otherwise be closed to them, such as construction and manufacturing. Family firms provide females with job security (Salganicoff, 1990). Godfrey (1992) suggested that family relationships provide a training ground for women entrepreneurs for later relationships with customers, investors, and employees. Finally, according to Hisrich and Fulop (1997), women are twice as likely as men to envision their daughters taking over the business. Therefore, hav-ing female CEOs at the head of family firms may have a positive impact on the next gen-eration of women in family firms.

Sample, Methodology, and Research Questions

In Canada, no nationwide statistics on family business are available, perhaps because no universally accepted definition of a family business exists. As Chrisman, Chua, and Sharma (1998) noted, empirical research must therefore rely on convenience samples, such as the membership lists of professional associations. In keeping with their approach, the sample examined for this study was taken from a database of 864 family owned firms in Canada, compiled by convenience sampling (Goldberg & Woolridge, 1993).

From that database, I identified 372 firms (43%) in which at least one female family member was actively working. In total, 702 women were working in these firms. For the purposes of this study, selection criteria included the following: actively working in the firm, having a significant management role in the firm, and having the potential to be a successor. I developed a survey that captured the organizational characteristics of the women and the family firms.

Several assistants and I conducted surveys by telephone. The questions kept in mind when surveying the 702 women in family-owned firms included the following: What paths do women take that further their participation and leadership in the family business? What factors influence their participation? What characteristics identify these women and their firms?

Comparative statistical analyses are currently being conducted; preliminary results of the survey are presented here.

Results and Discussion

Table 1 shows a breakdown of the characteristics of the organizations and the respon-dents. The demographics of this study are very similar to those of the Arthur Andersen survey and the MassMutual survey, both conducted in 1995. These similarities speak well for the validity of this sample. The 702 women were working in family firms that were founded between 1824 and 1990, with the average age being 39 years.

The majority of these businesses (70%) had fewer than 50 employees. Gross revenues reported by respondents exceeded $50 million, but typically ranged from $1 million to $5 million. The majority of the firms (53.6%) were involved in wholesale trade; retail trade, including the hotel and restaurant business; or service industries. Manufacturing and con-struction were the next most prevalent types of business (40.7%). Only a few of the firms

Table 1. Organizational and Individual Characteristics

Business Profiles (n = 372)

Business Type		Number of Employees	
Wholesale or retail trade	53.6%	< 50 = 70%	
Manufacturing and construction	40.7%	50 + = 30%	
Agriculture, fishing, forestry, mining	4.7%		
No response	1.0%		

Gross Revenue	
$50 million and up	4.8%
$20 million to $49.9 million	6.8%
$10 million to $19.9 million	13.1%
$5 million to $9.9 million	10.4%
$1 million to $4.9 million	31.2%
$999, 999 and less	21.4%
No response	12.3%

Respondent Profiles (n = 702)

Generation		Current Position in Firm	
1st	21.5%	No job title	20.5%
2nd	57.2%	Director of marketing or design	14.5%
3rd	17.4%	Vice president or manager	9.1%
4th	0.0%	Secretary, receptionist, clerk	7.9%
5th	0.7%	President or general manager	6.7%
6th	3.2%	Customer service, public relations	6.5%
		Supervisor, assistant, team leader	5.0%
		Part-time	4.8%

Family Characteristics	
Only daughters (no sons)	12.10%
More daughters than sons	26.36%
More sons than daughters	30.64%
Only child	8.30%
Same number daughters and sons	22.60%

studied (4.7%) were involved in agriculture, fishing, forestry, and mining.

The majority of the 702 respondents worked for companies in which two generations worked together. Approximately 57% worked for companies in which one succession had been completed. The companies in which nearly 17% of the women worked had undergone a second succession, whereas 1% worked in companies that had third or fourth generations, respectively, succeed into control. The remainder either had not yet gone through a succession process or were in their fifth generation or beyond.

Women Are Well Represented. This study confirmed that women are a strong presence in family-owned firms, particularly those founded during and after the 1950s. Of the women surveyed, 72% worked in family firms founded as far back as 1950. On average, 1.89 women per business were actively engaged in the business.

Women Do Not Have Substantial Ownership. Status was defined by the position or the activities undertaken in the business, and by the ownership rights of these women. Looking first at ownership, although women were well represented in the family firm, they did not have substantial ownership. For example, wives of CEOs were twice as likely to be active without ownership. Only 18.1% of these wives worked full-time in the business and had ownership. In contrast, 62.2% worked full-time in the business without ownership. Of those women who were daughters of CEOs, 43.6% worked full-time in the business, with or without ownership.

However, women CEOs and founders were an emerging phenomenon. In this sample 21, or 3%, were CEOs who founded or acquired their businesses. The majority of these women (85.7%) still worked full-time in the businesses they still owned. The remaining 14.3% had already passed the business on to the next generation but still played a managerial or an advisory role.

Women Who Are the Daughters of the CEOs Have an Advantage. I grouped positions and job titles around common themes because the definition of job titles can vary from business to business. Many of the women surveyed (20.5%) did not have specific job titles. The next largest job grouping dealt with marketing; 14.5% were either marketing directors or design directors. When I cross-tabulated status and position, I found that being the CEO' daughter played a central role in the position held. Approximately 27% of CEOs' daughters were active in the business, held ownership positions, and were in positions of responsibility such as marketing, design, accounting, and management. In addition, 14.4% of the daughters were active, had ownership, and were president, CEO, or director. Daughters who were vice presidents comprised 13% of the sample, whereas only 2.9% were employees who held such positions as secretaries. Of the 702 women surveyed, daughters of CEOs who were actively involved in the business full-time, had ownership, and higher level positions, outnumbered those who were actively involved, in higher level positions, but had no ownership. Daughters who were active with ownership also out-numbered wives with ownership who were presidents or general managers (17.8% and 12.85% , respectively).

Of the women in our sample, 57 (44.5%) were wives who held no ownership positions in the company and were secretaries, pay clerks, and billing clerks. These were almost four times more prevalent than any other job. Therefore, it appears that blood ties with the CEO, made more solid by ownership rights, had a greater impact than marriage on determining the position a woman held in the family business. For example, 57.5% of daughters were actively involved in the company, had ownership, and had jobs in upper management, whereas 42.5% of wives with ownership had such jobs.

There may be several reasons for these differences. First, cultural and social tradition make the "man-husband-father-provider" the traditional director of the family and of the business. In addition, this same patriarchal tradition and the marriage laws in effect at the time meant wives chose to stay away from official business positions to protect family property. These constraints don't exist for daughters. Daughter successors were the most visible in terms of full-time involvement and ownership in the family firm. These women seemed to take leadership roles even in families that had more sons than daughters.

A Framework for Participation and Leadership

The following is a descriptive framework that emerged in the analysis of the data (see Figure 1).

Initiation: According to our sample, when a parent had founded the business entry into the business actually began at home. In this stage, the owner-manager served as a role model for these women. This stage could last throughout the woman's childhood until she entered the business, depending on when the business was founded. The process was gradual, beginning at home when family members talked about the business over dinner – as one woman stated: "the business was like part of the furniture at home, it was always there" through visits to the business "just for fun – it was a game," to part-time work throughout school. During this time, the child was initiated into the values encouraged by the family as well as the decisions, experiences, behaviors, and relationships that occurred before the woman began working full-time at the company. As one woman put it:

> We learned to work and to shoulder our responsibilities from a very young age.

And another described it this way:

> The business was in my blood. I was always around the business from a very young age. I played there, then I went to work there.

This is the time when the child follows the owner-manager and becomes familiar with how the business works. Involvement in the company intensifies the development of technical, interpersonal and managerial knowledge, judgment, and skills. It is also a crucial time for the owner to foster in the daughter the desire to follow his or her footsteps, main-

Figure 1. Women's Pathways to Participation and Leadership in the Family-Owned Business: A Descriptive Framework

Initiation
- begins at home (+)
- owner is role model (+, -)
- a gradual process (+)
- consists of decisions, experiences, behaviors and relationships (+, -)
- allows girl to familiarize herself with how business works (+)
- develops technical, interpersonal, managerial knowledge, judgment, and skills (+)
- owner fosters girl's desire to follow in his or her footsteps, maintain family ties, work for success of business (+)

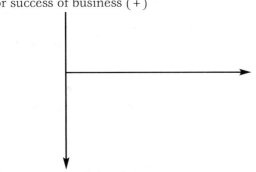

Pathways to Leadership
- evaluated by parents (+, -)
- circumstantial (+, -)
- transitional difficulties (+, -)
- family support, training (+)
- intrinsic and extrinsic motivators (+)
- team support (siblings, cousins, non-family members) (+)
- connected to interests, education (+)
- changes in family and business (+, -)
- uniqueness of opportunity (+)

Pathways to Participation
- starts her own business, or works up to greater responsibility in parent's company (+)
- begins in a managerial position (+)
- takes on special projects (+)
- visions of business: reactive (-), proactive (+, -), or evolving (+, -)

tain family ties, and work for the success of the family business. This is a period of training and learning about the business and has unparalleled benefit to the woman. There are few other such long-term job training opportunities. This training seemed to work best when the experience was either positive or at least constructive in helping the young woman define herself in relation to the business. If the experience and the relationship with the parent were negative, the initiation phase would be less likely to lead to participation in the business.

Pathways to Participation. The women surveyed tended to enter the business full-time in one of the following ways: started her own business; started at the lowest level and worked her way up to higher levels of responsibility; immediately began in a management position; or worked on special projects assigned by the current founder. As they took on increasingly more responsibility, while learning the business in greater detail, these women assessed the family business using three categories of vision: reactive, proactive, and evolving. How these women participated in the business was determined in part by her vision of the business, which was shaped during her initiation phase. If she had a reactive vision of the business, she would see the business in more utilitarian terms. Thus her participation in the firm would mostly involve doing her job, nothing more. The reactive vision was one in which the business was seen as "a means of making a living," and "you go in, do your job, let others do their job, that's all." In these cases, the women had no desire to go beyond the role of employee. These women would often focus on the difficulties of working in the business and on the burden of such responsibility. This vision of the business often led to greater participation in and possibly leadership of the business.

When the woman's vision of the business was proactive, she had a clear image of the business as her business, with an awareness of the changes needed, but not always the skills needed to make those changes. This perspective is usually based on a sense of the business's history, often coupled with a solid education or work experience and a desire to improve the business. In addition, a positive or constructive initiation phase usually fostered development of this vision of the business. Thus the woman would want to actively influence the business's success by taking an active role in the business.

Those with an evolving vision, saw the businesses and her own potential in it gradually. These women may have been aware of possibilities she envisioned for the business and herself, but she would only gradually see the business as hers. Her vision of the ways she could shape the business evolved. Two key elements in this case were a gradually increasing sense of self-esteem and a greater awareness of her skills through experience and education. If these two elements were not present, the woman tended not to believe that she could meet the challenges of leadership. In some cases, women had to help out when a family member, often the father, became ill or when parents got older. These women found the work interesting, and they often decided to stay on. They eventually began to see the possibilities and learn to love the work.

In other instances, the women became interested and began to see the potential when the business began to grow. These women then saw the opportunity to do something in the business beyond the narrower realm of what family members were currently doing. One woman described it this way:

> I have an MBA. I wanted to use it. The business started taking off and I could see that my mother and father needed to set up an employee training program to better market the business. That was something I could do.

If the perceived opportunity developed, these women participated actively in the business and contributed to the business. That would often lead to a leadership role in the business.

Pathways to Leadership. The process of choosing the successor varied depending on the family and the business. Sometimes parents needed to evaluate their daughter by her interest in the business, her skills, her education, her leadership ability, and prior experience. This evaluation process could be colored by biases the parents may have about the daughter's capabilities and potential. Other factors were more circumstantial, such as whether the daughter is the only one of their children who has taken an interest in a leadership position, or whether she is the oldest, or their only child. Such circumstances can lead to either a fortuitous or a limiting outcome.

Many of these women encountered a variety of problems when transitioning into the business, being accepted by customers and suppliers, or adapting to the long hours needed to commit to the business. However, for many, family support played an important role in guiding these women in the form of moral support, solidarity, and love. Family support also served to perpetuate family values, such as honesty, justice, happiness, and peace, which conveyed important messages about how these families lived their lives. These values informed the choices some women made to take over the family business and influenced their future commitment to the business. In addition, working in the family business provided intrinsic sources of satisfaction, such as interesting, challenging, and satisfying work; working for oneself and one's family rather than being employed by someone else; a variety of daily tasks; a comfortable lifestyle; and a flexible environment for raising children.

Women who chose to pursue the family business early on and who had followed that pursuit with a variety of training and education, expressed this career choice in positive, affirming terms. They described the paths they took in such terms as "challenging," "my future," "a family dream," "a chance to prove myself," and "giving back to the family." Still others saw the chance to take over the family business as an opportunity that was "too good to pass up" and "the best thing to come along," and "it's more satisfying to work for yourself than for someone else."

The opportunity to lead the family business, either alone or as a member of a team, was also a determining factor in their paths to leadership. Several themes emerged that were pivotal to making their decisions: connecting to their interests and educational training; grabbing the opportunity, especially when they experienced difficulties elsewhere; and finding unexpected changes in the family and the business. For some of the women, the end of their studies signaled a time to transition into the business and to apply their training, especially when their studies related to the family business. For others, the family business represented a chance to shine, prove their abilities, and excel in a way that they were unable to in outside employment. Finally, changes in the business and the family, such as the death of the founder; the departure of a family member, even a sibling; and the impending failure of the business or its growing success signaled an opportunity or a need to help the family and an opportunity for herself.

Leadership was sometimes determined by birth order and gender. In some cases, the woman was the only one interested in taking over the business. Other times, the founder was looking for a successor who shared his or her philosophy of life. The decision to lead sometimes depends on the presence of a team of either siblings, cousins, a spouse, or significant other to share the responsibilities of leadership. As one woman said, "Alone, it would be impossible. Together, we are stronger." Pathways to leadership also came in the form of training, guidance, and support by parents, family members, and even nonfamily members within and outside the business. One woman explained, "My mother gave me projects and let me run them. She would give me advice from time to time, when I asked." These women were given responsibilities with the express purpose of gaining experience and becoming autonomous. In addition, parents and other family members set the example by the way they approached their work and carried out various tasks. As one daughter learned from her father: "Work hard and you will have what you need." In one family, the founder asked his children what their dreams were and then supported them, financially and with his expertise, to help them create their businesses.

Pathways to leadership evolved as women became aware of the family firm as a means of earning a living and making a contribution. This awareness grew into a unique leadership opportunity for some. As one woman told me:

> Even if I were offered double my salary to work somewhere else, I wouldn't take it. I love working for my family business. It is ours. We work as a family and we have a wonderful quality of life.

Implications for Practice and Research

This study has useful implications for both practice and research. It is the first large-scale study of women in family firms. Therefore, it allowed us to develop our understanding of women's presence and contribution to the family firm. It also enabled us to better understand women's participation and leadership in these firms and what factors encouraged them.

One of the strongest implications for practice is the potential use of the framework as a diagnostic tool for evaluating women's decisions to participate in the family business, and to take a leadership role as well. This has particular importance to family-owned firms currently, given the large-scale leadership change anticipated in these businesses.

Specific implications exist at the three levels of analysis associated with the descriptive framework of this study. At the level of initiation, the study suggests that next-generation family members were influenced from an early age in their decision to participate in the family firm. This positive socialization helped women develop the skills and knowledge they would use as they participated in the family business. Family influence, support, and role modeling, along with long-term training at the firm, were important to women's participation in the company. Participation then became a natural outcome of the initiation experience. Leadership can also result from family support and modeling and, when circumstances allow, from extrinsic and intrinsic motivators.

We now know that women are a prominent force in family-owned firms. However, we need to take a longitudinal look at whether women will continue to have low levels of ownership in the family business. A large-scale comparative study of men and women in the family firm is needed to delve into this issue further.

A descriptive framework, such as the one presented in this paper, is very useful for identifying the factors that encourage women's participation and leadership in the family firm. Using this information when consulting to family businesses can potentially make a difference in family business ownership and its related issues.

Finally, the number of women who have founded family firms and who are CEOs is growing. Therefore, more research should focus on these women, developing longitudinal databases, and following this new generation of family business owners.

References

Aldrich, H. (1989). Networking among women entrepreneurs. In O. Hagan, C. Rivchun, & D. Sexton (Eds.), *Women-owned businesses* (pp. 103 –132), New York: Praeger.

Arthur Andersen & Co., S. C. (1995). *American family business survey*. Chicago: Author.

Barnes, L. B. (1988). Incongruent hierarchies: Daughters and younger sons as company CEOs. *Family Business Review, 1* (1), 9 –21.

Barnes, L. B., & Kaftan, C. (1990). *Organizational transitions for individuals, families, and work groups*. Englewood Cliffs, NJ: Prentice Hall.

Brush, C. (1992). Research on women business owners: Past trends, a new perspective and future directions. *Entrepreneurship Theory and Practice, 16* (4), 5 – 30.

Chrisman, J. J., Chua, J. H., & Sharma, P. (1998). Important attributes of successors in family businesses: An exploratory study. *Family Business Review, 11* (1), 19 –34.

Cole, P. (1997). Women in family business. *Family Business Review, 10* (4), 353 –371.

Dumas, C. (1989a). *Daughters in family-owned businesses*. An applied systems perspective. Unpublished doctoral dissertation, the Fielding Institute, Santa Barbara, CA.

Dumas, C. (1989b). Understanding of father-daughter and father-son dyads in family-owned businesses. *Family Business Review, 2* (1), 31 –46.

Dumas, C. (1990). Preparing the new CEO: Managing the father-daughter succession process in family business. *Family Business Review, 3* (2), 169 –181.

Dumas, C. (1992). Integrating the daughter into family business management. *Entrepreneurship Theory and Practice, 16* (4), 41 –56.

Dumas, C., Dupuis, J. P., Richer, F., & St. -Cyr, L. (1995). Factors that influence the next generation to take over the family farm. *Family Business Review, 8* (2), 99 –120.

Freudenberger, H. J., Freedheim, D. K., & Kurtz, T. S. (1989). Treatment of individuals in family business. *Psychotherapy, 26* (1), 47 –53.

Frishkoff, P. A., & Brown, B. M. (1993). Women on the move in family business. *Business Horizons*, March –April, 66 –70.

Gillis-Donovan, J., & Moynihan-Bradt, C. (1990). The power of invisible women in the family business. *Family Business Review, 3* (2), 153 –167.

Godfrey, J. (1992). *Our wildest dreams: Women entrepreneurs. Making money, having fun, doing good*. New York: HarperCollins.

Goldberg, S. D., & Woolridge, B. (1993). Self-confidence and managerial autonomy: Successor characteristics critical to succession in family firms. *Family Business Review, 6* (1), 55 –73.

Harveston, P. D., Davis, P. S., & Lyden, J. A. (1997). Succession planning in family business: The impact of owner gender. *Family Business Review, 10* (4), 373 – 396.

Hisrich, R. D., & Fulop, G. (1997). Women entrepreneurs in family business: The Hungarian Case. *Family Business Review, 10* (3), 281 –302.

Hollander, B. S., & Bukowitz, W. R. (1990). Women, family, culture and family business. *Family Business Review, 3* (2), 139 –151.

Iannarelli, C. (1992). *The socialization of leaders: A study of gender in family business*. Unpublished doctoral dissertation, University of Pittsburgh.

Jaffe, D. (1990). *Working with the ones you love: Strategies for a successful family business*. Emeryville, CA: Conari Press.

Keating, N. C., & Little, H. M. (1997). Choosing the successor in New Zealand family farms. *Family Business Review, 10* (2), 157 –171.

Lank, A. G. (1995). *Key challenges facing family enterprises.* Lausanne, Switzerland: IMD Publication.

Lyman, A., Salganicoff, M., & Hollander, B. (1985). Women in family business: An untapped resource. *SAM Advanced Management Journal, 50* , 46 –49.

Marshack, K. (1994). Copreneurs and dual-career couples: Are they different? *Entrepreneurship Theory and Practice, 19* (1), 49 –69.

Massachusetts Mutual Life Insurance Company. (1995). *1995 research findings of American family business.* Springfield, MA: Author.

National Foundation for Women Business Owners (1996). *Key facts about U. S. women-owned businesses.* Silver Spring, MD: Author.

Nelton, S. (1996). A coming sea change in leadership. *Nation's Business, 84* (4), 60.

Nelton, S. (1997). Major shifts in leadership lie ahead. *Nation's Business, 85* (6), 56 –57.

Salganicoff, M. (1990). Women in family business: challenges and opportunities. *Family Business Review, 3* (2), 125 –137.

Shanker, M. C., & Astrachan, J. H. (1996). Myths and realities: Family businesses' contribution to the U. S. economy – A framework for assessing family business statistics. *Family Business Review, 9* (2), 107 –123.

Starr, J., & Yudkin, M. (1996). *Women entrepreneurs: A review of current research.* Wellesley, MA: Wellesley Center for Research on Women.

Widows are a tremendous force in family businesses, but they often need more knowledge and preparation for the responsibilities that may be thrust upon them. The spouse of a family business owner needs to be involved in succession planning, not underrate her skills and get good advice. Eves are often better than their husbands at bringing children into the family business. A "Spouse Survival List" will help family businesses prepare for the possibility of the spouse's death.

When Widows Take Charge

By Sharon Nelton

If she had it to do all over again, says Seona T. Baldwin, she would become more involved in her husband's business earlier and would ask more questions

But she doesn't have it to do all over again. George Baldwin died in an automobile accident in 1981, and two years later she stepped in to run Baldwin Sanitary Service, Inc., the Portland, Ore., trash-collection company that her husband had founded in 1971. She knew little about the business, and she thought her involvement in it would be only temporary. She has been running it ever since.

Widows "are a tremendous force in the survival and growth of family businesses," says Matilda Salganicoff of the Family Business Consultancy in Philadelphia.

At first a widow may take over a business to preserve its founder's vision or because it offers the best livelihood for her family. Or she may see herself as the caretaker of the business until it can be passed to the next generation.

Joyce Signer, in Corvallis, Ore., owns Signer Motors, Inc., a General Motors dealership that her husband was buying when he died of a heart attack in 1970. Signer, then a housewife and former schoolteacher, used to tell herself, "If I can just keep this until my son is out of college and old enough to take over!" Her son was 19, and she also had two younger daughters to support.

In Detroit, Helen Keene McKenna's leadership of McKenna Industries was described in a 1956 story under the headline, "Fulfills Her Late Husband's Dreams." Three years earlier, after her husband, Patrick, was killed in an automobile accident, she took over the company he had founded in 1952. "I wanted to do it for him," says McKenna. At the time of her husband's death, her daughter was 14 and her son was 8. The company, now in Troy, Mich., makes production models for the automobile, aircraft and aerospace industries.

Rosemary S. Garbett, president of Los Tios Mexican Restaurants in Houston, was a 40-year-old housewife with four teenage children when her husband accidentally shot and killed himself in 1976. Garbett learned she could get only $800,000-half the book value for the three struggling restaurants he left behind and that she would have to payoff debts out of that. So she decided that keeping the restaurants and making them go would offer her family a better livelihood than living off the interest from the money she would get by selling the business.

Women are often the "supporters and enhances" of their husbands while the men are still alive, says Salganicoff, but they are more assertive and aggressive after they become widows. Under their leadership, she adds, the businesses often flourish because these women, though generally conservative, are open to new ideas. And they often come to realize that they are no longer running the businesses for their husbands or even for their children.

"That wonderful business I was saving for my son is still mine, and my son is a Buick dealer in Fremont, Calif.," Signer said recently at a family-business conference at Oregon State University.

McKenna Industries had five employees when Helen McKenna took over. She still says she doesn't know how to read a blueprint, but the business today comprises five companies, employs 150 and does $11 million in sales annually. Son Mike is now president and CEO, but McKenna stays on as chairman.

"When I took over the business, I was scared and had no confidence at all in my ability to do anything," recalls Rosemary Garbett. Her husband had occasionally "allowed" her to be a cashier at the restaurants, she says. But she also had done the bookkeeping. "I knew how every dollar was being spent. I knew every debt and how it was or was not being Paid."

She began to tighten controls to keep money from flowing out the door. She instituted other measures, such as centralized purchasing to hold down costs, and a centralized kitchen to assure product quality and consistency in all the restaurants.

"The original debt-ridden three Los Tios restaurants have grown to 10 successful, debt-free restaurants," says Garbett. She employs 375 people and has increased the company's annual sales to over $7 million from $2.5 million. The once-frightened homemaker has twice been honored by the city of Houston with a "Rosemary Garbett Day."

Taking over the businesses wasn't easy for any of these women. Baldwin gave up an 18-year telephone-company career to run Baldwin Sanitary Service, and she did so only after a buy-sell agreement transferring ownership to an employee fell through, and efforts to find a manager failed. The company was losing money when she took charge, but she turned it around.

Some of Los Tios' key employees quit to work for competitors, and a bank that had done business with the firm for years refused Garbett a loan. But what really put steel in her spine were the put-downs she got from people who thought she couldn't succeed Creditors, suppliers and landlords feared they wouldn't get paid, and Garbett heard comments such as, "If she doesn't sex, we'll have to eat a lot of enchiladas to get our money back."

Joyce Signer found that her husband's will was one of her biggest obstacles. It provided that the business be sold and the proceeds go to a trust, a plan that might have been practical had she not decided she wanted to run the business herself. She had to go to court to have the will set aside.

Yet a widow may find encouragement to step in and run her late husband's company. It was a family friend who first suggested to Signer that she could take over the business. And while McKenna found that some purchasing agents didn't want to deal with her in what was then an all-male field, she encountered many more who went out of their way to help.

Most family-business owners are men, and women tend to outlive men by about seven years. So it makes sense for a woman to consider ahead of time what will happen to the business after her husband dies. Experts on family businesses offer these tips:

Do succession planning, but don't lock yourself in-or out. Many wives do not realize, until they become widows, that running a business will be their best choice. She would not have been her husband's choice of a successor, says Signer. And if he had had a buy-sell agreement arranging for someone else to buy the company upon his death, she would not have the business today. "Keep all your options open," she advises.

Think of yourself, adds Jane Siebler, assistant professor of management at Oregon State. She urges wives to consider not only the founder's dreams for a business but their own dreams as well. And when it comes to determining who should succeed the owner, Siebler suggests, a wife should consider herself as a choice.

Don't underrate your skills. Widows who succeed at running the family business are often self-effacing, says Salganicoff. "They will say, 'I was lucky. I had good support. My brother-in-law helped me. My lawyer was great.'" They call on a lot of resources, says Salganicoff, not recognizing "that to get adequate help is a sign of mature management."

Garbett says she became a success "by transferring the homemaker's rules to business...A mother who manages a household with a tight budget and raises a family, while saving a little and paying off creditors, can do what I've done."

Be prepared to seek advice, but also be prepared to go against it. When Garbett decided not to sell Los Tios, she did so against the recommendations of her accountant and her lawyer.

Siebler says, "If your intuition is telling you one thing and your advisers are telling you another, you can trust your instincts."

Get involved in the business early. Seona Baldwin advises women to discuss the business with them husbands and to ask questions if thou husbands are "open-minded enough" to share information.

The presence of wives working in a family Sum helps guarantee the continuity of the business and makes it easier for children to gain access to it, according to Salganicoff.

Husbands often awe ambivalent about having children in the business, and older men may feel they are in competition with the younger generation. But women, she says, really want the children in the business.

So Salganicoff urges wives to become actively involved in the company. 'It's good for them husbands, it's good for the business, and it's good for the family."

Family businesses have the potential to be especially productive environments for women. However, as carriers family culture and processes that may contain gender bias, they can also be the last bastion of resistance to cultural change.

Women, Family Culture, and Family Business

By Barbara S. Hollander and Wendi R. Bukowitz

This article deals with the impact family culture has upon decision making in family businesses, especially as it relates to women in the family firm. The underlying theme is how family culture promotes or limits options for its female members, thereby expanding or restricting opportunities for both the family business system and for the female participants themselves. We will examine family culture through four components-structure, rules, roles, and triangles.

Before we begin our discussion, we would like to acknowledge an inescapable problem. When writing about women, the approach that intuitively suggests itself is to compare them with men, which can lead to unintended oversimplifications about both sexes and to polarization. Some writers have attempted to deal with these problems by making disclaimers. Carol Gilligan puts it very eloquently in her book, *In a Different Voice* (1982):

> The different voice I describe is characterized not by gender but by theme. Its association with women is an empirical observation, and it is primarily through women's voices that I trace its development. But this association is not absolute, and the contrasts between male and female voices are presented here to highlight a distinction between two modes of thought and to focus a problem of interpretation rather than to represent a generalization about either sex [p. 2].

Even Gilligan's attempt to deal with this problem is undercut by the language that she uses, which identifies different developmental patterns for women and men. The fact that she does not intend to make generalizations about the sexes becomes lost in the gender-based support of her concepts. We doubt that we will be any more successful than Gilligan in our attempts to describe distinct themes without creating gender-based polarization. However, that is our aim.

Historically, the concept of culture has been linked with ethnicity and religious ritual. In recent years, the notion of organizational culture has received close attention and is now a readily accepted "buzzword" in management literature and in the field of management science.

Schein describes organizational (business) culture as a "pattern of basic assumptions that a given group has invented, discovered, or developed in learning to cope with its problems of external adaptation and internal integration, and that have worked well enough to be considered valid, and, therefore, to be taught to new members as the correct way to perceive, think, and feel in relation to those problems" (1985, p. 262). These processes are embedded in the relationship system, both above and below the level of awareness of those involved. For this reason, most models of organizational culture use the construct of a continuum that runs between the visible and the invisible (Figure 1).

Family cultures can be represented by a similarly structured continuum. In our model of family culture, another component, emotional processes, exists beyond the "core beliefs" of Schein's model. Emotional processes exist at the least visible level and are powerful determinants of behaviors and decisions. As in organizational culture, acceptable patterns of behavior are developed over time and taught as the correct way to think, perceive, and feel. Family culture evolves from the establishment of patterns around major emo-

Figure 1. Organizational Culture

Invisible ◄——————————————————————————————► Visible

Core Beliefs	Values	Rites and Rituals	Artifacts
Human nature fairness and equality, authority	Slogans and sayings, norms, procedures	Myths and legends, language and humor, new-member socialization	Use of time and space, decor

Source: Adapted from Schein, 1985.

tional issues such as closeness and separation, independence and dependence, and submission and dominance. These patterns give rise to rules and organizing principles. They are automatic and unquestioned. When families also work together in business, the patterns that have been developed over time around these major emotional issues are passed down and played out in the arena of the family business.

When the family culture and the business culture merge in family businesses, they create both a context in which all decisions are made and the glue that holds the family business together. Family patterns, many of which are invisible, become automatic responses to "how we do things around here." The rules, roles, structure, and triangles that each family adopts are expressions of family culture. In the sections that follow, we examine how these four concepts affect the family in business.

Rules and Roles

Families use covert and overt rules governing acceptable and unacceptable behavior as guidelines for interaction among members. Families typically have rules about money, loyalty, togetherness, image, conflict, and roles. Some rules are gender-based; for example, the rule of primogeniture in the context of the family-owned business stipulates that the first-born son will inherit the mantle of family leadership.

Roles set out alternative behaviors that the family believes its members must choose from as they move into adulthood. Rules reinforce roles. To continue the above example, the rule of primogeniture reinforces the role of women as less visible than men. Rules and roles provide clues for family members about the paths they are expected to take as they move through their lives.

For many women and men, rules and roles tend to be polarized along gender-based lines. As Walters suggests in *The Invisible Web* (1988):

> Raising a son is not primarily about raising a father nor even a husband, although this may be a part of parental expectation. Rather it is about raising a man, a worker, a person of public pursuit and individual achievement, an autonomous individual. Raising a daughter is primarily about relationships, caretaking, homemaking, attachments and affiliation, private and interpersonal achievements...So mother's job is to affiliate their daughters with intrafamilial life and to affiliate their sons with the extrafamilial [p 35].

The rules and roles that operate in the family system are often transferred to the family business. To borrow from the above quote, the family business is a curious hybrid, encompassing both the intra- and the extra-familial aspects of its members' lives. More than a nonfamily business, the family business celebrates connection and community by virtue of the family values that pervade it.

The overt role connection plays in the family business lends itself to the strengths that are associated with women's traditional roles. However, some women find themselves locked into these roles, unable to develop the extrafamilial skills that they need to become successful businesspeople. Two roles that women often find difficult to escape are the overnurturer and the invisible women.

The Overnurturer. The concept of nurturing is intimately associated with the concept of mothering. We have used the term overnurturer to describe excessive immersion in this role and to emphasize that overnurturing is too much of a good thing rather than too much of a bad thing. The challenge raised by a term like overnurturing is to define nurturing, generally considered a healthy, balanced activity. We propose that nurturing in the business place combines providing support and encouragement with maintaining an acute awareness of boundaries-knowing where responsibilities start and where they end.

Overnurturing implies a smothering kind of caretaking. The woman who overnurtures is often blamed by others for holding them back or not letting them grow up. A study by Walters, Carter, Papp, and Silverstein (1988) examines women's roles in the family culture and proposes a non-blaming interpretation of typically female behaviors. Based on their study's findings, the authors argue that a higher value needs to be placed upon the active, connecting role of women in families.

Overnurturing can be viewed as an attempt to correct a situation that feels out of balance. Many women are intuitively aware that they are not supposed to be too successful in the business world and that too much success in business can compromise their success as a woman (attracting men, being a good mother, etc.). To counterbalance their success, many businesswomen assume an overzealous caretaking role to avoid being pegged as a "bitch," a term that is often applied to ambitious, aggressive women. Overnurturing serves as an antidote to a businesswoman's sense of guilt over her own success.

Women who are locked into the nurturing role to the point of overnurturing typically find themselves exhausted from trying to take care of the needs of so many others and have no time to take care of themselves. They often feel that if they don't continue to take care of everyone and everything, it will all fall apart. At the same time, others may resent what they see as intrusive meddling.

In a family business, the propensity toward overnurturing can be doubly seductive because of the family's immediate presence. Sheer proximity enforces rules and roles. For example, overnurturing can be a way that many daughters who enter the family business try to fulfill the implicit contract they feel they have with their fathers. When women negotiate the transition of power in the family business, they are often very concerned about "taking care" of their fathers. This can give rise to a form of protectionism that inhibits direct exchange and action regarding succession (see Dumas, this issue). Fathers who assume the role of protectors of their little girls are often reluctant to participate in decisions that will put their daughters on the firing line. In this way, the transition of authority is inhibited.

Nurturing is not solely a characteristic of women; it is also exhibited by men. Family businesses have the potential to bring out nurturing qualities in both male and female members.

Among husband-and-wife business teams in which both partners function as coequals, the women in their thirties with whom we have had contact describe a separation of the role of nurturer from the role of caretaker. These women reserve nurturing for their children; their husbands tend to assume the nurturing role in the business, as one woman we interviewed made clear.

> I think that [our employees] would approach [my husband] before they would approach me on any problem. He is the nice guy, and I am the person who usually says no. The pattern is just the opposite with the kids. They will come to me first to ask about something before they go to [my husband]. I tend to let them explore new things more than he does.

While nurturing may be reserved for their children, the domestic manager role is often transferred from the family to the family business. This generally takes the form of handling the finances and most of the details of running the business' day-to-day operations.

The Invisible Woman. Another example of how adherence to roles promulgates the family culture is the role of the invisible woman. In the family business, many women find that they are not viewed by others, whether within the business or outside, in the same way as male members of the business. For some, the degree to which they are not considered makes it seem as if they were simply not there-as if they were invisible.

Many female partners in husband-and-wife business teams find that they are less visible to the outside world than their spouses. It is often assumed that the only reason they hold their position is that they are married to the boss. As "the wife," they may be expected to play a subordinate role. Women go through an emotional struggle to cope with not being perceived in the same way their husbands are.

Even if they have equal or weightier credentials than their spouses, women often find that other businesspeople tend to look to their spouses for decisions. One woman described the problems she faced and how she and her husband worked to resolve them.

> The problem isn't so much how [my husband] views me, but how I think outsiders view me. I don't want to be viewed as "the wife." It used to bother me if [my husband took the lead in [business] situations, but now its okay. I think that's because now if I say that something is okay, then the perception among our employees is that it s okay. They don't feel that they have to ask [my husband].

> When we first started the business, customers would ask for [my husband] when there was a problem. He would either not return the call or return it and say that the customer would have to talk with me because l had the final say. He helped me carve out my own identity and legitimacy in the business.

> When l meet men [in business] who behave like jerks, I realize that that's their problem, not mine. I just don't take it on.

> We are really coequals in the creative process, but I do perform more of a support role. I am less visible to our clients in the negotiating process, even though I contribute to the process by discussing the details with [my husband].

For daughters in the family business, invisibility means that they are typically passed over when their fathers consider suitable successors. Fathers' passing over their daughters for consideration as successors is often a reflection of their family's cultural values. They tend to view women as not possessing the character traits and experience necessary for running a business.

Limited by this perceptual "blind spot," many fathers experience conflicting emotions over placing their daughters in a leadership role in business. Running a business can be a tough, grueling job, and many fathers want to protect their children from life's hardships. However, the way they protect their daughters often differs from the way they protect their sons.

While no parents want their children to suffer, most parents expect their sons to go out into the world and fend for themselves. On the other hand, a daughter is rarely expected to go it alone. She is frequently encouraged to find a husband who will take care of her and brave the outside world for both of them. The father who supports his daughter in the position of business owner often has difficulty resolving his own conflicts about sending a woman out to confront the world when he feels she should be protected.

The antidote to invisibility is often self-promotion. Daughters and sisters have to announce and support their own candidacies for the position of next-generation business owner. Wives who are partners have to assert their role as influential decision makers in the family business to associates in the outside world. The problem with choosing active self-promotion is that it is culturally stamped as "unwomanly" behavior. "Aggressive" plus "woman" most often equals "bitch." Daughters' self-promotion also activates their fathers' anxiety about encouraging them to assume business leadership. In these situations, women in the family business find themselves caught in a double bind.

A double bind is a situation in which both conformity and nonconformity carry penalties and rewards. The choice for women in family businesses is either self-promotion or accepting a more traditional role. Self-promotion might yield a satisfying career, but successful women must also cope with negative sanctions as well as their fathers' anxiety and perceived disapproval. Accepting a traditional role in the family might create more harmonious relations with family members but also contribute to personal feelings of inadequacy and frustration.

In order for women in family businesses to make themselves visible and escape the double bind, the entire family must be committed to accepting new roles for its members, both male and female. The woman may take the lead in this process, but change can be accomplished much more quickly when the entire family is aware of the process and participates actively.

Relieving the Double Bind. In the context of family business, the tension of choosing between traditional and nontraditional female roles is heightened for many women because they are exploring and experimenting with these roles on a playing field that combines both the family and the family business. The daughter who opts for roles in both the family business and her own nuclear family quite often finds herself stuck, so to speak, between a rock and a hard place. While she negotiates the business succession process whereby she will replace the current owner-leader, usually her father, she must also respond to her parents' expectations that she create a family of her own.

Relieving the pressure of double binds calls for heightened awareness and creativity on the part of the family and family business members. They need to construct new roles that blend the traditional and nontraditional and assign them to business members on the basis of ability and desire rather than gender.

Structure

Family systems have a hierarchical structure in which authority is determined by generational membership. Through childhood and adolescence, parents traditionally have more responsibility and authority than their children. During and after adolescence, the hierarchy begins to flatten out, allowing offspring the potential for an adult relationship with parental figures. Structure may then be viewed as a dynamically adaptive process in the family system. Violation of the generational hierarchy, whether felt or real, results in familial conflict and anxiety. Also, when the processes that sustain the structure become rigidified or get derailed in a tangle of parent-child roles, conflict arises. For example, what is structurally appropriate in the family may not be structurally appropriate in the business, particularly at the point of entry for the next generation.

The family hierarchy is usually respected and reflected in the business hierarchy; the founding owner generally maintains a higher title and status than his or her offspring. Typical roles for the founder and the successor might be president and vice-president, CEO and president, or chairman of the board and CEO.

The development and transfer of the leadership role from one generation to the next creates tension in the family business and may be viewed as a structural process. Many children enter the family business on a full-time basis when they are in their mid- to late twenties By that age, they are recognized by their families and the outside world as adults. However, when they enter the family business, they are often treated like children, forced to learn the business from the bottom up and submit to close monitoring by the owner of the business, usually their father.

Being treated at two different developmental levels – adult outside the business, child or adolescent inside the business – is difficult and confusing for the child as well as the parent. Passage through these stages can be eased by marking transitions to new roles in the business by acknowledging the difference between family roles and business roles.

Succession, whereby the younger generation aspires to the title and status of the preceding generation, is often experienced as a violation of generational hierarchy, especially in the case of a male successor. While the rite of passage for female successors is no less complicated, it tends to be characterized by a different process.

Male successors often pass through a ritual of overt encounter with the founder-CEO. This process has been romanticized into the fairy tale of the young hero displacing the old regime. On the other hand, female successors tend to avoid open conflict and displacement of the CEO by teaming up with him or by carving out a separate playing field that doesn't infringe on his. Avoidance of open conflict with their fathers might be related to the role that women have traditionally played within the family – the protectors of generational continuity.

While the imagery of warfare and squashing the old regime may not be very appealing, overt encounters between the senior and upcoming generations might be a necessary part of the succession process. Expressing disagreement with the CEO-founder and arguing for courses of action can be part of a process that creates a level playing field on which child and parent can meet as two businesspeople who are coequals. For female successors, not establishing a level playing field may result in business-related developmental detours that are not shared by their male counterparts.

Triangles

The paradigm of the triangle as a descriptor of the emotional pattern and emotional "charge" of family interactions is well established in family systems thinking. Triangles connect three individuals with emotional "legs" of varying "distance" or "closeness." Triangles are a basic fact of family life; they serve as a stabilizing force that configures the dynamics of family relationships.

Triangles may be envisioned as having varying shapes, as indicated in the examples in Figure 2. Equilateral triangles, in which legs of equal length maintain equidistant/equiclose connections among members of the triangle, are usually experienced as healthy, or functional. Members experience reasonably easy access to one another. The legs need not be exactly of equal length for the triangle to be perceived as functional. The "coach" triangle permits one point to buffer, coach, consult, or occasionally separate the other two points, especially during periods of high stress or tension. Once the difficult period has passed, the triangle usually resumes an equilateral shape.

In the "messenger" triangle, conflict between two points of a triangle is often suppressed or stabilized by the third, "noninvolved" leg. The third party may become the focus of a problem that permits the two principal parties to avoid dealing with the issues between them. Or, in another variation, conflict can be suppressed through creation of a messenger role. In this pattern, conflict between two points is mediated by the member at the third point who acts as a messenger, absorbing the electricity that passes between the two members who are at odds with each other.

Another common pattern can be coined the "insider/outsider" triangle. In this triangle, the outsider frequently experiences conflicting emotions – a strong desire to move inside, coupled with an equally strong resentment about being forced outside. The negative side of the outsider's reactions is often the only side seen by the two insiders. This perception serves to bring the insiders closer together, driving the outsider even further away. The negative cycle is reinforced, since the outsider's attempts to "get in" are perceived as negative or distancing behaviors.

The characteristics of functional triangles are related to the ability of those who occupy the "points" to experience accessibility to each other. This involves keeping the lines of communication open and the distances between the points in balance. When a triangulated relationship is creating pain or unhappiness for one of the three individuals of the triangle, intervention typically involves equalizing the triangle's three legs. The longer the history of a triangle, the more difficult the restructuring process can be.

When families also run family businesses, triangles have a way of migrating from the family system into the business system. In some cases, these triangles transfer healthy and harmonious interactions from the family into the family business; in others, they shift problems from the family to the family business.

When women participate in a family business, the triangles that they form frequently include the typically male CEO as the second point. The third point can be another family member, whether or not an active participant in the business, or a key nonfamily manager. The triangles that are described below are common to many women who are involved in or with family businesses.

Figure 2. Common (Triangular) Family Patterns

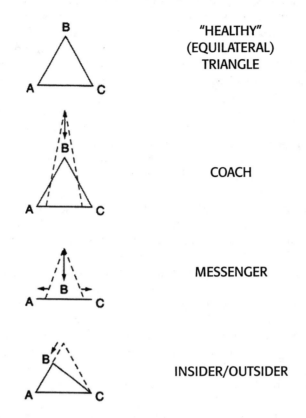

"HEALTHY"
(EQUILATERAL)
TRIANGLE

COACH

MESSENGER

INSIDER/OUTSIDER

Triangles with Mothers. We will first examine some healthy triangles that involve women in the "mother" role. In one common scenario, a triangle forms with the founder-family CEO, the spouse, and the successor. In its most traditional incarnation, these positions are held by a male founder-father, a wife-mother, and a first-born son-successor.

The triangle is often described as a healthy one by its participants when the wife-mother acts as a buffer between the CEO and the successor, sometimes defusing friction, other times redirecting it. Her role as informal coach and consultant is the glue that binds without suffocating, resulting in a "coach" triangle.

In a more modern configuration, the successor might be a daughter. Many daughter-successors describe the triangle that includes their mother and their father-CEO as healthy when they have been encouraged to identify with and model themselves after both their mothers and their fathers. In these instances, daughter-successors report feeling equally connected to both of their parents and describe themselves as having integrated both the female and male aspects of their personalities.

Triangles involving "mothers" become problematic in cases when the wife-mother is described in terms that use the prefix over-overnurturing, overinvolved, overfunctioning. Seemingly overfunctioning or overinvolved mothers often participate in triangles in which the connection between the wife-mother and the successor remains rigidly close, locking the founder into a distant, outside position. This triangle typically occurs when the founder has been an absent parent and the mother-wife has provided the main support system for the children. When the successor moves into the family business and experiences conflict with the founder, it often drives the founder into a more distant position from the successor. The farther out he is driven, the harder it is for the founder to develop a mentor relationship with the successor. In this scenario, the dynamics continue to distort the triangle; each cycle of conflict has a distancing effect.

When the successor is female, the wife-mother can find herself locked into the outside, distant position. In another disproportionate triangle, the daughter-successor overidentifies with her father in reaction to perceived attempts at control on the part of her mother. Female successors commonly report that they identify more strongly with their fathers than their mothers. They often complain that their mothers behave "like a victim" or that they have been "too passive." In their role as future business owner-leader, behaving like a victim and passivity are unacceptable. These daughters cannot and do not want to identify with their mothers. They may turn against the totality of the mother role and experience problems with their own femaleness. The challenge for female successors is to include in their developmental process both separating from their mothers and connecting with them.

Restructuring the triangle typically involves sending the daughter-successor back to discover the woman that is her mother. If the daughter-successor can expand her understanding of her mother beyond that of a role, she is often able to discover positive qualities in her mother that she would like to emulate and can ultimately find those qualities in herself. In addition to the female successor establishing a relationship with her mother, the family system legitimating the mother's role in the family business through a position on family councils or the board of the family foundation, if one exists, can also play a part in equalizing this triangle.

Triangles with Daughters. Daughter-successors are also commonly involved in two other triangles within the family business. One triangle includes the father-CEO and another sibling, usually a brother; the other triangle includes the father-CEO and a key nonfamily manager.

In the triangle that includes her father and brother, the daughter in the family business often de-escalates conflict between father and brother by playing either the role of knight in shining armor or a buffer. As the knight in shining armor, she stands in the number-two position, ready to become the successor if the founder and her brother cannot work out their differences. As a buffer, she runs interference between the founder and her brother, making sure that the conflict en between them never gets too hot to handle; this produces a messenger triangle.

The inevitable result of functioning in either of these roles for an extended period of time is burnout. The role of the white knight is a thankless one because it is based on a win-lose proposition. The daughter only gets a chance to shine if her brother fails. The role of buffer is equally thankless; both the role and the person assuming the role will self-destruct once the buffer has absorbed all it can. Restructuring the triangle, in these cases, involves putting the heat back where it belongs-between her father and her brother.

Colette Dumas calls the triangle that includes the daughter-successor, the father-founder, and a key nonfamily manager"the usurper." One woman whom Dumas interviewed expressed her strong distrust of the nonfamily manager. "I didn't trust the general manager. His conduct was unethical. I told my dad I had a hard time with him. I think he [the general manager] was envious of me, because he once tried to set up his own business, and it failed. I think he thought he was going to take over the business. [Dumas, 1989, p. 40].

Dumas's research indicated that conflict-ridden relationships between daughter-successors and nonfamily managers might be attempts to indirectly assert a claim to the leadership role, which daughters felt uncomfortable doing with their fathers directly. Dumas also speculates that daughters do not want to replace their fathers but want to work alongside them, a role that they feel must be reclaimed from the usurper, the nonfamily manager.

One way to restructure this lopsided triangle is for the management team (and the daughter if she is not on the team) to clearly define the daughter's current position within the business and the path that will lead her to her ultimate position within the business. This position should preferably not necessitate the ouster of an effective nonfamily manager; the path will define the nature of the relationship between the daughter and the nonfamily manager.

Predictions and Possibilities

America's romance with the large publicly held corporation has been waning for a number of years, displaced by a new fascination with entrepreneurship and small business. Many women who work outside the home are looking for careers and companies that allow them to incorporate both family and business into their lives. A recent article in *Working Woman* offered the criteria that it used to evaluate the "best companies for women" (Dusky, 1990). These criteria centered around corporate responsiveness to family needs as well as corporate recognition of the professional contributions women made to the business. Overt recognition of the importance of both the intra- and extrafamilial aspects of working people's lives has the potential to make the family business an especially congenial environment for working women.

However, as we have seen, family businesses are extensions of the family's culture, dynamics, and biases, many of them gender related. The family unit is often the last stronghold against social and cultural change. Family cultural processes can establish perceptions of who should be doing what in the family and the family business. It is important for family members to explore how they have internalized and played out these automatic processes, since they can lead to suboptimal family and business decisions. For example, the rule of primogeniture can often lead to placing the wrong person in the leadership role. This can be just as damaging for men as it is for women.

As family businesses grapple with the increasing number of women who are staking their claim to leadership roles in business, they are faced with a tremendous opportunity. Senior and next-generation members of family businesses will be challenged to rethink the validity of rules and roles in a changing social and organizational context. Family businesses can then lead the way toward building a business community that supports family and economic activity for both male and female participants.

References

Dumas, C. "Understanding the Father-Daughter and Father-Son Dyads in Family-Owned Businesses." *Family Business Review*, 1989, 2 (1), 31-46.

Dusky, L "How to Find the Companies Where women Succeed." *Working Woman,* Jan. 1990, pp. 81-88.

Gilligan, C. *In a Different Voice*. Cambridge, Mass.: Harvard University Press, 1982.

Schein, E. H. *Organizational Culture and Leadership: A Dynamic View*. San Francisco: Jossey-Bass, 1985.

Walters, M., Carter, B., Papp, P., and Silverstein, O. *The Invisible Web: Gender Patterns in Family Relationships*. New York: Guilford Press, 1988.

CHAPTER 13
THE YOUNGER GENERATION

To survive as a family business, business families must produce heirs with appropriate values, skills and motivations and who view active participation in the business as a meaningful life's work. Then the relationship between parents and children must survive the normal pressures of maturation plus the difficulties of working together.

This section deals with the dilemmas confronting the younger generation working and considering working in the family business. The decision to enter the business is a crucial one-both from the perspective of the younger generation's considerations and for the parents' who want to attract their children's real commitment to the business. Once the decision to join the business has been made, a strategy for gaining legitimacy and credibility still must be developed.

Deciding whether to join the family firm can be an agonizing experience This article raises the important questions that a young person should ask while making that decision, provides advice from leading experts and cites experiences of those who elected to join the family business.

Shaky About Joining the Family Firm?

By Sharon Nelton

Doris Mattus Hurley, 42, president of Haagen-Dazs Franchise, Inc., the nationwide chain of ice cream "dipping" stores based in Englewood Cliffs, N.J., was in her early 30s before she did it in 1974.

But Terry Squibb, 30, purchasing and inventory control manager of Welders Supply Inc., of Dallas, did it as soon as he got out of college.

So did Edward R. Schwinn, Jr., 34, president of the Schwinn Bicycle Company in Chicago.

What they did was join the family business. And although, as Schwinn warns, being a member of a family business is "not a piece of cake," the three are satisfied with their decisions. "Everyone is working together for a common goal, the success of the company, because it's ours," says Schwinn, whose great-grandfather started the firm in 1895.

Deciding whether or not to join a family firm can be an agonizing experience. Often children are tormented by feelings of disloyalty when they turn their backs on the business. Many parents feel betrayed or rejected when their children decide to do something else. One tough-minded Iowa company president admits that when his son finally decided to join the family firm, "I sat down and cried like a baby."

There are an estimated 12 million family-held businesses in the United States. Most experts agree that only 30 percent or so survive into the second generation as family firms; less than 15 percent make it into the third. Some are merged or acquired, and some simply go out of business.

Whatever a company's fate, employees are affected. According to Leon A. Danco, who heads the Center for Family Business, a consulting firm in Cleveland, a whole town maybe hurt by heirs' inability or reluctance to continue a large family enterprise.

Furthermore, the younger generation can be vital to the quality of management in a family firm, observes Peter Davis, director of the Wharton Applied Research Center at the University of Pennsylvania. It is often difficult for smaller companies to attract top-rate managers, he explains, and young family members are frequently brighter and abler than management the company can attract from outside.

Among the points a young person must consider in making the decision, experts generally agree, are these:

- Do you *really* want to join the family firm? Would you enjoy it? ("The world doesn't need a reluctant heir," says Danco.)
- Are you prepared to join it? Do you have the education? Experience from another company?
- What alternatives do you have?
- Can you work with your parents or other relatives in the company? (Says Schwinn: "We are a tight, loving family. We all like each other. It makes it a good deal easier. If you don't have those basics, you are not going to have a happy time.")
- Are you interested in the company's products or services? If not, are there other aspects of the business such as marketing or management that offer excitement?
- Are you comfortable with inherited wealth? (Not all family businesses result in wealth for the younger generation, but many do.)
- If you were eventually to take over the company, would you have the energy and commitment required?

For some heirs, joining a family business brings unexpected rewards, such as a strengthened bond with one's parents. Doris Hurley had little interest in joining Haagen-Dazs Ice Cream, founded by her parents, Reuben and Rose Mattus. Before her children were born, she worked in the office, and she had had enough of that.

After she thought her children were old enough, she went to work as a sales representative for another company. When she was offered a promotion a year later, her father made a more attractive bid, and she accepted. Not long after, she convinced him she should launch the franchise operation, which now numbers over 260 stores.

(The Pillsbury Company acquired the Haagen-Dazs companies earlier this year, but family members retain the top management positions. They include Kevin Hurley, who is president of Haagen-Dazs Ice Cream and who became Doris' husband three years ago.)

"As a child, you don't necessarily understand what is going on when you have parents who are completely dedicated to their business," says Doris Hurley. Because she had an opportunity to become part of the business, she says, resentments she felt as a girl have been dispelled, and she has a great deal more Understanding of the sacrifices her parents made in building the company. She admits it can be emotionally difficult for family members to work together. But, she says, "Our extraordinary feelings about the business and the product override any other consideration we have."

Just as hard as deciding to join the business is sticking with it. Welders' Terry Squibb admits to a period of unhappiness when there was just not enough communication between him and his brother, Randy, the firm's sales manager, and their father, Charley.

"My dad had told us he was going to retire in 1985," recalls Squibb. "I didn't think I was being prepared to take over. I wasn't sure he would teach us what we needed to learn." There was uneasiness between the brothers about who would succeed their father and how the stock would be shared.

The Squibbs got help. All three have attended seminars and programs at Danco's center. Terry Squibb also underwent aptitude testing that boosted his confidence by showing him how good he is at paper work and by indicating talents-like a potential for selling-that he did not know he had. His father listened to a taped analysis of the test and, Terry says, "we had a starting point." Now, he reports, the two of them can tall; to each other without getting angry within 10 minutes.

Charley Squibb still plans to retire in 1985, but he is no longer leaving his sons in the dark. He has laid out a stock transfer plan for the next 12 years that will result in the brothers' having a 50-50 partnership in the firm.

Once in the company, some young people cannot get up the courage to leave it, even if that would be best. Compounding their unease may be doubts they have about themselves – Could I really make it on my own? – and the stigma that often goes with being an heir. In some circles, heirs are said to belong to the "golden sperm club."

Indeed, notes Danco, some heirs have great difficulty dealing with wealth because they associate it with evil.

"Why are you hung up on the fact that you are inheriting money?" Danco asks young people who attend his seminars. He tells them that they should learn to handle wealth just as they might handle other unearned privileges, like health, good looks, athletic ability or being born in the United States. "Accept that you are privileged," he counsels, "and work like a dog to be worthy of it. You have to make a contribution."

But he adds: "If you can't be comfortable in the family business because of hang-ups, don't no into it."

People love to talk about the problems of being in family businesses, observes John Messervey, executive director of the National Family Business Council in Chicago. He illustrates with a chance encounter:

He was sitting in the anteroom of an auto repair shop while his car was being serviced. Also waiting was a young man who turned out to be the son of a sausage manufacturer whose company did $100 million or so a year in sales. The stranger began to unburden himself and finally lamented, "I don't want to make sausage the rest of my life!"

Messervey warns that a son's or daughter's decision to join the family firm carries heavy emotional freight, bound up as it is with their relationship with their parents. Unless the heirs understand what they are getting into, the decision could lead to disappointment and disillusionment that threaten not only the parent-child relationship but also the business. When the going gets tough for an heir or the family, it is time, Messervey says, to get professional help from a clinical psychologist specializing in family business issues.

One such specialist is Matilda Salganicoff in Philadelphia. In addition to her private practice, she is on the staff of the University of Pennsylvania Center for the Study of Adult Development.

"Unfortunately," she says, "Most of the people I work with remain in the family firm out of inertia or because they're afraid to go into the outside world. It's not a thought-out decision."

The main thing she says, is for the young person to know what he or she wants to do. And that can be extremely difficult if parents are pressing a son or daughter to go into the business.

Salganicoff advises young people to work outside the family business before they make a final decision. Outside experience will prove they can make it on their own; they need not be nagged by lingering doubts. It will also help them gain credibility with the family firm's employees. And they will learn things that they would not learn otherwise. "It's like going to a different country," Salganicoff says. "You always come back enriched "

Other ways to help determine what one really wants to do include a lot of talking about the issue with family and friends, reading and taking courses. Salganicoff also suggests simply making a list of what one likes to do best and what one likes to do least

"The essence of the whole process is not to betray yourself," she says. "Do what you really like to do."

She cautions both parents and children not to close the door. If the young person chooses the company initially, he should have the freedom to leave later. If he at first decides against the company, he should be allowed to change his mind.

Another major issue for the young person, she says, is the need to become independent. Everyone must gain independence no matter where he or she works, but it is more difficult to do so in a business where the owner is one's parent. For the offspring, she explains, it is like being an adolescent again. The parent may send double messages: "Be dependent but independent" or "Be creative but consult me first."

A young person may join the family firm because it offers an easy way to get employment in a tough job market, according to Leon Danco. "Add to that the potential for getting paid more than the going market rate, and you have a heavily baited hook. It looks like guaranteed security."

Danco warns, however, "that if an heir joins a family business with anything other then competent hard work and a sense of teamwork in mind, sooner or later he or she is going to get badly burned" The heir who does not make a contribution will be resented by those who do. Failing to attain a key management position, he may eventually have to live with the insecurity of having his fate in someone else's hands.

There are also wrong reasons for staying out of the business, Danco points out. Inability to get along with Dad (or Mom) tops the list. Danco urges young people to understand that the experiences the parent is going through "teaching a successor and preparing for retirement" are new to him and that he maybe just as confused as his offspring.

If joining the firm is attractive in most other ways, making the attempt to get along is worthwhile, Danco says.

With all the stigma and challenges and family conflict, why stick it out in the family business? Opportunity for self employment is the No. 1 reason, according to preliminary research conducted jointly by John L. Ward, professor of management at Loyola University in Chicago, and Donald J. Jonovic of the Business Succession Resource Center in Cleveland. Family expectations, an opportunity to share interests and commitments with loved ones and a sense of belonging are among other reasons cited.

Salganicoff points out that a family business offers an opportunity to be creative, even though the young person may not have the challenges of starting and building an enterprise, as his parents did. The heirs, she says, "are not condemned to do the same thing that was already done in the business " in style, process or products. There's flexibility." Adds

Danco: "The real fun of business lies in preparing for the future, in planning for change, adapting to conditions, moving a company toward its full potential," often in directions significantly different from its present products or services." Too few entrepreneurs, he contends, convey the fun and joy of business to their children.

This article was originally printed in *Nation's Business*, November 1983. Copyright 1983, U. S. Chamber of Commerce. Reprinted with permission of the publisher.

Literature indicates that succession is critical to the future of a family firm. However, little is known about how the next generation actually experiences the process of succession. An in-depth biographical study of thirty-two next-generation family members indicates specific factors critical to succession. The findings offer a framework that portrays these influences, their relationships, and the effect they have on the succession experience of next-generation family members.

Succession Experience of the Next Generation

By Wendy C. Handler

Studies of succession in family firms dating back to the early work of Christensen (1953) have commonly recognized its importance for business continuity. Traditionally, the focus has been on the founder or owner as the central person in the family business system. The literature indicates that it is the founder or owner whose responsibility it is to adequately manage the transfer of power (see Barnes and Hershon, 1976; Danco, 1980, 1982; Davis, 1968; Schein, 1983; Levinson, 1974). Individual members of the family have often been lumped together as "the family" or "the family system." Few empirical studies (see Birley, 1986; Blotnick, 1984; Patrick, 1985), anecdotal accounts (Correll, 1989), or conceptual analyses (Barnes, 1988; Friedman, 1991; Rogal, 1989) have focused on the experiences of next-generation family members and their relationship with their parent(s) (Davis, 1982; Dumas, 1990).

There are several important reasons for considering the members of the next generation associated with family businesses. First, one cannot assume that the motivation, desires, and concerns of next-generation family members are identical to or should be secondary to those of founders or owners in family firms. The specific nature of these individuals' needs and the ways they are met in the family firm require attention. Furthermore, there is general agreement that the participation of the next generation in the organization is critical to the transfer of power between generations (Barach, Gantisky, Carson, and Doochin, 1988; Davis, 1982; Longenecker and Schoen, 1975, 1978; Nelton, 1986; Patrick, 1985; Ward, 1987). A better understanding of the experience of next-generation family members in the family firm is therefore called for. Finally, the most practical reason for studying these individuals is related to the statistics that exist on family firm succession – only 30 percent of family firms are thought to survive the transition to the second generation (Beckhard and Dyer,1983). An inquiry into the experience of next-generation family members may increase awareness of what is needed to improve these odds.

For these reasons, the first systematic study of the next-generation family members' personal experience of succession in a family firm has been undertaken. The major product of the study is a framework that describes the factors shaping the succession experience from their perspective. This descriptive framework, which emerged through the systematic analysis of the personal accounts of next-generation family members, portrays two levels of influences on succession. In the next section, the research methodology is described briefly. The reminder of the article is a detailed analysis of the descriptive framework that emerged from the study; it outlines the factors that next-generation family members indicated were most critical to their experience in the family firm. In concluding, the implications of this study for research and practice are considered.

Research Method

The study involved the investigation of thirty-two next-generation family members associated with thirty-two firms. These individuals were interviewed with the intent of gaining an in-depth understanding of their experience. A description of the participants and of the data collection and analysis process follows. (Also see Appendix A for a more detailed discussion of the methodology.)

Participants. In designing the research, it was decided that a snowball sample (see Appendix) would be used made up solely of next-generation family members. Only one individual per organization was interviewed; this made it possible to do an in-depth study of next-generation family members across family businesses. In other words, the purpose of the research was to focus exclusively on what next-generation family members were experiencing personally. To interview more than one person from each firm would have changed the focus of the research from the individual to the relationship.

The sample was designed to be cross-sectional; it was made up of individuals at various points along two dimensions: (1) the life stage, and (2) the phase in the succession process. Designing the sample with reference to these variables (see Table 1) made it possible to address research questions associated with the influence of life stage and the nature of the succession process. A summary of the sample is presented in Table 2.

Data Collection and Analysis. The primary means of gathering data was through an in-depth clinical interview that was designed for the study (see Exhibit 1). The participants were interviewed on two separate occasions, each lasting one and one-half to two hours. The first interview session sought to learn about the family firm, the individual's career history and present involvement in the firm, and future expectations. The second interview session was an in-depth exploration of the family. Individuals were asked to complete a family tree between interviews, in preparation for the second meeting.

In this session, a discussion of the family tree led into questions about family get-together, structure, roles and relationships, and situations where there was a lack of agreement with authority figures. The existence of family discussions concerning succession, and the relationship between life in the family and in the business, was also explored. All sessions were tape-recorded. Participants were also asked to complete and send back a questionnaire concerning their family system (Williamson, Bray, and Malone, 1982) at the end of the interview process. Process notes were taken immediately following each part of the interview.

The data analysis process was an ongoing creative experience that began with the first data collected. This involved the preparation of coding sheets that paralleled the interview guide for each participant; data, impressions, and hypotheses were indicated on these sheets. The files compiled for each member of the sample were read and reread, coded, and analyzed for specific themes that were common across the individuals. These themes served as the basis for the development of the framework highlighting the experience of the next-generation family member.

Table 1. Classifying the Theoretical Sample

	Phase in the Succession Process		
Adult Life Stage	Personal Development	Business Involvement	Leadership Succession
Entering early adulthood (age 17-28)	n = 6	n = 8	
Early adulthood (age 29-39)		n = 6	
			n = 7[a]
Entering middle adulthood (age 40-50)		n = 5	
COLUMN TOTALS	N = 6	N = 19	N = 7

[a]The seven individuals in the leadership succession phase came from early adulthood and entering middle adulthood and therefore were ages 29-50.

Table 2. Summary of the Sample[a]

Individuals' Age		Phase of Succession Process	
17-28	14	personal development	6
29-39	10	business involvement	19
40-50s	8	leadership succession	7
		Career Interest[b]	
Gender		real estate	6
female	9	food	5
male	23	sales	5
		Wall Street	2
Total	32	architecture	2
		automotive	2
		insurance	2
		communications	2
		other	8
		Effectiveness of Succession[d]	
		low	5
		low-moderate	7
		moderate	9
		moderate-high	9
		high	2
Organizations Industry[b]		*Generation-Owner*[c]	
retail/wholesale	11	1	12
sales real estate	5	1 + 2	7
food/restaurant	4	2	4
insurance	3	2 + 3	5
automotive	2	3	2
printing	2	3 + 4	1
computer services	2	4 + 5	1
manufacturing	2		
other	3	*Years in Existence*	
Total	34	3-5	4
		5-10	2
		10-20	4
		21-30	6
		31-40	4
		41-50	2
		51-60	3
		61-70	3
		71 +	4
		Size (Revenue in Millions of Dollars)	
		< =1	6
		1-5	9
		5-10	4
		10-20	3
		20-50	2
		> 50	3
		Unsure	5

[a]All information was obtained through interviews-that is, self-reports.
[b]Some individuals have more than one career interest. Some families owned several firms in different industries.
[c]*Generation-owner* stands for the current generation that owns the firm.
[d]*Effectiveness of succession* was judged using a list of criteria generated from the literature as a checklist.

Exhibit 1. The Interview Guide

1. The family member's career history and present involvement in the business, as well as future expectations
    A. Background on the firm
    B. Career history and present involvement in the family firm
        1. If not presently working in the business
           If job outside the family firm
           If in school
        2. If have worked part time in the family business
        3. If presently working or have worked in the family business
    C. Future expectations

(Complete Family Chart in Preparation for Interview Part 2)

2. In-depth Exploration of the Family
    A. Family structure
    B. In-depth exploration of family roles/interaction given a typical situation
    C. Reflection on roles/relationships
    D. In-depth exploration of a situation where there was a lack of agreement with authority figures
    E. In-depth exploration of an experience in the business involving family member(s)
    F. Family member structure and interaction in the business and in the family
    G. Critical incidents/problems

Results: A Descriptive Framework

The major results of the study are portrayed in a descriptive framework (Figure 1). This diagram presents the influences most central to the next-generation family members' experience. Specifically, next-generation family members described various influences affecting the dependent variable-their quality of experience in the family firm. The *quality of succession experience* is defined as the degree to which one's ongoing involvement in the family business is satisfying and productive from the perspective of the next-generation family member. Quality of succession experience considers how the next-generation family member personally experiences the succession process and therefore is a measure of internal fit.

The influences or independent variables affecting the quality of succession experience were categorized as individual influences and relational influences. *Individual influences* are forces from within the individual and therefore represent the *intra*personal level of analysis. *Relational influences* describe the individual in relation to others – specifically, other individuals in the family and the business. Relational influences thus represent the *inter*personal and group levels of analysis. The purpose of the remainder of the article is to explain the range of influences impacting the experience of succession and to provide examples of these influences-individual (that is, within the individual) and relational (that is, the individual in relation to others) from the perspective of the next-generation family member.

Individual Influences. Individual influences are those influences within the individual that impact one's personal experience of the succession process. There are two individual influence – *personal need fulfillment* and *personal influence* (Figure 1). There are three components of personal need fulfillment associated with three distinct, yet related needs – career, psychosocial, and life stage. Each of these needs is explored, and the ability to personally influence their fulfillment in the context of the family business is also addressed.

Personal Need Fulfillment. Personal need fulfillment refers to the degree to which an individual's needs can be met given opportunities in the context of the family business. The research finding associated with the concept of personal need fulfillment is stated as follows:

Figure 1. The Descriptive Framework

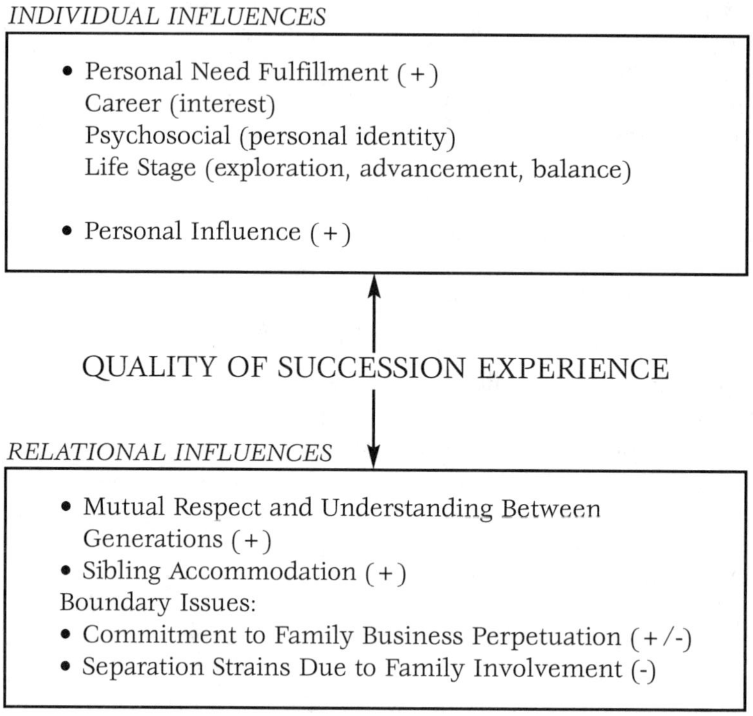

INDIVIDUAL INFLUENCES

> • Personal Need Fulfillment (+)
> Career (interest)
> Psychosocial (personal identity)
> Life Stage (exploration, advancement, balance)
>
> • Personal Influence (+)

QUALITY OF SUCCESSION EXPERIENCE

RELATIONAL INFLUENCES

> • Mutual Respect and Understanding Between
> Generations (+)
> • Sibling Accommodation (+)
> Boundary Issues:
> • Commitment to Family Business Perpetuation (+/-)
> • Separation Strains Due to Family Involvement (-)

FINDING 1. The more a next-generation family member has achieved fulfillment of three needs (career, psychosocial, and life stage) given opportunities in the context of the family firm, the more likely it is that the individual will have a positive succession experience.

Individuals indicated three aspects of personal need fulfillment that impacted their quality of succession experience. The first component, known as *career need fulfillment,* is defined as the degree to which one's career needs were satisfiable in the context of the family business. Furthermore, the clarity or crystallization of career interest does increase as individuals move through life stages. Ten of the fourteen individuals entering adulthood (ages seventeen to twenty-eight) were unclear about what their plans for the future included. Five individuals at this early life stage talked generally about being successful or comfortable in the future but were unable to be more specific. And, interestingly, only seven of these individuals mentioned the family business as a possibility for five to twenty years in the future without being prompted.

Over time, individuals become aware of their own career interests and how well they can be met in the context of the family firm. Some individuals realize that there is a fit (or lack of fit) early in their career development. For example, one twenty-one-year-old individual recently tried working in the family textile business and quit after two days. She quit largely because of her lack of interest in business. Instead, she is majoring in communications in college, and she anticipates getting a job in public relations and eventually starting her own business. She feels she has given the business an adequate chance and has no interest in pursuing further involvement, given the poor fit between her interest in communications and the context of the family textile business. She explained that:

> Business is just not my thing. Business per se, like that. True business – hard business, like you go into work everyday like "I'm going to make money." That's his kind of business: "I'm selling to make money." Communications to me is more like "I'm going to do what I like to do, and in turn, I'll be making money."

Other next-generation family members may have had interests other than the family business, but they decided not to pursue them because they did not seem realistic. One individual (age twenty-one) was always interested in architecture and indicates that he would have studied it if the family furniture business had not been an option. He never did, however, because of his mediocre grades as well as the apparent interest he and others in his family had in the family business. He also indicated that what he personally likes about architecture-the opportunity to be creative, to build, and to design using space – can be satisfied in the family furniture business.

> In the office furniture business, a lot is presentation. And I like presentation a lot. I love working on the computer; I have one at home. I've been working on programs for the company, presentation programs.

Another individual (age twenty) explained that it would be hard to be interested in something different from the family's interests. It seems that next-generation family members are often "socialized" into the family business; in other words, they become accustomed to what the family is accustomed to in terms of career interests. This was a common finding; at least half of the sample suggested that they would be involved in the same type of business even if there were no family business. This suggests that the family socialization process is a strong force influencing the development of the individual's career interest or anchor (Schein, 1978). Even a twenty-year-old male who had never worked in the family's store display business indicated that working, in business would be appropriate for him.

> I find that...all my friends – regardless of if there's a family business or whatever – want to do what their family wants to do just by virtue of the fact that that's what they know. I could never see myself as being a doctor. I have one relative that's a doctor and none of my parents' friends are doctors...Business is something that I've grown up with, and it seems totally normal to me as a way of life and as what people do.

Those who have high career need fulfillment within the context of the family firm tend to be personally invested, enthusiastic, and generally satisfied with their experience in their family firm. One individual (age forty-four) has been president and publisher of his family's newspaper business for eight years and involved in the business for thirty-two years. He indicated that he always enjoyed the newspaper business and feels that he would be working in publishing even if his family did not have a business. He remembers "hanging around" in the business when he was only about ten years old and reflects on these earlier years.

> I can remember when I was in fourth grade I used to ride my bicycle down to the old building...after school every day and just sort of hang around and be a general pain in the neck, I'm sure. In the *fourth grade* I did that, and I'm looking at my children now – one's just finishing the third grade and the other one's just finishing the fifth grade - and that's when I was already, *really* involved...I *loved* it.

The second component associated with meeting one's personal needs has to do with one's *psychosocial need fulfillment* – that is, the degree to which an individual's need for personal identity is satisfiable in the context of the family business. Other studies have suggested that sons and daughters can have difficulty building their own identity in their father's shadow (Aberman, 1988; Davis, 1982; Dumas, 1988; Rosenblatt, de Mik, Anderson, and Johnson, 1985). This study found, in addition, that next-generation family members at each life stage tend to contemplate the question of whether they can meet their identity needs in the context of the family firm.

When psychosocial need fulfillment is low, individuals talked about feeling unimportant and without adequate responsibilities or ways of contributing to the organization.

One's individuation or differentiation from one's parents (Williamson, Bray, and Malone, 1982) has important implications for one's quality of experience. For example, one individual (age twenty-one) described how his role in the family is very much a function of his relationship with his parents.

> Although my relationship with my parents has developed and has grown tremendously over the years, I still see myself, to a very large extent, being a child, and them being my parents. That's a role that you re born into and is very difficult to escape from, try as hard as one might.

This individual's inability to conceptualize his role in the family as distinct from his parents has an important effect on his personal experience in the family business. In the firm, he has worked small jobs, helping to answer the phone and thumbing through resumes, and has attended occasional meetings with his father. However, given the highly technical nature of the consulting firm and the level of training required, he understands that achieving a sense of personal identity and making a contribution to the organization would be unlikely after he graduates from college.

Furthermore, because individuals at this life stage have not established adequate boundaries with their parents, they find it hard to feel good about their contributions to the business. For example, while one individual (age eighteen) admitted that he liked to work, he indicated that this did not include working for his father.

> I just like working in general. I don't like working for my father yet because in my opinion I haven't been given enough responsibility or been treated well enough where I can really enjoy it. I just enjoy working. I won t say it's for my father...

Even next-generation family members who had already become president and in charge of their family firm were prone to feelings of low psychosocial need fulfillment. This was particularly likely when they lacked a sense of personal ownership of the business. One individual (age thirty-five) talked about the reasons for his "lack of psychological good feelings."

> I was running my father's business, and I wasn't personally owning the business, in my own mind, in my own heart. Now, I am. Now it s becoming my business, and I'm looking at it as my business...Psychologically I was just *running* "the family business." Now I'm running *my* business, and the benefits of that business go to my family.

One's sense of psychosocial development is potentially enhanced when an individual is able to look at his or her development in time. For example, one college senior talked about how his father, grandfather, and uncle are grooming him to take over the top position. He also indicated that he was proud of his own personal accomplishments toward this goal (for example, learning the overall market, getting an undergraduate degree in business, and going to work for the company whose product they sell). However, twenty-one individuals in the study chose to work outside the family firm to establish their own identity. In addition, two individuals started their own business within the family firm as a way of establishing their own sense of self. Therefore, just nine individuals attempted to meet early psychosocial needs directly within the family firm. When these needs are satisfied, self-doubt and self-questioning are minimized.

The third component associated with meeting one's personal needs has to do with *life-stage need fulfillment*. This is the degree to which the need for exploration (while entering adulthood), for advancement (in early adulthood), and for balance (in middle adulthood) can be satisfied in the context of the family business. Individuals entering adulthood who are in the late teens through late twenties (fourteen members of the sample) indicated a strong desire or need for exploration. They talked about "the freedom to do what I want to do" and "the need for doing my own thing" and about disliking the feeling that "my job is too secure" in the family business. Only eight individuals in the study had entered or were entering the family business having received no prior outside work experience. One-fourth of these individuals were to start working in the business several months after graduating from college. The remaining three-fourths of the individuals admitted that if they could relive the entering adulthood stage again, they would get experience outside the family business.

The need for exploration, while critically important, can be a paradox for next-generation family members. The reason is that the need for exploration implies personal independence, while the family business is a context that implies family involvement. Thus, the majority of individuals entering adulthood tended to see the effects of entering the family business too early as potentially negative; one individual summarized that it can "limit your exposure" to the range of experiences available. With their focus on personal exploration, they typically thought of the family business as an option for the future or as a last resort. Having this option provides a "safety net" that actually enables exploration. One college student (age twenty) explained:

> In case I don't like to work someplace else and I want to be my own boss, I can always come back here. And that's what my father has been telling me all the time: "Go out, do whatever you want and this is a safe boat."

Individuals in early adulthood (ages twenty-nine to thirty-nine; ten members of the sample) expressed a strong interest in their own advancement. They talked about a desire to "see things get achieved," to realize "the potential," and to "prove out what I see for this business." They used terms like *opportunity, challenge, planning, succeeding,* and *momentum*. They seemed to think about their own advancement in terms of the business's growth and development. For example, when the thirty-six-year-old vice-president of operations of a successful restaurant chain was asked about where he would like to be five years from now, he responded that he has been doing some creative map work that could take them down the road toward the future.

> I don't think we should operate a mundane business. I've always thought we should have fun in what we re doing. But still addressing the needs that we need to grow and make money. Those are the challenges; you want to have fun, you want to enjoy what you're doing. we want to be a forerunner in the business. Those are goals. How do we do that? Growing a business and making money. So that becomes a challenge. If those can be successfully integrated, our – or *my* – mission I feel has been accomplished, anyway.

Individuals in middle adulthood (ages forty to fifty; eight members of the sample) indicated a growing desire for a stable life structure (Levinson and others, 1978) where there is a balance between work and other activities. Next-generation family members at or nearing this stage of life talked about looking forward to slowing down, spending time outside the business, and retiring. Achieving a sense of balance appeared especially important for individuals who were between forty and fifty and in the business involvement phase of the succession process. These individuals had each become involved and stayed in the family firm for reasons associated with personal security and safety. A career anchor perspective (Schein, 1978, p. 149) would suggest that the family business allowed them to have "stable membership in a given organization," which was important for their security. Six individuals attributed their involvement in the business to a sickness or disability. And three individuals had worked in their family's business for over twenty-five years.

The implications of having life-stage needs met in the context of the family business are noteworthy. Satisfying exploration needs while entering adulthood is important for individual development. Those next-generation family members that do not have their exploration needs met either within or outside the business can feel trapped or closed in and can experience a sense of despair during the course of their involvement in the family firm. Similarly, those individuals that cannot meet advancement needs in the business can experience negative feelings, including a sense of ongoing failure or lack of fulfillment as well as anger, resentment, and despair. Finally, because of the sample's boundary in terms of age, the effects of achieving balance between work and other activities outside work are uncertain. However, it does seem that a sense of balance between work and activities outside work is achievable for many in the context of the family firm.

Personal Influence. A next-generation family member has the potential to use personal influence to the degree he or she feels personally able to influence or effect change so that personal needs are met in the context of the family business. The research finding associated with the concept of personal influence is stated as follows:

> *FINDING 2.* The more a next-generation family member has the potential or ability to exercise personal influence given the family business, the more likely it is that the individual will have a positive succession experience.

Thus, the potential to exercise personal influence is important for a high quality of succession experience. Even though this influence reflects both an individual's ability to influence other individuals and his or her own situation, it is classified as an individual influence rather than a relational influence. The reason is that personal influence is largely a matter of personal style. Individuals with low personal influence tend to talk passively about themselves, using expressions like "They expect me to do [xyz]" or "I was running my father's business." Individuals with high personal influence use active verbs. They are likely to describe situations where they were catalysts of change and are likely to say that their own development took place because of their active pursuit of goals.

Furthermore, personal influence is highly related to one's posture toward authority. Dependent (conforming) individuals are least likely to exercise personal influence as next-generation family members. Instead, they tend to be highly concerned with pleasing others and are likely to downplay their own personal needs. Thus, the inability to use personal influence is likely to have a negative effect on their quality of succession experience. Counter-dependent (rebellious) individuals typically rely heavily on personal influence to get their needs met. However, there is often a negative feeling associated with this use of influence; for example, they see themselves as having to be forceful to get what they want.

Finally, individuals with an interdependent (situational) posture are most likely to exercise personal influence in a way that is productive both personally and for the organization. The use of influence in this case is a neutral action and appears devoid of the underlying negative energy typical of the counter-dependent individual. For example, one individual (age forty-four) talked about how he took charge of his own career development. Managing his career path not only enabled his own advancement but also led to the ongoing growth and expansion of the family newspaper business.

> [T]he path was my choosing. I was a bookkeeper, and then I was a business manager. That was my father's plan. And...as I started doing things, I was business manager, when there was still a general manager who was my father, I didn't have the authority to tell anybody else anything. So I "manipulated" the "Assistant General Manager" [position], and then at one point, I can't remember why, but I became general manager...[and finally] publisher.

He explained that the change in title was not that important because it was really the same job he was performing all along until he became publisher. However, what achieving these new titles did was to send out a message; he was indicating that he was capable of exercising personal influence. He could be an effective successor to the leadership of the family newspaper business.

Personal influence is highly related to personal need fulfillment. While the fulfillment of personal needs provides a sense of internal fit for the next-generation family member, the potential to exercise personal influence enables the ongoing adjustment of this internal fit. Personal influence therefore is a dynamic influence; for those who can exert personal influence, there is the opportunity to increase their self-concept through the fulfillment of personal needs. Thus, one's ability to exercise personal influence may aid in triggering a cycle of psychological success (Hall, 1976). For this reason, both the fulfillment of personal needs *and* the potential to exert personal influence are necessary for the highest quality of succession experience.

Furthermore, individuals at different stages of life manifest personal influence in distinctive ways. For next-generation family members entering adulthood, exercising personal influence means creating options for exploration. In early adulthood, personal influence is manifested to the extent that the next-generation family member can enable his or her own advancement along a life course. Finally, in middle adulthood, one uses personal influence by creating balance between work and other activities in one's life. This often means cutting back one's responsibilities, spending more time with family, and beginning to groom family members from the next generation.

Relational Influences. Four relational influences are central to the next-generation family member's experience of succession (Figure 1). Each of these four influences involves the next-generation family member in relation to another individual or group. The first two influences are interpersonal: (1) mutual respect and understanding between the next-generation family member and the founder or owner, and (2) sibling accommodation between the next-generation family member and other siblings or relatives from the same generation. The other two influences are intergroup or boundary issues, because their existence is a function of the overlap between family and business systems or groups. The first boundary issue is represented by the (3) commitment to family business perpetuation. This is manifested by the family's contributing, helping, and sharing in the business. It is considered a "boundary issue" because it is a family value that manifests itself through the contribution of family members within the business. The second boundary issue is manifested in (4) separation strains due to family involvement. In other words, the difficulty separating family and business puts a strain on family and business functioning. Each will be discussed in turn.

Mutual Respect and Understanding Between Generations. The research finding associated with mutual respect and understanding between the next-generation family member and the founder or owner is stated as follows:

> *FINDING 3.* The more a next-generation family member achieves mutual respect and understanding with the predecessor in succession, the more likely it is that the individual will have a positive succession experience.

The evolution of a relationship between current and next-generation family members based on mutual respect and understanding is one of the most important influences on the quality of succession experience for the next-generation family member. "It's an extension of the parent-child relationship; the business acts as a powerful amplifier" (Jonovic, 1982, p. 71; also see Bernstein, 1985). At its best, it encompasses the qualities of mutuality, earning of respect, trust, support, feedback, learning, friendship, and sharing. At its worst, these relationships between current and next-generation family members were described in terms of the parent's criticism, judgment, conservatism, lack of support, narcissism, and lack of trust. In addition, communication difficulties typically underlie these inter-generational relationships.

Next-generation family members who have positive working relationships with their predecessor indicate a range of effects on their experience in the family firm. These include enrichment, growth, and further strengthening of their relationship with the current-generation family member. The development of confidence, trust, and comfort with one another is an important part of this process, as one woman (age twenty-eight) explained:

> [My position] has evolved...through trust-a good working relationship with my father. He wanted his hands in everything. He didn't feel as if I knew enough to be left alone to make certain decisions. Now he has a lot of trust in me, and I make a lot of decisions, and he asks me quite a bit for my input. And that's nice – it's taken me many years to develop to that point and have that kind Of relationship with him. And that has been – more than money, more than ben-

efits, more than having a piece of the rock – that has been the most reward-ing part of my being involved in this family business.

This woman is representative of the individuals whose relationship changes and grows through their working together. Before entering the family firm, she had always looked up to her father and considered herself to be her father's "kid." She had the qualities and man-nerisms of her father. However, during her early involvement in the family printing busi-ness, there were many rocky times.

> There was a lot of aggravation. I quit twenty times. He fired me twenty times. I fired him twenty times. We fired each other – we both walked out – we were gonna close the whole place...

She explained that working for him required an important transition-the evolution of a father-daughter relationship into a working association. A key characteristic of this rela-tionship is that the respect be mutual. For this to happen, next-generation family members must have the confidence in themselves in order to build their parent's respect. The devel-opment of this mutual feeling derives from both individuals' experience, knowledge, and involvement in the family firm together (Handler, 1990).

When the working relationship between generations lies on the negative end of the continuum, the possibility of a highly satisfying experience in the firm is severely ham-pered. In addition, next-generation family members are likely to feel resentment, anger, frustration, and lack of recognition while involved in the firm. And though exercising per-sonal influence can improve their overall experience in the firm, it is doubtful that it can alter the relationship.

There are several possible reasons why some relationships are better than others. One reason for good working relationships stems from the owner's positive self-concept and healthy attachment to his organization (Kets de Vries, 1985; Levinson, 1971; Zaleznik and Kets de Vries,1985). In his study of family companies, Davis (1982, p.184) found that "in the best father-son relationships...the father demonstrates a strong desire, unqualified by his attachment to his company, to see his son grow into all that he can be." This parallels findings in the career development literature that indicate that capable mentors tend to be those individuals who feel good about their own accomplishments (Kram, 1985).

Another explanation for good work relationships is based on the relative life stages of the parent and the next-generation family member. Specifically, Davis (1982) found that the quality of the relationship between father and son is generally harmonious when the father is in his fifties and the son between the ages of twenty-three and thirty-two. This study validates Davis's explanation for the findings; the reason for the harmony may lie in the ability of both individuals to satisfy personal needs as well as goals associated with the business. In other words, compatibility of needs, as well as the ability to compromise or adjust expectations (Davis, 1982) and to resolve conflict (Patrick, 1985), may be key com-ponents of the harmonious relationship at this life stage for father and son.

This study suggests that the significant improvement of a relationship where there is a low level of mutual respect and understanding between generations is rare and that it is highly dependent on the predecessor's openness to learning. Those next-generation fami-ly members that remain involved in the family firm in anticipation of an improved rela-tionship are typically disappointed. This was the case for one individual in his early fifties. For thirteen years, he was his father's errand boy in the family oil business. He explained how his father expected this service but never showed any sense of recognition, praise, or respect in return.

> I had a tremendous affinity with my father-mind you, still not earning his approbation...[My father is a man in a small company who's a big shot. He's got a son who runs around and does all the paperwork he doesn't like, all the dirty work he doesn't like. He loved it...And I never got the picture. I was so damn dumb that I kept trying to please someone whose goal was not to be pleased. He won. The day he died, he died *not* being pleased with me. And that was the way he lived.

Sibling Accommodation. The research finding associated with sibling accommodation is stated as follows:

> *FINDING 4.* The more siblings can accommodate rather than conflict with one another given the family business, the more likely it is that the individual will have a positive succession experience.

Sibling accommodation occurs when siblings or other relatives of the same generation working in the business agree on their relative positions of responsibility and power. When a next-generation family member has siblings, certain aspects of the relationship while growing up may carry over into the business association. These include attributes due to birth order as well as the extent of sibling conflict and sharing. At its best (and in about five reported situations), sibling accommodation enables the development of a team feeling within the business. For example, one daughter (age twenty-nine) recalled:

> In my first couple of months here [working for my family real estate firm, my father took my sister, my husband, and me walking on Park Avenue [New York], looking at the buildings we have owned...and pointing out different aspects of other buildings and then walking us through a rehabilitated one and feeling like the three of us were so in tune and learning, and here are my sister and I learning. I'm learning from Susan, Susan is learning from my father, and I'm learning from both really.

On the other hand (and in approximately six reported situations), sibling relationships can be manifested by rivalry, having potentially damaging effects on the succession process. For example, one individual's (age nineteen) family owns a chain of department stores that generate yearly sales revenue of $200 million. Since the business is so large, the family wants more than one family member involved in the future if it is going to stay in the family. The two oldest brothers appear to be the likely pair. However, the younger of the two admits:

> I don't enjoy working with my brother. That would probably be one of the reasons – if I don't go into the business – he'd be it. He's a nice guy and everything, but he enjoys bothering me, making me mad...even when I'm working.

In the remaining twenty-one situations, sibling accommodation within the business was either not an issue or was managed adequately. Dividing responsibilities between siblings within the business was an approach used in twenty-four of the family firms in the sample; the effect was to minimize the likelihood of comparisons between siblings (also see Crane, 1982; Ward, 1987). Sibling accommodation can signify, too, that an understanding exists (although often not explicit) concerning who will be the successor. For example, one individual (age thirty-two) is the middle of three sons; all are vice-presidents in charge of the family restaurant business. Despite his strong leadership ability, when asked to talk about his desire to be successor, he admitted he could not think of being in charge of his older brother, who has worked in the business longer than he has:

> I really can't be boss here because I have an older brother as well as a younger brother. For me to step in and be the boss with my older brother [in the business] just won't work. I mean, I've come to terms with it. I understand it...It's just the kind of thing I can't do.

The input of siblings not working in the firm is also important to the succession issue; their concerns often focus on the division of the company's assets and stock.

Boundary Issues. Miller and Rice (1967, p. 163) have singled out the family business as an example of "when the boundary of a system of [family] activities crosses enterprise boundaries." The two boundary issues described by next-generation family members exist due to the overlapping boundaries between family and business systems. Miller and Rice found that these overlapping boundaries can produce certain tensions experienced by individuals involved in either system. According to the findings of this research, there appear to be positive as well as negative influences on the quality of succession experience for those involved. The first boundary issue is the commitment to family business perpetuation, which is a family value that manifests itself through the contributions of family members within the business. The second boundary issue is represented by separation strains due to family involvement. These strains occur because of the difficulty of achieving separation between family and business tasks; they can produce observable effects in both arenas.

Commitment to Family Business Perpetuation. The research finding associated with commitment to family business perpetuation is stated as follows:

> *FINDING 5.* The greater the commitment to family business perpetuation as a family value, the more likely it is that the individual will have a positive succession experience (except when the commitment is to business means rather than business ends).

Commitment to family business perpetuation, as a family value, is generally manifested through family helping, sharing, and contributing for the sake of the business. It is similar to family values associated with honesty, justice, happiness, and peace in that they represent important messages about how families live. However, this value associated with the family's intentionality (Davis, 1983) is practiced within the business, and that is why it is considered a "boundary issue." In addition to guiding the next-generation family member's earliest decision around joining, the value shapes future actions concerning long-term involvement and succession and can have positive or negative effects on an individual's quality of succession experience.

Commitment to perpetuation was discussed in terms of family pride in the business, ownership, commitment, accountability, and longevity of family involvement. It also manifests itself in certain norms or business policies. When these norms are associated with *business ends*, such as success, growth, or other values related to the organizational mission, they enable family members to work together toward their achievement. For example, one individual (age thirty-six) explained how the family restaurant business evolved out of his grandfather's interest in quality and consistency of food. He called this the beginning of "the family food culture."

> My grandfather had a philosophy of always using the best – finest quality. And so what we've tried to strive for – no matter what we get involved in – we want it to be *the* very *best* in terms of quality, and consistency. And *that's* where I think the beginning of the culture started.

On the other hand, when norms or traditions that are passed down through generations are associated with *business means*, or the details of operating the business, they can be detrimental to the organization and the individuals involved. In fact, such family traditions appear to explain why many family firms are slow to modernize with new technology and more formalized systems. In their commitment to perpetuate the business, there may be an unspoken underlying desire to maintain certain methods of operation, even those that are antiquated. For example, there was a common belief that firing a family member or having him or her quit was wrong.

> That [firing] could *never* happen in my family. It could *never* happen. If my father thought I was doing a terrible job, was a rotten employee and wanted to fire me, he would catch *SUCH* a wrath from my mother – "You *fired* your own *SON*?! This is my *flesh* and *blood* – you *fired* my *flesh* and *blood*!?!" It would be such a nightmare. That could *never* – and I say that with utmost conviction – that could never, never happen.

It is doubtful that such policies concerning family member involvement and disengagement from the organization are useful to either the firm or the family member (who might be better off not working in the organization).

However, not all of the next-generation family members talked about the perpetuation of the family firm with such conviction. In fact, ten of the individuals interviewed mentioned the possibility of selling the firm. This was typically considered as an option if the next generation was not interested or could not run it effectively, and if the business was undergoing difficulties. One individual (age thirty-three) indicated that selling the family drugstore would be a possibility if he and his sister were unable to manage the business through future business downturns.

> We would *like* to keep the business and run it, but we also are in no illusions; if things get bad, we would sell out in a *heartbeat*. I would sell this business so fast it would make your eyes blink. I have no intentions of taking substantial assets and running them down the tubes.

Several individuals also indicated how complex and difficult the recent business environment had become. Contemplating the option to sell the business seemed necessary for the realistic next-generation family member. Mention of the rules, regulations, tax considerations, legal and business expenses, and tight employment pool indicated an awareness of the potential risks of operating a family business.

Separation Strains Due to Family Involvement. The research finding associated with separation strains because of family involvement is stated as follows:

> *FINDING 6.* The greater the existence of separation strains due to family involvement in the business, the less likely it is that the individual will have a positive succession experience.

Separation strains occur when the family and business overlap and permeate each other, so that they produce tensions in the family and/or the business. Although the intensity and type of strain varied depending on the nature of the family and business relationship, all of the individuals in the sample indicated that separation strains existed. All of them mentioned some type of *business strain* associated with separating business and family. These included family conflict, emotionality, heated arguments, unrealistic expectations for family members, arbitrary rules, and informal policies. About ten of the participants indicated that such strains were marked, so that they had a negative effect on the quality of succession experience. One individual (age fifty-three) indicated how the infighting in his family had taken away valuable energy from necessary business decisions and planning.

> It's a shame because all the infighting and all this psychological stuff took 50 percent of the energy that if I had directed it at the business – you know, if we had all been pulling in the same direction – we might have had a good business.

An example of how business strains can be manifested in terms of informal and arbitrary policies is provided by another individual (age thirty-five), who is president of the family insurance business. When he was asked if he reported to anybody, he responded:

> Are you kidding? Are you *kidding*? Ask the next questions – "how are raises determined – particularly for me? " I'll tell you when I got a raise; I got a raise when I got married. I got a raise when I bought a house. I got a raise when my first child was born...My sales haven't made any difference – nothing I do makes a difference. There is *no* performance relationship. And the same thing with everybody else [in the organization].

Approximately ten of the participants also suggested that there were *family strains* due to business issues being brought home, so that there was little separation between family and business outside of work. When poorly managed, these strains can intensify into family battles as severe as in the accounts of the Binghams (*New York Times*, Jan. 19, 1986), the Mondavis (*Money*, July 1983), the Lorentzens of Levolor (*New York Times*, May 15,

1988), the Tompkins of Esprit Corp. (*Newsweek*, May 23, 1988), and the Shoens of U-Haul (*Business Week*, Aug. 29, 1988).

Implications for Research and Practice

This study has valuable implications for research and practice. In terms of research, it furthers our presently limited understanding of successful or likely successions (Lansberg, 1986; Malone, 1989; Stempler, 1988) by delineating significant influences affecting the experience of the next generation. Further investigation will be necessary to better understand the nature of these influences-at the individual and relational levels of analysis-and to test propositions indicated by this study. Also, various perspectives in addition to that of the next-generation family member will add further richness and integrity to these findings. Finally, the qualitative grounded theory approach used in this study seems applicable to future studies of family business issues, given the opportunity it allows to access one's depth of experience.

A major implication for practice is the potential use of the framework as a diagnostic tool for evaluating next-generation family members' experience of succession. The relevance of the study's findings for many individuals is worth noting. According to the literature, at least 90 percent of businesses in the United States are family owned or controlled (Beckhard and Dyer, 1983). This suggests that the vast majority of the United States' next generation are affiliated with a family firm. And since many other countries also rely on family businesses for economic growth (Gallo and Pont, 1988; Okochi and Yasuoka, 1984; Thomassen, 1988), the number of next-generation family members on the international level is also extensive.

Specific implications exist on the two levels of analysis associated with the descriptive framework. On the individual level, the study suggests that next-generation family members judge their experience in the family firm in terms of the degree to which needs associated with individual development are satisfied. Specifically, the importance of meeting needs associated with one's career, psychosocial development, and life stage are critical for the next-generation family member. The ongoing assessment of these needs through personal reflection and planning is necessary.

In terms of career needs, individuals should ask themselves: In what ways does working in the family firm satisfy my career interests? In addressing their own psychosocial development, individuals should consider the extent to which they are capable of their own accomplishments and accountable to themselves while involved in the family firm. Finally, in meeting life-stage needs, individuals should consider the question: In what ways are my needs changing over time, and how can they be satisfied through the family firm? Individuals also should consider whether they can exert personal influence and should evaluate relational influences associated with their experience.

On the family level, the study suggests that mechanisms are required to strengthen family relationships through improving communications both within and between generations, as well as to manage boundaries between family and firm. Working on communication between family members is necessary to institutionalize succession planning in family firms by reducing the conspiracy (Lansberg, 1988) or resistance (Handler and Kram,1988) associated with succession planning. Increasing awareness in families of the existence of an overlapping system between family and business is also necessary. Related to this is the creation of family values associated with the business mission or goals and the establishment of norms for minimizing the interference of family issues in business (see Ward,1987) .

Finally, the major implication for succession planning lies in recognizing the perspectives of the next-generation family members. Strategic planning associated with succession should incorporate their needs. These individuals should be actively involved in planning for the future, particularly given that the leadership of the organization is likely to depend on them. Thus, this study suggests that the challenge for organizations lies in managing succession as a means of enhancing the continuity of organizations as well as the quality of experience of the individuals involved.

Appendix A. Detailed Discussion of the Research Methodology

To generate theory through the determination of general categories and properties, a grounded theory approach was used (Glaser and Strauss,1967). This approach relies on letting theory emerge or unfold, rather than solely verifying or disputing existing hypotheses. Clinical field methods (Berg and Smith, 1985; Schein, 1987) were also utilized to achieve a rich portrayal of the influences on the succession experiences of next-generation family members.

The participants were gathered through the use of "theoretical sampling" (Glaser and Strauss, 1967). The research was developed and controlled by the structure of the emerging theory, as explained by Glaser and Strauss (1967, p.45): "Theoretical sampling is the process of data collection for generating theory whereby the analyst jointly collects, codes, and analyzes his data and decides what data to collect next and where to find them, in order to develop his theory as it emerges. This process of data collection is *controlled* by the emerging theory...The [researcher] may begin the research with a partial framework of 'local' concepts, designating a few principal or gross features of the structure and processes in the situations that he will study."

The adult or life stage was broken down into three periods, based on the literature on adult development (Erikson,1963; Gould, 1978; Levinson and others,1978; Super and others,1957; Vaillant,1977). The first phase, called *entering early adulthood*, extends from age seventeen to twenty-eight and involves the tasks associated with moving into the adult world by exploring its possibilities. The second phase, extending from age twenty-nine to thirty-nine, is labeled *early adulthood*; its tasks involve establishing one's place in society and working at advancement. The third phase, extending from age forty to fifty, is labeled *entering middle adulthood*. Achieving a sense of balance between work and life's other activities is critical to individuals at this stage (Levinson and others, 1978).

Three phases in the succession process were also designated. These phases are consistent with work done by Longenecker and Schoen (1978) as well as by Churchill and Hatten (1987). The phases are as follows: (1) the personal development period, where the individual works at most part time in the business; (2) the business involvement period, where the individual is actively involved working full time in the business; and (3) the leadership succession phase, where the individual is in charge and/or has the title of president. Another variable critical to the development of the sample was the effectiveness of succession. A list of criteria associated with effective successions generated from the literature was used as a checklist to determine the effectiveness of succession. Thus, the rating that the succession process was given was based on the self-report of individuals, using the checklist as a guide. Other variables noted were the gender and career interests of the individual and the generation, size, and age of the firm. Also, to further bound the sample, only individuals from private firms were selected. (A summary of the sample is presented in Table 2.)

The sampling process took place over a five and one-half month period, during which a file of possible referrals was created and updated. This file was developed through contacting colleagues, students, and associations with members consisting of family firms. In all cases, my initial contact with the potential participant was through a phone call. The phone conversation was considered the first step in establishing rapport and was critical to the participants' agreement to participate. The conversation would begin by indicating the source of referral. Following this, the nature of the study, the time involved, and the confidentiality and anonymity of responses was discussed. Questions were then asked about the nature of the firm, the individual's degree of involvement, and the age range of the individual. This allowed me to target the individual in terms of the appropriate sampling cell (see Table 1) or to rule out the individual based on the need or lack of fit with sampling criteria. The referral system of sampling was successful; only one individual flatly turned down participation, claiming his family business situation was too unpleasant to discuss. Another individual indicated that she could not participate because of time pressures.

The data analysis stage actively involved myself as researcher in a back-and-forth process between the data and the development of grounded theory (Glaser and Strauss, 1967) . There were certain distinct yet overlapping steps, beginning with the detailed coding of the data. The cumulative coding of each three- to four-hour interview took between six and twenty-two hours, depending on the length and richness of the information. Individual folders for each of the thirty-two members of the sample were set up. These folders were reviewed many times, and common themes were coded and tabulated. Through my review of all the folders and because of my familiarity with each individual, the influences began to emerge from the data. The descriptive framework presented in Figure 1 is the integration of these themes.

References

Aberman, R. "Dynamics and Stresses Within the Family and the Family Business." Paperpresented at the Research Day of the Family Firm Institute Conference, Boston, Oct. 1988.

Barach, J. A., Gantisky, J., Carson, J. A., and Doochin, B. A. "Entry of the Next Generation: Strategic Challenges for Family Business." *Journal of Small Business Management*, 1988,26, 49-56.

Barnes, L. B. "Incongruent Hierarchies: Daughters and Younger Sons as Company CEO's." *Family Business Review*, 1988,1(1), 9-21.

Barnes, L. B., and Hershon, S. A. "Transferring Power in the Family Business." *Harvard Business Review*, 1976, 54(4), 105-114.

Beckhard, R., and Dyer, W.,Jr. "Managing Change in the Family Firm-Issues and Strategies." *Sloan Management Review*, 1983,24, 59-65.

Berg, D., and Smith, K. (eds.). *Exploring Clinical Methods for Social Science Research.* Newbury Park, Calif.: Sage, 1985.

Bernstein, P. *Family Ties, Corporate Bonds.* Troy, Mo.: Holt, Rinehart & Winston, 1985.

Birley, S. "Succession in the Family Firm: The Inheritor's View." *Journal of Small Business Management*, 1986,24, 36-43.

Blotnick, S. "The Case Of the Reluctant Heirs." *Forbes*, 1984,134, 180.

Christensen, C. *Management Succession in Small and Growing Enterprises.* Boston: Division of Research, Harvard Business School, 1953.

Churchill, N. C., and Hatten, K.J. "Non-Market-Based Transfers of Wealth and Power: A Research Framework for Family Businesses." *American Journal of Small Business*, 1987,11 (3), 51-64.

Correll, R. W. "Facing Up to Moving Forward: A Third-Generation Successor's Reflections." *Family Business Review*, 1989,2(1), 17-29.

Crane, M. A. "How to Keep Families from Feuding." *Inc.*, Feb. 1982, pp. 73-74, 78-79.

Danco, L. *Inside the Family Business.* Cleveland: University Press, 1980.

Danco, L. *Beyond Survival: A Guide for the Business Owner and His Family.* Cleveland: University Press, 1982.

Davis, P. "The Influence of Life Stage on Father-Son Work Relationships in Family Companies." Unpublished doctoral dissertation, Harvard Business School, 1982.

Davis, P. "Realizing the Potential of the Family Business." *Organizational Dynamics*, 1983,12(1), 47-56.

Davis, S. "Entrepreneurial Succession." *Administrative Science Quarterly*, 1968,13, 402-416.

Dumas, C. "Succession Dyads in Family-Owned Businesses: A Comparison of Sons and Daughters." Paper presented at the Research Day Of the Family Firm Institute Conference, Boston, Oct. 1988.

Dumas, C. "Preparing the New CEO: Managing the Father-Daughter Succession Process in Family Business." *Family Business Review*, 1990, 3(3), 169-181.

Erikson, E. *Childhood and Society.* New York: Norton, 1963.

Friedman, S. D. "Sibling Relationships and Intergenerational Succession in Family Firms." *Family Business Review*, 1991, 4(1), 3-20.

Gallo, M. A., and Pont, C. G. "The Family Business in the Spanish Economy." Paper presented at the Research Day of the Family Firm Institute Conference, Boston, Oct. 1988.

Glaser, B. G., and Strauss, A. L. *The Discovery of Grounded Theory*. Hawthorne, N.Y.: Aldine, 1967.

Gould, R. *Transformations*. New York: Simon & Schuster, 1978.

Hall, D. T. *Careers in Organizations*. Pacific Palisades, Calif.: Goodyear, 1976.

Handler, W. C. "Succession in Family Firms: A Mutual Role Adjustment Between Entrepreneur and Next-Generation Family Members." *Entrepreneurship Theory and Practice*, 1990, 15(1), 37-51

Handler, W. C., and Kram, K. E. "Succession in Family Firms: The Problem of Resistance." *Family Business Review*, 1988,1(4), 361-381.

"International Perspectives on Family Business." *Family Business Review*, 1991, 4 (entire issue 2) .

Jonovic, D. *The Second Generation Boss*. Ottawa, IL.: Jameson Press, 1982.

Kets de Vries, M.F.R. "The Dark Side of Entrepreneurship." *Harvard Business Review*, 1985,63, 160-167.

Kram, K. E. *Mentoring at Work: Developmental Relationships in Organizational Life*. Glenview, IL.: Scott, Foresman, 1985.

Lansberg, I. S. *Program for the Study of Family Firms: Survey on Succession and Continuity*. New Haven, Conn.: School of Organization and Management, Yale University, 1986.

Lansberg, I. S. "The Succession Conspiracy." *Family Business Review*, 1988,1 (2), 119-143.

Levinson, H. "Conflicts That Plague the Family Business." *Harvard Business Review*, 1971,49, 9 > 98.

Levinson, H. "Don't Choose Your Own Successor." *Harvard Business Review*, 1974,52, 5342.

Levinson, D. J., and others. *Seasons of a Man's Life*. New York: Knopf, 1978.

Longenecker,J. G., and Schoen, J. E. "An Empirical Investigation of Pre-Entry Socialization of Successors for Leadership in Family-Controlled Businesses." Paper presented at Management Perspectives on Organizational Effectiveness, Southern Management Association Meetings, 1975.

Longenecker,J. G., and Schoen, J. E. "Management Succession in the Family Business." *Journal of Small Business Management*, 1978,16, 14.

Malone, S. C. "Selected Correlates of Business Continuity Planning in the Family Business." *Family Business Review*, 1989,2(4), 341-353.

Miller, E.J., and Rice, A. K. *Systems of Organization*. London: Tavistock, 1967.

Nelton, S. "Making Sure Your Business Outlasts You." *Nation's Business*, Jan. 1986, pp. 32-38.

Okochi, A., and Yasuoka, S. (eds.). "Family Business in the Era of Industrial Growth: Its Ownership and Management." Proceedings of the Fuji conference. Tokyo: University of Tokyo Press, 1984.

Patrick, A. "Family Business: The Offsprings' Perception of Work Satisfaction and Their Working Relationship with Their Father." Unpublished doctoral dissertation, Fielding Institute,1985.

Rogal, K. H. "Obligation or Opportunity: How Can Could-Be Heirs Assess Their Position?" *Family Business Review*, 1989,2(3), 237-255.

Rosenblatt, P. C., de Mik, L., Anderson, R. M., and Johnson, P. A. *The Family in Business: Understanding and Dealing with the Challenges Entrepreneurial Families Face*. San Francisco: Jossey-Bass, 1985.

Schein, E. H. *Career Dynamics*. Reading, Mass.: Addison-Wesley, 1978.

Schein, E. H. "The Role of the Founder in the Creation of Organizational Culture." *Organizational Dynamics*, 1983,12(1), 13-28.

Schein, E. H. *The Clinical Perspective in Fieldwork*. Newbury Park, Calif.: Sage, 1987.

Stempler, G. "The Study of Succession in Family Owned Businesses." Unpublished doctoral dissertation, George Washington University, 1988.

Super, D. E., and others. *Vocational Development: A Framework for Research*. New York: Teachers College Press, 1957.

Thomassen, A. J. "Succession in Family Business." Paper presented at the Research Day of the Family Firm Institute Conference, Boston, Oct. 1988.

Vaillant, G. *Adaptation to Life*. Boston: Little, Brown, 1977.

Ward, J. L. *Keeping the Family Business Healthy: How to Plan for Continuing Growth, Profitability, and Family Leadership*. San Francisco: Jossey-Bass, 1987.

Williamson, D. S., Bray, J. H., and Malone, P. E. *Personal Authority in the Family System Questionnaire*. Houston: Houston Family Institute, 1982.

Zaleznik A. and Kets de Vries. M.F.R. *Power and the Corporate Mind*. Chicago: Bonus, 1985.

How does the next generation earn legitimacy in the family firm? How do offspring gain credibility? This report on interviews with 30 family business executives suggests that to succeed, boss's children should 1) Start early with summer jobs; 2) demonstrate competence by sound handling of day-to-day work and decisions; 3) take time – five to ten years – to gain thorough knowledge of all aspects of the business. Alternatively, next generation executives sometimes gain credibility through innovative behavior that improved current operations. Even in cases where innovators' actions hastened executive credibility, however, the groundwork was laid with experience gained through day-to-day work. Exploring the advantages and disadvantages of low-level vs. delayed entry strategies, the authors point out the risks involved in the approach usually advocated by family business experts.

Entry of the Next Generation: Strategic Challenge for Family Business

By Jeffrey A. Barach, Joseph Gantisky, James A. Carson, Benjamin A. Doochin

Planning for the integration of the younger generation into the family firm is an issue of strategic importance, although offering chat cages and finding a place for younger family members, or adjusting the organization to the new generation's inputs and demands are issues not usually included as goals for sound business planning.[1] In fact, business theorists generally point out the drawbacks of constraining business decisions by any criteria other than profit. While arguments can be made both for and against nepotism,[2] Harry Levinson, who has written thoughtfully about family businesses, notes:

> It is obvious common sense that when managerial decisions are influenced by feelings about and responsibilities toward relatives in the business, when nepotism exerts a negative influence, and when a company is run more to honor a family tradition than for its own needs and purposes, there is likely to be trouble.[3]

For owner-manager firms, successful integration of offspring into the firm is almost always an issue. As one family business owner said:

> I started this firm to gain freedom and security not available elsewhere. The success I have had is something I would like to pass on to my children. I hope they come into the firm, but they must have the patience to learn the business before they take over.

Patience is a two-way street. To succeed in transferring the business to their offspring, family business CEOs must be ready to adjust the organization to the skills, perspectives, and values of the next generation as part of the implementation of strategy. The successful integration of new family members is a goal for many family firms as important as profit targets, business niches, and other determinants of the firm's business policy. Incorporating new family members into the firm, however, is complicated by the blurring of the boundaries between the family and the family business.[4]

Strategy for the owner-managed firm requires that economic success be achieved in a context that includes presently and prospectively employed family members. Owner/managers have often changed their organization's structure to reflect the needs of children entering the business. For example, entrepreneurial firms have been structured to provide territories for siblings in the firm; and separate divisions have been started in some firms to give offspring a place to thrive under the family banner.[5] It can sometimes be beneficial to split the original firm into a family of enterprises in order to achieve the twin goals of family continuity and financial success.

Owner/managers of family businesses face the dual challenges of rearing children who want to join the family business and to shape a work environment where the young person can "earn legitimacy": the confidence and ability to make significant contributions and the trust of others.

The purpose of this article is to report the results of interviews with executives in family businesses in order to explore ways in which the introduction of family members can be accomplished successfully. In this context, "success" refers to favorable outcomes for both the family members and the firm. The focus of the analysis is on how the next generation achieves a position of power within the firm, not necessarily on replacement of the older generation. This process is termed "earning legitimacy."

Background

Earning Legitimacy

The present article reviews the literature on entry strategies and presents results from interviews with 30 family business executives. The interviews focused on strategies for gaining credibility once the family offspring entered the firm. These can be classified as career paths which are primarily innovative or non-innovative. The various career strategies were examined in the light of the situation that prevailed in the firm.

Early writing described legitimacy as based on such factors as tradition, attitudes about the propriety of a particular order, or a rational belief in a particular social structure.[6] Legitimacy, for purposes of this article, has both tangible and intangible elements, most of which must be present before legitimacy can be said to be achieved. Both the boss and scion must feel the scion has executive status. The scion must feel that he or she plans an important role in the firm, and not only the boss (whether father, mother, or relative), but other family members, employees and significant others must see the scion as having earned rather than inherited the responsibility and respect of his or her position. This legitimacy is demonstrated to the potential successor by the actions of others.

Literature Review

Many writers have suggested strategies for the younger generation's entry into the family firm. Most agree that children should work elsewhere early in their careers.[7] Some writers have pointed out that entry into the family business via summer or low-level jobs is less than ideal in creating the image of a competent leader in the eyes of other employees, customers, and other groups significant to the transition. Yet 80 to 90 percent of fam-

Exhibit 1. Succession in the Family Business

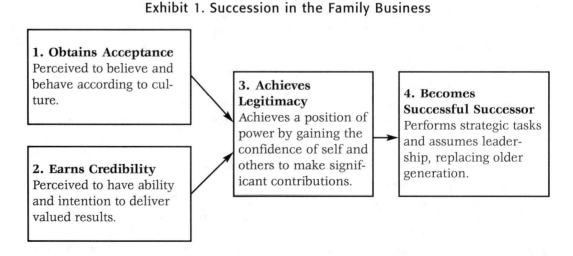

1. Obtains Acceptance
Perceived to believe and behave according to culture.

2. Earns Credibility
Perceived to have ability and intention to deliver valued results.

3. Achieves Legitimacy
Achieves a position of power by gaining the confidence of self and others to make significant contributions.

4. Becomes Successful Successor
Performs strategic tasks and assumes leadership, replacing older generation.

ily members do enter the firm through summer jobs or low-level employment.

Sathe advised managers in general to be aware of the level of acceptance and credibility they enjoy in the organization, with acceptance defined as "the extent to which others perceive one believes and behaves as prescribed by the culture," and credibility as "the perception of others in the organization of his or her ability and intention to deliver valued results."[8] Sathe feels that long-term success may be determined by the level of acceptance and credibility the scion has achieved. He concludes that acceptance and credibility are achieved independently of each other, but neither alone is sufficient for success.

Credibility can be the key to legitimacy. If the older and younger generations are not willing to accept each other, and if they do not recognize each others' abilities, then successful entry to the firm may be impossible. Credibility is therefore crucial to successful integration into the firm. Without credibility, the potential successor cannot attain legitimacy (see exhibit 1).

Christensen has noted that:

> The newcomer must be able to prove his ability to the other executives and win their confidence. In their eyes, at least, he is on trial. Although he has legal authority of the name and future ownership, [of the firm] he must earn the real respect of his associates. The father can appoint the son to the office, but he cannot force acceptance by the organization.[9]

How a family member enters the firm affects credibility, and therefore the attainment of legitimacy. Donald Jonovic proposes these rules:

1. The child should work elsewhere and act as if he or she did not have the family firm to fall back on
2. He or she should be treated like any other employee, instead of as the heir to the company throne.[10]

This rationale for working outside the family firm is justified, Jonovic says, because "an entry-level successor is not just a new employee in the office. He is the next vice-president or the next president. What would be normal mistakes for anybody else will be looked upon as signs of incompetence."

Most successors join the family firm upon completing their education. MBAs who come from families which own businesses usually say they don't intend to join the family firm when they graduate, but when they get their degrees, most do go on to Work for the family firm at some point.[11] (Jonovic notes that almost 85 percent of ad successors go to work for the family firm immediately after graduation.)[12]

Tagiuri and Davis counsel delay in entering the family firm due to the stressful period of the life-cycle which the CEO may be experiencing, pointing out that as the successor is finishing college, the parent may be in his or her early forties-a time when many business owners (and others) evaluate their accomplishments and look to the future. When business owners enter their fifties, they have generally weathered this crisis and are better able to teach the successor about the management of the business.[13]

There are strategic reasons for determining the timing of both entry into the firm and succession to power. Barnes and Hershon show how strategic changes can facilitate succession.[14] Well planned strategic changes can also create a place for the next generation. The timing of strategic events can pressure an offspring into the firm or allow time for broader experience. A variety of reasons are offered for why the potential successor should delay his or her entry into the family firm. The basis for most is that the delay permits a gain in outside experience and objective recognition. But there are problems with the "outside entry" thesis. One is that expertise developed elsewhere may be less valuable in the family business than in other locations; it may conflict with existing resources and/or the power structure of the family business; or it may not be needed at all at the time of entering the family business. (Later, however that expertise could provide management flexibility in the face of strategic challenges.)

It would appear, however, that summer and low-level jobs can often be a viable strategy for entering family firms-one which can work when the potential successor can devel-

BARACH, GANTISKY,
CARSON, DOOCHIN

op relevant expertise in a fashion consistent with the culture, resources, and priorities of the firm.

By entering the family firm through summer jobs and low-level employment, credibility can be achieved in the eyes of those important to the success of the new entrant. This manner of entry can also provide the successor with knowledge of the firm's operations which helps generate a feeling of confidence and respect.

A summary of the advantages and disadvantages of two common entry strategies (low-level and delayed entry) is depicted in exhibit 2.

Sample and Method

Family executives in thirty family businesses were questioned at length on their ideas about optimal succession strategies and about their own succession. Since the selection was necessarily based on accessibility and willingness to cooperate, the sample cannot be considered random. However, the businesses represented a wide cross-section of firm types and sizes. Nine had fewer than 50 employees; eleven had between 50 and 200, and eight had over 200. Annual sales ranged from under $10 million to more than $50 million. The businesses were equally divided between those in second generation of leadership and those which were moving into the third.

There is a natural bias in the sample toward success, since only those family members who had made a successful transition into the business and those businesses which had successfully weathered the transition have survived to give the interviews. No data ar available from this study on businesses which failed.

The interviews were designed to yield insight into the following four propositions:

Proposition I: Summer and low-level jobs are viable ways for future managers to begin learning the business and earning respect.

Proposition II: Most successful managers and entrants advocate a non-innovative career path, earning legitimacy by "learning the ropes and not rocking the boat," except in uncertain situations.

Exhibit 2. Comparison of Entry Strategies for Succession in Family Business

Low-Level Entry Strategy

Advantages	Disadvantages
1. Intimate familiarity with the nature of the business and employees is acquired.	1. Conflict results when owner has difficulty in teaching or relinquishing control to successor.
2. Skills specifically required by the business are developed.	2. Normal mistakes tend to be viewed as incompetence in the successor.
3. Exposure to others in the business facilitates acceptance and the achievement of credibility.	3. Knowledge of the environment is limited and risks of inbreeding are incurred.

Delayed Entry Strategy

Advantages	Disadvantages
1. Successor's skills are judged with greater objectivity.	1. Specific expertise and understanding of organization's key success factors and culture may be lacking.
2. Development of self-confidence and growth independent of familial influence are achieved.	2. Set patterns of outside activity may conflict with those prevailing in the family firm.
3. Outside success established credibility and serves as a basis for accepting the successor as a competent executive.	3. Resentment may result when successors are advanced ahead of long-term employees.
4. Perspective of the business environment is broadened.	

Proposition III: In times of transition or uncertainty, innovative behavior may be a means of bypassing the slow path to credibility.

Proposition IV: Prior, successful non-innovative behavior may place the entrant in a position to innovate successfully.

Results

Start Early

Of those offspring who joined the firm after having summer jobs, most felt that they were received favorably by employees. Furthermore, they showed strong agreement on how to start a successor in the business (even among those who themselves entered through management positions). They agreed that they would introduce their heirs via summer jobs, a finding which supports Proposition I.

Several successors who began their involvement with the family firm in summer jobs felt they gained valuable insight into the basic operation of the firm that could not be gained in management position. As one stated: "Washing grease off nuts and bolts didn't teach me much, but I learned a lot about the mentality of the people who worked on production lines that way."

Slow and Steady Wins the Race

Ninety percent of the interviewees advocated a succession strategy whereby the newcomer earns credibility "by having the necessary experience to do the job better than anyone who could be hired." All agreed that the potential successor should "demonstrate competence," and 92 percent agreed that the potential successor should "earn spurs." Nine to one, respondents advocated sound handling of day-to-day work and decisions, rather than innovative behavior, as a proper means of gaining credibility.

Time to Credibility

There were differences in the time taken to achieve credibility. The average, in the judgment of interviewees, was five years (for those who followed the non-innovative path); two years for those using innovative behavior. But these differences did not depend on prior outside work experience-the average for those with and without prior experience was the same-four years. In some instances, however, the process can take longer, as observed by one who entered the firm as its chief executive: "It takes about ten years before employees defer to your knowledge instead of your position." The point made was that it may take a very long period before the successor gains thorough knowledge of all aspects of the business.

The Innovators

A minority of next-generation executives attained credibility through innovative behavior early in their careers with the family firm. Two who did innovate told of experiences that support the proposition that innovative behavior may be a good means of establishing credibility in times of change. One executive who joined the firm during a time of adversity said, "No one knew what was going on. I applied cost accounting stuff I learned in school, just basic things. It made me look like a star. From then on Dad listened to me; everyone listened to me." Another executive implemented simple marketing techniques which saved a major unit of the family firm.

There are pitfalls in attempting to be innovative before credibility is well established, but the executives who achieved credibility through initial innovative behavior brought something to the firm which improved current operations. It is probably easier to do this during times of high flexibility, when the firm can afford to pursue new ideas, or during times of turbulence, when change is necessary.

Earning the "Right to Innovate"

In the interviews, the executives were asked, "Did you have a critical incident or turning point in your career?" This was asked immediately after asking how credibility was achieved. One respondent captured the tone of all participants. After stating that he had gained credibility through day-to-day work, he described a critical incident in his career. "I worked on all the background for the introduction of a new product line. Suddenly I became the expert on what no one else knew about. But I never would have been given the project if I had not proven myself in the past." This statement demonstrates the feeling among many successful successors that experience gained through day-to-day work prepares the way to grasp opportunities for innovation, supporting Proposition IV.

Discussion and Conclusions

The data base was not sufficient to draw any conclusions about management level entrants, but data for those entering through summer and low-level employment were sufficient to permit some inferences.

Most future successors join the family firm immediately after completing their education. One viable strategy is to use summer and low-level jobs as methods of entry. Most writers in the field argue for the rarer course of external employment after school and prior to working for the family firm, a course which has value for numerous reasons. In many cases, the young person may not feel a sense of personal accomplishment or self-confidence in a family environment, and thus should start out independently. Non-family firms may provide more objective opportunity and judgment of a young person's achievement. Experience in other companies can also provide a broader perspective on business and develop capacity to adapt to radical environmental change. Furthermore, achievement on the outside can win the entrant credibility and respect when joining the family firm.

What is not considered by advocates of this course, however, is that the young family member entering from the outside and transferring credibility can also make mistakes. These mistakes may be damaging for an outsider not yet familiar with the intricate operations and relations of the firm. After a brief honeymoon, he or she may fail to develop a support system among managers and employees. To regain credibility after a mistake is more difficult than building it day by day. For this reason, early exposure to the family business may be as critical for those coming into the firm after outside experience as for those who enter just after college.

The successor with experience from summer and low-level jobs has had the opportunity to become familiar with the business and its workers, and to build a central network within the ongoing organization. One family firm executive stated: "Everyone who intends to enter the family business should get some early experience from that business. You need to know what's going on and you learn by being there."

The real importance of succession strategies is their impact on the strategic planning of the firm. The founder must determine whether or not his or her children will play a role in the firm. If the answer is "no," arrangements should be made to hire professional management or sell the business. If the answer is "yes," one must determine how to arrange for the entry of the younger generation. This article does not argue for the desirability of one entry strategy over the other in specific cases. Such decisions as how to bring family members into the firm must be made by weighing the numerous and complex criteria which affect the likelihood of success in each instance.

But it can be argued that succeeding generations can achieve legitimacy in family firms by rising through summer and low-level jobs, as well as by gaining credentials outside the firm. Whichever entry strategy is used, an early introduction to the firm through low-level and summer jobs may be desirable by giving successors a valuable working knowledge of the firm.

CEOs of family firms and their successors can benefit from thoughtful career planning for the next generation, because goals of both the firm and the individual are involved. Care given to the career path of the next generation is an essential part of the implementation strategy of family firms.

Notes

1. D. M. Ambrose, "Transfer of the Family-Owned Business," *Journal of Small Business Management*, (January 1983), pp. 49-56.

2. D. W. Erwing, "Is Nepotism So Bad?" *Harvard Business Review*, (January/ February, 1965), pp. 22-40 and 156-160.

3. H. Levinson, "Conflicts That Plague Family Businesses," *Harvard Business Review* (March/April 1971), pp. 90-98.

4. For a more thorough discussion of familial factors in business, see the fob lowing: P. Davis and D. Stern, "Adaption, Survival, and Growth of the Family Business: An Integrated Systems Perspective," *Human Relations*, vol. 34 no. 4 (1980), pp. 207-224; W. G. Dyer, Jr., *Cultural Change in Family Firms: Anticipating and Managing Business and Family Transitions* (San Francisco: Jossey Bass, 1986); P. G. Holland and W. R. Boulton, "Balancing the 'Family' and 'Business' in Family Business," *Business Horizons*, Vol. 27, no.2 (1984), pp. 16-21; and E. Kepner, "The Family and the Firm: A Coevolutionary Perspective," *Organizational Dynamics*, vol. 49, no. 2 (1983), pp. 57-70.

5. J.A. Barach, "Is There a Cure for the Paralyzed Family Board?" *Sloan Management Review* (Fall 1984), pp. 312.

6. J. P. R. French, Jr., and B. Raven, "The Bases of Social Power," *Studies in Social Power*, ed. D. Cartwright (Ann Arbor: University of Michigan, 1959); Max Weber, *On Charisma and Institution Building*, (Chicago: The University of Chicago Press, 1986).

7. See, for example, Renato Tagiuri and John Davis, "Life Stages and Father-Son Work Relationships," Working Paper 9-784-026 (Boston: Division of Research, Harvard Business School, 1984); Leon Danco, *Beyond Survival*, 5th ed. (Cleveland: The University Press, 1979); and "A Lot of Enterprise Is Staying in the Family These Days," *Business Week* (July 1, 1985), pp. 62-63.

8. V. Sathe, *Culture and Related Corporate Realities* (Homewood, III.: R. D. Irwin, Inc., 1985), pp. 264-261.

9. R. C. Christensen, *Management Success in Small and Growing Enterprises* (New York. Arno Press, 1979), p. 182.

10. Donald Jonovic, *The Second Generation Boss* (Cleveland: The University Press, 1982), pp. 113-115.

11. W. Kiechel, "How to Relate to Nepotism," *Fortune* (Feb. 6, 1984), pp. 143-144

12. Jonovic, *The Second Generation Boss*, p. 99.

13. Tagiuri and Davis, "Life Stages and Father-Son Work Relationships."

14. L B. Barnes and S. A. Hershon, "Transferring Power in the Family Business," *Harvard Business Review* (July/August 1976), pp. 105-114.

A universal disparity in values exists around the use of time and money between first and second generations in family businesses. This "silver spoon syndrome" is a prime source of conflict. To combat the syndrome, have children work elsewhere before joining the family business and set clear guidelines and evaluation criteria upon entry.

Silver Spoon Syndrome

By Barbara S. Hollander

A common saying in the world of family business is "shirt sleeves to shirt sleeves in three generations." The generalized scenario is that the first generation makes it, the second generation spends it, and the third generation buries it.

As I have worked with family business members over time, this old saw has been both proven and disproven. However, what seems universal is the seeming disparity in values around the use of time and money between the first and second generation members in a family firm. This seems to emerge as a prime source of conflict between founder and successor.

Folklore blames the successor – pointing to lack of healthy work ethic, commitment, twisted values, and the generalized "born with a silver spoon in the mouth" syndrome. Indeed, I often see behaviors which reinforce these notions.

However, the damning of the second generation needs to be looked at as an outcropping of a process rather than an intentional revolt.

What I often see in the family-held corporation that contributes to the "silver spoon syndrome" is the seeming inability of the founder to take a stand where it counts. Undoubtedly, there is most often ample advice about car allowances, paper clips, what color tie to wear, how often to call Mom or Grandma. What I often don't see are guidelines and ground rules around expectations for performance, feedback, mentoring, training, and career development goals.

The lack of these all important guidelines seems to be traceable to a common dynamic. Often, the "old man" as we affectionately call the founder, was an absentee father. This became and continues as an issue in the family. The founder has been blamed repeatedly for lack of attention to family matters, particularly as the children were growing up. Mom was the disciplinarian.

The entry of the second generation into the business may indeed be the first time that the founder is primarily responsible for discipline or guidance. Often, founders feel guilty about their previous absenteeism. To compensate, they offer free rein to the entrant. I call this the "nosing around" training program. The next generation is invited to sniff around and identify an area where they would like to work. Little guidance and few ground rules are established at the outset. The next generation often flounders as a result.

Another aspect of the reluctance of the founder to take a stand on the big issues often has to do with Mom. The demands of the founding of the business (in second generation businesses, at this point in time, most founders have been males) have left his spouse with most of the home responsibilities. She has learned to focus on them as intently as he has learned to focus on the business. Taking on junior, therefore, often seems to mean taking on Mom, who is often highly invested in the progress and success of the next generation, and may have some different ideas about the management of the offspring.

In the face of these powerful forces, the founder backs off. The next generation swims around in the business often without direction and therefore accomplishment. The founder complains about shortcomings and the successor feels less and less competent. The cycle escalates to the point where the successor develops a "what the hell" attitude, the onset of the "silver spoon" syndrome.

How to Break the Cycle

Some antidotes to this cycle are the following:

1. The successor spends the first few years of his/her career working outside the family business, perhaps in a related field.
2. Upon entry, guidelines, ground rules, expectations are established based on acceptable business practices, and all key parties are informed, including Mom.
3. A mentoring relationship is established and encouraged. The mentor may be a key person in the business, not in line for succession.
4. Periodic evaluation and discussion of progress about business performance and working relationships is scheduled.
5. Criteria for being a "good son or daughter" are distinguished from criteria for being an effective manager.

Reprinted with permission. Originally printed in *In Business*, March/April, 1987. Copyright 1987, Barbara S. Hollander. All rights reserved.

A psychological disease afflicts many who inherit wealth. Characterized by lack of motivation, low self-esteem and loneliness, the author of this article calls it "affluenza." It results in those who have the opportunity to live "the good life" to do so without purpose or enthusiasm Worse, it too frequently results in drug abuse, divorce or even suicide. Psychologists estimate that as many as 80 percent of heirs have problems with their inherited wealth.

Affluenza

By Robert Farago

Carl contemplated the plunging Alpine slope. One little push and the sole inheritor of an $8-million stock portfolio would be flying down an endless carpet of hip-deep snow. Carl would then be free-free from the aimlessness, the doubt, and the failed relationships that had plagued him since he graduated from Harvard University in 1977. The fact that the ski slope was strictly off-limits – a well-known avalanche hazard – only added to the appeal.

"I had a real death wish," Carl admits. "I'd never come to terms with whom I was or what I wanted from life. My net worth was somehow always more important than my self-worth."

In a very real sense, Carl was not alone on that mountaintop. Every day, thousands of young inheritors face identical problems: lack of motivation, low self-esteem and loneliness. Society might callously dismiss them with a sarcastic comment such as "poor little rich kids," but these young men and women often face serious-sometimes life threatening-psychological trauma. Carl was not the first troubled inheritor to risk his life for a moment of escape. Nor is he likely to be the last.

There is an epidemic of profound unhappiness among young inheritors. Lurid media stories about rich kids' drug abuse, violence, and perversion reveal but the most obvious evidence of their deep troubles. Spend some time in any one of 100 affluent U.S. suburbs from Long Island to Bel Air. Talk to middle-aged parents. Soon you'll hear strikingly similar stories about children who drift from job to job, marriage to marriage-kids who live the "good life" without apparent purpose or enthusiasm. This condition is as socially pervasive as it is individually devastating. Yet it's also treatable and preventable. Thanks to those who are addressing the problems of inherited wealth, "it" now has a name: affluenza.

"About four out of five (heirs) have problems with major inherited wealth," claims psychologist John Levy. "The problems are essentially inevitable."

Levy, director of San Francisco's Carl G. Jung Institute, is also an independent consultant on inherited wealth; he has spent five years investigating the psychology of inheritance. Levy began his study at the urging of a father who was worried about his offspring's unhappiness. Suspecting that his children's generous inheritance somehow caused their depression, the concerned parent paid Levy $20,000 to study the wider implications of inherited wealth. After talking with money managers, psychologists, psychiatrists, and more than 30 Bay area inheritors, Levy compiled his findings in "Coping with Inherited Wealth," an unpublished article.

Levy's research indicates that inheritance is a mixed blessing. Inherited wealth often buys children a reprieve from the aggravations of earning a weekly paycheck. It opens up a world of fulfilling, noncommercial career possibilities – everything from painting to public service. Yet unearned money can also shield inheritors from the financial and emotional challenges that are critical to developing self-confidence and maturity. Using their bankroll as a cushion against hardship, emotionally immature inheritors simply walk away from careers and relationships that require serious commitment. As a result, they often feel board, lonely, and listless.

"If I had to boil it down, these inheritors lack self-esteem," Levy says. "You have to meet challenges to feel good about yourself. If you have a lot of inherited money, you're never quite sure if you could exist without it."

Simply put, affluenza stems from too much, too soon. John Sedgewick, author of *Rich Kids*, compares the stress experienced by poorly adjusted inheritors to an overwhelming Christmas.

"It's like coming downstairs Christmas morning and instead of finding a few presents, suddenly facing a whole roomful" he says. "To say the least, it's very unsettling."

Many Americans dream of such a bounty or of a distant relative suddenly leaving them a large fortune. They imagine a life of leisure-a life free from everyday struggle and toil. What they fail to consider is the barrage of emotional moral and financial questions inheritance brings with it. Jennifer's experience is typical.

"When I turned 18, I got a call from my trust of finer," she recalls. "In these nice somber tones he quietly informed me that I was now worth $2 million. I said, oh, that's great. No one in my family had ever discussed money with me, so it just wasn't real.

"Suddenly I had to make all these decisions. Should I work 9 to 5? Should I work for money? Who controls my money? What are all these papers they want me to sign? What kind of investments do I want to make? How much do I spend? Where do I live?

"Then the deeper issues surfaced. Should I tell my friends? Who do I trust? Do I deserve this money? For years I had no idea what to do."

Compounding the problem, less-affluent people and the media view inheritors' psychological stress with little or no sympathy. "Most people believe that if they only had enough money they would live in a state of constant bliss," Levy explains.

"They tend to respond disdainfully to any suffering by the affluent, particularly if these people didn't earn their fortunes," he says. "For the inheritors that means they feel badly and think they shouldn't feel this way."

The contagious respiratory disease influenza got its name because it was believed to be influenced by the stars. Abandoning superstitious astrology in favor of rational analysis was the first step to devising a cure. So, too, inheritors often view their unearned money as being "heaven-sent" – the fruits of a divine birth lottery – and thus feel that the attendant problems are inescapable.

For affluenza-stricken inheritors who are willing to take a good look at themselves and for parents who don't want their money to ruin their children's lives, professional help is available. A growing cadre of therapists and money managers is sensitive to the problems inheritors face and is skilled at finding solutions. Locating a sympathetic listener who is familiar with the problems of inherited wealth is the first step to recovery.

"The first thing to do," counsels San Francisco psychologist, author, and teacher Judy Barber, "is to articulate the problem so a therapist can understand. Say 'I need someone who's willing to talk to me about practical reality as well as symbolic meaning.'

"Many psychologists say money is symbolic and ignore practical realities," she says. "They don't want to consider budgets, taxes, or wills. They don't understand trusts or the mechanics of inherited wealth."

Inheritors face two sets of overlapping issues: financial and psychological. Separating the two may not only be impractical, but undesirable. Says Barber: "I had a woman client – a teacher in her mid-30s. She received a large portfolio from her father that included substantial holdings in nuclear power plants. Her father didn't approve of her academic lifestyle and she didn't approve of the nuclear stocks.

"She wanted to invest in something she loved: oriental rugs. But guilt and a sense that the money wasn't really hers prevented her from acting.

"After counseling, she decided to confront her father first. Eventually," Barber continues, "she made more money in oriental rugs than she had with the stocks. In the end their relationship improved."

When a donating parent or grandparent is still alive, such issues of control can arise. As Jennifer discovered, however, even independently controlled inheritance brings family relationships sharply into focus. Frequently major inherited wealth arrives after a parent's or grandparent's death – the culmination of a lifetime of work. When trying to administer what they consider "my family's money," inheritors can feel guilty or just plain incompetent. Therapists need to consider an inheritor's family relationships as well as their financial experience or, more commonly, lack of experience.

Inheritors who are reasonably secure with the circumstances of their inheritance still may need money advice that is tailored to their emotional needs. Even therapists like Barber, who specializes in the psychology of money, don't recommend particular investments or investment strategies. That task falls to money managers, financial planners, and trust officers. However, all too often these professionals fail to consider their clients' state of mind. The result: confrontation, miscommunication, apathy – in short, more affluenza.

Lawrence A. Krause, owner of a San Francisco-based personal financial planning service, maintains that inheriting money forces heirs to assume responsibilities they may not be ready to handle, which in turn creates anxiety. Unless inheritors' financial advisers are sensitive to the often-hidden psychological motivations of their clients, financial advice falls on deaf or uncooperative ears.

"Sooner or later most people who inherit money they're not used to become insecure," Krause says.

"I had one client who was earning about $50,000 a year. One day he inherited $2 million. When he became a client, he had a very hard time writing checks for $100,000 or $200,000. That would aggravate some financial planners, but they have to realize that if a client has a $50,000-a-year mentality, he needs to mature into the million-dollar mentality. It's not easy."

San Francisco tax attorney David L. Gibson concurs: "Sometimes inheritors put off issues of inheritance. They don't file tax returns, pretending the responsibility doesn't exist. I kept seeing clients who'd get things fixed up, then go right back and get them messed up again. I began to understand that these problems came from unresolved emotional questions. My background and training as a tax lawyer didn't prepare me for dealing with the emotional issues around money."

The success of Victoria Felton-Collins' financial planning service is proof that inheritors want money managers with training in psychology. Says Collins, a psychologist and a certified Financial Planner: "My counseling background helps me understand what my clients' goals really are. Then I can help translate those goals into a financial strategy."

Most money managers are problem solvers who focus on the bottom line. It's no surprise then that they have trouble dealing with inheritors who have ambivalent feelings about money. In order to shake the affluenza paralysis, inheritors must learn not to assume that financial advisers are better qualified than they are to make the final investment decisions.

Inheritors must begin by examining their own values and taking control. Obviously they have a better chance of finding a cure for their malady if they establish a relationship of mutual respect with a sensitive financial professional

Collins recommends inheritors interview three or four planners to find one with whom they can develop a sense of security. This, she says, is "one of the best investments an inheritor can make."

Inheritors who start actively managing their money soon find they need a whole new set of skills in order to communicate with their advisers. On one level they're unaccustomed to the jargon of the investment world. On a deeper level, like Barber's client, they confront for the first time the ethical questions raised by having wealth. Acquiring the communication skills and exploring their investment options often lead inheritors to the emotional support necessary to overcome affluenza.

More than a dozen ethical-investment foundations are administered nationwide. Philadelphia's Bread and Roses Community Fund, New York City's North Star Fund, San Francisco's Vanguard Public Foundation, and Boston's Haymarket People's Fund are examples of progressive groups that advise inheritors. They work with inheritors to stimulate social change through the support of grass roots organizations, environmental groups, and community causes. The groups also provide peer support and workshops that focus on their members' emotional needs.

"It's easier to call for investment information than to call and say, 'I'm having trouble dealing with my wealth,'" says inheritor Paul Haible, coordinator of Vanguard. "It's not easy to admit your problems with money when the whole society is set up to perpetuate wealth. But isolation is a real problem. When inheritors come in, they look around and say, 'Wow, a whole group of people I can talk to.'"

Curing affluenza is not just a matter of determining that it's OK to be rich. Inheritors must also confront the implications of having money-emotional, financial, and moral. If inherited wealth makes some people feel guilty, inheritors must address these feelings in order to live a happier life. Progressive funds demonstrate that society can benefit Tom inheritors who work to cure their affluenza.

"For an inheritor with a social conscience, guilt is an appropriate response," says Haymarket development coordinator Hillary Smith. "But at what point does the guilt become immobilization? Haymarket helps people become unstuck, to take responsibility and control of their lives. At the same time we help people who weren't born with as many advantages."

In addition to its grants, newsletters, and referral service, San Francisco's

Women's Foundation runs a Managing Inherited Wealth program. At a series of monthly meetings, attending female inheritors choose two discussion topics. The topics are evenly split between technical and emotional issues. On a typical evening, inheritors might choose Mutual Funds or Money and Relationships and Comparing Tax Strategies or Your Contribution to Social Change. Throughout emphasis is on empowerment-the need for women to take control of their lives and their money.

Affluenza can be cured. Unfortunately, only a small percentage of inheritors are willing or able to examine their unhappiness. The rest drift along, waiting and hoping for their lives to take direction. For parents, that's a very disturbing image. Money managers, psychologists, and other experts agree, however, that there's nothing intractable about affluenza; there's a great deal parents can do to spare their children this unenviable fate. Most of it, of course, is common sense

"Money is like sex to most people," says Levy. "It's something dirty they don't discuss in front of the kids. Parents need to prepare children to be inheritors. They need to tell kids about money from an early age."

Greg, like Jennifer, grew up disoriented "I never even knew where the money came from until I was a teenager," he says. "I mean, my dad put on a suit and tie and went downtown, but I never knew where or what he did. Whenever my family needed money he just wrote a check. When I came into my inheritance, it was like joining this club – except I didn't know the rules."

If Greg's parents didn't give him the skills he needed later in life, at least they were there to offer support. Many inheritors report an appalling lack of parenting. From his research for *Rich Kids*, Sedgewick is convinced that absentee parenthood is a major cause of affluenza. "If kids are being fobbed off with money or servants, it's going to really mess them up," he says. "Your psychological development is completely wound up in your parents. Parents need to spend quality time with their kids."

Then there is the money itself. Today, many wealthy parents are giving children their inheritance later, are spreading payments over a long period of time, and are reducing the size of the inheritance to a more sane, manageable amount; the rest usually goes to charity. These parents want their children to have certain important advantages-a house to live in, private education for their children-but not so many advantages that they won't find challenging work. They recognize that too much of a good thing-an overwhelming Christmas-is no good at all.

One millionaire father, a man who worked his way up from the streets of Brooklyn to the top level of a *Fortune* 500 company, puts it this way. "No way I want my kids to have to go through what I did. But I'm not giving them a Ferrari or trips to Club Med every other week, and I'm not leaving them the kind of money that buys those things. If they want that kind of extra, that's fine; let them earn it on their own.

"My responsibility is to keep them sane and happy. For that they need two things: love and some kind of job that makes them feel useful."

Affluenza may not be the scourge of the Western world. Yet realizing that there are psychological ramifications of wealth and that there is a limit to money's benefits is critical to understanding a productive economy. Eradicating affluenza – and saving the Carls of this world from an ugly and untimely end – mandates that everyone involved contemplate the true nature of money and how it affects their lives and the lives of those around them. As the committed inheritors at Vanguard and Bread and Roses will tell you, that kind of thinking is the first step to creating a better world for everyone.

One of the greatest dilemmas facing successful business families is dealing with the impact of wealth on children. As megabillionaire Curtis Carlson puts it "How the hell do we keep our money from destroying our kids?" When FORTUNE surveyed 30 multibillionaires, 20 percent planned to give their children minimal inheritances and half plan to leave as much to charity as to heirs. Many successful people fear that large inheritances will allow offspring to do nothing with their lives. Psychologists suggest that many wealthy children have little self-respect because they can't take much satisfaction from their accomplishments. Of course, not passing money to your children can also cause problems and resentment, particularly when the decision not to give is based on parental disapproval rather than understood principle.

When the legacy is a family business, estate planning is especially difficult. Keeping the business whole, in family hands and successful is very difficult. Strategies used by Chicago's Crown family and Colorado's Coors are presented.

Should You Leave It All to The Children?

By Richard I. Kirkland Jr.

Warren Buffett, 56, the chairman and guiding genius of Berkshire Hathaway, the phenomenally successful holding company, is worth at least $1.5 billion. But don't bother being jealous of his three children. Buffett does not believe that it is wise to bequeath great wealth and plans to give most of his money to his charitable foundation.

Having put his two sons and daughter through college, the Omaha investor contents himself with giving them several thousand dollars each at Christmas. Beyond that, says daughter Susan, 33, "If I write my dad a check for $20, he cashes it."

Buffett is not cutting his children out of his fortune because they are wastrels or wantons or refuse to go into the family business – the traditional reasons rich parents withhold money. Says he: "My kids are going to carve out their own place in this world, and they know I'm for them whatever they want to do." But he believes that setting up his heirs with "a lifetime supply of food stamps just because they came out of the right womb" can be "harmful" for them and is "an antisocial act." To him the perfect amount to leave children is "enough money so that they would feel they could do anything, but not so much that they could do nothing." For a college graduate, Buffett reckons "a few hundred thousand dollars" sounds about right.

How much should you leave the kids? Agonizing over that question is a peculiarly American obsession. In much of the world custom and law dictate that children, unless they have committed some heinous crime, automatically receive most of the parents' wealth when they die. Only Britain and her former colonies – common-law countries all – give property owners the freedom to leave their children whatever they want.

And nowhere is the feeling about inherited wealth so ambivalent as in the U.S. No country so readily celebrates the self-made man; no culture is more suspicious that the silver spoon contains something vaguely narcotic. Says Curtis L. Carlson, 72, the Minnesota travel and real estate magnate (Radisson Hotel Corp., TGI Fridays restaurants, and the Ask Mr. Foster travel agency), who has a net worth of $700 million and two married daughters: "There's nothing people like me worry about more – how the hell do we keep our money from destroying our kids?"

Certainly nowhere else in the world do so many parents enjoy the privilege of grappling with this dilemma. The Federal Reserve Board estimates that some 1.3 million U.S. households enjoy a net worth of at least $1 million. The vast majority of millionaires inherited their wealth or built it on a business they founded Plenty of corporate careerists have also racked up seven-figure estates by taking advantage of profit-sharing and pension plans. But concern for how best to provide for the offspring is not exclusive to the millionaires' club. Estate planning is fast becoming a major concern of the middle class.

Whatever their misgivings about inheritance, most Americans – rich, poor, or somewhere in between – keep the bulk of their estates in the family. Once formed, the chain of inherited wealth is rarely broken-until the money runs out. It has pretty much run out for some of the great names of U.S. business: the Dodges, Reynoldses, and Vanderbilts. The sons of Texas oil tycoon H. L. Hunt, whose fortune was once estimated at $8 billion, have just filed for bankruptcy protection for the family's corporate jewel, Placid Oil Co.

Of 30 multimillionaires recently surveyed by *Fortune*, six say their children will be better off with only minimal inheritances. Almost half plan to leave at least as much to charity as to their heirs. In an area where almost no research exists, Alexander Sanger, a partner with the law firm White and Case, New York, offers a revealing statistic. Of 20 wills Sanger has drawn up for newly-wealthy parents with net worths of $1 million or more, 16 left at least half their estates to charity. Of 12 comparable old-money estates, only one gave so much away.

Old money tends to keep its wealth in the family. "After a generation or more, inheritance becomes a stewardship kind of thing," says Alexander Forger, head of estate law at the New York firm Milbank Tweed Hadley & McCloy. Sometimes, as in the case of one of the firm's clients, the Rockefeller family, the progenitor already fattened some foundation with a big endowment years ago.

Even inheritors who want to give their money away feel dub-bound to pass on some of their wealth to their children. George Pillsbury Jr., 37, a scion of the Midwestern baking family, inherited more than $1 million while still in college. He has spent his adult life building and bankrolling a network of foundations that tap young inheritors for a variety of liberal causes. "Robin Hood was Right," declares one foundation pamphlet. Pillsbury believes in "much, much higher" inheritance taxes. Yet despite his politics, he says "it seems unfair" not to leave his two young children at least a few hundred thousand dollars.

Why shouldn't parents leave it all to the children? Newspaper headlines shriek the more lurid reasons – drugs, derangement, even murder. In July a Pennsylvania judge ruled Lewis du Pont Smith, 29, heir to $1.5 million of the du Pont fortune, "mentally incompetent" to manage his affairs; Smith had been handing over thousands of dollars to political extremist Lyndon H. LaRouche Jr. This month a Florida judge sentenced Steven Benson, 35, heir to a $10-million tobacco fortune, to 72 years in prison for killing his mother and her adopted son with a car bomb.

What usually troubles successful entrepreneurs and executives, however, is the mundane but far more likely prospect that large inheritances will encourage their offspring to do nothing useful with their lives. They worry that Commodore Vanderbilt's grandson William, heir to some $60 million in 1885, was right when he declared that "inherited wealth...is as certain death to ambition as cocaine is to morality." (An indifferent businessman and dedicated bon vivant, William suffered a fatal heart attack at a fashionable French race track in 1920.) Says centimillionaire Curt Carlson: "I know one extremely wealthy Minnesota family that has 63 heirs in the fourth generation, and none is gainfully employed. I think that's terrible."

One self-made multimillionaire wants to ensure that his heirs are leading productive lives before they get a share of his estate. He has set up trusts for each of his children – a sound estate planning practice even for middle-income families. None of the trusts pays a penny until the child turns 30. Until then, the entrepreneur says, he expects his sons and daughters, all still under 30, to "live on the salaries that young adults who are college graduates can make." The terms of his trusts also allow him or his executors to withhold the kids' patrimony in certain situations. Says he: 'I believe you've got to be doing right, or you don't get anything. If I end up with a 30-year-old who's not worth a plugged nicked all his money goes to my personal foundation."

Encouraging rich children to be self-supporting can be good for them. John L. Levy, executive director of the C. G. Jung Institute of San Francisco, has spent the past five years studying the effects of inherited wealth on 30 families. He concludes that many wealthy children experience "considerable suffering and deprivation" because they have little self-respect. "It's hard for them to take much satisfaction in their accomplishments since they always suspect that their successes are at least partly the result of the wealth and position they inherited."

To let children grow up free of their parents' long shadows is the main reason rich individuals choose to withhold or limit their legacies. New Yorker Eugene Lang, 67, for example, built a fortune of more than $50 million by founding REFAC Technology Development Corp., a high-tech licensing company. Lang paid for the education of his three children and after college handed each "a nominal sum" – she won't say how much. Since then he has given them nothing but encouragement. Says Lang: "To me inheritance dilutes the motivation that most young people have to fulfill the best that is in them. I want to give my kids the tremendous satisfaction of making it on their own." Now in their 30s, his children are a lawyer, an actor and an investment analyst. They will get nothing from their father's estate. Lang plans to provide "adequate security" for his wife and bequeath the rest to a charitable foundation. He has already given away more than $25 million to hospitals, colleges, and a scholarship program for Harlem schoolchildren.

Californian Gordon Moore, 57, who co-founded semiconductor maker Intel and is worth $200 million, agrees that "children ought to have a sense of accomplishment for what they've done." Moore set up small trusts for his two sons when they were young the sort of thing that let my older boy make a down payment on the house-but does not plan to do much more. He expects to leave "almost everything" to charity.

Still the urge to heap most of the wealth upon the family continues to be powerful "I'd rather give my money to my kids than do anything else with it," says Jackson T. Stephens, 63, chairman of Stephens Inc. of Little Rock, Arkansas, the largest investment bank outside New York "If my heirs want to clip coupons, that'll be their business. I can't control the future, and I'm not going to worry a whole bunch." Stephens, who has four children, and his older brother Wilton, who also has four children, share a net worth of at least $500 million.

Some entrepreneurs and their heirs argue that rather than being a disincentive to work, an inheritance can give a child a target to outstrip. "I feel I've got to make my mark equal or better than my Other," said Warren Stephens, 29, Jackson's son. California real estate developer M. Larry Lawrence, 60, who has three children and a fortune worth more than $200 million, concurs. Says he, "If the children have been brought up right, they end up attempting to outdo the parents."

Inevitably those who hand on their wealth see proper upbringing as the ultimate safeguard against potential problems. Says Katherine Graham, 69, chief executive of the Washington Post Co. and head of a family whose fortune totals some $350 million: "My instinct would be to just pass the money on and hope that in doing so you also pass on your values-how to use it, the life to lead, the standards to have."

Besides, some rich individuals argue, not giving it to the children can cause problems too. Says one: "If you're the child and you see your father with all this dough and you get some but not much, I just can't help thinking resentment will enter in." Susan Buffett, who works in Washington as an administrative assistant to the editor of U.S. News & World Report and is married to a public interest lawyer, admits her father's position is tough to live with. "My dad is one of the most honest, principled, good guys I know," she says. "And I basically agree with him. But it's sort of strange when you know most parents want to buy things for their kids and all you need is a small sum of money – to fix up the kitchen, not to go to the beach for six months. He won't give it to us on principle. All my life my father has been teaching us. Well, I feel I've learned the lesson. At a certain point you can stop."

Parents who disinherit not on principle but because they disapprove of their young heir's behavior might face a troubling prospect-they might be making a mistake. Just days before committing suicide in 1963, R. E. Turner Jr., the father of maverick television mogul Ted Turner, arranged a quick sale of his Atlanta billboard business to Curt Carlson. Recalls Carlson, who had no idea that the elder Turner was planning to kill himself, "He told me he wanted to have some money to leave his wife when he died, but that everything he had was tied up in his business. He said he was sure if Ted got his hands on the business, he would run it into the ground." Within days of Turner's death, Carlson got a call from his widow, Florence, and a visit from Ted, then 24. Says Carlson, "His mother wanted Ted to have the business back, and Ted, who can be very convincing, talked about how this was his one chance to get going in life." Persuaded, he sold the business back to Ted, who has been going fast ever since.

Estate planning is particularly tough when the legacy is a family business. Most entrepreneurs do not plan to sell out, as R. E. Turner did, but try to keep the business in the family. Says Curt Carlson, whose privately held Carlson Cos. brought in revenues of more than $3 billion last year: "You think of your company as your own baby. You hate to think of someone buying it and then the name is gone."

But leaving it to the children will not guarantee that the business stays in family hands. Because of fraternal fights, the Bingham family's Louisville newspaper and broadcasting empire went up for sale last January. Destructive squabbles are most likely to break out when family members try to sell company stock to outsiders, an act viewed as disloyal by those desperate to keep control. In St. Louis the heirs of legendary Joseph Pulitzer staged a noisy row this year over the attempted sale of some Pulitzer Publishing Co. stock. The family members who wanted to sell backed a takeover bid by Alfred Taubman, a Detroit-based real estate developer. Chairman Joseph Pulitzer Jr., his half brother and a cousin struck a deal to buy out the dissidents' shares at three times the pre-feud price. Taubman is still fighting in the courts.

Chicago centimillionaire Lester Crown, 61, worries that mercenary motives among family members could one day force the breakup of his very private business empire. The Crowns' holdings range from building materials, hotels, and real estate to 23 percent of General Dynamics, one of the largest U.S. defense contractors. Over the years, says Lester, he and his father, Henry, 90, have "always treated our operations as a common pot." They have handed out voting shares and limited partnerships in the various businesses to Lester's uncles, cousins, brothers, nieces, and nephews, as well as his seven children. Lester predicts that "one of these days we're going to get hit in the back of the head because we did this." If he could do it over again, he would still give the family "the ability to enjoy the good life" by setting up a single trust to pay out a guaranteed income to everyone. But he would make sure that control of the companies was "retained by those who operate the business."

The Coors family of Colorado has kept its brewery bubbling with just such an arrangement since 1969. All the company's voting stock sits in a trust, whose trustees can only be family members active in the business. Says Bill Coors, 70, chairman of Adolph Coors Co. and grandson of the founder: "We've minimized family feuds by concentrating control in the hands of those most dedicated to preserving the family values."

Warren Buffett argues that most proprietors should forget trying to keep the management of their beloved companies in the family, he assumes current nonfamily management will continue running Berkshire Hathaway after he is gone. He grants that occasionally an heir may be the most suitable candidate to manage a company but believes the odds are against it. Says Buffett: "Would anyone say the best way to pick a championship Olympic team is to select the sons and daughters of those who won 20 years ago? Giving someone a favored position just because his old man accomplished something is a crazy way for a society to compete."

Buffett especially admires how fellow Omaha businessman Peter Kiewit solved his legacy problem. Kiewit arranged his affairs so that when he died in 1979 his 40 percent stake in the family's enormously successful construction company was sold to employees. The proceeds from the sale then went to a charitable foundation that he had established to promote education and social services in Nebraska. Kiewit left approximately three percent of his $186-million estate to his widow, his son, Peter Jr., 60, and other relatives. Peter, a successful Phoenix lawyer, was surprised by the $1.5-million legacy he received at age 53. Says he, "I was raised to expect nothing, and supported myself all my life. In the end, I think my father was saying from the grave that he approved."

For wealthy parents, and even for those with more modest estates, the question of how much to leave the kids is a highly subjective matter. But here are a few points worth keeping in mind.

Don't Play Hide-and-Seek

Forget locking your will away in mystery like some 19th-century miser. Bring the family finances into the daylight, so the children will know what they are getting and where it came from, and will have some idea of how to hold on to it. They should also, of course, know if they are not getting anything. For example George Pillsbury knew that he would get more than $1 million when he turned 21 – "It's tough to be unaware of your wealth when you have a brand name," he says. But many of his friends had no idea what was coming to them. "A lot of them were shocked," he recalls, and some had trouble coping with their new fortunes.

John Train, whose investment firm claims to be the largest in New York City serving rich families, recommends that talks about money, like those about sex, begin as early as possible. These can evolve into full-scale sessions on the family finances. Lester Crown is a big booster of this idea: "We started when the kids were young and put the dollar signs in as they got older."

Former Treasury Secretary William Simon, who has made tens of millions in leveraged buyouts since leaving Washington, says that at one of his family's regular meetings, his seven children had to read and discuss 19th century steel magnate Andrew Carnegie's essay "The Gospel of Wealth." (Carnegie argued that by giving away their great fortunes, rich men would produce "an ideal state in which the surplus wealth of the few will become, in the best sense, the property of the many.")

Though the children of Eugene Lang will not share in his estate, they and Lang's wife are trustees of his private foundation and join in deciding where to give. Says Lang: "In a way they're spending their inheritance with me here and now and getting a lot of satisfaction and joy from it."

No amount of family talk will guarantee that the children will not turn out like Tommy Manville, the asbestos heir who went through 13 marriages and millions of dollars, or Huntington Hartford of the A&P fortune, who has lost a reported $90 million in a lifetime of bad business deals. But it should help.

Shelve the Silver Spoon

Psychiatrists say the lack of work experience not only alienates heirs from humanity, but also contributes to insecurity about their ability to survive without their inheritance. H. Ross Perot, 56, the Texas billionaire who founded Electronic Data Systems, a computer services company, and sold it to General Motors, puts it this way: "If your kids grow up living in fairyland thinking they're princes and princesses, you're going to curse their lives."

T. Boone Pickens Jr., chairman of Mesa Petroleum and worth tens of millions of dollars, remembers his middle-class upbringing as "the best a boy could have." When he graduated from college, Pickens thought his father, a buyer of oil leases for Phillips Petroleum, might give him $500 or so. Instead, all he got was "good luck." Pickens plans to leave at least half his estate to charity; he has arranged what he considers small trusts for his five children and three stepchildren. Says he: "If you don't watch out, you can set up a situation where a child never has the pleasure of bringing home a paycheck."

Don't Be Afraid To Experiment

Robert D. Rogers, chief executive officer of Texas Industries, a manufacturer of cement and steel, swears by a Texas-sized version of every parent's basic financial training tool-the allowance. At 18, each of his three children began receiving annual stipends that covered living expenses and then some – college costs, clothing, travel. The youngsters were not accountable for the money, but if it ran out, tough luck. As an incentive to save, the children could claim whatever remained when they reached 25. "My oldest son ran through his first year's income in nine months and had to go to work," recalls Rogers, who credits a Texas Instruments co-founder, Eugene McDermott, with the idea. Young Rogers never ran out again. If you are going to leave money to your children, a generous living allowance should give you a good idea what they will do with it.

Parents who want to encourage their offspring to work, and provide them a little extra money besides, can create incentive income trusts designed to match or double the child's salary. The trusts also can be set up to pay out principal if a child achieves some objective, such as attaining tenure at a university or even holding down a steady job.

Give Later Rather Than Sooner

Most estate advisors now agree that 21, the age of majority, is too early for most children to reap a windfall. Warns John Train: "Very large sums handed over to children who have done nothing to deserve them almost inevitably tend to corrupt them." Ross Perot, as usual, is more blunt: "Anybody who gives kids a lot of money at 21 doesn't have much sense." Bill Simon suggests that "sensible parents" put a reasonable amount in a trust that only starts paying interest at, say, 35, and then allows access to principal in two installments at 40 and 45. What's a reasonable amount? Says Simon: "Everybody has to define that for himself."

Trust in God and Take Short Views

It's 2075. Do you know who your great great-grandchildren are? Do you really care? Louis Auchincloss, the novelist, estate lawyer, and scion of one of America's most prominent families, believes the "dynastic impulse" is on the wane in America. "When I came out of law school, people were always deeply concerned about their great-grand children," he says. "Not now." That may be no bad thing; the U.S. is littered with indolent people who were ruined by trusts set up by adoring grandparents.

Besides, Congress has tightened tax loopholes that encourage generation skipping trusts. If you want to ensure some accountability among your heirs, you might consider Ross Perot's advice to make bequests one generation at a time. Says he: "Let your children decide how much to give their children."

Don't Live and Die in Louisiana

The Bayou State adheres to the Napoleonic Code, which requires forced heirship: A single child is entitled to one-quarter of any estate, two or more children split half. If you want to give more, that's no problem. If you want to disinherit, Baton Rouge lawyer Gerald Led Van says the state recognizes a few reasons as valid-attempted assault against the parent, conviction for a felony, and a debatable rule, just passed by the legislature last session, "failure to communicate for two years without just cause." If you want to give it all to charity, Le Van advises moving to another state.

Put Child-Rearing Before Estate Planning

Child psychoanalyst Roy Grinker Jr. worked with the children of the very rich for 15 years. Often the problem in wealthy households, he says, is that parents pay too little attention to their children's upbringing. "Rather than give rich parents money advice, I would give them child-rearing advice," says Grinker. "I would say, 'Pay attention to your kids, spend some time with your kids, love your kids.'" Warren Buffett cheerfully agrees: "Love is the greatest advantage a parent can give."

CHAPTER 14
CONSULTING AND EDUCATION
FOR FAMILY BUSINESS

A special breed of consultants, thoroughly understanding both business and family processes, now offer services to family firms. In addition, nearly 100 colleges and universities – as well as trade associations and others – provide special education programs for families in business. This section explores who these consultants are, the problems they confront and their approaches to family business systems.

The circumstances of the family firm a consultant works with does much to determine the circumstances that will be confronted. In any case, consultants would do well to question the perspective of family business participants. Consultants should work to clarify purposes, roles, expectations and norms, helping members to find common ground and manage differences.

One of the key factors determining the success of family businesses is the extent to which they are willing to study and understand their own circumstances. Indeed, many families are able to be their own consultants by using the many educational resources available.

It is the responsibility of those who consult to business-owning families to have as much knowl-edge about themselves as they do about their clients. A framework is offered for the consultant to understand self and others. A case study and implications for consultative practice evolve from the framework described in this paper.

The "Softer Side" of Consulting to Business-Owning Families: Understanding Our Clients and Ourselves

By Fredda Herz Brown

Introduction

Perhaps it is typical in the growth phase of a field that there is a focus on the development of technical knowledge to the general exclusion of process or "soft" information. For the evolving field of study of business-owning families there has been much to learn; it is a field that is truly interdisciplinary, requiring not only the participation of other disciplines but also the knowledge and language from other disciplines. The Family Firm Institute's Body of Knowledge Task Force has focused its work on defining the knowledge and skills necessary to function with business owning families; its effort is to assist learners in defining what they know and what they don't know, including knowledge of self. Knowledge of self is necessary for the development of self – the development of who we are as people and as consultants. To develop ourselves as consultants we must be aware of the impact of what we bring to the work and what we leave in our wake. I believe that involving self in people's lives bears the responsibility to have as much clarity and control over the impact a consultant has on a client system.

What follows has evolved from my years of work with families that own businesses and families that do not. It also has evolved from years of learning about managing myself in relation to others. I have always enjoyed watching human interaction and have made the study of it the focus of my life work. What I write about here is an attempt to define the principles that I have found useful in dealing with families who own businesses; it is somewhat philosophical in base and has become a set of guidelines that I work and live by. How we understand and explain the behavior of others and ourselves is important in setting a framework for how we are to function with them. What I have learned overtime is that often knowledge regarding ourselves can make the difference between a successful interaction and an unsuccessful one. It is only with the knowledge of what brings us to our work and what we bring to it that we can learn to be sensitive to changes that we need to make in our approaches to clients.

Self and Perception

We all grew up in families of varying sizes and structures, and we all generally continue to live in at least nuclear families for the majority of our adult lives. Whether we acknowledge it or not, our family is the primary emotional/psychological influence in our lives. It is in our families of origin that we learn the patterns, both good and bad, of relating to others that will form the foundation of our relational styles. In our nuclear families and other relationships are both the propensity for repetition and the opportunity for change. It is also in our families of origin that we learn how to relate to gender and authority. We learn how to view and value various characteristics and emotional commodities, such as money, power, education, and time. Our birth order or ordinal position effects how we view our family and is our first experience of ourselves in relation to others, especially at the peer level. The context of our family's life, such as, position in society, socioeconomic status; ethnicity, and geography all have an effect on how we perceive ourselves and the world. Contextual aspects of our early life become more observable once we are moving about in the world and begin to notice the differences between ourselves and others. Because each of these variables has a great impact on how we perceive others and ourselves, they are described separately below.

The Past

There is a saying that the past is always present, that it continues to be active in our current context. As the nuclear family moves through its life cycle in a horizontal dimension, its movement is also affecting and being affected by the generations that precede and follow it. Family patterns and themes tend to repeat from generation to generation. Sometimes it is easier to see these patterns as they exist or existed in previous generations than to try to examine such patterns in the current generation. Thus to see how the past is really active in the present, it is helpful to do a genogram of the family for three generations. The genogram should include the structure of the family and the important dates and events in its past and present. It should also be able to reflect the closeness/distance (alliances and alienations) patterns as they have existed over the generations. Such patterns usually repeat over the generations as they are replicated in the family triangles that become part of the family fabric. Central family issues and/or themes are often played out in the positions family members take in various situations. Take, for example, birth order and gender.

Birth Order and Gender

Birth order and gender are two variables that are "givens" in the family of origin. There has been great debate of how birth order exactly effects perception and behavior but no one generally would generally disagree that firstborn children, middle born and last born have very different characteristics and behavior. For instance, who has not heard an oldest son in a family firm complain that his younger brother doesn't take things seriously enough or work hard enough. Or who has not heard a younger child complain that no positions are left for him/her because the others were there first? One's position in the family profoundly effects how you will relate to your parents and to your siblings. In turn these will impact how you relate to authority and peers.

Not only is the "spot" you hold in the family lineup that is important but also the gender of the siblings who are born around you. For example, if you are a first-born female with a second-born brother, your experience will be different than if you were born after your brother. Being an oldest sister of a brother or brothers is very different from being a younger sister of brothers. Not only are your concerns different, but you have a different relationship with your parents and your siblings. An older sister of brother(s) is usually a caretaker; in addition, depending on your ethnic group, the position of older female is a less-prized position than that of the older male. While being a younger sister is no better in terms of the gender issue, it is a "darling" position for the female. Younger females of males are often catered to and/or protected by their older male siblings. You can only imagine the different expectations these two females experience in their male relationships later in life.

Gender and birth order also seem to affect the emotional alliances that form in families and thus affect relationships in family-owned firms. As Tagiuri and Davis found in their study (1996), cross-generational family alliances tend to form first across gender lines – that is, if a daughter is born first, she is usually more likely to be allied with her father. If a son is born first, he is usually more connected to his mother, and in the family firm he tends to struggle with his father as he has generally done throughout his growing up. In both instances, the next child, regardless of gender, tends to become emotionally allied with the other parent. This pattern is disturbed only when some previous family pattern or alliance is carried into the present situation. Who you ally with in your family often affects your position on a variety of issues, and it is not uncommon for a child who is allied with a particular parent to take that parent's point of view, sometimes in direct opposition to the other parent.

Alliances can also influence the degree of power that a child has in the family. If the father is viewed as the most powerful family member or at least more influential, the child most allied with him often has some of that power slide onto him or her. This does not necessarily have an impact on how powerful the child may feel because having a very powerful parent can create a sense of powerlessness in others. It should be clear, however, that such alliances often lead to positions of distance with the other parent, and thus triangles are born and become the threads for future triangles. More on this later.

Our Reaction to Anxiety

People tend to adjust their behavior to feel more comfortable, and feeling more comfortable means feeling less anxious. Most of us learn about anxiety early in our families. We also learn ways of dealing with anxiety, and one of the most frequent ways in which individuals deal with their anxiety is by triangling. Although triangling temporarily decreases the tension between people, it does not solve the original tension-creating situation. Rather it tends to act as a valve for a pressure cooker, releasing the steam but still allowing the "cooking" to continue. This is how triangling works: As anxiety increases in an individual or between two individuals, one or both of the people move away from the situation. Movement can either be toward another person, in the form of sharing the anxious experience or telling a story (gossiping) about the other's behavior. Or one can move toward an object or thing, such as spending more time at work or becoming involved with substances. Triangles also have some consequences vis-à-vis the overall system functioning.

One of the major effects of triangling is that using a particular form of triangling becomes fairly patterned and therefore inflexible over time. In other words, every time one person becomes anxious that individual will tend to involve the same person or object to decrease the anxiety, and over time this becomes a fairly knee-jerk reaction, needing little thought. For the person who gets drawn into the triangle, the process also becomes automatic; little or no thought is required for the particular situation or issue at hand. Defining self becomes less a focus or a possibility the more a person is drawn into the issues. For instance, if over time a mother shares her thoughts with her child regarding the father' behavior toward her or her worry about him, the child will learn to respond to the mother's anxiety without her talking with the child and to form some opinion about the father from her.

These opinions will not necessarily be based on reality because reality should also include at least the father's view on the situation. Thus the child takes a position based on the parent's view and on their relationship, which is connected to the mother's anxiety. Over time chances are that this position may tend to affect the child's view of men and his or her tendency to side with women. This may be a greater tendency for the individual when he or she is feeling anxious. The less the individual is able to think in anxious situations, the more emotionally immature and reactive that person will appear to others. The more triangles that the individual has been involved with the family of origin, the more likely it will be that this individual is pulled into situations on the basis of increasing comfort.

Triangles are also the major way in which issues and patterns get transmitted over the generations in families. We learn to take positions on money, power, gender, and authority by the way these issues were handled in our family. Our alliances with and distances from various members of our family often define positions on these issues. For instance, if your mother and father always fought about money and your mother, with whom you are allied, felt strongly that your father was foolhardy with money, it is likely that you share her view. The tendency is for you to adopt her view of how to deal with money.

There is also a tendency in families for triangles to repeat over the generations with certain repetitions of alliances and misalliances. For instance, in my own family my mother was the oldest daughter in her family; in that position she not only served as the caretaker of her sister but also of her mother with whom she also served as confidant. When she had her firstborn daughter, she expected her daughter to serve the same functions in their relationship. This kind of pattern transfer is called a flip flop, with my mother taking her mother's position in the next generation. Because she herself received little caretaking, she looked to her daughter for that. There could have been a more direct transfer, with my mother continuing her role as the caretaker with her daughter as she had with her own mother and sister. It is often difficult to predict which transfer will occur, but it is important to know that an individual seeks to complete what had been missing in the previous generation. In other words, dealing with our anxieties once again motivates the way we act in relation to others.

Issues in System Change

Perception Is Biased. We all know the story of the elephant in the room and the variety of descriptions given by blind people, depending on where they are positioned in relation to the elephant. The same is true for other situations; what you "see" depends on your view of the issue at hand and/or your connection and/or alliance with the individuals involved in the situation. Truth is somewhere in the middle of the room, and, depending on where you are sitting, your view of truth will vary from another person' who has a different vantage point. We tend to put boundaries around situations to understand them, and we tend to do this in ways that are familiar to us. When positions are based on the emotional connection to someone, then the person is just tending to react to a situation rather than to think about it.

Not only does this apply to situations with which we are familiar, but it can even apply to familiar situations in which the players are unfamiliar. When engaged professionally with clients or colleagues, it is important to take positions that are based in thoughtful deliberation. If our reactions are based on biases from our own past, which may or may not have anything to do with the situation, we are not going to be as helpful as we could be. If we do so without awareness that it is our bias or reaction we are introducing, we may find the situation heading in a direction that seems unplanned or uncharted. At least if we are able to declare our bias and where it comes from, client can then define where they stand in relation to it.

An inexperienced consultant who was working with our group recently provided one example. He was the older brother of sisters and in client situations often felt compelled to jump to a daughter's aid when the young woman's father or brother criticized her actions. It was only when he was able to laughingly state how hard it was for him not to want to protect her that he was able to stop himself. Sometimes the simple act of declaring something makes doing it much less difficult.

My mother used to have this practice that if one of us complained to her about another, asking her to intervene on our behalf, then the complainer would be punished along with the one being complained about. This was her way of encouraging us to work things out for ourselves. This was lifesaving for her because with five children, resolving disputes could have been a fulltime job. However, it was also based on her belief that if she were not present, she couldn't know what truly was going on. If asked to make such a decision she would be basing her view on factors unrelated to the situation, such as the way in which the story was told or the previous history of the participants or her relationship with them. Rather than do so, she used a method I would guess is familiar to a lot of parents. It is also a philosophy that applies to other situations in which we are asked to take one or another person's side. An awareness of being pulled into such a situation and what taking a position could do to the relationship between the other two and their relationship with you is very important.

Context Defines Behavior. It is really quite easy to view the behavior of an individual as being part of that person's personality. It sort of fits with the natural tendency to look to another for the source of difficulties. But whereas most of us may have particular behavioral characteristics that when put together can be called a personality, a great number of our personality characteristics do not surface unless a specific context encourages them. For example, when I used to do marital therapy, clients would frequently complain that their spouses behaved just fine when they were courting but after marrying another side emerged. The context of marriage, which requires unreserved intimacy and a level of responsibility to another, often creates a situation of fairly high tension. It is in this setting that certain behavior exhibits itself. It is not that the person changed personalities or that deception occurred intentionally. Rather, parts of a person' personality or certain behaviors are drawn out by particular situations.

Furthermore, when you define behavior as personality derived, causality is defined as belonging inside the person and therefore out of one' reach and ability to change. If the other person "houses" the reason for the behavior internally, then I bear no responsibility for looking at myself in the context of the situation. In fact, defining causality as being inside the other means that there is really little that anyone can do to change things because you can't change another person. Thus not only is the idea of personality-driving behavior less important to understanding a situation, it is also less significant, as we shall see below, in trying to change it also.

Shared Responsibility. Each participant shares in a problem, not always equally and not always at the same volume. My father would always say to be wary of the quiet ones. I would wonder what he would mean, and he would explain that the quiet ones are often just as much of the difficulty as the ones who are noisily voicing or creating difficulty. With kids he would say that the quiet one was frequently in the background stimulating the difficulties, the "plunger" as he called it.

Things do not occur in isolation so it is likely in most situations that there are multiple participants, some of whom may not even be present at the time. For instance, how many consultants have had the experience of a father-son conflict in the business that involves both mother and daughter-in-law behind the scenes. Sometimes their participation is intentional, and sometimes it is unwitting.

The importance of this idea is manifold: First, it suggests that although a father and son may change some aspect of their relationship, the involvement of the other parties may also need to be addressed. Second, it suggests that if each individual has a part in the process, then any one of them is a point of change. In fact, I usually suggest that each of us is a leader for change because if we each have some ownership of the process then we, as individuals, can change the process. Third, the idea that each participant has a part of the action and that some participants may not be as obvious also suggests that an expanded lens will provide a better understanding of a situation.

Fourth, pinning a difficulty on one person, especially the one who is most verbal about it, often misses many other opportunities for understanding and changing a situation. For example, if a son keeps threatening to resign and creates a brouhaha while making his threats, it would be easy to view that behavior as the problem and see him as creating an untenable situation for the family. However, with a broadened lens it is possible to discover that the threats occurred after the son's repeated attempts to get his boss/father to listen to his suggestions and complaints about the division he is dealing with and how he is being treated by other nonfamily employees. Looking more broadly helps to understand the sequence of events leading up to the son's threat and to see other participants' parts in the outburst, which initially seemed to belong totally to the son. A completely different view of the son is therefore possible, and some other points of change emerge.

In our own families, we are often not privy to all aspects of a situation and as a result grow up believing in a view that holds one person more responsible for a situation than another. Typically this situation involves our parents. We generally come out of our families believing that one parent was a greater participant in a difficulty than the other; this likely occurs when we are more connected or allied with one parent than the other. The more this happens the more the view is reinforced, and the more we tend to carry this view to other similar situations. We therefore may fail to see that the father is not the only one at fault in the issues with his son, but that the son and the mother have also contributed to the process. Recognizing that one person is not the "wicked witch" or the evil one helps in understanding the broader and often complex aspects of life's dilemmas, challenges, and opportunities.

Change Is Solitary and Strategic

If any number of people can have a part in a situation, then any one of them can show leadership in changing it. One of the most important principles that governs change is that it is impossible to change another person; you can only change yourself. If that's true, how do organizations go about changing? My answer: one person at a time. Organizations do not change, rather the people in organizations are asked to change their way of doing or thinking about things. The desire and/ or need for change must override the risk. If it doesn't, then no one would feel the need to change. It has been said that no one changes until they are in pain. I would agree, if "pain" means experiencing the need to do so. Change takes both courage and energy.

In families and other relationship systems with long histories, the pulls to remain the same are fairly intense. It is as if the energy just continues to pull in one direction for so long, it becomes more difficult to shift the direction. For this reason, anyone seeking to change a pattern or way of relating in his/her family must plan and prepare for the shift. Planning and preparing mean planning what to do differently, thinking through the system reactions to the change in your behavior, and planning for your reaction. Change is a three-step process and will not occur unless you are able to deal with the reactions to that shift. If you do not plan your responses to others' reactions, then you will go back to your old ways of responding and no change will be made. If, on the other hand, you have planned ways to deal with others' responses and do not fall into your old patterns of relating, then change will occur.

People we know usually respond to differences in our behavior by trying to get us to change back. They do this by indicating that the way we are acting is either bad or wrong and certainly not in keeping with their expectations. Family members usually particularize their way of letting you know you are out of line.

If you want to understand how hard change is, think about how hard it is to change how you relate to your family during a particular event, like holiday dinners. You seemingly get caught up in a script to which you automatically know your lines without even thinking about or studying them. I remember sitting in mourning at my parental home after my father's recent death. I became totally aware of how my siblings and I had shifted back to some earlier time and had begun, without thinking, to act as we did when we were all at home. It took a lot of thinking and planning for me not to get caught up in the old sibling issues.

Change tends to endure when it occurs on a variety of fronts. That is, changing behavior in regard to extended family, nuclear family, and friends is more likely to last. Viewing change in this way also points out how many opportunities there are to change patterns of behavior. One assumption underlying this perspective is that we basically carry the same behaviors into a variety of situations and therefore have a variety of opportunities for shifting them if we so choose.

Homeostasis

We all grow older, and change is inherent to that process. In fact, succession is driven by a biological clock in which time demands some shift in how people relate to one another. Even though change is inevitable, we all tend to resist it. We want things to be different and the same at once.

I will frequently hear a young successor suggest that no matter what the senior person says, he or she wants to keep things as they are. And this is said with complete sincerity and candor. Of course seniors say and do two different things. Don't we all at some points? Aren't we all, including the successors, just as afraid of moving ahead as we are of staying put? At any point in time we've all felt as if we're being pulled in two directions at once —that which impels us to move forward and that which seems to hold us back. Any process of change involves mobilizing the forces to move ahead to a greater extent than those forces that prefer to maintain the status quo. Experiencing these forces can provide very useful learning experiences for those of us who make our livings by assisting business-owning family members change.

Examining and changing should be an ongoing part of all our lives but especially those of us whose professional lives involve being a change agent. Making this a systematic part of our own existence —either with or without help —should be a requirement of anyone seeking to work with others in their lives.

Faith, Generosity, and Forgiveness

It may seem like these three words have little relationship to a system's or our own change. They all relate to a general positive attitude that is useful for change. In terms of faith, it is easy to see that initiating change can be difficult when a repetition of patterns has decreased each person' ability to be resilient. In terms of forgiveness it is often hard to accept that, while we may all try our best and start out with the best of intentions, things do not always go as planned. A corollary of this notion is that people do the best with what they have —that is, most people are not purposely mean to others, and that goes for parents. Most people generally try to do their best in raising their children.

In fact, it is often as we grow older (and perhaps have children of our own) that we learn of our tendencies to make mistakes and even to repeat those we regret the most. Although we cannot forget what others have done, we can be more forgiving of others at this point. However, our culture is more supportive of the notion that our parents are responsible for what we have become, and, if you believe what you read, all of us grew up in dysfunctional families and may even have "toxic" parents. Such beliefs run counter to the idea of accepting responsibility for one's own behavior and fully lay the responsibility elsewhere. As long as blaming exists, forgiveness is impossible to achieve. True forgiveness involves accepting that person really did the best that he or she could have done within the context

It has been my experience that being generous and forgiving toward others is important in understanding and overcoming resistance or ambivalence regarding change. Thinking about what the other person needs to feel more comfortable is about the closest we can get to assist them to change. Generosity involves asking yourself: "What does this person need from me so that he or she is more able to participate with me in this process? Or to give me what I need and/ or want." Being forgiving of the back and forth movements that are natural in the process of change is necessary to keep the forward momentum going.

Being too forgiving and generous can put individuals in situations where others take advantage of them. This tends to happen when the individual attributes fault/blame to self rather than sharing it with others. This can create difficulties, an extreme of which is abuse. However, it is my belief that change of any magnitude requires this triumvirate of attitude.

These principles offer ways of understanding our own and others' legacies. If we are able to apply them to our clients as well as to ourselves, our view will be much broader and more generous toward others. Because "we are more simply human than otherwise," we must, in our consultative practices, include ourselves in the equation. That is, we need to consider ourselves as part of the dynamics of the client situation. Because we cannot change another directly, we need to focus more on changing our relationships with others, which means managing ourselves so that we improve our interactions with others. In addition, understanding triangles and how they operate in relationships assist consultants in positioning self in the context of a client triangle. The following example illustrates both client and consultant legacies and their interaction.

Case Example

The Casey family sought the assistance of James Cook, a 43-year-old family business consultant. One of the reasons the family chose Cook was his 10-year track record as a financial consultant to businesses. Although his experience in working with the particular issues of family firms was not initially discussed, it was his understanding of ownership-transfer issues and his ability to work with numbers that lead the Caseys to hire him.

For his part, James decided to accept the assignment based on his interest in the manufacturing area and his empathy for the kinds of father-son issues that seemed to be the basis of some of the family's conflictual areas. James himself was the oldest of a family of three sons and two daughters. Although he always desired to go into an entrepreneurial enterprise, he hesitated because of his father's warnings regarding attempting a startup. The senior Mr. Cook had some knowledge of what was necessary for a startup, having started a machine manufacturing company almost 20 years ago. James and his father were somewhat close, but it was clear to James that his father would not have chosen to share his firm with him. Rather, his father seemed to prefer the next oldest brother, Paul, to join the firm. The third brother, Seth, and his two sisters were not generally interested in the business and had sought postgraduate degrees in accounting and law. James's interest in the details of his family's business continued with frequent conversations between he, his father, and his brother. James readily acknowledged and promoted this interest and involvement in his family's firm as a criterion, which made him particularly suited for family business work.

The Caseys were a third-generation family business, which manufactured boxes and other containers for the packaging industry. Sean Casey, who passed the business along to his son William, began the firm. William was currently seeking to make the transition of the business to the next generation. Part of the dilemma for William was that his three children were currently working in the business. Sean, 41 years old and his oldest son, had been with the firm since completing his degree in packaging engineering. Eleanor, 39, his second-oldest child, had served the business as a successful salesperson for the last eight years. Kerry, William's youngest child and second son, had been working in customer relations at the company for the last five years; like their elder brother, both Kerry and Eleanor had completed their college education before entering the firm. For William, it seemed that he faced an impossible dilemma of choosing one successor from his three children. He did believe that it was his responsibility to choose, but he felt that doing so was a no-win situation: No matter whom he chose, the other children would be very disappointed. In addition, he did believe that daughters should not be CEOs if they intended to have children. He did not see this as a gender-biased statement because if his sons chose to take time out for a baby, he would feel the same way about one of them taking the helm.

The initial phone call requesting James's service came from Kerry, who believed that the family needed assistance in developing some management structure that would be in keeping with the business's size and functional areas. Kerry wanted to make sure the business was in a position to prosper after their father retired, which was planned for the year 2000. Kerry also expressed concern that he and his siblings learn how to function together without their father's interventions. He believed that his brother did not value his contributions to the firm. He also stated that both he and his brother did not see their sister as a real contender for the CEO position.

After explaining his services to Kerry, James agreed to conduct an organizational assessment of the Casey family business to understand better the three different areas – management, family, and ownership. He estimated the amount of time and energy that this would take and based his proposal on a fee commensurate with the workload.

He arrived with one of his junior consultants for the first day of the assessment process and began interviewing the family members involved in the business. It did not take long for Sean and Eleanor to communicate their lack of interest and that they did not buy into the early evaluation process. They both felt that Kerry was looking for an ally in a consultant; neither of the older siblings were pleased with their brother' performance in the firm and felt that Dad expected them to keep him on because he was their brother. William believed that there could only be one boss and resisted his children's view that newer management theories suggested that it was possible for a team to lead a company.

Seeing the sibling rivalry and sensing that it might be difficult to get them together, and also sensing that William was the boss, James concluded that it was better to align himself with the father and to work with him to choose the next leader. James believed that once this was done, the next generation leader would be able to establish a more functional organizational structure that was in keeping with the vision and mission of the firm. With this working hypothesis, James began to meet with William to help him define the criteria he was going to use to choose the next leader. He suggested that William ask his advisors for their sense of important criteria for a leader of the family firm. James also suggested that William begin to establish an independent board of directors to assist him in the transition process. William resisted this idea because he felt that managing such a board would demand too much time and energy. In addition, William believed that "no one else but I will run my business."

William also believed that his oldest son, Sean, should be the leader of the business, but he was also clear that Sean was not a manager but rather someone who understood technology, product development, and production. Sean was not comfortable with people and often engendered animosity when he interacted with peers or subordinates. Eleanor was much more comfortable with people, having honed some of her innate skills in her role as a salesperson. She too had no skills (or interest) in management and felt that her father should hire an outside CEO for whom her brothers and she would work. Kerry disagreed and felt that the three of them together could run the business in an office of the president. He did not intend to continue in the business if his father appointed his brother CEO. William did not want to lose Kerry from the firm but felt that if necessary he was willing to let him leave if it was good for the company. James thought how much this reminded him of his own father's attitude toward the next generation entering the firm. He also thought Sean was "crazy" to want to work with his father rather than go out on his own. With this in mind James began to have William also review what were the necessary knowledge and skills in his job and what he felt would be necessary to maintain his future vision for the business.

As time went on, it seemed to James that William was not taking him seriously; he did not complete the tasks that James had assigned and would often be late for or cancel appointments. Perhaps the next generation was correct that William really had no intention of retiring. When James asked him about his apparent lack of interest in the project and/or his lack of regard for his comments, William said that he was really busy running the company and wasn't all that interested in giving up all of his functions. As for his regard for James, he assured him that he did think what he said was important, but he was also aware that James had less experience and knowledge than he did. James was struck by how similar this was to the way William treated his own offspring in the business. For no matter how much William believed that his children were capable of running their areas of the business, he did not hesitate to second-guess them and to change their decisions when he felt they were not in keeping with his thoughts. This matched the next generation's view of their father's behavior toward them in the business.

James was just about ready to give up the consultation, thinking he was clearly unsuccessful and that further attempts at success would be unlikely. He believed that he could have assisted William in the selection of a successor, helping protect Sean from what he viewed as an impending disaster and encouraging the others to reexamine what they wanted to do with their professional lives.

Case Summary and Conclusions

So what happened? If James had been able to examine his behavior in terms of his own family dynamics and his interactions with the client family, he might have been able to shift what he was attempting to do or to change the method he was using to do it. James, like most of us, clearly went into the situation with biases based on his own experiences. However, he failed to identify his biases to the family members with whom he was dealing. In point of fact, James did not recognize that his "solution" to the problem the Caseys faced did not evolve from the Casey family but rather from James's family. He decided that Sean was making a big mistake and that the other siblings should also examine what their professional choices should be. Certainly it is not clear from the example that James received any of this information from the siblings. Rather it seems more likely that he based his ideas on what worked in his own family's business situation. Although that situation might be helpful, it is more likely to be useful to James and the family if it is examined in terms of pros and cons and in terms of some other options that are available.

In addition, James's decision to align himself with the father in the Casey family may have proved to be one of his challenges. Although he would have been a peer to the next generation who were not as powerful as the senior generation, the position he chose was one that tended to place him in a younger male/son position with the senior generation. From such a position it became more difficult to maintain a sense of power, particularly when he was likely to be treated much as the next generation was being treated. The belief that William was the only one who could choose a successor was based more on his own experiences with his father than on the reality of the situation. Clearly, James was unable to even consider the next generation's idea of a sibling team. Without ever meeting with them, James was unable to maximize his options when William seemed to pull back from the work.

If we were observers to this situation we might also be able to examine the ways in which James's nonverbal behavior also communicated his biases and alliances with the family members. Certainly, we would also be able to observe how he positioned himself physically with William and how he interacted with him during their meetings. In addition, we would be able to help James focus more of his ongoing attention on his own behavior as it affected client behavior and postures. For James, clarifying his own viewpoint regarding such issues as power, authority, leadership, money, and gender would have helped him be more cognizant of his biases.

Implications for Consultation Practice

Having these ideas in mind, I believe, leads to some fundamentals regarding the conduct, structure, and process used in consulting in general and to business-owning families in particular. I have derived five basic ideas that I believe begin to define a mode of practice with clients.

The Complexity of Consulting. One of the first implications is that consulting is a very complex process, which by its very nature is difficult for one individual to keep track of. It has been my experience that assigning two individuals to a particular consulting assignment is important in helping the consultant track the process and maintain objectivity in working with the client. Assigning two individuals does not mean that two need to be on site, but rather that the two consult regularly on the progress of the case and the strategies for dealing with the case.

The importance of objectivity cannot be underscored enough. By objectivity I do not mean remaining rational. A lot of things are hidden under the term "rational," including a stalwart attempt to remain contained while feeling extremely tense. "Objectivity" means remaining calm or nonreactive to the anxiety in the system —not letting the anxiety define how you behave or think. It means not getting triangled into the situation on one side or the other. This can usually be determined by the degree to which you see one side of an argument more than another or view one person as a victim or a tyrant. It is necessary to maintain a broad enough perspective, which permits you to see both sides at the same time and to entertain two seemingly disparate thoughts or ideas simultaneously. Having two consultants available to work on client situations permits each the opportunity to gain perspective.

Working on Process and Structure. Consulting means working on process and structure at the same time. A few months ago, a young woman whose father, husband, and brother were in business together called to ask me to work with them. In the course of the conversation it became clear that they already had a consultant who helped them to establish both a board of directors and a family council. When I asked what the problem was, since it seemed that they had all the right things in place, she said "Yes, but my father, brother, and husband fight the same way in all of these places." My experience is much like this young person's – family interaction patterns continue in whatever structure they are given if the patterns are not worked on or changed. In some ways it is fairly easy to establish structures, at least in family firms that welcome the opportunity.

Structure accomplishes what it suggests: It helps the family develop appropriate places and mechanisms to have discussions of note. Systems, however, are dictated by blood and history and are therefore emotional by nature. As we discussed earlier, these kinds of systems have patterns of relating that have developed and endured over time. It takes more than establishing structure to break the patterns; it takes frequent meetings that permit the access to patterns. It also takes the structure to provide the opportunity for access. We have found that work with family firms may require jump starting the process part by having more frequent contact in the first several months. As they get more adept at changing the ways in which they relate, the frequency of meetings with the consultant can decrease. Every interaction between various family members creates an opportunity for change to occur. However, it also provides an opportunity for the repetition of patterns, and, in the beginning of a consultation when the anxiety tends to run high, repetition also tends to increase. With each repetition of a pattern, the resilience of the system tends to diminish. When clients experience decreased resilience, they lose hope and, sometimes, trust in each other.

Strategizing the Work

It is primarily because families repeat patterns that it is necessary for consultants to utilize strategy in dealing with them. When consultants "wing it," that is, meet with clients without anticipating and planning for the process and content of the meeting, the family patterns tend to take over. In addition, a family's emotional process is stronger than any connection that a family member will have to a consultant. Therefore consultants who view their personality or their power as enough to shift a particular person or viewpoint often find themselves perplexed when confronted by the power of the family relationships, even those that are negative in nature.

Without planning for the impact of what you say about the alliances and cutoffs in the family, it is often difficult to convey a message in the manner in which it was intended. Planning how to say what you need to say and who to say it to is just as important as what to say. Often this means that the consultant is not doing what feels comfortable at the moment because often what feels comfortable is to say nothing or to respond to the moment. Helping clients change how they relate involves being able to change how you, the consultant, relates. The motto here is *plan, plan, plan!*

A Leap of Faith

Working with families who own businesses often requires a leap of faith on the part of the family members and the consultant. The longer the family has unsuccessfully struggled with issues, the less capable they will feel of making things different. Resilience is lowered, and the family responds by losing faith or hope that they can change the situation. Many consultants tend to join the bandwagon by viewing families in which hope and resilience are down as dysfunctional and incapable of changing. The term "dysfunctional" is overused and has really lost its meaning. All families are dysfunctional to a certain degree because they have patterns of relating that don't work well. However, dysfunctionality does not mean change is not possible but rather that patterns are fairly entrenched and resilience is low, with no one willing to risk being the first to change. For these kinds of families, a consultant without an understanding of family dynamics will feel anxious and may view the family as hopeless. Collaboration with a colleague who is more experienced in this area will be of great help to the family and the consultant.

Defining the Consultant's Personal Agenda

It is often said in a fairly negative manner that someone has a hidden agenda. My experience suggests to me that each of us has personal agendas that we carry with us into situations and are more or less hidden. The degree to which they are hidden may depend in part on the situation, the degree to which the individual is able to articulate and be in touch with the agenda, and the valence attached to having an agenda. What I mean by personal agenda is a need or wish that, when satisfied, will make the individual more amenable to the situation at hand. In family firms, each family member has a personal agenda that, if not satisfied, may impede the transition process. For the senior generation this agenda generally focuses on the need to be acknowledged for what they have accomplished and provided for the family, particularly the successors. For the successors, it may focus on the need to be appreciated. However, no matter what the focus, it is important that these agendas be clear and be dealt with in the family business consultation. The same is true for the consultant.

A consultant needs to be aware of why the family asked for this particular consultation and what their needs are in relation to it. It can be said that consultants have a general need to help or seek approval, which may be underlying all of their work. It is important to examine any other agendas that are at play, such as resolving some old family issue or reworking a family theme. It is the consultant's responsibility to manage self in relation to his or her clients. This includes understanding the issues that are "hot buttons" and/or understanding their reaction to money, power, and authority. Consultants can often figure out what their hot buttons are by examining how anxious they get when the family mentions a particular topic. Or, alternatively, consultants can focus on these issues as themes in their own family work.

The Use of Self

Being able to stay calm in the wake of a family' battles not only permits them to talk about the situation or issue more calmly but also makes it easier for the consultant to avoid getting caught in their battles. The idea of modeling for the client seems to be a long-overused idea. Being a model could just as easily mean modeling negative behavior as well as positive. Remaining a calm presence in the face of some anxious situations goes a long way toward demonstrating a process or mechanism for dealing with difficult situations. A calm presence permits the consultant to think more broadly about an issue and to thus assist the client to do the same as well. Looking beyond the obvious is only possible when feelings are fairly calm. I believe that business-owning families have the solution to their own difficulties, but that the inability to remain calm (and thus to decrease the automatic patterns) does not afford the opportunity for them to surface.

Using these ideas in consultative practice with business-owning families has permitted me the opportunity to learn as much about myself as about my clients. Certainly my clients are not paying me to learn about myself, but if learning about myself allows me to work better with them and affords them the chance to explore their situation in ways they have been unable to, then they have gained a lot.

References

Tagiuri, R, and Davis, J. (1996). Bivalent attributes of the family firm. *Family Business Review, 9* (2), 199–208.

Papers concerning interprofessional collaboration meant for interprofessional audiences are difficult to write. Business owners, accountants, lawyers, economists and managers are interested in an emphasis on the business of family business. Those psychologically trained, like family therapists, would emphasize the family in family business.

This paper was originally written for a conference that brought together family business professionals and family therapists. We would ask its readers to open their frames of reference, perhaps departing from the traditional. Both family and business make up a family business. No single consulting discipline can understand a family business as an entity unto itself. Family businesses may have some similarities with families and businesses as they are discussed in textbooks. But they are different in important ways. These differences with traditional notions of family and business are, at a very basic level, what makes multi-disciplinary collaboration essential if we are to understand and provide effective aid to family businesses.

Family Business: The Challenges and Opportunities of Interprofessional Collaboration

By Joseph H. Astrachan and Boris M. Astrachan

Prevalence and Performance of Family Businesses

Family business can be defined broadly. Few who work with or research family business would limit their definition to small, "mom & pop," businesses. Generally, when we talk of family businesses we are speaking of companies whose ownership is controlled by a family, or which have more than one family member significantly involved in the management of the company.

Contrary to what Berle and Means (1932) predicted sixty years ago, family business is the primary form of organization throughout the world, North America included. Some important statistics show how prevalent family business is in the United States. Similar results are reported in Great Britain (Stoy Hayward, 1992).

- It has been estimated that there are as many as 13 million family businesses in the United States (Dreux, 1990).
- 175 of the *Fortune* 500 companies were controlled by families (Dyer, 1986, Zeitlin, 1976).
- From 40 to 60% of our country's largest publicly held company's are under family control (Burch, 1972).
- Family businesses produce over half the nation's Gross Domestic Product (Becker & Tillman, 1978, Hershon, 1975).
- They account for more than half the nation's employment and new job creation (Becker & Tillman, 1978, Hershon, 1975).
- Family businesses are large as well as small. A single family business, like Wal-Mart or Ford, accounts for about 1 percent of the GDP.

These are large numbers. If we removed government spending, these numbers – percentage of GDP, employment and new job creation – would be substantially higher.

Family businesses can be highly effective and efficient economic entities. Early results from a study being conducted at Kennesaw State College by Bob Desman and Gene Hennsler (1992) indicate that over the last ten years, publicly traded family businesses outperformed the Standard & Poor's 500 stock index by more than 50%. Similar results were found by the Pitcairn Financial Management Group (Moscatello, 1990), whose Family Universe index out-performed the S & P by 2 to 1 over the past 25 years or so.

Longevity of Family Businesses

But despite the importance of family business, the statistics about the number of family businesses that survive in the family from one generation to the next are startling. John Ward (1988b), in his seminal study of family business, looked at 200 manufacturing companies in the state of Illinois, and found that:

- Fewer than 20% of first generation family businesses survived beyond the second generation, and
- Only 13% of first generation family businesses remained in the family beyond the second generation.

Others have found that only 30% of family businesses survive their founders, and make it to the second generation (Beckhard & Dyer, 1983). In Great Britain, the accounting firm of Stoy Hayward (1992) found that:

- Fewer than 25% of first generation family businesses remained in the family into the second generation, and
- Only 14% of first generation family businesses survived beyond the second generation.

What accounts for these bleak statistics? Bankers and lawyers can attest to the fact that among the most important reasons for the failure or limited longevity of a family business are issues with the family. It is common for an attorney to create perfect estate plans or buy-sell agreements tailored to business and family needs, and yet the family cannot agree and will not sign.

Effecting collaboration and reaching agreement among family members who do not have a business is always an accomplishment. Family unity is an even loftier goal. When the complexities and high stakes of a business are enmeshed with family dynamics, collaboration and reaching agreement seem next to impossible.

For example, as a member of a family, worrying about sibling and in-law relationships after parents die is difficult enough. As a member of a family business, added to that worry, is worry about whether or not your brother-in-law is capable of looking after the business that bears your name, as well as your wealth that is tied up in the business. Family business family members worry about the implications of being seated at the other end of the family dinner table, "does it mean no raise, no promotion?"

The connections among family in a business are much greater, they are structured into the very economic relationships that sustain life through old age. This is not only confounding to the legal and accounting communities, but it is confounding to the psychological and family therapy communities as well. In traditional western thought over the past century, an ideal business is not complicated by a family. The business hires the best and the brightest and discards those who no longer add value. Most importantly, the "ideal" business does not have owners who interfere in the daily operational decisions of the organization. In the hypothetical world, a family is not tied together by such a consequential entity as a business. In the ideal, psychologists might say, children are free to find their own sense of self, they can leave parents, and brothers and sisters, unencumbered by perceived and real obligations to what many calls another member of the family: the business.

One can see that in consulting to family businesses, there is a need for collaboration between those with traditional business skills, and those with family and psychological skills. There are multiple issues that require interdisciplinary collaboration in order effectively understand what is taking place and offer any effective assistance (Swartz, 1989). These include family and business issues such as:

- estate planning
- succession planning
- the entry of family members into the business
- salary, bonus, promotion, and dividend policy
- strategic planning for the family and business.

Again, each of these has implications for the family and the business. Without an understanding of the interaction of the dynamics of families with the work of businesses, or of businesses controlled by a family, we are limited in our ability to prevent problems and provide aid.

Within the last ten years, there has been a growing movement in academic and professional circles which targets family businesses as entities that are separate from nonfamily businesses (cf. Kepner, 1983). With the help of the Family Firm Institute (Lansberg, Perrow & Rogolsky, 1988), the field of family business is about where entrepreneurship was some fifteen years ago (Astrachan, 1993, Wortman, 1992). The Family Firm Institute's scholarly has been reporting on the issue of multi-journal, the *Family Business Review*, disciplinary collaboration for several years, and important work is being done (Swartz, 1989, Ward, 1990, Davidow & Narva, 1990).

To help us understand the developments in the family business field, We will first discuss the characteristics that make family business unique -from both the family and business perspectives.

Characteristics of Family Businesses

We have already mentioned one of the most important unique characteristics of family businesses: the family and the business are all part of one highly interconnected and complex system (Whiteside & Brown, 1991, McCollom, 1990, Lansberg, 1988, Swartz, 1989, Kepner, 1983). Many of the features of family business discussed in the literature stem from this one. We will list some examples of this complex system in order to demonstrate that different disciplines have much to say to one another.

- The identity of every family member is, in part, defined by their relationship, or lack of relationship, to the family business (Miller and Rice, 1967; Guzzo and Abott, 1991). Family members who feel left out and neglected by the business are often recompensed by the family in other ways. This may be a partial explanation for why some estate plans are not constructed with the best interests of the business at heart.

- The family has the power to pursue its own objectives even when these are at a variance with generally accepted business practice (Donnelly, 1964). This may include promotion of a family member who is incompetent, or establishing family members' salaries above market rates. Again, without an understanding of how the family and business function as a unit, legal and accounting consultants, for example, might not be able to suggest alternative schemes that would satisfy the tenuous balance in family firms.

- Families often structure their relationships in the business in ways that fill a void in their family relationships outside of the business (Lansberg, 1991). For example, brothers whose relationship is conflicting, who don't regularly communicate about family issues, and who live in different cities might both commute to work where they have a partner's desk and share the same office. Family therapists who are unaware of the way in which family relationships may serve business needs maybe at a disadvantage when working with a family. For example, if fraternal conflict external to the business were reduced in this situation, it might alter well-established patterns of behavior at work that have led to business success.

- Family members often feel obligated to hold stock in the family company especially when there are losses (Donnelly, 1964), and family generally feel some obligation to one another in times of crisis. The demands of family loyalty, when measured against business exigencies can lead to dramatic feelings of unfairness and resentment that can threaten long-term family unity. Miller and Rice (1967) have identified family unity as being of central importance to keeping the business healthy.

- The position of a family member in the family business will influence their position in the family (Donnelly, 1964). Those who are looked up to in the business are also well respected in their family. Those who have dominant roles in the business may seek to dominate family. In general, the business can define relationships among family members. For example, a young sibling with excellent technical skills useful to the business may be given a more senior role in the business than a much older sibling. Within the family, the younger sibling's advancement may be entirely understood as reflecting family dynamics. Alternately, promotion may be denied the younger sibling because of family issues and he may experience resentment that may also be misidentified in the family. Again, without understanding this dynamic, a therapist might be at a loss to explain ambiguous boundaries that often exist between siblings or between parental and child generations of family in a family business. Likewise, business consultants might seriously overestimate the ability of a successor to establish his or her legitimacy in the business if the successor is not also doing so in the family.

- Family business leaders have multiple bases of authority. The business leader is generally the family leader and a leader in the community as well. Family roles and business roles also are intimately linked in other ways. For example, the brother who plays an emotionally supportive role in the family will likely play one in the business as well. Again, we can see that action in the business will affect the family and vice versa. Without taking this fact into account, effective or acceptable interventions cannot be designed.

- Family businesses are characterized by personal sacrifice, especially of family members' time and money (Donnelly, 1964; Abott & Guzzo, 1991). This too can lead family members to resent the business. The business often accepts and even expects generosity from family members with little short term acknowledgment or reward.

- The family's reputation and the business' reputation often are tightly interconnected. The business has access to and may draw upon all of the family's social connections. The business has access to family knowledge and skills that can be mobilized during periods of need. Likewise, the family can act as a strong symbol of corporate purpose. The continuity of a single owning family can provide a psychological anchor that eases large scale organizational change. Often, during times of crisis and change, the founder's legacy is revived with fanfare (Donnelly, 1964, Guzzo & Abott, 1991).

- Employees in family businesses tend to have a good deal of loyalty and a high sense of security. Having a visible family owning the company engenders a sense that the business will be around as long as the family is alive. As the famous business strategist, Michael Porter (1992) recently has pointed out, the overlap of ownership and management also leads a business to have an interest in long-term survival and long-term goals. Loyalty is also enhanced in those businesses where employees believe that they are in some sense members of the owning family.

- Family businesses tend to have a large interest in the well-being of their surrounding communities (Donnelly, 1964, Astrachan, 1988). Even the impact on the local community often needs to be considered when consulting with family businesses.

- Family businesses tend to have multiple independent feed back loops running from the bottom to the top of the organization. Family members throughout the business have access to senior management during family occasions. Working in the family and business can alter these feedback mechanisms, having a direct impact on business and family functioning.

- Family businesses place a high regard on business independence and business and family secrecy (Donkels & Frolich, 1991, Lansberg, 1992). Secrecy is twofold: the family does not want its dynamics, financial or other information shared with non-family, and family often does not want information shared within the family. Both of these secrecy issues concern, in part, the desire to maintain stable relationships in and out of the family. The appropriate sharing of information within the family is something about which the field of family therapy provides tremendous insight. Not wanting to share information with outsiders makes entry into a consultation, as well as interviews or other work with family members, extremely difficult for consultants. This fact of family business life also influences our ability to work with family business, both independently and as consulting teams.

All of these characteristics of family business indicate that issues of family structure and business always are interacting with one another. No single professional perspective is adequate to understand a family business. Clearly, an individual or team that can successfully integrate the variety of perspectives contained in a family business will be able to help the family business do the same. This is a strong argument for having interdisciplinary teams working with family businesses.

Consulting with Family Business

Consulting with family businesses is a less straightforward affair than consulting with other kinds of organizations (Rosenblatt, de Mik, Anderson, & Johnson, 1985). It requires that the consultant possess a wide range of skills (Poza, 1989) due to the inherent complexity of the family business system. Defining who is the client is a major issue for family business consultants (Kaye, 1992). Who is being looked after first and foremost by the consultant? The advisor could be concerned primarily with the business, with the family, or with some subset of the family. Often, consultants try to balance these many needs with varying degrees of success.

Families and family businesses tend to be secretive (Levinson, 1983). Rarely do they feel comfortable in revealing their secrets and family relationships to strangers (Lansberg, 1992). Indeed, family businesses often use the same accountant and attorney long after their business has outgrown the expertise of their original advisors. A further complicating issue is that family businesses often do not acknowledge that they are a family business.

Under such circumstances, how does a family business consultant enter the family business system? How does a team of consultants develop sufficient trust with a client to enter the system? These are questions to which there are no easy answers. In the absence of a crisis, developing trust and credibility, and being accepted by a family, takes great effort and even more time.

Family businesses tend to have an active emotional system (Swartz, 1989). Consultants are often used as pawns in the emotional life of the system. It is common for a consultation to be actively terminated or terminated via omission due to family business politics. There is generally great pressure on the consultant to side with one of the many groups in the system. Secrets are often revealed to consultants with the proviso that they not be shared with anyone. In many situations, a consultant becomes thought of as a member of the system or an ally of a member, threatening the consultant's expert status and stance of impartiality.

Family business families are often organized in a way that makes explicit conflict and disagreement taboo (Miller & Rice, 1967). The necessity for the family to stay together in order to ensure mutual financial security makes family conflicts a serious threat to personal well-being. Consultants often need to understand and resolve tacit disagreements and misunderstandings among family members during the course of a consultation. When a family Will does not acknowledge those disagreements that impact work, the probability of a successful consultation is severely diminished. It is common for a consultant who surfaces conflict to be terminated, purportedly for not having the best interests of the family at heart. Creating a safe environment for the discussion of disagreement is a challenging task. So too is the task of intervening in a family business in ways that reduce misunderstandings without openly surfacing them.

Family business systems have dual hierarchies that are not always aligned and that are often in transition. The heads of the family and the leaders of the business are not always the same people, especially during times of leadership succession that is when consultation is sought. During periods of succession, new family coalitions may be formed and new leaders identified. The needs of future leaders also must be considered. The balance of power among these leaders and leaders-to-be is often fragile. Successful work in the family business system requires the consultant to be cognizant of the multiple leaders. Successful work also requires political acumen so that the consultant does not slight one leader while talking to another, nor upset the balance of power in unintentional ways.

Family businesses tend to have rigidly defined boundaries between the family business system and others, and vaguely defined boundaries among ownership, leadership, management, employees, and other stakeholders. In family businesses, people occupy many roles simultaneously. Boundaries can be loosely defined in other respects as well. Senior non-family management will often report feeling like they are truly members of the family. Consultants often get swept into the many facets of the system, losing their identities as independent outsiders.

Alderfer (1980) describes the many problems of consulting to an under bounded system. In such organizations, implementation of projects and the attainment of goals is complicated by a diffuse sense of responsibility. Likewise, disagreements and conflict tend to spread quickly through this type of system and is one reason family business families have strong norms against conflict and disagreement. Alderfer suggests using interventions that are designed to strengthen boundaries early during the consultation. This is a complicated task in a family business where the overlap in roles is real and relatively fixed. It requires that system members become conscious of the multiple boundaries and abide by them. For example, a father who has turned over the management of the business to his son needs to recognize that, on the one hand, reasserting decision making in the business represents an overstepping a boundary in the business. On the other hand, asserting decision making influence in other parts of his son's life may be within the boundary of a father-son relationship. Similar boundary confusion can occur between siblings, or other family groups. In real terms, recognizing which boundary is appropriate to enforce at any given time means that behavior must be rigidly defined by the situation and by the people with whom the system member is interacting.

The high level of interconnectedness within a family business system also can be an advantage to a consultant. Effecting change in one part of the systems will impact other, generally more stable, parts of the system (Lansberg, 1992). However, this route to system change tends to be slower than a more direct approach.

Team Consulting

Consulting as a team to a family business is even more complicated than individual consultation. In this section, we will address multi-disciplinary consultation that takes place where all members of a consulting team interact with a client as a team. Other models of multi-disciplinary consultation will be discussed later. There are several distinct benefits and many potential problems of team consulting.

The most important benefit of team consulting is that more than one perspective on the client is available (Swartz, 1989). This allows the consultants to maintain impartiality and greater emotional distance from the family business. In conflicted situations, team consulting enables each team member to mirror the particular positions held in the family business and to work on resolution in the less complicated environment of the consulting team. The team can use its expertise, distance, and experience to work through otherwise intractable issues.

The consulting team has the ability to go back to the client and reveal the logic and deliberations used to reach potential solutions and recommendations. In this sense, the consulting team can provide a model for teamwork that is helpful to the client system (Swartz, 1989). Likewise, by having multiple perspectives on the same issues, consultants can demonstrate that there may be many routes to a correct answer (Roller & Nelson, 1991). This can be particularly helpful, especially where family businesses have a dominant leader.

Another benefit is that individual team members can more quickly establish trusting relationships with individuals in the family business. This can facilitate the acceptance of new ideas and the implementation of change. It also enables the consultants to gain more valid information from the client system (Hoy, Isaacs, Neuman, Schwerzler, & Sidwell, 1990).

The caveat to this approach is that the team members can become too identified with particular positions held by family members and therefore are unable to reach any resolutions. In that case, the team merely reflects the conflicts in the family business. This issue alone can cause a team to have a conflicted and argumentative demise.

A multi-disciplinary team can have the capacity to understand and focus on the business and the family at the same time. The team can maintain the clarity needed for effective business consulting while being attentive to the ambiguity of emotional systems and family life. Here again, the team members can conflict if members of the team become too focused on different aspect of the family business system.

The ability for team members to quickly establish trusting relationships with individuals in the client system can also be an advantage in terms of entering the family business system. A team can become closer to a client in a shorter period than an individual consultant (Roller & Nelson, 1991). Unlike the individual consultant, a team does not have to maintain the same high degree of distance and the face of impartiality as long as the team is balanced in its relationships to individuals in the family business.

The entry advantages of team consulting are particularly evident in those cases when the consultants are called into the situation by a low ranking member of the system. In such cases, one member of the team can tend to the inquiring person's needs, while other members can focus on developing trusting relationships with more influential members of the system.

Team consulting also has other benefits for the consultants involved in the consultation. A team can provide valuable social and technical support, enabling consultants to maintain a higher level of confidence in a complex situation (Swartz, 1989). Team members can also aid with the pernicious problem of consultants who have an overactive ego or who behave defensively with clients (Swartz, 1989). Some consultants maintain an air of invulnerability with their family business clients. Often, this is a mechanism for coping with uncertainty and the great emotional and intellectual demands of a family business consultation. Team members can serve as a check on one another's egos, reducing the probability that inappropriate or damaging advice will be given.

Drawbacks of Team Consulting

The list of potential problems for team consulting is longer than the few caveats mentioned above. There are issues to be considered both in terms of consulting with family businesses and in terms of team operations.

At times, entry into the client system can be greatly complicated by using team consulting. It has already been mentioned that family businesses value privacy. Opening the family business' issues to a team of people can be a more threatening, difficult, and time-consuming proposition in some settings. Trust needs to be established with several people instead of a single consultant.

Similarly, there can be a lack of clarity around whom the lead consultant is, especially when one member of the team makes initial contact with the family business. This ambiguity increases dramatically when one of the consultants has a preexisting relationship with the client.

Determining who will and can have what relationship with a client after the consultation project ends also can be a thorny issue. If it is not resolved before a consultation, it can lead to competition among team members during the consultation as each consultant vies for future business. In such a situation, the client may find themselves asking who, if anyone, is the real expert in the team.

Multi-disciplinary teamwork is further compounded by the fact that there is no common professional language for dealing with family businesses as of yet. Lawyers, accountants, psychologists, strategists, and therapists all have a particular jargon that is not always understandable to the layman. Working together is time consuming for it often involves much translation and education across the disciplines.

A related issue is the philosophies of the various disciplines are sometimes at odds (Swartz, 1989). The behavioral sciences tend to be process oriented-helping the client to solve their own problems and to develop their own action plans. Other disciplines tend to be prescriptive and action oriented -preferring to analyze the situation and give the solutions. Some consultants desire to help with the implementation of plans, while others prefer to provide a plan and leave the client to their own devices regarding implementation. Another philosophical difference is that some advisors like to take a "big picture" approach, helping the family business define and realize long term goals. Other consultants would prefer to work on a specific task. Some advisors believe in major, "deep-structure" change, while others are concerned with fine tuning the family business. Finally, some disciplines seem more naturally oriented towards the needs of the family, while others orient themselves toward the needs of the business. Currently, there is no established discipline that is concerned with the needs of the entire family business system.

Aside from the difficulties of team consulting in a family business, there are a variety of potentially disruptive dynamics that occur in any type of team consulting. Most of these issues revolve around the issues of money, ego, and control.

Roller and Nelson (1991) describe many complications of team consulting. They describe power struggles, competition, and the need to be seen as an expert as all too frequent, and quite pernicious dynamics of team consulting. When a reasonable and mutually acceptable balance and sharing of power exists, consulting is made possible. Otherwise, they note, consulting teams can do more harm than good for their clients.

Roller & Nelson (1991) also describe the dynamics of splitting and countertransference. Splitting is where the client sees some member(s) of the team as all good, while viewing other(s) as all bad. Consultants sometimes unwittingly promote this view of the team, especially when the power and ego component of the team is unbalanced.

Countertransference is where the consultant unconsciously makes assumptions about the client and other consultants that are not based in fact, but are based on prior experiences with others. For example, a junior consultant may misinterpret the behavior of a senior consultant as being critical and demanding-perhaps like the junior consultant's parents and other authority figures. Such incorrect assumptions lead to dramatic communication failures and misunderstandings between consultants.

In other situations, a consultant may try to make up for something they lacked in their own families with the client. For example, consultants in a team may unconsciously strive for the love of family members in the client system. This can occur at the expense of the consulting team and client.

Models of Collaboration

Collaboration among advisors is not a new idea. Accountants, lawyers and others routinely collaborate on transactions. Though usually in such collaborations, the role of each discipline is tightly defined and the overall goals of the consultation are clearly articulated. Generally, in these cases the nature of the project is transaction based. That is to say that professionals collaborate for the purpose of bringing a deal to fruition such as the sale of a business, creation of an estate plan, or the raising of capital.

Another model of collaboration is the board of directors or board of advisors (Ward, 1991). Currently, fewer than 10 percent of closely-held businesses have boards with outside directors (Ward, 1988a). In the case of a board, the advisors typically do not work together serving other clients. Entry is managed by the fact that board members are selected by the owners. Problems are generally defined by the company leadership and not by the board.

Boards can be a very effective model for problem solving and planning for a family business that does not need more intensive consulting time and advice than a board traditionally provides. There are some other drawbacks to boards. Typically, they are only as good as the chairman and chief executive who manages them. They generally do not probe to discover unacknowledged organizational and system problems. In addition, boards generally do not concern themselves with issues of less importance than corporate policy and executive leadership.

Family Business Forums are another model of collaboration. In this case, family businesses join an educational organization that has regular meetings at which they receive general advice from experts in the family business field (Astrachan, 1990). In this setting, family members can learn from multiple cooperating experts whom each have an individual effect on the family. Family businesses have the opportunity to hear from multiple disciplines. The experts do not generally collaborate in consultation to a specific family business about specific family business issues. In the family business forum model, there is no need for experts to work together beyond logistical considerations.

The supervision model of collaboration involves a single consultant to a family business who calls on the expertise of others to aid the consultative process. In this case, the team is essentially behind the scenes. The multiple perspectives are filtered through the primary consultant. It relies on the consultant to know when and how to seek advice from other experts. The model has some advantages of team consulting-multiple perspectives, a check on ego and power, and support-without the disadvantages of having to manage a team.

This model is similar to a subcontracting model. Subcontracting is a fairly familiar form of collaboration. It generally takes the form of a trusted lawyer or accountant who calls on other experts to help the family business as needed. The subcontracted experts generally do not need to work in close collaboration with one another. It is more common for a specific issue to be taken by a single consultant. This model has one important advantage over a single consultant hired directly by the family business. The lead consultant/attorney can provide oversight of the subcontractor's activities. A drawback is that the lead consultant/attorney may not be qualified to provide appropriate oversight.

There are two other models of team collaboration that have been used in consulting with family business. One is where there is an intact team with a definite leader and a definite protocol for the consultation (LeVan, 1991). In the other, there is no defined hierarchy in the team and the team may include people who have not worked together in the past (Swartz, 1989).

The intact team with a defined leader has the advantage of multiple perspectives and an intact team. Another advantage is that most of the power, ego and financial issues are resolved before the consultation begins. It is an open question as to whether having an established protocol and a definite leader allows for the full benefits of collaboration as described by Swartz (1989) and Roller & Nelson (1991). When it works well, the flexible team with no leader model has all the advantages of team collaboration. However, the difficulties of managing this type of team are significant, as outlined above. In addition, it is difficult for a team to resist the gradual encroachment of a hierarchy as differing abilities become apparent over time.

Prospects for Collaboration: Making the Team Work

There are a large variety of issues that need to be attended to in team consulting. The following summarizes my attempt to combine the work of previous authors into a helpful framework for multi-disciplinary collaboration.

1. Before engaging in a consultation, there needs to be clarity about how leadership and agenda setting will be handled. If leadership will be shared or rotated, then a procedure for doing so needs to be established.
2. Before engaging in a consultation, there should be a clearly articulated mechanism for dealing with differences among team members. This can include a process and a mediator. In addition, rules for disagreeing in front of clients should be prearranged. Such rules can be simple, such as, "we never disagree," or complex, such as, "we only disagree when all the members we are consulting to are in the room and only around a defined list of topics."
3. A mechanism for identifying and resolving competition between consulting team members needs to be established.
4. A method should be established for identifying and resolving situations where consultants are becoming too involved with a minority perspective in the client system. Likewise, a way of pointing out scapegoating among team members should be created.
5. Team members must have a willingness to learn new approaches and perspectives. Team members also need to open about their philosophies of consultation. For example, consultants should be open to the idea that prescriptive interventions may be better in some situations than process interventions.
6. Consultants must be open and honest about their limitations. The relationships among team members should allow for the comfortable identification of others' limits.
7. Frequent coordination and discussion of clients should take place, ideally after every meeting with the client. This can serve to keep the team from developing large differences in how the client is viewed. Such differences tend to become entrenched over

time, and can threaten the unity of the team. Similarly, routine time should be scheduled for consultants to acknowledge what they have learned from one another. This is a helpful ritual for reaffirming the value of the team.

8. Guidelines about sharing of clients and involvement with a client after the bulk of the consultation is complete should be prearranged.

9. Procedures and criteria for how to leave the team, how to remove someone from the team, and for terminating the consultation should be established prior to the consultation.

10. Teams should have a trusted and impartial outsider with whom they consult regularly. This will help to keep the team from overlooking important issues in the client and team systems.

11. Finally, if the team or consultation has a probable ending point, the team should prearrange a ritual and a time for saying goodbye.

An important trend on the horizon is the development of a pool of cross-trained people who have the necessary understanding of multiple disciplines needed to effectively work together. Multi-disciplinary knowledge, combined with an understanding of the potential pitfalls of collaboration can provide the basis from which effective team consulting can occur. In the last several years, the Family Firm Institute has been studying the issue of certifying or credentialing family business consultants (Davidow & Narva, 1990). At a minimum, the process should require that certified consultants have a basic understanding of all the disciplines that are important to working with family business. This will enable better individual and team consultation. Education will help create a common language and will provide the basic understanding needed to effectively work together. Such a process moves the primary education out of the consultative team, and into a sphere that can handle teaching and learning without negatively affecting an individual consultation project.

Perhaps as family businesses are better understood, the urgent need for multi-disciplinary collaboration will diminish. At that point, like a medical team dealing with a unique condition where each specialist knows their role and how they must work together to succeed, each discipline will have a better understanding of what a family business is and each discipline will be forever changed.

References

Alderfer, C. 1980. *Consulting to Underbounded Systems. Advances in Experiential Social Processes*, Volume 2, Edited by C. Alderfer and C. Cooper. John Wiley & Sons, Ltd.: London, England.

Astrachan, 1. 1988. Family Firm and Community Culture. *Family Business Review*, 1(2), Jossey-Bass: San Francisco, California.

Astrachan, J. 1990. An Interview with Craig Aronoff, Founder of the Kennesaw State College Family Business Forum. *Family Business Review*, 3 (1), Jossey-Bass: San Francisco, California.

Astrachan, J. 1993. Preparing the Next Generation for Wealth: A Conversation with Howard H. Stevenson. *Family Business Review*, 6 (1), Jossey-Bass: San Francisco, California.

Becker & Tillman, 1978. *The Family Owned Business* (second edition). Commerce Clearing House, Inc.: Chicago, Illinois.

Beckhard, R. & G. Dyer, Jr. 1983. Managing Continuity in the Family Owned Business. *Organizational Dynamics* (summer).

Berle, A., J. & G. Means. 1932. *The Modern Corporation and Private Property*. Macmillan: New York City, New York.

Burch, P., Jr. 1972. *The Managerial Revolution*. D.C. Heath: Lexington, Massachusetts.

Davidow, T., & R. Narva. 1990. Credentials: A Commentary. *Family Business Review*, 3 (3), Jossey-Bass: San Francisco, California.

Desman, R & G. Hennsler. 1992. The Family-Business Stock Index. Unpublished Manuscript, Kennesaw State College: Marietta, Georgia.

Donkels, R. & E. Frolich. 1991. Are Family Businesses Really Different? European Experiences from STRATOS. *Family Business Review*, 4 (2), Jossey-Bass: San Francisco, California.

Donnelly, R. 1964. The Family Business. *Harvard Business Review* (July/August).

Dreux, D. 1990. Financing the Family Business: Alternatives to Selling Out or Going Public. *Family Business Review*, 3 (3), Jossey-Bass: San Francisco, California.

Dyer, W.G., Jr. 1986. *Cultural Change in Family Firms: Anticipating and Managing Business and Family Transitions*. Jossey-Bass: San Francisco, California.

Guzzo R. & S. Abott, 1991. Family Firms as Utopian Organizations. *Family Business Review*, 3 (1), Jossey-Bass: San Francisco, California.

Hershon, S. 1975. The Problem of Management Succession in Family Businesses. Unpublished Doctoral Dissertation. Harvard University: Cambridge, Massachusetts.

Hoy, F, L. D. Isaacs, H. Neiman, D.A. Schwerzler, & P. P. Sidwell . 1990. A Multi-disciplinary Application of Intervention Theory in a Family Firm. Paper presented at the Family Firm Institute Annual Conference (October): Atlanta, Georgia.

Kaye, K. 1992. Who is the Client? *Family Firm Institute Newsletter*. Fall, Family Firm Institute: Boston, Massachusetts.

Kepner, E. 1983. The Family and the Firm: A Coevolutionary Perspective. *Organizational Dynamics* (summer).

Lansberg, I. 1988. The Succession Conspiracy. *Family Business Review*, 1 (2), Jossey-Bass: San Francisco, California.

Lansberg, I. 1991. Fairness and Justice in the Family Business. New England Family Business Forum Quarterly Meeting: Newport, Rhode Island.

Lansberg, I. 1992. Family Business: Field or Fad? Second International Symposium on Family and Closely-Held Business, John E. Anderson Graduate School of Management, UCLA: Los Angeles, California.

Lansberg, I., E. Perrow & S. Rogolsky. 1988. Family Business as an Emerging Field. *Family Business Review*, 1 (1), Jossey-Bass: San Francisco, California.

LeVan, G. 1991. Lawyers, Families and Feelings: Representing the Family Relationship. *Private Business Advisor* (Fall). U.S. Trust: New York City, New York.

Levinson, H. 1983. Consulting with Family Businesses: What to Look for, What to Look out for. *Organizational Dynamics*, Summer.

McCollom, M. 1990. Problems and Prospects in Clinical Research on Family Firms. *Family Business Review*, 3 (3), Jossey-Bass: San Francisco, California.

Miller, E.J. & A.K. Rice, 1967. *Systems of Organization: The Control of Task and Sentient Boundaries*. Tavistock Publications: London, England.

Moscatello, L. 1990. The Pitcairns Want You. *Family Business Magazine* (February).

Porter, M. 1992. *Capital Choices: Changing the Way America Invests in Industry*. Harvard Graduate School of Business Administration: Cambridge, MA.

Poza, E.J. 1989. *Smart Growth*. Jossey-Bass: San Francisco, California.

Roller, B. & V. Nelson. 1991. *The Art of Co-Therapy: How Therapists Work Together*. Guilford Press: New York City, NY.

Rosenblatt, P.C., L. de Mik, R.M. Anderson, & P.A. Johnson. 1985. *The Family in Business*. Jossey-Bass: San Francisco, California.

Stoy Hayward. 1992. Family Business: Splits, and Survival (article on research report by the accounting firm of Stoy Hayward). *The Economist*, October 31.

Swartz, S. 1989. The Challenges of Multidisciplinary Consulting to family owned Business. *Family Business Review*, 4 (4), Jossey-Bass: San Francisco, California.

Ward, J. L. 1988a. The Active Board with Outside Directors and the Family Firm. *Family Business Review*, 1(3). Jossey-Bass: San Francisco, California.

Ward, J. 1988b. *Keeping the Family Business Healthy*. Jossey-Bass: San Francisco, California.

Ward, J. 1990. Should We Professionalize Family Business Consulting? A Commentary. *Family Business Review*, 3 (3), Jossey-Bass: San Francisco, California.

Ward, J. 1991. *Creating Effective Boards for Family Owned Business*. Jossey-Bass: San Francisco, CA.

Whiteside M. & F.H. Brown. 1991. Drawbacks of a Dual Systems Approach to Family Firms: Can We Expand Our Thinking? *Family Business Review*, 4 (4), Jossey-Bass: San Francisco, California.

Wortman, M., Jr. 1992. Typology of Family Firm Strategies: A Reprise from Strategic Management. Second International Symposium on Family and Closely-Held Business, John E. Anderson Graduate School of Management, UCLA: Los Angeles, California.

Zeitlin, M. 1976. Corporate Ownership and Control. *American Journal of Sociology*, 79, 1073-1119.

This article discusses recently altered mandates for auditors considering an entity's ability to continue as a going concern. The authors evaluate the appropriateness of these standards in engagements involving family firms and conclude that existing procedures are inadequate to assess the risks unique to family businesses. A detailed checklist of questions is proposed as warning signals in family businesses about problems affecting the going-concern status.

Evaluation of Auditors' Going Concern Risk in Family Businesses

By Michael A. Schaefer and Patricia A. Frishkoff

Is this family business a going concern? Are there conditions that would prevent it from continuing to operate as a going concern? Answering these questions comprises part of the attestation function any time auditors are involved with the financial statements of a family business.

This article will consider going-concern risk in family businesses with three objectives: to detail specific rules of practice for one type of family business practitioner, the auditor; to identify current responsibilities related to one area of attestation, evaluation of going-concern risk; and to offer a plea to auditors to expand their evaluation by considering factors that may involve risk unique to family businesses.

Introduction

That the business will continue to operate is a basic tenet of financial accounting and underlies all financial reports with which an auditor is involved. Users depend on auditors to assure that the accounting data are reliable. Auditors are the only group licensed to express such an opinion.

Certified Public Accountants as Family Business Practitioners. Family business practitioners come from many disciplines. The nature of business operations dictates that members of at least two professions will be involved in almost every family firm: accountants and attorneys. Accountants have the advantage of recurring activity with family business clients, "a regular calendar of interventions" (Ward, 1990).

Although technical and advisory family business literature includes vast contributions from these professionals, almost none of the research in the field points to the significant involvement of accountants in serving family firms.

What Is an Auditor? Auditors are specialists in the accounting profession. During an audit, the auditor examines financial statements in accordance with detailed standards of practice prescribed by the American Institute of Certified Public Accountants (AICPA), the rule-making body of the auditing profession in the United States. The objective of an audit is to write an opinion on the fairness, consistency, and conformity of the business with established principles.

Assessing whether a business is a going concern is an important responsibility of auditors, because users of financial statements assume a going concern status unless the auditor's report signals the contrary.

Why the Interest in Going Concern Now? The American Institute of Certified Public Accountants (AICPA) Auditing Standards Board (ASB) has recently addressed this issue in its series of new statements on auditing standards (SASs). A review of existing standards was undertaken, and new standards were issued in an attempt to close a gap between the expectations of public users of financial statements about the responsibility of the auditor and what the auditor believes that responsibility to be.

The recent adoption of Statement of Auditing Standards No. 59 has increased the responsibilities of the auditor to assess going-concern risk (Ellingsen, Pany, and Fagan,

1989). Prior to SAS No. 59, the auditor assumed continuation unless evidence pointed to the contrary; if such evidence emerged, the auditor would add audit procedures to examine the situation. Now auditors must consider whether there is substantial doubt about the entity's ability to continue as a going concern on every audit engagement; in other words, they must undertake certain procedures even if there is no evidence of inability to continue as a going concern.

Certainly the frequency of business failures and the publicity about them increase the concern of the public and the profession. The new requirements are intended to provide greater assurances to users of financial statements about the long-term viability of the entity in question. That is good news for users. But there are things that the new requirements do not do, especially with respect to family businesses. The ASB determined that new auditing procedures were not needed to make the going-concern assessment. It also reaffirmed that the new requirements do not make auditors responsible for predicting future events. This means that, while an explanatory paragraph following the opinion paragraph in an auditor's report could question the ability of the entity to continue as a going concern for a reasonable period of time, "the absence of reference to substantial doubt in an auditor's report should not be viewed as providing assurance to an entity's ability to continue as a going concern" (AICPA, 1988, par. 4). In other words, auditors have been charged to be on a close watch for problems, but specific new audit steps have not been defined to make that watch proactive. So, while there is a hint of extended responsibility in the new standards, further assurance is needed, especially in family business.

Why Does This Matter with a Family Company? Privately held family businesses would have their financial statements audited if audited statements were required by lending institutions, contractors, bonding companies, franchisors, or suppliers; if owners, including family shareholders, wanted the assurance that auditor attestation adds to the quality of reporting; and if managers desired them. In family firms, relatives assume financial risk simply because of their membership in the family. Involvement on the part of auditors adds assurances about financial longevity. Besides enhanced usefulness, audits help promote and guarantee stewardship. Key managers and owners want the credibility that an audit adds to the facts represented in financial statements.

Is This Any Different from Public Companies? Evaluation of going concern risk must occur on each audit engagement, whether it involves a family business client or a publicly traded company (many of which also happen to be family businesses). Little attention, however, is usually given to the unique and critical issues that affect confidence in the family business as a going concern. Accountants have so far all but ignored many essential risk factors. It is impossible to determine whether this omission rests on failure to consider the unique problems of family business or stems from avoidance of assessments behind which there could be lawsuits.

Old and new auditing standards seem to assume that all firms are homogeneous and that similar standards and procedures will work in all cases. We argue that the family business provides a unique set of risks. Methods to evaluate these risks are currently outside normal audit procedures. Users may rely on the financial statements of family businesses assuming that assessments have been made when in fact they have not.

A leading authority in the field of family business describes keeping a family business alive as perhaps the toughest management job of all (Ward, 1987) and underlines the low rates of survival for such firms.

Intent of This Article. This article examines the going-concern concept as it applies to family-owned businesses and pleads with auditors to add procedures that will enhance the reliability of financial statements for such firms. What does going concern mean for a family business? Businesses often survive but lose their family business context by being sold to outside parties or by going public. Such transitions do not threaten the going concern status even though the enterprises are no longer family businesses.

We will first review the authoritative literature on the going-concern concept and then illustrate how the authoritative position applies to reporting on the family-owned business by linking the requirements to the unique problems that cause family businesses to fail. Then we will propose a checklist of warning signals for family businesses, arguing that the auditor should, at minimum, raise questions with the client about situations that threaten the viability of the family firm.

Authoritative Background

Although the going-concern concept did not generate a great deal of authoritative and professional literature until SAS No. 34 (AICPA, 1981) was issued, the last few years have seen an increasing interest in the practical application of this accounting concept (Clark and Newman, 1986; Ellingsen, Pany, and Fagan, 1989; Rubin, 1986). Earlier authoritative pronouncements include APB Statement No. 4 (AICPA, 1964), which recognizes the going-concern concept as a basic feature of financial accounting, and International Accounting Standard No. 1 (AICPA, 1989), which acknowledges it as a fundamental accounting assumption.

The most recent authoritative pronouncement is SAS No. 59, The Auditor's Consideration of an Entity's Ability to Continue as a Going Concern, issued by the Auditing Standards Board in April 1988 (AICPA, 1988). SAS No. 59 applies to audits of financial statements prepared in accordance with generally accepted principles or in accordance with a comprehensive basis of accounting other than generally accepted accounting principles.

SAS No. 59 provides guidance in evaluating whether there is substantial doubt about the entity's ability to continue as a going concern. As stated previously, the continuation of an entity as a going concern is assumed in financial reporting in the absence of significant information to the contrary. However, significant information that would indicate an inability to continue in existence extends far beyond the measurement principles that CPAs are trained to observe. SAS No. 59 recognizes this difficulty by segregating contrary information into two categories (Exhibit 1).

The type of information in category A is the most obvious to the trained eye of the CPA because it is quantitative and therefore measurable and because it is contained within the body of the financial statements. Most audit checklists and procedures should bring these types of problems to the fore. It is easy to leave an audit trail to substantiate an opinion based on such evidence.

However, the types of information in category B are more qualitative and subjective, and traditional audit procedures are not designed to identify them. Yet, surprisingly, SAS No. 59 indicates that existing procedures should be appropriate to evaluate the entity's

---

Exhibit 1. Two Categories of Contrary Information from SAS No. 59

A. *Information that may indicate solvency problems*
   Recurring operating losses
   Working capital deficiencies
   Negative cash flows
   Adverse key financial ratios

B. *Information that may raise questions about continued existence without necessarily indicating potential solvency problems*
   Internal matters
      Loss of key management
      Labor difficulties
      Substantial dependence on a project
      Uneconomic long-term commitments

   External matters
      Legal proceedings
      Legislation
      Loss of a key franchise, license, or patent
      Loss of a principal customer or supplier

Source: AICPA, 1988.

ability to continue as a going concern.

One of the challenges ahead for the CPA is to develop procedures that will help him or her to identify category B information when performing fieldwork. This paper primarily emphasizes the review of category B problems as identified by SAS No. 59 and as applied to the family business.

Causes of Family Business Failure

Family firms suffer high failure rates. Granted, failure – the inability to continue operating, whether as a family business or not – results from causes that strike businesses in general: Businesses mature, markets and technologies change, suppliers and customers alter their plans, competitors steal good ideas, and premiums lure owners to sell (Ward, 1987).

But beyond these typical business problems, family businesses face unique problems. Family business lack of financial capabilities, thin management expertise, conflicts between family and business demands, the absence of a successor, and lack of long-term vision and planning on business issues and the family's interrelationship to those issues (Ward, 1987).

Benjamin Benson, a family business specialist recently retired from the Boston office of the public accounting firm Laventhol & Horwath (itself a case in going concern), describes a process triggered by entrepreneurial qualities that create a successful beginning but which break down when the business grows and endures. "It is hardly coincidental that the average life cycle of a family-owned business and the average time between startup of the company and death of the founder are both twenty-four years" (Benson, 1984, p. 3). 68 Schaefer, Frishkoff

Going-Concern Problems in Family Versus Nonfamily Businesses

All businesses face risks that affect their ability to continue in operation. The category B concerns highlighted in Exhibit 1 must be addressed when auditing any company large or small, publicly traded or privately held, family-owned or not.

Many causes of failure would affect small businesses in general. Others, especially loss of key management, apply to large publicly traded firms. It is the link of the family to the business that makes this collective list of causes for failure unique. In particular, the family business faces risks related to leadership continuation, cash demands, family involvement, and absence of checks and balances. Every business audit needs procedures with which to evaluate going-concern potential. These procedures are now unspecified in the code of auditing practice. A principal objective of this paper is to provide a checklist of such procedures. At least some of these checks are uniquely necessary in family business. Procedures for forms of business other than family businesses have not been considered in the literature (although they may be employed in practice), and they are beyond the scope of this paper.

Category B Problems in Family Firms

Accountants must learn to identify and address the unique problems of family firms as part of their normal procedures. Problems in the family owned business have special characteristics that are due to the very nature of the family business: The family and the business are interwoven and cannot be separated. It is this web of connectedness that is the primary source of questions about the ability of the family-owned business to continue in existence.

In order for problems to be solved, they must first be identified. To this end, we will discuss the general categories of family business problems and provide a list of questions that can serve to identify warning signals about family businesses (see Exhibit 2).

Warning Signals Checklist. Exhibit 2 proposes questions to evaluate the potential risk of failing to continue as a going concern. Two levels of inquiry are presented. The first level

Exhibit 2. Warning Signals in Family Businesses

Item	Level 1[a]	Level 2[b]	Unique to Family Business?
Section 1: Risk of Leadership Disruption			
If the founder were to die today, could this business be effectively managed on a continuing basis without jeopardizing the business?		X	
How old is the principal owner-manager?	X		
How good is the principal owner-manager's health?	X		
Is there a named successor-manager for this firm included in franchise and distributorship agreements?	X		
Did the naming of the successor-manager occur only because it was required, or is that person the one whom the founderi ntends to be his or her successor?		X	
Is the founder intent on having one of his or her children be the successor?		X	X
How old is the intended[c] successor?	X		
Does the intended successor have three to five years of experience in a management capacity in a similar industry?	X		
Does the intended successor have training and education related to this business?	X		
Is the intended successor active now in the business?	X		
Section 2: Risks Related to Ownership			
Does the founder have a will?	X		X
Does the intended successor know the terms of the founder's will?	X		X
If there are other owners, is there a buy/sell agreement?	X		X
If there are other owners, do all the other owners have wills?	X		X
Do those wills follow the intent of the buy/sell agreement?		X	X
Is there sufficient liquidity or insurance to effect an ownership transition of this business?		X	X
Has there been a valuation of this business in the past eighteen months?	X		X
Is there a valuation in the buy/sell agreement that has been set or adjusted in the past eighteen months?	X		X
Could ownership by other family members become a problem for this company?		X	X
Could ownership by nonfamily members become a problem for this company?		X	X
Section 3: Cash Demands			
Are the will and the estate documents set forth so that the $600,000 exclusion can be used for both the founder and the spouse if applicable?	X		X
If a principal owner and spouse, if applicable, were to die suddenly today, could the family afford to pay the estate taxes without jeopardizing the business?		X	X
Have potential estate obligations been estimated?	X		X

Exhibit 2. (Continued)

Item	Level 1[a]	Level 2[b]	Unique to Family Business?
Is there a plan for funding those taxes?	X		X
Is there key man life insurance on the founder?	X		X
Is there key man life insurance on other principal owners?	X		
Have resources been targeted to provide continued living expenses for surviving family members of principal owners?	X		X
Are all the immediate family members covered by health insurance?	X		X
Is that insurance adequate?		X	X
Is the founder covered by a long-term disability policy?	X		X
Is that insurance adequate?		X	X
Do the principal owners have personal financial statements?	X		X

Section 4: Risk Created by Family Involvement

Item	Level 1[a]	Level 2[b]	Unique to Family Business?
Is family conflict impairing business practices and operations?		X	X
Does this family have a mechanism, such as family meetings or a family council, to talk about sensitive issues, such as death, divorce, rivalry, conflict?		X	X
Are family members granted concessions or treated in a differential manner so that business operations, liquidity, and morale are affected?		X	X

Section 5: Checks and Balances

Item	Level 1[a]	Level 2[b]	Unique to Family Business?
Does this family have a formal board of directors?	X		X
Are there any nonfamily members on the board of directors?	X		X
Are the directors involved in making major policy decisions, evaluating top management, and guiding significant changes in the business?		X	X
Have legal documents and ownership plans, such as the buy/sell agreement, ever been reviewed by a second professional consultant, other than the individual who prepared them?	X		X
If the founder died today, would his or her spouse know where to find key documents?	X		X

[a]Level I factors require objective judgments based on observable data.
[b]Level 2 factors require subjective judgments and are based upon behaviors, assumptions, situations, and intuition.
[c]The intended successor is not necessarily the named successor but rather the person whom the owner really expects to replace him or her.

of questions, based on factual information and observable data, requires only objective evaluations. The second level of inquiry, demanding much more subjective judgments, clearly steps beyond the intent of SAS No. 59. Use of this list of warning signals will be discussed later in this paper.

Because going concern is an issue for all firms, Exhibit 2 identifies the warning signals that are unique to family businesses. Other questions on the list might also apply to small or publicly traded companies.

Leadership Continuation. Leadership continuity is vital to the family business. The family business typically is dominated by a single manager or management group. Those individuals tend to work long hours and perform most tasks themselves. They delegate little real authority, provide no documentation for most of their decisions, and do not train anyone to succeed them. They are tight-fisted about control and tight-lipped with information. If in due course they turn over the reins, there is a tough period of adjustment and transition. If they die before the shakedown period, considerable information and all management's intent is buried. Even if succession plans are developed, the pool of candidates is often restricted to family members, regardless of experience and expertise. The questions in Section 1 of Exhibit 2 are intended to assess risks of leadership disruption.

Ownership Issues. The next area of assessment centers on whether the owner or owners have developed transfer plans to move the business into the next generation of owners. Family business owners often fail to plan for either leadership or ownership succession. Those who manage to effect leadership succession sometimes keep the trump card by holding ownership control. They may treat their children unequally in their action of selecting a sole successor and then treat them equally upon death by dividing the business equally, thereby diluting the control that comes with ownership. Or, worse yet, the owner leaves no will providing instructions for handling ownership transfer. The transfer is then effected, by default, according to state law. The questions in Section 2 of Exhibit 2 assess plans for continued family ownership of the business.

Cash Demands. Family needs and business needs will often conflict in family firms. When the founder is ready for retirement, creating a potential cash drain on the firm, the business is often in a time when revitalization is essential, which also creates need for cash. Or the owners die, and estate taxes strip away all growth-targeted resources.

Another sorry case occurs if family members are forced to sell off pieces of a family business to pay for medical expenses because there is no insurance. Unless the business, the family, or both are flush with dollars, conflict about the use of resources arises.

Each of these situations creates a contingent liability that could necessitate cash outlays. Although accounting rules provide for disclosure of contingent liabilities (Statement of Financial Accounting Standards No. 5 [FASB, 1984]), potential estate taxes or medical costs are family liabilities, not business liabilities, and they do not need to be disclosed on business financials. However, the outlays necessary could severely tax business resources because the family funds and business funds are usually considered one pool by the business family. Questions to evaluate the risk of cash drain are presented in Section 3 of Exhibit 2.

Risks Created by Family Involvement. Family involvement can be the root of family business failure, and it is therefore important in evaluating the going-concern nature. Family members allow family conflicts to override the use of sound business practices. If evidence can be seen in the financial information (because they define the boundaries of the audit), the auditor may recognize poor or thin management. Family problems may be masquerading as business problems. Special treatment of family members can have a negative impact on business results. Failure to control family use of business assets or to fire family employees with substandard performance are examples of differentiation. The questions in Section 5 of Exhibit 2 address problems of family involvement.

Checks and Balances. Audits require an assessment of internal control. The purpose is to provide assurances about the quality of information and to determine the extent to which checks and balances exist in the system. Checks and balances also protect businesses from failure. Section 6 of Exhibit 2 suggests questions that can be used to evaluate checks and balances in family business situations.

Publicly held corporations must have a board of directors, but no such requirement exists for privately held enterprises. Therefore, a logical control mechanism is a board dominated by outsiders (rather than the typical family board) that reviews major policy decisions and significant changes.

Expanding the Scope of Auditor Responsibility

SAS No. 59 (AICPA, 1988) requires auditors to question the ability of businesses to continue to exist. This paper has proposed that existing audit procedures are not sufficient to assess that issue when the client is a family business. Exhibit 2 lists some questions that should be addressed during audits of family firms. The first level of these questions rests on observable, objective data. We recommend that the Auditing Standards Board give consideration to providing categories of contrary information addressing the unique issues of family firms.

Robert H. Temkin, a member of the Auditing Standards Board, dissented on SAS No. 59 because he was concerned that evaluating an entity as a going concern without providing new auditing procedures to help fulfill this responsibility would widen the so-called expectation gap (AICPA, 1988, p. 11). His dissent supports our argument that expanded procedures are needed for family firms.

But our concern for family firms goes beyond the kinds of issues that can be addressed with level 1 types of questions. Often the accountant is one of a very small number of advisers allowed access to the family business system. Attorneys also fall into this category. The family business situation presents two problems with which we believe the auditor should assist. First, the owner is often unwilling to face the tough issues, so he or she chooses to avoid needed decisions. Second, management team members, because of their familial relationships, are unwilling to press these issues-to force decisions. Therefore, unless an outsider raises these issues, nothing will happen. Lack of decisions will only magnify the prospects of failure. The auditor is already poised in a position to ask questions that might promote needed planning. If auditors did make the effort, they could really help the business, the owners, the employees, and even the community – who all have a stake in the continuing success of the firm.

Philosophically, it would be nice to argue that the audit should involve extensive investigation into aspects of the system in question. In truth, audits are based on objective evidence traceable in the audit process. Who explores these issues, particularly the issues that are primarily behavioral in nature, and how are the questions. For example, if this checklist were adopted, how would investigation of the issue of familial concessions as a detriment to business be addressed?

In an ideal world, the auditor would bring in an organizational psychologist to perform an assessment. The field of family business is already moving toward that through consulting teams and cooperative efforts. In a practical world, a staff accountant would probe the system, examine evidence, and document responses in a manner similar to that used to evaluate access to cash or to test internal controls of the information system. The partner managing the engagement, by nature of a relationship built on trust, is already poised to conclude the investigation, to run through the checklist gathering evidence.

The main vehicle by which the auditor would report concerns is a final written report to management. This final report is different from the report of opinion that accompanies the financial statements. The terminology and format of the auditor's report in the financials are fixed. A final report to management, however, is not rigid in structure. It is here that areas of deficiency, as identified by use of the checklist and related questioning, would be enumerated and recommendations offered to the client. In other words, the auditor would point to areas of deficiency important enough to mention but cumulatively insufficient to necessitate a going-concern exception in the auditor's opinion to the financials. Substantial risks of failure would however, mandate the additional paragraph.

An Uphill Battle. Since SAS No. 59 (AICPA, 1988), even with its expanded review, does not mandate additional audit procedures, we recognize that asking the auditor to accept responsibility for evaluating the long-run viability of a family firm is an uphill battle.

SAS No. 59 requires an explanatory paragraph in the audit opinion even when substantial doubt about such ability has been adequately disclosed in the financial statements. Four members of the twenty-one-member Auditing Standards Board dissented on the statement because they believed that this explanatory paragraph would expand expectations for assurances. Conrad A. Kappel dissented because he feels that insufficient guidance is provided for auditors to address such risks and uncertainties (AICPA, 1988, p. 11). His dissent seems to argue for expanded auditor conservatism because of the legal threat. However, business owners should recognize that when an auditor publicly raises questions about going-concern status, it can have a negative impact on the firm, especially in the eyes of lenders.

SAS No. 59: Compilation and Review. Two types of auditor involvement provide less assurance to the user than a formal audit. A compilation involves presenting, in the form of financial statements, information that is the representation of management. The auditor does not undertake to express any assurance on the statements. In other words, the accountant has assembled the information, but he or she has not tested for fairness as he or she would during an audit.

A review involves performing inquiries and analyses that allow the auditor to express limited assurance that there are no material misrepresentations. For privately held companies, unless a financial institution demands a formal audit, many firms involve an auditor only to the extent of compilation or review. Although the requirements of SAS No. 59 (AICPA, 1988) only indirectly affect compilation and review services, accountants assess the adequacy of disclosures about going concern in these engagements. As such, the concerns addressed in this paper extend also to compilation and review services.

Summary

Family businesses face unique problems, many of which threaten their long-term viability. As auditors question the continued existence of family entities, they must consider not only typical business problems but those unique to family firms.

This paper has presented a checklist of warning signals-questions for the auditor to investigate. While some of the findings might affect the auditor's report that accompanies the financial statements, the greatest impact would come from raising the issues with owners, from questioning the need for plans and procedures that could increase the chances of survival. If family businesses are to remain going concerns, the auditor must be willing to accept full responsibility for his or her involvement with the family in business.

References

AICPA "Accounting for the Investment Credit." *Opinions of the Accounting Principles Board.* New York: American Institute of Certified Public Accountants, 1964.

AICPA. *The Auditor's Considerations When a Question Arises About an Entity's Continued Existence.* Statement of Auditing Standards No. 34. New York: American Institute of Certified Public Accountants, Mar. 1981.

AICPA. *Codification of Statements of Auditing Standards.* New York: American Institute of Certified Public Accountants, 1985.

AICPA. *The Auditor's Consideration of the Entity's Ability to Continue as a Going Concern.* Statement of Auditing Standards No. 59. New York: American Institute of Certified Public Accountants, Apr. 1988.

AICPA. *International Accounting Standard 1.* New York: American Institute of Certified Public Accountants, 1989.

Benson, B. "The Enigma of the Family-Owned Business." *L&H Perspective,* 1984, 10 (1), 3-6.

Clark, R. L., and Newman, M. S. "Evaluating Continued Existence." *CPA Journal,* Aug. 1986, pp. 22-30.

Ellingsen, J. E., Pany, K., and Fagan, P. "SAS No. 59: How to Evaluate Going Concern." *Journal of Accountancy,* Jan. 1989, pp. 24-31.

FASB. *Statement of financial Accounting Concepts No. 5*. New York: Financial Accounting Standards Board, 1984.

Killough, L. N., and Koh, H. C. "The Going-Concern Concept." *CPA Journal*, July 1986, pp. 24-33.

Rubin, S. "Risk and Uncertainties: Disclosing More." *CPA Journal*, Dec. 1986, pp. 81-83.

Ward, J. L *Keeping the Family Business Healthy: How to Plan for Continuing Growth, Profitability, and Family Leadership*. San Francisco: Jossey-Bass, 1987.

Ward, J. L. Master Class, Tape 10. Family Firm Institute Annual Conference, 1990.

CHAPTER 15
FAMILY BUSINESS IN SOCIETY

Business and family as Western institutions have grown together such that family business is the root of society's wealth and innovation. This reality has not always been appreciated by economists and sociologists who have thought they recognized the end of family capitalism, when in fact it remains a potent force in both advanced and developing socioeconomic systems.

Placing family business in historical perspective shows how family firms shape and are shaped by the society in which they are embedded. Indeed, family firms are so much a part and product of their communities, that when new owners with different values take over a family firm, negative impacts are felt in terms of productivity, turnover and profitability.

This article presents a framework for assessing commonly accepted family business statistics, based on the criteria used to define a family business. Using existing research from multiple fields and sources, a range is extrapolated for the total number of family businesses in the US, their contribution to Gross Domestic Product (GDP) and employment.

Myths and Realities: Family Businesses' Contribution to the US Economy – A Framework for Assessing Family Business Statistics

By Melissa Carey Shanker and Joseph H. Astrachan

Introduction

Family businesses are important contributors to the US economy, but the extent of their impact has been a matter of debate. The most commonly cited figures claim that family businesses represent 90-98% of all US businesses (Beckhard & Dyer, 1983; Hershon, 1975; Stern, 1986), that they employ over half the work force, create over half of all new jobs and generate 40-60% of the GDP (Becker & Tillman, 1978; de Visscher & Bruel, 1994). Closer analysis of these statistics reveals that a large portion of these family business "facts" have been cited so often that original sources cannot be located.

In an effort to gain a more accurate empirically-based understanding of US family businesses' collective economic impact, we reviewed the family business literature to identify quoted economic statistics. We then traced statistics to their origin. The majority of statistics identified were not rooted in formal research. In addition, the definitions used to qualify a business as a "family business" were ambiguous, or omitted altogether. Our investigation revealed four categories of family business statistics. The first category is "Street Lore" statistics and is comprised of those statistics which lack evident research origins or coinciding family business definitions. The majority of quoted family business statistics fits the "Street Lore" definition. The second largest portion of family business data consists of "Educated Estimates" based on expert knowledge and experience in the field. The third statistical category —a smaller portion of family business statistics —is comprised of extrapolations based on known data or small samples of family businesses that have been projected out to the entire universe. The last and smallest set, based on actual empirical research which uses a precise definition of a family business, can be termed "family business facts."

Our initial analysis raised several questions: Are the majority of economic statistics we read in family business literature reliable?Can such statistics be meaningful in the absence of precise family business definitions?Are the "Street Lore" statistics representative of reality or are they simply an example of the old adage that "if you say anything enough times, people will believe it" ?

Reasons for Lack of Quantitative Research

Although much qualitative research exists on family-owned businesses, few quantitative studies have been sought to determine their precise cumulative size and economic impact. The lack of substantial data is not surprising. Until recently few academics, governmental agencies, or data gathering enterprises, regarded families in business as characteristically distinct entities (Lansberg, Perrow & Rogolsky, 1988). Most research on family business is less than 10 years old.

Another reason that more extensive quantitative research has not been accomplished

Figure 1. Family Business Definitions by Degree of Family Involvement

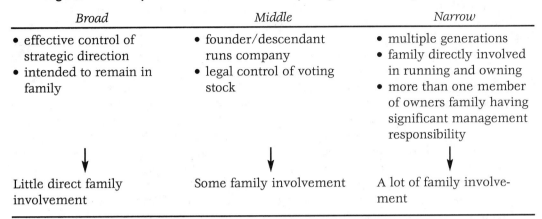

Broad	Middle	Narrow
• effective control of strategic direction • intended to remain in family	• founder/descendant runs company • legal control of voting stock	• multiple generations • family directly involved in running and owning • more than one member of owners family having significant management responsibility
↓	↓	↓
Little direct family involvement	Some family involvement	A lot of family involvement

is the difficulty in defining and identifying family businesses (Handler, 1989). Given the private nature of most family businesses, accurate information about them is not readily available. But even if all pertinent information were available, a common definition of what constitutes a family business does not exist. Unlike impartial measurements that separate small businesses from Fortune 500s, such as number of employees or sales revenues, there is no standard of measurement for specifying a family business. Without a precise definition or formula for distinguishing family run businesses from their non-family counterparts, research regarding their prevalence and economic contributions is difficult.

Family Business Definitions

Economic measurement of US family businesses is obviously linked to their definition. While anyone can intuitively recognize a "family business," even the field's experts find the task of defining precisely such businesses difficult. Family business scholars lack consensus on which criteria are most important in identifying a family business (Handler, 1989). The criteria used to define family business include: percentage of ownership, voting control, power over strategic direction, involvement of multiple generations, active

Figure 2. The Family Universe Bull's Eye

Little direct involvement

Some involvement

A lot of involvement
• >1 mgmt position

• family directly involved

• multiple generations

• control of strategic direction

• founder/ descendant runs company

• legal control of voting stock

• intended to remain in family

management by family members, and others.

Figure 1 divides the criteria used to define family businesses into three groups: broad, middle and narrow definitions. The broadest and most inclusive definition requires that the family have some degree of effective control over strategic direction, and that the business is at least intended to remain in the family. This definition includes businesses where a family member is not in direct daily contact with the business but influences decision-making, perhaps through board membership or significant stock ownership. The middle division would include all the criteria of the broadest group and would require that the founder or descendant runs the company. Again, this definition would include those businesses where only one member of the family is directly involved in the day-to-day operations. The narrowest family business definition would require that the business have multiple generations involved, direct family involvement in daily operations, and more than one family member having significant management responsibility.

The three rings of the "Bull's Eye" in figure 2 show how definitions can affect the size of the family business universe. Note that we do not suggest that the center ring is the real or best family universe —only the narrowest and most tightly defined. A looser definition will ultimately include more businesses and result in larger economic contributions. While the outer ring of businesses appears to be legitimate "family businesses," many people working in the field of family business prefer more restricted family business definitions. One should distinguish the "type" of family business to which one refers before blindly accepting general statistics about family businesses' size and impact. .

Framework for Assessing Family Businesses' Contribution to the Economy

Our objectives are to review the state of current family business statistics and to establish a framework for understanding the size of the family business universe based on various criteria. This framework will help to put frequently quoted family business statistics into perspective. We have used existing information to extrapolate and make educated estimates on the size and impact of the family business universe, e. g. , total number of family businesses, and contributions to GDP, employment and job creation. A range of statistics based on the broad, middle and narrow family business definitions established earlier are provided, and permit us to offer general statistical boundaries of the family business universe.

Size of the Family Business Universe

Family business "Street Lore" statistics state that 90-98% of all US businesses are family run (Rosenblatt, de Mik, Anderson & Johnson, 1985; Beckhard & Dyer, 1983; Barnes & Hershon, 1976). In order to determine the reliability of these statistics, US businesses were broken down into various subgroups (public and private corporations, partnerships, and sole proprietorships) and existing research was used to assess the propensity of each subgroup to include family businesses.

Public Companies

Only three research studies have been conducted that examine the number of family businesses in well-known groups of public companies. These studies have been given the rare distinction of being labeled "Family Business Facts" because each statistic is based on empirical research, and each uses a precise family business definition. The earliest study located was Philip Burch's 1972 "Managerial Revolution Reassessed." Burch's study, based on the 1965 *Fortune* 500 , examines the top 300 manufacturing firms and the top 50 merchandising, transportation and commercial banking companies. His definition used the following criteria: (1) 4-5% or more of voting stock held by a family or group of families or one affluent individual; and (2) inside or outside representation on the part of the family on the board of directors, generally over a period of time. Burch found that not only were close to half (47%) of these publicly held firms family controlled, but that the family had been wielding its power for many generations. Dan McConaughy from the University of Cincinnati (1994) researched the *Business Week* 1000 list and found that 21% of those publicly held businesses had top managers that were direct descendants of the founding family and used the following definition: a family business is one in which the CEO, President, or Chairperson is a descendant of the founding family. Hasnehn Jetha from Loyola University based his 1993 unpublished research on the 1992 *Fortune* 500 list and discovered that 37% of that list qualify as family businesses according to his definition, which is one that involves a member from at least the second generation who was a descendant of the founding family and who is a key officer, director, or owner. This research seems to point in the direction of approximately one-third of the largest publicly held companies being family-run operations.

Yet this is not the entire picture. According to the National Association of Security Dealers, there are approximately 54, 000 public companies. The three studies we referred to deal with only the largest publicly-traded companies. There are only 3, 000 stocks traded on the New York and American Stock Exchanges, leaving another 51, 000 to be traded in the over-the-counter market (OTC). The OTC market typically caters to smaller, closely-held companies as well as high tech and bio tech start-ups. Most of these smaller publicly-traded stocks remain in family control, and are only traded to give the family businesses access to equity capital. Taking this into consideration, an estimate that 60% of all public companies are family operated businesses would be conservative. However, public companies represent less than 2% of all US companies. A valid picture of family businesses requires focus on private companies.

Privately-held Companies

The IRS provides one of the very few accessible sources of information on privately held companies (US Department of Treasury, IRS, 1993). Every legally operating business in the US, large or small, public or private, family or Myths and Realities: Family Businesses' non-family, files a tax return with the IRS. Looking at each component separately, logical judgments were made about each group's propensity to include family businesses.

There are approximately 17 million sole-proprietorships in the US. It can be argued that a sole-proprietorship (an unincorporated business owned by a single person) is a type of family business; and many scholars have incorporated this idea into their definitions (Alcorn, 1982; Barnes & Hershon, 1976). In support of this theory, it is likely that there is a high occurrence of family members helping out in such enterprises. A study by Kirchoff & Kirchoff (1987) found that smaller family businesses very often use both paid and non-paid family labor, especially when first starting out. Depending on the strictness of the family business definition used, it is probable that sole proprietorships as a whole has the

Figure 3. Breakout of Total Business Tax Returns in 1991

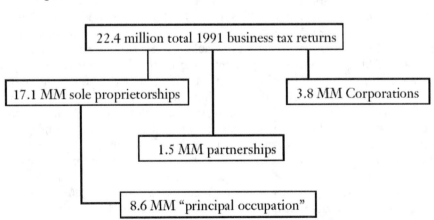

potential to include a large number of family-run businesses. An important distinction to note regarding sole proprietorships is that the 17 million total includes 1.9 million schedule F tax returns, or farmers. Non-farm sole proprietors total 15.2 million. For our purposes we have included farmers, because farms are traditionally family-run operations.

Of course, not all of the sole proprietorships represent the main occupation of the tax filer. In fact only 8.6 million called their sole proprietorship their "principal occupation" (Dennis, 1993). This distinction is addressed in the formulation of the statistical range for a narrower definition of a family business which includes "multiple family members in management" as one of its criteria.

Partnerships made up 1.5 million of total business tax returns in 1991. Partnerships possess many of the same business dynamics as sole proprietorships in that they are often small and have the potential to include high levels of family involvement.

The last category is the private corporation, of which 3.8 million filed tax returns in 1991. It is more difficult to make assumptions about the degree of family-involvement inherent in a corporation. Based on these three categories of US businesses and the research available, the authors extrapolated estimations of the size and impact of family businesses in the US that coincide with the high and low family involvement definitions established earlier (see Figure 1).

Model for Low Family Involvement (Broad) Definition

The broadest and most inclusive definition of a family business consists of all sole proprietorships based on the belief that although only one family member is officially running the business, the family dynamics involved in businesses of this type qualify it as a family business. As discussed earlier, many small businesses involve the contributions of non-paid family members. Partnerships and private corporations may be somewhat less likely to involve this level of direct family involvement. In keeping with the public corporation estimate formulated earlier, the authors estimate that 60% of all partnerships and private corporations can be deemed family businesses. This is a conservative estimate based on years of experience working with these types of family entities. Adding these figures to the 60% of all public companies estimated earlier as family businesses results in 20.3 million total family businesses in the US, or 92% of all US businesses (see Appendix 1 for calculations). This estimate is based on the broadest definition of a family business, with the outer ring of the bull's eye as its parameters. This estimation is quite close to the "Street Lore" estimation that claims 90-98% of all businesses are family businesses.

Model for High Family Involvement (Narrow) Definition

In comparison, the stricter criteria of the narrow definition disqualifies a majority of the 20.3 million family businesses in the broad group. As mentioned before, only 8. 6 million of the total 17.1 million sole proprietors that filed tax returns claimed that the business was their "principal occupation" (Dennis, 1993). In the model's narrow definition more than one family member must have significant managerial responsibility. Only the group of 8. 6 million "principal occupation" sole proprietors are included in the narrow definition. If the business is not the principal source of income for the family unit, it is unlikely that more than one family member has taken an active role in its management. In addition, the narrow definition requires that multiple generations be involved in the business. According to John Ward' research on succession (Ward, 1987), approximately one-third of post-start-up family businesses survive and reach the second generation of ownership. *The MassMutual 1994 Family Business Study* (Rosenblatt, 1985), which surveyed 1002 family businesses via telephone, supported Ward' statistic by finding that 35% of the businesses contacted had multiple generations working in the business. Weeding out the 35% of probable multiple generation family businesses results in 3.01 million "principal occupation" sole proprietors that can reasonably be considered potential family businesses under the narrow definition. Applying this same model to partnerships, corporations and public companies, results in 1.1 million potential family-run partnerships and private corporations and 11,340 publicly owned, but family operated businesses. Tallying the sole proprietors, partnerships, corporations and publics, we find 4.1 million family businesses which meet the criteria of the stricter definition, i.e. , multiple generations and more than one family member with significant managerial responsibility (see Appendix 1 for calculations).

Depending upon the criteria used, there may be a vast difference (16.2 million) in the total number of family businesses. Even though these estimates may be inexact, they illustrate that when "Street Lore" claims that over 90% of all US businesses are family-run, many businesses with little direct family involvement are included. Therefore, a lenient definition of a family business must be accepted if "Street Lore" statistics on the number of family businesses are to be considered.

The same logic has been employed to scrutinize the other commonly quoted statistics regarding family businesses' contribution to Gross Domestic Product (GDP), employment and job creation. The established ratio of 100% sole proprietors to 60% partnerships and corporations to 60% public companies will be the model for the broad definition, and 35%/21%/21% respectively for the narrow family business definition. (see Appendix 1 for calculations)

Family Businesses' Contribution to the GDP

Family business "Street Lore" claims that between 40-60% of the US GDP is generated by family businesses (Hershon, 1975; Becker & Tillman, 1978; de Visscher & Bruel, 1994). First, it must be noted that there is really no way to calculate the exact amount of GDP that family businesses — or for that matter, any business — directly contributes to GDP. There are many extraneous factors that go into determining the Gross Domestic Product (personal consumption + private domestic investment + government purchases + net exports). Yet estimations can be made based on the total output of goods and services that various business types generate. For example, the Department of Commerce (US Small Business Administration, 1993) reports that government spending is estimated to account for 36% of Gross Domestic Product. The Small Business Administration estimates that 38% of the GDP is generated by small (less than 500 employees) businesses. Thus we may assume that big businesses (500+ employees) account for the remaining 26% of GDP.

According to the US Department of Commerce (US Small Business Administration, 1993), there are 22 million small businesses (less than 500 employees) in the US and approximately 14,000 big businesses (500+ employees). Small businesses can consist of all three types of IRS subgroups: sole proprietorships, partnerships and corporations. It is, however, assumed that the 14,000 large businesses are primarily public or private corporations.

Dividing the small and large businesses into IRS categories and applying the broad definition model established earlier in this paper results in the following: under the broad definition, an estimated 50% of the GDP — or $3339.6 billion in 1993 dollars of goods and services — were generated by family businesses. The higher family involvement criteria of the narrow definition for qualifying a family business established in this paper results in the following: an estimated 12% of total goods and services, or approximately $830.9 billion in 1993 dollars (see Appendix 2 for calculations). Again, "Street Lore" is slightly on the high side of probable reality, with its claims that family businesses generate 40-60% of US GDP. Based on this analysis, a truer family business range falls closer to 20-40% of total GDP. Because of the very complex make-up of GDP, these are only estimations, but help provide a more meaningful understanding of existing family business statistics and GDP statistics in general.

Family Business Employment

Family business literature suggests that family businesses employ over half of the US work force (Becker & Tillman, 1978; de Visscher & Bruel, 1994). Workforce statistics for 1994 state that there are approximately 130 million people employed in the US (US

Department of Labor, Bureau of Labor Statistics, 1994). The US government employs close to 15% of all American workers. Of the remaining 111 million workers employed by other public and private enterprises, 54 million work for businesses employing 500 employees or less and 48 million work for larger businesses employing 500 or more.

Using the narrow and broad family business models defined earlier, we can estimate the number of small and large businesses that are family run and then extrapolate the number of workers employed by each category from the work force information provided by the Department of Labor (US Department of Labor, Bureau of Labor Statistics, 1994). Using the broadest definition model, family businesses employ 59% of the total US work force, or approximately 77 million people. The narrower definition would result in 15% of the work force or approximately 20 million people employed by family firms (see Appendix 3 for calculations). In our literature review, "Street Lore" suggested that family businesses employ over half of the US work force. Once again, the broader family business definition must be used for "Street Lore" statistics to be valid.

Family Business Net Job Creation

Job creation statistics regarding family businesses are not as prevalent in family business literature as other economic statistics because of controversy related to job growth calculations. Various sources have attempted to quantify job creation and attribute growth to a particular sector. It is a complicated procedure and there are several conflicting views in terms of the reliability of databases used and the differences between service and manufacturing industries. Nevertheless, there is some consensus among economists that small businesses have been responsible for the majority of new jobs during the past two decades. This bodes well for family businesses' role in job creation.

In 1979, David Birch published the first empirical evidence that small firms (fewer than 100 employees) created the most new jobs (Birch, 1979). His 1994 research (Birch, Haggerty & Parsons, 1994) proposes that the very small businesses, employing less than 20 employees, accounted for virtually all new net job growth from 1989-1993. The Small Business Administration (US Small Business Administration, 1993) reports that small businesses (fewer than 500) created 2/3 of all new net jobs from 1976-1990. Dun & Bradstreet's Dun' 5000 survey (Dun & Bradstreet Corporation, 1994) projects that this trend will continue, and that 73% of new (net) jobs will come from businesses with less than 100 employees.

Figure 4. Family Business Bull's Eye

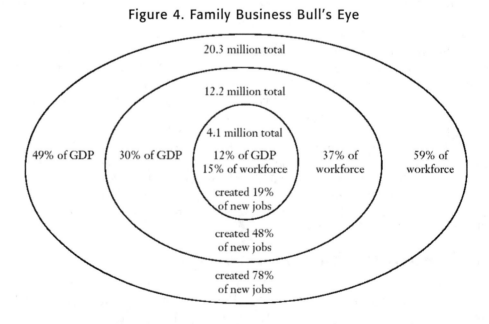

The US Small Business Administration calculates share of jobs created by firm size for the years 1976-1990 (US Small Business Administration, 1993). Based on these numbers we were able to apply our broad definition and narrow definition models to extrapolate the share of jobs created by family businesses.

Based on the broad definition, family businesses generated 78% of all new net jobs from 1976-1990, whereas only 19% of new jobs were created by family businesses that fit the narrower definition (see Appendix 4 for calculations). Such an example illustrates yet again how economic statistics vary depending upon the criteria used to define the family business universe.

Conclusion

The difficulty in identifying and defining a family business has lead to a lack of general economic profile information regarding the size and impact of this important segment of the US economy. The criteria used to define a family business will directly affect the size of the universe and therefore family business' overall apparent impact on the economy. The research of this paper is summarized in Figure 4.

We found that most family business statistics quoted in literature are a form of "Street Lore" or commonly accepted estimates — estimates that in fact are not derived from primary research. Despite the lack of research foundations, "Street Lore" statistics tend to be reasonable when viewed through the prism of a broad and inclusive definition of a family business. If a more rigorous definition is used, however, "Street Lore" statistics can be considered inflated and invalid estimates.

This paper provides a framework to assess available statistics based on the criteria chosen to include in a family business definition. In addition, using existing data, a more realistic range of economic contributions made by family businesses was extrapolated.

Implications of Findings on US Economy

Whatever the definition, family businesses represent a substantial portion of the US economy and have a massive impact on the economy as a whole. According to the MassMutual Survey, 13% of family businesses have members 65 years or older who direct the business. According to the Department of Health, life expectancy for a 65 year old white male is 13 additional years. Applying these facts to the total number of family businesses based on our broad definition model suggests that in the next 10-20 years approximately 3 million US businesses may be forced to transfer ownership (or 533, 000 businesses using the narrow definition). How much capital will be taken out of the business sector to pay estate taxes in the next two decades? Will the economy be adversely affected by a "estate tax bubble?" What will be the domino effect on the entire economy? Are only large family businesses hurt by estate taxes? How does estate taxes' capital drain affect the development and perpetuation of small family businesses in the US? If family businesses represent 90% of all US businesses, how much in total taxes do they pay? To what extent are family businesses funding the US government?

Answers to these important questions are not currently available. Clearly, there is a need for more research and study regarding family business' importance in the US economy, particularly for policy reasons. Developing accurate information is an expensive proposition. Yet the evidence in this paper strongly supports the value of further study of this crucial sector of the US economy.

References

Alcorn, P. B. (1982). *Success and survival in the family-owned firm*. New York: McGrawHill.

Barnes, L. B. , & Hershon, S. A. (1976). Transferring power in the family business. *Harvard Business Review* , 54 (4), 105-114.

Becker, B. M. , & Tillman, F. A. (1978). *The family owned business*. Chicago: Commerce Clearing House Inc.

Beckhard, R. , & Dyer, W. (1983). Managing continuity in the family-owned business. *Organizational Dynamics* , Summer, 5-12.

Birch, D. (1979). *The job generation process.* Unpublished Report, Massachusetts Institute of Technology, prepared for the Economic Development Administration of the US Department of Commerce, Washington D. C.

Birch, D., Haggerty, A., & Parsons, W. (1994). *Who's creating jobs?*: 1994. Cambridge, MA: Cogentics, Inc.

Burch, P. (1972) *Managerial revolution reassessed: Family control in America's largest corporations.* Lexington, MA: Lexington Books

Dennis, W. J. (1993). A small business primer. The NFIB Foundation: Washington, D. C., August. .

deVisscher, F., & Bruel, M. (1994). The adolescence of the American family business. *FBN Newsletter*, 9.

Dun & Bradstreet Corporation. (1994). *Dun's 5000 survey: 1994 employment survey.*

Handler, W. (1989). Methodological issues and considerations in studying family businesses. *Family Business Review*, 2 (3), 257-276.

Hershon, S. (1975). *The problem of management succession in the family business.* Unpublished dissertation, Harvard Business School.

Jetha, H. (1993). The industrial fortune 500 study. Unpublished Research, Loyola University, Chicago.

Kirchoff, B. A., & Kirchoff, J. J. (1987). Family contributions to productivity and profitability in small business. *Journal of Small Business Management*, 24-31.

Lansberg, I., Perrow, E. L., & Rogolsky, S. (1988). Family business as an emerging field. *Family Business Review*, 1 (1), 1-8.

Massachusetts Mutual Life Insurance Company. (1994). *1994 research findings of American family businesses.*

McConaughy, D. (1994). Founding-family-controlled corporations: An agency-theoretic analysis of corporate ownership and its impact upon performance, operating efficiency and capital structure. Doctoral dissertation, University of Cincinnati.

Rosenblatt, P. C., de Mik, L., Anderson, R. M., & Johnson, P. A. (1985). *The family in business: understanding and dealing with the challenges entrepreneurial families face.* San Francisco, CA: Jossey-Bass.

Stern, M. H., (1986). *Inside the family-held business.* New York: Harcourt Brace Jovanovich.

US Department of Treasury, Internal Revenue Service. (1993). *Statistics of income.* Washington, DC: US Government Printing Office.

US Small Business Administration, Office of Advocacy, Small Business Data Base: 19761986, 1984-1988, 1988-1990 USELM files, version 8.

US Small Business Administration. (1993). *The state of small business.* Washington, DC: US Government Printing Office.

US Department of Commerce. (1991). *Enterprise statistics.* Washington, DC: US Government Printing Office.

US Department of Labor, Bureau of Labor Statistics. (1994). *Employment in perspective: earnings and job growth.* Washington, DC: US Government Printing Office, August.

Ward, J. L. (1987). *Keeping the family business healthy: how to plan for continued growth, profitability, and family leadership.* San Francisco, CA: Jossey-Bass.

Appendix 1. Total Number of Family Businesses in the US

Model for total number of family businesses based on broad and narrow definitions of a family business

Broad Definition Model	total (000)
100% of Sole Proprietorships	17,100.0
60% of partnerships & private corporations	3,200.0
60% of publicly owned co.s	32.4
Total #of F.B.s	20,332.4
Narrow Definition Model	
"35% of "principal occupation"	
Sole Prop.(8.6 million)	3,010.0
21% of partnerships* & private corporations	1,113.0
21% of publicly owned co.s*	11.3
Total #of F.B.s	4,134.3

*35% (multi-generational businesses)of the 60% of total partnerships and corporations that were determined to be family businesses under the broad definition.
SOURCES: "1991 IRS income statistics,1994 Mass Mutual Family Business Survey"
National Association of Securities Dealers

Appendix 3. Family Business Employment

Total Workforce as of 8/94 = 129,866,000

Small Business = 53,769,000	Farm Workforce = 9,402,000
Big Business = 47,682,000	Government = 19,013,000

Broad Def'n Model:	100% of Sole Proprietors/60% partnerships & corp./60% public corp.	
formula: IRS category share of employment x broad model index total		(000)
Sole Prop. (total)	76% of employment by small businesses x 100% =	40,864
Part. & Corp. (<500)	24% of employment by small businesses x 60% =	7,743
Public/Private Corp. (500+)	100% of employment by big businesses x 60% =	28,609
Family Business Workforce		77,216
% of total US workforce		59%

Narrow Def'n Model:	35% of "principal occupation" Sole Prop./21% Part. & Corp./21% Public co. s"	
formula: IRS category share of employment narrow model index		total (billion)
Sole Prop. ("principal occupation")	38% of employment by small businesses x 35% =	7,151
Part. & Corp. (<500)	24% of employment by small businesses x 21% =	2,710
Public/Private Corp. (500+)	100% of employment by big businesses x 21% =	10,013
Family Business Workforce		19,874
% of total US workforce		15%

SOURCE: Department of Labor Statistics, August 1994

Appendix 4. Family Business Contribution to Job Creation

IRS Categories		Total Businesses (000)	Share of Job Growth Broad Def'n	Narrow Def'n
Small business (less than 500 employees)	=	22,386	100%	100%
- Sole Prop. (principal occupation)	=	8,600	38%	38%
- Sole Prop. (not principal occupation)	=	8,500	38%	n/a
- Partnerships &				
Corporations (<500)	=	5,300	24%	24%
Big Business (500+employees)		14	100%	100%
-Corporation(500+)		14	100%	100%

Broad Def'n Model: 100% of Sole Proprietors/60% Part. & Corp./60% Public co. s
Formula: IRS category share of job growth x broad model index

Sole Prop.	76% of jobs created by small business x 100%
Part. & Corp. (<500)	24% of jobs created by small business x 60%
Corp. (500+)	100% of jobs created by big business x 60%

Narrow Def'n Model: 35% of" Principal Occupation " Sole Proprietors/21% of Part. & Corp./21% of Public Co.s"
Formula: IRS category share of job growth x narrow model index
"Principal occupation"

Sole Prop. (8. 6 million)	38% of jobs created by small business x 35%
Part. & Corp. (<500)	24% of jobs created by small business x 21%
Corp. (500+)	100% of jobs created by big business x 21%

Family Business Job Creation 1976-1990

	US SBA DATA Small Business	Big Business	EXTRAPOLATIONS Family Broad	Family Narrow
1976-78				
jobs created	4407	1655	4977	1172
share	73%	27%	82%	19%
1978-1980				
jobs created	2605	3172	4285	1153
share	45%	27%	74%	20%
1980-1982				
jobs created	1473	69	1373	290
share	95%	4%	89%	19%
1982-1984				
jobs created	3312	1006	3597	830
share	77%	23%	83%	19%
1984-1986				
jobs created	2411	2199	3499	913
share	52%	48%	76%	20%
1986-1988				
jobs created	2770	3399	4543	1231
share	45%	55%	74%	20%
1988-1990				
jobs created	2664	-501	2408	498
share	119%	-19%	90%	18%
Total Job Growth	19642	11500	24656	6086
	63%	37%	78%	19%

SOURCE: US SBA,Office of Advocacy, Small Business Data Base.

This paper presents U. S. prevalence figures and their relationship to various family business definitions offered in literature to date. The percentage of households that own at least one family business where its owner or manager resides in the residential family/household was 13.8%. Results yielded a 10.0% prevalence rate for households having a business that qualified for this 1997 National Family Business Survey. The level of prevalence was shown to be associated with gender, ownership/management, involvement of family members, and generation of owner. These findings are useful for refining family business definitions. This paper also offers implications for future research, teaching, and practice relative to family businesses.

The Prevalence of Family Business from a Household Sample

By Ramona K. Z. Heck and Elizabeth Scannell Trent

Introduction

Even though family businesses undergird and sustain our economy and society, their pervasiveness often goes unnoticed (Cox, 1998). Notwithstanding some previous conceptual work defining family businesses (Litz, 1995), this type of business is so unnoticed and understudied that there are few serious efforts to count or determine the prevalence of family businesses accurately (Shanker & Astrachan, 1996; Upton & Heck, 1997). The lack of definitional precision, sound sampling, and methodology precludes such efforts. Litz (1997) suggested a tenure track professor's 6-year academic time line for publishing as an additional reason for the lack of empirical studies: It may limit inquiries into privately or closely held family firms given the availability of data on large, publicly held corporate enterprises (Litz, 1997).

Several estimates, though crude but improved upon with the sampling, methodology, and analyses herein, suggest that the majority of all firms in the United States are family-owned and family-operated businesses. These family firms contribute about half of both the nation's GDP and total wages (Barnes & Hershon, 1976; Hershon, 1975; Holland, 1981; Ibrahim & Ellis, 1994; Ward, 1987). Yet, the focus of attention is mainly on large, publicly held corporate enterprises. Even the extant family business literature often focuses on large-scale family firms (NE-167R Technical Committee, 1993). However, most of our economy operates around the small-to medium-scale, closely held enterprise that is nearly always a business that is owned and/ or managed by one or more individuals who can be designated as a member or members of a family – namely, the family business.

In fact, much of what is designated as entrepreneurship is often synonymous with or very closely related to family business (Casson, 1991; International Family Business Program Association [IFBPA], 1995; Kent, Sexton, & Vesper, 1982; Sexton & Kasarda, 1992; Sexton & Smilor, 1997). Entrepreneurs rarely operate alone or in a vacuum. Whether born of necessity, attribute driven, or emerging from environmental milieus (Ibrahim & Ellis, 1994), entrepreneurs are usually family members maneuvering in concert or disharmony with an array of other family members, sometimes even within the nonresidential, extended family arena (Butler & Greene, 1997; Moen, 1998; Upton & Heck, 1997).

Admittedly, the number of family firms or prevalence will depend on the definition. The purpose of this paper is threefold: first, to review operational definitions used to delineate and study households with a family firm; second, to offer prevalence estimates from the national study entitled, "Family Businesses: Interactions of Work and Family Spheres" and its 1997 National Family Business Survey (1997 NFBS), a nationally representative sample of U. S. family businesses; and third, to examine in detail selected characteristics of family businesses.

Generally, there are at least three major reasons to better define and count family businesses. First, few previous studies clearly define the entity of a family business, and previous research fails to sample or count family businesses correctly. This is the main reason for the analyses herein. Second, development of a useful empirical definition of a family business and a proper sampling procedure using households is necessary for further in-depth research and study of the interface of family and business functions within a single family. And third, a proper definition and count of family businesses is important to future research and current policy, practice, service, and education: Promoting definitional consensus among researchers may increase the likelihood of theory development, in-depth empirical analyses, comparative studies, and replication.

Previous Research

Definitions Used in Previous Empirical Research. Family business research literature is riddled with definitional issues as well as major methodological and empirical concerns (Handler, 1989; Upton & Heck, 1997). Most research suffers from lack of an integrated theoretical model and weak empirical efforts (Wortman, 1994; Upton & Heck, 1997). Clearly, the lack of high quality and comprehensive data hampers family business research.

Although it is probable that there will be multiple definitions of family business, it is imperative that these definitions have external validity, clarity, and generalizability among researchers, educators, policy makers, and practitioners. Most definitional literature is conceptually based, with no empirical evidence to support the choice or use of a particular definition. Most empirical study sampling frames are selected based on the type and size of the businesses. Such circumstances expose the research to a high probability of bias and statistically inadequate results (i.e., sample selection bias) (Heckman, 1979). Moreover, sampling family business from the population of businesses severely limits the research focus and the ability to examine the complexity of the family in relation to its business and, in particular, the interdependency of the family and the business. Studies completed to date by MassMutual (1993, 1994, & 1995) and the latest survey with MassMutual and Arthur Andersen (1997) are examples of such limited research. These studies further limit their samples based on the number of employees, amount of annual revenues, and number of years in business.

Handler (1989) developed a useful classification of family business definitions, including those that were based on ownership/management, interdependent subsystems, generational transfer, and multiple conditions. Herein, previous family business research was reviewed and classified according to the family business definition used by and relative to Handler's classifications.

Ownership/management. Although most researchers address the ownership and management of the family business, some studies emphasize ownership and control by a family entity (Alcorn, 1982; Barry, 1975; Dyer, 1986; Hershon, 1975; Kleiman, Petty, & Martin, 1995; Lansberg, 1988; Lansberg, Perrow, & Rogolsky, 1988; Rue & Ibrahim, 1996; Sharma, Chrisman, & Chua, 1997; Stern, 1986) (see Table 1). Other researchers define specifically that at least one or more family members must own and manage the business (Barnes & Hershon, 1976; Hollander & Elman, 1988; McConaughy, 1994; Winter & Morris, 1998). Still others infer that multiple (i.e., two or more) family members must own, and/or manage, the family firm (Daily & Dollinger, 1992; Daily & Thompson, 1994; Dunn, 1996).

Interdependent subsystems (family involve-ment in the business). Researchers note that the family firm involves a general interacting of two systems – namely, the family and the business (Goldberg & Wooldridge, 1993; Harvey & Evans, 1995; Kepner, 1983; Kirchhoff & Kirchhoff, 1987; Narva & Dreux, 1996) (see Table 1). Other researchers specify that interactions between the family and the business must involve multiple family members (Covin, 1994; Davis, 1983; Tagiuri & Davis, 1996). Finally, other studies specify very detailed interactions, such as influence over major decisions, board membership, and succession planning for the business (Beckhard & Dyer, 1983; Handler, 1992). The 1997 NFBS reported in this paper invokes the specific length and intensity criteria of at least 1 year of being in business and a minimal time involvement of 312 hours per year (i.e., about 1 day per week) (Winter, Fitzgerald, Heck, Haynes, & Danes, 1998).

Generational transfer. Several researchers further specify that there must be an intent to transfer or an actual generational movement of the business in addition to ownership and management control. These definitions involve multiple conditions and are categorized here specific to their generational transfer criteria (Barach & Ganitsky, 1995; Birley, 1986; Churchill & Hatten, 1997; Fiegener, Brown, Prince, & File, 1994; Litz, 1995; Ward, 1987, 1988) (see Table 1). Businesses that have not transferred or have no intent or potential to transfer may be entrepreneurial firms that have gone public or hired professional management, or existing family businesses that have done the same and do not retain control over the ownership and/or management (Litz, 1995).

Multiple conditions. Several researchers apply multiple criteria to define family businesses. Some use only two criteria of ownership/management and involvement of family members (Blake & Saleh, 1995; Cox, 1998; Lyman, 1991) (see Table 1). Still other studies define family business according to a variety of additional criteria (Astrachan & Kolenko, 1994; Dannhaeuser, 1993; Donnelley, 1964; Rosenblatt, deMik, Anderson, & Johnson, 1985).

Definitional Works. Determining a prevalence rate of family firms necessitates a level of definitional precision not achieved to date in the family business literature. Wortman's (1995) survey of the literature yields more than 20 different definitions of a family firm, and he notes the singular and ad hoc nature of many definitions. Earlier work by Handler (1989) describes a variety of definitions for a family business, each varying relative to family ownership, involvement of family members, control or management by a family member, and the family's intent to transfer. Litz (1995) attempts to identify family businesses conceptually, based on ownership, management, and intent to transfer. He develops a 3 x 3 matrix, or nine business types, based on ownership and management and then examines the intent to transfer notion. Litz identifies four of the nine business types as either family businesses or potential family businesses. Although his conceptual work helps to develop further possible definitions of family business, it does nothing to test these definitions, for he does not apply or tie his definitions to empirical data.

Upton and Heck (1997) note the pressing need for a consistent family business definition. Such definitional refinement would allow comparative studies and replications as well as precursor work leading to the development of a conceptual framework for the family firm. To date, definitions have been inconsistent, and important dimensions, such as the degree or intensity of ownership, involvement, and management, have not been fully conceptualized or empirically explored. Previous research bears out that a definitive family business definition is likely to remain elusive. Only a few studies specify in detail the family aspect of their definitions by including criteria that relate to the family as well as the business (Kepner, 1983; Rosenblatt et al., 1985).

Early writings of Hollander and Elman (1988), relative to a systems approach, suggest that a family business is a business that is owned and/or managed by one or more family members. This simple definition was used herein for this national study. The Methods section of this paper further discusses definitional issues.

Previous Counts of Family Businesses. Most previous studies (Barnes & Hershon, 1976; Hershon, 1975; Holland, 1981) that offer counts of family businesses are based on U. S. Small Business Administration (SBA) reports derived from its own data sources. These data sources do not differentiate between family and nonfamily firms. Dreux (1990 & 1994) used Dun & Bradstreet data, excluding sole owners, to develop estimates of the number of family businesses. Dun & Bradstreet data include only those who file detailed financial information with this source and, so, result in a biased sample of businesses. Still other researchers, such as Ward (1987), collected their own data using various business lists; in most cases, the quality of such lists and the resulting counts could be questioned.

Shanker and Astrachan (1996) recently reviewed these previous research claims and conclude that most are questionable in their scope, methods, and generalizations. Although primary data was not collected, Shanker and Astrachan used extant business data sources, such as those from the SBA, to infer the validity of these previous definitions, prevalence, and associated economic contributions of family business. They found a range from a narrow definition resulting in 4.1 million family businesses contributing 12% of the

GDP, 15% of the workforce, and 19% of new jobs to the broadest definition resulting in 20. 3 million contributing 49% of the GDP, 59% of the workforce, and 78% of the new jobs.

Methods

The 1997 NFBS used a household sampling frame. The sample was limited to families (defined as a group of people related by blood, marriage, or adoption who shared a common dwelling unit) in which at least one person owned or managed a family business. Another criterion of the sample was work intensity in the business as assessed by length of time in business and number of hours per week of involvement. To qualify for this study, the owner-manager had to have been in business for a least 1 year, worked at least 6 hours per week year-round or a minimum of 312 hours a year in the business, be involved in its day-to-day management, and reside with another family member.

Data collection involved four instruments. The first, the screening instrument, was piloted and developed to ascertain whether the household contained a family business (Heck & Scannell, 1997). Three interview schedules formed the core data collection instruments – one schedule for the household manager, one for the business manager, and one combined interview if the household manager and the business manager were the same individual. After verifying eligibility, the respondent was asked to identify the household manager, the business manager, and the family financial manager. The household manager was defined as "the person who actually manages the household, that is, the one who takes care of most of the meal preparation, laundry, cleaning, scheduling of family activities, and overseeing of child care." The instruments were administered to household members that met the study criteria.

The national sample was purchased from Survey Sampling in Fairfield, Connecticut, a commercial firm that provides samples based on specified sampling frames. Because the interviews were administered by telephone, the sample frame consisted of all households with a listed telephone.

During 1997, the Iowa State University Statistical Laboratory screened 14,115 U.S. households, resulting in 1,116 eligible family households. At the completion of interviewing, the 1997 NFBS consisted of 794 families with a family business, a 71% response rate. The response rate for the 708 completed business interviews was 63.4%. Households with a family business that completed both the business and household interviews numbered 673, a 60.3% response rate. Missing data were imputed. For further details concerning the methods of the 1997 NFBS, see Winter et al. (1998).

Data. The focus of this research paper is to report the prevalence and selected characteristics of 1,116 (9,858,666 weighted frequency) family households that completed a screen interview. These screen data are used to identify the prevalence of households owning or managing one or more businesses and with more than one person in the household. In addition, the 708 (9,747,103 weighted frequency) households that completed the business interview schedule are also delineated by the definitional classifications that Handler developed (1989).

Analysis. Data were analyzed using descriptive statistics of frequency counts, percentage, mean, and standard deviations. In addition, tests for equality of variances were made using Levene's (1960) test. If variances were found to be unequal, then two sample T-tests for equality of means were made. Data were analyzed using the 95% confidence interval, with the level of significance set at $p < .05$.

Strengths and Limitations of the Research Methods.

Household sampling frame. The advantages of the household sampling frame are threefold. First, by interviewing households to find businesses, respondents will include agricultural, newer, smaller, and minority businesses that may be underrepresented in business lists such as Dun & Bradstreet's. Second, because the authors are members of a research team that has studied home-based businesses extensively, the literature on this subset of family businesses can be expanded through this study. Third, one objective of the research is to examine the relationships between the family and the business. The household is the logical place to contact family members concerning both family and business issues.

A household sampling frame may undercount the number of businesses to the extent a household owns multiple businesses. Households were eligible for this study on the basis of participation by the business manager in the main or primary business, defined as the one in which the business manager spent the most hours working. If more than one business qualified on hours, the one generating the higher gross income was chosen. If more than one business qualified on hours and had the same gross income, then the one owned or managed by the household manager was chosen. The number of households with multiple businesses was low and, in most cases, these additional businesses were minor relative to the business that the interview covered.

The limitations of using a purchased sampling list relate to the quality of the list. The decision to use a listed sample rather than random digit dialing (RDD) was economic. RDD is substantially more expensive to use both in terms of time and money due to telephoning nonhouseholds and nonworking numbers. Survey Sampling, a widely used commercial sampling firm, supplements their telephone listings with a variety of lists, including magazine subscription, voter registration, and vehicle and driver registration lists. Of the 14,115 screened households, 14.7% of the telephone numbers were ineligible because they were either not in service or were not the telephone numbers of households. Of the 12,046 eligible households, 12.6% that were assumed to be households were not screened because of refusal or language barrier and about 5.1% never answered or had answering machines. The 9,910 completed screen interviews represent an 82.3% response rate. Such a response rate is acceptable for a telephone interview and reflects the quality of the purchased sample list.

Family business definition. The 1997 NFBS employed a broad definition of a family business, namely, a business that is owned and/or managed by one or more family members. Such a family business definition was chosen for three reasons. First, the conceptual underpinnings of the 1997 NFBS were based on systems theory (Stafford, Duncan, Danes, & Winter, 1999). Systems theory is sensitive to the interrelationships and perspectives of all subsystems, parts, or individuals within the whole system. Thus, both the business and the family systems are important to understanding the family business. In addition, any individual in either system may affect parts of both systems or the family business. Therefore, ownership per se cannot define a family business and may, in fact, be irrelevant to the family and business dynamics.

Second, many family business issues may affect all family members whether they are in or out of the business. For example, tensions or conflicts stemming from the business may affect family members regardless of which or how many family members work in the business. Or, if an entrepreneur owns a business with no family members involved (other than himself or herself) and the business fails, this business failure will no doubt affect the family dramatically. Further, the lack of involvement of family members in a business that another family member owns may be arbitrary, not by mutual consent, and important in and of itself. Dumas (1989) and Cole (1997), among others, documented the exclusion or discounting of females relative to the family business. Spouses and other family members might be less formally involved in the business or involved on an unpaid basis (Heck & Walker, 1993; Rosenblatt et al., 1985).

Third, using a broad definition of family business allows for a more comprehensive examination of both the family and business characteristics of the phenomena under study. In addition, it affords the researchers flexibility in examining the variations in family businesses (Winter et al., 1998). Note that this study's 12-month, 312-hour criteria exclude nascent and new startup businesses. As a result, the businesses in this study are sufficiently established and occupy a sufficiently large enough proportion of the business manager's time for meaningful interactions to occur between the family and the business. Thus, using a broad definition of family business along with these eligibility requirements does not limit the 1997 NFBS. Rather, it makes the 1997 NFBS more useful in examining a number of family business definitions, often cited in previous family business literature but never tested empirically.

1997 National Family Business Survey: Screen Data

Prevalence of Households Owning a Family Business. In determining the prevalence of family businesses in the United States, results differ based on the operational definition. Looking just for the prevalence of businesses in households, 18.3%, or 18,037,000 households, responded that someone in the household owns one or more businesses of some kind (Table 2). This general prevalence for business-owning households is reasonably comparable to the SBA figures that are total business counts (U.S. Small Business Administration, 1996) and to counts related to the broadest family business definition that Shanker and Astrachan (1996) use. In addition, 4.4% replied that a business manager resides in the household. However, only a small number of the managers are related to the owner of the business that they manage.

Without using the work measures of length and intensity for family household definition, 13.8%, or 13,667,000 households, own at least one business that is owned or managed by a family member living in the residential unit. The majority of these households are families; only 1.4% of the households are nonfamilies. In addition, 1,863,000 (1,465,000 plus 374,000 owners plus 24,000 managers) households own/manage two or more businesses. Families held the vast majority of these multiple businesses.

Work intensity was the first part of the definition. A business owner-manager had to have owned the business for at least 1 year and worked at least 312 hours per year. In applying these criteria, 19.6%, or 2,688,000, did not fulfill the defined work intensity, 11.5% worked less than 312 hours, and 8.1% were in business for less than 1 year, as shown in Table 2. These criteria lowered the prevalence to 11.1%

A family was defined as a household with two or more people related by blood, marriage, or adoption and included partners living as married. Adding this family requirement to the business owner-managers' findings reduced the eligibles by 1.1%, or 1,120,000 households. Family households owning at least one business that met the study's work intensity and years in business requirements numbered 9,859,000 out of the total 98,754,000 households in the United States, yielding a prevalence rate of 10.0%. These prevalence figures and rates reported herein compare favorably with Shanker and Astrachan's (1996) middle and narrow definitions for family business and their corresponding prevalence figures.

Sample Characteristics.

Work intensity. The length of time in business ranged from 1 year to 80 years, with the average being 13.2 years. For reporting consistency, hours worked per week were top coded. It was reasonable to assume that no one could consistently work more than 18 hours per day or 126 hours per week. Business owner-managers reported working an average of 44.6 hours per week. They reported working between a minimum of 6 hours to a maximum of 126 hours per week. When asked how long the owner-manager worked per month and per year, the averages reported working were 193.3 hours per month and 2,319.7 hours per year. Clearly, the business managers were working longer hours than the average 40-hour workweek.

Family characteristics. The business owner/managers reported on average having three household members (Table 3). The size of the household ranged from the minimum of two to a maximum of nine persons. The percentage of the business owner-managers who are male was 75.8%, and 24.2% are female.

Multiple businesses. Only 16.0% of the family owner-managers reported having more than one business in the household. When examining these multiple businesses by business type, all industrial sectors were represented. The household's first and second businesses were compared by industry. The results indicated that 65% of the second businesses are in a different sector from the primary business. For example, the first business might be as a financial service consultant and the second one might be making and selling gifts retail. Overall, households owning more than one business were less likely to have a secondary business in construction and manufacturing and more likely to own a service business compared to other industrial sectors.

Two Sample T-Test Findings. There were significant differences found using a two sample T-test to compare the gender of the owner-managers to the mean number of years in business and the mean number of hours worked per week, month, and year. As shown in Table 4, males reported being in business significantly more years (M = 14.0, SD = 11.7) than females (M = 10.5, SD = 9.7). There were differences by gender for the reported number of hours worked per week, per month, and per year. When asked how much they worked per week, female business owner-managers reported working significantly fewer hours per week (M = 38.0, SD = 21.2) on average than male owner-managers (M = 46.7, SD = 24.1). This relationship of males working more than females was also significant for hours per month and hours per year. In addition, male owners had significantly larger households (3.3) than females owners (3.1).

Prevalence of Households Owning a Family Business by Definitions. Using the data from the main interviews, 9,747,103 households can be described and categorized by the four main criteria developed by Handler's (1989) typology: ownership/management, independent systems, generational transfer, and multiple conditions. Thus, the prevalence of households that owned or managed a family business can be examined in terms of the selected variables in Table 5 under these four definitional criteria.

The predominant ownership status was sole proprietorships, although subchapter S-corporations amounted to 18.0% of the family businesses under study (Table 5). One-owner businesses were 79.7% of the family businesses, whereas 20.3% had multiple owners. Relative to multiple owners, 14.6% were owned with other family members living in the household, and 12.7% were owned with other family members not living in the household. The business manager owned on average 85.0% of the family business, with the owned share worth $295,586.

The major decision makers were most often the business owner or spouses. Parents, adult children, and other relatives sometimes were involved in the decision making, but all participated at about 5% levels.

Family members working in the business was commonplace, with 19.9% of the family businesses under study having three family members working in the business. Two family members working in the business was the highest rate – 42.6%, or 4,149,219 households. The rates of having a relative not living in the household and working in the business as either an employee or unpaid worker were much lower – 11.0% and 15.5%, respectively. There were more households with family businesses where these relatives (not living in the household) were unpaid workers rather than employees.

The generation owning or managing the family business was predominantly the founder or the first generation at 86.6%. However, 10.3%, or 1,003,454 households, were second generation, and the third and fourth generations had much lower percentages. A sizable number of the businesses, 2,228,041, or 22.9%, expected to change ownership during the next 5 years. Within this ownership change group, about one-half thought that retaining family ownership was very unlikely, whereas the other half thought otherwise.

The multiple-conditions criteria lowered the prevalence figures incrementally. Starting with the 9,747,103 households, imposing the criteria of 50% or greater ownership reduced the prevalence to 8,795,104, or 90.2% of households with family businesses. Sequentially, if only family members were the major decision makers for the business, the prevalence was further reduced to 7,949,742, or 81.6%. In addition to these two criteria, requiring that two or more family members or relatives be involved in the business caused the prevalence to fall to 6,205,896, or 63.7%. If the business was either a second-generation or higher business, or there was a likelihood that changing ownership would stay in the family, the prevalence was substantially reduced to 807,995, or 8.3% of the households.

Discussion and Conclusions

Results from a nationally representative sample of households indicate a 10.0% prevalence rate of at least one family owned/managed business for the population of U. S. households when the business is more than 1 year old and the owner/manager works a minimum of 312 hours. That is, a family business owner-manager resides in approximately 10 out of every 100 households. The screen data indicate that fewer women owned/managed businesses and they worked fewer hours per week, per month, and per year than those owned by men. It may be that the longer established businesses owned/managed by women have circumstances that justify their working fewer hours than men, or they may choose to do so.

Because of the careful sampling and the national scope of the 1997 NFBS, the nature of family business was examined in great depth by this prevalence analysis. Although ownership status showed that a little over one-half of the family businesses in this study were sole proprietorships, one-owner businesses predominated at nearly 80%. However, spouses, parents, adult children, and other relatives often played a major decision making role in the business. Ownership does not completely depict the nature of the family business. The majority of businesses had two or more family members of the residential household working in the business. Also, extended family members were involved in about one-quarter of the businesses on both a paid and unpaid basis. Multiple conditions were imposed to reveal the prevalence numbers associated with various family business definitions. Clearly, the more restrictions imposed, the lower the prevalence rate. However, the uniqueness of the 1997 NFBS will allow the stratification of family businesses by various definitions, thereby enabling further examination.

The prevalence and characteristics of business owners are important to policy makers for establishing practices for family businesses. Moreover, practitioners, family business programs, and service providers can better meet the demand for keeping these businesses healthy and vibrant. Educators can use the information to assist students in making career decisions. Finally, researchers will benefit from definitional clarity and established estimates in developing theory, in-depth empirical analyses, comparative studies, and replication.

Beyond this prevalence rate analysis, the 1997 NFBS will allow for more in-depth examination of the family business. These family business data, collected in conjunction with community and family data, provide rich and unique information. Many additional topics are being explored relative to the business, the family, and the interaction between the two. Results from the 1997 NFBS will contribute to the understanding of individual and group well-being in family, business, and community settings. Such understanding will enhance the stability and security of families who own and operate businesses, aid in developing policies and programs that foster family firms, and quantify the family businesses' contributions to local, state, and national community and economic development. The research produced from analyses using the 1997 NFBS will add significantly to the empirical literature on work and family life as well as to general family business literature. The research efforts developed and tested empirically precise definitions of family versus nonfamily businesses and, in turn, established precise empirical estimates of their prevalence. A comprehensive examination of family factors and business factors that are associated with both family viability and business viability can be explored for the first time.

References

Alcorn, P. B. (1982). *Success and survival in the family owned firm.* New York: McGraw-Hill.

Arthur Andersen & MassMutual. (1997). *American family business survey, 1997.* Springfield, MA: Author.

Astrachan, J. H., & Kolenko, T. A. (1994). A neglected factor explaining family business success: Human resource practices. *Family Business Review, 7* (3), 251262.

Barach, J. A., & Ganitsky, J. B. (1995). Successful succession in family business. *Family Business Review, 8* (2), 131-155.

Barnes, L. B., & Hershon, S. A. (1976). Transferring power in the family business. *Harvard Business Review, 54* (4), 105-116.

Barry, B. (1975). The development of organization structure in the family firm. *Journal of General Management, 3,* 42-60.

Beckhard, R., & Dyer, W. G. (1983). Managing change in the family firm: Issues and strategies. *Sloan Management Review, 25,* 59-65.

Birley, S. (1986). Succession in the family firm: The inheritor's view. *Journal of Small Business Management, 24* (3), 36-43.

Blake, C. G., & Saleh, S. D. (1995). A model of family owned small business performance. *Family Business Annual, 1* (Section I), 22-30.

Butler, J. S., & Greene, P. G. (1997). Ethnic entrepreneurship: The continuous rebirth of American enterprise. In D. L. Sexton & R. W. Smilor (Eds.), *Entrepreneurship: 2000* (pp. 267-289). Chicago, IL: Upstart Publishing Company.

Casson, M. (1991). *The entrepreneur: An economic theory.* Hampshire, England: Gregg Revivals.

Churchill, N. C., & Hatten, K. J. (1997). Non-market-based transfers of wealth and power: A research framework for family business. *Family Business Review, 10* (1), 53-67. (Originally published in *American Journal of Small Business*, Winter, 1987.)

Cole, P. M. (1997). Women in family business. *Family Business Review, 10* (4), 353-371.

Covin, T. J. (1994). Perceptions of family-owned firms: The impact of gender and education level. *Journal of Small Business Management, 32* (3), 29-39.

Cox, E. S. (1998). The family as a foundation of our free society: Strengths and opportunities. In R. K. Z. Heck (Ed.), *The entrepreneurial family* (pp. 8-15). Needham, MA: Family Business Resources, Inc.

Daily, C. M., & Dollinger, M. J. (1992). An empirical examination of ownership structure in family and professionally managed firms. *Family Business Review, 5* (2), 117-136.

Daily, C. M., & Thompson, S. S. (1994). Ownership structure, strategic posture, and firm growth: An empirical examination. *Family Business Review, 7* (3), 237-249.

Dannhaeuser, N. (1993). The survival of family-operated firms under developed conditions: The case of Hassfurt, Germany. *The Journal of Developing Areas, 27*, 307-328.

Davis, P. (1983). Realizing the potential of the family business. *Organizational Dynamics, 12* (1), 47-56.

Donnelley, R. G. (1964). The family business. *Harvard Business Review, 42* (4), 93-105.

Dreux, D. R. (1990). Financing family business: Alternatives to selling out or going public. *Family Business Review, 3*, 225-243.

Dreux, D. R. (1994, December 7). *Business communication from U. S. Trust Company using Dun & Bradstreet Market Indicators.*

Dumas, C. (1989). Understanding the father-daughter and father-son dyads in family-owned businesses. *Family Business Review, 2* (1), 31-46.

Dunn, B. (1996). Family enterprises in the UK: A special sector? *Family Business Review, 9* (2), 139-156.

Dyer, W. G., Jr. (1986). *Cultural change in family firms: Anticipating and managing business and family transitions.* San Francisco: Jossey-Bass.

Goldberg, S. D., & Wooldridge, B. (1993). Self-confidence and managerial autonomy: Successor characteristics critical to succession in family firms. *Family Business Review, 6* (1), 55-73.

Fiegener, M. K., Brown, B. M., Prince, R. A., & File, K. M. (1994). A comparison of successor development in family and nonfamily businesses. *Family Business Review, 7* (4), 313-329.

Handler, W. C. (1989). Methodological issues and considerations in studying family business. *Family Business Review, 2* (3), 257-276.

Handler, W. C. (1992). The succession experience of the next generation. *Family Business Review, 5* (3), 283-307.

Harvey, M., & Evans, R. (1995). Forgotten sources of capital for the family-owned business. *Family Business Review, 8* (3), 159-176.

Heck, R. K. Z., & Scannell, E. (1997). Defining and counting family businesses: Results from a national pilot study. *Proceedings of the 1997 Annual Conference of the International Family Business Program Association*, Amherst, MA, July 10-12.

Heck, R. K. Z., & Walker, R. (1993). Family-owned home businesses, their employees, and unpaid helpers. *Family Business Review, 6* (4), 397-415.

Heckman, J. (1979). Sample selection bias as a specification error. *Econometrica, 47*, 153-161.

Hershon, S. A. (1975). *The problem of management succession in family businesses.* Unpublished doctoral dissertation, Harvard University, Business Administration.

Holland, P. J. (1981). *Strategic management in family business: An exploratory study of the development and strategic effects of the family-business relationship.* Unpublished doctoral dissertation, University of Georgia.

Hollander, B. S., & Elman, N. S. (1988). Family-owned businesses: An emerging field of inquiry. *Family Business Review, 1* (2), 145-164.

Ibrahim, A. B., & Ellis, W. H. (1994). *Family business management: Concepts and practice.* Dubuque, IA: Kendall/Hunt.

International Family Business Program Association, Task Force. (1995). Family business as a field of study. *Family Business Annual, 1* (Section II), 1-8.

Kent, C. A., Sexton, D. L., & Vesper, K. H. (1982). *Encyclopedia of Entrepreneurship.* Englewood Cliffs, NJ: Prentice-Hall.

Kepner, E. (1983). The family and the firm: A coevolutionary perspective. *Organizational Dynamics,* (Summer), 57-70.

Kirchhoff, B. A., & Kirchhoff, J. J. (1987). Family contributions to productivity and profitability in small business. *Journal of Small Business Management, 25,* 24-31.

Kleiman, B., Petty, J. W., & Martin, J. (1995). Family controlled firms: An assessment of performance. *Family Business Annual, 1* (Section I), 1-13.

Lansberg, I. (1988). The succession conspiracy. *Family Business Review, 1* (2), 119-143.

Lansberg, I., Perrow, E. L., & Rogolsky, S. (1988). Family business as an emerging field. *Family Business Review, 1* (1), 1-8.

Levene, H. (1960). Robust test for equality of variance. In I. Olkin (Ed.). *Contributions to Probability and Statistics* (pp. 278-292). Palo Alto, CA: Stanford University Press.

Litz, R. A. (1995). The family business: Toward definitional clarity. *Family Business Review, 8* (2), 71-81.

Litz, R. A. (1997). The family firm's exclusion from business school research: Explaining the void; addressing the opportunity. *Entrepreneurship Theory and Practice, 21* (3), 55-71.

Lyman, A. R. (1991). Customer service: Does family ownership make a difference? *Family Business Review, 4* (3), 303-324.

MassMutual. (1993). *Family business: 1993 research findings.* Springfield, MA: Author.

MassMutual. (1994). *Family business: 1994 research findings.* Springfield, MA: Author.

MassMutual. (1995). *Family business: 1995 research findings.* Springfield, MA: Author.

McConaughy, D. (1994). *Founding-family-controlled corporations: An agency-theoretic analysis of corporate ownership and its impact upon performance, operating efficiency and capital structure.* Doctoral dissertation, University of Cincinnati.

Moen, P. (1998). A life course approach to the entrepreneurial family. In R. K. Z. Heck (Ed.), *The entrepreneurial family* (pp. 16-29). Needham, MA: Family Business Resources, Inc.

Narva, R. L., & Dreux, D. R. (1996). What's in store for the family business market? *Proceedings of the Cornell University Conference on the Entrepreneurial Family: Building Bridges,* March 17-19, 1996, New York.

NE-167R Technical Committee. (1993). *Family businesses: Interaction of work and spheres.* Unpublished research grant proposal, Cornell University, Department of Policy Analysis and Management.

Rosenblatt, P. C., deMik, L., Anderson, R. M., & Johnson, P. A. (1985). *The family in business: Understanding and dealing with the challenges entrepreneurial families face.* San Francisco: Jossey-Bass.

Rue, L. W., & Ibrahim, N. A. (1996). The status of planning in smaller family-owned business. *Family Business Review, 9* (1), 29-43.

Scannell, E., & Heck, R. K. Z. (1998). The prevalence of businesses owned and operated by families. In I. Leech (Ed.), *Proceedings of the 44th Annual Conference of the American Council on Consumer Interests* (p. 194). Columbia, MO: American Council on Consumer Interests.

Sexton, D. L., & Kasarda, J. D. (Eds.). (1992). *The state of the art of entrepreneurship.* Boston: PWSKENT.

Sexton, D. L., & Smilor, R. W. (Eds.). (1997). *Entrepreneurship: 2000.* Chicago, IL: Upstart Publishing Company.

Shanker, M. C., & Astrachan, J. H. (1996). Myths and realities: Family businesses' contribution to the US economy -A framework for assessing family business statistics. *Family Business Review, 9* (2), 107-123.

Sharma, P., Chrisman, J. J., & Chua, J. H. (1997). Strategic management of the family business: Past research and future challenges. *Family Business Review, 10* (1), 1-35.

Stafford, K., Duncan, K. A., Danes, S. M., & Winter, M. (1999). *A research model of sustainable family businesses.* Unpublished manuscript.

Stern, M. H. (1986). *Inside the family-held business.* New York: Harcourt Brace Jovanovich.

Tagiuri, R., & Davis, J. A. (1996). Bivalent attributes of the family firm. *Family Business Review, 9* (2), 199208. (Originally published by Davis, J. A., & Tagiuri, R., Santa Barbara, CA: Owner Managed Business Institute, 1982.)

U. S. Bureau of the Census. (1996, March). *Current population survey.* Washington, D.C.: U. S. Government Printing Office.

U. S. Bureau of the Census. (1997, August 21). Population estimates program, population division. < http://www. census. gov/population/ >.

U. S. Small Business Administration. (1996). *The state of small business: A report to the President.* Washington, D. C. : U. S. Government Printing Office.

Upton, N. B., & Heck, R. K. Z. (1997). The family business dimension of entrepreneurship. In D. L. Sexton & R. W. Smilor (Eds.), *Entrepreneurship: 2000* (pp. 243-266). Chicago, IL: Upstart Publishing Company.

Ward, J. L. (1987). *Keeping the family business healthy: How to plan for continuing growth profitability and family leadership.* San Francisco, CA: Jossey-Bass.

Ward, J. L. (1988). The special role of strategic planning for family businesses. *Family Business Review, 1* (2), 105-117.

Winter, M., Fitzgerald, M. A., Heck, R. K. Z., Haynes, G. W., & Danes, S. M. (1998). Revisiting the study of Family Businesses: Methodological challenges, dilemmas, and alternative approaches. *Family Business Review, 11* (3), 239-252.

Winter, M., & Morris, E. W. (1998). Family resource management and family business: Coming together in theory and research. In R. K. Z. Heck (Ed.), *The entrepreneurial family* (pp. 30-47). Needham, MA: Family Business Resources, Inc.

Wortman, M. S. (1994). Theoretical foundations for family-owned business: A conceptual and research based paradigm. *Family Business Review, 7* (1), 3-27.

Wortman, M. S. (1995). Critical issues in family business: An international perspective of practice and research. In *Proceedings of the ICSB 40th World Conference* (pp. 53-76). Sydney, Australia: Institute of Industrial Economics.

This paper reports results from the Cooperative Regional Research Project, NE-167R, "Family Businesses: Interaction in Work and Family Spheres," partially supported by the Cooperative States Research, Education and Extension Service (CSREES) ; U. S. Department of Agriculture; the experiment stations at University of Hawaii at Manoa, University of Illinois, Purdue University (Indiana), Iowa State University, Michigan State University, University of Minnesota, Montana State University, University of Nebraska, Cornell University (New York), North Dakota State University, The Ohio State University, Pennsylvania State University, Texas A & M University, Utah State University, University of Vermont, and University of Wisconsin Madison; and the Social Sciences and Humanities Research Council of Canada (for the University of Manitoba). An earlier version of this paper was presented at the Annual Conference of the American Association for Consumer Interests, Washington, D. C., March 25-28, 1998, as a part of the symposium, "Concepts and Challenges: Surveying Families in Business" (Scannell & Heck, 1998). The authors are grateful to Kathryn Stafford and Mary Winter for their reviews of the paper's early drafts. The authors are also appreciative of comments by peer reviewers relative to the journal's review process.

Table 1. Summary of Family Business Definitions from Previous Literature Based on Handler's (1989) Typology, Relative to Operational Variables in the 1997 National Family Business Survey

Conceptual Definitions by Authors	*Operational Variables from 1997 National Family Business Survey*
Alcorn (1982); Barnes & Hershon (1976); Barry (1975); Daily & Dollinger (1992); Daily & Thompson (1994); Dunn (1996); Dyer (1986); Hershon (1975); Hollander & Elman (1988); Kleiman, Petty, & Martin (1995); Lansberg, Perrow, & Rogolsky (1988); McConaughy (1994); Rue & Ibrahim (1996); Sharma, Chrisman, & Chua (1997); Stern (1986); Winter & Morris (1998)	Ownership status; multiowners; who are multiowners; decision making or control; percentage ownership; worth of share owned
Interdependent Subsystems (family involvement in the business) Beckhard & Dyer (1983); Covin (1994); Davis (1983); Goldberg & Wooldridge (1993); Handler (1992); Harvey & Evans (1995); Kepner (1983); Kirchhoff & Kirchhoff (1987); Narva & Dreux (1996); Taguiri & Davis (1996); Winter, Fitzgerald, Heck, Haynes, & Danes (1998)	Number of residential household members working in business; paid and unpaid employees who are relatives not living in the household
Generational Transfer Barach & Ganitsky (1995); Churchill & Hatten (1997); Litz (1995); Ward (1987, 1988)	Generation; ownership change in next 5 years; likelihood ownership stays in family
Multiple Conditions Astrachan & Kolenko (1994); Birley (1986); Blake & Saleh (1995); Cox (1998); Dannhaeuser (1993); Donnelley (1964); Fiegener, Brown, Prince, & File (1994); Lansberg (1988); Lyman (1991); Rosenblatt, deMik, Anderson, & Johnson (1985)	Several measures from above imposed simultaneously

Table 2. Prevalence of Family Business, 1997 (weighted data)

Population/Sample/Subsample	All Count	All % Sample/Subsample	All % Population	Families Count	Families % Sample/Subsample	Families % Population	Nonfamilies Count	Nonfamilies % Sample/Subsample	Nonfamilies % Population
U.S. households (HH)	98,754[a]			N/A	N/A	N/A	N/A	N/A	N/A
HH sample interviewed	9,910*			N/A	N/A	N/A	N/A	N/A	N/A
HH w/someone who owns or manages	18,037		18.3	N/A	N/A	N/A	N/A	N/A	N/A
HH w/owner	14,202[b]	78.7	14.4	N/A	N/A	N/A	N/A	N/A	N/A
HH w/nonresident manager	748[b]	5.3	0.8	N/A	N/A	N/A	N/A	N/A	N/A
HH w/nonowner-manager	4,347[b]	24.1	4.4	N/A	N/A	N/A	N/A	N/A	N/A
HH w/nonowner-manager, not related	3,665[b]	84.3	3.7	N/A	N/A	N/A	N/A	N/A	N/A
HH w/at least one owner who manages or one manager (owner related)	13,667		13.8	12,243		12.4	1,424		1.4
HH w/an owner who manages	13,306[b]	97.4	13.5	11,902[b]	97.2	12.1	1,404[b]	98.6	1.4
HH w/1 business owned	11,467	86.2	11.6	10,232	86.0	10.4	1,234	87.9	1.2
HH w/2 businesses owned	1,465	11.0	1.5	1,346	11.3	1.4	119	8.5	.1
HH w/3+ businesses owned	374	2.8	.4	323	2.7	.3	58	4.1	.1
HH w/a manager who is owner related	413[b]	3.0	.4	407[b]	3.3	.4	6[b]	.4	.01
HH w/1 business managed	389	94.2	.4	383	94.1	.4	6	100.0	.01
HH w/2 businesses managed	24	5.8	.02	24	5.9	.02	0	0	0.0
HH w/3 businesses managed	0	0.0	0.0	0	0	0.0	0	0	0.0
HH w/at least one owner who manages or one manager (owner related)	13,667		13.8	12,243		12.4	1,424[c]		1.4
HH w/length < 1 year	1,110	8.1	1.1	996	8.1	1.0	114	8.0	.1
HH w/time < 312 hours	1,578	11.5	1.6	1,388	11.3	1.4	190	13.3	.2
HH w/nonfamilies < 2 people	1,120[c]	8.2	1.1	0	0.0	0.0	1,120	78.7	1.1
HH w/at least 1 eligible business	9,859		10.0	9,859		10.0	0		0.0
Male owner-manager	7,470[d]	75.8	7.6	7,470[d]	75.8	7.6	0	0.0	0.0
Female owner-manager	2,389[d]	24.2	2.4	2,389[d]	24.2	2.4	0	0.0	0.0

Note. Reported numbers are in thousands of households, except " * ", which is the actual number of 9,910 households administered a screen interview. "N/A" means not applicable because data is not available.
a Source: U.S. Bureau of the Census: http:\\www.census.gov\population\estimates\housing. b Some households have both an owner and a manager of different businesses. These are included in both places. c Actually, 1,424,000 of the 13,667,000 households were nonfamilies (one person households). However, households were eliminated from eligibility first by length of time (< 1 year), then by hours worked (< 1 year), then by household size (< 312), and then by household size (< two people). Only 1,120,000 households were eliminated due to household size; 304,000 were eliminated for length of time and hours worked. d Numbers for male and female reflect the gender of the owner (who manages) or manager (owner related) of the selected business, i.e., the business selected for the main interviews.

Table 3. Selected Characteristics of Family-Owned and Family-Managed Businesses, 1997, N =9,858,666

Characteristics	Count	Percent	Mean	Standard Deviation
Number of years in selected business	--	--	13.2	11.3
Hours per week worked in selected business	--	--	4.6	23.8
Hours per month worked in selected business	--	--	193.3	103.1
Hours per year worked in selected business	--	--	2, 319.7	1,237.2
Household size	--	--	3.3	1.3
Business manager gender:				
Female	2,388,821	24.2		
Male	7,469,845	75.8		

Note.Data are weighted to be nationally representative.

Table 4. Two Sample T-Tests for Business Manager's Gender by Number of Years in Business; Hours Worked per Week,Month,and Year; and Household Size,1997,N =9,858,666

Variable	Mean	Standard Deviation	T-Value
Years in business:			
Female	10.5	9.7	467.0***
Male	14.0	11.7	
Hours worked per week:			
Female	38.0	21.2	540.7***
Male	46.7	24.1	
Hours worked per month:			
Female	164.3	92.2	540.2***
Male	202.6	104.7	
Hours worked per year:			
Female	1,971.5	1,106.2	540.2***
Male	2,431.0	1,256.0	
Household size:			
Female	3.1	1.3	241.9***
Male	3.3	1.3	

Note.Data are weighted to be nationally representative.
***p <.001.

Table 5. Counts and Percentages of Family Businesses Relative to Handler's (1989) Typology of Definitions, 1997,N =9,747,103

Conceptual Definition Criteria	Count	% Sample/ Subsample	% Population[a]	% Mean	SD
Ownership/Management					
Ownership status					
Sole proprietorship	5,367,511	55.1	5.4	--	--
Legal partnership	1,027,720	10.5	1.0	--	--
C-corporation	1,261,367	12.9	1.3	--	--
Subchapter S-corporation	1,755,114	18.0	1.8	--	--
Limited liability partnership	41,683	.4	.04	--	--
Limited liability corporation	90,916	.9	.1	--	--
Other	202,792	2.1	.2	--	--
Number of owners					
One	7,773,004	79.7	7.9	--	--
Multiple[b]	1,974,099	20.3	2.0	--	--
Family member living in household	1,425,659	14.6	1.4	--	--
Family member not living in household	1,235,341	12.7	1.3	--	--
Nonfamily member	613,435	6.3	.6	--	--
Stockholders	150,125	1.5	.2	--	--
Percentage of ownership	--	--	--	85.0	28.3
Worth of share	--	--	--	$295,586	$1,001,632
Decision makers					
Business owner	4,593,870	47.1	4.7	--	--
Spouses	2,924,954	30.0	3.0	--	--
Parents	499,999	5.1	.5	--	--
Adult children	388,857	4.0	.4	--	--
Other relatives	764,110	7.8	.8	--	--
Nonfamily members	992,028	10.2	1.0	--	--
Family Board of Directors	383,400	3.9	.4	--	--
Nonfamily Board of Directors	188,531	1.9	.2	--	--
Interdependent Subsystems					
Number of residential household members working in business				2.2	1.0
1	2,622,399	26.9	2.7	--	--
2	4,149,219	42.6	4.2	--	--
3	1,939,818	19.9	2.0	--	--
4	695,303	7.1	.7	--	--
5	315,462	3.2	.3	--	--
6	18,771	.2	.02	--	--
7	6,131	.1	.01	--	--
Number of relatives not living in household who are employees				0.4	0.8
None	7,400,662	75.9	7.5	--	--
1	1,075,118	11.0	1.1	--	--
2	894,155	9.2	.9	--	--
3	174,734	1.8	.2	--	--
4 or more	202,434	2.1	.2	--	--
Number of relatives not living in household who are *unpaid workers*				0.5	0.9
None	7,123,292	73.1	7.2	--	--
1	1,508,316	15.5	1.5	--	--
2	501,768	5.1	.5	--	--
3	358,409	3.7	.4	--	--
4 or more	255,318	2.6	.3	--	--

Table 5. (continued)

Conceptual Definition Criteria	Count	% Sample/ Subsample	Population[a]	% Mean	SD
Generational Transfer					
Generation					
Founder or first	8,444,018	86.6	8.6	--	--
Second	1,003,454	10.3	1.0	--	--
Third	243,391	2.5	.2	--	--
Fourth or more	56,240	.6	.1	--	--
Expect ownership change next 5 years					
Yes	2,228,041	22.9	2.3	--	--
No	7,335,482	75.3	7.4	--	--
Do not know	183,580	1.9	.2	--	--
Probability of remaining in family					
1 = very likely	489,882	5.0	.5	--	--
2 = somewhat likely	196,764	2.0	.2	--	--
3 = uncertain	239,961	2.5	.2	--	--
4 = somewhat unlikely	344,673	3.5	.3	--	--
5 = very unlikely	1,042,295	10.7	1.1	--	--
No change expected	7,249,948	74.4	7.3	--	--
Do not know	183,580	1.9	.2	--	--
Multiple Conditions					
Percent of ownership ≥50%	8,795,104	90.2	8.9	--	--
Plus family member control	7,949,742	81.6	8.1	--	--
Plus family members or relatives involved in business ≥2	6,205,896	63.7	6.3	--	--
Plus second generation and higher or intent to stay in family	807,995	8.3	.8	--	--

[a]Count divided by population of 98,754,000 households. [b]Multiple owners categories may not be mutually exclusive and, therefore, counts and percents for subsamples will not add up to the count for multiple owners.

Many entrepreneurs stay too long in the role of owner-manager of their family business because of confusion about alternatives, the desire to continue achieving, and fear of losing control of hard-earned wealth and authority. This article suggests that setting up a family foundation affords the aging business owner a new, challenging career. Arguments in favor of philanthropy are presented, including social responsibility and resource utilization. The article concludes with an outline of the basic steps in establishing a foundation.

Beyond Success: The Continuing Contribution of the Family Foundation

By Lèon A. Danco and John L. Ward

Note: We use the pronoun "he" in this article to refer to the business owner. While the bulk of the experience supporting this article is with mature male entrepreneurs, we believe the same personality characteristics and philanthropic motivations are held by female business owners.

As they approach late middle age, many successful American family business founders and owners face new challenges with no clear idea of how to meet them. The business owner resists giving up control of the business as the usual retirement age nears. Self-made, self-reliant, and driven by a powerful desire to remain in charge of his life, he typically is not satisfied with any potential successor. No one, he believes, can do it like he can. Despite his success, the business owner wrestles with a continuing desire for recognition and social esteem. Although he may have amassed wealth beyond his wildest dreams, his neighbors may not even know what his business does. Commonly, he keeps struggling for recognition by doing what he has always done best – creating and building and making even more money. This effort to achieve even more success can distract him from laying the plans essential to the future of his family and his business. Confusion about how to pass on his wealth further clouds the future. He has no intention of leaving the bulk of his hard-earned estate to the Internal Revenue Service. He hates relinquishing control of his money to charities that may not share his social concerns and philosophy. At the same time, he is deeply worried about passing on too much passive wealth to his children for fear of destroying in them the value system he prizes hard work, initiative, and self-reliance. He knows a huge inheritance can encourage recipients to be lazy, unappreciative, unaccomplished, and undisciplined, and he has no desire to foster those traits in his offspring.

Seeing no attractive alternative, many aging family business owners cling too long to their business and holdings. Often they stifle and harm those around them by avoiding crucial succession and estate planning. Those who do relinquish control to a successor or sell their businesses may set out in unfamiliar and often disastrous directions, starting a new business outside their area of expertise or undertaking questionable investment ventures.

A Promising Potential Solution

Missed by these hard-working business owners is a unique opportunity for a rewarding, creative new career: establishing a family foundation. Setting up and running a foundation to support cherished causes and social goals can be an exciting entrepreneurial venture for the business owner at the height of his abilities. It can afford him another chance to develop a new enterprise with courage and determination. With the family foundation as an option, the business owner is not ending his business career at retirement; he is taking it in a challenging new direction.

In many ways, setting up a family foundation is the natural final product of the entrepreneur's lifetime of building and creating. It challenges him to devote the same energy, astuteness, and wisdom to its success as he invested in his business, and it offers a continuing opportunity to be a creator, a maverick, and an innovator. Setting up a foundation often suits the owner's vision of himself as a nonconformist mounting a lonely but triumphant battle against the nay-sayers. It also can help ease his fear of surrendering control of his life's principal creation, the business.

The head of one fast-growing food manufacturer found tremendous satisfaction in his new role as philanthropist. While still in his fifties, he relinquished the titles of president and CEO to a successor, retaining only the chairman's role. Then he turned eagerly to developing a new career in financing nutritional research that would enable him to give back to society some of the riches he had earned. He made learning the business of philanthropy – screening proposals, evaluating the results of giving, deter mining appropriate funding levels, and so on – his new professional goal.

The foundation also allows the business owner to maintain control over his destiny and his money. It affords him far more influence over his contributions than outside foundations, community trusts, or organized charities. Most are too big, bureaucratic, or resistant to external influence to accept the counsel of a successful family business owner, a fact that can be extremely frustrating to an entrepreneur with a lifetime of business knowledge and wisdom to offer.

The foundation's activities can win the business owner the recognition and social esteem he desires. While philanthropy does not have to thrust him into the public eye, it can win him acknowledgment by an important circle of business and social contacts. This peer recognition can heighten the business owner's sense of self-worth and elevate the family's image in the community. Two-thirds of America's independent foundations emphasize giving within a particular geographic locale, at least partly to satisfy benefactors' need for local recognition

A foundation can also help the business owner deflect requests for charitable donations. He can refer solicitations to his foundation's trustees or, if he chooses, merely refuse requests by explaining that they do not fit the mission of his foundation.

Finally, the foundation can minimize taxes while avoiding the pitfall of leaving too much wealth to the next generation. An individual may make tax-deductible contributions to his foundation of up to 30 percent of his income plus 20 percent of appreciated property. Taxes usually amount to 1 or 2 percent of the foundation's investment earnings.

Social Argument

Harnessing the founder's desire for recognition and implementing his vision can hold great benefit for society. Too often, the task of identifying society's most pressing needs is left to large, centralized, and often bureaucratic organizations, such as government or big social agencies. While these entities can accomplish much that is worthwhile, they may lack a sense of changing and diverse community needs.

The business owner brings a unique perspective to the task of identifying society's needs. He deals daily with a wide range of age, ethnic, social, economic, and political groups. His long experience with constituencies ranging from vendors and employees to customers and community residents can afford unusual social insight. And he is deeply invested in the future. Few people have a larger stake in the economic, social, educational, civic, and political health of their particular community, and few have been more deeply touched by its needs.

Growth in family foundations can bring this perspective to bear on philanthropy in a highly constructive way. It encourages many and varied charitable activities by a wide range of business owners. The result may be that more social needs are met in a more creative and diverse way. This can only strengthen and help perpetuate a strong, pluralistic political system.

In many ways, the business owner represents the best of society. Typically, he prizes hard work, thrift, respect for family, good works, and other fundamental Judeo-Christian values. Manifesting those values in the community through foundation work can be of great benefit. At the same time, the business owner's innate abilities can magnify the impact of his giving. He has much to contribute. He has an outstanding ability to spot needs and move to fill them. He is opportunistic, creative, courageous, innovative, and insightful-qualities frequently lacking in large, bureaucratic philanthropic organizations. And he brings tremendous personal skill to bear on the task of managing a philanthropic enterprise. Society at large is certain to benefit as these entrepreneurs turn to philanthropy in their latter years, often as they reach the apex of their abilities.

An Untapped Resource

Despite their strengths, family business owners remain an enormous untapped philanthropic resource. Few family business owners have taken advantage of the opportunity to set up a foundation, and few advisers have promoted it. Only 7,000 foundations had assets of $1 million or more in 1988 (Rens, 1990).

Nevertheless, according to the Foundation Center, a nonprofit New York organization that tracks foundation giving, the total number of private grant-making U.S. foundations has risen 10 percent over the past five years to about 30,000. About 27,000 foundations are independent, set up by an individual, group, or family rather than a corporation. These foundations typically make donations to narrow fields of interest; about 90 percent are so small that they make annual payouts of less than $100,000.

The climate suggests continued growth. An estimated 20,000 family business owners have sufficient surplus funds to set up their own foundations, and that number should grow as much as fivefold in the next decade. Americans age sixty and over have a collective net worth of nearly $7 trillion, and their numbers are expanding rapidly, according to a new Cornell University study (Farnham, 1990). Many of them are members of a large, post-World War II generation of family business owners who have made their fortunes and are ready to retire. An estimated one in three of these owners lack family successors, and many more face other succession problems, increasing the pressure to sell the business and find other activities.

The Wall Street scandals of the 1980s have helped create a positive climate for the family foundation by prompting many wealthy Americans to reexamine their contribution to society. Many are concerned by the widespread perception that capitalism equals greed. Rising pressure on the private sector to meet society's growing needs for housing, welfare, education, environmental, and other programs has accelerated the trend.

Psychological Hurdles

Despite these factors, the idea of setting up a private family foundation is alien to many family business owners. The cultural and makeup of the family business owner is not always fertile soil for the idea. For the most part, he is a loner consumed by a relentless compulsion to build and achieve. To him, charity is structuring a strong company and taking good care of its employees.

The retiring founder and owner of one successful food processing business strongly resisted establishing a foundation. He saw the idea posed by his advisers-setting up a family foundation devoted to nutrition and health research – as a sham, a gimmick to remove him from the day-to-day operations of his business. Only after long discussion and reflection did he begin to see it as an opportunity to help the company – both by promoting its name and products and by freeing his successors to do their jobs while putting his money to the best and loftiest use.

The family business owner is distrustful by nature of "good causes." He may assume that all foundations have a liberal social agenda at odds with his conservatism. He may also lack interest in the activities of local charities or even disagree with their goals. The owners of one third-generation food service concern decided to focus their philanthropic efforts on strengthening Judaism in America. But that course took them far afield from charities in their medium-sized southern city, which expected routine donations for the local civic center, the community chest, and so on. In order to pursue their own philanthropic goals, the family had to delicately turn down requests from some local charities and deal with the disappointment of local leaders and associates.

Philanthropy is uncharted turf for most business owners. Even after identifying philanthropic goals, the entrepreneur may face unfamiliar and intimidating issues in carrying them out. One successful retailing family decided to endow university chairs on entrepreneurship. But the academic environment was so alien to them that they sought the help of professional advisers to implement the plan. Evaluating proposals, limiting the scope of their giving, and deciding between endowments and outright donations were among the issues they tackled and resolved.

The business owner may also believe that he lacks adequate wealth to set up a foundation. After starting out with almost nothing and driving himself for years to overcome privation, he made most of his money in a relatively short time. He still may not believe he has any surplus cash at all; in fact, he may feel as though he is teetering on the brink of poverty. The idea of giving away money, versus creating and conserving it, seems unnatural. To him, foundations are the exclusive preserve of elite families like the Fords and the Rockefellers. In fact, $1 million can be enough to set up an effective foundation. Even the smallest family foundations can have a significant impact by managing their activities in a disciplined way. The owners of one safety equipment company chose occupational safety research as the mission for their foundation. While the field was too broad to permit the foundation to cover all the bases, the family nevertheless was able to have an impact by making some tough decisions about focusing their giving.

Private by nature, the business owner may also fear the visibility that often comes with organized philanthropic effort. The owner of a successful medical equipment concern knew he wanted to use some of his hard-earned wealth to set up and fund substance abuse programs in his region. But he lacked confidence in his ability to speak in public and to cope with the other kinds of visibility such activities would bring. He worried that putting the family's name on a foundation would attract a flood of solicitations from charities already too eager for donations. "How am I going to turn all these people down?" he wondered.

With help from professional advisers, this business owner realized that he was already visible in his community. Everyone knew who he was, his name sometimes appeared in the local papers, and he served on various boards. He decided the added exposure afforded by philanthropic activity could be managed, particularly if he used the family name selectively. To fend off unwanted solicitations, he developed a clear, highly focused mission for the foundation. This made it easier to turn down most requests, which were from charities active in other areas.

Other business owners find that they actually enjoy the increased exposure. The retailing family mentioned above found that their philanthropic endeavors yielded tremendous personal growth opportunities. The founder, once a highly private man, came to enjoy speaking in public and answering media questions on entrepreneurship education. His wife, a longtime homemaker, increased her self-confidence and developed new capabilities as a speaker as well.

As these family business owners found, the business of giving money can be as challenging and satisfying as the business of making money.

Where Do We Start?

The mechanics of setting up a family foundation can raise questions even for the most experienced business owner. Once the founder is persuaded that a foundation can benefit everyone concerned, advisers can help him lay the groundwork. Ideally, this should take place long before he plans to retire. By communicating early to family and employees his desire to set up a foundation in his lifetime, the business owner can avoid potential emotional upheaval and legal trouble and reduce the possibility that his children and spouse might contest his will.

First, the business owner and his advisers should carefully and thoughtfully brief both the family and employees. Allowing plenty of time to defuse potential problems is particularly important in reaching older children who might feel they were neglected in their youth by a hard-driving father and now feel they are entitled to a huge inheritance. With careful explanation, many of these heirs can be helped to understand that they are not automatically entitled to all the family wealth. In fact, a foundation can bolster family members' self-esteem by sharing that inheritance with worthy causes and affording them an opportunity to prove self-reliance. As mentioned, it can also boost the family's standing in the community. The business owner should discuss his plans with the company's board of directors and seek its support as well.

The next step is to commit to paper a statement of mission, purpose, or philosophy for the foundation. Often, owners select goals that complement the mission of the family business. The owners of the safety equipment company mentioned above found that their foundation's work in occupational safety enhanced the image of the family business as vitally interested in protecting workers from injury. Another owner of a food business devoted his family foundation partly to research on heart disease, fostering a public perception of his products as healthy foods. Other families choose deeply felt personal causes. After the founders of Fannie Mae Candies lost several family members to cancer, they dedicated their foundation in large part to cancer research.

The next step is to create the foundation as a legal entity. Most entrepreneurs find the optimum time to do this is around age sixty. By then, most have finished preparing and teaching their business successors, and they are ready for a new challenge. The business owner should seek out an attorney knowledgeable in foundation law to help set up the organization and ensure compliance with the law.

The business owner must next select trustees for the foundation. Most foundation boards have four to six members. Ideally, the board should be made up of mutually respecting, independent peers of the founder. A business owner can appoint his children, spouse, or other family members as trustees. But their selection should depend on their qualifications-not on any attempt to create work for a bored spouse or an unmotivated child. In many ways, foundation trustees can serve the same purposes as an effective corporate board of directors, offering accountability, objective advice and counsel, and help with plans for orderly succession and continuity of the enterprise.

The role of trustees is to fulfill certain important fiduciary and social responsibilities, as well as to keep the founders' vision alive in a changing world and assure that funds are disbursed in accordance with the foundation's mission. Their duties include distribution and investment of the foundation's funds. While trustees can invest the money virtually as they see fit, they must limit payouts to nonprofit organizations qualified by the Internal Revenue Service as Section 501(c)(3) recipients or to businesses that aid the foundation in its mission. The donor, his family, or the foundation's trustees must not benefit financially from the foundation. Among other things, the trustees must also make a full report of investments, distributions, and administrative costs to the Internal Revenue Service each year.

Around the same time, the business owner must decide how the foundation is to be administered. Most smaller family foundations do not have a full-time staff and probably will not need a professional administrator. Usually that work can be done by the benefactor himself or someone he designates. Often, the business owner wants the experience and emotional rewards of managing the foundation as well as directing its efforts as a trustee. Larger foundations, however, might require a full-time administrator, at least in the time-consuming start-up phase. One midwestern food products business owner hired a full-time executive director to help organize his foundation, write a mission statement, counsel on investment strategies, review grant applications, and fill out tax forms.

Final Reward: Continuity

The desire for continuity-a yearning to create a lasting memorial, to make an additional contribution beyond hard work and earning more dollars is absolute in most business owners. Like the successful family business, the family foundation affords the business owner another chance to create a structure that can survive and do even more good after he is gone.

The founder has some alternatives in considering whether to perpetuate his foundation beyond his lifetime. He may choose to turn the foundation over to a community trust, which may either exhaust its resources or manage it as a continuing enterprise. He may choose to pass it on to a family member or members. As in the business, this decision should be based on the potential successor's ability to identify with the foundation's mission and share the values that underlie it. The successor should be as carefully informed and prepared to take the reins of the foundation as he would be for corporate management.

In any case, the founder of an active family foundation must once again face the need to let go at the appropriate time. As in the family business, an active board of respected trustees can be of help to him in preparing for this step and evaluating alternatives. Whatever his decision, he can retire from the foundation with vast satisfaction that he has used his skills and resources to the fullest, throughout his years; that he has, in effect, borne yet another new child in the latter stages of life.

References

Farnham, A. "The Windfall Awaiting the New Inheritors." *Fortune*, 1990, 121 (10), 72-78.

Rens, L. (ed.). *Foundations Today: Current Facts and Figures on Private and Community Foundations.* (7th ed.) New York: Foundation Centers 1990.

In this early article, noted sociologist Daniel Bell recognizes the central role of the family in the capitalistic system. Modern society's loosening of the traditional relationship between property and family has led to a decline of "family capitalism." "Private productive property, especially in the U. S., is largely a fiction..." Bell writes.

While it is true that the American economy is no longer dominated by a small number of wealthy dynasties, Bell's contention that "the system of family control is finished" is belied by today's economic reality. While family businesses coexist with corporations not controlled by specific families, the renaissance in family business clearly shows Bell's conclusion in error. The article, nonetheless, is quite worthwhile for its analysis and as a product of its era.

The Break-up of Family Capitalism

By Daniel Bell

The story of the rise and fall of social classes in Western Society, as Pirenne and Schumpeter have pointed out, is that of the rise and fall of families. Without understanding that fact, as many American sociologists, accustomed to viewing class position in individualistic terms, have failed to do, one cannot understand the peculiar cohesiveness of dominant economic classes in the past, or the sources of the break-up of power in contemporary society today. A bold statement, perhaps, but one which the following sketch attempts to prove.

Capitalism is not only, as Mans saw it, an economic system with employer worker relations and classes formed on strictly economic lines, but a social system wherein power has been transmitted through the family, and where the satisfactions of ownership lay, in part, in the family name by which the business enterprise was known. The social organization of the family rested on two institutions: property and the "dynastic" marriage. Property, sanctioned by law and reinforced by the coercive power of the state, meant power; the "dynastic" marriage was a means of conserving, and through inheritance laws of transmitting property and so preserving, as the case might be, the continuity of the family enterprise. Through the fusion of the two institutions, a class system was maintained: people met at the same social level, had similar educations mingled in specific milieux-in short, created a distinctive style of life.

The singular fact is that in the last seventy-five years the old relationship between the two institutions of property and family, which, Malthus maintained, represented the "fundamental laws" of society, has broken down. The specific reasons for this breakdown are too complex to describe here, but the process is clear. In bourgeois society, marriage was a means of keeping sex relations within bounds; in bourgeois marriage, as Denis de Rougemont wittily observed, every woman had a husband and desired a lover; the great Continental novels of the nineteenth century, Tolstoy's *Anna Karenina*, Flaubert's *Madame Bovary*, with their geometry of adultery, pointed up this paradox. The growth of romanticism, the high premium on individual attachment and free choice, the translation of passion into secular and carnal terms all worked against the system of "dynastic" marriage. The emancipation of women meant, in one sense, the disappearance of one of the stable aspects of bourgeois society. If women could marry freely, crossing class lines if they so desired, then the economic enterprise with which the "dynastic" marriage was intertwined would lose some of its staying power.

But there are also reasons more indigenous to the nature of the economic system for the mode of family capitalism having given way. Some are general: the decline of the extended family or clan narrowed the choice of heirs competent to manage the enterprise; the increasing importance of professional techniques placed a high premium on skill rather than blood relationships. In the United States one can point to even more specific factors. The break-up of family capitalism came, roughly, around the turn of the century, when American industry, having over-extended itself, underwent a succession of crises. At this point, the bankers, with their control of the money and credit market, stepped in and reorganized and took control of many of the country's leading enterprises. The great mergers at the turn of the century, typified by the formation of United States Steel, marked the emergence of "finance capitalism" in this country.

By their intervention, the investment bankers, in effect, tore up the social roots of the capitalist order. By installing professional managers – with no proprietary stakes in the enterprise, therefore unable to pass along their power automatically to their sons, and accountable to outside controllers – the bankers effected a radical separation of property and family. The "young men from the provinces" passing through the classrooms of the Harvard Business School, now had an avenue by which to ascend to high social as well as economic positions. In time, however, the power of the bankers, too, declined as the managers became able, especially in the last twenty years, to detach themselves from financial controls, and win independent power in their enterprises. In some cases they were able to do this because they, the corporate organizers, were strong individuals; even more important was the enforced separation, by the New Deal measures, of investment and banking functions, which limited the investment bankers' control of the money market; but most important of all, perhaps was the fact that the tremendous growth of American corporations enabled them to finance their expansion from their own profits rather than by borrowing on the money market.

The breakdown of family capitalism may explain, in part, the "dynamic" nature of modern American capitalism, for the establishment of independent managerial controls has produced a new impetus and new incentives. Unable to withdraw enormous sums of wealth from their corporations, as, say, Andrew Carnegie did from his steel company, the chief status drives of the managers have been performance and growth. Such aims, combined with the changed tax laws, have stimulated a high and constant degree of reinvestment of profits. Whereas only 30 per cent of corporate profits in 1929 were reinvested, about 70 per cent of corporate profits in the postwar years were plowed back for expansion.

The fact that the new managers have lacked a class position buttressed by tradition has given rise to a need on their part for an ideology to justify their power and prestige. In no other capitalist order, as in the American, has this drive for an ideology been pressed so compulsively. In other orders it was less needed. Private property was always linked, philosophically, to a system of natural rights; thus, property itself provided a moral justification. But private productive property, especially in the U. S. is largely a fiction, and rarely does one hear it invoked any longer as the moral source of the corporate executive's power. As we have had in the corporation the classic shift from ownership to managerial control, so, on the symbolic level, we have the shift from "private property" to "enterprise" as the justification of power. And, as with any ideology, the symbol itself sometimes becomes a propelling force, and "performance" for its own sake has become a driving motive of the American corporate head.

Sociologically, the break-up of family capitalism is linked to a series of shifts in power in Western society as a whole. No longer are there America's "Sixty Families" (or even France's "Two Hundred"). Family capitalism meant social and political as well as economic dominance: the leading family used to live in the "house on the hill." It does so no longer. Many middle-sized enterprises are still family owned, with son succeeding father (e. g., breweries), and many towns, like St. Louis and Cincinnati, still reveal the marks of the old dominance by families, but by and large the system of family control is finished. So much so that a classic study of American life like R. S. Lynd's *Middletown in Transition*, with its picture of the"X" family dominating the town, has in less than twenty years become completely outmoded.

Two "silent" revolutions in the relations between power and class position in modern society seem to be in process. One is a change in the *mode of access* to power insofar as inheritance alone is no longer all-determining; the other is a change in the *nature of powerholding* itself insofar as technical skill rather than property, and political position rather than wealth, have become the basis on which power is wielded.

The two "revolutions" proceed simultaneously. The chief consequence, politically, is the break-up of the "ruling class." A ruling class maybe defined as a power-holding group which has both an established *community* of interest, and a *continuity* of interest. In effect, there is an "upper class" and a "ruling group." Being a member of the "upper class" (i.e., having differential privileges, and being able to pass those privileges along to one's designees) no longer means that one is a member of the ruling group, for rule is now based on other than the traditional criteria of property, the modern ruling groups are essentially coalitions, and the means of passing on the power they possess, or the institutionalization of any specific modes of access to power (the political route, or military advancement) is not yet fully demarked and established.

How do dynastic families adapt to social and economic forces restricting attempts to transmit family wealth from one generation to the next?

A Historical Overview of Family Firms in the United States

By Peter Dobkin Hall

Writing in the 1850s, the physician and novelist Oliver Wendell Holmes summed up the problems faced by Americans who hoped to pass their firms and fortunes intact to their children and grandchildren: "It is in the nature of large fortunes to diminish rapidly, when subdivided and distributed. A million is the unit of wealth, now and here in America. It splits into four handsome properties; each of these into four good inheritances; these, again, into scanty competencies for four ancient maidens, – with whom it is best that the family should die out, unless it can begin again as its great-grandfather did. Now a million is a kind of golden cheese, which represents in a compendious form the summer's growth of a fat meadow of craft or commerce; and as this kind of meadow rarely bears more than one crop, it is pretty certain that sons and grandsons will not get another golden cheese out of it, whether they milk the same cows or turn in new ones. In other words, the millioncracy, considered in a large way, is not at all an affair of persons and families, but a perpetual fact of money with a variable human element" (Holmes, 1961[1860], pp. 15-16).

Holmes knew what he was talking about, for he was heir to two venerable family dynasties. His mother's family, the Wendells, of Portsmouth, New Hampshire, had reaped the "fat meadow of craft and commerce" of the eighteenth-century West Indies trade. His father's family belonged to a New England Brahmin caste of clergymen scholars.

Combining these two dynastic strands in a secular and industrial age, Holmes practiced medicine, taught at Harvard, and wrote for his own amusement. As a healer, he ministered to the bodies and minds of Boston's elite, who were struggling to run, pass on, and inherit family firms and fortunes. He distilled their experiences and distinctive outlook into popular poems, novels, and essays that, in a significant sense, gave voice to the critical problems faced by nineteenth-century Boston merchant families. Though preeminently concerned with Boston, which Holmes dubbed the "hub of the solar system" in one of his essays, Holmes's conception of the predicament faced by family dynasties in a democratic and capitalist society held true for the United States as a whole.

This paper will give a historically informed, multidisciplinary account of the obstacles to dynastic success in the United States and discuss some of the special means that families have used to surmount them. The following topics will be considered: the impact of the law of inheritance on family property, including its role in dividing and consolidating family interests; the impact of economic and technological processes on ties between families and firms; ideological and political obstacles to dynastic formation; the resolution of the conflict between dynasty and dominant democratic and meritocratic values; and the significance of the family firm and the dynastic process in American social and economic life. Although this paper deals with the past, the purpose is not historical. Rather, it is to provide a cultural framework that helps us to understand some of the problems that family business managers, advisers, consultants, and therapists face today.

The Law of Inheritance

When Alexis de Tocqueville visited the United States in the late 1820s, he wanted not only to observe how the world's first modern democracy worked but also to discover how it had become a democracy in the first place. As a French aristocrat, he was exquisitely sensitive to dynastic issues, which for centuries had shaped the political and social life of

Europe but which appeared to be entirely absent from the New World. Not only were Americans able to do without a titular aristocracy, they also lacked the sentimental and legal ties that bound European families of all classes to land, crafts, and occupations.

Tocqueville could easily understand how the patchwork character of early settlement, the heterogeneity of the colonists, and the privations of life on the frontier had prevented the establishment of feudalism and its apparatus of family succession. More puzzling was the failure of dynasty to establish itself – even in an informal way, based on wealth or political alliances – once the colonies had advanced beyond the stage of pioneering.

Tocqueville came to view the law of inheritance as the most important single factor shaping American life and character (1945 [1835],I, pp. 50-51): "When the legislator has once regulated the law of inheritance, he may rest from his labor...When framed in a particular manner, this law unites, draws together, and vests property and power in a few hands; it causes an aristocracy, so to speak, to spring out of the ground. If formed on opposite principles, its action is still more rapid; it divides, distributes, and disperses both property and power. Alarmed by the rapidity of its progress, those who despair of arresting its motion endeavor at least to obstruct it by difficulties and impediments; they vainly seek to counteract its effect by contrary efforts; but it shatters and reduces to powder every obstacle, until we can no longer see anything but a moving and impalpable cloud of dust, which signals the coming of democracy." The division of estates broke up family holdings, transforming land from patrimony to commodity and family from corporate group to collections of autonomous individuals. Individualism and the ability to buy and sell property freely created the basis for the democratic state and a capitalist economy.

Americans were curiously ambivalent about the inheritance of property. As responsible citizens, virtually all Americans agreed that accumulation of vast fortunes was inimical to democracy, and for that reason they supported the passage of laws favoring the division of estates. However, as individuals, they continuously sought ways of passing their farms, firms, and fortunes on to the next generation intact. They devised a variety of adaptive strategies to counteract the erosion of family resources by the system of partible inheritance (Farber, 1972; Hall, 1982).

In the eighteenth century, kin-marriage was a basic means of preserving land, labor, skill, and capital from the inheritance system. Kin-marriage circumvented the partition of estates with elegant simplicity. Visualize a three-generation family: generation one consists of two grandparents, generation two of their four children and generation three of their eight grandchildren. In the normal process of estate partition, generation one's estate would be divided eight ways by the time it was distributed to generation three. However, if the grandchildren were encouraged to marry one another rather than nonfamily members, their one-eighth shares in their grandparental estates would be recombined. The number of divisions of the grandparent's estate would be reduced by half from eight to four.

Another method, sibling exchange, worked even more efficiently. It involved encouraging siblings in one family to marry siblings in another family. Imagine two business partners, each with four children. If each child married outside his or her family, the estates of the partners would be divided eight ways on their deaths. But, if the eight children of the partners married one another, the number of divisions would be reduced to four, and assuming that each couple produced two children, it would only increase to eight in the next generation. Sibling exchange had the particular virtue of both consolidating existing wealth and combining resources that had hitherto been separate.

Cousin-marriage, sibling exchange, the marriage of widows to their husband's brother, and delaying or preventing marriage were among the estate-preserving strategies in common use throughout the colonies by the early 1700s (Farber, 1972; Hall, 1982). The strategy used depended on the needs of the group using it. Farmers and artisans, whose primary interest was preserving land, labor, and skill, encouraged alliances between related male lines: Sons tended to marry the daughters of the father's brothers. Merchants, whose primary interest was increasing capital and extending commercial contacts, favored marriages linking previously unrelated males, such as sibling exchanges between the children of partners, and encouraged sons to marry the daughters of their mother's sisters, which tied the unrelated maternal uncle into the family. Having a widow marry her late husband's brother kept her dower right (one-third share) of his estate as well as the shares of his children within control of the paternal line. Preventing marriage, especially of daughters, assured that their share in their parents' estates would be distributed among their male siblings. This practice had much to do with the large number of unmarried women among elite New England families in the nineteenth century.

Dynasty and Democracy

The use of marriage for dynastic purposes was ultimately limited in its effectiveness. Kin-marriage slowed, but did not stop, the partible division of estates. As holdings became smaller, more effective means of keeping estates intact had to be devised. In any event, children in the post-Revolutionary era were less willing to allow their parents to dictate their marital choices. Under these circumstances, farmers and artisans increasingly left the "family place" or the craft to their younger sons as a trade-off for caring for parents in their old age (Waters, 1978). In more affluent families, older children were provided with educations, with apprenticeships in other crafts, or with farms in other places. Poorer families simply sent them off to seek their fortunes, a practice that had much to do with the growth of the free labor force in the first decades of the nineteenth century.

While farmers and artisans had little to lose by sending their children out to seek their fortunes, those who already possessed fortunes could not afford to take such risks. Each child remained a potential legatee. And, even if a child was disinherited, he or she could challenge a parental will with a fair hope of success. For purely instrumental reasons, elite families had an interest in reigning [sic] in their children. Beyond this, the social styles of the Enlightenment and the Romantic period promoted the sentimentalization of relations between parents and children. This sentimentalization produced emotional bonds that made it difficult for parents to allow their children to go their own way, and it sapped the desire of children to do so. Finally, because wealthy Americans modeled themselves on their aristocratic European counterparts, they began to view themselves as family founders, as dynasts. The 1780 declaration of Massachusetts nouveau riche John Adams typified this sensibility (Smith, 1962, pp. 468-469): "I must study war, that my sons may have liberty to study mathematics and philosophy. My sons ought to study mathematics and philosophy, geography, natural history and naval architecture, navigation, commerce, and agriculture, in order to give their children a right to study painting, poetry, music, architecture, statuary, tapestry, and porcelain."

The urban merchants of the New Republic, rather than leaving their children to fate, turned to formal legal mechanisms to preserve their estates and to keep their children in dynastic orbits. Their wealth enabled them to be more sophisticated about the law and its uses. They rediscovered English law and introduced to America doctrines and practices that their forebears had left behind in the Old World or that had failed to develop when first brought here. One of the most important of these involved equity jurisprudence (Scott, 1939). In equity jurisprudence, it was possible for one person to hold legal title to a piece of property, while another was entitled to receive the benefits of it. This division of ownership and use was the basis for *trusts*. Trusts made it possible to keep capital intact for generations in the legal possession of a trustee; the earnings of that capital could be partibly divided among descendants, the holders of equitable title. Trusts, which could be set up between living persons, under wills, or as perpetual charitable endowments, opened new vistas for the founders of trading and industrial fortunes.

The Massachusetts merchants of the post-Revolutionary era spearheaded the legal innovations that would eventually be adopted everywhere, laying the foundation for dynasties of national significance (Hall, 1973; Marcus, 1983). The changes wrought by these men in the law of inheritance were not, notwithstanding John Adams's assertion, intended to create a European-style aristocracy. They appear to have understood that, in the American setting, the survival of family dynasties depended on continuing commercial, industrial, and financial eminence. This is evident in some of their key contributions to the law of trusts, particularly the introduction of the rule against perpetuities and the prudent man rule.

The rule against perpetuities had its roots in Tudor England. The rising middle class of the sixteenth century had feared that the use of trusts by the aristocracy and the monasteries would ultimately make it impossible to buy or sell property, thus strangling commerce. The English courts began to hand down decisions limiting the length of time that a trust could run before its principal ultimately "vested" in an individual. The basic rule, as handed down in 1682 in the Duke of Norfolk's Case, stated that the limitation on the duration of a trust was "a life or lives in being" at the time the trust took effect, plus twenty-one years, plus nine months (Newhall, 1942). This seemed to strike a reasonable balance between the desire of families to keep capital intact for two generations and the public good of freely circulating property. By the nineteenth century, however, elites on both sides of the Atlantic had become more dynastically minded. The phrase *life or lives in being*, which comprised the most flexible element in the formula, came to be stretched to the point of absurdity: One will specifying the group to be all the lineal descendants of Queen Victoria living at the time the will was made was upheld by the British courts. This version of the rule was accepted in Massachusetts.

Although the rule against perpetuities strengthened trusts, it still conceded the ultimate necessity of freeing family property from testamentary restrictions. To this extent, it acknowledged the mandates of a triumphant capitalism as well as the extent to which all dynasties both sprang from and returned to the world of market relations.

The prudent man rule, which was enunciated by the Massachusetts courts in 1830, dealt with the investment of trust capital. Much as they wished their capital to be safe, the Massachusetts merchants also wanted it to be available for investment in the region's economic growth. When a group of beneficiaries sued a trustee for investing in the shares of manufacturing corporations, which the beneficiaries regarded as unsafe securities, the court, after reviewing all the possible ways in which money could be invested, declared that there was no perfectly safe investment vehicle. All that could be required of a trustee was that he be guided by the practice of "men of prudence" in managing their own affairs "in regard to the permanent disposition of their funds" (*Pickering's Reports*, 1830, p. 461). This decision had a twofold effect. First, it protected trustees from legal action by beneficiaries, thereby enabling them to pursue their dynastic purposes more effectively. Second, it made trust capital available for investment in the industrial economy. This enabled Massachusetts to lead the nation in industrial growth and to its role as an early center of investment banking.

A third feature of the Massachusetts trust doctrine was the development of charitable endowments. While such endowments dated from Puritan times, their establishment became tied in the early nineteenth century to the mercantile effort to conserve and consolidate family capital. Charitable endowments, whether held by organizations like Harvard College or free-standing like the Lowell Institute, served not only the long-term goal of preventing the division of estates but also the short-term goal of providing for the needs of children and grandchildren. The creation of charitable endowments was the most complex of the dynastic strategies used by Massachusetts families.

The basic business organization used by these families was the partnership firm, in which all members were related by blood or marriage. Before the Revolution, sons generally entered their father's firms and daughters married partners, reducing the erosion of operating capital caused by death and subsequent divisions of estates. Business practice began to change after independence. Freed from the restrictions of British mercantilism, merchants who once traded only with the West Indies and England now expanded to India, China, and Latin America. Such large scale trade was risky. It was also expensive, often requiring nonfamily capital. For these reasons, firms not only had to begin to admit unrelated partners, who brought their capital with them, but competence became more important than blood.

Responding to these changes in economic life, the merchants began to encourage vocational diversity. Those with an aptitude for business became businessmen; those without such an aptitude were encouraged to enter the law, medicine, or some other respectable occupation. Endowment trusts played a key role in this process. Endowing colleges and professional schools made alternatives to business careers more attractive by raising the status of the professions and by creating positions of influence for family members (Hall, 1973; Story, 1981). Endowments themselves constituted important pools of investment capital that were not only managed by family members of governing boards but also used in underwriting family businesses (White, 1955; Hall, 1973). Family involvement in the governance of endowed charitable corporations, usually via business members, perpetuated intergenerational control and authority and created arenas in which the competence of relatives and in-laws could be assessed.

In devising special means to overcome the centrifugal and individuating dynamic of the inheritance system, the Brahmins never forgot that they were, first and foremost, a business class whose preeminence depended on active participation in the new nation's exponentially growing economy. The portrayals of aristocratic disdain for commerce so favored by fictioneers mask the long traditions of managerial and entrepreneurial leadership maintained by some patrician families (Kolko, 1967). The genius of the institutional system devised by the Bostonians and adopted by other urban patriarchates lies in its capacity to sort family members for fitness, recruit and maritally coopt talented outsiders, and constantly produce "golden cheeses" by farming ever new "fat meadows of craft or commerce."

All Americans in the eighteenth and early nineteenth centuries struggled to keep farms, firms, and fortunes intact against the divisive force of the law of inheritance. Not only were some groups more successful than others, but the relative degrees of success profoundly shaped the emerging hierarchy of wealth, power, and influence (Hall, 1982).

Farmers fared worst. Although they were the most numerous group in the population, they became steadily more impoverished and powerless. Land holdings were often successfully preserved through such strategies as kin-marriage and leaving family farms to the youngest son. But, the price of success was enormous. Providing the other sons with apprenticeships and farms in new settlements cost money, which could be earned only by shifting away from self-sufficiency toward commercial agriculture and participation in markets over which the farmers had little control. The out-migration of all but the youngest sons meant that farm families lost invaluable human capital. The most ambitious went West or gravitated to the cities. What remained was the pathetic spectacle of ingrownness, isolation, and poverty so accurately depicted in novels like Wharton's *Ethan Frome* (1911).

The effectiveness of the adaptive strategies that artisan families used is more difficult to assess, because rapidly changing technology and the changing character of the markets played so important a role in shaping relations between family and productive enterprise. In highly skilled and highly capitalized occupations like printing, ties between family and craft were unusually long-lasting. For example, the Green family of Boston remained closely identified with the printing trade for more than five generations (Thomas, 1970). To maintain such enduring ties between family and craft required considerable geographical mobility, since colonial cities could not support an unlimited number of printers. To remain printers, the Greens sent sons to establish shops in Connecticut, Nova Scotia, Maryland, and Virginia.

Other artisans chose to stay where they were, even if it meant altering their occupations. Such highly skilled artisans as silversmiths and cabinetmakers developed a specialized and cooperative division of labor. The woodworkers often became upholsterers, coachmakers, or japanners – all interdependent crafts. In a similar fashion, silversmiths became jewelers, engravers, or clock and instrument makers (Jobe and Kaye, 1984). A few craftsmen became entrepreneurs, moving out of production into financing and marketing the work of others.

Of the major occupational groups in early America, only the merchants succeeded in using the major adaptive strategies – occupational diversification and kin-marriage – to long-term advantage. But, their success in maintaining continuities of family, firm, and fortune depended on their ability to create unified institutional infrastructures that both collectivized their human and financial capital and served as a mechanism for coopting talented new blood. This was not possible everywhere. In cities like Boston, where institutional development was relatively integrated, elite families not only displayed remarkable continuity but remained economic leaders into the twentieth century. However, in New York and Philadelphia, many of the families that were prominent in the late eighteenth century were either swept away or left the great commercial and industrial achievements of the nineteenth century to more ambitions strivers (Baltzell, 1979).

The great industrial fortunes created in the decades after the Civil War were the substance of the final development of dynastic machinery in the United States. These fortunes presented their founders with unique problems, not only because of their enormous size but also because their creation coincided with the appearance of mass poverty and unemployment. For this reason, the final development in the legal machinery of dynastic formation was the charitable foundation, which combined features intended to maintain family control of wealth with socially concerned philanthropy. The emergence of foundations was also tied to the changing structure of family firms, which, as they increased their scale of operations and capital requirements, came to be incorporated enterprises. In this setting, ostensibly charitable foundations served as holding companies that removed control of the firm from the testamentary process, permitting division of income while at the same time perpetuating and formally collectivizing family and inheritance taxes, foundations also became a major means of tax avoidance (Hall, 1986).

For many wealthy families, philanthropy itself became an important occupational alternative involving both altruistic and self-interested components. The Rockefeller "family office" in Room 5600 at Rockefeller Plaza served as the nerve center for managing the family's assets, coordinating its public relations, and overseeing its numerous charitable interests (Collier and Horowitz, 1976). As family holdings diversified and as family members scattered occupationally and geographically, it also played a central role in sustaining the family identity and mission (Marcus, 1983).

We should not make too much of the ability of some families – the Rockefellers, the Du Ponts, the Cabots, and others – to resist the divisive dynamic of the inheritance system, because even

for the largest and most enduring family fortunes, each new generation presents the challenge of successful transmission. For example, it is by no means clear that the Rockefeller family will continue to exist in any dynastic sense a century from now. Collier and Horowitz (1976, p. 624) point out the problems posed when the number of heirs to a fortune increases from six siblings to twenty-two cousins: "Instead of the family, there will be five families – those of each of the male heirs of the Brothers. Long after the Brothers have died, their grandchildren – the fifth generation – will finally inherit the vestige of Senior's fortune, the '34 Trusts, which terminate by law when they reach maturity. The aging Cousins will no doubt worry over the impact this sudden wealth will have on their children and what it will portend for the Rockefellers and their concept of service. But by that time the sense in which this has been the most royal of America's families will have passed, and the question will be largely academic." As Tocqueville wrote a century and a half ago in the passage quoted earlier, the law of inheritance in the end "shatters and reduces to powder every obstacle" placed in its path.

From Firm to Fortune

The perpetuation of a fortune and the perpetuation of a family's ties to a particular business constitute distinct but overlapping issues. Because those who seek guidance from consultants and therapists are often closely tied to the enterprises from which they derived their wealth, it is tempting to focus exclusively on the ties between family and firm. However, doing this arbitrarily excludes those who have successfully diversified their interests beyond a particular enterprise but for whom family economic interests remain centrally important. What makes an activity a family enterprise is the degree of family involvement in the sources of family wealth, however diverse those sources may be.

Diversification, like partible inheritance, is tied to the fundamental dynamics of American economic life. As the inheritance system detached families from the land, it also detached artisans from their crafts. Profits rather than perfection became the artisan's goal, and earning profits – even survival itself – demanded continuous technological and organizational innovation. In this rapidly changing and intensely competitive environment, maintaining close ties to a single productive activity and retaining wealth became virtually incompatible. As the nineteenth-century industrial system grew more complex, success even in a single area"for example, steel" required the control of coal, ores, railroads, and construction companies, as survival increasingly hinged on strategic control of raw materials, market access, and markets themselves. To be sure, many small firms found niches for themselves, either by producing specialty products or by establishing client relationships with larger enterprises. But, over the longer term survival inevitably required the dissolution of ties between family and firm or, under special circumstances, the development of interrelated and interdependent clusters of enterprises, such as those created by the Du Ponts.

The changing scale of market activity also worked against family firms. Until the early nineteenth century, most markets were local, and most enterprises were familial. Economic activity was noncompetitive, and consumer choices were governed not by rational choice but by kinship and loyalty (Jobe and Kaye, 1984). The growth of trans-local markets was accompanied by the growing use of money, which provided a standard for making rational economic choices. As market relations grew more impersonal, they also became more competitive, because successful firms depended increasingly on mechanical efficiency, the quality of decision making, and the rational division of labor.

Under these circumstances, the factors that had made family firms so vital a part of the colonial social and economic pattern became in many instances obstacles to their survival. As capital markets grew and as family firms began to compete with publicly held corporations, depending solely on the family for financing became a disadvantage. Resistance to employing nonrelatives and reluctance to promote newcomers to positions of responsibility deprived family firms of the talents and skills of these individuals, many of whom became commercial rivals. Unless family firms were fortunate enough to find a niche through control of resources and industrial processes, as did the anthracite coal operators and iron makers of northeastern Pennsylvania (Folsom, 1981), they found it increasingly difficult to succeed in the emerging national economy of the nineteenth century.

In the aggregate, such factors could affect the destinies of towns and cities as they struggled for market dominance in the heady antebellum economy. Nineteenth-century Boston, despite its reputation for Old Family exclusiveness, was remarkable for its ability to attract and provide places for the talented. As lesser cities came within its intellectual range, it drained off their wealth and talent, their promising authors, rising lawyers, large capitalists, and prettiest girls (Holmes, 1957 [1859]).

Where Boston succeeded, other cities failed. Middletown was the largest city in Connecticut in 1800, but its economic life was closely controlled by a small group of traditionally minded families. As early as 1806, a letter in the *Middlesex Gazette* (1806) complained of the unwillingness of "older and wealthier citizens" to "induce young men of property, industry, and enterprise to become inhabitants." Instead of attracting them, the writer noted, "they have actually been driven from the place." By 1860, Middletown had fallen from first in population to seventh, and, in spite of its strategic location on the Connecticut River, the industrial and commercial growth that had enriched the state's other cities largely passed it by.

Dynasty and the Polity

The third force that has persistently worked against family firms is political. In a certain sense, this is the most important force, since it is the political process that shapes the legal and tax environments so central to the survival of family firms. Political opposition to dynasticism is embedded in the earliest legal codes, and it has arisen episodically as a component of electoral appeals.

Partible inheritance was not introduced to the British colonies of North America in order to prevent the intergenerational transmission of farms and firms. On the contrary, its original purpose was to assure patriarchal and patrilineal continuities of authority and property. But, as extraordinary population growth severed the ties between families, land, and traditional occupations, it began to serve a contrary purpose.

In this setting, some families proved more adept than others at operating in the emerging market system, and the countryside witnessed the emergence of a class of landed entrepreneurs (Sweeney, 1984). In the towns and cities, the merchants benefited both from the rise of colonial markets and from the integration of these markets into an international mercantilist system. By the mid-eighteenth century, significant differences in economic and political interests had begun to divide American society. It was at this point that anti-dynastic political sentiments began to be voiced.

The revolutionary legislatures abolished entail, the English law that in some colonies had perpetually tied lands and families. Many legislatures also repealed the entire body of English common law and with it the statute of uses (the juridical basis of trusts) and the statute of charitable uses (the basis for endowment). As the propertied worked to form for-profit and not-for-profit corporations, they were opposed at every step of the way by their political enemies, who understood the dynastic implications and the larger political consequences of incorporation, private charity, and testamentary trusts (Hall, 1982).

Thomas Jefferson was the most eloquent spokesman for the populist, anti-dynastic "Virginia Doctrine." He opposed industrial and commercial development, describing market dependency as "a canker which soon eats to the heart of [a republic's] laws and constitution" (Koch, 1965,

p. 393). More important, he believed that every generation should be free to work out its own destinies unencumbered by the past. "The earth belongs to the living," Jefferson declared, "the dead have neither power nor rights over it" (Koch, 1965, pp. 329-330). This position was the kernel of the Virginia Doctrine and the basis for anti-dynastic legislation and court decisions throughout the United States (Miller, 1961).

The Virginia Doctrine distorted the institutional and economic life of the early republic. In spite of its large population, the Jeffersonian South had few business corporations or cultural institutions. In contrast, Federalist New England possessed two thirds of the business corporations and most of the colleges in the United States (Davis, 1917). These institutional differences were paralleled by advances in economic development which were in turn closely tied to the use of testamentary and endowment trusts, the fundamental legal mechanisms of dynastic formation.

In the 1820s, Jacksonianism represented the final crystallization of anti-dynastic politics. This development was especially evident in states like New York, which enacted laws limiting the proportion of estates that could be left to charity, made the size of institutional endowments subject to the will of the legislature, and established governmental oversight of charitable organizations (Scott, 1951). Although the federal courts eased some of these strictures, anti-aristocratic doctrines remained strong. As late as the 1880s, New York courts enforced the Jacksonian statutes against the trustees of Samuel J. Tilden, who had left the bulk of his fortune to establish the New York Public Library. Only a national outcry spearheaded by reformers concerned about the need for private wealth to serve the public good led to a change in the state's laws (Ames, 1913).

Anti-dynasticism was not the exclusive property of populist politicians. Social Darwinism influenced some founders of the great post-Civil War industrial fortunes to question the wisdom of passing on huge accumulations of wealth. Andrew Carnegie was the most outspoken of these. Proclaiming that he who dies rich dies disgraced, he became the greatest philanthropist of his generation. He advocated a progressive income tax and confiscatory inheritance laws (Carnegie, 1889). Carnegie was echoed by Boston legal scholar John Chipman Gray. In criticizing the legitimation of spendthrift trusts, Gray (1895, p. vi) denounced mechanisms through which the rich could "assure undisturbed possession of wealth to their children, however weak or wicked they may be."

Politically impelled opposition to dynasties and the institutions that produced them continued into this century. Efforts to obtain a federal charter for the Rockefeller Foundation in 1910 led to three years of congressional hearings, which ended only when Rockefeller withdrew from the battle. The New Deal's 1935 revision of the tax code was explicitly framed to "soak the rich." And, the Temporary National Economic Committee

(TNEC) investigations conducted by Congress in the late 1930s devoted volumes both to the vast size and to the extraordinary influence of the nation's dynastic families. In 1969, a decade of enquiry into the charitable foundations led to changes in the federal tax code affecting self-dealing, excess business holdings, reinvestment of income, and public accountability. These changes came close to eliminating the usefulness of foundations as dynastic mechanisms (Andrews, 1968, 1970; Neilson, 1972, 1985).

Ambivalence

In Europe, aristocratic dynasties were protected by a special legal status. The law of inheritance required lands and titles to be passed undivided to the eldest son. Entail prevented the sale or seizure of dynastic property by nonfamily members, however indebted the family might be. In America dynasties enjoyed no special standing. That they could exist at all was due to the adeptness of family founders and their successors in preserving and renewing their wealth and sense of special purpose – really the only things that set the so-called "great families" apart from the others. In the end, the survival of the great families depended on their ability to participate effectively in the capitalist economy and to defend their place in the democratic polity. Neither their own sense of special purpose nor their standing in the eyes of others exempted them from accountability to the marketplace. As one nineteenth-century dynast put it (Hall, 1892, p. 3), "No amount of good blood can make a fool other than he is, but family pride may stimulate a person of respectable origin and but limited capacity to exertions that will bring success in life."

The absence of special legal status meant that the children of dynastic families, like the children of lesser families, had to live in society and exert themselves in order to succeed. These were the only ways of assuring the survival of the dynasty. The rich could be exclusive, but only up to a point. The economic and political skills essential to dynastic survival could not be learned from private tutors; they could only be acquired in schools where merit, not manners, was the standard of excellence. The wealthy in America could not live idly when their self-interest required activity and engagement. They could not set themselves apart, either from society in general or from people like themselves, because the perpetuation of wealth was a matter of collective action to deploy political and economic resources.

However great a family's wealth and however compelling its sense of special destiny, no dynasty could be indifferent to the dominant democratic and meritocratic values of American society. Dynastic survival depended not only on institutional effectiveness in the marketplace but also on the ability of members, who as Americans were influenced by the dominant values, to reconcile the privileges of wealth with social expectations of individual achievement. Because a dynasty is ultimately an affair of persons, its continuation has depended less on its wealth than on the willingness of individuals in each succeeding generation to carry on the family mission. Individual responses to the conflict between dominant values and the family myth ultimately determine the fate of dynasties.

In dealing with this conflict between family and society, each child faces choices about how to use the family myth and the fortune that accompanies it. It can be a source of strength, a crippling burden, or an excuse for failure. The Adams family is a case in point. George Washington Adams (1801-1829), the son and grandson of presidents, lived a short and miserably failed life. He drowned himself in Long Island Sound when, during a psychotic break, he hallucinated that the engine of the steamship on which he was a passenger was speaking reproachfully in his father's voice (Nagel, 1983). In contrast, his brother Charles Francis (1807-1886) accepted both the assets and the liabilities of dynasty and built a brilliant career as a lawyer and diplomat in the mold of his forebears.

Eli Whitney, Jr. (1825-1895), son of the famous inventor and industrial pioneer, represented an interesting variation on this theme in which even children who forge successful careers and fulfill dynastic expectations remain incapable of valuing their achievements. Although his father died when Whitney was an infant, the son spent most of his life in the shadow of the great man's reputation. It was predetermined that he would take over management of the Whitney Armory, which his uncles operated during his minority. Whitney took over the firm shortly after graduating from Princeton. He was phenomenally successful in an intensely competitive industry. But, he was incapable of seeing himself as a success. Through the decade of the 1850s he kept a diary in which, between notes on spectacular transactions, he endlessly reiterated his sense of personal failure (Whitney, 1852-1860, p. 2): "July 9, 1852: I am very blue and possessed of a feeling of uncertainty as to my future business prospects and standing as a man...I seem to have been continuously putting my hand to the plow and looking back all my life long. My mistakes in life have been many. I am called somewhat energetic but lack energy more than anything else." The tone of the diary begins to change when, in the late 1850s, Whitney becomes involved in the effort to organize the New Haven Water Company. Initially an outsider to the project, he eventually not only became its largest stockholder but built the waterworks itself. What began as an effort to secure a greater power source for his father's factory became in the end a means of creating his own identity as a person and as an entrepreneur. Only by making his work his own could he have a sense that it had any real value. At the same time, it is significant that his self-affirmation came not from rejecting the dynastic burden but from accepting it and building his own life on and beyond it.

As the wealthy in America coalesced into a class at the end of the nineteenth century, the conflict between dominant values and dynastic claims came increasingly to be institutionally mediated. This was no accident, for, as the Holmes quote that began this paper suggests, dynastic families were becoming deeply concerned about their prospects for survival. After the Civil War, private education in America underwent a fundamental restructuring that was largely underwritten by dynastic families. Although they were motivated by the obvious need for an educational system appropriate to a national industrial economy, they were no less concerned with ensuring their own place in that new world.

The keystone of the new elite boarding schools and great private universities was an ethos of public service. This ethos not only legitimated the wealthy as a class but also created a matrix in which members of dynastic families could work to resolve the family-society conflict in a reasonably regulated way. Surrounded by people like themselves who were undergoing the same kinds of stresses, the sons and daughters who filled the prep schools played an especially important role in institutionalizing the intrapersonal struggle and guiding its resolution in socially productive directions. This development probably accounts for the fact that most dynastic families in America ended up accommodating the conflict between dynasty and democracy through public service and philanthropy rather than through exile or Bohemianism.

Conclusion

In spite of the social, economic, and political forces arrayed against them and in spite of individual ambivalence and family conflict, the dynastic process continues. It involves not only the heirs to great eighteenth- and nineteenth-century mercantile or industrial fortunes but any parent who, having succeeded in business, hopes to found a family and any child who faces a future in which expectations and resources garnered in the past have set him apart from his contemporaries.

Although social commentators, from Tocqueville in the nineteenth century through Weber and Parsons in the twentieth, have assured us that the future lay with impersonally and professionally managed bureaucratic enterprises, family firms and the dynastic processes that they often set in motion continue to play a dominant part in American life.

The persistence of family firms suggests that they are not merely holdovers or throwbacks. They can do things that more formally structured business organizations cannot. Proprietors accountable to themselves and their sense of family responsibility can act more flexibly and imaginatively than managers beholden to accountants and anonymous stockholders. The importance of family firms in the newspaper business is not a coincidence. Family control gives editors and publishers the independence of marketplace accountability that permits them to take unpopular or unprofitable stands. And, the family tie to the community makes these stands influential. Family firms have a capacity to make long-term investments and resist the pressure of financial analysts for short-term returns that currently bedevil many publicly held corporations.

The persistence of the family firm, together with evidence of the roles that it plays in industrial innovation, community leadership, and philanthropy, has important implications not only for therapists and management consultants but also for students of economic development and public policy. The larger social, technological, and political forces working against family firms have not been forces of nature but products of legislation and jurisprudence. Investigating them may lead both to a clearer understanding of the dynamics of family firms and to changes that will alter those dynamics.

An earlier version of this paper was presented to the Family Business Conference, the Wharton School, University of Pennsylvania in October 1986. The research from which this paper was drawn has been supported by the American Council of Learned Societies, AT&T Foundation, the Ellis Phillips Foundation, Equitable Life Assurance Society of the United States, Exxon Education Foundation, General Electric Foundation, the Teagle Foundation, and the Program on Nonprofit Organizations, Yale University.

References

Ames, J. B. *Lectures on Legal History and Miscellaneous Legal Essays.* Cambridge, Mass.: Harvard University Press, 1913.

Andrews, F. E. *Patman and the Foundations: Review and Assessment.* New York: The Foundation Center, 1968.

Andrews, F. E. *Foundations and the Tax Reform Act of 1969.* New York: The Foundation Center, 1970.

Baltzell, E. D. *Puritan Boston and Quaker Philadelphia: Two Protestant Ethics and the Spirit of Class Authority and Leadership.* New York: Free Press. 1979.

Carnegie, A. "The Gospel of Wealth." *North American Review*, 1889, 148, 653-664, 149, 682-698.

Collier, P., and Horowitz, D. *The Rockefellers: An American Dynasty.* New York: New American Library, 1976.

Davis, J. S. *Essays in the Earlier History of American Corporations.* Cambridge, Mass.: Harvard University Press, 1917.

Farber, B. *Guardians of Virtue: Salem Families in 1800.* New York: St. Martins Press, 1972.

Folsom, B. W. *Urban Capitalists: Entrepreneurs and City Growth in Pennsylvania's Lackawanna and Lehigh Regions, 1800-1920.* Baltimore, Md.: Johns Hopkins University Press, 1981.

Gray, J. C. *Restraints on the Alienation of Property.* Boston: Boston Book Company, 1895.

Hall, P. D. "Family Structure and Class Consolidation Among the Boston Brahmins." Unpublished doctoral dissertation, Department of History, State University of New York, Stony Brook, 1973.

Hall, P. D. *The Organization of American Culture, 1700-1900: Institutions, Elites, and the Origins of American Nationality.* New York: New York University Press, 1982.

Hall, P. D. "An Historical Overview of the Private Nonprofit Sector." In W. W. Powell (ed.), *The Nonprofit Sector: A Research Handbook.* New Haven, Conn.: Yale University Press, 1986.

Hall, T. P. *Family Records of Theodore Parsons Hall and Alexandrine Louise Godfroy.* Detroit, Mich.: W. C. Heath, 1892.

Holmes, O. W. *Elsie Venner: A Romance of Destiny.* New York: Signet, 1957 [1859].

Holmes, O. W. *Autocrat of the Breakfast Table.* New York: Sagamore Press, 1961 [1860].

Jobe, B., and Kaye, M. *New England Furniture: The Colonial Era.* Boston: Houghton Mifflin, 1984.

Koch, A. *The American Enlightenment.* New York: George Braziller, 1965.

Kolko, G. "Brahmins and Businessmen." In B. Moore and K Wolfe (eds.), *The Critical Spirit: Essays in Honor of Herbert Marcuse.* Boston: Beacon Press, 1967.

Marcus, G. "The Fiduciary Role in American Families and Their Institutional Legacy: From the Law of Trusts to Trusts in the Establishment." In G. Marcus (ed.), *Elites: Ethnographic Issues.* Albuquerque: University of New Mexico Press, 1983.

Middlesex Gazette (Middletown, Connecticut), May 16, 1806.

Miller, H. S. *The Legal Foundations of American Philanthropy.* Madison: State Historical Society of Wisconsin, 1961

Nagel, P. C. *Descent from Glory: Four Generations of the Adams Family.* New York: Oxford University Press, 1983.

Neilson, W. *The Big Foundations.* New York: Columbia University Press, 1972.

Neilson, W. *The Golden Donors.* New York: Dutton, 1985.

Newhall, G. *Future Interests and the Rule Against Perpetuities in Massachusetts.* Boston: Hildreth, 1942.

Pickering's Reports, Boston, Mass.: 1830, 9, 461.

Scott, A. W. "Charitable Trusts in New York." *New York University Law Review*, 1951, 26 (2), 251-265.

Scott, A. W. *The Law of Trusts.* Boston: Little, Brown, 1939.

Smith, P. *John Adams.* Garden City, N. Y.: Doubleday, 1962.

Story, R. *The Forging of an Aristocracy: Harvard and Boston's Upper Class, 1800-1870.* Middletown, Conn.: Wesleyan University Press, 1981.

Sweeney, K M. "Mansion People: Kinship, Class, and Architecture in the Mid-Eighteenth Century." *Winterthur Portfolio*, 1984 19 (4), 231-255.

Thomas, I. *History of Printing in America, with a Biography of Printers and an Account of Newspapers.* Barre, Mass.: Imprint Society, 1970.

Tocqueville, A. de. *Democracy in America.* New York: Vintage Books, 1945 [1835].

Waters, J. "American Colonial Stem Families: Persisting European Patterns in the New World." Unpublished paper presented at the History Department Faculty Seminar, Wesleyan University, April 1978.

Wharton, E. *Ethan Frome.* New York: Scribners, 1911.

White, G. T. *History of the Massachusetts Hospital Life Insurance Company.* Cambridge, Mass.: Harvard University Press, 1955.

Whitney, E., Jr. "Business Diary. 1852-1860." Whitney Family Papers, Yale University Library, Box 11, Folder 173.

When a family business is acquired by new owners, success will depend on whether the firm is managed in harmony with local culture. Though an extensive case study relationships between ownership, firm and community are explored.

Using a cultural perspective, this article investigates the proposition that family businesses acquired and managed in a manner that is at odds with the local culture win suffer, while firms that are acquired and managed in harmony with the local culture win have a higher level of morale and long-run productivity.

Family Firm and Community Culture

By Joseph H. Astrachan

Family Firm, Community Bureaucratic, and Urban Culture

Basic assumptions, which constitute the deepest level of culture, can be broken into five categories: humanity's relationship to nature, the nature of reality and truth, the nature of human nature, the nature of human activity, and the nature of human relationships (Schein, 1985; Parsons, 1951). The idea that bureaucracies are not like family firms is neither new nor controversial (Weber, 1947). Family firms often struggle to balance the cultural elements of families with the cultural elements of bureaucratic organizations (Lansberg, 1983). An analogue to the divergence of family firm and bureaucratic needs can be found in the tension that exists between communal and business needs in developing communities (Stein, 1973).

Figure 1 displays the five cultural categories with respect to family firms, bureaucracies, urban settings, and dose community settings. Figure 1 shows that the only two combinations of firm and environment culture that appear to be wholly compatible are family firm with community culture and bureaucracy with urban culture. It should be noted that the description of bureaucratic culture explored here is consistent with what Walton (1985) defines as "control driven." It is not meant to be representative of emerging "commitment-driven" bureaucratic forms. While the long-term results are not yet in, such forms frequently attempt to integrate the cultural elements described here as communal with large corporate size and attendant diversity.

Figure 1 is presented as an aid to understanding the case that follows; it considers forms of organization theoretically. As we well know, actual organizations may fit the idealized forms considered here only imperfectly. Further, the point is not the relative merits of one form over another. Rather, these assumptions are elaborated to gauge their consistency and degree of contradiction.

Railtown and the Quality Commodity Company

To study the relationship between family firm and community culture empirically, I was fortunate to be given access to Quality Commodity Company, a business located in America's Midwest. (Names and many of the details have been altered to protect the firm's identity.) The firm exists in a community of fewer than 10,000 people. When it was founded by the Alden family around the turn of the century, there was one other major employer in Railtown. After prospering as a family firm for over fifty years, the company was purchased by Corporal Industries, a large conglomerate. Approximately ten years later, Corporal Industries sold the business to its current owners, the Newcastle family. At the time I completed the fieldwork, the Newcastle had owned the firm for more than nine years. They are not related to the original owning family, and they had never lived in the surrounding community. Currently, Railtown has five large employers. Quality

Figure 1. Cultural Archetypes

Category of Cultural Assumption	Community and Family firm Culture	Urban and Bureaucratic Culture
Humanity's Relationship to Nature	Harmony with nature; emphasis on maintaining a delicate balance with nature	Domination of nature; even the bureaucratic form seeks to shape and control nature
The Nature of Reality and Truth	Testable truth is pragmatically defined	Truth is to be found in the next higher level of the hierarchy, in specialists who have expertise, and in "careful" analyses.
	For firms, untestable truth is defined by council of elders ownership	Highest form of truth is that which survives conflict and debate
	For communities, untestable truth is defined by council of elders of the "town fathers"	
	Polychronic or diffuse sense of time; open and unlocked space	Time and space are rigidly defined and compartmentalized
The Nature of Human Nature	Basically good, trustworthy, capable of substantial development, responsible, and accountable unless proved otherwise	Capable of limited growth, untrustworthy, self-seeking, and greedy; can only individually be proved otherwise
The Nature of Human Activity	Reactive; little emphasis on specific or detailed planning	Always planning and forecasting for future activity; actions are evaluated on the basis of plans; most behavior is made explicit prior to its implementation
	Highest-priority activities are those that benefit the collective	Highest-priority activities are those which benefit self
	Long-range time orientation	Short-range time orientation
The Nature of Human Relationships	Highly emotional, diffuse in nature, particularistic, sharing, cooperative, ascription and collectivity oriented	Emotionally neutral, specific in nature, impersonal, universalistic, achievement and self orientation

Note: The descriptions and assumptions in this figure are based on Ben-Prath, 1980; Bendix, 1956; Blood and Hulin, 1969; Braverman, 1974; Clark and Mills, 1979; Dyer, 1984; Etzioni, 1968; Gouldner, 1954; Hall, 1966; Hofstede, 1980; Merton, 1968; Milgram, 1970, Miller and Rice, 1967; Miklofsky, 1981; Parsons, 1951; Shein, 1985; Simmel, 1950; Taylor, 1947; Toennies, 1963; Weber, 1947.

Commodity employs about 500 people and has sales of between $20 million and $50 million.

This interesting case provides a rich source for learning. It has many characteristics of the so-called natural experiment. The company and its community have essentially remained intact, because there have been no large emigrations to or immigrations from the community during the years covered by this investigation. This fact makes comparisons of the three ownership periods valid.

With the exception of the conglomerate's corporate headquarters, whose members declined to be interviewed, I talked with people at all levels of the firm. The interviewees included line personnel who had worked at least fifteen years in the firm, the current owning family, and the former chairman and chief executive officer (the founder's son) who had sold the firm to the conglomerate. Historical and archival data were collected to corroborate the interview material.

The case examination of the proposition that firm productivity and morale are closely related to the compatibility of company and community culture will occur in several steps. Each of the three eras in the Quality Commodity Company's history Alden family, Corporal Industries, and Newcastle family will be examined, and data relevant to the multiple culture categories will be provided. After the three time periods are compared in terms of culture, morale, and productivity, some implications for firms going through management changes and for organizations that are acquiring firms will be outlined.

Quality Commodity: The Early Years

Shortly after the turn of the century, the Quality Commodity Company settled in Railtown. The company began operations with the explicit intention of becoming the town's company. Its leaders publicly offered minority ownership interest in the company to the townspeople. As an article in the local newspaper stated, "It is the intention of the men at the head of this company to make it a substantial asset to the city of Railtown and the community and to only increase growth along the lines that experience has shown to be conservative...This is a local institution, and the stock should be owned and controlled in the community." To Mr. Alden, the company's founder, being the town's company meant both that the company's primary responsibilities lay with the town and that the town had a mutual responsibility toward the company. As the eighty-year-old unofficial historian of Railtown explained to me during an interview, "Mr Alden had the idea that not only should a company have a conscience about its people, but also the people should have one about the way they should handle their company. It was, I think Mr. Alden would say, a two-way street." During these early years, Quality Commodity shaped and reflected Railtown's community culture.

Mr. Alden's direction was congruent with beliefs already existing in Railtown. The community's traits, which came from its "notable fathers," included "having the good judgment to open the door when opportunity knocked," punctuality, honesty, trustworthiness, donating of self, teaching by example, and having a firm idea of right and wrong and making that idea understandable.

From its founding until the end of this first period, Quality Commodity had the express goal of slow and cautious growth. The desire was to maintain harmony with the community and citizens of Railtown. For example, Quality Commodity helped many employees to buy homes, and it gave annual picnics for the entire community. Neither firm nor town attempted to dominate its members. As an article in the local newspaper put it, "For many years, the personnel policies of Quality Commodity carried out a 'one big family concept. Group insurance, profit sharing, a liberal pension plan, and other benefits were set up for employees...Mr. Alden believed that business should be ruled by principles of integrity, fair treatment of employees, and the manufacture of a quality product." The wish to harmonize with employees is manifest in the company's early adoption of many liberal personnel policies. These policies included a five-day work week, company cafeterias, no time clocks, and seven-and-one-half-hour days with no reduction in pay.

As in many family firms and close communities, pragmatism was a high priority. Quality early move into an automated manufacturing process was also a pragmatic decision. Initially, a line employee convinced Mr. Alden to try a small automation experiment in one small step of the manufacturing process. When this experiment was demonstrated to be successful, other parts of the line were automated. Quality Community occasionally suffered because of its trial-and-error method of decision making. Projects were canceled when a series of trial-and-error experiments failed.

From the very start, Quality had an open sense of time and space. Few meetings were scheduled, and they occurred as needed. Although space was not abundant, it was open. Since its founding, the company had, on the average, added a new building more than once every five years.

Mr. Alden had strong beliefs about the good in people. As one interviewee phrased it, "Mr. Alden was a faithful human being; he had faith in things and in people." Born in Appalachia, Mr. Alden was self-educated, and he had worked on the family farm in his youth. Within the business, his beliefs about the developmental capacity of human beings were evident in his policy of promotion from within.

Every person from this first era whom I interviewed acknowledged that the highest-priority activities were those that ultimately benefited the firm and, through the firm, the community. A concrete example of Mr. Alden's altruism occurred during the depression:

He used his own life insurance policy as collateral to borrow money to secure the payroll. During that period, employees worked without pay for company-issued scrip, which was honored in stores more than four towns away; employees could exchange the scrip for shares in the company. In the community, people were reported to have pulled together, not to have separated or left the town.

There was generally little precise advance planning. The earliest example of advance planning comes from the decision concerning the type of product that the firm would manufacture. The original plan was that the firm would produce a product that would compete in a new, fast-growing, yet increasingly congested market. When it finally began production, the company used a similar advanced technology to produce an entirely different (though not a new) item. The company's decision to enter this niche was a reaction to limited financial resources not to market research. There was no evidence in Railtown of community planning, even during the depression. Although activities related to survival during the depressions were not planned, they did involve the entire community, and they were usually initiated by the town's business leaders.

Perhaps because of the size of Rail town, people knew each other in many contexts. A retired employee informed me that "in the earlier days things were simplified because most of the people were local people, so you know a lot about them, their families, and their backgrounds."

People were generally treated independently and in a particularistic manner. One former manager said, "We tried to treat all the people based on what the person and the work called for." Particularism within the firm is evidenced by the firm's practice of al; lowing employees to arrange their own schedules in a manner that resembles what is now known as flex time. Everyone reported that, up until the end of this period, there had been a large degree of caring for individual people.

Cooperation was the rule in the company. One manager said, "We had real team work. You'd work with the guys using each other's ideas, and then we'd do the best job possible." If people on the line needed help, it was common for management to give assistance.

Ascription (rights and responsibilities based not on merit but on birth) was also accepted. The succession from first to second-generation Alden proceeded smoothly. The employees saw the succession from one generation to the next as a legitimate and necessary transfer of ownership and managerial responsibilities. No fighting for top positions was reported. One common comment was, "If I had children, I think that it'd be natural that they come into the business." When Mr. Alden's son came into the business, the employees sought to improve his skills and build cooperative relationships with him rather than challenging his right to the job. Only a few years after the junior Alden joined the firm, he was asked to accept full responsibility for the company when his father suddenly died of a heart attack.

The Alden family reduced some of the tensions that can accompany a strict adherence to ascription by frowning on displays of class differences or other symbols that imply a separation between people. Family members worked to create a feeling that everyone was in the firm together for equal reward and for benefit to all The Aldens lived in an average house. During the depression, even the Aldens did not buy clothing for more than eight years. They chose instead to save for times of greater despair and for others. Although the sale of the firm to Corporal Industries created millionaires in the town, as an article in a national newspaper reported, no displays of affluence could be found except in the "local banks' balance sheets."

The Aldens labored to create a powerful sense of community in both the Quality Commodity Company and Railtown. They encouraged their employees to participate in management and ownership of the company and in committees in town. The Aldens felt that people would be especially motivated to work by the feeling that they were working for themselves, their families, and their community. They believed that a sense of family benefitted everyone in Railtown. The Aldens' influence in the community was demonstrated by the view of many that they were one of the town's founding families, although they had arrived more than a generation after the town was founded.

Until shortly before the business was sold, Quality Commodity maintained its high level of morale and prosperity under the direction of Mr. Alden's son. In the years preceding the sale, employees began to have doubts about the future of the company and its management. This short period of discontent was brought about by the declining health of the junior Alden. President for more than twenty-five years, the junior Alden had suffered at least one heart attack and was contending with a very painful and visible angina condition. Following his physician's advice, he withdrew from the business. It was speculated in town that his condition had been brought about by his own son, who had refused to take over the business and left Railtown to seek his fortune elsewhere.

Employees, who had come to expect openness from management, began to inquire about succession plans. The belief that the junior Alden was not functioning well enough to ensure the future of the firm and community after his departure spread. With succession unplanned and the future threatened, company morale began to decline. This decline was not reflected in sales or profit figures. However, many employees remembered it, and it was reflected in the success of the union's fifteenth organizing drive. Townsfolk and employees who doubted the future of the firm accepted unionization because it seemed to promise survival Employees were far more concerned with the firm's future than they were with wresting day-to-day control from management. They became concerned with influencing management only after the next owners had instituted bureaucracy.

The period that included the fifteenth unionization drive and the sale of the business was acknowledged by all to have been a very dark time in Railtown's history. Reports of that time include stories of how every other window in the company's buildings had been broken during one riot. One onlooker said that she ran home crying after witnessing the senseless destruction. "It was like a war had broke out in our town," she said. The union was formalized, and with it the separation between management and employees; deep divisions withing the community formed and were openly acknowledged. Quality was sold that same year. Emotion were reported to have cooled down a bit after the firm's sale was announced. Anticipation of a new era in the company's history replaced anger and hostility. Nevertheless, many people felt a sense of loss and grief at the departure of the junior Alden. These feelings increased as employees and other community members alike learned that ensuring the future through unionization and bureaucracy had substantial costs.

The Corporal Industries Years

Corporal Industries and the Aldens had very different styles of management. The first words spoken to me during many interviews are an indication of how culturally inconsistent Corporal Industries was with Railtown and prior management: "So, you've come to study something to do with Corporal and us? it should give about the best lesson there is in how not to manage a company." The junior Alden made a statement that is consistent with the theoretical position taken in this paper. He said, "The problem was that people who were sent here didn't know how to manage a small company in a small town."

The very idea of being sold as part of a company was distasteful to many of Quality's employees. (In the remainder of this paper, Alden-era employees are referred to as *Quality's* or as the *Quality employees*. Corporal Industries' managers are referred to as *Corporal, Corporal managers* and *Corporal people*.) They felt dominated almost from the start. The Corporal manager who was put in charge of operations had been instrumental in closing the deal. He was replaced within weeks of the sale. As soon as his replacement arrived, Corporal imposed its management structure on Quality Commodity. Of Corporal's style, one returned manager said, "They never heard the old Chinese proverb that you start a journey of one thousand miles with a single step...When they came in, they pretty much rode roughshod. They developed a pretty good resentment because us country boys didn't like that."

Further evidence of Corporal's unwillingness to harmonize with local culture was provided by one interviewee, who reported that corporal's people "didn't try to fit into Railtown; they didn't care to." When individuals from Corporal's headquarters came to visit the factories, they refused to stay in either of the two local motels. Instead, they chose lodging in a larger city more than an hour from Railtown.

The biggest symbol of domination and the thing that hurt Railtown citizens the most was that Corporal destroyed every trace of the old company. This "cleansing" included the destruction of paintings of the founding family, machinery, files, and several buildings. Old, though not obsolete, equipment that Quality employees had crafted was melted down and transferred to other divisions in the Corporal conglomerate. Employees loyal to the Alden family scrambled to ferret away mementos as soon as they learned of Corporal's actions.

Corporal also attempted to implement typically bureaucratic policies. Overall direction for Quality Commodity was defined by Corporal's headquarters in the form of a five-year plan. The five-year plan included multiple operational and sales goals. Corporal seemed to require a forecast for everything.

Quality's employees did not understand the methods that Corporal used to make decisions. The goals and other results of the many analyses were nonsensical to those who had experience in the company. One manager explained that "they bogged you down in paperwork." Another reported that "they tried to turn us into paper pushers." Too much time seemed to be spent deciding what to do and too little on doing it.

Corporal placed very strong boundaries on time and space. Time was scheduled in detail. Routine meetings seemed to take precedence over substantive issues occurring on the shop floor or in the sales field. Space was also more clearly defined, and it was accorded new meaning. Corporal managers fought over office space and furniture. Office doors were locked for the first time in company history.

Perhaps the most divergent assumption about human nature that Corporal people displayed was that employees were only capable of limited growth. A Corporal manager who had been at Quality for a number of years once stated that "people in corporate headquarters told me that the people in Railtown are dumb SOBs, but after I'd been here a while I learned that they [Corporal headquarters] are the dumb SOBs." The general feeling at Quality was that the majority of Corporal people thought they were smarter and better than Quality veterans.

Corporal policies also assumed that people were basically not good. That is, people were untrustworthy, irresponsible, and self-seeking. This assumption was implied in the elaborate system of controls that Corporal tried to foster.

Another indication was that Corporal people "would not take any suggestions or ideas." One manager reported, "You couldn't tell them when you knew that they were wrong." Quality people observed dishonest and disingenuous behavior on the part of a few Corporal managers and then assumed that Corporal management was untrustworthy and self-interested.

Corporal did not want local employees to become involved with company wide issues. Through directives and other actions, Corporal made it clear that local employees were to deal only with their specific tasks. For example, managerial offices were separated, and on time and unscheduled meetings and informal communication were discouraged. In creased conflict accompanied Corporal's attempted separation of people. One person reported that Corporal managers would "build little kingdoms, buy their people, and in two years' time, they're gone." Corporal also removed several functions from Quality control, including research, advertising, and accounting.

Quality's identity in the community also changed. Nearly all the activities that Quality had performed for the community were discontinued. Informal representation of Quality ownership ceased on town committees, money was no longer given to the community, advertisements disappeared from the local papers. Activities that would benefit the community were not considered a priority. As one resident stated, "Corporal had a very saddening effect on Railtown. Quality and Railtown were synonymous." Another reported that, while Corporal may have had a somewhat depressing effect, "the town pretty much acclimated itself to the new industrial companies that characterize modern corporations...We couldn't go to the industries anymore to get things done for the community." To some people, Corporal seemed like a deadly parasite that had no real interest in the well-being of Railtown.

Quality people had a difficult time understanding why Corporal managers acted impersonally and without feeling. Most Quality people interpreted impersonality as an indication of lack of caring. Other facts validated this interpretation. One Corporal manager often did not show up to work until 11 A.M. and left well before 4:30 P.M. Rumors, bolstered by powerful feelings, suggested that Corporal "didn't care about us. We were under them, just one of their plants." Others were convinced that Corporal was going to liquidate Quality. Several large layoffs and wholesale firings occurred. One manager stated that "there was a real lack of security; you didn't know who was going to go next. It was the same in the town; people were waiting for us to go under."

Teamwork and cooperation diminished. Relationships with Corporal management were specific in nature, occurring only in the business context. Unlike the Alden family days, when people shared ideas and knowledge freely, under Corporal, "if someone said that they wanted to pick your brain, that would mean that you were about to be fired." Corporal discouraged participatory behavior. Outside associations among Quality people decreased. There were no reported instances of Corporal people befriending Quality employees. There were a few Corporal people with whom Railtown folk were comfortable. However, "they didn't make up for the obnoxiousness of others."

Corporal practiced universalism. Several people described its hiring method as consisting of putting names into a hat and pulling them out at a random. Corporal people had no regard for the diffuse character of relationships within Railtown. For example, people were hired who had demonstrated irresponsibility in other settings within the community, and the new hires, as well as Corporal management, were subsequently resented. Life outside Quality was unimportant to Corporal.

Short-run, self, and achievement orientations were prevalent in Corporal. Corporal managers never stayed at Quality's facilities for more than two years. More than one Quality employee said, "They came to establish a track record, and they didn't care how they did it." Once interpretation of high turnover among Corporal management became popular among Quality's employees: Quality had become the last stop before Corporal managers were fired. The combination of repeated failures initiated by Corporal and Corporal managers' limited understanding of how decisions were made prompted one Quality employee to state, "I don't think any of us could remember all the stupid things that were being done." Another employee said, "the Corporal image stood for failure, incompetence, and the like." Eventually, Quality was put up for sale. While the citizens of Railtown were apprehensive and uncertain about having yet another owner became involved in Quality, they believed that with change there was hope. Within a matter of months, the Newcastle family was making the final arrangements to acquire Quality.

Quality Commodity and the Newcastle Family

At first glance, Mr. Newcastle's academic and practical education seemed well suited to bureaucratic culture. An Ivy League graduate with an M.B.A. from a prestigious school he had begun his career as a manager in a multinational corporation. Mrs. Newcastle was college educated. She had been primarily a homemaker until her children reached high school age. Her family had a history of female entrepreneurs. Her mother was a major contributor to recent world changing technologies. Dissatisfaction with the management practices and politics of corporate America had led Mr. and Mrs. Newcastle to go out on their own.

Before acquiring Quality Commodity, the Newcastle had started several smaller ventures, which provided mediocre returns at best. Prompted primarily by the desire to manage a larger organization, the Newcastles began to hunt for an acquisition. Like those who had founded Railtown, the Newcastles had a history of making the most of opportunities. When Quality became available, the Newcastles quickly gauged its potential. Using a combination of intuition and financially based analyses, they decided to purchase the company.

In defining the division of labor, the Newcastle decided that Mr. Newcastle was to have primary responsibility for financial and operational management. Mrs. Newcastle was to be responsible for personnel human resources, and marketing. They firmly decided, long before their purchase of Quality, that all major decisions about product development, company expansion, or major change would be made jointly. After mutual agreement on such decisions, they would then ask key players from the rest of the company to help them make the final decision and develop implementation plans.

The Newcastle's first actions established a dear difference between themselves and Corporal Industries. They held a factory wide meeting to explain their proposed purchase and to discuss what life would be like with new owners in control According to employees' reports, the Newcastle, in contrast to Corporal, actually solicited listened to, and acted on advice from everyone in the plant.

One thing that consciously bothered the Newcastles was that by purchasing the firm they were, in a philosophical sense, dominating the employees. Mr. Newcastle expressed discomfort that he had been part of a transaction in which "the workers were sold like cattle." When the Newcastle first purchased the firm, they left policies and personnel intact. Any changes that were made occurred only after consultation with the people who would be affected. As one manager put it, Mr. Newcastle "really wants people to get along with each other; he really wants to make it a team effort." Another stated, "This is the most harmonious office I've ever worked in."

The Newcastles returned pragmatic management to the company. Several people stated that Mr. Newcastle had "a real open mind" He was willing to allow people to try things without "a hundred pages of justification." Product and production ideas once again flowed from the bottom of the hierarchy.

In the Newcastles' Quality, untestable truth was defined largely by the owner, as is typical in patriarchal systems. As Mr. Newcastle said, "Ultimately, I am the boss of my business." Without any testing or discussion, the Newcastle returned the firm to its previous goals of quality products and customer service. Shortcuts in the production process that Corporal had implemented were eliminated. The attitude that everyone in the plant was member of the quality control department was adopted.

These changes were well accepted at Quality. People remembered their past prospering as being largely the result of high quality and customer service. In a manner that resembled Mr. Alden's, Mr. and Mrs. Newcastle also sought innovations that, while costing more, noticeably improved quality. Quality's products once again became the highest-quality products in the industry.

The Newcastles also returned the sense of time and space that Quality had once enjoyed. New offices were built both at the factory and at the corporate headquarters. Both buildings are characterized by open spaces and open office doors where doors exist at all. The Newcastle also blurred the lines that existed between Quality and Railtown. For example, the local high school's yearbooks are proudly placed on a conference room bookshelf in front of popular books on management, such as *In Search of Excellence* and *The One Minute Manager.*

Time returned to its polychronic state. Many meetings were unscheduled, all were informal, and the number of routine meetings was so few that appointment calendars were not seen anywhere. For example, the director of quality control intermittently met with the general manager early in the morning over coffee. Further evidence came from my own experience. When I asked people if I could schedule an interview, almost everyone said, "Sure, how about now?"

Mr. and Mrs. Newcastle frequently expressed their beliefs about human nature. They believed that trust went hand in hand with the granting of autonomy. The Newcastle also felt that, when people are allowed, they are naturally good, most are honest, and all are capable of substantial learning and growth. These beliefs were best illustrated by the amount of time and effort devoted to explaining each decision, especially the decisions that affected the overall direction of the company.

The Newcastle's style of management was reactive. While planning did occur, it was not emphasized. As one employee described the orientation toward activity at Quality, "The way we do things around here is someone asks for something to be done, and, if it's at all possible, we do it and I don't remember too many things that were impossible!" One example of reactivity in the company as a whole was the frequency with which someone

Figure 2. Culture of Railtown and the Quality Commodity Company

Category of Cultural Assumption	Railtown	Quality Commodity: The Alden Years	Corporal Industries	Quality Commodity: The Newcastle Years
Humanity's Relationship to Nature	Harmonize with nature	Harmony: goal of slow and cautious growth; acted as a citizen in Railtown; liberal policies toward employees	Domination: made many policy and product changes without seeking advice; relations with town halted	Harmony: acted on workers' concerns, no initial changes in personnel; restored Quality's role in town; created new markets
The Nature of Reality and Truth	Testable truth defined pragmatically	Pragmatism: trial-and-error decision making; autonomy given for all testable decisions	Rigid Analyses: extensive documentation and forecasting required	Pragmatism: trial-and-error decision making; autonomy given for testable decisions
	Untestable truth defined patriarchically, by a council of elders	Defined by founder: Mr. Alden made all important decisions about company policy and direction	Defined in next-highest level of hierarchy; five-year plans; all decision making about policies occurred in corporate headquarters	Defined by owner: Newcastles made most of the important decisions regarding overall policy and firm's direction
	Time and space are diffuse	Difuse: no time clocks; appointments and meetings largely unscheduled; space open, and doors unlockcd	Fixed: appointments formally scheduled; fights occurred over office space; doors lockcd	Diffuse: open offices and spaces; unscheduled meetings; no appointment books visible
The Nature of Human Nature	Basically good, capable of development, trustworthy, responsible and accountable	Good: Mr. Alden was self-made; management never hired from outside firm; workers had high autonomy; employees held ownership in company	Bad: not concerned with employees outside work; no advice seeking; elaborate controls implemented; white collar crime	Good: time is taken to explain all decisions; teaching orientation; autonomy promoted at all levels; employees listened to, and their opinions solicited
The Nature of Human Activity	Reactive, little emphasis on planning, seizes opportunities	Reactive: no formal forecasting; new products discovered by accident	Planning: five-year plans required; quarterly forecasting	Reactive: purchase of firm and product development were responses to opportunity
	Participatory in nature	Participatory: involved employees in decision making	Individual orientation: separation of functions and offices; informal communications discouraged	Participatory: concerned with creating a "family feeling" in firm and community
	Highest-priority activities are those that benefit the collective	Benefit the collective: helped arrange housing; sponsored company activities that included the town	Benefit company: all community support disappeared	Benefit community: reestablished community support and work study programs
	Long-range time orientation	Long-range: instrumental in bringing new business to Railtown	Short-range: high turnover of management; short-term goals specified	Long-range: concern with quality products; invested in equipment that depressed profit in short run
The Nature of Human Relationships	Highly emotional, diffuse, particularistic, ascription and collectively oriented	Diffuse, emotional: people interacted in many contexts, and the firm supported this; people judged in terms of who they were and how they related to the whole comany; succession of son was well accepted	Specific, impersonal: teamwork replaced by destructive competition; positions in company became a rung on career ladder; community role of employees discouraged	Diffuse, emotional; sanctioned hiring of families; no formal organization chart; organization-wide meetings held; people judged on basis of who they were in relation to whole company

returned from a convention filled with ideas for new products, and many of the ideas were implemented.

The Newcastle were explicit about their desire for most activities to be participatory in nature. Many employees explained that they spent a good deal of time working with others. The team feeling, which had disappeared under Corporal, returned to Quality. The Newcastle were very concerned with creating a sense of family within their firm and with benefiting the community of Railtown in both the long and the short term. As Mr. Newcastle said, "I want very much to create a family system...I have attempted to allow for an environment in which a community could form. This will help me and the business and therefore the community. Quality Commodity is part of the community. It has an established place but does not take up the whole environment. It is recognized that part of them is Quality."

One action in particular symbolizes Quality return to the community. During the Alden family days, the firm used an old steamship whistle to signal the changes of shifts and breaks. Many people in town were fond of the sound, which had become a beloved tradition. Corporal had removed the whistle early in its ownership. After the Newcastle gained control, the general manager remembered that they had hidden the whistle to preserve it from being melted down. When he returned the whistle to active duty, one newspaper headline read, "Lots of memories called up by a steam whistle's toot." An editorial in another paper gave "special thanks to those whose effort restored the old Quality whistle."

The Newcastles accepted nearly all the responsibilities that the Aldens and their company had assumed for the community. Quality once again sponsored local sports teams, bought advertisements in the local paper, made donations to local organizations, and contributed to the community in many other ways. The newspaper advertisements stressed quality, community, and teamwork; for example: "Congratulations Flames [high school-team] on another Super Season Quality Efforts of quality young men building community pride." In coordination with the local high school, the Newcastle began a work study program.

The Newcastles displayed their assumption that relationships should be diffuse by example. The entire Newcastle family worked for Quality. Moreover, Quality employed two or more members of more than fifteen local families. There was no formal organization chart. Mr. Newcastle maintained that "people have spheres of influence." People must report to many others and must individually determine to whom to give information. In this way, Mr. Newcastle tried to establish a system in which people were required to think about their role in, and their relationship to the whole company.

Particularism also worked its way back into the Quality Commodity Company. Mr. Newcastle stated that "people are judged on the basis of who they are and how they are relating to the whole and not how they are doing in their own separate sphere; their separation is de-emphasized." One employee said, 'It's more like old times now than ever before; there's more interest in ya." Another commented, 'We've grown so large, I'm afraid that if we grow any more, things might become impersonal." Aware of this, the Newcastle met their growth needs by expanding in other communities as well as by gradually enlarging their operations in Railtown.

Perhaps the most impressive evidence for the Newcastle' impact was union relations. Less than two years after the Newcastle family took control of the business, an internal drive started for union decertification. However, Mr. Newcastle stated that he could not endorse a decertification drive, because the union was not interfering in the daily activities of the company, because decertification drive might cause conflict among employees, and because the union still might provide some benefits and long-run security to the employees. The Newcastle' competitors were particularly distressed by this news, as the Newcastle' operation had regained the reputation of being very generous and caring toward employees. In other words, the Newcastle were setting bargaining standards that competitors had difficulty matching.

Under the Newcastle family, Quality's culture stabilized and largely returned to its state in the days before Corporal. This happened because the Newcastle' assumptions were similar to those that historically had operated in Railtown. Figure 2 summarizes Railtown's culture and the culture of Quality Commodity during each of the three ownership periods.

The descriptions of the cultures provided here cannot be complete. It may not be possible to express the richness of culture adequately in words. This paper has attempted to provide a brief sketch of some of the important cultural aspects. The next step is to examine the effects that the various cultures had on Quality Commodity's performance.

Effects of Culture on Quality Commodity

Under Corporal, the Quality Commodity Company was often caught in the cultural cross fire between its owners and Railtown. This position led to many misinterpretations of behavior and in turn to inappropriate responses.

We have already witnessed several results of the situation in which one culture asserts itself over another culture that is incompatible, strong, and well entrenched. These results included confusion, helplessness, and anger. A dramatic example of how these conflicts affected people personally was that a manager who "didn't fit in" with Corporal and was subsequently fired committed suicide.

There were many other organizationally relevant effects. When people were asked about loyalty during Corporal's ownership, they would laugh. 'What loyalty?" they asked. One manager was quite clear about the period when Corporal controlled Quality: "Loyalty was to the past rather than to Corporal or its management. I can't recall any [loyalty]. I'm talking about the people who were local. People were responsible people. Supervisors and up, salaried people. But not because of Corporal. It was in spite of them." Several top managers and sales people quit because of cultural and managerial differences with Corporal policies.

The return of family ownership brought a return of loyalty and commitment. As a testament to the similarity in cultures, one manager who quit during the Corporal days returned to the company when the Newcastle requested his services. Employees stated that they were committed to the Newcastle and their ideals. Because the Newcastle were operating from assumptions similar to Railtown's, it was easy for townspeople to understand and support their actions, policies, and decisions. As Figures 3 through 6 indicate, the company and the employees benefited in many ways when the Newcastle family reintroduced a managerial culture that was similar to the community's culture.

Common measures of employee morale and productivity include absenteeism, turnover, and scrap rates. As Figure 3 shows, during the Alden family era, the yearly scrap rate never exceeded 11 per cent. In sharp contrast, Corporal attained an unbelievable 50 percent scrap rate. As one manager stated, "Morale went bad. People were deliberately turning out a bad product. They were putting very derogatory notes in packages [that were to be shipped]." Under the Newcastle family, the scrap rate returned to the 10 percent

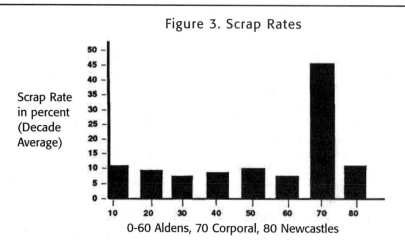

Figure 3. Scrap Rates

Scrap Rate in percent (Decade Average)

0-60 Aldens, 70 Corporal, 80 Newcastles

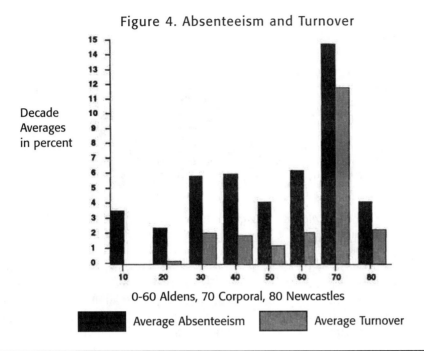

Figure 4. Absenteeism and Turnover

Decade Averages in percent

0-60 Aldens, 70 Corporal, 80 Newcastles

Average Absenteeism   Average Turnover

range. Corporal's scrap rate is even more surprising than it looks because Corporal shipped goods that the Alden and Newcastle families would have considered to be scrap.

As Figure 4 shows, the pattern of absenteeism is very similar to the pattern for scrap rates. Starting with a rate of between 2 and 9 percent under the Aldens, it increased to well over 15 percent for Corporal and then returned to between 2 and 9 percent once again. (Until the year before the fieldwork for this study was conducted, when the work force was increased by 25 percent the absenteeism rate under the Newcastle had been between 1 and 5 percent.) Figures for employee turnover were not readily available from Corporal, and they were distorted by Corporal's layoffs. Setting death and retirements aside, turnover was well under 3 percent a year during the Alden period. Under Corporal, it may have jumped to between 10 and 20 percent, not including layoffs. Again the pattern reversed under the Newcastle, with turnover dropping to 3 percent or less.

Company prosperity can be measured by such indicators as sales growth and number of people employed. (Profits are not used, because they were unavailable from Corporal, and they could not be reconstructed from interview material. Indicators that rely on financial data were not adjusted for inflation. Financial data are reported in standardized terms to protect confidentiality.) As Figure 5 shows, sales growth steadily increased under the

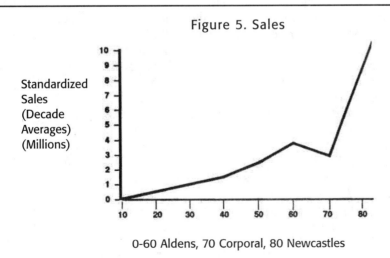

Figure 5. Sales

Standardized Sales (Decade Averages) (Millions)

0-60 Aldens, 70 Corporal, 80 Newcastles

Figure 6. Employment

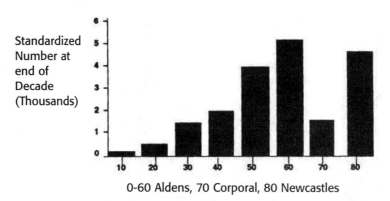

Standardized Number at end of Decade (Thousands)

0-60 Aldens, 70 Corporal, 80 Newcastles

Alden family. In the first five years after the company's founding, sales increased 758 percent. By the time Corporal purchased the firm, sales had increased more than 25,000 percent. Sales decreased more than 20 percent during Corporal's ownership. However, under the Newcastle family, sales quickly rebounded. In the first year alone, sales were up 35 percent. By the end of 1985, sales had increased more than 450 percent since the Newcastle had taken control.

As Figure 6 shows, the number of employees under the Alden family grew 5,600 percent from Quality first year of operation. During the lowest point of Corporal's cutbacks, the number of people employed dropped by more than 75 percent. Employment under the Newcastles grew 20 percent in the first year, and it had grown 300 overall as of December 1985. Employment figures also reflect community well-being and morale, because high employment reduces unemployment, increases the tax base, and increases local property values.

Other measures of growth and productivity, including total building space, number of production lines, money spent on new equipment, contributions to employee pension funds and insurance, dollars spent on advertising and promotion, new products introduced, and product enhancements, show a similar trend. The patterns just described vividly illustrate the relationship between ownership and a firm's prosperity.

Conclusion

This paper has explored the idea that the compatibility between firm and community culture has consequences for both the firm and the community. The case of Railtown and the Quality Commodity Company support the premise remarkably well. The firm was initially composed entirely of people from the local community. Its owners and managers lived in Railtown. Quality Commodity firmly held and indeed shaped the cultural assumptions that were alive in Railtown. Comfortably situated within Railtown's culture, Quality Commodity was seen by the community as a resource and as a responsible and influential community member, As a result, the employees and the town displayed a great deal of loyalty and commitment to Quality. The company was treated like a trusted friend by its employees and the community, and this trust was reflected in Quality's success. Through their own behavior, the Newcastle family promoted practices, norms, and working relationships that were consistent with the assumptions of Quality Commodity, Railtown and the Alden family.

Corporal Industries' culture was incompatible with both Railtown's culture and with the Alden's basic assumptions, which had shaped Quality's culture. Corporal's influence acted as a force that pulled the Quality Commodity Company out of the community in which it had been born. Quality personnel had difficulty understanding and responding appropriately to Corporal management. Quality's cultural assumptions led employees to misinterpret Corporal's actions. The result was low morale and the rapid failure of Corporal's operations in Railtown.

This paper suggests not only that the firm is part of a larger system but that the host places cultural constraints on the firm. Cultural and organizational change is therefore limited by factors that may be beyond the organization's control. Within a highly interconnected system, a change in one part of the system, such as the firm, is accompanied by changes elsewhere, such as in the community.

This paper also shows how differences in assumptions between people and between groups who must interact within larger organizational and societal contexts results in discomfort, stress, and inappropriate behavior. The paper does not intend to state that one culture is better than another culture. What its findings suggest is that cultural similarity between firm and environment is less stressful and problematic for the community and the firm than dissimilarity is.

Other factors, such as firm size, industry technology, and history and nature of the work force, may provide complementary explanations. By definition, the nature of the work force is manifested in the culture. In this case, the work force was comprised of individuals who had a fairly stable set of existing relationships. Culture also expresses history. The technology issue seems to have little bearing on the results seen in this case. Industry technology remained stable, as is evidenced by the many other firms that used similar technology.

This examination does not rule out the possibility that bureaucracies have cultures like the firms they acquire. One successful entrepreneur has started at least two large conglomerates that acquire only family businesses (Simon, 1985). And, this exploration does not rule out the possibility that family and community-like cultures exist elsewhere than in rural areas. Research suggests that similar subcultures can be found in and around large cities (Dobriner, 1958). My research also does not say that all close communities and family firms have the culture described here. Further studies are needed to examine these other possibilities and to elaborate the factors that differentiate among situations.

One very important question that also needs further study is, Does the firm's relevant community include more than just the geographic locale and ownership? Owners and managers may also need to consider the influence of the cultures of their suppliers, distributors, and customers when managing their firms.

This line of inquiry has several implications for firms acquiring family firms, for family firms that are being sold to other firms, and for family firms that are undergoing a transfer of management. These implications spring from the central theme that sensitivity to the existing culture is critical to the success of a firm. Perhaps most important, the acquiring firm should evaluate the way in which it intends to manage the acquired firm and its community and the fit between these intentions and the cultural assumptions already in place. To do this requires an in-depth study of the cultures of all systems involved. The model types of culture presented here are a particularly useful starting point for such a study. Cultural diagnosis is a difficult and important task whenever change is planned. It is advisable to seek expert guidance.

References

Alderfer, C. P., and Klein, E. B. "Affect, Leadership, and Organizational Boundaries." *Journal of Personality and Social Systems*, 1976, 1 (3), 19-33.

Astrachan, B. M. "Organizational Boundary Management for Value Congruence." Unpublished manuscript, Yale University School of Medicine, 1975.

Bendix, R. *Work and Authority in Industry*. Berkeley: University of California Press, 1956.

Ben-Prath, Y. "'The F Connection' Families, Friends, and Firms in the Organization of Exchange." *Population and Development Review*, 1980, 6(1), 130.

Blood, M. R., and Hulin, C. L. "Alienation, Environmental Characteristics, and Worker Responses." *Journal of Applied Psychology*, 1969, 51, 284 290.

Clark, M. S., and Mills, J. "Interpersonal Attraction in Exchange and Communal Relationships." *Journal of Personality and Social Psychology*, 1979, 37(1), 1224.

Dobriner, W. (ed.). *The Suburban Community*. New York: Putnam, 1958.

Dyer, W. G., Jr. "Cultural Evolution in Organizations: The Case of a Family Owned Firm." Unpublished doctoral dissertation, Sloan School of Management, Massachusetts Institute of Technology, 1984.

Dyer, W. G., Jr. *Cultural Change in Family Firms: Anticipating and Managing Business and Family Transitions*. San Francisco: Jossey-Bass, 1986.

Etzioni, A. *The Active Society*, New York: Free Press, 1968.

Gouldner, A. W. *Patterns of Industrial Bureaucracy: A Case Study of Modern Factory Administration*. New York: Free Press, 1954.

Hall, E. T. *The Hidden Dimension*. New York: Doubleday, 1966.

Hofstede, G. *Culture's Consequences*, Newbury Park, Calif.: Sage, 1980.

Kanter, R. M. *Commitment and Community*, Cambridge, Mass.: Harvard University Press, 1972.

Lansberg, I. S. "Managing Human Resources in Family Firms: The Problem of Institutional Overlap." *Organizational Dynamics*, Summer 1983, pp. 39-46.

McCollom, M. "Organizational Culture: A Literature Review and Analysis." Unpublished manuscript, Yale School of Organization and Management, New Haven, 1983.

Merton, R. K. *Social Theory and Social Structure*, Glencoe, Ill.: Free Press, 1968.

Milgram, S. "The Experience of Living in Cities." *Science*, 1970, 167 (13), 14611468.

Miller, E. J., and Rice, A. K. *Systems of Organization*. London: Tavistock Publications, 1967.

Milofsky, C. "Scarcity and Community A Resource Allocation Theory of Community and Mass Society Organizations." Unpublished working paper, Program on Nonprofit Organizations, Institute for Social and Policy Studies, Yale University, New Haven, Conn., 1981.

Parsons, T. *The Social System*. New York: Free Press, 1951.

Schein, E. H. *Organizational Culture and Leadership: A Dynamic View*. San Francisco: Jossey-Bass, 1985.

Simmel, G. *The Sociology of George Simmel*. (K. H. Wolff, trans.) New York: Macmillian, 1950.

Simon, R. "Thou Shalt Not Waste Deals." *Forbes*, Dec. 2, 1985, pp. 62-66.

Stein, B. A. "The Centerville Fund, Inc." A Case Study in Community Economic Control." *Journal of Applied Behavioral Science*, 1973, a 243-260.

Taylor, F. W. *Scientific Management*. New York: Harper & Row, 1947.

Thomas, D. A. "The Relationship Between Organizations and Their Environments: A Micro Level Perspective." Unpublished manuscript, Yale School of Organization and Management, New Haven, Conn., 1984.

Toennies, F. *Gemeinschaft und Gessellschaft [Community and Society]* C. P. Loomis, trans.) NewYork: Harper & Row, 1963.

Walton, R. E. "From Control to Commitment in the Workplace. *Harvard Business Review*, 1985, 63 (2), 76-84.

Weber, M. *From Max Weber: Essays in Sociology*. H. H. Gerth and C. W. Mills, trans.) New York: Oxford University Press, 1947.

Wells, L Jr. "Misunderstandings of and Among Cultures: The Effects of Transubstantive Error." In D. Vails-Weber and J. Potts (eds.), *Sunrise Seminars: Volume 2*. Arlington, Va.: NTL Institute, 1985.

CHAPTER 16
CULTURE, VALUES
AND ETHNICITY

Culture and values are the invisible glue that holds families and businesses together across generations. They provide guidance about right and wrong, priorities, directions and relationships. In this chapter, the role of values and culture are explored. Examples are given of family businesses that have committed to paper their values and cultural legacy. They show the critical relationship of articulated values to business success.

Which values a family business should pursue depends greatly on history and family and business needs. As seen here, sometimes it becomes necessary to modify or even change values. This process can pull at the core of a family business even as it seeks to strengthen the firm's foundation. Articulating values is a difficult enough task – redefining or changing values must be handled with extreme care.

What becomes clear in this chapter is that circumstances and surroundings play an enormous role in the development of values and closeness of family. And it is this closeness of family and strength of shared values that enable many of these businesses to survive and even prosper in very demanding business environments.

A dialogue with the founder of Black Enterprise *magazine and his son illustrates some traditional concerns for family businesses and underscores the significance of race for all family firms.*

A Dialogue with Earl Graves and Earl G. Graves, Jr.

By James I. Herbert and Joseph H. Astrachan

Earl G. Graves is an internationally recognized authority on black business development. He is president and chief executive officer of Earl G. Graves Ltd., parent corporation for the Earl G. Graves Publishing Company, which publishes *Black Enterprise* magazine – a business service publication targeted to up-scale black professionals, executives, entrepreneurs, and policymakers. Earl Graves also heads the Minority Information Business Institute, a not-for-profit resource library on black business development located in the company's corporate headquarters in New York City. He earned his B.A. in economics from Morgan State University in Baltimore, Maryland, and has received numerous honorary degrees.

Earl G. Graves, Jr., "Butch," is vice-president of advertising and marketing for *Black Enterprise* magazine. He earned his B.A. in economics from Yale University and his M.B.A. from Harvard University. Butch is the oldest of three children (he has two brothers) of Earl G. Graves, Sr., and is currently the only son working in the family business.

This interview sought to capture the portrait of a family publishing business and the relationships within it. The issues were allowed to emerge during the conversation, and many are common to many family firms. Most notable among these are the relationship between the owner-manager/parent and successor/offspring, the successor's decision to enter the business, succession planning and business vision, and the family/business interface.

The importance of race in family business dynamics is underscored in this interview. Even after twenty years of profitable operations – *Black Enterprise* magazine celebrates its twentieth anniversary in August 1990 – Earl G. Graves, Ltd., continues to be powerfully affected by considerations of race, which are reported to be critical in every element of the Graves's family firm. The comments made during this interview about race and racism come from the minority perspective of a black family. This interview does not address how race affects white family businesses. In general, the white majority thinks racial issues are the concern of minorities only. In our view, that attitude stems from the belief commonly held by the white majority that their racial identity does not affect them. In other words, the majority often overlooks its own whiteness. The concerns raised by this interview affect not just minorities but the white majority as well. Those who study and work with family businesses may wish to use this interview and their experiences to explore the impact of race – beneficial, harmful, and otherwise – on all family businesses.

HERBERT: Earl, since you will be celebrating your twentieth anniversary this year I could go off in a thousand different directions, but I'd like to start with your relationship with Butch. How has your relationship evolved especially with regard to how Butch became involved with the business.

EARL: There are a couple of high-water marks in terms of our relationship as father and son. One mark happened at age about thirteen. We had just moved to Scarsdale and Butch was down in the mouth one day. I said, "What's the problem?" At this point, we had already started to have allowances – my family comes from the West Indies where the work ethic is not open to discussion, everybody works to earn money, you have to own something, you have to get an education. "Well," he said, "You know I've been going to all these bar mitzvahs and these guys get all this money for being thirteen years old." He said, "I'm thirteen, you know, and I'm blowing it." So I said, "Well you can't get bar mitzvahed, but why don't you let me think about it a little bit and maybe we'll come up with a solution."

My wife and I decided that we would give him a piece of money. It was about $500, all in stock. I found a broker, who was indeed black, because I wanted Butch to be able to get on the phone with this guy and talk with him about his stock. I explained that "Whatever you put in the bank or add to this stock portfolio, we will double." Offering him that challenge was an enormous mistake. In the first year he had saved over $250, which is phenomenal. So we indeed had to double that. He really has never looked back in terms of his involvement with stocks. So much so that I would tell you to the point that he is our financial adviser.

ASTRACHAN: So you saw that Butch's interests in business needed to be developed at a young age?

EARL: Yes. I also remember a time when we were somewhere out in Brooklyn or Bedford-Stuyvesant and he asked, "Why can't we own a pro basketball team?" That was another high-water mark. It showed that his interests clearly needed to be directed in the area of business. Butch was interested in making money, and he had interest in ownership and doing well for himself. And I think you really have to have that in your gut. I think that I saw in him a hustle that you've gotta have to be successful, even though he clearly came from a situation where he didn't have to hustle the way I had to hustle.

I grew up in different circumstances. My parents sent me $55 in four years of college. That was all they could afford – my father died in my sophomore year. My wife and I used to send our children money. But we only sent them money for what was within reason: room and board, books, and a very modest subsidy. We didn't subsidize being in love. If you wanted to be in love you had to do that one yourself. They had to work during the summer and clearly have saved at least $3,000 so that they could see their way through the year.

HERBERT: Working for the firm or working outside of the firm?

BUTCH: None of us ever worked with the firm – that was by design.

HERBERT: Whose design?

BUTCH: I think it was really out of my father's design, but it was really for our own good. In college, everyone is fighting for the few jobs that there are. The reality is that most people are getting jobs through the connections that their fathers and mothers have. Often they are creating a job when there really is none. One thing I always remember my father always saying from when we were very very young was that "connections, in the business world, are everything. Don't let anyone kid you that they got where they are based only on their merits." So, he set up whatever interviews we needed to set up. I worked at all types of different things: IBM, Manufacturers Hanover, and Chase Manhattan Bank. All of which gave me a perspective on business that most kids would never have. It's unfortunate that that is the reality. In college, some kids get the opportunity to do that and others get to be lifeguards for the summer.

HERBERT: Earl, did you ever consider having them struggle through?

EARL: No, I didn't see anything redeeming in that. I remember once, when I was an ITT director, Geneen – the CEO – saying to me, "Geez, it must be terrific. You struggled, you lifted yourself up by your bootstraps and had all that pain and struggle – and then to have made it! That must have been great!" And I said, "You know, having seen the other side, I think I could have forced myself to have done it the other way." So, no, I didn't think that since we were financially in a position to pay for tuition that we had to tell them, "You gotta go out and earn your tuition." They knew that we were not going to pay for certain things, for those things we said, "You have to earn it!"

HERBERT: So the orchestration of summer jobs was, in part, to get them to assume certain degrees of responsibility?

EARL: I wanted them to know that they had to start now to plan ahead for where they were going to be and for what they were going to have. For instance, Butch got married, bought himself a house, and he and his new wife moved into that house. He did that on his own. I didn't do that-he did.

HERBERT: Earl, was another reason for tapping into your network to give your children a diversified experience in the business world and in business departments?

EARL: No. I wanted Butch to work at Morgan Stanley because I wanted to have him exposed to the market, and he really was. He worked at Morgan Stanley twice. He worked there once on the "gopher" floor and another time after he graduated from Yale. He was really working there. Interestingly enough, the guy who was his supervisor ended up working for him.

Another part of it also has to do with what black people have to do. I really think that all black people who have the leverage have to use their clout in a way that makes a difference. We really have got to reach out and be sure that what I did for my kids we continue to do for all our kids. You know, the poor kids in Bedford-Stuyvesant think that the kids in Scarsdale are getting those jobs just because they're smart. The reality is they're getting those jobs because somebody's picking up the phone and saying, "Hey, my kid's coming home for the summer – look out for him." We should use that system to our advantage, at least for minority kids who are more fortunate. Then we've got to try to help others who are not at all fortunate.

HERBERT: You've talked about how Butch was prepared for the business world. How was the decision made that Butch would come into the firm?

EARL: He made that decision. That would have been a mistake if we made that decision. In fact I didn't know that he was coming.

HERBERT: Butch, what led up to your wanting to join *Black Enterprise*?

BUTCH: Part of it was a responsibility that was set before me. When people ask, "What is the single greatest thing that your parents have given you, it would not be any material thing. The best thing that they ever gave to any of us – or that any kid could hope to get – is an opportunity. Opportunity to go to the best schools, get a good education, to have things, and to be exposed to things. At a young age, we were exposed to politicians, business leaders, doctors, and lawyers. They were all black or happened to be black.

So we didn't grow up in a world in which the media shows you that everything positive going on in this country is being done by whites. We were exposed to successful people who happened to be black. Therefore, it was not a daunting task for us to make the natural progression into whatever profession we chose. When I say opportunity; I mean that my father always made us feel, or at least made me feel, that there was nothing that I could not do if I set my mind to doing it. Nothing at all.

This is important because, whether in academics or in athletics, I had to believe that I was better than everyone else. That is the single greatest thing that my parents gave to us. It gave us self-confidence so that we could prosper in high school and prosper in college and not feel that we had less ability than our white peers. He was constantly making us feel proud to be black. He made us feel that we did not have to apologize for being black, and not have to apologize for our parents being successful. That always happens: people always want you to apologize somehow. People used to want me to apologize while at Yale for having a successful mother and father.

HERBERT: Did you feel pushed or pulled into the business?

BUTCH: Never did my father say to us, "I expect you, upon graduation from college, to come join the company," or, "I expect you, upon graduation of business school, to come into the business," to any of the three of us. He never said that that was his expectation. He would do things to encourage us. Like tell us that the business was doing well and that, one day this business would be ours to have. He wanted us to go out and pursue what we wanted to pursue. It actually was a smart way of doing it, because it lets you evaluate and come up with what it is that you want to do. My decision to join the company was just that-entirely my decision.

Frankly, when you grow up and the business is a family business, the business is very much part of your family life. We were constantly getting involved. As young kids, we would come into the office. We went to see the plant for the first time at age five. So we got an opportunity to see things, but it was more of a subtle push.

ASTRACHAN: Was it like an invitation?

BUTCH: Yes, it was an invitation as opposed to a demand. It was never, "Listen, this is the way the family business is going to be run. You're going to be put in this position. And this is what the succession is going to be."

HERBERT: It sounds as if there was a lot of input from family members into forming the direction of the company. Earl, you have a vision of the company, the family, and their futures. How has that vision developed, and is it the Earl Graves vision that we're operating on or is it some combination of Earl and Butch Graves?

EARL: I think it is clearly a combined vision today. I would hope that part of the vision has come from some goals and some direction that I initially set.

My wife has played a significant part in this also. She is a very strong, very smart, and very able person. She has been a very very solid citizen in terms of setting a moral tone for where we're going, what we're doing, and who we are. She doesn't allow us to get off the track. It's not grey about who we are, what we're supposed to be doing, and how we're supposed to be thinking. She helps set that tone.

The reason we have the credibility that we do, as far as the magazine is concerned, is that we have had the same story for twenty years. It has not wavered in terms of what we think are the inequities, what we think are the pluses, and where we think things have to get better. You know, when Reagan was a disaster – he was a disaster – it wasn't that we were against Republicans. We were against people who were tearing down the fabric of this country. We have the wherewithal to be sounding the clarion of saying, "Here is what is good, and here is what is bad, and here's what needs to be fixed." That's a direction that we've been trying to set for twenty years.

We also have some things that you just believe in. You believe in a God. You believe in trying to help people who are less fortunate. You try to do that with your own family first, and then you go from there. And I've told my three sons that I don't expect any nonsense about the three of them not getting along. That just can't be one of the options. Life is too short, the options and opportunities are too great, and the contributions I expect them to make are too significant to not be getting along.

HERBERT: You have stated that you began *Black Enterprise* with a goal of promoting the black business. Did you have a clear vision of getting along with your potential competitors in the black business community when you first started?

EARL: You have to run a business with some degree of moral character. Because of this, I have historically not shot down Ebony or Jet as entities. You go out and you sell. My competition is Business Week and Forbes and the other business publications, not Ebony and Jet. Therefore, Ed Lewis, publisher of Essence, and I have been pretty good friends over the years and the friendship has grown. But with John Johnson, publisher of Ebony and Jet, it's a different matter. His people were always working against us. They would say to advertisers, "You don't have to buy *Black Enterprise* because if you buy Ebony and Jet you buy all black people." Then I would come and say to the advertisers, "I think that is unfortunate, because I think that John has done a job that makes it possible for me to be able to sit here before you today, because he got beat up on for a long time and I happen to think that his is a good publication and I think that if you'll buy in a mix, you could buy me as a business book or buy him as a general publication."

Well, that went on for about ten years. About five years ago John called one day and said, "I want to come and see you." He came in and I closed the door and said "What's up?" And he said, "You win." And I said, "What was the bet?" And he said, "It wasn't a bet at all," he said, "I've been kicking your book around for a long as I can remember. I don't think I need to do that anymore You were right. You've been a person who's done it with dignity and character, and every time I tried to kick your head in – you didn't do that to me. I want you to know that I appreciate it." And he said, "You have set a tone for all of us, and you've made us all creditable by the things you've done and you've written about me. From now on in anything that you want to do together that's going to make black business better and our own publications better, I'm prepared to do that." Well that's a very important benchmark, I think, in terms of the things we achieve.

HERBERT: Do you have a vision of how your and Butch's activities fit into the larger community?

EARL: Vision is where you're thinking everyday, "Could we do something else, still be giving something back and still get on with what we've got to do?"

My sons have always known they had to give something back. Butch is doing a "Hope for the Homeless" benefit basketball game, which will be in Scarsdale. In the history of Scarsdale's basketball they have had two statewide championship teams – he was on one, and ten years later they had another one. Those teams are going to play against each other and half the village of Scarsdale is coming. All the money will go to the homeless in Westchester. That's Butch's origination and Butch's idea. So, what he sees us doing by giving to education and to Boy Scouts and to you just name it-I'm just overwhelmed by the enormity of the entities that seem to be calling us for everything. It just seems to be unending. There's the political side, the Dinkinses, and the Wilders, and the Youngs, and then there are the civil rights organizations.

My children know they have an obligation to that. But there is a limitation to what we can do, because we are not IBM. However, to the extent that we can do it, we are on the cutting edge. We gave to eighty-three different entities last year, starting with $500. That's a big hit for any one company. But that is giving something back. I think Butch understands that.

HERBERT: I'd like to hear a little about the moving from one generation to the next. Where is the company headed?

BUTCH: I don't think that when my father started the business he could have envisioned that it would be as successful as it has become in as short a period of time as it did. It happened relatively quickly.

I think what the transition now is – and part of it went on with the hiring of myself – is taking the company from being an entrepreneurially run company, where the decisions are made by my father and mother only, to having a professionally managed company. The board of directors meetings, as he used to say, were not very long – my parents were laying in bed.

In order for us to grow the way I see us growing, we have to bring in people from outside that are professional managers, put them into positions, let them manage, and take away part of the day-to-day stress that used to fall on my father and my mother. The company is established. The magazine is established. Now those things should be passed on to other people who should be able to take care of those things. Which means my father can get on to the next phase or the next thing that he wants to do. However, I don't, frankly, ever see him retiring and going on to do different things. I think that a person who starts a business from scratch really can't leave; it's almost like giving up a part of yourself. I see him always, always, having a role in the business. It may be diminished over time, but I don't ever see him ever saying, say at age seventy, "I think I've just had about enough."

HERBERT: Earl, I read that you are prepared to turn over the reigns to one of your sons in a defined period of time. What does your plan look like?

EARL: We haven't worked through the transition in our minds. I think it's something to sit down and do. As Butch said, I'm never going to retire. I probably would sit home and go crazy. So, I've always wanted to do something. I've wanted to give speeches and encourage kids to do something, or be somewhere in the Caribbean or Africa to try to see what I can do for black business. But there is a transition time coming.

I think Butch reached the benchmark last week. He doesn't think so, though. He closed what I consider a fairly large deal on the day he went out to do it. That's a measure of his not getting screwed around and it speaks to the fact that I will be able to go on to other things and have a level of comfort.

HERBERT: Can that also be a mixed bag for you, Earl? While it's a relief on one hand that Butch has done well so far, it also suggests that Butch can take on some areas of responsibility that you may not be ready to yield at this point?

EARL: No, that doesn't bother me at all. There is so much to do out there, that I would be delighted to have him just go do more.

HERBERT: Do you feel that you're such a big deal, Butch, and that you've prepared to handle the responsibilities you're gaining?

BUTCH: Well I shouldn't say that I think it's such a big deal. I think that for my father there are two things. People say to me, "Is it difficult working with your father? Because I know he's a very demanding person and will expect a lot of you." Well, no, it's not because, frankly, I expect a lot of myself. So therefore forget about whether or not he would be disappointed: I would be disappointed if I didn't do or obtain certain things.

As far as that's concerned, I am responsible for all the advertising that goes on in the magazine, therefore the revenue stream of the company falls in my responsibilities. It's not something I shirk or am afraid of. I accept it and want to be successful at it. As far as the deal that he is talking about – I guess it was a benchmark for him because in the past he had to sell anything large like a $150,000 sponsorship. It wouldn't even be a question of who had to sell that.

EARL: Particularly if you're black. It is a never-ending battle, because the general community still does not want to accept the credibility of the black race. That's the reality of it, though-get a copy of our magazine and you won't find ads in there for air conditioning, and you won't find ads for golf clubs, and we obviously don't wear watches. Somebody white buying an ad from somebody black for $150,000 is a big big deal. It is not a big deal if a white guy shows up at the golf club and talks with his buddy Harry because they've been growing up together.

On the other hand, we go to see white people who've never had a conversation with a black person. Let me be very clear to you. We have tried, and stopped a long time ago, having cocktail parties and inviting white people, because they become very uncomfortable – they look around and don't know what they should do next. They think, "I haven't been mugged yet." That's an exaggeration, but there is a lack of comfort with white people getting along with black people, which definitely rolls over into the business.

When I go to talk to a person who is a lower-level person in business, I do not discuss where I vacation. I do not discuss where I live. I do not discuss what car I drive. I do not even discuss that my kids went to Ivy League schools. I don't want to give anyone hangups. I want to keep the conversation very simple. I want to be able to cut through it, get the order and get out of there and not have him or her get all hung up on that. And in that respect, we have the most problems selling ads to white women-I think they often have to prove that they have brass in addition to being like white men. Now that's a double hit! So some of the white women in this world are a disaster to pitch and that's a big problem for somebody who's black or Hispanic.

ASTRACHAN: Butch, you must have dealt with a lot of these issues at Yale. What was it like going to school in the Ivy League? Do you think it gave you a different perspective from your father's?

BUTCH: One thing I find fascinating is what we used to call the black kids I went to school with who were not black in their heads. Somehow or another they thought that because they didn't grow up in a black neighborhood, were not disadvantaged, or whatever it might be, that they were somehow removed from being black. They were beyond that. I knew people I went to business school with who said, "Now that I got this Harvard Business School degree nobody can deal with me." But I don't care if you came in with suspenders and you were the cleanest cat in the world or if you're a bum on the street who happens to be black. What the white person sees is your blackness first. They don't see your degree. They don't see how you speak. They don't see any of that. So to me, the only thing that the Ivy League provided me was the confidence to know that I myself could do it. But it gives me no clout or no greater "in" to the person I'm going to speak with than someone who really has no education.

EARL: Initially.

BUTCH: Initially. The difference is that when I do get in to see someone, I'm that much more confident about what I'm speaking about. Then what happens – and I've always found it amazing – is that at the end of a sales call they will spend five minutes complimenting me on how wonderfully I spoke. And, "How nice you look today." Well, that's wonderful if I want to go home and say, "Damn, I really speak well and I look good!" But it's not that. It's that the expectations of me coming in the door are so low, they are amazed that I am able to carry on a conversation with them, speaking the same language they do.

Then, as my father said, I try to avoid as best I can getting into any discussion of where I went to school. I don't want to give anyone any hangups about where I went to school, because that becomes, "Oh, where did you go to school?" And through my hand I say, "Well I went to Yale and to graduate school." "You went to business school?" And I say, "Yes I did." And they say, "Where did you go?" And again I have to cover my mouth when I say, "I went to Yale and Harvard," because you don't want to get anyone half crazy as to what it is that you have in fact done or not done.

But going back to that original quote – because that is a poignant quote – I don't care who you are if you are black, because at some point along the line you are going to meet somebody who is not going to give a damn what you think you might be. They are going to evaluate you as someone black. It always happens. I'm sure it's happened to you many times. You're in a grocery store. You think you're dressed clean. You could be in a tuxedo and the person walks up to you and says, "Excuse me, where are the eggs?" You know, "Where are the eggs?" Like you're stocking shelves in the grocery store. It's mind-boggling to you, but they're not seeing anything else. All they're seeing is color. It happened to us in the gas station. We drove up and happened to be in my father's car. I think I'm clean, and a woman comes up to me. She hands me a water bucket and asks me to put some water in the car. And I'm in a bow tie with clean shoes on.

I don't get hung up about the problems though, because I don't think every person wakes up in the morning and says let me be the racist of the week. There's nothing to stick your head in the mud about and say, "This person doesn't like me because of whatever." You got to get past that because you will never be successful, I believe, if you spend all the time with negative energy about how everyone is doing me in and this one is not doing anything about it. You got to get past that. You charm them. You get by the thing. You work with it too, so it doesn't become an issue and you get it done.

HERBERT: You both have raised some interesting points here about how the closeness of the family and firm can influence family members to enter the business. To what extent are there demarcation lines between the family as a family and the family as a business?

BUTCH: I think that whether we like it or not they will be always intertwined. The family may, in fact, become even more intertwined as additional members of our family, if they choose or so desire, join the business. At this moment, it's really my father, my mother, and myself who have joined. My middle brother is a lawyer now at a big firm here in New York City. He may decide five years out or three years out-and it is my hope in fact that at some point he does-that he wants to become involved with the business. My younger brother is now working at Pepsi in Washington, D.C. Which will mean in a short period of time that he will be working for us because we're going to be the owners of the Washington, D.C., Pepsi franchise in another month or so.

So, as we're expanding into other things, there will be other opportunities and roles for family members. But, as I was saying, they will be intertwined. This does not mean that somehow or another my father is easier on us because, well, it's family. There is a clear distinction between what is business and what is family. And in fact, I think he would probably expect more of us, because we are family and because we should have more of a vested interest in what is going on. But I would not see for even a moment my father saying, "Well, let me lower my expectations for a particular job so that I can give this job to a family member." That just would not fit his type of personality.

HERBERT: One of the things I'm trying to get at, Earl and Butch, is how business considerations may drive family considerations and family considerations may drive business considerations.

EARL: Let me give you a quick object lesson of how family can drive things and yet make it work in a positive way. I got a call from our youngest son, Michael, who had gone into the Pepsi business and he was in a little bit of a huff. He is supposed to be sitting at somebody's knee learning all there is to know about a certain phase of the business. The person whose knee he is supposed to be sitting by, who happens to be white, has enormous hang-ups about having a black kid, who happens to be very bright, who went to the University of Pennsylvania, who's a whole twenty-two years old, learning what it took this guy six years to learn.

So Michael sent us a memo yesterday that he was sending to the general manager running the Pepsi business, who happens also to be white. The memo outlined that Michael wasn't happy with the way things were moving. I had heard him a month ago say that it was not going as well as it needed to go. But I said, "Let me stay out of this because I don't want the guy who is working for me to think that every time Michael sneezes, I'm jumping into it."

But I read Michael's memo yesterday and I said, "Enough of this because we've only got another month before we become the owners of the franchise." So I called the general manager and I said, "Look, let me explain something to you, one of the raps was that Michael was there only because he was the boss's son. My kid's been hearing that for a lifetime. You can assume I did not get where I am by my putting yo-yos in the way of what I've got to get on with doing. And that certainly holds true more for my own kids." I think this is the object we're coming around to that has to do with what you're asking. I said, "Now, if the guy you've assigned him to has his head screwed on wrong, that's that guy's problem. I've only got a month and a half to get on with this and you work for me. Get my son out of there and get him someplace where he can learn what he has to do. You are going to be the manager of that business, and he's going to be reporting to you, so I'm going to hold you responsible to ensure that he doesn't screw up. Now, as long as we understand each other, why don't we find a city where there is somebody who's not going to have these hang-ups? Michael's going to do a good job. I remind you I put him there because I think he will do it." I said, "He has crawled around the floor. He's proved he knows how to crawl on the floor, now he's going to stand on his feet, and you're going to help him do it."

Now, I really think that speaks to the issue of family and business. What you've got to understand is we're going into a business that is literally all white. It's the second time in the history of Pepsi that they will have a black franchise. There is a small franchise in a place in Michigan.

But anyway, I had a forty-five-minute conversation with this guy. When we were finished it was clear. I said, "If you can't fix it, I can."

All right, now that's a part of what you asked. And by the way, I took his memo home last night and showed it to his mother. I said, "What do you think of this? Here is what I'm going to do." She said, "That is exactly what I would do." So it is that kind of relationship. We're not confused in the family about what we've got to do. If we have one of them who's not pulling at the oars on the boat, we will tell him. And if he is doing what he's supposed to do, then we'll also let him know that. Now, that didn't give you a historical perspective, but it gives you an object lesson.

ASTRACHAN: We've been discussing the interface between family and business and a part of that is how the business can make a family feel closer. I know this is kind of an unfair question, but I want to ask it anyway. Does the racism you face interact in terms of making the family a different kind of family or a closer family?

BUTCH: No, it's not an unfair question. I think that when you deal with racism it brings any black family closer together. I'm assuming there is a family unit there to be together. I think that if you face – I don't know if the word obstacle is right – but if you go through experiences together it draws you closer together. You have a commonality.

ASTRACHAN: Is this the case with your family?

BUTCH: Oh, it's clearly the case in our family. One of the things that I think is great in terms of growing up is that we all generally like each other and generally like being around one another. I get along fabulously with both my brothers. They are absolutely my two best friends. If you ask them they would say the same exact thing. So, we enjoy each other's company. We enjoy doing things together. We're not jealous of one another. We want each of us to do well and all of us to do well. That does make a difference.

ASTRACHAN: Your family being together is clearly part of the future. Earl, how do you envision the involvement of your sons in the business in the future?

EARL: I think that each son will be differently involved. If you ask me what I see in the company five years out? I envision Butch doing deals for us. But I think he'd have to learn it by knowing what's involved. He will eventually turn the selling of the advertising to somebody else and he'll just be doing it by playing golf. I envision him doing more what it is that Malcolm Forbes did as it's much easier. Because he'll have a platform that I didn't have. He's got the network of people who did go to Yale and did go to Harvard. That will mean something. I can't imagine the world's going to stay as screwed up as it is forever in terms of how people get along with each other. I see a situation where he can leverage that in a much different way from what I have been able to. Although I see him running through some of the same aggravation I have.

HERBERT: Where do you see your sons in the corporate picture?

EARL: Sooner or later, I'll become chairman of the holding company and each one of them will become president of some entity within a freestanding entity and company.

ASTRACHAN: Coordinating through you or with themselves?

EARL: Among themselves. I mean, in ten years they'll be doing it by themselves. I intend to be selling the advertising the way Malcolm Forbes was in ten years. Maybe not on the High Lander [the Forbeses' yacht] though.

HERBERT: I know our time is running out and we're very appreciative of your taking the time to be with us. Butch, you're about to become a dad of twins? Earl a granddad? A third generation may be coming into the business.

BUTCH: It's a very exciting time for us because these are the first grandchildren we've had. As far as my own kids would be concerned, I would probably do much the same thing that my father did. I will encourage them, be they sons or daughters, to look at our business and what it is that we do on a day-to-day basis so that it can pass to the next generation. They often say that the third generation is where things break down within a family business. We're just entering into the second generation. We'll be able to encourage our children to explore things to do on their own.

ASTRACHAN: Thank you both for sharing your time with us.

EARL: I hope this has been helpful in some way.

HERBERT: I think it has been great.

ASTRACHAN: A milestone.

Reprinted with permission of the publisher from *Family Business Review*, Fall 1990. Copyright 1996, Family Firm Institute.

Management literature claims Japanese firms act like families while anthropological works report families in Japan function like firms. This article considers Kikkoman Shōyu Company Limited, which provides a 300-year history of the combined efforts of family and firm for entrepreneurial success. Japanese kinship systems were used for the organization of economic relationships and the promotion of social solidarity. In modern times corporate structures have made "family" more ideological than genealogical or biological.

The Family as a Firm and the Firm as a Family in Japan: The Case of the Kikkoman Shōyu Company Limited

By W. Mark Fruin

Family and Firm in Japan: The Basis for the Analogy

It is argued often that the key relationship in Japanese social structure and psychology in both preindustrial and industrial periods is that of kinship. This assertion follows from the observable preference of the Japanese to work out their deliberations and aspirations in small groups which often have family-like characteristics. It does not hold logically, however, that small groups are synonymous with families or that groups described as "family-like" are indeed like families. One of the most frequent uses of the analogy involves the relationship between family and firm. On one hand, management writings often allege that Japanese firms behave like families, while on the other, anthropological works report that families in Japan function like firms.

My contention is that the family-firm analogy in Japan is often misleading and generally overworked; its character is usually symbolic or ideological rather than descriptive. I would like to examine the relationship between family and firm in light of the history of one of Japan's larger and older enterprises, Kikkoman Shōyu Company Limited, which is known in Japan as a "family firm" and which offers for our examination a nearly three-hundred-year history of the combined efforts of family and firm for entrepreneurial success.

In discussing the "family as a firm" or the "the firm as a family," it is necessary to distinguish between the nuclear family (conjugal family unit), which is not the basis for the analogy, and the stem family, which is. The nuclear family, known in Japanese as *setai* or *kazoku*, is limited in size, scope, and space-time, while the stem family or *ie* is a descent group considered to endure forever. *Ie* persists by virtue of the continuity of property and genealogy through current family members with past and future generations. A *dōzoku* is a large lineage or clan composed of several *ie*, with a main household and a number of branch households where descent from the main house is traced through males (Befu, 1971: 38-46).[1]

According to Smith, a leading expert on Japanese kinship, the residential unit of the *ie* or stem family

> ...consists of a senior married couple and a married child with his or her own spouse and children. Such a family unit may include as many generations as are alive, but there can be only one married couple in each generation...Among the sacred duties of the head, who controlled the destiny of its living members, was that of preserving the descent line unbroken. He was responsible for passing on, enlarged if possible, the goods and property that he had inherited, and it was his task to see to the proper veneration of the ancestors...(Smith, 1978: 45-46).

It should be clear already that the *ie*, the "family" in the Japanese family-firm analogy, is not the family with which we in Western Europe and North America are familiar. Contemporary American family households are not formed primarily to preserve continuity of property and genealogy through time. Marriages are alliances based partly on affection and partly on implicit contractual obligations to share in housework, child rearing, and breadwinning. When one says that he firm is a family or the family is a firm in Japan, however, the metaphor does not refer to the family as a volitional or even contractual alliance. Instead, as most often conceived, the family is a kin-based unit where property ownership and descent relationships are exclusively mail-centered and where power and dignity are enjoyed preponderately by mail heads of household. As a result, the *ie* apportions obligations and concentrates authority hierarchically by sex and descent.

This characterization is clouded by the existence of family members in the *ie* who are not biologically related to the household head. The distinction between kin and non-kin, often so important in the Chinese and Western family, is not always emphasized in the Japanese stem family; and as a result non-kin and fictive kin, most often the adopted, have frequently constituted a substantial part of the total household membership. Rather than a genealogical or biological definition of a family, ie is often determined by who contributes to the economic welfare of the group. Usually the nucleus of such economic groups are kinsmen in the genealogical sense, but kinship is neither the absolute nor exclusive criterion of membership. Logically, therefore, the *ie* is not purely a kinship unit, but often an economic organization dressed up in family trim (Befu, 1971: 39). It us useful, then, to conceive of the Japanese *ie* in terms of concentric circles of "kinsmen": an inner core of consanguines where genetic descent is presumed and an outer core of the consanguines where genetic descent is implied but not required.

Such variations in the composition and structure of *ie* and *dōzoku* have fascinated and puzzled many. This has been reflected in a continuing debate among social scientists as to whether kinship in Japanese stem families and lineages should be defined *primarily* by descent or by contributions to corporate property, tools, and knowledge. Most often, ie and *dōzoku* are viewed as patrilineal descent groups where economic ties have frequently overshadowed genealogical relationships (Ariga, 1956; 199-207; Nagai, 1953). Other scholars, however, have emphasized the genealogical relationships over economic ties, arguing that kinship (Kitano, 1962; Brown, 1966). Moreover, one well known Japanese social scientist has taken the extreme view that ie and *dōzoku* are not patrilineal descent groups at all, but instead groups based solely on residence and locality (Nakane, 1962: 133-67). Examples of households organized around common residence and occupation may be found in traditional Japan, as they are for that matter in modern America, but such households are the exception, not the rule.

Most social scientists, therefore, have recognized the importance of both genealogical relationships and economic ties in defining ie and *dōzoku*, although each researcher tends to emphasize one or the other in practice. Apparently both views have validity, depending on what part of rural Japan is studied. The northeast in particular is noted for a strong economic content in kinship relations, so strong in fact, that genealogical ties are sometimes created to buttress established economic dependencies. The northeast is an area of limited economic resources, single rice cropping, and skewed personal income. The southwest, by contrast, is characterized by a more highly developed commercial economy, double rice cropping, agricultural land reclamation, and more evenly distributed personal income. In the southwest, the kinship relationship normally overshadows the economic content of household composition and structure.

Economic geography, therefore, helps to clarify the nature of membership in Japanese stem families. It is also useful conceptually to separate the question of the family as descent group from the question of the family as a corporate group, for it is this distinction which so often puzzles non-Japanese. Yet there is really no need for the perplexity since most institutions have multiple purposes, and Japanese households are no exception. Where a variety of tasks are required, different sets of rules can be created to achieve different goals within the same institutional framework. Rules for the maintenance and continuity of kinship relations defined by descent can be sustained in the face of rules for the maintenance and continuity of kinship defined by property relations.

In short, the Japanese household can be both a descent and a corporate group although in practice, I suspect, one is emphasized over the other. The latter concept and practice undoubtedly have many origins, most of which are lost to historical documentation. I will attempt to sketch the barest historical justification here in order to make the practice more comprehensible. From the thirteenth to the seventeenth centuries, the country passed through a period of internecine warfare and economic disruption. If one was a solider, a violent and early death was likely. If a cultivator, the prospects were often not better, given the dangers from malnutrition, epidemics, and tyrannical government. Among warriors and peasants alike, a rule of primogeniture evolved during this era as a means of preserving family and property.[2] However, small an inheritance, chances for survival and perhaps for eventual accumulation and transmission to future generations were enhanced when the inheritance remained intact and was passed to and through the head of the household, the socially and legally designated heir.

Often in such turbulent times inheritances must have gone unclaimed. Property outlasted its possessors and pursuers, in the sense that property did not pass in an orderly fashion between parties, be they related or not through descent. To circumvent this, the household head was thought to occupy a kind of office, the functions of which outlasted the individual occupant. Over many years of civil and economic turbulence, then, the idea of the household as a corporate group, distinct but not necessarily different in personnel from the household conceived as a kinship group, was joined with the concept of the office of household head. In this case, *ie* and *dōzoku* were corporate entities managed by a household head who was nominated to that office on the basis of merit and promise rather than descent. The head was usually referred to by that title, "household head," and this position, indeed that membership in the corporate household itself, could exist without any current incumbents.[3] The household was, in this sense, a legal fiction awaiting the appointment of an executor to carry out its corporate functions, primarily the maintenance and continuity of property and genealogical office.

In short, the traditional stem family in Japan was and is now a flexible institution. While it could be solely focused on genealogical descent, it could be partially or even wholly concerned with corporateness, that is, with property and its management, independent of kinship. Since anthropologists have done most of the research on Japanese households and since their field work has taken to various parts of Japan, they tend to emphasize one side or the other of the household equation depending on where their research was done. Those going to the southwest find relatively egalitarian villages where agnatic, and occasionally cognatic, descent defines the character of family groups. Sojourners to the northeast, by contrast, find an area of relative economic backwardness where households are often linked more by economic than by kinship ties. Since the Japanese household, it would appear, can be either a kinship or a corporate group, or both, an historical approach to *ie* and *dōzoku* in Japan would permit the unveiling of family strategy and structure over time in response to those features, internal as well as external, which permit and at times compel a household to act as if it were a kinship group at one moment and a corporate group at another.

Thus, the broad definition of family and household in Japan is very different from that in the West, and this elasticity of concept and meaning is one reason why the Japanese have effectively handled the management of single firms and groups of firms within a "family" contest. Needless to say, such malleability in the definition of who belongs to a family contributes to the inconsistent use of the family-firm analogy in Japan.

The Family-Firm Analogy

If kinship is the *ie* or *dōzoku* is to be determine principally by descent, a number of anomalies immediately appear in the case of those families most closely associated with the Kikkoman Shōyu Company Limited or its antecedent enterprises. Although traditional Japanese households practiced single son inheritance, it was not always the eldest or even one's natural son who inherited. Adoption was widely practiced in order to provide male heirs when none existed, to substitute a more promising male heir when one's own did not measure up, or to attract a husband for a nubile daughter. In this last case it was common to adopt a son for the combined purposes of marrying one's daughter as well as providing a household successor.

Given the flexibility of recruitment and membership in households provided by adoption, it would be accurate to say that, in the case of households and lineages associated with Kikkoman, economic considerations sometimes overwhelmed kinship considerations. This can be seen most clearly when households divided or branched for purpose of initiating a new economic venture. (Branching was a device wherein a main household would establish a separate related household with its own genealogical and corporate identity.) In only one of six cases of adopted son-in-law marriage did the adoption and marriage coincide with a household branching for the purpose of founding a new *shōyu* enterprise (shown in Figure 1 by a dotted line connecting the households involved). In the five cases, however, adopted son-in-law marriages sustained the continuity of family ownership and control in a *shōyu* enterprise. In the case of male adoption and marriage, therefore, economic considerations, namely the founding and organizing of branch households in the *shōyu* business, appear to have directly dominated kinship decision involving household division about 17 percent of the time (1 out of 6 cases of adopted son-in-law marriage). Where household division was not the concern but household maintenance and continuity in *shōyu* manufacture were, 83 percent of son-in-law adoptions were linked to economic concerns (five out of six cases).

The uses of kinship for economic ends is apparent in other ways as well. The following is a summary of a larger figure detailing kin exchange with 18 families which were involved for nearly three centuries, 1688-1978, in on way or another in the Noda Soy Sauce business.[4] In order of frequency, the summary lists: 25 daughter marriages, 11 son branchings, 6 son marriages, 3 son adoptions, 3 daughter branchings, and 2 daughter adoptions.

It is immediately apparent that more than half of these events are female centered. Combining marriages and adoptions (adoptions are really a form of betrothal) by sex, we find 27 such events for women and only 9 for men. This difference in frequency is highly significant statistically, indicating that the imbalance was planned and not accidental.[5] I am not implying that the frequency of these events should coincide with the sex ratio of the general population. Far from it. These tallies were taken from family tablets maintained at local Buddhist temples; they were kept not to inform government officials but to record family relationships that were considered significant to the *ie* in either its genealog-

Figure 1. Branching Relationships in Mogi, Takanaghi and Horikiri Dōzoku

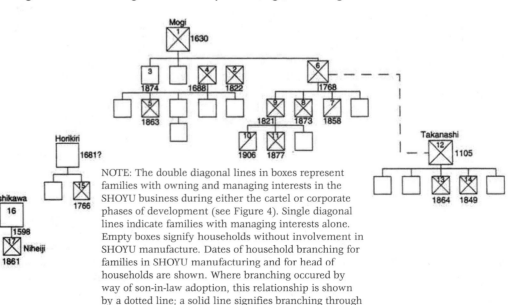

NOTE: The double diagonal lines in boxes represent families with owning and managing interests in the SHOYU business during either the cartel or corporate phases of development (see Figure 4). Single diagonal lines indicate families with managing interests alone. Empty boxes signify households without involvement in SHOYU manufacture. Dates of household branching for families in SHOYU manufacturing and for head of households are shown. Where branching occured by way of son-in-law adoption, this relationship is shown by a dotted line; a solid line signifies branching through a natural son.

ical or corporate manifestation. That the imbalance should be so striking is intriguing, and the reasons for it, I believe, have to do with political and economic considerations in the exchange of kinsmen for enterprise development.

Why would families choose to record female-centered events so frequently? These families, it should be emphasized, recorded these activities for their own purposes and from their own points of view, and herein lies the key. A marriage of a daughter involved neither power or property in a formal or institutional sense. In a patriarchally organized society, power was a privilege of men, notwithstanding occasional deviations from the rule. Likewise property was concentrated, by custom, in the hands of men. Female marriages, therefore, risked neither power nor property and so were ideally suited to the initiation and maintenance of family alliances within the soy-sauce business. In the same way other sorts of family-to-family interactions might be analyzed, as shown below:

	Property	Power
25 daughter marriages	no	no
11 son branchings	yes	yes
6 son marriages	no	no
3 son adoptions	no	yes
3 daughter branchings	yes	no
2 daughter adoptions	no	no

Of these 50 events, 14 occur between lineages, 19 within the extended Mogi Lineage, 3 within the Takanashi, and only 1 in the Ishikawa. Additionally, 13 events transpire within sublineages of the Mogi lineage and do not involve the main Mogi house of Mogi Shichizaemon. Reviewing the frequency of these events reveals that as a rule main houses of lineages and sublineages send out more household members for marriage and adoption than they take in. In effect, main houses implant their offspring in subsidiary houses. Between *dōzoku* the same rule applies. In fact, the number of women a house is successfully able to offer out for marriage may be interpreted as a measure of dominance, gauged by the genealogical rank order of donor and recipient households and the frequency of in- and out-marriages. This may be related to the desire of the main houses to keep their children close to home and the willingness of subordinate house to take in family members from genealogically prior and therefore socially superior households.

Within *dōzoku*, male rather than female placement in subordinate households assumes importance. This makes sense given the desire of main houses to control the timing and number of minor houses established within its own line through branching principally and through marriage secondarily. Branchings normally involve "sons," while marriages concern "daughters." If this summary and analysis of kin exchange may serve as a guide to the role of biology in family and enterprise development, then the following epigram may capture the essence of the relationship.

> It's better to give than receive,
> Between *dōzoku*, dispatch daughters,
> Within *dōzoku*, secure sons.

One family, the so-called Kashiwa house of the Mogi lineage founded by Mogi Shichirouemon in 1768, has been conspicuous in the execution of the strategy outlined above; and the preeminence of its power and position in the Noda soy sauce business has not been equaled since the mid-nineteenth century. The success of the Kashiwa house must be viewed in perspective, however. Since different development strategies have been pursued by other lineages associated with the soy sauce industry in Noda, the wisdom of their investment choices should be weighed against their probable success in the manufacture and marketing of *shōyu*. The sublineage headed by Mogi Saheiji, for example, diversified into local commercial and professional endeavors. Although the main house of the Mogi Saheiji *dōzoku* continued to work successfully in the soy sauce business, subhouses moved into such occupations as cereal commodity sales, pharmacy, optometry, jewelry, and watch-making. Although these endeavors have certainly been less financially rewarding than management in the *shōyu* enterprise, working within the community has provided economic security, civic respectability, and personal satisfaction for many members of the Mogi-sa lineage.

The Takanashi lineage's move into the Tokyo warehousing and distributing business offers another example of diversification outside of *shōyu* manufacture which, on the whole, has compared favorably with the economic success of Kikkoman. A considerable portion of the canned food as well as the alcoholic and carbonated beverages destined for Tokyo is handled by Takanashi branch households. *Shōyu* producers located in Choshi, another well known site of *shōyu* manufacturer in Chiba prefecture, have diversified in much the same manner. One of the two Hamaguchi households making *shōyu* in Choshi established a branch household in Edo (Tokyo) in 1645 for wholesaling *shōyu* and marine foods products. This branch of the Hamaguchi family, along with the Tokyo branch of the Takanashi family from Noda, account for a large share of the *shōyu* sold and distributed in Tokyo today.

The success and failure of any family strategy of either diversified or concentrated investment, however, depends in large part upon luck; and it was bad luck in the form of two disastrous fires in 1871 and 1908 which has accounted for the declining fortunes of Mogi Shichizaemon, head of the oldest Mogi lineage and once the principal investor in the Noda soy sauce industry (Ichiyama, 1968: chronological appendix 3,5). But such misfortune was not unique. Earlier in the mid-nineteenth century, for example, bad luck, including successive years of poor harvests, declining business, and famine from 1836 to 1838, reduced the number of soy sauce breweries in Noda from eighteen to eleven (Ichiyama, 1975:41).

Understandably in a era when raw material availability, the fermentation process, and even transportation were to a considerable degree dependent on weather, climatic fortune

Figure 2. Kin Exchange, 1688-1978

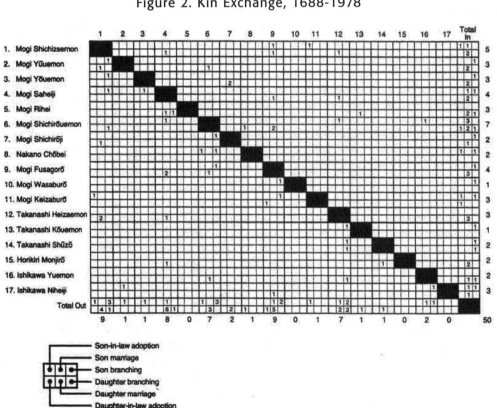

was a crucial concomitant of enterprise success. The unpredictability of weather, harvests, commodity markets, and consumer demand cautioned against too great an investment in any one line of endeavor, like *shōyu* manufacture. Yet the costs of making *shōyu* were considerable, for the most part fixed in the form of fermentation tanks, brewing and extracting equipment, storage and shipping facilities. Moreover, the fixed nature of this rather large investment in plant and equipment did not facilitate either production at the plant or turnover in the marketplace. Fermentation required eighteen to twenty-four months for completion, and market sales were controlled by the *tonya* system of wholesaling and distributing which denied manufacturers direct access to consumers. Accordingly, Noda *shōyu* manufacturers were presented with a difficult investment decision, namely, how much to invest in manufacturing capacity given the lumpiness of investment and the unpredictability of supply and demand markets. Too little invested might result in insufficient capitalization to take advantage of a rise in prices, whereas too much invested might lead to an inadequate return in a poor market and possible bankruptcy as a result.

In this context, the advantages of a large kinship network to support business activities become immediately obvious. In addition to opportunities for sharing information concerning raw material costs, labor availability, and production know-how, kin support in financing *shōyu* manufacturing and shipping facilities was a noteworthy advantage of the Mogi-Takanashi group. Not only did they aid each other in the establishment of enterprises, but they frequently sold and traded all or part of their operations to each other. They also stood ready to purchase the facilities of non-kinsmen in the Noda area. Although such financial dealings were not handled in a formal sense by the combined Mogi and Takanashi families until the days of cartel and incorporation in the late nineteenth and twentieth centuries, such deals were struck informally most often between the head and branch households of a single genealogical line. Where intermarriage and adoption may have created strong ties between households of different lines of descent, close business dealings could be expected to develop over time.

Further examination of the pattern of marriages, adoptions, and household branchings within the four main Kikkoman lineages reveals another way in which the organization of economic relationships and promotion of social solidarity were primary ends to which the kinship system was employed. The histogram or bar graph which summarizes the frequency of kin exchange between and within the Mogi, Takanshi, Horikiri, and Ishikawa

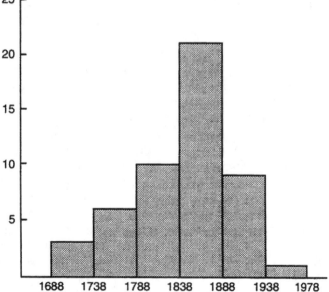

Figure 3. Historical Frequency of Marriages, Adoptions and Household Branchings

discloses that the frequency of such events increased regularly until the end of the nineteenth century, at which point a noticeable drop occurs; in the twentieth century, interlineage alliances almost disappear (see Figure 3).

The decline in frequency coincides directly with the formation of a *shōyu* manufacturing cartel in 1887 and the founding of Noda Shōyu Company Limited in 1918, the precursor of Kikkoman Shōyu Company Limited. In other words, once the organization and regulation of economic relationships and activities could be handled by formal institutions designed for such purposes, the kinship system essentially gave up such functions. The promotion of social and economic solidarity, the protection of property, and the continuity of family enterprise were turned over to the cartel and eventually to its corporate successors, with the result that non-economic matters became more salient for descent groups: children married out of the business; natural offspring, and not adopted scions, assumed family headships; affection and attraction played a greater part in courtship and marriage. Families were less economic and calculating, and they cultivated more personal emotional matters instead.

Although interlineage alliances in the form of *dōzoku*-based marriages, adoptions, and household branchings no longer play a dominant role in the organization and operation of Kikkoman, family as opposed to lineage membership continues to count for a great deal within the company. Kinship is now employed not for interfamily cooperation but for interfamily rivalry. Household membership has become all important in determining access to the upper reaches of corporate power. Consider the following statistics on family membership and corporate power and privilege. There are 28 main and branch households in the three Mogi, Takanashi, and Horikiri *dōzoku*. Of these 28 households, 3 (11 percent) were of the Horikiri lineage, 6 (21 percent) of the Takanashi, and 19 (68 percent) of the Mogi. Within each *dōzoku*, 13 percent of the Horikiri households engage in *shōyu* manufacture, 50 percent of the Takanashi and 53 percent of the Mogi.

Clearly the Mogi lineage has spawned the largest number of households and spurred the highest rate of participation in the soy sauce business. But within the Mogi clan a main and two branch households contend. The importance of the subdivisions within the Mogi lineage is revealed by the fact that, although all eight of the company presidents to date have been Mogis (to the exclusion of Horikiri and Takanashi aspirants), within the greater Mogi lineage 63 percent of the company presidents can be traced to the Kashiwa branch household of Mogi Shichirouemon, 25 percent from the Mogi-sa group of Mogi Saheiji, and only 12 percent from the main house of Mogi Shichizaemon. Household hegemony was reflected as well on the first Board of Directors, with 67, 22, and 11 percent representation for the households of Mogi Shichirouemon, Saheiji, and Shichizaemon, respectively.

The reasons for differential success rates within the firm according to family membership have been discussed earlier. In sum, the position and privilege of the main house were consumed by conflagration; the Mogi-sa and Takanashi households have chosen to diversify family investments outside of the firm, while the Kashiwa family has plowed back human and capital resources into the *shōyu* business. The Horikiri group was never committed to the soy sauce enterprise in a major way, and it has not played an important owning or managing role in the firm. Likewise, the Ishikawa family has not been active in *shōyu* manufacture since the early twentieth century; it did not continue its representation with the corporation after the cartel was relinquished.

Thus, if one looks at the three *dōzoku*, those of Mogi Shichirouemon, Mogi Saheiji and Takanashi Heizaemon, which were most directly associated with Kikkoman or its antecedent enterprises, the analogy between the family and the firm describes accurately the priority sometimes given to social and economic cooperation for enterprise development within the kinship framework. This was most true in the eighteenth century, when in the absence of other devices, the family was institutionalized as a social and economic control group in the management and maintenance of *shōyu* manufacture. Since that time, however, the analogy has become less and less appropriate as individual families have come to pursue social and economic advancement *within* the framework of the corporation.

The family no longer behaves like a firm because the corporation's characteristics of limited liability, perpetual succession, organized and concentrated management, and standard operating procedures make the functioning of a kinship system in these areas redundant. Families now rely upon the firm, rather than vice versa, for economic security and advancement; and enterprise endogamy which once decided the compatibility of interfamily alliances no longer determines the choice of marriage partners.

The Firm-Family Analogy

The three-hundred-year history of the manufacture of soy sauce by Kikkoman Shōyu Company Limited or its antecedent enterprises may be divided into four major phases, each characterized by different styles of ownership and management and by different levels of suitability in using the firm-family analogy. The first phase, the longest, lasted from the late seventeenth through the nineteenth century, and was characterized by the nearly complete separation of ownership and management. Such a separation is usually considered a unique feature of modern managerial capitalism, which boasts a high level of specialization in functions and consequently the divorce of ownership from professional management. Yet in this early modern period, overall management was divided between separate spheres of ownership, general management (sales, finance, and purchasing), operations management (the production process itself), and labor management (the hiring and contractual conditions of workers). In effect, four different kinds of authority existed "one financial and three managerial" each distinct and relatively independent of the others. This complex managerial system evolved when the sizes of various facilities producing soy sauce were small, on the order of several hundred full- and part-time workers per factory (Noda Shōyu kumiai shi, 1919: 16 – 19).

The separation and specialization of functions, such as sales, personnel, and production, had less to do with the size of the firm or the speed of production than with the failure of owners to manage. Owners did not actually operate or even oversee their production facilities. By custom, they entered their plants no more than twice a year, and on such occasions, they entered in full ceremonial dress and ritually inspected the soy sauce brew in various stages of fermentation. Otherwise, they stayed out of the way, far from production.

Owners in a real sense did little more than finance the operation and "supervise" the front office. They could, if they wished, inspect the books, but records, such as they were, constituted listings of what goods were bought and sold by *banto*, the office managers and personal retainers of the owning families. It was not possible to calculate costs of unit production, profit margins, or any other refined measure of efficiency or profitability from such records. To consolidate with information was available could prove difficult, moreover, for owners would have to petition their *banto, toji* (factory foremen), and *oyakata* (labor recruiters) to pull their lists, journals, and notebooks together. And such as effort on the part of owners would have been entirely out of character, even if it had been possible.

With so little direct involvement of the part of owners and with so many separate yet equal spheres of management, workers suffered. *Oyakata* benefited mainly by fees paid for placing workers, *toji*, concerned themselves with technique and not with industrial relations, and *banto* were in the front office where they never worried about workers' welfare. The only hint of worker identification came through an association with a production plant based on a particular patrilineal organization. But since owners involved themselves so little in the actual operation and no one else assumed overall responsibility for enterprise management, a sense of association felt by workers rarely matured into an identification with family and enterprise. Obviously, at this stage of development, no firm-family analogy would appropriately describe an enterprise so fragmented and divided.

A second phase of growth began with the banding together of owners in order to reduce risk and uncertainty. Diverse and separately owned enterprises, numbering as many as 19 different production facilities, were joined together for the purchase of raw materials, the standardization of wages, and the distribution and shipping of finished goods. The owners, in effect, formed in 1887, a cartel, the Noda Shōyu Manufacturers' Union; and during the next thirty years met regularly twice a year, and irregularly more

Figure 4. Organizational Change and Enterprise Development

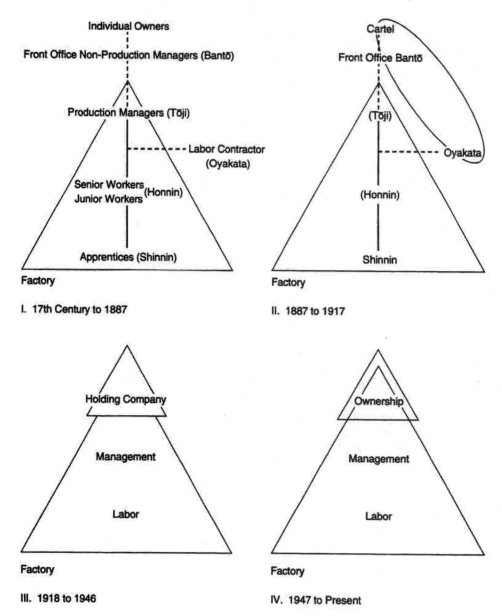

often, to buy raw materials and to fix costs and shipping schedules (*Noda shōyu kumiai shi*, 1919: 11, 19). The regularly scheduled meetings on January 8 and June 20 coincided roughly with the traditional dates of ritualized inspection of factory facilities. Although the tour of the breweries was largely ceremonial, the cartel meetings were not. The January meeting was concerned with fixing labor costs and estimating production levels, while the June assembly set the amount and cost of raw material purchases. Administrative coordination, in the sense of combining and rationalizing processes internal to the enterprise, was not a cause of the cartel. The reasons for collaboration were almost all external to the actual manufacture of *shōyu*. The functions of the *banto, toji,* and *oyakata* changed not at all as a result of the cartels. The chasm between owners and workers remain vast, and it was not alleviated by paternal concern. Workers lacked job security and their wages were arbitrarily set by cartel agreement. When prices fell so did wages. Wage manipulation was one of the most obvious means to control costs and owners took full advantage of it. Owners did not yet enter the factories that they owned, except upon the New Years and all Souls celebrations, and they continued to leave day-to-day management to others. Thus, even though enterprise-owning families were collaborating to a degree, family operations remained distinct in what counted the most: internal costs of production.

The formation of a cartel, in an important sense, represented the communal regulation of an already existing competition over production costs and production levels between individual *shōyu* makers; these, as pointed out already, the cartel left alone. What it did was to combine the separate factories, really family-owned breweries, into a collusive network to fix some but not all their shared costs, thereby mitigating but not eliminating the competitive struggle. Nevertheless, the cartel forced families of owners to assume some managerial functions themselves, such as the purchasing of raw materials, the setting of wages, the sorting out of distribution and shipping channels, and the determining of marketing territories in the country side but not in the cities, the latter was left to the *tonya* for determination. In short, this phase, although families began to cooperate in certain important aspects, they still remained relatively competitive with each other and uninvolved in the internal operation of their own enterprises. As a consequence, the family analogy could not be fairly applied to the collection of enterprises manufacturing *shōyu* in Noda; the families of owners were still quite distinct in organization and operation from their own breweries, those of their associates, and from men who labored in them.

In 1918, a third period of enterprise development unfolds. That year a joint stock company was formed through the merger of some but not all of the cartel members and their assets. At first, eight and then nine families joined to form the Noda Shōyu Company Limited, named for the town in Chiba Prefecture where most of the facilities were located. All nine families were related through descent or marriage; previously all had been independent manufacturers of *shōyu*, *miso*, or *sake*, products made from fermented soy beans or rice. For the first time, owners became managers. Owners made up the majority of senior company officers and member of the Board of Directors. Through the mechanism of a holding company, actual ownership of the firm remained somewhat distinct from the operation of the enterprise, yet ownership and management were merged as never before. The disarray of managerial interests was finally ordered within the structure of the firm, although it would be wrong to suggest that the new structure was easily accomplished, given the long standing tradition of independent organization and operation on the part of the families concerned, within a decade consolidation and coordination characterized the management of the greatly enlarged enterprise.

Only at this point does the firm-family analogy begin to be truly appropriate. Most top managers in the firm were "family," that is, they were from the firm's founding *dōzoku*; and many middle managers, who were the *banto* of individual entrepreneurs in prior phases, now came into the newly established corporation along with their family enterprise heads as "lifetime employees" (Fruin, 1978: 273-274, 289). In other words, the firm's management was composed largely of family members and family followers. Accordingly, the appropriateness of the firm-family analogy at this point is mainly biological, or perhaps, genealogical, in view of the importance of adoption in Japanese kinship. Eighty-five percent of the Board of Directors were family, and 63 percent of the first 80 managerial employees come to the company tied to individual family members on the Board.

Of course, it was possible for the firm-family analogy to be valid without Kikkoman's genealogical underpinning. Especially in joint stock companies which were independent of any *zaibatsu* association, it was rather common to have both dispersed ownership and paternalistic management. In fact, the lack of concentrated ownership in such cases probably inclined professional managers toward paternalistic management as a means of securing worker compliance. The best examples of this sort of firm-family analogy come from the textile industry where firms like Kanebo Spinning were well known for paternalistic management (of a largely female work force) and widely dispersed stock-ownership. Thus, in the early twentieth century, it was possible to have a paternalistic firm with a "family-style" but without family management or even closely held ownership. Such firms were more the exception than there rule, however, in the view of the prevalence of family-owned and close-held enterprises in prewar Japan. In the case of Kikkoman, the suitability of the analogy in the genealogical sense soon faded, as the firm grew in size and as nonkinsmen came to outnumber kinsmen in management. Within a decade of incorporation, the number of employees doubled from one to two thousand; sheer size dulled the aptness of the genealogical analogy. Then an extraordinary thing occurred which made the family-firm analogy even more appropriate than previously.

In 1927-28, a strike of 218 days, the longest labor strike in prewar Japan, erupted at Noda Shōyu Company. The strike was not only long, it was bitter, politically motivated, and received national attention. It took an appeal to the emperor himself, among others, to bring the strike to settlement.[7] In the end, 1,300 employees were fired, although two-thirds eventually came back, and the company was faced with the need to rebuild its public image and its internal morale. The firm-family analogy was employed to these ends.

The first public announcement of the firm-family *ideology* which I have been able to find occurred within weeks following the strike settlement. The company began a campaign of employee education which preached that all employees, from Board members to shop sweepers, were members of one "family" (*ikka*) united in a spirit of industry and common purpose. For Kikkoman, spiritual kinship, as symbolized by the firm-family analogy, was the road to company rejuvenation following the labor strike of 1927-28.

The transmutation of a biological or genealogical analogy into an ideological one at Kikkoman was not and isolated event. It happened commonly at other companies in the country generally. Kikkoman's analogical transformation coincided with efforts of the Japanese government to instill in all citizens the belief that Japan was a patriarchical state, whose people were related to one another and to the emperor, the supreme father of the nation. The theory of the patriarchical state with the emperor as father is usually known as *kokutai*, and it became the central belief of modern Japanese ideology from the late 1880s until 1945. The thesis of Hozumi Yatsuka (1860-1912), who is credited with being the chief architect of the state-as-household ideology, was simple and direct: the state is the household writ large; the household is the state in microcosm; they differ only in size, and they are made one through the medium of ancestor worship (Duus: 1976: 118).

More precisely, that part of the *kokutai* theory concerned with the identity of state and household was known as *kokka*. This concept stressed the equivalence of state and household in both a biological sense. Officially, the correspondence of state and household was not made by way of any intermediary institution. Nevertheless, firms like Kikkoman sought to juxtapose themselves between the state and household with the following construction; state – firm – household. In spite of the attempts of many enterprises to provide a bridge betweens state and households in their programs of employee education and socialization, the state never sanctioned their efforts, and many right-wing groups were publicly critical of such endeavors. But concepts of *kokka* and *kokutai* remained extremely useful to enterprise owners and managers in their efforts to secure the loyalty and the labor of the employees.

Insofar as businessmen were effective in their use of the firm-family analogy, it was largely because officials at all levels of society were employing the ideas of *kokka* and *kokutai* to counter the growing political and economic unrest which disturbed Japan from the first decade of the twentieth century onward. In 1906, the government began its "Every Village a Family" campaign to consolidate the deities worshipped on the local level into one shrine. About the same time, slogans like *kigyo ikka* or "the enterprise as a family" became widely current. Kikkoman's employees education program in the aftermath of the great Noda strike was representative of a national effort to enshrine the family ideologically (Hirshmeier and Yui, 1975: 206-211). Unlike a biological or genealogical analogy, an ideological analogy is infinitely expandable in space and time, since it is symbolic rather than substantive. This accounts in part for the enthusiasm with which Japanese leaders pressed such family-based political and ideological analogies on their own as well as on colonial peoples before and during the Pacific War period (Maruyama, 1963: 1-24).[8]

Since World War II, Kikkoman has entered a fourth phase of enterprise growth where the legal, ideological, and even genealogical foundations of the firm-family analogy have disappeared. Holding companies, which provided the device by which family ownership in the firm was concentrated and protected, have been abolished legally. The emperor has been demythologized, no longer providing the essential element in the ideological analogy. The household, *ie* is no longer a legal entity, and its head has been stripped of his power and authority. As a result, firms today cannot presumptuously appropriate power among kinsmen, be they real, fictive (adopted), or symbolic, as in the case of the emperor. A new egalitarian ethos of democracy undercuts the traditional patriarchal attitudes and polices. It coexists surprisingly well with a host of paternalistic benefits which Japanese firms provide for their regular employees. But such benefits as medical plans, housing subsidies, annual pay increases, and job security should not be misunderstood. They derive from postwar employee rights, not patriarchal or even paternalistic gratuity. They are as much in evidence in large American and European companies as they are in Japanese firms (Taira, 1790: 184-203).

Though large companies may continue to espouse managerial ideologies that speak vaguely of "the firm as a family," the legal, political, and biological-genealogical scaffold behind the analogy is gone. Without formal underpinning, the firm-family analogy no longer requires respect or even lip service. Yet, as a cultural ideal and as a characterization of the flexibility in *ie* structure and membership, the analogy remains viable. A genealogical basis for the analogy continues to be found in prevalence of family-based enterprise in Japan even today. Ninety-nine percent of Japanese firms, by absolute number, are classified as small- and medium-sized enterprises. They continue the tradition of family identification with enterprise, since the core of self-employed and nonpaid family members in such operations amount to 15 percent of all gainfully employed Japanese (Small and Medium Enterprise Agency, 1975: 50; Chusho Kigyocho-hen, 1975: 337-347).[9] In these firms, size, control, and management make the firm-family analogy apt, just as it was appropriate in the earliest days at Kikkoman following incorporation. For Kikkoman today, however, its four thousand employees, performing mostly specialized and professional jobs, make even an unofficial and informal use of the firm-family analogy inappropriate.

Yet problems of interpersonal relations and organizational behavior are most salient in large firms. As a result, they devote a far larger share of their earnings for employee socialization and corporate welfare programs that do small firms. They can, of course, more easily afford to do so, but size of enterprise rather than per capita cost seems to determine the necessity of such efforts. Paradoxically, therefore, it is in large Japanese firms rather than small ones that the firm-family analogy has greater currency today. In use, however, it is less an analogue than a simile. The prewar analogy of genealogical and ideological equivalency of firm and family has been transformed into a postwar simile of cultural proclivity. That is to say, the firm has become like a family in an emotional sense because company employees in Japan tend to identify themselves emotionally as well as intellectually with their firms or, more accurately, with their work mates. This tendency is understandably more evident in firms that provide more extensive in-company training and fringe benefits. The Japanese display a cultural preference for effective as well as instrumental work commitment which large firms are more easily able to take advantage of through their considerable emphasis on corporate welfare and paternalism. In this cultural sense, therefore, the firm *as* a family when used to describe the spirit or feeling of a firm has a certain validity in postwar Japan (Marsh and Mannari, 1976: 199, 202, 213, 253).

Finally, in a more subtle way the "firm-family" analogy mirrors the continuing competition among the Mogi and Takanashi families for position and prestige within the corporation. Since World War II the competition is not carried out under the guise of cartels, *kigyo-ikka*, or other firm-family analogy. As employment and promotion within the firm for family members are no longer patriarchal duties or rights, families have had to become more frankly competitive with each other within the context of the corporation. By agreement, only one son—most often, the elder—from each family in each generation has been allowed to join the company in the postwar period (although two out of nine families have managed to circumvent this rule). As a result, families carefully groom that scion, for a family's corporate prospects are anchored on his future. Recently, a prestigious postgraduate education in business and economics from the finest universities of Japan and the United States has been commonly added to a son's natural talents. The competition among families has produced what has been called in other situations "whiz-kids," and it is through the extraordinary socialization as well as the abilities and efforts of such sons that family stakes within the firm are maintained and, if successful, advance. In short, since the Pacific War, the firm is no longer an extension of family property and pride; instead, families have come full circle to rely upon the firm for purpose and direction. In this sense families follow the firm, and the firm-family analogy has a certain authenticity for the relatively few Mogi and Takanashi family members in Kikkoman today.

Conclusion

Comparisons are odious and analogies are never perfect—or so we are told. But there is no denying the close and constant interaction of family and firm for over three centuries in the case of Kikkoman Shōyu Company Limited. And yet in spite of the plasticity of form and function displayed by the traditional Japanese stem family, family and firm were and are different and distinguishable. The genealogical, and ideological, the cultural, and the socioeconomic uses of the family analogy in Japan must be descriptively and conceptually separated. Otherwise, reliance on the family analogy by Westerners and even Japanese to describe small and occasionally large group behavior in Japan will result in ambiguity and imprecision. Such analogizing has been historically inappropriate in most cases when applied to Kikkoman, and accordingly it is particularly misleading and misinformed when aimed at the larger, more mature, more diversified, and internationally-minded firms which characterize Japanese enterprise in the world today.

Bibliography

Ariga, Kizaemon, 1956, "Introduction to the Family System In Japan, China, and Korea." Transactions of the Third World Congress of Sociology 4:199-207.

Befu, Harumi, 1971, *Japan: An Anthropological Introduction*, San Francisco; Chandler Press.

Brown, Keith, 1966, *"Dōzoku and the Ideology of Descent in Rural Japan."* American Anthropologists 68:1129-1151.

Chusho Kigyocho-hen, 1975, *Chushp Kigyo Hakusho* (White Paper on Small and Medium Enterprise). Tokyo.

Duus, Peter, 1976, *The Rise of Modern Japan*. Boston: Houghton-Mifflin Company.

Fruin, W. Mark, 1978, "The Japanese Company Controversy." *Journal of Japanese Studies* 4-2:267-300.

Hirschmeier, Johannes and Yui, Tsunehiko, 1975, *The Development of Japanese Business*, Cambridge: Harvard University Press.

Ichiyama, Morio, 1968, *Kikkoman shōyu shi* (A History of Kikkoman Shōyu). Tokyo.

Ichiyama, Morio, 1975, *Noda no rekishi* (A History of Noda). Nagareyama.

Kitano, Shiichi, 1962, "Dōzoku and Ie in Japan: The Meaning of Family Genealogical Relationships." In R.J. Smith and R.K. Beardsley, eds. *Japanese Culture: Development and Characteristics*. Chicago: Aldine.

Marsh, Robert and Mannari, Hiroshi, 1976, *Modernization and the Japanese Factory*. Princeton: Princeton University Press.

Maruyama, Masao, 1963, *Thought and Behavior in Modern Japanese Politics*. London: Oxford University Press.

Nagai, Michio, 9153, " Dōzoku: A Preliminary Study of the Japanese Extended Family Group and its Social and Economic Functions." *Interim Technical Report No. 7*. Columbus: Ohio State University Research Foundation.

Nakane, Chie, 1962, "Analysis of Japanese dōzoku Structure." *Toyobunka Kenkyojo Kiyo* 28:133-167.

Nakano, Takashi, 1964, *Shoka dozokudan no kenkyo*. Tokyo: Miraisha.

Noda Shōyu Kumiai shi, 1919, (n.p.) *Noda Shōyu kumiai-shi*. Noda.

Olson, Lawrence, 1963, *Dimensions of Japan*, New York. Small and Medium Enterprise Agency.

Olson, Lawrence, 1975, *The Shift to an Economy of Slow Growth and Small Business.* Tokyo.

Smith, Robert J., 1978, *Kurusu: The Price of Progress in a Japanese Village, 1951-1978.* Stanford: Stanford University Press.

Taira, Koji, 1970, *Economic Development and the Labor Market in Japan.* New York: Columbia University Press.

Footnotes

1. Probably the best historical work in Japan on the changing structure and function of *ie* over time is being done by Professor Akira Hayami of Keio University in Tokyo. For seminal study of Japanese lineage and enterprise development, see Nakano, 1965. Most students of *ie* and *dōzoku* emphasize patrilineal descent, but Keith Brown does not. He argues instead for cognatic, not agnatic, descent; see Brown, 1966.

2. Primogeniture was modified to the degree that, although one son and only one son inherited, he was not necessarily the eldest son or even one's natural son.

3. I owe a great deal of my thinking on the office of the household head, and on Japanese household more generally, to an unpublished paper by Laurel Cornell, "Patterns of Succession to Household Headship in Japan." (October 20, 1976), Dept. of Anthropology, Cornell University.

4. Noda is located in Chiba Prefecture at the confluence of the Edo and Tone Rivers about one day's sailing distance from Tokyo. Access and ease of river transportation proved to be an important factor in the success of the soy sauce industry in Noda.

5. Using a chi-square test, the difference in frequency was significant at the 99.99 confidence level.

6. In the case of son-in-law adoption, even though he brought little property with him, he soon became the heir apparent of the house into which he was adopted and married. This is a case, then, of delayed property transfer.

7. The emperor became involved, in part, because Kikkoman has been a supplier of *shōyu* products to the Imperial Household.

8. The patriarchal authority of the family and state could be transferred to the corporation because the distinction between government and household (public and private), so basic to modern Western European thought, was undeveloped in Japan. As a result, Japanese managers enjoyed an authority which derived from more than their economic and managerial responsibilities; their positions carried moral weight and great social and political importance as well. Accordingly, the divisiveness which characterized labor conditions and colored labor-management relations in the West could only be repeated superficially in prewar Japan because managers, as heads of enterprise, combined the private authority of owner-operators with the public power of state officials.

9. A delightful description of the family character of small industry in Japan may be found in Olson, 1963: 13-33. It should be noted that the official definition of what constitutes a small- and medium-sized enterprise in Japan has changed. Before World War II, a firm with less than 100 employees fell into the category; from 1945-65, the cutoff grew to 300 employees, and since 1966, the upper limit has been moved to 500 employees.

The family business is being rediscovered as the embodiment of the management practices and business values needed to help the nation's industries regain their competitive edge. Family businesses offer many benefits including commitment to product quality, better employee relations and longer-term perspectives. They also better accommodate the next generation's talents and ambition while providing a more tolerant and supporting environment.

In the following article which originally appeared as a three-part series, the author also relates family business problems: conflicts in family businesses are dealt within the context of familial relationships and emotions, with much of the trauma centered in the succession process; in large family businesses, maintaining family control means dealing with additional stockholder and estate tax pressures.

Rediscovering Family Values

By Steven Prokesch

The wallflower is becoming the belle of the ball. A decade-long debate over what is wrong with American business and how to cure it has produced a surprising model for success: the family business.

As old as America itself, the family business is being rediscovered as the embodiment of the management practices and business values needed to help the nation's industries regain their competitive edge.

The best family companies have long cared about product quality, treated employees with respect and focused on more lasting concerns than the next quarter's results. These values, business critics say, are exactly what Japan has cultivated and America has generally neglected.

"There is a tremendous amount of interest in family businesses," said James O'Toole, a management professor at the University of Southern California. "If you start looking around at well-run companies that have been around for a long time, you often find they are the work of a single individual or a family."

Family businesses, large and small, account for a majority of the jobs in the United States and for nearly half of all that America produces. Many, of course, are very small. But a great many of the nation's largest and best-known businesses are also all, or nearly all, in the family.

The family empires include Cargill, the dominant force in grain trading; S. C. Johnson & Son, popularly known as Johnson Wax; Estée Lauder, the cosmetics and fragrances company; Levi Strauss, the company that invented blue jeans, and Bechtel, the construction giant. Tabasco sauce, Mars candy bars, Stroh's beer and Schwinn bicycles are also made by family companies. Families also hold sway over many large, publicly traded companies. The family influence at companies such as Du Pont may have withered over the decades as the family's holdings have dwindled or been diffused among the generations. Yet in many large companies families that own as little as 15 percent of the stock still remain dominant by holding prominent management positions, seats on the board and special voting privileges.

By this measure, Dow Jones & Company, the Times Mirror Company, the Washington Post Company and The New York Times Company remain family companies. The Corning Glass Works, one of the oldest enterprises in the United States, is headed by a fifth-generation member of the Houghton family, which founded the company. Descendants of the founders are still in charge at Anheuser-Busch, Marriott and McDonnell Douglas.

A growing number of universities – including Brigham Young, Pennsylvania, Southern California and Yale – are offering programs and sponsoring research on family business.

Major corporations in many industries are trying to create family-like environments in their factories and offices in an attempt to get employees to work harder and smarter.

Books singing the praises of family business are starting to appear. In *The Big Time: the Harvard Business School's Most Successful Class and How It Shaped America*, one member of the famous class of '49 suggests that American industry might be much better off today if it had fewer of the sort of high-powered executives that Harvard turned out and more family-run companies "driven by a value system that's an extension of family values."

Consumers Prefer Family Companies

True or not, the public believes that products manufactured by family businesses are of higher quality than those made by companies that are not family affairs, according to a study of large and medium-size companies by John L. Ward, a professor of private enterprise at Loyola University of Chicago. Last year's sale of Richardson-Vicks Inc., which makes cosmetics and cold remedies, and this year's attempt to buy the Pulitzer Publishing Company demonstrate that the contenders in the merger-and-acquisition wars have also discovered the allures of family businesses.

In a sharp departure from the 1960's and 1970's, droves of ambitious young people are now returning to the fold of their families' businesses, both large and small. As restructurings, mergers and acquisitions have swept American corporations, tens of thousands of white-collar jobs have been eliminated and it has become much tougher to climb the corporate ladder. And these events have coincided with a surge in demand for young managers at the family businesses created after World War II, whose founders are approaching retirement age.

"There is a perception that opportunities may not be as great in big corporations," said Peter Davis, the director of executive education at the University of Pennsylvania's Wharton School and a leading authority on family business.

At the same time, America's infatuation with the entrepreneur has turned family businesses – the vast majority of which are small or medium-sized companies – into respectable places to work. Only a decade ago, business school graduates who entered their families' businesses were often dismissed by their classmates as people who could not make it in the real world. Now their classmates are now more likely to view them with envy.

"I never realized how lucky I was until I went to business school," said Lisa M. Witomski,30 years old, the director of marketing at her family's company, T. Frank McCall's Inc. of Chester, Pa., a distributor of janitorial supplies with sales of about $5 million. "When I described my family's business to everyone, they oohed and ahhed."

In interviews, several young men and women who had decided to go into their family businesses cited not only the security – always an allure – but also the opportunities to attain higher positions, wield more responsibility, earn more money and, of course, some day own the show.

Miss Witomski, who worked at the Pillsbury company for two years before she joined her family's business, said: "When you're working for a company like Pillsbury, the chances of reaching the top are very slim. There's security working for your family business."

Opportunities for Women

Family businesses are especially attractive to women, experts say, because of their limited success in penetrating the senior ranks of most large, publicly held corporations. In big companies, "women feel only lip service is given them regarding promotions and growth," said Dr. Matilde Salganicoff, a psychologist and family business consultant who runs a workshop at Wharton for women in family businesses.

A study of 91 women who attended the Wharton workshop found that women in family-owned businesses earn more money and hold higher management positions than do women at publicly held corporations.

Many young men and women also believe that their families' businesses are more willing than nonfamily corporations to accommodate their lifestyles and values.

"There is a resurgence of the desire for family ties," said Dr. Abraham Zaleznik, a psychoanalyst and Matsushita Professor of Leadership at the Harvard Business School, "especially given the impersonal and superficial human relationships perceived to exist in large corporations."

But Dr. Zaleznik and many other experts said that those who return to family businesses should beware. Of 59 families who operate businesses that were studied by a University of Minnesota research team, 52 reported tension or stress in their relationships because of their business involvement.

Some family businesses have been in the spotlight lately because of the well-publicized traumas that have been ripping the business – or at least their families – apart. To put an end to bitter fighting among his three children, Barry Bingham Sr., the patriarch and chairman of the company that owned the *Louisville Courier-Journal* and the *Louisville Times*, put the family-owned newspaper and broadcasting on the auction block. Dissident family shareholders of Pulitzer Publishing tried to force the management members of the family to sell the company. And in the wine country of California, members of the Sebastiani family have feuded publicly over operation of their winery.

Family businesses have to deal with the generational disputes, sibling rivalries and the jealousies and tensions that divide so many families in addition to normal business problems. And in a family business, the death of the patriarch may not just be a personal trauma, but may set off a power struggle for control of the business.

A Respect for Tradition

The current fascination with family businesses, however, runs deeper than the public's love of a good family spat. It is also an appreciation of their values.

At Levi Strauss, S. C. Johnson, Marriott, L. L. Bean and other widely admired family companies, concern with quality, employees and the communities in which they have roots are not fads to be adopted today and abandoned tomorrow. They are family values handed down from one generation to the next and preserving them is often deemed as important as anything else.

Leon L. Bean, who founded the 74-year-old mail-order house that bears his name, died in 1967. But his grandson, Leon A. Gorman, the company's president, keeps alive the founder's tenet that the customer is always right. Even temporary employees go through a training program that includes a film on "L. L." and his philosophy. And to this day, dissatisfied Bean customers have the same privilege as those who bought L. L.'s original Maine hunting shoes: They may return merchandise with no questions asked.

Levi Strauss & Company is widely known for philanthropy and enlightened treatment of its employees. For Robert D. Haas, the president and chief executive, and his cousin Peter Haas Jr., a company executive and director, these are not beliefs learned at business school, but the values with which these two great-great-grand-nephews of the founder, Levi Strauss, were raised.

Both were expected, when growing up, to donate a portion of their allowances to charities. And when Robert's father, Walter Haas, Jr., was running the company, the kinds of business-related matters he discussed at home were the company's moves to integrate its plants in a still-segregated South or the ashtray that a worker had brought him from the Kentucky Derby. "What I drew from that was there aren't big and little people, just people, in an organization, and everybody counts," Robert said.

Certainly not all family businesses are well run. The Marriott Corporation may rank as one of the best-managed hotel and food-services companies around, but J. Willard Marriott Jr., its chairman and the son of its founders, said it took him 20 years to ease out unproductive relatives and family friends.

The late August Sebastiani may have built Sebastiani Vineyards into the nation's 11th-largest winery. But to hear his sons tell it, he was a tyrant who mistreated employees, family and nonfamily alike. He did not especially care about the welfare of the community in which he did business, they said, and he grossly underinvested in plant, equipment and staff, a practice that has come back to haunt the winery.

Some of the most venerable family-controlled or – run businesses – including Levi Strauss, S. C. Johnson, Corning Glass Works and the Weyerhaeuser Company, the timber and wood products giant – have had their share of troubles in recent years. To varying degrees, all four allowed bureaucracies to take root, tolerated mediocre or sloppy performance and were slow to adapt to changes in their industries. As a result, some of these companies had to restructure extensively and a couple had to resort to layoffs.

An examination by *Fortune* magazine of 10 large family-run companies whose stock is publicly traded found that their return to shareholders in the past decade in many instances lagged behind the average return in their respective industries. The mediocre earnings and stock performance of Richardson-Vicks, which had been run by the Richardson family for 80 years before it was sold last year to the Procter & Gamble Company, undoubtedly helped make it a takeover target.

On the other hand, several family companies were among those that had returned the most to their shareholders in the past decade. Shareholders of Hasbro Inc., the toy maker, fared the best of any *Fortune 500* company. Two other family companies – Herman Miller Inc., the office-furniture company based in Zeeland, Mich., and Tyson Foods of Springdale, Ark. – ranked fourth and fifth, respectively.

Some management experts insist that the larger, publicly traded family companies tend to outperform their competitors over the long haul. "If I'd want to make a quick killing, I'd probably not invest in them," Professor O'Toole of the University of Southern California said of family companies. "But if I wanted to have a secure investment that I could pass on to my children or grandchildren, I probably would."

Chief executives of nonfamily corporations, of course, often argue that they would like to take a long-term view toward their business. They want to take more risks in developing new products, they say, and they would show more commitment to their employees and communities if they could. Wall Street, with its pressure to keep up earnings, is the villain, they say.

Most family businesses, though, also have to contend with pressure to increase short-term earnings. Many have stock that is publicly traded. Even privately held family companies often have passive investors to worry about: relatives and foundations who may have no interest in management, but plenty of interest in their dividends. Yet many of these companies believe they answer to a higher authority – to family traditions and the communities in which they live and conduct business.

That was a key reason why after 14 years as a public company, the descendants of Levi Strauss took the company private last year in a leveraged buyout. The family feared that Levi – and its long history of placing social concerns above profits – would fall victim to the acquisition wars sweeping corporate America, Robert D. Haas said.

The story is similar at other family companies. In selling their Louisville newspapers, one condition that the Binghams established was that the buyer express a willingness to continue to contribute five percent of the newspapers' pretax profits to local charities and maintain their pay, benefits and employment levels. When the Gannett Company agreed last month to buy out the Binghams, it offered the most assurances of any prospective buyer, the family said.

Take Care of Employees

Although Marriott has grown in the past 59 years from a single root-beer stand to a hotel and food-service giant with sales of $4.24 billion, its guiding philosophy has not changed: "Take care of employees and customers," Mr. Marriott said. "My father knew if he had happy employees, he would have happy customers and then that would result in a good bottom line."

The philosophy appears to be working. The driver of an airport-shuttle van in the Washington area said the simple reason why he feels lucky to be a Marriott employee is that "they take care of their people." Customers apparently feel the same: Corporate travel managers and travel agents surveyed last year by *Business Travel News* ranked Marriott hotels as "the best over all in the United States."

Other family companies view their responsibility to employees with equal importance. The century-old Johnson Wax – one of the nation's largest family-owned and – run companies, with sales of $2 billion – was one of the first companies in the country to give its employees paid vacations, pensions, profit-sharing and group life insurance. And it still has a no-layoff policy. Herman Miller has a program that encourages workers (or "participative owners" as it calls them) to suggest ways to lower costs and raise productivity by giving them a portion of the savings. All of its 3,000 full-time employees in the United States who have been with the company a year or more are shareholders.

While many other apparel companies have moved production overseas, where labor costs are much lower, the Phillips-Van Heusen Corporation maintains half of its production in the United States. "These people have worked for this company for generations," Lawrence S. Phillips, the company's president and the great-grandson of the Polish immigrant who started the company by selling woolen shirts to Pennsylvania coal miners, said with emotion.

Passions run equally high when the family business executives talk about the products and services their companies provide. Why do they seem to care more about their products than other companies? And why do consumers perceive their products to be of higher-quality than those that non-family companies turn out? "It's your name on the product," said Professor Ward of Loyola. "It's your pride. It's your integrity. It's your love. That's why."

The pride was evident as Mr. Phillips explained why his company refuses to sell its apparel lines to discounters. "We didn't spend all this time and money to build a brand just to make a quick buck by selling opportunistically and materialistically," he said.

Such family concerns as Herman Miller and Estée Lauder will often spend years developing new products or markets and will stick with them long after most other companies would have given up on them. Estee Lauder, for instance, swallowed losses for 10 years in Japan, until it became "a very, very successful" market for the company, said Leonard A. Lauder, the president and chief executive of the cosmetics company named for his mother.

Often, the most venerable family businesses are led by men who know their companies inside and out because they grew up with them. Max O. De Pree, the chairman and chief executive of Herman Miller, swept floors at the company "as a kid," he said, and later was a master upholsterer. So was his older brother, Hugh, who succeeded his father, D. J. De Pree, as chief executive in the early 1960's and then stepped down himself at the end of 1979.

Leonard Lauder's career began at age 10, when he collected sales receipts from beauty salons that sold his mother's cosmetics. In high school, he helped with bills and taking orders. Mr. Marriott's first "real job," at age 14, was clipping invoices together in the finance department, he recalled. But his first big contribution came during the gas-rationing days of World War II, when his father asked him to help him figure out how to lure bus riders into the company's drive-in restaurants. He was then nine years old.

When the Relatives Fall Out

His wife, Vicki, stands stone-faced and silent, but Sam Sebastiani cannot hide his anguish as he chews a Tums in his home in the hills of California's wine country and mourns the loss of his job and his family. After he spent six years struggling to save his family's winery following his father's death, he said bitterly, his mother, brother and sister have rewarded his efforts by throwing him out.

Ernest D. Key Jr., the owner of the Atlanta Belting Company, is a man with a shattered dream: to pass on his small manufacturing company to his children, even as his father had passed it on to him. After disputes with two sons-in-law and a daughter, they quit the business. Now, he talks about selling it to employees.

"I thought the family that worked together, stayed together," he said. "I have proved that when a family works together, it is destroyed."

Family businesses. They can be the stuff that American dreams are made of. But as

Sam Sebastiani, Ernest Key, and plenty of others can attest to, they can turn into nightmares as well.

Only 30 percent of family businesses survive their founders and make it into the second generation, according to most authorities on the subject. The rest are sold or go bankrupt. And the statistics grow grimmer with the passage of time. Only half of these companies that live through the transition to the second generation will survive as a family business into the third or fourth generations.

Moreover, just because they survive does not mean they thrive. John L. Ward, professor of private enterprise at Loyola University of Chicago, studied what happened to 200 family businesses during a 60-year period. He found that while 26 survived as privately owned family businesses, only six continued to grow and prosper.

Businesses run by families face many of the same challenges that confront non-family companies: handling leadership succession; keeping shareholders happy without milking the business dry; attracting and developing capable managers; forging a management consensus on the company's direction, and treating all employees, including women, fairly in terms of promotion and pay.

But in family businesses these issues can quickly assume highly emotional dimensions because they involve two distinctly different but equally demanding organizations: the family and the business.

"Often we tend to think of family businesses as some kind of unified structure in which what's good for the family is good for the business and vice versa," said Paul C. Rosenblatt, professor of family social science and psychology at the University of Minnesota and co-author of *The Family in Business*. "But the goal of the business is profitability, survival and cornering a share of the market, and the goal of the family is to keep people sane and getting along O.K. The actions you might take to make sure that everyone gets along, such as keeping relatives in the business who aren't doing the job, might undermine the profitability of the business," he said.

When Decisions Must Be Made

If anything, being in business together makes it tougher – not easier – for relatives to get along, Professor Rosenblatt and other experts said. Doling out raises or selecting a successor may be a difficult decision for any chief executive.

It is doubly difficult when the boss has to choose a son over a daughter – or reject both in favor of a more deserving outsider. All chief executives complain about how hard it is to keep investors happy. It is much more complicated when those shareholders are siblings, uncles or cousins.

When power, money and prestige are mixed in with the personal tensions common to most families, all too often the family business turns into a battleground that pits fathers against children, brothers against sisters and cousins against cousins.

"One of the biggest problems, if not the biggest problem, in family business is family members getting along with each other," said J. Willard Marriott Jr., chairman, chief executive and son of the founder of the Marriott Corporation, the multibillion hotel and food-service company of which the Marriott family owns 21 percent.

The well-publicized fight for control of the Louisville-based media empire owned by the Bingham family may have looked like an instance of women struggling to claim their rightful place in a business world that still largely discriminates against them. But in this case the man denying them their place, on the board happened to be their brother. To try to restore family peace, their father decided to sell the business.

Relatives Judged by Relatives

Mr. Key of Atlanta Belting said that his family blowup illustrated how difficult it could be for one family member to sit in judgment on the performance of another. When he criticized the work of his two sons-in-law, his daughters sided with their husbands, and Mr. Key's wife sided with the children, he said.

After his father, August Sebastiani, died in 1980, Sam Sebastiani became head of

Sebastiani Vineyards. But he did not succeed his father in becoming the company's major stockholder. And perhaps even more important, he did not succeed him in becoming the head of the family. From accounts provided by both Sam and his younger brother Don, Sam's difficulties in getting along with his brother and sister quickly turned the business into a battleground.

But his fatal mistake may have been the way he handled his relationship with his mother, Sylvia. He acted more like a chief executive than the attentive son she had wanted following her husband's death. Sam began to communicate with her by memos, sent by intermediaries to keep her posted on the business. And he made his wife the winery's first lady, a role his mother had held.

All this not only hurt his mother's feelings. It also lost him the support of the company's controlling shareholder, his mother. And that cost him his job. "I should have seen the signal," he now says.

The Trauma of Succession

To varying degrees, the trauma that the Sebastiani family business suffered is well known to thousands of other family businesses: the trauma of succession. Because so many of the G.I.'s who came back from World War II to start up a business are nearing retirement age, an unprecedented number of family businesses are in the process of being passed from one generation to the next.

But to hear psychologists, consultants, academic experts and those in family businesses tell it, the vast majority of these companies will handle the transfer miserably. And as the statistics indicate, most of these businesses will leave the family fold.

Peter Davis, director of executive education at the University of Pennsylvania's Wharton School and a leading authority on family business, said succession was "the most difficult transition" that family companies face. Dr. Norman L. Paul, a Boston psychiatrist, called it "the main problem" for family businesses and one "that is sloppily handled in general."

The same business owners who say that their dream is to pass on the fruits of their labor to their children somehow cannot bring themselves to groom a successor and minimize estate taxes – both vital steps for insuring that the business stays in the family and thrives.

Why? Because many business founders view the task of giving up the enterprise as tantamount to planning for their own funerals.

"They look upon retirement as somewhere between euthanasia and castration," said Léon A. Danco, president of the Cleveland-based Center for Family Business, a consulting firm. Ivan L. Lansberg, an organizational behavior specialist at Yale University, said that many equate stepping down from the family business with surrendering their power, compromising their standing in the community and losing their identity.

Another Battle in Oedipal War

Some psychiatrists and psychologists see the struggle for control of the family business that often occurs between fathers and sons in particular as but another battle in their unresolved Oedipal war. Only now, the company is the mother figure both are fighting to possess.

John A. Davis, an organizational behavior specialist at the University of Southern California, said the best time to begin dealing with succession is when a father is in his 50's and his children are in their late 20's or early 30's. "Match them in this period, and you've got a teacher and a student," he said.

But match a father in his 40's who is undergoing midlife crisis and a son in his early 20's who is trying to assert his independence and the results can be disastrous. Another bad mix: When a father is in his 60's or older and is suddenly confronted with the frightening fact that his life is nearing an end, and his son is in his late 30's and is obsessed with making his own mark.

In many successful situations, Professor Davis said, "The son wants to take control of his own life and the father happens to be in the way." He added, "The father wants to maintain control over his own life and live out his dreams. What we have here is a battle between the two men's developmental needs."

This may explain why Dan Bishop, the 34-year-old vice president of operations of a Los Angeles-based rubber products company founded by his great-uncle, is full of anxieties. Succession plans at the company are in limbo. Meanwhile, Mr. Bishop favors an aggressive diversification program to reduce the company's dependence on its traditional product line of tire-repair materials. But his 60-year-old father, and boss, favors a slower approach.

"Change is harder for him," the younger Mr. Bishop said. "He did his risk-taking 50 years ago. I'm starting my risk-taking now." He added that "out of my frustration" he founded with his wife, Carol, a therapist, the National Family Business Association, one of many support groups for people in family businesses that have sprung up in recent years.

The Concern for Security

The problem is common. As business leaders enter their 60's, they often become risk-aversive. Financial security suddenly becomes of paramount importance. Handing over the business to a son or daughter eager to prove him or herself will jeopardize that security, they fear.

The story of John Paul Getty, the billionaire who was frightened to let go of his money, is legendary. But it seems that every consultant who works with family businesses has a comparable tale to tell.

The impact of not reinvesting in the business and not permitting the up-and-coming generation to spread its wings can be devastating, Professor Ward of Loyola said. He found that those few family companies that have managed to prosper and grow over the decades also were the ones that had given each new generation the room to prove itself by taking the business in a new direction.

As his official biography puts it, J. Willard Marriott Sr., the co-founder of Marriott, "shunned credit like the spotted fever." Nonetheless, he decided to let his oldest son, Bill, take on the debt needed to finance a big push into the hotel business – and transform a business with sales of less than $100 million into a corporation whose sales hit $4.24 billion last year.

While still in his 20's, Samuel C. Johnson, the current chief executive of S.C. Johnson & Son Inc. and great-grandson of the company's founder was allowed by his father to orchestrate the company's entry into the insecticide business. Today, insecticides are one of its most profitable businesses, with sales of more than $200 million.

Now he wants his children to carry on the tradition. So far, Mr. Johnson has coaxed two of his four children to join the company: His eldest son, S. Curtis Johnson 3rd, who is 31, is involved in a new venture capital business that he convinced his father to create. And a daughter, Helen, 29, is marketing new hair products. "I'm looking to the fifth generation to bring new perspectives and new inputs into the company," Mr. Johnson said.

Only too often, though, fathers cannot or will not face the fact that the son or daughter who is a manager in the business is capable of handling responsibility. Until his death in 1980, August Sebastiani ran what had become the nation's 11th-largest winery as a virtual one-man show.

"You had to be 55 before you could gain business credence with my father," Sam Sebastiani said. "If you did something 99 percent perfect, he concentrated on the one percent that was wrong."

Keeping Control Gets Harder

Last year's sale of Richardson-Vicks Inc. to the Procter & Gamble Company for $1.22 billion sent shock waves through other family businesses. If Richardson-Vicks was vulnerable, their leaders reasoned, what family company was not?

The Richardson family had managed the 80-year-old maker of cold remedies and personal-care products for four generations and had been united in its desire to keep the company independent. It controlled directly and indirectly a third of the company's stock. In times gone by, that would have been more than enough to quash the fancies of any would-be acquirer. But now even family-controlled businesses are vulnerable if their performance falls short in the eyes of the market.

As the fall of Richardson-Vicks amply demonstrated, times have radically changed. In a period when the values and traditions of family businesses are being held up as a model for American industry, it has never been tougher for families to hang on to their companies and to manage them the way they want. Judging from what the leaders of the biggest private and public family companies say, there is no safe haven for a family business of any size from the takeover wars and intensifying competition sweeping corporate America.

S. C. Johnson & Son Inc. may be one of the largest privately held family companies, with sales of $2 billion. Even so, its chairman, Samuel C. Johnson, worries about his century-old consumer-products company being overpowered in the marketplace by what he called "agglomerating competitors" such as Procter & Gamble, which can rely on the stock market to finance its mega-mergers.

On the other hand, J. Willard Marriott Jr. the chairman of the publicly traded Marriott Corporation, envies the likes of S. C. Johnson. Although his family controls 21 percent of the company, Mr. Marriott complains about the compromises he must make to raise his company's stock price. He would like to own more of his hotels, rather than just manage them. And he would spend more on advertising, if only he dared. "If we were a private company, we would do a lot of things differently," he said.

As the family leaders of companies, ranging from the giant Marriott to the relatively small McIlhenny company, the maker of Tabasco sauce, readily acknowledge, this is an age that honors merit. In an era when the takeover sharks will start circling at the first sign of weakness and shareholders – even those who are relatives – may be more than willing to sell for the right price, lineage and tradition are no longer deemed an adequate substitute for raw talent and outstanding performance. A high stock price and a healthy dividend seem to be all that matter these days.

"One of the reasons we're around is we are profitable and pay a good dividend," said Edward M. Simmons, the president and a member of the fourth generation of the founding family to manage McIlhenny, based in Avery Island, La., which is owned by 90 descendants of the company's founder or their spouses.

Estate Taxes are Burdensome

Even before the merger and acquisition boom, family tensions and the weakening of family bonds over time made it exceedingly difficult for most business families to maintain their ownership and management grip on their companies. If family squabbles did not cause the sale or breakup of a family business, estate taxes often would.

To settle with the tax man, the Wrigley family had to sell the Chicago Cubs baseball team. The Coors family had to sell shares in its beer company to the public. And confronted with the double whammy of five years of losses and a steep estate tax bill, the Sebastiani family of Sebastiani Vineyards has had to consider selling its winery.

Of course, the family influence at Du Pont, Procter & Gamble and thousands of other one-time family businesses has withered as their founders' descendants became too numerous or simply lost interest in the company over the years. As the business passed to the third, fourth or fifth generation, the priority of family members not active in management often becomes maximizing income rather than holding on to the business. That is why the Rockefeller family recently decided to cash out of Rockefeller Center by, in essence, selling a large portion of the famed Manhattan complex to a real estate investment trust. And it is a major reason why such newspaper publishing companies as the Tribune company of Chicago have gone public.

Another reason so many family companies are selling these days is because of the lofty premiums that acquirers are now frequently willing to pay. "Family members are saying: `Our business may never be worth this much again. Maybe we ought to sell while we're at the top of the market,'" said John L. Ward, professor of private enterprise at Loyola University of Chicago and an authority on family businesses.

At the Mercy of the Market

Even if a family wants to keep its businesses, the trusts and foundations that often hold their shares for them may have no choice but to sell if the bid is high. In a legal case arising from the LTV Corporation's attempt to buy the Grumman Corporation in 1981, a judge ruled that pension fund trustees who helped Grumman thwart LTV were personally liable for not acting in the best interest of their beneficiaries. Although an appeals court dismissed the case (because a rise in Grumman's stock price had eliminated the fund's paper loss and rendered the issue moot), the lower court ruling was still seen as setting a precedent.

"That scared the dickens out of a lot of family businesses," said Martin A. Siegel, a managing director and co-head of the mergers and acquisitions department at Drexel Burnham Lambert Inc. "Now unless 51 percent of the company is in the hands of one person who is young, in good health, has money outside of his investments in the company and doesn't live in a community property state, it's vulnerable."

If Richardson-Vicks failed to take precautions before it was too late, plenty of other companies are fighting back.

Mr. Johnson of S. C. Johnson plans eventually to transfer his majority ownership to one of his four children to protect the private company from family squabbles that have sparked the sale of other family businesses.

The descendants of the founder of Levi Strauss & Company, the blue jean and apparel maker, took their company private in a $2 billion leveraged buyout last summer. The move pre-empted any possible takeover attempt and also allowed the company to buy out 60 percent of its family shareholders. As a result, the worry of family shares passing into possibly unfriendly hands "is going to be a problem for another generation to contend with," said Robert D. Haas, the president and chief executive and a great-great-great-nephew of the company's founder.

Marriott purposely keeps its debt level high and requires that any acquirer has to obtain the backing of two-thirds of its shareholders. The Phillips-Van Heusen Corporation, which has been considering going private, just this week adopted a "stockholder rights" plan aimed at making it prohibitively expensive for an unfriendly suitor to buy the company.

Dow Jones & Company, the publisher of *The Wall Street Journal*, recently adopted a bylaw mandating its directors to take into account non-economic issues in considering any takeover bid. In a more dramatic move that has stirred controversy, Dow Jones is in the process of issuing a special class of stock to shareholders aimed at insuring that voting control of the company remains with the Bancroft family, which owns 54.7 percent of the company.

Companies Alter Voting Structures

Many other companies, non-family as well as family-run, are doing the same. "At least 50 companies on the three major stock exchanges have substantially altered their voting structures over the past two years and a number of others have proposed similar changes," said John Pound, a senior financial economist at the Securities and Exchange Commission.

Many family businesses have long had various classes of stock with different voting rights to insure that even if family ownership fell below the 50 percent mark, it would still control the company. But several of these businesses, including the New York Times Company, created their separate classes of stock before they went public.

What is controversial about what Dow Jones and other companies have done or are doing is that they are changing the rules in the middle of the game," said Mr. Pound, who is involved in an S.E.C. study of whether such changes hurt shareholders.

For its part, Dow Jones "feels very strongly that the journalistic independence that we operate under as a result of the Bancroft ownership is something very critical to the company's continued success," said Lawrence A. Armour, Dow Jones' director of corporate relations. Under increasing pressure from competing exchanges, the New York Stock Exchange, which had frowned on such recapitalizations, is reconsidering its regulations.

Even as family businesses are embracing these protective measures, though, many are taking steps to improve the quality of their management. At a time when thousands of young men and women are rediscovering their families' businesses as great places to work, many would-be successors are expected to "prove themselves" first in the outside world.

Giving Children Some Choices

Fathers who had been forced by their fathers to go into the business are now going to extremes to make sure that their children are not torn by the same doubts that they endured.

Lawrence S. Phillips, the president and chief executive of Phillips-Van Heusen, lamented that he had "no choice" about going into his family's apparel company. And he recalled his "embarrassment" at being made a vice president at age 29 because "I didn't deserve to be vice president nearly as much as executives who were not related to my father," Seymour J. Phillips, now the company's chairman. Now, he said, he will consider allowing his son, David, 26 years old, to join the business only after he has worked for five to 10 years someplace else.

William and Gary Lauder, the two sons of the president of Estée Lauder Inc., decided to get some career training outside the family. William, 26, is an associate merchandiser for Macy's, while Gary, 24, is a venture capital analyst for a small investment bank.

In another sign of the times, many family business leaders of bigger companies assert that no child of theirs should assume that he or she has an automatic claim to the throne. Mr. Marriott noted that his two sons and a son-in-law are beginning in low management positions and "there have been no promises" one will ever get to the top job.

Attracting and retaining outside management talent is also critically important for family businesses, and it is often a difficult task.

Some executives shun family companies for fear of getting caught in a family fight. Don Sebastiani, the chairman and chief executive of Sebastiani Vineyards, said he thought such fears were one reason why several executives he had approached about becoming president of the winery would not consider the job.

Non-family managers are frequently reluctant to devote themselves to a company in which they will never be able to obtain an ownership stake or have a shot at the top job. "A lot of professional managers say, `This is a good place to get started in but I wouldn't want to stay here for a career,'" said W. Gibb Dyer Jr., an organizational behavior specialist at Brigham Young University who has studied professional managers in family businesses.

Some family companies have been able to keep high-powered executives by paying them a premium. One such company is Mars, the family-owned candy giant, according to Peter Davis, the director of executive education at the University of Pennsylvania's Wharton School and a leading authority on family business. At Mars, he said, "managers know they will never own part of the company, but they are paid above the industry norms and in some cases, significantly above industry norms."

At least one family company has decided that not even money is enough of an incentive. When Max O. De Pree, the 61-year-old chief executive of Herman Miller Inc., retires, management control of the successful furniture maker will pass from the family, which has run the company since 1919.

What is unusual about this transfer is that it stems from neither a lack of heirs nor family interest. Rather, the De Prees decided that only by barring the third generation from the business could they attract the management talent that Herman Miller needed to grow.

Actions by Four Family-Owned Companies to Safeguard Family Control

Levi Strauss & Company: The Haas family, descendants of the company's founder, took the business private in a $2 billion leveraged buyout in 1985.

Phillips-Van Heusen: The board adopted a stockholder rights plan this week to make an unfriendly acquisition bid prohibitively expensive. The company has also been considering a leveraged buyout.

S. C. Johnson & Son: Samuel C. Johnson plans to transfer his majority ownership to one of his four children to protect this private company from family squabbles that have sparked sales of other family businesses.

Dow Jones & Company: The company announced plans in 1984 to issue a second class of stock with special voting rights that will maintain control by the Bancroft family, which now owns 54.7 percent of the company. A shareholder suit delayed the move but the case was settled in the company's favor on May 29.

Note:

On April 16, [1986] Dow Jones changed its bylaws to discourage unfriendly suitors. It staggered the terms of its board; required any prospective buyers to make the same dollar offer to all stockholders, and allowed the board to consider non-economic issues in a takeover offer.

Ethnicity is an important variable for practitioners in understanding family business systems, since ethnicity influences patterns of communication, values, relationships, and preferences in business practices.

Ethnicity, Families, and Family Business: Implications for Practitioners

By Monica McGoldrick and John G. Troast, Jr.

This article connects concepts about ethnicity developed in the family systems field with experiences in family businesses, some documented by others and some observed by us in our work with family businesses. In this article, we consider five ethnic groups: Irish, Italians, Jews, African-Americans, and Anglo Saxons or British-Americans (including descendants of English, Scottish, and Scots Irish immigrants). This work, like much that has been written on the subject of ethnicity, is based primarily upon experience. We believe, however, that the subject has potential for future research, as exemplified by the studies of Chinese, African-American, Jewish, and American Indian family businesses assembled in the Winter of 1992 issue of *Family Business Review*. What we offer here are descriptions of ways in which family businesses in the United States tend to operate in the context of their ethnic origins.

Defining Ethnicity

When we think of ethnicity, we think of people's religion, culture, geography, and language. Ethnic groups have been defined as "those who conceive of themselves as alike by virtue of their common ancestry, real or fictitious, and who ¹are so regarded by others" (Shibutani and Kwan, 1965, p. 23). Ethnicity refers to the concept of a group's peoplehood, which is based on a combination of race, religion, and cultural history, whether or not its members realize their commonalties with one another. However, it is more than just race, religion, and national and geographic origin. Ethnicity describes a commonality transmitted by families over generations and reinforced by the surrounding community. It encompasses those who are united by their common ancestry or history, and it involves a multilayered sense of group identification – of shared values and understandings – that fulfills a deep psychological need for identity and historical continuity (Giordano and Giordano, 1977). In no way do we mean to minimize the significance of race or the profound problems posed by racism in American culture.

Many factors influence the extent to which traditional ethnic patterns surface within a particular family and in turn affect its business relationships. The factors include the family's reasons for immigration (what was the family seeking – adventure, opportunity – and what was it leaving behind – religious or political persecution, poverty?); the length of time since immigration and the impact of generational acculturation conflict on the family; the family's place of residence (does the family live or has it lived in an ethnic neighborhood?); the order of migration (did one family member migrate alone, or did a large portion of the family, community, or nation arrive together?); the class background, socioeconomic status, education, and upward mobility of family members, the family's political and religious ties with the ethnic group; the languages spoken by family members, their age at the time of immigration, and their relative mastery of the English language; the extent to which family members have intermarried with or formed other connections with other ethnic groups; the attitudes of family members toward the ethnic group and its values; and the differences between the values of the culture of origin and the values of the dominant culture in the United States.

Most families in this country have experienced the complex stresses of immigration and migration. These may have been "buried" or forgotten, but they subtly continue to influence a family's outlook. Also, the pressure of accommodating to the new situation has forced many immigrant groups to abandon much of their ethnic heritage, and thus they have lost a part of their identity. The effects of this cutting off from the family may be all the more powerful for being hidden (McGoldrick, Pearce, and Giordano, 1982).

Cultural Stereotypes and Generalizations

Describing ethnic patterns necessitates the use of cultural generalizations – simplified pictures of the culture. These paradigms are frameworks within which we can explore our understanding; they are not truths but maps. While they cover only limited aspects of the terrain, they may nevertheless provide an explorer seeking a path with guidelines. By no means do we wish to advance any tendency toward negative labeling or stereotyping of people. We consider it essential to be able to describe group differences rooted in culture and ethnicity, recognizing that their truth is limited and that every family, business, and individual is unique. In working with any given family or individual, we must regard our assumptions about the influences of ethnicity as hypotheses to be explored.

Ethnicity and Family Business

The relationships among family members who work together in business are made doubly complex by the management and interpersonal requirements of their work together. Four issues affecting family businesses are likely to be influenced by ethnicity: patterns of interaction, involvement, management succession, and ownership.

Patterns of Interaction. How does the family communicate? How are conflicts that arise in the family business dealt with? Are they discussed openly? Are they submerged? Is the organization formally structured? Are outsiders brought in to negotiate? Are outsiders kept out of family conflicts?

Involvement. Which family members are involved in the business, and how are their roles defined? How does working together in the family business affect the relationships of family members over the life cycle? What values do family members hold most dearly: family loyalty, material success, togetherness? What criteria does the family use to judge performance, and how do these judgments affect compensation?

Management Succession. What are the rules by which management of the business is transferred? Will management go to another family member? If so, who is expected to succeed? Are daughters and sons considered differently? The oldest child? The brightest child? Are non-family members considered if they are more qualified? How is the succession timed? Is there an orderly plan for succession? Can family members discuss or even mention succession?

Ownership. Who will ultimately control the company? Will ownership be passed on equally to all children, or will one individual have a controlling advantage? What about family members who are not active in the business? Do daughters and sons receive equal shares? What happens if a child divorces a spouse who has become part of the business?

Interrelationships and Survival. Survival of the family business is ultimately influenced by decisions concerning the interrelationship of family members, involvement, succession, and ownership. Survival is a significant issue in that fewer than one-third of all family firms succeed to the second generation, and fewer than 15 percent survive into the third generation (Koselka, Meeks, and Saunders, 1989). Edward Welles (1991, p. 77), describing the trials and tribulations of New York's Starr family, owners of the Artkraft Strauss Sign Company (responsible for much of the neon in Times Square and beyond), suggested that families of different ethnic backgrounds have long recognized the potential seeds of destruction in multigenerational patterns. "Family businesses are so programmed to failure that there has arisen a consensus from one culture to the next that it takes no more than three generations to kill one.

In Mexico, one maxim reads "Father: merchant; son: playboy; grandson: beggar." The Chinese say, "From peasant shoes to peasant shoes in three generations." And in the

United States, one folk saying goes, 'From sleeveless to sleeveless in three generations.'"

Retaining the family name is itself an issue that influences how family members and outsiders perceive the firm. In a survey of some 1,000 family businesses conducted by Carin Rubenstein (1990), almost half of all firms used their family name as part of the company name. This tendency was more pronounced within certain industries, such as construction (75 percent); financial services, insurance, and real estate (58 percent); wholesale and retail trade (49 percent); and manufacturing (41 percent). This tendency probably reflects the values of the ethnic groups that have gone into these businesses, just as the values of those who choose not to use family or ethnic names reflect different priorities. Interestingly, the businesses with family names have survived somewhat longer (twenty-eight years) than family firms that do not make use of the name (twenty-four years). The survey found that 20 percent of family businesses using the family name identified respect for the family name as one of the firm's three key priorities. Only 9 percent of the firms that did not make use of the family name cited this as a priority (Rubenstein, 1990). Probably families that preserve their names in business place a higher value on family continuity than those that choose other names. Whatever the values of pride or tradition that prevail, a family's ethnic past is a part of the identity defining its family firm.

Patterns of Social Interaction

Those who work with family businesses know that the family's ongoing relations are influenced by a number of different factors, such as communication patterns, the ways in which differences are handled and conflicts are resolved, preferences for certain organizational structures, and the influence accorded outsiders. Sometimes the characteristic patterns of a group can be useful in framing particular transactions or interactions with or among group members.

Communication Patterns. The Irish have a tremendous bravado, but inwardly they tend to assume that anything that goes wrong is the result of their sins. Their basic belief is that problems are a private matter between themselves and God. They are therefore unlikely to seek or expect help when they have trouble (McGoldrick, 1982; Sanua, 1960; Zborowski, 1969; Zola, 1966). Among the Irish much is left unexpressed, especially hurts and conflicts, which can linger unspoken for years. Hostility and resentment are often dealt with indirectly in the family through sarcasm or innuendo. Feelings are so often hidden that it is hard for anyone to know exactly what is going on. While in poetry the Irish have a highly developed cultural skill with words, they may be at a loss to communicate, or even to understand, their own inner feelings of love, sadness, or anger. They have more phrases for the ways in which words can be used to color reality than any other ethnic group: *blarney, hooey, malarkey, palaver, shenanigans,* to name just a few. The Irish seem not to dare to be clear at either a verbal or nonverbal level, even with each other, and when they are mystified they can rarely ask for clarification (McGoldrick, 1982). For the many centuries of their oppression, clear speech could have meant death, so they have come to place a high value on complex, convoluted mystification and on double entendre in their use of language (McGoldrick, 1982).

Among the Irish, family relationships are often emotionally distant. Irish families, for example, may get together for duty visits on holidays and act jovial, even clannish (McGoldrick, 1982) yet not experience emotional connection when they work together. This can present a dilemma for multigenerational Irish family businesses. Because family members tend not to deal with conflicts directly or rely on one another for support, a family member who has a problem may see it as an added burden and embarrassment if the family finds out (McGoldrick, 1982). In our experience, Irish-Americans in family businesses tend not to discuss their relationships, which creates serious problems for succession.

Like the Irish, African-Americans use rich and colorful language, a practice that evolved as a way of coping with a culture in which direct speech could cost lives. But unlike the Irish, African-Americans have a highly developed ability to read nonverbal messages and the subtle contexts of speech, and they rarely confuse anyone unless they mean to.

Parents in Jewish families tend to have more open, democratic relationships with their children (Zuk, 1978) and less rigid generational boundaries than parents in most other groups (Herz and Rosen, 1982). They place high value on verbal explanations and use reasoning to teach their children how to behave. In providing for an orderly business succession at Frieda's, Inc., a Los Angeles based food company, Karen Caplan and her mother Frieda exemplify the generally open attitude in dealing with disagreements that we find among Jewish families. "We both make a lot of decisions on the gut level. I feel in my elbow that something is right," Frieda says. "If Karen doesn't agree, we sit down and talk about it." If they don't reach agreement, they may seek a mediator. Karen described her relationship with her sister Jackie in these terms: "We criticize each other freely. There never is any hollering or hurt feelings" (Klein, 1992, p. 26).

In Italian-American culture, communication tends to be much more ritualistic. Italians have learned to take maximum advantage of the present. They have a tremendous ability for intensely enjoying the experiences of eating, celebrating, fighting, and loving. They take great pleasure in festivals and fiestas. Church rituals have typically been prized for their pageantry, spectacle, and value in fostering family celebrations and rites of passage. Within the family context, all emotions are viewed as understandable. Italians do not have the problem with disallowed feelings that some cultural groups do, although there are clear values about right and wrong behavior. These values are based primarily on how such behavior affects the family (Rotunno and McGoldrick, 1982).

Handling Differences and Conflict. The differing communication styles among ethnic groups lead to differing styles of conflict and conflict resolution in family businesses of different ethnic origins. Some groups – for example, Jews – believe in talking things out. Others, like Anglo-Saxons, rely on form, convention, and fairness, while Italians may appeal to family loyalty to resolve differences.

Irish-Americans have been described as not communicating well about their differences (McGoldrick, 1982; Diner, 1983). As a result of built-up bad feelings, family members may silently cut one another off (McGoldrick, 1982). Problems can go unacknowledged for years until a succession or financial crisis makes some communication necessary. In some cases, it may be almost too late to help the family repair buried resentments and hurts. As a business moves into succeeding generations, unresolved conflicts from the past can cause deepening resentment. We have found that a decision to cease communications with other family members is particularly likely in Irish-influenced family businesses between those actively involved in the business and those with passive interests.

The Thomas Murray family illustrates the complexities of underground resentments across generations in Irish families. Born in 1860, Thomas Murray was a brilliant inventor. At his death in 1929, he left eight children, forty-eight grandchildren, a $9 million fortune, 1,100 patented inventions, and a record of industrial accomplishment that included the creation of Consolidated Edison.

Thomas Murray, Sr., had started a partnership with another self-made Irishman, Anthony Nicholas Brady, but the partnership and the family relationships began to erode during the succession process. Murray fell out with one of the Brady's sons, who tried to close him out of Consolidated Edison. Murray directed two of his sons, Joseph and Thomas, Jr., to make a private deal with Brady's son and buy him out separately from the other Murray family members. Thomas, Jr., was the third son. Serious, intelligent, and the most like his father, he became his father's surrogate, growing rich and celebrated. He succeeded his father in managing and controlling the family fortune.

After the senior Murray died, the youngest son, Jack, who had grown up with claustrophobia and a stammer, wanted to sue his brothers for what he believed should have been his share of the deal. "Jack decided to forsake the Murray family enterprises. They confined him, he said, scarcely allowing him the room or the opportunity to become the man he ought to become. Besides, they were too much of a family thing. It is difficult enough to be the youngest son in any large family; it was even harder in the Irish Catholic Murrays. They had a hierarchy, and Jack was at the bottom; everything came down on him...He began to drink...He was a type, really, this youngest son of a prominent Irish Catholic family, and his reach would always exceed his grasp. He carried baggage of which he was hardly aware" (Corry, 1977, p.49).

In Jewish family businesses, differences are more likely to be direct and overt. Conflict with the extended family often occurs over money or loyalty, and it can become extremely bitter (Rotunno and McGoldrick, 1982). Because conflicts and hostility are generally expressed in Jewish families, someone from a more restrained culture (such as Anglo-Saxon or Irish-American) may be uncomfortable with the intensity of Jewish criticism and verbal aggression (Herz and Rosen, 1982). Perhaps the values of success and family create conflicts for Jews in business because both values are strong. Individuals may be torn between the need for individual success and the need to be with and for the family. In this they contrast with the Italians, for whom individual success has little or no value apart from the family.

In a fair number of Jewish families, a child's marriage to a non-Jew can precipitate a cutoff. Preservation of the Jewish heritage, although not necessarily of Jewish religious practices, is crucial to the Jew's sense of identity. Inter-marriage, which is most frequent among Jewish males, may create great pain for parents. There is considerable pressure for Jews to identify with the group, and if a family member rejects his or her cultural background, it may be a serious issue for others in the family (Yaffe, 1968). These problems are naturally more prominent in the Northeast than in areas of the United States where the percentage of Jews is much smaller and patterns of intermarriage are less pronounced (Sanua, 1978). The presence of non-Jewish sons-in-law in a Jewish family business can be another source of family and business conflict. Experience suggests that cutoffs occur between sons and sons-in-law at the time of succession in the business. The overt conflicts focus on money and business practices. We have seen lawsuits develop between the branches of a family. Wives get caught up in the "men's" affairs more often than they do in Italian-American business culture.

Organizational Structure. Ethnicity can also be expressed in preferences for some organizational structures over others. In Italian culture, for example, where family unity and loyalty are strong, organizational structures can be relatively informal even in large organizations. In the fragmented grocery empire with more than $2 billion a year in sales. Although the company is publicly traded and it has provided shareholders with handsome returns (a 1,400 percent increase over ten years), the business has maintained its Italian ethnic traditions in management:

> From a nearly three-foot-high crucifix hanging in the lobby of the company's suburban Birmingham, Alabama, headquarters, to the oil portraits of family patriarch Vincent and his wife Theresa that adorn the boardroom, to the litter of family photographs in every executive office, you are constantly reminded that this is a family-run business. In an interesting way, this had enabled Bruno's to do without the layers of M.B.A.s, middle management, and merchandise managers that clog the decision-making pathways of larger chains. When food manufacturers want to sell their products in Bruno's, they still troop to the company's modest two-story prefab concrete and brick executive headquarters in Oxmoor, outside of Birmingham, and make their presentations to a committee of family members. If the family decides to buy, they buy in massive quantities, often for a year at a time. This 'forward buying' guarantees that Bruno's always gets every volume discount on the books, savings which are then passed on to the customers. [Kindel, 1990, p.23]

Among Irish-American family businesses, the so-called Irish solution is to divide business roles among family members. Perhaps this harkens back to a tradition of marriages for which divorce was not an option, and distance and separation became the primary solutions to marital conflict. In an analogous way, business diversification often provides a means of separating members of members of a business so as to reduce conflict and mutual dependence. Diversification can give siblings an opportunity to work in the business while reducing the conflicts of working together. This pattern may have governed the evolution of the Rooney family, owners of the Pittsburgh Steelers football team. Faced with the prospect of having five sons enter the business, Art Rooney, Sr. developed diversified interests in Shamrock Farms in Maryland and a variety of racetracks. The senior Rooney was very much in control yet enabled his sons to be independently involved in various opportunities (Alcorn, 1982).

Influence of Outsiders. Individuals outside the family play many different roles in family businesses. The way in which a family business deals with trusted advisers, other non-family employees, purveyors of goods and services, of professional service providers can be influenced by its ethnic traditions and beliefs. For example, since the Irish are uncomfortable with direct communication, consultation to an Irish family business can best be done by meeting separately with each family member until a good deal about the underlying workings of the family has been ascertained. Unlike Jewish, African-American, or Italian families, where the family bonds – and probably the conflicts as well-are so overt that meeting together will seem the obvious way to solve a problem, and it will not lead to any major revelations – one member of an Irish family may have been silently nursing grudges against others or even planning the breakup of the family business for years – even to the point of beginning discussions with lawyers – without mentioning a thing to anyone else in the family. In spite of the Irish tendency not to give much feedback about personal matters, the consultant needs to remember that the deep sense of personal responsibility for whatever goes wrong makes Irish-Americans very likely to continue efforts started with the consultant, even if they do not openly admit either their fault or their resolve to try to remedy it (McGoldrick, 1982).

Jewish families have a number of strengths that are important in consultation. One is their ability to see the humor in their own situation, which offers a release as well as some perspective on themselves and their foibles (Herz and Rosen, 1982). Generally they also have an openness to new ideas and new ways. They are foremost among American ethnic groups in their willingness to explore new ideas. Their verbal skills and willingness to talk about troubles and feelings are important assets (Herz and Rosen, 1982; Zuk, 1978). Their drive for success, as well as their profound acceptance of conflict as part of life, makes them ideal candidates for family business consultation. They are likely to have very little difficulty accepting the reality that relationships take time and need nurturing in order for a business to be run successfully. However, Jewish families can also become so preoccupied with the need to analyze and understand their experience that they are immobilized. The need to appear insightful, interesting, and successful, can in the extreme make them unable to experience anything without being concerned with what they are accomplishing. Professionals should be warned against applying solutions that might seem simplistic.

In consultation with Italian-American families, one must be cognizant of intense family loyalty. Anyone who tries to break the close bonds of an Italian family collides with Italian cultural norms. Consultation with Italian families has less to do with helping them to deal with any particular emotional issue than it does with facilitating the renegotiation of system boundaries, which tend to hold insiders (family members) in and outsiders (everyone else) out. Italian families have some difficulty turning to an outsider for consultation (Rotunno and McGoldrick, 1982). They tend to turn first to the family for support. While the enmeshment of Italian families certainly creates difficulties and conflicts for their members, it also provides much that family members from less supportive cultural environments lack. Their charm and skill in interpersonal expressiveness and their sense of the colorful and dramatic in their talk can give them a distinct advantage in dealing with others. However, outsiders sometimes see these gifts as manipulative. For Italians, words give expression to the emotion of the moment, and they therefore do not take them as seriously as others – for example, Anglo-Saxons – might (Rotunno and McGoldrick, 1982). Their expressiveness may be overpowering for a professional from a more restrained culture, one, for example, in which powerful expressions of hostility are interpreted literally. Consultants may also be frustrated by the Italian family's demand for immediate solutions. If one operates on the assumption that change occurs through long evaluation and discussion of problems, Italian families will be exceedingly difficult to help. The professional who focuses on mobilizing the family's own natural supports (as noted, this is the preferred Italian solution) and does not try to be the expert in relating to the family's relationships has a much better chance of constructive intervention.

As both authors of this article are white, our experiences in consulting with African-American family businesses reflect the historical relationships between white and black people in the United States. The institutional racism of our culture has profound implications for non-African-American consultants working with African-American family businesses. Since white institutions have been basically "foreign" to blacks and since racism is so pervasive in our society a certain level of mistrust of any "outsider" is natural (Grier and Cobbs, 1968; Hines and Boyd-Franklin, 1982). In the early stages of consultation, black families may keep their distance, participate with some reluctance, and offer minimal information. This withholding may reflect a natural sensitivity about the specific context of the consultation rather than discomfort about their own feelings or about communication in general. It may also relate to fears that any problems will be perceived as confirming negative stereotypes that have been applied to their group. They may feel pressure to act competent even if they do not feel competent because they are defensive and suspicious about how they will be judged.

Ethnicity and Involvement

Decisions to become involved in a family business are shaped by many different factors. These factors include the strength of filial relationships, birth order, gender roles, and basic family values. Since ethnic patterns can influence all these factors, it is useful to attempt to understand some possible differences among groups.

Loyalty and Independence. Certain ethnic groups may place a higher premium on family loyalty than others. This tendency can create expectations about who becomes involved with a family business. While all cultures value the family, the family is the primary orientation for some ethnic groups. Among Italians, for example, loyalty to the family is everything. It is seen as the protection against all troubles. Italians tend to believe that without your family you might as well be dead. Working together with your family is an obvious extension of this value (Gambino, 1974; Rotunno and McGoldrick, 1982). The family provides such an intense and wide network of support that developing away from it, even for education or achievement, is perceived as a major problem (Ragucci, 1981;Vecoli, 1978). Italian values of commitment to the group contrast strongly with the core values of the dominant U.S culture, which emphasizes independence, individualism, and personal achievement over affiliation (Rotunno and McGoldrick, 1982).

A problem is likely to arise in an Italian family business if a family member does not want to enter the business. Italians have one of the strongest informal community networks of any ethnic group (Fitzpatrick, 1969), and they are less likely to leave the neighborhood in order to get ahead. When they do break away, it is often very stressful for both the individuals involved and their families. In contrast, Anglo-Saxons raise their children to be independent and self-sufficient and think themselves failures if their children do not leave home on schedule (McGill and Pearce, 1982). Italians raise their children to be mutually supportive and to contribute to the family. Separation from the family is not expected. This ethnic contrast between dependent and independent value systems within a family business is well documented in the differences between Lee Iaocca and the Ford family:

> Iacocca was different...He was more driven, more self-assured, and, most crucially for future events, more distant from Henry himself. While Henry had been growing up in Grosse Point, separated from others in his family by large WASP distances and taboo subjects, Iacocca had been a boy in Allentown Pennsylvania, so close to his immigrant mother and father and his sister that the family felt like one person with four parts,' If the Fords embodied one part of the American myth, the one having to do with self-reliance and rugged individuality, the Iacoccas represented the other, having to do with upward striving and the attempt to crawl out of the melting pot into the mainstream. [Collier and Horowitz, 1987, p. 304]

Iacocca, of course, left Ford. Ultimately, he achieved notoriety at Chrysler. Despite his success in the corporate world, Iaocca maintained strong family ties, always taking daily telephone calls from his adult daughters, providing them with a private line and constant access despite his demanding business schedule.

Although expectations of family loyalty may be similar across different groups, the expressions of that sentiment may be very different. In Italian families, the expectations are apt to be articulated clearly. In contrast, this expectation is rarely acknowledged or openly discussed in Irish families. For this reason, feelings of betrayal and hurt and fear of abandonment are common among the Irish. Family members may enter the business against their interests or desires, while submerged resentment about the covert demands of family loyalty may simmer unacknowledged and ignored for years.

In the African-American culture, loyalty as a family value is often strongly interwoven with the need to survive in a world of prejudice. For black families, working together can provide a powerful force to counter the racism to which they are subjected. As Marion Wright Edelman (1992. P.3) recalls in her recent "public letter" to her children, "there were no black homes for the aged in Bennettsville, so [my father] began one across the street for which and Mama and we children cooked and served and cleaned. And we children learned that it was our responsibility to take care of elderly family members and neighbors and that everyone was our neighbor. My mother carried on the home after Daddy died, and my brother Julian has carried it on to this day behind our church since our mother's death."

The Wright family business, like so many black family businesses, grew out of the necessity that black communities faced to provide for their own. Black families have traditionally lived embedded in a wide network of extended kin and community, a pattern that appears to be rooted in both African traditions of strong community and in African-Americans' slave history, which systematically broke up biological families and forced blacks to turn to a wider network for support (Hines and Boyd-Franklin, 1982). In line with the value that they place on an extended kinship network, African-Americans may integrate more members of the extended family into the business than other groups do. The concept that everyone helps out is likely to be rotted in the need for cooperation in order to survive. Typical African-American family values that pervade family firms include loyalty, thrift, and shared responsibility. "For African-American families, these values resonate more deeply than the profit-and-loss column: They have meant survival itself in the face of enormous odds" (O'Connor, 1992, p.68).

Family 7, Inc., so named because it was founded by seven members of the same family, began as an investment club composed of the family of Reverend and Mrs. Irving Evans. With the efforts of two sons, three daughters, and their respective sons- and daughters-in-law, the family business enterprise parlayed a $700 monthly savings plan into a $2.3 million investment portfolio in five years. Everyone played a role in this part-time endeavor, assuming such functions as research, management, and administration. The varied roles and personalities balanced the effort and enabled this family enterprise to outperform the Dow Jones by a margin of three to one, returning 30 percent annually. One of the sons, Dr. Therman E. Evans, described the objective of the family operation as creating a solid, family-controlled dynasty in the tradition of the Hearsts, Fords, and Kennedys (Whittingham-Barnes, 1990).

Family businesses are quite common among Jewish families in the United States. Loyalty and success are highly valued. Intellectual ability and achievement are emphasized. Parents are expected to make great sacrifices for their children, and when children grow up, they are expected to repay their parent in "naches," a special pleasure one gets only from the success and happiness of one's children (Herz and Rosen, 1982). Non-Jewish professionals may be puzzled by the upset that Jewish parents feel when their children do not provide them with such rewards. In contrast, while Anglo-Saxons expect their children to be productive and a credit to the family and while they may take pride in their children's accomplishments, they do not experience the same kind of personal pleasure in their children's achievements.

To members of other cultures, Anglo-Saxons may appear self-centered (Greven, 1977; Penfield, 1967). For example, Donald Newhouse, heir to the vast media empire that includes Conde Nast, Random House, and scores of newspapers, describes his perception of the contrast between his Jewish orientation and that of the Hearst family: "What was important within the Newhouse family culture was that we not fall into the Hearstian trap of developing big egos and rich habits and that we continue to keep earnings in the company and build the company because we were building for ourselves, and we were building for our children and our children's children" (Mahar, 1989, p.34).

In working with family businesses, it is important to recognize the influences of ethnic values as well as the relative importance that the group places on family, as opposed to individual, achievement. Expectations of loyalty and independence will vary among family firms of different ethnic backgrounds. One must maintain an awareness of one's own ethnic norms when working with a family from a different ethnic background.

Gender Roles. In the same way in which ethnic value affect involvement in family business, ethnic traditions and beliefs may also have important implications for gender roles in family businesses. Professionals must be careful to heed how different ethnic groups view gender in their consultations and dealings with family firms.

The recent opportunities for women to succeed in business have offered a chance for Jewish women, who had already internalized the values of success and education, to flourish in their own right. Successful family business successions among women are evident in several Jewish family businesses. Doris and Morton Levin have structured an arrangement to sell the business to their daughter Frieda, the only one of five children to show an interest in the family's wholesale book-distributing company. Two daughters of Frieda Caplan, Karen and Jackie, have made a successful transition into management of Frieda's Inc. Kathryn Klinger has inherited much of her mother Georgette Klinger's strong will and conviction as she accedes to control of the successful skin care company, which has locations through out the country (Klein, 1992). Renee Edelman has worked to achieve a successful balance with her older brother Richard in developing her role in her family's public relations firm, Edelman Public Relations Worldwide, which is run by her father. With $36 million in revenues, it is the largest privately owned public relations firm in the nation (Edelman, 1990). The relative acceptance for the success of Jewish women in family businesses reflects the generally more democratic values of this ethnic group. Indeed, Jewish women descended from Eastern Europeans have a long history of maintaining the family economically through small business ventures while their husbands dedicated their lives to study and prayer (Zborowski and Herzog, 1952).

Women in African-American families tend to be strong and independent, and their sphere of activity often extends beyond the home to work situations and community activities. The numbers of African-American families headed by women are increasing to about the same proportion as two-parent families. Given the economic and social pressures on their families and the special pressure of racism directed against black men, black women have generally been employed outside the home to help support the family. They are much more likely than black men to attend college and to succeed academically. These developments seem to be very much related to the way in which racism is directed particularly against black men (Pinderhughes, 1982), a tendency that has led to the epidemic "invisibility" of black men within our culture. They are pushed to the periphery, as they were even in slave times, when the only record of their existence was in records of sale. Marriages were not validated by law, and fathers were not mentioned in birth records.

The ethnic tendency for black women to be strong and independent has had obvious implications for black family-owned businesses. At *Black Enterprise*, Earl Graves works closely with his wife Barbara, who is vice president and general manager (Whigham, 1990). Also in the publishing world, Linda Johnson Rice, age thirty-one, is president and chief operating officer of the family firm that owns *Ebony* and *Jet* magazines, employs 1,800 people, and posts in excess of $200 million in annual gross revenues. Her parents have been in business together since 1942, and the business has expanded into radio, television, cosmetics, and hair care products. Interestingly, it was Ms. Rice who was groomed for the position, not her older brother John, Jr., who subsequently died tragically. Linda Rice and her husband Andre balance child-rearing responsibilities for their young daughter with their careers (Edelman, 1990). *Coupreneurship*, a term meaning a couple in business together, has grown significantly in the past decade, particularly among black-owned businesses, such as Soft Sheen Products, Inc., the *Black Enterprise* company of the year in 1989 (Thompson, 1990). Because blacks have a longer history of gender role flexibility than many other groups, they may be better able to avoid the conflicts typical among working couples from groups with more rigid gender boundaries.

Italian families define women's roles quite narrowly and center these roles on the family. Italian families differentiate sharply between sons and daughters in a variety of ways – for example, with regard to premarital behavior. Sons clearly have greater latitude before marriage than daughters do. A bit of acting out is expected even subtly encouraged as a measure of manliness. Daughters are much more restricted socially. In particular, they are taught to eschew personal achievement in favor of respect and service to the role as family caretakers (Rotunno and McGoldrick, 1982). Traditionally, Italian males have been trained to be relatively understated in their emotional reactions with outsiders, while within the family they may be expressive to the point of losing control without much fear of sanction from others. Their ability to remain stone faced with outsiders reflects the historical need to protect oneself against dangerous exposure to strangers, while women are allowed to express their emotions freely but encouraged to stay out of "men's business" and the public sphere.

Italian family businesses appear to be dominated more by males than do the family businesses of some other groups, with the possible exception of businesses relating to food preparation and service. A manufacturing firm in the Northeast with sales of approximately $200 million demonstrates the gender pattern common to Italian family firms. The family patriarch anglicized both his forename and surname when he immigrated at the turn of the century in order to avoid prejudice. Nevertheless, he maintained a strong sense of ethnic pride, which he passed on to his only son. Although the patriarch was self-educated, he was a brilliant man who developed some fifty patents during his career. His only son had visions of other careers, yet he joined the family business and assumed his father's strong-willed work ethic. Following the Italian tradition, both men were dominant outside the home. The third generation consisted of three sons and three daughters. The three sons followed their father and grandfather into the business, where they now work with two sons-in-laws. The third son-in-law serves as the families outside counsel. Thus, all the males are involved in the family business, while the daughters remain outside the operation. This is very typical of Italian family traditions: All males go into the business, while the daughters are pressed into service as mothers and hearts of the home.

Succession

Succession is invariably a two-sided issue, involving as it does the transfer of management as well as of ownership. The transfer of each aspect can be affected by ethnicity. For example, Irish- and Italian-influenced family businesses sometimes name the eldest son the management successor but in the spirit of "fairness" leave the shares equally to all the children. Such a distribution can create problems for the future of the firm. In Italian-American family businesses, succession can also be affected by the strong role played by the Italian family patriarch and the tendency toward male dominance. For example, a highly successful construction-related business owned by an Italian family was left entirely to two sons. They shared the equity in the company, which was worth millions, while the daughter inherited only the modest family home.

Ethnic groups differ in their attitudes about primogeniture. There seems to be a greater tendency for family firms of some ethnic origins to address both management and ownership consistently from generation to generation. For example, Anglo-American culture has often passed the business on to the eldest son. This practice is reflected in dynastic families like the Vanderbilts and the Rockerfellers. More recently, Malcolm S. Forbes, Jr., inherited control of Forbes magazine on his father's death. As the oldest of four brothers and a sister, he tells the story in a recent interview: "My father took a lesson from his father in what not to do. My grandfather gave Pop and his brother Bruce equal shares of the magazine when he died. He saw Bruce on the Sales and marketing side, my father on the editorial side. I think when you have two strong personalities, they tend to fight and clash, to have major differences. My father learned that one person should have ultimate responsibility" (Pearl, 1990, p. 382).

The Irish traditionally did not follow a strict rule of primogeniture, perhaps naming the favorite or the most capable child to take over the farm (Arensberg, 1937; Arensberg and Kimball, 1968). Take the case of David Donovan, who worked hard to build a small cotton and soybean farm into a 1,000 acre family business plantation. He hoped that both his sons would seek a proper education and help advance the farm with their knowledge. Although the older son, Perry, entered the business directly after leaving high school, Donovan chose to leave the business to his younger son Art, who had a college degree in agriculture and who he saw as the gifted one. Over time, the decision proved faulty, since Art had poor interpersonal skills. Conflicts developed with many employees, resulting in enormous friction between the two sons. David Donovan coordinated a management change providing Perry with operational authority over the farm, while Art was put in charge providing Perry with operational authority over the farm, while Art was put in charge of the office in town to monitor new agricultural technology as well as follow the commodities futures markets (Alcorn, 1982). Experience shows that the Irish solution is often to divide roles and responsibilities as a means of resolving conflict. Parental disappointment may be intense if the children do not want the business, echoing the disappointment that fathers in Ireland felt when no child really wanted the farm (McGoldrick, 1982).

Members of Jewish families may attempt to get others to side with them for the wrongs they have withstood (Herz and Rosen, 1982). The overt view of life and work as suffering is sometimes implied in the ways in which Jewish family firms handle succession issues. Jacob Starr, the family patriarch of the Artkraft Strauss Sign Company, used a strong, self-indulgent work ethic as his trademark in dealing with his son Mel and other family members. A relative described Jake as "a self-made man of the school that the only way to succeed is if things are not easy for you; he went out of his way not to make things easy – particularly for his relatives" (Welles, 1991, p. 77). Ultimately, he deprived his son of learning some critical aspects of the business. Nonetheless, Mel carried the business into the next generation, more through romanticism and reputation than from a strong understanding of the business.

A recent study of African-American businesses in Los Angeles (Dean, 1992) suggests that African-American family businesses operate very much as closed systems, focused on the individual success for the firm rather than on political and community issues. The author suggests that a business may be regarded less as a family legacy than as a means for providing children with upward mobility by increasing their access to education. Thus, succession issues have low priority.

Conclusion

Understanding ethnicity is part of developing the history of a family and of its family businesses. Tools for gathering information on cultural and family patterns range from the asking of simple background questions to the more complex task of developing genograms (McGoldrick and Gerson, 1985). Those who gather a family history need to ask questions concerning the factors that influence traditional ethnic patterns, such as immigration, migration, religion, class, marriage, sibling patterns, conflicts, alliances, cutoffs, and so forth. When we appreciate the ethnic traits that pattern some of the ways in which families operate personally and in business, we become aware of some potential strengths as well as of areas in which they can use assistance.

This article directs the attention of practitioners to the ethnic dimension of family business, a rich and relatively unexplored area. The authors hope that this perspective can help families and family business consultants gain a new understanding of patterns that they may not have fully recognized were influencing their behavior and communication. Finally, the authors again emphasize that the descriptions provided are meant to serve practitioners only as guides in creating provisional hypotheses that must be tested in any particular circumstance.

References

Alcorn, P.B. *Success and Survival in the Family-Owned Business.* New York: McGraw-Hill, 1982.

Arensberg, C. *The Irish Countryman.* Garden City, N.Y.: Natuarl History Press, 1937.

Arensberg, C., and Kimball, S. *Family and Community in Ireland.* (2nd ed.) Cambridge, Mass.:Harvard University Press, 1968.

Collier, P., and Horowitz, D. *The Fords: An American Epic.* New York: Summit Books, 1987.

Corry, J. *The Golden Clan.* Boston: Houghton Mifflin, 1977.

Dean, S. M. "Characteristics of African Family-Owned Businesses in Los Angeles." *Family Business Review,* 1992, 5 (4), 373-395.

Diner, H. *Erin's Daughters in America.* Baltimore MD.: Johns Hopkins University Press, 1983.

Edelman, M. W. *The Measure of Our Success.* Boston: Becon Press, 1992.

Edelman, R. "When Little Sister Means Business." *Working Woman,* 1990, 15 (2), 82-85.

Fitzpatrick, J. *"The Role of White Ethnic Communities in the Urban Adjustment of Newcomers."* Paper presented at the Chicago conference on ethnicity, 1969.

Gambino, R. *Blood of My Blood: The Dilemma of Italian-Americans.* New York: Doubleday, 1974.

Giordano, J., and Giordano, G.P. *The Ethno-Cultural Factor in Mental Health: A Literature Review and Bibliography.* New York: Institute on Pluralism and Group Identity, 1977.

Greven, P. *The Protestant Temperament: Patterns of Child Rearing, Religious Experience, and the Self in Early America.* New York,: Vintage Books, 1977.

Grier, W., and Cobbs, P. *Black Rage.* New York: Bantam Books, 1968.

Herz, F., and Rosen, E. "Jewish Families." In M. McGoldrick,J.K. Pearce, and J. Giordano (eds.), *Ethnicity and Family Therapy.* New York: Guilford, 1982.

Hines, P., and Boyd-Franklin, N. "Black Families." In M. McGoldrick, J.K. Pearce, and J. Giordano (eds), *Ethnicity and Family Therapy.* New York: Guilford. 1982.

Kindel, S. "Rebel Self." *Financial World,* 1990, 159 (1), 22-24.

Klein, E. "My Mother, The Founder; My Daughter, The Boss." *D & B Reports,* 1992, 40 (2). 24-27.

Koselka, R., Meeks, F., and Saunders, L. "Family Affairs." *Forbes,* 1989, 144 (13), 212-218.

McGill, D., and Pearce, J.K. "British Families." In M. McGoldrick, J.K. Pearce, and J. Giordano (eds), *Ethnicity and Family Therapy.* New York: Guilford, 1982.

McGoldrick, M., and Gerson, R. *Genograms in Family Assessment.* New York: Norton, 1985.

McGoldrick, M., Pearce, J.K., and Giordano, J. (eds.). *Ethnicity and Family Therapy.* New York: Guilford, 1982.

Mahar, M. "All in the Family: How to the Newhouses Run Their Vast Media Empire." *Barrons,* 1989, 69 (48). 8-9, 32-36, 39-43.

O'Connor, B. W. "Management: Family Matters." *Black Enterprise,* 1992, 22 (6), 68-74.

Pearl, J. "The Forbes Mystique: An Interview with Malcom Forbes, Jr." *Forbes,* 1990, 146 (2), 380-383.

Penfield, W. *The Difficult Art of Giving: The Epic of Alan Gregg.* New York: Little, Brown, 1967.

Pinderhughes, E. "Afro-American Families and the Victim System." In M. McGoldrick, J.K. Pearce, and J. Giordano (eds.), *Ethnicity and Family Therapy.* New York: Guilford, 1982.

Ragucci, A.T. "Italian-Americans." In A Hargood (ed.), *Ethnicity and Medical Care.* Cambridge, Mass.: Harvard University Press, 1981.

Rotunno, M., and McGoldrick, M. "Italian Families." In M. McGoldrick, J.K. Pearce, and J. Giordano (eds.), *Ethnicity and Family Therapy.* New York: Guilford, 1982.

Rubenstein, C. "Power and Priorities." *Family Business,* 1990, 1 (2), 41-48.

Sanua, V.C. "Sociocultural Factors in Response to Stressful Life Situations: The Behavior of Aged Amputees as an Example." *Journal of Health and Human Behavior,* 1960, 1, 17-24.

Sanua, V.D. "The Contemporary Jewish Family: A Review of the Social Science Literature." In G. Babis (ed.), *Serving the Jewish Family*. New York: KTAV, 1978.

Shibutani, T., and Kwan, K. M. Ethnic Stratification. New York: Macmillian, 1965.

Thompson, K. "Married...with Business." *Black Enterprise*, 1990, 20 (9), 47-54.

Many families who own businesses benefit from an explicit statement of goals, values and guiding principles. Here is the century-old creed of the Mogi family, owners/operators of the Kikkoman foods business since 1630.

Kikkoman's Mogi Family Creed

Get a bottle of Kikkoman Soy Sauce and look at the label – you'll see the date 1630. That's when the Mogi family began the business and they've owned and operated it for the 17 generations since.

Current CEO Yuzaburo Mogi recently traveled from Japan to speak to Loyola University Chicago's Family Business Forum. As part of his presentation, he shared his family's creed written over a century ago and still used to guide the family and its business. Here it is, translated from Japanese:

Article I: All family members desire peace. Never fight, and always respect each other. Ensure progress in business and the perpetuation of family prosperity.

Article II: Loving God and Buddha is the source of all virtue. Keeping faith leads to a peaceful mind.

Article III: All family members should be polite to each other. If the master is not polite, the others will not follow. Sin is the result of being impolite. Families – young and – old, masters and workers-govern themselves by politeness; then peace will be brought of their own accord.

Article IV: Virtue is the cause, fortune the effect. Never mistake the cause for the effect. Never judge people on whether they are rich or not.

Article V: Keep strict discipline. Demand diligence. Preserve order, young and old, master and workers.

Article VI: Business depends on people. Do not make appointments or dismissals using personal prejudices. Put the right man in the right place. Loving men who do what they should, bring peace to their minds.

Article VII: Education of the children is our responsibility to the nation. Train the body and mind with moral, intellectual and physical education.

Article VIII: Approach all living beings with love. Love is fundamental to human beings and the source of a life worth living. Words are the door to fortune and misfortune. A foul tongue hurts oneself and others. A kind tongue keeps everything peaceful. Be careful in every word you speak.

Article IX: Keep humbleness and diligence, which have been handed down over the years from our forefathers. Make every effort to do as much as you can.

Article X: True earning comes from the labor of sweat. Speculation is not the best road to follow. Don't do business by taking advantage of another's weakness.

Article XI: Competition is an important factor in progress, but avoid extreme or unreasonable competition. Strive to prosper together with the public.

Article XII: Make success or failure clear, judge fairly punishment and reward. Never fail to reward meritorious service, and don't allow a mistake to go unpunished.

Article XIII: Consult with family members when starting a new business. Never try to do anything alone. Always appreciate any profit made by your family.

Article XIV: Don't carelessly fall into debt. Don't recklessly be a guarantor of liability. Don't lend money with the purpose of gaining interest, because you are not a bank.

Article XV: Save money from your earnings, and give to society as much as you can. But never ask for a reward nor think highly of yourself.

Article XVI: Don't decide important affairs by yourself. Always consult with the people concerned before making a decision. Then employees will have a positive attitude in their work.

Reprinted with permission from *The Family Business Advisor.* Copyright 1993, Family Enterprise Publishers.

John L. Ward uses his experience working with family businesses in India to stimulate thinking about family businesses in general and to reinforce application of the rich complexity of family firms. Ward proposes that the economic and cultural context of a nation significantly influences the strategic decisions and family policy decisions of the family firms of that nation.

Reflections on Indian Family Groups

By John L. Ward

Introduction

When I accepted the opportunity to write this article, I welcomed the chance to collect and share my thoughts from several recent consulting and speaking engagements in India. Then, as the commitment and deadline approached, I – as a total cultural outsider with very limited experience in the country – became uncomfortable attempting to offer my views. My reflections include much naiveté and oversimplification. However, I hope that some of the ideas and issues presented stimulate ways of thinking about family businesses in general and reinforce appreciation of the rich complexity of family firms.

India itself is incredibly complex. In the view of many, it is a state contrived by the British, made up of very different regions, states, languages, communities, religions, and geographies. Family cultures will, therefore, vary greatly. For example, I've been told that the south is more conservative, with closer families than the north, which is more aggressive and competitive. Through the ages, the north was invaded and at war many, many times. The south, however, was never invaded or lost lives in a war on Indian soil. That helps me understand why the business families in the south seem to embrace more family members for more generations.

Some social-religious communities have traveled and traded more and are, therefore, more open to outside ideas. Some find it easier to trust nonfamily managers. Some have deep traditions of high levels of education and/or service to those in need.

Given the differences among families throughout India and the world over, I hope to show some systematic influences on the challenges to and opportunities for the family businesses of this nation.

This article is more of a diary than it is research. Perhaps it is a bit journalistic. It is based largely on the following:

- Four visits to India over the past two years, including five speaking engagements and three ongoing consulting experiences
- Multiday speaking programs that provided many opportunities to listen to questions, hear about issues raised in discussion groups, benefit from the views of business-owner presenters, and meet individual families for breakfast or tea
- Several excellent recent Harvard Business School cases about Indian family groups (I draw more on their stories rather than risk exposing clients.)
- India's *Business Today*, which regularly features profiles on prominent families that dominate the economic landscape

A Contextual Model

When entertaining the factors that shape a particular family business's family and business decisions, there is a model that I find helpful (see Figure 1). For example, I have long felt that systematic family factors are at least as powerful in shaping the strategy of a family firm as its particular business environment (Harris, Martinez, & Ward, 1994). I also believe that the strategic environment is an important influence on the make-up of a family's family constitution or protocol, as portrayed in Figure 1. The conceptual intervening variable is the dominant ownership and leadership vision among the family (Ward, 1996).

For example, an enmeshed family with only two twin children who are both in the

Figure 1. Factors Affecting Business Strategy and Family Constitution

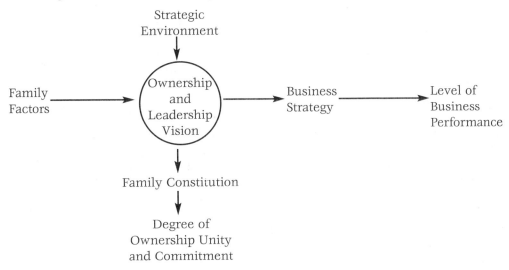

company (say, a distribution business) will likely pursue an equal ownership, share a joint leadership vision, ignore geographically distant business growth opportunities, and develop policies of equal pay and equal public relations exposure.

Perhaps an adaptation of the model in Figure 1 can help organize thinking about the family businesses of a nation. National economic policy is a distinguishing future of the strategic environment, and national culture is a distinguishing influence on the family factors that shape a business family's ownership and leadership vision. Therefore, Figure 2 may be a useful way to organize the analysis of the family businesses of India.

In this paper, I look at the national economic policies and the changing of those policies that seem most influential in shaping particular family and business decisions of Indian groups. I also examine specific cultural factors and changes in those factors that similarly seem to shape the family and business decisions of Indian groups.

In summary, I propose that the economic and cultural context of a nation significantly influences the strategic decisions and family policy decisions of the family firms of the nation. These factors also reflect themselves in how the business family forges its vision of its family ownership structure and the form of its business leadership.

Early Economic Environment

Old-line business families in India have seen both great opportunity and great hardship as socialistic governments struggled with economic control and economic develop-

Figure 2. The Analysis of Indian Family Businesses

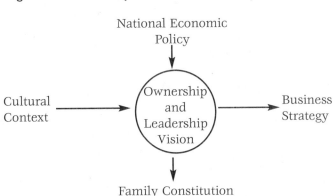

ment. Understanding how the economy evolved offers great insight, I think, into the issues facing many Indian family business groups today.

There are five categories of business in India: (a) government-controlled business (e.g., AirIndia); (b) multinational corporation (MNC) controlled businesses; (c) small-scale industries sector (SSI); (d) widely held, anonymously owned Indian companies (e.g., Proctor and Gamble), which are common on the U. S. stock markets; and (e) large family companies (e.g., groups).

There are fewer and fewer government companies, and relatively few MNCs and anonymously owned companies, although the latter are slowly growing in number. There are about 6 million SSIs with less than $500, 000 net worth or about 100 employees – and almost all are family businesses. The family business groups are the backbone of the economy, making up most of the GDP and nearly all of the industrial economy.

A group is a large, diversified collection of different businesses – frequently from 5 to 50 different businesses. Such groups are also prevalent in Latin America, Africa, and throughout Asia. They have become prevalent for several historic reasons common to developing countries. The family role in a group-type company in today's economy and the business challenges into the future for the family groups are two key forces affecting the Indian family business landscape.

Prior to its independence in 1947, India saw the founding of several of its largest family businesses (e. g. , the two largest today, Tata and Birla). Many of them were 19th century traders who brought to India the industrialization of the West, with great care for the development of the country they loved. This passion for corporate charity and a sense of social purpose is still prevalent in family business groups today.

Their entrepreneurial and social drive created some very large enterprises with interests in commodities like textiles, chemicals, steel, auto parts, plantation products, food processing, and insurance. These businesses were usually passed on to the oldest son, a practice that was unquestioned by social custom. Family frictions were largely invisible, as family members respected elders, married within their small social-religious communities, and hired management of similar values who were extremely loyal to the family due, in part, to generous paternalism in times of otherwise vast poverty and limited career opportunities.

Given an underdeveloped economy and the government's hold on most of the keys to business opportunity, family groups became the solution to otherwise inefficient markets. Their government contacts and social goodwill led to more investment opportunities. Their access to capital from past profits was a unique resource in a country with virtually no financial markets. Their reputations and training drew the most competent managers. Their diversity helped them survive economic cycles. In short, the family business groups were the economy and, most interestingly, the economy's market infrastructure as well.

But two key years – 1971 and 1991 – shook the destiny of this tranquility. In 1971, India's socialistic experiment reached peak proportions. The government nationalized several industries, most especially the financial institutions of insurance and banking. Further, the government all but prohibited foreign investment into the country; set import duties at more than 100%; limited equity positions of the MNCs in joint ventures to typically 26%; controlled new business starts via government licensing; and, pivotally, raised corporate and personal income taxes to near 100%.

There were two especially important consequences for the groups. First, those with satisfactory government relations were virtually the only source of new enterprises. They would obtain government permission to enter into or expand a venture opportunity, putting up 20% to 80% of the money and getting the rest from the government's financial institutions. To do as much of this as possible while retaining management control of each enterprise, they pursued "pyramid investments." For example, the group would invest 35% in a company for control and finance the rest. That company would then invest 51% or so in another company, and so on. In other words, the group could effectively control a large number of enterprises, each of which had government-sponsored financial institution investors and, perhaps, a few public shareholders (as few people had much to invest). To leverage this concept, the companies had to be publicly traded so that the financial institutions could hold more equity than debt. Public ownership would eventually raise other issues, but, for now, individual family members could buy more personal shares than their interests and means suggested. Different siblings could own different amounts of shares, depending on their private investing.

In summary, although socialistic government policy choked off external trade and the development of financial markets, family groups grew and dominated the Indian economy. On the other hand, the discouragingly high income tax rates drove all family members into company positions to protect their standard of living by using tax-deductible company resources for housing and personal expenses.

The typical picture became all male family members working in the family business, with each heading one or more of the particular companies in the group and exercising near autonomy in doing so. The individual businesses became like fiefdoms, and the senior generation leaders would beseech their children to join them in their particular business rather than in one led by an uncle or cousin.

Cultural Context

This business system was reinforced by the cultural mores of the times. Simply put, most Indians lived in "Hindu joint families" where three generations lived together in one home – parents, adult children, spouses, and grandchildren. All resources and income were shared equally. Daughters left their families of origin when they married into their new families through arranged marriages to husbands of equal means. Oldest sons assumed family leadership responsibility and maintained a posture of full espect for their parents. Culture kept family conflicts unspoken and unaddressed. When a daughter did, rarely, go into the business, it was in the absence of any sons. Daughters-in-law would manage the family's charitable interests – sometimes supervising significant schools or hospitals.

But these traditions changed quickly during the 1990's. Over the past 10 to 15 years, significantly fewer prosperous families live together in one home. In addition, daughters leave their family of origin less often and more often become employees and owners of the business. Or they, too, are interested in active leadership of the family charities. Emotional differences among siblings are more public. Numerous groups have gone to court to address their sibling conflicts.

Partitions

One common way business families attempted to minimize conflict was to have each son responsible for his own business. However, such an approach seems frequently to lead to strong conflicts and the eventual division of the group into different, independent businesses owned separately and wholly by each son. I call this phenomenon the "partitioning of fiefdoms."

The problem with fiefdoms is that different brothers perform differently in their businesses. And different brothers take different amounts of money out of their businesses and live different lifestyles (in the absence of the "Hindu joint family" system). As some sons become wealthier than others, they might buy more of a company's shares on the undervalued stock market. Then, of course, different brothers would have different ownership stakes with which to wield different positions of power and to provide different levels of wealth for themselves. Sons will want their own sons in their own business – hardly the most rational allocation of management human resources. The result is often to partition the business, which is hard to do while preserving family harmony. Some groups partitioned every generation. These breakups are typically very intense and appear in the press.

When I asked six daughters-in-law why sibling breakups seemed so frequent and intense in families known, culturally, for their family orientation and unexpressed conflict, they offered three reasons: (1) lack of transparency in salaries and finances, (2) repressed emotions, and (3) each sibling wanting to take care of their own male offspring.

In my mind, the fundamental Indian family business problem is the establishment of fiefdoms and the proprietary attitude on the part of each CEO toward "his" business's purpose and esources.

Some Indian families are highly aware of these temptations and problems. These families demonstrate a different model for second-and later generation involvement in the business – namely, to avoid fiefdoms and minimize partitioning.

These families rotate the next generation among several divisions of the business to provide them with breadth of experience and to avoid individuals feeling proprietary about any one division. Then, as the next generation becomes ready for general management, they move into overseeing governing positions. They do not become president of an operating company. Instead, they, along with their other siblings or cousins, become full-time observers of all of their businesses and counselors to all of their presidents. They also set corporate, total group strategy as a team and together recruit excellent nonfamily leadership for the individual operating companies. I call these "family-governed enterprises."

The families I have met who take this approach to avoid fiefdoms seem to distinguish themselves with their strong sense of family – a family first attitude – and their foresight to anticipate the business issues that often lead to family fractiousness and business partitions.

Changing Economic Times

Whereas the Indian family culture has changed significantly over the past decade, so, too, has the economic and strategic environment. Around 1991, after long economic doldrums, a new government pushed through substantial economic liberalization. Tariffs and quotas began to come down, now falling to as low as 10% to 20% and with no quantitative, quota restrictions after the year 2001. Income tax rates fell to 35%, with long-term capital gains tax rates only about 10%. Estate and inheritance taxes are zero. In addition, foreign investors are more welcome and can now control 51% of a company. Mutual funds have been introduced.

The result of these changes is tremendously tougher competition for the once-protected domestic family business groups. They are now required to change the way they do business or fail. As these businesses work to compete, they have upgraded quality and management systems tremendously. But they are also forced to achieve world-class cost structures by reducing labor and becoming more marketing oriented, which is not among their strengths.

More Changing Times

The "new economy" is revolutionizing India. It's a hotbed of new infotech startups. In addition, foreign companies (for example, Ford and Citibank) are setting up their data processing and customer service operations in India, which provides an English-speaking, well-educated, inexpensive labor market. Stock options and IPOs are becoming the rage. Young entrepreneurs are amassing substantial wealth. They are the heroes of the media and popular culture.

The new economy contrasts sharply with the old economy of commodity, inexpensive basic products, and slow-to-respond interlocking family group decision making. To make matters worse, the MNCs now want to control their positions in India and not settle for a minority equity position. In summary, the old family groups face tougher competition for domestic and global markets and more competition for talented management and capital.

To make matters even worse, the groups pay a 20% tax on dividend transfers among their cross-holdings, and their stock is at relatively low values to the market. Additionally, debt cost at about 13% is high by global standards, and their international joint venture (jv) partners are being bought and sold in consolidating global industries. (Managing jv partners is hard enough when they are stable in their management and intentions.) Families have limited access to personal financial nest eggs or growth capital.

Many of these new economic forces are affecting all kinds of businesses the world over. But the intensity of all these forces, compressed into just the past 10 years, along with the changes in Indian family culture, make change seem especially intense in India. As the CEO of a large group and recent past president of India's largest business association, M. V. Subbiah said at a seminar in 1999, "The forces of westernization combined with the evolving socialist framework have resulted in fragmenting the family."

I sense great stress and despondency among the family business sector as the business environment, as well as the structure and definition and comfortable stability of family, have changed so dramatically.

Other Related Business Issues

As competition intensifies and capital becomes both more important and scarcer for family businesses, groups will need to address the size and diversity of their portfolios. Consultants will tell them to focus more on fewer core businesses and capabilities. Family relatives may make that extremely difficult decision – whether to sell the businesses or whether the businesses will be deemphasized or run by family members or outsiders. Even if the businesses are not run by family members, what if different family members have a different equity interest in the different businesses?

As attracting new, talented nonfamily executives becomes more challenging due to new competition for talent, attracting the next generation of family becomes more challenging as well. Many are being educated in U. S. business schools and lured into e-commerce startups in the United States or India, where there is more promise of personal wealth and individual public recognition.

Other issues facing family Groups in India are classic to almost all family firms. They include the following (Advani, 2000):
- "The Group's insularity complicates"
- "A company that long put loyalty over competence"
- "[He]has a difficult act to follow in that his father was extremely successful. Tradition and the tendency to compare his performance must be weighing over him heavily."

Other Related Family Issues

The privilege of sons is threatened. Sisters are increasingly well educated and accepted into the business and ownership. Even sons-in-law are becoming more involved and important. Sons, especially eldest sons, are pressing for their historic entitlements. Conflict among siblings is increasing.

Daughters with careers are less inclined to be drawn to voluntary positions in the family's charities. New leadership and new energy will be needed to keep these activities successful and important.

The most senior generation increasingly despairs over the decline of unquestioned authority and the changes in traditional family structure and roles. Where once they felt relatively unthreatened turning over business responsibility, even control, to the younger generation, now some play more powerful, disruptive roles behind the scenes.

Conclusion

In these reflections, I hope to have shown how the economic environment and cultural context shape family business strategy and issues and family policies and problems. The dramatic compressed changes in both business and family circumstances in India make these forces apparent. (Many economies in Latin American and Asia have experienced similar changes. For example, Mexico deregulated in 1996 and Brazil in 1991.) It seems to me that the greatest challenges facing the family groups in India, and perhaps elsewhere, are as follows:
- Reconsolidating the business into a "one business" concept, where the business has the freedom to make necessary resource allocation decisions without alienating family interests and while building a single public identity.
- Reconsolidating the family around a "one family "concept that relates proudly to the entire company and pursues charitable and business activities together, not according

to branches or roles.

- A more visible investment in philanthropy even though family financial resources are tighter and gaining family consensus is more problematic.
- Attracting nonfamily and next-generation management talent to an old-economy business without exciting stock options and quick wealth prospects.

Addressing these challenges will be especially difficult given the divergence of family branch and member economic and equity interests over the years. It will also be particularly difficult because most families in India have never learned to convene as a multi-generation family to discuss difficult issues, and the role of family leader becomes more ambiguous. It is possible that family groups will lose popular support due to their effort to restructure and reduce employees. This restructuring and reduction will mean fewer investments in social capital. Family business publicity will likely focus more on family squabbles, whereas new start-up businesses will be acclaimed for creating new jobs. These start-ups will become the new social heroes.

In the meantime, a whole new generation of family businesses is emerging. Just this year the Indian government expanded its definition of "small-scale "enterprises to include companies up to five times larger than before. These businesses enjoy very favorable preferential tax treatment as well as no estate taxes and a rapidly growing economy. Some predict that the number of these small-scale enterprises will increase 300% over the next 10 years.

Whereas third-and fourth-generation family groups dominated the past, perhaps first- and second-generation private enterprises will dominate the future. Currently, however, there is no way to reach these 6 million family businesses to help them prepare for the future as ongoing, adaptable family businesses. Perhaps an important element of an economy's infrastructure is effective family business education and best-practice role models.

In addition, it may be of great value for government policy makers to arrive at a better understanding of their affect on the family business segment of the economy.

I believe the more diverse the makeup of an economy's business landscape – assuring a balance of efficient MNCs, spirited and innovative new enterprises with intense values, and purposedriven and long-lasting diverse family groups – the better. India may have been overly dependent on family groups in the past. Perhaps in the future there will be too few.

References

Advani, A. (2000, June 26). Business India: Editorial, *Business India*, p. 3.

Ghemawat, P. (1998). Ballapur Industries, (N9-798067). Boston: Harvard Business School Publishing.

Harris, D. , Martinez, J., & Ward, J. (1994). Is strategy different for the family-owned business? *Family Business Review*, 7 (2), 159-174.

Khanna, T. (1997). RPG Enterprises, (9-797-106). Boston: Harvard Business School Publishing.

Nanda, A. , & Austin, J. (1992). The House of Tata, (9-792-065). Boston: Harvard Business School Publishing.

Ward, J. (1996). Family Vision, Ownership Structure and Strategy Formulation for Family Firms, Annual Meeting of Academy of Management.

Families attempt to communicate their values across generations in many ways. The last effort of specific members of a given generation may take the form of an "ethical will." Here's how to write one.

So That Your Values Live On: Ethical Wills

As leaders of family businesses contemplate the "big transitions" that affect their families and businesses, they are increasingly embracing an ancient custom. In the effort to summarize life's meaning and to pass a precious legacy of values and beliefs to the next generation, they are writing what is known as an "ethical will." As one such will stated:

> *"Here we take inventory of precept instead of property, of concern instead of cash, of love in lieu of legacy."*

An ethical will usually takes the form of a letter or perhaps is a codicil to one's legal will. Its intent is to bequeath a spiritual legacy. While usually read after its author's death (sometimes as a part of the funeral) the ethical will is sometimes shared with children during life

"Ethical wills are windows into the souls of those who write them," explains Rabbi Jack Riemer, co-editor of *So That Your Values Live On: Ethical Wills And How To Prepare Them.* Such documents often become a cherished family artifact, passed from generation to generation. Some families reread ethical wills on the anniversary of their loved one's death. The words can become powerful guides or reminders for life.

Ethical wills are intensely personal. No prescribed format is required. Many people are moved to record thoughts for their progeny without ever knowing about the tradition of ethical wills. Writing one requires little more than the impulse to do so.

Riemer and co-editor Nathaniel Stampfer make some suggestions on how to write your ethical will. Some items they offer for consideration as you begin: the important lessons learned during your life; people and causes for which you feel a sense of responsibility; mistakes in your life you hope your children will not repeat; your definition of true success. Frequent themes in ethical wills include family unity, ethical conduct, charity, and when a family business is involved, business relationships and conduct. Expressions of gratitude, hope, faith and such are quite common. To evoke times together and to reinforce moral points, many wills repeat favorite sayings or stories. As you would with your material will, you should periodically review and perhaps revise your ethical will.

So That Your Values Live On is largely a collection of Jewish ethical wills written by people from many walks of life. Several are from people engaged in business, and one written by Samuel Lipsitz resonates for members of family businesses. Written in 1950-51, it says in part:

> "Being together daily in business has its disadvantage as far as a father wanting to be noble in the eyes of his children. The aggravations and heavy pressure in our business cause friction and annoyance with one another. Maybe we said things at such times that in calm retrospect we are sorry for. I was as guilty of these things as anyone. I hope such things will not stand out in your memory of me...“

The book referred to in this article is available from Jewish Lights Publishing, P.O. Box 237, Sunset Farm Offices, Route 4, Woodstock VT 05091. Phone: 802-457-4000.

Century-old Hatfield Quality Meats is a case study of how family values have sustained a substantial family business into its fourth generation. The Clemens family's belief in quality, fairness, integrity, ethical behavior and building good will translates into innovation, accountability, and an adaptive, satisfied, productive workforce. Here's how Hatfield does it.

Hatfield Quality Meats: "Just Taking Care of the Place"

John S. Clemens, a second-generation owner of Hatfield Quality Meats Inc., loved the outdoors and enjoyed tending the lawn around headquarters – even at the age of 89, after he had helped guide the family business as a manager and director to more than a quarter-billion dollars in sales.

When a salesman came by one day and saw the elderly gentleman trimming weeds, the salesman asked, "Sir, how long have you worked for the company?"

"I've been here over 50 years," Mr. Clemens replied.

"And you've only gotten to the level where you're just taking care of the place?" the incredulous salesman asked.

"Yup. Just taking care of the place," Mr. Clemens said.

That unpretentious sense of stewardship is just one of the many deeply felt family values that guide Hatfield Quality Meats. As the company nears its 100th anniversary of family ownership in 1995, it continues to forge new retail and food-service markets for its high-quality pork products in 16 Eastern states, posting sales of $289.3 million for the year ended April 30.

Yet through all the changes demanded by growth and the passage of the business from generation to generation, one trait of Hatfield Quality Meats remains the same: The ability of family shareholders, now in the third and fourth generation, to translate family values into business success. The family's belief in quality, fairness, integrity, ethical behavior and building good will transcends other goals for the business. The business translation of those values includes continuing innovation, accountability, adaptation to changing markets and a satisfied, productive workforce.

"We try to take family values and infuse them into every aspect of our business, whether we're dealing with employees, customers or vendors," says Philip A. Clemens, executive vice president and designated successor in 1995 to his cousin, current President and CEO Clair W. Clemens. "We like to treat people the way we ourselves want to be treated."

That isn't always easy. Phil Clemens recalls one particularly thorny negotiation in which Hatfield decided during a due-diligence investigation of a proposed deal that it didn't want to complete the transaction. Though Hatfield was well within its legal rights, the other party responded angrily, threatening a lawsuit and attacking Hatfield's integrity.

"When you challenge our ethics, you're going right to the heart of what makes us who we are," Mr. Clemens told the man. "If you feel we made a promise we aren't keeping, we will go through with the deal" and liquidate the assets purchased. Though completing the deal didn't prove necessary, the incident shows "that we will go to any length to protect our ethical stance. That's our heart and soul, Mr. Clemens says.

Similar core values are woven throughout the culture of the business. Hatfield's four-point philosophy – stressing product quality, fairness to employees, applying principles to business and supporting the community-is simply stated on a one-page handout, explained to all employees and imprinted on a pocket-size card for each to carry with them. Accompanying it is a "Four-Way Test" (borrowed from the Rotary International civic organization) for employee behavior in dealing with others:

1. Is it the truth?
2. Is it fair to all concerned?
3. Will it build goodwill and better friendships?
4. Will it be beneficial to all concerned ?

Hatfield safeguards product quality by building accountability into management. The company plows $14 million to $16 million back into the business each year, and "we ask employees to hold us as families and owners accountable for what we say we're trying to do," Mr. Clemens says. For instance, employees sometimes have questioned the company's definition of product quality. "We've kicked that around at our company quite a bit. We define it as meeting a set standard on a consistent basis," Mr. Clemens says. Then, managers re-examine "whether all products are meeting the consistent standards that we want."

The family is building more accountability into its management structure, adding outside directors to its board and setting up an 11-member committee to oversee day-to-day operations. Mr. Clemens speaks frequently to family business audiences, declining fees, partly "because I hear questions we may have never faced. People share some things that might work well, or that we might do differently. It's a two-way street," he says.

In pursuit of fairness to employees, another tenet of the Hatfield philosophy, the family treats Hatfield's 1,200 workers much like family members. The company shares one-third of its profit with employees and seeks employees' suggestions in upgrading and redesigning plant facilities. Workout facilities and athletic trainers help employees build the physical strength needed for demanding jobs in the plant, and a day-care center helps families with young children. Workers get the use of certain company tools and moving trucks on weekends.

In turn, family members face the same disciplines as others in the business. Management meetings start at 5:30 a.m., reflecting the industry's predawn plant startup times. "We feel it's important that the family doesn't ask employees to come in at ungodly hours if we don't do it," Clemens explains. "We make the same policies for family and nonfamily."

Hatfield also puts Christian principles to work in its business dealings. The company sets aside 10 percent of profit for charity, via matching gifts with employees. It encourages volunteerism and pays employees for the time they need to serve as volunteer firefighters or ambulance workers. When a flood forced a competitor 40 miles away to shut down, Hatfield sent a maintenance crew and some additional employees over to help clean up. Instead of saying, "Whew, they're out of business, let's take advantage of that...we felt, hey, if we had a problem, we would certainly hope other people would help us," Mr. Clemens says.

Building family harmony is another goal that demands conscious, hard work. With 38 third, fourth and fifth generation family members working in the business full- or part-time, friction sometimes arises, especially among younger family members who may feel they deserve special treatment. "How do you keep 38 family members happy? You don't try," Mr. Clemens says.

The family uses several techniques to cultivate consensus. The 23 family members employed full-time in the business attend an annual retreat where they air issues and hear speakers on such topics as resolving conflict, curbing jealousy and improving communication-as well as socializing and sharing family memories. "The goal is to unite family members who work in the business," Mr. Clemens states.

He and another senior family member conduct annual interviews with individual family members, setting aside two to four hours for a frank, confidential, two-way discussion of personal goals and opinions, as well as career plans and objectives for the business. The family also conducts a confidential family survey every few years, asking members their opinions and feelings about everything from corporate goals to the impact of the business upon their spouses. If problems surface in the survey, the results provide an anonymous starting point for a family discussion.

Openness is viewed as a tool for seeking consensus. To keep disputes from erupting into major battles, the family has set up a procedure for airing problems before a family council. "We don't feel it's wrong to confront each other," Mr. Clemens explains. In doing so, "we avoid the backlash that often occurs when problems aren't confronted."

When a family member's behavior causes concern, the person is asked to talk about how his or her values conflict with those the family has established as guiding principles.

"We will say, 'listen, if you feel your values supersede what we as a family have set up, how about if we bring the entire family together and you talk about your values to them?' In almost every case," Mr. Clemens says, "the family will say that person has to change." He stresses that "passing down values from generation to generation isn't easy, but it is very important."

To promote shareholder unity, the company holds an annual meeting for stockholders, including dinner and an informative presentation. The company also pays an annual dividend and allows family members to cash in some stock yearly.

For Mr. Clemens, strengthening the family and the business are goals well worth the effort. "I look at family business as a way of life that I would like to continue," he says. But with only 15 percent of family businesses surviving beyond the third generation of family ownership, "that poses a great challenge." he believes. As the youngest member of the third generation of family owners of Hatfield Meats, he says he works hard to answer the question, "How do we enable that business to continue to survive?"

The Hatfield story offers several valuable lessons in that regard:

- Acknowledge the potential for conflict in the family business and develop mechanisms for resolving it before it occurs. When disagreements happen, encourage family members to make them amicable ones.
- Realize that decision-making in a mature family business demands teamwork. "We make very few one person decisions at this company," says Mr. Clemens, who was selected CEO-designate by a team of top family and nonfamily employees. "We seek consensus-not unanimity, but consensus ."
- Recognize that openness, used properly, can be a tool for achieving family consensus, rather than a threat to family business stability.
- Examine and express the values that are important to you in the family business and work consciously to pass them on to the next generation. "If you don't pass your values on to the next generation, who will?" Mr. Clemens asks.
- Respect the steep odds against family business survival, and build accountability into management to improve those odds. "If a family business is to be successful, it will take hard work. It takes making the tough decisions." And, Mr. Clemens emphasizes, "It takes asking the tough questions of yourself."

Reprinted with permission from *The Family Business Advisor,* February 1994. Copyright 1994, Family Enterprise Publishers.

A responsible steward sees wealth as a resource to be used for the benefit of all of a business's constituents. Stewardship is among the most important values in families who experience multi-generational business success.

The Critical Value Of Stewardship

By Craig E. Aronoff and John L. Ward

"Our father passed the business he started down to us." The speaker was an 80-year-old, talking at a family meeting attended by nearly 30 people representing three generations.

"My brother and I never paid a penny for the business," he continued, "but we spent our lives building on what he began. Now you have a much more substantial enterprise. What we want for you is the kind of happiness and accomplishment we've known. But most of all, we want for future generations of our family to have the opportunities we've had. It is your responsibility to make that possible."

What that octogenarian was talking about is stewardship, the value we've found to be the most important in families that experience business success from one generation to the next.

A steward, according to one dictionary definition, is "one who manages another's property; trustee, chief servant." One family we know includes stewardship in its family creed, defining it as "the duty to enhance the family's resources for the benefit of employees and the community, as well as future generations of family."

The results of responsible stewardship provide the moral basis of private enterprise and justify the privilege of inheritance of private property.

The best business leaders we have met share several special characteristics:

- They wish to leave an enduring institution.
- They want to prove a personal philosophy of management.
- They are willing to have the business serve as a model company – open for others to evaluate and to learn from.
- They see themselves as stewards of the firm's resources.

A devotion to continuous improvement is common to all these characteristics. As a result, these leaders' motivations typically include the desires to build companies that last beyond their own lifetime; to accept personal responsibility for the organizations' management problems; to test themselves against other excellent businesses; and to add to their businesses' wealth and value.

We find that less successful leaders tend to just want to hold on to what they already have. They are conservators rather than stewards in that they seek not to maximize resources but simply to avoid losing their inheritance.

Stewardship is progressive, not just protective. Stewardship not only encourages constantly "adding value" but also depersonalizes wealth and family money. If one sees wealth in terms of one's own money, one often becomes protective and risk-averse. Money is viewed as a means for supporting one's lifestyle and providing personal economic security.

Stewards, on the other hand, see wealth as an economic resource to be applied to creating additional wealth for the benefit of all of a business's constituents. Taking the risks necessary to constantly strengthen a business seems more natural and less threatening. From this perspective, the long-term view makes sense.

Those who inherit family businesses need to understand and become comfortable with the privileges they have received.

How does a successor justify receiving a family business? Stewardship is one answer. Leaders of an earlier generation created value – jobs, an institution, a reputation, perhaps wealth. It was their responsibility to pass on not only the wealth they generated but also the talents and values that made them successful. Having received the resources to continue creating value, subsequent generations must also accept responsibility and transmit talents and values.

The result is good for society. Family firms are characterized by the family values that sustain us as a society. They are diverse, adding to the rich mosaic that distinguishes our nation. By preserving our family businesses, we maintain competition, assuring that wealth and power are broadly distributed.

The result is also good for the family. Family members learn the importance of fulfilling their potential and using their talents to contribute to the greater good.

The owners of the best family businesses we know reflect on and discuss these issues. "How is owning a business together good for the family?" they ask. "How is the business better off because of the family's ownership?"

The best leaders we know are constantly seeking to improve. They understand that they must take risks themselves and risk their firms' resources. But, of course, they do so in a responsible fashion – and for the benefit of others.

Motivation inspired merely by increasing personal power and wealth fails to sustain families through the generations. Perpetuating the family business is both a great challenge and a great privilege. Stewardship helps it all make sense for everyone.

This article was originally printed in *Nation's Business*, April 1992. Copyright 1992, U.S. Chamber of Commerce. Reprinted with permission of the authors.

This article summarizes the initial findings of a research project that explored violations of ethics in Spanish family businesses. The main results indicated that the most frequently perceived ethics violations were delaying succession processes, avoiding complex strategic planning, and building an organization based on the buying of loyalties. The age of the respondent affected the way in which these behaviors were perceived.

Ethics in Personal Behavior in Family Business

By Miguel Angel Gallo

Introduction

During the last 10 years, many institutions have been conducting research on family businesses. Among them, the Family Firm Institute and the Family Business Network have been making strides to help understand the unique characteristics of and the problems involved in running a family business.

As a result of these efforts, many articles have appeared that comment favorably on the extraordinary contributions that family businesses have made to economies throughout the world. These contributions include the creation of jobs and production of wealth. Despite this, there is a general opinion about family businesses that is not very flattering and is clearly seen in the following expressions:

"You know, 'A' is the typical family business where the owner does what he/she wants regardless of what anyone thinks."

"In 'B', as in so many other family businesses, the most important thing is to make the family happy."

"Company 'C' needs to become more professional from top to bottom, or what happens to all family businesses will happen to it."

These points of view are consistent with a recent report about university graduates' resistance to joining a family business. These graduates view family businesses as an insufficiently attractive professional path (Gallo & Cappuyns, 1996).

For those who work in the field of family business, there is no doubt that during the last 10 years important steps have been taken in understanding family businesses. Testimony to that are the 44 issues of the specialized journal *Family Business Review* as well as contents of the *Family Business Sourcebook II* (Aronoff, Astrachan, & Ward, 1996). However, judging by these publications and the proceedings of the annual Family Firm Institute Conference and the Family Business Network Conference, work in the field of family business ethics is still in its initial stages (Adams, Tashchian, & Shore, 1996; Hoover & Lank, 1997; Riemer, 1994).

Summarized here are the initial findings of a research project I am currently conducting. The goal of this research is to understand the viewpoints of a diverse group of individuals, including owners and their employees, regarding ethics violations in family businesses. The research presented here was exploratory, meaning it was not based on previously established hypotheses. Rather it sought to discover the areas in which ethics violations were most strongly perceived and possible differences in viewpoints among the groups of people studied.

The results have so far indicated that the areas in which ethics violations were most frequently perceived are the following:

- Delaying succession to stay in power
- Avoiding a strategic plan that would go beyond existing capacities and desires
- Building an organization based on the buying of loyalties

These perceptions differed widely, depending on the age of the person judging them.

The Study Questionnaire

The research was based on the information from a closed two-part questionnaire (see the Appendix). As we know, opinions on family businesses are usually related to the characteristics of the person offering them (Poza, Alfred, & Maheshwari, 1997). For this reason, the first part of the questionnaire asked for personal information (age, sex, education, percentage of capital owned in the family business, etc.)along with how business capital is structured, years in operation, and sector of activity.

Using a Likert scale of five anchors, the questionnaire asked how frequently ethics violations appeared in family businesses, according to the respondent's own experience. The questions addressed 33 types of behavior grouped around five basic topics.

The first two questionnaire topics were directly related to property and power – two traditional realms of basic motivation:

(1) Access and the transference of the owner's capital

(2) The use of power in the company

The use of power in the company essentially determines strategic orientation in areas such as growth and change versus continuity, long-term profits, etc. , and also in growing the organization, selecting the collaborators, and the manner of working with them. The next two topics in the questionnaire covered the following issues:

(3) Strategic changes

(4) The manner in which the organization advanced

Finally, given that in a family business the owners have a very extensive and intense relationship with the company, the final topic in the questionnaire was

(5) The behavior of the stockholders

The questionnaire did not include areas such as relations with clients and suppliers, relations with other employees, environmental concerns, and fulfillment of other types of social responsibilities. These were omitted to keep the questionnaire a manageable length and because conduct in these areas is more a result of teamwork by the company directors than by one person.

The questionnaire was tested and revised several times until it was easy to understand, which resulted in very few questionnaires being declared invalid.

Methodology

The questionnaire was sent out the first week in April of 1998 to a sample group of about 1,800 people, of whom 1,367 were owners and general managers of family businesses who have maintained contact with me over the last 10 years; approximately 100 were members of the Instituto de Empresa Familiar, and were the owners and managers of the largest Spanish family businesses, and some 350 were family businesses belonging to the four regional Spanish family businesses associations that were the most active in 1997. In comparison to all Spanish family businesses, one can safely confirm that this sample pool was made up largely of relatively important and multigenerational businesses.

In all, 265 questionnaires were received; however, 12 were eliminated, 5 that were inconsistent and 7 that were from nonfamily members who were not even shareholders. Altogether, 253 questionnaires were accepted from individuals directly related to family businesses by being either the owner or working there, this 13% response rate is consistent with prior large-scale studies of family businesses, such as Arthur Andersen and MassMutual (1997).

The Sample

Women made up only 22% of the sample. This low percentage will make future research on how gender affects perception difficult. Because the mailing of the questionnaire was indiscriminate, it is quite possible that this low representation corresponds to the low number of women in government positions or in management positions in Spanish family businesses.

The average age of the respondents was 46, and more than 80% were older than 35 (see Table 1). The sample, therefore, comprised mature adults whose values and scruples have already been formed and whose behavior patterns are usually stable. Of all the respondents, 84% have university degrees, which may imply that, having been through the halls of higher learning, they have had the opportunity to analyze other points of view, compare and contrast opinions, and achieve a heightened knowledge of ethical principles.

Age, education level, and the characteristics of the positions held (see Table 2) all indicate that the respondents had a good understanding of what goes on in the family business and had the information necessary to evaluate personal behavior, which was the objective of the second part of the questionnaire. Seventy-three percent (24% + 17% + 13% + 19%) were members of boards of directors and/or were chief executive officers of their businesses. In addition, 36% (17% + 19%) functioned as chief executive officers of the business – one of the most influential positions.

The capital structure data found in Table 3 helps support the assumption that the respondents had a good understanding of their business situations. In fact, 61% (14% + 6% + 41%) had an ownership level high enough to provide them ample information about the performance of the company.

Finally, only 11% were first-generation family business members (see Table 4), which would indicate that the vast majority of respondents probably knew how their business performed over a long period of time.

Results

Perceived Personal Behavior: Frequencies. The answers to each of the 33 questions in the second part of the questionnaire were weighed in accordance with how often ethics violations were perceived in each of the behaviors, using a fivepoint scale: very high = 5, high = 4, medium = 3, low = 2, very low = 1.

Table 1. Ages

Age	Number	%
Younger than 35	45	18
35 – 44	80	32
45 – 54	58	24
55 – 65	51	23
Older than 65	19	3
Total	**253**	**100**

Table 2. Position in the Family Business

Position	Number	%
Member of board of directors	59	24
Member of board of directors and chief executive officer	44	17
Member of board of directors and manager	33	13
Chief executive officer	49	19
Manager	52	21
Other	10	4
None	6	2
Total	**253**	**100**

Table 3. Capital Structure

% of Property Owned or Represented	Number	%
More than 50%	36	14
50%	15	6
Between 5% and 49%	120	47
No stockholders own >50% (n = 104)		
One stockholder owns >50% (n = 16)		
Less than 5%	43	17
Not a stockholder	39	16
Total	**253**	**100**

Table 4. Generation

Last Generation	Number	%
First	28	11
Second	111	44
Third	78	31
Fourth	28	11
Fifth or more	8	3
Total	**253**	**100**

The value of the frequency averages that correspond to each of the behaviors appears in Table 5. Three types of frequency are clearly identified in this table. First, "delaying succession, "the clearest among all behaviors, averaged 4 points, a high occurrence in terms of ethics violations. The number of respondents who perceived that behavior as very high equaled those who perceived it as medium, low, and very low.

Second, respondents believed eight types of behaviors occur with a medium frequency (3 points). The first three – 3.1, prevent necessary development and evolution of the company; 3.2, put the company on automatic pilot, leaving it to continue as is to dedicate time to other things; and 3.3, prevent the contrasting opinions of others in strategy formulation – relate to creating difficulties that make the business's strategic plan seem difficult and a challenge to whomever is responsible for it. Three other types of behavior are as follows: 4.1, to put incapable people in important positions (nepotism); 4.2, to provide unjust or inadequate compensation; and 4.3, to use favoritism and discrimination. These three types are all related to surrounding the person in power with people who allow that person to do whatever he or she wants. Last, the two other behavior types (2.2.4, to promote personal image and status, and 5.6, personal appropriation of company funds) are specific examples of using the company for one's own benefit.

Third, a large group of 24 behaviors (73% altogether) had a low frequency of occurrence. That is, the number of respondents who perceived a very low frequency was equal to the number of respondents who perceived medium, high, and very high frequencies. Because the questionnaire comprised five different groups of questions, there was a risk that respondents misinterpreted the question groupings. The cross-tab analysis of the questions in each group was significant in all cases (all correlations >0.7).

It is, however, important to emphasize that the lowest averages of the frequencies lower than 2.1 points corresponded to behaviors that were described using such terms as "force," "defraud," "deceive," "reveal," "falsify,"and "demand"and consequently were easily identified with poor ethical behavior. Additionally, most respondents considered these behaviors to clearly represent ethics violations and to be clearly associated with established responsibilities in the business bylaws, legislation, and legal practice. (These behaviors were; 1.1.1, forcing property rights from other people; 1.2.1, defrauding legitimate heirs; 2.1.1, deceiving legal power holders; 4.8, making confidential information public; 4.9, withholding or falsify information; 5.2, obliging the company to pay dividends that were not earned; and 5.4, divulging inappropriate information.)

The Age Factor. The most significant variable influencing respondents' perceptions of ethics violations was age. Statistically significant findings have also been found in the variables "studies"and "capital structure."

Breaking down the 253 survey respondents into two groups (45 and younger, n = 125 and older than 45, n = 128) shows some important differences in the medians. Table 6 contains median frequencies of how ethics violations in each behavior was perceived differently according to age. Respondents 45 and younger perceived ethics violations under the category "delaying succession processes" (question 4.6) as being at a high instead of medium frequency. Likewise, they considered the other five behaviors indicated in the table to occur with medium frequency instead of low. Possibly these responses related to their future position as managers of the family business.

In addition, the younger group of respondents perceived a greater lack of ethics regarding ownership. The younger respondents perceived that "underpricing shares' value"(question 1.1.2), occurred at a medium (as opposed to a low) frequency. They rated "defraud legitimate heirs" (question 1.2.1) at a low as opposed to very low frequency.

Analysis of the averages with statistically significant differences (see Table 7) indicated that the younger group judged ethical behavior more critically. They attributed a higher rate of ethics violation to failing to plan development strategies (questions 3.1, 3.2, and 3.3), lacking a capable organization (questions 4.1, 4.2, 4.3, and 4.5), delaying succession processes (question 4.6), using the company for personal benefit (questions 5.2, 5.4, 5.5, and 5.6), and postponing the transference of ownership to the next generation (questions 1.2.1 and 1.2.2).

Observations

Power is absolutely necessary to manage a business. In and of itself, power is neither good nor bad, but rather it depends on the way in which it is wielded. When a company correctly fulfills all of its social responsibilities, those who govern and manage the company have made good use of their power. However, when the company does not fulfill its social responsibilities, and this lack of compliance is not due to outside or unforeseeable factors, there is reason to suspect that power was used poorly. On occasion, that poor use of power may be a result of the ignorance of those who govern and manage the company. On other occasions, what frequently takes place is an abuse of power resulting from the refusal to solve a problem, the lack of knowledge, or a bad decision made intentionally.

Table 5. Median and Average Frequency of Ethics Violations in Each Behavior

Question	Median Total	Average Total	Question	Median Total	Average Total
1.1.1	2	1.8	4.3	3	2.7
1.1.2	2	2.4	4.4	2	2.2
1.2.1	2	1.7	4.5	2	2.4
1.2.2	2	2.4	4.6	4	3.3
2.1.1	2	1.8	4.7	2	2.3
2.1.2	2	2.2	4.8	2	2.0
2.1.3	2	2.4	4.9	2	2.1
2.2.1	2	2.3	4.10	2	2.5
2.2.2	2	2.2	4.11	2	2.2
2.2.3	2	2.5	5.1	2	2.3
2.2.4	3	2.8	5.2	2	2.1
3.1	3	2.8	5.3	2	2.3
3.2	3	2.6	5.4	2	2.1
3.3	3	3.0	5.5	2	2.5
3.4	2	2.5	5.6	3	2.9
4.1	3	2.8	5.7	2	2.4
4.2	3	2.8			

Table 6. Changes of Frequency in the Perception of Ethics Violations According to Age

Question	Behavior	Median Frequency 45 and Younger	Older Than 45
4.6	Delaying succession processes High Medium		
1. 2. 2	Setting up an ownership structure that results in difficult governance of the company.	Medium	Low
3. 2	To put the company on "automatic pilot", it to continues as it is, in order to dedicate time to other things.	Medium	Low
3. 4	Lack of thought for the interest for the next generations	Medium	Low
4. 5	Impede professional careers of capable executives	Medium	Low
4. 10	Excessive expenses	Medium	Low

In many family businesses, there is a high risk of misusing power because the owners of the business also run it. The owners have the power to control the company, and these owners give the managers the power to run the company. In family businesses, those in power are not usually held accountable for their decisions, which also increases the risk of abusing power. They can also act like someone who "does what he wants with what is his." In these cases, ethics violations can occur when family business leaders forget that the business, as an "organized community of people," is much more than its owners, and that those who control and run it also have responsibilities to the people working there as well to clients, suppliers, other institutions, and society in general.

Moreover, the owner and manager of a family business may be the same person, and that person may have been at the head of or had a key position in the company for many years. As a result, managers may become convinced of their own infallibility. At times they may believe – on some level – that by delaying the processes of succession they can avoid their own death.

Unnecessarily delaying succession is undoubtedly an ethics violation. It damages the successor, other members of the organization, and the family. It also puts the continuity of the company at risk. Similarly, impeding the development of the company by putting it on "automatic pilot" or by leaving it in a dangerously mature sector is another ethics violation. This behavior can cause the company to lose capital and put jobs at risk, damaging all parties involved. Yet another ethics violation involves giving management responsibilities to those who are incapable of handling such tasks. In accordance with these initial research results, people directly involved with the family business owners and managers, because of their position, maintain a certain perspective about ethical behavior, which showed that the most frequent violations relate to gaining and maintaining power (see Figure 1).

In fact, delaying succession, the behavior perceived most frequently as an ethics violation, has a direct impact on an owner-manager's temptation to remain in power. The argument behind this behavior may be summed up as follows: "If I delay succession, I can continue in power, and if I continue in power I can delay succession!"

Delaying succession also leads to the family business following an unchallenging strategy, which was also frequently perceived as an ethics violation. In this case the thinking may well be, "Because I am not prepared or motivated enough, I will devise an easy strategy. Because the strategy is easy and the important members of the organization don't argue with it, nobody can doubt that I'm fully capable of carrying it out." The result of delaying succession and following an unchallenging strategy is a weak organization made up of incapable or ineffectual managers who are both bound by their loyalties and have been bought with favors and money. Managers who are only able to carry out an unchallenging strategy will not oppose delaying succession.

The underlying logic behind the most frequent ethics violations is that power is used to increase personal status and to pass on personal expenses to the family business. It is therefore no wonder that younger people are quite a bit more critical. Unlike their older counterparts, they do not usually hold high positions with any considerable power, they

Table 7. Average Frequency in which Ethics Violations Are Perceived in Relation to Age and Particular Behavior

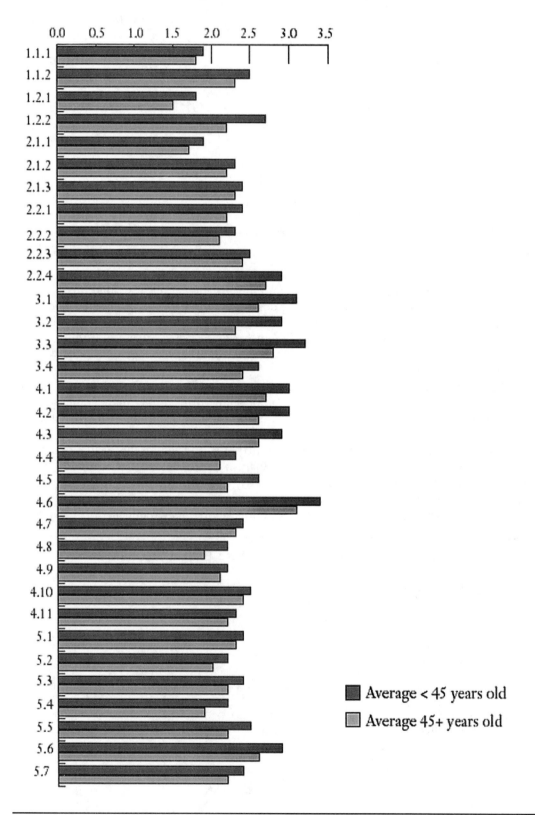

Note. With reliability index 95% , p < 0. 05

Figure 1. Gaining and Maintaining Power

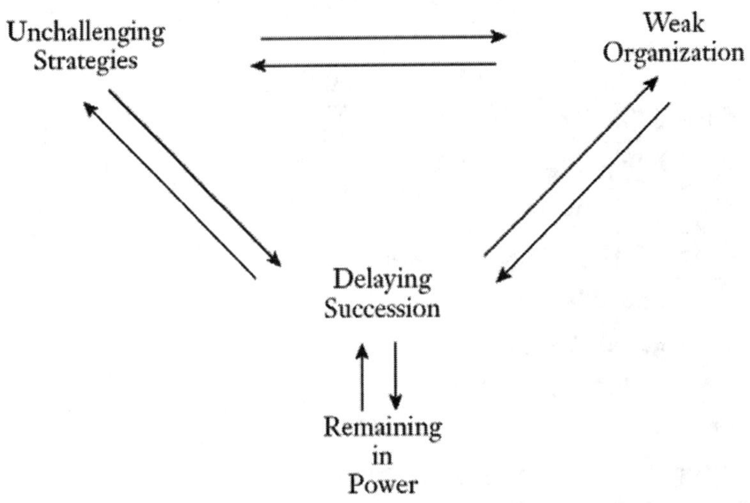

Unchallenging Strategies → Weak Organization

Delaying Succession

Remaining in Power

also suffer more direct consequences of their older colleagues' ethics violations.

Sometimes, those who have the power don't communicate the reasons behind many of their actions to the younger members of the family. A lack of communication may cause those with less power to speculate about certain actions. Likewise, if these actions have a negative impact on those with the least amount of power, they will perceive these actions as unethical.

The way to improve the ethical standards of these behaviors should come from the application of several "best practices" by Ward (1997). For example, management should regularly challenge initiatives, keep the organization innovative and flexible, and encourage the business to foster leadership (see Figure 2).

The importance of these best practices is further supported by the results of a recent study that examined success in 25 of the top Spanish family businesses from 1972 to 1997 (Gallo, Cappuyns, & Vilaseca, 1998). In that study, it was seen that, among all of the successful businesses, the presence of all of the values in the acronym ELISA were found. The first three – exigency, laboriousness, and initiative – are clearly opposed to the unchal-

Figure 2. Use of Power to Increase Ethical Standards

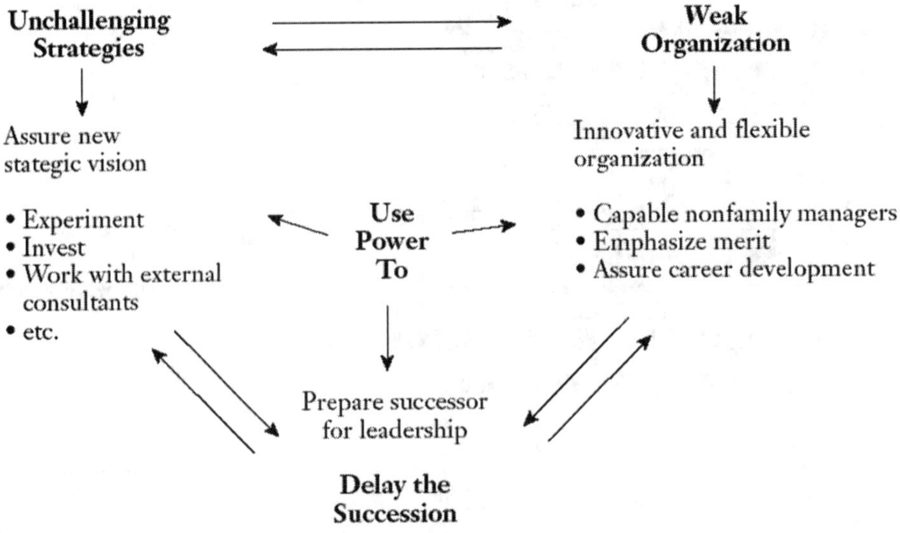

Unchallenging Strategies → **Weak Organization**

Assure new stategic vision

Innovative and flexible organization

Use Power To

- Experiment
- Invest
- Work with external consultants
- etc.

- Capable nonfamily managers
- Emphasize merit
- Assure career development

Prepare successor for leadership

Delay the Succession

lenging strategy and of the powerless organization. The last two – simplicity and austerity – clearly oppose the practices of using power for personal gain and status and passing on personal expenses to the company.

Because the least-frequent ethics violations involved carrying out of legislation and by-laws (also the easiest behaviors to observe), the owner-managers of family businesses must be encouraged to make commitments as to how they plan to use their power. This can be done, for example, by establishing an explicit strategic plan, succession and crisis policies, rules and regulations for boards of directors, codes of conduct, family protocols, and the like. They would then have to be accountable to a system of checks and balances (internal and external audits, formal evaluations and compensation systems, board of directors, family councils, etc.).

Conclusion

In the first part of this investigation we studied the differences in perception related to the different characteristics of the questionnaire's respondents. Two of these characteristics were especially interesting in view of the evolution most family businesses undergo: The first is the influence education had on the respondent. Today there are more and more opportunities to study and more information is available about family businesses. The second characteristic is related to the capital structure of the company. Today an increasing number of second-and third-generation family businesses are considering different types of business partnerships and are publicly traded.

Future Research

In future studies, we will examine the opinions of diverse groups of people who are not involved in a family business. These will include executives in nonfamily businesses, lawyers, finance people, bankers, consultants, and public administrators. We will interview these individuals in an effort to increase the awareness of those who own or work in family businesses of the existing perceptions of the ethics of their behavior.

Finally, two suggestions: The first of these concerns family businesses in countries with governments that support them. If these companies don't adhere to excellence in ethics in their activities, they stand the risk of being monitored by stricter laws. The second of these is to motivate family business consultants to diagnose in earnest the problems of postponing succession, pursuing unchallenging strategies, and managing powerless organizations and to challenge their clients by helping them initiate and carry out the necessary changes.

References

Adams, J. S. , Tashchian A. , & Shore, T. H. (1996). Ethics in family and nonfamily-owned firms: An exploratory study. *Family Business Review, 9* (2), 157 – 170.

Aronoff, C. E. , Astrachan, J. H. , & Ward, J. L. (Eds.). (1996). *Family business sourcebook II*. Marietta, GA: Business Owners Resources.

Arthur Andersen/MassMutual. (1997). *American family business survey*. Springfield, MA.: Author.

Gallo, M. A. , & Cappuyns, K. (1996). *Bringing university graduates into the family business*. (IESE Research Paper No. 304). University of Navarra, Spain.

Gallo, M. A. , Cappuyns, K. , & Vilaseca, A. (1998, September). *Successful family businesses*. Paper presented at the Family Business Network Ninth Annual World Conference, Paris.

Hoover, E. H. , & Lank, A. G. (1997, September). Right versus right: Ethics in the family business. Paper presented at the Family Business Network Eighth Annual World Conference, Hague, Netherlands.

Poza, E. J. , Alfred, T. , & Maheshwari, A. (1997). Stakeholders' perceptions of culture and management practices in family and nonfamily firms - A preliminary report. *Family Business Review, 10* (2), 135 –155.

Riemer, J. (1994). So that your values live on: Ethical wills. *The Family Business Advisor.*

Ward, J. L. (1997). Growing the family business: Special challenges and best practices. *Family Business Review, 10* (4), 323 –337.

Appendix. Ethics in Family Business: Questionnaire

Part I. Basic Data

1. Age_____   Gender: male/female_____   Education_____

2. Your position in the family Business
❑ Board of Directors
❑ Chief Executive Officer
❑ Manager
❑ Other
❑ None

3. Are you a shareholder?   ❑ Yes   ❑ No

4. What percentage of Equity do you own or represent?
❑ Less than 5%
❑ Between 5 and 49%
❑ 50%
❑ More than 50%

5. Is there a shareholder that owns more than 50%?   ❑ Yes   ❑ No

6. Does the company have shareholders who are not family members?   ❑ Yes   ❑ No

7. Approximately, what percentage of the capital do they own?

8. Last generation already incorporated in the family business:
❑ First
❑ Second
❑ Third
❑ Fourth
❑ Fifth or more

9. Main sector of activity is_____

Part II. Behaviors and Frequencies

In relationship with family business, according to your experiences, with what frequency do you think the following ethical faults in personal behavior occur?
The following scale was used:
very often =5, often =4, some times =3, rarely =2, never =1

1. Ownership of capital.
       1.1 Ways to achieve ownership:
              1.1.1 Force property rights from other people
              1.1.2 Underpricing shares' value
       1.2 Ways to transfer ownership.
              1.2.1 Defraud legitimate heirs
              1.2.2.Setting up an ownership structure that results in difficult governance of the company

2.Power
- 2.1 Ways to gain power.
  - 2.1.1.Deceive legal power holders.
  - 2.1.2.Threaten with a position of leverage due to a control of shares, vital information, etc.
  - 2.1.3.Use of delaying tactics to immobilize the exercise of legal power
- 2.2.General ways to exercise power
  - 2.2.1 To promote personal economic interest
  - 2.2.2.Taking strategic stand that can cause great risk
  - 2.2.3.Following personal preferences that can cause great risk
  - 2.2.4 To promote personal image and status

3.Business strategy

3.1 Prevent necessary development and evolution of the company (dangerous continuity in mature business, imprudent lack of diversification, etc.)

3.2 To put the company on automatic pilot, leaving it to continue as it is, in order to dedicate time to other things

3.3 Prevent the contrasting opinions of others in strategy formulation

3.4. Lack of thought for the interest of the next generations

4.Company organization.

4.1 To put incapable people in important positions (nepotism)

4.2 Unjust or inadequate compensation

4.3 Use of favoritism and discrimination

4.4 Blackmailing, buying executives through compensation or threats

4.5 Impede professional careers of capable executives

4.6 Delaying succession processes

4.7 Lack of time devoted to the company

4.8 Make public confidential information

4.9 Withhold or falsify information

4.10 Excessive expenses

4.11 Unnecessary luxury

5.Shareholders

5.1 Shareholders alliances at the expense of other shareholders

5.2 Obliging the company to pay dividends that were not earned

5.3 Requesting favors contrary to the interest of the company

5.4 Obliging to divulge inappropriate information

5.5 Make personal inappropriate use of company assets

5.6 Personal appropriation of company funds

5.7 Imprudent failure to exercise shareholder rights

Reprinted with permission of the publisher from *Family Business Review*, December 1998. Copyright 1998, Family Firm Institute.

INDEX